FUND
ACCOUNTING:
THEORY AND PRACTICE

INTERGOVERNMENTAL REVENUE

second edition

FUND ACCOUNTING:
THEORY AND PRACTICE

EDWARD S. LYNN
The University Of Arizona

ROBERT J. FREEMAN
Texas Tech University

PRENTICE-HALL, INC., *Englewood Cliffs, New Jersey 07632*

Library of Congress Cataloging in Publication Data

LYNN, EDWARD S.
    Fund accounting.

    Includes bibliographical references and index.
    1. Municipal finance—Accounting.
2. Local finance—United States—Accounting.
3. Finance, Public—United States—Accounting.
4. Fund accounting—United States.   I. Freeman, Robert J.
II. Title.
HJ9777.A3L95 1982   657'835'00973   82-21587
ISBN 0-13-332411-7

Editorial/production supervision and
interior design: LINDA C. MASON
Cover design: Wanda Lubelska
Manufacturing buyer: RAY KEATING

Printed in the United States of America

10 9 8 7 6 5 4 3 2 1

ISBN 0-13-332411-7

Prentice-Hall International, Inc., *London*
Prentice-Hall of Australia Pty. Limited, *Sydney*
Editora Prentice-Hall do Brasil, Ltda., *Rio de Janeiro*
Prentice-Hall Canada Inc., *Toronto*
Prentice-Hall of India Private Limited, *New Delhi*
Prentice-Hall of Japan, Inc., *Tokyo*
Prentice-Hall of Southeast Asia Pte. Ltd., *Singapore*
Whitehall Books Limited, *Wellington, New Zealand*

CONTENTS

Property Damaged or Destroyed/Statements of General Fixed Assets
GENERAL LONG-TERM DEBT
Overview of General Long-Term Debt Accounting/Relation to Term
Debt/Relation to Serial Debt/Relation to Non-GLTD Issuances/
Defaulted Bonds/GLTD Records/GLTD Statements, Schedules, and
Statistical Tables
INTERFUND RELATIONSHIPS

11/Trust and Agency (Fiduciary) Funds   404

THE ACCOUNTABILITY FOCUS
TRUST FUNDS
Budgetary Considerations/Expendable Trust Funds/Nonexpendable Trust
Funds
AGENCY FUNDS
Simpler Agency Funds/More Complex Agency Funds
PENSION AND TRUST FUNDS
Accounting Standards
RETIREMENT FUND EXAMPLE
NCGA ACCOUNTING STANDARDS REVISITED
SFAS No. 35/The Government and Its Pension Obligation

12/Internal Service Funds   453

OVERVIEW OF ACCOUNTING PRINCIPLES
Cost Accounting in the IS Fund/Creation of the IS Fund/Pricing
Policies/Pricing Methods/Relation to the Budget
IS FUND ACCOUNTING ILLUSTRATED
A Central Automotive Unit/A Central Stores Fund
DISPOSITION OF PROFIT OR LOSS   DISSOLUTION OF AN IS FUND
ACCOUNTING FOR BUDGETARY OPERATIONS
Accounting for Appropriations/Charging Expenditures and
Encumbrances to Appropriations/Trial Balance before Closing Entries/
Closing Entries for the Budgetary Group/Balance Sheet—Budgetary
Accounts

13/Enterprise Funds; Summary of Interfund
Accounting   487

ENTERPRISE FUND ACCOUNTING
Characteristics of Enterprise Fund Accounting/Enterprise Fund
Accounting Illustrated
A GENERAL COMMENT ON REPORTING FOR PROPRIETARY FUNDS
SUMMARY OF INTERFUND ACCOUNTING
Independent Fiscal and Accounting Entities/Types of Independent Fiscal
Entities/Differences in Budgetary Control Emphasis/Separation of
Related Assets and Liabilities/Differences in Recording Assets and
Liabilities/Differences in the Basis of Accounting/Accounts of Funds v.
Accounts of the Governmental Unit

PREFACE

Major changes have occurred in the accounting and reporting standards for state and local governments, hospitals, and universities since the previous edition of this text. A new body of knowledge and principles for voluntary health and welfare organizations and other not-for-profit organizations has come into print in that same period. This second edition is in many respects a new book dealing with new topics.

These developments in generally accepted accounting principles are by no means complete. For example, at this writing the organizational responsibility for establishing principles of accounting for state and local governments appears to be in transition. In any event, the generation of new principles is likely to continue at an accelerated pace. (We believe that users of this text will be greatly benefited by periodic updatings of materials in the text as new pronouncements are made, and accordingly we plan to provide them.)

We are the same authors with the same objectives and have, we believe, produced the same kind of text as the first edition. We believe that a text should be very "teachable." We believe that graphic illustrations for such things as fund purposes, the life cycles of funds, budgetary accounting, budget processes and procedures, and adaptations and changes in the accounting equation are helpful to the students. We continue to emphasize the environment of fund accounting; the evolution of its theory, both past and future; and its alternative accounting, reporting, and budgetary approaches and techniques.

The successful device of introducing the interfund entry problem before all the funds and account groups have been discussed has been continued. The student is by this device encouraged to recognize interfund relationships at an early point. He is thus spared, to some extent, the shock that interfund transactions bring when he has gone through the accounting for ten funds and account groups and suddenly has to integrate the several kinds of accounting.

The text is designed to be adaptable to the needs of a variety of course types and instructor preferences, as well as the needs of practitioners who desire a reference work. Its breadth and depth of coverage, its balanced treatment of theory and practice, and its wealth of assignment material provide an ample basis for the graduate level or two-term undergraduate courses, where readings and the preparation of student papers are desirable. It is equally suited for use in the more traditional one-term course, affording the instructor wide latitude in selecting those topics, approaches, and emphases that fit his objectives for the course.

In recent years it has become more common for public administration students to be required to take a fund accounting course. *Introduction to Fund Accounting*, by Edward S. Lynn and Joan Thompson, both of the University of Arizona, has been developed for those students without previous knowledge of accounting. The *Introduction*, together with this major text, provide appropriate materials for the first course in fund accounting for public administration students, both at the undergraduate and graduate levels. Such courses are being taught at the University of Arizona and we shall be glad to provide syllabi and other information.

Many users of the previous edition of the text have offered helpful suggestions for improvement. We thank them and solicit comments and constructive criticism on this edition. Our special thanks go to:

- Our students
- Professors Alan Berger, Daniel Kyle, Fred Mueller, D. D. Ray, and Gary Siegel for their reviews of the first edition and recommendations for the current edition; and Professor Craig D. Shoulders for his assistance on the revision while a doctoral student at Texas Tech University.
- Professor David W. Phipps of the University of Alabama, Ronald J Points of the U.S. General Accounting Office, and P. Douglas Powell of Ernst & Whinney for reviews of early drafts of chapters. (They bear none of the blame for whatever flaws may remain.)
- Our wives, Marcille and Beverly, for their assistance and encouragement.

E.S.L.
R.J.F.

GOVERNMENTAL AND INSTITUTIONAL ACCOUNTING: ITS ENVIRONMENT AND CHARACTERISTICS

Accounting is the art of analyzing, recording, summarizing, evaluating, and interpreting an organization's financial activities and status, and communicating the results. This book deals with accounting and reporting concepts, standards, and procedures applicable to (1) state and local governments, including counties, cities, townships, and villages, (2) the Federal government, and (3) not-for-profit institutions such as universities, hospitals, voluntary health and welfare organizations, and other nonprofit organizations. Financial management considerations and problems peculiar to the not-for-profit (NFP) sector receive emphasis throughout. In addition, unique aspects of auditing in this environment are discussed from the standpoint of both organization management and the independent auditor.

CHARACTERISTICS AND TYPES OF NFP ORGANIZATIONS

Governments and other not-for-profit organizations are unique in that:

1. The profit motive is not inherent in their inception or operation.
2. They are usually owned collectively by their constituents; i.e., ownership is not normally evidenced by individually owned equity shares which may be sold or exchanged.
3. Those contributing financial resources to the organization do not necessarily receive a direct or proportionate share of its goods or services; e.g., the welfare recipient most likely did not pay the taxes from which his benefits are paid.

A not-for-profit organization exists because a community or society considers it necessary or desirable to provide certain goods or services to its group as a whole, often without reference to whether costs incurred will be recovered through charges for the goods or services or whether those paying for the goods or services are those benefiting from them. In most instances NFP organizations provide goods or services which are not commercially feasible to produce through private enterprise and/or which are deemed so vital to the public well-being that it is felt that their provision should be supervised by elected or appointed representatives of the populace.

The major types of not-for-profit organizations may be classified as follows:

1. **Governmental:** Federal, state, county, municipal, township, village, and other local governmental authorities, including special districts.

2. **Educational:** kindergartens, elementary and secondary schools, and colleges and universities.

3. **Health and welfare:** e.g., hospitals, nursing homes, orphanages, the American Red Cross, and the USO.

4. **Religious:** churches, YMCA, Salvation Army, and other church-related organizations.

5. **Charitable:** Community Chests, United Appeals, United Funds, and other charitable organizations.

6. **Foundations:** private trusts and corporations organized for educational, religious, or charitable purposes.

The above is a general classification scheme, and much overlap occurs. Many charitable organizations are church-related, for example, and governments are deeply involved in education, health, and welfare activities.

Growth and Importance of the NFP Sector

Governments and other not-for-profit organizations have experienced dramatic growth in recent years and have emerged—individually and collectively— as major economic, political and social forces in our society. Of rather minor consequence thirty or forty years ago, the NFP sector now generates over *one-third* of all expenditures within our economy, and many "growth industries" may be found within it. The total value of resources devoted to this sector is gigantic, both absolutely and relatively.

Governments have experienced particularly dynamic growth both in the scope and in the magnitude of their activities. Despite some efforts to curb the growth of governments in our society, over 15,000,000 people work in government positions—about 20 percent of the employed civilian labor force—and total and per capita expenditures and debt of governments have increased dramatically in recent years.

Sound financial management—including thoughtful budgeting, appropriate accounting, meaningful financial reporting, and timely audits by qualified auditors—is at least as important in the not-for-profit sector as in the private sector. Furthermore, because of the scope and diversity of its activities, proper management of the financial affairs of a city or town, for example, may be far more complex than that of a private business with comparable assets or annual expenditures.

The NFP Environment

Not-for-profit organizations are in many ways similar to profit-seeking enterprises. For example:

1. They are integral parts of the same economic system and utilize similar resources in accomplishing their purposes.
2. Both must acquire and convert scarce resources into their respective goods or services.
3. Financial management processes are essentially similar in both and each must have a viable information system—of which the accounting system is an integral component—if its managers and other interested persons or groups are to receive relevant and timely data for planning, directing, controlling, and evaluating the use of its scarce resources.
4. Inasmuch as their resources are relatively scarce—whether donated, received from consumers, acquired from investors or creditors, or secured through taxation—least-cost analysis and other control and evaluation techniques are essential to assuring that resources are utilized economically, effectively, and efficiently.
5. In some cases, both produce similar products, e.g., both governments and private enterprise may own and operate transportation systems, sanitation services, and electric or gas utilities.

There are also significant differences between profit-seeking and not-for-profit organizations. Although there are many types of NFP organizations and broad generalizations about such a diversified group are difficult, the major differences may be classified for discussion purposes as arising from differing organizational objectives, sources of resources, and regulation and control.

Organizational Objectives. Expectation of income or gain is the principal factor motivating investors to provide resources to profit-seeking enterprises. On the other hand, a not-for-profit organization exists to provide certain goods or services to a community or society as a whole, often without reference to whether costs incurred are recouped through charges levied on those receiving them and without regard to whether those receiving the goods or services are those paying for them. There is no profit motive; there are no individual shareholders to whom dividends are paid.

The objective of most not-for-profit organizations is to provide as many goods or as much service each year as their financial and other resources permit. NFP organizations typically operate on a year-to-year basis, raising such resources as they can and expending them in serving their clientele. They may seek to increase the amount of resources made available to them each year—and most do—but this is to enable the organization to provide more or better goods and services, not to increase its wealth. In sum, whereas private businesses seek to increase their wealth for the benefit of their owners, NFP organizations seek to expend their available financial resources for the benefit of their clientele. Financial management in the NFP environment thus typically focuses on acquiring and using financial resources—upon sources and uses of working capital, budget status, and cash flow—rather than on net income or earnings per share.

Sources of Financial Resources. The sources of financial resources differ between business and not-for-profit organizations, as well as among not-for-profit organizations. And, in the absence of a net income determination emphasis, no distinction is generally made between invested capital and revenue. A dollar is a resource whether acquired through donation, user charge, sale of assets, loan, or in some other manner.

Governments have the unique power to force involuntary financial resource contributions through taxation—of property, sales, income, etc.—and all levels rely heavily upon this power. Grants and shared revenue from other governments also are important state and local government revenue sources—those from the Federal government exceed $80 billion per year—as are charges levied for goods or services provided, such as those of utilities.

Other not-for-profit organizations also derive financial resources from a variety of sources. Religious groups and charitable organizations usually rely heavily on donations, though they may have other revenue sources. Some colleges and universities rely heavily upon donations and income from trust funds; others depend primarily upon state appropriations and/or tuition charges for support. Finally, hospitals generally charge their clientele, though few select their patients on the basis of ability to pay and many rely heavily upon gifts and bequests.

There are other, more subtle, differences in sources of not-for-profit organization financial resources as compared with profit-seeking businesses. For example:

- User charges, where levied, usually are based on the cost of the goods or services rendered rather than upon supply-and-demand-related pricing policies common to private enterprise.
- Many services or goods provided by these organizations are monopolistic in nature and there is no open market in which their value may be objectively appraised or evaluated.
- Charges levied for goods or services often cover only part of the costs incurred to provide them; e.g., tuition generally covers only a fraction of the cost of operating state colleges or universities, and token charges (or no charges) may be made to a hospital's indigent patients.

Regulation and Control. The goods or services offered the consuming public by unregulated profit-seeking enterprises will be modified or withdrawn if they are not profitable. The direct relationship between the producer and the consumer allows every consumer to cast his dollar vote for that firm providing the goods or services most suitable to him. In this situation a firm whose management is inept or unresponsive to the desires of the consuming public will be unprofitable and will ultimately be forced out of business. Therefore, the profit motive and profit measurement constitute an automatic regulating device in our free enterprise economy.

This profit test/regulator device is not present in the usual not-for-profit situation, and most NFP organizations must strive to attain their objectives without its benefits. In addition, as noted earlier, many not-for-profit organizations provide goods or services having no open market value measurement by which to test consumer satisfaction because (1) the goods and services are unique or (2) the consumers are receiving "free" (to them) goods or services for which the community or society as a whole is paying, i.e., the consumers have no "dollar vote" to cast.

Unless alternative controls are employed, (1) the absence of the need to operate profitably, (2) the lack of an open market test of the value of the organization's output, (3) the remote and indirect relationship, if any, between the resource contributor and the goods or services recipient, and (4) in the case of governments, the ability to force resource contributions via taxation, might make it possible for an inefficient, uneconomical, or even ineffective not-for-profit organization to continue operating indefinitely. Not-for-profit organizations, particularly governments, are therefore subject to more stringent legal, regulatory, and other controls than are private businesses.

All facets of a NFP organization's operations may be affected by legal or quasi-legal requirements (1) imposed externally, as by Federal or state statute, ruling, grant stipulation, or judicial decree, or (2) imposed internally by charter, bylaw, ordinance, trust agreement, donor stipulation, or contract. Furthermore, operational and administrative controls may be more stringent than in private enterprise because of the need to assure compliance with legal and other requirements. Among the aspects of a NFP organization's operations that may be regulated or otherwise controlled are:

1. *Organization structure:* form; composition of its directing board or similar body; the number and duties of its personnel; lines of authority and responsibility; which officials or employees are to be elected, appointed, or hired from among applicants.

2. *Personnel policies and procedures:* who will appoint or hire personnel; tenure of personnel; policies and procedures upon termination; extent of minority group representation on the staff; levels of compensation; promotion policies; and types and amounts of compensation increments permissible.

3. *Sources of resources:* the types and maximum amounts of taxes, licenses, fines, or fees a government may levy; the manner in which user charges are to be set; tuition rates; debt limits; the purposes for which debt may be incurred.

4. *Use of resources:* the purpose for which resources may be used, including "earmarking" of certain resources for use only for specific purposes; purchasing procedures to be followed; budgeting methods, forms, or procedures to be used.

5. *Accounting:* any or all phases of the accounting system, e.g., chart of accounts, bases of accounting, forms, procedures.

6. *Reporting:* type and frequency of reports; report format and content; to whom reports are to be furnished.

7. *Auditing:* frequency of audit; who is to perform the audit; the scope and type of audit to be performed; the time and place for filing the

audit report; who is to receive or have access to the audit report; the wording of the auditor's report.

Thus, managers of NFP organizations may have limited discretion compared with managers of business enterprises. For example, it may be difficult to (1) modify an organization's structure, no matter how archaic, awkward, or ineffective; (2) attract qualified employees at prescribed pay rates, discharge or demote incompetent employees, or reward outstanding employees; (3) acquire sufficient resources or use available resources as management deems most appropriate; or (4) improve the existing budgeting, accounting, reporting, or auditing arrangements. The role and emphasis of financial accounting and reporting may be correspondingly altered, therefore, as compared with the profit-seeking enterprise environment.

OBJECTIVES OF NFP ACCOUNTING AND FINANCIAL REPORTING

According to a major committee of the American Accounting Association, the objectives of accounting are to provide information for:

1. Making decisions concerning the use of limited resources, including the identification of crucial decision areas and determination of objectives and goals.
2. Effectively directing and controlling an organization's human and material resources.
3. Maintaining and reporting on the custodianship of resources.
4. Contributing to the effectiveness of all organizations, whether profit-oriented or not, in fulfilling the desires and demands of all society for social control of their functions.[1]

As part of its "conceptual framework" project, the Financial Accounting Standards Board (FASB) issued *Statement of Financial Accounting Concepts No. 4* (SFAC 4), "Objectives of Financial Reporting by Nonbusiness Organizations" in December 1980. The FASB emphasized that SFAC 4 applies to general purpose external financial reporting, not to accounting per se, and that:

— The objectives stem primarily from the needs of external users who generally cannot prescribe the information they want from an organization.
— In addition to information provided by general purpose external financial reporting, managers and, to some extent, governing bodies need a great deal of internal accounting information to carry out their responsibilities in planning and controlling activities. That information and information directed at meeting the specialized needs of users having the power to obtain the information they need are beyond the scope of this Statement.[2]

---

[1] American Accounting Association, Committee to Prepare a Statement of Basic Accounting Theory, *A Statement of Basic Accounting Theory* (Evanston, Ill.: AAA, 1966), p. 4.

[2] Financial Accounting Standards Board, *Statement of Financial Accounting Concepts No. 4*, "Objectives of Financial Reporting by Nonbusiness Organizations." (Stamford, CT: The FASB, December, 1980), p. xii. (Hereafter cited "SFAC 4.")

The financial reporting objectives set forth in SFAC 4 state that:

— Financial reporting by nonbusiness organizations should provide information that is useful to present and potential resource providers and other users in making rational decisions about the allocation of resources to those organizations.
— Financial reporting should provide information to help present and potential resource providers and other users in assessing the services that a nonbusiness organization provides and its ability to continue to provide those services.
— Financial reporting should provide information that is useful to present and potential resource providers and other users in assessing how managers of a nonbusiness organization have discharged their stewardship responsibilities and about other aspects of their performance.
— Financial reporting should provide information about the economic resources, obligations, and net resources of an organization, and the effects of transactions, events, and circumstances that change resources and interests in those resources.
— Financial reporting should provide information about the performance of an organization during a period. Periodic measurement of the changes in the amount and nature of the net resources of a nonbusiness organization and information about the service efforts and accomplishments of an organization together represent the information most useful in assessing its performance.
— Financial reporting should provide information about how an organization obtains and spends cash or other liquid resources, about its borrowing and repayment of borrowing, and about other factors that may affect an organization's liquidity.
— Financial reporting should include explanations and interpretations to help users understand financial information provided.[3]

CHARACTERISTICS OF NFP ACCOUNTING

There are many similarities in the accounting for profit-seeking and not-for profit organizations. A double-entry system of accounts is recommended for both. The general mechanics of record keeping are the same: documents form the basic record, books of original entry (journals) are kept and posted to general ledgers and subsidiary ledgers, trial balances are drawn to prove the equality of debits and credits, a chart of accounts properly classified and properly fitted to the organization's structure is essential to good accounting, and, of course, uniform terminology is highly desirable in both fields.

Some NFP organization activities (such as utilities, public transportation, and parking facilities) parallel those of some profit-seeking enterprises. In such cases the accounting parallels that of their privately owned counterparts. In most of their operations, however, governments and other not-for-profit institutions are not concerned with profit measurement. (In even the cited activities the NFP organization may not seek to maximize profits, but only to assure continuity and/or improvement of service.)

[3] SFAC 4, pp. XIII-XIV.

Accounting is a service function and must evolve to meet the information demands in a given environment. In the NFP environment decisions concerning resource acquisition and allocation, managerial direction and control of resource utilization, and custodianship for resources have traditionally been framed in terms of social and political objectives and constraints rather than profitability. Legal and administrative constraints have been used as society's methods of directing its NFP institutions in achieving those objectives. Thus, NFP organization accounting and reporting have correspondingly evolved with a distinctive emphasis on control of and accountability for expendable resources. The two most important types of legal and administrative control provisions affecting accounting in this environment are (1) the use of funds and (2) the distinctive role of the budget.

Funds and Fund Accounting

It has been observed that the resources made available to a not-for-profit organization may be restricted; i.e., their use may be limited to specified purposes or activities. For example, a church may receive donations for a building addition; a hospital may receive a grant for adding an intensive care facility; a city may borrow money to construct a sewage treatment plant or may receive state gasoline tax "shared revenues" that are earmarked for local road improvement; a university may receive a Federal grant for research purposes or may be the custodian of resources to be used only for making student loans. All such *external* restrictions carry significant accountability obligations. Management also may "designate" specific purposes for which certain resources must be used; e.g., they may wish to accumulate resources for equipment replacement or facility enlargement. Since management designations are *internal* restrictions and may be changed by management, they carry only internal accountability requirements. In any event, using the resources in accordance with stipulations inherent in their receipt and reporting on this compliance to others is an essential custodianship obligation.

Not-for-profit organizations establish funds to control earmarked resources and both ensure and demonstrate compliance with legal or administrative requirements. In the early days of fund accounting, "funds" meant "cash funds." Each might be housed in a separate cash drawer; some bills would be paid from one drawer and others from another drawer, in accordance with the use to which the cash in each could be put. Today, "funds" are separate fiscal and accounting entities, and noncash resources as well as related liabilities are accounted for therein. A fund is:

> a fiscal and accounting entity with a self-balancing set of accounts recording cash and other financial resources together with all related liabilities, and residual equities or balances and changes therein, which are segregated for the purpose of carrying on specific activities or attaining certain objectives in accordance with special regulations, restrictions, or limitations.[4]

[4] National Council on Governmental Accounting, *Statement 1*, "Governmental Accounting and Financial Reporting Principles" (Chicago: Municipal Finance Officers Association of the United States and Canada, 1979), pp. 5-6. Hereafter cited "NCGAS 1."

Two basic types of fund accounting entities are used by NFP organizations:

1. *Expendable (governmental) funds:* to account for the current assets, related liabilities, changes in net assets, and balances that may be expended in its not-for-profit activities (e.g., for fire and police protection).

2. *Nonexpendable (proprietary) funds:* to account for the revenues, expenses, assets, liabilities, and equity of its "business-type" activities (e.g., utilities, cafeterias, or transportation systems) and some trust funds.

The fund concept involves an accounting segregation, not necessarily the physical separation of resources; however, resources are often also physically segregated—for example, through use of separate checking accounts for cash resources of various funds.

Use of the term "fund" in not-for-profit situations should be sharply distinguished from its use in private enterprise. A fund of a commercial enterprise is simply a portion of its assets that has been restricted to specific uses, not a separate and distinct accounting entity. Revenue and expense related to such funds are part of enterprise operations; i.e., fund revenue and expense accounts appear side by side in the general ledger with other enterprise revenue and expense accounts. On the other hand, a fund in the not-for-profit sense is a self-contained accounting entity with its own asset, liability, revenue, expenditure or expense, and fund balance or other equity accounts—and with its own ledger(s) (see Figure 1-1).

Figure 1-1

SINGLE ENTITY VERSUS MULTIPLE ENTITY ACCOUNTING

SINGLE ENTITY
(PROFIT-SEEKING ENTERPRISE)

MULTIPLE ENTITY
(NOT-FOR-PROFIT ORGANIZATION)

A = L + NW

FUND 1
A = L + FB

FUND 2
A = L + FB

FUND 3
A = L + FB

FUND 4
A = L + FB

FUND 5
A = L + FB

FUND n
A = L + FB

FIXED ASSETS
(Original Cost)

LONG-TERM DEBT
(Principal Owed)

Legend:

A = Assets
L = Liabilities
NW = Net Worth (of the enterprise)
FB = Fund Balance (of the individual fund)
— — — = The not-for-profit organization as a whole — for which statements are generally not prepared

Although experts agree that the fund device is essential to sound financial management of not-for-profit organizations, its use has an unfortunate fragmenting effect upon their accounting and reporting. The statements of a profit-seeking enterprise present in one place the information regarding that enterprise. It is possible, by looking at its balance sheet, to determine the nature and valuation of its assets, liabilities, and net worth. The nature and amounts of the components of change in net worth occasioned by enterprise operations are presented in its periodic operating statements.

The financial reports of most not-for-profit organizations, however, consist of a series of independent or combined (columnar) fund entity balance sheets and operating statements. Consolidated statements are not in widespread use in the not-for-profit sector.

Budgets and Appropriations

The creation of an expendable fund ordinarily does not carry with it the authority to expend its resources. In most not-for-profit organizations, expecially governments, expenditures may be made only within the authority of appropriations, which are authorizations to make expenditures for specified purposes.

A fixed-dollar budget is commonly prepared for each expendable fund. When approved by the directing board or enacted by the legislature, the budgetary expenditure estimates become binding appropriations—both authority to make expenditures and limits thereon. Appropriations must indicate the fund from which the expenditure may be made and specify the purposes, the maximum amount, and the period of time for which the expenditure authority is granted. A department or activity may be financed from several funds. In such cases at least one appropriation must be made from each supporting fund in order to provide the requisite expenditure authority.

In order to control and demonstrate expendable fund budgetary compliance, it is common for governments, in particular, to establish budgetary accounts within expendable fund ledgers. Through this technique, explained in detail subsequently, managers are able to determine their remaining expenditure authority at any time during the period. The technique of integrating budgetary accounts is particularly helpful in those cases where budget "overruns" subject officials to fine, imprisonment, impeachment, dismissal, or other punishment. Proprietary funds, on the other hand, are usually controlled by flexible budgets such as those used in businesses, and budgetary accounts are rarely needed.

Some Other Distinguishing Characteristics

As noted, the emphasis upon fund and budgetary controls causes the accounting for most not-for-profit organizations to more closely resemble cash flow or working capital change analysis than commercial accounting, in which net income determination is a paramount consideration. The focal point of most not-for-profit accounting and reporting is expendable resources, accounted for in expendable fund entities and allocated by the budget and appropriation process.

"Expenditures" are defined as "the cost of goods delivered or services rendered, whether paid or unpaid, including [current] expenses, provision for debt retirement not reported as a liability of the fund from which retired, and capital outlays."[5] Thus, the term "expenditures"—the term that is significant in expendable fund accounting—should not be confused with "expenses" as defined for accounting for profit-seeking enterprises.

Fixed assets normally are not appropriable resources and are commonly listed and accounted for separately from the expendable fund accounting entities. Similarly, long-term debt that is not a liability of a particular fund (but of the unit as a whole) may be listed in a separate nonfund accounting entity. Furthermore, since net income determination is not a consideration in most NFP organizations, (1) inventory valuation may receive only passing attention, and (2) depreciation of fixed assets usually is not accounted for, even though it is an expense, because it does not require the use of appropriable resources during the current period. Contrariwise, a fixed asset acquisition is considered an "expenditure" (use of current resources) in the period in which it occurs, as is the retirement of maturing long-term debt, since they reduce the net (current) assets of an expendable fund.

Summary Comparison with Commercial Accounting

Though commercial-type accounting is employed where NFP organizations are engaged in commercial-type activities (e.g., electric utilities), accounting and reporting for not-for-profit endeavors have evolved largely in view of these key differences from profit-seeking enterprises:

1. **Objectives:** acquiring resources and expending them in a legal and appropriate manner, as opposed to seeking to increase—or even maintain—its capital.
2. **Control:** substitution of statutory, fund, and budgetary controls in the absence of the profit regulator/control device inherent in profit-seeking endeavors.

These factors—objectives and control—underlie the major differences between commercial and not-for-profit accounting. The primary consideration in this environment is upon compliance—and accounting, reporting, and auditing have developed principally as tools of compliance control and demonstration.

The student should constantly take note of the similarities and differences between commercial and not-for-profit accounting in concept, approach, and terminology. He should be particularly cautious and observant in those cases where the same concepts and terms are used in both, but with different connotations. In not-for-profit accounting, for example:

1. The *entity* concept relates to the separate fund or fund type entities, not the organization as a whole; generally, there is no unified accounting or reporting entity for the organization in its entirety.

---

[5] National Committee on Governmental Accounting, *Governmental Accounting, Auditing, and Financial Reporting* (Chicago: The Municipal Finance Officers Association of the United States and Canada, 1968), p. 160.

2. The *periodicity* concept typically relates to the flow of funds during the budgetary period and to budgetary comparisons, rather than to income determination.

3. The *matching* concept as understood in commercial accounting is used similarly for commercial-type activities of NFP organizations. In all other cases reference is to matching revenue and expenditures—current operating, capital outlay, and debt retirement—and to matching estimated (budgeted) and actual revenues and expenditures. *Expendable fund accounting emphasizes the inflows, outflows, and balances of expendable resources rather than the determination of revenue, expense, and net income.*

4. The *going-concern* concept usually is considered relevant only when commercial type or self-supporting activities are involved in NFP organizations. Expendable resource funds exist on a year-by-year or project-by-project basis and may be intentionally exhausted and "go out of business." Little thought has been given to applying the going-concern concept to the NFP organization as a whole.

AUTHORITATIVE SOURCES OF NFP ACCOUNTING PRINCIPLES

NFP accounting and reporting principles (standards) have evolved separately from those for business enterprises and, to a large extent, separately for the several major types of NFP organizations. The American Hospital Association has fostered their development for hospitals, for example, and the National Association of College and University Business Officials has led in the development of those for colleges and universities. Similarly, the National Council on Governmental Accounting has led their formulation for state and local governments, and the U.S. General Accounting Office has been at the forefront at the Federal government level. In addition, each field has its own journals, newsletters, and professional societies.

The separation of business and NFP accounting principles was formalized in the 1930s when the first accounting standards-setting bodies were established in this country. The Securities Acts of 1933 and 1934 created the Securities and Exchange Commission (SEC), charged it with overseeing the financial reporting of business enterprises under its jurisdiction, and empowered the SEC to establish accounting and reporting standards for those business enterprises. The American Institute of Accountants (now the American Institute of Certified Public Accountants) then established a senior Committee on Accounting Procedure (CAP), the predecessor to the Institute's Accounting Principles Board and the Financial Accounting Standards Board. The CAP considered and made recommendations on business accounting and reporting issues, particularly those of concern to the SEC, and the SEC relied heavily on the CAP in determining what constituted generally accepted accounting principles for business enterprises. In view of its focus on business enterprise financial accounting and reporting, CAP pronouncements were accompanied by the following statement:

> The committee has not directed its attention to accounting problems or procedures of religious, charitable, scientific, educational and similar non-profit institutions, municipalities, professional firms, and the like. Accordingly . . . its opinions and recommendations are directed primarily to business enterprises organized for profit.[6]

Although the AIA directed the CAP to concentrate on business accounting and reporting, its leaders also recognized the need for nonbusiness accounting and reporting principles to be codified and further developed. Accordingly, the AIA encouraged the appropriate college and university, hospital, and municipal professional organizations to sponsor committees similar to the CAP to focus on accounting and reporting concerns of those types of NFP organizations. Thus, several separate NFP accounting standards-setting bodies were established, each charged with responsibility for a specific subset of the NFP sector. They have provided leadership in the development of NFP accounting and reporting principles since the 1930s, through many changes in names, sponsorship, structure, and roles.

The AICPA's Accounting Principles Board (APB), which succeeded the CAP in 1959, similarly focused its attention on business enterprises. Only one of its pronouncements (*Opinion 18*, "Disclosure of Accounting Policies") was specifically directed to not-for-profit as well as to for-profit organizations.

Several AICPA auditing committees studied the pronouncements of the various NFP accounting standards bodies in depth in the course of preparing a series of audit guides during the late 1960s and early 1970s. Each of these audit guides—for state and local government, college and university, hospital, and voluntary health and welfare organization audits—recognized the principles set by the several NFP standards-setting bodies as "authoritative." But in several instances AICPA audit guides took exception to certain NFP principles or stated that alternative methods were also acceptable. As might be expected, these conflicting views of the several NFP standards bodies and the several AICPA auditing committees proved disconcerting to practitioners. All substantive differences between the AICPA committees and the various NFP standards setting bodies were resolved by the late 1970s, however, and the various standards pronouncements and audit guides were amended accordingly.

The AICPA audit guides were of immense significance to the NFP standards-setting process. Whereas the several NFP standards bodies had functioned independently of the AICPA for forty years, now NFP accounting standards were in essence being established jointly by concurrence of the respective NFP standards bodies and their counterpart AICPA committees. Further, the AICPA issued a Statement of Position in 1978 (SOP 78-10) setting forth its views with respect to what constituted generally accepted accounting principles and reporting practices for those types of NFP organizations which did not have separate standards-setting bodies and audit guides.

[6] American Institute of Certified Public Accountants, *Accounting Research and Terminology Bulletins*, final ed. (New York: AICPA, 1961), p. 8.

The Financial Accounting Standards Board (FASB), which succeeded the APB in 1973, is quite different from the APB and CAP. The FASB is financed and overseen by a multisponsored Financial Accounting Foundation rather than by the AICPA, for example, and its seven members serve full time, whereas APB and CAP members served only part time. The FASB is not limited by its charter or rules of procedure to business accounting standards setting, but is also authorized to establish NFP accounting and reporting standards. The accounting and auditing profession recognizes the FASB as the most authoritative standards-setting body in the United States and Rule 203 of the AICPA Code of Professional Conduct requires compliance with FASB pronouncements in virtually all circumstances.

The Board devoted its efforts exclusively to business accounting concepts and standards during its first several years in operation, and deferred the decision on what role, if any, it would play in the NFP standards area. In 1977, the FASB commissioned Professor Robert N. Anthony of Harvard University to conduct impartial research on the objectives and basic concepts of nonbusiness organization financial accounting and reporting. The Anthony study was published as an FASB Research Report in 1978, and the Board promptly added an "Objectives of Nonbusiness Organization Financial Reporting" project to its agenda. After issuing a discussion memorandum based on the Anthony Report and holding a series of public hearings, the FASB decided in early 1979 to issue one or more statements of financial accounting *concepts*—such as SFAC 4 discussed earlier—but continued to defer the assumption of responsibility for NFP accounting and reporting *standards*.

Later, in 1979, the Board agreed to exercise responsibility for all specialized accounting and reporting principles and practices set forth in AICPA statements of position, accounting guides, and audit guides *except those dealing with state and local governments (Statement of Financial Accounting Standards No. 32)*. The FASB designated the principles and practices described in the AICPA pronouncements—including those related to colleges and universities, hospitals, voluntary health and welfare organizations, and other nonprofit organizations—as "preferable," and noted that it planned to extract them and, after due process, issue them as FASB statements. Thereafter, the Board would assume responsibility for amending and interpreting such standards in the future. The effect of the FASB's "specialized industry" action was to change the roles of the AICPA and the various bodies that previously had set standards for NFP organizations (other than state and local governments) from standards setting to serving in an advisory capacity to the FASB standards-setting process.

The Board deferred action with respect to state and local government standards in view of discussions under way with interested parties, including the National Council on Governmental Accounting and the AICPA, regarding the appropriate standards-setting structure for such governmental units. At issue was whether state and local government accounting standards should continue to be established by the National Council on Governmental Accounting (NCGA) or should be set by the FASB, a separate Governmental Accounting Standards Board (GASB) modeled after the FASB, a modified NCGA, or some other body. These discussions led to formation of an ad hoc Governmental Accounting Standards

Board Organizing Committee (GASBOC), which issued a tentative report exposure draft, held public hearings, and issued its final report in 1981.

Further discussion led to the final GASBOC report recommending that a new Governmental Accounting Standards Board (GASB) be established under the auspices of the Financial Accounting Foundation (FAF) which finances and oversees the FASB. As discussed further in Chapter 15, the FAF agreed to establish and oversee the new GASB, to succeed the National Council on Governmental Accounting as the authoritative standards setting body for state and local government accounting and financial reporting in 1983.

NCGA *Statement 1*, "Governmental Accounting and Financial Reporting Principles,"[7] issued in 1979, has been recognized as authoritative by the AICPA *(Statement of Position 80-2)*, as has NCGA *Statement 2*, and both are accepted in practice. Further, the NCGA-GASB transition agreement specifies that all NCGA Statements and Interpretations remain in effect until modified by the GASB.

Although the FASB issued a statement of financial accounting concepts on "Objectives of Financial Reporting by Nonbusiness Organizations" in 1980, and some of its recent statements apply to both business and nonbusiness organizations, the FASB has not yet had a major impact on NFP accounting and reporting standards. Thus, there continue to be several sources of authoritative pronouncements concerning NFP accounting and financial reporting. This text is based on the most authoritative pronouncements relevant to each of the several types of NFP organizations discussed. Sources of authoritative support are cited as appropriate throughout the text.

▶ **Question 1-1.** What characteristics differentiate not-for-profit organizations from profit-seeking organizations?

Question 1-2. How does society determine which goods or services will be provided by not-for-profit organizations?

Question 1-3. List four factors that cause society to subject NFP organizations to more stringent legal, regulatory, and other controls than it imposes on private businesses.

Question 1-4. Define "fund" as used in not-for-profit organizations. Contrast that definition with the same term as used in a profit-seeking organization.

Question 1-5. Distinguish between "expendable" funds and "nonexpendable" funds.

Question 1-6. Discuss the funds-flow concept as it applies to the operations of not-for-profit organizations.

Question 1-7. Contrast the terms "expense" and "expenditure."

Question 1-8. Contrast the following concepts as they are used in commercial and fund accounting: (a) entity; (b) periodicity; (c) matching; and (d) going concern.

Question 1-9. Some accountants feel that supplementary consolidated statements should be prepared for not-for-profit organizations in which activities are financed through numerous funds. Assess the merits of this suggestion.

[7] NCGAS 1.

Question 1-10. Does the creation of a fund constitute authority to spend or obligate its resouces? Explain.

Question 1-11. It was noted in this chapter that most of the differences between commercial accounting and that for not-for-profit organizations result from differences in (1) organizational objectives and (2) methods of fiscal control employed. Explain.

Question 1-12. Which professional association or other agency or group has played the major role in the development of accounting and reporting practices of (a) municipalities? (b) hospitals? (c) the Federal government? (d) colleges and universities?

Question 1-13. What types of problems might arise from accounting and reporting for an organization such as a municipal government as a set of several entities instead of as a single entity?

Question 1-14. Discuss the roles of the AICPA and the FASB in standards setting for NFP organizations.

Question 1-15. Legal and administrative constraints are society's tools for directing NFP institutions in achieving their objectives. This results in a control-of and accountability-for expendable resources emphasis in NFP organization accounting and reporting rather than an income determination emphasis. Explain why the profitability measure cannot provide this direction and identify various legal and administrative control provisions unique to NFP organizations and their impact on accounting and reporting for such organizations.

Question 1-16. Discuss (a) the similarities in accounting for profit-seeking and NFP organizations, and (b) the unique aspects of accounting for NFP organizations designed to help assure compliance with budgeted spending limits.

Question 1-17. The revenues of profit-seeking organizations are based on user charges. Users may be charged for various services provided by NFP organizations as well. However, differences often exist in the nature and purpose of user charges of NFP organizations and those of profit-seeking organizations. Explain.

PART I

STATE AND LOCAL GOVERNMENT ACCOUNTING AND REPORTING

2

STATE AND LOCAL GOVERNMENT ACCOUNTING PRINCIPLES

State and local government is truly "big business." The fifty states and over 79,000 local governments within these United States employ over 13 million persons—well over four times as many as are employed by the Federal government—and spend over $300 billion annually. Although the Federal government accounts for over half of all government expenditures, state and local governments spend substantially more than the Federal government for nondefense purposes. Furthermore, state and local government revenue, expenditures, debt, and employment—both in total and per capita—have been increasing at higher rates than those of the Federal complex in recent years. Today it is common to find that the state government is the largest industry within a state or that city hall houses the biggest business in a town.

Figure 2-1

TYPES OF LOCAL GOVERNMENTS: 1977

Counties	3,042
Municipalities	18,862
Townships	16,822
School districts	15,174
Special districts	25,962
Total	79,862

Source: 1977 Census of Governments, Governmental Organization, Vol. 1, p. 1.

The types and numbers of local governments are shown in Figure 2-1. Not obvious from this table, however, is the extent of local government jurisdictional overlap. It is common for a given geographical area to be served by a municipality, a school district, a county, and one or more special districts. In fact, many metropolitan areas have 100 or more separate and distinct local government units. This overlap, which frequently results in jurisdictional disputes and administrative complexities, is illustrated in Figure 2-2.

State and local governments have increased both the types and levels of goods and services provided their citizens in recent years and many have become among the most complex and diversified organizations in existence. No doubt the scope and diversity of their activities, the financial management and accounting

Figure 2-2

LAYERS OF GOVERNMENT, FRIDLEY, MINNESOTA

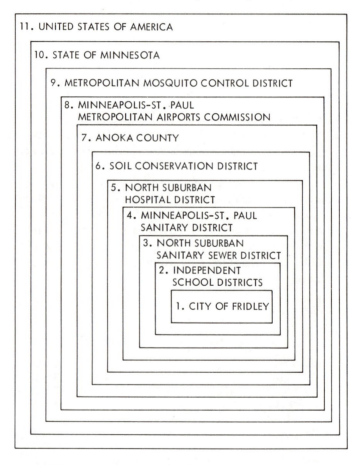

Believe it or not: A citizen of Fridley, Minnesota, is expected to exercise informed control, through the electoral franchise, over eleven separate superimposed governments, and is taxed for their support.

Source: Adapted from Committee for Economic Development, Modernizing Local Government (New York: CED, 1967), p. 12.

complexities involved, their total and per capita expenditures, and their relative importance in our economy and society will continue to grow as our society becomes increasingly urban and governments at all levels attempt to meet the demands of their constituencies for more and better goods and services.

EVOLUTION OF ACCOUNTING PRINCIPLES

Although the origin of the profession of accountancy is sometimes traced to ancient governments, modern municipal accounting is a development of the twentieth century—its beginning inseparably woven within the municipal reform movement which peaked near the turn of the century. About that time attention was focused on scandalous practices in the financial administration of many cities, the National Municipal League suggested uniform municipal reporting formats, and the Census Bureau was working toward building interest in obtaining uniformity in city accounts and reports.

A flurry of change in accounting and reporting practices occurred during this first decade. In 1901 the firm of Haskins and Sells, Certified Public Accountants, made an investigation into the affairs of the City of Chicago at the request of the Merchants' Club, and subsequently installed a completely new system of accounting for that city. The cities of Newton, Massachusetts, and Baltimore, Maryland, published annual reports during 1901 and 1902 along lines suggested by the National Municipal League, and the States of New York and Massachusetts passed legislation in the areas of uniform accounting and reporting in 1904 and 1906, respectively. There were many other examples of progress during this period as other cities and states followed suit.

During this era Herman A. Metz was elected Comptroller of the City of New York on a "business man for the head of the city's business office" slogan. When Metz assumed office it was estimated that one-fourth of New York's $80 million personal services budget was being lost through collusion, idleness, or inefficiency; and city departments commonly issued bonds to finance current operating expenditures.

Although his work as New York City's comptroller was said to have been outstanding, Metz's most important contribution was the formation of the Bureau of Municipal Research. One of its purposes was "to promote the adoption of scientific methods of accounting [for] and of reporting the details of municipal business. . . ."[1]

The *Handbook of Municipal Accounting*, commonly referred to as "The Metz Fund Handbook," was called "the most significant contribution of the 1910 decade . . . [because] it brought together for the first time many of the basic characteristics and requirements of municipal accounting and outlined methods of appropriate treatment."[2] Similarly, the Bureau's publications were referred to

[1] Bureau of Municipal Research, *Making a Municipal Budget: Functional Accounts and Operative Statistics for the Department of Greater New York* (New York: BMR, 1907), p. 5.
[2] Lloyd Morey, "Trends in Governmental Accounting," *Accounting Review*, 23 (July 1948), p. 224.

as the "first organized materials that could be called a treatise in Municipal Accounting."[3]

As others became more interested in the subject, pamphlets, articles, and a few textbooks appeared. Municipal leagues were formed in various states and, as Newton expressed it, "we soon began a very serious development of the specialized field of Municipal Accounting."[4]

Although some work continued, interest waned during the 1920s and early 1930s. In a study of Illinois cities during 1931 and 1932, W. E. Karrenbrock found that few had accounting systems adequate to segregate transactions of different activities and none had budgetary accounts coordinated within the regular accounting system.[5]

Writing in 1933, R. P. Hackett observed that:

> The first fact that we are confronted with when searching for recent developments, or any developments, in governmental accounting, particularly that of municipal governments, is the marked absence of any general improvement. . . . it must be admitted that there is very little development in the actual practice of governmental and institutional accounting.[6]

The National Committee on Municipal Accounting was organized in 1934 under the auspices of the Municipal Finance Officers Association of the United States and Canada in order to bring together representatives of various groups concerned with municipal accounting and to put into effect sound principles of accounting, budgeting, and reporting. Its membership included representatives of the American Association of University Instructors in Accounting; the American Institute of Accountants; the American Municipal Association; the American Society of Certified Public Accountants; the International City Managers' Association; the Municipal Finance Officers' Association; the National Association of Cost Accountants; the National Association of State Auditors, Controllers, and Treasurers; the National Municipal League; and the Bureau of the Census.[7] Each group represented also had a subcommittee on municipal or governmental accounting within its own ranks.

At its organizational meeting the Committee tentatively adopted certain principles as a guide to its activities and set out a fourteen point program of municipal accounting research. The Committee's formation was hailed as "the first effort on a national scale to establish principles and standards for municipal accounting and actively promote their use."[8] No doubt it was the major event in municipal accounting until that time; and the Committee's principles were offi-

---

[3] W. K. Newton, "New Developments and Simplified Approaches to Municipal Accounting," *Accounting Review*, 29 (October 1954), p. 656.

[4] Ibid.

[5] R. P. Hackett, "Recent Developments in Governmental and Institutional Accounting," *Accounting Review*, 8 (June 1933), p. 122.

[6] Ibid., pp. 122, 127.

[7] Carl H. Chatters, "Municipal Accounting Progresses," *Certified Public Accountant*, 14 (February, 1934), p. 101.

[8] Ibid.

cially recognized by the American Institute of Accountants, predecessor of the American Institute of Certified Public Accountants.[9]

Numerous publications defining proper or improved municipal accounting and financial administration practice have come from the Committee and the Municipal Finance Officers Association (MFOA) since 1934. In 1948, Morey stated:

> There is no longer any doubt as to what constitutes good accounting, reporting, and auditing for public bodies. The work of the National Committee on Municipal Accounting in particular, in establishing standards and models in these subjects, provides an authority to which officials, accountants, and public may turn with confidence.[10]

In 1951, the Committee, by then known as the National Committee on Governmental Accounting (NCGA), issued *Municipal Accounting and Auditing*. This book combined and revised the major publications of the Committee and became the basis for the major textbooks in the area as well as for many state laws and guides relating to municipal accounting, auditing, and reporting. This "Bible of municipal accounting," as it came to be called, was succeeded in 1968 by *Governmental Accounting, Auditing, and Financial Reporting* (GAAFR),[11] often referred to as "the blue book."

In 1974, the AICPA issued an audit guide, *Audits of State and Local Governmental Units*[12] (ASLGU), to assist its members in the conduct of governmental audits. ASLGU recognized GAAFR as authoritative and stated that, except as modified in ASLGU, the principles in GAAFR constituted generally accepted accounting principles.

The National Committee on Governmental Accounting was not a staff-supported, permanent body that met regularly. Rather, a new NCGA was formed of appointees of various government agencies, public administration groups, and accounting organizations whenever deemed necessary—historically about every ten years—and served in an advisory and review capacity with respect to revisions proposed by its consultants.

Recognizing the need for an ongoing body to reconcile the differences between GAAFR and ASLGU and continually evaluate and develop state and local government accounting principles, the MFOA established the National *Council* on Governmental Accounting (NCGA) in 1974. The Council consisted of 21 members who served four-year terms on a part-time voluntary basis, meeting for two days two to four times annually.

[9] American Institute of Accountants, *Audits of Governmental Bodies* and *Accounts of Governmental Bodies* (New York: AIA, 1934 and 1935).

[10] Morey, op. cit., p. 231.

[11] Published by the Municipal Finance Officers Association of the United States and Canada, 180 North Michigan Avenue, Chicago, Illinois 60601. © Municipal Finance Officers Association, Chicago, 1968. Hereafter cited as GAAFR (68).

[12] Committee on Governmental Accounting and Auditing, American Institute of Certified Public Accountants, *Audits of State and Local Governmental Units* (New York: AICPA, 1974). Hereafter cited as ASLGU.

Its 1982 membership included:

3	State finance officers.
7	Local government finance officers.
3	Practicing CPAs.
2	Educators.
1	Canadian finance officer.
1	City chief executive.
2	At large.
2	Federal government financial executives.
21	

The NCGA was assisted by a 28-member Committee of Advisors—one appointed by each of various U.S. and Canadian accounting and public administration associations and national government agencies. The NCGA maintained close liaison with the FASB, AICPA, and other organizations concerned with state and local government accounting and financial reporting standards.

The NCGA's charge was to:

> develop, promulgate, and interpret principles of accounting, financial reporting, and related financial activities for governments in the United States and Canada [and to] develop and promulgate appropriate methods, practices, and procedures for the effective implementation of such principles.[13]

In keeping with this charge, the NCGA undertook what it termed the GAAFR Restatement Project, the objective of which it described as "a modest revision to update, clarify, amplify, and reorder GAAFR in order to provide immediate guidance for governmental accounting and financial reporting." An important related objective was to incorporate pertinent aspects of ASLGU and reconcile any significant differences between GAAFR and ASLGU.

In 1976, as the NCGA proceeded with the GAAFR Restatement Project, it issued its first pronouncement, *Interpretation 1*, "GAAFR and the AICPA Audit Guide."[14] *Interpretation 1* stated, in essence, that the NCGA:

- Endorsed the GAAFR (68) principles until such time as it might modify them.
- Agreed that certain ASLGU modifications were valid clarifications or improvements of GAAFR (68) and endorsed those modifications.
- Pending resolution of other GAAFR–ASLGU differences in the course of the GAAFR Restatement Project, recognized as acceptable options the different approaches recommended in GAAFR (68) and ASLGU. State and local government financial statements should disclose which alternative method was used.

In keeping with "due process" procedures set forth in its rules of procedure, the NCGA issued a GAAFR Restatement Principles working draft for comment

---

[13] National Council on Governmental Accounting, *Rules of Procedure* (Chicago: Municipal Finance Officers Association, 1975), p. 2.

[14] National Council on Governmental Accounting, *Interpretation 1*, "GAAFR and the AICPA Audit Guide" (Chicago: Municipal Finance Officers Association, April 1, 1976).

in 1977 and an exposure draft in 1978. NCGA *Statement 1*, "Governmental Accounting and Financial Reporting Principles," commonly known as the GAAFR Restatement Principles, was issued in 1979. The NCGA had worked closely with the AICPA State and Local Government Accounting Committee during the principles restatement and, as planned, the two groups had reconciled the GAAFR–ASLGU differences. Accordingly, the AICPA issued a statement of position in 1980 (SOP 80-2)[15] amending ASLGU to incorporate NCGA *Statement 1* by reference and provide additional guidance to auditors of state and local government financial statements.

The NCGA issued the following pronouncements during 1974-82:

INTERPRETATION 1,	"GAAFR AND THE AICPA AUDIT GUIDE," APRIL 1, 1976.
STATEMENT 1,	"GOVERNMENTAL ACCOUNTING AND FINANCIAL REPORTING PRINCIPLES," WHICH RESTATED AND SUPERSEDED THE PRINCIPLES IN GAAFR68, MARCH 1979.
STATEMENT 2,	"GRANT, ENTITLEMENT, AND SHARED REVENUE ACCOUNTING AND REPORTING BY STATE AND LOCAL GOVERNMENTS," MARCH 1979.
INTERPRETATION 2,	"SEGMENT INFORMATION FOR ENTERPRISE FUNDS," JUNE 1980.
INTERPRETATION 3,	"REVENUE RECOGNITION — PROPERTY TAXES," JUNE 1981.
STATEMENT 3,	"DEFINING THE GOVERNMENTAL REPORTING ENTITY," DECEMBER 1981.
INTERPRETATION 4,	"ACCOUNTING AND FINANCIAL REPORTING FOR PUBLIC EMPLOYEE RETIREMENT SYSTEMS AND PENSION TRUST FUNDS," DECEMBER 1981. (EFFECTIVE DATE DEFERRED UNTIL YEARS BEGINNING AFTER JUNE 15, 1982 CONCURRENT WITH FASB DEFERRAL OF APPLICATION OF FASB *STATEMENT 35*, "ACCOUNTING AND REPORTING BY DEFINED BENEFIT PENSION PLANS," TO SLGS PER FASB *STATEMENT 59*, MARCH 1982.)
INTERPRETATION 5,	"AUTHORITATIVE STATUS OF GOVERNMENTAL ACCOUNTING, AUDITING, AND FINANCIAL REPORTING (1968)," MARCH 8, 1982.

[15] Audit Standards Division, American Institute of Certified Public Accountants, Inc., *Statement of Position 80-2*, "Accounting and Financial Reporting by Governmental Units" (New York: AICPA, June 30, 1980).

CONCEPTS

STATEMENT 1, "OBJECTIVES OF ACCOUNTING AND FI-
NANCIAL REPORTING FOR GOVERNMEN-
TAL UNITS," 1982

STATEMENT 4, "ACCOUNTING AND FINANCIAL REPORT-
ING FOR CLAIMS AND JUDGMENTS AND
COMPENSATED ABSENCES," MAY 1982.

INTERPRETATION 6, "NOTES TO THE FINANCIAL STATEMENTS
— DISCLOSURE," MAY 1982.

The AICPA issued five SLG-related Statements of Position during the same period:

SOP 75–3, "ACCRUAL OF REVENUES AND EXPENDITURES BY
STATE AND LOCAL GOVERNMENTAL UNITS,"
JULY 31, 1975

SOP 77-2, "ACCOUNTING FOR INTERFUND TRANSFERS OF
STATE AND LOCAL GOVERNMENTAL UNITS,"
SEPTEMBER 1, 1977

SOP 78-5, "ACCOUNTING FOR ADVANCE REFUNDINGS OF TAX-
EXEMPT DEBT," JUNE 30, 1978

SOP 78-7, "FINANCIAL ACCOUNTING AND REPORTING BY
HOSPITALS OPERATED BY A GOVERNMENTAL UNIT,"
JULY 31, 1978

SOP 80-2, "ACCOUNTING AND FINANCIAL REPORTING BY
GOVERNMENTAL UNITS," JUNE 30, 1980

SOPs 75-3, 77-2, 78-5, and 78-7 were incorporated in NCGA *Statement 1* directly or by reference, and SOP 80-2 amended the AICPA state and local government audit guide to recognize NCGA *Statement 1* as authoritative.

NCGA pronouncements, endorsed by the AICPA and accepted by the GASB, constitute the most authoritative and widely accepted statements of municipal accounting and reporting principles. Hence, the chapters of this text dealing with state and local government accounting and reporting are (unless otherwise noted) based upon and consistent with the recommendations of the National Council on Governmental Accounting and those recommendations of the predecessor national committee(s) still in effect.

The NCGA's *Concepts Statement 1*, "Objectives of Accounting and Financial Reporting for Governmental Units,"[16] was not intended to be authoritative or to establish standards but to guide future standards setting activities by the NCGA and/or GASB. Discussion of the NCGA "objectives" statement is deferred until Chapter 15 so that the objectives may be compared with contemporary governmental accounting and reporting concepts, principles, and procedures discussed in Chapters 2-14. The balance of this chapter is based on NCGA *Statement 1*.

---

[16] National Council on Governmental Accounting, *Concepts Statement 1*, "Objectives of Accounting and Financial Reporting for Governmental Units" (Chicago: NCGA, 1982). Hereafter cited as "NCGA Objectives."

The National Council on Governmental Accounting defined accounting principles as:

> specific fundamental tenets which, on the basis of reason, demonstrated performance, and general acceptance . . . are generally essential to effective management control and financial reporting.[17]

Its twelve principles may be conveniently divided into the following seven groups for ease of discussion: (1) Generally Accepted Accounting Principles and Legal Compliance, (2) Fund Accounting, (3) Fixed Assets and Long-Term Liabilities, (4) Basis of Accounting, (5) The Budget and Budgetary Accounting, (6) Classification and Terminology, and (7) Financial Reporting.

GAAP and Legal Compliance

Governments must comply with the many and varied legal and contractual requirements, regulations, restrictions, and agreements that affect their financial management and accounting; and such compliance must be demonstrable and reported upon regularly. Compliance is necessary even though legal requirements may be archaic, useless, or even detrimental to sound financial management. Governments should also prepare financial statements in conformity with generally accepted accounting principles (GAAP), which provide uniform minimum national standards of and guidelines to financial reporting.

The first NCGA principle recognizes that governmental accounting systems must provide data both for reporting in conformity with GAAP and for controlling and reporting on finance-related legal compliance matters.

ACCOUNTING AND REPORTING CAPABILITIES

1. A governmental accounting system must make it possible both: (a) to present fairly and with full disclosure the financial position and results of financial operations of the funds and account groups of the governmental unit in conformity with generally accepted accounting principles; and (b) to determine and demonstrate compliance with finance-related legal and contractual provisions.

In some instances the only finance-related legal compliance provision is that the government prepare financial statements in conformity with GAAP. In such cases legal compliance provisions and GAAP do not conflict, and the accounting system can be established on a GAAP basis.

In other instances certain finance-related legal provisions conflict with GAAP. The state may require cash-basis budgets and financial statements of its cities, for example, whereas GAAP requires use of the accrual and modified accrual bases of accounting. In these cases, the accounting system must provide

---

[17]National Council on Governmental Accounting, *Statement 1*, "Governmental Accounting and Financial Reporting Principles" (Chicago: Municipal Finance Officers Association, 1979), p. 2. Hereafter cited as "NCGAS 1."

data for both legal compliance and GAAP reports. This requirement does not necessitate two accounting systems. Rather, the accounts will be kept on one basis and the system will also provide the additional data needed to convert the accounts to the other basis.

GAAP statements are necessary to assure proper reporting and a reasonable degree of comparability among the statements of governments across the nation. Preparation of statements in conformity with GAAP assures that the financial reports of all state and local governments, regardless of their legal provisions and customs, contain the same types of financial statements and disclosures for the same categories and types of funds and account groups, and are based on the same measurement and classification criteria.

Fund Accounting

The significance the NCGA attributed to fund accounting, probably the most distinctive feature of governmental accounting, is indicated by the fact that three of its twelve principles directly concern this topic. They deal with: the need for fund accounting and definition of the term "fund" (Principle 2), the types of funds recommended for state and local governments (Principle 3), and the need to limit the number of fund entities employed in order to avoid undue accounting, reporting, and analytical complexities (Principle 4).

The second NCGA principle is:

FUND ACCOUNTING SYSTEMS

2. Governmental accounting systems should be organized and operated on a fund basis. A fund is defined as a fiscal and accounting entity with a self-balancing set of accounts recording cash and other financial resources, together with all related liabilities and residual equities or balances, and changes therein, which are segregated for the purpose of carrying on specific activities or attaining certain objectives in accordance with special regulations, restrictions, or limitations.

In discussing this principle the NCGA noted that the diverse nature of government operations and the necessity of assuring legal compliance preclude recording and summarizing all governmental financial transactions and balances in a single accounting entity. Unlike a private business, which is accounted for as a single entity, a governmental unit is accounted for through several separate fund and account group entities, each accounting for certain assets, liabilities, and equity or other balances. Thus, from an accounting and financial management viewpoint, a governmental unit is a combination of several distinctly different fiscal and accounting entities, each having a separate set of accounts and functioning independently of the other funds and account groups.

Three categories of funds and two types of nonfund account groups are employed in governmental accounting:

1. *Governmental funds.* "General government" functions typically are financed through one or more fund types in this expendable fund category. The sources, uses, and balances of the government's expendable financial resources and the related current liabilities (except

those accounted for in proprietary funds) are accounted for through governmental funds (General, Special Revenue, Capital Projects, Debt Service, and Special Assessment Funds).

Expendable assets are assigned to the several governmental funds according to the purposes for which they may (or must) be expended. Current liabilities are accounted for in the fund from which the expenditures giving rise to the liabilities were made, and thus from which they are to be paid. The difference between governmental fund assets and liabilities, the fund equity, is known as the "Fund Balance."

Governmental fund accounting measures fund financial position and changes in fund financial position—*sources, uses, and balances of fund financial resources*—rather than net income. The statement of revenues, expenditures, and changes in fund balance is the primary governmental fund operating statement.

2. *Proprietary funds.* These nonexpendable funds are used to account for a government's continuing organizations and activities that are similar to private business enterprises (Enterprise and Internal Service Funds). All assets, liabilities, equities, revenues, expenses, and transfers pertaining to these business (and quasi-business) organizations and activities are accounted for through proprietary funds. Proprietary fund accounting measures *net income, financial position, and changes in financial position.* The generally accepted accounting principles here are those applicable to similar private businesses.

3. *Fiduciary funds.* These funds are used to account for assets held by a government in a trustee or agency capacity, whether for individuals, private organizations, other governmental units, or other funds of the government. Expendable Trust Fund accounting parallels that for governmental funds; Nonexpendable Trust Fund and Pension Trust Fund accounting is similar to that for proprietary funds. Agency Funds are purely custodial (assets equal liabilities), and Agency Fund accounting is concerned only with recording the changes in fund assets held for others.

A government's "general fixed assets" and "general long-term debt" are accounted for through nonfund accounting entities called "account groups" (General Fixed Assets and General Long-Term Debt Account Groups). The government's "general fixed assets"—all fixed assets not related to (and hence not accounted for in) proprietary funds or Trust Funds—are *not financial resources available to finance governmental fund expenditures.* Similarly, the unmatured principal of a government's "general obligation long-term debt"—long-term liabilities not related to (and hence not accounted for in) proprietary funds, Special Assessment Funds, or Trust Funds—does not require a governmental fund expenditure (use of financial resources) until the liabilities mature and must be paid, perhaps many years in the future. Thus, neither general fixed assets nor general long-term debt are accounted for in the governmental funds, but in nonfund account groups. These account groups are not funds since they do not contain or account for available financial resources and related liabilities. Rather, they are self-balancing sets of accounting records of the general fixed assets and general long term debt, respectively.

The third NCGA principle recognizes eight specific types of funds within the three broad fund categories.

TYPES OF FUNDS

3. The following types of funds should be used by state and local governments:

Governmental Funds

(1) *The General Fund*—to account for all financial resources except those required to be accounted for in another fund.

(2) *Special Revenue Funds*—to account for the proceeds of specific revenue sources (other than special assessments, expendable trusts, or for major capital projects) that are legally restricted to expenditure for specified purposes.

(3) *Capital Projects Funds*—to account for financial resources to be used for the acquisition or construction of major capital facilities (other than those financed by proprietary funds, Special Assessment Funds, and Trust Funds).

(4) *Debt Service Funds*—to account for the accumulation of resources for, and the payment of, general long-term debt principal and interest.

(5) *Special Assessment Funds*—to account for the financing of public improvements or services deemed to benefit the properties against which special assessments are levied.

Proprietary Funds

(6) *Enterprise Funds*—to account for operations (a) that are financed and operated in a manner similar to private business enterprises—where the intent of the governing body is that the costs (expenses, including depreciation) of providing goods or services to the general public on a continuing basis be financed or recovered primarily through user charges; or (b) where the governing body has decided that periodic determination of revenues earned, expenses incurred, and/or net income is appropriate for capital maintenance, public policy, management control, accountability, or other purposes.

(7) *Internal Service Funds*—to account for the financing of goods or services provided by one department or agency to other departments or agencies of the governmental unit, or to other governmental units, on a cost-reimbursement basis.

Fiduciary Funds

(8) *Trust and Agency Funds*—to account for assets held by a governmental unit in a trustee capacity or as an agent for individuals, private organizations, other governmental units, and/or other funds. These include (a) *Expendable Trust Funds,* (b) *Nonexpendable Trust Funds,* (c) *Pension Trust Funds,* and (d) *Agency Funds.*

As noted earlier, fund accounting evolved because portions of a government's resources may be restricted as to use because of grantor or donor stipulation, by law, by contractual agreement, through action by the legislature or council, or for some other reason. The several fund types recommended in NCGAS 1 vary primarily in accordance with (1) the extent of budgetary control normally employed and (2) whether the resources of the fund may be expended or are to be maintained on a self-sustaining basis. Furthermore, the various types of *governmental and similar fiduciary* funds suggested differ principally according to the uses to which the resources accounted for therein may be put: (1) general operating, (2) special purpose or project, or (3) merely transferred to those for whom the government is acting as a trustee or agent. The types of fund and nonfund accounting entities recommended in NCGAS 1 are summarized in Figure 2-3; typical governmental and similar fiduciary fund resource flow patterns are indicated in Figure 2-4. Note that a state or local government will have only *one* General fund, *one* General Fixed Asset Account Group, and *one* General Long-Term Debt Account Group. It may have one, none, several, or many of the other types of funds.

Finally, the NCGA cautioned against using too few or too many funds in its fourth principle:

NUMBER OF FUNDS

4. Governmental units should establish and maintain those funds required by law and sound financial administration. Only the minimum number of funds consistent with legal and operating requirements should be established, however, since unnecessary funds result in inflexibility, undue complexity, and inefficient financial administration.

The government must establish and maintain those funds required by law or contractual agreement. Also, the unit should maintain other funds that assist in

Figure 2-3

TYPES OF STATE AND LOCAL GOVERNMENT FUNDS AND ACCOUNT GROUPS (NCGA RECOMMENDATIONS)

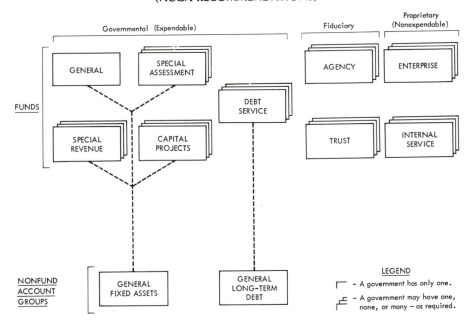

Figure 2-4

TYPICAL RESOURCE FLOW PATTERN—GOVERNMENTAL AND SIMILAR FIDUCIARY FUNDS*

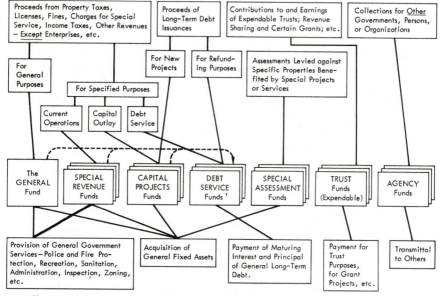

* Flows to and from proprietary and similar fiduciary funds are excluded.

† As indicated by ----, resources may be transferred to the Debt Service Funds from other funds; also, General Long-Term Debt may be serviced directly from other governmental funds.

Flows to and from proprietary and similar fiduciary funds are excluded.
†As indicated by ---, resources may be transferred to the Debt Service Fund from other funds; also, General Long-Term Debt may be serviced directly from other governmental funds.

assuring effective control over its finances. However, maintaining too many funds is as detrimental as maintaining too few funds.

Selecting the specific funds a government needs requires professional judgment, and the funds in use should be reviewed from time to time to assure that all funds needed are in use and that no unneeded funds are in use. In amplifying the fourth principle the NCGA offered the following guidance to the exercise of professional judgment in determining the fund structure of a state or local government:

> Some governmental units often need several funds of a single type, such as Special Revenue or Capital Projects Funds. On the other hand, many governmental units do not need funds of all types at any given time. Some find it necessary to use only a few of the specified types. For example, a government which does not finance improvements or services by special assessments obviously does not need Special Assessment Funds; nor do many small governmental units require Internal Service Funds. Moreover, resources restricted to expenditure for purposes normally financed from the General Fund may be accounted for through the General Fund provided that applicable legal requirements can be appropriately satisfied; and use of Special Revenue Funds

is not required unless they are legally mandated. Debt Service Funds are required if they are legally mandated and/or if financial resources are being accumulated for principal and interest payments maturing in future years.

The general rule is to establish the minimum number of separate funds consistent with legal specifications, operational requirements, and the principles of fund classification discussed above. Using too many funds causes inflexibility and undue complexity in budgeting, accounting, and other phases of financial management, and is best avoided in the interests of efficient and economical financial administration.[18]

Caution must be exercised in opting to account for resources restricted for current operating or debt service purposes in the General Fund. These resources typically are accounted for in Special Revenue and Debt Service funds, respectively, to assure that applicable legal requirements are met, and inadequate accountability may result when these resources are accounted for in the General Fund in governments with less than excellent accounting systems.

Fixed Assets and Long-Term Liabilities

In a fund accounting environment specific fund fixed assets and long-term debt, which are accounted for in the appropriate funds, must be distinguished from those related to the government in its entirety, which are accounted for in the account groups. The fifth NCGA Principle emphasizes this important distinction:

ACCOUNTING FOR FIXED ASSETS AND LONG-TERM LIABILITIES

5. A clear distinction should be made between (a) fund fixed assets and general fixed assets and (b) fund long-term liabilities and general long-term debt.
    a. Fixed assets related to specific proprietary funds or Trust Funds should be accounted for through those funds. All other fixed assets of a governmental unit should be accounted for through the General Fixed Assets Account Group.
    b. Long-term liabilities of proprietary funds, Special Assessment Funds, and Trust Funds should be accounted for through those funds. All other unmatured general long-term liabilities of the governmental unit should be accounted for through the General Long-Term Debt Account Group.

In discussing the reasons underlying the need to distinguish fund and nonfund fixed assets and long-term debt the Council noted:

General fixed assets do not represent financial resources available for expenditure, but are items for which financial resources have been used and for which accountability should be maintained. They are not assets of any fund but of the governmental unit as an instrumentality. Their inclusion in the financial statements of a governmental fund would increase the fund balance, which could mislead users of the fund balance sheet. *The primary purposes for a* [sic] *governmental fund accounting are to reflect its revenues and expenditures—the sources and uses of its financial resources—and its assets, the related liabilities, and the net financial resources available for subsequent appropriation and expenditure.* These objectives can most readily be achieved

[18] Ibid., p. 8.

by excluding general fixed assets from the governmental fund accounts and recording them in a separate General Fixed Assets Account Group.

. . .

The general long-term debt of a state or local government is secured by the general credit and revenue-raising powers of the government rather than by the assets acquired or specific fund resources. Further, just as general fixed assets do not represent financial resources available for appropriation and expenditure, the unmatured principal of general long-term debt does not require current appropriation and expenditure of governmental fund financial resources. To include it as a governmental fund liability would be misleading and dysfunctional to the current period management control (e.g., budgeting) and accountability functions.[19]

The sixth principle specifies that cost is the basic valuation method for both fund fixed assets and general fixed assets:

VALUATION OF FIXED ASSETS

6. Fixed assets should be accounted for at cost or, if the cost is not practicably determinable, at estimated cost. Donated fixed assets should be recorded at their estimated fair value at the time received.

Estimated cost is allowed because some governments have not maintained adequate fixed asset records before deciding (or being required) to report in conformity with generally accepted accounting principles. This principle allows a government to estimate the original cost of its fixed assets for which costs cannot reasonably be determined, but requires that its other fixed assets and all fixed assets acquired subsequently be recorded at cost (or estimated value, if donated).

Accounting for depreciation of a government's fixed assets is the subject of the seventh principle:

DEPRECIATION OF FIXED ASSETS

7. a. Depreciation of general fixed assets should not be recorded in the accounts of governmental funds. Depreciation of general fixed assets may be recorded in cost accounting systems or calculated for cost finding analyses; and accumulated depreciation may be recorded in the General Fixed Assets Account Group.

   b. Depreciation of fixed assets accounted for in a proprietary fund should be recorded in the accounts of that fund. Depreciation is also recognized in those Trust Funds where expenses, net income, and/or capital maintenance are measured.

The NCGA rationale for this principle is as follows:

Depreciation accounting is an important element of the income-determination process. Accordingly, it is recognized in the proprietary funds and in those Trust Funds where expenses, net income, and/or capital maintenance are measured.

Expenditures, not expenses, are measured in governmental fund accounting. To record depreciation expense in governmental funds would inappropriately

[19] Ibid., p. 9.

mix two fundamentally different measurements, expenses and expenditures. General fixed asset acquisitions *require* the use of governmental fund financial resources and are recorded as expenditures. General fixed asset sale proceeds *provide* governmental fund financial resources. Depreciation expense is neither a source nor a use of governmental fund financial resources, and thus is not properly recorded in the accounts of such funds.[20]

Further, the Council emphasized that:

The recommendation that depreciation not be recorded in the governmental fund accounts neither denies its existence nor precludes calculating depreciation to determine total and/or unit costs (expenses) of all or certain governmental activities and/or programs. The Council encourages use of cost accounting systems or cost finding analyses for such activities—e.g., vehicle operation, garbage collection, and data processing services—either routinely, in the process of "make or buy" or "do or contract for" decision analyses, or for such purposes as determining reimbursable costs under grant provisions, establishing fee schedules, or analyzing activity or program cost. Maintaining governmental fund and account group records in the manner recommended facilitates such calculations.[21]

Basis of Accounting

Consistent with its distinction between governmental fund accounting methods and those for proprietary funds, the NCGA specified different methods of applying the accrual concept in accounting for governmental funds and proprietary funds.

ACCRUAL BASIS IN GOVERNMENTAL ACCOUNTING

8. The modified accrual or accrual basis of accounting, as appropriate, should be utilized in measuring financial position and operating results.
   a. *Governmental fund* revenues and expenditures should be recognized on the modified accrual basis. Revenues should be recognized in the accounting period in which they become available and measurable. Expenditures should be recognized in the accounting period in which the fund liability is incurred, if measurable, except for unmatured interest on general long-term debt and on special assessment indebtedness secured by interest-bearing special assessment levies, which should be recognized when due.
   b. *Proprietary fund* revenues and expenses should be recognized on the accrual basis. Revenues should be recognized in the accounting period in which they are earned and become measurable; expenses should be recognized in the period incurred, if measurable.
   c. *Fiduciary fund* revenues and expenses or expenditures (as appropriate) should be recognized on the basis consistent with the fund's accounting measurement objective. Nonexpendable Trust and Pension Trust Funds should be accounted for on the accrual basis; Expendable Trust Funds

---

[20] Ibid., p. 10.
[21] Ibid.

should be accounted for on the modified accrual basis. Agency Fund assets and liabilities should be accounted for on the modified accrual basis.

    d. *Transfers* should be recognized in the accounting period in which the interfund receivable and payable arise.

In discussing this principle the Council noted that:

> "Basis of accounting" refers to *when* revenues, expenditures, expenses, and transfers—and the related assets and liabilities—are recognized in the accounts and reported in the financial statements. Specifically, it relates to the *timing* of the measurements made, regardless of the nature of the measurement, on either the cash or the accrual method. For example, whether depreciation is recognized depends on whether expenses or expenditures are being measured rather than on whether the cash or accrual basis is used.[22]

The "modified accrual" method is, in essence, the accrual method of accounting for the flows and balances of financial resources, usually working capital of governmental funds and similar trust funds, as contrasted with the cash basis of accounting. The term "accrual" basis refers to accounting for revenues earned and expenses incurred, as commonly done for business enterprises, in proprietary and similar trust funds. The application of the modified accrual and accrual bases is discussed and illustrated throughout this text.

The Budget and Budgetary Accounting

The importance of budgeting, budgetary control, and budgetary accountability is recognized in the ninth NCGA principle:

BUDGETING, BUDGETARY CONTROL, AND BUDGETARY REPORTING

    9. a. An annual budget(s) should be adopted by every governmental unit.
       b. The accounting system should provide the basis for appropriate budgetary control.
       c. Budgetary comparisons should be included in the appropriate financial statements and schedules for governmental funds for which an annual budget has been adopted.

Budgeting is considered in depth in Chapter 3 and in the chapters that deal with funds for which budgeting and budgetary control are particularly important.

Classification and Terminology

The needs (1) to classify accounting data in different ways to fulfill different information needs, and (2) to distinguish internal shifts of resources and long-term borrowings from revenues, expenditures, and expenses are the subjects of the tenth NCGA principle.

---

[22] Ibid., p. 11.

TRANSFER, REVENUE, EXPENDITURE, AND EXPENSE ACCOUNT CLASSIFICATION

10. a. Interfund transfers and proceeds of general long-term debt issues should be classified separately from fund revenues and expenditures or expenses.
    b. Governmental fund revenues should be classified by fund and source. Expenditures should be classified by fund, function (or program), organization unit, activity, character, and principal classes of objects.
    c. Proprietary fund revenues and expenses should be classified in essentially the same manner as those of similar business organizations, functions, or activities.

Four types of interfund transactions commonly encountered in state and local government are defined as follows:

(1) *Quasi-External Transactions.* Transactions that would be treated as revenues, expenditures, or expenses if they involved organizations *external* to the governmental unit—e.g., payments in lieu of taxes from an Enterprise Fund to the General Fund; Internal Service Fund billings to departments; routine employer contributions from the General Fund to a Pension Trust Fund; and routine service charges for inspection, engineering, utilities, or similar services provided by a department financed from one fund to a department financed from another fund—should be accounted for as revenues, expenditures, or expenses in the funds involved.

(2) *Reimbursements.* Transactions which constitute reimbursements of a fund for expenditures or expenses initially made from it which are properly applicable to another fund—e.g., an expenditure properly chargeable to a Special Revenue Fund was initially made from the General Fund, which is subsequently reimbursed—should be recorded as expenditures or expenses (as appropriate) in the reimbursing fund and as reductions of the expenditure or expense in the fund that it reimbursed.

(3) *Residual Equity Transfers.* Nonrecurring or nonroutine transfers of equity between funds—e.g., contribution of Enterprise Fund or Internal Service Fund capital by the General Fund, subsequent return of all or part of such contribution to the General Fund, and transfers of residual balances of discontinued funds to the General Fund or a Debt Service Fund.

(4) *Operating Transfers.* All other interfund transfers—e.g., legally authorized transfers from a fund receiving revenue to the fund through which the resources are to be expended, transfers of tax revenues from a Special Revenue Fund to a Debt Service Fund, transfers from the General Fund to a Special Revenue or Capital Projects Fund, operating subsidy transfers from the General or a Special Revenue Fund to an Enterprise Fund, and transfers from an Enterprise Fund other than payments in lieu of taxes to finance General Fund expenditures.[23]

Proper accounting and reporting for these types of interfund transaction is summarized in Figure 2-5.

Quasi-external interfund transactions are the only interfund transactions for which it is proper to recognize fund revenues, expenditures, or expenses that are not revenues, expenditures, or expenses of the governmental unit. The NCGA

[23] Ibid., pp. 15–16.

Figure 2-5

SUMMARY OF INTERFUND TRANSACTIONS

Category of Interfund Transaction	Distinguishing Characteristics	Reporting Treatment	
		Payee (Recipient) Fund	Payer Fund
Quasi-external transaction	The department or activity financed by each fund *both* gives *and* receives consideration.	Revenue	Expenditure or expense, as appropriate.
Reimbursement	Expenditure or expense of department or activity financed from payer fund was initially recorded in payee fund, which is now being reimbursed from payer fund.	Reduce expenditures or expenses, as appropriate.	Expenditure or expense, as appropriate.
Residual equity transfers (RETs)	a. The department or activity financed by each fund only gives *or* receives consideration, not both. b. Purpose is to increase (decrease) operating capacity of departments or activities financed by Proprietary funds or to discontinue a fund. c. Significant amounts involved; non-routine occurrence.	Residual Equity Transfers In (1) In Governmental and Trust funds—reported after operations, separate from revenues, bond issue proceeds, and operating transfers in, or after beginning fund balance. (2) In Proprietary funds—increase in contributed capital.	Residual Equity Transfer Out (1) In Governmental and Trust Funds—reported after operations separate from expenditures or expenses and operating transfers out, or after beginning fund balance. (2) In Proprietary funds—reported as a change in retained earnings or contributed capital, depending on circumstances.
Operating transfers	a. The department or activity financed by each fund only gives *or* receives consideration, not both. b. Purpose is to support the normal level of operations of the payee fund. c. All transfers that are not RETs are operating transfers.	Operating Transfers In reported (1) in "Other Sources (Uses) of Financial Resources" section of the Governmental funds operating statement and (2) separately as "Operating Transfers In" in the Proprietary funds operating statement.	Same as for Payee Fund except report "Operating Transfers Out".

viewed accounting for quasi-external transactions as fund revenues, expenditures, and expenses as essential both (1) to proper determination of proprietary fund operating results and (2) to reporting accurately the revenues and expenditures of programs or activities financed through governmental funds.

Reimbursements are necessary when an expenditure attributable to one fund initially was made from another fund. Accounting for interfund reimbursements as specified ensures that such transactions are reflected only once—and in the proper fund—as expenditures or expenses, as appropriate.

All interfund transactions except loans or advances, quasi-external transactions, and reimbursements are **transfers:**

- *Residual equity transfers* are reported separately after the beginning fund balance or after the results of operations in the statement of revenues, expenditures, and changes in fund balances of governmental funds. Residual equity transfers to proprietary funds are reported as additions to contributed capital of the proprietary fund; those from proprietary funds are reported as reductions of retained earnings or contributed capital, as appropriate.
- *Operating transfers* are reported in the "Other Financing Sources (Uses)" section in the statement of revenues, expenditures, and changes in fund balance (governmental funds) and in the "Operating Transfers" section in the statement of revenues, expenses, and changes in retained earnings or equity (proprietary funds).

The NCGA also stated that proceeds of long-term debt issues not recorded as fund liabilities—e.g., proceeds of bonds or notes expended through Capital Projects or Debt Service Funds—should be reported as "Bond Issue Proceeds" or "Proceeds of Long-Term Notes" in the "Other Financing Sources" section of the operating statement of the recipient governmental fund.

NCGA *Statement 1* recommends classifying expenditures by fund, function or program, activity, organization unit, character, and major object classes (1) to facilitate assembling data for internal analysis purposes in manners that cross fund and departmental lines and (2) so that data required for various intergovernmental comparisons and analyses will be readily available. Classification of governmental fund revenues and expenditures is discussed in detail in Chapters 5 and 6.

Consistent classification and terminology among the budget, the accounts, and the budgetary reports is a prerequisite to valid comparisons. In addition, effective budgetary control and accountability require that the accounts and budgetary reports, particularly those related to appropriations and expenditures, be in at least as much detail as appropriation control points. The NCGA recognized the necessity of such consistency and comparability in its eleventh principle:[24]

---

[24] Principle 11 is not relevant to (1) commercial-type activities of a government, which should be accounted for in a manner similar to that of commercial organizations, or (2) government-operated hospitals, libraries, schools, airports, transit authorities, or other facilities for which account classifications have been developed by organizations other than the National Council on Governmental Accounting.

COMMON TERMINOLOGY AND CLASSIFICATION

11. A common terminology and classification should be used consistently throughout the budget, the accounts, and the financial reports of each fund.

Financial Reporting

The final NCGA principle emphasizes the importance of both interim internal financial reporting and external annual financial reporting.

INTERIM AND ANNUAL FINANCIAL REPORTS

12. a. Appropriate interim financial statements and reports of financial position, operating results, and other pertinent information should be prepared to facilitate management control of financial operations, legislative oversight, and, where necessary or desired, for external reporting purposes.

b. A comprehensive annual financial report covering all funds and account groups of the governmental unit—including appropriate combined, combining, and individual fund statements; notes to the financial statements; schedules; narrative explanations; and statistical tables—should be prepared and published.

c. General purpose financial statements may be issued separately from the comprehensive annual financial report. Such statements should include the basic financial statements and notes to the financial statements that are essential to fair presentation of financial position and operating results (and changes in financial position of proprietary funds and similar Trust Funds).

No generally accepted accounting principles have been promulgated for interim financial reporting, the topic of Principle 12a. Interim reporting is discussed and illustrated at various points throughout the text, however, as is annual financial reporting in conformity with generally accepted accounting principles, the topic of Principles 12b and 12c. Financial reporting is covered comprehensively in Chapter 14.

A unique feature of state and local government financial reporting is that three categories of financial statements—of balance sheets, operating, and other statements—are used: (1) individual fund and account group statements, (2) combining statements, and (3) combined statements:

1. *Individual fund and account group statements,* as the name implies, present status or operating data for a single fund or account group, often in detail and/or with budget-to-actual or current year-to-prior year comparative data.

2. *Combining fund statements* present, in adjacent columns, data for all funds of a type (e.g., Special Revenue Funds), an "all funds" total, and perhaps a current year-to-prior year comparative total. Combining statements typically are in less detail than individual fund statements.

3. *Combined fund and account group statements,* known as the ***General Purpose Financial Statements (GPFS),*** present in adjacent columns data by fund type and account group, perhaps with memorandum only

total and comparative columns. Combined statements have only one column for each fund type and account group. Where there is more than one fund of a type the total data from the combining statement for that fund type would appear in the combined statement. Combined statements typically are more summarized than combining or individual fund and account group statements.

The distinction between combined and combining statements is important, and is illustrated in Figure 2-6. All three types of statements are illustrated in the following chapters.

State and local government units are required to issue an annual Comprehensive Annual Financial Report (CAFR), which includes the combined General Purpose Financial Statements (GPFS) as well as combining and, usually, individual fund and account group statements. The CAFR is viewed as the "official" annual financial report of the government and includes introductory materials and statistical data as well as financial statements and schedules. The GPFS can be separately issued for readers not requiring the detail in the CAFR, as long as the reader is made aware of the CAFR in the event he needs more detailed data. The combined statements required in the GPFS are:

1. *Combined Balance Sheet:* All Fund Types and Account Groups.
2. *Combined Statement of Revenues, Expenditures, and Changes in Fund Balances:* All Governmental and Expendable Trust Fund types.
3. *Combined Statement of Revenues, Expenditures, and Changes in Fund*

Figure 2-6

Combined v. Combining Statements

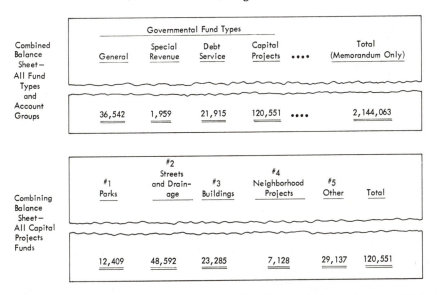

Note: Individual fund statements would contain data for only a single fund, e.g., Capital Projects Fund #3, Building.

Balances—Budget and Actual: General and Special Revenue Fund Types (and similar fund types for which annual budgets have been legally adopted).

4. *Combined Statement of Revenues, Expenses, and Changes in Retained Earnings (or Equity):* All Proprietary (and Nonexpendable and Pension Trust) Fund Types.

5. *Combined Statement of Changes in Financial Position:* All Proprietary (and Nonexpendable and Pension Trust) Fund Types.

Notes to the financial statements.

The comprehensive annual financial report (CAFR) and the general purpose financial statements (GPFS) for state and local governments are discussed and illustrated in Chapter 14.

SUMMARY AND OVERVIEW

Orienting oneself to state and local government accounting and reporting requires that particular attention be given to terminology, fund types, and budgetary control techniques.

New and unique terms should be noted carefully. Familiar terminology also deserves analysis, as it may be used with either usual or unique connotations. Definitions of pertinent terms may be found in most chapters.

Adapting to a situation in which there are many accounting entities requires both concentration and practice. The nature, role, and distinguishing characteristics of each of the eight types of funds and the two nonfund account groups recommended by the NCGA must be understood thoroughly. Each is discussed in depth in later chapters.

As an introduction to later discussions it may be helpful to review the " 'General Government' (Governmental funds and account groups) Accounting Entities and Equations" diagram (Figure 2-7) prepared by a recent American Accounting Association committee.

A peculiarity of the multiple-entity approach of fund accounting is that a single transaction may require entries in more than one accounting entity; e.g., the purchase of a *general* fixed asset necessitates entries to record both the fund expenditure and the asset in the General Fixed Assets Account Group. Further, one must both accept and adapt to virtual personification of the fund accounting entities and the definition of "revenue" and "expenditure" in a fund accounting context.

Organizational units financed from different funds may buy from and sell to one another (interfund transactions) and resources of one fund may be owed to another (interfund relationships). Therefore, a fund may have revenues or incur expenditures that are not revenues or expenditures of the government as a whole (quasi-external transactions). For example, payment from the General Fund to the fund through which the government's central repair shop is financed (a quasi-external transaction) constitutes a General Fund expenditure and an Internal Service Fund revenue, even though the transaction does not result in an expenditure or revenue of the government as a whole.

Figure 2-7

"General Government" Accounting
Entities and Equations*

	Assets + Contra	=	Liabilities	+	Fund Balances + Contra
Expendable funds:					
Fund 1	CA	=	CL	+	FB
Fund 2	CA	=	CL	+	FB
Fund n	CA	=	CL	+	FB
Nonfund account groups:					
General Fixed Assets	FA	=			Investment in Fixed Assets†
General Long-Term Debt	Amount(s) Available and that must be provided in the future to retire NCL†	=	NCL		
Arithmetic Summation	$\Sigma CA + \Sigma FA + \Sigma NCL$† $= \Sigma CL + \Sigma NCL + \Sigma FB + \Sigma FA$†				

*CA, Current Assets; CL, Current Liabilities; FB, Fund Balance (CA − CL = Working Capital); FA, Fixed Assets (General Fixed Assets); NCL, Noncurrent Liabilities (General Long-Term Debt).
†Contra or offset accounts.
Source: Adapted from American Accounting Association, "Report of the Committee on Not-for-Profit Organizations, 1972-73," Accounting Review, *Supplement to Vol. 49 (1974), p. 229.*

Finally, the budget is of such importance in governments that governmental accounting is often referred to as "budgetary" accounting. It is appropriate, therefore, to examine the role of the budget and major budgetary approaches before delving into the details of fund accounting technique.

▶ **Question 2-1.** The terms "fund" and "funds" are used with varying connotations. For example, a college student may consider his cash and checking account balance to be his "funds" and his savings account his "fund." Indicate (a) the various meanings associated with these terms in business and (b) the principal manner in which these terms are used in state and local government accounting.

Question 2-2. A state or local government may employ only one of certain fund or nonfund account group entities but one, none, or many of other types. Of which would you expect a government to have only one? One, none, or many?

Question 2-3. The following are names of funds encountered in governmental reports and the purposes for which these funds have been established. You are required to indicate the corresponding fund type recommended by the National Council on Government Accounting.

(a) School Fund (to account for special taxes levied to finance the operation of schools).

(b) Bond Redemption Fund (to account for taxes and other revenues to be used in retiring sinking fund bonds).

(c) Bridge Construction Fund (to account for the proceeds from the sale of bonds).

(d) Park Fund (to account for special taxes levied to finance the operation of parks).

(e) Street Improvement Trust Fund (to account for the expenditure of money raised by special assessments on property deemed to be benefited by an improvement).

(f) Interdepartmental Printing Shop Fund (to account for revenues received from departments for printing done for them by the interdepartmental printing shop).

(g) City Bus Line Fund (to account for revenues received from the public for transportation services).

(h) Money Collected For The State Fund (to account for money collected as agent for the state).

(i) Operating Fund (to account for revenues not handled through any other fund).

(j) Electric Fund (to account for revenues received from the sale of electricity to the public).

(k) Federal Fund (to account for Federal construction grant proceeds).

(l) Bond Redemption Fund (to account for proceeds of bond refunding issue).

(m) Federal Fund (to account for shared revenue which may be used for any of several broad purpose categories).

(n) Bond Proceeds Fund (to account for proceeds of bonds issued to finance street construction).

(o) Employees' Pension and Relief Fund (to provide retirement and disability benefits to employees).

Question 2-4. Why are a municipality's general fixed assets and general long-term debt accounted for through nonfund account groups rather than within one of its funds, such as the General Fund?

Question 2-5. What differences would you expect to find between the accounting principles for the General Fund and for Special Revenue funds?

Question 2-6. Revenues or expenditures of a specific fund may not be revenues or expenditures of the government as a whole. Why is this true?

Question 2-7. It has been asserted that terms such as "sources" and "uses" should be substituted for "revenues" and "expenditures," respectively, in accounting and reporting for governmental (expendable) funds. Do you agree? Why or why not?

Question 2-8. It is said that one of the differences between government and business is that business expenditures create revenues, whereas governmental expenditures do not. Is this statement true? Explain.

Question 2-9. It is not uncommon to find the terms "expenditures" and "expenses" erroneously used as synonyms. How do "expenditures" differ from "expenses"?

Question 2-10. What is the difference, if any, between a revenue and expenditure statement prepared on a cash basis and a statement of cash receipts and disbursements?

Question 2-11. A governmental unit has a choice of adopting either a cash basis or a modified accrual basis of accounting for its governmental funds. Which method should it adopt and why?

Question 2-12. NCGA Principle 11 states that "A common terminology and classification should be used consistently throughout the budget, the accounts, and the financial reports." Why is this important?

Question 2-13. The principal financial statements of business enterprises are the Balance Sheet, Income Statement, and Statement of Changes in Financial Position (funds flow). What *similarities* are there, if any, among these statements and the operating and position statements of a proprietary (nonexpendable) fund? A governmental (expendable) fund?

Question 2-14. Fund accounting and budgetary control were deemed of such importance by the NCGA that four of its twelve "principles" deal directly with these topics and most of the others relate to them at least indirectly. Why?

Question 2-15. In what funds and account groups are (a) fixed assets and (b) long-term debt accounted for? Why are they not accounted for in the other funds and account groups?

Question 2-16. Discuss the current roles of the FASB, the AICPA, the NCGA, and the GASB in setting standards for governmental accounting and financial reporting.

Question 2-17. Harvey Township budgets its resources on the cash basis in accordance with state law. State law also requires financial statements prepared on the cash basis. To comply with this requirement, Harvey Township prepares its Comprehensive Annual Financial Report on the cash basis.

(a) Discuss the appropriateness of Harvey Township's report, and

(b) Explain what, if anything, Harvey Township should change in its report.

Question 2-18. Define the following interfund transaction terms and explain how each is accounted for and reported by a municipality: (a) Reimbursement; (b) Quasi-External Transaction; (c) Operating Transfers; and (d) Residual Equity Transfers.

Question 2-19. The City of Horner's Corner publishes general purpose financial statements (as described in NCGA *Statement 1*), but considers it unnecessary to publish a comprehensive annual financial report. The city's only funds are a General Fund, three Special Revenue Funds, two Capital Projects Funds, an Internal Service Fund, and two Enterprise Funds. A citizen has asked you if this practice is appropriate according to NCGA *Statement 1*. Discuss.

Question 2-20. Distinguish between (a) the comprehensive annual financial report and the general purpose financial statements of a government; and (b) combining and combined financial statements of a government.

▶ **Problem 2-1.** Select the lettered response which best completes the numbered statements.

1. The operations of a public library receiving the majority of its support from property taxes for that purpose should be accounted for in:
   a. The General Fund
   b. A Special Revenue Fund
   c. An Enterprise Fund
   d. An Internal Service Fund
   e. None of the above

2. The proceeds of a Federal grant made to assist in financing the future construction of an adult training center should be recorded in:
   a. The General Fund
   b. A Special Revenue Fund
   c. A Capital Projects Fund
   d. A Special Assessment Fund
   e. None of the above

3. The receipts from a special tax levy to retire and pay interest on general obligation

bonds issued to finance the construction of a new city hall should be recorded in a:
a. Debt Service Fund
b. Capital Projects Fund
c. Revolving Interest Fund
d. Special Revenue Fund
e. None of the above

4. The operations of a municipal swimming pool receiving the majority of its support from charges to users should be accounted for in:
a. A Special Revenue Fund
b. The General Fund
c. An Internal Service Fund
d. An Enterprise Fund
e. None of the above

5. The monthly remittance to an insurance company of the lump sum of hospital-surgical insurance premiums collected as payroll deductions from employees should be recorded in:
a. The General Fund
b. An Agency Fund
c. A Special Revenue Fund
d. An Internal Service Fund
e. None of the above

6. A transaction in which a municipality issued general obligation serial bonds to finance the construction of a fire station requires accounting recognition in the:
a. General Fund
b. Capital Projects and General Funds
c. Capital Projects Fund and the General Long-Term Debt Account Group
d. General Fund and the General Long-Term Debt Account Group
e. None of the above

7. Expenditures of $200,000 were made during the year on the fire station in item 6. This transaction requires accounting recognition in the:
a. General Fund
b. Capital Projects Fund and General Fixed Assets Account Group
c. Capital Projects Fund and the General Long-Term Debt Account Group
d. General Fund and the General Fixed Assets Account Group
e. None of the above

8. The activities of a central motor pool which provides and services vehicles for the use of municipal employees on official business should be accounted for in:
a. An Agency Fund
b. The General Fund
c. An Internal Service Fund
d. A Special Revenue Fund
e. None of the above

9. A transaction in which a municipal electric utility paid $150,000 out of its earnings for new equipment requires accounting recognition in:
a. An Enterprise Fund
b. The General Fund
c. The General Fund and the General Fixed Assets Account Group
d. An Enterprise Fund and the General Fixed Assets Account Group
e. None of the above

10. The activities of a municipal employee retirement plan which is financed by equal employer and employee contributions should be accounted for in:
    a. An Agency Fund
    b. An Internal Service Fund
    c. A Special Assessment Fund
    d. A Trust Fund
    e. None of the above

11. A city collects property taxes for the benefit of the local sanitary, park, and school districts and periodically remits collections to these units. This activity should be accounted for in:
    a. An Agency Fund
    b. The General Fund
    c. An Internal Service Fund
    d. A Special Assessment Fund
    e. None of the above

12. A transaction in which a municipal electric utility issues bonds (to be repaid from its own operations) requires accounting recognition in:
    a. The General Fund
    b. A Debt Service Fund
    c. Enterprise and Debt Service Funds
    d. An Enterprise Fund, a Debt Service Fund, and the General Long-Term Debt Account Group
    e. None of the above

(AICPA, adapted)

Problem 2-2. The City of Nancyville provides the following services:

Police and fire protection
Mass transportation
Garbage removal
Health services
Recreation facilities and programs
Water and sewer services
Street maintenance and improvements
Library services

Nancyville's primary revenue sources are property taxes, sales taxes, and fees for services.

The city has been awarded a Federal grant to build a fire station for the southeast portion of the city. Costs in excess of the grant will be financed from general revenues, as are police and fire protection operating costs.

The mass transit system is partially financed by charges levied on users, but the bulk of its financing is from general revenues. However, for management purposes the city administration believes it is essential to know the full cost of operating the system.

The city health services, garbage removal, and library services are financed primarily from general revenues. However, a small portion of the city property tax is restricted for library purposes and the ordinance requires that portion to be accounted for in a separate fund.

Street maintenance and improvements are financed by general revenues and by an annual state grant restricted to those uses. Water and sewer services are financed primarily by user charges, although the city finances any operating deficits that occur from time to time.

City vehicles are maintained in a central motor pool which charges departments on a full-cost-reimbursement basis. The central purchasing office and storehouse charges departments only for the actual costs of acquiring supplies and materials used by the departments plus a small overhead charge.

Four general obligation bond issues are outstanding. One was issued to finance construction of a new city hall downtown and a new outdoor recreational facility in the north part of town. Both projects are currently in progress. Another issue was for construction of sidewalks and a lighting system in a newly developed area of the city. Assessments levied against properties in the area are being used to retire this bond issue. This project has been completed. A third bond issue financed construction of the main fire and police facility (completed two years ago) in the north-central part of Nancyville. The fourth bond issue is being used to finance new library facilities.

One revenue bond issue—to be repaid from water and sewer revenues—was issued to finance major renovations of the water and sewer facilities, which are still under way.

All the bond issues are serial bonds except the library bonds, which are term bonds. Each general obligation bond ordinance requires a certain portion of property tax revenues or assessments to be set aside for debt service of the respective bonds. The fire and police facility bond indenture requires that the related debt service be accounted for in a separate fund.

Required:

(a) Indicate the various individual funds and account groups necessary to account for each of the activities, assets, and liabilities of the City of Nancyville. Use the following format for your answer

Activity, Asset, or Liability	Fund or Account Group to Be Used	Reason(s)

(b) NCGAS1 allows the number of funds necessary to be reduced, under certain conditions, by using the General Fund to account for resources restricted for current operating or debt service purposes. Discuss those instances where it would be possible for Nancyville to exercise this option and the advantages and disadvantages of doing so.

Problem 2-3. The following revenue and expense statement was prepared by a municipality's bookkeeper:

CITY OF *B*
INTERNAL SERVICE FUND

Revenue and Expense Statement
for the Fiscal Year Ended December 19XX

Sales to departments	$ 85,000	
Borrowed from other funds	17,500	$102,500
Less: costs of operating:		
Materials	$ 58,000	
Labor	5,000	
Heat	2,000	
Light and power	2,000	
Superintendent's salary	3,000	
Purchase of machinery	11,000	
Payment of liability to other fund	15,000	
Total cost of operating		96,000
Net income		$ 6,500

1. The cost of materials shown in this statement is the total amount paid for materials during the year. An inventory of $10,000 was carried over from last year; $5,000 was paid for materials purchased during the preceding year; materials costing $20,000 were purchased during the year but have not yet been paid for; the closing inventory is $24,000.

2. The amounts shown for labor, heat, light and power, and superintendent's salary represent actual payments. Charges incurred last year but not paid until this year include the following: labor $450; heat, $100; light and power, $225; superintendent's salary, $190. Charges incurred but not yet paid include the following: labor, $750; heat, $150; light and power, $300; superintendent's salary, $150.

3. The amount shown for sales represents actual receipts of cash from other funds; only $75,000 of the total collections is applicable to sales made this year; $20,000 is still due from other funds on account of sales made this year.

Required:

Prepare a correct statement of revenues and expenses for the Internal Service Fund on (a) a cash basis, (b) the accrual basis, and (c) a modified accrual basis. Assume that the modified accrual basis has been used since the inception of the fund because charges to departments are not calculated frequently, but through semiannual analyses each March and September.

Problem 2-4. In order to assure continuous and dependable bus service to its citizens "from now on," Mobiline County acquired the following assets of Mobiline Transit, Inc., a privately owned bus line in financial difficulty:

Assets	Amount Paid By County
Land	$ 10,000
Garage and office building	30,000
Inventory of tires and parts	15,000
Shop equipment	5,000
Buses	140,000
Total paid—February 1, 19X3	$200,000

Additional information:

1. The purchase was financed through the issue of 6 percent general obligation notes payable, scheduled to mature in amounts of $20,000 each February 1, for ten years. Interest is payable annually each February 1.

2. Bus line revenues and expenditures are accounted for through the General Fund. The fixed assets acquired were recorded in the General Fixed Assets Account Group and the notes payable were recorded in the General Long-Term Debt Account Group.

3. In November 19X3, following the close of the county's fiscal year on October 31, the Mobiline *Daily Banner* published a feature story about the county-owned

bus line under the heading "Bus Line Prospers under County Management." The following Operating Statement, prepared by the county clerk from the General Fund records, appeared within the newspaper article:

MOBILINE COUNTY BUS LINES

Operating Statement
for the Nine-Month Period Ending October 31, 19X3

Revenues:		
Passenger fares—routine route service	$77,000	
Special charter fees	3,000	$80,000
Expenditures:		
Salaries (superintendent, drivers, mechanics)	$52,000	
Fuel and lubrication	12,000	
Tires and parts	1,000	
Contracted repairs and maintenance	8,000	
Miscellaneous	1,000	74,000
Net profit		$ 6,000

The story quoted a county commissioner as saying:

> We are extremely pleased with our bus line operating results to date. Through sound management, we have turned a losing operation into a profitable one— and we expect an even greater profit next year. When we got into the bus line business we determined that the buses would last five years and the building and shop equipment would suffice for ten years—so we do not anticipate any capital outlay expense for some time. In addition, we have $3,000 worth of tires and parts on hand which do not appear in the Operating Statement but will help us hold down our expenses during the next few months, and we should collect another $500 fee for an October charter this week.

Required:

(a) Prepare an accrual basis Statement of Revenues and Expenses (Income Statement) for Mobiline County Bus Lines for the nine month period ending October 31, 19X3.

(b) Evaluate the propriety of the information contained within the *Daily Banner* feature story.

Problem 2-5. (a) Record each of the following transactions on (1) the cash basis, (2) the modified accrual basis, and (3) the accrual basis.

January	1	Billed customers $400 for services rendered
	3	Purchased $50 of supplies on account
	5	Purchased a truck costing $5,000 (to be paid for on February 3)
	11	Collected $200 from customers on account
	15	Recorded accrued wages to date, $1,000
	17	Paid for supplies
	21	Paid wages
February	3	Paid for the truck
	5	$20 of supplies have been used
	6	Depreciation on the truck for the month was $100

		Cash Basis		Modified Accrual Basis		Accrual Basis	
Date	Accounts	Dr.	Cr.	Dr.	Cr.	Dr.	Cr.

(b) Explain the similarities and differences between the modified accrual and accrual bases of accounting.

Problem 2-6. Using the appropriate fund abbreviations, indicate which governmental fund(s) might be used to account for the following items and give the reasons for your answer(s).

1. Revenues not restricted as to use
2. Revenues restricted for specified current operating purposes
3. Purchase of equipment, furniture, and fixtures
4. Depreciation of equipment used in general government functions
5. Payment of short-term debt interest and principal
6. Payment of maturing long-term debt interest and principal
7. Construction of a major capital facility or improvement
8. Charges for services
9. Revenues restricted to payment of general obligation long-term debt interest and principal
10. Proceeds of long-term debt issuances

GF	General Fund
SRF	Special Revenue Fund
CPF	Capital Projects Fund
DSF	Debt Service Fund
SAF	Special Assessment Fund

Solution Format

No.	Fund(s) to Be Used	Reason(s)

Problem 2-7. (a) Identify the type of each interfund transaction described below or indicate that it is not an interfund transaction. Indicate why you classified the transaction as you did.

1. $50,000 of General Fund cash was contributed to establish an Internal Service Fund.
2. A truck—acquired two years ago with General Fund revenues for $8,000—with a fair market value of $4,000 was contributed to a department financed by an Enterprise Fund.
3. The Sanitation Department, accounted for in the General Fund, billed the Municipal Airport, accounted for in an Enterprise Fund, $400 for garbage collection.
4. General Fund cash amounting to $40,000—to be repaid in 90 days—was provided to enable construction to begin on a new courthouse before a bond issue was sold.
5. A $1,000,000 bond issue to finance construction of an addition to the civic center was sold at par.

6. General Fund disbursements during May included payment of $30,000 to a Capital Projects Fund to help finance a major capital project.

7. After retirement of the related debt, the balance of the net assets of a Debt Service Fund, $1,500, were transferred to the General Fund.

8. General Fund cash amounting to $10,000 was contributed to a Special Assessment Fund as its portion of the financing of the special assessment project.

9. An Internal Service Fund department contributed $5,000 to the General Fund to repay it for Internal Service Fund supplies originally paid for by, and recorded as expenditures in, the General Fund.

10. $50,000 was allocated and paid from the General Fund to the Enterprise Fund to finance its budgeted operating deficit.

Solution Format

No.	Classification	Reason(s)

(b) Discuss how each type of interfund transaction should be reported in the Statement of Revenues, Expenditures, and Changes in Fund Balance.

(c) Why is it important to distinguish interfund transfers and bond issue proceeds from fund revenues, expenditures, and expenses?

Problem 2-8. William Bates is executive vice-president of Mavis Industries, Inc., a publicly held industrial corporation. Bates has just been elected to the city council of Gotham City. Prior to assuming office as a city councilman, he asks you to explain the major differences in accounting and financial reporting for a large city as compared to a large industrial corporation.

Required:

(a) Describe the major differences in the purpose of accounting and financial reporting and in the types of financial reports of a large city as compared to a large industrial corporation.

(b) Under what circumstances should depreciation be recognized in accounting for local governmental units? Explain.

(AICPA, adapted)

3

ACCOUNTING AND THE BUDGET PROCESS

Budgeting is the process of allocating scarce resources to unlimited demands, a dollars and cents plan of operation for a specific period of time. As a minimum, such a plan should contain information about the types and amounts of proposed expenditures, the purposes for which they are to be made, and the proposed means of financing them.

Although practices are by no means uniform, budgeting and budgets typically play a far greater role in the planning and control of governmental operations than in those of privately owned businesses. The NCGA recognized the importance of the budget process in the following principle:

9. a. An annual budget(s) should be adopted by every governmental unit.
   b. The accounting system should provide the basis for appropriate budgetary control.
   c. Budgetary comparisons should be included in the appropriate financial statements and schedules for governmental funds for which an annual budget has been adopted.[1]

The adoption of a budget implies that decisions have been made, on the basis of a planning process, as to how the unit is to reach its objectives. The accounting system then provides assistance to the administrators in carrying out the plans and in preparing the statements that permit comparison of operations with the budget.

The prominence to which the budgetary process has risen in government is a natural outgrowth of its environment. *Planning* is a special concern here since, as noted previously, (1) the type, quantity, and quality of governmental goods and services provided are not normally evaluated and adjusted through the open market mechanism; (2) these goods and services, e.g., education, police and fire protection, and sanitation, are often considered among the most critical to

[1] NCGAS 1, p. 3.

the public interest and well-being; (3) the scope and diversity of modern government activities have become so great that comprehensive, thoughtful, and systematic planning is a prerequisite to orderly decision making in this complex environment; and (4) governments are "owned" by their citizens; and planning and decision making are therefore generally a joint process participated in by citizens, either individually or in groups, by their elected representatives within the legislative branch, and by the members of the executive branch. The legislative-executive division of powers, the so-called "checks-and-balances" device, is operative in all states and in most local governments. In these and in most manager-council forms of organization, "the executive proposes, the legislature disposes"; i.e., the executive is responsible for drafting tentative plans, but final plans are made by the legislative body—often after public hearings in which interested citizens or groups are able to participate. Written budget proposals are obviously essential to communication, discussion, revision, and documentation of plans by those concerned with and responsible for planning.

Budgets are also widely used as devices of *control* in governments, both in regard to (1) control of the legislative branch over the executive branch, and (2) control of the chief executive over subordinate executive agencies or departments. As observed earlier, when a budget is enacted by the legislative branch, the expenditure estimates become appropriations—both authorizations to and limitations upon the executive branch. Appropriations may be enacted in very broad categorical terms or in minute detail. In the former case, the legislature exercises general or policy-level control only and the executive is given much managerial discretion in the conduct of government business; in the latter case, the chief executive may have almost no discretion, his role being restricted to that of carrying out various specific, detailed orders from the legislature. Similarly, the chief executive may restrict his subordinates by granting agency or departmental expenditure authority in more detailed or specific categories (allocations) than those approved by the legislature and/or by rationing expenditure authority to subordinate agencies or departments in terms of monthly or quarterly expenditure ceilings, referred to as "allotments." When allocations or allotments have been made, it is essential that the accounting system provide information that will enable (1) agencies or departments to keep their expenditures within limitations imposed by the chief executive and demonstrate compliance therewith and (2) the chief executive to keep the expenditures of the government as a whole within limitations imposed by the legislative branch and demonstrate such compliance. The budgetary authority extended one branch or level of government by another therefore becomes a standard for measurement of compliance or noncompliance. Appropriate financial reports serve as a basis for *evaluating* the extent of compliance with standards established by the various "dollar stewardship" relationships in this environment.

BASIC BUDGETARY TERMINOLOGY

Although the operating budget of each year stands alone from a legal standpoint, budgeting is a continuous process. Budget officials will be engaged during any given year in assuring that the prior year's budgetary reports are properly audited and appropriately distributed, in administering the budget of the current year, and in preparing the budget for the upcoming year(s). This is illustrated in Figure 3-1. The budget for any year (see Figure 3-2) goes through five phases: (1) preparation, (2) legislative enactment, (3) administration, (4) reporting, and (5) postaudit.

State and local governments typically prepare and utilize several types of financial plans referred to as "budgets." It is important, therefore, to distinguish among various types of budgets, to understand the phases through which each may pass, and to be familiar with commonly used budgetary terminology. For purposes of this discussion, budgets may be classified as: (1) capital or current, (2) tentative or enacted, (3) general or special, (4) fixed or flexible, and (5) executive or legislative.

Capital v. Current Budgets

Sound governmental fiscal management requires continual planning for several periods into the future. Most governments are involved in programs to provide certain goods or services continuously (or at least for several years); in acquisitions of buildings, land, or other major items of capital outlay that must be scheduled and financed; and in long-term debt service commitments. Although some prepare comprehensive multiyear plans which include all of these, a more common practice is for such plans to include only the capital outlay plans for the organization. Such a plan generally covers a period of two to six years and is referred to as a "capital program." Each year the current segment of the capital program is considered for inclusion as the "capital budget," in the "current budget." The current budget also includes the proposed expenditures for current operations and debt service, as well as estimates of all financial resources expected to be available during the current period. The NCGA defined the quoted terms as follows·

Figure 3-1

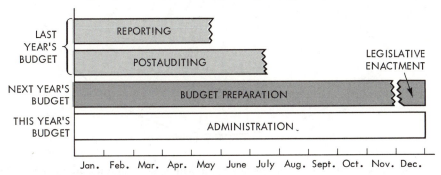

A GOVERNMENTAL UNIT

Budgetary Processes Occurring during a single Fiscal Year*

* Based on the assumption that the budget is prepared annually.
Note: Dates for the beginning and end of the several processes are illustrative only.
They will vary with the government's fiscal year, budget calendar, and other circumstances.

Capital Program. A plan for capital expenditures to be incurred each year over a fixed period of years. . . . It sets forth each project or contemplated expenditure in which the government is to have a part and specifies the full resources estimated to be available to finance the projected expenditures.

Capital Budget. A plan of proposed capital outlays and the means of financing them for the current fiscal period. It is usually a part of the current budget. If a Capital Program is in operation, it will be the first year thereof.

Current Budget. The annual budget prepared for and effective during the present fiscal year; or, in the case of some state governments, the budget for the present biennium.[2]

Figure 3-2

A GOVERNMENTAL UNIT

The Budget Cycle

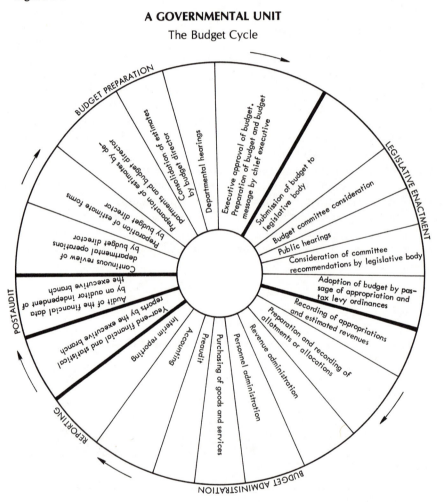

The typical interrelationships of a capital program, capital budget, and current budget are illustrated in Figure 3-3. The remainder of this chapter is concerned primarily with current or operating budgets.

[2] GAAFR (68), pp. 155, 157.

Figure 3-3

INTERRELATIONSHIP OF
CAPITAL PROGRAM—CAPITAL BUDGET—OPERATING BUDGET

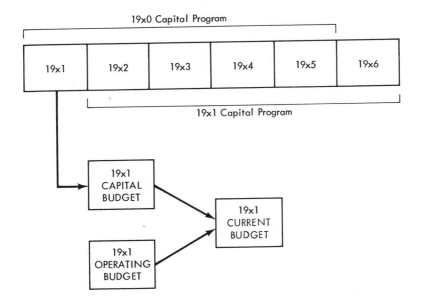

Tentative v. Enacted Budgets

One of the most important bases of distinctions between budgets is their legal status. Prior to approval by the legislative body various documents may be called budgets and have greater or lesser degrees of finality. Capital programs represent plans but not requests by the executive branch; they are subject to change from year to year. Similarly, a departmental budget request may be called a budget but may be changed several times by the department head or higher authority before it is included in the chief executive's final budget presented to the legislature. Enactment of an appropriation bill by the legislative branch is the basis of its control over the executive branch. Only the legislature may revise the terms or conditions of this final budget.

General v. Special Budgets

The budgets of general governmental activities, commonly financed through the General, Special Revenue and Debt Service Funds, are referred to as "general" budgets. A budget prepared for any other fund is referred to as a "special" budget. Appropriations are not normally required for Trust and Agency Funds since the government is acting merely as a fiduciary in such situations; consequently, formal budgets are rarely prepared for these types of funds. Special budgets are commonly limited to those for Capital Projects and Special Assessment Funds. Internal Service and Enterprise Funds are sometimes formally budgeted.

Fixed v. Flexible Budgets

Fixed budgets are those in which appropriations are for a specific (fixed) dollar amount and may not be exceeded because of changes in demand for governmental goods or services. On the other hand, expenditures authorized by **flexible budgets** are fixed *per unit* of goods or services, but are variable in total according to demand for either production or delivery of the goods or services.

Fixed budgets are relatively simple to prepare and administer, are more easily understood than flexible ones, lend themselves to the desire of "strong" legislatures to limit the discretion of the executive (or the executive of his subordinates), are more readily adaptable to integrating budgetary control techniques into accounting systems, and are in harmony with the intent of allocating a fixed amount of resources among various departments or programs. Governmental fund budgets are almost invariably of the fixed variety. Flexible budgets are more realistic when changes in the quantities of goods or services provided directly affect resource availability and expenditure requirements and when formal budgetary control (in the account structure) is not deemed essential. Flexible budgets are appropriate for Enterprise and Internal Service Funds.

Executive v. Legislative Budgets

Budgets are also sometimes categorized by preparer. As noted earlier, budget preparation is usually considered an executive function, though the legislature may revise the budget prior to approval. In some instances, however, the legislative branch prepares the budget, possibly subject to executive veto; in other instances, the budget may originate with a joint legislative-executive committee (possibly with citizen representatives) or with a committee comprised solely of citizens or constituents. Such budgets are frequently referred to by terms such as "executive budget," "legislative budget," "joint budget," or "committee budget."

BUDGETARY APPROACHES AND EMPHASES _____

Rarely does one find two governments with identical budgetary approaches and procedures. A government's budgetary system should be designed to fit its environmental factors, some of which may be unique. Its system should provide a planning and control balance that is appropriate to its circumstances.

The several general approaches to governmental budgeting have marked differences in their emphases on planning, control, and evaluation. As we discuss these approaches we shall point out their suitability for planning and control. At this point it may be useful to point out that the principal groups that exercise control are executive branch officials and the legislature. Citizens, creditors, officials of higher governments, and other groups may have control powers that only indirectly affect the planning and control processes.

The most common approaches to operating expenditure budgeting may be characterized as follows:

1. Object-of-expenditure
2. Performance
3. Program and planning-programming-budgeting (PPB)
4. Zero-base budgeting (ZBB)

A complete discussion of each approach—or possible combinations of approaches—is beyond the scope of this text. In the discussion of each that follows, one should bear in mind that budgetary nomenclature is far from standardized, that each approach may be implemented to varying degrees, that these approaches overlap significantly, and that elements of all four are often found in a single budget system. Furthermore, one must always look to the substance of a system rather than to the terminology used in reference to it, e.g., an object-of-expenditure budget may be referred to publicly as a performance or program budget, since these have been considered the more modern approaches in recent years.

The Budget as Information

Both in practice and in budgetary theory the budget is designed to provide information to decision makers and to indicate the decisions that have been made. Top officials in the executive branch develop policy guidelines for departmental supervisors to use in support of departmental budget requests. The chief executive, with the assistance of his budgetary staff, decides what information and budget requests will go to the legislative body. The ultimate example of the use of the budget to indicate the decisions that have been made is the appropriation bill, a law. What kinds of information may a budget contain to facilitate decision making by officials of the two branches of government?

1. Descriptions of programs, functions, and activities carried on by organizational units of the government.
2. Objectives of programs, functions, and activities.
3. Descriptions of and quantitative data regarding the outputs (services) of the programs, functions, and activities.
4. Benefits provided at increased (maximum?) levels of service.
5. Benefits provided at decreased (minimum?) levels of service.
6. Methods now in use for delivering services.
7. Alternative methods for delivering services.
8. Systems analyses and cost-benefit analyses of methods for delivering services.
9. Cost data
   a. By organization units
   b. By programs, functions, and activities
   c. By object of expenditure
   d. Per unit of service (output)
      (1) At present levels
      (2) At reduced levels
      (3) At expanded levels

It is safe to say that no budget provides all these kinds of information but that every budget provides some of them. The budget approach selected tends to determine the kinds of planning analysis that will be used and the data that will be provided.

The Object-of-Expenditure Approach

The object-of-expenditure approach to budgeting, often referred to as the "traditional" approach, has an expenditure *control* orientation. It became popular as the basis for legislative control over the executive branch. It continues to be the most widely used, though elements of newer approaches are often added.

Simply described, this method involves (1) subordinate agencies submitting budget requests to the chief executive in terms of the type of expenditures to be made, that is, the number of people to be hired in each specified position and salary level and the specific goods or services to be purchased during the upcoming period; (2) the chief executive compiling, modifying, and submitting an overall request for the organization to the legislature in the same object-of-expenditure terms; and, frequently though not necessarily, (3) the legislature making "line-item" appropriations, possibly after revising the requests, along object-of-expenditure "input" lines. Performance or program data may be included in the budget document, but they are used only to supplement or support the object-of-expenditure requests. The basic elements of this approach are illustrated in Figure 3-4.

Various degrees of appropriation control that might be exercised by a legislature through object-of-expenditure budgets may be illustrated by identifying the possible "**control points**" in the example in Figure 3-4. A great degree of legislative control will be typified if appropriations are stated in terms of the most detailed level. For example, the police department appropriation might be in terms of: one chief, $22,000; two captains, $39,000; etc. Alternatively, a lesser amount of control would result if appropriations are stated in terms of object classes, that is, Salaries and Wages, $341,000; Supplies, $29,000; Other Services and Charges, $9,000; and Capital Outlay, $6,000. In this case the detailed objects listed would be indicative of the types of goods and services to be secured, but the executive branch would have discretion as to an appropriate "input mix" so long as these expenditure category subtotals were not exceeded. Next, an even greater degree of executive discretion would be granted if appropriations are stated in "lump sum" at the departmental level, e.g., Police Department, $385,000. Only departmental totals would be legally binding upon the executive in such a situation. Finally, it is conceivable that the legislative branch would appropriate a "lump-sum" total, $1,801,720, for operation of the entire city. Again, the chief executive may refine the level of legislative control in order to achieve the degree of fiscal control he desires to exercise over his subordinates.

Defenders of the object-of-expenditure approach note its longstanding use, its simplicity, and its ease of preparation and understanding by all concerned. Too, they note that budgeting by organizational units and objects-of-expenditure closely fits patterns of responsibility accounting, that this method facilitates accounting control in the budget execution process, and that comparable data may be accumulated for a series of years in order to facilitate trend comparison. In addition, they contend that (1) most programs are of an ongoing nature; (2) most expenditures are relatively unavoidable; (3) decisions must, in the real world, be

Figure 3-4

SIMPLIFIED OBJECT-OF-EXPENDITURE BUDGET

(Classified by Organizational Unit and Object-of-Expenditure)

Mayor's Office

~~~~~~~~~~~~~~~~~~~~~~~~~~~~~~~~~~~~~~

Police Department

Salaries and Wages:

	Rate		
1—Chief	$22,000	$ 22,000	
2—Captains	19,500	39,000	
2—Sergeants	18,500	37,000	
12—Patrolmen	15,000	180,000	
3—Radio operators	15,000	45,000	
10—School guards (part time)	1,800	18,000	$341,000

Supplies:

Stationery and other office supplies	$ 2,200	
Janitorial supplies	1,100	
Gasoline and oil	23,000	
Uniforms	2,200	
Other	500	29,000

Other Services and Charges:

Telephone	$ 1,400	
Out-of-town travel	1,800	
Parking tickets	1,600	
Utilities	3,000	
Other	1,200	9,000

Capital Outlay:

1—Motorcycle (net)	$ 1,600	
1—Patrol car (net)	4,400	6,000
Total Police Department		$385,000

Fire Department

Salaries and Wages:

~~~~~~~~~~~~~~~~~~~~~~~~~~~~~~~~~~~~~~

Total Budget	$1,801,720

based on *changes* in programs, and attention can most readily be given to changes proposed, compared with prior year data; and (4) the object-of-expenditure approach does not preclude supplementing object-of-expenditure data with planning and evaluation information commonly associated with other budgetary approaches. Finally, they observe that, where activities are the basis for organizational units, costs for activities are accumulated as costs of the related organizational units. Identification of activity costs permit summations of program and function costs.

Despite its long-term and widespread use, the object-of-expenditure budget has been severely criticized. In its simplest form it provides no genuine information base for decision makers who read it. Figure 3-4 provides only a list of the proposed personnel to be hired and objects or services to be acquired. Only if the decision maker is familiar with the function and activities of a police department will he have some knowledge of the justifications for such expenditures. For example, former U.S. Senator Samuel J. Ervin, Jr., recounted the story of the Spruce Corporation. An appropriation bill in about 1948 contained amounts for a director, a staff, some secretaries, supplies, and the like for the Corporation. A reporter began asking questions and found that the "Corporation" had been created in 1918 to buy spruce for the construction of airplanes. Before it could buy any spruce, World War I was over and construction had ceased. But in the appropriation bills the Corporation lived on, as did its director, staff, etc. For 30 years they had done nothing—not even answer questions about their function. Nobody asked.

Some critics of the object-of-expenditure approach feel that it is overly control centered, to the detriment of the planning and evaluation processes. They assert that in practice a disproportionate amount of attention is focused upon short-term dollar inputs of specific departments (personnel, supplies, etc.); and, consequently, that both long-run considerations and those relevent to the programs of the organization as a whole usually receive inadequate attention. Too, they argue that crucial planning decisions tend to originate at the lowest levels of the organization and flow upward; whereas broad goals, objectives, and policies should originate in the upper echelon and flow downward to be implemented by subordinates. As a result, governmental goals tend to be stated in terms of uncoordinated aggregations of goals of the various department heads. It is also asserted that planning may be neglected, budgets being based upon hastily made requests based merely on present expenditure levels and patterns. This "budgeting by default" leads to perpetuation of past activities, whether or not appropriate, failure to set definite goals and objectives, and failure to consider all possible alternatives available to the organization in striving to accomplish its purposes. Further, it is asserted that the legislative branch is given so much object-of-expenditure detail that it cannot possibly assimilate it, yet it is not given data pertaining to the functions, programs, activities, and outputs of executive branch agencies. Consequently, the legislative branch tends to exercise control over such items as the number of telephones to be permitted or the salary of a particular individual, rather than focusing its attention upon broad programs and policies of the organization.

This approach is also criticized as being out of date. Line-item appropriations, encouraged by the approach, may have been a necessary reaction to the "boss rule" scandals of the turn of the century period; but critics assert that in today's complex environment the executive branch must have reasonable discretion and flexibility to manage diverse and complex programs. Finally, it is contended that this method encourages spending rather than economizing, and that department heads feel compelled to expend their full appropriations—whether needed or not—as (1) performance evaluation tends to be focused upon spending, and the manager is assumed to be "good" as long as he keeps his spending within budgetary limitations, and (2) a manager's subsequent budgets may be reduced if he spends less than he requests for a given year, as legislators often base appropriations on prior expenditures and also may consider the fact that a manager did not spend as much as he requested indicative of budget request "padding."

The Performance Approach

Although the performance approach originated near the turn of the century, it received its biggest impetus from the report of the first Hoover Commission in 1949 and came into popular usage in the fifties. The Hoover Commission report included the statement that:

> We recommend that the whole budgetary concept of the federal government should be refashioned by the adoption of a budget based on functions, activities, and projects: this we designate a "performance budget."[3]

Confusion accompanied the report of the Commission's Task Force, however, as it used the terms "performance" and "program" synonymously:

> A program or performance budget should be substituted for the present budget, thus presenting a document . . . in terms of services, activities, and work projects rather than in terms of the things bought.[4]

Although these terms have been used synonymously by many eminent authorities, the term "program budgeting" has recently taken on different connotations from that of "performance budgeting" and these terms will be distinguished here.[5]

The NCGA defined a **performance budget** as:

> A budget wherein expenditures are based primarily upon measurable performance of activities and work programs. A performance budget may also incorporate other bases of expenditure classification, such as character and object class, but these are given a subordinate status to activity performance.[6]

This approach embodies a shifting of emphasis from objects of expenditure to "measurable performance of activities and work programs." The primary focus is on *evaluation* of the efficiency with which existing activities are being carried out; its primary tools are cost accounting and work measurement. The gist of this method may be summarized as (1) classifying budgetary accounts by function and activity, as well as by organization unit and object of expenditure, (2) investigating

---

[3] Commission on Organization of the Executive Branch of the Government, *Budgeting and Accounting* (Washington, D.C.: U.S. Government Printing Office, 1949), p. 8.

[4] Task Force Report, *Fiscal, Budgeting, and Accounting Activities* (Washington, D.C.: U.S. Government Printing Office, 1949), p. 43.

[5] The confusion has arisen primarily over differing uses of the term "program." In performance budgeting the term has been applied generally to specific activities within a single department (street sweeping, police patrol, etc.), whereas in program or planning programming-budgeting (PPB) the term usually has a broader connotation (preservation of life and property, alleviation of pain and suffering, etc.) which may include activities of many departments of a government.

[6] GAAFR (80), p. 70.

and measuring existing activities in order to obtain maximum efficiency and to establish cost standards, and (3) basing the budget of the succeeding period upon unit cost standards multiplied by the expected number of units of the activity estimated to be required in that period. The total budget for an agency would be the sum of the products of its unit cost standards multiplied by the expected units of activity in the upcoming period. The enacted budget is viewed somewhat as a performance contract between the legislative branch and the chief executive.

Probably the most important contributions of the performance approach have been (1) its emphasis upon the inclusion within the proposed budget of a narrative description of each proposed activity, and (2) organization of the budget by activities, with requests supported by estimates of costs and accomplishments in quantitative terms, and (3) its emphasis on the need to measure output as well as input. The performance budget emphasizes the activities for which funds are requested, therefore, rather than merely how much will be spent, and requires answers to questions such as these:

1. What are the agency's objectives; for what reason does the agency ask for appropriations; what services does the agency render to justify its existence?
2. What programs or activities does the agency use to achieve its objective?
3. What volume of work is required in each of the activities?
4. What levels of services have past appropriations provided?
5. What level of activity or service may legislators and the taxpayers expect if the requested amounts are appropriated?

To provide the legislative body with a reasonable program, each department must do some clear thinking about what it is trying to do and how it can do it best. In addition, when the legislators fully understand the department's work, its objectives, and its problems, the appropriation ordinance achieves its full meaning as a contract between the executive and legislative branches.

In addition to assisting both the legislature and the public in understanding the nature of the activities undertaken by the executive branch, performance data also provide legislators additional freedom to reduce or expand the amounts requested for particular functions or activities. This additional freedom may be illustrated by contrasting the legislative position under the performance approach with that when an object-of-expenditure budget is used. The detailed listings of positions to be filled and things to be bought in object-of-expenditure budgets provide the legislative group with a wealth of detail. And, in the usual case, the appropriations are made in almost as great detail, so that any attempt to change the budget requests requires that the detailed items making up the budget be changed by the legislature. Decisions as to such changes are administrative, not legislative, in nature. The legislative body should make decisions concerning the distribution of limited resources in accordance with the relative importance of the several functions and activities for which funds are needed. Where information is available as to particular functions and activities, these may be readily expanded or contracted at the will of legislature; where only object-of-expenditure data are available, the legislature must deal with minutiae; it may be tempted to make changes arbitrarily, such as slashing all requests a given percentage. If the final appropriation under the performance approach provides more or less than was budgeted for a function or activity, the executive branch must, of course, revise its plans in order to make the most effective use of amounts appropriated.

The performance approach also provides the chief executive with an additional avenue of control over his subordinates. Rather than being restricted merely to how much his subordinates spend, he may evaluate the performance of activities in terms of both dollar and activity unit standards.

Although much has been written about the performance approach, it does not appear to have often been adopted in its "pure state," though performance data are frequently used to supplement or support object-of-expenditure requests and are essential to program budgeting. Although the approach is fundamentally sound, (1) few state and local governments have sufficient budgetary or accounting staffs to identify units of measurement, perform cost analyses, etc.; (2) many services and activities of governments do not appear readily measurable in meaningful output units or unit cost terms; and (3) accounts of governments have typically been maintained on a budgetary expenditure basis, rather than on a full cost basis, making data gathering difficult if not impossible. In practice, expenditure data often have been substituted indiscriminately for cost (expense) data; and input measures have been used in place of output measures. In addition, activities sometimes have been costed and measured in great detail without sufficient consideration being given to the necessity or desirability of the activities themselves—that is, without concern for whether the activity contributed to achievement of the government's goals or, if the activity was necessary, whether it could be accomplished in a better way. For these and other reasons, most attempts to install comprehensive performance budgeting systems were disappointing and the adverse publicity received by some attempts no doubt discouraged others from experimenting with the approach. Advocates of the performance approach feel that it has been successful in instilling an attitude of cost consciousness in government, however, and note the many governmental activities now being measured objectively. The approach has therefore proved extremely helpful, especially when its application has been limited to discrete, tangible, routine types of activities such as street sweeping, police patrol, and garbage collection.

The Program and Planning-Programming-Budgeting (PPB) Approaches

Another reason for the apparent demise of the performance budget (as such) was the shift in emphasis in the late fifties and early sixties to the program approach and then, in the mid-sixties, to what has come to be known as the Planning-Programming-Budgeting System, often referred to as PPB or PPBS. Here again, terminology is a problem. The term "program budget" is sometimes used to refer to PPB systems or approaches and at other times is used in distinctly different ways. The NCGA, for example, defined a **program budget** as:

> A budget wherein expenditures are based primarily on programs of work and secondarily on character and object . . . a transitional type of budget between

the traditional character and object class budget, on the one hand, and the performance budget, on the other.[7]

Others distinguish between "full program" and "modified program" budgetary approaches, the latter being essentially a performance approach in which unit cost measurement is attempted only selectively. The following definition is preferred by the authors:

> Program budgets deal principally with broad planning and the costs of functions or activities. A **full** program approach to budgeting would require that the full cost of a function, e.g., juvenile delinquency control, would be set forth under the *program* regardless of the organizational units that may be involved in carrying such programs into execution. Thus, in the juvenile delinquency "program," certain activities of the welfare agency, the police department, the juvenile courts, the law department, and the district attorney would be included. . . .
>
> A **modified** program budget approach would be organized solely within major organizational units, e.g., departments.[8]

As the term is used here, "program budgeting" refers to a *planning-oriented* approach which emphasizes programs, functions, and activities—with lesser emphasis upon evaluation or control. Performance measurement is not, therefore, a prerequisite to program budgeting, though it may be a useful adjunct. Too, the program approach is *communication-oriented*, with budgetary requests and reports summarized in terms of a few broad programs rather than in a myriad of object-of-expenditure or departmental activity detail—though such details may be provided in the executive budget and the final appropriation may be on a line-item basis.

The most elaborate version of program budgeting has come to be known as the Planning-Programming-Budgeting system (PPB or PPBS). As was the case with performance budgeting, PPB emphasis originated with the Federal government when concepts developed in the early part of this century were refined by the Rand Corporation in the late fifties and experimented with in the Department of Defense in the early sixties. The movement to PPB received its greatest impetus in 1965 when President Johnson instructed most Federal departments and agencies to apply this approach to their program planning and budgeting.

PPB or PPBS is not so much a new system or approach as a reordered synthesis of time-honored budgetary concepts and techniques, with additional emphasis on long-run considerations, systems analyses, and cost-benefit analyses of alternative courses of action. As Hatry observed:

> Its essence is development and presentation of information as to the full implications, the costs and benefits, of the major alternative courses of action relevant to major resource allocation decisions.
>
> The main contribution of PPBS lies in the *planning* process, i.e., the process of making program policy decisions that lead to a specific budget and specific

---

[7] Ibid.

[8] L. Moak and K. Killian, *Operating Budget Manual* (Chicago: Municipal Finance Officers Association, 1963), pp. 11–12. (Emphasis added.)

multi-year plans. The *budget* is a detailed short term resource plan for implementing the program decisions. PPBS does not replace the need for careful budget analysis to assure that approved programs will be carried out in an efficient and cost-conscious manner, nor does it remove the need for the preparation of the detailed, line-item type of information to *support* budget submission.[9]

The major distinctive characteristics of PPB, as described by Hatry, are:

1. It focuses on identifying the fundamental objectives of the government and then relating all activities to these (regardless of organizational placement).
2. Future year implications are explicitly identified.
3. All pertinent costs are considered.
4. Systematic analysis of alternatives is performed [e.g., cost-benefit analysis and systems analysis and operations research].[10]

Among the benefits to states and localities attributed to the PPB approach are these:

1. *Long range fiscal planning becomes routine.* All government programs have to be viewed in a perspective that considers not only the expenditures in the immediate budget period but for the years ahead.
2. *Plans and programs are reviewed continuously.* Under the system progress on each program will have to be reviewed each year, and the program revised, when new, previously unknown factors come into play, or when previous judgments have to be corrected. The periodic review helps to ascertain whether existing and proposed programs are the most effective ways of accomplishing a particular government mission. The most effective way is to be determined in terms of budgetary costs, the extent to which ample or scarce resources (for instance, highly skilled labor) are to be utilized, and whether a program has a positive or negative effect with respect not only to the primary but also to the secondary goals.
3. *Government activities are classified in terms of programs and their purposes.* Budgeting by programs rather than by administrative units, by budgeted positions, and by object expenditures has long been advocated. It permits a better understanding of the role of individual activities in meeting governmental objectives.
4. *Interagency coordination of programs is strengthened.* The system requires that each agency of the government engage periodically in meaningful self-examination both in terms of the specific function of the agency, and of the relation of this function to the activities of other agencies of the government. The latter requires interagency discussion and clarification, even prior to review in any office for program coordination.
5. *Intergovernmental planning is improved.* Federal aid programs will be viewed in the context of the jurisdictions' own program plans. The system will strengthen the federal effort toward improving budgeting and decision making by a counterpart effort in the state and local governments where the major portion of civilian public services are provided.
6. *A program evaluation cycle of program formulation, progress reporting,*

[9] Harry P. Hatry and John F. Cotton, *Program Planning for State, County, City* (Washington, D.C.: George Washington University, 1967), pp. 14–15. (Emphasis added.)

[10] Ibid., p. 15.

and program revision is established. Planning will be linked to budget decisions and program evaluation to planning. The budget process becomes a more meaningful tool of government.

7. *Each program is to be evaluated in terms of national goals.* This requires not only consideration of the appropriate functions of the various levels of government but also the relationship of government to private activities in the same field; activities which may either support these goals, or be in conflict with them.[11]

Those closely associated with PPB do not claim it to be a panacea. But this approach is designed to overcome criticisms that have been made of object-of-expenditure and performance budgeting. Both of these other approaches are based principally upon historical data and focus upon a single period, whereas PPB emphasizes long-range planning in which (1) ultimate goals and intermediate objectives must be explicitly stated, and (2) the costs and benefits of major alternative courses to achieve these goals and objectives are to be explicitly evaluated—in quantitative terms where practicable and narratively in all cases. PPB theory assumes that all programs are to be evaluated annually, so that poor ones may be weeded out and new ones added. Changes in existing programs are evaluated in terms of discounted marginal costs (and benefits), whereas object-of-expenditure budgets focus upon total expenditures and performance budgets are based upon an average cost or average expenditure concept. Program decisions are to be formulated at upper management levels under PPB, as illustrated in Figure 3-5, and department or agency heads are expected to gear their activities to fulfilling those agreed-upon objectives and goals. Finally, though PPB can be adapted to any level of appropriation specificity, many of its advocates hope to

Figure 3-5

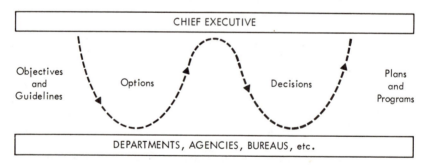

PPBS CYCLE

CHIEF EXECUTIVE

Objectives and Guidelines · Options · Decisions · Plans and Programs

DEPARTMENTS, AGENCIES, BUREAUS, etc.

Source: Harry P. Hatry and John F. Cotton, *Program Planning for State, County, City* (Washington, D.C.: George Washington University, 1967), p. 38.

encourage (1) decision making and appropriations by legislatures in broader policy terms, and (2) increased executive powers by use of "lump-sum" appropriations.

The broadened concept of a "program" under program budgeting is illustrated in Figure 3-6; the typical relationships among programs, subprograms, and

[11] *Ibid.*, p. 7. (Emphasis added.)

program elements are shown in Figures 3-7 and 3-8; and a multiyear program and fiscal plan format is illustrated in Figure 3-9.

Figure 3-6

STATE, COUNTY, CITY

Illustrative PPBS Program Structure

I. Personal Safety
   A. Law Enforcement
   B. Traffic Safety
   C. Fire Prevention and Control
   D. Safety from Animals
   E. Protection and Control of Disasters, Natural and Man-made
   F. Prevention of Other Accidents
II. Health
III. Intellectual Development and Personal Enrichment
IV. Satisfactory Home/Community Environment
V. Economic Satisfaction and Satisfactory Work Opportunities for the Individual
VI. Leisure-Time Opportunities

The focus of this categorization is the individual citizen—his needs and wants. Two category levels are shown (one represented by the roman numerals, the other by the capital letters). For a complete program structure, however, more levels are needed to display the applicable individual government activities.

Furthermore, the descriptions of each category (not shown here), including statements of major objectives, are an indispensable part of program structure preparation. The categories "Unassignable Research" and "Unassignable Support" might also be included for each of the eight program areas. These categories would contain activities directly related to the program area but which could not be related to individual categories within the program area.

Source: Harry P. Hatry and John F. Cotton, "Individual PPBS Characteristics," Program Planning for State, County, City (Washington, D.C.: George Washington University, 1967), p. 17.

Figure 3-7

EXAMPLE OF A PROGRAM STRUCTURE FORMAT

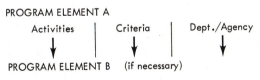

Source: H. Sternberger, J. Renz, and G. Fasolina, *Planning-Programming-Budgeting Systems (PPBS) in Nassau County, N.Y.," in Innovations in Planning, Programming, and Budgeting Systems in State and Local Governments* Washington, D.C.: U.S. Government Printing Office, 1969), p. 145.

Figure 3-8

PPB SYSTEMS: TYPICAL RELATIONSHIPS OF PROGRAMS, SUBPROGRAMS, AND PROGRAM ELEMENTS*

I. Human Resource Development
  A. Education: Elementary and Secondary
  B. Education: Higher
  C. Education: Special and Other
  D. Welfare: Public Assistance
  E. Welfare: Other
  F. Direct Payments to Individuals
  G. Employment Services
  H. Mental Health
  I. Health: General Services
  J. Health: General Facilities
    1. V.D. Control
    2. Communicable Disease Control
    3. Cancer Control
    4. Chronic Disease Control
    5. Health Education
    6. Tuberculosis Control
      a. X-Ray Services
      b. Laboratory Services
      c. Clinic Visits
      d. Non-Nursing Visits
      e. Examinations
      f. Social Work
      g. Nutrition Counseling
      h. Case Work
      i. Drug Services

Roman numeral: Objective level; capital letters: Major Program Area Level; arabic numerals: Program [Subprogram] Level; lowercase letters: Program Element Level. Adapted from Ernst and Ernst, Planning–Programming–Budgeting System for State and Local Governments (Olympia, Wash.: State of Washington, 1968), pp. 34–37.

Although the logic of PPB is convincing, there are many barriers to implementation of a complete PPB system.

1. It is quite difficult to formulate a meaningful, explicit statement of a government's goals and objectives that can be agreed upon by all concerned—regardless of how worthwhile such a statement may be.

2. Not only do goals change, but elected officials, in particular, often prefer not to commit themselves to more than very general statements lest they be precluded from changing their positions when politics dictates.

3. The time period considered relevant by an elected official may be limited to that remaining prior to the expiration of his current term of office; he may, at least subconsciously, be more interested in short run costs and results than in long run results or costs.

4. PPB, like performance budgeting, assumes both an adequate data base and a high level of analytical ability to be readily available to the

Figure 3-9

MULTIYEAR PROGRAM AND FINANCIAL PLAN
from Year 19X3 to 19X7 (Millions of Dollars)

Level		Program Categories*	FY 19X1 Actual	FY 19X2 Current Estimate	FY 19X3 Budget Year Estimate	FY 19X4 Program Estimate	FY 19X5 Program Estimate	FY 19X6 Program Estimate	FY 19X7 Program Estimate	Total Costs 19X3–X7
1st	2nd									
I		Personal Safety								
	A	Law Enforcement								
	B	Traffic Safety								
	C	Fire Prevention and Control								
	D	Safety From Animals								
	E	Protection and Control of Natural and Man-Made Disasters								
	F	Prevention of Other Accidents								
		Total Program Area I								
II		Health								
	A	Physical Health								
	B	Mental Health								
	C	Drug and Alcohol Addiction— Prevention and Control								
		Total Program Area II								

*In practice, more category levels would be needed to display the individual government activities/programs.
Source: Adapted from Harry P. Hatry and John F. Cotton, "Individual PPBS Characteristics," Program Planning for State, County, City (Washington, D.C.: George Washington University, 1967), pp. 20–21.

government. Relatively few state or local governments have sophisticated program data or the luxury of sophisticated staff analysts.

5. Finally, it should be noted that objective measurement is even more of a problem here than in the performance approach, as both costs and benefits, over a period of several years, must be estimated. Both are often quite difficult to measure and the ratio or relationship between two such estimates is apt to imply far more precision than is actually present.

The full PPBS approach requires the consideration of government-wide programs and their evaluation without regard to departmental assignments. That requirement, together with the habits of years of object-of-expenditure budgeting and a jealously guarded legislative power of the purse strings, has required that PPBS budgets contain explanations of the relationships between programs, program plans, and program budget requests, on the one hand, and units of government (agencies) and objects of expenditure, on the other. Such "crosswalks" are illustrated in Figure 3-10. Appropriations are likely to be made on the basis of organization units and objects of expenditure.

The implications of the preceding paragraph are that PPBS information appears to be used in practice more to supplement and support traditional budget information than vice versa, that there seems to be little or no accounting follow-up for comparisons of PPBS plans with results, that governmental accounting systems are geared first to budgetary accounting and only secondarily to supplemental data, and that PPBS is more useful for planning than for operation and control.

Zero-Base Budgeting

The newest approach to budgetary planning is zero-base budgeting (ZBB). It came on the scene about 1970 from the profit-seeking sector of the economy, was adopted by a few governments, and was popularized when President Carter, citing his Georgia experience with the approach, required its use for the Federal government. The essential idea of ZBB is that the continued existence of programs or activities is not taken for granted; each service must be justified in its entirety every year. Continued usage appears to lead to reductions in the rigor of the theory: (1) It may be recognized that full justification need be required of specific activities once every few years rather than for every budget (periodic "sunset reviews" of agencies fit nicely with this adaptation), and (2) it may be decided that some or all of the services provided by agencies must be provided at a minimal level and that crucial judgments need be applied only to the levels of service to be provided.

The basic processes of ZBB are as follows:

1. Divide all the operations of the government into *"decision units."* These are programs, activities, or relatively low level organization units. In general ZBB does not attempt to go outside major organizational units in its definition of program, though it can be combined with PPBS in this respect.

Figure 3-10

PPBS "Crosswalk"
19X1 Budget, All Departments

Department or Agency or Object of Expenditure	Total	Public Safety	Health	Education	Transportation	Recreation and Culture	Social Services	Legal, Fiscal Management	Community Welfare	Nonprogram Items
Mayor/Council										
City Clerk										
City Attorney										
Personnel										
City Planning										
Retirement Administration										
Office of Finance										
Office of Budget										
Police Department										
Fire Department										

Note: Totals of each column indicate program sums; totals for each organization unit indicate the amounts requested for each. If desired, the amounts requested for each unit may be broken down by classes of objects in varying degrees of detail.

2. Divide the operations of each decision unit into *"decision packages."* The bases for these may be specific activities, specific services rendered, organizational subunits of the decision unit, or alternative activities to be carried out to achieve, say, program goals.

3. Select the best option for providing service based on cost-benefit or other analysis (or on a political basis).

4. Divide the selected option into levels of service to be provided, such as last year's level, minimal, reduced, increased, or maximum. The levels of service should be costed and the costs compared with the services to be provided.

5. Rank the decision packages. As the budget requests move upward through the executive branch, managers at each level rank the decision packages in terms of governmental priorities. These priorities may have been developed through PPB; if not, a similar exercise at the highest levels should be available as assumptions to be used in ranking decision packages. The chief executive, having the priorities assigned by those below him in the administrative hierarchy, makes the ultimate decisions required to produce the executive budget.

ZBB is designed to force an annual review of all programs, activities, and expenditures; to save money by identifying outdated programs and unnecessarily high levels of service; to concentrate the attention of officials on the costs and benefits of services; to cause a search for new ways of providing services and achieving objectives; to improve the abilities of management to plan and evaluate; to provide better justification for the budget; and, finally, to improve the decisions made by the executive and legislative branches of the government. It is too soon to tell whether it will be successful in achieving these benefits. Certainly it requires a great deal of paperwork, staff time, and effort to identify and rank decision units and decision packages. Certainly it is difficult to obtain the data to compute costs of alternative methods of achieving objectives and of alternative levels of service.

To Sum Up

The budgetary approaches outlined here present, in theory, a record of changes from devices (object-of-expenditure budget and line-item appropriations) designed primarily to authorize and fiscally control expenditures through developments that have sought to bring program planning, analysis (systems, cost-benefit), and performance measurement into the process. The primarily incremental approach has given way to the consideration of complete programs and activities (program budgets, PPBS, ZBB). Techniques encouraging managerial control have been developed; legislative control has, in many instances, moved from minute control of details to broad control of functions, programs, and activities. Emphasis has shifted from input to output..

In practice the changes have not been as dramatic. Few budgets, no matter what their planning bases may have been, have avoided specification of objects of expenditures. Program planning on a government-wide basis, as in PPBS, must be related to agencies responsible for elements of the programs. The relationship may be stated in the executive budget or in the appropriation bill, but few legislative bodies are willing to appropriate without identifying agencies and objects of expenditure. PPBS has proved useful for planning, but not for execution, and has not been considered successful. Performance budgeting has led to gradual increases in the number of activities having defined units of output. Nonetheless, it has proved feasible in a relatively small number of such activities. ZBB, concentrating at the decision package level, may prove to be more easily convertible into appropriation bills and legislative control on program or activity bases within specific agencies. At this time the organization unit and objects of expenditure are the primary basis for financial reporting and managerial accountability.

The typical "good" budget for a municipality at this time, then, probably consists of program or activity descriptions *within organization units*, quantitative descriptions of levels of program activity where units of output have been defined, and object-of-expenditure units of input in dollars and numbers of employees.

Selecting an Appropriate Approach

Designing an appropriate approach to expenditure budgeting for a specific government requires (1) knowledge of the various general approaches that have been developed, (2) insight into the history and activities of the organization in question and the attitudes and capabilities of its personnel, in order to assess the proper planning-control-evaluation balance to be sought, (3) originality in combining the strengths of the object-of-expenditure, performance, program and ZZB approaches, while avoiding their weaknesses, and (4) patience in system design and implementation and the ability to adapt the system to changed circumstances. Experimentation with PPBS and ZBB analysis is highly desirable in the hope that they will be suited or adaptable to state and local government needs.

Because of its widespread use and adaptability to budgetary accounting, illustrations in the remainder of this text generally assume that an appropriation bill based on organization units and objects of expenditure is in use. The concepts and procedures illustrated apply generally to all budgetary systems, though expenditure account classifications may need to be changed and additional data gathered to achieve program or performance accountability and reporting. Even this change can be largely obviated if single activities are assigned to organization units for which expenditures are accumulated.

BUDGET PREPARATION

Sound financial planning requires that preparation of the budget be started in time for its adoption before the beginning of the period to which it applies. To insure that adequate time will be allowed, a budget calendar (see Figure 3-11) listing each step in the budgetary procedure and the time allowed for its completion should be prepared. The budget preparation then proceeds in a manner similar to that shown in Figure 3-12.

Budgeting has been described as the process of allocating scarce resources

Figure 3-11

A GOVERNMENTAL UNIT
Budget Calendar
For the Year Beginning January 1, 19X7

Date	Steps in Budget Procedure
Prior to October 1, 19X6	Budget officer prepares estimate forms and instructions.
October 1	Budget officer distributes estimate forms and instructions among departments.
October 1 to October 21	Departments prepare estimates. Budget officer prepares estimates of fixed charges and other nondepartmental items. Budget officer also prepares estimates of taxes and other nondepartmental revenues. Completed departmental estimate forms are returned to the budget officer by departments.
October 22 to November 1	Budget officer consolidates estimates.
November 2 to November 30	Budget officer conducts departmental hearings. Budget officer confers with chief executive, and the latter determines amounts to be finally recommended to the legislative body. Chief executive also determines amounts to be adopted as the official revenue estimates of the municipality for the budget year. Chief executive prepares budget message. Budget officer prepares final budget document for submission to legislative body.
December 1	Budget document, including message of chief executive, is turned over to legislative body.
December 2	Legislative body turns budget document over to its budget committee.
December 2 to December 15	Budget committee conducts public hearings and makes recommendations concerning the amounts to be appropriated.
December 16	Budget committee turns its recommendations over to the legislative body.
December 16 to December 23	Legislative body considers the committee's recommendations.
December 23	Legislative body adopts the budget by passing an appropriation ordinance. Legislative body levies taxes by passing a tax levy ordinance(s).
December 27	Request for allotments is sent out by chief executive through budget officer.
January 2, 19X7	Adopted budget is recorded on the books.
January 6	Departments submit work programs and allotment schedules to budget officer.
January 6 to January 15	Budget officer consolidates allotment schedules and presents them with recommendations to chief executive.
January 15	Chief executive makes final revisions.
January 16	Department heads are informed of the amounts alloted to them. Allotments are recorded on the books.

Figure 3-12

TRADITIONAL INFORMATION FLOW—BUDGET PREPARATION

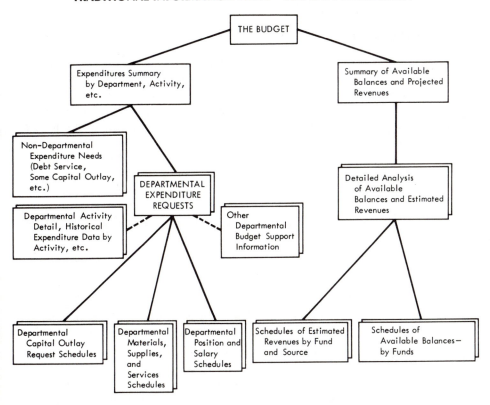

to unlimited demands. The typical formula for budget decision makers is as follows :

Estimated fund balance, beginning of budget year	$ X
Add: Estimated revenues, budget year	Y
Total appropriable resources, budget year	$ $X+Y$
Deduct: Estimated expenditures (appropriations), budget year	Z
Estimated fund balance, end of year	$\$X+Y-Z$

After making his best estimate of the fund balance at the beginning of the budget year, the chief budget officer must obtain estimates of the revenues that will be produced by all revenue sources at current rates of taxes, fees, and other charges. Having produced such estimates, the budget officer and the chief executive can compare them with revenues and expenditures of prior years and with their knowledge of changes in demands on the government and its programs. Such comparisons should provide an impression of the adequacy of estimated revenues to meet the needs for expenditures.

Revenue Estimates

The process of estimating revenues has almost as many facets as there are types of revenue. The general property tax, the chief reliance of most municipalities, is described in detail in Chapter 5. The revenue from the property tax is computed by applying a rate determined by the legislative body to a tax base of assessed property values. The latter may be expected to increase with building activity, inflation, and economic development. Since most assessments do not equal market value, property tax revenue may also be changed by changing the percentage of market value at which property is assessed. Thus the general property tax has a number of variables which must be considered in estimating revenues.

Nearly all revenues are determined by applying a rate to some base. Many municipalities now depend on an income tax, a tax form which has become an increasingly important revenue source of non-Federal governments in recent years. Here the rates expected to be in effect must be used to estimate expected revenue, which will be directly related to levels of economic activity and wage and salary rates. Licenses and permits, important revenue sources in many municipalities, require evaluation of the number of such licenses or permits to be issued and any rate changes contemplated. Other revenues, such as from fines and forfeitures, intergovernmental grants or shared revenue, and fees must be estimated on the best available basis.

After all of these estimates have been made, they are tabulated in a Statement of Actual and Estimated Revenues (Figure 3-13). This statement provides for the computation of total estimated revenues for the new year and for comparisons with prior years.

Expenditure Planning

In large organizations expenditure planning should be considered a year-round activity. The budget director and his budget examiners should be continually studying the agencies with whose budgets they will work because analyses of agency operations, including both what the agency does and how it does it, are essential if the budget office is to give proper consideration to agency requests. In many jurisdictions the budget office has been assigned responsibilities for doing work best described as that of an operations analyst. This assignment has come in many cases because of the qualifications of budget personnel; in other cases it has been a natural outgrowth of the intimate, yet independent, knowledge and viewpoint of the budget examiners. The budget office should also utilize relevant reports of the internal audit staff, independent auditors, management consultants, or others in familiarizing itself with agency operations.

The review of agency operations becomes a secondary (but still important) operation when the actual production of an expenditure budget begins. The first move in the latter process is to design forms that will make feasible the handling

Figure 3-13

A GOVERNMENTAL UNIT
General Fund
Statement of Actual and Estimated Revenues

	Actual 19X5	Actual First Nine Months of 19X6	Estimated Remainder of 19X6	Total Columns 2 and 3	Estimated 19X7
Taxes:					
General property taxes	$294,000	$291,000	—	$291,000	$288,000
Penalties and interest on delinquent taxes	1,100	800	$ 250	1,050	1,000
Total taxes	$295,100	$291,800	$ 250	$292,050	$289,000
Licenses and Permits:					
Motor vehicles	$ 31,000	$ 25,500	$ 7,000	$ 32,500	$ 34,000
Building structures and equipment	1,500	1,450	450	1,900	2,000
Alcoholic beverages	11,000	9,000	3,000	12,000	13,000
Professional and occupational	6,200	4,650	1,225	5,875	6,000
Amusements	1,350	990	300	1,290	1,300
Total licenses and permits	$ 51,050	$ 41,590	$11,975	$ 53,565	$ 56,300
Intergovernmental Revenues:					
Charges for Services:					
Court costs, fees, and charges	$ 1,100	$ 1,000	$ 200	$ 1,200	$ 1,000
Sale of ordinances— parking meters	1,200	925	250	1,175	1,000
Special police services	5,100	3,000	1,050	4,050	4,000
Health inspection	375	465	135	600	800
Total charges for services	$ 7,775	$ 5,390	$ 1,635	$ 7,025	$ 6,800
Fines and Forfeits	$ 6,000	$ 4,000	$ 500	$ 4,500	$ 5,100
Miscellaneous Revenue	4,000	3,000	1,200	4,200	4,300
Grand Total	$437,000	$397,000	$ 36,000	$433,000	$431,000

of the volume of work. The process continues as outlined in the budget calendar, Figure 3-11 and in Figure 3-12.

Budget Instructions. The instructions the budget officer sends to the agencies should include (1) the budget calendar; (2) a statement of executive goals, policies, and expectations relative to the upcoming budget period; (3) other appropriate comments or instructions explaining how decisions regarding amounts to be requested should be made, necessary supporting data, etc.; and (4) an explanation of how to perform the mechanics of filling out the budget estimate forms, with emphasis upon any changes from prior years. Policy statements to aid the heads of agencies or departments in deciding amounts of budget requests will include such matters as the following:

1. The type of budget to be prepared (see the "Budgetary Approaches and Emphases" section earlier in this chapter) and the character and quantity of explanatory material.
2. The general level of revenue and expenditures anticipated for the period and the attitude of the chief executive toward improved or expanded services, i.e., the major program thrusts and their appoximate magnitude.
3. The application of legal or administrative requirements to the departments. For example, new personnel regulations may drastically change the pattern for staffing the departments.
4. Relevant economic and other data bearing on subjects such as the expected state of the economy and its effect on commodity and labor prices and levels of business activity. For example, an estimate of the level and type of construction activity in a community will determine the number of building permits to be issued and the number of inspections that the government will have to make in the succeeding period. City-owned utilities will also obtain from such data their estimates of new connections.

Identity of Organizational, Budgetary, and Accounting Units. In the process of organizing the agencies or departments of a governmental unit the programs and activities of the organization should be the controlling factor. From the standpoint of managerial control through budgeting and accounting, it would be desirable for each program and activity to be within a single organizational unit. (At the lowest organization level, no more than one activity or subactivity should be assigned to each unit.) This is not to say that the city organization would have hundreds of small departments, or only a few large ones, but simply that the major functions should be assigned to departments and that activities and subactivities under each function should be charged to the organization subunits of the departments on the basis indicated. For example, the business office of the city should be broken down into such units as general ledger, accounts payable, accounts receivable, purchasing, and the like. (In small cities organizational patterns may have to be determined by technical skills rather than by functions and activities).

Under this concept organizational units are also budgetary planning units, budgetary accounting units, and, if cost accounting is used, cost accounting units. The accumulation of accurate past and current costs for a unit and its activity is necessary for the adequate and accurate calculation of future costs for that unit and its activity.

Call for Departmental Estimates. The chief executive's call for departmental estimates is one of the first steps in the preparation of the budget. Following the object-of-expenditure/performance combination approach illustrated here, a department's first move in preparing its estimate would be to accumulate and schedule workload data. A work program for the Bureau of Sanitation of the

Department of Public Works is presented in Figure 3-14. Actual and estimated workload and unit cost[12] figures are compiled and used both to produce and support the budget request. Note that there are slight changes in the unit cost figures used for estimating 19X7 expenditures. Such changes may be due to expected changes in the cost of labor, materials, or equipment. Unit cost figures will also fluctuate with volume as fixed costs are spread over a greater or lesser volume of work. (Capital outlay is treated separately to avoid distortion of year-to-year comparisons.) To avoid the influence of price level vagaries upon the measurement of efficiency, some cities use man-hours or other work measurement units rather than total cost as the measure, or indicator, of performance.

Many activities or a city or state are not susceptible to such exact costing as are those of the Bureau of Sanitation. Organizations responsible for such activities should nonetheless attempt to describe their activities in meaningful units. For example, the Patrol Division of a Police Department might provide comparative data by years for such significant activities as those indicated in Figure 3-15. Note also the information on the change from two-man to one-man prowl cars and the resulting improvement of service as indicated by (1) estimates of prowl car average response time and (2) the increase in the number of patrol beats. Progress is continually being made in relating such activity information to the cost of operations; activities previously considered unmeasurable are steadily subjected to analysis and control through newly devised criteria indicative of performance.

A series of several performance measures or indicators often proves superior to the use of a single compromise measure. It is essential in all cases to remember that such measures are merely *indicators* to guide management decisions, not substitutes therefor, and that such indicators must actually relate directly to either (or both) the *quality* or *quantity* of work performed in terms of organizational goals. The latter point is of particular importance because poorly selected indicators or failure to specify and control performance quality may lead to a decline in efficiency. To illustrate, should the purchasing department's performance be measured only in terms of the number of purchase orders issued one might find its performance "dressed up" through such tactics as making many unnecessarily small orders, e.g., ordering supplies in uneconomically small quantities in order to generate many purchase order "performance measures."

After work load and unit cost information for an organizational unit have been accumulated to the extent deemed practicable, this information should be converted into estimates of total costs for the upcoming budget period. Estimates should be made for each organizational unit and subunit (remember that insofar as possible organizational lines should be based on activities). Estimates for the supervisory activity of the Police Department are set out in Figure 3-16. The first eight columns are filled in by the finance officer; columns 9 through 11 are filled in by the chief of police. In some jurisdictions columns are provided following column nine in which the chief executive places his recommendation as to the number of employees, their rates of pay, and the total amount. If these latter

[12] The term "cost" and "unit cost," when used with reference to govermental funds, usually connotes *expenditure* rather than expense.

Figure 3-14

A GOVERNMENTAL UNIT

Work Program—19X7

Departmental Code: 4000

Fund: General
Function: Sanitation and Waste Removal
Department: Public Works
Bureau: Sanitation
Submitted by: M. A. Downs, Chief
Date: October 10, 19X6

Operation	Work Unit	Actual 19X5			Estimated 19X6			Estimated 19X7		
		No. of Units	Unit Cost	Total	No. of Units	Unit Cost	Total	No. of Units	Unit Cost	Total
Garbage Collection	Tons	158,319	$1.45	$229,562.22	168,000	$1.46	$245,280.00	170,000	$1.44	$244,800.00
Incineration	Tons	170,350	1.18	201,013.00	180,000	1.18	212,400.00	182,000	1.19	216,580.00

Figure 3-15

A GOVERNMENTAL UNIT—POLICE DEPARTMENT
Patrol Division Work Load Information

	Actual 19X4	Actual 19X5	Estimated 19X6	Estimated 19X7
Prowl car average response time	3.4	3.4	3.4	3.4 – 2.0
Mileage	1,763,900	1,837,000	1,936,000	2,800,000
Arrests	25,625	28,832	32,725	35,000
Citations	103,319	94,741	106,316	114,000
Investigations	9,078	10,604	11,600	12,650
Shakedowns	69,460	77,116	90,750	98,000

The prowl car is one of the basic elements in a modern police system, and the field operations of the Patrol Division during the coming year are scheduled for conversion to one-man prowl cars on all watches. The number of patrol beats during the two evening watches also will be increased from 24 to 48. This major change in operations will result in a higher utilization of existing manpower, and prowl car response time to radio calls should be reduced from 3.4 to 2 minutes. An improved level of crime prevention and traffic control is anticipated.

Conversion to one-man patrol car operations will require three additional positions of Sergeant to provide adequate field supervision. Also required is one position of Intermediate Stenographer Clerk, which would relieve the Patrol Division staff of a considerable volume of clerical work.

columns are provided, and if the chief executive's recommendations differ from departmental requests, the city council will be presented with conflicting information. Some feel that since the chief executive is responsible for planning and administration, it is better for the council to receive only his recommendations. Where this view prevails, the chief of police will fill out columns 9 through 11; but when the estimate is presented to the council, these columns will have been revised to contain the chief executive's recommendations, which may or may not be the same as those of the chief of police. Others feel that the council should have knowledge of departmental requests as well as executive proposals (where these differ) and include such information in the budget document or in notes thereto.

Column 12 contains the appropriation granted by the council. Note that in this case a lump sum of $71,500 was granted for personal services. The council could have made an appropriation for each line; in doing so it would have secured detailed control of expenditures, but would have sacrificed the advantages of executive flexibility.

Figures 3-17 and 3-18 illustrate forms used for estimating supervisory expenditures other than personal services. Figure 3-19 summarizes the estimates of the department's supervisory activity.

Figure 3-20 presents the departmental summary. Notice that the summary

Figure 3-16

A GOVERNMENTAL UNIT
Departmental Estimate Personal Services—19X7

Departmental Code: 2000

Fund: General
Function: Public Safety
Department: Police
Activity: Supervision
Submitted by: A. Johnson, Chief
Date: October 10, 19X6

Code No.	Classification	Actual						Proposed, 19X7			Appropriation by Legislative Body
		January 1, 19X6			October 1, 19X6						
		No.	Rate	Amount	No.	Rate	Amount	No.	Rate	Amount	Amount
1	2	3	4	5	6	7	8	9	10	11	12
01	Chief of Police	1	$22,500	$22,500	1	$22,500	$22,500	1	$23,500	$23,500	
01	Deputy Chief	1	17,500	17,500	1	17,500	17,500	1	19,000	19,000	
01	Clerk-Typist	2	8,000	16,000	2	8,000	16,000	2	9,000	18,000	
01	Policewoman	1	10,000	10,000	1	10,000	10,000	1	16,000	11,000	
	Total	5	......	$66,000	5	......	$66,000	5	......	$71,500	$71,500

Figure 3-17

A GOVERNMENTAL UNIT
Departmental Estimate
Current Expenses—Other than Personal Services
19X7

Departmental Code: __2000__

Fund: General
Function: Public Safety
Department: Police
Activity: Supervision
Submitted by: A. Johnson, Chief
Date: October 10, 19X6

Code No.	Classification	Actual 19X4	Actual 19X5	Actual First Nine Months of 19X6	Estimated Remainder of 19X6	Total Columns 5 and 6	Proposed 19X7	Appropriation by Legislative Body
1	2	3	4	5	6	7	8	9
	Supplies:							
02	Janitor Supplies	$ 95	$ 96	$ 77	$ 25	$ 102	$ 120	
02	Clothing	1,011	1,200	785	260	1,045	1,300	
02	Record Supplies	100	115	95	30	125	150	
02	Ammunition	427	431	335	115	450	500	
	Total	$ 1,633	$1,842	$1,292	$ 430	$1,722	$2,070	$2,000
	Other Services and Charges:							
03	Printing	$ 247	$ 255	$ 195	$ 65	$ 260	$ 280	
03	Gas	74	73	55	20	75	80	
03	Electricity	158	161	126	43	169	177	
03	Water	56	53	41	14	55	60	
03	Repairs to Office Equipment	293	300	235	80	315	363	
03	Rent	1,800	1,800	1,405	470	1,875	1,900	
03	Surety Bond Premiums	80	80	60	20	80	100	
	Total	$2,708	$2,722	$2,117	$ 712	$2,829	$2,960	$2,900
	Grand Total	$4,341	$4,564	$3,409	$1,142	$4,551	$5,030	$4,900

Figure 3-18

A GOVERNMENTAL UNIT
Departmental Estimate
Capital Outlays
19X7

Fund: General
Function: Public Safety
Department: Police
Activity: Supervision
Submitted by: A. Johnson, Chief
Date: October 10, 19X6

Departmental Code: 2000

| Code No. | Classification | Explanation | Proposed 19X7 | | | Appropriation by Legislative Body |
			Quantity	Unit Price	Cost	
1	2	3	4	5	6	7
04	Office Equipment	Desks	1	$ 90	$ 90	
		Total	—	—	$ 90	$ 90

in this example is by object-of-expenditure and by organizational subunit. In the object-of-expenditure summary the identity of the estimates of the supervisory activity has been lost, but in the summary by organizational subunit the estimate of supervisory activity appears as an identifiable figure. Appropriations could be made by granting the amounts shown in either summary. As observed previously, if the appropriation ordinance is drawn to appropriate a lump sum for each activity, the legislative body can very easily change the requested amounts; that is, the legislators can say, by increasing or decreasing amounts requested by the several activities, that they believe an activity should be stepped up or reduced. Such a decision gives the executive branch the responsibility of scaling operations to the level indicated as desirable by the legislative group.

Estimating Other Charges. Some expenditures are ordinarily not allocated to any program or activity of an organizational unit. Examples are interest, contributions to pension funds, retirement of serial bonds, and contributions to sinking funds. These expenditure estimates are therefore prepared by the budget officer. However, refinements of accounting and budgeting are continually reducing the number of unallocated expenditures. For example, contributions to pension funds may properly be charged to activities on the basis of the employees whose salaries caused the contributions.

Figure 3-19

A GOVERNMENTAL UNIT

Departmental Estimate
Activity Summary—Supervision
19X7

Departmental Code: 421

Fund: General
Function: Public Safety
Department: Police
Activity: Supervision
Submitted by: A. Johnson, Chief
Date: October 10, 19X6

Code No.	Classification	Actual 19X4	Actual 19X5	Actual First Nine Months of 19X6	Estimated Remainder of 19X6	Total Columns 5 and 6	Proposed 19X7	Appropria- tion by Legislative Body
1	2	3	4	5	6	7	8	9
01	Personal Services	$42,000	$44,000	$49,500	$16,500	$66,000	$71,500	$71,500
02	Supplies	1,633	1,842	1,292	430	1,722	2,070	2,000
03	Other Services and Charges	2,708	2,722	2,117	712	2,829	2,960	2,900
	Total Current Expenditures	$46,341	$48,564	$52,909	$17,642	$70,551	$76,530	$76,400
06	Capital Outlays	$ 150	$ 200	$ 100	$ 40	$ 140	$ 190	$ 190
	Total	$46,491	$48,764	$53,009	$17,682	$70,691	$76,720	$76,590

Figure 3-20

A GOVERNMENTAL UNIT
Departmental Estimate Summary 19X7

Departmental Code: 2000

Fund: General
Function: Public Safety
Department: Police
Submitted by: A. Johnson, Chief
Date: October 10, 19X6

Code No.	Classification	19X4	19X5	First Nine Months of 19X6	Estimated Remainder of 19X6	Total Columns 5 and 6	Proposed 19X7	Appropriation by Legislative Body
1	2	3	4	5	6	7	8	9
	By Object of Expenditure:							
01	Personal Services	$569,248	$680,299	$590,705	$176,610	$767,315	$774,990	$775,050
02	Supplies	43,831	45,941	39,795	8,925	48,720	50,100	50,100
03	Other Services and Charges	34,046	34,932	26,137	11,668	37,805	38,250	37,500
	Total Current Expenditures	$647,125	$761,172	$656,637	$197,203	$853,840	$863,340	$862,650
04-07	Capital Outlays	$ 21,590	$ 28,900	$ 26,148	$ 3,952	$ 30,100	$ 24,250	$ 24,250
	Total	$668,715	$790,072	$682,785	$201,155	$883,940	$887,590	$886,900

By Organizational Subunits:							
Supervision	$ 46,491	$ 48,764	$ 53,009	$ 17,682	$ 70,691	$ 76,720	$ 76,590
Training	4,675	5,560	4,723	1,376	6,099	7,000	7,000
General and Criminal Records	12,444	14,826	12,596	3,661	16,257	16,257	16,257
Identification Records	7,775	9,266	7,872	2,293	10,165	10,165	10,165
Custody of Recovered Property	3,111	3,707	3,149	917	4,066	4,075	4,075
Communications Systems	34,222	40,772	34,638	10,091	44,729	44,700	44,500
Detention and Custody of Prisoners	40,445	48,185	40,935	11,926	52,861	52,861	52,861
Motor Vehicle Inspection and Regulation	15,556	18,533	15,744	4,587	20,331	20,331	20,331
Criminal Investigation	49,778	59,305	50,382	14,678	65,060	65,000	65,060
Uniformed Patrol	224,000	266,871	226,719	66,050	292,769	289,731	289,525
Vice and Morals Control	21,779	25,946	22,042	6,422	28,464	28,464	28,350
Crime Prevention	28,000	33,359	28,340	8,256	36,596	36,500	36,500
Traffic Control	118,223	140,849	119,657	34,868	154,525	154,525	154,525
Special Detail Services	20,222	24,093	20,468	5,963	26,431	26,431	26,431
Auxiliary Services	24,889	29,652	25,191	7,339	32,530	32,530	32,530
Police Stations and Buildings	17,105	20,384	17,320	5,046	22,366	22,300	22,200
Total	$668,715	$790,072	$682,785	$201,155	$883,940	$887,590	$886,900

Revision of Departmental Estimates. As soon as department heads have filled out the budget estimate forms, and at any rate not later than the date designated in the budget calendar, they transmit the forms, together with work programs and other supporting data, to the budget officer. The latter notes whether the estimates have been properly prepared, summarizes the information received, and presents the schedules, together with the summaries and revenue estimates, to the chief executive, who must analyze all the data in order to prepare his recommendations to the legislative body.

Both the departmental estimate schedules and the work programs are of great help to the chief executive in preparing his recommendations. In addition, he confers with the budget officer and with department heads, whom he may ask to justify estimates of expenditures. In larger governmental units the chief executive may employ efficiency engineers, program consultants, or other specialists to make special investigations to determine whether departmental requests are justified.

The chief executive pays careful attention also to the revenue estimates. Whereas no single operating department head knows the relationship between total estimated expenditures and total estimated revenues, the chief executive has these data. If estimated expenditures exceed appropriable resources first estimated to be available during the budget period, (1) reductions may be made in the expenditure amounts requested, (2) additional revenues may be secured, or (3) a decision may be made to incur a deficit. A chief executive should not make arbitrary adjustments of expenditure requests at some fixed percentage. For example, if estimated expenditures exceed estimated revenues by 10 percent, he should not automatically reduce each department's request by this percentage but will consider each department individually. If he believes that a department's request is proper in the light of the number, volume, and quality of services projected for the budget year, his decision to increase, decrease, or approve the department's estimates will depend on his evaluation of the community's needs for the services and of the political effects of curtailing them.

The Budget Document. After the chief executive has considered the requests of the various departments and taken action on them, he is in a position to prepare the budget document to be submitted to the legislative body for consideration and adoption. The budget document may consist of the following:

1. A budget message, in which the principal budget items are explained, the governmental unit's experience during the past year and its financial status at the present time are outlined, and recommendations regarding the programs and financial policy for the coming year are made.

2. Budget summaries. Some of the possible schedules are summaries of revenues, all funds, by source; summaries of actual and proposed expenditures by major function, by major organizational unit, by major object of expenditure; summaries of actual and proposed staffing levels by organizational units. Figures 3-13 and 3-21 are examples of these summaries.

Figure 3-21

A GOVERNMENTAL UNIT
Budget Summary
General Budget—19X7

Estimated Revenues		*Estimated Expeditures*	
General Fund			
Taxes	$289,000	Personal Services	$219,000
Other Revenues	142,000	Other Current Expenditures	63,600
		Capital Outlays	109,400
		Debt Service	34,000
		Excess of Resources over Expenditures	5,000
Total General Fund	$431,000	Total General Fund	$431,000
Special Revenue Fund			
Taxes	$100,000	Personal Services	$ 75,000
Other Revenues	25,000	Other Current Expenditures	30,000
		Capital Outlays	20,000
Total Special Revenue Fund	$125,000	Total Special Revenue Fund	$125,000
Total General Budget	$556,000	Total General Budget	$556,000

Note: The estimated amount of Fund Balance at the beginning of the budget year, if any, would be added to the estimated revenues.

3. The departmental activity or work programs, request forms, and comments (Figures 3-14 through 3-20).

4. Schedules showing charges not applicable to any particular department, including such items as judgments and claims, interest on notes and bonds, maturing general serial bonds, contributions to debt service funds, contributions to pension funds, the governmental unit's share of special assessment costs, and estimated fund deficits.

5. Fund balance sheets showing estimated assets, liabilities, reserves, and available fund balances or deficits as of the close of the current fiscal year.

6. A statement of actual and estimated cash receipts, disbursements, and balances. This statement is prepared in addition to the revenue statement. The revenue statement shows merely the revenues estimated to be earned; some of these may not be collected during the year. On the other hand, the governmental unit will collect delinquent taxes and other receivables of the preceding years. Through a comparison of estimated total receipts with estimated total disbursements, it is possible to determine whether short-term borrowing will be necessary. An additional statement, showing both actual and estimated receipts and disbursements by months, would also be helpful.

7. If short-term borrowing is contemplated, a schedule showing short-term borrowing transactions during the past two years and the current year and the proposed short-term borrowing for the coming year.
8. A statement showing bonded debt outstanding (Figure 18-5).
9. Statements of tax collections (Figures 6-8 and 6-9).
10. A draft for an appropriation ordinance.
11. A draft for a tax levy ordinance (discussed in Chapter 5).

LEGISLATIVE CONSIDERATION AND ACTION

After receiving the executive budget document, the legislative body must adopt an official "budget," the appropriation bill. A legislature or the Congress usually turns the proposed budget over to a committee or committees to make investigations, to call on department heads and the chief executive for justifications of their requests, and to conduct public hearings. The committee then makes its recommendations to the legislature. At the municipal level the council or board of supervisors is likely to act as a committee of the whole in its consideration of the budget.

After completing the budget hearings and investigations, the legislative body adopts the budget by passing an appropriation act or ordinance. The amount of detail in which the act is expressed determines the flexibility granted to the executive branch by the legislative body. Lump-sum appropriations may be made for functions or activities, or, more likely, for organization units. If proper internal control, accounting, reporting, and postaudit procedures are used, the legislative body can retain control of operations without recourse to detailed appropriations. However, most legislative bodies will insist on fairly detailed object-of-expenditure data in the executive budget, and they may be appropriated in comparable detail.

The appropriation act or ordinance merely authorizes expenditures. It is also necessary to provide the means of financing them. Some revenues (for example, interest on investments) will accrue to the governmental unit without any legal action on its part. Other revenues will come as a result of legal action taken in the past. Examples of these are licenses and fees, income taxes, and sales taxes, the rates for which continue until they are changed by the legislative body. A third type of revenue—for example, the general property tax—requires new legal action each year (every two years in most states levying property taxes). Accordingly, as soon as the legislative body has passed the appropriation ordinance or act, it proceeds to levy general property taxes.

BUDGET EXECUTION

Just as the budget approved by the legislative body expresses in financial terms the government's planned activities, the process of budget execution includes every operating decision and transaction made during the budget period. For this reason Figure 3-2, "The Budget Cycle," lists the many activities of administration as aspects of budget execution. Accounting keeps a record of the results of the transactions and permits their summarization, reporting, and comparison with plans (the budget). Therefore, the following chapters that describe the accounting and reporting for the governmental funds are all devoted to, in a sense, budget execution.

The appropriations are such a controlling influence in government that, contrary to business practice, the budget is recorded as an integral part of the accounting system. In the general ledger, as well as in the subsidiary ledgers for revenues and expenditures, budgeted amounts are recorded and can be directly compared with their actual counterparts. Similarly, accountability for budget compliance is reported in the financial statements together with the information accountants expect from the financial statements of the profit-seeking sector of the economy.

▶ **Question 3-1.** Distinguish between the following terms:
(a) a fund and an appropriation; (b) a budget and an appropriation; (c) an appropriation and an allotment; (d) allocations and allotments; and (e) an expenditure and an encumbrance.

Question 3-2. Indicate at least three ways in which the term "budget" may be used correctly.

Question 3-3. Governmental budgeting and budgetary control was deemed so important by the NCGA that it devoted an entire "principle" to the subject. Why?

Question 3-4. Budgeting is a continuous process. Explain.

Question 3-5. Distinguish between the following types of budgets:
(a) capital and current; (b) tentative and enacted; (c) general and special; (d) fixed and flexible; and (e) executive and legislative.

Question 3-6. What are budgetary "control points"? How do they affect budgetary accounting and reporting?

Question 3-7. A municipality's budget is prepared on a cash basis. What basis of accounting would you recommend? Explain.

Question 3-8. What major strengths and weaknesses are generally associated with the (a) line-item or object-of-expenditure, (b) performance, and (c) program approaches to budgeting?

Question 3-9. What is a budgetary "crosswalk"?

Question 3-10. What are the major distinctive characteristics of the PPB approach to budgeting?

Question 3-11. Some persons contend that an inherent limitation of the line-item department or object-of-expenditure budget is that it is based on a "backwards" or "reverse" decision-making process. Explain and evaluate this assertion.

Question 3-12. What questions about the activities for which appropriations are requested in the executive budget should be answered in the budget?

Question 3-13. Why are General, Special Revenue, and other expendable funds typically controlled by fixed budgets integrated within the account structure, while Enterprise and other nonexpendable funds are subject to less formal control through flexible budgets not integrated within the account structure?

Question 3-14. A General Fund balanced budget has been amended to increase the total appropriations. From what sources may the increase be financed?

Question 3-15. What is the essential idea of ZBB?

Question 3-16. An ordinance provides that collections from the sale of dog licenses are "hereby appropriated for the maintenance of the dog pound." During the month of January, $5,000 was collected. Is another appropriation necessary to spend this money for the maintenance of the dog pound?

Question 3-17. What are the processes required to produce a ZBB?

Question 3-18. Discuss the meaning and implications of the following statements pertaining to budgeting:

(a) "A budget is just a means of getting money."

(b) "*Never* underexpend an appropriation—the more you spend, the more you get next year."

(c) "Budgeting is easy! You just take last year's budget and add 10%—or twice what you think you might need. The council will cut your request in half and you'll wind up getting what you wanted in the first place."

(d) "The traditional line-item budget only appears to provide an orderly and seemingly objective approach to financial planning and control. In too many instances, all it really provides is a uniform framework for establishing and maintaining a set of orderly records which comply with legal requirements, but which provide very little in the way of useful management information."

Question 3-19. Revenue estimates and appropriations enacted are "standards" against which performance is subsequently measured. What implications can be drawn at year end if there are variances from these standards? If there are no variances?

Question 3-20. Behaviorial scientists tell us that "the measurement employed affects the performance of the person or group measured." What implications for performance and program budgeting are contained in this statement?

Question 3-21. Most "performance measures" (number of arrests made, tons of garbage collected, miles of street cleaned, etc.) do not adequately measure the quantity or quality of performance but are only "indicators" of certain aspects of performance. Discuss (a) the validity of this statement and (b) how "performance measures" or "indicators" may be properly and beneficially employed in evaluating performance.

Question 3-22. Proponents of "zero-based" budgeting contend that a government's budgetary process should begin each year with the assumption that no program or department has a vested interest—that each should comprehensively justify its existence, its activities, and its appropriation requests annually as if it were a proposed program or department not in existence previously. Evaluate the merits of this approach.

Question 3-23. What are the difficulties that may prevent ZBB from achieving success and continuing application?

Question 3-24. What benefits is ZBB designed to produce?

▶ **Problem 3-1.** The following information is available from the 19X4 General Fund budget, the general ledger of the City of Epps, and calculations:

	General Fund	Park Fund	School Fund
Fund Balance, Estimated January 1, 19X4	$ 125,000	$ 25,000	$ 50,000
Estimated Revenues:			
Property taxes	1,400,000	100,000	400,000
Other revenues	1,200,000		300,000
Appropriations:			
Salaries and wages	1,800,000	65,000	435,000
Other operations	775,000	15,000	200,000
Capital outlay	75,000	19,000	70,000

Required:

(a) Prepare a budget summary for the 19X4 Budget of the City of Epps.

(b) Describe other methods by which proposed expenditures could be classified. Which method do you prefer? Which method is in agreement with the performance budget concept?

Problem 3-2. The following is a portion of a draft of the 19X5 budget for the City of Woodbridge which is being compiled by its administrator. The major programs and subprograms are indicated by notations in brackets; the departmental responsibility for program elements is indicated in parentheses.

CITY OF WOODBRIDGE

19X5 Budget (Draft)

Public Safety [Program]:
Prevent and Prosecute Crime [Subprogram]:
Community Police Surveillance (Police Department):

Salaries and Wages	$399,796
Materials and Supplies	34,023
Contractual Services	41,905
Permanent Property	1,734
	$477,458

Investigate and Prosecute Adult Crime (Police Department):

Salaries and Wages	$258,944
Materials and Supplies	7,760
Contractual Services	7,750
	$274,454

Investigate and Prosecute Juvenile Crimes (Police Department):

Salaries and Wages	$207,450
Materials and Supplies	1,100
Contractual Services	2,150
	$210,700

Detain Accused Law Violators (Police Department):

Materials and Supplies	$ 50
Contractual Services	750
	$ 800

Cooperate with Regional Law Enforcement Agencies
(Police Department):

Materials and Supplies	$ 50

Total	$963,462

Adjudication of Crimes [Subprogram]:
Litigate Civil Cases (Municipal Court):

Salaries and Wages	$ 6,468
Materials and Supplies	200
Contractual Services	494
	$ 7,162

Penalize Criminal Law Violators (Municipal Court):

Salaries and Wages	$ 14,325
Materials and Supplies	575
Contractual Services	644
Permanent Property	400
	$ 15,944

Total	$23,106

Community Development and Environmental Control [Program]:
Community Development [Subprogram]:
Planning Land Use (Director of Planning):

Salaries and Wages	$ 54,439
Materials and Supplies	2,422
Contractual Services	7,825
	$ 64,686

Grand Total—Public Safety [Program]	$7,261,500

The grand total budgeted (all programs) for the object-of-expenditure classifications
included above was:

Salaries and Wages	$5,126,197
Materials and Supplies	1,817,923
Contractual Services	291,060
Permanent Property	2,140,781
	$9,375,961

Required:

Using the data given, prepare a budget presentation in a program to object-of-expenditure
crosswalk format, with subprogram and program element detail.

Problem 3-3. Using the information contained in Problem 3-2, prepare a crosswalk
budgetary presentation relating programs, subprograms, and program elements to departments. (You need not include object-of-expenditure detail.) The grand total budgeted
for the departments with which this problem deals are as follows:

Police	$1,717,476
Municipal Court	81,050
Director of Planning	124,292

Problem 3-4. From the following information prepare a departmental estimate of
personal services (adapt Figure 3-16) for 19X4 for the Finance Department of the City of
X. Submission date: October 1, 19X3; appropriation granted January 2, 19X4.

INFORMATION AS OF JANUARY 1, 19X4

Code	No.	Job Description	Rate per Annum
1420–A1.1	1	Director of Finance	$15,000
1420–A1.2	1	Cashier	7,800
1420–A1.3	2	Revenue Clerk	6,400
1420–A1.4	2	Parking Meter Collector	5,640
1420–A1.5	1	License Clerk	5,800
1420–A1.6	2	Machine Operator	5,600
1420–A1.7	1	Accountant	8,400

Additional information:

1. As of September 1, 19X3, a stenographer-clerk (A1.8) was added to the staff at a salary of $5,800.
2. The Director of Finance, Adam Smith, recommended that for 19X4 all salaries be increased by 8 percent.
3. The chief executive recommended that the staff be reduced by one parking meter collector, that Mr. Smith's salary be increased by $700, and that all other salaries be increased by 5 percent.
4. The legislative body approved the recommended staff reduction and allowed a 6 percent increase in all salaries, including the salary of the Director of Finance.

Problem 3-5. From the information below prepare a departmental estimate of current expenditures—other than personal services (see Figure 3-17) for the Fire Department of the City of Z. Submission date: October 15, 19X3.

ACTUAL EXPENDITURES

Code	Classification	19X1	19X2	19X3 (First Nine Months)
	Supplies:			
2100–B11	Office	432	530	420
2100–B22	Coal	15,066	11,742	9,750
2100–B41	Clothing	840	1,030	798
2100–B51	Mechanical	648	364	300
2100–B52	Automotive	4,070	4,534	3,306
2100–B61	Chemical	206	200	234
2100–B62	Medical	216	364	138
2100–B71	Books and Reports	30	36	24
	Other Services and Charges:			
2100–C11	Transportation	70	84	150
2100–C12	Insurance	900	950	750
2100–C25	Pension Contribution	12,274	12,286	9,240
2100–C26	Hospital	230	1,396	750
2100–C31	Light and Power	6,138	5,090	3,876
2100–C43	Apparatus Repair	650	772	378
2100–C44	Automotive Repair	11,578	13,878	8,436

Additional information:

1. The expenditures for the first nine months of 19X3 are estimated to be 75 percent of the total expenditures for 19X3.

2. Fire Chief A. C. Carr proposed that the 19X4 appropriations for his department be 105 percent of the total 19X3 expenditures, with the exception of account 2100-C41, for which he proposed that $2,000 be appropriated.

3. City Manager Johnson made the recommendation that the amounts for 19X4 appropriations be the same as the actual (for the first nine months) plus the estimated (for the remaining three months) expenditures for 19X3, with the exceptions that only $1,000 be appropriated for clothing, that accounts 2100-B26, C22, and C52 be decreased 7, 10, and 5 percent, respectively, from 19X3 estimated and actual expenditures, and that accounts 2100-C61 and C62 be increased 10 percent over the 19X3 expenditures.

4. The City Council appropriated $1,000 for account 2100-B26, and for the remainder of the accounts it appropriated the amounts recommended by the City Manager.

Problem 3-6. From the following information, prepare a statement of actual and estimated revenues (see Figure 3-13) for the City of Q's General Fund. The percentages apply to the first column.

	Actual 19X3	Actual First Nine Months of 19X4	Estimated Remainder of 19X4	Estimated 19X5
General Property Taxes	$601,202	94%	—	101%
Interest and Penalties—				
Delinquent Taxes	13,450	84	—	110
Police Fines	1,410	80	30%	112
Concessions	1,750	42	21	50
Sewer Permits	2,500	75	25	105
Building Permit Fees	145	125	50	200
Vendors' Licenses	7,200	67	30	98
Share of State-Collected				
Franchise Taxes	18,530	84	27	140
Fire Protection Service	4,365	69	30	103
Rent of Public Properties	1,720	77	23	95

Problem 3-7. The comptroller of the City of Helmaville recently resigned. In his absence, the deputy comptroller attempted to calculate the amount of money required to be raised from property taxes for the General Fund for the fiscal year ending June 30, 19X7. The calculation is to be made as of January 1, 19X6, to serve as a basis for setting the property tax rate for the following fiscal year. The mayor has requested you to review the deputy comptroller's calculations and obtain other necessary information to prepare a formal statement for the General Fund which will disclose the amount of money required to be raised from property taxes for the fiscal year ending June 30, 19X7. Following are the calculations prepared by the deputy comptroller:

City resources other than proposed tax levy:
Estimated General Fund working
    balance, January 1, 19X6 .... $ 352,000

Estimated receipts from property taxes (January 1, 19X6–June 30, 19X6)	2,222,000
Estimated revenue from investments (January 1, 19X6–June 30, 19X7)	442,000
Estimated proceeds from sale of general obligation bonds in August 19X6	3,000,000
	$6,016,000

General Fund requirements:	
Estimated expenditures (January 1, 19X6–June 30, 19X6)	$1,900,000
Proposed appropriations (July 1, 19X6–June 30, 19X7)	4,300,000
	$6,200,000

Additional information:

1. The General Fund working balance required by the city council for July 1, 19X6, is $175,000.
2. Property tax collections are due in March and September of each year. Your review indicates that during the month of February 19X6 estimated expenditures will exceed available funds by $200,000. Pending collection of property taxes in March 19X6, this deficiency will have to be met by the issuance of 30-day tax-anticipation notes of $200,000 at an estimated interest rate of 9 percent per annum.
3. The proposed general obligation bonds will be issued by the City Water Fund and will be used for the construction of a new water pumping station.

Required:

Prepare a statement as of January 1, 19X6, calculating the property tax levy required for the City of Helmaville General Fund for the fiscal year ending June 30, 19X7. (*Hint:* Requirements − Resources other than property tax levy = Amount of the required levy.)

(AICPA, adapted)

4

GENERAL AND SPECIAL REVENUE FUNDS

The General Fund and Special Revenue Funds typically are used to finance and account for most "general government" activities of state and local governments, e.g., police protection, fire protection, central administration, schools, and street maintenance. They are discussed together because accounting and reporting for General and Special Revenue Funds are identical.

Special Revenue Funds are established to account for financial resources allocated by law or by contractual agreement to specific purposes. The General Fund is used to account for all financial resources not allocated to specific purposes. The General Fund is established at the inception of a government and exists throughout the government's life, whereas Special Revenue Funds exist as long as the government has resources dedicated to specific purposes. In the typical case the resources of both types of funds are expended wholly or almost wholly each year and are replenished on an annual basis.

Recall from the discussion of NCGA *Statement 1* principles in Chapter 2 that (1) resources restricted to expenditure for purposes normally financed from the General Fund may be accounted for through the General Fund as long as applicable legal requirements are met, and (2) use of Special Revenue Funds is not required unless they are legally mandated. Thus, some restricted resources may be accounted for through the General Fund rather than through Special Revenue Funds.

Because of the recurring nature of their revenues and commitments and the necessity of meeting current commitments from the currently expendable (appropriable) financial resources, the accounting principles for General and Special Revenue Funds are based on the funds flow concept rather than on the income determination concept of business accounting. For example, purchases of fixed assets with the financial resources of these funds decrease their fund balance. Expenditures for fixed assets have the same status within these funds as expenditures for wages and salaries, since fixed assets are not capitalized in the General or Special Revenue Funds. Similarly, if maturing general obligation bonds of the government—which are carried as liabilities in the General Long-Term Debt Account Group prior to maturity—are paid from the resources of these funds, the payment decreases their fund balance and is treated in the same manner as expenditures for salaries and wages.

As a result of the flow of funds concept, the General or Special Revenue Fund balance sheet at the end of the year presents the financial resources on hand, any related current liabilities, and the Fund Balance. The Fund Balance is expected to be available, together with the revenues and transfers in of the following year, to meet the needs of that year. Additional references to this concept will be made as transactions and statements of the funds are discussed.

Since accounting and reporting for the General Fund and Special Revenue Funds are identical, there is no need to discuss each fund type separately. The balance of this chapter deals with General Fund accounting and reporting, with only occassional reference to Special Revenue Funds. The principles, procedures, and illustrations are equally applicable to Special Revenue Funds, however.

OPERATION OF THE GENERAL FUND, 19X1

To illustrate the essential aspects of General and Special Revenue Fund accounting, let us assume that a new local governmental unit, which we shall call "A Governmental Unit," was founded late in 19X0 and adopted General and Special Revenue Fund budgets similar to that illustrated in the latter part of Chapter 3 and summarized in Figure 3-21 for the fiscal year beginning January 1, 19X1. Assume also that the trial balance of the General Fund of A Governmental Unit at January 1 appeared as in Figure 4-1.

Figure 4-1

A GOVERNMENTAL UNIT
GENERAL FUND

Trial Balance
January 1, 19X1

	Debit	Credit
Cash	4,000	
Accounts Receivable	2,000	
Vouchers Payable		5,000
Fund Balance		1,000
	6,000	6,000

The operation of the General Fund of A Governmental Unit begins with the adoption of the budget. The appropriations it contains, together with the revenue estimates on which the appropriations are based, provide the basis for the following *General Ledger* entry on the first day of the new year:

(1)	Estimated Revenues	431,000	
	Appropriations		426,000
	Fund Balance		5,000
	To record appropriations and		
	revenue estimates.		

Note that (1) both the Estimated Revenues account and the Appropriations (estimated expenditures) account are general ledger control accounts, (2) the budgetary entry above causes the Fund Balance account to be stated at its $6,000 ($1,000 beginning balance plus $5,000 planned increase) planned end-of-period balance, (3) subsidiary ledgers are maintained in which detailed records of revenues and appropriations and expenditures are recorded, and (4) these subsidiary records provide the basis for budgetary control of the operations of the agencies of the governmental unit.

Entry (1) compounds two possible separate budgetary entries:

(1a)	Estimated Revenues	431,000	
	Fund Balance		431,000
	To record estimated revenue and		
	the expected fund balance increase		
	to result during the period.		

(1b)	Fund Balance	426,000	
	Appropriations		426,000
	To record appropriations and the		
	expected fund balance decrease to		
	result during the period.		

Should the revenue estimate be revised upward during the period the increase would be debited to Estimated Revenues and credited to Fund Balance; a decrease in estimated revenues would be recorded by debiting the expected decrease to Fund Balance and crediting Estimated Revenues. Similarly, if additional appropriations are made during the year, Fund Balance would be debited and Appropriations credited for the increase; the opposite would be true should appropriations be decreased.

This chapter focuses on General Ledger accounting and budgetary control procedures. Detailed discussions of the Revenue and Expenditure Subsidiary Ledgers and detailed budgetary control procedures are contained in Chapters 5 and 6.

Property taxes usually are a major revenue source of the General Funds of cities. They accrue when they are formally levied by the legislative body of the city. (The assessment date is the date on which the value and ownership of property is determined for purposes of assigning tax liability and usually precedes the date of levy by a substantial period.) On the date that A Governmental Unit's taxes are levied, the following entry is made:

(2)	Taxes Receivable—Current	300,000	
	Allowance for Uncollectible		
	Current Taxes		3,000
	Revenues		297,000
	To record accrual of taxes.		

The Allowance for Uncollectible Taxes figure is the portion of the tax levy not expected to be collected. At this time the city does not know which specific tax bills will not be collected. As specific amounts are discovered to be uncollectible they are written off by charging the Allowance for Uncollectible Taxes account and crediting Taxes Receivable. Since such taxes are a primary lien on the property, no loss is incurred until the city has gone through foreclosure proceedings that result in the sale of property for taxes. The accounting for tax liens and for such disposition of property is discussed in Chapter 5.

Observe in entry (2) that only the net expected tax collections are credited to Revenues. This *net revenue* approach differs from business accounting, where the gross receivable is credited to revenues and the estimated uncollectible amounts are debited to expense. But governmental funds account for expenditures, not expenses; and the amount of taxes levied that is uncollectible does not constitute an expenditure but is considered a deduction from revenue.

As other revenues accrue, the following entries are made:

(3)	Accounts Receivable	36,000	
	Allowance for Uncollectible		
	Accounts Receivable		1,000
	Revenues		35,000
	To record accrual of miscellaneous		
	revenues and to set up an		
	allowance for estimated losses		
	thereon.		

The foregoing revenues might, for example, represent charges for services rendered. Those revenues that do not accrue, or are not deemed sufficiently measurable to be accrued in the accounts prior to collection, are debited to Cash and credited to Revenues at the time of collection.

A primary objective of governmental accounting is to assist the administration in controlling the expenditures, including the control of overexpenditure of appropriations. Thus, accounts must be kept both for total expenditures (General Ledger) and for expenditures chargeable to each appropriation (Expenditure Subsidiary Ledger). Usually a record of the estimated amount of "in process" expenditures is maintained—in total in the General Ledger and by each appropriation in the Expenditure Subsidiary Ledger—through the use of an Encumbrances account. As orders are placed, entries are made setting up encumbrances; a comparison of appropriations with expenditures and encumbrances indicates the amount of uncommitted appropriations available for expenditure. When the actual expenditure is determined, the entry setting up the encumbrances is reversed and the actual expenditure is recorded. Thus, if we assume that an order is placed for materials and equipment estimated to cost $30,000, the General Ledger entry at the time the order is placed would be:

(4)	Encumbrances	30,000	
	Reserve for Encumbrances		30,000
	To record encumbering of		
	appropriation.		

Assume, however, that when the materials and equipment and the bill are subsequently received, they cost only $29,900. The entries will be:

(5a) Reserve for Encumbrances	30,000	
Encumbrances		30,000
To reverse the entry encumbering the Appropriations account.		
(5b) Expenditures	29,900	
Vouchers Payable		29,900
To record expenditures.		

These entries accomplish two things. The balance of the Appropriations control account in the General Ledger and of the individual appropriation account(s) in the Expenditure Subsidiary Ledger (Chapter 6) against which the expenditures for materials and equipment are chargeable was temporarily reduced—while the order was outstanding—by the estimated amount of the expenditure, the encumbrance. Now, however, the exact amount of the expenditure is known; accordingly, the entry setting up the encumbrances is reversed and the actual expenditure is recorded. The effects of these entries are as follows:

	After Entry 1	After Entry 4	After Entries 5a and 5b
Appropriations	$426,000	$426,000	$426,000
Less: Expenditures	-0-	-0-	29,900
Unexpended Balance	$426,000	$426,000	$396,100
Less: Encumbrances	-0-	30,000	-0-
Unencumbered Balance	$426,000	$396,000	$396,100

If an expenditure is controlled by devices other than encumbrances, the appropriation is not encumbered first but the amount of the available appropriation is reduced only at the time of the expenditure. This is usually true with payrolls. Thus, if the payroll at the end of a pay period was $40,000, the entry at the time the payroll was approved for payment would be:

(6) Expenditures	40,000	
Vouchers Payable		40,000
To record approval of payroll.		

Additional entries illustrating the operation of the General Fund of A Governmental Unit follow:

(7) Cash	245,000	
Taxes Receivable—Current		230,000
Accounts Receivable		15,000
To record collection of taxes receivable and accounts receivable.		
(8) Taxes Receivable—Delinquent	70,000	
Taxes Receivable—Current		70,000
To record taxes becoming delinquent.		

(9) Allowance for Uncollectible
      Current Taxes   3,000
      Allowance for Uncollectible
      Delinquent Taxes   3,000
    To record reclassification of
    allowance for estimated losses on
    taxes.

(10) Cash 105,000
      Revenues   105,000
    To record receipt of miscellaneous
    revenues not previously accrued.

(11) Vouchers Payable   40,000
      Cash   40,000
    To record payment of payroll
    voucher.

(12) Encumbrances   20,000
      Reserve for Encumbrances   20,000
    To record reduction of
    appropriation available for future
    expenditure by amount of
    estimated cost of purchase orders
    placed.

(13) Cash   50,200
      Taxes Receivable—Delinquent ..   50,000
      Revenues   200
    To record collection of delinquent
    taxes, together with interest and
    penalties thereon that had not
    been accrued.

(14) Interest and Penalties
      Receivable—Delinquent
      Taxes   550
      Allowance for Uncollectible
      Interest and Penalties   50
      Revenues   500
    To record interest and penalties
    accrued on delinquent taxes
    outstanding and to provide for
    estimated losses.

(15) Expenditures   30,000
      Due to Stores Fund   30,000
    To record supplies provided by an
    Internal Service Fund.

    (Note: This is a **quasi-external
    transaction;** revenues would be
    credited in the Stores Fund.)

(16) Due from Special Revenue Fund ..   1,500
      Expenditures   1,500
    To record reimbursement due
    from Special Revenue Fund for
    expenditure made initially from
    the General Fund.

    (Note: This is an interfund
    reimbursement transaction.)

(17) Operating Transfer to Debt
        Service Fund 4,000
        Due to Debt Service Fund 4,000
    To record annual transfer to Debt
    Service Fund to meet debt service
    and fiscal charges.

    (Note that **interfund operating
    transfers** must be reported
    separately from Revenues and
    Expenditures.)

(18) Due from Special Revenue Fund .. 10,000
        Operating Transfer from
        Special Revenue Fund 10,000
    To record interfund transfer from
    Special Revenue Fund ordered by
    governing board.

(19) Residual Equity Transfer to
        Enterprise Fund 6,000
        Cash 6,000
    To record residual equity transfer
    to provide contributed capital to a
    new Enterprise Fund.

    (Note that **interfund residual
    equity transfers** must be reported
    separately from Revenues,
    Expenditures, and Operating
    Transfers.)

(20) Expenditures 300,000
        Vouchers Payable 300,000
    To record expenditures for which
    no encumbrances had been set up.

(21) Vouchers Payable 320,000
        Cash 320,000
    To record payment of vouchers.

(22) Due to Stores Fund 22,500
        Cash 22,500
    To record partial payment of
    amount due the Stores Fund.

(23) Cash 13,000
        Accounts Receivable 13,000
    To record collections of accounts
    receivable.

(24) Allowance for Uncollectible
        Accounts Receivable 400
        Accounts Receivable 400
    To record write-off of accounts
    receivable determined to be
    uncollectible.

(25) Fund Balance 300
        Vouchers Payable 300
    To record **correction of prior
    period (19X0) error** (failure to

record 19X0 expenditure and
liability at December 31, 19X0).

(26) Investments 10,000
    Cash   10,000
To record temporary investment of
excess cash.

In reviewing the illustrative general journal entries above, note particularly entries 15 through 19. Entry 15 records an interfund *quasi-external transaction*, while entry 16 reflects an *interfund reimbursement;* entries 17 and 18 are for *interfund operating transfers,* and entry 19 records an *interfund residual equity transfer.* Further, note that while separate General Ledger accounts are used for each operating transfer and residual equity transfer for illustrative purposes, it is *equally acceptable* to (1) record all operating transfers in Other Financing Sources and Other Financing Uses accounts or in a single Other Financing Sources (Uses) account in the General Ledger, perhaps supported by an Other Financing Sources (Uses) Subsidiary Ledger containing an account for each operating transfer; and (2) record all residual equity transfers in Residual Equity Transfers In and Residual Equity Transfer Out accounts or in a single Residual Equity Transfers account in the General Ledger, perhaps supported by a Residual Equity Transfers Subsidiary Ledger containing an account for each residual equity transfer. Other acceptable methods of recording interfund transfers in the accounts are discussed and illustrated in Chapters 5 and 6.

Figure 4-2 presents the trial balance of the accounts after the preceding illustrative journal entries are posted.

Figure 4-2

A GOVERNMENTAL UNIT
General Fund
Preclosing Trial Balance
December 31, 19X1

	Debit	Credit
Cash	18,700	
Investments	10,000	
Taxes Receivable—Delinquent	20,000	
Allowance for Uncollectible Delinquent Taxes		3,000
Interest and Penalties Receivable on Taxes	550	
Allowance for Uncollectible Interest and		
Penalties		50
Accounts Receivable	9,600	
Allowance for Uncollectible Accounts		
Receivable		600
Vouchers Payable		15,200
Due to Stores Fund		7,500
Due to Debt Service Fund		4,000
Due from Special Revenue Fund	11,500	
Reserve for Encumbrances		20,000
Fund Balance (1,000 + 5,000 - 300)		5,700

	Debit	Credit
Estimated Revenues	431,000	
Revenues		437,700
Appropriations		426,000
Expenditures	398,400	
Encumbrances	20,000	
Operating Transfer to Debt Service Fund	4,000	
Operating Transfer from Special Revenue Fund		10,000
Residual Equity Transfer to Enterprise Fund	6,000	
	929,750	929,750

This trial balance is the basis for the closing entries discussed in the following section and for the statements later in the chapter.

CLOSING THE BOOKS, 19X1

At the end of the fiscal year, entries are made closing the accounts. The closing process summarizes the results of operations in the Fund Balance account.

Closing The Revenue Accounts

The General Ledger revenue closing entry is:

(C1) Revenues	437,700	
Estimated Revenues		431,000
Fund Balance		6,700
To close actual and estimated revenues.		

The entry closes the Estimated Revenues and (actual) Revenues accounts, compares the totals of those accounts, and adds the difference to Fund Balance—to adjust that account for the variance between planned and actual revenues. In this case actual revenues exceeded the estimate; if the converse had been true, Fund Balance would have been debited.

Closing the Expenditure and Encumbrance Accounts

The procedure for closing Expenditures and related accounts is determined by the government's legal and policy provisions pertaining to the lapsing of appropriations and to the treatment of encumbrances outstanding at year end. An appropriation is said to lapse when it terminates, i.e., when it no longer is an authorization to make an expenditure. The illustration for A Governmental Unit is completed on the assumption that the law and policy state that (1) all unexpended appropriations lapse at the end of the year, even if encumbered; (2) the Unit is committed to accepting the goods or services on order at year end; (3) expenditures resulting from encumbrances outstanding at the end of the year must be charged against appropriations of the next year; and (4) the closing entry should leave on the books a Reserve for Encumbrances account to indicate the commitment of the resources of the fund. We shall call this Assumption A1; other types of laws and policies relating to appropriations and encumbrances are discussed later in this chapter.[1]

Under the foregoing assumptions, the General Ledger closing entry for the appropriation, expenditure, and encumbrance accounts is:

(C2) Appropriations	426,000	
Expenditures		398,400
Encumbrances		20,000
Fund Balance		7,600
To close appropriations, expenditures, and encumbrances.		

This entry (1) compares Appropriations with Expenditures and Encumbrances, (2) closes those accounts, (3) converts the Reserve for Encumbrances account from an offsetting memorandum account in the General Ledger to a reservation of Fund Balance, and (4) adjusts the Fund Balance account for the variance between planned and actual expenditures. Since expenditures cannot legally be made without an authorizing appropriation and therefore cannot legally exceed appropriations, the balancing element in the entry should never be a debit to Fund Balance. However, both in practice and in problems an excess of expenditures, or expenditures and encumbrances, over appropriations may occur. In problems, the excess may be charged to Fund Balance; in practice, a supplementary appropriation should be secured from the legislative body to cover the excess.

Some accountants prefer to separate closing entry C2 into its two primary components, as follows:

(C2a) Appropriations	426,000	
Expenditures		398,400
Fund Balance		27,600
To close appropriations and expenditures.		
(C2b) Fund Balance	20,000	
Encumbrances		20,000
To close encumbrances and establish the reserve for encumbrances as a fund balance reserve.		

This approach separates (a) the closing of Expenditures and Appropriations to Fund Balance from (b) the entry closing Encumbrances to Fund Balance in order to establish the Reserve for Encumbrances (no longer offset by Encumbrances) as a true reservation of fund balance. It also emphasizes that the Encumbrances account is not being closed as if encumbrances outstanding at year end are in substance equivalent to expenditures—as some might conclude erroneously from casually observing entry C2—but to decrease the *unreserved* fund balance (Fund

---

[1] Assumption A2, discussed later in this chapter, is the same as A1 except that encumbrances outstanding at year end are disclosed in the notes to the financial statements instead of in a Reserve for Encumbrances account reported in the balance sheet. Assumptions A1 and A2 are often alternatives in practice.

Balance account) by an amount equal to the Reserve for Encumbrances (now *reserved* fund balance).[2]

Closing the Transfer Accounts

The transfer accounts would be closed at year end as follows:

(C3)	Operating Transfers from Special Revenue Fund	10,000	
	Operating Transfer to Debt Service Fund		4,000
	Residual Equity Transfer to Enterprise Fund		6,000
	To close transfer accounts.		

In this case the transfers out equaled the transfers in and no entry to Fund Balance was required. Had transfers out exceeded transfers in, the difference would have been debited to Fund Balance; had transfers in exceeded transfers out, the difference would have been credited to Fund Balance.

This illustration assumes that only revenues and expenditures are subject to formal budgetary accounting control procedures. This is often the case as the governing board directly controls interfund transfers. Alternatively, budgetary accounts such as Estimated Operating Transfers In, Estimated Operating Transfers Out, and Estimated Residual Equity Transfers Out could have been used and would be closed at this time. Accounting procedures where interfund transfers and debt issue proceeds are subject to formal budgetary accounting control are considered in Chapters 5 and 6.

Alternative Closing Entry Approaches

The closing entry sequence presented above to close the Revenue accounts (C1) and Expenditure and Encumbrance accounts (C2) is logical and widely used in practice. It is by no means the only acceptable approach, however. Any reasonable entry or sequence of entries to close the General Ledger accounts is acceptable as long as (1) the Fund Balance account is updated to its proper balance at the end of the period, (2) the temporary proprietary accounts that should be closed are closed, and (3) the account balances that should be carried forward to the succeeding period are properly carried forward.

[2] Entry C2b is in essence a compounding of the following two entries:

(C2b1)	Reserve for Encumbrance	20,000	
	Encumbrances		20,000
	To close the offsetting encumbrances and reserve for encumbrances memorandum accounts.		
(C2b2)	Fund Balance	20,000	
	Reserve for Encumbrances		20,000
	To reduce unreserved fund balance and increase reserved fund balance (for encumbrances).		

Some accountants prefer to alter the closing entry sequence illustrated by (1) reversing the effects of the budgetary entry or entries on the Fund Balance account, then (2) closing (actual) Revenues, Expenditures, and Encumbrances balances to Fund Balance; and then (3) closing the transfer accounts. This approach is illustrated below.

(C1)	Appropriations	426,000	
	Fund Balance	5,000	
	Estimated Revenues		431,000
	To close the budgetary accounts and bring the Fund Balance account to its actual preclosing balance.		
(C2)	Revenues	437,700	
	Fund Balance		39,300
	Expenditures		398,400
	To close the Revenues and Expenditures accounts to Fund Balance.		
(C3)	Fund Balance	20,000	
	Encumbrances		20,000
	To close the Encumbrances account and establish the Reserve for Encumbrances account as a reservation of fund balance.		
(C4)	Operating Transfer from Special Revenue Fund	10,000	
	Operating Transfer to Debt Service Fund		4,000
	Residual Equity Transfer to Enterprise Fund		6,000
	To close transfer accounts.		

Other accountants prefer to prepare a single *compound* General Ledger closing entry. A compound General Fund closing entry for A Governmental Unit at December 31, 19X1, under the assumptions illustrated so far, would appear as follows:

Revenues	437,700	
Appropriations	426,000	
Operating Transfers from Special Revenue Fund	10,000	
Estimated Revenues		431,000
Expenditures		398,400
Encumbrances		20,000
Operating Transfer to Debt Service Fund		4,000
Residual Equity Transfer to Enterprise Fund		6,000
To close the accounts.		

Reserve for Encumbrances

At this point a review of the nature of the Reserve for Encumbrances account is appropriate. It started life as an offset to the Encumbrances account in the General Ledger. Throughout 19X1 both accounts contained a balance representing the amount to be deducted from the Appropriations account to arrive at the estimated spendable balance of appropriations. In other words, the Encumbrances and Reserve for Encumbrances accounts were offsetting *memorandum* accounts in the General Ledger. The closing entry for expenditure accounts closed the Encumbrances account but not the Reserve for Encumbrances; the Reserve for Encumbrances was converted into a *reservation of fund balance.* It and the Fund Balance account should be added to obtain the total fund balance at year end.

Reserves usually indicate that a portion of the total fund balance is not applicable for appropriation, that only the *unreserved* fund balance may be appropriated. Under Assumption A1, however, the Reserve for Encumbrances indicates the amount of total fund balance that must be appropriated next year (19X2) to authorize completion of transaction in process at year end (19X1). Thus, under Assumption A1 the amount in the Reserve for Encumbrances is available for 19X2 appropriation, but only to provide for past commitments, while the unreserved fund balance is available to finance new 19X2 expenditure commitments. Since the amount represented by the Reserve for Encumbrances is available for appropriation under Assumption A1, many accountants prefer to disclose encumbrances outstanding at year end in the notes to the financial statements rather than in a Reserve for Encumbrances account in the balance sheet. Assumption A2, discussed later in this chapter, is the same as Assumption A1 except that it provides for disclosure of encumbrances outstanding at year end in the notes to the financial statements rather than by a Reserve for Encumbrances.

Postclosing Trial Balance

Following the posting of the 19X1 closing entries, the trial balance of the General Fund appears as in Figure 4-3.

OPERATION OF THE FUND, 19X2 ⎯⎯⎯⎯⎯⎯⎯⎯⎯⎯⎯⎯⎯⎯⎯⎯

The only new subject that must be covered for the operation of the Fund in 19X2 is the treatment of the Reserve for Encumbrances account and the related expenditures made in 19X2. At the first of 19X2 the entry that closed Encumbrances to Fund Balance to establish the Reserve for Encumbrances as a true fund balance reserve is reversed:

Encumbrances	20,000	
Fund Balance		20,000
To return the Encumbrances account to its usual offset relation with the Reserve for Encumbrances and increase unreserved Fund Balance accordingly.		

Figure 4-3

A GOVERNMENTAL UNIT

General Fund
Postclosing Trial Balance
December 31, 19X1

	Debit	Credit
Cash	18,700	
Investments	10,000	
Taxes Receivable—Delinquent	20,000	
Allowance for Uncollectible Delinquent Taxes		3,000
Interest and Penalties Receivable on Taxes ...	550	
Allowance for Uncollectible Interest and Penalties		50
Accounts Receivable	9,600	
Allowance for Uncollectible Accounts Receivable		600
Due from Special Revenue Fund	11,500	
Vouchers Payable		15,200
Due to Stores Fund		7,500
Due to Debt Service Fund		4,000
Reserve for Encumbrances		20,000
Fund Balance		20,000
	70,350	70,350

This entry reestablishes the Encumbrances and Reserve for Encumbrances accounts in their usual offset relationship, causing the Reserve for Encumbrances to no longer be a true fund balance reserve, and increases the Fund Balance account to the total appropriable fund balance amount so that 19X2 appropriations for encumbrances outstanding at the end of 19X1 can be recorded. When the goods or services are received in 19X2 the usual "reverse the encumbrances, record the actual expenditures" entries are made and the expenditure is charged against the 19X2 appropriations. Assuming that the goods or services actually cost $21,000, the entry to record their receipt would be:

Reserve for Encumbrances	20,000	
Expenditures	21,000	
Encumbrances		20,000
Vouchers Payable		21,000
To record expenditures for goods and services and reverse the related encumbrance entry.		

If the government wanted to account separately for the goods or services received during 19X2 that were ordered in 19X1, it could use separate General Ledger and/or Expenditure Subsidiary Ledger accounts as discussed in Chapter 6.

The essential character of the General Fund should be kept constantly in mind as balance sheets and balance sheet accounts are discussed. Though the General Fund presumably will exist as long as the governmental unit exists, the operation of the Fund is on a year-to-year basis. Each year the problem of financing a new year's operations with financial resources on hand and the new year's revenues and other financial resource inflows (e.g., transfers) is the central concern of those managing the finances of the Fund. The balance sheet is prepared to provide information that assists in the solution of this problem.

The Interim Balance Sheet

Transactions that are not in all cases the same as those illustrated earlier have been assumed in order to prepare the balance sheet prepared *during* a fiscal year that is presented in Figure 4-4. Note that the estimated revenues figure appears on the debit side and is reduced by the actual revenues to date to derive

Figure 4-4

A GOVERNMENTAL UNIT

General Fund
Balance Sheet
During the Fiscal Year 19X1*

Assets and Estimated Revenues

Cash		$ 25,000
Accounts receivable	$ 36,000	
Less: Allowance for uncollectible accounts		
receivable	1,000	35,000
Estimated revenues	$431,000	
Less: Revenues	115,000	316,000
		$376,000

*Liabilities, Appropriations, Reserves,
and Unreserved Fund Balance*

Liabilities:		
Vouchers payable	$122,500	
Due to Stores Fund	7,500	$130,000
Appropriations:		
Appropriations	$426,000	
Less: Expenditures $186,000		
Encumbrances 10,000	196,000	230,000
Reserve for encumbrances		10,000
Fund balance		6,000
		$376,000

The transactions assumed to have produced this interim balance sheet bear no necessary relationship to the transactions discussed earlier.

the net amount expected to be earned during the balance of the year—an estimated fund "resource." Similarly, the appropriations figure appears on the credit side reduced by the expenditures and encumbrances to date; the net figure presents the net unencumbered expenditure authority (unencumbered appropriations) at the statement date.

An interim balance sheet presents a picture of the Fund at a point within the planned year of operations. Inclusion of both budgetary (showing the results of budget transactions) and proprietary (showing actual financial condition or operations) accounts for the Fund helps the reader analyze the financial position of the Fund in a way that would not be possible without them. For example, a midyear balance sheet showing an expenditure figure that is two-thirds that of appropriations tells the reader that planned expenditures (and hence the planned incurrence of liabilities) for the last half of the year are expected to be only one-third of the appropriations figure. Similarly, a midyear balance sheet that shows an actual revenue figure only one-fourth the amount of estimated revenue tells the reader that future revenue accruals or collections are expected to occur at a much faster rate than that of the first half-year. In all probability the preceding situation applies to a city that levies its annual property taxes in the last half of the year.

A reader who wants to review the position of the Fund without the Revenue and Expenditure accounts must, mentally or otherwise, transfer the balances of these accounts to Fund Balance. But, one might, as in the cases assumed in the preceding paragraph, receive a misleading impression from the resulting Fund Balance figure if he or she took the data from Figure 4-4 and calculated the Fund Balance figure as follows:

Fund balance per Figure 4-4			$ 6,000
Add:			
Appropriations		$426,000	
Less:			
Expenditures	$186,000		
Encumbrances	10,000	196,000	230,000
			$236,000
Deduct:			
Estimated revenues		$431,000	
Revenues		115,000	316,000
Deficit			$ 80,000

The deficit is by no means an accurate indication of the General Fund's financial position. A further look at the assets reveals no taxes receivable. Evidently, the tax levy has not yet been recorded, and the Fund may well be operating exactly as planned.

The Year-End Balance Sheet

The balance sheet of the General Fund of A Governmental Unit at December 31, 19X1 (Figure 4-5) is based on the trial balance at that date and on the closing entries that were illustrated. The statement is for the most part self-explanatory, but comments on some of the accounts will help to produce a clear picture of its characteristics. The comments deal with (1) the significance of the Fund Balance account, (2) the nature of several fund balance reserve accounts, and (3) the exclusion of fixed assets and long-term (noncurrent) liabilities from the General Fund accounts and its Balance Sheet.

Figure 4-5

A GOVERNMENTAL UNIT

General Fund
Balance Sheet
December 31, 19X1

Assets

Cash		$18,700
Investments		10,000
Taxes receivable—delinquent	$20,000	
Less: Allowance for uncollectible delinquent taxes	3,000	17,000
Interest and penalities receivable on taxes	$ 550	
Less: Allowance for uncollectible interest and penalities	50	500
Accounts receivable	$ 9,600	
Less: Allowance for uncollectible accounts	600	9,000
Due from Special Revenue Fund		11,500
		$66,700

Liabilities and Fund Balance

Liabilities:		
Vouchers payable	$15,200	
Due to Stores Fund	7,500	
Due to Debt Service Fund	4,000	$26,700
Fund balance:		
Reserved for encumbrances	$20,000	
Unreserved	20,000	40,000
		$66,700

Fund Balance

As previously indicated, the General Fund is a current fund. Its fiscal operations are concerned with the current year revenues and other financing sources and the current year expenditures and other uses of financial resources. As a general rule the Fund is intended to show neither a surplus nor a deficit. A credit balance in the Fund Balance account after closing entries does not in any sense represent retained earnings. Rather, it indicates an excess of the assets of the fund over its liabilities and fund balance reservations, if any, and would more properly be titled "Unreserved, Unappropriated Fund Balance." Accordingly, the legislative body is likely to use the available assets, as indicated by the credit balance, in financing the budget for the succeeding year. But, as noted earlier, under

Assumption A1 the budget officials and the legislative body should realize that the Reserve for Encumbrances also is available for 19X2 appropriation for the 19X1 commitments.

During a fiscal year the balance of the Fund Balance account may be of a nature substantially different from that of the year-end balance. Suppose that the year-end Fund Balance (postclosing) is $5,000, and that in the following year budgeted revenues are $100,000 and appropriations total $97,000. The Fund Balance account will be carried at $8,000 after the recording of the budget, i.e., at the planned balance at period end. The exact nature of the balance can be determined only by examining all the facts. Its balance is neither exclusively budgetary nor exclusively proprietary.

If the General Fund has a deficit, the amount of the deficit should be exhibited on the balance sheet in the same position as the Fund Balance and called a "Deficit." Typical municipal financial administration policy requires that the deficit be eliminated in the following fiscal year and that the necessary revenues for this purpose be provided in the budget.

Fund Balance Reserves

Since assets in an amount equal to the Fund Balance account are assumed to be available to finance appropriations for expenditures of the succeeding year, it is desirable to remove from the account any portions that are not available for that purpose. The Reserve for Encumbrances left on the books by the closing entries made has already been discussed as a fund balance reserve at the end of the year. This reserve indicates that some of the General Fund assets are not available to finance *new* purchase commitments in 19X2 because they will be needed to pay for the 19X2 expenditures that result from the outstanding 19X1 purchase commitments. It also serves to remind those preparing the 19X2 budget to make sufficient appropriations to provide for the expenditures to result in 19X2 from the 19X1 purchase commitments.

Frequently, some of the General Fund assets need to be maintained at a certain level rather than expended. For example, such assets as petty cash and inventories of materials and supplies may not be available for financing expenditures of a subsequent period because they must be maintained at or near the required level. The entries to account for materials and supplies and the related Reserve for Inventories are discussed in Chapter 6. Entries for petty cash are as follows:

Petty Cash	2,000	
Cash		2,000
To record the creation of a petty cash fund out of general cash.		
Fund Balance	2,000	
Reserve for Petty Cash Fund		2,000
To record a reservation of fund balance in the amount of the petty cash fund.		

As another example, suppose that a $5,000 loan to be repaid in 19X3 had been made from the General Fund to a Special Revenue Fund at the end of 19X1.

Entries at the end of 19X1 would be:

Advance to Special Revenue Fund	5,000	
Cash		5,000
To record interfund loan to be repaid in 19X3.		
Fund Balance	5,000	
Reserve for Advance to Special		
Revenue Fund		5,000
To record a reservation of fund balance in the amount of the interfund advance.		

The Reserve for Advance to Special Revenue Fund indicates that the General Fund asset represented by the Advance to Special Revenue Fund is not available to finance 19X2 expenditures. The Reserve for Advance to Special Revenue Fund will be canceled at the end of 19X2 since the loan will be repaid in 19X3.

Similar reservations may be made for other assets that are not expected to be available to finance current operations. Examples of such assets are deposits and long-term accounts and claims receivable. Fund balance reserves are reported in the "Fund Balance" section of the balance sheet as shown in Figure 4-4. Alternatively, separate "Reserved Fund Balance" and "Unreserved Fund Balance" categories may be used, especially when there are several reserves. But a "Total Fund Balance" amount should be reported and reserves should **not** be reported with liabilities or between the liabilities and fund balance sections of the balance sheet.

Exclusion of Fixed Assets and Long-Term Debt

Although some General Fund expenditures represent outlays that should be capitalized, fixed assets are not included in the balance sheet of the General Fund. For example, let us assume that $2,000 of the total expenditures of $29,900 shown in entry 5b on page 104 was for equipment. In commercial accounting this $2,000 would be shown in the general balance sheet as part of the assets. In governmental fund accounting the fixed assets are capitalized in a separate nonfund account group rather than as assets of the General Fund (see Chapter 10). Even if general obligation long-term debt (such as bonds) is ultimately payable out of the General Fund, and even if it has been issued to eliminate a deficit in the General Fund, unmatured general obligation long-term debt is not recorded as a liability of the General Fund but in a separate nonfund account group (see Chapter 10). The only long-term debt included in the General Fund is that which has matured and is payable from the current resources of the General Fund (an unusual occurrence, since matured bonds and other long-term debts are ordinarily repaid from a Debt Service Fund).

Fixed assets are excluded from the General Fund balance sheet because they do not represent financial resources with which the government intends to finance its current activities or pay its liabilities. These assets are not acquired for resale, but for the purpose of rendering service over a relatively long period of time.

Bonds and other long-term general obligation debts payable are not included as part of the liabilities of the General Fund because the existing resources of the Fund are not expected to be used for their payment. The governmental unit's future taxing power will ultimately provide resources to pay them. Taxes designated for debt service usually are treated as revenues of a Debt Service Fund and do not affect the General Fund. In specific cases, however, the taxes may be collected through the General Fund and used to service debt directly from the General Fund. Alternatively, such taxes may be transferred to the Debt Service Fund. In the latter case they would be accounted for as General Fund revenues and as an operating transfer to the Debt Service Fund.[3]

Combining Balance Sheet

A government with more than one Special Revenue Fund will present both the balance sheets and the statements of revenues, expenditures, and other changes in fund balance in combining statements. A recent combining balance sheet for the Special Revenue Funds of the City of Indianapolis appears in Figure 4-6.

STATEMENT OF REVENUES, EXPENDITURES, AND CHANGES IN FUND BALANCE

The second major General and Special Revenue Fund financial statement is the Statement of Revenues, Expenditures, and Changes in Fund Balance. As its title indicates, this statement presents the revenues, expenditures, and other items that increased or decreased fund balance during a year (or other time period) and reconciles the beginning and ending fund balance.

The Statement of Revenues, Expenditures, and Changes in Fund Balance may present data pertaining to either the Fund Balance account, the unreserved fund balance, or to the total fund balance, including reserves. The former requires a "changes in reserves" section within the statement and reconciles the beginning and ending Fund Balance *account* balances. The latter (Figure 4-7) presents only the items that changed total fund balance, excluding changes in reserves, and reconciles beginning and ending *total* fund balances. Significant changes in reserves are disclosed in the notes to the financial statements.

Total Fund Balance Approach

The general format for a Statement of Revenues, Expenditures, and Changes in Fund Balance is presented in Figure 4-7.[4] The detailed classifications of rev-

---

[3] It is also permissible to report the transfer to the Debt Service Fund as a deduction from General Fund gross revenues and report the revenues in the Debt Service Fund.

[4] Former NCGA pronouncements, superseded by NCGA *Statement 1*, required three separate governmental fund "operating" statements: (1) an Analysis of Changes in Fund Balance, prepared similarly to Figure 4-7 but with no revenue or expenditure detail, that is, only one total revenue amount and one total expenditure amount; (2) a Statement of Expenditures, in which expenditure (and perhaps encumbrance) detail data was compared with Appropriations; and (3) a Statement of Revenues, in which estimated and actual revenues by source were compared. The Statement of Revenues, Expenditures, and Changes in Fund Balance essentially combines these three statements into a single statement.

Figure 4-6

CITY OF INDIANAPOLIS
Special Revenue Funds
Combining Balance Sheet
December 31, 1980

	Community Services	Manpower Federal Programs	Trustee for the Secretary of HUD	Unsafe Building	Sanitary District General Improvement	Junk Vehicle	Arterial Roads and Streets	Parking Meters	Historic Preservation	Park Land	Interfund Eliminations	Totals 1980	Totals 1979
Assets													
Cash	$1,917,003	$ 560,963	$ 31,901	$ 15,417	$ 6,127	$ 6,980	$ 8,060	$ 10,570	$ 360	$ 7,242	$	$ 2,964,623	$ 1,915,101
Investments (note 1H)			661,134	195,965	2,773,259	79,169	4,946,909	338,266		203,192		9,197,894	8,248,639
Due from Federal, state, and local governments (note 4)		1,612,311			51,222		39,261					1,702,794	2,971,284
Due from other funds (note 5)	29,477								8,091		$(37,568)		13,090
Total assets	$1,946,480	$2,573,274	$693,035	$211,382	$2,830,608	$86,149	$4,994,230	$348,836	$ 8,451	$210,434	$(37,568)	$13,865,311	$13,148,114
Liabilities and Fund Balances													
Liabilities:													
Accounts payable	$ 304	$ 63,472	$	$	$	$	$	$ 8,869	$ 304	$	$	$ 72,949	$ 85,071
Note payable			511,872			495		79	5,000			511,872	
Contracts payable	259,258	2,247,032			24,095		1,597,303					4,133,262	2,831,647
Accrued payroll and payroll taxes	2,066	256,776						7,881	2,430			269,153	565,968
Other accrued liabilities		2,585						616	30			3,231	65,400
Due to other funds (note 5)	1,684,852	3,409		30,732			5,270	267			(37,568)	1,686,962	1,886,679
Total liabilities	1,946,480	2,573,274	511,872	30,732	24,095	495	1,602,573	17,712	7,764		(37,568)	6,677,429	5,434,765
Fund balances (note 1E)													
Reserved for encumbrances					114,376		3,185,531	607	38,129	500		3,339,143	5,266,274
Unencumbered (overencumbered)			181,163	180,650	2,692,137	85,654	206,126	330,517	(37,442)	209,934		3,848,739	2,447,075
Total fund balances			181,163	180,650	2,806,513	85,654	3,391,657	331,124	687	210,434		7,187,882	7,713,349
Total liabilities and fund balances	$1,946,480	$2,573,274	$693,035	$211,382	$2,830,608	$86,149	$4,994,230	$348,836	$ 8,451	$210,434	$(37,568)	$13,865,311	$13,148,114

See notes to combined financial statements.

enues and expenditures are discussed in Chapter 5 and 6, respectively, as indicated in Figure 4-7. However, observe the major components of this statement and the order in which they appear:

Revenues
− Expenditures
Excess of revenues over (under) expenditures
± Other financing sources (uses)
Excess of revenues and other sources over (under) expenditures and other uses
+ Fund balance, beginning of period
± Residual equity transfers
Fund balance, end of period

Observe also in Figure 4-7 that (1) the beginning fund balance is reported as originally reported, followed by the error correction and the restated amount; (2) operating transfers are reported separately from revenues and expenditures—as "Other Financing Sources (Uses)"; (3) residual equity transfers are reported separately from operating transfers; and (4) the statement explains the change in *total* fund balance during the period.

Unreserved Fund Balance (Account) Approach

Some accountants prefer to prepare the Statement of Revenues, Expenditures, and Changes in Fund Balance in a manner that explains the changes in the beginning and ending Fund Balance *account* balances. Statements prepared under this acceptable alternative approach are structured like that presented in Figure 4-7 except that a "Changes in Reserves" section is inserted after "Excess of revenues and other financing sources over (under) expenditures and other uses of financial resources." To illustrate, the last part of Figure 4-7 would appear as follows in a Statement of Revenues, Expenditures, and Changes in Fund Balance that focuses on changes in the Fund Balance *account:*

Excess of revenues and other financing sources over (under) expenditures and other uses of financial resources		$45,300
Decreases (increases) in reserves:		
Increase in reserve for encumbrances		(20,000)
		$25,300
Unreserved fund balance, January 1, 19X1:		
As previously reported	$1,000	
Correction of 19X0 error	(300)	
As restated		700
Residual equity transfer to Enterprise Fund		(6,000)
Unreserved fund balance, December 31, 19X1		$20,000

Figure 4-7

A GOVERNMENTAL UNIT

General Fund
Statement of Revenues, Expenditures, and Changes
in Fund Balance (Total)
for the Fiscal Year Ended December 31, 19X1

Revenues:				
Revenue 1 ⎫	(Classified by	$	xx	
. . . ⎬	Source:		xx	
Revenue *n* ⎭	Chapter 5)		xx	$437,700

Expenditures:				
Program 1 ⎫	(Classified by		xx	
. . . ⎬	Program:		xx	
Program *n* ⎭	Chapter 6)		xx	

-or-

Operations ⎫	(Classified by		xx	
Capital outlay ⎬	Object Class:		xx	
Debt service ⎭	Chapter 6)		xx	398,400

Excess of revenues over (under) expenditures .... $ 39,300

Other financing sources (uses):*
Operating transfer from Special Revenue Fund $10,000
Operating transfer to Debt Service Fund .... (4,000) 6,000

Excess of revenues and other financing sources over
expenditures and other uses of financial resources .... $ 45,300

Fund balance, January 1, 19X1:

As previously reported .... $ 1,000
Correction of 19X0 error .... (300)

As restated 700
Residual equity transfer to Enterprise Fund .... (6,000)

Fund balance, December 31, 19X1 .... $ 40,000

Any bond or other general obligation long-term debt issue proceeds accounted for in the General Fund—for example, if long-term bonds were issued to finance a General Fund deficit—would be reported as "Other Financing Sources."

Alternative Statement Formats

The Statement of Revenues, Expenditures, and Changes in Fund Balance illustrated in Figure 4-7 is presented in the format used for illustrative purposes by the National Council on Governmental Accounting in NCGA *Statement 1.* That format emphasizes the comparison of revenues and expenditures, and the excess of one over the other, and provides for presenting all other changes (bond issue proceeds, operating transfers, residual equity transfers) in specified places in the statement.

Professional accountants have different opinions, however, as to what order of data presentation and emphasis results in the most meaningful statement. Recognizing these differences of opinion, the NCGA provided for flexibility in the design of the Statement of Revenues, Expenditures, and Changes in Fund Balance.

One acceptable alternative design of the Statement of Revenues, Expenditures, and Changes in Fund Balance is to present the other financing sources (but not residual equity transfers) immediately after revenues, to derive a "Total Revenues and Other Sources" subtotal, and to report other financing uses after expenditures. Such a statement format (total fund balance approach) would appear:

> Revenues
> + Other financing sources (e.g., bond issue proceeds
>   and operating transfers from other funds)
> ———————————————————————
> Total revenues and other financing sources
> ———————————————————————
> Expenditures
> + Other uses (e.g., operating transfers to other funds)
> ———————————————————————
> Total expenditures and other uses
> ———————————————————————
> Excess of revenues and other financing sources over
>   (under) expenditures and other uses
> + Fund balance, beginning of period
> ± Residual equity transfers
> ———————————————————————
> Fund balance, end of period
> ═══════════════════════

This format emphasizes the total financing resource inflows and outflows and the excess of one over the other rather than a direct comparison of only revenues and expenditures.

Still another acceptable alternative design of the Statement of Revenues, Expenditures, and Changes in Fund Balance is to open the statement in the alternative format above with the beginning fund balance amount. Such a statement format (total fund balance approach) would appear:

> Fund balance, beginning of period
> ———————————————————————
> Revenues
> + Other financing sources (e.g., bond issue proceeds
>   and operating transfers from other funds)
> ———————————————————————
> Total revenues and other financing sources
> ———————————————————————
> Total resources available
> ———————————————————————
> Expenditures
> + Other uses (e.g., operating transfers to other funds)
> ———————————————————————
> Total expenditures and other uses
> ———————————————————————
> Excess of total resources available over (under)
>   expenditures and other uses
> ———————————————————————
> ± Residual equity transfers
> ———————————————————————
> Fund balance, end of period
> ═══════════════════════

This format highlights the total resources available, the total expenditures and other uses of financial resources, and the excess of one over the other, as well as the beginning and ending fund balances.

Note that, regardless of the format of the Statement of Revenues, Expenditures, and Changes in Fund Balance, residual equity transfers are reported separately after the results of operations, whereas operating transfers enter the determination of operating results.

Comparative Statements, Residual Equity Transfers, and Restatements

Comparative Statements. Financial statements presenting data for two or more years are helpful in comparing financial position and operating results over time and in assessing trends in financial position and operating results. A *comparative* statement of Revenues, Expenditures, and Changes in Fund Balance, 19X2 and 19X1, for the General Fund of A Governmental Unit, prepared on a fund balance *account* approach using assumed data for 19X2, is presented in Figure 4-8.

In studying Figure 4-8 observe that:

1. The 19X2 beginning fund balance is equal to the 19X1 ending fund balance.
2. The Reserve for Encumbrances account has a $30,000 balance at the end of 19X2, an increase of $10,000 over its balance at the end of 19X1. Only the *change* in the reserve appears in the statement.
3. An advance was made from the General Fund to a Special Revenue Fund during 19X2 that is not expected to be repaid until 19X4 or later. Thus, a corresponding reserve was established.
4. The only 19X2 operating transfer was for $5,000 to a Debt Service Fund; no residual equity transfers occurred during 19X2, nor were any restatements necessary.

Residual Equity Transfers. NCGA *Statement 1* says at one point that "residual equity transfers should be reported as additions to or deductions from the beginning fund balance of governmental funds."[5] At another point *Statement 1* says that "residual equity transfers should be reported after the results of operations"[6] and illustrates presentation of residual equity transfers after "Excess of revenues and other sources over (under) expenditures and other uses" and immediately before ending Fund Balance. Either presentation approach is acceptable: (1) as the last item in the Statement of Revenues, Expenditures, and Changes in Fund Balance before the Fund Balance section, or (2) as the last item before the ending Fund Balance. We have chosen to illustrate the latter approach because it seems preferable in NCGAS 1 and is most in keeping with current practice.

[5] NCGAS 1, p. 16.
[6] Ibid., p. 23.

Figure 4-8

A GOVERNMENTAL UNIT

General Fund
Statement of Revenues, Expenditures, and Changes in Fund Balance (Account)
for the Fiscal Years Ended December 31, 19X2 and 19X1

	19X2	19X1
Revenues:		
(Classified by source, Chapter 5)	$475,000	$437,700
Expenditures:		
(Classified by program, function, or object class, Chapter 6)	460,000	398,400
Excess of revenues over (under) expenditures	15,000	39,300
Other financing sources (uses):		
Operating transfer from Special Revenue Fund	—	10,000
Operating transfer to Debt Service Fund	(5,000)	(4,000)
Total other financing sources (uses)	(5,000)	6,000
Excess of revenues and other financing sources over (under) expenditures and other uses	10,000	45,300
Decreases (increases) in reserves:		
Increase in reserve for encumbrances	(10,000)	(20,000)
Increase in reserve for advance to Special Revenue Fund	(5,000)	—
Increase (decrease) in fund balance (account)	(5,000)	25,300
Unreserved fund balance (account), January 1, as restated*	20,000	700
Residual equity transfer to Enterprise Fund	—	(6,000)
Unreserved fund balance (account), December 31	$ 15,000	$ 20,000

The January 1, 19X1, balance is restated from $1,000, as previously reported, to $700 to reflect the correction of a 19X0 accounting error which resulted in Vouchers Payable being understated by $300 in the December 31, 19X0, General Fund balance sheet and expenditures being understated by $300 in the General Fund Statement of Revenues, Expenditures, and Changes in Fund Balance for the year ended December 31, 19X0.

Restatements. Occasionally, a governmental fund Statement of Revenues, Expenditures, and Changes in Fund Balance for an accounting period must be restated to show the correction of an error or the change to a preferable accounting principle. Regardless of the placement of the beginning fund balance in the statement, that amount should be noted as being "as previously reported" and followed by the restatement amount and a restated beginning fund balance, presented as follows:

Fund balance, beginning of period,
as previously reported
± Restatements (e.g., correction of
prior period errors)
_____

Fund balance, beginning of period,
as restated

Alternatively, the restated beginning fund balance amount may be presented in the statement, as in Figure 4-8, and the restatement explained in the notes to the financial statements. In comparative statements covering two or more periods (1) the cumulative restatement effect on periods prior to the earliest period being reported on should be reported as a restatement of the beginning fund balance of that period, and (2) the data reported for later periods should be restated to reflect the changed accounting principle or error correction.

Combining Statement of Revenues, Expenditures, and Changes in Fund Balance

A government with more than one Special Revenue Fund will present a combining statement of revenues, expenditures, and changes in fund balance as well as a combining balance sheet. The Combining Statement of Special Revenue Fund Revenues, Expenditures, and Changes in Fund Balance from a recent annual financial report of the City of Indianapolis appears as Figure 4-9.

STATEMENT OF REVENUES, EXPENDITURES, AND CHANGES IN FUND BALANCE—BUDGET AND ACTUAL

A third statement required for General and Special Revenue Funds, and for similar governmental funds that finance the annual operating budget, compares budgeted and actual operating results. This Statement of Revenues, Expenditures, and Changes in Fund Balance—*Budget and Actual* may be presented in any of the alternative formats discussed earlier for the Statement of Revenues, Expenditures, and Changes in Fund Balance. However, it would have columns headed:

Budget	Actual	Variance— Favorable (Unfavorable)

If the legally adopted budget is prepared on a basis consistent with GAAP, the "actual" data on this statement will correspond with the data presented in the Statement of Revenues, Expenditures, and Changes in Fund Balance (Figure 4-7). However, if the budget is prepared on a basis other than GAAP—for example, on the cash receipts and disbursements basis—both the "budget" data and the "actual" data should be presented on the **budgetary** basis so that the statement will display an accurate budgetary comparison and the "variance—favorable (unfavorable)" comparison will be meaningful. Where the budget is prepared on a basis other than GAAP, and thus the Statement of Revenues, Expenditures, and Changes in Fund Balance—Budget and Actual is prepared on a non-GAAP basis, the notes to the financial statements should contain an explanation of the budgetary basis employed and a reconciliation of the budgetary data with the GAAP data

Figure 4-9

CITY OF INDIANAPOLIS
Special Revenue Funds
Combining Statement of Revenues, Expenditures and Changes in Fund Balances
for the Year Ended December 31, 1980

	Community Services	Manpower Federal Program	Trustee for the Secretary of HUD	Unsafe Building	Sanitary District General Improvement	Junk Vehicle	Arterial Roads and Streets	Parking Meters	Historic Preservation	Park Land	Interfund Eliminations	Totals 1980	Totals 1979
Revenues:													
Taxes	$	$	$	$	$	$	$5,397,274	$	$	$	$	$5,397,274	$8,082,368
Other federal funds (note 4)	16,801,760	24,879,185	693,035		99,187		42,113		148,267		(154,799)	42,508,748	36,652,913
Other operating revenues	740,900	2,237		56,938	51,322	20,380	1,069,595	474,374		137,892		2,553,638	1,507,161
Total revenues	17,542,660	24,881,422	693,035	56,938	150,509	20,380	6,508,982	474,374	148,267	137,892	(154,799)	50,459,660	46,242,442
Other financing sources:													
Transfers (note 5)	689,148				2,004,458						(36,936)	2,656,670	355,451
Total revenues and other financing sources	18,231,808	24,881,422	693,035	56,938	2,154,967	20,380	6,508,982	474,374	148,267	137,892	(191,735)	53,116,330	46,597,893
Expenditures:													
Current:													
Community cultural and recreation													7,500
Community development and welfare	18,231,808	24,862,591	511,872						169,099		(154,799)	43,620,571	36,899,795
Transportation and related services							3,788,151	353,511				4,141,662	1,897,375
Environmental services					95,889	7,563						103,452	359,302
Total current expenditures	18,231,808	24,862,591	511,872		95,889	7,563	3,788,151	353,511	169,099		(154,799)	47,865,685	39,163,972
Debt service								6,034	3,352			9,386	13,408
Capital outlays		18,831			1,238		5,699,031	26,412		2,433		5,747,945	2,883,002
Total expenditures	18,231,808	24,881,422	511,872		97,127	7,563	9,487,182	385,957	172,451	2,433	(154,799)	53,623,016	42,060,382
Other uses:													
Transfers (note 5)				36,936	18,781						(36,936)	18,781	4,889,859
Total expenditures and other uses	18,231,808	24,881,422	511,872	36,936	115,908	7,563	9,487,182	385,957	172,451	2,433	(191,735)	53,641,797	46,950,241
Excess of revenues and other financing sources over (under) expenditures and other uses			181,163	20,002	2,039,059	12,817	(2,978,200)	88,417	(24,184)	135,459		(525,467)	(352,348)
Fund balances at beginning of year (note 1A)				160,648	767,454	72,837	6,369,857	242,707	24,871	74,975		7,713,349	8,065,697
Fund balances at end of year (note 1A)	$	$	$181,163	$180,650	$2,806,513	$85,654	$3,391,657	$331,124	$687	$210,434	$	$7,187,882	$7,713,349

See notes to combined financial statements

presented in the Statement of Revenues, Expenditures, and Changes in Fund Balance. A *combined* Statement of Revenues, Expenditures, and Changes in Fund Balance—Budget and Actual—General and Special Revenue Funds is illustrated in Figure 14-7. One approach to preparing the budgetary statement where the budget is not prepared on a GAAP basis is shown in Figure 4-10, which presents the General Fund budgetary comparison statement from a recent City of Tucson, Arizona annual financial report.

SOME ALTERNATIVE PROCEDURES

To this point in the chapter we have, for the most part, demonstrated only one way to account for various transactions and events affecting General and Special Revenue Funds. Numerous variations in the accounting mechanics by which transactions are recorded may be encountered in practice, however. Alternative approaches may arise from legal provisions, policies, or personal preferences of governmental accountants and are acceptable if they accomplish the required results.

Variations in accounting mechanics vary from quite simple—e.g., some governments do not subclassify Allowance for Uncollectible Taxes applicable to current taxes, delinquent taxes, tax liens, etc.—to quite complex and pervasive. Three types of fairly common variations warrant mention here. These relate to (1) closing entries, (2) use of a Budgetary Fund Balance account, and (3) recording transfers and bond issue proceeds. Others are discussed in Chapters 5 and 6.

Closing Entries

The closing entries illustrated earlier in the chapter were based on certain assumptions about the laws and policies of A Governmental Unit, which we referred to as "Assumption A1."

> *Assumption A1.* (1) All unexpended appropriations lapse at year end, even if encumbered; (2) the unit is committed to accept the goods or services on order at year end; (3) expenditures resulting from encumbrances outstanding at the end of a year must be charged against the next year's appropriations; and (4) the Reserve for Encumbrances should be left open and be reported as a reservation of fund balance in the year-end balance sheet.

Under Assumption A1, the Reserve for Encumbrances balance reported in the 19X1 year-end balance sheet serves (1) as a reminder to those preparing the 19X2 budget to include $20,000 appropriations for 19X2 expenditures expected to result from encumbrances outstanding at the end of 19X1 as well as (2) to inform readers of the financial statements of the commitments outstanding at the end of 19X1 that are expected to result in expenditures in 19X2. The entry at the start of 19X2

Encumbrances	20,000	
Fund Balance		20,000

returns the Encumbrances and Reserve for Encumbrances accounts to their usual offsetting relationship in the General Ledger, causing the Reserve for Encumbrances to no longer be a true Fund Balance reserve, and increases the Fund Balance account accordingly.

Another legal and policy situation that may be encountered is one where all appropriations lapse, whether or not encumbered, as in Assumption A1—but there is no statutory or policy requirement that the Reserve for Encumbrance be reported in the balance sheet. This variation of Assumption A1, which we shall call Assumption A2, may be summarized:

> *Assumption A2.* (1) All unexpended appropriations lapse at year end, even if encumbered; (2) the unit is committed to accept the goods or services on order at year end; and (3) expenditures resulting from encumbrances outstanding at the end of a year must be authorized by and charged against the next year's appropriations; and (4) a Reserve for Encumbrances is **not** required to be reported in the year-end balance sheet.

Under Assumption A2, management may choose to report the Reserve for Encumbrances in the balance sheet as required by Assumption A1. If so, the entries illustrated earlier for the end of 19X1 and the beginning of 19X2 are applicable. Alternatively, management may choose to report the encumbrances outstanding only in the notes to the financial statements and not by a Reserve for Encumbrances in the 19X1 year-end balance sheet. In this case it is permissible either to (1) close both Encumbrances and Reserve for Encumbrances accounts, or (2) leave both open in their usual offset relationship in the General Ledger, since they are not reported in the financial statements, and disclose any material amounts of encumbrances outstanding in the notes to the financial statements. The General Ledger closing entry for appropriations, expenditures, and encumbrances on page 109 might appear in either of the following ways in this case:

CLOSING BOTH ENCUMBRANCES AND RESERVE FOR ENCUMBRANCES:

Appropriations	426,000	
Reserve for Encumbrances	20,000	
Expenditures		398,400
Encumbrances		20,000
Fund Balance		27,600
To close the accounts at year end.		

-or-

CLOSING NEITHER ENCUMBRANCES NOR RESERVE FOR ENCUMBRANCES:

Appropriations	426,000	
Expenditures		398,400
Fund Balance		27,600
To close the accounts at year end.		

Note that the Fund Balance account would reflect total fund balance (except for any other reserves) in this case, and no Reserve for Encumbrances would be reported in the General Fund balance sheet. Note also that if both Encumbrances

Figure 4-10

CITY OF TUCSON
General Fund
Statement of Revenues, Expenditures and Changes in Fund Balance - Budget and Actual
(Budgetary Basis at Variance With GAAP)
for the Year Ended June 30, 1981

	Actual	Adjustment to Budgetary Basis	Actual on Budgetary Basis	Budget	Variance— Favorable (Unfavorable)
Revenues:					
Taxes	$44,557,085	$ —	$44,557,085	$44,068,206	$ 488,879
Licenses and Permits	1,627,774	—	1,627,774	1,625,000	2,774
Fines and Forfeitures	1,656,872	—	1,656,872	1,597,000	59,872
Use of Money and Property	183,585	—	183,585	1,645,000	(1,461,415)
Other Agencies	29,341,371	—	29,341,371	29,606,000	(264,629)
Charges for Current Services	6,930,799	—	6,930,799	7,055,000	(124,201)
Miscellaneous Revenue	1,595,448	600,748	2,196,196	4,157,436	(1,961,240)
Total Revenues	85,892,934	600,748	86,493,682	89,753,642	(3,259,960)

	Actual	Adjustment to Budgetary Basis	Actual on Budgetary Basis	Budget	Variance— Favorable (Unfavorable)
Expenditures:					
General Government	18,435,559	(1,391,124)	17,044,435	17,130,807	86,372
Police	21,843,212	(120,829)	21,722,383	21,568,850	(153,533)
Fire	12,686,369	210,069	12,896,438	12,657,000	(239,438)
Operations	14,130,904	(196,231)	13,934,673	16,624,349	2,689,676
Transportation	13,318,759	554,818	13,873,577	15,465,099	1,591,522
Parks	6,202,091	76,723	6,278,814	6,307,537	28,723
Total Expenditures	86,616,894	(866,574)	85,750,320	89,753,642	4,003,322
Excess (Deficiency) of Revenues Over Expenditures	(723,960)	1,467,322	743,362		
Other Changes in Unreserved Fund Balance:					
Net Decrease in Reserves for Advances, Deposits and Inventory	669,848	—	669,848		
Decrease (Increase) in Reserve for Encumbrances	1,467,322	(1,467,322)	—		
Total Other Changes in Unreserved Fund Balance	2,137,170	(1,467,322)	669,848		
Unreserved Fund Balance July 1, 1980	2,619,246	—	2,619,246		
Unreserved Fund Balance—June 30, 1981	$ 4,032,456	$ —	$ 4,032,456		

See notes to the financial statements.

and Reserve for Encumbrances are closed at the end of 19X1 both must be reestablished in the accounts, by the reverse of the closing entry, at the start of 19X2:

Encumbrances 20,000
    Reserve for Encumbrances   20,000
To reestablish these accounts at the
beginning of 19X2.

If neither Encumbrances nor Reserve for Encumbrances was closed at the end of 19X1, no entry is required at the beginning of 19X2 since the necessary balances are in the accounts.

A third variation in the legal status of appropriations at year end, which we shall call Assumption B, may be summarized:

Assumption B. (1) All unexpended appropriations lapse, even if encumbered; and (2) all encumbrances are null and void after year end.

The essence of this legal circumstance is that each year stands clearly apart. Vendors must perform by 19X1 year end or seek new 19X2 contracts, which may or may not be approved, to provide the goods or services in 19X2. Purchase orders typically carry a notice to this effect in bold face type in this situation. While the essence of Assumption B differs markedly from that of Assumptions A1 and A2, the accounting entries at the end of 19X1 are the same as those for the "Closing Both Encumbrances and Reserve for Encumbrances" variation of Assumption A2, illustrated above. Under Assumption B neither Encumbrances nor Reserve for Encumbrances would be reported or disclosed in the statements at year end. There would be no Encumbrances and Reserve for Encumbrances entry in 19X2 until new 19X2 encumbrances were incurred.

Other variations in closing entry technique are apt to be encountered when all appropriations do not lapse at year end, as illustrated earlier in the chapter. For example, assume that the charter of A Governmental Unit provides that:

Assumption C1. Encumbered appropriations continue (do not lapse at year end) to the next period; that is, only unencumbered appropriations lapse at year end.

In this case the closing entry would leave on the books Appropriations, Encumbrances, and Reserve for Encumbrances in the $20,000 amount of the encumbrances outstanding and the General Ledger closing entry for appropriations, expenditures, and encumbrances on page 109 would appear instead as:

Appropriations [$20,000 left]   406,000
    Expenditures   398,400
    Fund Balance   7,600
To close the accounts at year end.

This would result in the same balance in the Fund Balance account as in Assumption A1 but (1) Appropriations, or "Appropriated Fund Balance," would appear in the Fund Balance section of the balance sheet rather than Reserve for Encumbrances, and (2) the Encumbrances and Reserve for Encumbrances accounts would not appear in the financial statements but would be ready for use in the subsequent period. The encumbrances outstanding would be disclosed in the notes to the financial statements or parenthetically in the balance sheet, e.g., by reporting "Appropriations (Encumbered)" in the fund balance section of the balance sheet.

As another example, assume that the charter of A Governmental Unit provides that:

> *Assumption C2. Unexpended appropriations continue* (do not lapse at year end) *to the next period(s);* that is, only expended appropriations lapse at year end.

In this case, assuming that the Encumbrances and Reserve for Encumbrances accounts were not closed, the General Ledger closing entry for the appropriations, expenditures, and encumbrances of the General Fund at page 109 would appear:

Appropriations [$27,600 left]	398,400	
Expenditures		398,400
To close the accounts at year end.		

In this case the fund balance section of the balance sheet (Figure 4-5) might appear:

Fund Balance:	
Appropriated ($20,000 encumbered)	$27,600
Unappropriated (unencumbered)	12,400
	$40,000

Alternatively, the fund balance section might appear:

Fund Balance:		
Appropriated:		
Reserved for encumbrances (or		
Encumbered)	$20,000	
Unencumbered	7,600	$27,600
Unappropriated		12,400
		$40,000

Budgetary Fund Balance Account

Some accountants prefer not to let the budgetary entries change the balance of the Fund Balance account. Rather than letting the Fund Balance account become a "mixed" (part actual, part budgetary) account, they carry the *planned change* in Fund Balance in a separate Budgetary Fund Balance account during the year. Following this approach the budgetary entry illustrated earlier in this chapter would appear:

(1) Estimated Revenues 431,000
     Appropriations   426,000
     Budgetary Fund Balance   5,000
    To record appropriations and
    estimated revenue.

At the end of the year the budgetary entry (perhaps as amended) would be closed by reversal:

Appropriations 426,000
Budgetary Fund Balance   5,000
    Estimated Revenues   431,000
    To close the budgetary accounts.

Transfer and Bond Issue Proceeds

The illustrative entries in this chapter were based on the assumption that separate operating transfer, residual equity transfer, and bond issue proceeds accounts were used in the General Ledger to distinguish such items from Revenues and Expenditures. Generally accepted accounting principles require that such items be *reported* separately from fund revenues and expenditures, but this does not mean that they must necessarily be *accounted* for separately in the fund General Ledger. Thus, an acceptable alternative approach is to account for all fund revenues, expenditues, transfers, and bond issue proceeds in General Ledger control accounts such as "Revenues and Other Resource Inflows" and "Expenditures and Other Resource Outflows" and classify them separately only in the subsidiary ledger accounts. This approach—which should *not* be used in working text, course examination, or CPA examination problems unless explicitly required—is discussed more fully and illustrated in Chapters 5 and 6.

CONCLUDING COMMENTS ──────────────────────

The General and Special Revenue Funds typically account for significant portions of the financial resources of state and local government units. A thorough understanding of General and Special Revenue Fund accounting thus is important to governmental accountants, auditors, and systems specialists.

Moreover, accounting and reporting for the other governmental funds (Capital Projects, Debt Service, Special Assessment, and Expendable Trust Funds) closely parallel that for the General and Special Revenue Funds and can be understood largely by analogy. Thus, a firm foundation in General and Special Revenue Fund accounting and reporting is essential for both students and practitioners.

▶ **Question 4-1.** Why is there no chapter in this text devoted to describing operations and accounting procedures of Special Revenue Funds?

Question 4-2. What are the characteristics of "expenditures" that distinguish them from "expenses" in the financial accounting sense?

Question 4-3. What is the nature of the Fund Balance account as it appears (a) in the interim balance sheet? (b) in a postclosing trial balance?

Question 4-4. You are the administrator of a large department of a city in which appropriations lapse at the end of the year. Near the end of the year you find that part of your appropriation is unspent and will not be required for current operations. Under what circumstances should you (a) spend all of the appropriation? (b) permit a substantial part of your appropriation to lapse?

Question 4-5. Discuss the legal assumptions as to the lapsing of appropriations for the benefit of a committee to write the charter for a newly incorporated village.

Question 4-6. The postclosing trial balance of the General Fund contains, in three different cases, balances for the following accounts, among others:

Case 1: Reserve for Encumbrances   Case 2: Fund Balance
   Fund Balance   Case 3: Reserve for Encumbrances
   Appropriations   Fund Balance
   Encumbrances

On which legal assumptions may the closing entries have been based in each case?

Question 4-7. The appropriations of a certain government for current expenditures lapse at the end of the fiscal year for which made, while appropriations for capital outlay lapse two years later. Discuss the desirability of this dual arrangement.

Note to Instructor: All problems in the text that require recording and posting transactions, taking a preclosing trial balance, recording and posting closing entries, and taking a postclosing trial balance may be solved by the use of a worksheet. The authors recommend that the first problem assignment or two require journals, ledgers, and trial balances. After the students have been exposed to this cycle, worksheets may be used for as many subsequent problems as the instructor thinks desirable.

▶ **Problem 4-1.** (a) Prepare general journal entries to record the following transactions:

1. On November 4, 19X1, the Town of Hopper's Haven ordered, for its police department, supplies costing $2,700.
2. Hopper's Haven received the goods ordered on November 4 and an invoice for $2,700 on November 11.
3. Hopper's Haven paid for the goods on November 21.
   (b) Record the transactions above assuming that the invoice price for the goods was $2,500.
   (c) Record the transactions above assuming that the invoice price for the goods was $2,800.

Problem 4-2. Prepare general journal entries to record the following transactions in the general ledger of the General Fund or a Special Revenue Fund, as appropriate.

1. $50,000 of General Fund cash was contributed to establish an Internal Service Fund.

2. A truck—acquired two years ago with General Fund revenues for $8,000—with a fair market value of $4,000 was contributed to a department financed by an Enterprise Fund.

3. The Sanitation Department, accounted for in the General Fund, billed the Municipal Airport, accounted for in an Enterprise Fund, $400 for garbage collection.

4. General Fund cash of $40,000—to be repaid in 90 days—was provided to enable construction to begin on a new courthouse before a bond issue was sold.

5. A $1,000,000 bond issue to finance construction of an addition to the civic center was sold at par.

6. General Fund disbursements during May included payment of $30,000 to a Capital Projects Fund to help finance a major capital project.

7. After retirement of the related debt, the balance of the net assets of a Debt Service Fund, $1,500, was transferred to the General Fund.

8. General Fund cash of $10,000 was contributed to a Special Assessment Fund as the city's portion of the financing of the special assessment project.

Problem 4-3. (a) On January 1, 19X0, the Kiblersville city council adopted the following General Fund budget for 19X0:

Estimated Revenues	$270,000
Estimated Operating Transfers In	45,000
Appropriations	300,000

(b) Estimated revenues were revised downward by $8,000 on April 11, 19X0.

(c) Spiraling operating costs resulted in amending the General Fund budget on May 21, 19X0, to increase General Fund appropriations by $6,000.

(d) The budget was amended on May 30, 19X0, to shift $4,000 of the fire department supplies appropriation to the police department.

(e) The budget was amended on September 14, 19X0, to decrease the general government appropriation for supplies by $200 and increase the general government appropriation for capital outlay by $200.

(f) On December 31, 19X0, the budgetary accounts were closed.

Required:

(a) Prepare general journal entries to record the transactions above in the Kiblersville General Fund general ledger without using a Budgetary Fund Balance account.

(b) Prepare general journal entries to record the transactions above using a Budgetary Fund Balance Account.

Problem 4-4. The trial balance of the General Fund of the City of W on January 1, 19X0, was as follows:

Cash	$15,000	
Taxes Receivable—Delinquent	20,000	
Allowance for Uncollectible Taxes—		
Delinquent		$ 3,000
Interest and Penalties Receivable on Taxes ...	1,000	

Allowance for Uncollectible Interest and Penalties		75
Accounts Receivable	10,000	
Allowance for Uncollectible Accounts		1,000
Vouchers Payable		20,500
Reserve for Encumbrances (Assumption A1) ..		10,000
Fund Balance		11,425
	$46,000	$46,000

The following transactions took place during 19X0:

1. Revenues were estimated at $110,000; appropriations of $108,000 were made.
2. An order placed at the end of the preceding year and estimated to cost $10,000 was received; the invoice indicated an actual cost of $9,500.
3. Taxes of $110,000 accrued; an allowance of 5 percent was made for possible losses.
4. Collections were made as follows:

Current Taxes	$90,000
Delinquent Taxes	10,000
Interest and Penalties Receivable on Taxes	300
Accounts Receivable	5,000

5. Taxes amounting to $20,000 have become delinquent; the balance of Allowance for Uncollectible Taxes—Current was transferred to Allowance for Uncollectible Taxes—Delinquent.
6. Delinquent Taxes amounting to $2,000 were written off; Interest and Penalties Receivable on Taxes of $20 were also written off.
7. An order was placed for materials estimated to cost $20,000.
8. Delinquent Taxes amounting to $200, which were written off in preceding years, were collected with interest and penalties of $35, $25 of which had been previously accrued and written off.
9. Payments were made as follows:

Vouchers Payable	$15,500
Payrolls	20,000

10. The materials ordered (in 7) were received; a bill for $21,000 was also received.
11. An order was placed for an automobile for the police department; the estimated cost was $8,000.
12. Payrolls of $25,000 were paid.
13. The automobile ordered for the police department (in 11) was received; the actual cost was $8,000.
14. Serial bonds in the amount of $10,000, to be repaid through the General Fund, matured.
15. The matured serial bonds were paid.
16. Interest amounting to $5,000 was paid from the General Fund.

17. Interest of $600 accrued on Delinquent Taxes, and an allowance for uncollectible losses thereon of 10 percent was provided.

18. An order was placed for materials estimated to cost $19,000.

Required:

(a) Post the opening trial balance to "T" accounts.

(b) Prepare journal entries.

(c) Post to "T" accounts.

(d) Prepare closing entries.

(e) Post to "T" accounts.

(f) Prepare a postclosing trial balance at December 31, 19X0.

(g) Prepare a balance sheet at December 31, 19X0.

In lieu of requirements (a)–(g) you may complete a worksheet headed as follows:

Columns	Heading
1–2	Trial Balance, 1/1/19X0
3–4	19X0 Transactions
5–6	Preclosing Trial Balance, 12/31/19X0
7–8	19X0 Operations/Closing Entries
9–10	Postclosing Trial Balance, 12/13/19X0

Problem 4-5. At December 31, 19X1, the City of X had in certain of its accounts the following balances: Appropriations, $200,000; Expenditures, $190,000; Encumbrances, $7,500; Reserve for Encumbrances, $7,500. On February 15, 19X2, the only item represented by the $7,500 encumbrance was billed to the City at $7,350. On the basis of the information above, prepare the closing entry, December 31, 19X1; entries required to be made January 1, 19X2, and February 15, 19X2; and the closing entry December 31, 19X2, for each of the five law and policy assumptions pertaining to the lapsing of appropriations and encumbrances outstanding at year end.

Problem 4-6. Presented below are the balances of selected accounts of the Town of Bettinger's Haven General Fund at December 31, 19X5 before preparing year-end closing entries:

Fund Balance	$ 5,000
Appropriations	1,000,000
Estimated Revenues	1,020,000
Expenditures	920,000
Encumbrances	50,000
Operating Transfers In	30,000
Revenues	980,000
Reserve for Advances	10,000
Reserve for Encumbrances	50,000

Required:

(a) Prepare the closing entry(ies) under each of the five law and policy assumptions pertaining to the lapsing of appropriations and encumbrances outstanding at year end.

(b) Prepare the fund balance section of the year end balance sheet under each of the five assumptions.

(c) Indicate what footnote disclosures related to encumbrances are required under each assumption.

(d) Assuming the goods on order at year end were received January 15, 19X6 at an invoice price of $50,900, prepare the general journal entries required on January 1 and January 15, 19X6 under each of the five assumptions.

Problem 4-7. The following is a trial balance of the General Fund of the City of Lynnville as of December 31, 19X0, after closing entries (Interest and Penalties on Taxes are not accrued):

Cash	$33,600	
Taxes Receivable—Delinquent	25,400	
Allowance for Uncollectible Delinquent Taxes		$ 5,900
Accounts Receivable	15,500	
Allowance for Uncollectible Accounts ..		2,500
Vouchers Payable		42,000
Reserve for Encumbrances		16,000
Fund Balance		8,100
	$74,500	$74,500

The following transactions took place during 19X1:

1. The budget for the year was adopted. Revenues were estimated at $216,000; appropriations of $229,000 were made, including an appropriation of $16,000 for materials ordered in 19X0, covered by the Reserve for Encumbrances.

2. Delinquent Taxes amounting to $2,800 were declared uncollectible and written off.

3. Taxes of $210,000 accrued; a 3 percent allowance for estimated losses was provided.

4. Uniforms estimated to cost $15,000 were ordered.

5. The materials ordered in 19X0 and set up as an encumbrance of that year for $16,000 were received; the actual cost was $15,000.

6. Collections were made as follows:

Current Taxes	$182,000
Delinquent Taxes	8,500
Interest and Penalties on Taxes	200
Accounts Receivable	7,300

7. Received a bill for $3,000 from the central printing shop.

8. Payroll vouchers for $100,000 were approved.

9. The uniforms (ordered in 4) were received; the invoice was for $16,000.

10. Approved an upcoming transfer of $38,000 to a Debt Service Fund to cover serial bond debt service.

11. Delinquent Taxes of $350, written off in preceding years, were collected.

12. Current Taxes became delinquent; the balance of Allowance for Uncollectible Current Taxes was transferred to Allowance for Uncollectible Delinquent Taxes.

13. Paid to the Special Revenue Fund $200 for supplies acquired for General Fund purposes, but originally paid for from (and recorded as expenditures in) the Special Revenue Fund.

14. An order was placed for a snowplow estimated to cost $3,500.
15. Vouchers paid amounted to $60,000.
16. The snowplow was received; the invoice was for $3,800.
17. The $38,000 transfer (transaction 10) due the Debt Service Fund was paid.
18. Miscellaneous revenues of $5,000 were collected.
19. An order was placed for civil defense equipment estimated to cost $24,000.
20. Received $5,000 from a discontinued Capital Projects Fund.
21. The payroll vouchers were paid.

Required:

(a) Post the opening trial balance to "T" accounts.
(b) Prepare journal entries.
(c) Post to "T" accounts.
(d) Prepare a preclosing trial balance at December 31, 19X1.
(e) Prepare closing entries.
(f) Post to "T" accounts.
(g) Prepare a postclosing trial balance at December 31, 19X1.
(h) Prepare a balance sheet at December 31, 19X1.

In lieu of requirements (a)–(g), you may complete a worksheet headed as follows:

Columns	Heading
1–2	Trial Balance, 1/1/19X1
3–4	19X1 Transactions
5–6	Preclosing Trial Balance, 12/31/19X1
7–8	Closing Entries, 12/31/19X1
9–10	Postclosing Trial Balance, 12/31/19X1

Problem 4-8. A Statement of Revenues, Expenditures, and Changes in Fund Balance for 19X2 for the General Fund of the consolidated government of the City of Hatfield and McCoy County is presented below. The independent auditor has discovered that $2,000 of encumbrances outstanding at the end of 19X1 were reported as expenditures in 19X1. The subsequent purchases are also included in the 19X2 expenditures reported below. The auditor also discovered that operating transfers out reported for 19X2 includes $800,000 of General Fund resources used to establish an Internal Service Fund.

CITY OF HATFIELD/MCCOY COUNTY
Consolidated Government
General Fund
Statement of Revenues, Expenditures,
and Changes in Fund Balance
for the Fiscal Year Ended
December 31, 19X2

	19X2
Revenues:	
Taxes	$21,554,027
Licenses and permits	384,213
Intergovernmental	766,884

Charges for services	1,485,653
Fines and forefeitures	1,266,261
Miscellaneous	1,065,094
Total revenues	$26,522,132

Expenditures:
Current operating:

Personal services	$20,001,982
Materials and supplies	2,214,655
Contractual services	1,500,000
Capital outlay	3,428,911
Debt service	1,428,713
Total expenditures	$28,574,261

Excess of revenues over (under) expenditures	($2,052,129)

Other financing sources (uses):

Operating transfers in	3,490,137
Operating transfers out	(1,704,637)
Excess of revenues and other sources over (under) expenditures and other uses	($ 266,629)
Fund balance, January 1, ...	6,658,504
Fund balance, December 31	$6,391,875

Required:

(a) Revise the City of Hatfield/McCoy County General Fund 19X2 Statement of Revenues, Expenditures, and Changes in Fund Balance to correct for the auditor's findings.

(b) Prepare two other fiscal year 1982 statements of Revenues, Expenditures, and Changes in Fund Balance for the City of Hatfield/McCoy County General Fund in different acceptable formats.

(c) Analyze each of the three statements and discuss the attributes of each format that might cause it to be preferred by certain people or in certain situations.

Problem 4-9. The March 31, 19X5 trial balance of the City of Andrew General Fund is presented below. Taxes and accounts receivable are shown net in the interest of brevity.

CITY OF ANDREW
General Fund
Trial Balance
March 31, 19X5

Cash	$ 285,500
Investments, at cost	65,000
Taxes Receivable (net)	58,300
Accounts Receivable (net)	8,300
Due from Other Funds	2,000
Advances to Internal Service Funds	65,000
Inventory of Supplies, at cost	7,200

Vouchers Payable		$ 118,261
Contracts Payable		57,600
Due to Other Taxing Units		24,189
Deferred Revenue		15,000
Reserve for Encumbrances		18,000
Reserve for Inventory		7,200
Reserve for Interfund Advances		65,000
Fund Balance		332,350
Revenues		698,300
Expenditures	685,200	
Encumbrances	18,000	
Estimated Revenues	1,314,500	
Appropriations		1,237,400
Operating Transfers In		10,200
Operating Transfers Out	74,500	
Totals	$2,583,500	$2,583,500

Required:

(a) Compute the beginning balance of the unreserved fund balance account assuming that there were zero beginning balances in all reserve accounts except Reserve for Encumbrances, which had a $20,000 beginning balance. Assume that all appropriations lapse at year end and that a reserve is established for encumbrances outstanding at year end.

(b) Prepare an interim balance sheet for the City of Andrew as of March 31, 19X5. Assume that estimated transfers are included in Estimated Revenues and in Appropriations, as appropriate.

Problem 4-10. The beginning balances of the General Fund of the City of Marshall on January 1, 19X5 were as follows:

Cash	$2,000	
Taxes Receivable—Current	2,000	
Estimated Uncollectible Current Taxes		$ 100
Vouchers Payable		900
Fund Balance		3,000
	$4,000	$4,000

The following transactions occured during 19X5:

1. Taxes Receivable—Current that were not collected by December 31 became delinquent as of January 1.

2. Revenues were estimated at $200,000. Appropriations of $197,000 were made.

3. Property Taxes of $150,000 were levied. It was estimated that 1 percent of these taxes will not be collected.

4. The accountant was notified that the appropriations total covered a 19X4 order for materials estimated to cost $25,200. (The city follows Assumption B, but honors most prior year encumbrances.)

5. The materials ordered in 19X4 were received at an actual cost of $25,000.

6. Citizens paid $130,000 of taxes, of which $1,000 was for delinquent taxes.

7. Miscellaneous revenue of $50,000 was received.

8. The voucher for the materials and the beginning balance in Vouchers Payable were paid.

9. Salaries of $120,000 were paid.
10. Materials and supplies estimated to cost $30,000 were ordered.
11. The materials and supplies ordered were received at an actual cost of $31,000.
12. Office equipment estimated to cost $20,000 was ordered.
13. The City wrote off $100 of delinquent taxes as uncollectible.
14. The office equipment ordered was received at an actual cost of $20,000.
15. Vouchers were paid, $31,000.
16. The City received $14,000 in payment of 19X5 property taxes.
17. The City ordered $1,500 of supplies.

Required:

(a) Record the beginning balances in "T" accounts.
(b) Journalize the transactions.
(c) Post to "T" accounts.
(d) Prepare a preclosing trial balance at December 31, 19X5.
(e) Prepare closing entries.
(f) Prepare a postclosing trial balance at December 31, 19X5.

In lieu of requirements (a)–(f), you may prepare a worksheet headed as follows:

Columns	Heading
1–2	Trial Balance, 1/1/X5
3–4	19X5 Transactions
5–6	Preclosing Trial Balance, 12/31/X5
7–8	Closing Entries, 12/31/19X5
9–10	Postclosing Trial Balance, 12/31/X5

Problem 4-11. The December 31, 19X1, preclosing trial balance of the City of Bakersville Parks Special Revenue Fund is presented below:

CITY OF BAKERSVILLE
PRECLOSING TRIAL BALANCE
PARKS SPECIAL REVENUE FUND
December 31, 19X1

Cash	$ 110,000
Investments	645,739
Due from other governments	649,371
Advances to other funds	80,000
Vouchers payable	241,930
Due to other funds	70,000
Reserve for advances to other funds	80,000
Fund balance	999,872
Property tax revenues	675,000
Intergovernmental revenues	550,000
Charges for services	50,408
Operating transfers in	181,332
Personal service expenditures	908,753
Materials and supplies expenditures	159,247

Contractual services expenditures	22,000
Capital outlay expenditures	10,000
Operating transfers out	85,692
Residual equity transfers out	200,000
Encumbrances	150,000
Reserve for encumbrances	150,000
Estimated revenues	1,390,000
Appropriations	1,412,260

Additional information:

1. The January 1, 19X1, balance in Reserve for Advances to Other Funds was $56,000 and in Reserve for Encumbrances was $182,000.

2. All appropriations lapse. Bakersville closes its Encumbrances account but leaves the related reserve account balance and reports it in the financial statements.

3. The 1/1/X1 balance in Due from Other Funds, $23,271, was received on October 5, 19X1.

4. Bakersville includes interfund transfers in its estimated revenues and appropriations.

Required:

(a) Prepare a preclosing trial balance at December 31,19X1 in proper form.

(b) Analyze the unreserved fund balance account to determine its 1/1/X1 balance.

(c) Prepare the general journal entry(ies) to close the accounts.

(d) Using a six-column worksheet, prepare in the first two columns a Statement of Revenues, Expenditures, and Changes in (Unreserved) Fund Balance for the Bakersville Parks Special Revenue Fund for the year ended 12/31/19X1.

(e) Indicate in the third column of the worksheet how the statement would differ if it presented changes in *total* fund balance instead of in unreserved fund balance.

(f) Indicate in column 4 how the statement prepared in C would differ assuming that only unexpended appropriations lapse at year end.

(g) Indicate in column 5 how the statement presenting charges in *total* fund balance [see (d)] would differ assuming all appropriations lapse at year end and encumbrances outstanding are disclosed only in the footnotes.

Problem 4-12. The City of Happy Hollow has engaged you to examine its financial statements for the year ended December 31, 19X1. The city was incorporated as a municipality and began operations on January 1, 19X1. You find that a budget was approved by the city council and was recorded, but that all transactions have been recorded on the cash basis. The bookkeeper has provided an Operating Fund trial balance.

CITY OF HAPPY HOLLOW
Operating Fund
Trial Balance—December31,19X0

	Debit	Credit
Cash	$ 238,900	
Expenditures	72,500	

	Debit	Credit
Estimated Revenues	114,100	
Appropriations		$102,000
Revenues		108,400
Bonds Payable		200,000
Premium on Bonds Payable		3,000
Fund Balance		12,100
	$ 425,500	$425,500

Additional information:

1. Examination of the Expenditure Ledger revealed the following information:

	Budgeted	Actual
Personal services	$ 45,000	$38,500
Supplies	19,000	11,000
Equipment	38,000	23,000
	$102,000	$72,500

2. Supplies and equipment of $4,000 and $10,000, respectively, had been received, but the vouchers had not been paid at December 31.

3. At December 31, outstanding purchase orders for supplies and equipment not yet received were $1,200 and $3,800, respectively.

4. The inventory of supplies on December 31 was $1,700 by physical count. The decision was made to record the inventory of supplies. A city ordinance requires that expenditures are to be based on purchases, not on the basis of usage.

5. Examination of the revenue subsidiary ledger revealed the following information:

	Budgeted	Actual
Property taxes	$102,600	$ 96,000
Licenses	7,400	7,900
Fines	4,100	4,500
	$114,100	$108,400

It was estimated that 5 percent of the property taxes would not be collected. Accordingly, property taxes were levied in an amount so that collections would yield the budgeted amount of $102,600.

6. On November 1, 19X1, Happy Hollow issued 8 percent General Obligation Term Bonds with $200,000 face value for a premium of $3,000. Interest is payable each May 1 and November 1 until the maturity date of November 1, 19Y5. The city council ordered that the cash from the bond premium be set aside and restricted for the eventual retirement of the debt principal. The bonds were issued to finance the construction of a city hall, but no contracts had been let as of December 31.

Required:

(a) Prepare the general journal adjusting entries required to convert the "Operating Fund" trial balance to a correct General Fund preclosing trial balance at December 31, 19X0. Use six (or more)-column analysis paper headed as follows:

Columns	Heading
1–2	"Operating Fund" Uncorrected Trial Balance, 12/31/19X0
3–4	Adjustments and Corrections
5–6	General Fund Preclosing Trial Balance, 12/31/19X0

(b) Identify the financial statements that should be prepared for the General Fund. (You are not required to prepare these statements.)

(c) Draft formal closing entries for the General Fund at December 31, 19X0.

(AICPA, adapted)

Problem 4-13. The following information was abstracted from the accounts of the General Fund of the City of Ragus after the books had been closed for the fiscal year ended June 30, 19X2:

	Postclosing Trial Balance June 30, 19X1	Transactions July 1, 19X1 to June 30, 19X2 Debit	Credit	Postclosing Trial Balance June 30, 19X2
Cash	$700,000	$1,820,000	$1,852,000	$668,000
Taxes receivable	40,000	1,870,000	1,828,000	82,000
	$740,000			$750,000
Allowance for uncollectible				
taxes	$ 8,000	8,000	10,000	$ 10,000
Vouchers payable	132,000	1,852,000	1,840,000	120,000
Fund balance:				
Reserved for				
encumbrances	—	1,000,000	1,070,000	70,000
Unreserved	600,000	140,000	60,000 { 30,000 {	550,000
	$740,000			$750,000

Additional information:

The budget for the fiscal year ended June 30, 19X2, provided for estimated revenues of $2,000,000 and appropriations of $1,940,000.

Required:

Prepare general journal entries to record the budgeted and actual transactions of the General Fund of the City of Ragus for the fiscal year ended June 30, 19X2.

(AICPA, adapted)

Problem 4-14. The controller of Pacter Township has prepared the trial balance presented on page 147 and has asked your advice on which of the several alternative formats should be used in preparing the Statement of Revenues, Expenditures, and Changes in Fund Balance for the Pacter Township General Fund for the year ended June 30, 19X5.

PACTER TOWNSHIP
General Fund
Trial Balance
June 30, 19X5

Capital outlay	(320,000)
Contractual services	(300,000)
Correction of prior year errors	(200,000)
Debt service	(480,000)
Fines and forfeits	250,000
Fund balance, 7/1/19X4	600,000
Intergovernmental	400,000
Licenses and permits	800,000
Materials and supplies	(200,000)
Personal services	(2,800,000)
Operating transfers—Debt Service Fund	(80,000)
Operating transfer—General Fund	800,000
Other	120,000
Other	(100,000)
Residual equity transfer—Capital Projects Fund	10,000
Taxes	2,000,000
To balance	(500,000)

Required:

(a) Prepare three Statements of Revenues, Expenditures, and Changes in Fund Balance for the Pacter Township General Fund for the year ended June 30, 19X5, each in a different acceptable format.

(b) Analyze each of the three statements and discuss the attributes of each format that might cause it to be preferred by certain people or in certain situations.

5

REVENUE ACCOUNTING— GOVERNMENTAL FUNDS

Revenue accounting in government parallels that for business enterprises in many respects. In both, revenue must be distinguished from nonrevenue resource inflows, and accounting guidelines have been established regarding the timing of revenue recognition. Proprietary fund revenue recognition is virtually identical to that in business accounting.

Significant differences and unique considerations are also involved, however, particularly in revenue accounting for governmental (expendable) funds. These differences and special considerations provide the principal focus of this chapter. Specifically, this chapter addresses (1) the definition of revenue in the governmental environment and the revenue recognition criteria used, (2) classification of revenue accounts, (3) accounting for revenue sources that are unique to governments, (4) use of the Revenue Subsidiary Ledger in government, and (5) revenue statements.

REVENUE DEFINITION AND RECOGNITION

Revenues may be operationally defined in a governmental fund accounting context as all increases in fund net assets except those arising from interfund reimbursements, interfund operating and residual equity transfers, or long-term debt issues. Only quasi-external transactions involve the recognition of fund revenue that is not revenue of the government as a whole.

Governments have a wide variety of revenue sources. Some revenues, such as property taxes, are levied in known amounts prior to collection and uncollectible amounts usually can be estimated with reasonable accuracy. Such revenues are recorded on the accrual basis, as are other revenues billed by the government. On the other hand, it is not practicable to accrue other types of government revenues. For example, sales taxes theoretically accrue to the government as retail merchants sell goods and collect sales taxes on behalf of the government. However, the government has no knowlege of the amount of the sales taxes until merchants file sales tax returns. Thus, it is not practicable to accrue the sales tax revenues prior to receipt of the sales tax returns, which normally coincides with payment of the taxes due, and sales taxes are recorded essentially on the cash basis.[1] Similarly, the amounts of self-assessed income taxes and business licenses are not known prior to receipt of the tax return or license application by the government, and it is not practicable to accrue them prior to that point.

The modified accrual basis of governmental fund revenue recognition takes into account the diversity of government revenue sources and the varying degrees to which government revenues can be recorded on the accrual basis. Under the modified accrual basis, only those revenues that are "susceptible to accrual" are recognized on the accrual basis; others are recognized on the cash basis.

Revenues are considered susceptible to accrual if they are both (1) objectively *measurable* and (2) *available* to finance current period expenditures. An item is "available" only if it is legally usable to finance current period expenditures and is to be collected in the current period or soon enough thereafter to be used to pay liabilities of the current period. Thus, governmental fund revenues are recognized conservatively on a "cash or near cash" approach under the modified accrual basis.

The NCGA noted that application of the "susceptibility to accrual" criteria requires (1) judgment, (2) consideration of the materiality of the item in question, (3) due regard for the practicality of accrual, and (4) consistency in application.[2] In commenting further on revenue accrual the Council observed that:

> some revenues are assessed and collected in such a manner that they can appropriately be accrued, whereas others cannot. Revenues and other increases in governmental fund financial resources which usually can and should be recorded on the accrual basis include property taxes, regularly billed charges for inspection or other routinely provided services, most grants from other governments, interfund transactions, and sales and income taxes where taxpayer liability has been established and collectibility is assured or losses can be reasonably estimated.[3]

The Council also stated that:

> The susceptibility to accrual of the various revenue sources of a governmental unit may differ significantly. Likewise, the susceptibility to accrual of similar revenue sources (e.g., property taxes) differs among governmental units. Thus, each governmental unit should (1) adopt revenue accounting policies that appropriately implement the susceptibility to accrual criteria, (2) apply them

---

[1] But note that "Sales taxes collected and held by one government agency for another at year end should be accrued if they are to be remitted in time to be used as a resource for payment of obligations incurred during the preceding fiscal year." (AICPA *Statement of Position 75-3*). In this case they would be deemed both measurable and available.

[2] NCGAS 1, p. 11.

[3] Ibid.

consistently, and (3) disclose them in the Summary of Significant Accounting Policies.[4]

Applying the susceptibility to accrual criteria—particularly the "availability" criterion—often proves difficult in practice. Application of the criteria is discussed further at several points in this chapter, in later chapters dealing with specific governmental fund types, and in Chapter 15.

CLASSIFICATION OF REVENUE ACCOUNTS

A chart of accounts is designed to provide a vehicle for summarizing information in a useful form. Revenues are classified by source in the accounts in order to produce information that management may use to (1) prepare and control the budget, (2) control the collection of revenues, (3) prepare financial statements for reporting to the public, and (4) prepare financial statistics. The revenue accounts provide the basic data for revenue statements used for all these purposes.

General Fund Revenues

The following are the main revenue source classes for the General Fund:

Taxes (including property, sales, income, and other taxes; penalties and interest on delinquent taxes).

Licenses and Permits.

Intergovernmental Revenues (including grants, shared revenues, and payments by other governments in lieu of taxes).

Charges for Services (excluding revenues of public enterprises).

Fines and Forfeits.

Miscellaneous Revenues (including interest earnings, rents and royalties, sales of and compensation for loss of fixed assets, contributions in lieu of taxes from the government's own public enterprises, escheats, and contributions and donations from private sources).

The classes given above are not account titles. They are broad group headings which are useful for reporting purposes just as Current Assets and Fixed Assets are category groupings on the balance sheet of a private enterprise. For example, no account would be set up for fines and forfeits. Instead, individual accounts would be provided for each type of revenue falling in that class, including Court Fines, Library Fines, and Forfeits. The total revenue accrued or received from fines and forfeits would be the sum of the balances of these accounts.

Revenues of Other Funds

The revenue classes described for the General Fund also are suitable for the other governmental funds of a governmental unit. For example, taxes may be a revenue source of Special Revenue Funds and Debt Service Funds, while a special assessments category may be added to either the taxes or miscellaneous

[4] Ibid., p. 12.

150   Lynn/Freeman   FUND ACCOUNTING, second edition

revenue classification, as appropriate, for the Special Assessment Funds. Clearly, no other fund is likely to have as many different revenue sources as the General Fund. Enterprise and Internal Service Funds use revenue accounts and revenue recognition principles similar to those of business enterprises.

Distinction between Revenues of a Fund and Revenues of a Governmental Unit

A distinction must be made between the revenues of a fund and the revenues of the governmental unit as a whole. As noted earlier, transfers and reimbursements are not reported as revenue. Only quasi-external transaction receipts or accruals constitute fund revenues but are not revenues of the governmental unit; i.e., they increase the equity of the fund but not that of the unit. To illustrate, charges for services rendered to departments financed out of the General Fund are revenues of the Internal Service Fund but not of the governmental unit as a whole, since these charges must be paid from the General Fund. Quasi-external transactions are the only instance where fund revenues (and related expenditures or expenses, as appropriate) should be recognized when they are not revenues of the government as a whole.

In classifying revenues for the purpose of statewide or national financial statistics, only those revenues of the governmental unit as a whole should be included. These usually consist of the revenues of the General Fund and the Special Revenue Funds, special assessment and interest revenue of Special Assessment Funds, Debt Service Fund tax revenue and interest earnings, and the revenues of enterprises operated by the governmental unit. Ideally, any material amounts arising from quasi-external transactions would be eliminated. Further, some accountants prefer to supplement the fund statements with consolidated or consolidating statements for these funds, the unit as a whole, or its major subdivisions, where interfund revenues are significant in amount.

This chapter is concerned with accounting for the principal revenue sources of the General Fund and Special Revenue Funds. Those types of revenue that are peculiar to another fund, such as special assessments, are discussed with the related fund.

TAXES

A tax is a forced contribution made to a government to meet public needs. Typically, the amount of tax bears no direct relationship to any benefit received by the taxpayer.

The amount of any tax is computed by applying a rate or rates set by the governmental unit to a defined base, such as value of property, amount of income, or number of units. From the standpoint of administration, taxes may be divided into two groups—those that are self-assessing and those that are not. The latter group, of which the general property tax on real and personal property is the chief representative, requires that the governmental unit establish the amount of the tax base to which the rate or rates will be applied. Taxes on income, inheritance, severance of natural resources, gasoline, general sales, tobacco, alcoholic beverages, and chain stores are self-assessing; that is, the taxpayer is expected to determine the amount of the tax base, apply the proper rate or rates thereto, and submit the payment with the return that shows the computation.

When the taxpayer assesses his own tax, verifying the amount of tax requires (1) determining that the tax base has been properly reported by the taxpayer and (2) determining that the proper rates have been applied accurately to the tax base to arrive at the total amount of the tax. The first is the most difficult problem, of course. For example, in the case of the income tax it is necessary to ascertain that all income that should have been reported has been disclosed. Furthermore, investigation should not be limited to those taxpayers who file returns. The governmental unit must also make certain that all taxpayers who should pay taxes have filed returns.

Self-assessed taxes are usually accounted for on a cash basis because the return and the remittance are ordinarily received at the same time. Further, there may be no objectively measurable basis upon which to set up accruals because the amount of tax is not known before the return is filed. In some jurisdictions income tax returns are filed at a specified time and the tax is paid in installments. In such a case, since the amount of the tax is known, the revenues are accrued as soon as the return is filed. Some taxes require the attachment of stamps to an article to indicate that the tax has been paid. For example, liquor taxes and tobacco taxes are frequently paid through the purchase of stamps to be affixed to bottles or packages. In such cases the taxes are considered to be revenue as soon as the stamps are sold to the manufacturer, dealer, or other businessman, even though the articles to which the stamps are affixed may not be sold for an indefinite period following the purchase of the tax stamps.

General Property Taxes

General property taxes are ad valorem taxes in proportion to the assessed valuation of real or personal property. The procedure for administering general property taxes is as follows: (1) The assessed valuation of each piece of real property and of the taxable personal property of each taxpayer is determined by the local tax assessor; (2) a local board of review hears complaints regarding assessments; (3) county and state boards of equalization assign equalized values to taxing districts; (4) the legislative body levies the total amount of taxes which it needs, but not in excess of the amount permitted by law; (5) the tax levy is distributed among taxpayers on the basis of the assessed value of property owned by them; (6) taxpayers are billed; (7) tax collections are credited to taxpayers' accounts; and (8) tax collections are enforced by the imposition of penalties and the sale of property for taxes. Each of these steps in general property tax administration is discussed below.

Assessment of Property.   Valuing property for purposes of taxation is called assessment. Assessment of property for local taxes usually is performed by an elected or appointed official known as an assessor. The assessed value of each piece of real property or of the personal property of every taxpayer is recorded on a sheet known as an assessment roll, which typically contains columns entitled as follows for the tax roll of real property:

Taxpayer's Name and General Description of Property
Block and Lot Number
Value of Land
Value of Improvements
Total Assessed Valuation

Each such sheet contains the assessed value of several pieces of property or the assessed values of the personal property of several owners. In the case of real property, for each piece of property there will be a separate continuing record on which the assessed valuation for that piece alone, together with its full description, is recorded.

Not all real and personal property in the jurisdiction of a government will be subject to real or personal property assessment and taxation. Properties owned by governments and religious organizations usually are exempt from such taxes and are referred to as "exempt properties."

The total assessed value of real estate in the governmental unit is the sum of the assessed values of the individual pieces of property within its jurisdiction; the total assessed value of personal property is the sum of the assessed values of the personal property of the individual owners residing within the limits of the governmental unit. Thus several governmental units, such as a state, county, city, and school district, may tax each piece of property. Ordinarily only one of these jurisdictions will have the assessment responsibility, and separate assessment rolls are prepared for each of the governmental units for the property within its jurisdiction.

Review of Assessment. After each property owner is notified of the assessment of his property, he is permitted to protest his assessment to a local reviewing board, which may be composed of officials of the government or of nonofficial residents of the governmental unit. The board hears objections to assessments, weighs the evidence, and changes the assessment if it considers a change to be proper. A taxpayer who is not satisfied with board action may appeal his assessment to the courts.

Equalization of Assessments. In most states the assessment of property is made by a local government. The taxes of the state and perhaps even the county are, therefore, levied on the basis of assessments made by a number of different assessors, each of whom may have different ideas as to the valuations that should be assigned to property. The law usually requires that the assessment be made at a figure which is the equivalent of "fair market value" in the accountant's terminology, but in practice the actual valuations in a state or even a county will cover a wide range of percentages of market value. Lack of equalization or poor equalization leads to "competitive underassessment" in the several assessing districts and to widespread dissatisfaction with the property tax as a revenue source.

Levying the Tax.   Taxes are levied through the passage of a tax levy act or ordinance, usually passed at the time the appropriation act or ordinance is passed. The levy is ordinarily applicable to only one year.

Tax levies are made in one or two lump sums in some governmental units, whereas in others the levies are very detailed. A statute or even a charter may require that certain taxes are to be levied for specified purposes. In that event the legislative body must indicate specifically the amount levied for each purpose. Another effect of detailed tax levies is to require the creation of Special Revenue Funds. For example, if a special levy is made for parks, it usually is necessary to create a Special Revenue Fund for parks to ensure that the taxes collected are not used for any other purposes.[5]

Determining the tax rate.   As indicated above, the tax rate is determined by dividing the amount of taxes levied by the assessed valuation. Thus, if a government has an assessed valuation of $10,000,000 and its total tax levy is $250,000, the tax rate is 2.5 percent of, or 25 mills per dollar of, assessed value ($250,000 ÷ $10,000,000). The total tax rate consists of the tax rate for general purposes and special tax rates, if any, for particular purposes. For example, if we assume that the total levy of $250,000 consisted of $150,000 for general purposes, $10,000 for park purposes, $50,000 for schools, and $40,000 for debt service, the tax rates would be as follows:

Purpose	Rate (mills per dollar of assessed value)
General	15
Parks	1
Schools	5
Debt Service	4
	25

Maximum tax rates are frequently prescribed for governmental units by the constitution, statutes, or charters. The legislative body must recognize such limitations as it plans the total levy. If the amount the legislative body would like to produce from the tax will require a rate higher than the maximum permitted by law, the amount of the levy must be reduced. When a government finds itself thus limited in the amount of taxes it can levy, it would ordinarily review the assessment process in the hope that the total assessed valuation, the tax base, could be increased.

Determining the amount due from each taxpayer.   The amount of tax due from each taxpayer is arrived at by multiplying the assessed value of his property by the tax rate. For example, if a taxpayer owns real estate with an assessed value of $10,000 and the city tax rate is 25 mills per dollar of assessed value, his city tax will be $250 ($10,000 × 0.025).

[5] Recall that NCGA *Statement 1* (p. 8) states that "use of Special Revenue Funds is not required unless they are legally mandated." Property tax authorization legislation typically specifies that a separate fund be maintained, however, and many accountants feel that Special Revenue Funds are needed to assure sound financial administration of property taxes even if not legally mandated.

Setting Up Taxes Receivable and Billing Taxpayers. As soon as the amount due from each taxpayer is determined, it is entered on the tax roll.

The tax roll. A tax roll is a record showing the amount of taxes levied against each piece of real property and against each owner of personal property. The assessment roll previously described may be used for this purpose by adding several columns, or tax rolls may be prepared separately. The tax roll provides a record of each parcel of real or personal property—including its assessed value, taxes levied against the property, and property tax collections and balances owed with respect to the property—and also serves as a subsidiary ledger supporting the Taxes Receivable control accounts in the General Ledger. If interest and penalties on delinquent taxes are accrued at the end of each year, provision is made for showing the accruals.

Recording taxes on the books. Some of the entries to record taxes on the books have already been introduced in Chapter 4. For example, when taxes are levied, the usual entry in each fund is a debit to Taxes Receivable—Current and credits to Allowance for Uncollectible Current Taxes and to Revenues. (If the tax is levied prior to the year to which it applies, a Deferred Revenue account is credited initially.) Later, when the taxes become delinquent, an entry is made debiting Taxes Receivable—Delinquent and Allowance for Uncollectible Current Taxes and crediting Taxes Receivable—Current and Allowance for Uncollectible Delinquent Taxes.

It should be emphasized at this point that separate Taxes Receivable accounts should be set up for each kind of taxes, such as real property taxes, personal property taxes, and income taxes that may have been accrued. Further, all these taxes should be recorded in a way that allows the amount applicable to each year to be readily determined. One way to accomplish this objective is to set up control accounts for each kind of taxes receivable by years.

Because the proportion of the total tax levy made for each purpose may vary from year to year, it is important to be able to identify each year's levy so that the proper Taxes Receivable accounts may be credited and the proceeds of tax collections may be allocated to the proper fund. For example, suppose that the tax levy is $100,000 both for this year and for last year but that the levies are divided as follows:

	This Year		Last Year	
Fund	Amount Levied	Percentage of Total	Amount Levied	Percentage of Total
General Fund	$ 46,700	46.7	$ 40,000	40.0
Parks Fund	13,300	13.3	13,300	13.3
School Fund	26,700	26.7	33,400	33.4
Debt Service Fund	13,300	13.3	13,300	13.3
	$100,000	100.0	$100,000	100.0

The General Fund portion of the proceeds of this year's tax levy is found by multiplying the amount collected from the levy by 46.7 percent. Thus, if $90,000 is collected, $42,030 is placed to the credit of the General Fund ($90,000 × 46.7

percent). On the other hand, the amount of collections from last year's levy that is for General Fund purposes is obtained by multiplying the collections from that levy by 40 percent. For example, if collections total $10,000, $4,000 ($10,000 × 40 percent) is for the General Fund. Collections from other year's levies are allocated to the proper funds in the same manner. Clearly, tax collections cannot be applied to the proper funds unless the amount collected from each year's levy is known.

Recording Tax Collections. Assume that if full details regarding delinquent taxes were to be shown on the balance sheet, the Taxes Receivable account for a governmental unit would appear as follows:

Real Property Taxes Receivable—
Delinquent:

Levy of 19X9	$30,000		
19X8	20,000		
19X7	10,000		
19X6	5,000		
19X5 and prior	3,000	$68,000	
Less: Allowance for Uncollectible Delinquent Taxes		10,000	$58,000

Personal Property Taxes Receivable—
Delinquent:

Levy of 19X9	$20,000		
19X8	15,000		
19X7	10,000		
19X6	4,000		
19X5 and prior	5,000	$54,000	
Less: Allowance for Uncollectible Delinquent Taxes		15,000	39,000
Total Taxes Receivable Delinquent			$97,000

As taxes are collected, the entry in the recipient fund is as follows:

Cash	100,000	
Taxes Receivable—Current		80,000
Taxes Receivable—Delinquent		20,000

To record collection of current and delinquent taxes, as follows:

Year of Levy	Amount
19Y0 (Current)	$ 80,000
19X9	10,000
19X8	5,000
19X7	3,000
19X6	1,000
19X5	500
19X4	500
	$100,000

Collection of a government's taxes by another unit. Frequently one governmental unit acts as collecting agent for other units. In that case, each governmental unit certifies its tax levy to the collecting unit, which in turn bills the taxpayers. These taxes are handled by the collecting unit in an Agency Fund, for which the accounting procedures are discussed in Chapter 11.

The accounting procedure outlined thus far for governmental units that collect their own taxes also applies to those that do not. In the latter case the collecting unit transmits a report indicating the amount collected from each year's levy of real property taxes and of personal property taxes. The receiving unit, on the basis of this report, distributes the proceeds among the various funds and credits the proper General Ledger accounts. Thus the only difference between the accounting procedure for a governmental unit that collects its own taxes and one that does not is that the latter does not prepare a tax roll and probably does not keep a record of the amounts paid or owed by the individual taxpayers. The latter records are kept for it by the collecting governmental unit.

Discounts on taxes. Some governmental units allow discounts on taxes paid before a certain date. These discounts should be considered as revenue deductions; that is, an Allowance for Discounts on Taxes account should be provided and pthe tax revenues should be credited only for the net amount of the tax. For example, if the tax levy was $300,000, on which it is estimated that $9,000 will be uncollectible and discounts of $2,000 will be taken, the entry to record the levy of the tax and the estimated discounts and uncollectible taxes is:

Taxes Receivable—Current	300,000	
Allowance for Uncollectible Current Taxes		9,000
Allowance for Discounts on Taxes		2,000
Revenues		289,000
To record levy of taxes, estimated losses, and estimated discounts to be taken.		

As taxes are collected and discounts are taken, the discounts are charged against the Allowance account. For example, if tax collections amounted to $150,000 and discounts of $1,500 had been taken, the entry to record the transaction would be:

Cash	150,000	
Allowance for Discounts on Taxes	1,500	
Taxes Receivable—Current		151,500
To record collection of taxes and net discounts thereon.		

As the discount period is passed, the following entry is made:

Allowance for Discounts on Taxes	500	
Revenues		500
To record increase in revenues by amount of estimated discounts which were not taken.		

Had discounts properly taken exceeded the balance of the Allowance for Discounts on Taxes account, the excess would be debited to Revenues.

In a few governmental units the law requires that discounts be authorized by appropriations. In such cases the levy of taxes is recorded by the standard entry—with no discount allowance—and the collection of taxes as above would signal the following entry:

Cash	150,000	
Expenditures	1,500	
Taxes Receivable—Current		151,500

To record collection of taxes and the
allowance of discounts.

This method of accounting for discounts has the effect of overstating both revenues and expenditures and is therefore not desirable. It should be used only where the law makes it impossible to use the first method.

Taxes collected in advance.   Sometimes a taxpayer will pay his subsequent year's taxes before they are due, possibly before the tax has been levied or billed. Such tax collections are subsequent period revenue, not revenue of the period in which they are collected. They may be recorded either in the General Fund or in a Trust Fund, the entry in either case being:

Cash	2,500	
Taxes Collected in Advance		2,500

To record collection of taxes on next year's
roll.

These tax collections represent a deferred credit to revenues, and the Taxes Collected in Advance account is therefore shown as a deferred revenue in the balance sheet. Subsequent entries when the taxes are levied and the Taxes Receivable accounts are set up depend on where the transaction is originally recorded. If the cash from the advance tax collections was recorded in a Trust Fund, an entry must be made transferring the money out of that fund to the proper fund(s). This Trust Fund entry is as follows:

Taxes Collected in Advance	2,500	
Cash		2,500

To record paying to each fund of proper
amount of taxes belonging to it.

Assuming that the current year's tax levy has been recorded, and revenue recognized, the corresponding entry in each of the funds receiving the cash parallels that for the General Fund, which we assume received $1,000 of the $2,500.

Cash	1,000	
Taxes Receivable—Current		1,000

To record receipt of cash from Trust Fund
representing share of taxes collected in
advance applicable to this fund.

If, on the other hand, the taxes collected in advance are recorded in the General

Fund, and the taxes are also applicable to other funds, the entry after the Taxes Receivable accounts are set up is:

Taxes Collected in Advance	2,500	
Taxes Receivable—Current		1,000
Cash		1,500

To record application of taxes collected in
advance to reduce General Fund taxes
receivable and to record payment of cash
to other funds on account of advance tax
collections applicable to them.

In each of the other funds affected, an entry is made debiting Cash and crediting Taxes Receivable—Current.

If the amount of taxes collected in advance exceeds the amount levied, the excess is either refunded or continues as a deferred revenue until the next levy is made. If, on the other hand, the amount collected is less than the amount levied, the taxpayer is billed for the difference.

Taxes levied but not available. In some governments taxes are levied in one year but are not available, and hence not revenue, in that year because (1) the taxes were levied to finance the next year's operations, and thus are not legally available in the year of levy, or (2) the taxes will not be collected until well into the next period* and thus are not available to finance current year expenditures. The entry upon levy of taxes in either case would be:

Taxes Receivable—Current	100,000	
Allowance for Uncollectible Current		
Taxes		3,000
Deferred Revenues		97,000

To record levy of taxes not available to
finance current period expenditures.

At the start of the next period the Deferred Revenues would be reclassified as revenues by the following entry:

Deferred Revenue	97,000	
Revenues		97,000

To record the taxes levied last period
becoming available.

Enforcing the Collection of Taxes. The laws for most jurisdictions prescribe a date after which unpaid taxes become delinquent, whereupon they are subject to specified penalties and accrual of interest. Taxes, interest, and penalties in most states become a lien against property without any action by the governmental unit. At the expiration of a specified period of time the governmental unit can sell the property to satisfy its lien. Any excess of the amount received from the sale of the property over the amount of taxes, interest, penalties, and the cost

* NCGA *Interpretation 3*, "Revenue Recognition-Property Taxes," states that property taxes collected within approximately 60 days after year end would be considered "available" at year end and thus recognized as revenue in the year preceding collection.

of holding the sale is turned over to the property owner. If the proceeds from the sale of the property are less than the amount due, the law may or may not make the property owner liable for the difference.

The property owner usually is given the privilege of redeeming the property within a certain period of time. If the property was purchased by an individual, it can be redeemed by payment to the buyer of the purchase price plus interest. If it was bid in by the governmental unit, the property can be redeemed by payment of the taxes, interest, penalties, and other charges. If the property is not redeemed by the specified date, the acquirer secures title.

Typically, more than one governmental unit is involved in the process of selling property for delinquent taxes and in the related redemption of the property. If each government were left to enforce its own lien and sell the property for taxes, not only would the cost of sale greatly increase but considerable confusion would result. Accordingly, the statutes ordinarily provide for transfering delinquent tax rolls to a single governmental unit. This unit attempts to collect the delinquent taxes and performs all the steps necessary to enforce the lien. In the absence of statutory provisions, each unit receives from the collecting unit its proportionate share of tax collections, net of collection costs.

Recording interest and penalties on taxes. Some governmental units accrue interest and penalties on delinquent taxes, while others do not record them until they are collected. If they are accrued, they are added to the tax roll or other subsidiary record. The entry to record the accrual of interest and penalties, the preferable practice, is:

Interest and Penalties Receivable	15,000	
Allowance for Uncollectible		
Interest and Penalties		1,000
Revenues		14,000
To record revenues from interest and penalties on delinquent taxes net of the amount that is estimated will never be collected.		

If the "available" criterion is not met when interest and penalties receivable are accrued, Deferred Revenues would be credited (rather than Revenues) and revenue would be recognized when the receivable becomes "available," usually upon collection.

If interest and penalties are not accrued, but are recorded as revenues only at the time the cash is received, the entry to record revenues from this source is:

Cash	10,000	
Revenues		10,000
To record receipt of interest and penalties on delinquent taxes.		

In both of the foregoing cases, it is essential to identify the revenues from interest and penalties with the particular tax levy to which they apply. The reasons for this distinction are the same as those given for recording taxes receivable by year of levy.

Accounting for tax sales. When the period specified by law has passed without payment of taxes, penalties, and interest, the assets are converted into tax liens:

Tax Liens Receivable 28,000		
Taxes Receivable—Delinquent	25,000	
Interest and Penalties Receivable on		
Taxes	3,000	

To record conversion of delinquent taxes and of interest and penalties thereon to tax liens, as follows:

Levy of	Taxes	Interest and Penalties	Total
19X8	$10,000	$1,000	$11,000
19X7	15,000	2,000	17,000
	$25,000	$3,000	$28,000

Subsidiary taxes receivable records (including penalties and interest) for each piece of property are credited at this time; and subsidiary records of the individual tax liens are established.

Court and other costs are ordinarily incurred in the process of converting property into tax liens and in the subsequent effort to sell the properties. In some jurisdictions the costs of holding a tax sale are charged to expenditures because the law provides that such costs are covered by interest and penalties levied against the property. In most cases, however, the cost should be added to the amount of the tax lien:

Tax Liens Receivable	1,000	
Cash		1,000

To record court costs and other costs required in the conversion of delinquent taxes and interest and penalties thereon into tax liens.

When the assets are converted into tax liens, the related Allowance for Uncollectible Accounts is converted into Allowance for Uncollectible Tax Liens. The amount to be reclassified is necessarily based on an estimate of the results of the tax sale.

Allowance for Uncollectible		
Delinquent Taxes	2,000	
Allowance for Uncollectible Interest		
and Penalties	100	
Allowance for Uncollectible Tax		
Liens		2,100

To transfer the allowances for estimated uncollectible taxes, interest, and penalties to the allowance for uncollectible tax liens.

The proceeds from the sale of the property may be more than, less than, or exactly the same as the amount of the tax liens. If they are the same there is simply a debit to Cash and a credit to Tax Liens Receivable. If the property is sold for more than the amount of the liens, the entry would be:

Cash	30,000	
Tax Liens Receivable		29,000
Due to Property Owners Trust Fund ...		1,000
To record sale of tax liens for an amount in excess of their carrying value.		

The amount due to the Property Owners Trust Fund would be paid to that fund and would be held there in trust for subsequent payment to the property owner.[6]

On the other hand, if the cash received from the sale of the property is not sufficient to cover the tax liens, and if taxes are a lien only against the property, the difference is charged to Allowance for Uncollectible Tax Liens:

Cash	27,000	
Allowance for Uncollectible Tax Liens	2,000	
Tax Liens Receivable		29,000
To record the sale of property for taxes and to charge the difference between cash received and the amount of the tax liens to the allowance for uncollectible tax liens.		

If the governmental unit *bids in* properties at the time of the sale, it becomes, as is any other purchaser, subject to the redemption privilege by the property owners. As properties are redeemed, an entry is made debiting Cash and crediting Tax Liens Receivable.[7]

If properties are not redeemed and the governmental unit decides to use them for its own purposes—for example, for playgrounds—the Tax Liens Receivable accounts are removed from the funds in which they are carried through

---

[6] A property owners' trust fund is usually established because it may be difficult to locate property owners, the money may not be claimed for many years, and the government holds the money in trust for the property owners in the interim. Where amounts involved are relatively small, payment is expected to be made soon after collection, and a Trust Fund is not required by law, it is acceptable to retain the collections in the General Fund (or other fund for which the tax is levied) and credit Due to Property Owners.

[7] Some governments reclassify Tax Liens Receivable as Tax Sale Certificates upon taking provisional title by bidding in property at tax sales and reclassify an appropriate amount from Allowance for Uncollectible Tax Liens to an Allowance for Loss on Tax Sale Certificates account.

the following entry:

Expenditures	1,000	
Allowance for Uncollectible Tax Liens	700	
Tax Liens Receivable		1,700
To record the removal of tax sale property		
from the asset category.		

The debit to Expenditures represents the estimated salable value of the tax liens, while the debit to Allowance for Uncollectible Tax Liens represents the difference between the salable value of the liens and the value at which they are carried in the accounts.

Since the property will be part of the governmental unit's general fixed assets, it must be recorded in the General Fixed Assets Account Group. The entry to record this transaction there is as follows:

Land	300	
Buildings	700	
Investment in General Fixed		
Assets—General Fund Revenues		1,000
To record property acquired at tax sale		
and not redeemed.		

Note that these fixed assets are capitalized at the market value of the tax liens outstanding against them (in this case, $1,000). The joint cost incurred should be allocated between the land and building in proportion to their relative fair values. The apportionment between land and buildings must sometimes be made arbitrarily, although an appraisal or the assessed values usually provide a reasonable allocation basis.

As noted earlier, several governmental units may have liens on the same piece of property. The accounting procedure for the sale of the property is the same as that for property sold to satisfy the lien of only one governmental unit. The proceeds from the sale of the property are distributed among the various units to satisfy their liens, and any remaining cash is turned over to the property owner. If the proceeds are not sufficient to cover all the liens, each governmental unit receives a proportionate share of the money realized, unless statutes specify another basis of distribution.

General Property Tax Statements

Property tax statements are prepared to provide adequate disclosure of the details of property taxes. These statements may be divided into two classes: (1) those that are directly integrated with the financial statements of the current period, and (2) those that show data for other periods as well as for this period.

The comprehensive annual financial report (CAFR) of a state or local government (see Chapter 14) contains a financial section and a statistical section. The general property tax statements and schedules that are directly related to the financial statements of the current period belong in the financial section of the annual report, while those that show data for a number of periods are known as statistical statements and appear in the statistical section. The first four statements illustrated here (Figures 5-1 through 5-4) are *financial statements* (or schedules) and the last four (Figures 5-5 through 5-8) are *statistical statements.* Each is discussed in detail below.

Statement of Changes in Taxes Receivable (Figure 5-1). This statement contains complete analyses of the Current Taxes and Delinquent Taxes Receivable accounts for the current fiscal year. It shows the transfers from current to delinquent status and provides an analysis of the total taxes receivable at the end of the year.

Figure 5-1

A GOVERNMENTAL UNIT

Statement of Changes in Taxes Receivable
For the Fiscal Year Ended December 31, 19X5

	Total	Current Taxes	Delinquent Taxes
Taxes receivable, January 1, 19X5	$ 160,000	$	$160,000
Add:			
Taxes levied	$8,000,000	$8,000,000	
Transfers from current taxes	100,000		$100,000
Total additions	$8,100,000	$8,000,000	$100,000
Total	$8,260,000	$8,000,000	$260,000
Deduct:			
Collections	$7,950,000	$7,900,000	$ 50,000
Transfers to delinquent taxes	100,000	100,000	
Cancellations and abatements	30,000		30,000
Total deductions	$8,080,000	$8,000,000	$ 80,000
Taxes receivable, December 31, 19X5	$ 180,000	$	$180,000

Statement of Taxes Receivable by Funds (Figure 5-2). This is an analysis of the Taxes Receivable account or accounts that appear in the year end balance sheets of the several funds. Taxes receivable are subdivided by years, and real estate and personal property taxes are shown separately.

Statement of Changes in Tax Liens Receivable (Figure 5-3). This statement shows a complete analysis of the Tax Liens Receivable account for the year. If tax liens relate to several funds, this statement could be prepared with columns for each fund (or fund type) and for the total.

Detailed Statement of Tax Liens (Figure 5-4). This statement shows a complete analysis of the tax liens receivable at the end of the year. The details making up the total amount of liens, the allowance for uncollectible amounts by years, and an analysis of liens according to fund type or fund complete the state-

Figure 5-2

A GOVERNMENTAL UNIT

Statement of Taxes Receivable by Funds
December 31, 19X8

	Total	General Fund	Debt Service Fund
Real estate taxes:			
19X8	$ 70,000	$55,000	$15,000
19X7	15,000	12,000	3,000
19X6 and prior	1,500	1,000	500
	$ 86,500	$68,000	$18,500
Personal property taxes:			
19X8	$ 7,000	$ 5,500	$ 1,500
19X7	2,000	1,500	500
19X6 and prior	5,000	4,000	1,000
	$ 14,000	$11,000	$ 3,000
	$100,500	$79,000	$21,500

Figure 5-3

A GOVERNMENTAL UNIT

Statement of Changes in Tax Liens Receivable
For the Fiscal Year Ended December 31, 19X9

Tax liens receivable—beginning of year		$ 78,000
Add:		
Tax liens acquired—		
Transfers from taxes receivable	$20,000	
Interest, penalties, and costs on taxes transferred	3,000	23,000
Total		$101,000
Deduct:		
Payments received	$22,000	
Tax liens canceled or abated	3,000	
Property transferred to General Fixed Assets	5,000	30,000
Tax liens receivable—end of year		$ 71,000

ment. The statement in Figure 5-5 is prepared on a fund type basis; one prepared on a fund basis would include data by fund for each fund type as well as fund type totals.

Statement of Assessed Value and Estimated Fair Value of All Taxable Property (Figure 5-5). This statement presents information over a period of time regarding the assessed and estimated values of both real and personal property and culminates in an annual ratio of total assessed value to total fair value. The

Figure 5-4

A GOVERNMENTAL UNIT

Statement of Tax Liens
December 31, 19X9

	Amount of Tax	Interest and Penalties Accrued to Date of Sale	Costs of Sale	Total Amount of Liens	Less Estimated Uncollectibles	Net Amount of Liens
Taxes of:						
19X8	$18,700	$2,800	$ 500	$22,000	$ 3,500	$18,500
19X7	12,800	1,800	400	15,000	2,500	12,500
19X6	8,500	1,300	200	10,000	1,500	8,500
19X5	6,800	1,000	200	8,000	1,000	7,000
19X4 and prior years	13,600	2,000	400	16,000	1,500	14,500
Total	$60,400	$8,900	$1,700	$71,000	$10,000	$61,000
Made up as follows:						
General Fund	$42,280	$6,230	$1,190	$49,700	$ 7,000	$42,700
Special Revenue Funds	12,080	1,780	340	14,200	2,000	12,200
Debt Service Funds	6,040	890	170	7,100	1,000	6,100
Total (as above)	$60,400	$8,900	$1,700	$71,000	$10,000	$61,000

Figure 5-5

A GOVERNMENTAL UNIT

Statement of Assessed Value and Estimated Fair Value
of All Taxable Property
For the Fiscal Years Ended December 31, 19X3-19Y2

Assessment Period	Real Property (thousands of dollars)		Personal Property (thousands of dollars)		Ratio (%) of Total Assessed Value to Total Fair Value
	Assessed Value	Estimated Fair Value	Assessed Value	Estimated Fair Value	
19X3	$ 25,000	$ 50,000	$ 9,000	$ 18,000	50
19X4	50,000	100,000	15,000	31,000	50
19X5	55,000	110,000	25,000	50,000	50
19X6	57,000	114,000	27,000	56,000	50
19X7	63,000	126,000	31,000	60,000	50
19X8	92,000	150,000	40,000	75,000	59
19X9	120,000	190,000	53,000	81,000	64
19Y0	126,000	201,000	49,000	82,000	60
19Y1	150,000	240,000	57,000	95,000	62
19Y2	175,000	275,000	63,000	110,000	62

assessed value of property is an important determinant of the amount of taxes that can be raised, and it is therefore important to know the relationship between assessed value and fair value. If additional taxes are needed, they may be provided by increasing the ratio of total assessed value to total fair value or by increasing the tax rate, as well as by an increase in the total fair value of property. Therefore a rise or a fall in the tax rate must be judged in the light of the assessed valuation, for a fall in the tax rate may have been compensated for by increasing the ratio of assessed value to fair value. Further, unless the ratio of assessed value to fair value is known, comparable tax rates for different governmental units cannot be compiled.

Statement of Tax Rates and Tax Levies (Figure 5-6). This statement shows the tax rates and tax levies on property within the jurisdiction of a governmental unit for all the governmental units that levy taxes on property therein. It therefore provides an indication of the tax burden on property in A Governmental Unit.

Figure 5-6

A GOVERNMENTAL UNIT

Statement of Tax Rates and Tax Levies
For the Fiscal Years Ended December 31, 19X7-19Y6

		Tax Rates (mills)		
Assessment Period	City	County	School	Total
19X7	15	8	10	33
19X8	15	9	11	35
19X9	15	9	11	35
19Y0	16	9	14	39
19Y1	16	10	14	40
19Y2	16	10	14	40
19Y3	16	10	14	40
19Y4	16	10	14	40
19Y5	16	10	19	45
19Y6	18	10	17	45
		Tax Levies		
19X7	$ 375,000	$ 200,000	$ 250,000	$ 825,000
19X8	750,000	450,000	550,000	1,750,000
19X9	825,000	495,000	605,000	1,925,000
19Y0	912,000	513,000	798,000	2,223,000
19Y1	1,008,000	630,000	882,000	2,520,000
19Y2	1,472,000	920,000	1,288,000	3,680,000
19Y3	1,926,000	1,200,000	1,680,000	4,806,000
19Y4	2,016,000	1,266,000	1,764,000	5,046,000
19Y5	2,400,000	1,500,000	2,850,000	6,750,000
19Y6	3,150,000	1,750,000	2,975,000	7,875,000

Statements of Tax Levies and Tax Collections (Figures 5-7 and 5-8). One of the most important factors in the financial strength of a government is its success in collecting taxes.

No matter what its taxing power, a government will suffer financial embarrassment if it cannot collect the taxes it levies. These statements provide information regarding both tax levies and tax collections. The main difference between them is that the first (Figure 5-7) is prepared during the year, primarily for internal use, and shows collections from the beginning of the year to the date of the statement and for the current month. The second (Figure 5-8) is prepared at the end of the fiscal year, for both internal and external use, and shows information regarding the success with which each year's levy has been collected, collections of delinquent taxes during each fiscal period, and accumulated delinquent taxes. These data are important in evaluating the financial health of the government and the trend of that health.

LICENSES AND PERMITS

Goverments have the right to permit, control, or forbid many activities of individuals or corporations. The privilege of performing an act that would otherwise be illegal is granted by means of licenses or permits. Revenues from them may be divided into business and nonbusiness categories. In the business category are alcoholic beverages, health, corporations, public utilities, professional and occupational, and amusements licenses, among others. In the nonbusiness category may be found building permits and motor vehicle, motor vehicle operator, hunting and fishing, marriage, burial, and animal licenses.

The rates for licenses and permits are established through legislative action, that is, by the passage of an ordinance or statute. In contrast to property taxes, however, completely new rates need not be established each year. Instead, the legislative body usually adjusts the rates of particular licenses from time to time as the need arises.

Revenue from most licenses and permits is not recognized until it is received in cash, since the amount is not known until the licenses and permits are issued and cash is collected upon their issuance. Proper control over these revenues must insure not only that the revenues actually collected are properly handled but also that all the revenues which should be collected are collected. In other words, the governmental unit must see that all those who should secure licenses or permits do so. For example, if a license is required for the operation of a motor vehicle, the governmental unit must see that no vehicle is operated without one. Of course, the governmental unit must also assure that the revenues actually collected are recorded. This feature of control is accomplished in part by using sequentially numbered financial stationery. The numbers on the licenses, permits, or other documents are recorded when they are given to the employees who issue them. Thereafter, employees must account for the documents either with cash or with unused and spoiled documents.

INTERGOVERNMENTAL REVENUE

Integovernmental revenues consist of grants (grants-in-aid), entitlements, shared revenues, and payments received from other governmental units in lieu of taxes. NCGA *Statement 2*, "Grant, Entitlement, and Shared Revenue Accounting and

Figure 5-7

A GOVERNMENTAL UNIT

Statement of Tax Levies and Tax Collections
For the Fiscal Years Ended December 31, 19X1-19Y0

| | Total Tax Levy for Year | Uncollected at Beginning of This Year | Amount Collected This Month | Amount Collected from Beginning of This Year to Date | Amount Uncollected at This Date | Ratio (%) of: | | |
| | | | | | | Column 3 to Column 2 | Column 5 to Column 3 | Column 6 to Column 2 |
	2	3	4	5	6	7	8	9
19X1	$500,000	$ 30,500	$ 1,567	$ 5,093	$25,407	6.1	16.7	5.1
19X2	450,000	35,750	1,789	6,613	29,137	7.9	18.5	6.5
19X3	425,000	45,475	2,140	9,868	35,607	10.7	21.7	8.4
19X4	400,000	53,600	2,560	13,024	40,576	13.4	24.3	10.1
19X5	430,000	68,370	3,429	19,553	48,817	15.9	28.6	11.4
19X6	460,000	87,860	5,223	29,257	58,603	19.1	33.3	12.7
19X7	500,000	108,500	9,342	45,244	63,256	21.7	41.7	12.7
19X8	505,000	123,725	10,355	53,820	69,905	24.5	43.5	13.8
19X9	504,000	140,350	11,960	66,385	73,965	27.8	47.3	14.7
19Y0	505,000	150,420	13,197	75,360	75,060	29.8	50.1	14.9

Figure 5-8

A GOVERNMENTAL UNIT

Statement of Tax Levies and Tax Collections
For the Fiscal Years Ended December 31, 19X5-19Y4
(thousands of dollars)

Tax Year	Total Tax Levy	Collections of Current Year's Taxes during Fiscal Period	Proportion of Levy Collected during Fiscal Period	Collections of Prior Years' Taxes during Fiscal Period	Total Collections	Ratio (%) of Total Collections to Tax Levy	Accumulated Delinquent Taxes	Ratio (%) of Accumulated Delinquent Taxes to Current Year's Tax Levy
19X5	$ 500	$375	75%	$150	$ 525	105%	$125	25
19X6	600	425	71	120	545	91	180	30
19X7	750	550	73	150	700	93	230	31
19X8	850	600	71	225	825	97	255	30
19X9	900	650	72	265	915	102	240	27
19Y0	1,000	750	75	270	1,020	102	220	22
19Y1	1,050	800	76	200	1,000	95	270	26
19Y2	1,100	825	75	250	1,075	98	295	27
19Y3	1,200	900	75	325	1,225	102	270	23
19Y4	1,300	950	73	170	1,120	86	450	35

Reporting by State and Local Governments," defines grants, entitlements, and shared revenues as follows:

> A *grant* is a contribution or gift of cash or other assets from another government to be used or expended for a specified purpose, activity, or facility. *Capital grants* are restricted by the grantor for the acquisition and/or construction of fixed (capital) assets. All other grants are *operating grants*.
>
> An *entitlement* is the amount of payment to which a state or local government is entitled as determined by the federal government (e.g., the Director of the Office of Revenue Sharing) pursuant to an allocation formula contained in applicable statutes. A *shared revenue* is a revenue levied by one government but shared on a predetermined basis, often in proportion to the amount collected at the local level, with another government or class of government.[8]

Payments in lieu of taxes are amounts paid to one government by another to reimburse the payee for revenues lost because the payer government does not pay taxes. The maximum amount usually would be computed by determining the amount that the receiving government would have collected had the property of the paying government been subject to taxation.

Intergovernmental Revenue Account Classifications

A total of twelve possible classifications of intergovernmental revenues may be prepared for a municipality by listing the four kinds of intergovernmental revenue under Federal, state, and local unit categories. For example, there would be Federal grants, state grants, local grants, Federal entitlements, etc.

As already indicated, grants ordinarily are made for a specified purpose(s). Entitlements and shared revenues may also be restricted as to use, but frequently are not. Accordingly, all grants and restricted entitlements and shared revenues—whether from Federal, state, or local government sources—should be recorded in the appropriate fund and classified according to the function for which the grants are to be spent. Grants and restricted entitlements and shared revenues may be classified both by source and by such functions as general government, public safety, highways and streets, sanitation, and health. On the other hand, unrestricted entitlements and shared revenues should be classified into accounts according to the source of the revenue since they may be used for a variety of purposes. Similarly, payments in lieu of taxes are classified only by governmental source—Federal, state, or local unit—since they ordinarily are not restricted as to use.

Accounting for Intergovernmental Revenue

Intergovernmental receivables should be accrued, whether or not the revenue is earned, as they become due from the paying government. First, the fund in which the revenue is to be recorded must be determined.

---

[8] National Council on Governmental Accounting, *Statement 2*, "Grant, Entitlement, and Shared Revenue Accounting and Reporting by State and Local Governments" (Chicago: Municipal Finance Officers Association, 1979), p. 1. Hereafter cited as NCGAS 2.

Fund Identification. The purpose and requirements of each grant, entitlement, or shared revenue must be analyzed to identify the proper fund(s) to be utilized. Existing funds should be used where possible; it is not always necessary to establish a separate fund for each grant, entitlement, or shared revenue.

NCGA *Statement 2* provides that:

> Grants, entitlements, or shared revenues received for purposes normally financed through the General Fund may be accounted for within that fund provided that applicable legal requirements can be appropriately satisfied; and use of Special Revenue Funds is not required unless they are legally mandated. Such resources received for the payment of principal and/or interest on general long-term debt should be accounted for in a Debt Service Fund. Capital grants or shared revenues restricted for capital acquisitions or construction, other than those associated with Enterprise and Internal Service Funds, should be accounted for in a Capital Projects Fund.
>
> Grants, entitlements, or shared revenues received or utilized for Enterprise or Internal Service Fund operations and/or capital assets should be accounted for in these fund types. A Trust Fund should be used for such resources that establish a continuing trustee relationship. Such resources received by one governmental unit on behalf of a secondary recipient ("pass through"), governmental or other, should be accounted for in an Agency Fund. Pass through resources are received by a government to transfer to or spend on behalf of another entity in accordance with legal or contractual provisions. The receipt or disbursement of such resources does not affect the operations of the agent government except for the imposed accounting and reporting requirements. Pass through resources should be reported as revenues or contributed capital and as expenditures or expenses, as appropriate, by the secondary recipient.[9]

Further, NCGA *Statement 2* observes that:

> Some grants, entitlements, and shared revenues may be used in more than one fund at the discretion of the recipient. Pending determination of the fund(s) to be financed, such resources should be accounted for in an Agency Fund. When the decision is made about the fund(s) to be financed, the asset(s) and revenues should be recognized in the fund(s) financed and removed from the Agency Fund. Revenues and expenditures or expenses are not recognized in Agency Funds. Assets being held in Agency Funds pending a determination of the fund(s) to be financed should be disclosed in the notes to the financial statements.[10]

Presumably, the receiving government would record payments in lieu of taxes in the same fund(s) and manner as it records its taxes revenues. State collected, locally shared taxes should be identified in the subsidiary Revenue Ledger as to to the kind of tax being received.

Revenue Recognition. Regarding governmental fund revenue recognition for grants, entitlements, and shared revenues, NCGA *Statement 2* states that:

[9] Ibid., p. 2.
[10] Ibid.

Grants, entitlements, or shared revenues recorded in governmental funds should be recognized as revenue in the accounting period when they become susceptible to accrual, i.e., both measurable and available (modified accrual basis). In applying this definition, legal and contractual requirements should be carefully reviewed for guidance. Some such resources, usually entitlements or shared revenues, are restricted more in form than in substance. Only a failure on the part of the recipient to comply with prescribed regulations will cause a forfeiture of the resources. Such resources should be recorded as revenue at the time of receipt or earlier if the susceptible to accrual criteria are met. For other such resources, usually grants, expenditure is the prime factor for determining eligibility, and revenue should be recognized when the expenditure is made. Similarly, if cost sharing or matching requirements exist, revenue recognition depends upon compliance with these requirements.[11]

Where revenue is not properly recognized at the time the grant, entitlement, or shared revenue is received or accrued, the following entry is appropriate:

Cash or Receivable	100,000	
Deferred Revenues		100,000
To record receipt or accrual of grant,		
entitlement, or shared revenue prior to		
revenue recognition.		

When the conditions of the grant, entitlement, or shared revenue restrictions have been met, the deferred revenue is recognized as revenue. For example, assuming that any local matching requirements have been met and the remaining requirement is that the resources be expended for a specified purpose(s), the following entries are made upon incurring a qualifying expenditure:

(1) Expenditures	40,000	
Vouchers Payable		40,000
To record expenditures qualifying		
under restricted grant, entitlement,		
or shared revenue programs.		
(2) Deferred Revenues	40,000	
Revenues		40,000
To record recognition of revenues		
concurrent with expenditures meeting		
grant, entitlement, or shared revenue		
restrictions.		

Revenue recognition for grants, entitlements, and shared revenues restricted for proprietary fund purposes is discussed in Chapters 12 and 13.

Compliance Accounting. Grant, entitlement, and shared revenue provisions often require that special accounting procedures be followed and certain special reports that are not in confirmity with generally accepted accounting principles be made to grantors. Also, they may specify that reports be prepared for a fiscal year different from that of the recipient government or for a period

[11] Ibid.

other than a fiscal year, e.g., the duration of the grant. In this regard, NCGA *Statement 2* states that:

> In some instances, it may be necessary or desirable to record grant, entitlement, or shared revenue transactions in an Agency Fund in order to provide an audit trail and/or to facilitate the preparation of special purpose financial statements. The transactions are recorded as they occur in the Agency Fund utilizing "memoranda" revenue and expenditure accounts coded in accordance with specialized needs. The same transactions are subsequently recorded as revenues or contributed capital and expenditures or expenses, as appropriate, in conformity with GAAP in the fund(s) financed. The Agency Fund memoranda accounts are not reported as operating accounts. This "dual" recording approach may be especially helpful where a grant is received for multiple purposes and/or where the grant accounting period is different from that of the fund(s) financed, i.e., multiyear or different operating year awards. This "dual" recording approach is suggested only when a beneficial purpose is served. When an Agency Fund is utilized for this purpose, fund assets and liabilities should be combined with those of the fund(s) financed for financial statement presentation.[12]

Accounting for grants, entitlements, and shared revenues initially through an Agency Fund in this manner is discussed further and illustrated in Chapter 11.

CHARGES FOR SERVICES

These revenues consist of charges made by various general government departments for goods or services rendered by them to the public, other departments of the government, or other governments. The revenues of Enterprise Funds are also derived from the sale of goods or services, but because of their importance they are treated separately. Similarly, special assessments for improvements can in a sense be considered revenues of the department that constructs the improvements financed from them; but, because of their special nature, they are not so treated.

It is important to distinguish between revenues derived from departmental earnings and those from licenses and permits. Only those charges that result directly from the activity of the department and that are made for the purpose of recovering part of the cost of the department are considered charges for current services. Some of these charges may involve the issuance of permits, but the revenues should not be classed as coming from permits but rather as charges for services.

It is also important to distinguish charges for services rendered by one department to other departments, which constitute quasi-external transactions, from reimbursements. This is because *quasi-external* transactions result in revenue being recognized in the fund financing the provider department and an expenditure being recognized in the fund financing the department receiving the goods or services. Transactions classified as *reimbursements*, on the other hand,

---

[12] Ibid.

result in an expenditure being recognized in the fund from which the department receiving the goods or services is financed but an expenditure reduction (recovery) being recorded in the fund through which the provider department is financed. A quasi-external transaction should be deemed to occur when interdepartmental services (or goods) of the type routinely rendered to external parties are provided in the equivalent of an interdepartmental "arm's-length" transaction and charged for at established rates. Such instances are relatively few, except as between departments financed from governmental funds and those financed through Internal Service and Enterprise Funds; and most interdepartmental service (and goods) charges should be accounted for as reimbursements.

Some charges for services are not recorded until they are collected in cash. If collection does not occur at the time the services are rendered or immediately thereafter, revenue should be recorded as the persons or governments served are billed. The following entries illustrate some transactions that result in revenues being recorded as soon as they are earned:

Due from Other Governmental Units ..	25,000	
Revenues		25,000

To record earnings resulting from charges to other governmental units for patients in mental hospitals and for board of prisoners. Entries in subsidiary accounts: *Debit* each governmental unit. *Credit* Hospital Fees, $10,000; Prison Fees, $15,000.

Accounts Receivable	25,000	
Revenues		25,000

To record street lighting, street sprinkling, and garbage collection charges made to property owners. Entries in subsidiary accounts: *Debit* each person for whom service was rendered. *Credit* Street Lighting Charges, $5,000; Street Sanitation Charges, $10,000; Refuse Collection Fees, $10,000.

The following entry, on the other hand, illustrates some of the transactions in which revenues typically are not accrued:

Cash	38,200	
Revenues		38,200

To record receipt of cash representing charges for services. Entries in subsidiary accounts:

Credit

Sale of Maps and Publications	1,200
Special Police Services	3,000
Special Fire Protection Services	4,000
Building Inspection Fees	5,000

Plumbing Inspection Fees	5,000
Swimming Pool Inspection Fees	2,000
Golf Fees ......,...................................	7,000
Fees for Recording Legal Instruments	6,000
Animal Control and Shelter Fees	5,000
	38,200

As implied by the foregoing materials, the chart of accounts for charges for services should be based on the activity for which the charge is made. These activities can be classified according to the function of the government in which the activity is carried on. For example, under the general government function we would expect to find accounts for the following:

1. Court costs, fees, and charges
2. Recording of legal instruments
3. Zoning and subdivision fees
4. Plan checking fees
5. Sale of maps and publications

FINES AND FORFEITS

Revenues from fines and forfeits do not usually form an important part of a governmental unit's income and are usually accounted for on a cash basis. Fines are penalties imposed for the commission of statutory offenses or for violation of lawful administrative rules. Penalties for the delinquent payment of taxes are not included in this category of revenue, since they are considered part of tax revenues. Similarly, penalties for late payment of utility bills are considered utility operating revenues. Fines and other penalties included in this section are primarily those imposed by the courts.

The money from forfeits is usually first accounted for in a Trust or Agency Fund. For example, assume that a person has been released on bail and has forfeited the bail. When bail is received, it is recorded in a Trust Fund by debiting Cash or another asset account and crediting the proper Trust Fund Balance account. Unless the law provides otherwise, when bail is forfeited, the money is paid to the General Fund. The entries to record these transactions in the Trust Fund and General Fund, respectively, are:

Trust Fund:

Fund Balance	5,000	
Cash		5,000

To record reduction of Trust Fund Balance through transfer of forfeited bail to the General Fund.

General Fund:

Cash	5,000	
Revenues		5,000

To record receipt of money representing forfeited bail.

Included in the miscellaneous category are such sources of revenue as interest earnings, rents and royalties, sales and compensation for loss of fixed assets, contributions from the government's public enterprises, escheats, and contributions and donations from private sources. Notice that all the revenues discussed in this chapter may be found in General and Special Revenue Funds; some of them may also appear in other funds, as we shall see. In addition, other funds may have sources of revenue which have not been described here but will be treated in subsequent chapters. Most of the revenues in the miscellaneous category are self-explanatory, but a discussion of some of them may prove useful.

Interest Earnings. Short-term investment of cash available in excess of current needs has been authorized by legislative bodies throughout the country. Thus, in addition to interest on long-term investments of Debt Service and Trust Funds, for example, interest earned on short-term investments of idle cash has become a substantial general revenue source in many municipalities. Interest should be accrued as it is earned by the government unit.[13]

Sales and Compensation for Loss of Fixed Assets. Although fixed assets financed from General and Special Revenue Funds are not carried as part of the assets of such funds, the net proceeds from the sale and compensation for loss of these assets form a part of the revenue of these funds. As a general rule, such revenue should be recorded in the fund that financed the acquisition of the asset that has been sold or destroyed. Since identifying the source from which assets were financed may be difficult, and since in many instances the funds that financed the purchase of assets are abolished before the assets are disposed of, the net proceeds from the sale and compensation for loss of general fixed assets usually flow into the General Fund and are considered revenues of that fund. As we shall see, proceeds from the sale and compensation for loss of assets carried in Internal Service Funds, Enterprise Funds, and Trust Funds are ordinarily accounted for in those funds rather than in the General Fund.

Contributions from Public Enterprises. Payments made to the government by a publicly owned enterprise in lieu of property of other taxes from which they are legally exempt may be reported either as miscellaneous revenue or as tax revenues. Other contributions made by its Enterprise Funds should be classified as operating transfers or residual equity transfers, as appropriate in the circumstances.

---

[13] Government finance officers, accountants, and auditors should assure that any state or local regulations relating to short-term investments are observed, as well those of the federal government with respect to "arbitrage bonds" in Internal Revenue Code (IRC) section 130 and related regulations. Briefly, IRC 130 provides that a state or local government investing tax-exempt debt issue proceeds (interest exempt from federal income taxes) at rates materially higher than that being paid on the debt may have the tax exempt status of the government debt revoked. While the immediate and direct impact of such an action would adversely affect the investors in those debt securities rather than the government, its future debt issues would probably be difficult to sell and carry much higher interest rates than formerly.

Escheats. The laws of several states specify that the net assets of deceased persons who died intestate (without having a valid will) and with no known relatives revert to the state. Such laws result in what are referred to as escheats to the state. The cash or equivalent values of financial resources (e.g., cash, stocks, and bonds) received by escheat are recognized as revenues by the recipient state; fixed assets received by escheat are recorded in the General Fixed Asset Account Group at fair market value at time of receipt by the state.

Private Contributions. Occasionally, a state or local government will receive contributions or donations from private sources. Where these are unrestricted as to use, which is rare, they would be recognized as General Fund revenue. Restricted donations (except those in trust) usually would be recognized as Special Revenue[14] or Capital Projects Fund revenue, as appropriate to the operating or capital purpose; those in trust would be accounted for initially in a Trust Fund as discussed in Chapter 11.

REVENUE LEDGER

So far we have concentrated on General Ledger entries for revenues, other financing sources (operating transfers in and bond issue proceeds), and residual equity transfers in, although we illustrated subsidiary entries for charges for services to indicate the types of revenues in that category. We now turn our attention to the use of the subsidiary Revenue Ledger in state and local governments, considering first the usual approach and then an alternative approach that may be used (and useful) in practice.

Usual Approach

The subsidiary Revenue Ledger contains an account for each source of revenue; its general ledger control accounts are Estimated Revenues and Revenues. To minimize the number of accounts in the Revenue Ledger and also to facilitate comparisons of actual and estimated revenues, one account is used for each revenue source. For example, Figure 5-9 is the account for motor vehicle license revenues. When the Estimated Revenues general ledger account is debited at the beginning of the year to record revenue plans, the subsidiary Revenue Ledger accounts for the specific sources of that revenue also are debited. To illustrate, the "inflows" portion of the 19X1 budget in Chapter 4 (assuming some detail amounts) would give rise to this entry:

Estimated Revenues	431,000	
Fund Balance		431,000
To record adoption of the revenue part		
of the 19X1 budget.		
Debit (Revenue Subsidiary Ledger):		
General Property Taxes	297,000	

[14] Alternatively, restricted donations (except in trust) for purposes normally financed through the General Fund could be accounted for in the General Fund—initially as deferred revenue, then recognized as revenue when expended for the specified purpose(s).

| Penalties and Interest on Delinquent Property Taxes .... | 1,000 |
| Licenses and Permits—Motor Vehicle Licenses .... | 34,000 |

[wavy break]

Interest Earnings	2,200
Rents	5,000
Sales of Fixed Assets	9,400
Conscience Money	200
	431,000

At this point the sum of the various revenue subsidiary ledger accounts is $431,000, which agrees with the Estimated Revenues account balance. Each time the Revenues or Estimated Revenues accounts in the *general ledger* are debited or credited one or more *subsidiary ledger* accounts are debited or credited the same amount—so that the *sum* of the balances of the subsidiary accounts equals the *difference* between the balances of the Estimated Revenues and Revenues accounts in the general ledger.

As the Revenues account is credited, the corresponding revenue source accounts are credited in the subsidiary Revenue Ledger. Thus, the account balances present at all times a series of comparisons of plans and achievements. The General Ledger *control accounts* compare planned and actual revenue totals, while the *subsidiary accounts* present such comparisons with respect to *each revenue source*.

At the end of the fiscal period, the function of the Revenue Ledger has been fulfilled. If the Ledger is to be filed away—if new (physically) accounts are to be used in the next period—no subsidiary Revenue Ledger closing entries are required. The Revenue Ledger can be filed away with its year-end balances unchanged. But if the same manual or computer ledger accounts, sheets, or cards are to be used in the next period, the accounts must be closed.

Figure 5-9

			A GOVERNMENTAL UNIT Revenue Ledger		
			Account No.: 322.2 Class: Licenses and Permits Account Name: Motor Vehicle Licenses		
Date	*Reference*	*Folio*	*Estimated Revenue Dr.*	*Actual Revenue Cr.*	*Balance Dr. or (Cr.)*
19X6 Jan. 3	Budget Estimate	G. J. 1	$34,000	—	$34,000
June 30	Licenses Issued	C. R. 41	—	$34,500	(500)

The entry closing out revenues in both the General Ledger and Revenue Ledger, using the 19X1 General Ledger data from Chapter 4 and assuming detail amounts, is:

Revenues	437,700	
Estimated Revenues		431,000
Fund Balance		6,700

To record closing of actual revenues
and estimated revenue accounts.
Entries in Revenue Ledger subsidiary
accounts:

	Debit to Close Excess of Actual Revenues Over Estimated Revenues	Credit to Close Deficiency of Actual Revenues Under Estimated Revenues
Penalties and Interest on Delinquent Property Taxes		450
Motor Vehicle Licenses	500	
Street and Curb Permits	1,000	
Alcoholic Beverage Licenses	1,000	
Amusement Licenses	500	
Professional and Occupational Licenses	150	
Municipal Court Fines	100	
Interest Earnings	200	
Rents and Royalties	300	
Share of Income Taxes	5,350	
Share of Gasoline Taxes		2,700
Special Police Services	300	
Health Inspection Fees	450	
(Proof: $9,850-$3,150 = $6,700)	9,850	3,150

Note that the sum of the debits required to close the subsidiary Revenue Ledger accounts does not equal the sum of the credits. Rather, the *difference* between the total debits and total credits to the subsidiary Revenue Ledger accounts ($9,850 − $3,150 = $6,700) should equal the *difference* between the preclosing balances of the Estimated Revenues and Revenues accounts ($437,700 − $431,000 = $6,700). Further, note that under the General Ledger "variance" closing approach used here the difference between the sum of the debits and credits needed to close the Revenue Ledger accounts also equals the amount credited to Fund Balance in the General Ledger. If estimated revenues had exceeded actual revenues, the difference between the total debits and credits to close the Revenue Ledger accounts would equal the amount debited to Fund Balance in the General Ledger closing entry under this approach. This is one reason some accountants prefer this General Ledger closing entry approach over other closing entry approaches ("reverse the budget, close the actual" and compound entry closing approaches) illustrated in Chapter 4.

This "usual" Revenue Subsidiary Ledger approach assumes that operating transfers in, residual equity transfers in, and bond issue proceeds are accounted for in appropriately titled General Ledger accounts separate from the Revenues and Estimated Revenues accounts. Such items normally are few in number and subsidiary accounts detailing the balances of the Operating Transfers In, Residual Equity Transfers In, and Bond Issue Proceeds accounts in the General Ledger usually are not needed. This approach also assumes that Operating Transfers In, Residual Equity Transfers In, and Bond Issue Proceeds are not subject to formal budgetary accounting procedures—since there typically are few such items and they are controlled directly by the governing board—or that separate Estimated Operating Transfers In, Estimated Residual Equity Transfers In, and Estimated Bond Issue Proceeds accounts are established in the General Ledger. In the latter case budgetary and transaction entries would parallel those for Estimated Revenues and Revenues, subsidiary ledgers under joint control of the General Ledger "estimated" and "actual" accounts could be established if desired, and closing entries would parallel those illustrated for the Revenues and Estimated Revenues accounts in the General Ledger and for the detailed accounts in the related subsidiary ledger(s).

Alternative Approach

Some governments have numerous interfund operating transfers, residual equity transfers, or bond issues during a given accounting period and treat them as if they were revenues (or expenditures) for budget preparation and budgetary control purposes. The numerous estimated and actual General Ledger accounts (illustrated in Chapter 4) and the several subsidiary ledgers required by the usual Revenue Ledger accounting approach illustrated above may prove unwieldy in such cases.

The accounting procedures in such cases may be simplified by (1) using one Estimated Revenues and Other Resource Inflows account and one Revenues and Other Resource Inflows account in the General Ledger, to which are posted all estimated and actual revenues, operating transfers in, residual equity transfers in, and bond issue proceeds; and (2) separately identifying revenues, operating transfers in, residual equity transfers in, and bond issue proceeds only in the accounts of a single Revenue and Other Resource Inflows (or similarly titled) subsidiary ledger.

To illustrate this alternative approach, assume that the 19X1 budget for the General Fund of A Governmental Unit included a $9,000 estimated operating transfer to the General Fund from a Special Revenue Fund. In this case the budgetary entry for the estimated revenues and transfer in, under the alternative approach, would be:

Estimated Revenues and Other Resource Inflows ($431,000 + $9,000)	440,000	
Fund Balance		440,000
To record the revenues and other estimated resource inflows portion of the 19X1 budget.		

Inflows Subsidiary Ledger):

General Property Taxes	297,000
Penalties and Interest on General Property Taxes	1,000

Interest Earnings	2,200
Rents	5,000
Sales of Fixed Assets	9,400
Conscience Money	200
Operating Transfer from Special Revenue Fund	9,000
	440,000

The accrual of the operating transfer would be recorded:

Due from Special Revenue Fund	10,000	
Revenues and Other Resource Inflows		10,000

To record accrual of operating transfer in.

Credit (Revenues and Other Inflows Subsidiary Ledger): Operating Transfer from Special Revenue Fund, $10,000.

Revenue accruals and receipts would similarly be credited to the Revenues and Other Resource Inflows control account in the General Ledger and to appropriate Revenue and Other Resource Inflow subsidiary ledger accounts. The closing entry at the end of 19X1 with respect to revenues and other financing sources would be:

Revenues and Other Resource Inflows ($437,700 + $10,000)	447,700	
Estimated Revenues and Other Resource Inflows ($431,000 + $9,000)		440,000
Fund Balance		7,700

To record closing of actual and estimated revenues and other resource inflow accounts. Entries in Revenues and Other Financing Sources Subsidiary Ledger:

	Debit	Credit
Penalties and Interest on Delinquent Taxes		450
Motor Vehicle Licenses	500	
Special Police Services	300	
Health Inspection Fees	450	
Operating Transfer from Special Revenue Fund	1,000	
(Proof: $10,850 − $3,150 = $7,700)	10,850	3,150

Budgets usually are prepared several months before the beginning of the year to which they apply based on the best information available at that time. While preliminary estimates often are revised prior to formal adoption of the budget, it may also be appropriate to revise the estimates after adoption of the budget. For example, the government may find it is not going to receive a sizable grant it had expected to receive during the budget year or it may be granted a significantly less or greater amount than planned. Such an event may well signal a need to decrease or increase appropriations also, as discussed in Chapter 6.

The entry to record a revenue estimate *increase* upon its formal approval of the governing board would parallel the original budgetary entry for estimated revenue:

Estimated Revenue	75,000	
Fund Balance		75,000

To record an increase in estimated revenue.

Debit (Revenue Ledger):
Intergovernmental Revenues, $75,000.

The entry to record a *decrease* in estimated revenues formally authorized by the governing board would be the reverse:

Fund Balance	50,000	
Estimated Revenue		50,000

To record a decrease in estimated revenue.

Credit (Revenue Ledger):
Intergovernmental Revenues, $50,000.

In the event two or more significant revenue estimate revisions net to zero—for example, the estimate of general property tax revenues is reduced $30,000 but those for income taxes and for sales taxes are increased $20,000 and $10,000, respectively—the following entry is required:

Estimated Revenue	30,000	
Estimated Revenue		30,000

To record offsetting revenue estimate revisions.

Revenue Ledger: *Debit* Income Taxes, $20,000; sales taxes, $10,000; *Credit* General Property Taxes, $30,000.

The only effect of this entry, of course, is to change the estimated revenue amounts in the several Revenue Subsidiary Ledger accounts affected. The offsetting Estimated Revenue entries in the General Ledger are needed since the subsidiary ledger is normally accessed, in both manual and automated systems, through the General Ledger.

The entries appropriate to record changed estimates of operating transfers in, residual equity transfers in, and bond issue proceeds depend on (1) whether they are subject to formal budgetary control, and (2) if so, whether the "usual" or "alternative" accounting approach is employed.

REVERSING ENTRIES

At the beginning of a new fiscal year any accrual entries made in the adjustment process at the end of the preceding period should be reversed to simplify accounting procedures during the new fiscal year. For example, had $500 of interest earned been accrued at the end of 19X1 in the illustrative example in Chapter 4, the following entries would have been recorded at the end of 19X1 and the beginning of 19X2, respectively:

December 31, 19X1	Accrued Interest Receivable	500	
	Revenues		500
	To record accrual of interest earned. *Credit* (Revenue Ledger): Interest Earnings, $500.		

January 2, 19X2	Revenues	500	
	Accrued Interest Receivable		500
	To reverse interest earnings accrual at the end of 19X1. *Debit* (Revenue Ledger): Interest Earnings, $500.		

The interest earnings accrual having been reversed, any accruals or receipts of interest earnings during 19X2 can be recorded in the routine manner:

Cash (or Accrued Interest Receivable)	900	
Revenues		900
To record receipt (or accrual) of interest earnings. *Credit* (Revenue Ledger): Interest Earnings, $900.		

The ledgers will automatically reflect the proper 19X2 interest earnings amount. Had the reversing entry not been made at the beginning of 19X2 the person recording the 19X2 receipt or accrual of interest would have to check to see if any of the receipt or accrual was accrued at the end of 19X1 and, if so, make an entry such as the following:

Cash (or Receivable)	900	
Accrued Interest Receivable		500
Revenues		400
To record receipt (or accrual) of interest earnings, reduction of the accrued receivable recorded at the end of 19X1, and interest earnings attributable to 19X2. *Credit* (Revenue Ledger): Interest Earnings, $400.		

Since this procedure involves additional clerical effort, differs from the usual revenue receipt or accrual entry routine, and increases the probability of recording errors, the use of reversing entries at the beginning of a new fiscal year is preferable.

REVENUE STATEMENTS

The detailed data regarding estimated and actual revenues in the accounts of the Revenue Ledger are the source of information presented to administrators and the public in formal revenue statements and schedules.

The general purpose financial statements (GPFS) that a governmental unit issues annually include two statements that contain governmental fund revenue data: (1) the Statement of Revenues, Expenditures, and Changes in Fund Balance—All Governmental Fund Types; and (2) the Statement of Revenues, Expenditures, and Changes in Fund Balance—Budget and Actual—General and Special Revenue Fund Types.[15] These statements are illustrated in Chapter 14. A Statement of Revenues, Expenditures, and Changes in Fund Balance for the General Fund of A Governmental Unit was presented in Chapter 4 (Figure 4-6), as was a General Fund Statement of Revenues, Expenditures, and Changes in Fund Balance—Budget and Actual (Figure 4-10). Comparing estimated and actual revenues is extremely important in controlling and evaluating governmental finances, and several statements have been developed for annual financial reporting, often as schedules in the CAFR, and for internal reporting purposes.

Statement of Revenues—Estimated and Actual

This statement (Figure 5-10) is prepared only at year end, since there is no basis for comparisons of total estimates and actual data until the year has been completed. It is important because:

1. The comparison of estimated and actual revenues at year end is valuable in preparing future estimates. Usually the finance officer will be called upon to explain why the original estimates fell short of or exceeded actual revenues; and, if the estimation errors are due to failure to take certain factors into account, he will attempt to remedy the situation in making future estimates.

2. The statement is likely to prevent the finance officer from purposely overestimating or underestimating revenues over a period of years, for a series of such statements will make this practice evident. Overestimates lead to the making of appropriations in excess of revenues and may cause the governmental unit to end its operations with a deficit. Underestimates are most likely to occur in a government in which the estimating officer is administratively independent of the chief executive. In such cases the estimates may be continually un-

---

[15] The former normally includes Expendable Trust Fund data and the latter must include data for Expendable Trust Funds and any other governmental funds included in the annual operating budget adopted by the unit.

derstated, without any danger of administrative action, because of the estimator's political bias or because of a sincere belief that underestimation is the proper means of maintaining a balanced budget.

3. The comparison of estimated and actual revenues may reveal that actual collections have not been as great as they should have been. Investigation may reveal laxness or fraud in assessment or collection procedures.

Figure 5-10

A GOVERNMENTAL UNIT

General Fund
Statement of Revenues—Estimated and Actual
For the Fiscal Year

	Estimated Revenues	Actual Revenues	Actual over (under) Estimated
Taxes:			
General property taxes	$297,000	$297,000	$ —
Penalties and interest on delinquent general property taxes	1,000	550	(450)
Total taxes	$298,000	$297,550	$ (450)
Licenses and Permits:			
Business	$ 20,300	$ 21,950	$ 1,650
Nonbusiness	26,600	28,100	1,500
Total licenses and permits	$ 46,900	$ 50,050	$ 3,150
Intergovernmental Revenue:			
Share of state income taxes	$ 28,000	$ 33,350	$ 5,350
Share of state gasoline taxes	25,000	22,300	(2,700)
Total intergovernmental revenue	$ 53,000	$ 55,650	$ 2,650
Charges for Services:			
General government	$ 1,000	$ 1,000	$ —
Public safety	4,000	4,300	300
Health	1,800	2,250	450
Total charges for services	$ 6,800	$ 7,550	$ 750
Fines and Forfeits:			
Fines	$ 9,000	$ 9,100	$ 100
Forfeits	500	500	—
Total fines and forfeits	$ 9,500	$ 9,600	$ 100
Miscellaneous Revenues:			
Interest earnings	$ 2,200	$ 2,400	$ 200
Rents	5,000	5,300	300
Sales of fixed assets	9,400	9,400	—
Conscience money	200	200	—
Total miscellaneous revenues	$ 16,800	$ 17,300	$ 500
Total revenues	$431,000	$437,700	$6,700

Figure 5-11

A GOVERNMENTAL UNIT

General Fund

Statement of Actual and Estimated Revenue

For the Month Ending March 31, 19X2, and the Three Months Ending March 31, 19X2

Revenue Source	Total Estimated 19X2	March			Year to Date			
		Estimated	Actual	Over or Under* Estimate	Estimated	Actual	Over or Under* Estimate	Balance to Be Collected
Taxes:								
General property taxes	$290,600	$48,500	$46,990	$1,510*	$106,500	$103,435	$3,065*	$187,165
Penalties and interest on delinquent taxes	1,150	100	90	10*	300	250	50*	900
Total taxes	$291,750	$48,600	$47,080	$1,520*	$106,800	$103,685	$3,115*	$188,065
Licenses and permits	$ 56,300	$ 4,800	$ 7,000	$2,200	$ 15,000	$ 18,000	$3,000	$ 38,300
Fines and Forfeits:								
Fines	$ 6,500	$ 500	$ 550	$ 50	$ 1,600	$ 1,675	$ 75	$ 4,825
Forfeits	3,000	250	250	—	800	825	25	2,175
Total fines and forfeits	$ 9,500	$ 750	$ 800	$ 50	$ 2,400	$ 2,500	$ 100	$ 7,000

Intergovernmental Revenue:								
Federal grants	$ 15,000	$ —	$ —	$ —	$ —	$ —	$ —	$ 15,000
State grants	47,200	5,200	5,300	100	17,000	18,000	1,000	29,200
Total intergovernmental revenue	$ 62,200	$ 5,200	$ 5,300	$ 100	$ 17,000	$ 18,000	$1,000	$ 44,200
Charges for Services:								
Public safety	$ 6,800	$ 575	$ 550	$ 25*	$ 1,600	$ 1,550	$ 50*	$ 5,250
Highways and streets	5,200	440	450	10	1,300	1,375	75	3,825
Total charges for services	$ 12,000	$ 1,015	$ 1,000	$ 15*	$ 2,900	$ 2,925	$ 25	$ 9,075
Miscellaneous Revenue:								
Interest	$ 7,200	$ 610	$ 580	$ 30*	$ 1,800	$ 1,775	$ 25*	$ 5,425
Rents	5,100	1,000	1,010	10	2,000	2,015	15	3,085
Sale of fixed assets	4,300	500	500	—	1,500	1,550	50	2,750
Total miscellaneous revenue	$ 16,600	$ 2,110	$ 2,090	$ 20*	$ 5,300	$ 5,340	$ 40	$ 11,260
Total revenues	$448,350	$62,475	$63,270	$ 795	$149,400	$150,450	$1,050	$297,900

Statement of Actual and Estimated Revenue

It is important that the administration recognize during the year whether revenues are being collected at the proper rate. A comparison of monthly revenues with estimates will provide prompt notice when specific revenues are falling behind schedule. When the Statement of Actual and Estimated Revenues (Figure 5-11) provides such notice, the administration can take steps to satisfy itself as to the reasons for the deficiencies and, if necessary, adjust the rate and amount of expenditures. Interim statements of actual and estimated revenues may include percentages—e.g., the percentage of the year's estimate of each item that has been realized to date and the percentage realized at this point last year and/or the percentage the month's realization is of the annual estimate and the percentage the prior year's realizations this month were of the annual estimate. Such percentage data are valuable additions to these statements and give the statement users additional analysis and reference points.

CONCLUDING COMMENTS

Proper revenue administration, including revenue accounting and reporting, has never been more important to state and local governments. During periods of rapid economic growth, some governments became lax on revenue administration, assuming that growth in revenues would compensate for any administrative shortcoming. Well-managed governments, however, place equal emphasis on excellent revenue administration and expenditure administration.

Current rules for revenue recognition require that revenue be both measurable and available before it is recognized. Applying these criteria in practice requires judgment, consistency in application, and disclosure of the major judgments made in the notes to the financial statements. Too, intergovernmental grant revenue is subject to special revenue recognition criteria. Futher, it is important to distinguish revenues from reimbursements, bond issue proceeds, operating transfers in, and residual equity transfers in.

Several important revenue statements and schedules, for both internal and external use, were introduced in this chapter. Revenue reporting is discussed further in Chapter 14. Revenue Subsidiary Ledger accounting was considered in depth in this chapter. Proper subsidiary ledger accounting is vital for a sound revenue administration and accounting system.

Finally, budgetary revision entries and entries necessary to begin a new year's accounts were discussed and illustrated. These procedures and the concepts and procedures discussed above are essential in practice and will be applied throughout the upcoming chapters.

▶ **Question 5-1.** The term *competitive* underassessment is used in the "Equalization of Assessments" section of Chapter 5. What does the term mean? How does the process of equalization discourage underassessment?

Question 5-2. In a certain governmental unit, homesteads are exempt from taxation up to $2,500 of their assessed value except for taxes levied for the payment of bonds issued prior to enactment of the homestead exemption law and for the payment of the interest on such bonds. The assessed valuation of the municipality in 19X9 was $100,000,000, out of which properties with an assessed value of $20,000,000 were entitled to the exemption privilege. The tax levy for 19X9 was as follows: (1) for all expenditures excepting interest and bond retirements, $700,000; (2) for interest and bond retirements, $100,000, out of which $70,000 is applicable to bonds issued prior to the enactment of the homestead exemption act and $30,000 to bonds issued after passage of the act. Calculate the tax rate or tax rates of the governmental unit in question.

Question 5-3. Referring to Question 5-2, assume that taxpayer A resides in a homestead with an assessed valuation of $10,000. What is his 19X9 tax bill?

Question 5-4. Is it better to consider discounts on taxes as direct deductions from revenue or as expenditures? Why?

Question 5-5. Is it better to consider estimated uncollectible amounts of taxes receivable as direct deductions from revenue or as expenditures? Why?

Question 5-6. A municipality removes from the General Fund all taxes delinquent more than one year. As these taxes are collected, the proceeds are transferred to the General Fund. (a) What effect will the removal of the delinquent taxes have on the financial condition of the General Fund? (b) How will the revenues of the General Fund be affected by the collections of delinquent taxes? (c) Comment on the propriety of this practice.

Question 5-7. In some cases no provision for loss is made when uncollected taxes, interest, and penalties are transferred to tax liens. If there is a loss on such a lien, what accounts would you charge? How would you apportion the loss between those accounts?

Question 5-8. The taxes of City A are collected by County C, while City B collects its own taxes. In what respects will the tax accounting procedures for the two cities differ?

Question 5-9. For which of the following would you set up accounts in the Revenue Ledger?

Case 1: Taxes
    General Property Taxes
      Real Property
      Personal Property
        Tangible Personal
        Intangible Personal

Case 2: Intergovernmental Revenue
    State-Shared Revenues
      Property Taxes
      Individual Income Taxes
      Corporate Income Taxes

Question 5-10. (a) What is the difference between state-collected, locally shared taxes and grants-in-aid? (b) A statute provides that 50 percent of state motor vehicle license collections are to be distributed annually among the municipalities and counties (that is, county territory outside of municipalities) on the basis of the number of licenses issued to residents thereof during the year. Are such payments a distribution of state-collected, locally shared taxes or grants-in-aid? (c) Would your answer be different if the statute had provided, in addition, that the money received by the municipalities and counties was to be employed only for road purposes?

Question 5-11. (a) What is the difference between revenues from charges for current services and license revenues? (b) A department charges $10, the approximate cost of inspection, for issuing a building permit. Would you classify this as revenues from permits or as charges for current services?

Question 5-12. Both tax rates and license rates are established by legislative action. Which rates (license or tax) are likely to remain in effect over a longer period of time?

Question 5-13. The controller of the City of F, who is independent of the chief executive, purposely underestimates revenues and publishes revenue statements which show actual revenues only. (a) How can one discover the controller's practice? (b) The controller, when discovered in the practice, "points with pride" to the City's solvency and states that his underestimates have kept the City from overspending. Comment.

Question 5-14. What purposes do revenue statements serve in the administration of the General Fund?

Question 5-15. A recently elected city council member of the City of Lynne has returned from a two-day course on governmental accounting which he attended to assist him in understanding the city financial statements and budgeting process. He is perplexed by a point the instructor emphasized during the course, however, and asks the city finance officer about it. "Why did the instructor keep harping about the need to distinguish between fund revenues and the revenues of the governmental unit? It seems to me that if the governmental unit as a whole has a net increase in resources, one or more of the funds has to recognize net increases totaling the same amount. So, what's the big problem?" Respond.

Question 5-16. Mr. A acquired a tract of land at a Bethsville tax sale on January 15, 19X1. Two months later, however, the previous owner—upon learning the property had been sold to pay back taxes—told Mr. A that he was going to redeem the land. Mr. A was quite angry and insisted that the prior owner had no right to redeem the property. Who is right? Explain.

▶ **Problem 5-1.** The 19X5, 19X6, and 19X7 tax rates for the City of Coker are:

	Rate per $100 of Assessed Value		
	19X5	19X6	19X7
General Fund	$1.00	$1.10	$1.20
Library Fund	.09	.09	.09
Municipal Bonds—			
Redemptions	.20	.18	.16
	$1.29	$1.37	$1.45

The total assessed value for 19X7 was $88,400,000.

Compute the amount of taxes levied for each fund for 19X7.

Problem 5-2. In the City of Coker (Problem 5-1), collections were made in 19X7 as follows:

19X5 levy	$1,000,000
19X6 levy	100,000
19X7 levy	50,000
	$1,150,000

Compute the amount of collections applicable to each fund for each year.

Problem 5-3. On the basis of the following facts, determine the assessed value of the County of Z:

Kind of Property	True Value
Real Estate:	
Homesteads on platted property up to $4,000	$ 18,000,000
Homesteads on unplatted property up to $4,000	3,200,000
Homesteads on platted property in excess of $4,000	3,500,000
Homesteads on unplatted property in excess of $4,000.	100,000
Other real estate	192,300,000
Personal Property:	
Household goods and furniture	32,510,000
Livestock, agricultural products, stocks of merchandise, and so on	72,490,000
Other personal property	17,500,000
Money and Credits	175,000,000

Basis of Assessment

1. Real estate is assessed at 55 percent of true value. Homesteads on platted property up to $4,000 true value are assessed at 30 percent of true value, and homesteads on unplatted property up to $4,000 true value are assessed at 25 percent of true value.

2. Homesteads on platted property in excess of $4,000 true value are assessed at 52 percent of true value, and homesteads on unplatted property in excess of $4,000 true value are assessed at 40 percent of true value.

3. Household goods and furniture, including musical instruments, sewing machines, wearing apparel of members of family, and all personal property actually used by the owner for personal and domestic purposes or for the furnishing or equipment of the familiy residence are assessed at 30 percent of true value.

4. Livestock, poultry, all agricultural products, stocks of merchandise, together with the furniture and fixtures used therewith, manufacturer's materials and manufactured articles, and all tools, implements, and machinery which are not permanently attached to and a part of the real estate where located are assessed at 40 percent of true value. Other personal property is assessed at 55 percent of its true value.

5. Money and credits are assessed at 98 percent of their true value.

Problem 5-4. AAA City had the following transactions, among others, in 19X7:

1. The Council estimated that revenue of $150,000 would be generated for the

General Fund in 19X7. The sources and amounts of expected revenue are as follows:

Property taxes	$ 90,000
Parking meters	5,000
Business licenses	30,000
Amusement licenses	10,000
Charges for services	8,000
Other revenues	7,000
	$150,000

2. Property taxes of $91,000 were levied by the Council; $1,000 of these taxes are expected to be uncollectible.

3. The Council adopted a budget revision increasing the estimate of amusement licenses revenues by $2,000 and decreasing the estimate for business licenses revenues by $2,000.

4. The following collections were made by the City:

Property taxes	$ 80,000
Parking meters	5,500
Business licenses	28,000
Amusement licenses	9,500
Charges for services (not	
previously accrued)	9,000
Other revenues	9,000
	$141,000

5. The resources of a Capital Projects Fund being discontinued were transferred to the General Fund, $1,800.

6. Enterprise Fund cash of $6,000 was paid to the General Fund to subsidize its operations.

Required:

(a) Prepare general journal entries to record the transactions in the General Ledger and Revenue Ledger accounts.

(b) Prepare a trial balance of the Revenue Ledger after posting the general journal entries prepared in (a). Show agreement with the control accounts.

(c) Prepare the general journal entry(ies) to close the revenue accounts in the General and Revenue Ledgers.

(d) Repeat requirements (a)–(c) assuming the city uses the Revenue and Other Sources Ledger approach and that budgeted operating transfers in totaled $6,500.

Problem 5-5. The following are the estimated revenues for a Special Revenue Fund of the City of A at January 1, 19X0:

Taxes	$175,000
Interest and Penalties	2,000
Fines and Fees	700
Permits	300
Animal Licenses	900
Rents	500
Other Licenses	3,500
Interest	1,000

The city reports its transactions on a cash basis during the year and adjusts to the modified accrual basis at year end. At the end of January, the following SRF collections had been made:

Taxes	$90,000
Interest and Penalties	1,000
Fines and Fees	50
Permits	140
Animal Licenses	800
Rents	45
Other Licenses	2,000

An unanticipated grant-in-aid of $5,000 was received from the state. SRF collections for the remaining eleven months were as follows:

Taxes	$70,000
Interest and Penalties	800
Fines and Fees	400
Permits	30
Animal Licenses	70
Rents	455
Other Licenses	300
Interest	900

Accrued SRF revenues at year end were as follows:

Taxes	$20,000
Interest and Penalties	300
Rents	10
Interest	50

Required:

(a) Prepare the general and subsidiary ledger entries necessary to record the SRF estimated revenues, revenue collections, and revenue accruals.

(b) Post to SRF T-accounts and to subsidiary revenue accounts.

(c) Prepare SRF closing entries for both the general and subsidiary ledger.

(d) Post to the SRF general ledger T-accounts and to the subsidiary revenue accounts.

(e) Prepare a SRF statement of estimated revenues compared with actual revenues for 19X0.

Problem 5-6. On February 4, 19X6, selected accounts for the City of Robinson's Grove General Fund had the following balances:

	Debit	Credit
Taxes Receivable—Delinquent	$83,000	
Allowance for Uncollectible Delinquent Taxes		$26,500
Interest and Penalties Receivable	4,000	
Allowance for Uncollectible Interest and Penalties		1,500

Required:

Prepare general journal entries to record the following transactions:

1. Robinson formalized tax liens against properties with delinquent taxes of $9,000 and related interest and penalties of $1,000. The estimated salable value of the properties was $11,500.

2. Robinson sold the properties at a tax sale for $11,000. Costs of selling the property totaled $400.

3. How would your answers to items (1) and (2) differ if the estimated fair value of the properties was $9,000 and the property sold for $9,400?

4. How would your answers to items (1) and (2) differ if the estimated fair value of the property was $9,000 and the City of Robinson decided to use it for a playground development?

Problem 5-7. Prepare the general journal entries to record the following transactions in the general ledger accounts of a General or Special Revenue Fund:

1. The city levied property taxes of $1,000,000 with 5 percent estimated to be uncollectible. Also, 70 percent of the taxes expected to be collected are normally collected within the 2 percent discount period.

2. Current property taxes of $600,000 (gross) were collected within the recently expired discount period.

3. Assume current property taxes of $700,000 (instead of $600,000 in item 2) were collected before the discount period expired.

4. $100,000 of current taxes (not collected in item 3) were collected after the discount period and the balance of current property taxes became delinquent. Interest and penalties of $5,000—$\frac{1}{4}$ of which is estimated to be uncollectible—were assessed on delinquent taxes.

5. $110,000 of delinquent taxes and $1,400 of previously accrued interest and penalties were collected and $30,000 was collected on taxes not to be levied or due until the next fiscal year.

6. Taxes of $1,100,000 were levied to finance operations of the next year. $80,000 of the taxes are estimated to be uncollectible and there is no reason to expect the timing of collections to vary significantly from the historical collection cycle.

Problem 5-8. In auditing the City of Pippa Passes General Fund a staff member asks whether the following items should be reported as calendar year 19X4 revenues:

1. Property Taxes—which are levied in December and due the following April 30
   a. Levied in 19X3 and collected in April 19X4, $800,000
   b. Levied in 19X4 and collected in 19X5, $850,000
   c. Levied in 19X2 and collected in 19X4, $8,000
   d. Levied in 19X3 and collected in the first month of 19X5, $137,000
   e. Collected in 19X4 on taxes levied for 19X5, $22,000
   f. Levied in 19X3, not expected to be collected until 19X5 or 19X6, $12,000

2. Income Taxes
   a. 1973 returns filed during 19X4 and taxes collected in 19X4, $150,000
   b. 19X4 returns filed in 19X4 and taxes collected in 19X4, $18,000
   c. 19X4 returns filed in 19X4 and taxes not yet collected in mid-19X5, $4,000

3. Sales Taxes
   a. Returns filed and taxes collected in 19X4, $42,000
   b. Returns filed in 19X3 and taxes collected in June 19X4, $7,400
   c. Returns filed in 19X4 and taxes collected in the first week of 19X5, $6,200

4. Interest and Penalties
   a. Accruing and collected during 19X4, $2,200
   b. Accruing, but not recorded in the accounts, during 19X0–X3 and collected in mid-19X4, $7,800
   c. Accruing during 19X4 and expected to be collected in early 19X5, $3,400
   d. Accruing during 19X4 and expected to be collected in 19X6 and later, $1,200
5. Proceeds of 6 percent, 10-year general obligation bond issued December 28, 19X4, $540,000
6. Proceeds of 10 percent note payable, dated November 1, 19X4, and due March 1, 19X5, $15,000
7. Grant awarded in 19X4—received in full in mid-19X4 (Portion not used for designated purposes by 19X7 must be refunded.)
   a. Total amount of award, $250,000
   b. Qualifying expenditures made in 19X4, $172,000
8. Repayment in 19X4 of an advance made to the Internal Service Fund in 19X0, $72,300
9. Payment from Enterprise Fund in lieu of taxes, $2,500
10. Payment from the Captial Projects Fund of net assets after completion of the project, $3,000
11. Payment from a Special Revenue Fund to finance street improvements, $12,000

Required:

a. What is your recommendation for each of the items above? (Indicate how each item not reported as 19X4 revenue should be reported.) Explain your recommendation using this format:

Item	Recommendation(s)	Reason(s)

b. What total revenue amount should Pippa Passes report for 19X4?

Problem 5-9.

1. The cash receipts of the Robintown General Fund for the month of January, 19X1 included the following:

$ 800,000	Collection of current taxes receivable
150,000	Collection of delinquent taxes receivable
5,000	Collection of interest and penalties not previously accrued
6,000	Charges to departments financed by other funds for services rendered by departments financed by the General Fund—⅔ was for services rendered in 19X0, ⅓ for those in 19X1
20,000	Payment in lieu of taxes from the city water and sewer department
200,000	Proceeds of a grant from the state to be expended for street improvement and to be matched equally by the city
1,000	Fines and forfeitures
$1,182,000	

2. The cash disbursements of the Robintown General Fund for the month included:

$ 600,000	Payroll
200,000	Payments on accounts outstanding at 12/31/X0
50,000	To a Capital Projects Fund (City's contribution to project—not previously accrued)
75,000	To establish a fund to operate a new centralized print shop
80,000	For street improvements made from grant funds and matching funds; related liabilities of $32,000 remain outstanding at the end of the month
20,000	Purchase of police cars
120,000	To the Enterprise Fund to be repaid in 19X5
10,000	For supplies ordered in December 19X0 and reappropriated for and received in 19X1
$1,155,000	

Required:

Prepare general journal entries to record the Robintown General Fund cash receipts and disbursements for January 19X1 in the general ledger. December 31 is the fiscal year end. Also prepare any other General Fund general journal entries required by the foregoing information.

Problem 5-10. The City of Corky's Corner had the following transactions, among others, in 19X3:

1. The city council estimated that revenues and other financial resources of $249,000 would be generated for the General Fund in 19X3, as follows:

Property tax	$120,000
City sales tax	40,000
Parking meters	8,000
Business licenses	20,000
Amusement licenses	10,000
Fines and forfeitures	12,000
Interest earnings	2,000
Proceeds of five-year note	25,000
Transfer from Special Revenue Fund	12,000
	$249,000

2. Property taxes of $124,000 were levied by the council; $2,500 of these taxes are expected to be uncollectible and discounts of $1,500 are expected to be taken.
3. The following General Fund collections were made by the city:

Property taxes—current	$105,000
City sales tax	41,000
Parking meters	7,900
Business licenses	29,000
Amusement licenses	7,000

Fines and forfeitures	12,200
Interest earnings	1,100
Proceeds of five-year note	25,000
Transfer from Special Revenue Fund	12,000
	$240,200

4. Discounts of $1,400 were taken on property taxes before the discount period lapsed. Of the remaining balance of 19X3 taxes, $12,000 is expected to be collected by mid-19X4; the remainder is expected to be collected in 19X5 or later, or not collected.

5. The General Fund received $3,000 from issuance of a 30-day note dated September 30, 19X3.

Required:

(a) Prepare general journal entries to record the 19X3 transactions in the General Ledger and in the Revenue and Other Sources Ledger accounts.

(b) Prepare a trial balance of the Revenue and Other Sources Ledger after posting the entries in (a). Prove its agreement with the control accounts.

(c) Prepare general journal entries to close the revenue accounts in the General Ledger and in the Revenue and Other Sources Ledger at the end of 19X3.

(d) Repeat requirements (a)–(c) assuming that the city uses the Revenue Ledger approach.

6

EXPENDITURE ACCOUNTING— GOVERNMENTAL FUNDS

The budget prepared by the executive branch contains the activity and expenditure plans the chief executive wants to carry out during a fiscal year. The legislative branch reviews the plans, and by providing appropriations it enters into a contract with the executive branch for putting into effect those plans—or as much of the plans as it endorses. The executive branch is then charged with the responsibility of carrying out the contract in both a legal and an efficient manner.

Since the primary measurement focus of governmental funds is on financial position and changes in financial position, activities financed through such funds are usually planned, authorized, controlled, and evaluated in terms of expenditures. Therefore, the primary "outflow" measurement in governmental fund accounting is *expenditures*. Expenditures is a different measurement concept than expenses in that *expenditures* is a measure of fund current liabilities incurred during a period for operations, capital outlay, and debt service—whereas *expenses* is a measure of costs expired or consumed during a period.

This chapter focuses on expenditure accounting for governmental funds. Specifically, it addresses (1) the definition of expenditures in the governmental fund accounting environment and the expenditure recognition criteria used, (2) expenditure accounting controls and procedures, (3) classification of expenditure accounts, (4) use of the Expenditure Subsidiary Ledger, and (5) expenditure statements.

EXPENDITURE DEFINITION AND RECOGNITION

Expenditures may be defined in a governmental fund accounting context as all decreases in fund net assets—for current operations, capital outlay, or debt service—except those arising from operating and residual equity transfers to other

200

funds. Only quasi-external transactions result in the recognition of fund expenditures that are not expenditures of the government as a whole.

NCGA *Statement 1* provides in the eighth principle that:

> Expenditures should be recognized in the accounting period in which the *fund* liability is incurred, if measurable, except for unmatured interest on general long-term debt and on special assessment indebtedness secured by interest-bearing special assessments, which should be recognized when due.[1]

The *Statement 1* explanation of the eighth principle clarifies and extends that principle:

(1) When *interest* expenditures on special assessment indebtedness are approximately offset by interest earnings on special assessment levies, both may be recorded *when due* rather than being accrued.

(2) *Inventory* items (e.g., materials and supplies) may be considered expenditures either when purchased (*purchases method*) or when used (*consumption method*), but significant amounts of inventory should be reported in the balance sheet.

(3) Expenditures for insurance and similar services extending over more than one accounting period [*prepayments*] need not be allocated between or among accounting periods, but may be accounted for as expenditures of the period of acquisition.[2]

The reasons that interest expenditures on general long-term debt usually are not accrued at year end, and when they should be accrued, are explained in *Statement 1* as follows:

> The major exception to the general rule of expenditure accrual relates to *unmatured principal and interest* on general obligation long-term debt. Financial resources usually are appropriated in other funds for transfer to a Debt Service Fund in the period in which maturing debt principal and interest must be paid. Such amounts thus are not current liabilities of the Debt Service Fund(s) as their settlement will not require expenditure of existing fund assets. Further, to accrue the Debt Service Fund expenditure and liability in one period but record the transfer of financial resources for debt service purposes in a later period would be confusing and would result in overstatement of Debt Service Fund expenditures and liabilities and understatement of the fund balance. Thus, disclosure of subsequent year debt service requirements is appropriate, but they usually are appropriately accounted for as expenditures in the year of payment. On the other hand, if Debt Service Fund resources have been provided during the current year for payment of principal and interest due early in the following year, the expenditure and related liability *may* be recognized in the Debt Service Fund and the debt principal amount removed from the General Long-Term Debt Account Group.[3]

[1] NCGAS 1, p. 10. (Emphasis added.)
[2] Ibid., p. 12. (Emphasis added.)
[3] Ibid. (Emphasis added.)

The practical reason for the interest accrual exception in Special Assessment Funds is discussed in Chapter 9.

The NCGA permits inventories and prepayments to be charged as expenditures immediately because such items are not financial resources available for financing future expenditures. In essence, this alternative permits those governments that wish to do so to follow a "quick assets" concept of working capital in accounting for fund balance and changes in fund financial position. Also, many governments make appropriations in terms of the inventory to be acquired or insurance to be purchased during a fiscal year. Permitting them to account for such items on the budgetary basis in the governmental fund Statement of Revenues, Expenditures, and Changes in Fund Balance (but not in the Balance Sheet) avoids a potential conflict between budgetary accounting procedures and generally accepted accounting principles that would have to be explained and reconciled in the notes to the financial statements. Governmental fund inventory accounting procedures are discussed further later in this chapter.

EXPENDITURE ACCOUNTING CONTROLS

The accounting system is a powerful tool for control of both legality and efficiency. Though its obvious role is financial, it may also be used to record and report quantitative data of all kinds. The statistical data that must be estimated and accumulated to plan and control virtually all the operations of a government are best used in conjunction with financial data, and it is frequently feasible to accumulate the two kinds of data simultaneously. The accounting system will be discussed in relation to the following problems:

1. Misapplication of assets
2. Illegal expenditures
   a. Overspending of appropriations
   b. Spending for illegal purposes
3. Use of improper methods and procedures
4. Unwise or inappropriate expenditures
5. Allocation and allotments of appropriations

Discussing these problems and control methods serves as an excellent introduction to expenditure accounting principles and procedures. In general the expenditure control principles are those of internal control, and an exhaustive discussion of that topic is not presented here.[4]

Misapplication of Assets

Governments and other not-for-profit organizations own many assets, starting with but not restricted to cash, that are desirable to those who do not own them. The accounting system is a principal means of preventing the misuse or

[4] See Auditing Standards Board, American Institute of Certified Public Accountants, *Codification of Statements on Auditing Standards*, sections 320 and 321, and related interpretations (New York: AICPA 1979), and Committee on Auditing Procedure, American Institute of Certified Public Accountants, *Internal Control* (New York: AICPA, 1949).

theft of assets. Control to prevent misapplication of assets is provided by a combination of operational procedures, including the entire set of preaudit procedures, and by the postaudit. Sound operational procedures are founded on the separation of responsibility for operation, for custody, and for control. For example, a large storeroom for office supplies should be under the care of a storekeeper who is given adequate personnel and appropriate physical facilities for maintaining control over the supplies. The operating personnel who need office supplies should be able to obtain them only through requisitions that become the basis for reducing the storekeeper's responsibility. The accounting department, exercising the control function, should maintain a record of supplies for which the storekeeper is responsible, and periodic physical inventory counts and analyses should be performed to reconcile the goods on hand and the goods listed in the control records.

The preaudit is usually the responsibility of the chief accounting officer of the governmental unit and is designed to determine whether prescribed procedures are being followed in acquiring goods and services. Preaudit procedures are discussed later in this chapter.

Finally, the examination of the financial statements and their supporting records by an independent postauditor is a powerful deterrent to misapplication of assets. Chapter 21 is devoted to auditing.

Illegal Expenditures

Expenditures are illegal if they exceed the appropriations that authorize them or if they are made for purposes not contemplated by the appropriation. Control of overspending of appropriations is, of course, basically the responsibility of the individual department head; but ultimate control is ordinarily exercised by the chief accounting officer.

The accounting system provides records that permit the comparison of expenditures with appropriations or allotments and also provides current information regarding the encumbrances outstanding. The department head can exercise control only if current information is provided as to the unexpended and unencumbered balances of the department's allotments or appropriations. Expenditures that are made on purchase orders are ordinarily subject to approval by the chief accounting officer at the time the order is placed. Other expenditures are ordinarily controlled by the preaudit work of the accounting department; however, in some cases it may be desirable to encumber the appropriations for amounts that are obviously committed, such as certain contractual services and even payroll. Certainly, payroll expenditures should be controlled in part at the time of hiring and again in the preaudit procedure.

Expenditures may legally be made only for purposes contemplated by the legislators when they make appropriations. For example, the purchase of liquor for the entertainment of highway contractors would not legally be made out of governmental funds unless the legislative body had appropriated funds for that purpose. In some cases the legislature may specifically prohibit purchases of certain items, such as passenger cars. Again the primary responsibility for preventing illegal expenditures rests with the operating agency, but the final control as to legality is usually exercised by the chief accounting officer in the central administration. Such control typically is imposed at the purchase order point as orders are presented for approval and encumbrance; expenditures that are not encumbered should be controlled at the preaudit point.

Use of Improper Methods and Procedures

Assuring the use of proper methods and procedures is an integral part of the internal control process. The central financial administrative agencies, including those of the chief accounting officer, the treasurer, the purchasing agent, and the budget officer, should work together in specifying the forms, methods, and procedures to be used within the framework of applicable law. Examples of specific procedures are discussed in a later section of this chapter.

Responsibility for operational control necessarily belongs to the operating units of the government, and the heads of such agencies are primarily responsible for compliance with specified methods and procedures. The ultimate responsibility rests with the central agencies; the chief accountant's control is exercised through preaudit procedures, which provide an overview of methods and procedures in use.

Unwise or Inappropriate Expenditures

A situation encountered frequently in governments is that in which the operating agencies have an appropriation against which a proposed expenditure may legally be charged but the central financial administrative agencies question the wisdom or appropriateness of the expenditure. Lump-sum appropriations provide substantial flexibility to the operating agency and for that reason usually are highly desirable. A sound accounting and reporting system generates reliable comparisons of plans and accomplishments that provide an after-the-fact control on the agency in such cases, and the head of the agency should have ultimate responsibility for his decisions. This responsibility is removed if the agency head is subject to veto by a central purchasing agent, a central budget officer, or the chief accountant. *The central financial administrative agencies should not have authority to prevent such expenditures where the agency head may be in a better position to judge their propriety and necessity.* They should certainly be free to suggest the possibility of a mistake, of course, and possibly to veto agency head decisions which are clearly irresponsible, such as if an operating agency is ordering what is known to be a three-year supply of an item or is ordering Cadillacs to be used as highway patrol cars.

The foregoing discussion of expenditure controls should be tempered by acknowledging that the size of the government has a substantial effect on the ways that these controls are exercised. A very small governmental unit may have highly centralized control because of the ease with which central financial administrative officers, or even the chief executive, can review operations. As the size of the government expands, responsibility tends to be concentrated in the departments. Larger department size, higher-quality supervisory personnel, and decreased ability of a central officer to be conversant with all operations tend to shift power to the departments. This is particularly true in unintegrated, loosely knit governments such as those of many states.

Allocation and Allotment of Appropriations

A discussion of accounting controls would be incomplete without recognizing the importance of executive control of rates of expenditure (allotments) and purposes of expenditure (allocations). After the appropriation ordinance or act is passed, the executive branch of the government is expected to control the budget properly. The appropriation ordinance or act does not specify the rate at which expenditures are to be made throughout the year nor, in the case of lump-sum appropriations, does it specify the details of expenditure. Thus, *allotments* and *allocations*—executive assignments of appropriations to specific periods of time (e.g., months or quarters) or to specific subclassifications of expenditures, respectively—may be established to control the departments' use of the appropriations. When such assignments are made, only the assigned portion of the annual appropriation constitutes valid expenditure authority at the operating agency level.

The following schedule of events is typical of the process of control by allotments and allocations:

1. The chief executive calls for departmental allocation and allotment schedules. Each department head knows the maximum amount that the department may spend; he must determine how much of the appropriations should be spent during each period and must determine, if a lump sum of appropriation has been made, how the sum is to be spread among the department's activities. The latter distribution will be made in essentially the same way as the original budget estimates were made. Work programs showing both the allocation to activities and the allotment by periods may be utilized to support the schedules to be submitted to the chief executive.

2. The chief executive receives from the director of finance or the budget officer statements showing estimated receipts by months, quarters, or other planning periods.

3. The departmental allocation and allotment schedules are submitted to the chief executive with appropriate supporting schedules.

4. The departmental schedules are tabulated to show total allocations and allotments requested for each period of the year.

5. Adjustments are then made, as far as possible, to bring the amount of expenditures to be authorized within the actual resources available each period. The periodic work programs are helpful in this connection, and the chief executive will work with department heads to determine what adjustments are necessary and desirable.

6. The allocations and allotments are approved by the chief executive and certified to the finance officer, who sets up the proper accounts for each unit so as to show both the amounts allocated and the allotments into which the appropriation allocation is divided. To control the budget effectively, organization units must stay within both their appropriations allocations and the amounts alloted to them for a particular period.

None of the foregoing should be taken to mean that all governmental units use allotments or allocations or that very many use both time and expenditure classification assignments. In the case of detailed line-item appropriations, there may be no necessity for allocation by expenditure classification; and many governmental units may have no need to allot expenditures by periods. Allotments and allocations are important facets of the budgetary control process in many governments, however, and budgetary accounting procedures for them are discussed and illustrated later in this chapter.

EXPENDITURE ACCOUNTING PROCEDURES

Expenditures are classified and coded during the preaudit step of the expenditure control process. Preaudit consists of approving transactions before they occur, as in the case of purchase orders, or before they are recorded, as in the case of expenditures. Responsibility for the function is usually assigned to the chief accounting officer, although large departments, especially at the state and national levels, have accountants who perform some or all of the preaudit functions. The preaudit is, in the case of expenditures, directed to the control of methods and procedures involved in the expenditure process as well as to the prevention of illegal expenditures and the stealing and misuse of assets.

Most governmental units use some form of the voucher system which requires that all disbursements be authorized by an approved voucher. The voucher itself constitutes an outline of the work that must be performed in making sure that appropriate procedures have been followed in the process of requisitioning, purchasing, receiving, and approving invoices for payment.

Since accounting procedures for each of the main object of expenditure classes differ somewhat, the procedures for personal services, supplies, and other services and charges are discussed briefly in the following pages.

Personal Services

The steps in accounting for personal services are (1) determining rates of pay, (2) ascertaining the amounts earned by employees, (3) recording payments made to employees, and (4) charging the resultant expenditures to the proper accounts.

Determining Rates of Pay. When an employee is hired his pay rate is set by reference to the authority in use in the governmental unit. The legislative body has the ultimate authority and may determine rates of pay directly, or the power to do so may be delegated to the chief executive or to a civil service commission. Rates that are set legislatively may be expressed in an appropriation ordinance, an annual wage and salary ordinance, or in a continuing ordinance.

Determining Amounts Due Employees. Since an employee's pay depends both on his rate of pay and the amount of time he works, time or attendance records must be kept for employees. These records are the responsibility of each department head who may of course delegate the time-keeping duty. Mechanical time-recording devices may be used, especially where employees are paid hourly wage rates; but the typical record is a time sheet, which may or may not be a part of the same form used for the payroll.

In most cities the time records are submitted to a central payroll or accounting department. There is a substantial trend towards centralization of payroll preparation in state governments, and many state departments are large enough to support an efficient payroll department.

The payroll is not considered completed until it has been preaudited. Preauditing of payrolls consists of verifying (1) that employees have been placed on the payroll by the appropriate authority, (2) that persons listed actually worked the time for which they are being paid, (3) that calculations are correct, (4) that classes of positions and rates of pay correspond with the provisions of the salary and wage ordinance or other documents designating rates of pay for employees, and (5) that, in the case of salaries and wages subject to appropriation, a sufficient amount of the appropriation is available to absorb the salary and wage expenditures chargeable to it. This work may be performed by various departments. For example, the civil service commission may verify the classes of positions and rates of pay for civil service employees on the payroll. The budget officer may be required to ascertain that appropriations for particular departments have sufficient balances against which to charge the salary and wage expenditures. On the other hand, all these functions may be entrusted to the governmental unit's finance officer.

The above discussion relates primarily to permanent employees hired on either an hourly or salary basis. The primary difference in the payroll procedure for temporary employees is that master records may not be used. In this case, too, it is necessary to ensure that employees have been placed on the payroll by the appropriate authority, that employees worked the time they are being paid for, that the payroll has been properly calculated, that rates of pay are as authorized, that the expenditures, if subject to appropriation, have been appropriated for, and that a sufficient amount of the appropriation against which the expenditures are to be charged is available.

Recording Payments to Employees. After the payroll has been completed and approved, or in the process of payroll preparation, checks are made out for the employees and, at the designated time, are distributed. Under a proper system of internal control, employees having anything to do with the preparation of time reports, payrolls, or checks are not permitted to distribute the checks to employees. At frequent intervals, endorsements on checks are verified by comparison with the signature cards on file in the accounting department; and other preaudit and postaudit procedures are employed (see Chapter 21) to assure the propriety of payroll procedures and expenditures.

Charging Personal Service Expenditures to Proper Accounts. The costs of services of personnel that are chargeable directly to departments or other organizational units are accumulated in the payroll process by the account to be charged. Costs of maintenance and construction personnel may be assignable to numerous expenditure accounts, as may the cost of personnel whose duties cause them to move from one department or activity to another. In these latter cases supervisors or the individual employees may be required to keep and submit records indicating time spent in the several assignments so that payroll costs may be properly allocated to expenditure accounts. When the payroll has been approved, an entry is made to record the authorization of the liability and to charge the proper accounts, as follows:

Expenditures	10,000	
Vouchers Payable		10,000
To record payroll for period May 1-15, 19X1, chargeable as follows:		
Council	$ 1,000	
Executive Department	2,000	
Courts	2,000	
Board of Elections	200	
Etc.	4,800	
	$10,000	

The amounts shown in the explanation to the above entry would be posted to the "Expenditures" columns of the individual appropriation accounts in the Expenditures Ledger, discussed later in this chapter.

As employees are paid, an entry is made debiting Vouchers Payable and crediting Cash. Frequently, a special payroll bank account is provided, in which case one check is prepared for the amount of the entire payroll and is deposited to the credit of the account. The entry is made when the check for the total payroll is drawn, and the payroll checks are charged against this bank account.

Materials and Supplies

The accounting procedure for materials and supplies may be divided into two parts: (1) accounting for **purchases,** and (2) accounting for the **use of** materials and supplies.

Accounting for Purchases. The details of purchasing procedure vary according to whether (1) the materials and supplies are purchased directly by individual departments or through a central purchasing agency, and (2) the materials and supplies are purchased for a central storeroom or directly for departments. Nearly all city, county, and state governments, as well as the Federal government, use varying degrees of central purchasing. Throughout this chapter purchases are assumed to be made through a central agency. If a central storeroom is not used, all materials and supplies are delivered directly to the departments; and, even if a storeroom is used, many deliveries will be made directly to departments.

The purchasing procedure and the related accounting procedures consist of the following steps: (1) preparing purchase requisitions and placing them with the purchasing agent, (2) securing prices or bids, (3) placing orders, (4) receiving the materials and supplies, (5) receiving the invoice and approving the liability, and (6) paying the liability. All these steps, except paying the liability, are discussed below.

The first step in the purchasing procedure is filing a requisition with the purchasing agent, asking him to secure the desired supplies. If the governmental unit has a central storeroom, many purchase requisitions may be initiated by storekeepers when the amount of inventory items on hand has reached a predetermined minimum. Where no central storeroom exists, requisitions are filed by the organization units needing materials and supplies. Even if a central store-room is maintained, departments often file requisitions for materials or supplies that cannot be economically carried in stock.

Although the work of the purchasing agent is extremely technical, an understanding of the expenditure process requires an understanding of basic purchasing functions and methods. The purchasing agent is a specialist in acquiring personal property who is trained to identify and evaluate the goods that are available for various needs and to determine the best way to acquire the proper goods to fill those needs. These activities may readily be identified as staff services; that is, they are intended to assist operating officials and employees discharge their assigned responsibilities effectively. The purchasing function consists primarily of providing service to the other units of the government and assuring that certain controls are exercised over the purchasing process.

Responsibility for controlling purchasing is usually assigned to the purchasing agent. A twofold duty is imposed: first, the government should obtain the proper goods at the proper price; and second, safeguards should be maintained to prevent misappropriation of public moneys. The following discussion outlines some of the methods the purchasing agent should (and should not) use to discharge his responsibilities.

Upon receiving a requisition from a storeroom or department the purchasing agent first determines whether the item or items are described properly. The law usually requires all purchases over a minimum amount, ranging typically from $250 to $2,500, to be made by formal competitive bids; smaller purchases must in many jurisdictions be made by an informal competitive process such as obtaining bids by telephone. For bids to be truly competitive, bidders must understand precisely what is desired. Descriptions of articles, called "specifications," must state explicitly what is to be provided. Bidders then understand what they are expected to provide and can be held responsible for failure of their merchandise to conform to specifications.

The purchasing agent should not be assigned, and usually is not assigned, responsibility for the following: (1) control of overspending of appropriations, (2) control of unwise expenditures, and (3) control to assure that an appropriation exists for an expenditure of the nature contemplated. Basic responsibility for all of these rests with the department originating the requisition; the chief accounting officer usually must approve the purchase order with respect to responsibilities (1) and (3) above. In some governmental units the finance officer reviews requisitions for adequacy of appropriation and for legality of the nature of the expenditure, but usually these controls are exercised just prior to the placement of the purchase order.

After the specifications for the items to be bought have been properly selected or prepared, the purchasing agent sends out requests for bids. At the time specified in the request the bids are opened and the award is made to the lowest and best bidder. Normally the purchasing agent makes the award, but for purchases over a certain amount the approval of the chief executive and, in the case of local governments, sometimes also the legislative body may be required.

The next step is issuing a purchase order, prepared by the purchasing agent, to the vendor selected. As already indicated, to assure proper budgetary control purchase orders ordinarily are not valid unless approved by the finance officer. Accordingly, the finance officer must certify that a sufficient amount of the appropriation to which the purchase is chargeable is available. The finance officer will reduce the balance of the appropriation available (by encumbering it) when certifying the purchase order. The certified purchase order is then transmitted to the vendor. Even when materials and supplies are ordered for a central storeroom financed through an Internal Service Fund, and even though no appropriation is necessary for the expenditures made out of that fund, it is advisable to have the finance officer certify that funds are legally available for the expenditure.

The materials and supplies are received by the requisitioning departments or by the central storeroom. In either case a receiving report is filled out indicating the kinds and quantities of materials or supplies received. In an effective purchasing system the purchasing agent and the receiving agency work together to verify that the goods received conform to specifications. The receiving report is used later to compare the quantities received with the quantities ordered and the quantities billed. If the goods apply to a contract for delivery over a period of time, the receiving report is used also as the basis for making an entry on the bidding form, the order form, or some special form reducing the quantities of goods remaining to be received on the contract.

Since most vendors allow a cash discount for the prompt payment of bills, governmental units find it desirable to audit invoices promptly to assure payment within the discount period. To facilitate the work of auditing invoices, some governmental units furnish the vendor with invoice blanks. Auditing invoices consists of determining that (1) the purchase has been made as required by law, (2) each invoice is for goods or services actually received, (3) the quantities agree with the receiving report, (4) the unit prices are those indicated on the purchase order, (5) extensions and footings are correct, (6) the invoice price does not exceed the encumbrance or, if it does, the unencumbered balance of the appropriation is sufficient to cover the excess, (7) prescribed purchasing procedures were used, and (8) an appropriation is available to which the purchase may legally be charged.

After an invoice has been audited and the expenditures have been found to comply with all these requirements, a voucher is prepared signifying the approval of the liability and designating the expenditure or asset accounts to be charged.

The law, particularly of small governmental units, sometimes requires that vouchers be approved by the legislative body. Approval of vouchers is a function of the executive department but, in cases in which internal control is weak, legislative approval may enhance the control of expenditures.

Accounting for Materials and Supplies Used. As in all governmental activities, the law may to some degree determine the practices a government uses to provide and account for materials and supplies used by its departments, but the law and policy may allow substantial latitude. Two legal assumptions are dealt with in the following paragraphs: (1) The Expenditures account is to be charged with the amount of materials and supplies consumed (consumption basis) and (2) the Expenditures account is to be charged with the amount of materials and supplies purchased (purchases basis).

When stores accounting is on the *consumption* basis, the appropriation is provided on the basis of estimated usage and the Expenditures account is charged with actual usage. The inventory may be kept on either the periodic or the perpetual basis.

When the *periodic* inventory method is used with the *consumption* basis, typical entries (encumbrance and subsidiary ledger entries omitted) are as follows:

Expenditures	150,000	
Vouchers Payable		150,000
To record the purchase of stores for the year.		
Inventory of Supplies	2,500	
Expenditures		2,500
To record the increase in inventory during the fiscal period, or to record the inventory at the end of the first year of the fund's existence.		

These entries may be accompanied by an entry to adjust the reserve account, even though the supplies are available to finance subsequent period expenditures. The entry to adjust the Reserve for Inventory of Supplies to "fully reserve" fund balance for the inventory on hand would be:

Fund Balance	2,500	
Reserve for Inventory of Supplies		2,500
To adjust the reserve to equal the valuation of the supplies on hand.		

The debits and credits in the last two entries are reversed if the inventory has decreased.

When a *perpetual* inventory is used with the *consumption* basis, typical entries to be made after the inventory has first been recorded are as follows (encumbrances and subsidiary ledger entries again omitted):

Inventory of Supplies	150,000	
Vouchers Payable		150,000
To record the purchases of supplies.		
Expenditures	147,000	
Inventory of Supplies		147,000
To charge Expenditures with the amount of stores issued.		
Expenditures	500	
Inventory of Supplies		500
To record inventory shortage, per physical inventory. (If there is an overage, the accounts debited and credited in this entry are reversed.)		
Fund Balance	2,500	
Reserve for Inventory of Supplies		2,500
To adjust the reserve for the increase in inventory during the period. (If there has been a decrease in inventory during the period, the entry is reversed.)		

The foregoing entries affecting the Reserve for Inventory of Supplies are based on the assumption that the Reserve for Inventory of Supplies is to be maintained at an amount equal to the inventory. While this "fully reserving" is common in practice, theoretically only the normal minimum (base stock) amount of inventory need be reserved. This is because under the *consumption* method of inventory accounting inventory is not charged to Expenditures until consumed and hence may be viewed as a financial resource available to finance future expenditures. If the inventory varies substantially from normal levels, it may be desirable to maintain the Reserve for Inventory of Supplies account at the "normal" figure in order to indicate accurately the Fund Balance available for appropriation in the succeeding year.

The *purchases* basis is used when the appropriation is based on estimated purchases. The Expenditures account is charged with all actual purchases during the year. Assuming that the usual entry has been made encumbering the purchase order, the approval of the invoice gives rise to the following entry:

Reserve for Encumbrances	10,000	
Expenditures	9,500	
Vouchers Payable		9,500
Encumbrances		10,000

To record approval of invoice, cancellation of encumbrance, and reduction of appropriation by amount of actual expenditure. Subsidiary accounts:

Organization Unit	Encumbrances Canceled	Expenditure Charged
Department of Public Works	10,000	9,500

The amounts shown in the explanation to the entry are posted to the "Encumbrances" and "Expenditures" columns of the individual Expenditure Ledger accounts (see Figure 6-2). The foregoing entry would also serve to record in a General or Special Revenue Fund (or other governmental fund) the supplies received from a central storeroom operated through an Internal Service Fund, although Due to Internal Service Fund would be credited rather than Vouchers Payable.

Failure to record inventory leads to a management problem (perhaps unrecognized) because inventories are not likely to be subject either to custodial control or budgetary consideration. On the other hand, recording the inventory tends to point out to management the need for controlling the inventory in terms of both physical custody and total investment. Too, the budget authorities of the executive and legislative branches, as well as other statement users, need data concerning both the inventory and estimated consumption if they are to give intelligent consideration to budget requests. Thus, while generally accepted accounting principles permit the purchases method of inventory accounting, the inventory on hand at the end of the period should be reported in the balance sheet.

Each department should take a physical inventory of supplies at the end of the fiscal year. Assume that departments do not keep perpetual inventory records, that this is the first time that departments have taken a physical inventory, and that the cost of supplies on hand is ascertained to be $20,000. In that case, if the departments are all financed either from the General Fund or from some Special Revenue Fund, the following entry is made as soon as the value of materials on hand is determined:

Inventory of Supplies	20,000	
Reserve for Inventory of Supplies		20,000
To record inventories of supplies on		
hand in following organization units:		
Department of Public Works	$10,000	
Police Department	1,000	
Fire Department	1,000	
Etc.	8,000	
	$20,000	

The foregoing entry may be thought of as a combination of two entries: (1) debit Inventory of Supplies and credit Fund Balance and (2) debit Fund Balance and credit Reserve for Inventories. Inventories of future years will differ in amount; what change should be made in the two accounts in the preceding entry? Most authorities agree that both accounts should show the cost of the inventory on hand at the end of the year when the *purchases* basis is used. Thus, both the Inventory of Supplies and the Reserve for Inventories accounts should be adjusted at the end of each period for any change in the cost of the inventory on hand under the purchases method of inventory accounting.

Note that under the purchases method, the change in the Reserve for Inventory is not debited or credited directly to the Fund Balance account and is not reported in the Statement of Revenues, Expenditures, and Changes in Fund Balance prepared on the *account* basis. However, it must be reported (as an "other change") when that statement is prepared on a *total* basis in order to reconcile *total* beginning and ending fund balance.

Other Services and Charges

When services are acquired under contract, an entry is made encumbering appropriations for the amount of the estimated ultimate contractual liability at the time the contract is awarded. As services and the related invoices are received, the encumbering entries are reversed and the actual expenditures are recorded. When the cost of contractual services is small, or is a regularly recurring and relatively constant amount, the appropriations for them are not ordinarily encumbered.

Depreciation expense (not an expenditure) and interest expenditures present accounting problems that are discussed in subsequent chapters.

Fixed Assets and Retirement of Debt

The foregoing discussion of purchasing procedures applies also to the acquisition of relatively small fixed assets, such as furniture and minor equipment. It does not apply to major fixed assets or to the retirement of bonds or other long-term debts. These subjects are discussed in subsequent chapters.

Expenditures of a governmental unit are classified to serve several purposes. First, a government's financial resources are in various funds; the appropriations for the expenditures must necessarily be classified according to these funds, and as we have seen, the expenditures must be related to the appropriations. Second, appropriate classification provides information that is helpful in preparing budgets for succeeding years. Third, appropriate classification provides information to control the expenditure of funds. Fourth, proper classification permits aggregating expenditure data by fund type and for the general government as a whole for analyses and special purpose reports—e.g., by functions, programs, organization units, activities, object class. Fifth, the properly classified expenditures provide information for the financial statements and for financial statistics that may be used for comparative purposes.

Since appropriations are made in terms of specified funds, the basic classification of expenditures is by fund. To produce all the required information, the expenditures of a fund are also classified by function or program, activity, organization unit, character, and object class. In preparing non-GAAP statements that describe in a broad fashion the operation of a governmental unit the fund classification may be ignored, but it cannot be ignored in the accounting process.

The National Committee on Governmental Accounting, the predecessor of the National Council on Governmental Accounting, prepared a standard classification of accounts, including expenditure accounts.[5] That classification of accounts has been updated by the MFOA staff and is contained in *Governmental Accounting, Auditing and Financial Reporting,* issued by the MFOA in 1980.[6] The budgeting, accounting, and reporting systems of a governmental unit should utilize the same structure of accounts; and comparing and summarizing expenditure data for various purposes on a local, state, and national basis is facilitated if the same standard classification is used by all governmental units.

Classification by Function or Program

A governmental unit's functions are the broad purposes it strives to fulfill; its programs are groups of activities designed to achieve those purposes. NCGA *Statement 1* provides that a governmental unit that budgets on a program basis may use its program expenditure classification either in lieu of or in addition to functional expenditure classification.[7] A typical governmental unit provides a wide spectrum of services; many provide services that are also provided by other governmental units. For example, typical city, county, and state governments all provide for public safety. If they all select the accounts necessary to record their expenditures for public safety from a standard classification, a total figure may be accumulated for a state or for the nation as a whole. Further, it makes possible comparisons of expenditure data between and among cities and counties of com-

[5] GAAFR (68), "Appendix B: Use of Account Classifications," pp. 175–201.

[6] GAAFR (80), Appendix C, pp. 79–101.

[7] NCGAS 1, p. 16. Standard classifications of accounts by function are contained in GAAFR (68) and GAAFR (80).

parable size that have similar problems. The functional classification provides the basic structure for the classification of expenditures.

Figure 6-1 is a condensed standard classification of expenditures by function. Classifying expenditure data by function or program is essential for preparing both general purpose financial statements and special purpose summary financial reports to the general public.

Figure 6-1

EXPENDITURE CLASSIFICATION— BY FUNCTIONS

Broad Functions, Functional Classifications		Functions	
Code*	Title	Code*	Title
1000– 1999	General Government	1000	Legislative Branch
		1100	Executive Branch
		1200	Judicial Branch
		1300	Elections
		1400	Financial Administration
		1500	Other
2000– 2999	Public Safety	2000	Police Protection
		2100	Fire Protection
		2200	Correction
		2300	Protective Inspection
3000– 4999	Public Works	3000	Highways and Streets
		4000	Sanitation
5000– 6999	Health and Welfare	5000	Health
		6000	Welfare
7000– 7999	Education (Schools)		
8000– 9999	Culture-Recreation	8000	Libraries
		9000	Parks
10000–14999	Conservation of Natural Resources	10000	Water Resources
		11000	Agricultural Resources
		12000	Mineral Resources
		13000	Fish and Game Resources
		14000	Other Natural Resources
15000–15999	Urban Redevelopment and Housing		
16000–16999	Economic Development and Assistance		
17000–17999	Economic Opportunity		
18000–19999	Debt Service	18000	Interest
		19000	Principal
		19500	Paying Agent's Fees
20000–20999	Intergovernmental		
21000–21999	Miscellaneous		

For an explanation of code numbers, see the section headed "Coding Expenditure Accounts," which follows.

Classification by Activity

An *activity* is a specific line of work performed by a governmental unit as part of one of its functions or programs. Ordinarily, several activities are required to fulfill a function or program. The typical activities for the police protection and sanitation functions are given below:[8]

2000	Police Protection Function	
	2010	Police Administration
	2020	Crime Control and Investigation
		2021 Criminal Investigation
		2022 Vice Control
		2023 Patrol
		2024 Records and Identification
		2025 Youth Investigation and Control
		2026 Custody of Prisoners
		2027 Custody of Property
		2028 Crime Laboratory
	2030	Traffic Control
		2031 Motor Vehicle Inspection and Regulation
	2040	Police Training
	2050	Support Services
		2051 Communications Services
		2052 Automotive Services
		2053 Ambulance Services
		2054 Medical Services
		2055 Special Detail Services
		2056 Police Stations and Buildings
4000	Sanitation Function	
	4010	Sanitary Administration
	4020	Street Cleaning
	4030	Waste Collection
	4040	Waste Disposal
	4050	Sewage Collection and Disposal
		4051 Sanitary Sewer Construction
		4052 Sanitary Sewer Maintenance
		4053 Sanitary Sewer Cleaning
		4054 New Sewer Services
		4055 Sewer Lift Stations
		4056 Sewage Treatment Plants
	4060	Weed Control

Classifying expenditures by activity is essential to secure cost (expenditure basis) data for budget preparation and managerial control. Unit cost accounting (expenditure or expense basis) is possible only if (1) expenditures are classified by activities, and (2) statistics concerning units of output are accumulated. Even

---

[8] For an explanation of code numbers, see the section headed "Coding Expenditure Accounts," which follows. This illustration assumes that sewage collection and disposal is financed and accounted for as a general government function through a governmental fund. Alternatively, the sewage collection and disposal function may be financed and accounted for through a proprietary fund, such as a Water and Sewage Fund, as discussed in Chapter 13.

if unit costs are not to be computed, the costs (expenditure and expense bases) of an activity should be compared with the benefits expected from it as a basis for deciding whether the scope of the activity should be increased, decreased, or left unchanged. Accumulating cost data by activities also permits comparing such costs between governmental units and, by addition, accumulating cost data by function or program.

NCGA *Statement 1* notes that:

> *Activity* classification is particularly significant because it facilitates evaluation of the economy and efficiency of operations by providing data for calculating *expenditures* per unit of activity. That is, the expenditure requirements of performing a given unit of work can be determined by classifying expenditures by activities and providing for performance measurement where such techniques are practicable. These expenditure data, in turn, can be used in preparing future budgets and in setting standards against which future expenditure levels can be evaluated.[9]

It also observes that:

> Further, activity expenditure data provide a convenient starting point for calculating total and/or unit *expenses* of activities where that is desired, e.g., for "make or buy" and "do or contract out" decisions. Current operating expenditures (total expenditures less those for capital outlay and debt service) may be adjusted by depreciation and amortization data derived from the account group records to determine activity expense.[10]

This discussion of activity, function, and program classification also illustrates the need to distinguish the expenditure and expense measurement concepts, both conceptually and in practice, and to use appropriate terminology. Too often, the term "expense" is used (e.g., operating expense) when the measurement being described is "expenditures." Using these terms improperly, or interchangeably as if they were synonymous, causes confusion and should be avoided.

Classification by Organization Unit

Sound budgetary control requires that authority and responsibility for the activities of the government be assigned in a definite fashion to its officials. Assignment of appropriations and related expenditures to organization units is essential if department heads are to be held responsible for planning their activities and for controlling those activities authorized by the legislative body through the appropriations process. Classifying expenditures by organization unit is therefore important because it provides the means for controlling expenditures and for definitively allocating and evaluating expenditure responsibility. Stated differently, classifying expenditures by organizational unit is a prerequisite to effective "responsibility accounting" and to assuring and evaluating proper "stewardship" of public funds.

If the planning and execution of government functions, programs, and ac-

[9] NCGAS 1, p. 16. (Emphasis added.)
[10] Ibid., pp. 16-17. (Emphasis added.)

tivities are to be properly controlled, activities must be properly allocated to departments. Ideally, a major department would be assigned responsibility for a function or program and its subunits would be assigned responsibility for the several activities necessary to carry out the function or program. However, in some situations it may not be feasible to attain the ideal. For example, it may be appropriate to assign activities of a governmental unit so that those requiring engineering skill are in the same department, perhaps called the Department of Public Works. The Department head might be assigned responsibility for sanitation and streets, both of which are major functions, and also for building inspection, plumbing inspection, electrical inspection, gas inspection, air conditioning inspection, boiler inspection, elevator inspection, and weights and measures, all in the public safety function. Within that Department of Public Works each of the many activities involved in the two major functions, together with each of the other miscellaneous activities, should be assigned to individual organizational subunits. Again speaking ideally, each organizational unit (or subunit) in the Department of Public Works should have responsibility for a single activity. *A minimum requirement is that responsibility for an activity should be assigned to only one organization unit.* Those units that cover more than one activity should have their budgeting, accounting, reporting, and administration arranged so that assignments or allocations of costs can be made by activity. Organization by activity is highly desirable because it facilitates precise assignment of authority and responsibility and because it simplifies accounting for and controlling activities.

The foregoing description illustrates that no major difficulty arises from assigning a department responsibility for activities in more than one function or program. This arrangement may be highly desirable in order for a governmental unit to take advantage of the training and experience of officers or employees whose skills are in short supply. This arrangement also emphasizes that the functional (or program) classification's chief importance is in broad-scale planning and reporting rather than in controlling or evaluating operations.

Classification by Character

The character classification identifies expenditures by the period benefited. The three usual groupings are *current operating, capital outlays,* and *debt service.* A fourth category, *intergovernmental,* is needed where one government transfers resources to another, as when states transfer shared revenues to local governments. A state should account for pass through grants to local governments in an Agency Fund. Only the amount to be retained by the state would be recognized as state revenue; amounts remitted to local governments would not be recognized as state revenues nor expenditures.

Current operating expenditures are those expenditures expected to benefit primarily the current period. *Capital outlays* are those expenditures expected to benefit not only the current period but also future periods. Desks, trucks, and buildings are examples of capital outlays. Inasmuch as the distinction between capital outlays and current operating expenditures is sometimes difficult to make, policies are established for making these classification decisions. For example, whether test tubes for a laboratory are classified as a current operating expenditure or a capital outlay expenditure depends on experience with test tubes. If most of them, say 95 percent, are broken in the year acquired, they probably should be classified as current operating expenditures even though the other 5 percent may last for several years. The decision may also be made on the basis of cost; the fairness of financial reporting will not be impaired significantly if capital outlay items costing less than some arbitrary and relatively small sum are treated as current operating expenditures.

Maturing long-term debt principal, interest on debt, and related service charges are *debt service expenditures.* Payments made from the General Fund or Special Revenue Funds to Debt Service Funds for these purposes are operating transfers that ultimately will finance Debt Service Fund expenditures, perhaps many years hence. Though debt service expenditures are sometimes said to be expenditures that are made for past benefits, where debt proceeds were used to acquire capital outlay items, the expenditures may "benefit" past, present, and future periods.

Classification by Object Classes

The "object class" (object of expenditure) classification groups expenditures according to the type of article purchased or service obtained. The following is a standard classification of object classes related to the character classification as indicated:

Character		Object Class	
01–03* Current Operating		01	Personal Services
		02	Supplies
		03	Other Services and Charges
04–07 Capital Outlays		04	Land
		05	Buildings
		06	Improvements Other Than Buildings
		07	Machinery and Equipment
08–10 Debt Service		08	Debt Principal
		09	Interest
		10	Debt Service Charges
11 Intergovernmental		11	Intergovernmental

For an explanation of code numbers, see the section headed "Coding Expenditure Accounts," which follows.

The object classifications under Capital Outlays are obviously directly applicable to purchased assets rather than to those constructed by the governmental unit. In the latter case it may be useful to use the object-of-expenditure classification under current operating expenditures for controlling and accumulating costs. While these classifications are useful during construction, they culminate in a classification under capital outlay called "Buildings."

The object classes listed above under Current Operating are major classifications. A small municipality, or a small organizational unit in a larger municipality, might find that "personal services," "supplies," and "other services and charges" provide enough detail for administrative and reporting purposes. In most cases, however, each of those classifications would be subdivided into more detailed classifications. Personal services could be subdivided into salaries, wages, employer contributions to the retirement system, insurance, sick leave, terminal pay, and the like. The supplies category may be detailed in whatever way proves useful: at a minimum as among office supplies, operating supplies, and repair and maintenance supplies. Other services and charges include such costs as professional services, communication, transportation, advertising, printing, and binding. In certain circumstances it might be very useful to the administration to further subdivide some or all of the foregoing into even greater detail. For example, it might be useful to divide communication into such categories as telephone, telegraph, and postage.

The main object classes ordinarily provide sufficient detail for reports to the public. Providing greater amounts of detail by object of expenditure in the accounts should be based on administrative need for such information for planning, controlling, and evaluating the operations of the governmental unit.

CODING EXPENDITURE ACCOUNTS

To facilitate the accounting work and the preparation of financial statistics, accounts are coded—that is, assigned numbers or symbols that can be used in place of the account titles. The codes form a convenient shorthand for verbal, written, and machine reference. All accounts would be coded; but since the coding of expenditure accounts is more difficult than the coding of other accounts, only their coding is illustrated. The coding system shown here is only one of several that may be used.

In the preceding tables, numbers have been placed beside the several function, activity, character, and object class classifications. These numbers represent an assumed assignment of codes for A Governmental Unit. The following transactions and their coding illustrate the use of the code numbers assuming the several activities or subactivities listed earlier have been assigned to organizational units such as departments, bureaus, or sections:

1. Salaries were paid to the policemen in the Patrol division.
   Code No. 2023–01
   > Function: Public Safety (2000–2999)
   > > Police Protection (2000)
   > Activity: Crime Control and Investigation (2020)
   > > Patrol (2023)
   > Organization Unit: Patrol Division (2023)
   > Character: Current Operating Expenditures (01–03)
   > Object: Personal Services (01)
2. Travel expenditures of the head of the Sanitation Division were paid.
   Code No. 4010–03
   > Function: Public Works (3000–4999)
   > > Sanitation (4000)
   > Activity: Sanitary Administration (4010)
   > Organization Unit: Sanitation Division Administration (4010)

Character: Current Operating Expenditures (01–03)
Object: Other Services and Charges (03)

3. New benches were purchased for the City Court.
Code No. 1000–07
Function: General Government (1000–1999)
Activity: Legislative Branch (1000)
Organization Unit: City Court (1000)
Character: Capital Outlay (04–07)
Object: Machinery and Equipment (07)

The examples provide several instances in which additional information, and therefore additional coding, might be desirable. In the second example it might be desirable to have information regarding the specific object of expenditure for "Other Services and Charges." If so, an additional digit, let us say "5," could be added to the "03" to designate travel expenses, and Travel Expenses in the "Other Services and Charges" category would be coded "035." Such additional codings would apply throughout all the departments of the governmental unit. Similarly, in example 3 it might be desirable to divide machinery and equipment into various categories, of which "Furniture" might be one and might be assigned the number "3." The code to designate the purchase of the benches would then be "073."

The foregoing code provided no designation of fund. Two possible ways of providing this information might be used. First, a code of one or more digits to identify the funds might be placed ahead of the function and activity coding illustrated above. Another possibility is to assign all accounts bearing numbers between, let us say, 1000 and 22000 to the General Fund and develop additional code numbers for the other funds.

Codes similar to the one described above emphasize that the chart of accounts for expenditures is based upon two classifications: organizational unit and object class. Given the assignment of functions, programs, or activities to organization units, the organizational unit and object class become the basis for managerial planning and control. Data classified by organization unit and by object may be combined in various manners to produce summaries for the other types of classifications because the accounts have been coded to show fund, function or program, activity, and character. The following is a part of the heading of a subsidiary Expenditure Ledger account:

Code No. 2023–01
Function: Public Safety—Police Protection
Activity: Crime Control and Investigation—Patrol
Organization Unit: Police Department—Patrol Division
Character: Current Operating Expenditures
Object: Personal Services

The code provides full information regarding function or program, activity, organization unit, character, and object class. If data on the total expenditures for police protection are desired, all the accounts that bear numbers from 2000 through 2099 may be summarized. If data on the total expenditures of personal services for the Police Department are desired, all the personal services accounts (01) bearing numbers from 2000 through 2099 may be summarized. Total expenditures for public safety would be derived by summarizing the balances of all the accounts bearing numbers from 2000 through 2999; that is, after the expenditures for the Police, Fire, Corrections, and Protective Inspection Departments have been determined, those data may be added to obtain the total expenditures for the public safety function.

EXPENDITURE LEDGER

To this point we have focused primarily on General Ledger entries for expenditures, encumbrances, operating transfers out, and residual equity transfers out, though we have illustrated subsidiary Expenditure Ledger account entries on a few occasions. We now turn our attention to the use of the subsidiary Expenditure Ledger[11] in state and local governments, considering first the usual approach and then an alternative approach that may be used (and useful) in practice.

To illustrate the usual use of subsidiary Expenditure Ledger accounts, assume that allotments[12] of appropriations are not made, that is, the entire appropriation is available to the operating agencies from the start of the period. In this situation the total appropriation is recorded in the Appropriations account in the General Ledger. The Expenditures and Encumbrances accounts in the General Ledger contain the information on orders placed and expenditures made against the Appropriations. These three General Ledger accounts—Appropriations, Expenditures, and Encumbrances—are *control* accounts for the subsidiary Expenditure Ledger. Each Expenditure Ledger account shows not only the amount appropriated for a specified purpose but also the expenditures and encumbrances charged against that appropriation. Thus, all the information about a specific appropriation is recorded in one subsidiary account (see Figure 6-2) in order (1) to minimize the number of accounts needed to record expenditure information, and (2) more important, to provide better budgetary control. Such an account shows the status of each appropriation at any point in time.

The account illustrated in Figure 6-2 is for supplies for the Bureau of Fire Fighting in the Fire Department. There are other appropriations, not illustrated, for the Bureau's personal services, other services and charges, and, perhaps, capital outlay. At the beginning of the year, when the appropriations entry is made, the appropriation is entered in the "Appropriations" column and added to the "Unencumbered Balance" column. The unencumbered balance is reduced by expenditures and by purchase orders placed. This form of account provides valuable information to the finance officer as he controls the expenditures of the departmental units. Regulations are set up providing that no purchase order or contract is valid unless it is approved by the finance officer. An approved purchase order is the basis for an entry debiting Encumbrances and crediting Reserve for

[11] The Expenditures Ledger is sometimes referred to as the Appropriations-Expenditure Ledger.

[12] If allotments are made, only the allotted appropriations are credited to the "Appropriations" column of the Expenditure Ledger accounts and added to the "Unencumbered Balance" column.

Figure 6-2

A GOVERNMENTAL UNIT
Appropriation-Expenditure Ledger

Code No.: 2120–02
Function: Public Safety
Organization Unit: Fire Department
   Bureau of Fire Fighting
Activity: Fire Fighting
Character: Current Expenses
Object: Supplies
Year: 19X1

Cumulative Allotments

Original				Revisions
Jan.	$ 350	July	$2,300	July
Feb.	700	Aug.	2,600	Aug.
Mar.	1,000	Sept.	2,900	Sept.
Apr.	1,400	Oct.	3,250	Oct.
May	1,700	Nov.	3,550	Nov.
June	2,000	Dec.	3,800	Dec.

		Encumbrances				Expenditures				
		Order								
Date	Description	No.	Issued Dr.	Filled or Canceled Cr.	Balance Dr.	Voucher No.	Amount Dr.	Total Expenditures Dr.	Appropriations Cr.	Unencumbered Balance Cr.
1	2	3	4	5	6	7	8	9	10	11
1/3	Appropriation	—	—	—	—	—	—	—	3,800	3,800
1/3	Clothing	2	200	—	200	—	—	—	—	3,600
1/7	Lubricants	4	45	—	245	—	—	—	—	3,555
1/23	Clothing	2	—	200	45	39	205	205	—	3,550
12/10	Clothing	20	300	—	300	—	—	3,000	—	500
12/31	Closing Entry							—	(500)	—

6/Expenditure Accounting   223

Encumbrances in the General Ledger. The entry debiting Encumbrances in the General Ledger is supported by an entry recording the purchase order in the "Encumbrances—Order Issued" column of the subsidiary Expenditure Ledger account, which reduces the unencumbered balance by the amount of the encumbrance. When an expenditure is made for an item not encumbered previously (1) the Expenditures account in the General Ledger is debited, (2) the "Expenditures—Amount" column in the subsidiary Expenditure Ledger account is debited and (3) the "Unencumbered Balance" is reduced by the amount of the expenditure. Thus at any time the finance officer can determine whether there is an unencumbered balance sufficient to authorize a purchase order or an expenditure.

When an encumbered expenditure is made, it is necessary in the General Ledger to reverse the encumbering entry as well as to record the expenditure. The credit to Encumbrances in the General Ledger is supported by an entry in the "Encumbrances—Order Filled or Canceled" column in the Expenditure Ledger account. If the amount of the expenditure is not the same as the amount of the purchase order, it is also necessary to adjust the unencumbered balance. (This adjustment is made automatically in most mechanized accounting systems.) If the amount of the purchase order exceeds the expenditure, the difference is added to the unencumbered balance; if the expenditure exceeds the purchase order, the unencumbered balance is reduced.

Subsidiary Ledger Entries. We have observed that as soon as the appropriation ordinance is passed, an entry is made to record it. If the budgetary entry for the General Fund of A Governmental Unit for 19X1 illustrated in Chapter 4 is divided into its estimated revenue and appropriations components, the appropriations entry is as follows:

Fund Balance	426,000	
Appropriations		426,000

To record appropriations. Entries in subsidiary accounts are as follows (amounts to be posted to the subsidiary Expenditure Ledger accounts are indicated by an asterisk):

Credit Appropriations:
General Government:
  Council:
    Current Operating:

Personal Services	8,400*		
Supplies	600*		
Other Services and Charges ..	800*	9,800	
Capital Outlays:			
Equipment		1,500*	11,300
Executive Department:			
Current Operating:			
Personal Services	10,000*		
Supplies	1,200*		
Other Services and Charges ..	1,100*	12,300	

Capital Outlays:		
Equipment	1,500*	13,800

~~~

Research and Investigation:		
Current Operating:		
Personal Services	1,900*	
Material and Supplies	75*	
Other Charges	25*	2,000
Capital Outlays:		
Equipment	300*	2,300
Total General Government		57,030

~~~

Interest	14,400*
Retirement of Bonds	34,000*
Total Appropriations	426,000

Subsidiary ledger accounts would be established for these elements.

Even though expenditures are carefully planned, additions to certain appropriations may be necessary. Some governmental units are prohibited by law from making such changes, and other methods are available for taking care of contingencies that may arise. Sometimes a lump-sum contingent appropriation is made and assigned to the mayor or city manager. Either the chief executive or the legislative body may have legislative authorization to make transfers from the contingency appropriation to the several departments. Assuming that an $8,000 appropriations transfer is made to the executive department from the general appropriation for contigencies, the entry is:

Appropriations	8,000	
Appropriations		8,000
To record transfer of appropriations.		
Entries in subsidiary accounts: *Debit*		
Contingencies, $8,000. *Credit*		
Executive Department, $8000.		

Note that the Appropriations account carried in the General Ledger is not affected—the only change is in the subsidiary ledger accounts—but that, as noted earlier with respect to revenue estimate revisions, the simultaneous General Ledger debit and credit to Appropriations are made to signal the appropriation revision and, in many systems, to access the subsidiary Expenditure Ledger accounts affected. If no contingent appropriation has been provided, an additional appropriation may be desired and legal. Unless additional revenue is provided at the same time, the appropriation is debited to the Fund Balance account (it decreases the planned year-end balance) as follows:

Fund Balance	8,000	
Appropriations		8,000
To record additional appropriations.		
Entries in subsidiary accounts: *Credit*		
Executive Department, $8,000.		

To the extent that additional revenues are expected to cover the appropriation, the Estimated Revenues account is debited instead of the Fund Balance account.

Obviously, the need for amending specific appropriations is reduced if a lump-sum appropriation is made. Suppose that during the year it is found advantageous to have work done by the department's employees that was originally intended to be performed by contract. If additional employees must be hired to do the work, and if separate departmental appropriations for personal services and other services and charges were made, the appropriations will have to be changed to implement the decision. On the other hand, if the department has received a lump-sum appropriation, no change in the appropriation is needed and the departmental decision can be implemented without complication. Some have objected that such freedom of action is not desirable because it implies lack of legislative control over the executive branch . It is true that the executive branch in such circumstances has substantial latitude. On the other hand, if the accounting and reporting systems are properly designed to compare the budgeted and actual expenditures, the legislative body will have an opportunity to observe the change in plan through the reports and, if appropriate, to call the executive branch to account for the change. Since the executive branch obtains its funds from the legislative branch, the knowledge that it will be called to account for its decisions provides a powerful deterrent to inappropriate action.

Throughout the year the General Ledger entries to the three controlling accounts—Appropriations, Expenditures, and Encumbrances—will be supported by entries in the subsidiary Expenditure Ledger. At any point in time it should be possible to post all of the journals and prepare a list of account balances in the subsidiary ledger, the sum of which should equal the **net difference** in the three control accounts, computed as follows:

Appropriations		$X
Less: Expenditures	$Y	
Encumbrances	Z	Y + Z
Control figure		$X − (Y + Z)

This balancing process should be conducted at least monthly.

Closing Entries. At the end of the year the Expenditure Ledger accounts contain the information necessary for preparing the financial statements relating to expenditures. Accumulating that information concludes the functions of the subsidiary accounts and they are ready to be closed or, if new ledger sheets or cards are to be used for succeeding years, to be stored. The closing entry for the Appropriations, Expenditures, and Encumbrances controlling accounts of the General Fund of A Governmental Unit at the end of 19X1 was given in Chapter 4. It is repeated here, but subsidiary accounts have been added to show how they are affected by this entry if they are to be closed.

In the closing entry following, the total of the unencumbered balances is $7,600, which is both the sum of the subsidiary ledger account balances and the amount that is credited to the Fund Balance account by the closing entry. Note that the effect of the closing process in the General Ledger is to close the unencumbered appropriations [Appropriations − (Expenditures + Encumbrances)] to the Fund Balance account, thereby adjusting the Fund Balance account for the difference between planned and actual expenditures and for the fact that the Reserve for Encumbrances account has now become a Fund Balance reservation, i.e., it is no longer a memorandum offset account but a Fund Balance Reserve. The amount to be posted to each of the individual Expenditure Ledger accounts is the amount of the unencumbered balance of that Expenditure Ledger account. The journal entry, including instructions for closing the subsidiary Expenditures Ledger accounts, is given below. Note that the total debits and credits in the Expenditure Ledger closing entry do *not* balance, but that the difference equals the $7,600 closed to Fund Balance in the General Ledger.

Appropriations	426,000	
Expenditures		398,400
Encumbrances		20,000
Fund Balance		7,600

To record closing appropriations, expenditures, encumbrances. Entries (debits) in subsidiary accounts:

	Personal Services	Supplies	Other Services and Charges	Capital Outlays
General Government:				
Council		200		100
Executive Department		150	150	
Courts			100	100
Department of Finance:				
General Supervision		100		
Bureau of Accounts	75			
Bureau of Treasury		20		
Bureau of Purchases			75	
Department of Law	100			
City Clerk		100	55	
Planning and Zoning	50		75	
Civil Service Commission				100
Public Safety:				
Department of Police				
Administration		40		
Bureau of Records		100	60	
Bureau of Fire Fighting		500		
Department of Traffic Engineering			75	
Department of Licensed Occupations		25		
Highways and Streets	500	100	100	
Health and Welfare	1,000	350	100	500
Culture–Recreation	125	100	75	
Education	200			
	2,650	1,785	1,465	1,700
				1,465
				1,785
				2,650
Total				7,600

An example of the posting of one of the subsidiary ledger entries above is provided by Figure 6-2 for the Bureau of Fire Fighting. On December 10, 19X1, the account shows encumbrances outstanding amounting to $300 and an unencumbered balance of $500. This account is closed by the journal entry above by a $500 debit which is posted in the "Appropriations" column.

Alternative Approach

As noted in Chapter 5, some governments make numerous interfund operating transfers and residual equity transfers during a given accounting period and treat them as if they were expenditures (or revenues) for budget preparation and budgetary control purposes. The numerous estimated and actual General Ledger accounts (illustrated in Chapter 4) and the several subsidiary ledgers required (in such a situation) by the usual Expenditure Ledger accounting approach illustrated above may prove cumbersome in such cases.

The accounting procedures in such situations may be simplified by (1) using one Appropriations and Other Authorized Resource Outflows account and one Expenditures and Other Resource Outflows account in the General Ledger, to which are posted all appropriations, expenditures, operating transfers out, and residual equity transfers out; and (2) separately identifying expenditures, operating transfers out, and residual equity transfers out only in the accounts of a single Expenditure and Other Resource Outflow (or similarly titled) Subsidiary Ledger.

To illustrate this alternative approach, assume that the 19X1 budget for the General Fund of A Governmental Unit included a $4,100 estimated operating transfer to the Debt Service Fund and an $8,000 estimated residual equity transfer to provide contributed capital to an Enterprise Fund. In this case the budgetary entry for the appropriations and estimated transfers out, under the alternative approach, would be:

Fund Balance	438,100	
Appropriations and Other Estimated Resource Outflows ($426,000 + 4,100 + 8,000)		438,100
To record the appropriations and other estimated resource outflows portion of the 19X1 budget.		
Credit (Expenditure and Other Resource Outflow Ledger):		
The various expenditure accounts (by Department, Activity, Object Class)		426,000
Operating Transfer to Debt Service Fund		4,100
Residual Equity Transfer to Enterprise Fund		8,000
		$438,100

The accrual of the transfers would be recorded:

Expenditures and Other Resource Outflows	10,000	
Due to Debt Service Fund		4,000
Due to Enterprise Fund		6,000

To record accrual of operating and residual equity transfers out.

Debit (Expenditure and Other Resource Outflow Ledger): Operating Transfer to Debt Service Fund, $4,000; Residual Equity Transfer to Enterprise Fund, $6,000.

Expenditures would likewise be debited to the Expenditures and Other Resource Outflows account in the General Ledger and to appropriate Expenditure and Other Resource Outflow (subsidiary) Ledger accounts. The closing entry at the end of 19X1 with respect to the expenditures and other financial resource uses— assuming that all appropriations lapse and the Encumbrances account is closed but the Reserve for Encumbrances account is not closed—would be:

Appropriations and Other Estimated Resource Outflows	438,100	
Expenditures and Other Resource Outflows ($398,400 + $4,000 + $6,000)		408,400
Encumbrances		20,000
Fund Balance		9,700

To record closing of appropriations, expenditures and other estimated resource outflows, and encumbrances.

	Debit	*Credit*
Debit or Credit (Expenditure and Other Resource Outflow Ledger):		
The various expenditures accounts, the debit balances of which total		7,600
Operating Transfers to Debt Service Fund		100
Residual Equity Transfer to Enterprise Fund		2,000
		9,700

ACCOUNTING FOR CONTINUING APPROPRIATIONS

Recall that in some state and local governments some appropriations do not lapse at the end of each year, as assumed above, but either all *unexpended* appropriations (C2) or all *encumbered* appropriations (C1) continue to the following year(s) as authority for incurring expenditures. In such cases an appropriate balance should be left in the Appropriations account in the General Ledger, the Encumbrances account must be closed, and the Reserve for Encumbrances must be reported as a reservation of fund balance in the year-end balance sheet as discussed in Chapter 4.

When *unexpended appropriations continue* (do not lapse at year end) to the subsequent period(s), the Expenditure Ledger closing entries should result in the

"Unencumbered Balances" columns of the various accounts containing the *unencumbered* balances (unexpended appropriations less related encumbrances) carried forward to the succeeding period. When only *unencumbered appropriations continue* the Expenditures Ledger closing entries should, as illustrated earlier, result in the various accounts ending the year with zero in the "Unencumbered Balances" columns.

Some governmental units use only one series of Appropriations, Expenditures, Encumbrances, and Reserve for Encumbrances accounts in the General Ledger and one series of Expenditure Ledger accounts. They are not concerned with segregating appropriations by year or expenditures according to which year the appropriation authorizing them was made, but only with total appropriations, expenditures, and encumbrances of each period. Other governmental units consider it important (or it may be required) to segregate appropriations by year made and expenditures, encumbrances, and reserve for encumbrances according to the appropriations to which they relate. To do so, these governments either (1) use two or more appropriately dated (19X1, 19X2, etc.) series of Appropriations, Expenditures, Encumbrances, and Reserve for Encumbrances accounts in the General Ledger and establish separate Expenditure Ledgers subsidiary to each series of General Ledger control accounts; or (2) maintain only one series of General Ledger control accounts but establish separate, dated series of Expenditure Ledger accounts, e.g., Materials and Supplies, 19X1 and Materials and Supplies, 19X2. Segregating expenditures by year of authorization requires additional accounting control procedures, of course, such as separating receiving reports and invoices according to the year in which the expenditures were authorized.

ACCOUNTING FOR ALLOCATIONS AND ALLOTMENTS

Allocations, further executive branch subdivisions of legislative appropriations, do not cause any unique accounting procedures. Rather, they are accommodated in the Expenditure Ledger by establishing subsidiary accounts in at least as much detail as the allocations. To illustrate, assume that the legislative body made a lump-sum appropriation for the Police Department, but the executive branch then allocated specific maximum amounts by object of expenditure class. Only one subsidiary account (Police Department) would be needed to satisfy legislative budgetary control and accountability requirements in this instance, but a series of more detailed accounts (Police Department—Personal Services, etc.) would be needed to meet the more stringent executive branch budgetary control and accountability requirements. Hence, the subsidiary accounts must provide at least as much detail as is required to meet the more stringent requirements. They usually are established in even more detail than required in order to accumulate more detailed data for a variety of planning, evaluation, and decision-making purposes.

The chief executive may not allocate all the appropriations to the agencies immediately, but may hold back some expenditure authority for contingencies that might arise during the year. In such cases an account such as Unallocated Appropriations should be established in either the General Ledger or the Expenditure Ledger.

Allotments—divisions of appropriations authority by time period, usually months or quarters—require modification of the General Ledger accounts and accounting procedures discussed so far. To illustrate, assume that the annual General Fund appropriations of A Governmental Unit are allotted on a monthly basis, that $35,000 was allotted for the month of January 19X1, and that $350 of the total allotment was allotted to the Fire Department for supplies expenditures during January 19X1. Since only allotted appropriations constitute valid expenditure authority at the department or agency level, separate Unallotted Appropriations and Allotted Appropriations (or Allotments) control accounts are established in the General Ledger and the budgetary entry to record appropriations for the year and the allotments for January 19X1 would appear:

Fund Balance	426,000	
Unallotted Appropriations		391,000
Allotted Appropriation (or		
Allotments)		35,000
To record the 19X1 appropriations and		
January 19X1 allotments.		
Credit (Expenditures Ledger):		
Fire Department—Firefighting		
Supplies	350	
Fire Department—Other	XX	
Other Departments	XX	
	35,000	

Note that the Allotted Appropriations (or Allotments), Expenditures, and Encumbrances accounts in the General Ledger jointly control the Expenditure Ledger accounts where formal allotments are used. Thus, whereas the Expenditure Ledger account for Fire Department fire fighting supplies illustrated in Figure 6-2 assumes that allotments are made informally as guides to operating agencies—and thus the total annual appropriation was entered in the "Appropriations" column on January 3, 19X1—if a formal allotment was made as illustrated above, only the $350 January allotment would be entered into the "Appropriations" column, which would perhaps be retitled "Allotments."

At the beginning of each month (1) an appropriate amount will be reclassified from the Unallotted Appropriations account to the Allotted Appropriations (or Allotments) account in the General Ledger and, correspondingly, (2) appropriate amounts will be credited to the "Appropriations" (or "Allotments") columns of the various Expenditure Ledger accounts. Assuming that all appropriations have been allotted by the end of 19X1, the Unallotted Appropriations account will have a zero balance and will require no closing entry at the end of 19X1. If some appropriations have not been allotted—for example, some governments do not allot all appropriations so that they have a "cushion" in the event that contingencies occur—the balance of the Unallotted Appropriations account is closed at year end unless unexpended or unencumbered appropriations do not lapse.

EXPENDITURE STATEMENTS

The data contained in the individual Expenditure Ledger accounts are the basis for several different expenditure statements necessary to assist in managing and controlling the operations of the governmental unit and to report upon the operations at the end of each fiscal period. The following discussions pertain to both the General Fund and any Special Revenue Funds that the governmental unit may have.

Year-End Statements

Two financial statements required to be included in the general purpose financial statements (GPFS) of a state or local government by the NCGA are (1) a Statement of Revenues, Expenditures, and Changes in Fund Balance—All Governmental Fund Types, and (2) a Statement of Revenues, Expenditures, and Changes in Fund Balance—Budget and Actual—General and Special Revenue Fund Types.[13] Both of these statements are illustrated in Chapter 14 (Figures 14-6 and 14-7).

A Statement of Revenues, Expenditures, and Changes in Fund Balance for the General Fund of A Governmental Unit is illustrated in Chapter 4 (Figure 4-7), which also contains a discussion of that statement and its various acceptable formats. A Statement of Revenues, Expenditures, and Changes in Fund Balance—Budget and Actual for the General Fund of A Governmental Unit would be prepared similarly except that the data would be presented in columns headed "Budget," "Actual," and "Variance—Favorable (Unfavorable)."

A Statement of Expenditures and Encumbrances Compared with Appropriations, Figure 6-3, or a variant of that statement, often is prepared at year end for internal use by government managers or legislators and for presentation in the CAFR. Its principal purpose is to report on executive accountability for not spending more than the amount of appropriations. It also may have some value because of the historical record of the appropriations, expenditures, unexpended balances, and unencumbered balances that it contains.

Since the first column of the statement is for revised appropriations, the amount of detail presented in the statement is determined by the detail in which appropriations are made. If the legislative body provided appropriations on a lump-sum basis for each of the major departments in the city, the functional (or program) and departmental classifications would have been used. If the activities of the governmental unit had been assigned to the departments for which appropriations were made, the activity information would be available through the departmental classifications.

The appropriations information in Figure 6-3 is *after* revisions have been made. Detailed appropriations information may be provided in three columns entitled "Appropriations," "Revisions," and "Final Appropriations." When substantial changes have been made in appropriations, the supplemental information regarding changes may be useful and should be provided in the statement or in notes thereto.

[13] As discussed in Chapter 14, the former may include similar Expendable Trust Funds and the latter should include data on Expendable Trust Funds that are included in the annual operating budget adopted.

Figure 6-3

A GOVERNMENTAL UNIT

General Fund
Statement of Expenditures and Encumbrances Compared with Appropriations
For the Fiscal Year Ended December 31, 19X5

Function, Activity, and Object*	Appropriations (after revisions)	Expenditures	Unexpended Balance	Encumbrances	Unencumbered Balance
General Government:					
Legislative:					
Personal Services	$ 20,000	$ 19,000	$ 1,000	$ 400	$ 600
Supplies	3,000	2,750	250	—	250
Other Services and Charges	4,000	3,900	100	100	—
Capital Outlays	500	500	—	—	—
Total Legislative	$ 27,500	$ 26,150	$ 1,350	$ 500	$ 850
Judicial	25,000	23,000	2,000	1,750	250
Executive	75,000	73,000	2,000	1,250	750
Total General Government	$ 127,500	$ 122,150	$ 5,350	$ 3,500	$ 1,850
Public Safety†	200,000	198,500	1,500	1,000	500
Highways and Streets†	100,000	99,400	600	500	100
Sanitation†	60,000	57,500	2,500	2,000	500
Health†	50,000	49,225	775	575	200
Welfare†	40,000	38,750	1,250	1,000	250
Culture–Recreation†	55,000	54,000	1,000	1,000	—
Education†	500,000	495,000	5,000	3,000	2,000
Total	$1,132,500	$1,114,525	$17,975	$12,575	$5,400

* The amount and nature of detail to be included in this statement depend upon the amount and nature of the detail in which appropriations are made. For example, appropriations may be made in lump sum or in detail, for activities or for departmental units.
† Itemize by activity or organization unit and by object, if possible.

If the governmental unit uses lump-sum appropriations, the lack of detail in the Statement of Expenditures and Encumbrances Compared with Appropriations may make it desirable to present a statement in which a considerably greater amount of detail can be presented—the Statement of Expenditures, Classified by Function, Organization Unit, Character, and Object (Figure 6-4). The first column has been headed "Function and Activity (or Organization Unit)." Assuming that each activity has been assigned to a specific organization unit, the statement contains the fully classified historical detail of expenditures for a fiscal year. These kinds of data may be useful for planning, for comparison of expenditures with expected expenditures, and for the needs of those in such professions as economics and political science for information regarding the nature of expenditures. Accordingly, a statement of this type is often presented in the CAFR.

Interim Statements

The principal interim expenditure statement is the Statement of Actual and Estimated Expenditures, which provides both monthly and year-to-date figures for expenditures, presented in Figure 6-5. If this statement is to be published, summary data by functions and activities or organization units should be adequate. If it is prepared for management purposes, more detailed information regarding, for example, objects of expenditure would presumably be required.

To prepare this statement either appropriations must be made in the detail desired for the statement or the executive branch must make allocations of lump-sum appropriations in the degree of detail desired. For example, referring to Figure 6-5, if the judicial branch received a lump-sum appropriation for 19X5 in the amount of $27,500, the amounts in the appropriations column for Personal Services, Supplies, Other Services and Charges, and Capital Outlays might not have been provided. However, if the mayor or city manager approved allocations for those objects of expenditure, the allocation data can be used in lieu of appropriations. Under such circumstances, the first column should be retitled, perhaps as "Appropriations (Revised) and Allocations," with an asterisk being used to separate the two kinds of figures in the column.

Allotments are also assumed by the Statement of Actual and Estimated Expenditures. The two columns headed "Estimated" are the result of allotments of appropriations. The existence of allotments permits the statement to be used as a basis of managerial control; i.e., the chief executive and the city council can tell from the Statement whether the allotments are being heeded by the supervisors.

In many governmental units each supervisor is provided copies of his Expenditure Ledger accounts or with summaries of those accounts on a monthly basis. In others the supervisor may use the computerized central accounting system by remote terminal to review his departmental accounts and, in some cases, obtain a printout of any account or of all accounts for which he has responsibility. These account data or summaries keep the supervisor up to date as to his expenditure position. Many supervisors go even further and require personnel within their organizational unit to maintain a record that parallels the expenditure accounts for the unit. By this means the supervisor has information

Figure 6-4

A GOVERNMENTAL UNIT

General Fund

Statement of Expenditures, Classified by Function, Organization Unit, Character, and Object
For the Fiscal Year Ended December 31, 19X1

Function and Activity (or Organization Unit)	Grand Total	Current Operating Expenditures				Capital Outlays				
		Total Current Operating Expenditures	Personal Services	Supplies	Other Services and Charges	Total Capital Outlays	Land	Buildings	Improvements Other Than Buildings	Machinery and Equipment
General Government:										
Council	$ 5,100	$ 3,800	$ 3,500	$ 150	$ 150	$ 1,300	—	—	—	$ 1,300
Executive Department	46,730	40,200	37,350	1,300	1,550	6,530	—	—	—	6,530
Judiciary	2,200	2,000	1,900	75	25	200	—	—	—	200
Total General Government	$ 54,030	$ 46,000	$ 42,750	$ 1,525	$ 1,725	$ 8,030	—	—	—	$ 8,030
Public Safety	85,370	64,100	58,050	2,850	3,200	21,270	—	—	$ 6,000	15,270
Highways and Streets	28,300	18,000	15,000	1,800	1,200	10,300	—	—	9,000	1,300
Sanitation	26,700	16,000	13,500	1,500	1,000	10,700	—	—	8,700	2,000
Health	41,400	13,800	12,000	1,300	500	27,600	$5,000	—	12,000	10,600
Welfare	17,000	12,000	4,000	200	7,800	5,000	—	—	—	5,000
Culture–Recreation	17,400	8,500	7,500	200	800	8,900	2,000	—	1,500	5,400
Education	81,300	69,800	63,000	3,800	3,000	11,500	—	—	—	11,500
Interest	14,400	14,400	—	—	14,400	—	—	—	—	—
Total Current Operating Expenditures and Capital Outlays	$365,900	$262,600	$215,800	$13,175	$33,625	$103,300	$7,000	—	$37,200	$59,100
Retirement of Bonds	34,000									
Total	$399,900									

Figure 6-5

A GOVERNMENTAL UNIT
General Fund
Statement of Actual and Estimated Expenditures
For the Month of March 31, 19X5, and the Three Months Ending March 31, 19X5

Function, Activity or Organization, and Object	Appropriations (Revised)	March			January–March			Unexpended Balance	Encumbrances	Unencumbered Balance
		Estimated	Actual	Actual (Over) Under Estimated	Estimated	Actual	Actual (Over) Under Estimated			
General Government:										
Judicial*										
Personal Services ..	$ 20,000	$ 1,667	$ 1,667	$ —	$ 5,000	$ 5,000	$ —	$ 15,000	$ —	$ 15,000
Supplies	3,000	300	275	25	800	770	30	2,230	400	1,830
Other Services and Charges	4,000	333	350	(17)	1,000	990	10	3,010	75	2,935
Capital Outlays	500	—	—	—	500	500	—	—	—	—
Total Judicial	$ 27,500	$ 2,300	$ 2,292	$ 8	$ 7,300	$ 7,260	$ 40	$ 20,240	$ 475	$ 19,765

Legislative	25,000	2,500	2,400	100	6,000	5,900	100	19,100	1,100	18,000
Executive*	75,000	7,500	7,550	(50)	18,000	17,500	500	57,500	2,500	55,000
Total General Government...	$ 127,500	$ 12,300	$ 12,242	$ 58	$ 31,300	$30,660	$ 640	$ 96,840	$ 4,075	$92,765
Public Safety*	200,000	21,000	20,500	500	50,000	49,000	1,000	151,000	10,800	140,200
Highways and Streets*	100,000	8,500	8,400	100	24,000	23,850	150	76,150	4,100	72,050
Sanitation*	60,000	7,500	7,200	300	15,000	15,100	(100)	44,900	3,800	41,100
Health*	50,000	5,000	4,950	50	12,000	11,750	250	38,250	2,250	36,000
Welfare*	40,000	3,500	3,600	(100)	10,000	9,500	500	30,500	4,500	26,000
Culture–Recreation*	55,000	4,500	4,250	250	14,000	13,425	575	41,575	4,125	37,450
Education*	500,000	40,000	39,150	850	120,500	119,750	750	380,250	15,900	364,350
Total	$1,132,500	$102,300	$100,292	$2,008	$276,800	$273,035	$3,765	$859,465	$49,550	$809,915

*Information by activity or organizaton unit and by object if possible (see the text for comment regarding the degrees of detail desirable when the statement is used for various purposes).

available on a basis even more timely than can be provided by the central accounting office. The duplication of records is undesirable, but it may be necessary unless the supervisor can be given day-to-day information regarding his appropriations, expenditures, and encumbrances.

CONCLUDING COMMENTS

We noted earlier, without comment, that NCGA *Statement 1* says that governmental fund expenditures should be recognized when governmental fund liabilities are incurred. Only current liabilities are recognized in governmental funds, of course; and, by definition, current liabilities are those whose settlement will require the use of existing current assets. Further, many liabilities considered current in the business environment are not considered current liabilities in the government environment because they will be paid from the next year's taxes or other revenues—and thus will not require the use of existing current assets. Accordingly, in practice many general government "near-current" liabilities are recorded directly in the General Long-Term Debt accounts rather than as governmental fund expenditures and liabilities. This approach was adopted in NCGA *Statement 4*, which states that (1) the total liability for claims, judgments, and compensated absences should be estimated at year end, (2) the amount that "normally" would be liquidated with "expendable available financial resources" should be recorded as a governmental fund expenditure and liability, and (3) the balance of the liability should be recorded in the GLTD accounts.[14]

We do not believe that such a narrow "fund expenditure" definition results in optimal accounting, reporting, and disclosure. Governmental fund expenditure recognition is discussed further in Chapters 10 and 15.

▶ **Question 6-1.** Designate the functions to which the following activities apply.

Granting aid to libraries	Rendering aid to dependent children
Operating a museum	Activities of parole boards
Retirement of debt	Personnel administration
Enacting laws	Providing Pasteur treatments
Judicial activities	Operating a hospital for the blind
Detecting crime	Operating a school
Preventing fires	Operating an old soldiers' home
Supervising banks	Constructing and maintaining highways
Maintaining a sewer system	Fighting fires
Operating hospitals	Prosecuting offenders
Payment of old age assistance	Administering elections
Operating a jail	Rendering legal advice to the legislative body
Operating a park	Payment of interest
Payments for pupils attending schools of another governmental unit	Inspecting buildings
	Keeping accounts

[14]National Council on Governmental Accounting, "Accounting and Financial Reporting Principles for Claims and Judgments and Compensated Absences" (Chicago: NCGA, August 1982), pp. 2–3

Question 6-2. The following is a part of an expenditure statement. Set up account headings to designate the function, organization unit, and so forth, with which the accounts are identified. You may disregard code numbers for the accounts.

Public Safety:
  Police Department:
    Current Operations:

Personal Services	$40,000		
Materials and Supplies	2,000		
Other Services and Charges	2,000	$44,000	
Capital Outlays:			
Equipment		6,000	
Total Police Department			$50,000

  Fire Department:
    Current Operations:

Personal Services	$30,000		
Supplies	1,500		
Other Services and Charges	2,000	$33,500	
Capital Outlays:			
Equipment		6,500	
Total Fire Department			40,000
Total Public Safety			$90,000

Question 6-3. Distinguish between an expenditure in the governmental accounting sense and an expense in the commercial accounting sense.

Question 6-4. Explain how an accounting system can be designed to produce informaton for all the bases of expenditure classification and still produce information useful for managerial purposes.

Question 6-5. Name the controlling accounts which one might expect to find in use in the General Fund.

Question 6-6. In a certain municipality the purchase of materials is charged against an appropriation set up for that purpose. Subsequently, as materials are withdrawn, their cost is charged to the appropriations of the departments by which they are withdrawn. What is wrong with this procedure, and what remedy would you propose?

Question 6-7. (a) Should the inventory of materials and supplies carried in the General Fund of a governmental unit be recorded at cost, at lower of cost or market, or on some other basis? (b) Would your answer be different if the inventory was owned by a municipal water utility?

Question 6-8. On January 2, 19X1, materials costing $100 were transferred from perpetual inventory to the Police Department. Give the journal entry or entries to be made.

Question 6-9. A governmental unit takes advantage of purchase discounts by paying its bills promptly. Should the full purchase price be recorded in the records with the discounts treated as revenue, or should the purchases be recorded at their net cost (i.e., after deduction of discounts)?

Question 6-10. It has been suggested that the amounts paid from the General Fund to a pension fund for the city's share of pension fund contributions be charged to the departments in which the covered employees work. Do you agree? Explain.

Question 6-11. In one municipality vouchers must be approved not only by the finance officer but also by the four members of the finance committee of the city council. In your opinion is the approval of the finance committee desirable? Give reasons.

Question 6-12. Explain how you would decide whether or not a planned expenditure should be encumbered.

Question 6-13. The newly elected mayor of the Town of Dewey is a well-respected businessman. He is perplexed because the town's finance director has given him an interim financial statement which reports repayment of a ten-year note through the General Fund as an expenditure. The mayor is aware that several short-term notes were repaid during the interim period as well, and these are not reported. "Two things puzzle me," says the mayor. "First, why should repayment of a note be reported as an expenditure? We decreased our assets and liabilities by equal amounts; therefore, the city's equity did not change. Second, why is only part of the principal retirement reported as expenditures if such a practice is appropriate?" Respond to the mayor.

Question 6-14. Why would an executive branch make allocations and/or allotments of appropriations authorized by the legislative branch? How do (a) allocations and (b) allotments of appropriations affect accounting for a Governmental Fund's expenditures?

Question 6-15. An accountant for the Town of Don's Grove previously worked for the City of Carlisle. Don's Grove records purchases of materials and supplies as expenditures and reports any change in the inventory of materials and supplies in its Statement of Revenues, Expenditures, and Changes in (Total) Fund Balance. The accountant recalls, however, that the City of Carlisle recorded expenditures for materials and supplies when they were used, not when they were purchased. Also, Carlisle did not report changes in inventory on its Statement of Revenues, Expenditures, and Changes in (Total) Fund Balance. The accountant asks his supervisor which way is correct. Respond.

Question 6-16. When is "fully reserving" Fund Balance for inventory on hand appropriate? Explain.

Question 6-17. The clerk of the City of Wilmaton is revising the city accounting system so that she can report expenditures by function, organization unit, activity, character, and object class as well as by fund. Her assistant is perturbed because he considers all these classifications unnecessary and, he states: "It will take five extra sets of books to record expenditures this way. Every expenditure will have to be recorded six times!" Explain to the assistant (a) the purpose of each expenditure classification and (b) how to implement the multiple classification scheme without multiplying the work required to record expenditures.

Question 6-18. Distinguish between and among the four character classifications.

Question 6-19. When should General Fund expenditures be recognized? What are the major exceptions?

▶ **Problem 6-1.** The portion of the proposed 19X5 budget applicable to Titusville's Department of City Manager follows:

Major Classification	Proposed Budget 19X5
Personal Services:	
Salaries and Wages:	
City Manager	$18,000
Administrative Assistant ..	10,500
Secretary	7,000
	$35,500

Contractual Services:

Travel and Training	$ 2,400
Telephone and Telegraph ...	600
Equipment Maintenance	100
Professional Services	800
	$ 3,900

Materials and Supplies:

Supplies	$ 1,000
Gasoline and Oil	250
Tires	150
Parts for Equipment	400
	$ 1,800

Fixed and Sundry:

Taxes and Licenses	$ 50
Memberships and Subscriptions	350
	$ 400

Capital Outlay:

Office Machinery	$ 6,000
Office Furniture	2,000
	$ 8,000
Total	$49,600

Required:

Prepare the *subsidiary* Expenditure Ledger entry necessary to record enactment of appropriations by the council as follows: (a) by department; (b) by major object-of-expenditure categories; and (c) by detailed object-of-expenditure line items.

Problem 6-2. The following General Fund appropriations were made for 19X4 by the City of L:

City Council	$ 15,000
Mayor	15,000
Courts	30,000
City Clerk	15,000
Department of Finance	30,000
Department of Police	75,000
Department of Fire	60,000
Department of Public Works .	30,000
Interest	15,000
Retirement of bonds	15,000
	$300,000

The following transfers between appropriations were subsequently authorized:

Transferred from:	Transferred to:	Amount
City Council	City Clerk	$ 750
City Clerk	Mayor	1,500
Department of Finance	Department of Public Works	1,500
Department of Public Works	Courts	1,000

Transferred from:	Transferred to:	Amount
Reserve for Contingencies	{ Department of Police	1,500
	Department of Fire	2,200
	City Council	750
	Department of Public Works	3,000

Estimated revenues are $350,000; the Council reserved $30,000 for contingencies.

Required:

(a) Prepare the GF journal entry necessary to record the adoption of the budget, showing both the General Ledger and the Subsidiary Ledger accounts.

(b) Prepare the GF journal entry to record the transfers between appropriations, showing both the General Ledger and the Subsidiary Ledger accounts involved.

(c) Prepare a statement showing the appropriation balances after the transfers have been made effective.

Problem 6-3. The following appropriations and first quarter allotments for 19X4 were made by Dogwood City's council and manager, respectively:

	19X4 Appropriations	First Quarter Allotments
City Council	$ 12,000	$ 3,000
Manager	40,000	11,000
Courts	30,000	7,000
City Clerk	20,000	5,000
Finance Department	35,000	10,000
Police Department	80,000	20,000
Fire Department	75,000	16,000
Public Works Department .	45,000	12,000
Interest	15,000	—
Retirement of Bonds	25,000	—
	$377,000	$84,000

Required:

Prepare the journal entry necessary to record the appropriations and first quarter allotments, showing both the General Ledger and the Subsidiary Ledger accounts.

Problem 6-4. The following information pertains to the operations of the General Fund of County X. Functions of this county government include operating the county jail and caring for the county courts.

Funds to finance the operations are provided from a levy of county tax against the various towns of the county, from the state distribution of unincorporated business taxes, from board of jail prisoners assessed against the towns and against the state, and from interest on savings accounts.

The balances in the accounts of the Fund on January 1, 19X0, were as follows:

Cash in savings accounts	$ 60,650
Cash in checking accounts	41,380
Cash on hand (undeposited prisoners' board receipts)	320
Inventory of jail supplies	3,070

Due from towns and state for board of	
prisoners	3,550
General Fund balance	108,970

The budget for the year 19X0 as adopted by the county commissioners provided for the following items of revenue and expenditure:

(1) Town and county taxes	$20,000
(2) Jail operating costs	55,500
(3) Court operating costs	7,500
(4) Unincorporated business tax	18,000
(5) Board of prisoners (revenue)	5,000
(6) Commissioners' salaries and costs	8,000
(7) Interest on savings	1,000
(8) Miscellaneous expenditures	1,000

General Fund balance was appropriated in sufficient amount to balance the budget. At December 31, 19X0, the jail supply inventory amounted to $5,120, cash of $380 was on hand, and $1,325 of prisoners' board bills were unpaid. The following items represent all of the transactions which occurred during the year, with all current bills vouchered and paid by December 31, 19X0:

Item (1) was transacted exactly as budgeted.	
Item (2) cash expenditures amounted to	$55,230
Item (3) amounted to	7,110
Item (4) amounted to	18,070
Item (5) billings amounted to	4,550
Item (6) amounted to	6,670
Item (7) amounted to	1,050
Item (8) amounted to	2,310

During the year, $25,000 was transferred from the savings accounts to the checking accounts.

Required:

From the information above, prepare a worksheet providing columns to show:

(a) The balances at the beginning of the year.

(b) The transactions for the year. (Journal entries are not required.)

(c) Variances between budgeted and actual revenues and expenditures for the year.

(d) Balance sheet of the General Fund, December 31, 19X0.

(AICPA, adapted)

Problem 6-5. The account on page 244 appears in the Expenditures Ledger of the City of X. Restate the account to show the correct recording of the transactions and to show correct balances.

Problem 6-6. The following information summarizes the operation of the Library Fund of the City of Hillsdale:

1. The account balances at December 31, 19X0, were as follows:

Cash	$2,350
Reserve for Encumbrances	1,000
Fund Balance	1,350

CITY OF X
Expenditure Ledger

Acc. No. 1110–02
Office of the Mayor
Supplies

19X2 Date	Description	Encumbrances Dr.	Encumbrances Cr.	Expenditures	Appropriations	Balance
Jan. 1	Budget				$3,800	$3,800
5	Purchase Order 8—Stationery	$ 500				3,300
10	Invoice 498—telephone bill			$ 20		3,280
25	Invoice for P.O. 8		$ 495	495		3,280
Feb. 1	Bill from Stores Fund	200				3,080
8	Returned Stationery				50	3,130
9	Purchase Order 250—Supplies	100				3,230
Mar. 5	Invoice for P.O. 250		100	105		3,230
15	Allowance on Supplies				5	3,225
June 10	Transferred Supplies to Fire Department				50	3,175
15	P.O. 2561—Printing and Supplies	2,000				1,175
Aug. 15	Invoice for P.O. 2561		2,000	2,100		1,075
Nov. 15	Transfer of Appropriation to City Manager's Office			500		575

2. Effective January 1, 19X1, the city council dedicated a portion of the property taxes of the city, together with all receipts from parking meters, to the Library Fund. The council's estimate of revenues from these sources follows:

Property Taxes	$ 50,000
Parking Meters	135,000
	$185,000

3. Planned expenditures for 19X1 were as follows:

General Administration	$ 50,000
Library-on-Wheels	40,000
Books	90,000
	$180,000

The council's approval of expenditures included $1,000 for books ordered in 19X0.

4. Taxes of $52,500 were levied. It was expected that $2,000 would prove uncollectible.

5. Receipts during the year consisted of the following items:

Property Taxes	$ 51,500
Parking Meter Collections	136,000
Refund on Books Bought This Year	300
	$187,800

6. The following purchase orders were placed:

General Administration	$ 30,000
Library-on-Wheels	10,000
Books	80,000
	$120,000

7. Certain of the orders placed in 19X0 and 19X1 were received. The vouchers, together with amount of the related purchase orders, are summarized below:

	Ordered	Vouchered
General Administration	$ 20,000	$ 21,500
Library-on-Wheels	10,000	10,000
Books	80,000	85,000
	$110,000	$116,500

8. Additional vouchers were prepared for the following purposes:

General Administration	$27,000
Library-on-Wheels	30,000

Books	....	6,000
Refund of Overpayment of Taxes	....	400
		$63,400

9. Vouchers were paid in the total amount of $178,000.

10. A physical inventory of $2,000 was taken on December 31, 19X1, and the city council directed that it be properly recorded. (Use the purchases method.) The $2,000 is applicable to General Administration.

11. Expenditures must be charged against appropriations of the year in which the expenditures are made. Any outstanding orders at year end must be honored, however, and are to be reported as fund balance reserves.

Required:

(a) Prepare a worksheet(s) that will show the Library Fund closing entries and balance sheet information at December 31, 19X1, and will summarize the information needed for the Statement of Revenues, Expenditures, and Changes in Total Fund Balance.

(b) Prepare the statements mentioned above.

Problem 6-7. Waynesville had the following General Fund trial balance on January 1, 19X1:

Cash	$ 7,000	
Taxes Receivable, Delinquent	48,000	
Allowance for Uncollectible Delinquent		
Taxes		$ 4,000
Due from Water Fund	500	
Vouchers Payable		11,000
Due to Taxpayers		1,000
Encumbrances	3,000	
Reserve for Encumbrances		3,000
Appropriations		3,000
Fund Balance		36,500
	$58,500	$58,500

The following information summarizes the transactions of the General Fund during 19X1:

1. The city council approved the following budget for 19X1:

Expenditures:		
City Manager	....	$20,000
Police Department	....	10,000
Fire Department	....	10,000
Streets and Roads	....	20,000
		$60,000

Revenues:

Property Taxes	$75,000
Fines and Fees	5,000
Miscellaneous	5,000
	$85,000

2. The council approved the levy of taxes in the amount of $75,000. It was estimated that $2,000 of the amount would never be collected.

3. Cash collected during the year may be summarized as follows:

Prior years' levies	$45,000
19X1 levy	46,000
Fines and fees	4,000
Taxes written off in prior years	500
Interest	500
Service charges	2,000
	$98,000

4. The council approved borrowing $5,000 on a 90-day note.

5. Orders placed during the year were as follows:

City Manager	$ 4,000
Police Department	3,000
Fire Department	3,000
Streets and Roads	5,000
	$15,000

6. Payrolls vouchered during the year were as follows:

City Manager	$15,000
Police Department	7,000
Fire Department	6,500
Streets and Roads	14,000
	$42,500

7. Invoices vouchered during the year are listed as follows:

City Manager	$ 4,500
Police Department	6,100
Fire Department	3,000
Streets and Roads	4,000
Repayment of note plus interest (see item 4)	5,200
	$22,800

The invoices above completed all orders except one dated June 1, 19X1, for an attachment for the road grader for $950.

8. Payments to other funds:

Fund	Purpose	Amount
Debt Service Fund	Provide for payment of bond principal and interest	$ 8,000
Capital Projects	City contribution to construction of city park facilities	15,000
Water Fund	Water supply for Streets and Roads Department	1,500
		$24,500

9. Analysis of collections revealed that taxpayer A, to whom the city owed $1,000 on January 1, 19X1, for overpayment of taxes, had paid his tax for 19X1 less $1,000.

10. The Streets and Roads Department rendered services in the amount of $250 to the Water Fund.

11. The city council made an additional appropriation in the amount of $5,000 (including $600 interest) for a long-term note maturity which was overlooked in preparing the budget.

12. The note matured and was vouchered.

13. Vouchers of $70,000 were paid.

14. Delinquent Taxes in the amount of $500 were written off on the authority of the council.

15. Current taxes became delinquent.

Required:

(a) Prepare a worksheet or worksheets summarizing the year's operations in such a way that the required statements may be easily prepared.

(b) Prepare the required closing entry(ies) for the General Ledger and Subsidiary Ledger accounts at year end.

(c) Prepare a Statement of Revenues, Expenditures, and Changes in (Unreserved) Fund Balance for the General Fund of Waynesville for the year ended December 31, 19X1.

Problem 6-8. The City of Bettinger's Bend General Fund had a beginning inventory of materials and supplies of $6,000. The beginning balance of Fund Balance Reserved for Inventory was also $6,000.

1. Materials and supplies costing $74,000 were ordered during the year.

2. The materials and supplies ordered were received; actual cost, $72,800.

3. According to the physical inventory, $5,400 of materials and supplies were on hand at year end.

Required:

(a) Prepare general journal entries to record the information above using the ***purchases*** method of accounting for inventories.

(b) Prepare general journal entries to record the information above using the **consumption** method assuming (1) a perpetual inventory system and (2) a periodic inventory system.

Problem 6-9. The City of Beverly Heights General Fund had the following transactions, among others, in 19X7:

1. Appropriations were made as follows:

Personal Services	$111,400
Contractual Services	8,700
Materials and Supplies	8,500
New Patrol Cars	21,000
Other	12,000
	$161,600

2. $2,000 of General Fund cash was paid to the Debt Service Fund to provide for debt service.

3. A long-term note of $8,300, including interest of $1,300, and a short-term note of $2,500 (including $150 interest) came due. The Beverly Heights Council had not made appropriations for these items. The necessary action was taken and the notes were repaid.

4. $100,000 of General Fund cash was paid to the Enterprise Fund to finance construction of a new auxiliary generator and $50,000 was contributed to establish a central motor pool facility. The Enterprise Fund will repay the General Fund in ten equal annual installments beginning January 1, 19X9.

5. The council increased the appropriation for personal services by $500.

6. Materials and supplies are accounted for on the purchase basis. The beginning inventory was $200; $8,500 of materials and supplies were ordered during the year. New patrol cars costing $20,000 were also ordered.

7. The following expenditures were made by the city:

Personal Services	$111,700	
Contractual Services	8,700	
Materials and Supplies	7,500	(encumbered for $7,600)
New Patrol Cars	21,200	(encumbered for $20,000)
Other	11,800	
	$160,900	

The council passed the amendments to its appropriations necessary to make the foregoing expenditures legal.

8. Materials and supplies on hand at year end amounted to $1,000.

Required:

(a) Prepare and post the general journal entries required to record the transactions in the General Ledger and in the Expenditure Ledger. Assume that there were no outstanding encumbrances at the beginning of 19X7.

(b) Prepare a trial balance of the Expenditure Ledger and prove its agreement with the control accounts.

(c) Prepare the general journal entries required to close the expenditure accounts in the General and Expenditure Ledgers. Assume that all appropriations lapse, but a reserve is reported for encumbrances outstanding at year end.

(d) Prepare the general journal entries required to close the expenditure accounts in the General and Expenditure Ledgers assuming that unexpended appropriations do not lapse.

(e) Repeat requirements (a)–(c) assuming (1) Beverly Heights uses the Expenditure and Other Outflow Ledger approach, (2) budgeted transfers for debt service were $12,000, and (3) budgeted transfers to establish a central motor pool facility were $60,000.

Problem 6-10. The Town of Dee's Junction General Fund was affected by the following transactions, among others, in 19X4:

1. Appropriations were made as follows:

Personal Services	$222,800
Contractual Services	17,400
Materials and Supplies	17,000
Firefighting Equipment	42,000
Other	24,000
	$323,200

The appropriation for materials and supplies covers a $1,800 order outstanding at the end of 19X3. An appropriate fund balance reserve is on the books.

January transactions (2–8):

2. Allotments for the month of January (fiscal year ends December 31) were:

Personal Services	$20,800
Contractual Services	1,600
Materials and Supplies	3,000
Firefighting Equipment	35,000
Other	500
	$60,900

3. $15,000 of General Fund cash was paid to the Debt Service Fund to provide for debt service.

4. The Dee's Junction Council amended the budget, increasing the contractual services appropriation by $5,000 and decreasing the materials and supplies appropriation by $1,700.

5. Materials and supplies of $200 were acquired for cash and $1,200 of supplies were ordered during January. Materials ordered in 19X3 were received on January 8 at their estimated cost of $1,800. Materials and supplies are accounted for on the purchases basis.

6. The supplies ordered were received, with an invoice for $1,180.

7. Firefighting equipment costing $35,000 was ordered.

8. Other expenditures during January 19X4 were:

Personal Services	$20,800
Firefighting Equipment (included in January order—estimated cost $31,800)	32,000
Other	400
	$53,200

February through December transactions (9–11):

9. Allotments for the remainder of the year were sharply reduced from the earlier plan because of financial difficulties:

Personal Services	$202,000
Contractual Services	15,800
Materials and Supplies	12,000
Firefighting Equipment	7,000
Other	11,500
	$248,300

10. Expenditures for the remainder of the year were:

Personal Services	$200,000
Contractual Services	12,000
Materials and Supplies	11,000
Firefighting equipment	1,000
Other	11,500
	$235,500

11. In addition to the encumbrances for firefighting equipment, encumbrances of $1,000 for materials and supplies and $2,000 for contractual services were outstanding at year end. The inventory of materials and supplies decreased by $1,100 during the year.

Required:

(a) Prepare the general journal entries to record the transactions in the General Ledger and in the Expenditure Ledger and post the Expenditure Ledger accounts.

(b) Prepare a trial balance of the January 31, 19X4, balances in the Expenditure Ledger. Show its agreement with the General Ledger control accounts.

(c) Prepare a preclosing trial balance of the year end balances in the Expenditure Ledger and show its agreement with the General Ledger control accounts.

(d) Prepare the general journal entries to close the expenditure accounts in the General and Expenditure Ledgers assuming that (1) all appropriations lapse and (2) a reserve is reported for encumbrances outstanding at year end.

(e) Repeat requirements (a)–(d) assuming that (1) Dee's Junction uses the Expenditure and Other Outflow Ledger approach, and (2) budgeted transfers for debt service were $15,000.

Problem 6-11. The bookkeeper for the Town of Hopper's Corner has accumulated the following information relating to the General Fund for the 19X0–19X1 fiscal year ending June 30, 19X1.

Source	Revenues	
	Estimated	Actual
General Property Taxes	$120,974	$121,000
Franchise Taxes	62,897	61,900
Licenses and Permits	17,934	18,000
Fines and Penalties	16,474	16,400
Interest Earnings	1,234	1,500
Contributions from Other Funds	8,736	8,700
Other	480	500
	$228,729	$228,000

Classification	Expenditures	
	Budgeted	Actual
Personal Services	$111,400	$111,200
Contractual Services	8,700	8,400
Materials and Supplies	8,500	8,500
Contributions to Other Funds	18,000	42,000
Capital Outlay	3,000	2,950
Debt Service	15,000	15,300
Other	850	800
	$165,450	$189,150

Further analysis of the Town of Hopper's Corner records revealed the following:

1. The amount listed as actual franchise taxes includes $1,500 of 19X1–19X2 taxes levied on July 15, 19X1, and due July 31, 19X1.
2. Actual "Contributions from Other Funds" were:
   a. $2,000 received from a department financed by an Internal Service Fund for charges for services rendered by a department financed by the General Fund.
   b. $3,700 from a discontinued Capital Projects Fund.
   c. A $1,000 payment in lieu of taxes from an Enterprise Fund.
   d. $2,000 of Enterprise Fund cash contributed to subsidize operations financed by the General Fund.
3. Actual "Contractual Services" expenditures include $1,000 encumbered at year end for contractual services. Other encumbrances outstanding at June 30, 19X1, totaled $1,500.
4. Hopper's Corner records and reports actual "Materials and Supplies" expenditures when the goods are acquired rather than when they are used. Materials and Supplies Inventory increased by $500 during the 19X0–19X1 fiscal year.
5. Actual "Contributions to Other Funds" consists of General Fund cash used to expand the operating capacity of an Internal Service Fund. $20,000 is to be repaid to the General Fund on June 30, 19X5; the remainder is not intended to be repaid.
6. Actual "Debt Service" expenditures listed by the bookkeeper includes a $7,000 payment of principal on a 90-day note which matured June 1, 19X1, plus the related interest and $8,000 contributed to a Debt Service Fund through which the town's general obligation term bonds (due in 19Y9 will be repaid).

7. The July 1, 19X0 Fund Balance of the Hopper's Corner General Fund included:

Fund Balance Reserved for:
Encumbrances	$ 2,000
Inventory	3,000
Interfund Advances	22,000
Total Fund Balance Reserves	$27,000
Unreserved Fund Balance	$84,000

8. The June 30, 19X1 balance of Fund Balance Reserved for Advances is $19,000, and the balance of Fund Balance Reserved for Encumbrances is $1,500.

Required:

(a) Prepare a Statement of Revenues, Expenditures, and Changes in *(Total)* Fund Balance for the Town of Hopper's Corner General Fund for the year ended June 30, 19X1. Show supporting computations in good form.

(b) How would the statement prepared in (a) differ if it reported changes in unreserved fund balance?

Problem 6-12. (Review Problem) The City of K has adopted the following General Fund budget for its 19X5 fiscal year, beginning February 1, 19X4:

Estimated revenues, $790,000, consisting of the following:
Real property taxes	$390,000
Interest on investments	2,000
Motor vehicle licenses and fees	20,000
Portion of sales tax to be received from state	10,000
Interest on bank deposits	500
Grants-in-aid to be received from state	5,000
Other revenues	169,500
Court fines	5,000
Personal property taxes	140,000
Income taxes	25,000
Alcoholic beverage licenses	15,000
Interest and penalties on taxes	5,000
Building permits	3,000
	$790,000

Appropriations, $787,000, consisting of the following:
Civil Service Commission	$ 5,000
Department of Police—Bureau of Uniformed Patrol	40,000
Department of Fire—Bureau of Fire Fighting	40,000
Court	20,000
Department of Police—Bureau of Supervision	20,000
Department of Police—Bureau of Communication System	20,000
Interest	40,000
Department of Fire—Bureau of Supervision	15,000
Board of Elections	5,000
Department of Law	25,000
Department of Fire—Bureau of Prevention	20,000

Retirement of Bonds	100,000
Department of Finance—Bureau of Administration	10,000
Department of Finance—Bureau of Purchases	6,000
City Clerk	10,000
Department of Finance—Bureau of Accounts	15,000
Mayor	15,000
Department of Finance—Bureau of Assessment ...	15,000
Department of Fire—Bureau of Training	10,000
Department of Police—Bureau of Criminal Investigation	20,000
Department of Police—Bureau of Police Training	8,000
Department of Finance—Bureau of Treasury	8,000
City Council	20,000
All Other Departments	300,000
	$787,000

Required:

(a) Prepare a journal entry to record the adoption of the General Fund budget, showing both the General Ledger accounts and all the Subsidiary Ledger accounts involved, the latter properly classified.

(b) Post the General Ledger accounts to T-accounts.

(c) Post the estimated revenues for Real Property Taxes to a revenue account similar to the account illustrated in Figure 5-9.

(d) Post the appropriations for the City Clerk to an appropriation account similar to the account illustrated in Figure 6-2.

Problem 6-13. (Comprehensive Review Problem) The Oakleysborough General Fund trial balance at July 1, 19X8, is presented below:

OAKLEYSBOROUGH

General Fund
Trial Balance
at July 1, 19X8

	Debit	Credit
Cash	$ 65,000	
Taxes receivable—delinquent	300,000	
Allowance for uncollectible delinquent taxes .		$ 25,000
Material and supplies inventory (public works)	22,000	
Due from other funds	6,000	
Advances to other funds	25,000	
Vouchers payable		212,000
Taxes collected in advance		13,200
Due to other funds		15,700
Reserve for inventories		22,000
Reserve for encumbrances		19,000
Reserve for advances		25,000
Fund balance		86,100
	$418,000	$418,000

1. The budget was passed as follows:

Estimated Revenues:
Taxes	$1,500,000
Interest and penalties	18,000
Permits and licenses	150,000
Fines and forfeitures	80,000
Intergovernmental grant	300,000
Charges for services	20,000
Other revenue	8,000
	$2,076,000

Appropriations:
General government	$ 200,000
Public safety	870,000
Public works	500,000
Health and welfare	297,000
Other functions	190,000
Capital outlay	30,000
Grants to special districts	10,000
	$2,097,000

2. Taxes for 19X8–19X9 were levied. The total levy was $1,575,000 with estimated discounts of $23,000 and estimated uncollectible taxes of $52,000.

3. Encumbrances were established against the various appropriations as follows:

General government	$ 20,000
Public safety	131,000
Public works	200,000
Health and welfare	60,000
Other functions	19,000
Capital outlay—for furniture and equipment	30,000
	$460,000

4. $20,000 was received from the Special Assessment Fund to repay an advance made by the General Fund three years ago.

5. Tax collections for the year were $1,580,000 (including $280,000 of delinquent taxes). Discounts of $22,000 were taken before the discount period expired. $15,000 of interest and penalties were collected on the delinquent taxes.

6. The remaining 19X8–19X9 taxes became delinquent.

7. Salaries and wages (which were not encumbered) paid during the year totaled $1,597,400, as follows:

General government	$ 153,400
Public safety	739,000
Public works	298,000
Health and welfare	237,000
Other functions	170,000
	$1,597,400

8. Orders placed in April 19X8 and encumbered at year end were received and invoices were approved for payment. The total cost, $19,300, was charged to the general government function.

9. Tax liens were formalized against properties with back taxes of $8,200 and related interest and penalties of $400. The estimated fair market value of the properties is $9,400.

10. Items encumbered during the year that were received by year end and vouchered are listed below:

	Amount of:	
	Encumbrance	Expenditure
General government	$ 18,000	$ 18,200
Public safety	115,000	113,400
Public works	200,000	200,000
Health and welfare	51,000	54,500
Other functions	18,000	17,100
Capital outlay	30,000	29,800
	$432,000	$433,000

11. Grants of $10,000 were awarded to special districts serving the Oakleysborough area.

12. Other collections during the year were:

Permits and licenses	$147,000
Fines and forfeitures	81,000
Intergovernmental grants	450,000
Charges for services	18,000
Other revenues	1,200
	$697,200

(The intergovernmental grants must be expended for the designated purposes or refunded to the grantors. Oakleysborough expenditures included $291,000 of qualifying expenditures which are included in amounts noted earlier. It is anticipated that the remaining grant funds will be used over the next year and a half. Nothing is expected to be refunded to the grantors.)

13. The council approved the issue of a five-year note of $100,000. The proceeds of the note were used to establish an Internal Service Fund, and the note will be serviced through the General Fund.

14. Other interfund transactions included the following:

Fund	Purpose	Amount
Capital Projects	General Fund contributions to project	($20,000)
Enterprise	Payment in lieu of taxes	78,000
Debt Service	Provide for debt service	(15,000)
Special Revenue	Repay short-term loan	(15,700)
	Reimburse General Fund expenditures for special health and welfare purposes	18,000

Fund	Purpose	Amount
Special Assessment	To cover General Fund expenditures (for general government purposes) originally recorded by and paid from Special Assessment Fund	(3,500)

15. All but $150,200 of vouchers payable were paid.
16. The year-end physical inventory of materials and supplies amounted to $18,200. (The consumption method is used to account for Oakleysborough inventories.)
17. $2,000 of 19X9–19Y0 taxes were collected.

Required:

(a) Prepare the general journal entries needed to record the transactions above in the General Ledger and Subsidiary Ledgers.
(b) Establish the necessary General Ledger "T" accounts for the Oakleysborough General Fund.
(c) Post the transactions in both the General Ledger and the Subsidiary Ledger(s) accounts.
(d) Prepare a General Ledger preclosing trial balance and reconcile the Subsidiary Ledger accounts with the General Ledger control accounts.
(e) Prepare general journal entries to close the General Ledger and Subsidiary Ledger accounts assuming all appropriations lapse at year end but the Reserve for Encumbrances account is not to be closed.
(f) Prepare a balance sheet for the Oakleysborough General Fund at June 30, 19X9.
(g) Prepare a Statement of Revenues, Expenditures, and Changes in Unreserved Fund Balance for the Oakleysborough General Fund for the 19X8–X9 fiscal year.

[Note: Appropriate worksheets may be prepared to satisfy requirements (a)–(d).]

7

CAPITAL PROJECTS FUNDS

Capital Projects Funds are established to account for resources that are to be used to acquire major long-lived capital facilities. Their principal purpose is to assure the economical and legal expenditure of the resources, but they also serve as cost accounting mechanisms for the accumulation of the cost of major capital outlay projects.

Not all fixed asset acquisitions are financed through Capital Projects Funds. Fixed assets of limited cost may be acquired with resources of almost any fund; and major fixed assets may be financed by proprietary funds, Special Assessment Funds, and Trust Funds. Major fixed assets also may be acquired through the General or Special Revenue Funds when long-term debt or special purpose grants are not involved. Since the accounting systems of Capital Projects Funds are designed to control the expenditure of resources for major assets, it may be desirable to transfer resources of General nd Special Revenue Funds to Capital Projects Funds rather than to account for their expenditure through systems oriented to current operations.

Similarly, not all bond issue proceeds are accounted for in Capital Projects Funds. The NCGA recommends that the proceeds of long-term debt issues should be accounted for in the following funds:

- Proceeds that are to be used to acquire capital assets should be accounted for in a Capital Projects Fund.
- Proceeds of refunding issues should be accounted for in a Debt Service Fund.
- Proceeds of issues of proprietary, Special Assessment, and Trust Funds should be accounted for in those funds because such liabilities are the primary responsibility of and will be serviced by the issuing funds.

The NCGA recommendations are silent with respect to debt issued for other

258

purposes. It seems appropriate for proceeds of debt issued to fund a deficit to be accounted for in the fund that has the deficit. It would seem that the proceeds of debt issued to provide disaster relief might properly be accounted for in Capital Projects or Special Revenue Funds, or even the General Fund.

SOURCES OF RESOURCES

Typical sources of Capital Projects Fund resources are bond or other long-term general obligation debt issues, grants or shared revenues from other governments dedicated to the acquisition of fixed assets, transfers from other funds, and interest from temporary investments. The classification of resource inflows is significant for reporting purposes because the government as a whole should be considered the entity for which reports are made. Capital Projects Fund inflows from intergovernmental grants and from interest on investments should be considered revenue. But two typical sources do not represent revenues to the government as a whole: (1) Interfund transfers should be classified as operating transfers (or as residual equity transfers if appropriate), and (2) proceeds of the issue of long-term debt should be labeled as what they are, since from the standpoint of the government as a whole they cannot be viewed as revenue. Operating transfers and bond issue proceeds are reported in the "Other Financing Sources" section of the Capital Projects Fund statement of revenues, expenditures, and changes in fund balance.

NUMBER OF FUNDS REQUIRED

Separate Capital Projects Funds are usually established for each project or debt issue because the nature of such projects varies widely, they typically involve significant amounts of resources, they are usually budgeted on an individual project or debt issue basis, and legal and contractual requirements differ significantly among such projects. Where debt issues or grants are involved, a major purpose of the Capital Projects Fund is to show that the proceeds were used only for authorized purposes and that unexpended balances or deficits have been handled in accordance with applicable contractual agreements or legal provisions. A single Capital Projects Fund will suffice, however, where a single debt issue is used to finance several projects or a series of closely related projects is financed through a single grant or by internal transfers from the General or Special Revenue Funds. Combining statements are used to present financial operation or position data where a government has more than one Capital Projects Fund in operation during a given year.

CAPITAL PROJECTS FUND LIFE CYCLE

A Capital Projects Fund is authorized by action of the legislative body on either the project or debt issue. The accrual and inflows, expenditures and encumbrances, and balances of project-related resources are then recorded in the Fund accounting records. The Fund is abolished at the conclusion of the project and the accounting records retained to evidence the fiscal stewardship of the government.

THE BUDGET

The projects financed through Capital Projects Funds are usually planned in the government's long-term capital budget. The case illustration in this chapter assumes that full budgetary control is desirable, but there are cases in which control is provided without the budgetary process. Reasons for not budgeting include (1) projects are appropriated on a project rather than on an annual basis; (2) control is provided by specifications, bids, inspections, and the like; and (3) only one project is financed from a single fund. On the other hand, budgetary control is important where several projects are accounted for through a single CPF, where the government budgets the CPF in detail, and where the CPF is budgeted annually.

COSTS CHARGED TO PROJECTS

All expenditures necessary to bring the facility in question to a state of readiness for its intended purpose are properly chargeable as Capital Projects Fund costs. In addition to the direct cost of items such as land, buildings, materials, and labor, total project cost would therefore include such related items as engineering and architect fees, transportation costs, damages occasioned by the project, and other costs associated with the endeavor.

Although it may be contended that a share of general government overhead is a proper project cost, it is rarely charged to the project unless it is reimbursable, such as under terms of the grant through which the project is financed. Where costs such as overhead are reimbursable, the reimbursable amount is frequently calculated in accordance with a predetermined formula rather than by being derived from cost accounting or similar records.

This is not to say that no overhead costs are charged to the project unless reimbursable. Overhead is charged to the project, for example, to the extent that such costs are included in charges for goods or services provided for the project through Internal Service Funds. Because of past manipulation abuses, however, and since intergovernmental grants are often intended only to supplement existing resources, charges for overhead may be specifically excluded from "project cost" as defined by statute, contractual agreement, or administrative determination.

Interest incurred on debt during the construction of a project has not usually been recorded as a project cost, but in *Statement 1* the NCGA said that: "The accounting policy with respect to capitalization of interest costs incurred during construction should be disclosed and consistently applied."[1]

In recent years it has been possible for governments to earn substantial interest by investing idle cash. If the bonds to finance a project are sold at the beginning of the project, interest revenue will at least partially offset interest expenditures. The NCGA favored the net method (expenditures less revenues)

[1] NCGAS 1, p. 10.

of determining amounts to be capitalized in the General Fixed Assets Account Group, but it did not issue a pronouncement on the matter. FASB *Statement 62* specifies the net method of interest capitalization where tax exempt debt issues are involved.[2] Its major impact is on proprietary fund and GFA interest capitalization, however; it does not directly affect amounts reported as CPF interest expenditures or project costs.

In general a Debt Service Fund will be responsible for payment of interest, while bond proceeds will be recorded in, and perhaps invested in, the Capital Projects Fund. Thus, the accountant for the government may have to collect data from two sources to determine the net addition to the cost of the projects arising from interest capitalization.

ESTABLISHMENT OF FUND

In the following illustration a $400,000 project has been authorized, to be financed from four sources: A General Fund transfer of $50,000, a county contribution of $50,000, a Federal grant of $200,000, and a bond issue of $100,000. No formal journal entry is needed or recommended to record the authorization; a narrative memorandum entry is sufficient.

If the number or complexity of projects, project details, or financing sources justify budgetary accounting, the following entry will be made:

(A)	Estimated Revenue from County Contributions	50,000	
	Estimated Revenue from Federal Grant	200,000	
	Estimated Operating Transfer from General Fund	50,000	
	Estimated Bond Issue Proceeds	100,000	
	Appropriations		400,000
	To record the budget.		

If there had been a difference between the debits and credits of the entry above, Fund Balance (or Budgetary Fund Balance) would have received the difference.

The accrual and receipt of assets, as planned except that the bonds were sold at a premium of $1,000, are summarized as follows:

(B)	Cash	101,000	
	Due from County	50,000	
	Due from Federal Government	200,000	
	Due from General Fund	50,000	
	Revenue from County Contribution		50,000
	Revenue from Federal Grant		200,000
	Operating Transfer from General Fund		50,000
	Bond Issue Proceeds		101,000
	To record receipt of bond proceeds and accrual of assets, revenues, and other financing sources.		

[2] Financial Accounting Standards Board, *Statement of Financial Accounting Standards No. 62,* "Capitalization of Interest Cost in Situations Involving Certain Tax-Exempt Borrowings and Certain Gifts and Grants" (Stamford: FASB, June 1982).

Since grants and shared revenues from other governments are revenues, they are subject to the modified accrual basis specified by the NCGA for governmental funds. To be recognized as revenues, they must be both measurable and available. These two qualities are determined by the legal and contractual requirements of each case. Two grants are illustrated in this chapter; their restrictions are assumed to be such that the grant commitments may be treated as assets and revenues.

Some contributions from one government to another must be earned by the grantee's incurring of expenditures that qualify under the terms of the grant or other contribution. If at the time of the receipt of resources appropriate expenditures have not been made (the usual case), recognition of the asset results in deferral of the related revenue. As appropriate expenditures are made, revenue is recognized. In any case in which the assets should not be recognized, the potential resources should be disclosed in notes to the financial statements. Accounting for contractual or legal arrangements of this type is illustrated in Chapter 9.

In the preceding journal entry bond premium was included with bond proceeds. In theory premium is, of course, a factor in determining interest expense; since interest on the bonds will be paid by a Debt Service Fund, the authors believe the premium (and any payment received for accrued interest) should be transferred to that fund. Indeed, premiums and interest received upon bond issuance are sometimes recorded directly in a Debt Service Fund. In such cases a clear audit trail should be maintained.

A discount on issuance of bonds must usually be written off because of legal or financial difficulties that prevent transfer of money from other funds to offset the discount. If the amount of the discount is not offset by the acquisition of resources (from other funds, for example, or from interest earned on temporary investments of the Capital Projects Fund), the project authorization must be reduced.

Laws or contracts will determine the disposition of any balance remaining unused in the Capital Projects Fund at completion of its mission. It may, for example, have to be refunded on a pro rata basis to the grantors who participated in financing the project. The city's portion is usually transferred to the fund that will service and pay off debt created to finance the project (usually a Debt Service Fund). If the premium is kept in the Capital Projects Fund in conformity with legal or debt indenture requirements, it will, if unused, be transferred to a Debt Service Fund as the balance of the Capital Projects Fund is closed out.

THE OPERATING CYCLE

As noted earlier, a Capital Projects Fund continues in existence until its projects are completed and the related resources have been expended or transferred to other funds.

In extremely simple situations, such as where the project consists of purchasing existing facilities for a single payment or transferring resources to another fund (e.g., to finance a deficit or establish an Enterprise Fund), the life of the

Capital Projects Fund may be brief and its entries uncomplicated: (1) Receipts of all resources will occur and revenues or other financing sources will be credited, (2) Expenditures will be recorded and paid for, (3) the temporary fund balance accounts will be closed to Unreserved Fund Balance, and (4) any remaining resources and the balance of the Fund will be closed out as the assets are transferred to another fund (or disposed of in some other way as required by law or contract).

In other cases, however, a Capital Projects Fund is used to finance construction projects where the government acts as a general contractor, possibly using its own employees and equipment for part or all of the work. In this situation accounting procedures are more complicated and closely resemble those of the General Fund.

CAPITAL PROJECTS FUND CASE ILLUSTRATION

Typical Capital Projects Fund transactions and entries will now be illustrated through use of an extended case example. Only general ledger accounts are used in the illustration, though one or more subsidiary ledgers may be employed if warranted by a need for more detailed data. The following trial balance of the Bridge Capital Projects Fund is based on the assumptions that the preceding journal entries A and B have been posted and that cash has been collected in full from the General Fund, the County, and the Federal government.

Cash	401,000	
Estimated Revenue from County Contribution	50,000	
Estimated Revenue from Federal Grant	200,000	
Estimated Operating Transfer from General Fund	50,000	
Estimated Bond Issue Proceeds	100,000	
Revenue from County Contribution		50,000
Revenue from Federal Grant		200,000
Operating Transfer from General Fund		50,000
Bond Issue Proceeds		101,000
Appropriations		400,000
	801,000	801,000

Transactions and Entries—First Fiscal Year

Let us assume that this project involves a bridge to be constructed partly by a contractor and partly by city labor.

A contract is entered into with Jones & Company for construction of certain parts of the bridge, at an estimated cost of $300,000.

(1)	Encumbrances	300,000	
	Reserve for Encumbrances		300,000
	To record encumbrance for contract let.		

Orders were placed for materials estimated to cost $5,000.

(2)	Encumbrances	5,000	
	Reserve for Encumbrances		5,000
	To record encumbrances for orders placed.		

Payroll, $16,000, was paid.

(3)	Expenditures	16,000	
	Cash		16,000
	To record payment of payroll.		

A bill for $120,000 was received from Jones & Company for part of the work.

(4)	Reserve for Encumbrances	120,000	
	Encumbrances		120,000
	To record reversal of a part of the encumbrance for the contract.		
(5)	Expenditures	120,000	
	Contracts Payable		120,000
	To record expenditures.		

The materials previously ordered were received; the bill was for $4,800.

(6)	Reserve for Encumbrances	5,000	
	Encumbrances		5,000
	To reverse entry setting up encumbrances.		
(7)	Expenditures	4,800	
	Vouchers payable		4,800
	To record expenditures.		

Payment of $120,000 was made to Jones & Company.

(8)	Contracts Payable	120,000	
	Cash		120,000
	To record payment on contract.		

An order estimated to cost $12,000 was placed.

(9)	Encumbrances	12,000	
	Reserve for Encumbrances		12,000
	To record encumbrances on order placed.		

The premium from the bond issue was remitted to a Debt Service Fund because the DSF will pay the interest on the debt.

(10) Operating Transfer to DSF 1,000
    Cash 1,000
    To transfer the premium on bonds
    to a Debt Service Fund.

Preclosing Trial Balance

Upon posting the numbered entries above to the Capital Projects Fund accounts, the following unadjusted, preclosing trial balance could be drawn at the close of the first year's activities:

Cash	264,000	
Vouchers Payable		4,800
Reserve for Encumbrances		192,000
Estimated Revenue from Federal Grant	200,000	
Estimated Revenue from County Contribution	50,000	
Estimated Bond Issue Proceeds	100,000	
Estimated Operating Transfer from GF	50,000	
Bond Issue Proceeds		101,000
Revenue from Federal Grant		200,000
Revenue from County Contribution		50,000
Operating Transfer from GF		50,000
Appropriations		400,000
Encumbrances	192,000	
Expenditures	140,800	
Operating Transfer to DSF	1,000	
	997,800	997,800

Adjusting Entries—Project Incomplete

The accounts should be adjusted, as appropriate, prior to preparation of year-end statements. Most of the usual types of adjusting entries have already been presented and need not be discussed again here. One problem warrants special attention, however, as it is unique to project- and purpose-oriented funds such as Capital Projects and Special Assessment Funds.

If expenditures as of the end of the period in which the project is incomplete exceed the sum of revenues and other financing sources, or even if expenditures plus encumbrances are greater, the (Unreserved) Fund Balance will show a deficit. For example, if in the foregoing case the bond issue had not yet been sold at year end, the sum of expenditures and encumbrances, $332,800, would exceed the sum of revenues and the transfer from the General Fund, $300,000. The effect of this temporary deficit, if indeed it is temporary, on the reader can be ameliorated by full footnote disclosure of appropriations, encumbrances, and the financing source that is expected to eliminate the deficit.

Closing Entries—Project Incomplete

The Capital Projects Fund, unlike the General Fund, has a natural life cycle determined by the life of the project. General Fund appropriations are typically limited by time; those of the Capital Projects Fund normally continue until the project is complete. But when a year end occurs before the project is completed, reporting must occur. Should closing entries be prepared? The preferred approach is to close. Closing facilitates the summarization of operating results to date and the Fund's financial status at year end, and closing the Expenditures account annually signals the need to capitalize cost of construction (or acquisition) in the General Fixed Assets Account Group. The most logical set of entries appears to be the following:

(C1)	Revenue from County Contribution	50,000	
	Revenue from Federal Grant	200,000	
	Operating Transfer from General Fund	50,000	
	Bond Issue Proceeds	101,000	
	Estimated Revenue from County Contribution		50,000
	Estimated Revenue from Federal Grant		200,000
	Estimated Operating Transfer from General Fund		50,000
	Estimated Bond Issue Proceeds		100,000
	Fund Balance		1,000
	To close the revenue and other financing sources accounts.		
(C2)	Appropriations	140,800	
	Fund Balance	1,000	
	Expenditures		140,800
	Operating Transfer to Debt Service Fund		1,000
	To close expenditures and other financing uses accounts.		

This set of closing entries disposes of the Revenue and other financing sources accounts and closes the Expenditures and Operating Transfer to Debt Service Fund accounts. Equally important, it leaves the continuing appropriation on the books, together with the memorandum Encumbrances and Reserve for Encumbrances accounts. The Appropriations account is, of course, an Appropriated Fund Balance account.

Major Statements at Close of the Fiscal Year— Project Incomplete

If the journal entries illustrated thus far are posted to the accounts, the statements in Figures 7-1 and 7-2 can be prepared.

Note particularly that neither the long-term debt incurred to finance the project nor the fixed assets acquired thereby appear in Capital Projects Fund balance sheet. The long-term debt is recorded in the General Long-Term Debt Account Group upon incurrence; fixed assets are capitalized at year end in the General Fixed Assets Account Group.

In some cases bond anticipation notes are issued for periods of over one year in the expectation that bond interest rates will decline in the future. In such cases it is proper to record the note liability in the General Long-Term Debt Account Group. When the bonds are issued, they should be considered a refunding issue. The proceeds should be handled through a Debt Service Fund, where they will be expended to retire the notes.

Revenues and expenditures should be itemized in appropriate detail in either the Statement of Revenues, Expenditures, and Changes in Fund Balance or in schedules cross-referenced to that statement. Supplementary schedules should use the same column headings as the master statement.

Note that the format of Figure 7-2 is not the only one that may be used. Refer to the alternative formats of the Statement of Revenues, Expenditures, and Changes in Fund Balance presented in Chapter 4. The authors believe that the format of Figure 7-2 is the most appropriate, however, since it groups and summarizes the sources of project resources.

Figure 7-1

A GOVERNMENTAL UNIT
Bridge Capital Projects Fund
Balance Sheet
At Close of Fiscal Year (Date)
(Project Incomplete)

Assets

Cash		$264,000

Liabilities and Fund Balance

Liabilities:		
Vouchers payable		$ 4,800
Fund balance, fully appropriated:		
Reserved for encumbrances	$192,000	
Unencumberered	67,200	$259,200
		$264,000

Transactions and Entries—Second Fiscal Year

To conclude the illustration, let us assume that the project was completed in the next fiscal year. Since unexpended appropriations have not lapsed and were not closed out last year, they are on the books at the beginning of the second year of project life to authorize expenditures. The encumbrances that were not fulfilled in the first year are still in effect and were left on the books with their related Reserve for Encumbrances by last year's closing entries. No entries, then, were needed to establish, or reestablish, these account balances. The Second

Figure 7-2

A GOVERNMENTAL UNIT

Bridge Capital Projects Fund
Statement of Revenues, Expenditures, and
Changes in Fund Balance
For the Fiscal Year Ended (Date)
(Project Incomplete)

	Budget	Actual	Variance— Favorable (Unfavorable)
Revenues and other financing sources:			
Revenues:			
County contribution	$ 50,000	$ 50,000	$ -0-
Federal grant	200,000	200,000	-0-
Total revenues	$250,000	$250,000	$ -0-
Other financing sources:			
Transfer from General Fund	$ 50,000	$ 50,000	$ -0-
Proceeds of general obligation bond issue ...	100,000	101,000	1,000
Total other financing sources	$150,000	$151,000	$ 1,000
Total revenues and other financing sources	$400,000	$401,000	$ 1,000
Expenditures and other financing uses:			
Expenditures	$400,000	$140,800	$259,200
Transfer to Debt Service Fund	-0-	1,000	(1,000)
Total expenditures and other financing uses	$400,000	$141,800	$258,200
Excess of revenues and other financing sources over expenditures and other financing uses	$ -0-	$259,200	$259,200
Fund balance, beginning of year	-0-	-0-	-0-
Fund balance, end of year, fully appropriated	$ -0-	$259,200	$259,200

Note: It has been assumed in this case that the GAAP and budgetary bases coincide. If they do not, then both GAAP-basis and budgetary-basis statements are needed.

Fiscal Year transactions or events, and the corresponding entries, were as follows:

The materials ordered were received with an invoice for $12,400.

(11) Reserve for Encumbrances   12,000
          Encumbrances   12,000
      To reverse entry setting up
      encumbrances.

(12) Expenditures   12,400
          Vouchers Payable   12,400
      To record expenditures.

Jones & Company completed its part of the work; its bill was for $180,000.

(13)	Reserve for Encumbrances	180,000	
	Encumbrances		180,000
	To reverse remaining encumbrances.		
(14)	Expenditures	180,000	
	Contracts Payable		180,000
	To record expenditures.		

Total additional payments for labor amounted to $60,000.

(15)	Expenditures	60,000	
	Cash		60,000
	To record expenditures.		

Jones & Company's bill was paid, except for 5 percent of the total contract, which was retained pending inspection and final approval of the completed project.

(16)	Contracts Payable	180,000	
	Contracts Payable—Retained Percentage		15,000
	Cash		165,000
	To record payment of the contract less retained percentage of 5 percent of the total contract.		

All other outstanding bills were paid.

(17)	Vouchers Payable	17,200	
	Cash		17,200
	To record payment of vouchers.		

Closing Entry—Project Completed

When the project is completed, the budgetary and other temporary fund balance accounts are closed as follows:

(C)	Appropriations	259,200	
	Expenditures		252,400
	Fund Balance		6,800
	To close the temporary fund balance accounts.		

Balance Sheet—Project Completed

After the entries above have been posted, the balance sheet in Figure 7-3 can be prepared.

Note again that the resulting fixed assets are not set up in the Capital Projects Fund even when the project is completed. Instead, as already indicated, they are shown as part of the General Fixed Assets Account Group. Again, bonds payable are not shown in the Capital Projects Fund balance sheet but are carried as part of the General Long-Term Debt accounts.

Since the project is completed, the Fund has accomplished its purpose.

Figure 7-3

A GOVERNMENTAL UNIT

Bridge Capital Projects Fund
Balance Sheet
During, or at Close of, Fiscal Year (Date)
(Project Completed)

Assets

Cash $21,800

Liabilities and Fund Balance

Contracts payable—retained percentage $15,000
Fund balance 6,800
$21,800

From the above Balance Sheet (Figure 7-3) it is evident that, were it not for the fund balance, the Fund could be abolished as soon as the completed project was approved and the retained percentage on the contract paid.

Disposing of Fund Balance or Deficit

Frequently, the legislative body specifies what shall be done with the fund balance. In the absence of legislative restrictions, however, the balance is usually transferred to the Debt Service Fund from which the bonds or other related debt will be retired. The rationale for such action is that the balance arose because project expenditure requirements were overestimated, with the result that a larger amount than necessary was borrowed. Where resources were provided by intergovernmental grants or intragovernmental transfers, it may be either necessary or appropriate to refund a portion of these resources in disposing of the fund balance.

If we assume that the completed project was approved and that it was decided that contract and grant terms permitted a "residual equity transfer" of the fund balance to a Debt Service Fund, the following entries would be made to close out the Bridge Capital Projects Fund:

(18) Contracts Payable—Retained
Percentage 15,000
Cash 15,000
To record payment of the portion
of contracts payable held to
guarantee completion of the
project.

(19) Fund Balance 6,800
Cash 6,800
To record the transfer of the
Fund's residual equity to the
DSF.

In lieu of journal entry (19), the following entries might have been made:

Residual Equity Transfer to DSF	6,800	
Cash		6,800
To record the transfer of the residual equity.		
Fund Balance	6,800	
Residual Equity Transfer to DSF		6,800
To close the Residual Equity Transfer account.		

Government managers are well advised to provide in project authorizations, bond indentures, or otherwise for the possibility that costs have been overestimated and a fund balance might need to be disposed of at the conclusion of the project. In the absence of written authorization to rebate unneeded monies or transfer them to the related Debt Service Fund, officials may be precluded from doing so and forced to hold them, possibly indefinitely, until they are needed for the express purpose for which they were secured. Such situations have arisen occasionally, for example, in cases in which money was borrowed "for the sole and exclusive purpose of extending existing waterlines and no other purposes." Should the waterlines now extend well beyond the urban area and a fund balance remain, it is obviously preferable to transfer or rebate the unneeded balance rather than be forced to retain the money—possibly without even being able to invest it if the terms cited above are literally interpreted—until such time as population growth might justify further waterline expansion.

A Capital Projects Fund deficit would ordinarily be disposed of in one of two ways. If small, it would probably be eliminated by transferring money from the General Fund; if large, it would probably be disposed of by additional borrowing.

Operating Statement—Project Completed

The major operating statement for Capital Projects Funds is the Statement of Revenues, Expenditures, and Changes in Fund Balance. A statement similar to Figure 7-4 would be prepared if we assume that transactions 11-19 occurred in the second year of the Bridge Fund's life. The residual equity transfer illustrated in Figure 7-4 was assumed to occur at *year end* after the amount of the (unused) fund balance was determined. Such transfers probably occur most often *during* a fiscal year and then clearly should be deducted from the beginning of the year fund balance in the statement, as illustrated in the alternative treatment for Figure 7-4.

Compare the format of Figure 7-4 with that of Figure 7-2. Although any of the formats illustrated in Chapter 4 for the Statement of Revenues, Expenditures, and Changes in Fund Balance would be acceptable here, the format of Figure 7-2 has the advantage of producing a subtotal of total resources available.

Figure 7-4

A GOVERNMENTAL UNIT

Bridge Capital Projects Fund
Statement of Revenues, Expenditures, and Changes in Fund Balance
For the Fiscal Year Ended (Date)
(Project Complete)

	Budget	Actual	Variance—Favorable (Unfavorable)
Fund balance, beginning of year, fully appropriated:			
Reserved for encumbrances	$192,000	$192,000	$ -0-
Unreserved	67,200	67,200	-0-
Total	$259,200	$259,200	$ -0-
Revenues	-0-	-0-	-0-
Total financial resources available	$259,200	$259,200	$ -0-
Expenditures	259,200	252,400	6,800
Fund balance, end of year, before transfer ...	$ -0-	$ 6,800	$ 6,800
Transfer to Debt Service Fund	-0-	6,800	(6,800)
Fund balance, end of year	$ -0-	$ -0-	$ -0-

INVESTMENT OF IDLE CASH

Significant sums of cash are commonly involved in capital project fiscal management. Cash receipt, investment, and disbursement therefore warrant careful planning, timing, and control.

Prudent financial management typically requires that loan transactions not be closed (and interest charges begun) until the cash is needed. There often are exceptions to this rule, of course, as in cases where investments yield the government more than enough to cover the related interest costs. Similarly, significant sums should not be permitted to remain on demand deposit, but should be invested until such time as they are to be disbursed.[3]

Both the authority to invest idle cash and the disposition of investment earnings should be agreed upon and documented in the project authorization ordinance and in contractual agreements. Investment earnings might be used, for example, to reduce the government's share of the project cost or to increase the project expenditure authorization. Where monies have been borrowed and interest expenditures are being incurred, however, investment earnings should normally be transferred to the appropriate Debt Service Fund.

[3] Note the discussion of Section 130, Internal Revenue Code, in footnote 13 of Chapter 5.

FINANCING SEVERAL PROJECTS THROUGH ONE FUND

Earlier in this chapter it was noted that a single Capital Projects Fund may be used to finance several projects where only one debt issue or grant is involved or the projects are financed through internal transfers from other funds. For example, the capital project may consist of several "general improvements," possibly financed through a general obligation bond issue. Each project undertaken may be separately budgeted in such cases and, in any event, each must be separately controlled and accounted for within the CPF accounts.

Separate project control and accounting within a single CPF is best done by using Appropriations, Expenditures, and Encumbrances control accounts and a set of appropriately named subsidiary ledger accounts. Accounting for this type of fund corresponds with procedures discussed above.

Financial statements for a multiproject fund should show data for each project. If assets, liabilities, and fund balance are identified by projects, the balance sheet may be presented in this columnar form:

A GOVERNMENTAL UNIT

Capital Projects Fund
Balance Sheet
(Date)

Total	Completed Projects Project A	Incomplete Projects Project B	Projects Not Yet Determined

A supplemental schedule like that shown in Figure 7-5 may be prepared in "pancake" form to show operating data for individual projects. Information for it would be provided by the subsidiary Expenditures Ledger.

Figure 7-5

A GOVERNMENTAL UNIT

Capital Projects Fund
Statement of Appropriations, Expenditures, and Encumbrances
For the Fiscal Year Ended (Date)

	Appropriations	Expenditures	Encumbrances	Unencumbered Balance
Project A				
Total Project A	$ 500,000	$200,000	$ 10,000	$290,000
Project B				
Total Project B	$ 700,000	$600,000	$ 90,000	$ 10,000
Total—All Projects	$1,200,000	$800,000	$100,000	$300,000

Figure 7-6

A GOVERNMENTAL UNIT

Capital Projects Funds
Combining Balance Sheet
(Date)

	Completed Projects	Incomplete Projects			Totals	
Assets	Bridge Fund*	Sewer System Fund	Civic Center Fund	General Improvements Fund	This Year	Last Year
Cash		$10,000	$ 5,000	$ 9,000	$ 24,000	$ 50,000
Investments			450,000	100,000	550,000	600,000
Due from other funds (itemize)			30,000	20,000	50,000	40,000
Due from county			15,000	10,000	25,000	35,000
Total assets		$10,000	$500,000	$139,000	$649,000	$725,000

Liabilities and Fund Balances

Liabilities:					
Vouchers payable			$ 60,000	$ 60,000	$ 55,000
Contracts payable			50,000	50,000	57,500
Contracts payable—retained percentage		$10,000		10,000	27,500
Due to other funds (itemize)			10,000	10,000	10,000
Total liabilities	$ ____	$10,000	$120,000	$130,000	$150,000
Fund Balance, fully appropriated:					
Reserved for encumbrances	$490,000		$ 10,000	$500,000	$550,000
Unencumbered	10,000		9,000	19,000	25,000
Total fund balances	$500,000	$ ____	$ 19,000	$519,000	$575,000
Total liabilities and fund balances	$500,000	$10,000	$139,000	$649,000	$725,000

*The Bridge Fund has been closed; see Figures 7–4 and 7–9.

Figure 7-7

A GOVERNMENTAL UNIT

Capital Projects Funds

Combining Statement of Revenues, Expenditures, and
Changes in Fund Balances
(Period)

	Completed Projects		Incomplete Projects		Totals	
	Bridge Fund	Sewer System Fund	Civic Center Fund	General Improvements Fund	This Period	Last Period
Initial project authorization	$ 400,000	$ 575,000	$ 500,000	$ 700,000	$ 2,175,000	$3,000,000
Less: Discount on bonds				2,000	2,000	
Net project authorization	$ 400,000	$ 575,000	$ 500,000	$ 698,000	$ 2,173,000	$3,000,000
Revenues [Itemize or reference statement of]	$	$ 200,000	$	$ 300,000	$ 500,000	$2,000,000
Expenditures [Itemize or reference statement of]	252,400	550,000	490,000	541,000	1,833,400	1,500,000
Excess (deficit) of revenues over expenditures	$(252,400)	$(350,000)	$(490,000)	$(241,000)	$(1,333,400)	$ 500,000
Fund balance, beginning of period, fully appropriated:						
Reserved for encumbrances	$ 192,000	$ 150,000	$	$ 115,000	$ 457,000	$ 250,000
Unreserved	67,200	200,000	500,000	135,000	902,200	610,200
Total	$ 259,200	$ 350,000	$ 500,000	$ 250,000	$ 1,359,200	$ 860,200
Fund balance, end of year, before transfer	$ 6,800	$	$ 10,000	$ 9,000	$ 25,800	$1,360,200
Residual equity transfer to Debt Service Fund	6,800				6,800	
Fund balance, end of year	$	$	$ 10,000	$ 9,000	$ 19,000	$1,360,200

CAPITAL PROJECTS FUNDS COMBINING STATEMENTS

In order to focus attention on capital projects activities as a whole and to reduce the number of separate statements required, statements of the several Capital Projects Funds of a government are usually presented in combining form. With adequate disclosure, such combining statements fulfill the requirement for separate statements for each fund. In general, combining totals should be shown with the details applicable to each fund either being presented in the statement itself or being incorporated by reference therein to a statement or schedule containing the separate fund details. The totals are properly presented alone only in certain combined statements discussed and illustrated in the "Financial Reporting" chapter (14).

A Combining Balance Sheet for several Capital Projects Funds is shown in Figure 7-6. The Bridge Fund illustrated in this chapter has been closed; the information for other funds is assumed for illustrative purposes. As indicated in this statement, a distinction is frequently made between complete and incomplete projects in combining balance sheets as well as in combining statements of revenues, expenditures, and changes in fund balance.

A combining Statement of Revenues, Expenditures, and Changes in Fund Balances is illustrated in Figure 7-7. In addition to the statements for each fund there are total columns for the current and immediately preceding years.

If a government has numerous Capital Projects Funds (i.e., more than six or seven), it may be desirable to prepare combining schedules for groups of funds and use such combining data, appropriately described and referenced to the schedules, in preparation of the combining balance sheet for all Capital Projects Funds. A similar technique often proves useful in connection with statements of multiproject funds.

▶ **Question 7-1.** A Capital Projects Fund is, in essence, a special type of Special Revenue Fund. Explain.

Question 7-2. Must all municipal capital outlays be financed and accounted for through Capital Projects Funds? Explain.

Question 7-3. What is the "life cycle" of a Capital Projects Fund?

Question 7-4. Why is each identifiable capital project of material proportions usually financed and accounted for through a separate Capital Projects Fund?

Question 7-5. In what situations might several capital projects properly be financed and accounted for through a single Capital Projects Fund?

Question 7-6. The governing board of a city recently levied a gasoline tax "for the express purpose of financing the construction of a civic center, servicing debt issued to do so, or both" and instructed the Comptroller to establish a Gasoline Tax Fund to account for the receipt, expenditure, and balances of the tax proceeds. What type fund should be established?

Question 7-7. Why might the term "revenues" be objected to when used to describe inflows of Capital Projects Fund resources from debt issues or interfund transfers?

Question 7-8. A municipality sold bonds and then, finding that it would not need the money for several months, invested it. (a) Assuming that interest in the amount of $500 was received, give the entry to record this transaction. (b) Now assume that the bonds had originally been sold at a discount of $300 and give the entry to record the receipt of such interest. (c) Finally, assume that the appropriations amounted to $100,000, that the bonds were sold at par, but that it now appears that the project will cost $100,500. Can the $500 be used to finance the additional expenditures without authorization from the legislative body?

Question 7-9. Why are statements for several Capital Projects Funds presented in combining form?

Question 7-10. What type of statement presentation is appropriate to present the details of Capital Projects Fund revenues and expenditures of a particular period?

Question 7-11. Why might a grantor not permit general municipal overhead to be charged to a capital project financed by its grant, or insist that allowable (reimburseable) overhead be calculated by means of a predetermined formula related to direct project costs?

Question 7-12. Is it permissible to record bond premiums and accrued bond interest received upon the issuance of bonds directly in the accounts of a Debt Service Fund rather than recording them initially in the Capital Projects Fund and subsequently transferring them to the Debt Service Fund?

Question 7-13. At the beginning of the year $100,000 of an issue of serial bonds to be used to finance a capital project was sold at a discount of $1,000. Subsequently there was a rise in the price of the bonds so that the remaining $200,000 of the same issue was sold several months later at a premium of $2,000. How should these premiums and discounts be recorded? Give entries.

Question 7-14. Assume the same facts as in Question 7-13, except that the bonds were sold at a discount of $2,000 and at a premium of $1,000, respectively. Give the necessary entries.

Question 7-15. Assume the same facts as in Question 7-13, except that the first sale was in one year and the second sale was during the following year. Would the premiums and discounts be handled in the same way as those described in Question 7-13? If not, in what way should they be handled? Give entries.

Question 7-16. Why should a competent governmental accountant or auditor review proposed bond indentures, ordinances establishing Capital Projects Funds, and similar instruments or agreements before they are agreed to or enacted?

Question 7-17. In certain Capital Projects Funds accounting situations it might be appropriate to (1) employ complete budgetary accounting in a manner paralleling that of General Fund accounting; (2) debit and credit the Fund Balance account for expenditures incurred and revenues received or accrued, respectively; or (3) utilize only the Fund Balance, Expenditures, Encumbrances, and Reserve for Encumbrances equity accounts. Briefly describe a situation in which each of these approaches would be appropriate.

Question 7-18. What similarities exist between and among the Fund Balance, Appropriations, and Revenues accounts?

Question 7-19. What problems might one encounter in attempting to determine the proper disposition of a Capital Projects Fund balance remaining after the project has been completed and all Capital Projects Fund liabilities have been paid?

Question 7-20. What disposition should be made of a Capital Projects Fund *deficit* remaining at the conclusion of the project?

Question 7-21. Neither the fixed assets acquired through a Capital Projects Fund nor the long-term debt issued to finance capital projects are normally accounted for therein. Why? Where are such fixed assets and long-term debt accounted for, and are there exceptions to this general rule?

Question 7-22. Proceeds of certain general obligation long-term debt issues are not accounted for through Capital Projects Funds. When is this the case? Through which funds or fund types are such debt proceeds accounted for?

Question 7-23. Balance sheets prepared in the past used the caption "Liabilities, Reserves, and Fund Balance" for the credit side. Why is this caption now considered objectionable?

Question 7-24. Should expenditures and/or encumbrances relating to construction in progress being financed through a Capital Projects Fund be capitalized in the General Fixed Assets Account Group?

Question 7-25. In the past some accountants have preferred to close Capital Projects Fund Revenues, Expenditures, and Encumbrances accounts of incomplete projects at year end, whereas others preferred that they not be closed until the project is complete. Are both approaches acceptable? Why?

▶ **Problem 7-1.** The following transactions and events occurred in Lanesburg Township during 19X4:

1. The township assembly agreed that a new police and fire department building would be constructed at a cost not to exceed $150,000, on land owned by the township.

2. Cash with which to finance the project was received from the following sources:

Transfer from General Fund	$ 10,000
State–Federal grant	50,000
Bank of Lanesburg (long-term note)	90,000
	$150,000

3. Cash was disbursed from the Capital Projects Fund as follows:

Construction contract	$140,000
Architect fees	5,000
Engineering charges	1,000
Transfer to General Fund	4,000
	$150,000

Required:

Prepare general journal entries to record the foregoing facts.

Problem 7-2. The following transactions and events relating to a capital project undertaken by Williams County occurred during 19X4.

1. The Board of Commissioners approved a street improvement program expected to cost $500,000 and authorized a $300,000 bond issue to partially finance the improvements; the remaining resources needed are to be provided by a Federal grant and an interfund transfer. Capital Projects Fund accounting records were

established and the plans and authorizations recorded therein by memorandum entry.

2. Proceeds of the bond sale, $303,000, were recorded in the Capital Projects Fund.

3. A purchase order was issued for materials estimated to cost $120,000.

4. Engineering costs were paid, $15,000.

5. Right-of-way acquisition costs, $30,000, were paid.

6. The Board of Commissioners was notified that a $125,000 Federal street improvement grant had been approved and would be received in two equal installments. The first installment will be received in 19X4, the second in 19X5.

7. The bond premium (2) was transferred to the appropriate Debt Service Fund.

8. The materials ordered above (3) arrived, except for items expected to cost $10,000, which were delayed temporarily, together with an invoice for $112,000.

9. Freight charges paid on the materials received, $700.

10. Materials expected to cost $40,000 were ordered.

11. The first installment of the Federal grant was received.

12. The interfund transfer due from the General Fund was established as a receivable in the Capital Projects Fund accounts.

13. Equipment rental costs paid during 19X4 were $20,000; in addition, $3,000 of such costs are accrued at year end.

14. Wages paid workers on the project during 19X4 totaled $90,000; an additional $6,000 is accrued at year end.

15. The Revenues, Expenditures, and Encumbrances accounts were closed at year end.

Required:

Prepare a columnar worksheet to reflect the foregoing transactions and events and from which a CPF preclosing trial balance; Statement of Revenues, Expenditures, and Changes in Fund Balance; and Balance Sheet may be prepared. Set up separate accounts (e.g., revenue accounts) to provide appropriate detail in the statements. Key your worksheet entries to the numbered transactions in the problem.

Problem 7-3, Part I. The following transactions took place in the village of Alffton during 19A:

1. A bond issue of $120,000 was authorized for the construction of a library.

2. The bonds were sold at a premium of $900.

3. The cost of issuing the bonds, $800, was paid.

4. An order was placed for materials estimated to cost $65,000.

5. Salaries and wages amounting to $5,000 were paid.

6. The premium was transferred to a Debt Service Fund.

Required:

(a) Prepare all entries, including closing entries, to record the Capital Projects Fund transactions for 19A.

(b) Post to T-accounts.

(c) Prepare a CPF balance sheet as of December 31, 19A.

(d) Prepare a CPF Statement of Revenues, Expenditures, and Changes in Fund Balance for the year ended December 31, 19A.

Problem 7-3, Part II. The following transactions took place during 19B:

7. The materials were received; the actual cost was found to be $65,850.
8. Salaries and wages amounting to $40,100 were paid.
9. All bills outstanding were paid.
10. The project was completed. The accounts were closed and the remaining balance was to be transferred to a Debt Service Fund.

Required:

(a) Prepare all journal entries, including closing entries, to record the CPF transactions for 19B.
(b) Post to T-accounts.
(c) Prepare a CPF Statement of Revenues, Expenditures, and Changes in Fund Balance for the year ended December 31, 19B.

Problem 7-4. From the data in Problem 7-3, Parts I and II: Prepare a columnar worksheet for the two-year period ending December 31, 19B, using the following columnar headings:

1. 19A Transactions
2. Closing Entries, 12/31/19A
3. Postclosing Trial Balance, 12/31/19A
4. 19B Transactions
5. Closing Entries, 12/31/19B
6. Postclosing Trial Balance, 12/31/19B

Problem 7-5, Part I. The following transactions took place in Mills County during 19X4.

1. A bond issue of $500,000 was authorized for the construction of a bridge.
2. One-half of the bonds were sold at par.
3. The cost of handling the bonds, $700, was paid from, and charged as an expenditure of, the Capital Projects Fund.
4. A contract was entered into with White & Company for the construction of the bridge at a cost of $420,000.
5. A bill for $175,000 was received from White & Company for work done on the bridge to date.
6. Salaries of state engineers amounting to $5,350 were paid to the state.

Required:

(a) Prepare CPF journal entries.
(b) Post to T-accounts.
(c) Prepare CPF financial statements as of December 31, 19X4.

Problem 7-5, Part II. The following transactions took place during 19X5:

7. The bill due White & Company was paid.
8. A bond issue of $400,000 was authorized for the purpose of constructing a garage;

another Capital Projects Fund was established. The bond issue authorization was recorded in the accounts.

9. Bonds (garage) of $200,000 were sold at a $4,000 premium.

10. The cost of handling the bonds, $2,500, was paid.

11. Orders were placed for materials (garage project) estimated to cost $52,000.

12. A bill for $125,000 was received from White & Company for further work performed on the bridge contract.

13. Salaries and wages paid amounted to $51,000; of this total $4,000 applies to the bridge project and the remainder to the garage project.

14. The materials ordered (11) were received; the actual cost, $53,000, was vouchered for later payment.

15. An order was placed for materials (garage project) estimated to cost $100,000.

16. The net bond premium was transferred to the appropriate Debt Service Fund.

Required:

(a) Prepare CPF journal entries.

(b) Post to T-accounts.

(c) Prepare a Combining Balance Sheet for the Capital Projects Funds as of December 31, 19X5.

(d) Prepare a CPF Combining Statement of Revenues, Expenditures, and Changes in Fund Balance for the year ended December 31, 19X5.

Problem 7-6. From the data in Problem 7-5, Parts I and II, prepare columnar worksheets for the two-year period ended December 31, 19X5. The worksheet for the Bridge (Capital Projects) Fund should have columnar headings as follows:

19X4 Transactions		Trial Balance, 12/31/19X4		19X5 Transactions		Trial Balance, 12/31/19X5	
Debit	Credit	Debit	Credit	Debit	Credit	Debit	Credit

The worksheet for the Garage (Capital Projects) Fund should contain similar headings relating to 19X5 transactions and balances. Entries should be keyed to the numbered items in Problem 7-5. (If statements were not prepared for Problem 7-5, they may be assigned here.)

Problem 7-7. The City of Westgate's fiscal year ends on June 30. During the fiscal year ended June 30, 19X2, the city authorized the construction of a new library and sale of general obligation term bonds to finance the construction of the library. The authorization imposed the following restrictions: (1) Construction cost was not to exceed $5,000,000; and (2) the annual interest rate was not to exceed 8½ percent. The following transactions relating to the financing and construction of the library occurred during the fiscal year ended June 30, 19X3:

1. On July 1, 19X2, the city recorded the budget for the project.

2. On July 1, 19X2, the city issued $5,000,000 of 30-year 8 percent general obligation bonds for $5,100,000. The semiannual interest dates are December 31 and June 30. The premium of $100,000 was transferred to the Library Debt Service Fund.

3. On July 3, 19X2, $4,900,000 of Library Capital Projects Fund cash was invested in short-term commercial paper. These purchases were at face value with no accrued interest. Interest on Library Capital Projects Fund investments must be transferred to the Library Debt Service Fund. During the fiscal year ending June 30, 19X3, estimated interest to be earned is $140,000.

4. On July 5, 19X2, the city signed a contract with F & A Construction Company to build the library for $4,980,000.

5. On January 15, 19X3, the Library Capital Projects Fund received $3,040,000 from the maturity of short-term notes purchased on July 3. The cost of these notes was $3,000,000. The interest of $40,000 was transferred to the Library Debt Service Fund.

6. On January 20, 19X3, F & A Construction Company properly billed the city $3,000,000 for work performed on the new library. The contract calls for 10 percent retention until final inspection and acceptance of the building. F & A was paid $2,700,000 from the Library Capital Projects Fund.

7. On June 30, 19X3, the proper adjusting entries (including accrued interest receivable of $103,000) and closing entries were made for the Library Capital Projects Fund.

Required:

(a) Prepare journal entries to record the preceding sets of facts in the Library Capital Projects Fund. Do not record journal entries in any other fund or account group.

(b) Prepare a Balance Sheet for the City of Westgate—Library Capital Projects Fund as of June 30, 19X3.

(c) Prepare a Statement of Revenues, Expenditures, and Changes in Fund Balance for the City of Westgate—Library Capital Projects Fund for the year ended June 30, 19X3.

(AICPA, adapted)

Problem 7-8. A bond issue utilized to finance a capital project of Smithson Township sold at a $3,000 discount. Although for several months the council was uncertain as to whether any or all of the deficiency would be financed from other sources, it subsequently ordered that $2,000 be transferred to the Capital Projects Fund from the General Fund and reduced the project authorization by the remaining $1,000. The clerk carried out the council's mandate immediately. What journal entries did he make if the order was transmitted in the year the bonds were sold? In the year after the bonds were sold?

DEBT
SERVICE
FUNDS

The purpose of Debt Service Funds is "to account for the accumulation of resources for, and the payment of, *general long-term debt* principal and interest."[1]

Not all general long-term debt must be serviced through Debt Service Funds. NCGA *Statement 1* provides that "Debt Service Funds are required [only] if they are legally mandated and/or if financial resources are being accumulated for principal and interest payments maturing in future years."[2]

Thus, serial debt might properly be serviced directly from the General Fund or a Special Revenue Fund—rather than from a Debt Service Fund to which resources are transferred from these funds—if a Debt Service Fund is not required legally or contractually and debt service resources are not being accumulated beyond those needed currently. Of course, such debt could be serviced through a Debt Service Fund, and many government accountants prefer to account for all general long-term debt service through one or more Debt Service Funds (1) so that all general long-term debt is serviced through the same fund type, and (2) to enhance control over and accountability for these resources.

The responsibility of providing for the retirement of long-term general obligation debt is ordinarily indicated by the terms of the debt indenture or other contract. The term "general obligation" indicates that the "full faith and credit" of the governmental unit has been pledged to the repayment of the debt.

Liabilities of specific funds are not general long-term debt, even if "full faith and credit" debt; and they are normally serviced through those funds rather than the Debt Service Fund(s). For example, when improvements are to be paid for by owners of benefited property, bonds and other debt issued to finance the improvements are expected to be repaid by the special assessments levied against

---

[1] NCGAS 1, p. 7. (Emphasis added.)
[2] Ibid. p. 8.

the property benefited (Chapter 9). Similarly, when general obligation bonds are issued for the benefit of a public enterprise, the enterprise frequently has primary responsibility for repayment of the bonds (Chapter 13). Similarly, some Trust Funds (Chapter 11) may have long-term debt. In all three of these situations the debt is *specific fund debt*—not general long-term debt to be serviced through Debt Service Funds—and is accounted for in and serviced through those funds.

TYPES OF LONG-TERM DEBT

Four types of long-term debt are frequently incurred by state and local governments: bonds; notes; time warrants; and capital leases, lease-purchase agreements, and installment purchase contracts.

A *bond* is a written promise to pay a specified principal sum at a specified future date, usually with interest at a specified rate. Bond issues often are for many millions of dollars since bonds are a major source of long-term financing of capital improvements of most governments. Bonds usually are issued in $1,000 and $5,000 denominations with maturities scheduled over 15 to 25 years and interest paid semiannually or annually. *Term bonds* are those for which all of the principal is payable at a single specified maturity date. *Serial bonds,* by far the most widely used, provide for periodic maturities ranging up to the maximum period permitted by law in the respective states. Specific arrangements of maturities vary widely. Regular serial bonds are repayable in equal annual installments over the life of the issue. In some cases the beginning of the repayment series is deferred a specified number of years in the future, after which equal annual installments are to be paid. In some cases the indenture provides for increasing amounts of annual principal payments, computed so that the total annual payment of interest and principal is constant over the life of the issue. Other arrangements also may be provided in the bond indenture.

Notes are less formal documents than bonds that indicate an obligation to repay borrowed money at interest. Notes have a single maturity date, as do term bonds, but their maturity typically ranges from as few as 30 to 90 days to as long as three to five years after issuance. Too, a single note usually evidences the borrowing transaction, whereas bonds are generally issued in $1,000 and $5,000 denominations. *General Obligation notes* to be repaid within one year of the date of issue normally are carried as liabilities of the General Fund, whereas those to be repaid over a longer period are carried in the General Long-Term Debt Account Group and are serviced through Debt Service Funds.

Warrants are orders by authorized legislative or executive officials directing the treasurer to pay a specific sum to order or bearer. If these warrants are to be paid more than one year after the date of issue, they also are recorded in the General Long-Term Debt Account Group and serviced through a Debt Service Fund.

Capital leases, lease-purchase agreements, and installment purchase contracts have come into widespread use in government recently. Where the substance of these transactions indicates that a purchase (or capital lease) and liability exist, they should be recorded as General Fixed Assets and General Long-Term

Debt, and may require a Debt Service Fund.[3] Arrangements of maturity dates of notes, warrants, leases, and similar debt may have substantial diversity. Debt Service Funds for notes, warrants, and other types of General Long-Term Debt are not discussed separately because the accounting for them is similar to that for bonds.

TIMING OF DEBT SERVICE PAYMENTS

Interest expenditure is an annual cost and is directly proportional to the principal amount of debt outstanding. Since a common debt service planning objective is to keep the drain on each year's resources relatively constant, the pattern of debt service payments for long-term debt usually is designed so that total annual debt service requirements will not fluctuate materially. Regular serial bonds meet the objective fairly well, and both serial bond issues and lease agreements may be structured to meet the objective extremely well. On the other hand, a term bond maturing twenty years in the future requires the governmental unit to accumulate the amount of principal due twenty years hence through annual contributions that, together with earnings on the invested contributions, will equal the principal amount. The operation of a Debt Service Fund for a term bond issue will therefore differ substantially from that of a Debt Service Fund for a serial bond issue.

SOURCES OF FINANCING

The money for repaying long-term debt may come from numerous sources with varying legal restrictions. The typical source is property taxes. A special tax rate may be assessed for a single bond issue, or a total annual rate may be used with the proceeds prorated to several debt issues. Legislative bodies may earmark a tax for a specified purpose, with a proviso that the proceeds may be used for current operating expenditures, capital outlay, or to repay debt incurred to finance the specified purpose. In such cases the proceeds of the tax would be accounted for in a Special Revenue Fund; the portion of the proceeds allocated to debt service would be transferred to a Debt Service Fund.

Still another method of providing for debt service is required by bond indentures or other contracts that specify that the debt shall be repaid out of "the first revenues accruing to the treasury." Such agreements require the government to contribute the necessary amounts to the Debt Service Fund from the General Fund; the obligation has first claim on the revenues of the General Fund.

When a term bond issue is to be repaid through a fund in which resources are being accumulated to retire the principal at maturity, the assets of the fund will be invested in income-producing securities. Similarly, some serial bond Debt Service Funds have investable resources. The income from these securities constitutes still another form of Debt Service Fund revenue.

Finally, maturing bonds may be refunded, that is, they may be retired by either (1) exchanging new bonds for old ones or (2) selling a new bond issue and

---

[3] If such agreements relate to Trust, Internal Service, or Enterprise Funds, the assets, liabilities, and debt service are recorded in those funds.

using the proceeds to retire an old issue. The new bond issue constitutes the financing source in refunding transactions.

DEBT SERVICE FUND FOR A REFUNDING ISSUE ————————————

A Debt Service Fund is not needed where new bonds are simply exchanged for old ones and no cash changes hands. The only accounting requirement in this case is that the General Long-Term Debt Account Group (Chapter 10) be adjusted to reflect the retirement of the old bonds and issuance of the new ones.

A Debt Service Fund is needed, however, if the new bonds are sold and the proceeds are used to retire the maturing issue. The Debt Service Fund may exist only for a few moments in this situation, as its function is merely to record the receipt of the new issue proceeds and their use to retire the old issue. Assuming that a $1,000,000 bond issue was sold at par to refund an old bond issue in that amount, the Debt Service Fund entries would be:

Cash	1,000,000	
Bond Issue Proceeds		1,000,000
To record receipt of the proceeds from sale of the new issue.		
Expenditures	1,000,000	
Cash		1,000,000
To record expenditure of the proceeds to retire the old issue.		
Bond Issue Proceeds	1,000,000	
Expenditures		1,000,000
To close the accounts of the Debt Service Fund for the bonds retired and to abolish the fund.		

The refunding entries above assumed that the new issue yielded par, the old issue was matured and could be retired at par, and there were no significant issue costs of the new issue or acquisition costs related to the old issue. To illustrate a more complex refunding situation, assume the same facts as above except that (1) $10,000 of costs related to the refunding were incurred, and (2) the old bonds were bought at a discount, at 95, on the open market. The first entry above would be the same, but the second would be:

(2) Expenditures (Par of bonds retired)	1,000,000	
Gain on Refunding		40,000
Cash ($950,000 + $10,000)		960,000
To record retirement of old bond issue at a gain.		

This entry records the total expenditures in two amounts: (1) the principal of the debt retired and (2) the gain or loss on refunding—and is in substantial conformity with AICPA *Statement of Position 78-5*, "Accounting for Advance Refundings of Tax-Exempt Debt." A literal interpretation of SOP 78-5 would indicate that (1) the related costs should be charged to a separate expenditure account, and (2) the gain or loss reported should be the difference between the amount paid to retire the old bonds and their par value. That would not be in conformity with the cost principle and, further, would result in a $50,000 gain being reported in the example. The authors prefer the more conceptually correct and conservative approach illustrated. In any event, the gain reported would be closed to Fund Balance at year end. Again, the General Long-Term Debt Account Group (Chapter 10) must be adjusted to record the new issue outstanding and the retirement of the old issue.

Another type of refunding situation occurs where the old debt has not matured and cannot be called for retirement except at a high call premium. Some bond issues have defeasance provisions that specify terms by which the debt may be legally satisfied, and any related liens released, without actually retiring the debt. Such provisions usually include these factors, among others:

- The issuer is irrevocably committed to refund the old debt.
- The funds used to consummate the advance refunding are placed in an irrevocable trust with a reputable trustee for the purpose of satisfying the old debt at a specified future date(s).
- The funds used to consummate the advance refunding are invested in qualifying securities with maturities that approximate the debt service requirements of the trust.
- The invested funds used to consummate the advance refunding are not subject to lien for any purpose other than in connection with the advance refunding transaction.

The essence of these defeasance provisions, paraphrased from AICPA SOP 78-5, is that a government can put sufficient money and investments in an irrevocable trust and, if it meets these criteria, consider the debt defeased even though the debt is not paid until its regularly scheduled maturities for many years in the future. If the debt is defeased, (1) the Debt Service Fund entries are similar to those illustrated and (2) the old debt is removed from the General Long-Term Debt accounts and replaced by the new debt. If defeasance is not achieved, both the old debt and the new debt must be reported as general long-term debt and the amount placed in trust to retire the old issue will be reported as an asset of a Debt Service Fund and as an Amount Available in Debt Service Funds for future debt service in the General Long-Term Debt accounts. SOP 78-5 contains additional guidance on accounting for advance refundings, which are quite complex in all but the simplest situations, such as those illustrated above.

DEBT SERVICE FUND FOR A SERIAL ISSUE

To illustrate the operation of a Debt Service Fund for a serial issue assume that A Governmental Unit issued $1,000,000 of 5 percent Flores Park Serial Bonds on January 1, 19X1, to finance the purchase and development of a park. The bond indenture requires annual payments of $100,000 to retire the principal. The debt service requirements (principal and interest) are to be financed by a property tax levied for that purpose. The following journal entries record the transactions for the first year of operation of the Flores Park Debt Service Fund, assuming budgetary accounts are used.

(1)	Estimated Revenues	155,000	
	Appropriations		150,000
	Fund Balance		5,000
	To record the budget for the fund for the fiscal year.		
(2)	Taxes Receivable—Current	156,000	
	Allowance for Uncollectible Current Taxes		1,000
	Revenues		155,000
	To record the taxes levied for the year.		
(3)	Cash	151,000	
	Taxes Receivable—Current		151,000
	To record collection of taxes for the year.		
(4)	Expenditures	100,000	
	Matured Bonds Payable		100,000
	To record the fund's liability for payment of the first annual serial maturity.		
(5)	Expenditures	50,000	
	Matured Interest Payable		50,000
	To record the accrual of interest payable at the end of the year.		
(6)	Matured Bonds Payable	100,000	
	Matured Interest Payable	50,000	
	Cash		150,000
	To record payment of liabilities.		
(7)	Taxes Receivable—Delinquent	5,000	
	Allowance for Uncollectible Current Taxes	1,000	
	Taxes Receivable—Current		5,000
	Allowance for Uncollectible Delinquent Taxes		1,000
	To record the change of taxes receivable and the related allowance for uncollectible taxes from current to delinquent status.		

Closing Entries

(C1)	Revenues	155,000	
	Estimated Revenues		155,000
	To close the revenue accounts.		
(C2)	Appropriations	150,000	
	Expenditures		150,000
	To close the expenditure accounts.		

Note that the operations of the Debt Service Fund for the Flores Park Serial Bonds could have been financed by any one or a combination of the revenue sources described earlier in this chapter, or by interfund transfers. Further, since the amounts required to service the debt are known and the revenue and other financing sources are few, many governments do not employ budgetary accounting in simple serial bond Debt Service Funds.

SINKING FUND REQUIREMENTS

Term bonds ordinarily are repaid from a fund in which resources are accumulated over the life of the bonds by means of annual additions to the fund and by earnings of the fund assets. A "Schedule of Sinking Fund Requirements," (Figure 8-1) has been prepared for the City Hall bonds of A Governmental Unit. These are 9 percent, 20-year term bonds issued January 1, 19X0 to be repaid out of "the first revenues accruing to the Treasury." Recall that the latter terminology indicates that the source of financing for the Debt Service Fund for these bonds is the General Fund of A Governmental Unit.

The first payment to the sinking fund is scheduled for the end of year 1 (19X0). A similar payment will be made at the end of each succeeding year until, when the twentieth payment has been made, fund resources should total $1,000,000. An estimated earnings rate of 10 percent has been used in developing Figure 8-1. The amount of the required annual additions was determined by selecting from a table the amount of an ordinary annuity of $1 per period at 10 percent for twenty periods. This amount, $57.274999 is the amount to which an annual annuity of one dollar would accumulate in twenty years at 10 percent. Since the desired amount to be accumulated is $1,000,000, that amount is divided by $57.274999 to obtain $17,460, the amount of the required annual additions. As indicated in the schedule, the last addition is somewhat less than the preceding ones because of rounding errors. In any event, the final payment in 19Y9 will be in the amount that brings the sinking fund resources to $1,000,000, the amount required to retire the term bonds.

The schedule of sinking fund requirements provides the amounts of the budgetary requirements for the Debt Service Fund for the duration of the Fund, provided the accumulation process proceeds as planned or departs from the plan by immaterial amounts. The required fund balance at the end of each year (Figure 8-1) provides a standard against which the actual accumulation may be compared. If the actual accumulation falls short or exceeds the required fund balances by substantial amounts, a new schedule of sinking fund requirements should be computed by starting from actual accumulation and computing the annual additions and fund earnings required to produce $1 million by the end of the twentieth year. The calculation of the new schedule may be based on an altered expected annual earnings rate.

Several reasons may underlie differences between the actual and planned accumulation of a sinking fund. Contributions or revenues may fall short or exceed those planned, as may earnings on investments. Capital gains or losses on the disposition of investments are not contemplated in the accumulation schedule (except as they may be included in the expected earnings rate). Finally, a Debt Service Fund's resources may be used to purchase some of the bonds it is set up to service. If the bonds are kept "alive" in the Fund, with interest being paid to

Figure 8-1

SCHEDULE OF SINKING FUND REQUIREMENTS
$1 Million 20 Year Term Bond Issue
(Assuming an Annual Earnings Rate of 10 Percent)

Year	Required Annual Additions	Required Fund Earnings	Required Fund Increases	Required Fund Balances
1 (19X0)	$ 17,460		$ 17,460	$ 17,460
2 (19X1)	17,460	$ 1,746	19,206	36,666
3 (19X2)	17,460	3,667	21,127	57,793
4 (19X3)	17,460	5,779	23,239	81,032
5 (19X4)	17,460	8,103	25,563	106,595
6 (19X5)	17,460	10,660	28,120	134,715
7 (19X6)	17,460	13,472	30,932	165,647
8 (19X7)	17,460	16,565	34,025	199,672
9 (19X8)	17,460	19,967	37,427	237,099
10 (19X9)	17,460	23,710	41,170	278,269
11 (19Y0)	17,460	27,827	45,287	323,556
12 (19Y1)	17,460	32,356	49,816	373,372
13 (19Y2)	17,460	37,337	54,797	428,169
14 (19Y3)	17,460	42,817	60,277	488,446
15 (19Y4)	17,460	48,845	66,305	554,751
16 (19Y5)	17,460	55,475	72,935	627,686
17 (19Y6)	17,460	62,769	80,229	707,915
18 (19Y7)	17,460	70,792	88,252	796,167
19 (19Y8)	17,460	79,617	97,077	893,244
20 (19Y9)	17,432*	89,324	106,756	1,000,000
	$349,172	$650,828	$1,000,000	$1,000,000

The last year's addition needs to be only $17,432 because of rounding errors.

itself, the planned accumulation is not affected by the purchase. But both the National Committee on Governmental Accounting and the AICPA Committee on Governmental Accounting and Auditing have recommended that such bonds be retired unless legal or contractual provisions prohibit retirement. Bond retirement removes assets originally intended to be held to maturity of the debt issue and hence removes some of the Fund's earning capacity. This in turn requires recalculation of the accumulation schedule and, in many cases, an increase in the annual revenues or contributions other than earnings on investments that build the Fund Balance.

DEBT SERVICE FUND FOR A TERM ISSUE

To illustrate the operation of a Debt Service Fund for a term issue we shall use the City Hall bonds described above and the schedule of sinking fund requirements presented in Figure 8-1. At the end of the first year of the Fund's operation, 19X0, there would have been a balance of $17,460 in both the Fund Balance and Cash accounts of the Debt Service Fund. These would have resulted from the first payment to the sinking fund of the required annual additions. The following journal entries record the transactions of the City Hall Bonds Debt Service Fund for the second year of operation, 19X1, assuming that budgetary accounts are employed:

(1)	Required Additions	107,860	
	Required Earnings	1,746	
	Appropriations		90,400
	Fund Balance		19,206
	To record the budget for 19X1.		

The budget for 19X1 is calculated as follows:

Required transfers (from the General Fund) ..	107,860	
Required earnings	1,746	109,606
Appropriations:		
Annual interest charges	90,000	
Fiscal agent's fee	400	90,400
Required Fund increase		19,206

The required additions figure is computed as follows:

Required additions to sinking fund	17,460
Annual interest charges (9% x $1,000,000)	90,000
Fiscal agent's fee	400
	107,860

The term "Required Additions" is the account title used by the National Committee on Governmental Accounting in GAAFR (68); GAAFR (80) does not illustrate budgetary accounting for Debt Service Funds. In any event, in this set of circumstances perhaps a better term would be "Required Transfers." Note that the credit to Fund Balance is the amount of "Required Fund Increases" for year 2 (19X1) in Figure 8-1 and causes the Fund Balance account to be carried during the year at its planned end-of-year balance.

(2)	Investments	17,000	
	Unamortized Premiums on Investments	270	
	Interest Receivable on Investments	120	
	Unamortized Discounts on Investments		80
	Cash		17,310
	To record the purchase of investments,		
	together with the related premiums, accrued		
	interest, and discounts.		

[Alternatively, (1) the interest receivable on investments at the time of purchase may be debited to Interest Earnings rather than Interest Receivable on Investments; (2) entry 5 omitted except in the year-end adjustment process, after which it would be reversed; and (3) interest collections credited to Interest Earnings.]

(3) Due from General Fund 107,860
      Operating Transfers from
        General Fund 107,860
    To accrue the contribution from
    the General Fund.

(4) Cash 107,860
      Due from General Fund 107,860
    To record the receipt of the
    contribution from the General
    Fund.

(5) Interest Receivable on
        Investments 1,480
      Interest Earnings (or Earnings) . 1,480
    To record accrual of interest
    revenue on investments.

(6) Cash 1,600
      Interest Receivable on
        Investments 1,600
    To record collection of interest
    receivable.

(7) Unamortized Discounts on
        Investments 20
    Interest Earnings 10
      Unamortized Premiums on
        Investments 30
    To record amortization of
    premiums and discounts on
    investments and the resultant
    correction of interest earnings.

(8) Expenditures 90,400
      Matured Interest Payable 90,000
      Vouchers Payable 400
    To record accrual of interest
    payments on the bonds and the
    payment of agent's fees.

(9) Cash with Fiscal Agent 90,000
      Cash 90,000
    To record transfer of cash for
    payment of interest on the bonds
    to the fiscal agent.

(10) Matured Interest Payable 90,000
      Vouchers Payable 90,000
    To record the vouchering of the
    interest liability.

(11) Vouchers Payable 90,000
      Cash with Fiscal Agent 90,000
    To record payment of the interest
    by the fiscal agent.

(12) Vouchers Payable 400
      Cash 400
    To record payment of the fiscal
    agent's fee.

(13) Interest Receivable on		
Investments	420	
Interest Earnings (or Earnings) .		420
To accrue interest receivable at		
year end.		
(14) Investments	18,000	
Cash		18,000
To record purchase of investments		
at face value, with no accrued		
interest.		
(C1) Operating Transfers from General		
Fund	107,860	
Required Additions		107,860
To close the Operating Transfers		
and Required Additions accounts.		
(C2) Interest Earnings (or Earnings)	1,890	
Required Earnings		1,746
Fund Balance		144
To close the earnings and		
estimated earnings accounts and to		
transfer the difference to Fund		
Balance.		

When the budget was recorded in journal entry number 1, the credit to Fund Balance was $19,206, the amount of the required fund increase for the second year according to Figure 8-1. The $144 difference between estimated and actual earnings for year 2 will produce a higher figure for Fund Balance at the end of year 2 than that required by the schedule of sinking fund requirements.

(C3) Appropriations	90,400	
Expenditures		90,400
To close the estimated and actual		
expenditures accounts.		

Again, we have chosen to illustrate Debt Service Fund accounting with budgetary control accounts. Where formal budgetary control is not exercised, the budgetary entries are omitted.

ACCRUAL OF INTEREST PAYABLE

The National Council on Governmental Accounting does not recommend accrual of the year-end balances of interest payable on term or serial bonds unless the resources to pay the interest have been accrued or received in the Debt Service Fund. If a fund is on a calendar year basis and the annual interest on its bonds was paid as scheduled on October 31, 19X1, the Debt Service Fund clearly would be obligated, as of December 31, 19X1, for the interest for the last two months of 19X1. On the other hand, the 19X1 budget typically would provide for the payment of the interest expenditure falling due in the current year, and the following year's budget would provide for payment of interest due in 19X2. Since the resources that will be used to pay the interest for the months of November and December 19X1 cannot be accrued as of December 31, 19X1, accruing that interest expenditure and liability could result in (1) an unwarranted deficit being reported in the serial bond Debt Service Funds and (2) an unwarranted fund balance deficiency being reported in term bond Debt Service Funds. Thus, interest payable at year end normally is not recorded in Debt Service Funds.

On the other hand, if Debt Service Fund resources have been made available at the end of 19X1 to pay debt interest and/or principal maturing early in 19X2, the expenditure and related liability may be recorded in the Debt Service Fund in 19X1. In this case the amount of the debt principal that is recorded as a Debt Service Fund liability should be removed from the General Long-Term Debt accounts.

BALANCE SHEET PRIOR TO MATURITY

Separate balance sheets for each of the Debt Service Funds of A Governmental Unit could be prepared, but where a number of funds exists it is customary to combine them as shown in Figure 8-2. The balance sheet might include such additional assets as Cash with Fiscal Agents, Taxes Receivable—Current, Tax Liens Receivable, and Interest and Penalties Receivable on Taxes. In addition, the unamortized premiums and discounts on investments may be presented in the balance sheet rather than showing the investment figure at net amortized cost. Similarly, there may be such liability accounts as Matured Bonds Payable and Matured Interest Payable. In the case of term bonds, the actuarial requirement for the fund should be footnoted so that statement users may compare the actual status of the fund with the actuarial requirement.

If the number of Debt Service Funds exceeds seven or eight, the format of Figure 8-2 becomes unwieldy. One option in such cases is to present a Combining Debt Service Funds Balance Sheet with a column for each major Debt Service Fund and an "Other Debt Service Funds" column presenting the combined data for the other Debt Service Funds. This should be accompanied by a Combining Balance Sheet for the "other" Debt Service Funds, the total of which agrees with the "Other Debt Service Funds" column of the main Combining Balance Sheet.

BALANCE SHEET AT MATURITY

The Balance Sheet of A Governmental Unit's City Hall Term Bonds Debt Service Fund at the date of maturity of the bonds, December 31, 19Y9, is presented in Figure 8-3. It presents two problems. First, though the fund has assets in excess of the matured bonds payable, some of the assets have not yet been converted into cash. Therefore, the cash balance is not sufficient to pay the matured bonds. Second, the Fund Balance remaining after retiring the bonds must be disposed of.

The first problem is a minor one if the investments are readily marketable at or above cost. The Interest Receivable on Investments will also be liquidated upon sale of the investments. A more difficult problem is presented when the

Figure 8-2

A GOVERNMENTAL UNIT

Debt Service Funds
Combining Balance Sheet
December 31, 19X1

	Total	19Z0 Flores Park	19Y9 City Hall
Assets			
Cash	$ 2,210	$1,000	$ 1,210
Taxes receivable—delinquent (net of estimated uncollectible taxes)	4,000	4,000	
Investments (net)	35,180		35,180
Interest receivable on investments	420		420
Total assets	$41,810	$5,000	$36,810
Liabilities and Fund Balances			
Fund balances	$41,810	$5,000	$36,810*

*The actuarial requirement is $36,666.

source of revenues for the Debt Service Fund is property taxes. Delinquent taxes receivable of a Debt Service Fund at maturity may ultimately be collected, but cash is required immediately for the payment of the bonds. If the government has other Debt Service Funds, and if the law permits, cash may be borrowed from other Debt Service Funds. When delinquent taxes are collected, the inter-fund loan is repaid. Alternatively, money may be loaned to the Debt Service Fund from the General Fund, or the delinquent tax receivables may be transferred to the General Fund when the necessary money is provided to the Debt Service

Figure 8-3

A GOVERNMENTAL UNIT

City Hall Bonds Debt Service Fund
Balance Sheet
December 31, 19Y9

Assets	
Cash	$ 975,000
Investments	26,000
Interest receivable on investments	1,500
Total assets	$1,002,500

Liabilities and Fund Balance	
Matured bonds payable	$1,000,000
Fund balance	2,500
Total liabilities and fund balance	$1,002,500

Fund from the General Fund. If the law prohibits such interfund loans or interfund "sales" of delinquent receivables, short-term borrowing from nongovernment sources may be necessary.

The second problem is the disposition of the Fund Balance. If the law permits, the balance will be transferred (a residual equity transfer) to another Debt Service Fund, especially if the latter's contributions or earnings are short of requirements. Similarly, if the Fund had a deficit, it might be made up by transfers from the General Fund, by an additional tax levy, or by transfers of balances of other Debt Service Funds. Normally the fund balance or deficit of a Debt Service Fund will be small because adjustments will have been made from time to time throughout the life of the Fund. Deficits are sometimes large, however, because of failure to make contributions at proper intervals, failure to compute actuarial requirements properly, or losses on investments. A special tax may have to be levied in such instances; or, if the deficit is quite large, the bonds may have to be refunded; and there may even be a default.

STATEMENT OF OPERATIONS

Those managing Debt Service Funds, the investing public, and taxpayers are interested in the results of operations of Debt Service Funds. A Statement of Revenues, Expenditures, and Changes in Fund Balances is prepared for this purpose. A Combining Statement of Revenues, Expenditures, and Changes in Fund Balances for the Debt Service Funds of A Governmental Unit is presented in Figure 8-4. Additional revenue accounts that might appear in the statement include Interest and Penalties on Property Taxes; Revenue from Other Agencies, such as shared taxes from higher governments; and Gains or Losses on Disposition of Investments. Also, additional operating transfers and residual equity transfers may have increased the fund balance during the period. All users will be interested in comparing the actuarially required increases in fund balances with the actual increases; thus, the actuarially required increases are footnoted. The actuarially required balances may be footnoted here also, as well as on the balance sheet.

Interim financial statements may be prepared for the benefit of management. However, the few expenditures of a Debt Service Fund are more precisely budgetable than those of, for example, the General Fund and hence are more easily controlled.

SINGLE DEBT SERVICE FUND FOR SEVERAL BOND ISSUES

As a general rule, the number of Debt Service Funds should be held to a minimum. The law or contractual requirements may in some cases require a separate Debt Service Fund for each bond issue; in other cases they permit a single Debt Service Fund to service several or all issues. The latter arrangement is particularly desirable for all the issues to be financed from the general property tax. In such cases the budget for the single Debt Service Fund would be prepared by analyzing the debt service requirements for each bond issue. That is, the Required Addi-

Figure 8-4

A GOVERNMENTAL UNIT

Debt Service Funds
Combining Statement of Revenues, Expenditures, and Changes in Fund Balances
For the Year Ended December 31, 19X1

	19Z0 Flores Park	19Y9 City Hall	Total
Revenues and other financing sources:			
Property taxes	$155,000		$155,000
Operating transfers from General Fund .		$107,860	107,860
Interest on investments		1,890	1,890
Total revenues	$155,000	$109,750	$264,750
Expenditures:			
Redemption of serial bonds	$100,000		$100,000
Interest on bonds	50,000	$ 90,000	140,000
Fiscal agent's fees		400	400
Total expenditures	$150,000	$ 90,400	$240,400
Excess (deficit) to fund balance	$ 5,000	$ 19,350	$ 24,350
Fund balances, January 1, 19X1		17,460	17,460
Fund balances, December 31, 19X1	$ 5,000*	$ 36,810†	$ 41,810

*The actuarial requirement for 19X1 was $0.
†The actuarial requirement for 19X1 was $19,206.

tions, Required Earnings, and Appropriations accounts would be set up in the sum of the amounts they would have been set up for in individual Debt Service Funds for each issue. No attempt is made to allocate revenues or transfers in to specific issues in such cases, nor are assets and liabilities segregated by bond issue, though fund balances may be.

When a balance sheet is prepared for a single Debt Service Fund that is servicing several issues, two sections of the balance sheet may require specific identification of debt issues: (1) If a matured debt issue is reported as a liability of the Fund, it should be identified by name, and (2) the Fund Balance figure(s) should be supported by a schedule of the actuarial requirements, if any, for each debt issue.

POOLING OF ASSETS

Even though the law, contractual agreements, or administrative judgment may require several Debt Service Funds, it may be feasible to pool the investments of the Debt Service Funds to achieve maximum efficiency and safety in the investment program. For example, a single investment counsel may be able to serve as easily for a major investment as for several minor ones. More important, the investments may be diversified when a substantial sum is involved and economies of purchase may result from investing large sums rather than small ones.

Also, higher yields may be earned and less of the total assets of all of the Funds may need to be kept in cash (nonearning) if the investable assets of the Debt Service Funds are pooled. In such cases well-defined rules for determining the equity of each Debt Service Fund in the assets and in the profits and losses from investments must be established and detailed records must be maintained.

CONCLUDING COMMENTS

Most government bond issues in recent years have been serial issues; term bond issues have been less popular, though they still are encountered in practice. Further, since many serial bonds have been serviced by annual transfers from the General or a Special Revenue Fund(s) to a Debt Service Fund(s)—and Debt Service Funds are no longer required by GAAP in such cases—some governments now record such debt service directly in the General and Special Revenue Funds instead of making annual operating transfers to Debt Service Funds. On the other hand, the law or contractual agreements often require Debt Service Funds for serial bonds or other long-term debt, and many finance officers prefer to control and account for all "general government" general obligation debt service through Debt Service Funds.

Finally, the use of various forms of lease arrangements—including capital leases and lease-purchase agreements as well as operating leases—has increased significantly in recent years. Those finance officers who prefer to centralize the control of and accounting for general long-term debt service in Debt Service Funds use them to service major capital leases, at least, and possibly other significant lease arrangements. Those finance officers who prefer to control and account for as much of the general operations of government as possible through the General and Special Revenue Funds do not use Debt Service Funds to service any lease arrangements unless required to do so by law or contractual agreement. Thus, the use of Debt Service Funds for leases—and for serial bonds, notes, and warrants—varies widely among state and local governmental units.

▶ **Question 8-1.** What is the nature of the Fund Balance account in the Debt Service Fund at year end?

Question 8-2. A sinking fund was established for the purpose of retiring Dorchester Street Bridge bonds, which have a twenty-year maturity. In the fifth year $10,000 of Dorchester Street Bridge bonds were acquired by the Debt Service Fund. Should these bonds be canceled, or should they be held "alive" until maturity? Why?

Question 8-3. Why might a governmental unit want to refund an outstanding bond issue (a) at maturity? (b) prior to maturity?

Question 8-4. City Z's Debt Service Fund pays interest on the City Hall Bonds on February 1 and August 1. Should interest payable be accrued at December 31, the end of the Fund's fiscal year? Why?

Question 8-5. (a) General sinking fund securities have risen in value. Should the appreciation in value be recorded in the accounts of the Debt Service Fund? (b) Would your answer be different if the securities had declined in value?

Question 8-6. A fund was established for the retirement of bonds of $100,000 maturing at the end of ten years. Annual contributions of $10,000 are to be made to the fund, but all earnings on the contributions are to be transferred to the General Fund. Is this fund a sinking fund in the sense in which the term is used in this chapter? Give reasons for your answer.

Question 8-7. A certain municipality provides that its sinking fund is to be built up from various licenses and fines. The revenues from these sources have been as follows: 19X7, $5,000; 19X8, $3,000; 19X9, $8,000. Can you see what is wrong with such a provision?

Question 8-8. What disposition should be made of the balance remaining in a Debt Service Fund after the bonds mature and are paid?

Question 8-9. What is meant by defeasance? What conditions are necessary to achieve defeasance or defeasance in substance?

Question 8-10. What are the advantages of pooling the investments of a city's Debt Service Funds?

Question 8-11. What are the main sources of assets for a Debt Service Fund?

Question 8-12. Some accountants believe that budgetary control of Debt Service Fund operations such as those illustrated in this chapter is unnecessary unless required by law. Others disagree. What do you think?

Question 8-13. When would bond interest or principal due soon in the next year be accrued as expenditures and current liabilities of a Debt Service Fund? When would they not be accrued?

Question 8-14. Why might a government use a Debt Service Fund for a serial bond issue when it is not required to do so?

▶ **Problem 8-1.** Set up a schedule showing the required sinking fund contributions and required earnings if it is assumed that a $100,000 term bond issue is to be retired in ten years and contributions are to earn 9 percent interest compounded annually. The required annual addition of $6,582 is made at the end of each year.

Problem 8-2. Gotham City issued $500,000 of 8 percent regular serial bonds at par (no accrued interest) on January 2, 19X0, to finance a General Fund deficit. Interest is payable semiannually on January 2 and July 2 and $50,000 of the principal matures each January 2 beginning in 19X1. Resources for servicing the debt will be made available through a special tax levy for this purpose and transfers as needed from a Special Revenue Fund. The Debt Service Fund is not under formal budget control; the city's fiscal year begins October 1.

Required:

Prepare general journal entries for the Debt Service Fund to record the transactions and events described below.

1. June 28, 19X0—The first installment of the special tax was received, $12,000.
2. June 29, 19X0—A Special Revenue Fund transfer of $8,000 was received.
3. July 2, 19X0—The semiannual interest payment on the bonds was made.
4. December 10, 19X0—The second installment of the special tax levy was received, $40,000.
5. December 12, 19X0—A $30,000 Special Revenue Fund transfer was made to the Debt Service Fund.

6. January 2, 19X1—The semiannual interest payment and the bond payment were made.

7. January 2, 19Y0—At the beginning of 19Y0, the Debt Service Fund had accumulated $30,000 in investments (from transfers) and $25,000 in cash (from taxes). The investments were liquidated at face value and the final interest and principal payment on the bonds was made.

8. January 3, 19Y0—The Debt Service Fund's purpose having been served, the council ordered the residual assets transferred to the Special Revenue Fund and the Debt Service Fund terminated.

Problem 8-3. The City of B, pursuant to state law, consolidated all of its Debt Service Funds into one Fund, the balance sheet for which was as follows:

CITY OF B

Debt Service Fund
Balance Sheet
December 31, 19X9

Assets

Cash		$150,000
Taxes receivable—delinquent	$ 90,000	
Less: Estimated uncollectible delinquent taxes ..	10,000	80,000
Investments	$276,000	
Less: Discounts on investments	1,000	275,000
		$505,000

Fund Balance

Fund Balance:	
School bonds	$252,500
Library bonds	176,750
Recreation bonds	75,750
	$505,000

The state Supreme Court subsequently held the law authorizing consolidated Debt Service Funds unconstitutional.

Required:

Recast the balance sheet above so as to comply with the court decision (i.e., show the financial condition of *each* fund).

Problem 8-4. Shoulders Village, which operates on the calendar year, issued a five year, 8 percent $100,000 note to the Bank of Shoulders on January 5, 19X4. The proceeds of the note were recorded in the General Fund. Interest and one-tenth of the principal is due semiannually, on January 5 and July 5, beginning July 5, 19X4. A Debt Service Fund has been established to service this debt; financing will come from General Fund transfers and a small debt service tax levied serveral years ago.

Required:

(a) Prepare the general journal entries needed to record the following transactions and events and (b) prepare a balance sheet at December 31, 19X4, and a statement of revenues, expenditures, and changes in fund balance for the year then ended for the Debt Service Fund.

1. January 6—The Debt Service Fund budget for 19X4 was adopted. The General Fund contribution was estimated at $10,000; the tax levy was expected to yield $18,000.
2. The tax levy was received, $20,000.
3. The July 5, 19X4, payment of principal and interest was accrued on June 25.
4. The July 5, 19X4, payment was made.
5. The General Fund contribution of $10,000 was received.
6. The residual balance of a discontinued Capital Projects Fund, $6,000, was transferred to the Debt Service Fund.
7. Since resources had been made available, the January 5, 19X1, payment was accrued.
8. Closing entries were prepared at December 31, 19X4.

Problem 8-5. The City of Andrew had outstanding $1,000,000 par of 12 percent Series A bonds issued several years ago when interest was high. The finance officer proposes to refinance the issue with a new 8 percent Series B issue and some cash to be transferred from the General Fund. Since the Series A bonds are now selling at a substantial premium and, in any event, it does not appear feasible to buy all of them back, the finance officer proposed to place sufficient monies in an irrevocable trust and meet all other conditions as set forth in the Internal Revenue Code and Regulations and in AICPA SOP 78-5 to achieve defeasance in substance. The council approved the plan and the following transactions occurred during 19X8:

1. A new 8 percent Series B serial bond issue was sold at par, $1,000,000.
2. A General Fund transfer of $150,000 was made to the Debt Service Fund.
3. It was determined that the amount that must be placed in the irrevocable trust to service the Series A issue until maturity and pay the principal at that time was $1,140,000.
4. The payment to the trustee was made, as were payments of $5,000 of consultation fees and travel costs necessary to consummate the transaction.
5. Its function served, the Debt Service Fund was terminated and the remaining balance transferred to the General Fund.

Required:

Prepare the general journal entries required in the Debt Service Fund to record the transactions described above.

Problem 8-6. A N City Debt Service Fund has the following trial balance on January 1, 19X0:

Cash	10,623.00	
Investments (Net of discount of $312.50)	45,687.50	
Interest Receivable	498.66	
Fund Balance		56,809.16
	56,809.16	56,809.16

The following information is available for the calendar year 19X0:

1. The accumulation schedule for the fund shows $8,723 as the required annual addition and $1,692.72 as the required fund earnings.
2. Interest expenditures will be $9,000 during the period.
3. On January 15 a $10,000, 10 percent bond, interest dates January 1 and July 1, is purchased for 101 plus accrued interest.
4. The General Fund contribution of the required annual addition is received.
5. Interest is received on July 2 on the bonds bought in transaction 3.
6. Other interest collected during the year totals $1,400.
7. Interest expenditures paid on the outstanding term debt, $9,000
8. On December 31 the accrued interest on investments other than those bought this year totals $475.80.
9. Amortization of the discounts on investments is $73.50; of premiums, $10.00.

Required:

(a) Prepare a worksheet summarizing the activities of the Debt Service Fund for the year. Include closing entries.
(b) Prepare a DSF balance sheet at December 31, 19X0.

Problem 8-7. On January 1, 19X1, Central City issued bonds amounting to $100,000 and maturing in five years. At the same time an appropriation was made for the first year's contribution to a sinking fund on December 31, 19X1, to be paid from the General Fund. A similar contribution was to be made from the General Fund each year thereafter to maturity, and interest on the bonds is paid directly from the General Fund.

Additional information:

1. Each year the contribution and earnings were received on December 31 and the cash in the fund on January 1 was invested. The city's fiscal year is the calendar year.
2. The investments all had the same maturity date as did the sinking fund bonds.
3. At maturity sinking fund bonds were set up in the sinking fund, and cash for their retirement was transmitted to fiscal agents. The remaining cash was transferred to the General Fund.
4. A comparison of sinking fund earnings with requirements showed the following:

Year	Excess of Earnings over Requirements	Deficiency of Earnings over Requirements
19X2	$300	
19X3		$500
19X4	400	
19X5	200	

Required:

(a) Prepare a schedule showing required contributions and earnings. (Assume that sinking fund investments will earn 7 percent per year, compounded annually. According to sinking fund tables, the required annual contribution on the basis of this rate of interest is $17,389.) Round all amounts to the nearest whole dollar.

(b) Prepare DSF journal entries, including closing entries, to be made each year.

(c) Prepare a DSF balance sheet as of December 31 of each year.

Problem 8-8. A serial Debt Service Fund of the State of Texona had the following postclosing trial balance at September 30, 19X7, the end of its fiscal year:

STATE OF TEXONA

Serial Debt Service Fund No. 2
Postclosing Trial Balance
September 30, 19X7

Cash	10,600,000	
Investments	7,600,000	
Matured Bonds Payable		5,000,000
Matured Notes Payable		2,000,000
Matured Interest Payable		3,500,000
Reserve for Bond Debt Service		6,000,000
Unreserved Fund Balance		1,700,000
	18,200,000	18,200,000

The Debt Service Fund is financed by a share of state sales tax revenues, transfers from other funds, and interest earnings. Significant debt service payments fall due on October 1 each year and are provided for in the appropriations of the previous year.

The following transactions and events affected the State of Texona Serial Debt Service Fund No. 2 during the 19X7-X8 fiscal year:

1. The matured bonds, notes, and interest payable were paid.
2. State sales taxes collected for the Debt Service Fund totalled $12,000,000.
3. All but $10,000 of the cash was invested.
4. The Reserve for Bond Debt Service was increased to $7,000,000 as required by the bond indenture.
5. Debt service maturities were:

Bonds	$5,000,000
Notes	2,000,000
Interest	3,000,000

6. Temporary investments of $9,200,000 were liquidated to pay the debt service due; the proceeds were $10,500,000. (Accrued interest receivable is debited to the Investments account at year end.)
7. The debt service payments due were made.
8. A $1,400,000 transfer was received upon termination of Debt Service Fund No. 6.
9. An $8,000,000 transfer was received from the General Fund.
10. A capital lease obligation, $1,500,000, was paid.
11. Debt service maturities at year end, on which payment is due October 1, 19X8, were:

Bonds	$5,000,000
Notes	2,000,000
Interest	2,500,000

12. Accrued interest receivable on investments at year end, $900,000.

Required:

1. Prepare DSF general journal entries to record the above transactions and events.
2. Prepare a preclosing trial balance for the Debt Service Fund at September 30, 19X8.
3. Prepare DSF closing entries at September 30, 19X8.
4. Prepare a balance sheet for the Debt Service Fund at September 30, 19X8.
5. Prepare a statement of revenues, expenditures, and changes in unreserved fund balance for the Debt Service Fund for the 19X7-X8 fiscal year.

Alternatively, in lieu of requirements 1-4, prepare a worksheet headed as follows:

Columns	Heading
1–2	Postclosing Trial Balance, 9/30/19X7
3–4	19X7-X8 Transactions
5–6	Closing Entries, 9/30/19X8
7–8	Postclosing Trial Balance, 9/30/19X8

Problem 8-9. Everett County services all of its general obligation serial indebtedness through one Debt Service Fund. Its serial indebtedness at August 31, 19X4, the end of its fiscal year, was:

$20,000,000—8% serial bonds, series F, interest and $1,000,000 principal payable January 1 and July 1

$30,000,000—10% serial bonds, series G, interest and $2,000,000 principal payable April 1 and October 1

$12,000,000—9% time warrants, interest and $600,000 principal payable quarterly on March 31, June 30, September 30, and December 31

$ 4,000,000—11% lease-purchase (capital lease) obligation, interest and $400,000 principal payable annually on November 1.

The trial balance of the Everett County Serial Debt Service Fund at August 31, 19X4, was:

Everett County

Serial Debt Service Fund
Postclosing Trial Balance
August 31, 19X4

Cash	5,000	
Cash with Fiscal Agent	55,000	
Investments	940,000	
Taxes Receivable—Delinquent	100,000	
Allowance for Uncollectible Taxes		10,000
Matured Bonds Payable		50,000
Matured Interest Payable		5,000
Fund Balance		1,035,000
	1,100,000	1,100,000

1. The fund is financed by a $5,000,000 General Fund transfer, made September 1, and a $10,000,000 property tax levy, of which 1% is expected to prove uncollectible. The taxes are levied September 1, and are payable on or before November 15, after which time they become delinquent. Tax collections as of November 15, 19X4 were:

Delinquent taxes	$ 92,000
Current taxes	9,600,000
	$9,692,000

Any uncollected 19X3-X4 taxes are written off at the end of 19X4-X5.

2. All cash is invested immediately in $10,000 increments and earns 1% per month, compounded quarterly on the average Investments balance. Interest accrued is debited to the Investments account and credited to Interest Revenue. Disinvestments may be made in any amount.

3. Cash with Fiscal Agent normally clears 30 days after the debt service due date. The Cash with Fiscal Agent reported in the August 31, 19X4 trial balance cleared September 15, 19X4; however, $100,000 of bond principal and $5,000 of interest of the April 1, 19X5 bond debt service payment had not cleared by year end.

4. Budgetary control accounts are not employed in the Everett County Serial Debt Service Fund.

Required:

A. Prepare (1) a schedule of Debt Service Fund requirements for 19X4-5 and (2) a chronological debt service schedule for 19X4-5.

B. Prepare general journal entries to (1) record the various transactions and events affecting the Everett County Serial Debt Service Fund during the 19X4-5 fiscal year, and (2) close the accounts at year end.

Alternatively, prepare a worksheet headed as follows:

Columns	Heading
1–2	Postclosing Trial Balance, 8/31/19X4
3–4	19X4-X5 Transactions
5–6	Preclosing Trial Balance, 8/31/19X5
7–8	Closing Entries, 8/31/19X5
9–10	Postclosing Trial Balance, 8/31/19X5

C. Prepare for the Everett County Serial Debt Service Fund (1) a balance sheet at 8/31/19X5, and (2) a statement of revenues, expenditures, and changes in fund balance for the year ended 8/31/19X5.

9

SPECIAL ASSESSMENT FUNDS

The typical services rendered by a government are beneficial to the general public, but some improvements or services are so evidently of primary benefit to a citizen or group of citizens that all or a part of their cost is charged to the properties or persons benefited. Special Assessment Funds are established to account for the financing of such improvements or services through special charges levied against the properties or persons benefited. Typical improvements are sewers, street paving and widening, curbs, and sidewalks; typical services are street cleaning and street lighting.

This chapter deals with *improvements* financed through special assessments for three reasons: (1) Special Assessment Funds are used to finance construction projects more often than services, (2) most services provided on a continuing basis are best financed and accounted for through Enterprise Funds, and (3) accounting procedures for improvement projects are more complicated than for services.

SPECIAL ASSESSMENT FUND LIFE CYCLE

A construction-related Special Assessment Fund normally must originate with a petition requesting the improvement. Most states have laws requiring that, to be effective, the petition must be signed by owners of more than 50 percent of the property in the improvement district. The local government acts on behalf of the property owners to authorize the project, conduct the improvement (usually through a contractor), and approve the completed construction.

Because the assessments against the properties are likely to be relatively large, the government generally extends the owners the privilege of paying their assessments in installments over a number of years. For major projects, assessments are not usually levied until construction is completed and all costs iden-

307

tified. The government is responsible for arranging and administering the financing of construction. Construction may be financed by bonds, notes, or advances from an Internal Service Fund; deferred assessments are usually financed by notes or bonds.

The Special Assessment Fund is, on the basis of the preceding description, a combination of a Capital Projects Fund and Debt Service Fund. Construction records must be kept in order to control and determine the cost of the project, as in the Capital Projects Fund. The Debt Service Fund aspects include determining and accounting for the sources of funds for debt service, accumulating the funds, and paying the debts and interest thereon.

The more complex funds may go through the following distinct processes:

1. Authorization of the project
2. Financing the construction
3. Construction of the improvement
4. Assessment determination and levy
5. Collection of assessments and interest thereon
6. Servicing debt principal and interest
7. Disposing of fund balances or deficits and terminating the fund

Some special assessment projects follow this order exactly, but not all projects involve all phases, nor are the phases always sequenced as in the foregoing list. In simpler situations where (1) construction is to be done under a fixed-price contract and (2) costs are assessed and collected prior to payment being made to the contractor, the Special Assessment Fund functions only as a Capital Projects Fund and phases 2 and 6 are eliminated. In other cases (1) assessments are levied before all project costs are known, (2) some assessments may be designated for construction use and others for debt service, and (3) construction, assessment and collection, and debt service activities may be carried on simultaneously (see Figure 9-1). In the third situation just noted—where construction, assessment and collection, and debt service activities overlap—particular care must be taken to assure that assets designated for one purpose are not used for another. Separate Cash and Fund Balance accounts prove especially useful in such cases.

The Project Authorization

Authorization of the project begins the Special Assessment Fund life cycle. Authorization is a function of a local legislative body or of special district commissioners and is usually the result of a petition from owners of more than 50 percent of the property in the improvement district. In some cases the government may initiate the project to take care of problems that threaten the general public. For example, the Health Department might order installation of sanitary sewers when septic tanks in the assessment area are a threat to the public health. In all cases legal requirements such as due notice and hearings must be complied with and the authorization should be a formal action.

Figure 9-1

ILLUSTRATIVE SPECIAL ASSESSMENT
FUND PHASES AND ACTIVITIES

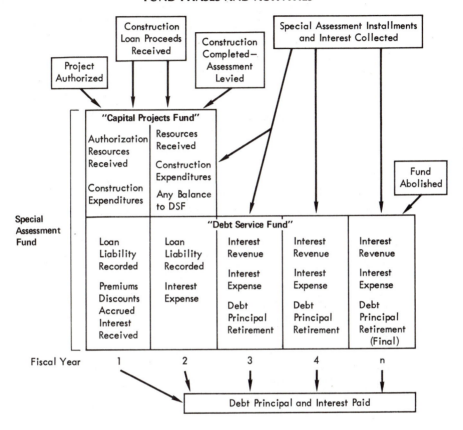

Budgeting and Accounting

Special Assessment Funds are of the governmental type and hence must use the accounting recommended for governmental funds; its application to the SAF is discussed in following paragraphs.

The modified accrual basis must be used; Fund revenues should be recognized when the related assets are both measurable and available. The process of assembling assets may occur at the start of the project; in other cases the levy of assessments may be deferred until the project is completed. In either case, revenues are considered earned and are recognized only as appropriate expenditures are made. If assets had been assembled at the start of the project and if the project were not carried out, the assets would have to be returned to the property owners who were assessed, to the other governmental units that may have contributed, and even to the General Fund if it has contributed. Hence the government stands in a trust relationship to the contributors, and *revenue is earned and recognized only as expenditures are made for the expressed purpose. Statement*

1 is silent on how the modified accrual basis should be applied to recognition of special assessment revenue. This reasoning was derived in large part from the NCGA position adopted in *Statement 2* pertaining to grants, entitlements, and shared revenue. Indeed, the SAF may be partially financed from such sources, and thus the presumed NCGA position as to SAF accounting is consistent. Other interpretations of how the modified accrual basis should be applied to SAFs are discussed later in this chapter.

Another revenue modification is derived from the NCGA position that:

> unmatured interest on . . . special assessment indebtedness secured by interest-bearing special assessment levies . . . should be recognized when due.[1]

The NCGA went on to observe that:

> as a practical matter, interest earned on special assessment levies may be accrued when due, rather than when earned, if it approximately offsets interest expenditure of such projects that is also recorded when due.[2]

The latter position was justified on both cost-benefit and materiality grounds. The former position was justified on the same basis used to justify recognition of interest on general long-term debt, which is discussed in Chapter 8.

The reporting focus, as with all governmental funds, is on the fiscal year. The project as a focus of fund operation may be reported on by supplementary, special purpose statements and by footnotes to the SAF financial statements.

All special assessment notes and bonds are liabilities of the Special Assessment Fund, and they are the sole exception to the general rule that only short-term liabilities are included in the balance sheets of governmental funds. The proceeds of notes or bonds, then, are not "other financing sources" as in, for example, the CPF; and payments of the debt are not expenditures.

Budgetary accounting for the SAF is discussed later in this chapter, but for the moment several observations can be made. Revenue sources are invariably few in number, well known, and do not need much administrative supervision (except for the collection of assessments). Usually the projects are major, there is one project per fund, and the expenditure is made by contract (not, for example, by the government's own work force). These circumstances imply that administrative control is simple. For these reasons, we have chosen to present our principal illustration without budgetary accounting.

Interim Financing of the Special Assessment Project

Since few property owners are financially able to pay the total amount of a major assessment immediately, provision is usually made for installment payments. But the construction work must be paid for upon completion, and therefore must be financed from other sources. Several interim financing possibilities are available.

---

[1] NCGAS 1, pp. 2 and 10.
[2] Ibid., p. 12.

Interfund Loans. In some instances cash may be borrowed from other funds of the government, either pending or in lieu of the issuing notes or bonds. Such loans are usually considered investments from the standpoint of the lending fund, and interest is paid on them. Where such loans are considered temporary, they are repaid from the proceeds of special assessment bond or other debt issues. If interfund loans are made in lieu of issuing special assessment bonds or other indebtedness, they will be repaid from special assessment collections.

Interfund loans should not be made unless they are both legal and properly authorized, and intermediate- or long-term loans from General or Special Revenue Funds are rarely used in special assessment project financing. Interfund loans are frequently made from Debt Service, Enterprise, or Trust Funds, however, and are generally an extremely safe form of investment. Furthermore, they may provide a higher yield than other investments of comparable safety and involve no brokerage or similar costs.

In other instances, governments may establish an Internal Service Fund (see Chapter 12) for the express purpose of providing interim financing for Special Assessment Funds. Internal Service Fund capital may be provided in such cases through a special tax levy, through issuance of bonds, or through a transfer from the General Fund. As money is repaid, it is used to finance other special assessment projects.

Issuance of Notes. Long-term interim financing is ordinarily obtained from the sale of bonds or the issuance of long-term notes, which are usually not issued until the costs of the project have been determined. Financing needed before the bond proceeds become available may be provided by the issuance of short-term notes—open notes from a local bank or more formal "bond anticipation notes."

Sale of Bonds. Special assessment project interim financing may be secured through bond issues. Either general-special assessment bonds or special-special assessment bonds may be issued. A general-special assessment bond is secured by the full faith and credit of the governmental unit; that is, maturing interest or principal payments must be met from other resources of the unit if assessment collections are inadequate to do so. A special-special assessment bond is one that may not become a charge against the governmental unit as a whole but is secured only by the assessments collected or the properties benefited. Technically, the government's responsibility in the case of special-special assessment bonds is merely to enforce collections and to handle proceeds properly. In practice, a government normally will be equally vigilant in enforcing collection of assessments relating to either type of bond issue and will see that neither type is permitted to be in default. Default of any bond issue with which it is even casually associated may severely affect a government's credit rating and, hence, both its ability to borrow for other purposes and the interest rate it must pay.

Serial bonds usually are issued with maturity dates arranged so that part of the issue may be retired as soon as a special assessment installment is collected. Specific bonds may be payable from particular installment collections. In that case, bonds may be payable only from the collections of the installment to which they apply and no other. Bonds are sometimes made liens against specific pieces of property. In that case, each bond is payable only from the assessments levied against the particular pieces of property with which it is identified.

Authority for Sale of Bonds. Appropriate authority must be secured and documented if bonds are to be issued or other debt is to be incurred in the course of the project. A narrative memorandum entry will suffice, though some accountants prefer preparation of a formal entry to record the authority to incur debt. Formal bond authorization entries are often used to establish accounting system control over unissued bonds. In this case the unissued bonds, or records thereof, constitute a subsidiary ledger under general ledger control.

Several approaches to entering debt issuance authority in the accounts may be encountered in practice, but the simplest is that used in accounting for business enterprises:

Bonds Authorized—Unissued	350,000	
Bonds Payable		350,000
To record authorization of the bond issue.		
Cash for Construction	100,000	
Bonds Authorized—Unissued		100,000
To record sale of a part of the bond issue.		

Under this method, the par or face value of bonds outstanding at any time is the difference between the balances of the Bonds Payable and Bonds Authorized—Unissued accounts, less any treasury bonds held.

Contractor Financing. The most widely used interim financing provides that cash will be paid at the end of the project, after it passes inspection. (A variant is to require the contractor to take, at the conclusion of the project, the *long-term* notes or bonds that provide permanent financing.) This practice simplifies the later accounting, since interest on deferred assessments and interest on long-term financing are the major remaining problems. Any arrangement that permits levy of assessment at the end of the project makes interim interest an implicit part of the cost of construction. Capitalization of interest during construction is in conformity with GAAP.

Cash Accounts

All SAF cash is to be used for specified purposes, including (1) construction, (2) payments of notes and interest, (3) bond payment, and (4) interest payments on bonds. The NCGA has not made segregation of cash by purpose mandatory, but we illustrate segregation in journal entries in the principal example.

There may be cases in which segregation is required by law, by contracts with creditors, or by action of local authorities. In simple cases nothing is to be gained from segregation; but if financing is complicated the authors recommend segregation. A schematic arrangement indicating possible sources of the several categories of cash is presented in Figure 9-2. This figure is a useful reference guide to the analysis and recording of cash collections.

Fund Balance

As in the case of separate cash accounts, separate fund balance accounts are not required by NCGA. Where they are used, they indicate positive or negative fund balances resulting from construction, interest, and bond payment activities.

Figure 9-2

SPECIAL ASSESSMENT FUND
Typical Sources of Cash

Case A: The project is financed by contribution from the government and by assessment. The governmental unit pays its share of the costs promptly. Bonds are issued to permit deferral of assessment payments.

Case B: The project is financed by contribution from the government and by assessment. The governmental unit defers one-half of its payments to future years. Notes are issued to finance construction and to permit the issuance of bonds for the exact amount necessary to finance the deferred assessments. Assessments are levied upon completion of the project.

Cash Account Debited	Source of Cash	
	Case A	*Case B*
Cash for Construction	Governmental unit's share of cost First assessment installment(s) Bond proceeds (excluding premiums)	One-half of governmental unit's share of cost Note proceeds
Cash for Payment of Notes and Interest		Installment(s) of governmental unit's share of cost Bond proceeds (excluding premiums) Installment(s) of assessments receivable
Cash for Payment of Bonds	Assessment Collections	Assessment Collections
Cash for Payment of Interest	Bond premium Interest on assessment installments	Bond premium Interest on assessment installments

Such information will indicate, for example, the relationship between interest revenues and expenses for time periods and at the ends of reporting periods. It may, of course, be provided by analyses rather than by separate accounts.

Proponents of multiple fund balance and cash accounts argue that, where they are not utilized, (1) resources intended for debt service may be illegally used for construction, (2) legally authorized construction cost ceilings may be exceeded, (3) the security of fund creditors may be endangered, (4) bond indenture provisions or other contractual agreements may be violated, (5) supplemental assessments may have to be levied against the persons or properties benefited by the project, if possible, or (6) the public at large may be forced to bear more than its fair share of the project cost when General Fund resources must be used to "bail out" the Special Assessment Fund. Though not everyday occurrences, situations such as these do arise.

The decision should be based on an analysis of the cost of maintaining separate accounts compared to the benefits derived therefrom—or the costs of not maintaining them. Any doubtful case should be resolved in favor of separate fund balance accounts.

Levying and Collecting Assessments

Assessments are levied in some cases when the project is completed and in others as soon as construction is authorized. A brief description of assessment procedures will help in understanding special assessment accounting.

Assigning the Cost. The cost of an improvement is levied on the basis of benefit. Though in theory all properties considered to be benefited by the improvement will be assessed a part of the cost, in the usual case only those properties contiguous to the improvement will be assessed. The methods of determining the incidence of benefit, the total benefit, and the distribution of cost among benefited parties and between them and the governmental unit are governed by many arbitrary laws and rules.

As implied above, the governmental unit may bear part of the cost because property owners are not expected to pay more than the amount of benefit accruing to their properties (they may not be legally required to do so under terms of usual state or local statutes). If the total of the estimated assessments (based on presumed benefits) is less than the cost of the improvement, the government will make up the difference; but if the total of these estimated assessments equals or exceeds the estimated cost of the improvement, the government may assume no part of the cost.

The governmental unit may also bear part of the cost of an improvement because it receives some of the benefits. For example, if one of the streets in an improvement district is a traffic artery, its paving benefits all the citizens, not just adjacent property owners.

Finally, the governmental unit may share in the cost of the improvement in the capacity of a property owner. If a police station or fire station lies in the improvement district, the owner should share in the cost of the improvement as the citizen property owners do. Unless statutes specifically permit a city to assess the property of another governmental unit lying in the district, assessments cannot be so levied. The city may bear the cost in such cases.

Assessment Rolls and Records. Detailed records of special assessments and interest receivable must be maintained for each piece of property. The identification (legal description) of the property, information about the owner, the amounts of assessments and interest receivable, and a record of payments are minimum information to support the various asset accounts for assessments and interest receivable.

Allowance for Uncollectible Assessments. In spite of the fact that some of the assessments may prove to be uncollectible, usually no allowance for uncollectible assessments is set up. This is because the government is acting in a trustee capacity; as such, its duty is to see that the assessments are collected and properly disbursed. If delinquent assessments are not paid, the government may secure a lien against the property, and it may have the property sold to satisfy the lien. The accounting procedure involved in such cases is described later in this chapter.

The trust character of Special Assessment Funds is especially evident in those instances where bonds are a lien against specific properties. Here the government may use the proceeds from the assessments levied against these properties only for the payment of such bonds. Further, certain bonds may be payable from specified installments of assessments levied against particular pieces of property. Even if general-special assessment bonds are issued, an allowance for uncollectible assessments is often considered impractical in such situations. If an allowance for uncollectible assessments is established, all assessments must be increased proportionately. Not only might this be considered inequitable, it might also be illegal—since properties may not be assessed for more than the amount of the benefit accruing to them as a result of the project. For these reasons, deficiencies resulting from uncollectible assessments usually must be made up by the governmental unit.

Financing the Government's Contribution

The governmental unit may finance its contributions to project cost in various ways. If the amount is small, an operating transfer from the General Fund will probably be authorized. If the government's share of the cost is too large to be financed from current revenues, it may pay its share in installments or by the issuance of general bonds.

Interest Income and Expense

Interest costs on bonds or notes arise because (1) assessments usually are not levied until the project is complete and (2) property owners are permitted to pay by installments. The property owners are expected to bear the interest cost. The interest rate set by the government on deferred assessments may be higher than the rate on special assessment bonds or notes for at least two reasons: (1) After financing arrangements are complete, some property owners may want to pay in full. If the bonds or notes are not callable, the government may have to continue to pay interest on them; it may or may not be able to earn enough on the money paid by property owners to meet interest payments on the debt. (2) Even if bonds or notes are issued well before the project is completed, assessments usually cannot be levied until completion. The interest costs during the construction period should either be included in the assessments or recovered by having the rate on the assessments exceed that on the debt. As recommended by the NCGA and discussed earlier in this chapter, where interest on long-term debt and interest on special assessments are approximately offsetting, they should be recorded when due.

Bond Premium or Discount

As indicated previously, premiums and discounts on long-term investments or arising from the sale of bonds represent interest-rate adjustments. The NCGA has consistently recommended that premiums and discounts on special assessment bonds be amortized in a systematic and rational manner over the life of the bond issue in order properly to report interest expense. Presumably it would also favor amortization of premiums or discounts on long-term Special Assessment Fund investments in order to properly compute interest income and, hence, Fund Balance—Interest. Thus, the illustrations and examples in this chapter assume that bond premiums or discounts are amortized in some rational and systematic manner rather than written off directly to a Fund Balance account.

TRANSACTIONS AND ENTRIES—FIRST FISCAL YEAR _____

The following transactions are typical of the first year of operation of a Special Assessment Fund. They are based on the following assumptions, among others:

- The assessments will be levied when the work of the contractor is complete and accepted.
- Bonds will be sold to pay the contractor.
- The SAF has only one project and a few sources of resources, and therefore formal budgetary accounting is not necessary.

Transactions

1. The legislative body authorized a special assessment project in the amount of $500,000. The governmental unit was to pay $100,000 and the remainder was to be provided by assessments against property owners.
2. A construction contract was awarded for $440,000.
3. The governmental unit paid $50,000 of its share of the cost; the remainder was considered due and payable.
4. A contractor's bill of $100,000 was approved for payment.
5. Property was condemned and the judgments of $40,000 were paid.

(1) No entry.

(2) Encumbrances 440,000
    Reserve for Encumbrances   440,000
    To record the awarding of a
    contract.

(3) Cash—Construction 50,000
    Due from GF 50,000
        Operating Transfer from GF—
        Construction   100,000
    To record the receipt of cash and
    the recognition of a receivable from
    the General Fund.

Transaction (3) has been recorded on the assumption that the first $100,000 of expenditures is to be attributed to the operating transfer and hence the transfer is recognized in the period it arises. Under this assumption all additional expenditures will justify recognition of revenue [see entry (A-1)]. Another accounting policy option would be to attribute expenditures to operating transfer and revenues on the ratio (80–20) of assessments to the governmental unit's share of the cost. The note to the financial statement that describes significant accounting policies should include a description of the revenue recognition method that is used.

(4a) Reserve for Encumbrances 100,000
      Encumbrances   100,000
    To reduce, by the amount of an
    approved progress report, the
    memorandum amount of the
    contract.

(4b) Expenditures—Construction 100,000
      Contracts Payable   100,000
    To record receipt and approval of
    a progress report from the
    contractor.

(5) Expenditures—Construction 40,000
    Cash—Construction   40,000
    To record payment of judgments
    based on condemnation awards to
    property owners.

Adjusting Entry

At the end of the year an adjusting entry was needed and made to recognize the revenues that had been justified by the incurring of appropriate expenditures:

(A-1) Assessable Costs 40,000
      Revenues—Construction   40,000
    To recognize revenues equal to
    expenditures in excess of the
    amount of the operating
    transfer. [See the discussion of
    entry (3).]

Since assessments were not to be levied until the project was completed, they could not be set up as assets. But to the extent of the amount of assessable expenditures in excess of the amount of the operating transfer there is an asset, assessable costs, that should be set up. It represents the right of the government to levy assessments in the future. This right justifies recognizing revenues.

Trial Balance before Closing Entry

On the basis of the transactions and adjusting journal entries, the preclosing trial balance of the SAF would appear as follows:

Cash—Construction	10,000	
Due from General Fund	50,000	
Assessable Costs	40,000	
Contracts Payable		100,000
Reserve for Encumbrances		340,000
Revenues—Construction		40,000
Operating Transfer from GF—Construction		100,000
Encumbrances—Construction	340,000	
Expenditures—Construction	140,000	
	580,000	580,000

Closing Entry at End of Fiscal Year

The Revenues, Operating Transfer, and Expenditures accounts should be closed out at year end. The closing entry is the signal for an entry in the General Fixed Asset Account Group to record the cost of work in process at that date. The Encumbrance and Reserve for Encumbrance accounts do not require closing, since the contract continues.

(C-1) Revenues—Construction	40,000	
Operating Transfer from GF— Construction	100,000	
Expenditures—Construction		140,000
To close the temporary fund balance accounts.		

Balance Sheet for Uncompleted Project

After the closing entry, the SAF balance sheet would appear as shown in Figure 9-3. It has been assumed that the General Fund will pay the remainder of the governmental unit's share of the project cost early in the next period, and hence the receivable from the GF is shown as a current asset.

The "Assessable costs" figure is shown as current. Such costs will be the basis for the levy of assessments upon completion of the project, and presumably some estimatable sum will be paid on the assessments shortly after the levy. More important, in this case the levy will support the issue of bonds; and the bond proceeds, together with the operating transfer from the GF, will be used to pay the current liability. A note to the financial statements should explain the nature of this asset and how it was calculated.

The year-end closing of the Fund accounts left Encumbrances and Reserve

Figure 9-3

A GOVERNMENTAL UNIT

Special Assessment Fund
Balance Sheet
At Close of First Fiscal Year

Assets

Current assets:	
Cash for construction	$ 10,000
Due from General Fund	50,000
Assessable costs	40,000
	$100,000

Liability and Fund Balance

Current liability:	
Contracts payable	$100,000
Fund balance	-0-
	$100,000

for Encumbrances accounts on the books. These memorandum accounts need not be shown on the balance sheet—but the contractual commitment should be described in a note thereto—unless a formal SAF continuing appropriation has been made, in which case the Reserve for Encumbrances should appear in the CPF balance sheet.

When the financing plan for an SAF project is not clear from amounts in the financial statements, a footnote should present the plan to statement readers.

Statement of Revenues, Expenditures, and Changes in Fund Balance for Uncompleted Project

After the closing entry, the Statement of Revenues, Expenditures, and Changes in Fund Balance presented in Figure 9-4 can be prepared. Because of the assumption regarding the recording of the budget, it is quite simple. The

Figure 9-4

A GOVERNMENTAL UNIT

Special Assessment Fund
Statement of Revenues, Expenditures, and Changes in Fund Balance
For the Year Ended (Date)
(Project Incomplete)

Project authorization	$500,000
Revenues and other financing sources:	
Revenues—construction	$ 40,000
Operating transfer from General Fund	100,000
Total	$140,000
Expenditures—construction	140,000
Excess of revenues and other financing sources over expenditures	$ 0
Fund balance, end of year	$ 0

delay in levying assessments until completion of the project and the GAAP provision that revenue may be recognized only upon the incurring of assessable expenditures contribute to the simplicity of the statement.

TRANSACTIONS AND ENTRIES—SECOND FISCAL YEAR

The following lists of transactions and entries illustrate the operation of the Fund during the second year:

Transactions

R. Adjusting entry (A-1) of the first year was reversed.

1. The remainder of the governmental unit's share of the cost was paid from the General Fund.

2. Supervisory costs of engineers, $5,000, were paid.

3. The project was completed and a bill was received from the contractor for $340,000.

4. Final approval of construction was given, and assessments were levied against property owners for the cost of the project not absorbed by the governmental unit. Current assessments were $50,000; deferred assessments, $335,000.

5. Bonds totaling $335,000 were sold at a premium of $1,000.

6. Current assessments of $50,000 were collected.

7. The amount due on the contract was paid.

8. The second installment of assessments came due in the amount of $40,000.

9. Interest in the amount of $17,000 became due on assessments.

10. Interest in the amount of $15,750 became due on bonds; premium of $200 was amortized.

11. Interest on assessments was collected in the amount of $17,000.

12. Interest on bonds was paid in the amount of $15,750.

13. Current assessments were collected in the amount of $36,000.

14. The unpaid part of the second installment became delinquent.

15. Bonds in the amount of $35,000 were retired.

Entries

(R)*	Revenues—Construction	40,000	
	Assessable Costs		40,000
	To reverse the adjusting entry made at the end of the first year.		

* The reversing entry is not essential. If it were not made, entry (4) would appear as follows:

	Assessments Receivable—Current	50,000	
	Assessments Receivable—Deferred	335,000	
	Assessable Costs		40,000
	Revenues—Construction		345,000
	To record the levy of assessments, the elimination of assessable costs, and the resultant revenue.		

(1)	Cash—Construction	50,000	
	Due from General Fund		50,000
	To record final payment of the governmental unit's share of the cost.		

(2)	Expenditures—Construction	5,000	
	Cash—Construction		5,000
	To record payment of supervisory costs of engineers.		

(3a)	Reserve for Encumbrances	340,000	
	Encumbrances		340,000
	To reverse the encumbrances at completion of the project.		

(3b)	Expenditures—Construction	340,000	
	Contracts Payable		340,000
	To record the remainder of the contract expenditures upon completion of the project.		

(4)	Assessments Receivable—Current	50,000	
	Assessments Receivable—Deferred	335,000	
	Revenues—Construction		385,000
	To record the levy of assessments and the resultant revenue [realized revenue because appropriate expenditures had been made at the time of levy].		

(5)	Cash—Construction	335,000	
	Cash—Payment of Interest	1,000	
	Bonds Payable		335,000
	Unamortized Premium on Bonds		1,000
	To record sale of bonds at a premium.		

(6)	Cash—Construction	50,000	
	Assessments Receivable—Current		50,000
	To record collection of the first installment of assessments.		

(7)	Contracts Payable	440,000	
	Cash—Construction		440,000
	To record payment of the contract.		

(8)	Assessments Receivable—Current	40,000	
	Assessments Receivable—Deferred ..		40,000
	To record the maturity of the next installment of assessments.		

(9)	Interest Receivable	17,000	
	Interest Revenue		17,000
	To record accrual of interest on *due* date.		

(10)	Expenditures—Interest	15,550	
	Unamortized Premium on Bonds	200	
	Interest Payable		15,750
	To record accrual of interest on *due* date.		

(11)	Cash—Payment of Interest	17,000	
	Interest Receivable		17,000
	To record collection of interest.		

(12)	Interest Payable	15,750	
	Cash—Payment of Interest		15,750
	To record payment of interest.		

(13)	Cash—Bond Payments	36,000	
	Assessments Receivable—Current		36,000
	To record collection of a part of the second installment.		

(14)	Assessments Receivable—Delinquent ..	4,000	
	Assessments Receivable—Current		4,000
	To record the delinquency of the unpaid part of the second installment.		

(15)	Bonds Payable	35,000	
	Cash—Bond Payments		35,000
	To record the retirement of bonds.		

If the foregoing entries are posted to the Fund's General Ledger, the following trial balance may be drawn:

Cash—Interest Payments	2,250	
Cash—Bond Payments	1,000	
Assessments Receivable:		
Deferred	295,000	
Delinquent	4,000	
Bonds Payable		300,000
Unamortized Premium on Bonds		800
Revenues:		
Construction		345,000
Interest		17,000
Expenditures:		
Construction	345,000	
Interest	15,500	
	662,800	662,800

Closing Entries

The following closing entries are needed:

(C-1)	Revenues—Construction	345,000	
	Expenditures—Construction		345,000
	To close the construction-related temporary fund balance accounts.		

(C-2)	Revenues—Interest	17,000	
	Expenditures—Interest		15,550
	Fund Balance—Interest		1,450
	To close the interest-related temporary fund balance accounts.		

Balance Sheet—Project Completed

After the foregoing closing entries are posted, the balance sheet of the Special Assessment Fund will appear as indicated in Figure 9-5.

Figure 9-5

A GOVERNMENTAL UNIT
Special Assessment Fund
Balance Sheet
At Close of Fiscal Year

Assets

Cash:		
For interest payments	$ 2,250	
For bond payments	1,000	$ 3,250
Assessments receivable:		
Deferred	$295,000	
Delinquent	4,000	299,000
Total assets		$302,250

Liabilities and Fund Balance

Bonds payable	$300,000
Unamortized premium on bonds	800
Total liabilities	$300,800
Fund balance—interest	1,450
Total liabilities and fund balance ..	$302,250

Note that there are no fund balances for construction or bond payments. Construction has been completed and there was no balance left; the assets dedicated to bond payments equal the bond liability (see Figure 9-6).

The fixed assets acquired through Special Assessment Fund expenditures are general assets of the government and their entire cost should be recorded in the General Fixed Assets Account Group even though the projects are, to a great extent, financed by the owners of the assessed private property. The improvements cannot be considered the property of assessment payers, and the city is responsible for the maintenance and repair of the improvements. For all practical purposes the government is the owner of the improvements. A record is maintained in the General Fixed Assets Account Group of the portions of project costs financed by the governmental unit and by the group of property owners.

Balance Sheet Classified by Purposes. If special assessment projects are financed from the sale of special assessment bonds, the Special Assessment Fund may consist of three funds: (1) a Capital Projects Fund that accounts for the proceeds from the sale of the bonds or notes used to finance construction, (2) a Debt Service Fund that accounts for the special assessments used to retire the bonds or notes, and (3) a Debt Service Fund that accounts for interest collected on deferred special assessments and used to pay interest on the bonds or notes.

Figure 9-6 illustrates how the segregation may be shown in balance sheet form. In this case construction was completed and no column, "Fund for Construction," is necessary.

Figure 9-6

A GOVERNMENTAL UNIT

Special Assessment Fund
Balance Sheet (Alternative Form)
At Close of Fiscal Year

Assets	Total	Fund for: Payment of Bonds	Payment of Interest
Cash	$ 3,250	$ 1,000	$2,250
Assessments receivable	299,000	299,000	
Total assets	$302,250	$300,000	$2,250
Liabilities and Fund Balance			
Bonds payable	$300,000	$300,000	
Unamortized premiums on bonds	800		$ 800
Total liabilities	$300,800	$300,000	$ 800
Fund balance	1,450		1,450
Total liabilities and fund balance	$302,250	$300,000	$2,250

Subsidiary Schedule of Installments Receivable and Bonds Payable. If bonds are identified with and are made payable from particular installments, a subsidiary schedule similar to the one illustrated in Figure 9-7 must be prepared. This schedule shows for each installment the amount of cash and other assets that will ultimately be used in paying bonds and interest, the amount of bonds and interest payable, and the related balance or deficit.

Operating Statement—Project Completed

The Statement of Revenues, Expenditures, and Changes in Fund Balances that would be prepared at the end of the second fiscal year is shown in Figure 9-8. Note that the interest expenditure reported there is neither "pure" expenditure data—since SAF debt security premiums and discounts are amortized—nor "pure" expense data—since interest on SAF debt securities is recognized "when due" rather than accrued. This hybrid SAF interest cost recognition method is appropriate given the "matching" of interest revenues and expenditures objective, however, and rarely results in a materially different interest cost being reported as compared with the modified accrual method.

Figure 9-7

A GOVERNMENTAL UNIT

Special Assessment Fund

Schedule of Installments to Be Applied
to Payment of Bonds and Interest

(Date)

	Total	Years			
		19—	19—	19—	19—
		Installment No.			
		2	3	4	5
Cash for bond payments	$ 1,000	$ 1,000			
Cash for interest payments	2,250	1,650	$ 200	$ 200	$ 200
Assessments receivable:					
Delinquent	4,000	4,000			
Deferred	295,000	70,000	75,000	75,000	75,000
	$302,250	$76,650	$75,200	$75,200	$75,200
Bonds payable	$300,000	$75,000	$75,000	$75,000	75,000
Premium on bonds	800	200	200	200	$75,000
Fund balance, interest	1,450	1,450			200
	$302,250	$76,650	$75,200	$75,200	$75,200

Figure 9-8

A GOVERNMENTAL UNIT
Special Assessment Fund
Statement of Revenues, Expenditures, and Changes in Fund Balances
For the Fiscal Year Ended (Date)
(Second Fiscal Year—Project Completed)

	Total	Construction	Interest
Revenues	$362,000	$345,000	$17,000
Expenditures	360,550	345,000	15,550
	$ 1,450	$ -0-	$ 1,450
Fund balance, beginning of year	-0-	-0-	-0-
Fund balance (deficit), end of year	$ 1,450	$ -0-	$ 1,450

EARLY LEVY OF ASSESSMENTS

The primary example of SAF operation assumed that assessments would be levied at the conclusion of the project. This pattern permits the costs of the project, including the cost of interim financing, to be determined before the levy. Thus, the amount of the levy is accurately determinable, the cost of interest during construction can easily be capitalized, and there should be no construction fund balance or deficit. Only if the costs of the project are known should the levy be made at the start. Inaccurate cost estimates result in supplemental assessments (if legal), abatements of assessments, or payment by the governmental unit of unexpected costs.

If assessments are the sole financing source, and if the levy occurs at the beginning of the project, the following entry would be made, using assumed amounts and maturity dates:

(S1)	Assessments Receivable—Current	100,000	
	Assessments Receivable—Deferred	400,000	
	Deferred Revenues		500,000
	To record the levy based on an		
	estimate of the cost of the project.		

As the expenditures of the project are recorded, equivalent amounts of deferred revenues would be recognized as revenues up to the maximum amount of assessments that qualify as measurable and available for payment of current liabilities. If it is assumed that expenditures of $500,000 have been made and recorded, the following entry would be made with respect to revenues:

(S2)	Deferred Revenues	500,000	
	Revenues		500,000
	To recognize revenues in the amount		
	of expenditures incurred.		

BUDGETARY ACCOUNTING

For reasons discussed earlier in the chapter, budgetary accounting is ordinarily not required for effective administration of the SAF. It is always theoretically appropriate and it may be desirable when operations of the fund are complicated. If there are multiple sources of financing, or multiple projects are financed by the same fund, or the governmental unit's own work force rather than a contractor is used for construction activity, budgetary accounting may be desirable for expenditures. There would ordinarily be no need to budget revenues.

The budgeting of construction payments must be distinguished from the planning of the ultimate financing of the project when a SAF's financial plan is like the one in the primary example of the chapter (and in many other cases). In the primary example, resources for the payment of the contractor were provided by transfer from the GF and by the sale of bonds. From a practical viewpoint the budgeting for construction included the transfer, which would be shown in the operating statement as an "other financing source," and proceeds of the sale of bonds, which would not be shown on a GAAP operating statement.

Some accountants have advocated budgeting as if proceeds of the sale of bonds were an "other financing source," as they are in the CPF. (The mechanics of recording the budget in the accounts would parallel those of the CPF.) These accountants would then prepare a "Statement of Revenues, Expenditures, and Changes in Fund Balance" *on the budgetary basis* that would show bond proceeds as an other financing source. Although this might be useful for internal purposes, presentation of two SAF operating statements, one on the GAAP basis and one on a budgetary basis, would confuse most municipal statement readers and is undesirable. Further, budgetary comparison statements are required only for *annually* budgeted governmental funds and SAFs are usually budgeted on a project life basis. The Statement of Revenues, Expenditures, and Changes in Fund Balance (Figure 9-8) is presented on the GAAP basis; and in the authors' view it provides sufficient indication of control over construction and financing of the Special Assessment Fund.

ACTIVITIES SUBSEQUENT TO PROJECT COMPLETION

The Capital Projects Fund aspects of the Special Assessment Fund life cycle have been concluded upon completion of construction and payment of construction costs. The Special Assessment Fund will continue to function in a Debt Service Fund capacity until all assessments receivable have been collected and all Special Assessment Fund debt has been liquidated. At that time, any fund balance will be appropriately disposed of and the fund terminated.

Disposing of Positive Fund Balances

At any time prior to abolition of the Fund there may be three distinct types of fund balances. First, a fund balance may result from an excess of authorized expenditures over actual expenditures. Second, an excess of interest revenues over interest expenditures gives rise to fund balance during or at the end of the fund's life cycle, or both. Third, a fund balance may result from an excess of assets earmarked for debt principal retirement over debt principal owed. These are referred to as *construction balance, interest balance,* and *debt principal balance,* respectively, in the discussions which follow.

The disposal of a *construction balance* varies according to the interim financing method and with the assessment procedure employed. Where interim financing is involved the construction balance would normally be reclassified as debt service balance. Where interim borrowing is not involved and the levy is made *after* the project is completed, there will be no balance, since the assessment will be made large enough to recover only the actual cost of construction. If assessments are levied *before* the project is completed, rebates may be granted in the form of cash or a reduction of the unpaid assessments. However, either statutes or sound management may prohibit the payment of rebates or the reduction of assessments until all outstanding debt has been paid, so that, in the event some assessments prove uncollectible, the balance may be applied to the retirement of the debt.

In cases where (1) the timing of assessment and interest collections coincides with debt service requirements, and (2) an excess of interest revenues over interest expenditures is expected to recur each year, it may be appropriate to reduce the interest rate charged on assessments receivable so that the *interest balance* is eliminated or minimal by the time the fund is to be terminated. The relevant balance is that *anticipated* immediately prior to fund termination, however, not the amount of the Fund Balance—Interest account at an earlier date. Since the Fund Balance—Interest account is not actuarially based, it may have a credit balance, particularly in the early years of the Special Assessment Fund life cycle, in situations in which an ultimate interest deficit is virtually assured. This would result, for example, if 9 percent bonds were sold to yield 8 percent, assessments yield 6 percent, and the premium is closed to Fund Balance—Interest rather than being amortized. (This is an excellent example of why both the NCGA and the authors recommend amortization of premiums and discounts.)

Some property owners may pay their assessments early. Investment of these monies may yield more or less than the rate charged on assessments. Reduction of interest charges or disposal of an interest balance is usually deferred until all debt principal and interest have been paid. Interest balance remaining after all debt is liquidated should generally be rebated or used to make up a deficit in another aspect of the Fund's activities. Alternatively, it may be transferred to another Special Assessment Fund or to the General Fund, particularly if the interest balance is small or is deemed to be attributable to the government's contribution to the special assessment project.

Bondholders may insist that assessments receivable in an amount greater than bond principal owed be earmarked for bond retirement. A Fund Balance—Bonds would be reported in such cases and, assuming that collections of assessments so designated exceed the bond principal owed, would require disposition after the bonds are paid. One would expect in such a case that a Fund Balance—Construction deficit resulted from this excessive earmarking of assessments receivable and that the *debt principal balance* would be used to offset that deficit.

In any event, a debt principal balance would normally be disposed of in the same manner as a construction balance.

Disposing of Deficits

Instead of having positive balances, a Special Assessment Fund may have three deficits—a *construction deficit*, an *interest deficit*, or a *debt principal deficit*.

Most construction deficits arise where assessments are levied *before* the completion of the project. If assessments are levied *after* the project is completed, the total construction cost is known—and the assessments plus the governmental unit's share of the cost are made large enough to cover the actual construction costs. More specifically, a *construction deficit* remaining upon termination of a Special Assessment Fund might indicate one of these:

1. If assessments were levied *before* completion of the project—that (a) actual costs exceeded the amount authorized and assessed or (b) some assessments proved uncollectible; or,

2. If assessments were levied *after* completion of the project—that actual construction costs exceeded (a) the estimated and authorized amount that had been borrowed and/or (b) the assessable amount, or (c) that the project authorization was not properly scaled down following the sale of bonds at a discount.

The deficit may be made up through the levy of *supplemental assessments.* If the assessments are payable in installments, the latter may be adjusted to reflect the supplemental levy or a separate supplementary roll may be made. Frequently a supplemental levy will not be deemed politically feasible, however, particularly where elected officials forced (or encouraged) the project to be undertaken. The project may have become an emotional issue of concern to some or all of the property owners in the district, for example, many of whom may be quite vocal, influential, or both. In such cases the government may make up the deficit through an additional contribution or from interest or debt principal balances.

Interest deficits for any one year are disposed of by charging them against accumulated Fund Balance—Interest. If it appears that an interest deficit will exist at the conclusion of the Fund's debt service function, it may be necessary to raise interest rates. On the other hand, interest deficits may be made up by a transfer from the General Fund. Or, if legal, they may be eliminated by applying construction or debt principal balances against the interest deficit. Although the last method penalizes those who have paid their assessments in full, it has the advantage of eliminating the ill feeling or litigation that may accompany a rise in the interest rate. As noted earlier, in many instances those assessment owners who have paid in full are responsible for the decline in interest earnings. That is, if bonds cannot be retired as soon as collections are made from those paying in full—or the money cannot be invested promptly at a yield commensurate with the interest paid on the bonds—the government will continue to pay the same amount of interest on the outstanding bonds, but its interest earnings will be reduced.

A *debt principal deficit* would be disposed of as appropriate in the circumstances. If the debt is of the special-special assessment type and is secured only by the delinquent assessments levied against certain properties, the government would have no legal obligation to see that creditors receive full payment. As discussed earlier, however, default on any obligation with which a government is even casually associated may have a significant detrimental effect on that government's credit standing. Thus, if possible, the government might make up the deficit in some manner, even though it was not legally obligated to do so. Accounting and other procedures related to delinquent assessments are discussed in more detail in the concluding section of this chapter.

Transactions and Entries Illustrating Disposal of Fund Balances and Deficits

The following transactions and entries illustrate the accounting procedure involved in disposing of construction, interest, and debt principal balances and deficits.

Transactions

1. Construction balance amounted to $62,000. Rebates were made in cash as follows: to property owners, $10,000; to the governmental unit, $2,000. A reduction of $50,000 was made in assessments.
2. Cash representing construction balance of $50,000 was used to retire bonds.
3. Construction balance was $10,000 and was applied toward eliminating an interest deficit of a corresponding amount.
4. A construction deficit of $100,000 was eliminated through supplemental assessments of $90,000, together with a supplemental contribution by the governmental unit of $10,000.
5. Interest and debt principal balances of $1,000 and $9,000, respectively, were transferred to the General Fund.

Entries

(1)	Fund Balance—Construction		62,000	
	Cash—Construction			12,000
	Assessments Receivable—Deferred			50,000
	To record making of cash rebates and reduction of assessments.			
(2)	Fund Balance—Construction		50,000	
	Bonds Payable		50,000	
	Cash—Construction			50,000
	Fund Balance—Bonds			50,000
	To record use of cash representing construction balance for the retirement of bonds.			
(3)	Fund Balance—Construction		10,000	
	Cash—Interest Payments		10,000	
	Fund Balance—Interest			10,000
	Cash—Construction			10,000
	To record application of construction balance to elimination of interest deficit.			

(4)	Assessments Receivable—Supplemental	90,000	
	Cash	10,000	
	Fund Balance—Construction		100,000
	To record levy of supplemental special assessments to eliminate deficit. (This entry assumes a residual equity transfer from another government fund.)		
(5)	Fund Balance—Interest	1,000	
	Fund Balance—Bonds	9,000	
	Cash—Interest		1,000
	Cash—Bond Payments		9,000
	To record transfer of cash representing interest and debt principal fund balances to the General Fund.		

COMBINING STATEMENTS

If a government has more than one SAF, it must prepare combining statements. The identity of each fund must be retained, ordinarily by providing a column for each fund. If there are too many funds to be presented in a single statement, the most important ones may be shown individually in the principal statement, with the others shown as "Others" and detailed on a supporting combining statement. Funds should also be classified as to whether their projects are complete or incomplete. The following is an illustration of the headings for a Combining SAF balance sheet:

A GOVERNMENTAL UNIT

Special Assessment Funds
Combining Balance Sheet
(Date)

	Completed Projects		Uncompleted Projects		
Assets	No. 59	No. 60	No. 61	No. 62	Total

A combining Statement of Revenues, Expenditures, and Changes in Fund Balance may also be prepared following these format modification guidelines. These guidelines are equally applicable to combining statements of cash receipts and disbursements or other Special Assessment Fund combining statements or analyses.

ACCOUNTING FOR DELINQUENT SPECIAL ASSESSMENTS

We have already discussed the accounting procedure for assessments receivable up to the time they become delinquent. In this section, we discuss the procedure relating to the collection of delinquent special assessments.

Special assessments are usually made, by statute, a lien against the property against which they are levied; and, at the expiration of a certain period of time, the property may be sold at a public sale and the proceeds used to satisfy the lien. Let us assume that the governmental unit incurred certain costs, such as advertising and auctioneer's fees, in holding the sale. The entry to record these costs would be as follows:

Cost of Holding Sale	200	
Accounts Payable		200
To record the costs of holding a sale of special assessment property.		

The entry to record the sale of property for unpaid special assessments is as follows:

Cash—Bond Payments	10,000	
Cash—Interest Payments	150	
Cash—Other Payments	200	
Assessments Receivable— Delinquent		2,000
Assessments Receivable—Deferred ..		8,000
Interest Receivable		150
Cost of Holding Sale		200
To record sale of property for nonpayment of special assessments.		

Note that the proceeds typically may be applied to satisfy not only the assessments receivable, but also the interest receivable up to the date of sale and the cost of holding the sale. However, specific authorization by ordinance or statute may be required to use the proceeds to cover interest and the cost of holding the sale.

The excess of the amount realized from the sale of the property over the amount of special assessments, interest, and the cost of holding the sale is held in a Trust Fund for the benefit of the property owner. The transaction is recorded in that fund by debiting Cash and crediting the Property Owner's Trust Fund Balance account. If, on the other hand, the proceeds are not sufficient to cover special assessments, interest, and the cost of the sale, the property owner would ordinarily not be called upon to make up the difference.

The proceeds realized by the governmental unit from the sale of property for delinquent assessments may be used for various purposes. If general-special assessment bonds have been issued, the governmental unit may have paid the bonds and interest as they fell due with money borrowed from other funds. The proceeds would then be used to pay off the loans. If special-special assessment bonds are used, neither bonds due nor the interest on bonds may have been paid, and the proceeds will in such cases be used to retire the bonds and pay the interest. If unmatured bonds are not callable, are callable only at a significant premium, or are not available at a reasonable price on the open market, the governmental unit may not be able or willing to retire them prior to maturity. Instead, bonds and interest will have to be paid as they fall due, and the governmental unit will invest the money in the interim.

If the amount realized from the sale of the property is insufficient to cover the principal of the bonds and the interest, and the property owner cannot be called upon to make up the difference, the procedure followed depends on whether special-special assessment or general-special assessment bonds were issued. If special-special assessment bonds were issued, the bondholder will bear the loss unless the government chooses to do so, often after first bidding in the property itself. On the other hand, if general-special assessment bonds were issued, the deficiency must be made up by the governmental unit. Frequently, if the property cannot be sold for a sufficient amount to meet bonds and interest, the governmental unit bids it in. The entry to record this transaction is as follows:

Assessment Sale Certificates	10,350	
Assessments Receivable—		
Delinquent		2,000
Assessments Receivable—Deferred ..		8,000
Interest Receivable		150
Cost of Holding Sale		200
To record bidding in of property for assessment.		

If the governmental unit bids in the property, payments on bonds and interest falling due often must be met, pending the disposition of the property, through interfund or bank loans.

The property owner usually has the right to redeem his property within a certain period of time by paying the purchaser the price paid at the public sale plus interest and costs. If the sales price was not sufficient to pay the assessments, the property owner often must also pay the remaining assessments in order to redeem the property.

If the property was purchased by a private buyer, the redemption is handled through a Trust Fund. On the other hand, if the property is bid in by the governmental unit, the transaction is handled in the Special Assessment Fund. For example, if the property was bid in by a municipality and a loan was made to finance maturing bonds and interest and to meet the cost of holding the sale, the entry to record the redemption of the property is as follows:

Cash—Payment of Loans	5,350	
Cash—Bond Payments	5,000	
Cash—Interest Payments	50	
Assessment Sale Certificates		10,350
Interest Revenues		50
To record redemption of property bid in by governmental unit.		

It should be noted that the Interest Revenues account consists of accrued interest from the time the property was bid in until the time of redemption. Interest prior to the date of bidding in the property is included in the Assessment Sale Certificates account.

If the property is not redeemed within the required period of time, the purchaser acquires title to it. If the property was bid in by the governmental unit, it gets title. No entries are necessary to record this fact, the next entry being made when the property is sold by the governmental unit and the proceeds are used to pay the bonds and interest. Since the entry would be similar to the one described immediately above, it will not be illustrated here.

If the governmental unit intends to keep the property, an entry must be made in the Special Assessment Fund to close out the Assessment Sale Certificates account. This will result in a deficit in the Fund unless an amount of money equal to the balance in the Assessment Sale Certificates account for the property is transferred, loaned, or otherwise paid from the General Fund (or another fund) to the Special Assessment Fund. The entry to record the receipt of the cash by the Special Assessment Fund is as follows:

Cash—Bond Payments	10,000	
Cash—Interest Payments	150	
Cash—Other Payments	200	
Assessment Sale Certificates		10,350

To record receipt of cash from the General Fund equal to the balance in the Assessment Sale Certificates account as a result of the bidding in of the delinquent property by this municipality.
[This is *not* an interfund transfer but the "sale" of assessment sale certificates to the General Fund.]

If money has already been advanced as a loan from the General Fund to the Special Assessment Fund, the loan will be canceled and only the difference between the loan and the amount of the assessment sale certificate will be transferred from the General Fund. If we assume that $5,350 had been borrowed from the General Fund, the entry to record the cancellation of the loan and the receipt of money to cover bond payments yet to be made is as follows:

Cash—Bonds Payments	5,000	
Due to General Fund	5,350	
Assessment Sale Certificates		10,350

To record cancellation of liability to General Fund and receipt of money from that fund for payment of bonds.
[This does not involve an interfund transfer since the General (or other) Fund expenditure is to obtain an asset.]

It is assumed immediately above that the entire amount of special assessment bonds outstanding is to be paid at one time. If bonds are to be retired in installments, two procedures might be followed. One procedure is to pay from the General Fund at one time cash equivalent to the full amount of the assessment sale certificate, as was assumed in the above entry. In that case, Special Assessment Fund cash is invested, and the earnings on investments are used to pay interest on bonds. The other procedure is to pay from the General Fund each year an amount sufficient only to retire that part of the bonds and interest falling due during that year which the Special Assessment Fund is unable to pay because of the transfer of the property. In this case Due from General Fund, rather than Cash—Bond Payments, would be debited in the preceding entry.

Two additional facts should be noted about special assessments. First, the law may provide for penalties on delinquent special assessments. These are accounted for in the same manner as interest on delinquent special assessments. In fact, an examination of the interest rates that governmental units are sometimes permitted to charge will reveal that these interest charges also include penalties, although they are referred to as *interest*. Sometimes the term *interest and penalties* is used.

Second, the same property will no doubt be subject to ad valorem real estate taxes as well as the special assessments, and unpaid taxes are also a lien against the property. Sometimes a single lien is secured against the property to cover both ad valorem taxes and special assessments. The proceeds from the sale of the property are in that event used to satisfy both liens. For example, the Illinois Supreme Court[3] has held that liens of general taxes and local improvement special assessments are on a parity, with no priority of one over the other.

ALTERNATIVE SAF ACCOUNTING METHODS

Special Assessment Fund usage and SAF accounting vary more in practice than is apparent in the preceding pages of this chapter. These variations relate to (1) nonuse of SAFs, and (2) SAF revenue recognition. Indeed, some suggest that SAFs should be abolished.

Nonuse of SAFs

Some SLGs do not finance projects by special assessments and obviously would not use SAFs. Others do finance projects by special assessments but do not establish Special Assessment Funds as discussed in this chapter. Rather, the project costs to be assessed are financed directly from the General (or another) Fund; assessment project expenditures are made through the General Fund or a Capital Projects Fund; the assessments levied are interest-bearing General Fund receivables and investments; and the General Fund investment is liquidated as assessments are collected. If long-term debt is issued to finance special assessment projects under this approach: (1) the debt would be recorded in the GLTD Account Group, (2) the debt issue proceeds would be expended through a Capital Projects Fund; and (3) the assessments receivable would be accounted for in a Debt Service Fund.

SAF Revenue Recognition

NCGA *Statement 1* requires that the modified accrual basis of accounting be used in SAF accounting. This means that SAF revenue should be recognized when (1) earned, (2) measurable, and (3) available. NCGA *Statement 1* is silent on how those criteria should be applied to SAF accounting, however, and differing

[3]People v. The Taylorville Sanitary District, et al., 371 Ill. 280 (1939), 20 N.E. (2d) 576.

interpretations of how to apply the criteria have resulted in various approaches to SAF revenue recognition in practice. The "earned" and "measurable" criteria usually are not the primary issue; rather, the varying practices arise primarily from differing interpretations of how the "available" criterion should be applied in SAF accounting. Three distinct interpretations on when assessments may be considered "available," and thus recognized as revenue, have emerged. These may be termed the (1) "when assessable costs are incurred," (2) "when assessments are levied," and (3) "when assessments become current" interpretations.

When Assessable Costs are Incurred. Those of this persuasion, including the authors, contend that revenues have been earned, and should be recognized, concurrent with the incurrence of assessable costs—whether before or after the assessments are formally levied. They note that *Statement 1* defines "available" as *collectible* within the current period or *soon enough thereafter to be used to pay liabilities of the current period.** Since in the usual SAF case payment of the liabilities is deferred through interim financing over the 5-15 years during which assessments are collected, they argue that incurring assessable costs gives rise to an available asset and revenue. They also note that both ASLGU and *Statement 1* say that if expenditure is the prime factor for determining grant eligibility, qualifying expenditures give rise to grant revenue recognition—and see special assessment projects and grant projects as being similar in that regard. Too, they note that (1) ASLGU says that billable amounts of valid receivables give rise to SLG revenue recognition, and (2) assessable SAF project costs are billable costs that are billed at or soon after the assessment levy. Finally, proponents of the "when assessable costs are incurred" approach note that it (1) is consistent with preferred private sector construction accounting, (2) is in keeping with the *Statement 1* position that accrual accounting should be followed to the fullest extent practicable, and (3) is the only method that produces meaningful and understandable SAF financial statements in all circumstances, whether the levy is made before or after project completion, and avoids reporting "artificial" operating and balance sheet deficits.

When Assessments Are Levied. Some accountants believe that revenue should be recognized, in total, when the special assessments are levied, whether before or after completion of the SAF project. They note that this method is illustrated in GAAFR (68), has not been explicitly withdrawn by the NCGA, and has long been used by many SLGs. Proponents of the "when assessments are levied" approach also contend that the SLG does not have a "claim certain" until assessments have formally been levied, and believe that revenue recognition prior to that point is premature. Like the "when assessable costs are incurred" proponents, they consider the assessments "available" when levied since payment for the project expenditures is typically deferred through interim financing until the assessments are collected. Finally, they note that once the assessments have been levied, the receivables serve as a "resource," if needed, for temporary borrowing to provide timely SAF debt service.

*NCGAS 1, p. 11, emphasis added.

When Assessments Become Current. Proponents of this approach, discussed and illustrated in the MFOA's GAAFR(80), believe that SAF revenue should not be recognized until—and as—the special assessments receivables become current assets, usually gradually over a 5-15 year period. They recognize that this approach causes the reporting of both operating and balance sheet deficits in the SAF construction phase that are only gradually reduced over its 5-15 year debt service phase. However, they note the frequent reference in NCGA *Statement 1* to terms such as current assets, current liabilities, and working capital, and believe that the "when assessments become current" interpretation is the most conservative and most consistent with *Statement 1*.

Example. The effects on the SAF operating statement and fund balance of the three described interpretations as to when assessments may be considered available and recognized as revenue are illustrated in Figure 9-9. The Statements of Revenues, Expenditures, and Changes in Fund Balance presented there are based on the following information:

    (1) $1,000,000 was borrowed long-term in 19X1 to finance SAF construction expenditures.

    (2) $400,000 was expended for construction during 19X1; $600,000 was expended during 19X2.

    (3) Assessments of $1,000,000 were levied in 19X2 to mature 10% each year over 10 years beginning in 19X3.

    (4) Interest is to be ignored.

Should SAFs Be Abolished?

Some accountants believe that SAFs—being combinations of Capital Projects and Debt Service Funds—are a superfluous governmental fund type that should be abolished. They include the "nonusers of SAFs," discussed above, as well as others who believe that SLG accounting and financial reporting should be simplified by deleting SAFs. Proponents of this approach would account for (1) special assessment long-term debt as GLTD, (2) the expenditure of debt issue proceeds and other special assessment project resources through Capital Project Funds, (3) the assessment levy and receivables through Debt Service Funds, (4) the resulting assets in the GFA accounts, as is done now.

Opponents counter that SAFs are frequently mandated by law or contractual agreement. Since the fourth basic *Statement 1* principle requires that funds required by law, including contractual agreements, be established, SAFs cannot simply be abolished as a fund type. Further, they argue, SAFs serve useful control and accountability roles and should not be abolished.

Still other accountants and auditors offer a "middle ground" suggestion: keep SAFs as *accounting entities* and for *internal* financial reporting purposes, but abolish their reporting in *external* financial statements. Proponents of this approach would report (1) any special assessment long-term debt in the GLTD Account Group; (2) any debt issue proceeds and other financing sources, and their expenditure, in Capital Projects Funds; (3) the assessments receivable in Debt Service Funds, when special assessment long-term debt is outstanding, otherwise

Figure 9-9

ASSESSMENT REVENUE RECOGNITION EXAMPLE

Special Assessment Fund
Alternative Statements of Revenues, Expenditures, and Changes in Fund Balance
(In Dollars)

	(1) Revenue Recognized When Assessable Costs Incurred			(2) Revenue Recognized When Assessments Levied			(3) Revenue Recognized When Assessments Receivable Become Current		
	19X1	19X2	19X3	19X1	19X2	19X3	19X1	19X2	19X3
Revenues	400	600	0	0	1,000	0	0	0	100
Expenditures	400	600	0	400	600	0	400	600	0
Excess of Revenues over (under) Expenditures	0	0	0	(400)	400	0	(400)	(600)	100
Fund Balance, Beginning	0	0	0	0	(400)	0	0	(400)	(1,000)
Fund Balance, Ending	0	0	0	(400)	0	0	(400)	(1,000)	(900)

in the General Fund or a Special Revenue Fund; and (4) the fixed assets acquired in the GFA Account Group, as is done now.

CONCLUDING COMMENTS

Instances of all the above variations and suggestions may be found in contemporary local government financial reports. It also has been suggested that SAFs should be reclassified as proprietary funds. The National Council on Governmental Accounting spent considerable time studying these and other SAF matters during 1980-1982, and issued two exposure drafts dealing with them. However, the NCGA was unable to attain the consensus required to issue a SAF statement or interpretation.

▶ **Question 9-1.** Inasmuch as special assessments may be levied to finance either routine services or special improvement projects, why does this chapter deal almost exclusively with the latter?

Question 9-2. "A construction-related special assessment fund will normally originate with a petition requesting the improvement or with an action taken by the government itself." Explain.

Question 9-3. A Special Assessment Fund may be, in essence, either a Capital Projects Fund or a combination Capital Projects–Debt Service Fund. Explain.

Question 9-4. Why might the use of a series of distinctively titled Cash accounts be appropriate in certain Special Assessment Fund situations but of little value in others?

Question 9-5. List the various means by which Special Assessment Fund interim financing may be secured and discuss the different manners in which notes may be employed for this purpose.

Question 9-6. Distinguish between general-special and special-special bonds.

Question 9-7. Why does a governmental unit frequently bear part of the cost of a special assessment improvement project?

Question 9-8. Despite the fact that some special assessments are expected to be uncollectible, an Allowance for Uncollectible Special Assessments is rarely established. Why is this so? Could such an allowance properly be established? Explain.

Question 9-9. Discuss the difference between the accounting for bond proceeds in the Capital Projects and Special Assessments Funds.

Question 9-10. How does the use of multiple Fund Balance accounts in Special Assessment Fund accounting differ from that in Capital Projects Fund accounting?

Question 9-11. Under what circumstances would it be appropriate to divide the accounts of a Special Assessment Fund into four "funds"? Describe the function of each "fund."

Question 9-12. Why do many governmental accountants insist that special assessment bond issue discounts be amortized, while they are less concerned about whether or not premiums are amortized?

Question 9-13. Though several capital projects might be financed and accounted for through a single Capital Projects Fund, a separate Special Assessment Fund is virtually always required for each special assessment project. Why is this so?

Question 9-14. Should the total cost of a special assessment project be capitalized in the General Fixed Assets accounts? Only the governmental unit's share of the cost? Why?

Question 9-15. Is the Fund Balance—Construction account likely to have a balance upon completion of an improvement project constructed on open account or under contract and paid for by assessments levied at the conclusion of the project and collected immediately? Why?

Question 9-16. Assuming that separate SAF fund balance accounts are used, why would an excess of authorization over expenditures remaining at the completion of construction normally be closed to the Fund Balance—Debt Principal account?

Question 9-17. When a government "bids in" property at a public sale held to satisfy liens against properties upon which assessments are delinquent, it receives an "assessment sale certificate." Explain the meaning of the term within quotation marks. How much cost (or disbursements) would be involved if a government bid in property for $5,000 and costs of holding the sale were $100?

Question 9-18. Discuss the equity of the use of the following methods of assigning the cost of a paving project to a developed assessment district: (a) footage of lots on paving; (b) per lot; and (c) per residence.

Question 9-19. A municipality plans to widen an existing two lane residential street into a four lane thoroughfare and assess the cost of the improvement to residents of the neighborhood in which the street is located. Might the residents raise valid objections to the plan from the standpoints of legality or equity? Explain.

Question 9-20. Why might the interest rate charged on deferred special assessments properly be set at a rate higher than that paid by the governmental unit on debt it incurs to finance the projects?

Question 9-21. Why should great care be exercised in determining special assessment benefit district boundaries? Why should assumption by the governmental unit of special assessments originally levied against privately owned properties be subject to action by its governing board and to special audit scrutiny?

Question 9-22. Suppose that it is decided to use interest on assessments to make up a discount on bonds in the amount of $1,000. Give the entries to record (a) the receipt of the interest and (b) its use in eliminating the discount.

▶ **Problem 9-1.**
The following transactions took place during 19X4 in the City of Flowersville:

1. The construction of street pavements for the Sunflower Addition was authorized at a cost of $150,000. It was to be financed by special assessments of $120,000 and a contribution from the General Fund of $30,000. Temporary financing of $90,000 was to be provided by the issue of notes, on which interest costs of $3,000 were expected.

2. Pending the collection of assessments, construction was financed through the issue of notes for $90,000.

3. A contract was entered into with Acher & Wallace for the construction of the pavements at a cost of $140,000.

4. Assessments to the amount of $120,000 were levied; the municipality agreed to contribute $30,000, as planned, as its share of the cost of financing the project.

5. A bill was received from Acher & Wallace for $50,000.

6. Supervisory engineering costs of $5,000 were paid.
7. Acher & Wallace was paid.
8. All assessments and the city's contribution were collected.
9. A bill was received from Acher & Wallace for the remaining amount due on the contract.
10. Notes payable outstanding and interest of $3,000 were paid.
11. The project was completed.
12. Acher & Wallace was paid in full, except for $10,000 which was retained pending the final inspection and approval of the project.

Required:

(a) Prepare SAF journal entries, including closing entries, and post to T-accounts.
(b) *Or* prepare a worksheet summarizing transactions and closing entries.
(c) Prepare a SAF Balance Sheet as of December 31, 19X4.
(d) Prepare a SAF Statement of Revenues, Expenditures, and Changes in Fund Balance for the year ended December 31, 19X4.
(e) What disposition should be made of the SAF Fund Balance?

Problem 9-2. A street improvement project expected to cost $200,000 and to be financed 70:20:10 by special assessments, a Federal grant, and General Fund contributions, respectively, was undertaken in 19X2. Assessments and contributions were levied and received based upon these estimates. Total expenditures incurred and encumbrances at year end were as follows:

	Expenditures (Cumulative)	Encumbrances (At Year End)
December 31, 19X2	$ 70,000	$35,000
December 31, 19X3	170,000	30,000
December 31, 19X4	195,000	0

A $10,000 state grant-in-aid was received for the project during 19X4, the year in which the project was completed. The resources remaining upon completion of the project were refunded pro rata to the Federal government and the General Fund.

Required:

Prepare SAF journal entries, including closing entries, for each year of the project's existence.

Problem 9-3, Part I. The following transactions took place in the City of N during 19X4:

1. The city commission authorized the paving of certain streets at an estimated cost of $200,000, the work to be performed by the city's own labor forces. The project is to be financed in the following manner:

City's share	$ 50,000
19X4 assessment installment	15,000
Deferred assessments (nine installments)	135,000
	$200,000

2. Special-special assessment bonds were sold at par, $135,000. These bonds will be paid from the deferred assessments.

3. Assessments were levied and the city's share of project costs was accrued.

4. The city paid over its share of the estimated cost.

5. Assessments of $13,000 were collected.

6. Materials estimated to cost $92,000 were ordered.

7. The Tact Company was paid $3,000 in surveying fees.

8. The materials ordered (6) were received. The actual cost was $92,500, and the invoice was approved for payment.

9. A $4,500 bill from the Petri Construction Company covering equipment rental charges was approved for payment.

10. Payrolls paid during the year amounted to $67,000.

11. Judgments for $10,000 on account of condemnation of property were awarded and paid.

12. Interest on bonds, $3,000, became due.

13. Vouchers payable amounting to $94,000 were paid.

14. Uncollected current assessments become delinquent.

15. Interest on deferred assessments, $3,500, became due.

Required:

(a) Prepare all SAF journal entries, including closing entries, and post to T-accounts.

(b) *Or* prepare a columnar worksheet to reflect the transactions of the Special Assessment Fund for the two years (see Problem 9-3, Part II) ended December 31, 19X5. Your worksheet headings should be as follows:

Columns	Heading
1–2	19X4 Transactions
3–4	19X4 Closing Entries
5–6	Trial Balance, 12/31/X4
7–8	19X5 Transactions
9–10	19X5 Closing Entries
11–12	Trial Balance, 12/31/X5

(c) Prepare for the year ended December 31, 19X4, a SAF Statement of Revenues, Expenditures, and Changes in Fund Balance.

Problem 9-3, Part II. Transactions taking place in 19X5 were as follows:

16. Another special assessment installment became due.

17. Collections were made as follows:

19X4 installments	$ 1,200
Current installments	10,500
Interest collected	3,300
	$15,000

18. Interest due on bonds was paid.
19. Uncollected current assessments became delinquent.
20. Payrolls of $5,000 were paid.
21. Interest on bonds, $4,000, became due.
22. Interest on assessments, $4,500, became due.
23. The cost of selling properties for unpaid special assessments, $65, was paid out of construction cash.
24. Property A, on which no assessments had been paid, was sold. Total unpaid special assessments on this parcel of property amounted to $1,200, accumulated interest was $70, and the cost of selling the property was $20. The property was sold for $1,290.
25. Properties E and L, on which no assessments had been paid, were offered for sale. The price offered was not satisfactory, and the governmental unit bid them in. Unpaid assessments, interest, and cost of holding the sale of these properties were as follows:

Property	Unpaid Assessments	Interest	Cost of Holding Sale
E	$2,000	$180	$25
L	2,200	135	20

26. Property E was redeemed by the owner, who paid, in addition to all other interest and charges due, interest of $40.
27. Bonds of $15,000 were called in and retired, and interest of $500 due thereon was paid.
28. Property L was taken over by the city and is to be used for recreation purposes. The city paid the full amount of the assessment certificate out of the General Fund.

Required:

(a) Prepare all SAF journal entries, including closing entries, and post to T-accounts.
(b) *Or*, prepare the worksheet described in requirement (b) of Problem 9-3, Part I.
(c) Prepare a SAF Balance Sheet as of December 31, 19X5.
(d) Prepare for the year ended December 31, 19X5, a SAF Statement of Revenues, Expenditures, and Changes in Fund Balance.

Problem 9-4. You were engaged as auditor of the City of Druid as of July 1, 19X4. You found the following accounts, among others, in the General Fund ledger for the fiscal year ending June 30, 19X4:

Special Cash

Date	Reference	Dr.	Cr.	Balance
8/1/X3	CR 58	301,000		301,000
9/1/X3	CR 60	80,000		381,000
12/1/X3	CD 41		185,000	196,000
2/1/X4	CD 45		9,000	187,000
6/1/X4	CR 64	50,500		237,500
6/30/X4	CD 65		167,000	70,500

Bonds Payable

Date	Reference	Dr.	Cr.	Balance
8/1/X3	CR 58		300,000	300,000
6/1/X4	CR 64		50,000	350,000

Construction in Progress—Main Street Improvement Project

Date	Reference	Dr.	Cr.	Balance
12/1/X3	CD 41	185,000		185,000
6/30/X4	CD 65	167,000		352,000

Interest Expense

Date	Reference	Dr.	Cr.	Balance
2/1/X4	CD 45	9,000		9,000
6/1/X4	CR 64		500	8,500

Assessment Income

Date	Reference	Dr.	Cr.	Balance
9/1/X3	CR 60		80,000	80,000

Premium on Bonds

Date	Reference	Dr.	Cr.	Balance
8/1/X4	CR 58		1,000	1,000

The accounts resulted from the project described below:

> The city council authorized the Main Street Improvement Project and a bond issue of $350,000 to permit deferral of assessment payments. According to the terms of the authorization the property owners were to be assessed 80 percent of the estimated cost of construction and the balance was made available by the city during October 19X3. On September 1, 19X3 the first of five equal annual assessment installments was collected in full from the property owners. The deferred assessments were to bear interest at 8 percent per annum from September 1, 19X3.

The project was expected to be completed by October 31, 19X4.

Required:

(a) Prepare a Special Assessment Fund worksheet in which you record the transactions of the Main Street Improvement Project as they should have been recorded by the city. A formal authorization entry should not be made; and the bond premium should be written off to Fund Balance—Interest. Show the closing entries at June 30, 19X4, and show the account balances at that date. (Formal journal entries are not required.)

(b) Prepare the formal journal entries that should be made to correct the General

Fund accounts and to record properly therein the results of transactions of the Main Street Improvement Project.

(c) Prepare a columnar Balance Sheet at June 30, 19X4, showing the balances of the various "funds" within the Special Assessment Fund.

(d) For the year ended June 30, 19X4, prepare a SAF Statement of Revenues, Expenditures, and Changes in Fund Balance.

(AICPA, adapted)

Problem 9-5, Part I. The following is a trial balance of the Special Assessment Fund of the City of Victorville as of January 1, 19X5.

Assessments Receivable—Deferred .	450,000	
Due from General Fund	80,000	
Bonds Payable		530,000
	530,000	530,000

Special assessments were levied after all construction had been completed. The special assessments and the city's share of cost are payable in ten equal installments beginning in 19X5. Collections from these sources are to be used to retire the serial bonds outstanding, which mature at a rate of $53,000 annually. Interest charged on deferred special assessments is to be used to pay bond interest.

The following transactions took place during 19X5:

1. The first installment became current.
2. Interest of $13,500 became due on assessments.
3. Collections of current assessments amounted to $44,000.
4. The city's 19X5 installment was paid from the General Fund.
5. Collections of interest amounted to $13,400.
6. Bonds in the amount of $53,000 matured; $52,000 of bonds were retired.
7. Interest paid on bonds amounted to $13,000.
8. Uncollected current assessments became delinquent.

The following transactions took place during the years 19X6 to 19Y2, inclusive:

9. The installments for 19X6–19Y2 became current.
10. Interest becoming due on assessments during this period amounted to $108,850.
11. Collections during this period were as follows:

Current assessments	$296,000
Interest on assessments	103.000
City's installments	56,000
Delinquent assessments	2,000

12. Payments were made as follows during these seven years:

Bonds	352,000
Interest	99,000

13. The uncollected current assessments became delinquent.

14. Cash for interest payments of $75 was used to pay the county for the cost of holding the sale of delinquent properties.

15. At the end of 19Y2, the properties listed below, on which the last two (19Y1 and 19Y2) installments had not been paid, were put up for sale. Property L was sold to an individual for $2,745, and properties M and N were bid in for this fund.

Property	Unpaid Assessments	Accrued Interest	Cost of Sale	Total
L	$2,500	$220	$25	$2,745
M	3,000	260	25	3,285
N	2,300	210	25	2,535

The following transactions took place during 19Y3:

16. The installment for this year became current.

17. Interest due on assessments amounted to $3,000.

18. Collections for this fund during the year were as follows:

19Y3 installments	$42,000
Delinquent assessments	10,000
Interest on assessments	5,200
City's installment	8,000

19. Bonds retired this year amounted to $59,000.

20. Interest on bonds paid, $6,200.

21. Property M was redeemed by the owner, who was charged additional interest of $15.

22. The uncollected portion of the 19Y3 installment became delinquent.

The following transactions took place during 19Y4:

23. The final installment became current.

24. Interest due on assessments amounted to $2,400.

25. Property N was transferred to the General Fixed Assets of the city, and this fund was reimbursed from the General Fund for the amount of the special assessment sale certificate.

26. Collections from assessments were as follows:

19Y4 installment	$42,050
City's installment	8,000

27. Cash for interest payments of $40 was used to pay the county for holding a delinquent assessment sale.

28. Property P, with a total unpaid assessment of $1,300, plus $200 interest (previously accrued) and $40 for cost of sale, was sold for $1,540.

29. All delinquent installments were collected.

30. All interest receivable was collected.

31. The remaining bonds were retired.

32. Interest paid on bonds amounted to $1,600.

33. The excess cash remaining was rebated and the fund was terminated.

Required:

Prepare a columnar worksheet to reflect the transactions affecting the Special Assessment Fund of the City of Victorville. Use a "debits over credits" worksheet with the following headings:

Columns	Heading
1	Trial Balance, 1/1/19X5
2–3	19X5 Transaction and Closing Entries
4	Trial Balance, 12/31/19X5
5–6	19X6–19Y2 Summary Transactions and Closing Entries
7	Trial Balance, 12/31/19Y2
8–9	19Y3 Transactions and Closing Entries
10	Trial Balance, 12/31/19Y3
11–12	19Y4 Transactions and Closing Entries
Optional 13	Trial Balance, 12/31/19Y4

Problem 9-5, Part II. Prepare the following financial statements for the Special Assessment Fund of the City of Victorville in columnar form:

(a) A Comparative Balance Sheet, setting forth the balances as of December 31, 19X4, 19X5, 19Y2, 19Y3, and 19Y4.

(b) A Comparative Statement of Revenues, Expenditures, and Changes in Fund Balance—Interest, with column headings as follows:

Year Ended December 31, 19X5	Seven (7) Years Ended December 31, 19Y2	Year Ended December 31, 19Y3	Year Ended December 31, 19Y4

Problem 9-6. The following transactions took place in the City of Dixonville during 19A:

1. The legislative body authorized the widening of a street at an estimated cost of $450,000.

2. Bonds of $300,000 were authorized and were sold at a discount of $1,300.

3. The city agreed to contribute $120,000 as its share of the estimated cost; the remainder was assessed against property owners. The assessments were made payable in installments, and *certain series of bonds were to be paid from certain installments and no others*. Assessment installments and bonds to be retired therefrom were as follows:

Nos.	Due Date	Amount of Installment	Amount of Bonds to Be Retired
1	19A	$30,000	—
2–9	19B-I	33,000	$33,000
10	19J	36,000	36,000

4. A contract was entered into with the Fane Construction Company for the construction of the project as a cost of $360,000.

5. Supervisory engineering costs of $10,000 were paid.

6. The city's contribution was received in full; and assessments of $27,000 were received.
7. The remainder of the first installment became delinquent.
8. Judgments of $120,000 were awarded for property condemned.
9. A bill for $100,000 was received from the Fane Construction Company.
10. Payments were made as follows:

Judgments payable	$120,000
Fane Construction Company	100,000

11. and 12. Interest of $8,200 became due; of this amount $7,500 was collected.
13. and 14. Interest of $6,100 became due; of this amount $4,000 was paid.

The transactions taking place in 19B were as follows:

15. Delinquent assessments of $1,500 were collected.
16. A bill was received from the Fane Construction Company for the remaining amount due on the contract.
17. Interest due at the close of the last fiscal year was paid.
18. and 19. Interest of $9,000 became due during this year; interest collected amounted to $8,900.
20. Assessments receivable coming due during 19B were reclassified accordingly.
21. and 22. Interest of $7,100 became due; of this amount, $3,550 was paid.
23. and 24. Current assessments amounting to $32,000 were collected; the remaining part of the second installment became delinquent.
25. The Fane Construction Company was paid the full amount of the contract, except for $50,000 which was retained pending final approval of the project.
26. Collections (transaction 23) were applied to the payment of bonds.

The transactions taking place in 19C were as follows:

27. Interest due at the close of 19B was paid.
28. The city agreed to contribute $10,000 for the purpose of eliminating the deficit.
29. The remaining part of the deficit was to be eliminated through the levy of supplemental assessments. Supplemental assessments were subsequently levied and were made payable in three equal annual installments, the first becoming due promptly.
30. Notes were issued to cover the last two annual installments of the supplemental assessments.
31. Assessments receivable coming due in 19C were reclassified as current.
32. Assessments (not supplemental) were collected as follows:

From first installment	$ 750
From second installment	750
From third installment	32,250

33. The proceeds, in so far as applicable, were used to retire bonds.
34. The uncollected portion of the third installment was reclassified as delinquent.
35. and 36. Interest on assessments of $7,900 became due during this year; interest receivable collected amounted to $7,750.

37. and 38. Interest on bonds of $6,240 became due; of this amount, $3,120 was paid.

39. The first installment of the supplemental assessment was collected in full, except for $800 which is now delinquent.

40. The city paid its contribution.

41. Interest on supplemental assessments collected was $464; and an additional $16 was due at December 31, 19C.

42. The project was found to be satisfactory and the Fane Construction Company was paid the amount due it. The additional cash necessary for this purpose was borrowed from the General Fund.

43. Interest on notes of $360 was paid.

Required:

(a) Prepare a columnar worksheet to reflect the transactions of the Dixonville Special Assessment Fund for the three years ending December 31, 19C. The columnar heading of the worksheet should be as follows:

Columns	Heading
1–2	19A Transaction and Closing Entries
3–4	Trial Balance, 12/31/19A
5–6	19B Transaction and Closing Entries
7–8	Trial Balance, 12/31/19B
9–10	19C Transaction and Closing Entries
11–12	Trial Balance, 12/31/19C

(b) Prepare a SAF Statement of Revenues, Expenditures, and Changes in Fund Balance for the three years ended December 31, 19C.

Problem 9-7, Part I. The City of Poseyton voted a bond issue for the purpose of constructing a modern sewer system in a section of the city. The cost is to be borne by general revenues of the city and by assessments levied against properties in the area of the improvement.

The following transactions and events related to this project occurred during 19X4:

1. February 1—The city engineer submitted to the city council an estimate of the construction cost of the project, showing a total of $445,000. Preliminary planning costs were expected to amount to $15,000. The council approved the estimate and project, subject to voter approval of the necessary bond issue.

2. April 1—A ten-year 6 percent special-general bond issue of $460,000 was approved by the voters of the city.

3. April 10—A contract covering preliminary planning (estimated to cost $15,000) was entered into by the project trustees.

4. April 15—The assessment roll was certified on the basis of $415,000, due in ten equal annual installments starting May 1, 19X5. Interest at 6 percent per annum from May 1, 19X4, is to be paid on each installment due date, based on the total assessment outstanding. Interest is charged at 10 percent per annum on delinquent assessments and interest receivable.

5. April 30—The preliminary plans were completed and an invoice of $13,700 was received from the planning contractor (in full). The trustees borrowed $25,000 from the General Fund of the city to pay this and other costs. The invoice was paid on May 5.

6. May 20—A contract for construction was entered into at a price of $420,000, subject to certain possible future adjustments.

7. June 1—$200,000 of the authorized bonds were sold at 101. The entire issue was dated June 1, 19X4, with interest payable December 1 and June 1 each year. The bonds mature at the rate of $46,000 per year, starting June 1, 19X5.

8. July 31—A partial payment of $26,100 was made to the contractor, which amount was 90 percent of the amount due based on percentage-of-completion. The balance is being held pending project completion, state inspection, and acceptance by the trustees. The loan from the General Fund was repaid.

9. November 1—The remaining bonds were sold at 98 and accrued interest.

10. August 1 to December 31—Payments to the contractor amounted to $284,400, 10 percent of the amount due having been withheld pending completion. Costs of $4,210 incurred in connection with administering the construction project were paid during the period. The bond interest was paid at due date. The city paid $2,300 on its part of the cost of the project.

Required:

Prepare the following:

(a) A columnar worksheet reflecting the transactions of the Special Assessment Fund of the City of Poseyton during the year ended December 31, 19X4. The worksheet should be headed as follows:

19X4 Transactions		Closing Entries 12/31/19X4		Postclosing Trial Balance 12/31/19X4	
Dr.	Cr.	Dr.	Cr.	Dr.	Cr.

Assume that budgetary accounts are not used and that interest should not be accrued but recorded when due. Worksheet entries should be keyed to the numbered items in the problem; a net bond premium is to be closed at year end to Fund Balance—Interest, but a net discount should be closed to Fund Balance—Construction.

(b) A columnar Balance Sheet at December 31, 19X4, presenting the assets, liabilities, and balances attributable to each "fund" within the Special Assessment Fund.

(c) A SAF Statement of Revenues, Expenditures, and Changes in Fund Balances for the year ended December 31, 19X4.

(AICPA, adapted)

Problem 9-7 Part II. The following transactions and events affected the Special Assessment Fund of the City of Poseyton during 19X5:

11. January 2—The assessment installment maturing in 19X5 was reclassified as current.

12. March 31—The project was completed and the contractor submitted a final invoice for $90,000, including the cost of modifications requested and agreed to by the trustees.

13. April 12—The contractor was paid $81,000 on the invoice above, the balance being withheld pending state inspection of the construction work and acceptance of the project by the trustees.

14. April 14—Landscaping and other costs not included within the construction contract were paid, $15,000.

15. April 18—A construction deficiency was discovered during the inspection. At the request of the contractor, who was now involved in an out-of-state project, the deficiency was repaired by Public Works Department employees at a cost of $4,000. The Public Works Department is financed through the General Fund.

16. April 28—The amount necessary to cover the excess construction costs to be borne by the city was appropriated from the General Fund. This amount, less the $4,000 due to the General Fund from the Special Assessment Fund, was paid to the Special Assessment Fund.

17. April 29—The amount due the contractor was paid.

18. May 1—December 30—Collections were made as follows: assessments, $47,000, including $8,000 from one person who paid the entire assessment levied against his property; interest was collected only from those property owners also paying their assessments. No additional interest was charged those paying by December 30.

19. June 1—The bond principal and interest due was paid.

20. December 1—The bond interest due was paid.

21. December 31—Unpaid current assessments and interest due as of May 1 were declared delinquent and interest at 10 percent per annum from May 1 was accrued thereon.

Required:

Prepare the following:

(a) A columnar worksheet reflecting the transactions of the Special Assessment Fund of the City of Poseyton for the year ended December 31, 19X5. The worksheet should be headed as follows:

Trial Balance 12/31/19X4		19X5 Transactions		Closing Entries 12/31/19X5		Postclosing Trial Balance 12/31/19X5	
Dr.	Cr.	Dr.	Cr.	Dr.	Cr.	Dr.	Cr.

Alternatively, you may continue using the worksheet prepared for Part I of this problem, adding the columns and headings required.

(b) A SAF Balance Sheet at December 31, 19X5, with comparative 19X4 year-end balances.

(c) A SAF Statement of Revenues, Expenditures, and Changes in Fund Balances for the two years ended December 31, 19X5. Show the beginning balances, changes, and ending balances for each year.

10

GENERAL FIXED ASSETS; GENERAL LONG-TERM DEBT; INTRODUCTION TO INTERFUND TRANSACTIONS AND RELATIONSHIPS

The funds for which accounting principles have been presented thus far have been separate, self-balancing entities that may have seemed unrelated to one another. Fixed assets purchased through the funds have mysteriously disappeared from the accounts, as has the liability for general obligation long-term indebtedness. These mysteries are explained in this chapter. The first part deals with the accounting procedure for General Fixed Assets and explains the relationship between them and the funds from which they are financed. The second part is concerned with the accounting procedure for a government's general obligation long-term debt and points out the relationship of the indebtedness to the General Fund, the Capital Projects Funds, and the Debt Service Funds. The third part provides a formal introduction to the subject of interfund transactions and relationships.

GENERAL FIXED ASSETS

Governments use many assets of a durable, long-term nature in their operations. Examples are land, buildings, and equipment. They possess physical substance and are expected to provide service for periods that extend beyond the year of acquisition. They are not physically consumed by their use, though their economic usefulness declines over their lifetimes. Their proper recording and control is necessary for efficient management and for financial reporting.

"General" Fixed Assets Defined

A clear-cut distinction is maintained between the accounting for fixed assets in the General Fixed Assets Account Group and that for fixed assets in specific fund entities. The NCGA has identified *general fixed assets* as "all fixed assets

352

except those accounted for in proprietary or Trust Funds."[1] In the Trust, Internal Service, and Enterprise Funds, fixed asset increases and decreases are accounted for in the same manner as in the accounts of profit-seeking enterprises.

The governmental funds, discussed in preceding chapters, are vehicles through which the sources and uses of appropriable financial resources are accounted for. Acquisition of fixed assets is a *use* of expendable fund resources because the fixed assets are not appropriable resources and belong to the organization as a whole, not to any specific fund. (The assets may or may not be used by agencies financed by the acquiring fund.) In none of the governmental funds are acquisitions of capital assets recorded in the fund as fixed assets; in all of the funds discussed in preceding chapters acquisition of fixed assets has been recorded as an *expenditure* of fund resources because the assets are considered *general* fixed assets to be capitalized in the General Fixed Assets Account Group.

Acquisition and Initial Valuation

A government's general fixed assets are initially recorded at cost. The cost principle used in fund accounting is the same as that included in generally accepted accounting principles (GAAP) for business enterprises. Cost is generally defined as the value of consideration given or consideration received, whichever is more clearly determinable. Cost includes all normal and necessary outlays incurred to bring the asset into a state of readiness for its intended use—including interest during construction, computed in conformity with FASB *Statement 62*.

The NCGA specifically states that "General fixed assets include those acquired, in substance, through noncancellable leases,"[2] and it may be assumed that the full range of GAAP is applicable to acquisitions of fixed assets.

In the past many governments failed to maintain records of fixed assets. As they became concerned about not complying with GAAP and missing other benefits of proper accounting, they began accumulating cost data and recording them. In some cases original records were not available and reconstruction of records was impossible or prohibitively expensive. In such cases the NCGA has approved recording *estimated* original cost on the basis of available information.[3] Although these estimates are less objective than the information usually available for recording cost, errors are gradually eliminated as the older assets are retired. The basis of fixed asset valuation, whether actual or estimated cost, should be clearly disclosed in the financial statements.

Governments acquire assets by three methods not customary for business enterprises. In cases of *foreclosure,* the valuation should normally be the lower of (1) the amount of taxes or special assessments due, related penalties and interest, and applicable foreclosure costs, or (2) the appraised value of the property. Both amounts should be included in the fixed asset records. *Eminent domain* is the power of government to seize private property for public use, compensation to the owner normally being determined through the courts. Property thus acquired is accounted for in the same manner as that acquired in a negotiated purchase.

[1] NCGAS 1, p. 6.
[2] Ibid., p. 9.
[3] Ibid., p. 10.

Acquisition by *escheat* occurs when title to property is vested in or reverts to the government because the rightful owner does not come forward to claim it or because he dies without known heirs. Fixed assets obtained in this manner are accounted for in the same manner as gifts; that is, they are capitalized in the General Fixed Assets accounts at estimated fair market value at acquisition.

Classification

The NCGA recommends that governmental fixed assets be classified as (1) Land, (2) Buildings, (3) Improvements Other Than Buildings, (4) Machinery and Equipment, or (5) Construction in Progress.

1. *Land.* The cost of land includes the amount paid for the land itself, costs incidental to the acquisition of land, and expenditures incurred in preparing the land for use.
2. *Buildings.* The "buildings" classification includes (1) relatively permanent structures used to house persons or property, and (2) fixtures which are permanently attached to and made a part of buildings and which cannot be removed without cutting into the walls, ceilings, or floors or without in some way damaging the building.
3. *Improvements Other Than Buildings.* Examples of items in this category are bridges, sidewalks, streets, dams, tunnels, and fences.
4. *Machinery and Equipment.* Examples are trucks, automobiles, pumps, desks, typewriters, and bookcases. Since much machinery and equipment is movable, it must be accounted for with particular care.
5. *Construction in Progress.* The cost of construction work undertaken but incomplete at a balance sheet date. These costs are appropriately reclassified upon project completion.

In order to record and report the manner in which fixed assets were acquired, both currently and cumulatively, the NCGA recommends that the credit side of the General Fixed Assets Account Group be classified according to the *source* of the resources used for fixed asset acquisition. In previous chapters we have observed that General Fixed Asset acquisition may be financed through three major fund types:

1. *Capital Projects Funds:* major facilities acquired through long-term borrowing, intergovernmental grants-in-aid, interfund transfers, or some combination of sources.
2. *Special Assessment Funds:* facilities or improvements partially or fully financed by property owners benefiting directly from them.
3. *General or Special Revenue Funds:* various general fixed assets, particularly equipment, from general or special revenues.

Inasmuch as general or special revenues may be transferred to Capital Projects and Special Assessment Funds, and since other governments often assist in fixed asset acquisition, it is not sufficient merely to classify fixed asset sources by fund or fund type. Rather, they should be classified by the original funding source, for example (1) general obligation bonds, (2) Federal grants, (3) state grants, (4) General Fund revenues, (5) Special Revenue Fund revenues, (6) special assessments, or (7) gifts. Therefore, a single acquisition may require credits to several Investment in General Fixed Assets (source) accounts. Figure 10-1 presents an overview of the accounting equation applicable to General Fixed Assets accounting.

Property Records

After the cost or other value of a fixed asset has been determined, it is recorded on an individual property record. The NCGA recommended recording the following information relative to each unit of property:

1. Class code
2. Sequence or payment voucher number
3. Date of acquisition
4. Name and address of vendor
5. Abbreviated description
6. Department, division, or unit charged with custody
7. Location
8. Cost
9. Fund and account from which purchased
10. Method of acquisition
11. Estimated life
12. Date, method, and authorization of disposition

A separate record is established for each "unit" of property. (A unit of property is any item which can be readily identified and accounted for separately.) These records of individual properties constitute the subsidiary accounts which support the General Fixed Assets accounts in the general ledger.

These subsidiary records must be available for classification in a number of ways:

1. They should permit a balancing operation to support the amounts in the Land, Buildings, and other control accounts in the general ledger.
2. The assets in use by the several organizational units of a government are the responsibility of the agencies, bureaus, departments, and so on; and the system should permit identification of such assets for custodial control purposes and any cost finding that is carried out.
3. Assets not in use should be easily identifiable so that requests for assets may be filled from assets on hand.
4. Assets should be classifiable by location so that custodial control by physical inventory will be feasible.

The foregoing list of classifications is intended to be illustrative, not exhaustive.

Figure 10-1

GENERAL FIXED ASSETS ACCOUNTING EQUATION

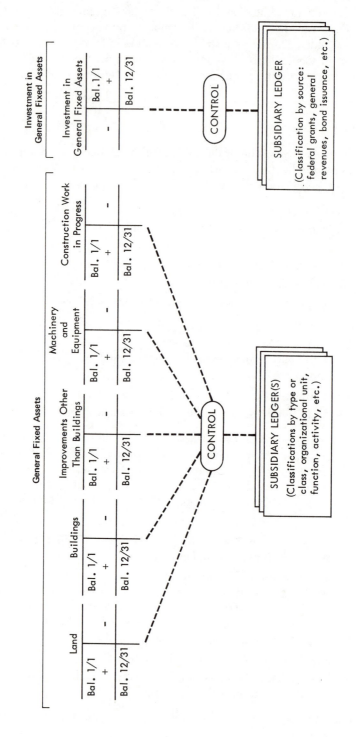

Inventory of Fixed Assets

A physical inventory of machinery and equipment should be taken on a regular basis for internal control purposes. The physical count can then be compared with recorded descriptions and quantities. All differences between counts and records should be investigated. Missing assets must be removed from the accounts, and significant shortages should be disclosed in the statements or notes. Management should correct the weaknesses in internal control or accounting systems revealed by the shortages and related investigations.

If a government has not maintained records of fixed assets, such records may be created from a physical inventory. The most difficult task is to arrive at a value at which to record the assets. Documents may be available to indicate cost. If not, the original cost should be estimated. Only as a last resort should appraisal values as of the inventory date be used.

Additions, Betterments, and Renewals

The costs of additions, betterments, and renewals are additional costs of general fixed assets; their capitalization is subject to GAAP. The costs will be incurred in one of the governmental funds, where the distinction between costs to be capitalized and those to be treated as expenditures must be made. Since expenditures for both purposes must be authorized by appropriations, the distinction should first be made in the budget.

Additions to fixed assets are not classified according to whether they are buildings, other improvements, or equipment until they are completed. As noted earlier, costs incurred are accumulated in the Construction Work in Progress account during the construction period and are reclassified by asset type following completion of the project.

Depreciation

A major distinction between the accounting for governmental funds and that for profit-seeking enterprises results from Principle 7a of the NCGA:

> Depreciation of general fixed assets should not be recorded in the accounts of governmental funds. Depreciation of general fixed assets may be recorded in cost accounting systems or calculated for cost finding analyses; and accumulated depreciation may be recorded in the General Fixed Assets Account Group.[4]

If accumulated depreciation is to be recorded in the General Fixed Assets Account Group, it should be directly related to the asset for which it is being recorded. The corresponding debit would reduce the Investment in General Fixed Assets account or accounts that are related to the asset.

The Council recognized the existence of depreciation (expense) as an economic fact, emphasizing its use as a part of the determination of net income and any calculation of total cost. But since governmental funds are intended to account for and report the sources and uses (expenditures) of financial resources and *not*

[4] Ibid., p. 3.

the measurement of income, the recording of depreciation therein is not appropriate. In fact, *acquisition* of general fixed assets requires resources of governmental funds; the *disposition* of general fixed assets may provide resources to governmental funds. "Depreciation expense is neither a source nor a use of governmental fund financial resources, and thus is not properly recorded in the accounts of such funds."[5]

This recommendation of the Council is a repetition of a long-standing but controversial principle. Many individuals and groups have argued that depreciation of general fixed assets should be recognized. For example, an American Accounting Association Committee recommended that:

1. The accounting records and related reports of a not-for-profit organization should disclose the cost of use or consumption of the assets allocated to services and/or time periods as appropriate by an acceptable depreciation technique;
2. Depreciation accounting should be recognized as an integral part of accounting for resources.[6]

A summary of the major issues of the depreciation controversy, as seen by the AAA committee, is contained in Figure 10-2.

Figure 10-2

THE DEPRECIATION CONTROVERSY: SUMMARY OF MAJOR ISSUES

Against Recognition	For Recognition
Serves no useful purpose. Depreciation accounting is necessary only to measure profit—NFP organizations are not organized for profit and *profit or loss determination is irrelevant.*	Accrual accounting is essential to an understanding of the financial status (and change in status) of all organizations—should be cognizant of total NFP resource availability, utilization, and capital implementation or diminution.
Taxes, not fixed assets, provide revenue—recognition would *violate the matching concept.*	Expenses need not physically "produce" revenue directly. In reality we *match* revenues and expenses *to periods,* often separately.
NFP organizations exist on a year-to-year basis—*are not going-concerns.*	Where power of self-perpetuation exists via taxes, NFP entities *are extremely "going"*—it is more necessary to give full accounting than in private enterprise because of this power and their broad social impact and responsibility.
Recognition would result in *double-charging* current generation.	Cost determination separate from "price determination." *Are now unaware of costs or who bears them*—may be triple charging or half charging. Cost determination and "price-setting" are separate problems—accrual cost data are often useful in setting pricing policies.

[5] Ibid., p. 10.

[6] American Accounting Association, "Report of the Committee on Accounting Practices of Not-for-Profit Organizations," *Accounting Review,* Supplement to Vol. 46 (1971), p. 119.

Figure 10-2 (continued)

Against Recognition	For Recognition

Recognition *might result in a deficit*—this would upset the public.

We should *report clearly* and *truthfully*—many organizations acquire excess resources in some periods and deplete these subsequently. Such should be reported.

Recognition would be *confusing*—fund and budgetary considerations dominate NFP accounting. *Expenditures* are *budgeted* and must be accounted for—*depreciation* expense is *not budgeted.*

Funds and budgets are control devices and adherence must be reported. A single report will suffice only where budget is expense-based. Otherwise, we must *separate* current *fund budgetary accounting from financial accounting* as is done in profit-oriented organizations. Alternatively, we can adjust budgetary statements for capital outlay and depreciation.

Recognition is *technically unmanageable* in fund accounting structure—a good place for a debit but no place for the credit as fixed assets are not in fund accounts.

Several *expedient alternatives* are *available*—for example, hospitals account for depreciation through expense-equity adjustment of fund structure and/or account classification.

Recognition of depreciation would be *misleading* as:

Failure to recognize depreciation is *more misleading.* The contra arguments are *irrelevant* because:

a. *"Reserve"* for depreciation *implies cash* availability.

a. This argument was settled years ago—it is a *nomenclature problem.*

b. *"Value"* of fixed assets *is academic question*—"Cost" is all that is of importance.

b. There is *no attempt to measure "value"* but rather costs consumed and the cost of service potentials remaining within the organization.

c. *Asset was donated*—NFP has no depreciation expense.

c. The *donation was a contribution of capital*—the source of capital does not determine the measurement of its consumption.

d. We *may not replace* fixed assets or will replace through public subscription or individual donation.

d. See c above—also, expense measurement and asset replacement are *separate problems.*

Fixed assets are a heritage of past administrations—is unfair to charge current administration with past mistakes.

Currently not accountable for use of them at all—should use or dispose of, clearly indicating reasons and effects.

Fixed assets *do not depreciate if properly maintained.*

Depreciation and maintenance are largely *separate problems.* Even so, who is to determine adequacy or propriety of current maintenance? Maintenance expenditures frequently are *deferable* to the next administration, or at least until after the next election.

Depreciation is an estimate—*it cannot be accurately computed.*

Informed *estimates* are certainly *preferable to nonaccounting.*

What purpose is served in reporting depreciation on the *White House?* the *Statue of Liberty?*

Probably none—infinite useful life and/or small initial cost may result in *immateriality,* and hence not require depreciation accounting.

Figure 10-2 (continued)

Against Recognition	For Recognition
No one (citizens, legislators, creditors, etc.) *is interested* in depreciation.	They *have not been "exposed"* to true accrual accounting for NFP organizations. Presented via readable, meaningful financial reports, information concerning total resource stewardship (as opposed to current line item dollar accountability) might awaken a generally apathetic citizenry. Many *managements now receive* unpublished data relating to depreciation.
The *expense* of depreciation accounting *would exceed* the *benefits*.	*Inexpensive* if there are reasonably accurate records essential to physical control of assets.
Can determine depreciation costs via memorandum records, special studies, etc.	*Current "non-accounting" practices based on this premise are disappointing.* In addition, control is established when integrated into system.

Source: American Accounting Association, "Report of the Committee on Accounting Practices of Not-for-Profit Organizations," Accounting Review, Supplement to Vol. 46 (1971), pp. 117–118.

Recording Fixed Asset Acquisitions

Practice varies considerably as to (1) the timing of the updating of the General Fixed Assets Account Group, and (2) the extent of subsidiary account use. Computerized systems may be programmed to generate General Fixed Asset entries continually, periodically, or at year end. In less than fully automated systems, (1) some accountants prefer to update the GFA ledger whenever a relevant transaction occurs; (2) others maintain a GFA journal which is posted to the GFA ledger periodically during the year or at year end; and (3) still others update the GFA ledger only at year end, perhaps based on worksheet analyses of fund capital outlay expenditures. Regardless of individual preference, there should be an established, workable system by which General Fixed Assets subsidiary records are prepared and the account group is updated prior to statement preparation, at least annually. Similarly, the extent to which subsidiary ledgers are employed is a matter of individual preference and the detailed information desired or required. Normally, the Land, Buildings, Improvements Other than Buildings, Machinery and Equipment, Construction in Progress, and Investment in General Fixed Assets accounts are *controlling* accounts and details of assets owned and the means by which they were financed are maintained in subsidiary ledgers.

Figure 10-1 illustrates the accounting equation (see "Classification" in this chapter) applicable to the General Fixed Assets Account Group and the subsidiary information necessary to support the principal accounts. The following trial balance further illustrates the account relationships:

Land	700,000
Buildings	2,500,000
Improvements Other than Buildings	1,100,000
Machinery and Equipment	619,200

Construction in Progress	480,800	
Investment in General Fixed Assets from:		
General Obligation Bonds		2,500,000
Federal Grants		1,500,000
General Fund Revenues		1,150,000
Special Assessments		250,000
	5,400,000	5,400,000

The entries to record the capital expenditures in each governmental fund have already been given. In order to illustrate more clearly the relationship between these funds and the General Fixed Assets accounts, some of the fund entries will be repeated and the corresponding entry in the General Fixed Assets Account Group will be indicated.

Assets Financed from the General or Special Revenue Funds. Let us assume that $103,300 was spent from the General Fund for fixed assets. The entry in the General Fund at the time the expenditure is made is:

Expenditures	103,300	
Vouchers Payable		103,300
To record purchase of land, buildings, and equipment.		

A companion entry would be made in the General Fixed Assets Account Group:

Land	7,000	
Buildings	37,200	
Machinery and Equipment	59,100	
Investment in General Fixed Assets .		103,300
To record cost of fixed assets financed from current revenues.		

Investment in GFA subsidiary accounts:	*Cr.*
General Fund Revenues	103,300

Assets Financed Through Capital Projects Funds. Construction expenditures may be closed out at the end of each year or they may not be closed out until construction is completed. Assuming that expenditures are closed annually, the entry in the Capital Projects Fund at the end of the first year (page 266) is:

Appropriations	140,800	
Expenditures		140,800
To close expenditures to date.		

Whether or not the foregoing entry is made, the following entry is required in the General Fixed Assets Account Group:

Construction in Progress	140,800	
Investment in General Fixed Assets .		140,800
To record construction in progress financed through Capital Projects Fund.		

Investment in GFA subsidiary accounts:

	Cr.
General Fund Revenues	17,600
County Grants	17,600
Federal Grants	70,400
General Obligation Bonds	35,200
	140,800

The distribution of sources as among General Fund revenues, county grants, Federal grants, and issuance of general obligation bonds would be made in proportion to the expected total contribution of each to the project. Note also that *encumbered* amounts, whether or not closed out at year end, are *not* capitalized; only *expended* amounts are capitalized.

When the project is completed, during the second year in our example, the entry in the Capital Projects Fund (page 269) is:

Appropriations	259,200	
Expenditures		252,400
Fund Balance		6,800

To close the temporary fund balance accounts.

In the General Fixed Assets Account Group, the entry is:

Improvements Other than Buildings ...	393,200	
Construction in Progress		140,800
Investment in General Fixed Assets .		252,400

To record the cost of completed project financed through Capital Projects Fund and to close the Construction in Progress account.

Investment in GFA subsidiary:

	Cr.
General Fund Revenues	32,400
County Grants	32,400
Federal Grants	129,600
General Obligation Bonds	58,000
	252,400

The subsidiary entry pertaining to sources was determined by the following calculation:

	Total	General Fund	County Grant	Federal Grant	Bond Issue
Final project revenues	$399,000	$50,000	$50,000	$200,000	$99,000
Less: Fund balance transferred to Debt Service Fund	(5,800)				(5,800)
Final project cost/sources	$393,200	$50,000	$50,000	$200,000	$93,200

	Total	General Fund	County Grant	Federal Grant	Bond Issue
Less: Amounts credited to sources in previous Construction in Progress entry(ies)	(140,800)	(17,600)	(17,600)	(70,400)	(35,200)
Balance to be credited to Investment in General Fixed Asset subsidiary ledger source accounts	$252,400	$32,400	$32,400	$129,600	$58,000

Assets Financed Through Special Assessment Funds. The procedure for recording general fixed assets acquired through Special Assessment Funds closely parallels that for Capital Projects Funds. Expenditures, but *not* encumbrances, incurred for uncompleted projects are capitalized currently; upon completion of the project, all costs are appropriately classified.

Assuming that expenditures were closed at year end, the following entry was made in the Special Assessment Fund (page 318):

Revenues—Construction	40,000	
Operating Transfer from GF— Construction	100,000	
Expenditures—Construction		140,000
To close the temporary fund balance accounts.		

The following entry should be made in the General Fixed Assets Account Group:

Construction in Progress	140,000	
Investment in General Fixed Assets .		140,000
To record construction in progress financed through a Special Assessment Fund.		

	Cr.
Investment in GFA subsidiary accounts:	
Special Assessments	112,000
General Fund Revenues	28,000
	140,000

Again, the source subsidiary ledger account entries were based on total expected revenue sources, that is, the government's share of this project was to be $100,000 of the $500,000 total cost, or 20 percent.

Upon completion of the project, the following closing entry was made in the Special Assessment Fund:

Revenues—Construction	345,000	
Expenditures—Construction		345,000
To close the construction-related temporary fund balance accounts.		

The following entry, supported by the schedule below, should be made in the General Fixed Assets Account Group:

Improvements Other Than Buildings	485,000	
Construction in Progress		140,000
Investment in General Fixed Assets		345,000
To record completion of special assessment project.		

	Cr.
Investment in GFA subsidiary accounts:	
Special Assessments	$273,000
General Fund Revenues	72,000
	$345,000

Calculation:

	Total	Special Assess- ments	General Fund Transfer
Final project financing sources	$485,000	$385,000	$100,000
Less: Amounts credited to sources at end of prior year	140,000	112,000	28,000
Balances to record, end of second year	$345,000	$273,000	$ 72,000

Assets Acquired Through Foreclosure. We noted earlier that fixed assets acquired through foreclosure should be recorded at the lower of (1) fair market value, and (2) the amount of taxes or assessments, penalties and interest due on the property, and costs of foreclosure and sale. To illustrate, assume that land with an estimated value of $2,000 was acquired through foreclosure. At the time of foreclosure, the following were due a Special Revenue Fund:

Taxes	$ 900
Penalties	100
Interest	75
Costs of foreclosure and sale	25
	$1,100

Further assuming that these receivables had been reclassified as Tax Liens Receivable prior to the decision to retain the property for the government's use, the following entry should be made in the Special Revenue Fund:

Expenditures	1,100	
Tax Liens Receivable		1,100
To record acquisition of land through foreclosure; estimated fair market value, $2,000.		

The accompanying entry in the General Fixed Assets Account Group would be:

Land	1,100	
Investment in General Fixed Assets .		1,100
To record acquisition of land through		
foreclosure of tax lien.		
Investment in GFA subsidiary accounts:	*Cr.*	
Special Revenue Fund Revenues	1,100	

Note that the Investment in General Fixed Asset subsidiary credit is to "Special Revenue Fund Revenues," rather than to Foreclosures (or some similar account). Note also that had the fair market value of the property been less than charges against it, say $800, the Special Revenue Fund expenditure would be recorded at $800 and $300 would be charged against the allowance for uncollectible taxes and interest (or tax liens) receivable.

In all of the examples cited thus far, there has been a clear-cut indication within a fund ledger that a fixed asset has been acquired and should be capitalized, that is, there has been a charge to the Expenditures account of some fund. Laws or custom in some jurisdictions do not permit charging fixed asset acquisitions through foreclosure to the Expenditures account, however. Rather, the uncollectible amount must be charged as a bad debt, and the following entry would appear in the fund ledger:

Allowance for Uncollectible Tax Liens .	1,100	
Tax Liens Receivable		1,100
To record acquisition of property through		
foreclosure, estimated fair market value,		
$2,000. (State laws do not permit		
charging the Expenditures account.)		

Thus, "bad debt" entries such as the above must be examined, as they may call for a General Fixed Assets entry. (Again, the Investment in General Fixed Assets subsidiary credit would be to Special Revenue Fund Revenues, since these were forgone to acquire the property.)

Assets Acquired Through Gifts. Inasmuch as no fund assets were relinquished in acquiring property donated to the government, transactions of this type are recorded *only* in the General Fixed Assets Account Group. Donated property should be recorded in the GFA accounts at estimated fair market value to the unit at the time of the donation:

Land	1,500	
Investment in General Fixed Assets .		1,500
To record land received by gift at		
estimated fair market value.		
Investment in GFA subsidiary accounts:	*Cr.*	
Private Gifts	1,500	

Sale, Retirement, or Replacement

If depreciation of General Fixed Assets is not recorded, an asset's carrying value in the accounts remains at original cost plus any additions and betterments throughout the period of its use. Removal of the asset's carrying value upon its disposal is simply a matter of reversal of the acquisition entry. The accounting procedure upon disposal is, in sum:

1. *General Fixed Assets.* Remove the asset carrying value by debiting the Investment in General Fixed Assets account(s) and crediting the asset account(s) in the general and subsidiary ledgers.
2. *Fund receiving proceeds of sale.* Record any salvage value, insurance proceeds, or other receipts as Revenue in the accounts of the recipient governmental fund.

Thus, if a fire truck with a book value of $10,000 is sold for $2,000, the following entries are made:

Entry in General Fund:		
Cash	2,000	
Revenues—Sales of Equipment		2,000
To record sale of fire truck.		
Entry in General Fixed Assets Account Group:		
Investment in General Fixed Assets—		
General Fund Revenues	10,000	
Machinery and Equipment		10,000
To record sale of fire truck with book value of $10,000.		

If the truck noted above is traded in on a new truck costing $12,000, and an allowance of $3,000 is made for the old truck, the transaction is recorded:

Entry in General Fund:		
Expenditures	9,000	
Cash		9,000
To record purchase of fire truck costing $12,000, net of trade-in allowance of $3,000.		
Entries in General Fixed Assets Account Group:		
Investment in General Fixed Assets—		
General Fund Revenues	10,000	
Machinery and Equipment		10,000
To record disposal (trade-in) of old fire truck with book value of $10,000.		
Machinery and Equipment	12,000	
Investment in General Fixed Assets—		
General Fund Revenues		12,000
To record purchase of fire truck at a cost of $9,000 plus trade-in allowance on old fire truck of $3,000.		

Thus far we have assumed that the assets were sold to private persons. Sometimes property accounted for in a proprietary or similar Trust Fund is sold to a department financed through a governmental fund. Let us assume, for example, that an enterprise sells equipment at book value to the public works department, which is financed from the General Fund. The following entries would be made:

ENTRY IN ENTERPRISE FUND:

Due from General Fund	15,000	
Allowance for Depreciation—		
Equipment	1,000	
Equipment		16,000

To record sale of equipment to department of public works at net book value.

ENTRY IN GENERAL FUND:

Expenditures	15,000	
Due to Enterprise Fund		15,000

To record purchase of equipment from Enterprise Fund for department of public works and liability owing to that fund.

ENTRY IN GENERAL FIXED ASSETS ACCOUNT GROUP:

Machinery and Equipment	15,000	
Investment in General Fixed		
Assets—General Fund Revenues ..		15,000

To record purchase of equipment for public works department.

The entries to record retirements are more complicated because it is important to take into account the cost of retirement as well as the proceeds received from the sale of salvage. For example, assume that a fire station was torn down, that the book value of the building was $60,000, that the cost of tearing it down was $1,000, and that $5,000 was realized from the sale of salvage. The entries to record these transactions are as shown below.

ENTRY IN GENERAL FIXED ASSETS ACCOUNT GROUP:

Investment in General Fixed Assets—		
Bond Issues	60,000	
Buildings		60,000

To record retirement of fire station.

ENTRIES IN GENERAL FUND:

Expenditures	1,000	
Cash		1,000

To record cost of dismantling building, such cost to be reimbursed from sale of salvage.

Cash	5,000	
Expenditures		1,000
Revenues		4,000

To record sale of salvage.

If a government has adopted the policy of recording accumulated depreciation on assets of the General Fixed Assets Account Group, the entries to record removal of an asset from the Group, for whatever reason, would include removal of the accumulated depreciation related to the asset being removed.

Transfer of Fixed Assets

When fixed assets are transferred from one agency to another, both financed by a governmental fund, or even from one location to another, a written authorization for the transfer should be issued by the proper authority. The authorization will be the basis for changes in the subsidiary records to permit continuing control. The general ledger accounts will not be affected.

Transfers of assets from agencies financed by governmental funds to agencies financed by proprietary funds affect both the general ledger and the subsidiary property records. For example, if equipment was transferred from the Water Fund to the Fire, Police, and Public Works Departments, the entries to record this transaction (assuming the three departments are financed from the General Fund) are as follows:

ENTRY IN WATER (ENTERPRISE) FUND:

Retained Earnings (or Governmental Unit's Contribution)	10,000	
Allowance for Depreciation— Equipment	20,000	
Equipment		30,000

To record transfer of equipment to other departments as follows:

Department	Cost of Equipment	Accumulated Depreciation	Net Book Value
Police	$ 5,000	$ 3,000	$ 2,000
Fire	10,000	6,500	3,500
Public Works	15,000	10,500	4,500
	$30,000	$20,000	$10,000

ENTRY IN GENERAL FIXED ASSETS ACCOUNT GROUP:

Machinery and Equipment	10,000	
Investment in Fixed Assets— Enterprise Fund Transfers		10,000

To record receipt of equipment.

A separate property record is established for this equipment in each department, of course. No entry is made in the General Fund accounts, however, since no appropriable General Fund assets were either provided or used as a result of the transfer.

Property Damaged or Destroyed

Expenditures for repairs necessary to restore damaged property to its former condition are charged to the Expenditures account in the fund from which the cost of repairs is financed and are classified as current operating expenditures. Let us assume that the total book value of a police station is $100,000, that the station is destroyed by fire, and that the governmental unit collects insurance of $90,000. The following entries would be made in the General Fixed Assets Account Group and in the General Fund, respectively, to record these transactions.

ENTRY IN GENERAL FIXED ASSETS
ACCOUNT GROUP:
Investment in Fixed Assets—Bond Issue	100,000	
Buildings		100,000
To record destruction of police station by fire.		

ENTRY IN GENERAL FUND:
Cash	90,000	
Revenues		90,000
To record receipt of proceeds of insurance policy on police station.		

If the government intends to use some or all of the proceeds for replacement purposes, a "Reserve for Restoring Police Station" could be created in the General Fund by a debit to Fund Balance. The intent of such a reserve is, of course, to make certain that the cash received from the insurance company is not appropriated for other purposes.

If a governmental fund's expenditures not only restore a damaged asset to its former condition but also result in bettering it, the excess of the total amount expended over the amount required to restore the asset to its former condition is classified as capital outlay. The amount of the capital outlay is then capitalized in the proper general ledger asset account in the General Fixed Assets Account Group and in the subsidiary individual property record for the asset.

The NCGA does not mention write-downs of General Fixed Assets because of damage, obsolescence, or abandonment. It would seem reasonable to write down an asset (say, a 1926 fire engine) to a much lower figure if it is now used for a purpose for which it was not purchased (say, a display in a park). Similarly, assets that are to be sold for scrap should be carried at salvage value.

STATEMENTS OF GENERAL FIXED ASSETS

The purpose of financial statements for the General Fixed Assets Account Group is to provide reports on what the NCGA has called "a management control and accountability listing." The implication of that term is that investors and the general public are not greatly interested in what assets are in use by the agencies financed by governmental funds. Be that as it may, the statements discussed in the following paragraphs are usually prepared.

The Statement of General Fixed Assets (Figure 10-3) presents a summary of the assets by major category and source. The supplementary Schedule of General Fixed Assets—By Functions and Activities (Figure 10-4) indicates where they are used. To be more useful to management, this schedule may be prepared on the basis of organizational units rather than along the broader function and activity basis illustrated. It then indicates departmental use of and responsibility for assets.

Figure 10-3

A GOVERNMENTAL UNIT
Statement of General Fixed Assets
(Date)

General fixed assets:

Land	$ 709,600
Buildings	2,487,200
Improvements other than buildings	1,978,200
Machinery and Equipment	643,100
Construction work in progress	300,000
Total general fixed assets	$6,118,100

Investment in general fixed assets from:

General obligation bonds	$2,558,000
Federal grants	1,629,600
County grants	50,000
Special assessments	650,000
General revenues	1,227,900
Private gifts	1,500
Special revenues	1,100
Total investment in general fixed assets .	$6,118,100

The NCGA has taken the position that the summary Statement of Changes in General Fixed Assets (Figure 10-5) should be included in the comprehensive annual financial report "unless sufficiently disclosed in the notes to the financial statements."[7] It serves as a connecting link between the Statements of General Fixed Assets at successive year ends. The Statement of Changes in General Fixed Assets—By Functions and Activities (Figure 10-6) is primarily useful for managerial purposes.

The NCGA has taken the position that:

> Reporting public domain or "infrastructure" fixed assets—roads, bridges, curbs and gutters, streets and sidewalks, drainage systems, lighting systems, and similar assets that are immovable and of value only to the governmental unit—is optional. The accounting policy in this respect should be consistently applied and should be disclosed in the Summary of Significant Accounting Policies. Appropriate legal and descriptive records (e.g., deeds, maps, and listings) should be maintained for *all* fixed assets, however, for both management and accountability purposes.[8]

[7] Ibid., p. 22.
[8] Ibid., p.9.

Figure 10-4

A GOVERNMENTAL UNIT

Schedule of General Fixed Assets—By Functions and Activities

(Date)

Function and Activity	Total	Land	Buildings	Improvements Other than Buildings	Machinery & Equipment
General government:					
Council	$ 20,000				$ 20,000
Executive department	13,080				13,080
Courts	100,148	$ 22,437	$ 72,700		5,011
Research and investigation	63,300				63,300
General government buildings	580,000	100,000	400,000	50,000	30,000
Total general government	$ 986,100	$141,600	$ 573,500	$ 90,000	$181,000
Public safety	643,600	124,000	305,000	11,700	202,900
Highways	2,310,000	200,500	270,000	1,819,400	20,100
Sanitation and waste removal	306,000	71,000	53,000	22,600	159,400
Public welfare	101,400	68,000	24,000	2,000	7,400
Schools	1,138,800	35,000	1,047,400	17,000	39,400
Libraries	202,000	47,000	122,600	3,500	28,900
Recreation	130,200	22,500	91,700	12,000	4,000
Total allocated to functions	$5,818,100	$709,600	$2,487,200	$1,978,200	$643,100
Construction work in progress	300,000				
Total general fixed assets	$6,118,100				

Figure 10-5

A GOVERNMENTAL UNIT

Statement of Changes in General Fixed Assets—By Sources
For the Fiscal Year Ended (Date)

	Total	Land	Buildings	Improvements Other than Buildings	Machinery & Equipment	Construction Work in Progress
General fixed assets (beginning of year)	$5,400,000	$700,000	$2,500,000	$1,100,000	$619,200	$480,800
Additions from:						
General obligation bonds	$ 168,200			$ 93,200		$ 75,000
Federal grants	225,000			200,000		25,000
County grants	50,000			50,000		
Special assessments	400,000			400,000		
General revenues*	238,300	$ 7,000	$ 37,200	135,000	$ 59,100	
Special revenues*	1,100	1,100				
Private gifts	1,500	1,500				
	$1,084,100	$ 9,600	$ 37,200	$ 878,200	$ 59,100	$100,000
Total balance and additions	$6,484,100	$709,600	$2,537,200	$1,978,200	$678,300	$580,800
Deductions:						
Cost of assets sold or traded	$ 32,800				$ 32,800	
Cost of assets lost by fire	50,000		$ 50,000			
Cost of assets worn out and written off	2,400				2,400	
Cost of construction work in process of prior year completed†	280,800					$280,800
	$ 366,000		$ 50,000		$ 35,200	$280,800
General fixed assets (end of year)	$6,118,100	$709,600	$2,487,200	$1,978,200	$643,100	$300,000

* Includes amounts transferred to and expended through Capital Projects and Special Assessment Funds.
† Included in costs capitalized to Land, Buildings, Improvements Other than Buildings, and Machinery and Equipment.

This option, like the permission to use estimated costs where necessary, is provided so that governments that have not maintained records of public domain assets may comply with GAAP; also, they may receive unqualified opinions from independent accountants without incurring the high costs of accounting for infrastructure assets. Inclusion of the details of infrastructure assets *in the accounts* is preferable to assure maintenance of essential records (e.g., deeds, maps).

GENERAL LONG-TERM DEBT

General long-term debt may be defined as the **unmatured principal** of bonds, warrants, notes, pension obligations, and other forms of debt that is secured by the full faith and credit of the government and is not a primary obligation of any fund. Excluded from the definition are debts to be paid by proprietary, Special Assessment, or Trust Funds, as well as matured general obligation debt that has been set up in and will be paid by a Debt Service Fund. The excluded debt is not recorded in the General Long-Term Debt Account Group, but it should be reported as a contingent liability if it is a general obligation of the government.

Thus we see that the same type of clear-cut distinction maintained between fixed assets of specific funds and general fixed assets is maintained between (1) long-term debt that is the primary responsibility of specific funds and (2) general long-term debt. The liability for unmatured *general* long-term debt is recorded in the General Long-Term Debt Account Group, not in the fund that may have accounted for the proceeds of its issuance (e.g., the Capital Projects Fund) or the fund that will eventually pay it (e.g., the Debt Service Fund).

Overview of General Long-Term Debt Accounting

Accounting for General Long-Term Debt may be divided into three phases:

1. **When debt is incurred.** The principal of the debt owed is credited to an appropriate liability account; the corresponding debit is to an "Amount to Be Provided for Payment of Debt Principal" or similar account, indicating the extent to which future revenues are committed to the retirement of debt principal.

2. **While unmatured debt is outstanding.** As resources for the retirement of General Long-Term Debt are accumulated, usually in Debt Service Funds, the "Amount to Be Provided . . ." account is reduced and an "Amount Available . . ." account established or increased to reflect their availability.

3. **When debt matures.** The matured debt is established as a liability of the fund through which it is to be paid—usually a Debt Service Fund—and the liability and related "Amount Available . . ." and/or "Amount to be Provided . . ." accounts are reversed from the General Long-Term Debt Account Group.

Though a distinction is made in the accounts as between term and serial indebtedness, the accounting process for General Long-Term Debt may be visualized as in Figure 10-7.

Figure 10-6

A GOVERNMENTAL UNIT

Statement of Changes in General Fixed Assets—By Functions and Activities
For the Fiscal Year Ended (Date)

Function and Activity	General Fixed Assets (Beginning of Year)	Additions	Deductions	General Fixed Assets (End of Year)
General government:				
Council	$ 18,400	$ 2,100	$ 500	$ 20,000
Executive department	11,580	1,500		13,080
Courts	98,548	2,200	600	100,148
Research and investigation	61,800	1,200		63,000
General government building .	516,000	84,000	20,000	580,000
Total general government ...	$ 923,500	$ 101,400	$ 38,800	$ 986,100
Public safety:				
Police protection	222,500	21,600	11,100	233,000
Fire protection	311,500	18,400	13,300	316,600
Protective inspection	6,100		100	6,000
Other inspection	2,000			2,000
Correction	81,800	4,600	400	86,000
Total public safety	$ 623,900	$ 44,600	$ 24,900	$ 643,600
Highways	$1,591,900	$ 718,100		$2,310,000
Sanitation and waste removal	298,000	10,000	2,000	306,000
Public welfare	101,400			101,400
Schools	1,070,000	84,000	15,200	1,138,800
Libraries	197,400	7,000	2,400	202,000
Recreation	113,100	19,000	1,900	130,200
Construction work in progress	480,800	100,000	280,800	300,000
	$5,400,000	$1,084,100	$366,000	$6,118,100

Practice varies somewhat as to the timing of the entries in the General
Long-Term Debt Account Group. As a general rule (1) entries to record incurrence
of debt are made immediately upon its incurrence, (2) entries to record accumulation of debt retirement resources are made in the course of the year-end
adjustment process, and (3) entries to record debt maturity are prepared at the
date the debt is due.

Relation to Term Debt

In order to illustrate the relationship among the Capital Projects and Debt
Service Funds and the General Long-Term Debt Account Group, recall the 19Y9
City Hall Bonds example of Chapter 7. Upon issuance of the debt instruments

Figure 10-7

GENERAL LONG-TERM DEBT ACCOUNT GROUP

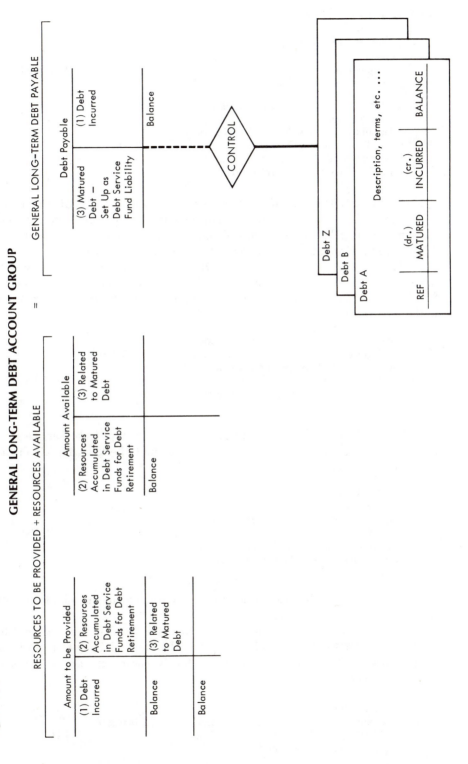

at par, entries would be required as follows:

ENTRY IN CAPITAL PROJECTS FUND
Cash 1,000,000
    Bond Issue Proceeds 1,000,000
To record receipt of bond issue proceeds.

ENTRY IN GENERAL LONG-TERM DEBT
ACCOUNT GROUP:
Amount to Be Provided for Payment of
    Term Bonds 1,000,000
    Term Bonds Payable 1,000,000
To record issuance of term bonds.

The liability is recorded at par or maturity value in the GLTD accounts, even if the debt is issued at a premium or discount. The proceeds are expended through the Capital Projects Funds and assets are capitalized in the General Fixed Asset Account Group following procedures previously discussed.

Recall, however, that a 19Y9 City Hall Bonds Debt Service Fund was established to service this debt. At the end of its first year there was a balance of $17,460 in that Fund, requiring the following adjustment to be made at year end in the GLTD accounts:

Amount Available in Debt Service Funds—
    Term Bonds 17,460
    Amount to Be Provided for Payment of
    Term Bonds 17,460
To record amount available for retirement of term bonds.

Similarly, at the end of the second year the 19Y9 City Hall Debt Service Fund had net assets (Fund Balance) of $36,810, occasioning the following GLTD adjustment for the amount of increase:

Amount Available in Debt Service Funds—
    Term Bonds 19,350
    Amount to Be Provided for Payment of
    Term Bonds 19,350
To record increase in the amount available for retirement of term bonds from $17,460 to $36,810.

Similar entries would be made at least annually throughout the life of the Debt Service Fund and the debt issue.

In the 19Y9 City Hall Bonds example, over $1 million had been accumulated in the Debt Service Fund—and reflected in the General Long-term Debt accounts—prior to bond maturity. When the bonds mature, the following related entries are needed:

ENTRY IN DEBT SERVICE FUND:
Expenditures 1,000,000
    Matured Bonds Payable 1,000,000
To record maturity of bonds.

ENTRY IN GENERAL LONG-TERM DEBT
ACCOUNT GROUP:
Term Bonds Payable 1,000,000
    Amount Available in Debt Service
      Funds—Term Bonds 1,000,000
To record term bonds maturing and
established as a liability of a Debt Service
Fund.

Had an amount less than the principal of the maturing bonds been accumulated in the Debt Service Fund (and been recognized in the "Amount Available . . ." account), a decision as to payment of the bonds would have to be made. If there is not to be a default, additional resources would have to be provided to the Debt Service Fund and recognized in the GLTD accounts.

Relation to Serial Debt

Most serial Debt Service Funds are essentially "flow-through" vehicles through which current period principal and interest requirements and payments are accounted for. Such funds are apt to have minimal (or zero) balances at year end and do not normally require entries in the General Long-Term Debt Account Group. The appropriate GLTD entry upon maturity of debt principal in such situations is simply the reverse of the entry made to record debt incurrence.

Where debt principal maturities are staggered over a period of years, the government may equalize its annual debt service provisions, thereby accumulating resources in "low requirement" years for use during "high requirement" years. Where a significant excess of serial Debt Service Fund assets over current year principal and interest requirements exists, the serial bond Debt Service Fund becomes similar to a term bond Debt Service Fund and should be accounted for similarly. The required annual adjustment to the GLTD accounts in such cases is again simply a matter of reclassifying from the "Amount to be Provided . . ." account to the "Amount Available . . ." account an amount sufficient to bring the latter into agreement with the Fund Balance account in the serial bond Debt Service Fund.

Relation to Non-GLTD Issuances

We have observed that long-term indebtedness of Special Assessment, Enterprise, and Trust Funds are usually specific fund liabilities rather than General Long-Term Debt. In many instances, however, governments have guaranteed the timely servicing of such indebtedness in order to make the issuances more saleable and/or to obtain a lower interest rate on such debt than would otherwise be possible. Though such arrangements usually do not call for formal GLTD entries—as the liability is shown in the balance sheet of the principal debtor fund—the organization's contingent liability on the debt should be disclosed by footnote in the Statement of General Long-Term Debt (Figure 10-8).[9] Should the servicing of such debt be in arrears, the contingent liability may become an actual liability, and would then be established in the GLTD accounts.

[9] Significant contingencies must be disclosed in notes to the GPFS.

As a general rule, then, a liability is accounted for in the fund primarily liable therefor, with disclosure required within the statements of the fund secondarily liable—or in GLTD statements if the government as a whole is secondarily liable. Application of this general rule proves difficult at times, and sound judgment and adequate disclosure often prove essential. For example, it may be difficult on occasion to determine (1) where the primary liability for a debt falls; (2) particularly where industrial revenue bonds or obligations of special boards or commissions are involved, which obligations the government should be—or might be—deemed contingently liable for under existing statutes or agreements; (3) where "moral" obligations to guarantee debt have been implied or acknowledged, which will prove enforceable and/or will be enforced against the government; or (4) at what stage a contingent liability becomes an actual liability.

Relation to Other "General Government" Liabilities

Recall that the *Statement 1* definition of the modified accrual basis of governmental (and similar trust) fund accounting states that a *fund expenditure* is recognized when a *fund liability* is incurred. Recall also that *Statement 1* provides that all unmatured indebtedness except specific fund indebtedness is GLTD; and GLTD "is not limited to liabilities arising from debt issuances *per se*, but may also include . . . other commitments that are not current liabilities properly recorded in governmental [or similar trust] funds."[10]

NCGA *Statement 4* on claims, judgments, and compensated absences states further that "in governmental (and similar trust) funds, liabilities usually are not considered current until they are *normally expected to be liquidated with expendable available financial resources.*"[11] It then provides direction for determining claims, judgments, and compensated absences liabilities, and changes therein, and directs that (1) the amount of the liability that would normally be expected to be liquidated with available expendable financial resources be recorded as a governmental (or similar trust) fund expenditure and liability, and (2) the excess be recorded in the GLTD accounts.

Such narrow interpretations of "fund expenditures" and "fund liability" have been criticized. These topics—and the direct recording of "near-current" liabilities in the GLTD accounts—are discussed further in Chapter 15.

Defaulted Bonds

When a government defaults on long-term debt, two accounting approaches are reasonable: (1) Leave defaulted debt in GLTD. Disclosure of the default in a note to the Statement of General Long-Term Debt (Figure 10-8) would be essential, and the debt should be segregated in the body of the statement and described as, say, "Bonds Payable in Default." (2) Record the maturity in a DSF on the grounds that the maturity causes an expenditure whether or not the related liability can be paid. The reporting of a deficit and of "Defaulted Bonds Payable"

---

[10] NCGAS 1, p. 9.

[11] National Council on Governmental Accounting *Statement 4*; "Accounting and Financial Reporting Principles for Claims and Judgments and Compensated Absences")Chicago: NCGA, 1982). p. 2

in the DSF would draw attention to the default, but the situation would also require a footnote in the Statement of General Long-Term Debt. In fact, it can be argued that the omission of the defaulted debt from the body of the statement would make the second approach less desirable than the first.

GLTD Records

A file should be established for each debt issue at an early date, preferably while it is in the planning stage. Here should be maintained copies of, or references to, all pertinent correspondence, ordinances or resolutions, advertisements for the authorization referendum, advertisements or calls for bids, bond indentures or other agreements, debt service schedules, and the like.

Subsidiary records should be established and maintained for each liability in the account group. The exact nature of each record will vary with the pertinent details of the debt, but typical information would include title and amount of the issue; nature of the debt; dates of issue, required interest payments, and maturity; denominations; nominal and effective interest rates; and premium or discount. If an issue is registered, provision must be made to record owners' names and addresses. The subsidiary record will support the liabilities recorded in the account group, together with the interest payments thereon.

The debt instruments should be prenumbered and carefully controlled at all stages of their life cycle. Most government bonds are "bearer" instruments with interest coupons attached, which makes strict control essential.

As debt principal and interest are paid, whether by the government or through a fiscal agent, paid coupons and bonds should be marked "Paid" or "Canceled," reconciled with reports of payments, and retained at least until the records have been audited. Paid bonds and coupons are typically destroyed periodically, usually by cremation, to conserve storage space and avoid even the slightest possibility of reissue or double payment. The number of each bond or coupon destroyed should be recorded, attested to by two or more responsible officials who have verified the accuracy of the list and witnessed the bond and coupon destruction, and filed for reference. Bonds and interest coupons may be destroyed by the fiscal agent. In this case, the certified statement of items destroyed (provided by the fiscal agent) should be recorded and filed for reference. As an extra safeguard, some governments require that canceled bonds and interest coupons be microfilmed prior to being destroyed.

GLTD Statements, Schedules, and Statistical Tables

A Statement of General Long-Term Debt (Figure 10-8) is prepared at each statement date. It is essentially a balance sheet of the GLTD Account Group; footnotes should disclose any obligations that, although primarily the responsibilities of some specific fund, are also full faith and credit responsibilities of the government as a whole. Footnote (2) of Figure 10-8 is an example of this kind of disclosure. This major statement should be supported by a Combined Schedule of Bonds Payable. This schedule is a detailed listing of all long-term debt of the governmental unit, divided into sections for GLTD, debt of Enterprise Funds, debt of Special Assessment Funds, and so on. It has headings such as Bond

Figure 10-8

CITY OF TUCSON

Statement of General Long-Term Debt
(in Thousands)
June 30, 1979

Amounts Available and to Be Provided for the Payment of General Long-Term Debt

General Obligation Bonds:		
Amount available in Debt Service Funds	$ 8,375	
Amount available from assets held in trust	10,235	
Amount to be provided	32,991	
Total general obligation bonds		$51,601
Street and Highway Bonds:		
Amount available in Debt Service Funds	$ 1,912	
Amount to be provided	12,193	
Total street and highway bonds		14,105
Purchase Contracts:		
Amount to be provided		20,788
Total available and to be provided		$86,494

General Long-Term Debt Payable

General obligation bonds payable	$41,366	
General obligation bonds payable from restricted assets held in trust	10,235 (1)	
Total general obligation bonds		$51,601
Street and highway bonds payable		14,105
Purchase Contracts Payable:		
Tucson Community Center Authority	$19,108	
Municipal buildings	292	
Municipal land	90	
Computer equipment	1,298	
Total purchase contracts payable (2)		20,788
Total general long-term debt payable		$86,494

(1) On June 30, 1975, the City issued $10,235,000 in General Obligation Bonds to refund the General Obligation Bonds, Project of 1973, Series B (1975) of the same amount. The proceeds of this bond issue are held in trust by the Valley National Bank.

(2) In addition to the long-term debt exhibited in this statement, the City of Tucson has a contingent liability against its full faith and credit on $3,266,796 of special assessment bonds recorded in the Special Assessment Fund. The general credit of the municipality is obligated only to the extent that liens foreclosed against properties involved in the special assessment district are insufficient to retire outstanding bonds.

Source: Adapted from Annual Financial Report, City of Tucson, Ariz.

Authors' note: The Comprehensive Annual Financial Report of the City of Tucson for the year ended June 30, 1981, contained no statement such as Figure 10-8 because detailed information concerning the City's general long-term debt was presented in footnotes to the General Purpose Financial Statements. See Chapter 14 for definitions of the capitalized terms.

Description, Purpose, Interest Rates, Interest Dates, Source of Payment, Principal Amount Issued, Principal Outstanding at Statement Date, and Year(s) of Maturity.

The NCGA has recommended preparation of a Statement of Changes in General Long-Term Debt (Figure 10-9) "unless sufficiently disclosed in the notes to the financial statements."[12] This statement, by accounting for increases and decreases, forms a connecting link between Statements of General Long-Term Debt at successive statement dates. Some governments prepare a statement of changes in total long-term debt.

Figure 10-9

A GOVERNMENTAL UNIT

Statement of Changes in General Long-Term Debt
(in Thousands)
For the Year Ended (Date)

General long-term debt, beginning of year		$82,000
Issues during the year:		
General obligation serial bonds payable:		
From ad valorem taxes	$5,000	
From sources other than ad valorem taxes	500	
Total additions	$5,500	
Retirements during the year:		
General obligation serial bonds payable	$2,000	
General notes payable	400	
Total retirements	$2,400	
Increase in GLTD		3,100
General long-term debt, end of year		$85,100

In addition to the foregoing financial statements, the comprehensive annual financial report ordinarily includes a number of detailed schedules that are designed to provide additional (usually unaudited) financial data. Several examples are presented in the following pages.

In order to present the resource requirements of the existing debt structure, for each future year and in total, a summary of Debt Service Requirements to Maturity—accompanied by a detailed schedule of the requirements of each issue of general obligation long-term debt—is recommended for inclusion in the statistical tables of the CAFR. Figure 10-10 is a typical summary statement. Summary disclosure of debt service requirements, perhaps more condensed than Figure 10-10, is required in the notes to the GPFS.

A number of other debt-related statistical tables are included in the CAFR of a governmental unit in order to assist bond holders, bond rating firms, and others in assessing the organization's debt structure and debt service ability and to demonstrate legal compliance. Both legal compliance and the amount of additional general obligation debt which may be issued in the future are indicated

[12] NCGAS 1, p. 22.

in the Computation of Legal Debt Margin (Figure 10-11). The calculation varies somewhat according to the laws governing a particular organization, but is typically made along the following lines:

1. *Calculation of Legal Debt Limit.* The general obligation debt issue ceiling is first calculated. In most jurisdictions, this is set forth by law as a percentage of the assessed value of taxable properties.

2. *Indication of Net Debt Outstanding Applicable to Debt Limit.* In the usual case the gross long-term debt is indicated, from which is subtracted (1) amounts available for debt retirement, and (2) debts which are not general obligations or that for other reasons are not covered by the debt limit statutes.

3. *Calculation of Legal Debt Margin.* This is the difference between the debt ceiling (1) and the debt outstanding in respect to the ceiling (2).

Figure 10-10

CITY OF TUCSON
Debt Service Requirements to Maturity
General Obligation Bonds
(in Thousands)
June 30, 1979

Fiscal Year	Principal	Interest	Total Principal and Interest Requirements
1979–80	$ 2,258	$ 2,139	$ 4,397
1980–81	2,333	2,025	4,358
1981–82	2,125	1,914	4,039
1982–83	2,125	1,809	3,934
1983–84	2,100	1,702	3,802
1984–85	2,675	1,591	4,266
1985–86	2,710	1,450	4,160
1986–87	2,500	1,305	3,805
1987–88	2,400	1,183	3,583
1988–89	525	1,056	1,581
1989–90	1,350	1,026	2,376
1990–91	1,375	954	2,329
1991–92	15,095	883	15,978
1992–93	615	103	718
1993–94	650	68	718
1994–95	530	30	560
Total	$41,366	$19,238	$60,604

Source: Adapted from Annual Financial Report, *City of Tucson, Ariz.*

Authors' note: The Comprehensive Annual Financial Report of the City of Tucson for the year ended June 30, 1981, contained no statement such as Figure 10-10; but debt service requirements to maturity for all types of long-term debt (e.g., general obligation, enterprise, and special assessment) were shown in footnotes to the General Purpose Financial Statements. See Chapter 14 for definitions of the capitalized terms.

Figure 10-11

CITY OF TUCSON

Computation of Legal Debt Margin (1)
(in thousands)
June 30, 1981
(Unaudited)

	Bonds Excluded From Limitation	General Obligation 6%	Utility Purpose & Open Space 20%	Total Bonded Debt
Legal Debt Limitation 1981 Assessed Valuation $680,386,981	$ —	$40,823	$136,077	$ —
Outstanding Bonded Debt By Purpose				
Fire Protection	—	3,660	—	3,660
Parks and Playground	—	—	8,455	8,455
Street and Highway	19,670	—	—	19,670
Sanitary Sewers	—	—	8,287	8,287
Water System	—	—	8,000	8,000
Drainage Sewers	—	—	12,668	12,668
Library	—	4,050	—	4,050
Police	—	1,705	—	1,705
Water System Revenue Bonds	73,890	—	—	73,890
Special Assessment Improvement Bonds	3,243	—	—	3,243
Major Thoroughfares	—	2,250	—	2,250
Other Various Purpose	—	6,610	—	6,610
	$96,803	18,275	37,410	$152,488
Less: Balance Held in Reserve		6,080	6,372	
		12,195	31,038	
Legal Debt Margin		$28,628	$105,039	

(1) Legal debt margin is calculated in conformity with Article 9, Section 8, Constitution of Arizona. The amount of general obligation bonded debt which may be issued and outstanding at any time is limited to a fixed percent of assessed valuation which is set at 20% for utility purposes and open space and 6% for other purposes.
Source: Adapted from Annual Financial Report, *City of Tucson, Ariz.*

The Computation of Direct and Overlapping Debt (Figure 10-12) indicates the total long-term debt burden or "debt saturation" of the populace within the unit's jurisdiction. Finally, the magnitude, relationship, and trends of the bonded debt burden and debt servicing ability are indicated in a ten-year historical presentation of the Ratio of Net General Bonded Debt to Assessed Value and Net Bonded Debt per Capita (Figure 10-13) and the Ratio of Annual Debt Service

Expenditures for General Bonded Debt to Total General Expenditures (Figure 10-14).

Figure 10-12

CITY OF TUCSON

Computation of Direct and Overlapping Debt
June 30, 1981
(Unaudited)

Name of Governmental Unit	Net Debt Outstanding	Percentage Applicable to City of Tucson	City of Tucson's Share of Debt
City of Tucson	$ 43,233	100.00%	$ 43,233
School District No. 1	5,079	79.17	4,021
School District No. 8	5,000	56.25	2,812
School District No. 10	17,068	31.37	5,354
School District No. 12	9,928	36.25	3,599
School District No. 20	1,627	1.97	32
Pima County	115,093	47.25	54,381
Pima Community College District	1,348	47.25	637
Pima County Flood Control District	20,467	54.36	11,126
Flowing Wells Irrigation District	151	52.00	78
State of Arizona	—	8.53	—
Total Direct and Overlapping Debt			$125,277

Source: Adapted from Annual Financial Report, *City of Tucson, Ariz.*

INTERFUND RELATIONSHIPS

Thus far in this chapter we have indicated how the transactions in the various governmental funds affect the General Fixed Assets and General Long-Term Debt Account Groups. The following entries illustrate how certain transactions in one fund affect another fund or account group:

Transactions Originating in the General Fund

1. A loan was made from the General Fund to the Debt Service Fund.

ENTRY IN GENERAL FUND:
Due from Debt Service Fund	40,000	
Cash		40,000

To record loan made to Debt Service Fund.

ENTRY IN DEBT SERVICE FUND:
Cash	40,000	
Due to General Fund		40,000

To record loan from General Fund.

2. A sinking fund contribution was made from the General Fund to the Debt Service Fund.

Figure 10-13

CITY OF TUCSON
Ratio of Net General Bonded Debt
to Assessed Value and Net Bonded Debt Per Capita
Last Ten Fiscal Years
(Unaudited)

Fiscal Year	Population	Assessed Value	Gross Bonded Debt	Less Debt Service Funds	Net Bonded Debt	Ratio of Net Bonded Debt to Assessed Value	Net Bonded Debt Per Capita
1971–72	281,798	$282,746,000	$16,872,000	$ 16,463	$16,855,537	.060	$ 59.81
1972–73	295,760	319,625,000	29,754,000	—	29,754,000	.093	100.60
1973–74	301,500	442,156,000	30,436,000	1,046,000	29,390,000	.066	97.50
1974–75	298,683	506,623,000	39,298,000	2,345,147	36,952,853	.073	123.72
1975–76	301,700	562,975,000	37,815,000	3,883,077	33,931,923	.060	112.47
1976–77	304,000	594,786,000	38,237,000	5,207,117	33,029,883	.056	108.65
1977–78	311,000	653,798,000	40,654,000	6,721,403	33,932,597	.052	109.11
1978–79	320,900	649,363,000	41,366,000	8,374,800	32,991,200	.051	102.81
1979–80	331,506	645,314,000	46,018,000	10,477,533	35,540,467	.055	107.21
1980–81	340,000	680,387,000	55,685,000	12,451,935	43,233,065	.064	127.16

Source: Adapted from the Annual Financial Report of the City of Tucson, Ariz., for the year ended June 30, 1981.

Figure 10-14

CITY OF TUCSON

Ratio of Annual Debt Service Expenditures for
General Bonded Debt to Total General Expenditures
Last Ten Fiscal Years (in Thousands)
(Unaudited)

Fiscal Year	Principal	Interest	Total Debt Service (1)	Total General Expenditures (2)	Ratio of Debt Service to General Expenditures
1971–72	$1,053	$ 562	$1,615	$32,889	4.9%
1972–73	1,263	594	1,857	38,383	4.8
1973–74	1,318	1,380	2,698	42,819	6.3
1974–75	1,373	1,324	2,697	47,084	5.7
1975–76	1,483	2,018	3,501	50,805	6.9
1976–77	1,978	1,921	3,899	55,910	7.0
1977–78	2,058	1,921	3,979	59,540	6.7
1978–79	2,183	2,066	4,249	69,223	6.1
1979–80	2,258	2,125	4,383	87,613	5.0
1980–81	2,333	2,455	4,788	85,750	5.6

(1) Excludes sinking fund expenditures.
(2) Includes only the General Fund.
Source: Adapted from the Annual Financial Report *of the City of Tucson, Ariz., for the year ended June 30, 1981.*

ENTRY IN GENERAL FUND:
Operating Transfer Out 50,000
  Cash 50,000
To record payment of contribution
to Debt Service Fund.

ENTRY IN DEBT SERVICE FUND:
Cash 50,000
  Operating Transfer In 50,000
To record receipt of contribution from
General Fund.

ENTRY IN GENERAL LONG-TERM DEBT ACCOUNT GROUP:
Amount Available for Retirement of
  Term Bonds 50,000
Amount to Be Provided for
  Retirement of Term Bonds 50,000
To decrease amount to be provided and
to increase the amount available for the
retirement of term bonds. [This entry is
necessary only at statement dates.]

3. The government unit is required to pay part of the cost of special assessment improvements.

ENTRY IN GENERAL FUND:
Operating Transfer Out 100,000
   Due to Special Assessment Fund   100,000
To record governmental unit's liability
for contribution toward construction of
special assessment improvements.

ENTRY IN SPECIAL ASSESSMENT FUND:
Due from General Fund 100,000
   Operating Transfer In   100,000
To record amount due from General
Fund for governmental unit's share of
cost of project.

4. Services were performed by a department financed through the General Fund for a special assessment project.

ENTRY IN GENERAL FUND:
Due from Special Assessment Fund 10,000
   Expenditures   10,000
To record reduction of expenditures by
cost of services rendered on special
assessment projects.

ENTRY IN SPECIAL ASSESSMENT FUND:
Expenditures 10,000
   Due to General Fund   10,000
To record cost of services performed by
a department financed through the
General Fund.

Transactions Originating in a Capital Projects Fund

1. Premiums on bonds were transferred to the General Fund.

ENTRY IN CAPITAL PROJECTS FUND:
Operating Transfer Out 1,000
   Cash   1,000
To record transfer of cash representing
premiums on bonds to the General Fund.

ENTRY IN GENERAL FUND:
Cash 1,000
   Operating Transfer In   1,000
To record receipt of cash representing
premiums on bonds.

2. Proceeds from the sale of bonds issued were transferred (immediately upon receipt) from the Capital Projects Fund to finance:
   a. The governmental unit's share of special assessment improvement costs.
   b. A deficit in the General Fund.

ENTRY IN CAPITAL PROJECTS FUND:
Operating Transfer Out 100,000
   Cash   100,000
To record immediate transfer of bond
proceeds out of Capital Projects Fund.

(a) ENTRY IN SPECIAL ASSESSMENT FUND:
 Cash—Construction 100,000
  Operating Transfer In 100,000
 To record receipt of cash representing
 governmental unit's share of cost.

(b) ENTRY IN GENERAL FUND:
 Cash 100,000
  Operating Transfer In 100,000
 To record receipt of proceeds from
 the sale of bonds issued to fund a
 deficit.

3. Services were rendered by workers paid from a Capital Projects Fund for a department financed through the General Fund.

ENTRY IN CAPITAL PROJECTS FUND:
 Due from General Fund 5,000
  Expenditures 5,000
 To record reduction of construction
 expenditures by cost of services
 rendered Department X.

ENTRY IN GENERAL FUND:
 Expenditures 5,000
  Due to Capital Projects Fund 5,000
 To record amount due to Capital Projects
 Fund on account of services rendered
 Department X.

4. Capital Projects Fund balance was transferred to the General Fund (or to a Debt Service Fund).

ENTRY IN CAPITAL PROJECTS FUND:
 Residual Equity Transfer Out 4,000
  Cash 4,000
 To record transfer of balance out of
 Capital Projects Fund to General Fund
 (or Debt Service Fund).

ENTRY IN GENERAL FUND (OR DEBT SERVICE FUND):
 Cash 4,000
  Residual Equity Transfer In 4,000
 To record receipt of Capital Projects
 Fund balance.

ENTRY IN GENERAL LONG-TERM DEBT ACCOUNT GROUP (if previous entry is in Debt Service Fund):
 Amount Available for Retirement of (Type
  of) Bonds 4,000
  Amount to Be Provided for Retirement
  of (Type of) Bonds 4,000
 To record receipt of Capital Projects
 Fund balance by Debt Service Fund
 and corresponding increase in amount
 available for retirement of bonds. [This
 entry is necessary only at statement
 dates.]

Since, at this point in the book, not all of the funds in governmental accounting have been presented, the foregoing entries are not illustrative of all funds. Additional funds are presented in the next three chapters, and in each case typical relationships of the fund with other funds are illustrated. Finally, a comprehensive "Summary of Interfund Accounting" is presented in Chapter 13.

▶ **Question 10-1.** Distinguish between *interfund transactions* and *interfund relationships*.

Question 10-2. Distinguish between a *fund* and an *account group* such as General Fixed Assets.

Question 10-3. What criteria must be met for an asset to be classified as a *fixed* asset? A *general* fixed asset?

Question 10-4. Generally speaking, what is meant by the term *cost* when determining what costs should be assigned to a fixed asset?

Question 10-5. A governmental unit acquired land, buildings, other improvements, and certain equipment for a single lump-sum purchase price. How should the portion of the total cost attributable to the various assets acquired be determined?

Question 10-6. Fixed assets may be acquired through exercise of a government's power of *eminent domain* and by *escheat*. Distinguish between these terms.

Question 10-7. A municipality was granted certain land for use as a playground. The property was appraised at $10,000 at the time of the grant. Subsequently, all land in the neighborhood rose in value by 20 percent. Should the increase be reflected in the records?

Question 10-8. A municipality owns a fire station and is required to pay assessments of $10,000 as an owner of property in the benefited area. As a result of the improvements, the property has risen in value by $15,000. Should the asset be written up, and, if so, by how much?

Question 10-9. At one time the current General Long-Term Debt Account Group was called the General Bonded Debt and Interest Account Group. Why was the name changed?

Question 10-10. What liabilities are accounted for through the General Long-Term Debt Account Group? Which items of long-term debt are excluded?

Question 10-11. Why are General Fixed Assets and General Long-Term Debt not shown in the same Account Group?

Question 10-12. What entries or disclosures should be made in the General Long-Term Debt Account Group, or statements pertaining thereto, with regard to general-special debt of Special Assessment Funds?

Question 10-13. A municipality's share of special assessment costs was $250,000. To finance these costs, the municipality issued bonds for a corresponding amount. Should these bonds be shown as part of the General Long-Term Debt Account Group or in the Special Assessment Fund? Explain.

Question 10-14. On June 1, 19W3, $300,000 par value of twenty-year term general obligation sinking fund bonds were issued by a governmental unit. Only $50,000 had been accumulated in the Debt Service (Sinking) Fund by May 30, 19Y4, the end of the unit's fiscal year, and there was no possibility of retiring the bonds from resources of other funds that year. Should the matured bonds be shown in the General Fund or in the Debt Service Fund, or should they continue to be carried in the General Long-Term Debt Account Group? Why?

Question 10-15. An asset was financed out of a Special Revenue Fund and was carried in the General Fixed Assets Account Group. Subsequently the asset was sold. To which fund would you credit the proceeds? Why?

Question 10-16. Assume that the asset referred to in the preceding question was financed from a Special Assessment Fund or a Capital Projects Fund. To which fund should the proceeds from the sale of this asset be credited? Explain.

Question 10-17. Records of fixed assets owned by Lucas County have never been maintained in a systematic manner, and the auditor has recommended that an inventory be taken and that a General Fixed Assets Account Group be established and maintained. The governing board agrees that it needs better fixed asset control, but has tentatively concluded that no action will be taken in this regard because the appraisal fee estimates provided by reputable appraisal firms far exceed the amount of resources available for such an undertaking. What suggestions or comments, if any, would you offer upon your advice being sought by members of the board?

Question 10-18. Near the end of 19X5, a city purchased an automobile at a cost of $6,000. The vehicle was wrecked during 19X6 and sold for salvage for $600. Assuming that the automobile was purchased from General Fund resources and the salvage proceeds were also recorded there, what entries would be made in 19X5 and 19X6 to reflect these facts? Might misleading inferences be drawn from the General Fund statements for 19X6?

▶ **Problem 10-1.** Prepare the entries that would be made in the General Fixed Assets Account Group at the end of each year to recognize the activities of the Special Assessment Fund described in Problem 9-2.

Problem 10-2. You have been engaged by the Town of Rego to examine its June 30, 19X8, balance sheet. You are the first CPA to be engaged by the town and find that acceptable methods of municipal accounting have not been employed. The town clerk stated that the books had not been closed and presented the following preclosing trial balance of the General Fund as at June 30, 19X8:

	Debit	Credit
Cash	$150,000	
Taxes Receivable—Current	59,200	
Allowance for Uncollectible Current Taxes		$ 18,000
Taxes Receivable—Delinquent	8,000	
Allowance for Uncollectible Delinquent Taxes		10,200
Estimated Revenues	310,000	
Appropriations		348,000
Donated Land	27,000	
Expenditures—Building Addition Constructed	50,000	
Expenditures—Serial Bonds Paid	16,000	
Expenditures	280,000	
Special Assessment Bonds Payable		100,000
Revenues		354,000
Accounts Payable		26,000
Fund Balance		44,000
	$900,200	$900,200

Additional information:

1. The estimated losses of $18,000 for current taxes receivable were determined to be a reasonable estimate.

2. Included in the Revenues account is a credit of $27,000 representing the value of land donated by the state as a grant-in-aid for construction of a municipal park.

3. The Building Addition Constructed account balance is the cost of an addition to the town hall building. This addition was constructed and completed in June 19X8. The payment was recorded in the General Fund as authorized.

4. The Serial Bonds Paid account reflects the annual retirement of general obligation bonds issued to finance the construction of the town hall. Interest payments of $7,000 for this bond issue are included in Expenditures.

5. Operating supplies ordered in the prior fiscal year and chargeable to that year were received, recorded, and consumed in July 19X7. The outstanding purchase orders for these supplies, which were not recorded in the accounts at June 30, 19X7, amounted to $8,800. The vendors' invoices for these supplies totaled $9,400. Encumbered appropriations lapse one year after the end of the fiscal year for which they are made.

6. Outstanding purchase orders at June 30, 19X8, for operating supplies totaled $2,100. These purchase orders were not recorded on the books.

7. The special assessment bonds were sold in June 19X8 to finance a street-paving project. No contracts have been signed for this project and no expenditures have been made.

8. The balance in the Revenues account includes credits for $20,000 for a note issued to a bank to obtain cash in anticipation of tax collections. The note was still outstanding at June 30, 19X8.

Required:

(a) Prepare the formal adjusting and closing journal entries for the General Fund for the fiscal year ended June 30, 19X8.

(b) The foregoing information disclosed by your examination was recorded only in the General Fund even though other funds or account groups were involved. Prepare the formal adjusting journal entries for any other funds or account groups involved.

(AICPA, adapted)

Problem 10-3. The City of Bergen entered into the following transactions during 19X4:

1. A bond issue was authorized to provide funds for the construction of a new municipal building estimated to cost $500,000. The bonds were to be paid in 10 equal installments, due March 1 of each year, beginning in 19X5.

2. An advance of $40,000 was received from the General Fund to underwrite a deposit on the land contract of $60,000. The deposit was made.

3. Bonds of $450,000 were sold for cash at 102 and the premium was transferred to a Debt Service Fund. It was decided not to sell all of the bonds because the cost of the land was less than was expected.

4. Contracts amounting to $390,000 were let to Michela and Company, the lowest bidder, for the construction of the municipal building.

5. The temporary advance from the General Fund was repaid and the balance on the land contract was paid.

6. Based on the architect's certificate, warrants were issued for $320,000 for the work completed to date.

7. Warrants paid in cash by the treasurer amounted to $310,000.

8. Because of changes in the plans, the contract with Michela and Company was revised to $440,000; the remaining bonds were sold at 101, and the premium was transferred to a Debt Service Fund.

9. The building was completed and additional warrants amounting to $115,000 were issued to the contractor in final payment for the work. All warrants were paid by the treasurer.

10. The Capital Projects Fund was closed, the balance being transferred to the Debt Service Fund.

Required:

(a) Record the foregoing transactions and closing entries in Capital Projects Fund T-accounts or on a transactions worksheet. Designate the entries by the numbers which identify the items above.

(b) Prepare applicable balance sheets of other funds and account groups of the City of Bergen as of December 31, 19X4, considering only the bond issue proceeds and expenditures from the Capital Projects Fund.

    (AICPA, adapted)

Problem 10-4. The City Hall (Capital Projects) Fund was established on July 1, 19X2, to account for the construction of a new city hall financed by the sale of bonds. The building was to be constructed on a site owned by the city.

The building construction was to be financed by the issuance of ten-year $2,000,000 general obligation bonds bearing interest at 4 percent. Through prior arrangements $1,000,000 of these bonds were sold on July 1, 19X2. The remaining bonds are to be sold on July 1, 19X3.

The only funds in which transactions pertaining to the new city hall were recorded were the City Hall Fund and the General Fund. The City Hall Fund trial balance follows:

CITY OF LARNACA

City Hall Fund

June 30, 19X3

	Debit	Credit
Cash	$ 893,000	
Expenditures	140,500	
Encumbrances	715,500	
Accounts payable		$ 11,000
Reserve for encumbrances		723,000
Appropriations		1,015,000
	$1,749,000	$1,749,000

An analysis of the Expenditures account follows:

	Debit
1. A progress billing invoice from General Construction Company (with which the city contracted for the construction of the new city hall for $750,000—other contracts will be let for heating, air conditioning, etc.) showing 10 percent of the work completed	$ 75,000
2. A charge from the General Fund for work done by Public Works Department employees in clearing the building site	11,000
3. Payments to suppliers for building materials and supplies purchases	14,500
4. Payment of interest on bonds outstanding	40,000
	$140,500

An analysis of the Reserve for Encumbrances account follows:

	Debit (Credit)
1. To record contract with General Construction Company	$(750,000)
2. Purchase orders placed for materials and supplies	(55,000)
3. Receipt of materials and supplies and payment therefor	14,500
4. Payment of General Construction Company invoice less 10 percent retention	67,500
	$(723,000)

An analysis of the Appropriations account follows:

	Debit (Credit)
1. Project authorization, 19X3	$(1,000,000)
2. Premium realized on sale of bonds	(15,000)
	$(1,015,000)

Required:

(a) Prepare a worksheet for the City Hall (Capital Projects) Fund at June 30, 19X3, showing:
   1. Preliminary trial balance
   2. Adjustments (formal journal entries are not required)
   3. Adjusted trial balance, before closing (closing entries are not required)

(b) Prepare the formal adjusting journal entries for the following funds and account groups (closing entries are not required).

1. General Fixed Assets
2. Debt Service Fund
3. General Long-Term Debt

(AICPA, adapted)

Problem 10-5. The accounts of the City of Daltonville were kept by an inexperienced bookkeeper during the year ended December 31, 19X5. The following trial balance of the General Fund was available when you began your examination:

CITY OF DALTONVILLE
General Fund
Trial Balance
December 31, 19X5

Cash	$ 75,600	
Taxes Receivable—Current Year	29,000	
Allowance for Uncollectible Current Taxes		$ 9,000
Taxes Receivable—Prior Year	4,000	
Allowance for Uncollectible Prior Taxes		5,100
Appropriations		174,000
Estimated Revenues	180,000	
Building Addition Constructed	25,000	
Serial Bonds Paid	8,000	
Expenditures	140,000	
Special Assessment Bonds Payable		50,000
Revenues		177,000
Accounts Payable		13,000
Fund Balance		33,500
	$461,600	$461,600

Your examination disclosed the following:

1. The estimate of losses of $9,000 for current year taxes receivable was found to be a reasonable estimate.

2. The Building Addition Constructed account balance is the cost of an addition to the municipal building. The addition was constructed during 19X5 and payment was made from the General Fund as authorized.

3. The Serial Bonds Paid account reports the annual retirement of general obligation bonds issued to finance the construction of the municipal building. Interest payments of $3,800 for this bond issue are included in Expenditures.

4. A physical count of the current operating supplies at December 31, 19X5, revealed an inventory of $6,500. The decision was made to record the inventory in the accounts; expenditures are to be recorded on the basis of usage rather than purchases.

5. Operating supplies ordered in 19X4 and chargeable to 19X4 appropriations were received, recorded, and consumed in January 19X5. The outstanding purchase orders for these supplies, which were not recorded in the accounts at year end, amounted to $4,400. The vendors' invoices for these supplies totaled $4,700.

Appropriations lapse one year after the end of the fiscal year for which they are made.

6. Outstanding purchase orders at December 31, 19X5, for operating supplies totaled $5,300. These purchase orders were not recorded on the books.

7. The special assessment bonds were sold at par in December 19X5 to finance a street paving project. No contracts have been signed for this project and no expenditures have been made.

8. The balance in the Revenues account includes credits for $10,000 for a note issued to a bank to obtain cash in anticipation of tax collections to pay current operating expenditures and for $900 for the sale of scrap iron from the city's water plant. The note was still outstanding at year end. The operations of the water plant are accounted for by a separate fund.

Required:

(a) Prepare the formal adjusting and closing journal entries for the General Fund.

(b) The foregoing information disclosed by your examination was recorded only in the General Fund even though other funds or account groups were involved. Prepare the formal adjusting journal entries for any other funds or account groups involved.

(AICPA, adapted)

Problem 10-6, Part I. From the information given in Problem 10-5, prepare a columnar worksheet to reflect the adjustments and corrections needed in order to establish appropriate funds and account groups for the City of Daltonville. Your worksheet headings should be as follows:

Column(s)		Worksheet Heading
1		General Fund Trial Balance (Uncorrected), 12/31/19X5
2–3		Adjusting and Correcting Entries, 12/31/19X5
4–5		Closing Entries, 12/31/19X5
6–9		Corrected Postclosing Trial Balances, 12/31/19X5
	6–7	General Fund
	8–9	Special Assessment Fund
10–12		Journal Entries Required, 12/31/19X5
	10	General Long-Term Debt
	11	General Fixed Assets
	12	Enterprise (Water) Fund

Problem 10-6, Part II. Assuming that the worksheet prepared in Part I will suffice for year-end statement preparation and as a basis for establishing ledgers for funds and account groups other than the General Fund, and that no adjusting or correcting entries have been made in the General Fund accounts, prepare a *compound* entry to correct the balance sheet accounts of the General Fund at December 31, 19X5.

Problem 10-7. The following transactions of the Village of Lakeside are not related unless the transactions are given under the same numeral or unless the connection is specifically stated; not all of the village's transactions are given. You are to make all of the journal entries to which each transaction gives rise. Use general journal paper and form; no explanation is required. Use the date columns to indicate the fund or account group in which each entry is made, using these abbreviations:

Fund or Account Group	Abbreviation
General	GF
Special Revenue	SR
Capital Projects	CP
Special Assessment	SA
Debt Service	DS
General Fixed Assets	GFA
General Long-Term Debt	GLTD

Separate the journal entries from each other by putting the transaction number and letter on the line above each entry.

1. Interest of $3,000 was paid on an issue of general sinking fund bonds.
2. A serial issue of general bonds matured in the amount of $50,000 and was paid.
3. a. General obligation sinking fund, 6 percent, twenty-year bonds were authorized in the amount of $500,000 (see item 7).
   b. The bonds were issued at a discount of $5,000 and the project authorization was reduced accordingly.
   c. The sole purpose of the bond issue was to acquire, for $490,000, a piece of property consisting of a parcel of land occupied by a building. The land was worth $50,000. The property was purchased and the fund closed, the balance being transferred to the sinking fund.
4. Ben E. Factor gave the Village eighty acres of land to be used as a park. The parcel had cost Mr. Factor $20,000 in 1945; its present market value is $80,000.
5. A fire truck, bought in 1948 at a cost of $4,000, was sold for $500; the proceeds were placed in the General Fund.
6. a. A special assessment project was approved in the amount of $75,000.
   b. The village borrowed $50,000 at 6 percent interest for three months to finance special assessment construction.
   c. The village's share of the cost was paid in the amount of $15,000.
   d. A contract for $74,000 was let to the ABC Company.
   e. The village engineer certified that the project was one-half completed. The contractor was paid one-half of the contract price, subject to a retained percentage of 5 percent.
   f. The contract was completed.
   g. The property owners were assessed for all costs.
   h. All assessments were collected in full.
   i. The fund's business was completed and it was terminated.
7. a. The schedule of accumulation for the Debt Service (sinking) Fund (see 3) showed an annual contribution requirement of $14,355 and estimated earnings of $985 for the current year.
   b. The contribution was received.
   c. The contribution was invested.
   d. Actual earnings totaled $960.
   e. The Debt Service (sinking) Fund books were closed.

Problem 10-8. Each of the following transactions is independent of the others. (a) Following each transaction a fund or account group is named. Prepare, without explanation, the entry or entries required to record the transaction in the designated fund or account group. (b) You are also to designate any other fund or account group in which the transaction gives rise to an entry or entries, either immediately or by year end, using the following symbols:

General Fund	GF
Special Revenue Fund	SR
Capital Projects Fund	CP
Special Assessment Fund	SA
Debt Service Fund	DS
General Fixed Assets	GFA
General Long-Term Debt	GLTD

1. A truck which was used for garbage disposal was sold for $400. The original cost of the truck was $8,500; it had an expected useful life of five years and was four years old at date of sale. General Fixed Assets.

2. An issue of $100,000 of twenty-year, 5 percent sinking fund bonds was authorized for the construction of a bridge over the Yahara River. General Long-Term Debt.

3. An anonymous donor gave the city 500 acres of land on the outskirts of the city. The City Council dedicated the land to park use. The original cost of the property to the donor was $500,000; he had paid taxes of $10,000 a year on it for ten years; the market value at date of donation was $750,000. General Fixed Assets.

4. The City Council ordered an inventory to be taken and an appropriate reserve to be placed on the books. It voted to consider appropriation expenditures to be based on purchases. The inventory was taken and found to total $10,000. General Fund.

5. Invoices totaling $15,700 were received and vouchered for goods which were ordered last year. Encumbered appropriations do not lapse. The invoices covered all of the orders outstanding at the end of the prior year; the orders had totaled $16,000. General Fund.

6. The postclosing trial balance of the General Fund at December 31, 19X4, contained a Reserve for Encumbrances of $20,000. The appropriations for 19X5 were $270,000, which included the orders which were placed in the preceding year. General Fund.

7. General obligation bonds of $100,000 par were sold at 101. Capital Projects Fund.

8. A bond issue was authorized in the amount of $50,000 for the payment of the total cost of a special assessment paving project. Special Assessment Fund.

9. The Expenditures account in the Capital Projects Fund has a balance of $129,000; Appropriations, a balance of $130,000. Construction has been completed. Closing entries are to be made for the Capital Projects Fund. Capital Projects Fund.

10. General obligation bonds of $100,000 were sold at 99. Capital Projects Fund.

11. A special assessment project of $100,000 was authorized. Special Assessment Fund.

12. A contract for a paving project was signed for $75,000. Special Assessment Fund.

13. The budget for the Debt Service Fund (contributions $20,000, interest $2,500) becomes available at the beginning of the year. Prepare the journal entry to record the budget. Debt Service Fund.

14. The sinking fund annual contribution of $20,000 from the General Fund became receivable. Debt Service Fund.

15. Bought a desk for the city attorney's office, $500, with General Fund cash. General Fund.

16. Prepare the closing entries, without dollar amounts, for a Debt Service (sinking) Fund that is completing a year that is neither its first nor its last. Debt Service (Sinking) Fund.

17. Last year a city building project was incomplete, but expenditures of $100,000 were closed. Now the project is complete and closing entries are made. This year's expenditures total $50,000. General Fixed Assets.

Problem 10-9. Insurance proceeds of $40,000, received after a fire damaged a municipal building, were recorded in a Capital Projects Fund while renovation was in process. A total of $70,000 was spent on the building, of which $50,000 was attributable to restoring it to its pre-fire condition, and the additional amount needed was transferred to the Capital Projects Fund from the General Fund. A billing error was discovered after the contractor was paid, and he refunded $1,500 to the Capital Projects Fund; this amount was later transferred to a Debt Service Fund, by order of the Council, ultimately to be used to repay the indebtedness incurred when the building was constructed five years earlier.

Required:

(a) What entries would be made in the city's accounts to reflect these transactions and events assuming that all occurred in 19X1?

(b) What entries would be made if (1) the fire damage occurred and the insurance proceeds were received in 19X1; (2) the General Fund transfer, completion of the project, and payment of the contractor's original bill occurred during 19X2; and (3) the billing error was discovered in 19X3 and the refund and transfer to the Debt Service Fund took place in that year?

Problem 10-10. You were engaged to examine the financial statements of the City of Homer for the year ended June 30, 19X9, and found that the bookkeeper had recorded all transactions in the General Fund. You were furnished the General Fund Trial Balance, which appears below:

CITY OF HOMER
General Fund
Trial Balance
June 30, 19X9

Debits

Cash	125,180
Cash for Construction	174,000
Taxes Receivable—Current	8,000
Assessments Receivable—Deferred	300,000
Inventory of Materials and Supplies	38,000
Estimated Revenues	4,135,000
Interest Expense	18,000
Encumbrances	360,000
Expenditures	4,310,000
Total Debits	9,468,180

Credits

Allowance for Estimated Uncollectible Current Taxes	7,000
Vouchers Payable	62,090
Interest Payable	18,000
Liability under Street Improvement Project	10,000
Bonds Payable	300,000
Premium on Bonds	3,000
Reserve for Inventory	36,000
Reserve for Encumbrances	360,000
Appropriations	4,450,000
Interest Revenue	21,000
Fund Balance	91,090
Revenues	4,110,000
Total Credits	9,468,180

Your audit disclosed the following:

1. Years ago the city council authorized the recording of inventories, and a physical inventory taken on June 30, 19X9, showed that materials and supplies with a cost of $37,750 were on hand at that date. The inventory is recorded on a perpetual basis.

2. Current taxes are now considered delinquent and it is estimated that $5,500 of such taxes will be uncollectible.

3. Discounts of $32,000 were taken on property taxes. An appropriation is not required for discounts, but an allowance for them was not made at the time the tax levy was recorded. Discounts taken were charged to Expenditures.

4. On June 25, 19X9, the State Revenue Department informed the city that its share of a state-collected, locally shared tax would be $75,000.

5. New equipment for the Police Department was acquired at a cost of $90,000 and the expenditure was properly recorded in the General Fund.

6. During the year 100 acres of land were donated to the city for use as an industrial park. The land had a value of $250,000. No recording has been made.

7. The city council authorized the paving and widening of certain streets at an estimated cost of $365,000, which included an estimated $5,000 cost for planning and engineering to be paid from the General Fund. The remaining $360,000 was to be financed by a $10,000 contribution from the city and $350,000 by assessments against property owners payable in seven equal annual installments. A $15,000 appropriation was made for the city's share at the time the annual budget was recorded, and the total $365,000 was also recorded as an appropriation. The following information is also relevant to the street improvement project:
   a. Property owners paid their annual installment plus a $21,000 interest charge in full.
   b. Special assessment bonds of $300,000 were authorized and sold at a premium of $3,000. An $18,000 liability for interest was properly recorded. The city does not amortize bond premium or discount.
   c. The city's $15,000 share was recorded as an expenditure during the year. The $5,000 for planning and engineering fees were paid. Construction began July 5, 19X8, and the contractor has been paid $200,000 under the contract for construction, which calls for performance of the work at a total cost of $360,000. This $360,000 makes up the balance in the Reserve for Encumbrances.

d. The Cash for Construction account was used for all receipts and disbursements relative to the project. It is made up of the proceeds of the bond issue and collection of assessment installments and interest minus payments to the contractor.

Required:

Prepare a worksheet to adjust (but not close) the account balances at June 30, 19X9, and to distribute them to the appropriate funds or account groups. It is recommended that the worksheet be in the order of the General Fund Trial Balance and have the following column headings:

1. Balance per books
2. Adjustments—debit
3. Adjustments—credit
4. General Fund
5. Special Assessment Fund
6. General Fixed Assets

(Number all adjusting entries. Formal journal entries or financial statements are not required. Supporting computations should be in good form.)

(AICPA, adapted)

Problem 10-11. The City of Patonton trial balances on January 1, 19X4, were as follows:

General Fund

Cash	7,000	
Taxes Receivable, Delinquent	48,000	
Allowance for Uncollectible Taxes Receivable, Delinquent		4,000
Due from Water Fund	500	
Vouchers Payable		11,000
Due to Taxpayers		1,000
Appropriations, 19X3		3,000
Fund Balance		36,500
	55,500	55,500

General Long-Term Debt

Amount to Be Provided for Payment of Bonds	75,000	
Bonds Payable		75,000
	75,000	75,000

The following information summarizes the transactions of the city during 19X4:

1. The city council approved the following General Fund budget for 19X4:

Expenditures	$60,000
Revenues	50,000

2. The council approved the levy of general property taxes of $40,000. It was estimated that $2,000 of the amount would never be collected.

3. Upon petition of the property owners in Foggy Bottom Subdivision, a paving project expected to cost $50,000 was authorized by the council. The city had been having such high maintenance costs for Foggy Bottom streets that the council agreed that the city should pay one-half of the cost of the project.

4. A contract for $40,000 was signed for the principal paving work.

5. The city engineer and the Street Department performed part of the work on the paving project at a cost of $10,000.

6. Property owners and the city were assessed on June 30, 19X4. Property owners are to pay one-fifth of their assessments each year starting January 1, 19X5, with interest at 6 percent from June 30, 19X4.

7. The paving project was financed by borrowing $50,000 from a local bank on short-term notes.

8. Bonds were authorized to pay the city's share of the cost of the paving project. The bonds carry an interest rate of 6 percent, and one-fifth of the face value matures annually starting one year from date of issue.

9. Some of the cash collections during the year are summarized as follows:

Prior years' levies	$45,000
19X4 levy	11,000
Fines and fees	4,000
Taxes written off in prior years	500
Interest	500
Service charges	2,000
	$63,000

10. Orders placed during the year totaled $15,000.

11. Payrolls vouchered during the year totaled $52,500.

12. The bonds referred to in transaction 8 were sold at 101. The proceeds were properly distributed and accounted for, the premiums being transferred to a Debt Service Fund, and the Capital Projects Fund for the issue was closed.

13. The paving contractor was paid $40,000 on the basis of the city engineer's statement of completion.

14. Bonds were sold at par to finance the property owners' share of the cost of the project. The bonds were dated July 1, 19X4, and bear interest at 5 percent.

15. The paving notes were paid without interest.

16. Invoices vouchered during the year in the General Fund were as follows:

Invoices for 19X4 orders	$14,500
Invoices for 19X3 orders	3,100
	$17,600

The above invoices completed all orders except one dated June 1, 19X4, for $950.

17. Analysis of collections revealed that taxpayer A, to whom the City owed $1,000 on January 1, 19X4, for overpayment of taxes, had settled the obligation by paying his tax for 19X4, less $1,000.

18. A department financed through the General Fund rendered services in the amount of $250 to the Water Fund.

19. The city council made an additional appropriation in the amount of $5,000 for a bond maturity which was overlooked in the preparation of the budget.

20. The bonds mentioned in transaction 12 matured and were vouchered.

21. Cash paid on vouchers payable totaled $65,000.

22. Delinquent taxes in the amount of $500 were written off on the authority of the council.

23. The General Fund was reimbursed from the Special Assessment Fund for the services rendered in transaction 5.

24. Included in General Fund expenditures is an amount of $1,500 for interest on bonded debt issued in 19X3.

Required:

For each fund (except the Water Fund) and account group needed to record properly the transactions above, prepare a worksheet to facilitate the preparation of statements describing the fund's operations and position at December 31, 19X4.

Problem 10-12. You have been engaged to examine the financial statements of the Town of Workville for the year ended June 30, 19X7. Your examination disclosed that, due to the inexperience of the town's bookkeeper, all transactions were recorded in the General Fund. The following General Fund Trial Balance as of June 30, 19X7, was furnished to you.

TOWN OF WORKVILLE
General Fund Trial Balance
June 30, 19X7

	Debit	Credit
Cash	16,800	
Short-Term Investments	40,000	
Accounts Receivable	11,500	
Taxes Receivable—Current	30,000	
Tax Anticipation Notes Payable		50,000
Appropriations		400,000
Expenditures	382,000	
Estimated Revenue	320,000	
Revenues		360,000
General Property	85,400	
Bonds Payable	52,000	
Fund Balance		127,700
	937,700	937,700

Your audit disclosed the following additional information:

1. The balance in Taxes Receivable—Current is now considered delinquent, and the town estimates that $24,000 will be uncollectible.

2. On June 30, 19X7, the town retired at face value, 6 percent General Obligation Serial Bonds totaling $40,000. The bonds were issued on July 1, 19X2, at a face value of $200,000. Interest paid during the year ended June 30, 19X7, was charged to Bonds Payable.

3. During the year supplies totaling $128,000 were purchased and charged to Expenditures. The town chose to conduct a physical inventory of supplies on hand

at June 30, 19X7, and this physical count disclosed that supplies totaling $44,000 were on hand. Appropriations were made on the consumption basis.

4. Expenditures for the year ended June 30, 19X7, included $11,200 applicable to purchase orders issued in the prior year. Encumbered appropriations do not lapse. Outstanding purchase orders at June 30, 19X7, not recorded in the accounts, amounted to $17,500.

5. On June 28, 19X7, the State Revenue Department informed the town that its share of a state-collected, locally shared tax would be $34,000.

6. During the year equipment with a book value of $7,900 was removed from service and sold for $4,600. In addition, new equipment costing $90,000 was purchased. The transactions were recorded in General Property.

7. During the year 100 acres of land were donated to the town for use as an industrial park. The land had a value of $125,000. No recording of this donation has been made.

Required:

(a) Prepare the formal reclassification, adjusting, and closing journal entries for the General Fund as of June 30, 19X7.

(b) Prepare the formal adjusting journal entries for any other funds or account groups as of June 30, 19X7.

(AICPA, adapted)

TRUST AND AGENCY (FIDUCIARY) FUNDS

A *Trust* Fund is established to account for assets received and held by a government acting in the capacity of trustee or custodian. An *Agency* Fund is established to account for assets received by a government in its capacity as an agent for individuals, businesses, or other governments.

In all trust or agency relationships the government acts in a **fiduciary** capacity; that is, it is managing assets that either belong to another agency or individual or must be handled in conformity with another agency or individual's directions. The difference between trust and agency relationships is often one of degree. Trust Funds, for example, may be subject to complex administrative and financial provisions set forth in trust agreements, may be in existence for long periods of time, and may involve investment or other management of trust assets. Thus, Trust Fund management and accounting may be very complex. Agency Funds, on the other hand, are primarily clearance devices for cash collected for others, held briefly, and then disbursed to authorized recipients. The essential equation for Agency Funds is that assets equal liabilities.

The similarity of the relationships and of the duties imposed by them justify considering Trust and Agency Funds as one category of funds. Enterprise trust and agency relationships (such as utility customer deposits) are accounted for in Enterprise Funds (Chapter 13) following the "funds within a fund" approach. Separate Trust or Agency Funds need not be established in such cases; all that is required is that the restricted asset and related liability accounts be distinctively titled as trust- or agency-related.

THE ACCOUNTABILITY FOCUS

The accountability focus in General and Special Revenue Fund accounting is primarily upon operating budget compliance within a specified time period. In

Capital Projects and Special Assessment Fund accounting, attention is generally focused mainly upon the project, rather than a specific period, and upon the capital program or capital budget. The accountability focus in Trust and Agency Fund accounting, on the other hand, is upon the manner in which the government fulfilled its fiduciary responsibilities during a specified period of time and upon those unfilled responsibilities remaining at the end of the period.

The aim in Trust Fund accounting is therefore to ensure that the money or other resources are handled in accordance with the terms of the trust agreement and/or applicable trust laws. The accounting procedure for Agency Funds must ensure that collections are properly handled and are turned over promptly to the party for whom they are collected. The net amount of resources in a Trust Fund is usually indicated in a Fund Balance account, though in some cases (see retirement and pension fund discussions following) different account titles may be used. The accounts of this type measure the *accountability* of the governmental unit as trustee for the use and disposition of the resources in its care. In the case of the Agency Fund the accountability concept is the liability concept, and even in the Trust Fund there is an obligation for the government to use Fund resources to discharge the assigned function. Failure to comply with trust terms would ordinarily be grounds for the forfeiture of Fund resources.

TRUST FUNDS

The NCGA classified Trust Funds as *expendable, nonexpendable,* and *pension.* In general they may also be classified as (1) proprietary or governmental, (2) internal or external, and (3) public or private.

Expendable Trust Funds are of a governmental nature. They are oriented to the inflow, outflow, and balances of resources much as are the General and Special Revenue Funds. In fact, many Trust Funds operate very much like Special Revenue Funds. An example would be a trust fund established to account for the use of income from endowments for purposes specified by a donor.

Nonexpendable Trust Funds require preservation of fund principal and the determination of net income or a similar figure. They are operated and accounted for in essentially the same manner as commercial counterparts in the private sector of the economy and hence are proprietary in nature. An endowment fund whose principal must be kept intact (while its earnings may be available to support a specified governmental activity and thus be accounted for in an expendable fund) is a good example of a proprietary or nonexpendable fund, as is a loan fund whose principal and earnings must be kept intact.

Pension Trust Funds are established (1) to accept payments made by the government, its employees, or others to fund pensions; (2) to invest fund resources; and (3) to calculate and pay pensions to beneficiaries. In its investment activities the pension fund is similar to the nonexpendable fund, but in its pension payment activities it is like the expendable fund.

Some Trust Funds are established *internally* for administrative expediency, whereas others are set up pursuant to formal agreements (e.g., trust indentures) with *external* persons or groups.

Trust Funds may also be classified as *public* and *private.* A public Trust

Fund is one whose principal, earnings, or both must be used for a public purpose. An example is a fund established to account for resources received by bequest which are to be used to provide health care for the indigent. A private Trust Fund is one that will ordinarily revert to private individuals or will be used for private purposes. A guaranty deposits fund is an example of a private Trust Fund. The accounting procedure is not determined by whether the Fund is public or private, however, but by whether it is expendable or nonexpendable.

An exhaustive treatment of trust law and accounting is beyond the scope of this text. Rather, the more usual types of Trust Funds found in state and local governments are briefly considered here and the fundamental accounting and reporting procedures applicable in typical situations are illustrated. The reader desiring a more comprehensive general knowledge of the subject should find the relevant chapter in any standard advanced accounting text helpful. Determination of appropriate systems and procedures in specific cases, however, may require a search of the more technical accounting, legal, and insurance literature or the assistance of specialists within one or more of these fields.

Budgetary Considerations

Because of the differences in complexity and purpose of Trust Funds, some should be formally budgeted and use budgetary control accounts and some should not. In the usual case the government manages or transmits fund resources in accordance with specific instructions or customary trust practices and does not need to budget. If a nonexpendable (proprietary) fund is of sufficient complexity, it may justify the flexible type of budget a business would use. Most expendable (governmental) funds are in essence Special Revenue Funds, and their resources may properly be budgeted as part of the government's operating budget and be subjected to formal budgetary control. No major budgetary problems are posed by Trust Funds, and hence their budgetary accounting is not illustrated.

Expendable Trust Funds

The most frequently encountered type of Expendable Trust Fund results from the government's agreement to accept resources and to spend them in ways specified by the donor. Assets may be donated to create a library or an intergovernmental grant may be received to fund a specific activity. These assets should be set up in a separate fund, a budget for the fund should be approved (frequently as a part of the government's operating budget), and expenditures should be controlled and recorded. The operation of such a fund is so like that of a Special Revenue Fund that no example is necessary.

A "guaranty deposits trust fund" is needed when, for example, contractors are required to post deposits with the government to guarantee satisfactory performance of their contracts. These deposits must be accounted for so that they may be returned to the depositors if contract performance is satisfactory or, if performance is not satisfactory, used to defray the costs of having the defective performance corrected. Although these may be called Guaranty (Expendable) Trust Funds, they are in essence Agency Funds. It is customary to call the credit portion of the accounting equation "fund balance," although it may more properly be considered a liability to depositors.

The accounting procedure for a guaranty deposits fund is simple. As deposits are received, Cash is debited and a Deposits Fund Balance account is credited. Subsequently, as deposits are refunded, these entries are reversed. The Balance Sheet of such a fund would, therefore, contain only a few accounts, as indicated by the statement presented in Figure 11-1.

Figure 11-1

A GOVERNMENTAL UNIT
Guaranty Deposits Trust Fund
Balance Sheet
At Close of Fiscal Year (Date)

Assets

Cash	$ 3,370
Investments	15,000
	$18,370

Fund Balance

Deposits fund balance	$18,370

Nonexpendable Trust Funds

There are two types of Nonexpendable Trust Funds: those in which neither the principal nor the earnings of the fund may be expended, and those in which earnings may be expended but principal must be kept intact. A loan fund is an example of the former type; examples of the latter type are some common forms of endowment funds. Where both expendable and nonexpendable aspects are involved (1) a careful distinction between trust principal (corpus) and income must be maintained, and (2) income determination procedures may be uniquely defined by the trust instrument or applicable laws. The same principles and distinctions apply as in trust accounting generally, that is, the creator or donor has the right to specify which items of revenue, expense, gain, or loss are to affect trust principal and which are deemed to relate to trust earnings. Where both expendable and nonexpendable trust aspects are involved, separate Expendable and Nonexpendable Trust Funds usually are established.

Loan Funds. The following transactions and entries are illustrative of the operation of a loan fund.

Transactions

1. A cash donation of $100,000 was received for the purpose of establishing a loan fund.
2. Loans amounting to $60,000 were made.
3. A loan of $1,000 was repaid with interest of $20.
4. Earnings were closed out.

1. Cash	100,000	
Loan Fund Balance		100,000
To record receipt of cash		
and establishment of loan fund.		
2. Loans Receivable	60,000	
Cash		60,000
To record loans made.		
3. Cash	1,020	
Loans Receivable		1,000
Earnings		20
To record repayment of loan		
with interest.		
4. Earnings	20	
Loan Fund Balance		20
To record closing of earnings and		
increase in loan fund balance.		

A Loan Fund balance sheet prepared after the transactions above had been posted would show cash and loans receivable as assets and contain a loan fund balance of $100,020. Only one amount for the balance would appear; there is no need to distinguish between the original capital and the $20 increase during the period because earnings increase the amount of Fund capital available for loans.

A question arises as to what would happen if the cost of administration were payable out of the Fund. In that case it would technically cease to be a nonexpendable fund, since administration expenses would reduce its balance. Provision is sometimes made, however, for meeting administration expenses out of earnings; and in that case, administrative expenses might be deemed deductible in determining *net* earnings. Strictly speaking, however, we have another type of Trust Fund, one whose principal must be kept intact but whose earnings may be expended. (This type of fund is discussed below.) Note also that though theoretically the loan fund illustrated above is nonexpendable, in actual practice the fund balance may be reduced through bad loans.

Endowment Funds. Some trusts are most easily accounted for by establishing both an Expendable (governmental type) Trust Fund and a Nonexpendable (proprietary type) Trust Fund. For example, an individual may donate money or other property with a view to having the income therefrom used to finance certain activities. Since the donor intended the principal to be held intact and the income alone expended, two funds may be established: (1) a Nonexpendable Trust Fund to account for the principal, and (2) an Expendable Trust Fund to account for the earnings.[1]

A trust agreement of the type just described imposes problems that are the same as, and require the use of the same principles as, those of accounting for

[1] Alternatively, a single Trust Fund having separate Fund Balance—Principal and Fund Balance—Earnings accounts may be established. In this case, the gains, losses, revenues and expenses attributed to principal (corpus) are closed to the Fund Balance—Principal account; those entering into the determination of trust income, and expenditures of earnings for their designated uses, are closed to Fund Balance—Earnings.

a trust that provides for payment of trust income to a life beneficiary with the principal payable to a remainderman at death of the beneficiary. As noted earlier, a discussion of the principles of trust accounting is found in standard advanced accounting tests and is beyond the scope of this book. Selected principles are illustrated in the following transactions and entries for an endowment fund:

Transactions

1. Cash of $210,000 was received to establish a fund whose income is to be used to grant scholarships.
2. Investments, par value $200,000, were purchased at a premium of $3,000 plus accrued interest of $400.
3. A check for $3,000 was received in payment of interest on the investments.
4. Premiums of $125 were amortized.
5. Securities, par value $1,000, to which unamortized premiums of $14 were applicable, were sold for $1,005 plus accrued interest of $10.
6. Securities, par value $2,000, to which $28 in unamortized premiums were applicable, were sold for $2,050 plus accrued interest of $25.
7. Interest receivable, $2,600, was recorded.
8. Premiums of $120 were amortized.
9. The total earnings to date were recorded as a liability of the Endowment Principal Fund to the Endowment Earnings Fund.
10. A $2,500 payment was made from the Endowment Principal Fund to the Endowment Earnings Fund.
11. A $2,000 scholarship grant was made out of the Endowment Earnings Fund. (Note: This is an outright grant, not a loan.)
12. Closing entries were prepared for both Funds.

Entries

1. ENTRY IN ENDOWMENT PRINCIPAL FUND:

Cash	210,000	
Fund Balance		210,000

To record receipt of cash for establishment of endowment fund.

2. ENTRY IN ENDOWMENT PRINCIPAL FUND:

Investments	200,000	
Unamortized Premiums on Investments	3,000	
Accrued Interest on Investments Purchased	400	
Cash		203,400

To record purchase of investments at a premium and accrued interest on investments purchased.

3. ENTRY IN ENDOWMENT PRINCIPAL
   FUND:

Cash	3,000	
Accrued Interest on Investments Purchased		400
Earnings		2,600

   To record collection of interest.

4. ENTRY IN ENDOWMENT PRINCIPAL
   FUND:

Earnings	125	
Unamortized Premiums on Investments		125

   To record amortization of premiums on
   investments.

5. ENTRY IN ENDOWMENT PRINCIPAL
   FUND:

Cash	1,015	
Fund Balance	9	
Investments		1,000
Unamortized Premiums on Investments		14
Earnings		10

   To record sale of investments at a loss
   of $9; also to record interest income of
   $10.

6. ENTRY IN ENDOWMENT PRINCIPAL
   FUND:

Cash	2,075	
Investments		2,000
Unamortized Premiums on Investments		28
Fund Balance		22
Earnings		25

   To record sale of investments at a gain
   of $22 and also to record interest
   income of $25.

7. ENTRY IN ENDOWMENT PRINCIPAL
   FUND:

Interest Receivable on Investments	2,600	
Earnings		2,600

   To record interest accrued on
   investments.

8. ENTRY IN ENDOWMENT PRINCIPAL
   FUND:

Earnings	120	
Unamortized Premiums on Investments		120

   To record amortization of premiums on
   investments.

9. (a) ENTRY IN ENDOWMENT PRINCIPAL
   FUND:

Operating Transfer to Endowment Earnings Fund	4,990	

Due to Endowment Earnings
Fund 4,990
To record liability of endowment
principal fund to endowment
earnings fund for earnings to date.

(b) ENTRY IN ENDOWMENT EARNINGS
FUND:
Due from Endowment Principal
Fund 4,990
Transfer from Endowment
Principal Fund 4,990
To record amount due from
endowment principal fund for
earnings to date.

10. (a) ENTRY IN ENDOWMENT PRINCIPAL
FUND:
Due to Endowment Earnings
Fund 2,500
Cash 2,500
To record payment of part of total
amount due to endowment
earnings fund.

(b) ENTRY IN ENDOWMENT EARNINGS
FUND:
Cash 2,500
Due from Endowment Principal
Fund 2,500
To record receipt of part of total
amount due from endowment
principal fund.

11. ENTRY IN ENDOWMENT EARNINGS
FUND:
Expenditures—Scholarship Grant 2,000
Cash 2,000
To record payment of scholarship.

12. (a) ENTRY IN ENDOWMENT PRINCIPAL
FUND:
Earnings 4,990
Operating Transfer to
Endowment Earnings Fund ... 4,990
To close earnings and transfer
accounts.

(b) ENTRY IN ENDOWMENT EARNINGS
FUND:
Operating Transfer from
Endowment Principal Fund ... 4,990
Expenditures—Scholarship
Grant 2,000
Fund Balance 2,990
To close transfer and expenditure
accounts.

After the preceding entries are posted to the accounts, the Endowment Fund Balance Sheets in Figures 11-2 and 11-3 may be prepared. Additional statements would be prepared, as required by NCGA *Statement 1*, with appropriate recognition that the Principal Fund is proprietary in nature and the Earnings Fund is governmental.

If endowments are in the form of fixed properties, these constitute the principal fund and the net income therefrom is transferred to an expendable fund. Both the revenues and the expenses of administering the property—for example, rents, repairs, decorating expenses, and janitor's wages—would be accounted for in the principal fund. The net earnings would be transferred to the earnings fund and expended for the purpose designated—for example, granting scholarships.

Figure 11-2

A GOVERNMENTAL UNIT

Endowment Principal Trust Fund
Balance Sheet
At Close of Fiscal Year

Assets

Cash		$ 10,190
Investments	$197,000	
Unamortized premiums on investments	2,713	199,713
Interest receivable on investments		2,600
		$212,503

Liabilities and Fund Balance

Due to Endowment Earnings Fund	$ 2,490
Fund balance	210,013
	$212,503

Figure 11-3

A GOVERNMENTAL UNIT

Endowment Earnings Trust Fund
Balance Sheet
At Close of Fiscal Year

Assets

Cash	$ 500
Due from Endowment Principal Fund	2,490
	$2,990

Fund Balance

Fund balance	$2,990

It is important, in such cases, to account carefully for the revenues and expenses of the principal fund so that the income may be properly computed. Whether depreciation is charged as an expense will depend on the provisions of the trust document or the implied intent of the donor. If the grant contemplates the replacement of worn-out property, depreciation must be charged in an amount sufficient to preserve the principal intact. On the other hand, if the property is not to be replaced, depreciation might not be charged as an expense in determining trust income. If the trust instrument is silent as to depreciation of fixed assets held in trust, and the donor's intent in this regard is unclear, state statutes control. If there are no relevant state statutes, the general rule is that depreciation or amortization of those assets comprising the original trust principal either is not recorded or is charged against trust *principal*, not earnings, as are gains and losses on sales of investments present when the trust was established. If depreciation and amortization are recorded, that related to assets acquired by the trustee with other trust assets is charged to *earnings*. Some authorities feel that this question has not been conclusively settled, however, and that the trend now appears to be toward charging depreciation in determining trust earnings. Obviously, accounting for such items as depreciation and investment gains and losses should be covered in the trust instrument. Competent legal advice should be sought whenever such questions are not explicitly treated in that document.

Pooled Investment Funds. Pooled Investment Trust Funds are "in-house mutual funds" through which the investment of resources of various governmental fund entities may be centrally administered. A government might set up a single pooled investment fund or it might employ a series of such funds to serve certain types of funds, such as a Special Assessment Fund pooled investment fund, a Trust Fund pooled investment fund, and so forth. The fund may be managed by an employee(s) of the government or by an individual or organization independent of the government.

Not every government would benefit from establishing a fund or funds of this type, though numerous advantages accompany their use where warranted by the potential magnitude of investments for the government as a whole. Among the benefits that may accrue through use of pooled investment funds are these:

1. *Improved investment management*—through giving high-level recognition to the need for investing idle cash, centralizing investment management authority and responsibility, and, to some extent, overcoming management problems occasioned by the necessity to manage resources of many separate fund accounting entities.

2. *Higher investment yield*—because (a) the time cash remains idle is minimized, that is, monies need not be accumulated in individual funds until they warrant investment, but may be invested collectively whenever total investable cash of the several funds warrants investment, (b) brokerage cost per dollar invested may be substantially reduced by investing larger sums and reducing the number of investment and disinvestment transactions, (c) some high yield, high grade securities are available only in rather large denominations, and

(d) the "average" investable cash of the government as a whole may be kept invested rather than only minimum amounts within various funds, that is, various funds may "buy in" and "sell out" as their cash requirements dictate.

3. *Diversification of investments*—which (a) permits the establishment of a reasoned investment policy and (b) spreads the benefits of unexpected gains and the risks of unexpected losses among many funds rather than attributing them to a single fund.

All pertinent legal or contractual provisions must be observed in establishing and operating pooled investment funds, of course. Beyond such compliance, it is essential that policies relating to issues and procedures such as those enumerated below be established, committed to writing, and followed consistently:

1. *Valuation of a participating fund's share in the pool*—upon investment, disinvestment, at year end.

2. *Distribution of earnings*—whether based upon average (simple or weighted) investment or upon some other method; the frequency with which the method is to be applied (annually, quarterly, daily); the effect of "buying in" and "selling out."

3. *Distribution of gains or losses*—valuation dates; whether gains or losses are to be distributed currently or averaged, possibly over a period of several years.

Practices vary widely in regard to questions such as these. A discussion of the ramifications and possible effects of alternative policies, though inviting, is beyond the scope of this text.

In order to illustrate the basic accounting procedures for pooled investment funds, let us assume that (1) a Special Assessment Funds pooled investment fund is established, and (2) Public Improvement Fund 726 (PI 726) participates in this investment pool. Some typical transactions are described below; to highlight the interfund aspects of this situation, entries are indicated both for the pooled investment Trust Fund and for PI 726, one of the member funds.

Transactions

1. The Pooled Investment Fund was established by transfers as follows: PI 726, $50,000; PI 741, $70,000; PI 750, securities (cost $75,000 to PI 750; fair market value upon pooling, $80,000).

2. Investments were made as follows: bonds, $105,000 (including $5,000 premium); certificates of deposit, $15,000.

3. Additional cash, $5,000, was received from PI 741.

4. Interest on bonds was received, $6,000; premium amortization of $1,000 for the period was recorded.

5. One fourth of the bonds were sold at the interest due date for $28,000 in order to meet cash needs of PI 750 (see below).

6. Cash, $25,000, was returned to PI 750 to meet its debt service requirements.

7. Accrued interest receivable on certificates of deposit at year end, $700.

8. Accounts were closed at year end; earnings and the investment gain were distributed (not disbursed) to member fund equity accounts in accordance with the agreed formula.

Entries

1. (a) ENTRY IN POOLED INVESTMENT FUND:

Cash	120,000	
Investments	80,000	
Fund Balance		200,000

To record original investments upon establishment of fund.

Both the Investments and Fund Balance accounts are control accounts in this example. The Investments account subsidiary ledger would contain details of each investment made; the individual member fund equities in the investment pool would be recorded in the Fund Balance subsidiary ledger. The transfer of securities from PI 750 must be recorded in the Pooled Investment Fund at fair market value upon transfer. Either the cost or equity method might be followed in recording the transaction in the accounts of PI 750.

(b) ENTRY IN PI 726:

Pooled Investments (or Equity in Investment Pool)	50,000	
Cash		50,000

To record transfer of cash to the investment pool.

2. ENTRY IN POOLED INVESTMENT FUND:

Investments	115,000	
Unamortized Premiums on Investments	5,000	
Cash		120,000

To record investments made.

3. ENTRY IN POOLED INVESTMENT FUND:

Cash	5,000	
Fund Balance		5,000

To record receipt of cash from PI 741.

4. ENTRY IN POOLED INVESTMENT FUND:

Cash	6,000	
Unamortized Premiums on Investments		1,000
Earnings		5,000

To record receipt of bond interest and premium amortization.

5. ENTRY IN POOLED INVESTMENT FUND:

Cash	28,000	
Investments		25,000
Unamortized Premiums on Investments		1,000
Gain on Sale of Investments		2,000

To record sale of one-fourth of the bonds at interest date.

6. Entry in Pooled Investment Fund:

Fund Balance	25,000	
Cash		25,000

To record disinvestment by PI 750.

7. Entry in Pooled Investment Fund:

Accrued Interest Receivable	700	
Earnings		700

To record interest accrued on
certificates of deposit at year end.

8. (a) Entry in Pooled Investment Fund:

Earnings	5,700	
Gain on Sale of Investments	2,000	
Fund Balance		7,700

To distribute earnings and gain to
member fund equity accounts per
agreed formula:

PI 726	$2,156
PI 741	2,695
PI 750	2,849
	$7,700

(b) Entry in PI 726:

Pooled Investments (or Equity in Investment Pool)	2,156	
Earnings		1,596
Gain on Sale of Investments		560

To record share of pooled
investment earnings and gains.

The transactions above have been recorded using the cost basis (but the additions to the fund were recorded at fair market value). Equity requires the use of fair market value in determining distributions of income and determining member fund equity at withdrawal dates. Therefore, where member funds "buy in" and "sell out" frequently, in whole or in part, there is strong support for regularly revaluing the pool's investments to fair market value as is common in accounting for mutual funds (regulated investment trusts).

A Pooled Investment Trust Fund Balance Sheet, prepared on a cost basis, appears in Figure 11-4. The equities of the member funds are identified. A Statement of Revenues, Expenses, and Changes in Fund Balance would also be prepared; and the composition of the investment portfolio would be disclosed in a separate schedule in the Comprehensive Annual Financial Report.

AGENCY FUNDS

Agency Funds are conduit or clearinghouse funds established to account for assets (usually cash) received for and paid to other funds, individuals, or organizations. The assets thus received are usually held only briefly; investment or other fiscal management complexities are rarely involved, except in situations such as that of the Tax Agency Fund illustrated later in this chapter.

Figure 11-4

A GOVERNMENTAL UNIT
Pooled Investment Trust Fund
Balance Sheet
At Close of Fiscal Year

Assets

Cash		$ 14,000
Investments	$170,000	
Unamortized premiums on investments	3,000	173,000
Interest receivable on investments		700
		$187,700

Fund Balance

Fund Balance—PI 726	$ 52,156
Fund Balance—PI 741	77,695
Fund Balance—PI 750	57,849
	$187,700

Not all agency relationships arising in the conduct of a government's business require that an Agency Fund be established. For example, payroll deductions for such items as insurance premiums and income tax withholdings create agency responsibilities which may often be accounted for (as liabilities) in the fund through which the payroll is paid. On the other hand, where payrolls are paid from several funds it may be more convenient to transfer withheld amounts to an Agency Fund in order that a single check and remittance report may be forwarded to the recipient. As a general rule, Agency Funds should be used whenever (1) the volume of agency transactions, the magnitude of the sums involved, and/or the management and accounting capabilities of government personnel make it either unwieldy or unwise to account for agency responsibilities through other funds, or (2) financial management or accounting for interfund transactions or relationships is expedited through their use.

Simpler Agency Funds

Though agency relationships are commonly viewed as arising between the government and individuals or organizations external to it, recall that each fund of the government is a distinct legal entity. Intragovernmental Agency Funds may prove useful in (1) alleviating some of the awkwardness occasioned by the use of numerous fund accounting entities in governments, and (2) establishing clear-cut audit trails where a single transaction affects several funds. Thus, though a special imprest[2] bank account will often suffice, some governments establish an Agency Fund where (1) receipts must be allocated among several funds or (2) a

[2] An imprest bank account is one to which deposits are made periodically in an amount equal to the sum of the checks written thereon; when all checks written have cleared, the bank account balance will equal a predetermined amount, often zero. Imprest bank accounts are often used to enhance cash control and/or to facilitate bank-book reconciliations.

single expenditure is financed through several funds. In the former case, a single check may be deposited in an Agency Fund and separate checks payable to the various funds drawn against it; in the latter, checks drawn against several funds are placed in an Agency Fund and a single check drawn against it in payment for the total expenditure. Similarly, some governments account for all receipts and disbursements through an Agency Fund, with interfund settlement being made periodically. Such a procedure is particularly useful in manual accounting systems as it (1) avoids the necessity of preparing separate deposit slips daily for each fund, as well as daily use of numerous different check forms, and (2) assists in centralization of the financial management function, such as through means of a single voucher system. Again, judgment should be exercised in deciding whether an Agency Fund is useful in such cases; a special imprest checking account may serve the government's needs adequately without necessitating the additional record-keeping occasioned by the establishment of an Agency Fund.

NCGA *Statement 2*, "Grant, Entitlement, and Shared Revenue Accounting and Reporting by State and Local Governments," notes three other situations where Agency Funds may be employed:

1. Where a government receives "pass through" grants—grants which the recipient government must transfer to, or spend on behalf of, another governmental unit—it should record the receipt and disbursement of the "pass through" grant in an Agency Fund rather than as revenues and expenditures.

2. Where a government receives a grant, entitlement, or shared revenue that may be used, at its discretion, for programs or projects financed through more than one fund, the resources should initially be accounted for in an Agency Fund. When decisions have been made as to which programs or projects—financed by which governmental and/or proprietary funds—the resources will be allocated to, the resources are removed from the Agency Fund and recorded in the governmental and/or proprietary fund(s). There they will be accounted for as revenues and as expenditures or expenses at the appropriate time.

3. When a grant, entitlement, or shared revenue must be accounted for in a prescribed way that differs from GAAP for purposes of reporting to the grantor government, the resources may be initially accounted for in an Agency Fund. The transactions are accounted for in the Agency Fund using "memoranda" accounts that accumulate data for the prescribed special purpose reports but are not reported in the GAAP financial statements, then are accounted for in the fund(s) financed as revenues or contributed capital and as expenditures or expenses, as appropriate, in conformity with GAAP.[3]

Whether the agency relationship is external or internal, the accounting in situations discussed thus far is not complicated. All that is required is that entries such as the following be prepared upon receipt and disbursement of monies:

Cash (or other assets) 100,000
    Due to Individual (or fund or organization) ..   100,000
To record receipt of assets.

[3] NCGAS 2, p. 2.

Due to Individual (or fund or organization) ...	100,000	
Cash (other assets)		100,000
To record payment of assets.		

Note that all Agency Fund assets are owed to some person, fund, or organization. The government has no equity in the Fund's assets.

More Complex Agency Funds

In the examples above, the Agency Fund required little management action or expertise. Other Agency Funds, such as the Tax Agency Fund illustrated below, may involve significant management responsibilities and more complex accounting procedures.

In order to avoid duplication of assessment and collection effort and to enforce tax laws as equitably and economically as possible, all taxes levied upon properties within a state, county, or other geographic area may be billed and collected by one of the governments. That unit therefore becomes an agent for the other taxing units and establishes an Agency Fund such as the Tax Agency Fund described below. In the usual case, the several taxing bodies (e.g., the state, county, school districts) certify the amounts or rates at which taxes are to be levied for them by the designated government. The latter then levies the total tax, including its own, against specific properties and proceeds to collect the tax. In addition, it normally makes pro rata payments of collections to the various taxing bodies during the year, often quarterly, and charges a collection or service fee to the other units.

The following example illustrates the general approach to Tax Agency Fund accounting. Though not illustrated here, detailed records of levies and collections relative to each property taxed, by year of levy, are required.[4] Collections pertaining to each year's levy are distributed among the taxing bodies in the ratio of each unit's levy to the total levy of that year.

Case of City A. City A serves as the property tax collecting agent for several governmental units. City A's levies and those certified by the other units for 19X2 and 19X3 are as follows:

	19X3		19X2	
	Amount Levied	Percentage of Total	Amount Levied	Percentage of Total
City A*	$100,000	25.0	$ 91,200	24.0
School Distict B	200,000	50.0	188,100	49.5
Park District X	50,000	12.5	49,400	13.0
Sanitary District Y	50,000	12.5	51,300	13.5
	$400,000	100.0	$380,000	100.0

*Although these taxes are the taxes of the collecting governmental unit, they are treated in the same manner as if they were being collected for it by another unit.

[4] These records are discussed and illustrated in Chapter 5.

The Tax Agency Fund trial balance at December 31, 19X2, consists of $75,000 of Taxes Receivable for Taxing Units and Due to Taxing Units, $75,000. These amounts arose entirely from the 19X2 levy. Transactions and entries illustrated for the General Fund of City A are similar to those of the other recipient governmental units.

Transactions

1. The 19X3 levies are placed on the tax roll and recorded on the books.
2. Collections of interest and penalties (not previously accrued in the Agency Fund) of $15,000 and taxes of $300,000 are received. Collections are identified by type, year, and governmental unit (see the explanation for the journal entry) so that distributions may be made in accordance with the original levies.
3. The collections (transaction 2) are paid from the Tax Agency Fund to the respective governmental units, except for a 2 percent collection charge levied upon the *other* governments.

Entries

1. ENTRY IN GENERAL FUND:

Taxes Receivable—Current	100,000	
Estimated Uncollectible		
Current Taxes		1,000
Revenues		99,000
To record the 19X3 tax levy.		

ENTRY IN TAX AGENCY FUND:

Taxes Receivable for Taxing Units.	400,000	
Due to Taxing Units		400,000

To record 19X3 taxes placed on the tax roll. *Credit* Due to Taxing Units subsidiary accounts:

City of A—Uncollected	100,000
School District B—Uncollected	200,000
Park District X—Uncollected ...	50,000
Sanitary District Y—	
Uncollected	50,000
	400,000

Taxes Receivable for Taxing Units may be classified into two accounts, Current and Delinquent, if desired. The distinction would be apparent in the subsidiary records, however, since (1) taxes are levied by year, and (2) a separate ledger account or column would be provided for each year's levy against each property. Appropriate subsidiary records for Taxes Receivable for Taxing Units by taxpayer would be maintained.

2. ENTRY IN TAX AGENCY FUND:

Cash	315,000	
Taxes Receivable for Taxing		
Units		300,000
Due to Taxing Units		15,000

To record collections of taxes and
interest and penalties classified as
follows:
Subsidiary taxpayer records would
be credited for appropriate amounts.
Debit Due to Taxing Units
subsidiary accounts:

City of A—Uncollected	74,250
School District B—Uncollected	149,625
Park District X—Uncollected ...	37,875
Sanitary District Y—	
Uncollected	38,250
	300,000

Credit Due to Taxing Units subsidiary
accounts:

City of A—Collected	77,850
School District B—Collected ...	157,050
Park District X—Collected	39,825
Sanitary District Y—Collected.	40,275
	315,000

3. ENTRY IN TAX AGENCY FUND:

Due to Taxing Units	315,000	
Cash		310,257
Due to General Fund		4,743

To record payment of amounts
collected, with the retention of a
2 percent collection charge for
taxes collected for *other*
governmental units.
Debit Due to Taxing Units
subsidiary accounts:

City of A—Collected	77,850
School District B—Collected ...	157,050
Park District X—Collected	39,825
Sanitary District Y—Collected .	40,275
	315,000

ENTRIES IN GENERAL FUND:

Cash	77,850	
Taxes Receivable—Current		56,250
Taxes Receivable—Delinquent .		18,000
Interest and Penalties		
Receivable on Taxes		3,600

To record receipt of collections of
taxes and interest and penalties
from Tax Agency Fund.

Due from Tax Agency Fund	4,743	
Revenues		4,743

To record revenues charged for
tax services rendered to other
governmental units.
Credit subsidiary revenue account:

Tax Collection Fees	4,743

The preparation of the tax roll, the accounting for taxes, and handling the collections involve considerable costs, and the collecting unit usually charges for these services. The charges are legitimate financial expenditures of the various units for which taxes are collected, and provision is made for them in the budgets. The usual practice, illustrated in the foregoing transactions, is for the collecting unit to retain a portion of the taxes and interest and penalties collected rather than to go through the process of billing the charges to the several governmental units. To further illustrate the procedure, the journal entry which School District B would make to record receipt of cash from the Tax Agency Fund (transaction 3 above) follows:

Cash	153,909	
Expenditures	3,141	
Taxes Receivable—Current		112,500
Taxes Receivable—Delinquent		37,125
Interest and Penalties Receivable on		
Taxes		7,425
To record receipts of amounts collected		
by City A less collection charge of 2		
percent.		

The Balance Sheet of the Tax Agency Fund of City A after the foregoing transactions have been recorded is presented in Figure 11-5.

Figure 11-5

CITY A

Tax Agency Fund
Balance Sheet
At Close of Fiscal Year

Assets

Cash	$ 4,743
Taxes receivable for taxing units	175,000
	$179,743

Liabilities

Due to General Fund	$ 4,743
Due to taxing units (for uncollected taxes)	175,000
	$179,743

A Statement of Changes in Assets and Liabilities for the Tax Agency Fund is presented in Figure 11-6.

PENSION TRUST FUNDS

Public employee retirement systems (PERS) provide examples of more complex Pension Trust Funds (PTFs) common to governments. These funds are likely to be the largest Trust Fund of a government unit. They are growing rapidly, the

Figure 11-6

CITY A

Tax Agency Fund
Statement of Changes in Assets and Liabilities
for the Year Ended December 31, 19X3

Assets	Balances, January 1, 19X3	Additions	Deductions	Balances, December 31, 19X3
Cash		$315,000	$310,257	$ 4,743
Taxes receivable for taxing units	$75,000	400,000	300,000	175,000
Total assets	$75,000	$715,000	$610,257	$179,743

Liabilities				
Due to General Fund ..		$ 4,743		$ 4,743
Due to taxing units for uncollected taxes	$75,000	415,000	$315,000	$175,000
Total liabilities	$75,000	$419,743	$315,000	$179,743

cost to the government of contributions to them is significant, and their ability to pay pensions on schedule is of vital importance to individual retirees and to the morale of the work force.

Many types of retirement plans are in existence in governments. Local governments often have retirement systems, though in some states employees of all governmental units of a certain type (e.g., municipalities) or all employees within certain functional fields (e.g., teachers, policemen, firemen) are included in a statewide retirement system. In some cases these plans are integrated with Federal social security benefits; in others, employees are not covered under that program. The administrative mechanisms established also differ widely. In some instances the retirement system is managed and accounted for by the finance department or some other executive agency of the government. In other cases an independent board, or even a separate corporation, is charged with retirement system management and accountability.

Of far more consequence to sound public finance policy and to the public interest generally is the disparate array of financial management practices relating to retirement systems. PERS are not subject to the Federal ERISA (Employee Retirement Income Security Act) regulations on vesting, funding, and the like, though various PERISA (Public Employee Retirement Income Security Act) and similar bills have been proposed in Congress in recent years. Some governments are on a virtual pay-as-you-go basis—pension payments are paid from current revenues. In such cases pensioners are dependent upon the flow of revenues and other demands for appropriations and thus on the uncertainties of the budget process. At the other extreme are those governments whose retirement systems are fully funded and actuarially sound. Most governments fall between these extremes. Perhaps the system is properly designed from an actuarial point of view but the government has fallen behind in payments. Or perhaps benefits have been raised as a result of increased salary levels or employee pressures on a pliant or uninformed political management. Or perhaps a new plan has been grafted onto an old one without appropriate actuarial consideration or without adequate funding.

It seems likely that retirement fund financial management practices and decisions are affected by the accounting and reporting systems in use. In many instances such funds have been operated on a cash receipts and disbursements basis and accounted for as a SRF when the nature of the plan required a long-run management and accountability focus. Where the government's legal obligation or intent is to manage and account for the retirement fund over a period of many years, "pay-as-you-go" and "terminal funding" procedures are inappropriate. They result at best in significant understatement of the government's liabilities; at worst, they lead to drastic increases in employee or employer contributions to the fund or to reduced payments being made to retirees.

Accounting Standards

The NCGA issued accounting standards for PERS and PTFs in both GAAFR (68) and NCGAS 1. In March 1980 the FASB issued "Accounting and Reporting by Defined Benefit Plans,"[5] which included plans of state and local governments.[6] The NCGA did not agree with all of the provisions of FASB *SFAS 35*, as applied to governments, and issued NCGA *Interpretation 4*, "Accounting and Financial Reporting for Public Employee Retirement Systems and Pension Trust Funds"[7] in December 1981. These two sources of standards are in some respects in conflict; and, after lengthy discussions, the NCGA and FASB agreed to defer application of FASB *Statement 35* and NCGA *Interpretation 4* to years beginning after June 15, 1982 (ending after June 15, 1983)—that is, they deferred the problem to the GASB.[8] The NCGA recommended that for the moment PERS continue to prepare financial statements for pension plans in accordance with the principles of *Statement 1* and *Interpretation 4*. We present a PERS example based on NCGA principles and follow it with a limited discussion of FASB *Statement 35* and NCGA *Interpretation 4*.

The NCGA determined that Pension Trust Funds are classified as proprietary rather than governmental (this despite the payments that such funds make to deceased, resigned, and retired employees and to their survivors). The accrual basis is used in accounting for their revenues and expenses, and net income is computed. Further, Pension Trust Funds and Nonexpendable Trust Funds are grouped in combining statements.

[5] Financial Accounting Standards Board, *Statement of Financial Accounting Standards No. 35* (Stamford, Conn.: FASB, 1980).

[6] *Ibid.*, p. 2.

[7] National Council on Governmental Accounting, *Interpretation 4*, "Accounting and Financial Reporting for Public Employee Retirement Systems and Pension Trust Funds" (Chicago: NCGA, December 1981.)

[8] Financial Accounting Standards Board, *Statement of Financial Accounting Standards No. 59*, "Deferral of the Effective Date of Certain Accounting Requirements for Pension Plans of State and Local Governmental Units: An Amendment of FASB Statement 35" (Stamford, FASB: April 1982). The NCGA suspended application of NCGA Interpretation 4 until the same date by resolution.

Retirement Fund Example

In order to illustrate the NCGA approach to accounting for a PTF, let us assume that the fund is already in operation and its beginning trial balance appears as in Figure 11-7. For purposes of this example, assume also that (1) the plan is financed by employer contributions, employee contributions, and investment earnings; (2) the equities of employees resigning or dying prior to retirement are returned to them or to their estates, but employer contributions on their behalf remain in the fund; (3) employer contributions and earnings thereon vest[9] to the benefit of the employee only upon retirement; (4) earnings of the fund are apportioned according to a predetermined formula among employee equity, employer equity, and retiree equity in the fund; and (5) actuarial requirements are recorded by year-end adjusting entries.

Figure 11-7

A GOVERNMENTAL UNIT
Pension Trust Fund
Trial Balance
At Beginning of Fiscal Year (Date)

	Debit	Credit
Cash	56,000	
Due from General Fund	8,000	
Interest Receivable	3,000	
Investments	980,000	
Unamortized Premiums on Investments	5,000	
Due to Resigned Employees		3,000
Annuities Payable		2,800
Reserve for Employee Contributions		470,200
Reserve for Employer Contributions		260,100
Actuarial Deficiency—Reserve for Employer Contributions		300,000
Reserve for Retiree Annuities		315,900
Fund Balance (deficit)		(300,000)
	1,052,000	1,052,000

The following transactions or events occurred during the year and would be recorded as indicated.

Transactions

Employer and employee contributions were accrued in the General Fund (a quasi-external transaction).

(1)	Due from General Fund	175,000	
	Revenues—Employee Contributions		125,000
	Revenues—Employer Contributions		50,000
	To record employee and employer contributions due from the GF.		

[9] Employer contributions or pension benefits "vest" when they are irrevocably owed to the employee or his estate. The trend is toward employer contributions being vested immediately or within a relatively short period (five to ten years), rather than only upon retirement, but this trend is less evident in government than in business.

Although the employer contribution would be budgeted in the GF through which payrolls are paid, the PERS in this example is not under formal budgetary accounting control. The levels of its activity are determined by factors such as levels of employment in the government and the changes in status of participants in the system.

A check was received from the General Fund.

(2)	Cash	170,000	
	Due from General Fund		170,000
	To record receipt of contributions from the General Fund.		

Accrued interest and premium amortization on investments was recorded.

(3)	Interest Receivable	45,000	
	Unamortized Premiums on Investments		200
	Revenues—Interest		44,800
	To record accrued interest receivable and amortization of premiums on investments.		

Investment premiums and discounts are amortized as a part of the accrual basis calculation of investment earnings.

A portion of the interest receivable was collected.

(4)	Cash	40,000	
	Interest Receivable		40,000
	To record receipt of interest receivable.		

An employee retired; employer contributions in his behalf vested and his retirement benefit formula was determined.

(5)	Reserve for Employee Contributions ...	10,000	
	Reserve for Employer Contributions ...	5,000	
	Reserve for Retiree Annuities		15,000
	To record reclassification of equities upon an employee's retirement and vesting of the government's contributions in his behalf.		

Three employees resigned and one died prior to retirement.

(6)	Expenses—Payments to Deceased Employee Estates	10,000	
	Expenses—Payments to Resigned Employees	15,000	
	Due to Deceased Employees' Estates		10,000
	Due to Resigned Employees		15,000
	To record amounts due upon employee resignations and the death of one employee prior to retirement.		

Checks were mailed to two of the resigned employees and to the estate of the deceased employee.

(7)	Due to Deceased Employees' Estates ..	10,000	
	Due to Resigned Employees	12,000	
	Cash		22,000
	To record payments to former employees and to the estate of a deceased employee.		

Annuities payable were accrued.

(8)	Expenses—Annuity Payments	24,000	
	Annuities Payable		24,000
	To record accrual of liability for annuities payable.		

Annuities payable were paid, except for that to one employee who is out of the country.

(9)	Annuities Payable	23,000	
	Cash		23,000
	To record payment of annuities.		

Additional investments were made.

(10)	Investments	150,000	
	Unamortized Discounts on Investments		7,000
	Cash		143,000
	To record the investments made.		

At year end the following adjusting and closing entries were made. The actuary indicated that the actuarial deficiency had increased by $20,000 during the year and additional contributions would need to be made if the fund were to be actuarially sound.

(11)	Fund Balance	20,000	
	Actuarial Deficiency—Reserve for Employer Contributions		20,000
	To record the change in the actuarial deficiency of the fund.		

The latter account title is often phrased "Reserve for Employer Contributions—Actuarial Deficiency."

Revenue and Expense Accounts were closed to Fund Balance.

(12)	Revenues—Employee Contributions ...	125,000	
	Revenues—Employer Contributions	50,000	
	Revenues—Interest	44,800	
	Expenses—Payments to Deceased Employees' Estates		10,000
	Expenses—Payments to Resigned Employees		15,000
	Expenses—Annuity Payments		24,000
	Fund Balance		170,800
	To close revenue and expense accounts.		

The amounts of contributions were added to the respective Reserve Accounts.

(13)	Fund Balance.	175,000	
	Reserve for Employee Contributions. .		125,000
	Reserve for Employer Contributions. .		50,000
	To increase reserves by the amounts of the respective contributions.		

The amount of interest earnings was apportioned among the respective reserve accounts.

(14)	Fund Balance	44,800	
	Reserve for Employee Contributions		18,300
	Reserve for Employer Contributions		15,700
	Reserve for Retiree Annuities		10,800
	To apportion the amount of interest earnings among the respective reserve accounts.		

The incurring of expenses was recognized by the reduction of the respective reserve accounts.

(15)	Reserve for Employee Contributions ...	25,000	
	Reserve for Retiree Annuities	24,000	
	Fund Balance		49,000
	To reduce the respective reserve accounts by the amount of expenses.		

The closing entries above (12-15) are theoretically correct. A less theoretically correct closing entry sequence often found in practice yields the same result:

(C1)	Revenues—Employee Contributions	125,000	
	Revenues—Employer Contributions	50,000	
	Reserve for Employee Contributions		125,000
	Reserve for Employer Contributions		50,000
	To close employee and employer contributions to related reserve accounts.		
(C2)	Reserve For Employee Contributions	25,000	
	Expenses—Payments to Deceased Employees' Estates		10,000
	Expenses—Payments to Resigned Employees		15,000
	To close expenses to related reserve accounts.		
(C3)	Reserve for Retiree Annuities	24,000	
	Expenses—Annuity Payments		24,000
	To close annuity expense to related reserve.		
(C4)	Revenue—Interest	44,800	
	Reserve for Employee Contributions		18,300
	Reserve for Employer Contributions		15,700
	Reserve for Retiree Annuities		10,800
	To allocate interest to the reserve accounts.		

Figure 11-8

A GOVERNMENTAL UNIT
Pension Trust Fund
Balance Sheet
At Close of Fiscal Year (Date)

Assets

Current assets:		
Cash	$	78,000
Due from General Fund		13,000
Interest receivable		8,000
Total current assets	$	99,000
Investments (at amortized cost; fair market value, $xx)		1,127,800
		$1,226,800

Liabilities and Fund Balance

Current liabilities:		
Due to resigned employees	$	6,000
Annuities payable		3,800
Total current liabilities	$	9,800
Fund balance:		
Reserve for employee contributions	$578,500	
Reserve for employer contributions	320,800	
Actuarial deficiency—Reserve for employer contributions	320,000	
Reserve for retiree annuities	317,700	
Unreserved fund balance (deficit)	(320,000)	
Total fund balance		1,217,000
		$1,226,800

A Pension Trust Fund is similar to proprietary funds in many respects, and the NCGA has said[10] that it should therefore have prepared for it a Balance Sheet; a Statement of Changes in Financial Position; and a Statement of Revenues, Expenses, and Changes in Fund Balance. In the authors' view, a statement analyzing changes in reserve accounts is also appropriate. These statements are presented, using data from the illustrated retirement fund, in Figures 11-8 to 11-12.

Figure 11-9

A GOVERNMENTAL UNIT

Pension Trust Fund
Statement of Changes in Financial Position
For the Year Ended (Date)

Sources of funds:		
Contributions from General Fund:		
Employees	$125,000	
Employers	50,000	$175,000
Interest accrued		45,000
Total funds provided		$220,000
Applications of funds:		
Investments (net)	$143,000	
Refunds due to:		
Death	10,000	
Resignation	15,000	
Annuities accrued	24,000	
Total funds applied		192,000
Increase in net current assets		$ 28,000

Schedule of changes in net current assets:

	Beginning of Year	End of Year	Working Capital Increase (Decrease)
Current assets:			
Cash	$56,000	$78,000	$22,000
Due from General Fund	8,000	13,000	5,000
Interest receivable	3,000	8,000	5,000
	$67,000	$99,000	$32,000
Current liabilities:			
Due to resigned employees	$ 3,000	$ 6,000	$(3,000)
Annuities payable	2,800	3,800	(1,000)
	$ 5,800	$ 9,800	$(4,000)
Working capital	$61,200	$89,200	$28,000

[10] NCGAS 1, p. 21.

Figure 11-10

A GOVERNMENTAL UNIT
Pension Trust Fund
Statement of Revenues, Expenses and Changes in (Total) Fund Balance
For the Fiscal Year Ended (Date)

Revenues:		
Interest		$ 44,800
Contributions (a quasi-external		
transaction)		175,000
Total		$ 219,800
Expenses:		
Benefit payments	$24,000	
Refunds	25,000	
Total		49,000
Excess of revenues over expenses		$ 170,800
Fund balance, beginning of year (date)		1,046,200
Fund balance, end of year (date)		$1,217,000

Note: NCGA Statement 1 asserts that "Pension Trust Funds are similar to proprietary funds (accrual basis) and should be reported as [are] proprietary funds" (p. 21).

NCGA Accounting Standards Revisited

The reserves shown as segregations of fund balance in Figure 11-8 are actually liabilities rather than equities. Under appropriate circumstances all of them will be paid out to participants in the plan; none of them represents ownership in the net assets by the sponsoring governmental unit. Indeed, as long as the governmental unit permits an "actuarial deficit" to exist, there is no fund balance. The authors believe that the following presentation of the liabilities and equity side of the balance sheet is more appropriate than that in Figure 11-8 (the usual balance sheet presentation) or in the condensed presentation of NCGAS 1 and GAAFR (80).

Liabilities and Fund Balance

Current liabilities:		
Due to resigned employees	$	6,000
Annuities currently payable		3,800
Total current liabilities	$	9,800
Long-term liabilities:		
Equities of annuitants in PERS		
resources	$317,700	
Equities of employees in PERS		
resources:		
From employee contributions	578,500	
From employer contributions	320,800	
From the acturial deficiency		
in employer contributions	320,000	
Total long-term liabilities		1,537,000
Total liabilities		$1,546,800
Fund balance (deficit)		(320,000)
Total liabilities, net of deficit		$1,226,800

Figure 11-11

A GOVERNMENTAL UNIT

Pension Trust Fund
Statement of Revenues, Expenses, and
Changes in (Unreserved) Fund Balance
For the Fiscal Year Ended (Date)

Revenues:		
Interest		$ 44,800
Contributions (a quasi-external		
transaction)		175,000
Total		$ 219,800
Expenses:		
Benefit payments	$24,000	
Refunds	25,000	
Total		49,000
Excess of revenues over expenses		$ 170,800
Changes in reserves:		
Increase in Reserve for Employee		
Contributions		$ 108,300
Increase in Reserve for Employer		
Contributions		60,700
Increase in Reserve for Retiree		
Annuities		1,800
Increase in Reserve for Employer		
Contribution-Actuarial Deficiency .		20,000
		$ 190,800
Increase (decrease) in unreserved		
fund balance		$ (20,000)
Unreserved fund balance, beginning		
of period		(300,000)
Unreserved fund balance, end of		
period		$(320,000)

If the "Reserve for" accounts are liabilities, their titles should not contain the word "reserve, " which is to be used for fund balance accounts only. Further, the "Fund balance (deficit)" is a receivable from the govermental unit rather than a deficit of the PTF, and that liability should be set up in the government's funds and/or in the GLTD Account Group. Indeed, some PTFs classify the Fund Balance deficit as a receivable from the government and some governments record the liability to the PTF in the GLTD accounts.

If the essential balance sheet relationship in a PTF is equality of assets and liabilities, this type of fund is similar to an Agency Fund and considerable doubt is cast on the propriety of identifying resource flows as revenues and expenses. Employees contribute to the system and (in our example) receive a promise that

Figure 11-12

A GOVERNMENTAL UNIT
Pension Trust Fund
Analysis of Changes in Retirement Reserves
For the Fiscal Year Ended (Date)

	Total	Reserve for Employee Contributions	Reserve for Employer Contributions	Actuarial Deficiency-Reserve for Employer Contributions	Reserve for Retiree Annuities
Balances, beginning of year	$1,346,200	$470,200	$260,100	$300,000	$315,900
Additions:					
Employee contributions	$ 125,000	$125,000	—	—	—
Employer contributions	50,000	—	$ 50,000	—	—
Interest earnings	44,800	18,300	15,700	—	$ 10,800
Total additions	$ 219,800	$143,300	$ 65,700	$ —	$ 10,800
Total balance and additions	$1,566,000	$613,500	$325,800	$300,000	$326,700
Annuities awarded	—	(10,000)	(5,000)	—	15,000
Actuarial adjustments	20,000	—	—	20,000	—
Total revised balances	$1,586,000	$603,500	$320,800	$320,000	$341,700
Deductions:					
Annuity payments	$ 24,000	—	—	—	$ 24,000
Refunds—deaths	10,000	$ 10,000	—	—	—
Refunds—resignations	15,000	15,000	—	—	—
Total deductions	$ 49,000	$ 25,000	$ —	$ —	$ 24,000
Balances, end of year	$1,537,000	$578,500	$320,800	$320,000	$317,700

if they resign or die the contribution and its accumulated earnings will be returned to them or to their estate. Has the PTF received revenue? The government incurs pension expense or expenditure in the several funds and pays—or fails to pay— the PTF. The accumulated resources are pledged to pay employees who retire. Has the PTF received revenue?

Such questions are even harder to answer in the affirmative in the case of disbursements. An employee dies or resigns and his equity in the PTF is paid out. Has the PTF incurred an expense? (In our example the PERS and the governmental unit are *better off* because the pension obligation to the employee is wiped out but the resources the government has contributed to the PTF on his account remain in the PTF.) If a payment is made to a retiree, has an expense been incurred? There has been a reduction in the obligation to the retiree; and such a result is more like a liability has been paid than that an expense has been incurred.

In summary, we believe that the PTF is *not* a proprietary fund and the NCGA made a mistake in so labeling it. It is true that the interest revenues, including amortization of premiums and discounts on investments, should be accounted for on the accrual basis. But this is necessary only to measure accurately the increase in the fiduciary responsibility of the system. Contributions to the fund by employer and employee, together with interest revenue, provide increases in assets and liabilities. Payments to employees and their estates represent decreases in assets and liabilities.

SFAS No. 35

As noted earlier, "Accounting and Reporting by Defined Pension Plans" was intended by the FASB to be applicable to plans that provide pensions for employees of state and local governments as well as employees of businesses and other organizations. The accompanying financial statements (Figures 11-13 and 11-14) summarize the FASB's point of view regarding the fundamental nature of such a fund and the essential information that should be provided regarding its financial position and results of operation. They provide quite different information from that in the preceding statements in this chapter, which are in conformity with NCGA pronouncements. A few examples of differences are the following:

- The financial statements are entirely different from the conventional proprietary fund balance sheet and operating statements.
- Accumulated plan benefits are "benefits that are attributable under the provisions of a pension plan to employees' service rendered to the benefit information date"[11] rather than a definition that takes into account benefits earned by both past and future service.
- Assets are presented at fair value rather than historical cost.

NCGA Interpretation 4. The NCGA moved slightly toward the FASB *Statement 35* recommendations in NCGA *Interpretation 4*. The NCGA did not endorse statements such as those in Figures 11-13 and 11-14, however. Rather, NCGA *Interpretation 4* first addresses asset valuation and PTF Fund Balance,

---

[11] FASB, *op. cit.*, p.115. This provision is being reconsidered by the FASB.

Figure 11-13

C&H COMPANY PENSION PLAN

Statement of Accumulated Plan Benefits
And Net Assets Available for Benefits

	December 31, 1981
Accumulated Plan Benefits [notes B(2) and C]:	
Actuarial present value of vested benefits:	
Participants currently receiving payments	$ 3,040,000
Other participants	8,120,000
	11,160,000
Actuarial present value of nonvested benefits	2,720,000
Total actuarial present value of accumulated plan benefits	13,880,000
Net Assets Available for Benefits:	
Investments, at fair value [notes B(1) and E]:	
United States government securities	350,000
Corporate bonds and debentures	3,500,000
Common stock:	
C&H Company	690,000
Other	2,250,000
Mortgages	480,000
Real estate	270,000
	7,540,000
Deposit administration contract, at contract value [notes B(1) and F]	1,000,000
Total investments	8,540,000
Receivables:	
Employees' contributions	40,000
Securities sold	310,000
Accrued interest and dividends	77,000
	427,000
Cash	200,000
Total assets	9,167,000
Accounts payable	70,000
Accrued expenses	85,000
Total liabilities	155,000
Net assets available for benefits	9,012,000
Excess of actuarial present value of accumulated plan benefits over net assets available for benefits	$ 4,868,000

The accompanying notes are an integral part of the financial statements.

Source: FASB, SFAS No. 35, p. 128.

Figure 11-14

C&H COMPANY PENSION PLAN

Statement of Changes in Accumulated Plan
Benefits and Net Assets Available for Benefits

	Year Ended December 31, 1981
Net Increase in Actuarial Present Value of Accumulated Plan Benefits:	
Increase (decrease) during the year attributable to:	
Plan amendment (Note G)	$2,410,000
Change in actuarial assumptions [note B(2)]	(1,050,500)
Benefits accumulated	895,000
Increase for interest due to the decrease in the discount period [note B(2)]	742,500
Benefits paid	(997,000)
Net increase	2,000,000
Net Increase in Net Assets Available for Benefits:	
Investment income:	
Net appreciation in fair value of investments (note E)	207,000
Interest	345,000
Dividends	130,000
Rents	55,000
	737,000
Less investment expenses	39,000
	698,000
Contributions (note C):	
Employer	780,000
Employees	450,000
	1,230,000
Total additions	1,928,000
Benefits paid directly to participants	740,000
Purchases of annuity contracts (note F)	257,000
	997,000
Administrative expenses	65,000
Total deductions	1,062,000
Net increase	866,000

Figure 11-14 (continued)

Increase in excess of actuarial present value of accumulated plan benefits over net assets available for benefits	1,134,000
Excess of actuarial present value of accumulated plan benefits over net assets available for benefits:	
Beginning of year	3,734,000
End of year	$ 4,868,000

The accompanying notes are an integral part of the financial statements.

Source: FASB, SFAS No. 35, p. 129.

then requires extensive additional footnote disclosures, many of which relate to FASB *Statement 35* statement data or footnote disclosures. Among the provisions of NCGA *Interpretation 4* are:

- Equity securities shall be reported at lower of cost or market, but debt securities are to be reported at amortized cost.

- Fixed assets are to be reported at cost and depreciated over their estimated useful lives.

- The difference between PTF assets and liabilities (usually short-term) shall be reported as Fund Balance.

- The *notes to the financial statements* shall include:

  (1) A description of the PERS or PTF accounting policies and disclosure of the significant assumptions and methods, including interest rate assumptions, used to determine the actuarial present value of accumulated plan benefits.

  (2) Information on the actuarial present value of accumulated plan benefits, computed in accordance with FASB *Statement 35,* including:
      (a) vested benefits of participants receiving payments,
      (b) vested benefits of current employees, and
      (c) nonvested accumulated benefits of current employees.
      In addition, anticipated increases in vested accumulated benefits based on *projected* salary increases from the current period to retirement shall be disclosed. (This differs from FASB *Statement 35.*)

  (3) Disclosure of the factors which affect the actuarial present value of accumulated benefits—as a minimum, including the date of actuarial valuation and the effects of:
      (a) plan amendments
      (b) changes in the nature of the plan, and
      (c) changes in actuarial assumptions.

  (4) The market value of both debt and equity securities, at both the balance sheet and actuarial valuation dates, and investments in any organization that are five percent or more of the net assets available for benefits.

(5) The government's policy for funding its accrued pension obligations and the extent to which it is implementing that policy.[12]

The Future.   The foregoing and other differences are being considered by the NCGA and FASB and will be considered by the GASB. For the interim, the NCGA asked that NCGA principles be followed. But those governments that are audited by independent accountants will doubtless find that their auditors will tend to favor the FASB's pronouncement, and at least some governments are willing to follow it. Some PERS report in accordance with the NCGA requirements and also make the disclosures required by FASB *Statement 35*. This is a sound interim solution to the problem.

The Government and Its Pension Obligation

The chapter's presentation of the PTF has focused on the accounting for the system—the fund. Another question related to pensions is: What disclosures are needed for the pension obligations of the government? Does NCGA's version of GAAP provide the information a user needs? NCGA apparently assumed that the PTF statements (including footnotes) provide sufficient data. The PTF statements are recommended for inclusion in "Combined Balance Sheets," "Combined Statements of Revenues, Expenses, and Changes in Retained Earnings/Fund Balances—All Proprietary Fund Types," and "Combined Statement of Changes in Financial Position—All Proprietary Fund Types and Similar Trust Funds."[13]

The illustrations cited above include no indication of the governmental unit's pension liability except for the PTF "Fund Balance" figure, which is shown to have a deficit. Presumably this is the actuarial deficiency—the amount by which the governmental unit has failed to contribute the proper amount to the PTF.

There is a question, now under consideration by NCGA, as to the propriety of including PTF financial statements in the financial statements of the government. What is the entity? The PTF has, essentially, an accounting equation of "assets equal liabilities," which is that of Agency Funds. If the PTF is not under the jurisdiction of the responsible officials of the governmental unit, why should the PTF be considered part of the governmental unit entity?

Clearly, if the PERS is a separate entity, (1) its PTF financial statements should not be presented with those of the governmental unit and (2) the governmental unit should provide information about the status and operation of its pension plan(s) in *its own* financial statements—presumably in the General Long-Term Debt Account Group and in the notes to its financial statements.

The FASB has issued a statement entitled "Disclosure of Pension Information"[14] in which it addresses the problem of employers' disclosures of information about their pension plans. SFAS No. 36 is not intended to apply to state and local governmental units, perhaps because of the inclusion of PTF statements in the CAFR and GPFS of governmental units. But financial reports of defined benefit pension plans are not considered to be part of the financial reports of

[12] NCGA *Interpretation 4*.
[13] NCGAS 1, pp. 30–32, 36–39. See Chapter 14.
[14] Financial Accounting Standards Board, *Statement of Financial Accounting Standards No. 36* (Stamford, Conn.: FASB, 1980).

business enterprises and may in some cases not be proper parts of financial statements of the governmental unit.

The FASB position with respect to disclosure of pension information in the financial statements of business enterprises is as follows:

The Board believes that pension plans are of sufficient importance to an understanding of financial position and results of operations that the disclosures set forth in this paragraph and paragraph 8 shall be made in financial statements or the notes thereto:

a. A statement that pension plans exist, identifying or describing the employee groups covered,
b. A statement of the company's accounting and funding policies,
c. The provision for pension cost for the period,
d. Nature and effect of significant matters affecting comparability for all periods presented, such as changes in accounting methods (actuarial cost method, amortization of past and prior service cost, treatment of actuarial gains and losses, etc.), changes in circumstances (actuarial assumptions, etc.), or adoption or amendment of a plan.

For its defined benefit pension plans, an employer shall disclose for each complete set of financial statements the following data determined in accordance with Statement 35 as of the most recent benefit information date* for which the data are available:

a. The actuarial present value of vested accumulated plan benefits,
b. The actuarial present value of nonvested accumulated plan benefits,
c. The plans' net assets available for benefits,†
d. The assumed rates of return used in determining the actuarial present values of vested and nonvested accumulated plan benefits,
e. The date as of which the benefit information was determined.[15]

*The benefit information date is the date as of which the actuarial present value of accumulated plan benefits is determined. In comparative financial statements, data disclosed for earlier periods shall be the data available when the earlier financial statements were originally issued.
† For purposes of this Statement, an employer's accrued pension liability, as of the benefit information date, shall be added to the plan's net assets to the extent that it exceeds contributions receivable from the employer included in the plan's net assets available for benefits.

The discussion of *Statements 35* and *36* presented here is not intended to be exhaustive. Rather, the intent is to indicate the unsettled state of accounting for PERS and PTFs and some of the variations of accounting thought and treatment that presently exist and are under consideration for the future.

▶ **Question 11-1.** Trust Funds and Agency Funds, though separate fund types, are treated in the same chapter in this text and are often spoken of collectively as "Trust and Agency" Funds. In what ways are they similar and how do they differ?

[15] Ibid., Paragraphs 7, 8.

Question 11-2. Compare the primary forms of accountability as among (1) the General and Special Revenue Funds, (2) Capital Projects and Special Revenue Funds, and (3) Trust and Agency Funds.

Question 11-3. A single trust agreement often gives rise to two separate Trust Funds. When is this so, and may a single trust agreement result in the establishment of three, four, or more separate funds?

Question 11-4. In certain situations an Expendable (governmental) Trust Fund may be virtually identical to a Special Revenue Fund and should be budgeted and accounted for as though it were a Special Revenue Fund. Explain.

Question 11-5. What is the difference between a Nonexpendable (proprietary) Trust Fund and an Agency Fund?

Question 11-6. Accounting for separate Trust and Agency Funds on a "funds within a fund" approach was not illustrated in this chapter. Is it possible and/or permissible to account for more than one type of trust or agency relationship within a single Trust or Agency Fund?

Question 11-7. Classify the following as to whether they are governmental (Expendable) Trust Funds, proprietary (Nonexpendable) Trust Funds, or Agency Funds:

(a) A fund established to handle tax collections by a governmental unit for other governments

(b) A pension fund

(c) A loan fund

(d) A fund whose principal is to be held intact but whose income must be expended for bravery awards

(e) A fund established to handle deposits

(f) A fund established to handle that part of the proceeds from the sale of property for taxes which is to be refunded to the property owner

(g) A fund whose principal and income are both to be used in granting scholarships

Question 11-8. How do the Trust and Agency Funds discussed in this chapter differ from those of business enterprises?

Question 11-9. A county's fee officers (sheriff, county clerk, etc.) deposit their collections with the county treasurer. Once a month, the county auditor determines the accounts to which such collections apply and makes the proper entries. Most of these collections apply to the General Fund, but some of them apply also to other funds. (a) Should these collections, pending their allocation, be handled through the General Fund or a Trust or Agency Fund? (b) Assuming that they are handled through the General Fund, what entry should be made in that fund (1) when the money is collected and (2) when the allocation is made? Assume that $14,000 applies to the General Fund and $1,000 to other funds.

Question 11-10. Although Fund Balance and Reserve accounts may be used in Trust and Agency Funds, they may actually be *liability* accounts. Explain.

Question 11-11. Taxes for Sanitary District R are collected by the County of C. The county clerk maintains the records of the individual taxpayers and enters in them the amount due from each taxpayer. For rendering this service, the clerk is permitted to add to each taxpayer's bill 2 cents for each governmental unit. For example, if a taxpayer is charged with taxes for the county, city, and sanitary district, 6 cents is added to his bill. Taxes are collected by the county treasurer, who is allowed a fee of 2 percent of the amount collected. Before transmitting the proceeds of any collections to a governmental unit, the treasurer deducts the county clerk's fee and his own fee. (a) Should the county clerk's fee be included as part of the sanitary district's tax levy? If not, should such fee be recorded at all on the sanitary district's books? (b) Should the treasurer's fees be included as part of the tax levy of the sanitary district? How would you treat such fees on the sanitary district's books?

Question 11-12. Why might the Balance Sheet prepared for a Pension Trust Fund report a Fund Balance *deficit* when it also reports assets far in excess of the amount shown as Pensions Payable?

Question 11-13. What is the difference between a Special Assessment Fund and a private Trust Fund?

Question 11-14. Why might a governmental unit establish a Pooled Investments Fund? What types of policies and procedures should be set forth clearly and adhered to consistently with regard to a fund of this sort?

Question 11-15. In what respects are a Pension Trust Fund and a Debt Service Sinking Fund similar and in what respects do they differ? (Assume that both are actuarially based and that budgetary entries are made in the accounts of both at the beginning of each year.)

Question 11-16. How might *internal* (interfund or intragovernmental) Agency Funds be used to facilitate a governmental unit's financial management and accounting processes?

Question 11-17. In accounting for a Tax Agency Fund, why is it necessary to maintain records of taxes levied and collected for each taxing authority involved by year of levy?

Question 11-18. According to the terms of A's will, the city is to become the owner of an apartment building. The net income from the building is to be added to the Policemen's Pension Fund. (a) Is this a governmental or proprietary trust fund? (b) Suppose that, in computing net income, the city does not take depreciation into account. Is the fund governmental or proprietary?

Question 11-19. The earnings of a proprietary (nonexpendable as to corpus) Trust Fund are used to support the operation of a municipal museum, art gallery, and park complex. Should these activities be accounted for through the General Fund, a Special Revenue Fund, or a Trust Fund?

Question 11-20. Should the financial statements of the PERS and PTFs be included in the combined statements issued as the GPFS of the governmental unit?

Question 11-21. A trust indenture states that the principal (corpus) of the trust is to be maintained intact in perpetuity. Yet, although the governmental trustee did not violate the terms of the trust agreement—and it was not subsequently revised—the principal (corpus) had decreased to less than half its original amount five years after the trust was created. Why or how might this have happened?

Question 11-22. How can the reader of a set of financial statements of a PERS PTF determine the governmental unit's liability for actuarial benefits under the system? If the statements of the PERS PTF are not included in the GPFS, how would the reader of the latter determine the city's liability for that actuarial deficit?

▶ **Problem 11-1.** Prepare the general journal entries required to record the following transactions in the general ledgers of the State, the County General Fund, and the County Tax Agency Fund. You may omit formal entry explanations, but should key the entries to the numbered items in this problem.

1. The County Tax Agency Fund has been established to account for the county's duties of collecting the county and state property taxes. The levies for the year 19X0 were $600,000 for the County General Fund and $480,000 for the state. It is expected that uncollectible taxes will be $10,000 for the state and $15,000 for the county.

2. Collections were $300,000 for the county and $240,000 for the state.

3. The county is entitled to a fee of 1 percent of taxes collected for other governments. The county sends the state the amount due.

4. The fee is transmitted from the Tax Agency Fund to the County General Fund.

5. Uncollectible taxes in the amount of $5,000 for the state and $6,000 for the county are written off.

Problem 11-2. The following is a trial balance of the Tax Agency Fund of the City of F as of June 30, 19X0:

Cash	$ 90,000	
Taxes Receivable for County X	22,500	
Taxes Receivable for City Y	48,000	
Taxes Receivable for School District Z	69,000	
Taxes Fund Balance—County X		$ 37,500
Taxes Fund Balance—City Y		78,000
Taxes Fund Balance—School District Z		114,000
	$229,500	$229,500

The following transactions took place:

1. Cash in the amount of $89,400 was paid over as follows:

Unit	Amount Due	Collection Fee	Amount Paid Over
X	$15,000	$100	$14,900
Y	30,000	200	29,800
Z	45,000	300	44,700

2. The collection fees were paid over to the General Fund.
3. Taxes were levied as follows:

Unit	Amount Levied
X	$ 50,000
Y	100,000
Z	150,000

Required:

(a) Prepare journal entries.
(b) Post to T-accounts.
(c) Prepare a Balance Sheet as of November 30, 19X0.
(d) **Or** prepare a worksheet from which requirement (c) might easily be fulfilled.

Problem 11-3. The City of Robinsburg collects, in addition to its own taxes, those of other units. The following are the tax levies for 19X1 and 19X2:

	19X1	19X2
City	$220,800	$249,000
School District	144,000	160,000
Park District	115,200	100,000
	$480,000	$500,000

Collections during 19X2 were as follows:

19X1 levy	$ 67,000
19X2 levy	464,000

The city tax levies are in turn distributed among the following funds:

Fund	Mills per Dollar of Assessed Value	
	19X1	19X2
General	8.76	8.51
Library	1.44	1.61
Debt Retirement	1.80	1.38
Total	12.00	11.50

Required:

(a) Compute the amount of the collection of each levy applicable to each governmental unit.

(b) Compute the amount of the collection from each city levy applicable to each city fund. (Assume that no collection fee is charged against City tax collections.)

(c) Prepare the journal entry to be made on the city's books to record the collection of taxes in 19X2 (that is, the collection of 19X1 and 19X2 taxes in 19X2).

(d) Assuming that the municipality charges a fee of 2 percent for collecting other units' taxes, prepare the entry to record on the city's books the collection of the fee and its payment to the General Fund. Prepare also an entry to record the transmittal of the money to the other units (districts) for which it is collected by the city.

(e) Prepare the entries to be made transmitting the city's collections to the proper city funds and the entries in each fund.

Problem 11-4. Prepare journal entries to record the following transactions:

1. Property A was sold for unpaid taxes covering 19X4 and 19X5 levies and interest and penalties, as follows:

Levy of	Taxes	Interest and Penalties
19X5	$7,500	$750
19X4	6,200	940

The cost of holding the sale was $65, and the property was sold for $17,500.

2. The taxpayer redeemed the property promptly; no additional penalties or interest were assessed.

3. Assume the same facts as in the first transaction except that the property was sold for $12,000.

4. Assume the same facts as in the first transaction except that the governmental unit bid in the property. (Note: Set up an allowance for estimated losses on tax sale certificates through debiting Allowance for Uncollectible Delinquent Taxes, $750, and Allowance for Uncollectible Interest and Penalties, $65.)

5. The governmental unit decided to use the property for recreational purposes. The taxes all belonged to the General Fund. (Assume that the salable value of the property is 85 percent of the amount of the tax sale certificate.)

Problem 11-5. The following is a trial balance of the Policemen's Retirement Fund of the City of Cherrydale at January 1, 19X0:

Cash	$ 6,000	
Interest Receivable	450	
Investments	52,000	
Pensions Payable		$ 150
Reserve for Employee Contributions ...		20,100
Reserve for Employer Contributions ...		22,200
Actuarial Deficiency—Reserve for Employer Contributions		15,000
Reserve for Retiree Pensions		16,000
Fund Balance (Deficit)		(15,000)
	$58,450	$58,450

The following transactions took place during the year:

1. Contributions became due from the General Fund, $38,000, and a Special Revenue Fund, $6,000. One-half of these amounts represents the employees' share of contributions.

2. Payments were received from the General Fund, $30,000, and the Special Revenue Fund, $4,000.

3. Securities were acquired for cash as follows:

a. First Purchase:	
Par Value	$20,000
Premiums	300
Interest accrued at purchase	200
b. Second Purchase:	
Par Value	15,000
Discounts	150

4. Interest received on investments amounted to $3,000, including interest receivable on January 1, 19X0, and the accrued interest purchased.

5. Premiums and discounts in the amounts of $50 and $30, respectively, were amortized.

6. An employee retired whose contributions and interest earnings since employment were $500. Employer contributions in his behalf vested in the amount of

$1,000; and his retirement annuity formula was determined to have a present value of $1,500.

7. An employee resigned prior to retirement and was paid $300, which is the amount of his contributions and interest thereon. Employer contributions do not vest until retirement.

8. Retirement payments of $500 were made; these included the 1/1/X0 accrual.

9. An actuary indicated that the actuarial deficiency at year end was $19,000.

10. The Plan states that all earnings of the fund must be allocated among the three funded reserve accounts according to the beginning balance in the accounts.

Required:

(a) Prepare a worksheet with columns for beginning trial balance, transactions and adjustments, ending trial balance, closing entries, and postclosing trial balance
or

(b) Prepare journal entries, including closing entries, and post to T-accounts.

(c) Prepare a Policemen's Retirement Fund balance sheet as of December 31, 19X0; a statement of revenues, expenses, and changes in fund balance; a statement of changes in financial position; and an analysis of changes in retirement reserves. The last three statements are for the year ended December 31, 19X0.

Problem 11-6. The following is a trial balance of the Public Employees Retirement Fund of Smith City:

Cash	$ 76,000	
Due from General Fund	12,000	
Interest Receivable	14,200	
Investments	1,450,000	
Unamortized Premiums on Investments	6,000	
Due to Resigned Employees		$ 14,500
Due to Estates of Deceased Employees		3,000
Annuities Payable		1,700
Reserve for Employee Contributions		840,000
Reserve for Employer Contributions		360,000
Actuarial Deficiency—Reserve for Employer Contributions		480,000
Reserve for Retirement Annuities		339,000
Fund Balance (Deficit)		(480,000)
	$1,558,200	$1,558,200

The employees' contributions are returned to them or to their estate upon resignation or death, respectively; vesting of employer's matching contributions occurs only at retirement. Interest revenue is apportioned equally among the reserve accounts.

During 19X4 the following transactions occurred:

1. Employees' contributions are 6 percent of gross payroll. The city's annual gross payroll for 19X4 was $2,000,000.

2. The General Fund paid $200,000 to the PERS.

3. Interest accrued in the amount of $169,000; $1,000 of premium was amortized.

4. Interest receivable of $168,400 was collected.

5. Three employees retired; their contributions were determined to have been $45,000.

6. Five employees resigned; their contributions were determined to have been $24,000. Two employees died prior to retirement; their contributions were determined to have been $36,000.

7. Checks mailed to retired employees during the year amounted to $34,500. Checks mailed to the estates of deceased employees totaled $33,000.

8. Annuities were accrued in the amount of $63,000; annuities in the amount of $62,700 were paid.

9. Additional investments were made as follows:

Bonds (at par)	$160,000
Accrued interest	30,000
Discounts	(8,000)
	$182,000

10. An actuary's report showed that the actuarial deficiency at year end was $520,000.

Required:

(a) Prepare a worksheet, or journal entries and T-accounts, showing transactions, adjustments, and closing entries for the Retirement Fund for 19X4.

(b) Prepare a PERF balance sheet as of December 31, 19X4; a Statement of Changes in Financial Position; Statement of Revenues, Expenses, and Changes in Fund Balance; and a statement analyzing changes in reserve accounts for the year ended December 31, 19X4.

Problem 11-7. The following is a trial balance of the Child Welfare Principal Trust Fund of the City of Sweeney Bluff as of January 1, 19X3:

Cash	$ 98,000	
Land	70,000	
Buildings	162,000	
Accumulated Depreciation		$65,000
Accrued Wages Payable		150
Accrued Taxes Payable		1,800
Due to Child Welfare Earnings Trust Fund		15,000
Fund Balance—Trust Principal		248,050
	$330,000	$330,000

The endowment was in the form of an apartment building. Endowment principal is to be kept intact, and the net earnings are to be used in financing child welfare activities.

The following transactions took place during the year:

1. Expenses and accrued liabilities paid in cash were as follows:

Heat, light, and power	$ 5,200
Janitor's wages (including $150 previously accrued)	3,000
Painting and decorating	3,750
Repairs	1,500
Taxes (including $1,800 previously accrued) ..	3,750

Management fees	4,500	
Miscellaneous expenses	1,500	
	$23,200	

2. A special assessment of $2,000 levied by the municipality against the property was paid.
3. Rents for 19X3 (all collected) amounted to $45,000.
4. The amount due to the Child Welfare Earnings Trust Fund at January 1, 19X3, was paid.
5. Expenditures of $15,000 were paid from the Child Welfare Earnings Trust Fund to finance 19X3 summer camp activities.
6. The following adjustments were made at the close of the year:

Depreciation	$6,000
Accrued Taxes	1,900
Accrued Wages	170

Required:

(a) Prepare a balance sheet as of December 31, 19X3, and a Statement of Revenues, Expenses, and Changes in Fund Balance for the fiscal year ended December 31, 19X3, for the Child Welfare Principal Trust Fund. (Support these statements with a worksheet, T-account, or other analysis.)

(b) Prepare a balance sheet as of December 31, 19X3, for the Child Welfare Earnings Trust Fund, and a Statement of Revenues, Expenditures, and Changes in Fund Balance for the year then ended. (Assume that the Child Welfare Earnings Trust Fund had no activities or balances other than those indicated in the problem.)

Problem 11-8. The city of New Arnheim has engaged you to examine the following Balance Sheet which was prepared by the city's bookkeeper:

CITY OF NEW ARNHEIM
Balance Sheet
June 30, 19X9

Assets

Cash	$ 159,000
Taxes receivable—current	32,000
Supplies on hand	9,000
Marketable securities	250,000
Land	1,000,000
Fixed assets	7,000,000
Total	$8,450,000

Liabilities

Vouchers payable	$ 42,000
Reserve for supplies inventory	8,000
Bonds payable	3,000,000
Fund balance	5,400,000
Total	$8,450,000

Your audit disclosed the following information:

1. An analysis of the Fund Balance account:

Balance, June 30, 19X8		$2,100,000
Add:		
Donated land	$ 800,000	
Federal grant-in-aid	2,200,000	
Creation of endowment fund	250,000	
Excess of actual tax revenue over estimated revenue	24,000	
Excess of appropriations closed out over expenditures and encumbrances	20,000	
Net income from endowment funds .	10,000	3,304,000
		$5,404,000
Deduct:		
Excess of Cultural Center operating expenses over income		4,000
		$5,400,000
Balance, June 30, 19X9		

2. In July 19X8 land appraised at a fair market value of $800,000 was donated to the city for a cultural center which was opened on April 15, 19X9. Building construction expenditures for the project were financed from a Federal grant-in-aid of $2,200,000 and from an authorized ten-year $3,000,000 issue of 6 percent general obligation bonds sold at par on July 1, 19X8. Interest is payable on December 31 and June 30. The fair market value of the land and the cost of the building are included, respectively, in the Land and Fixed Assets accounts.

3. The cultural center receives no direct state or city subsidy for current operating expenses. A Cultural Center Endowment Fund was established by a gift of marketable securities having a fair market value of $250,000 at date of receipt. The endowment principal is to be kept intact. Income is to be applied to any operating deficit of the center.

4. Other data:

a. It is anticipated that $7,000 of the 19X8–19X9 tax levy is uncollectible.

b. The physical inventory of supplies on hand at June 30, 19X9, amounted to $12,500.

c. Unfilled purchase orders for the General Fund at June 30, 19X9, totaled $5,000.

d. On July 1, 19X8, an all-purpose building was purchased for $2,000,000. Of the purchase price, $200,000 was allotted to the land. The purchase had been authorized under the budget for the year ended June 30, 19X9.

Required:

(a) Prepare a worksheet showing adjustments and distributions to the proper funds or account groups. The worksheet should be in the form of the City of New Arnheim's balance sheet and have the following column headings:

Column(s)	Headings
1	Balance per Books
2–3	Adjustments—Debit —Credit

Column(s)	Headings
4	General Fund
5–6	City Cultural Center Endowment Fund: Principal Revenues
7	General Fixed Assets
8	General Long-Term Debt

Number all adjusting entries. (Formal journal entries are not required.) Supporting computations should be in good form.

(b) Assuming that the amounts reflected in the Balance Sheet above were all in the General Fund, prepare the formal entry required, in compound form, to correct the accounts of the General Fund at June 30, 19X9.

(AICPA, adapted)

Problem 11-9, Part I. Cultura Township had not been operating a public library prior to October 1, 19X1. On October 1, 19X1, James Jones died, having made a valid will that provided for the gift of his residence and various securities to the town for the establishment and operations of a free public library. The gift was accepted, and the library funds and operation were placed under the control of trustees. The terms of the gift provided that not in excess of $5,000 of the principal of the fund could be used for the purchase of equipment, building rearrangement, and purchase of such "standard" library reference books as, in the opinion of the trustees, were needed for starting the library. Except for this $5,000, the principal of the fund is to be invested and the income therefrom used to operate the library in accordance with appropriations made by the trustees. The property received from the estate by the trustees was as follows:

Description	Face or Par	Appraised Value
Residence of James Jones:		
Land		$ 2,500
Building (25-year estimated life)		20,000
Bonds:		
AB Company	$34,000	32,000
C & D Company	10,000	11,200
D & G Company	20,000	20,000
Stocks:		
M Company, 6% preferred	12,000	12,600
S Company, 5% preferred	10,000	9,600
K Company, common (300 shares)	No par	12,900
GF Company (200 shares)	4,000	14,500

The following events occurred in connection with the library operations up to June 30, 19X2:

1. 100 shares of GF Company stock were sold on November 17, for $6,875.
2. Cash payments were made for: (a) Alteration of the house—$1,310, (b) General reference books—$725, (c) Equipment having an estimated life of ten years—$2,180. The trustees state that these amounts are to be charged to principal under the applicable provision of the gift.

3. The library started operation on January 1, 19X2. The trustees adopted the following budget for the year ended December 31, 19X2:

Estimated income from Trust Principal Fund earnings transfer	$5,000
Estimated income from fines, etc.	200
Appropriation for salaries	3,600
Appropriation for subscriptions	300
Appropriation for purchase of books	800
Appropriation for utilities, supplies, etc.	400

4. The following cash receipts were reported during the six months to June 30, 19X2:

a. Sale of C and D Company bonds, including accrued interest of $80	$11,550
b. Interest and dividends	3,100
c. Fines	20
d. Gift for purchase of books	200
Total	$14,870

5. The following cash payments were made during the six months to June 30, 19X2:

a.	Purchase of 100 shares of no-par common stock of L and M Company, including commission and tax cost of $50	$ 9,655
b.	Payment of salaries	1,500
c.	Payment of property taxes applicable to the year ended December 31, 19X1 based on an assessment as of June 30, 19X1	200
d.	Purchase of books	900
e.	Magazine subscriptions	230
f.	Supplies and other expense	260
	Total	$12,745

6. On June 30, 19X2, there were miscellaneous library expenses unpaid, but accrued, amounting to $90. Also there were outstanding purchase orders for books in the amount of $70.

Required:

Assuming that the township records budgetary accounts with respect to library operations, prepare in detail the worksheet(s) necessary to show the results of operations to June 30, 19X2, and the financial position of the Trust Fund(s) related to the library as of June 30, 19X2. Where alternative treatments of an item are acceptable, explain the alternative treatments and state the justification for your treatment. In designing your worksheet(s), you should observe the requirements of Part II of this problem in order that those requirements may be fulfilled readily from the worksheet(s) prepared here.

Problem 11-9, Part II. From the worksheet(s) prepared in Part I, construct the following formal statements relative to Cultura Township's library endowment and library operations:

(a) A Balance Sheet(s) for the Trust Fund(s) at June 30, 19X2.

(b) A Statement of Revenues, Expenditures, and Changes in Fund Balance—Budget and Actual—for the Library Endowment Earnings Trust Fund for the six months ended June 30, 19X2.

(c) A detailed Analysis of Changes in Fund Balance with respect to the trust principal for the nine-month period ended June 30, 19X2.

Problem 11-10. The City of Linde, organized on January 1, 19X1, has never kept accounts on a double-entry system. During 19X8 the city council employed you to install a system of accounts. You made a study and determined the values of assets and liabilities in order to inaugurate the proper system as of January 1, 19X9, the beginning of the city's fiscal year, as follows:

1.	City taxes receivable—19X8 and prior years (including 10 percent considered uncollectible)	$ 21,900
2.	Investment in securities:	
	a. Earmarked to bond retirement	136,680
	b. Donated by J. Stark on July 1, 19X8, the net income from which is to supplement library operations. The cost of all the stock to Stark was $50,000. Appraised value on July 1	65,400
3.	Cash:	
	a. For general operations, including $3,000 petty cash	18,000
	b. Earmarked to investments for bond retirement (represents interest earned over the actuarial estimate)	840
	c. Balance of cash donated by J. Stark, the net income from which is to supplement library operations	12,000
	d. Undistributed balance of cash received from J. Stark investments and apartment rents	3,000
4.	Buildings:	
	a. For general operations	235,000
	b. Apartment building donated by J. Stark on July 1, 19X8. Net rental income before depreciation is to be used in the operation of the library. Cost to Stark, July 1, 19X0, $96,000 (exclusive of cost of land); estimated life of 50 years, with no salvage value. Appraised value on July 1, 19X8	90,000
5.	Equipment:	
	a. For general use	280,000
	b. Apartment furniture purchased with donated cash, October 1, 19X8; estimated life ten years, with no salvage value. Cost	36,000
6.	Streets and curbs financed by special assessments levied in prior years (all collected). The city contributed one-third of the cost	300,000
7.	Land:	
	a. General use	60,000
	b. Apartment building site	10,000

8. Supplies:
    a. For general operation 1,800
    b. For apartment house operation, purchased by income
       cash 300
    c. Originally purchased for general operation, transferred
       to and used in library operations; no settlement has
       been made 2,400
9. Vouchers payable—for general operations 16,000
10. Five percent 30-year bonds payable, issued at par on Jan-
    uary 1, 19X6 (for purchase of land, buildings, and
    equipment) 400,000

Required:

List the funds or account group titles that would be required for the City of Linde on the basis of the above information, leaving at least fifteen lines between each title. Under each title make one summary journal entry to record all of the required accounts and amounts as of December 31, 19X8. You may omit formal entry explanations, but you should state any assumptions made and show calculations, as appropriate.

(AICPA, adapted)

Problem 11-11. Prepare a columnar analytical worksheet to serve as a basis upon which an appropriate double-entry accounting system may be established for the City of Linde (Problem 11-10). Use these headings.

Worksheet Column(s)	Heading
Date/Reference	Key
Account/Explanation	Account Titles
1–2	Combined Totals
3–4	General Fund
5–6	Proprietary (Principal) Trust Fund
7–8	Governmental (Earnings) Trust Fund
9–10	Debt Service Fund
11	General Fixed Assets Group
12	General Long-Term Debt Group

You are to cross-reference (key) your worksheet to the numbered and lettered items in Problem 11-10; other entries needed should be keyed A, B, C, etc.

12

INTERNAL
SERVICE
FUNDS

Internal Service (IS) Funds are established in order to finance, administer, and account for the provision of goods and services by one department of a government to its other departments (or to other governments) on a cost-reimbursement basis. The break-even objective has caused such funds to be referred to as "working capital" or "revolving" funds in many jurisdictions. This type of fund serves internal users primarily and should be distinguished from Enterprise Funds, through which provision of goods or services for compensation to the general public is financed and accounted for.

IS Funds are internal *intermediary* fiscal and accounting entities through which some of the expenditures of other departments are made. They are used (1) to attain greater economy, efficiency, and effectiveness in the acquisition and distribution of common goods or services utilized by several or all departments within the organization; and (2) to facilitate an equitable sharing of costs among the various departments served and, hence, among the funds of the organization. They may also be used to provide interim financing for Special Assessment and Capital Projects Funds.

Activities handled through IS Funds in practice vary widely both as to type and complexity of operation. Among the simpler types are those used (1) to distribute common or joint costs, such as the cost of telephone, two-way radio, or other communication facilities, among departments; (2) to acquire, distribute, and allocate costs of selected items of inventory, such as office supplies or gasoline; or (3) to provide temporary loans to other funds in deficit situations or prior to the receipt of debt issue or grant proceeds. Activities of a more complex nature accounted for through IS Funds include motor pools; data processing activities; duplicating and printing facilities; repair shops and garages; cement and asphalt plants; purchasing, warehousing, and distribution services; and insurance and other risk management services.

IS Funds are proprietary (nonexpendable) funds and their accounting is the same as that for a profit-seeking enterprise in the same business. They therefore use the accrual basis of accounting; their fixed assets are recorded in the Funds, as is any long-term debt for which they are responsible. Depreciation is recorded and net income or loss is computed. In short, they use the capital maintenance measurement focus of proprietary funds.

The full application of generally accepted financial accounting principles has the effect of facilitating the achievement of the Funds' typical objectives. First, the usual policy requires break-even pricing and the maintenance of the invested capital. Full information on revenues and expenses is essential to fulfilling this policy. Second, the Funds are usually created to provide goods or services at less cost than if they were procured commercially. Therefore, it is desirable to use full costing to provide appropriate information for the "make or buy" decision.

Failure to apply proper accounting may result in faulty decisions. For example, where all fixed assets utilized by the IS Fund activity are accounted for therein and are expected (properly or improperly) to be replaced through its resources, depreciation accounting results in the determination of full cost (historical) for reimbursement and other decision-making purposes. On the other hand, where only part of the fixed assets are capitalized in or to be replaced through the IS Fund—the balance usually being recorded in General Fixed Assets—depreciation is formally recorded *only* on these fixed assets in the IS Fund. The resultant "cost" in this latter case may be appropriate for purposes of reimbursement and maintenance of Fund capital, but it must be supplemented by depreciation expense data relative to non-IS Fund fixed assets if meaningful cost analyses and "make or buy" and similar decisions are to be made. As another example, consider the case of a machine shop in which special projects are undertaken for other departments. A department head, having seen a device advertised for $1,500, comes to the machine shop manager and asks for an estimate of the cost to manufacture the device. If the machine shop computes costs on the same basis as a private business, the department head receives a reply that permits an accurate direct comparison of total cost-to-produce with total cost-to-buy. But suppose that the machine shop has an appropriation that pays all labor costs and provides fixed assets for the shop and the manager computes the cost to the department head on the basis of direct materials cost plus a small percentage to cover minor overhead items. The department head will accept the lower price because it represents the lower charge to his own appropriation, but the total cost to the government may far exceed $1,500.

Finally, production of accurate cost data means that the departments that utilize the services of the IS Fund may be charged on an equitable basis for the cost of the services utilized. Recall again, however, that "reimbursable cost" and "full cost" may differ, e.g., where depreciation is not recorded on all fixed assets utilized by the IS Fund activities.

Cost Accounting in the IS Fund

The variety of activities that may be financed through an IS Fund indicates the variety of cost accounting systems that may be required for managerial control. Job order, process, or standard cost systems may be appropriate; the system used should produce accurate cost data and provide managerial control. Some of the simpler fundamental aspects of cost accounting systems are illustrated in Chapter 16; a more complete exposition is beyond the scope of this book.

Creation of the IS Fund

Ordinarily an IS Fund will be created by constitutional, charter, or legislative action, though the chief executive may be permitted by legislation to do so. Capital to finance IS Fund activities may come from appropriations from the General Fund, the issue of general bonds or other debt instruments, transfers from other funds, or advances from another government. Capital may also be augmented by confiscation of all, or excessive, inventories of materials and supplies that a fund's future "clients" (a governmental unit's departments) may have on hand at a specified time. Finally, IS Fund capital may be increased by setting prices which will produce a profit that is retained in the Fund.

If the General Fund provides permanent capital for the IS Fund, the following entries will be made:

ENTRY IN THE GENERAL FUND:

Residual Equity Transfer to IS Fund.	50,000	
Cash		50,000
To record capital provided to IS Fund.		

ENTRY IN THE IS FUND:

Cash	50,000	
Residual Equity Transfer from		
General Fund		50,000
To record receipt of capital		
from General Fund.		

If the General Fund is ultimately to be repaid from IS Fund resources, the following entries would be made rather than those above:

ENTRIES IN GENERAL FUND:

Advance to IS Fund	50,000	
Cash		50,000
To record capital advance to IS Fund.		

Fund Balance	50,000	
Reserve for Advance to IS Fund ...		50,000
To record reservation of fund		
balance because of advance to IS		
Fund.		

The terms "advance to" and "advance from" are used above rather than "due to" and "due from" to indicate intermediate- and long-term receivables and payables, whereas "due to" and "due from" connote short-term relationships. A reserve was established in the General Fund to indicate that the asset "Advance to IS Fund" does not represent currently appropriable resources.

If proceeds from the sale of bonds are transferred from a Capital Projects Fund to finance an IS Fund, the following entries will be made:

ENTRY IN CAPITAL PROJECTS FUND:
Residual Equity Transfer to IS Fund 100,000
 Cash   100,000
To record transfer of bond proceeds to provide IS Fund capital.

ENTRY IN IS FUND:
Cash 100,000
 Residual Equity Transfer from
  CP Fund   100,000
To record receipt of capital from sale of bonds.

Pricing Policies

The preceding discussions relative to pricing were based on the assumption that the prices charged by the IS Fund would be based on (historical) cost, and most authorities assume that cost is the proper pricing basis. Where IS Fund activities are very modest in scope and do not use full-time personnel or incur significant other costs, charges to user funds may be based on direct costs. This might be the case, for example, where (1) very limited group purchasing and warehousing is done only occasionally or as a small part of the overall purchasing operation, or (2) where the IS Fund is essentially a "flowthrough" or clearance device for common costs, such as two-way radio facility rentals. In the more usual case, however, the activity involves substantial amounts of personnel, space, materials, and other overhead costs that are recovered through billing user departments for more than the direct cost of the goods or services provided.

The IS Fund usually has a captive clientele, since in most governments the departments may not use another source of supply if a service or material is available through the IS Fund. This makes it possible for IS Fund prices to be set at levels that will produce profit or loss.

In some cases IS Fund capital has been built up by means of substantial annual profits. The increase in capital was paid for, of course, by the funds that financed the expenditures used to buy IS Fund services or supplies. There have even been instances in which the retained earnings of an IS Fund provided the basis for a cash "dividend" that was transferred as "revenue" to the General Fund. To the extent that IS Fund revenues were derived from departments financed by the General Fund, the profit thus transferred merely had the effect of offsetting excessive charges to it previously; but if departments or activities financed through other funds patronized the IS Fund, the effect of overcharging was to transfer resources from these other funds to the General Fund.

Use of IS Fund charges to divert restricted resources to other purposes cannot be condoned. Such practice erodes confidence in the organization's administrators and in the accounting system, constitutes indirect fraud at best, and at worst results in illegal usage of intergovernmental grant, trust, or other restricted resources.

Pricing Methods

The pricing method used by an IS Fund is usually based on estimates of total costs and total consumption of goods or services. From these two estimates a rate is developed which is applied to each purchase. If the cost of materials to be issued by a Stores Fund during the coming year was expected to be $300,000 and other costs of fund operation were estimated at $12,000, goods would be priced to departments at $1.04 for every $1.00 of direct cost of materials issued. Similarly, rental rates of automotive equipment may be based on time or mileage, or both. If a truck was expected to be driven 12,000 miles during the year at a total cost of $2,400, the departments would be charged $.20 per mile.

Where IS Fund charges to departments are based on predetermined price schedules, (1) IS Fund expenses are charged to appropriately titled expense accounts, and (2) IS Fund "sales" are credited to an account such as Billings to Departments and debited to a Due From (name) Fund account. Where goods or services provided are charged to user departments on the basis of direct cost plus estimated overhead, IS Fund overhead expenses incurred are debited to an Overhead account and amounts charged to user departments for overhead reimbursement are credited to Overhead or to an Overhead Applied account. The difference between overhead incurred and that billed to user departments during a period is referred to as "under-applied or -absorbed" or "over-applied or -absorbed" overhead.

The alternative to using predetermined rates such as those described in the preceding paragraphs is to charge the departments on the basis of actual costs determined at the end of each month, quarter, or year. Though this method is often used for uncomplicated IS Funds, a predetermined charge rate is generally used for more complex operations for the following reasons: (1) Some IS Fund expenses may not be determinable until the end of the month (or later), whereas it may be desirable to bill departments promptly so that they know how much expense or expenditure is charged to their jobs and activities at any time. (2) Charges based on actual monthly costs are likely to spread the burden unequally among departments. For example, assume that the costs of extensive equipment repairs made in June are included in the charges to the departments using the equipment during that month. In this situation, those departments that used the equipment in June would be billed for costs more properly allocated to several months or years, while the departments that used the equipment in previous or succeeding months would not bear their "fair share" of these costs. Furthermore, even if one department used the equipment throughout the year, charges based on actual monthly costs often would result in an unequitable distribution of costs among jobs and activities carried on by the department (as between June and other months in this example).

Relation to the Budget

The level of activity of an IS Fund will be determined by the demand of the user departments for its services. IS Fund appropriations are rarely made, and formal budgetary control is seldom introduced into IS Fund accounts, because

(1) the IS activity must be able to respond to service demands, not constrained by inflexible appropriation levels, and (2) the appropriations to the various user departments constitute an indirect budgetary ceiling on the IS activities.

Sound management requires that *flexible* budgetary techniques be employed in the planning and conduct of major IS Fund activities. Although the budget so developed may be formally approved, the expense element is not considered to have been appropriated. Budgetary control is exercised as in a business—the expenses incurred are compared with estimated expenses at the level of revenues actually earned.

Laws or custom in some cases prohibit the incurrence of obligations against or disbursement of cash from IS Funds without appropriation authority. Where this is the case, it is necessary to record not only those transactions that affect the actual position and operations of the fund (i.e., those transactions that affect the actual revenues, expenses, assets, liabilities, and capital) but also those relating to appropriations, expenditures, and encumbrances. Since this is the unusual case, rather than the usual one, the major examples that follow illustrate the accounting for proprietary accounts only; supplementary entries at the conclusion of the chapter illustrate the modifications necessary for budgetary accounting in IS Funds.

IS FUND ACCOUNTING ILLUSTRATED

Two illustrations of IS Fund activities, accounting, and reporting comprise the next section of this chapter. The Fund activities illustrated are a central automotive equipment operation and a Stores Fund.

A Central Automotive Equipment Unit

Assume that a Central Automotive Equipment Fund has been created and that some of the assets needed have been acquired. The IS Fund balance sheet prior to beginning operations is presented in Figure 12-1. Fund resources will

Figure 12-1

A GOVERNMENTAL UNIT

Central Automotive Equipment (IS) Fund
Balance Sheet
(Date)

Assets

Current assets:		
Cash		$ 75,000
Fixed assets:		
Land	$10,000	
Buildings	40,000	
Machinery and equipment	10,000	60,000
		$135,000

Contributed Capital

Contributed capital from General Fund	$135,000

be used to buy automobiles, trucks, tractors, and the like. The usage of each machine and the cost of operation on a per mile or per hour basis will be estimated and records of actual cost will be kept so that they may be compared with estimates and may be used in making estimates for coming years. Such records also are useful in making decisions concerning efficiency of management and economy of operation of various types and brands of equipment.

The following transactions and entries illustrate how a typical equipment bureau operates.

Transactions

1. Purchased equipment on credit for $40,000.
2. Materials and supplies purchased on credit, $10,000.
3. Salaries and wages paid, $19,000, distributed as follows:

Mechanics' Wages	$9,000
Indirect Labor	3,000
Superintendent's Salary	3,500
Office Salaries	3,500

4. Heat, light, and power paid, $2,000.
5. Depreciation:

Buildings	$2,400
Machinery and Equipment	9,200

6. Total billings to departments for services rendered, $42,800, of which $30,000 is chargeable to the General Fund and $12,800 is chargeable to the Enterprise Fund.
7. Vouchers payable in the amount of $42,500 were paid, of which $35,000 relates to the equipment purchased.
8. Office expenses paid, $200
9. Materials and supplies issued during the period, $7,000.
10. Accrued salaries and wages, $1,000, distributed as follows:

Mechanics' Wages	$500
Indirect Labor	150
Superintendent's Salary	175
Office Salaries	175

Entries

(1)	Machinery and Equipment	40,000	
	Vouchers Payable		40,000
	To record purchase of equipment.		
(2)	Inventory of Materials and Supplies	10,000	
	Vouchers Payable		10,000
	To record purchase of materials and supplies.		

(3)	Mechanics' Wages	9,000	
	Indirect Labor	3,000	
	Superintendent's Salary	3,500	
	Office Salaries	3,500	
	Cash		19,000
	To record salaries and wages expenses.		
(4)	Heat, Light, and Power	2,000	
	Cash		2,000
	To record heat, power, and light expenses.		
(5)	Depreciation—Buildings	2,400	
	Depreciation—Machinery and Equipment	9,200	
	Allowance for Depreciation— Buildings		2,400
	Allowance for Depreciation— Machinery and Equipment		9,200
	To record depreciation expenses.		
(6)	Due from General Fund	30,000	
	Due from Enterprise Fund	12,800	
	Billings to Departments*		42,800
	To record billings to departments.		
(7)	Vouchers Payable	42,500	
	Cash		42,500
	To record payment of vouchers payable.		
(8)	Office Expenses	200	
	Cash		200
	To record miscellaneous office expenses.		
(9)	Cost of Materials and Supplies Used	7,000	
	Inventory of Materials and Supplies ...		7,000
	To record cost of materials and supplies used.		
(10)	Mechanics' Wages	500	
	Indirect Labor	150	
	Superintendent's Salary	175	
	Office Salaries and Wages	175	
	Accrued Salaries and Wages Payable ..		1,000
	To record accrued salaries and wages.		

In the General Fund, Expenditures will be charged, while in the Enterprise Fund an expense or asset account will be charged. In both cases, the credit will be to Due to Central Automotive Equipment (Internal Service) Fund.

After these entries have been posted the trial balance of the accounts of the IS Fund will appear as follows:

Cash	11,300	
Due from General Fund	30,000	
Due from Enterprise Fund	12,800	
Inventory of Materials and Supplies	3,000	
Land	10,000	
Buildings	40,000	
Allowance for Depreciation—Buildings		2,400

Machinery and Equipment	50,000	
Allowance for Depreciation—Machinery and Equipment		9,200
Vouchers Payable		7,500
Accrued Salaries and Wages Payable		1,000
Contributed Capital from General Fund		135,000
Billings to Departments		42,800
Cost of Materials and Supplies Used	7,000	
Mechanics' Wages	9,500	
Indirect Labor	3,150	
Superintendent's Salary	3,675	
Depreciation—Buildings	2,400	
Depreciation—Machinery and Equipment	9,200	
Heat, Light, and Power	2,000	
Office Salaries	3,675	
Office Expenses	200	
	197,900	197,900

Closing entries may be made in a variety of methods. Some accountants prefer to make one compound entry closing all revenue and expense accounts directly to Retained Earnings. Others prefer a multiple-step approach through which (1) the various direct cost accounts are summarized in a single Direct Cost account, (2) the Direct Cost account and all other accounts are closed to a Cost of Services Rendered account, (3) the Cost of Services Rendered and Billings to Departments (and other revenue) accounts are closed to an Excess of Billings to Departments over Costs (or vice versa) account, and (4) the latter account is closed to Retained Earnings. Any reasonable closing entry or combination of entries will suffice that (1) updates the Retained Earnings account to its period end balance and (2) brings the temporary proprietary accounts to a zero balance so that they are ready for use during the succeeding period.

(11)	Billings to Departments	42,800	
	Cost of Materials and Supplies Used		7,000
	Mechanics' Wages		9,500
	Indirect Labor		3,150
	Superintendent's Salary		3,675
	Depreciation—Buildings		2,400
	Depreciation—Machinery and Equipment		9,200
	Heat, Light, and Power		2,000
	Office Salaries		3,675
	Office Expenses		200
	Excess of Net Billings to Departments over Costs		2,000
	To close revenue and expense accounts and determine the excess of net charges over costs of services for the period.		
(12)	Excess of Net Billings to Departments over Costs	2,000	
	Retained Earnings		2,000
	To close net income for the period to Retained Earnings.		

Figure 12-2

A GOVERNMENTAL UNIT

Central Automotive Equipment (IS) Fund
Balance Sheet
At Close of Fiscal Year (Date)

Assets

Current Assets:
Cash	$11,300	
Due from General Fund	30,000	
Due from Enterprise Fund	12,800	
Inventory of materials and supplies	3,000	$ 57,100

Fixed Assets:
Land		$10,000	
Buildings	$40,000		
Less: Accumulated depreciation .	2,400	37,600	
Machinery and equipment	$50,000		
Less: Accumulated depreciation .	9,200	40,800	88,400
Total assets			$145,500

Liabilities, Contributed Capital, and Retained Earnings

Liabilities:
Vouchers payable	$ 7,500	
Accrued salaries and wages payable	1,000	$ 8,500
Contributed capital from General Fund		135,000
Retained earnings (Figure 12-3)		2,000
Total liabilities, contributed capital, and retained earnings		$145,500

Figure 12-3

A GOVERNMENTAL UNIT

Central Automotive Equipment (IS) Fund
Statement of Revenues, Expenses, and
Changes in Retained Earnings
For (Period)

Billings to departments			$42,800
Less: Costs of materials and supplies used		$ 7,000	
Other operating costs:			
Mechanics' Wages	$9,500		
Indirect labor	3,150		
Superintendent's salary	3,675		
Depreciation—building	2,400		
Depreciation—machinery and equipment ..	9,200		
Heat, light, and power	2,000		
Office salaries	3,675		
Office expenses	200		
Total other operating costs		33,800	
Total cost of services rendered			40,800
Excess of billings to departments over costs			$ 2,000
Balance of retained earnings, beginning of period			0
Balance of retained earnings, end of period			$ 2,000

In Figures 12-2 to 12-5 are presented the Balance Sheet; the Statement of Revenues, Expenses, and Changes in Retained Earnings; and two Statements of Changes in Financial Position for the Central Automotive Equipment Fund based on the foregoing transactions. Note that the fixed assets of the Fund appear on the balance sheet with their related accumulated depreciation accounts. Since

Figure 12-4

A GOVERNMENTAL UNIT

Central Automotive Equipment (IS) Fund
Statement of Changes in (Working Capital) Financial Position
For (Period)

Source of working capital:		
Operations:		
Excess of billings to departments over cost		$ 2,000
Add, Expenses that did not require working capital:		
Depreciation of building	$2,400	
Depreciation of machinery and equipment	9,200	11,600
Resources provided by operations and total sources of working capital		$13,600
Use of working capital:		
Purchase of machinery		40,000
Net increase (decrease) in working capital		$(26,400)

	Increase (Decrease) in Working Capital
Changes in Components of Working Capital:	
Current assets:	
Cash	$(63,700)
Due from General Fund	30,000
Due from Enterprise Fund	12,800
Inventory of materials and supplies	3,000
Current liabilities:	
Vouchers payable	(7,500)
Accrued salaries and wages payable	(1,000)
Net increase (decrease) in working capital	$(26,400)

Note: This statement has been prepared to explain the sources and uses of "funds" defined as working capital. Another acceptable basis for its preparation is the cash concept—to explain the sources and uses of "funds" when "funds" are defined as cash. Such a statement is presented in Figure 12-5. Both the cash and working capital concepts are in conformity with GAAP; only one Statement of Changes in Financial Position should be presented.

Figure 12-5

A GOVERNMENTAL UNIT

Central Automotive Equipment (IS) Fund
Statement of Changes in (Cash) Financial Position
For the Year Ended (Date)

Cash, beginning of period (Figure 12-1)			$75,000
Cash was applied to:			
Operations—			
Excess of billings to departments over costs (Figure 12-3)		$ 2,000	
Adjustments to derive cash applied—			
Add: Depreciation expense	$11,600		
Increase in vouchers payable (operations)	2,500		
Increase in accrued salaries and wages payable	1,000		
	$15,100		
Less: Increase in billings receivable	$42,800		
Increase in inventories	3,000		
	$45,800		
Net adjustments—deduct		30,700	
Cash applied to operations			$28,700
Other applications—			
Purchase of equipment			35,000
Total cash applied (decrease in cash)			$63,700
Cash, end of period (Figure 12-2)			$11,300

departments are billed for overhead charges, including depreciation, part of the money received from departments represents depreciation charges. The money representing depreciation charges may be debited to a restricted cash account (set up in a separate "fund") to ensure its availability to replace assets; or it may be made part of the Fund's general cash and used for various purposes pending the replacement of the assets. In the present case, it is assumed that no segregation is made, nor is a retained earnings reserve established.

Long-term debt incurred for IS Fund purposes is not shown in the Fund balance sheet unless the resources of the Fund are to be used to service and retire the debt. Usually the debt will be paid out of general taxation or other sources, such as enterprise earnings in the case of IS Funds furnishing services to a utility department. However, if an IS Fund is dissolved, some of its assets may be used to retire outstanding debt.

The procedure described in this section applies to those cases where a central equipment bureau owns the equipment. However, the procedure would not be materially different if the equipment was owned by the individual departments or was classified in the General Fixed Assets category. In fact, the only difference is that billings to departments probably would be reduced by the amount of the depreciation charges. Depreciation should be computed in such an event; but the computation usually would be made primarily for statistical purposes, to determine the total cost (including depreciation) of operating each piece of equipment, and for determining total activity cost. Depreciation expense would not be formally recorded as part of the expenses of operating the central equipment bureau, nor would depreciation charges be included in the operating statement. No allowance for depreciation need be provided in such situations, but a record should be kept for each fixed asset indicating the cumulative amount of depreciation, based on the depreciation charges calculated for statistical purposes.

A Central Stores Fund

Another example of accounting for IS Fund transactions is to be found in a Central Stores Fund. Such a fund is established for the purpose of purchasing and storing materials for eventual distribution to departments; and, as in this example, departmental billings are usually based on direct inventory cost plus an overhead factor. To simplify the discussion it is again assumed that appropriations are not required for Fund expenditures.

The first step in the accounting process occurs here when an invoice for supplies of inventory items is approved for payment. At that time, an entry is made to record the purchase and to set up the liability. The entry is as follows:

Inventory of Materials and Supplies	20,000	
Vouchers Payable		20,000
To record the purchase of materials and supplies.		

Note that the debit is not made to a Purchases account but directly to an Inventory of Materials and Supplies account. The reason is that perpetual inventory records should be kept where a central storeroom is in operation.

Materials or supplies purchased for central storerooms are not charged against departmental appropriations until the materials or supplies are withdrawn from the storeroom. One procedure in withdrawing materials and charging appropriations is as follows: When a department needs materials, a stores requisition is prepared. This requisition is made out in duplicate (at least) and is presented to the storekeeper. The storekeeper issues the items called for on the requisition and has the employee receiving them sign one copy of the requisition. This copy is retained by the storekeeper as evidence that the materials have been withdrawn; it is also the basis for posting the individual stock records to reduce the amount shown to be on hand. Subsequently, individual items on the requisition are priced and the total cost of materials withdrawn on the particular requisition is computed. Sometimes requisitions are priced before they are filled, in order to see that the cost of materials requisitioned does not exceed a department's unencumbered appropriation, but this procedure is not always practicable.

In the perpetual inventory record, the unit cost should include the purchase price plus transportation expenses. If the IS Fund capital is to be kept intact, it is necessary also to recover overhead costs, such as the salary of the purchasing agent, wages of storekeepers, and amounts expended for heat, light, and power. As noted earlier, these expenses usually are allocated to each requisition based on a predetermined percentage of the cost of the materials withdrawn. The percentage is determined by dividing the estimated total stores overhead expenses by the total estimated cost of materials to be issued. Assuming that total stores overhead expenses for the forthcoming year are estimated to be $20,000 and that the cost of the materials to be withdrawn during the period is estimated at $500,000, the overhead rate applicable to materials issued is 4 percent ($20,000 ÷ $500,000). The amount of overhead to be charged upon the issue of materials that cost the Stores Fund $2,585 is $103.40 (4 percent of $2,585).

As soon as the requisition is priced, information is available for the purpose of billing the department withdrawing the materials. The entry to record the issue and billing is as follows:

Due from General Fund	2,688.40	
Inventory of Materials and Supplies .		2,585.00
Overhead Applied (or Overhead)		103.40
To record issuance of materials and supplies to Department of Public Works on Requisition 1405.		

Note that the General Fund is billed for both the cost of the materials and a portion of the estimated overhead expenses ($2,585.00 + $103.40). Alternatively, the gross Billings to Departments might be recorded and a Cost of Materials and Supplies Issued account used to record the direct cost of stores issued. The entry in this case would be:

Due from General Fund	2,688.40	
Cost of Materials and Supplies Issued ..	2,585.00	
Billings to Departments		2,688.40
Inventory of Materials and Supplies .		2,585.00
To record the billing and cost of materials issued to Department of Public Works on Requisition 1405.		

Entries to record actual overhead expenses in the IS Fund are made at the time the expenses are incurred, not at the time materials are issued. For example, at the time that storekeepers' salaries are approved for payment the following entry is made:

Overhead (or Operating Expenses)	1,000	
Vouchers Payable		1,000
To record storekeepers salaries. Subsidiary ledger: *Debit* Salaries and Wages, $1,000.		

At the end of the year, if overhead rates have been correctly estimated and the estimated operating level attained, the exact amount of overhead will have been recovered. Otherwise, the IS Fund will have either underabsorbed or overabsorbed overhead.

Under the system of accounting for materials described here, the inventory of materials and supplies on hand can be ascertained from the records at any time. To ensure that the materials and supplies shown by the records are actually on hand, a physical inventory should be taken at least annually. Usually the actual amount on hand will be smaller than the amount shown by the records. The variation may be due to such factors as shrinkage, breakage, theft, or improper recording. In any event, the records must be adjusted to correspond with the actual physical count by making entries on each perpetual inventory record affected. The Inventory of Materials and Supplies account in the general ledger must also be adjusted, of course. If the amounts according to physical count are less than the amounts shown on the records, the entry is as follows:

Overhead (or Operating Expenses)	2,000	
Inventory of Materials and Supplies .		2,000
To record inventory losses as		
revealed by actual physical count.		
Subsidiary ledger: *Debit* Inventory		
Losses, $2,000.		

Inventory losses must be recovered if the capital of the IS Fund is to be kept intact and should be taken into account in estimating the overhead expenses of the central storeroom for the purpose of establishing the overhead rate to be applied to requisitions.

Closing entries for the Stores Fund would parallel those illustrated earlier for the Central Automotive Equipment Fund. Similarly, a Balance Sheet, Statement of Revenues, Expenses, and Changes in Fund Balance, and Statement of Changes in Financial Position like those illustrated in Figures 12-2 to 12-5 should be prepared at least annually.

Thus far we have discussed the entries to be made in the IS Fund. Corresponding entries are, of course, made for the departments receiving the particular materials. In the case of a public works department, whose activities are financed from the General Fund, the entry is as follows:

Expenditures	2,688.40	
Due to IGS Fund		2,688.40
To record receipt of materials by the		
Department of Public Works and		
liability to IS Fund. Subsidiary ledger:		
Debit Department of Public Works,		
$2,688.40.		

Materials withdrawn by departments from a central storeroom and on hand in the departments at the close of the year should be treated the same as those acquired directly from vendors. Sometimes a storeroom system for a single department is financed through an IS Fund. Materials and supplies are accounted for in that case in the same manner as those handled through a central storeroom established for all departments.

DISPOSITION OF PROFIT OR LOSS

The necessity of basing charges to departments on estimates means that in the usual case an IS Fund, even one that is intended to break even, has a profit or loss at the end of a year. The profit or loss (or under- or overapplied overhead) may be disposed of in one of the following ways:

1. It may be charged or credited to the billed departments in accordance with their usage. If the intent is for the fund to break even, this procedure is theoretically the correct one.
2. The amount may be closed to Retained Earnings with the intent of adjusting the following year's billings to eliminate the balance. This procedure is a practical substitute for the first.
3. The amount may be closed to and left in Retained Earnings, or even Fund Capital—without subsequent adjustment of billing rates—on the theory that the Fund is to be increased or decreased in size. Reduction to Fund Capital should not be permitted without proper legislative or administrative authorization and supervision.
4. As indicated earlier, an amount of money equal to the profit may be transferred to the General Fund; occasionally this is required by law.

In the absence of specific instructions, the profit or loss should be closed to Retained Earnings. No refunds, supplemental billings, or transfers should be made in the absence of specific authorization or instructions in this regard.

DISSOLUTION OF AN *IS* FUND

When the services provided by an ISF are no longer needed, or when some more preferable method of providing them is found, the Fund is dissolved. The net current assets of a dissolved fund are usually transferred to the funds from which the capital was originally secured. However, as stated before, if capital was secured by incurring general obligation long-term debt, the net current assets usually are transferred to the Debt Service Fund that will retire the debt.

Fixed assets are usually transferred to departments financed from the funds that contributed the capital or to the departments that can best use them. Unless they are transferred to one of the governmental unit's enterprises, the assets are recorded in the General Fixed Assets accounts. If transferred to an enterprise, they are set up as part of the Enterprise Fund.

ACCOUNTING FOR BUDGETARY OPERATIONS

Thus far we have assumed that no appropriations were made by the legislative body of the governmental unit for IS Funds. The accounting procedure outlined is also applicable in its entirety to IS Funds subject to appropriations and budgetary control, but these require additional accounting. In this section, we point out the modifications in accounting procedure necessary to record ISF appropriations, expenditures, and encumbrances.

We have selected for illustration purposes *one* way in which budgetary requirements may be accounted for satisfactorily within the usual IS Fund accounting framework. There are other equally satisfactory approaches, such as through adaptation of the Federal government accounting approach to state and local government IS Fund accounting.

The approach illustrated is a dual expense/expenditure accounting system, a combination of the accounting equations for expendable and nonexpendable funds. It is shown graphically in Figure 12-6. Note that the left two-thirds of Figure 12-6 contains the usual commercial accounting equation, summarized here for ease of illustration; the right one-third contains the self-balancing budgetary account structure.

Accounting for Appropriations

If an activity financed from an IS Fund is to be operated as a self-supporting entity, appropriation accounts and the expenditures and encumbrances chargeable to them must be kept separate and distinct from the proprietary accounts, for many of the transactions affecting appropriations do not affect the profit or loss of the Fund and vice versa. For example, expenditures for fixed assets are capitalized and do not affect profits or losses, but they are charges against appropriations. On the other hand, depreciation expenses reduce profits, but usually no appropriation is made for them as they do not affect net appropriable assets.

It should also be evident from the discussion above that there is not necessarily any relationship between the estimated revenues of an IS Fund and the appropriations made for it. Thus, as we have seen, appropriations are frequently made for some expenditures that are not chargeable against revenues (e.g., the acquisition of fixed assets), and no appropriations are made for some expenses chargeable to revenues (e.g., depreciation expenses). Accordingly, appropriations are not offset by estimated revenues but by an account indicating budgetary requirements. For example, if we assume the figures illustrated, the entry setting up appropriations for an IS Fund is:

A. Budget Requirements 80,000
    Appropriations 80,000
    To record appropriations.

The Budget Requirements account is essentially a "plug" utilized in order to fit the budgetary accounts neatly within the IS Fund accounting equation. Since revenue estimates are not ordinarily subject to legal limitation or control, they need not be formally recorded. A memorandum account showing such estimates should be kept, however.

Charging Expenditures and Encumbrances to Appropriations

The following transactions and entries illustrate how appropriations are recorded and controlled. These transactions are similar to those given on pages 459–460. It is thus possible to note readily what *additional* entries are necessary

Figure 12-6

BUDGETARY ACCOUNTING WITHIN THE INTERNAL SERVICE FUND ACCOUNTING EQUATION

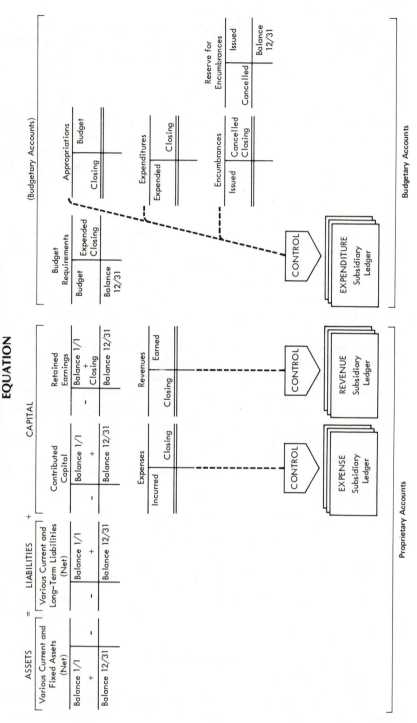

to record and to control appropriations. (To conserve space, the proprietary entries are *not* repeated here.) The transactions below are numbered to correspond with those of the Central Automotive Equipment Fund presented earlier in this Chapter. The letters A (above), B, C, and D identify budgetary transactions that have no proprietary accounting effect; transactions 5, 6, 7, and 9 in the example do not appear here because they have no budgetary accounting effect.

Transactions

B. Equipment estimated to cost $40,500 was ordered.

1. The equipment was received; the actual cost was $40,000.

C. Materials and supplies estimated to cost $9,700 were ordered.

2. The materials and supplies were received; the actual cost was $10,000.

3. Salaries and wages paid, $19,000.

4. Heat, light, and power paid, $2,000.

8. Office expenses paid, $200.

D. A purchase order was placed for materials estimated to cost $5,000.

10. Accrued salaries and wages, $1,000.

Entries

B.		Encumbrances	40,500	
		Reserve for Encumbrances		40,500
		To record placing order for equipment.		
(1)	(a)	Reserve for Encumbrances ..	40,500	
		Encumbrances		40,500
		To reverse entry setting up encumbrances.		
	(b)	Expenditures	40,000	
		Budget Requirements		40,000
		To record reduction of budget requirements and appropriations on account of equipment purchased.		
C.		Encumbrances	9,700	
		Reserve for Encumbrances		9,700
		To record order placed for materials and supplies.		
(2)	(a)	Reserve for Encumbrances ..	9,700	
		Encumbrances		9,700
		To reverse entry setting up encumbrances.		
	(b)	Expenditures	10,000	
		Budget Requirements		10,000
		To record reduction of budget requirements and appropriations on account of purchase of materials and supplies.		

(3)	Expenditures	19,000	
	Budget Requirements		19,000

To record reduction of budget requirements and appropriations on account of salaries and wages paid.

(4)	Expenditures	2,000	
	Budget Requirements		2,000

To record reduction of budget requirements and appropriations on account of heat, light, and power expenses paid.

(5–7) (No budgetary effect)

(8)	Expenditures	200	
	Budget Requirements		200

To record reduction of budget requirements and appropriations by amount of office expenses.

(9) (No budgetary effect)

D.	Encumbrances	5,000	
	Reserve for Encumbranes		5,000

To record purchase order placed for materials and supplies.

(10)	Expenditures	1,000	
	Budget Requirements		1,000

To record reduction of budget requirements and appropriations by amount of accrued salaries and wages.

The foregoing entries are based on the assumption that appropriations are charged as soon as expenditures are incurred, regardless of when they are paid, but that no adjustments are made for expenditures applicable to more than one year. For example, it is assumed that no adjustment is made in the budgetary accounts for materials purchased during the year that remain on hand at the close of the year (purchases basis). It is assumed also that depreciation is not charged to appropriations. These assumptions are in accordance with conditions existing in many governmental units.

Trial Balance before Closing Entries

Assuming that the foregoing entries had been posted, the trial balance of the *budgetary account group* would be as follows:

Budget Requirements	7,800	
Expenditures	72,200	
Encumbrances	5,000	
Reserve for Encumbrances		5,000
Appropriations		80,000
	85,000	85,000

Closing Entries for the Budgetary Group

The closing entries are made for the purpose of determining to what extent expenditures exceed or are under appropriations and to close out the budgetary accounts. However, if encumbered appropriations do not lapse and encumbrances are outstanding at the close of the fiscal year, a balance sufficient to cover these encumbrances must be retained in the Budget Requirements account. The closing entry here are is follows:

(13)	Appropriations	80,000	
	Expenditures		72,200
	Encumbrances		5,000
	Budget Requirements		2,800
	To close out appropriations, expenditures, and encumbrances.		

Balance Sheet—Budgetary Accounts

A postclosing trial balance or a balance sheet of the budgetary group of accounts after closing entries are posted contains only accounts to show budget requirements for encumbrances outstanding at the close of the fiscal year. If we assume the closing entry illustrated, the statement would appear as shown in Figure 12-7.

When the actual amount of the expenditure is determined during the following year, an entry is made debiting the Reserve for Encumbrances account and crediting the Budget Requirements account by the amount of the encumbrances (in this case, $5,000).

Figure 12-7

A GOVERNMENTAL UNIT
Internal Service Fund
Balance Sheet—Budgetary Group
At Close of Fiscal Year

Budget requirements	$5,000
Reserve for encumbrances	$5,000

▶ **Question 12-1.** Why are IS Funds often referred to as "revolving" or "working capital" funds?

Question 12-2. IS Funds are proprietary (nonexpendable) funds. How does this cause IS Fund accounting to differ from that for governmental (expendable) funds?

Question 12-3. The bookkeeper of a municipality asks your advice with respect to whether Due from IS Fund, Advance to IS Fund, Expenditures, Operating Transfer, or Residual Equity Transfer should be debited when General Fund resources are used to establish an Internal Service Fund. How would you answer?

Question 12-4. Resources from the General Fund were used to establish an IS Fund, and Advance to IS Fund was debited in the General Fund. What additional General Fund entry(ies) might be required at or before year end?

Question 12-5. How should the IS Fund temporary proprietorship accounts be closed at the end of the period?

Question 12-6. Why are terms such as "Billings to Departments" and "Excess of

Net Billings to Departments Over Costs" generally used in IS Fund accounting and reporting rather than more familiar terms such as "Sales " and "Net Income"?

Question 12-7. Why is an IS Fund not normally subject to fixed budgetary control?

Question 12-8. Accounting for an IS Fund that is controlled by a fixed budget may be referred to as "double accounting." Why?

Question 12-9. In what ways might the original capital required to establish an IS Fund be acquired?

Question 12-10. What advantages might a governmental unit expect from the use of an IS Fund to account for the acquisition, storage, and provision of supplies for the various departments?

Question 12-11. What major benefits should accrue from accurate cost data being maintained for activities accounted for through the IS Fund?

Question 12-12. Under what circumstances would the *direct* cost of the goods or services provided (with no additions to acquisition cost for items such as depreciation or overhead) be the appropriate basis for IS Fund reimbursement? Explain.

Question 12-13. Why are predetermined price schedules or overhead rates commonly used in IS Fund billings to user departments?

Question 12-14. An IS Fund established by a county is intended to operate on a break-even basis. How might profits or losses (or a retained earnings balance remaining at year end) be disposed of?

Question 12-15. A city operates a motor pool as an IS Fund. List and evaluate the ways that over- or under-absorbed overhead may be treated.

Question 12-16. Why might all of the fixed assets owned by a government and used in conducting activities financed through an IS Fund not be accounted for therein? Give examples and indicate where such assets would be accounted for.

Question 12-17. Under what circumstances would it be improper for an IS Fund to include depreciation in charges to other funds for services rendered or materials supplied?

Question 12-18. An IS Fund was established through the sale of bonds. What disposition should be made of the assets of the fund if it is dissolved?

Question 12-19. Referring to Question 12-18, suppose that the bonds are being retired from a DS Fund. Should the charges to departments for services include depreciation on buildings and equipment financed from these bonds, assuming (a) these departments are all financed from the GF, and (b) these departments are all financed from funds other than the GF?

Question 12-20. In a certain state a question has arisen as to whether the maintenance of one of the state office buildings should be financed by a single appropriation for maintenance or whether maintenance expenses should be financed through an IS Fund. If an IS Fund were established, the departments would be charged rent based on the amount of space occupied and an appropriation would be made to each department for this purpose. Which of the two methods would you recommend? Why?

Question 12-21. The mayor wants to increase the size of an IS Fund by setting a higher-than-cost rate of reimbursement. What response would you make to his suggestion?

Question 12-22. How should overtime premiums incurred in the conduct of IS Fund activities be charged to user departments where IS Fund charges are based on direct cost plus overhead?

(AICPA, adapted.)

► **Problem 12-1.** The following is a trial balance prepared for the Central Stores Department Fund of a state agency at December 31, 19X6.

Sales to Departments		$150,000
Sales Returns and Allowances	$ 2,000	
Purchases	100,600	
Freight In	1,000	
Wages	25,000	
Office Salaries	6,000	
Office Expenses	1,000	
Miscellaneous General Expenses	2,000	
Land	40,000	
Buildings	90,000	
Accumulated Depreciation—Buildings .		12,000
Equipment	65,000	
Accumulated Depreciation—		
Equipment		10,000
Cash	15,000	
Due from General Fund	48,000	
Notes Receivable	2,000	
Inventory	70,000	
Prepaid Insurance	700	
Accounts Payable		13,300
Bonds Payable		95,000
Contributed Capital		165,000
Retained Earnings		23,000
	$468,300	$468,300

Adjustments:

Insurance expired, $400
Accrued wages, $1,000; accrued salaries, $300
Accrued interest payable, $3,000
Closing inventory, $80,000
Depreciation
  Buildings, 4 percent
  Equipment, 8 percent

Required:

Prepare a Stores Fund Balance Sheet as of December 31, 19X6, and Statements of Changes in Financial Position and of Revenues, Expenses, and Changes in Retained Earnings for the year then ended.

Problem 12-2. The following is a trial balance of an Internal Service Fund of the City of Bevton at July 1, 19X0:

Cash	$ 50,000	
Land	55,000	
Buildings	32,000	
Accumulated Depreciation—Buildings .		$ 8,000
Machinery	26,000	
Accumulated Depreciation—		
Machinery		5,000
Equipment	36,000	
Accumulated Depreciation—		
Equipment		9,200

Due from General Fund	77,600	
Inventory of Materials	25,000	
Vouchers Payable		55,000
Capital Contributed from General Fund		200,000
Retained Earnings		31,400
Work in Process Inventory	7,000	
	$308,600	$308,600

The following transactions took place during the year:

1. Materials were received, together with an invoice in the amount of $63,000.

2. Payrolls were approved and paid as follows:

Direct labor	$12,000
Indirect labor	3,000
Plant office	6,000

3. Electric bills of $4,000 were paid.

4. The city treasurer paid cash from the General Fund to the IS Fund for the amount due to the IS Fund for past services.

5. Vouchers payable as of July 1, 19X0, were paid in full.

6. Telephone and telegraph charges of $500 were paid.

7. Plant office supplies were purchased on account for $200.

8. The General Fund was billed $95,000 for materials manufactured for and used by departments financed through the General Fund.

9. Materials used by the IS Fund activity during this period, all direct, $60,000.

10. Insurance premiums paid amounted to $500, of which $400 is applicable to succeeding years.

11. A small secondhand machine was purchased for $700 cash.

12. Repair bills incurred and paid during this period amounted to $1,200.

13. Depreciation charges:

Buildings	$1,600
Machinery	2,600
Equipment	3,600

14. Work in process on June 30, 19X1, amounted to $7,000.

Required:

Prepare a balance sheet for the IS Fund as of June 30,19X1, and Statements of Changes in Financial Position and of Revenues, Expenses, and Changes in Retained Earnings for the year then ended. Support the statements by a work-sheet, T-account analysis, or computation schedules.

Problem 12-3. The City of Morristown operates a printing shop through an Internal Service Fund to provide printing services for all departments. The Central Printing Fund was established by a contribution of $30,000 from the General Fund on January 1, 19X5, at which time the equipment was purchased. The after-closing trial balance on June 30,

19X8, was as follows:

	Debits	Credits
Cash	$35,000	
Due from General Fund	2,000	
Accounts Receivable	1,500	
Supplies Inventory	3,000	
Equipment	25,000	
Accumulated Depreciation—		
Equipment		$ 8,750
Accounts Payable		4,750
Advance from General Fund		20,000
Retained Earnings		33,000
	$66,500	$66,500

The following transactions occurred during fiscal year 19X9:

1. The Publicity Bureau, financed by the General Fund, ordered 30,000 multicolor travel brochures printed at a cost of $1.20 each. The brochures were delivered.

2. Supplies were purchased on account for $13,000.

3. Employee salaries were $30,000. One-sixth of this amount was withheld for taxes and is to be paid to the City's Tax Fund; the employees were paid.

4. Taxes withheld were remitted to the Tax Fund.

5. Utility charges for the year, billed by the Enterprise Fund, $2,200.

6. Supplies used, $10,050.

7. Other billings during the period were: Special Assessment Fund, $300; Special Revenue Fund, $4,750.

8. Inventory of supplies at year end, $5,900.

9. Unpaid receivable balances at June 30, 19X9, were: General Fund, $3,000; Special Revenue Fund, $750.

10. Printing press number 3 was repaired by the central repair shop, operated from the Maintenance Fund. A statement for $75 was received but has not been paid.

11. The Accounts Receivable at June 30, 19X8, were paid in full.

12. Accounts Payable as of June 30, 19X9, $2,800.

13. Depreciation expense was recorded.

Required:

(a) Journalize all transactions and adjustments required in the Central Printing Fund accounts.

(b) Prepare closing entries for the Central Printing Fund accounts as of June 30, 19X9.

(c) Prepare on after-closing trial balance of the Central Printing Fund accounts as of June 30, 19X9.

Problem 12-4. From the information in Problem 12-3, prepare a columnar work-sheet to reflect the beginning balances, transactions and adjustments, closing entries (results of operations), and ending balances of the Central Printing Fund of the City of Morristown for the year ended June 30, 19X9.

Problem 12-5. The following transactions took place during the fiscal year beginning July 1, 19X0, and relate to an Internal Service Fund of the City of Marcille.

1. Budget requirements for the year were estimated at $70,000 and an appropriation was made for this amount.

2. Materials were ordered as follows:

Sand	$ 6,200
Filter	7,200
Asphalt	16,400
Crushed rock	8,200

3. Telephone and telegraph charges of $300 were paid.

4. Plant office supplies were purchased for $100 cash.

5. The materials ordered were received together with an invoice. The actual cost of the materials ordered was as follows:

Sand	$ 6,000
Filter	7,200
Asphalt	16,500
Crushed rock	8,000

6. Payrolls were approved as follows:

Direct labor	$ 6,000
Indirect labor	2,000
Plant office	3,000

7. Electric bills for $2,000 were paid.

8. An order was placed for a small machine estimated to cost $280.

9. The equipment (machine) was received, together with an invoice for $300.

10. Repair bills paid this period amounted to $700.

11. Additional materials ordered amounted to $15,000.

Required:

(a) Prepare journal entries, including closing entries, for the budgetary transactions (only). You need not include subsidiary entries.

(b) Post to general ledger (control) T-accounts.

(c) Prepare a Balance Sheet for the budgetary group of accounts as of June 30, 19X1.

Problem 12-6. The following transactions and events occurred in Beatty County during its fiscal year ended September 30, 19X3:

1. An Internal Service Fund was established on October 1, 19X2, to account for the acquisition and issuance of materials and supplies. In addition to a General Fund contribution of $40,000, the following items on hand were transferred at cost to comprise IS Fund capital:

Department	Cost
Assessor	$ 3,300
Health	1,400
Highway*	48,600

Department	Cost
Administrative	1,700
Sheriff	800
	$55,800

* Financed through the Gasoline Tax Fund;
the remaining departments are financed from
the General Fund.

2. Storage bins and other furniture and equipment needed for the central storeroom were purchased on October 3, 19X2, for $6,000 and vouchered for payment. The storeroom is located in a small building adjacent to the courthouse. The small building was constructed several years ago at a cost of $18,000, and its useful life remaining at October 1, 19X2, was estimated at ten years; the bins and other furniture and equipment should last fifteen years. It is expected that within ten to fifteen years the central storeroom will be moved to the basement of the courthouse and the building in which it is presently housed will be demolished to provide additional parking space.

3. The general budget for Beatty County for the 19X3 fiscal year was adopted on October 15, 19X2. Departmental appropriations for materials and supplies included therein were as follows:

Department	Cost
Assessor	$ 5,000
Health	2,000
Highway	250,000
Administrative	3,000
Sheriff	1,500
	$261,500

The General Fund cash contribution to the IS Fund was included within the General Fund appropriations, but the inventories transferred were charged to the Fund Balance account(s) of funds from which they were contributed. The inventories transferred had been recorded properly and were fully reserved for in the accounts prior to their transfer to the IS Fund. No additional appropriation was made for the IS Fund, but the estimated departmental expenditures for materials and supplies from the IS Fund were shown as estimated revenues of that Fund in the budget, offset by estimated IS Fund expenditures.

4. Materials and supplies were issued during the first six months' operation of the central storeroom as follows:

Department	Inventory Cost to IS Fund	Billing to Department
Assessor	$ 1,800	$ 1,908
Health	400	424
Highway	80,000	84,800
Administration	1,300	1,378
Sheriff	300	318
	$83,800	$88,828

5. Materials and supplies estimated to cost $190,000 were ordered by central storeroom personnel during the year.

6. Costs of operating the storeroom during the year were vouchered as follows:

Salaries and wages	$ 9,000
Insurance	550
Heat, light, and power	700
Janitorial	300
Miscellaneous	450
	$11,000

7. Materials and supplies received and vouchered for payment during the year cost $187,000; goods on order at year end, included in item 5 above, were expected to cost $10,000.

8. Materials and supplies were issued from the central storeroom during the last six months of the 19X3 fiscal year as follows:

Department	Inventory Cost to IS Fund	Billing to Department
Assessor	$ 2,900	$ 3,074
Health	1,700	1,802
Highway	109,050	115,593
Administration	1,450	1,537
Sheriff	1,100	1,166
	$116,200	$123,172

9. At year end, $3,000 remained payable from the General Fund to the IS Fund.

10. Vouchers payable from the IS Fund at year end totaled $11,400.

11. Adjustment data:
   a. Salaries and wages accrued at year end, $150.
   b. It was determined that $300 of the insurance premiums paid during 19X3 were applicable to subsequent years:
   c. Inventory at hand (cost) per physical inventory taken at September 30, 19X3, $42,700.

Required:

(a) Prepare a worksheet to show the transactions and adjustments, preclosing trial balance, closing entries, and ending balances of the Internal Service Fund of Beatty County for the year ended September 30, 19X3. Use detailed revenue and expense accounts such as those illustrated in the Central Automotive Equipment Fund example in this chapter and incorporate such budgetary accounts as you deem necessary in the circumstances. Assume that a perpetual inventory system is in use, and that any excess of billings over cost (or vice versa) is to be retained in the IS Fund rather than being disposed of through supplemental billings or credit memorandums.

(b) Prepare the adjusting entry that would be made at year end in the IS Fund if any excess of costs over billings (or vice versa) must be reflected in supplemental billings or credit memorandums prior to closing the accounts. (Round to nearest one-half percent and to the nearest whole dollar.)

Problem 12-7. From the information in Problem 12-6:

(a) Prepare a worksheet to record the transactions and adjustments, preclosing trial balance, closing entries, and ending balances of Beatty County's Internal Service Fund for the year ended September 30, 19X3, under the assumption that Overhead and Overhead Applied control accounts similar to those illustrated in the Central Stores Fund example in this chapter are employed.

(b) Prepare the adjusting entry that would be made at year end in the IS Fund if any excess of billings over costs (or vice versa) must be disposed of by supplemental billings or credit memorandums prior to the accounts being closed. (Round to the nearest ½ percent and to the nearest whole dollar.)

Problem 12-8. The following is a trial balance of an Internal Service Fund established to finance the operations of a central garage of the City of Zeffler at January 1, 19X5:

Land	35,000	
Buildings	70,000	
Accumulated Depreciation—Buildings .		10,000
Equipment	180,000	
Accumulated Depreciation—		
Equipment		60,000
Cash	45,000	
Inventory:		
Gasoline	4,000	
Oil and Grease	2,000	
Tires	6,500	
Parts	13,500	
Due from General Fund	20,000	
Vouchers Payable		75,000
Contributed Capital		228,000
Retained Earnings		3,000
	$376,000	$376,000

1. Wages and salaries (all chargeable to 19X5) were as follows:

Salary of superintendent	$10,000
Mechanics' wages	39,000
Garage office salaries	6,500

2. Purchases (on account) were as follows:

Gasoline	$20,000
Oil and grease	2,000
Tires	16,000
Parts	30,000

3. Departments are charged at a predetermined rate based on mileage. During the year 19X5, billings to departments amounted to $140,000, all of which was payable from the General Fund. At December 31, 19X5, $25,000 was owed the Internal Service Fund from the General Fund.

4. Other expenses were as follows:
   Heat, light, and power, $10,000, which is due to the Enterprise Fund
   Depreciation
     Buildings, 5 percent of original cost
     Equipment, 10 percent of original cost
5. Vouchers payable paid, $35,000.
6. Closing inventories were as follows:

Gasoline	$ 7,000
Oil and grease	1,500
Tires	11,500
Parts	15,000

7. Accrued salaries and wages were as follows:

Salary of superintendent	$ 250
Mechanics' wages	830
Garage office salaries	180

Required:

(a) Prepare a worksheet showing the beginning balances, transactions and adjustments, operations, and ending balances of the Internal Service Fund of the City of Zeffler for 19X5.

(b) Prepare a Balance Sheet as of December 31, 19X5, and Statements of Changes in Financial Position and of Revenues, Expenses, and Changes in Retained Earnings for the year ended December 31, 19X5, for the Internal Service Fund of the City of Zeffler.

Problem 12-9. Cole County maintains an Internal Service Fund for financial control of a garage operated to serve several departments. It is the county's policy to maintain the Fund accounts so that the departments served will be charged their several shares of the operating cost for a fiscal year. Current billings are made to the departments for services based on charges for actual materials and supplies and actual direct labor plus estimated overhead. Differences between total overhead actually incurred and the estimated amounts billed to departments are adjusted through supplemental billing at the end of each fiscal year. Adjustments to physical inventories are handled through overhead.

1. Garage overhead for the fiscal year ended December 31, 19X9, was comprised of the physical inventory adjustments referred to and the following expenses: superintendence, $8,000; office salaries, $4,300; office supplies, $200; garage depreciation, $2,000; heat and light, $620; miscellaneous, $80.

2. Accounts payable at December 31, 19X9, amounted to $1,100. All payrolls had been paid.

3. The garage originally cost $50,000, financed by a capital advance from the General Fund; at January 1, 19X9, the accumulated depreciation thereagainst was $4,000. On that date, records of the Fund showed cash, $11,000; inventories of gas, oil, and grease, $1,050; inventories of repair and maintenance materials, $2,250; a balance of $900 on account of services previously rendered departments financed from the General Fund; accounts payable of $700; capital advances from the General Fund of $50,000; and a cumulative "surplus" account.

4. Physical inventories at December 31, 19X9, were as follows:

Gas, oil, and grease .... $ 890
Repair and maintenance materials ... 2,000

5. Summaries of certain transactions for the fiscal year ended December 31, 19X9, appear in journal entry form as follows:

a. Due from General Fund 11,300
   Due from Highway Fund 8,305
   Due from Police Fund 9,960
   Due from Fire Fund 5,585
   Billings for Services Rendered
   to Departments 35,150
   To record charges to departments
   for services billed, as follows:

Department	Total	Repairs and Maintenance			
		Actual Cost			Estimated Overhead (135% of Direct Labor)
		Gas, Oil, Grease (at Cost)	Materials	Direct Labor	
General	$11,300	$ 3,950	$1,240	$2,600	$ 3,510
Highway	8,305	2,460	910	2,100	2,835
Police	9,960	2,280	1,100	2,800	3,780
Fire	5,585	1,540	520	1,500	2,025
	$35,150	$10,230	$3,770	$9,000	$12,150

b. Cash 29,900
   Due from General Fund 10,400
   Due from Highway Fund 7,000
   Due from Police Fund 8,000
   Due from Fire Fund 4,500
   To record cash received for services billed.

c. Purchases—Gas, oil, and grease ... 10,100
   Purchases—Repair and main-
   tenance materials 3,580
   Accounts Payable 13,680
   To record purchases for the period.

Required:

Prepare a worksheet to record the beginning balances, transactions and adjustments, operations, and ending balances of the Internal Service Fund of Cole County for 19X9. The worksheet columnar headings should appear as follows:

Trial Balance January 1, 19X9		Transactions and Adjustments during the Fiscal Year Ended December 31, 19X9		Results of Operations, Fiscal Year Ended December 31, 19X9		Balance Sheet December 31, 19X9	
Debits	Credits	Debits	Credits	Debits	Credits	Debits	Credits

(AICPA, adapted)

Problem 12-10. The City of Merlot operates a central garage through an Internal Service Fund to provide garage space and repairs for all city-owned and operated vehicles. The Central Garage Fund was established by a contribution of $200,000 from the General Fund on July 1, 19X7, at which time the building was acquired. The after-closing trial balance at June 30, 19X9, was as follows:

	Debit	Credit
Cash	$150,000	
Due from General Fund	20,000	
Inventory of materials and supplies	80,000	
Land	60,000	
Building	200,000	
Allowance for depreciation—building		$ 10,000
Machinery and equipment	56,000	
Allowance for depreciation—machinery and equipment		12,000
Vouchers payable		38,000
Contribution from General Fund		200,000
Retained earnings		306,000
	$566,000	$566,000

The following information applies to the fiscal year ended June 30, 19Y0:

1. Materials and supplies were purchased on account for $74,000.
2. The inventory of materials and supplies at June 30, 19Y0, was $58,000, which agreed with the physical count taken.
3. Salaries and wages paid to employees totaled $230,000, including related costs.
4. A billing was received from the Enterprise Fund for utility charges totaling $30,000, and was paid.
5. Depreciation of the building was recorded in the amount of $5,000. Depreciation of the machinery and equipment amounted to $8,000.
6. Billings to other departments for services rendered to them were as follows:

General Fund	$262,000
Water and Sewer Fund	84,000
Special Revenue Fund	32,000

7. Unpaid interfund receivable balances at June 30, 1980, were as follows:

General Fund	$ 6,000
Special Revenue Fund	16,000

8. Vouchers payable at June 30, 19Y0, were $14,000.

Required:

(a) For the period July 1, 19Y9, through June 30, 19Y0, prepare journal entries to record all of the transactions in the Central Garage Fund accounts.
(b) Prepare closing entries for the Central Garage Fund at June 30, 19YO.

   (AICPA, adapted)

Problem 12-11. From the following information, prepare a worksheet for the City of Previtson for the year ended June 30, 19X8, showing opening balances, entries in the various accounts to reflect transactions for the year, closing entries, and fund balance sheets at the end of the year. The balance sheet of the City of Previtson at July 1, 19X7, is submitted as follows:

CITY OF PREVITSON
Combined Balance Sheet—All Funds
July 1, 19X7

General Fund

Assets

Cash	$50,000
Taxes receivable—delinquent	25,000
Long-term advance to Revolving Fund	15,000
	$90,000

Liabilities

Accounts payable	$30,000
Due to Revolving Fund	5,500
Reserve for encumbrances	4,500
Reserve for advance to Revolving Fund	15,000
Fund balance	35,000
	$90,000

Transportation Revolving Fund

Cash	$ 9,500	Long-term advance from	
Due from General Fund ...	5,500	General Fund	$15,000
	$15,000		$15,000

Transactions for fiscal year ended June 30, 19X8:

1. Estimated total General Fund revenues were $200,000, including $75,000 of miscellaneous revenues.
2. Appropriations made totaled $175,000.
3. The council levied property taxes of $125,000. Based on experience, the losses will be 5 percent.
4. Receipts from current tax revenues amounted to $85,000; receipts from miscellaneous sources were $80,000.
5. Delinquent taxes received, $23,500; the balance is considered uncollectible.
6. General Fund materials and supplies received and vouchered for payment amounted to $95,000, including $4,000 in complete fulfillment of all orders outstanding at July 1, 19X7; budgeted orders placed amounted to $100,000, and orders outstanding at the end of the year amounted to $4,000.
7. Salary and wage payments amounted to $72,000, as budgeted; vouchered bills paid were $90,000.
8. Collections on taxes written off in prior years were $1,650.
9. Taxes collected in advance were $1,000 (in addition to those collected earlier).

10. In order to finance the construction of certain local roadways, the council voted to set up a Special Assessment Fund and levied a special assessment of $75,000 on 1/1/19X8, collectible in equal proportions over a period of three years, with interest from date of assessment at the rate of 6 percent per year.

11. Pending collection of special assessments, 5 percent bonds in the amount of $25,000 were sold at a premium of $200 on January 1, 19X8. The premium is considered too small to be amortized over the life of the bonds.

12. Construction contracts were let in the amount of $50,000.

13. Contractors were paid $20,000, less 10 percent retained percentage.

14. Special assessments collected amounted to $23,000, representing $22,500 principal on current assessments due for the payment of bonds and $500 interest on deferred assessments to pay interest on outstanding bonds. Interest on special assessments is accounted for on the cash basis.

15. Outstanding bonds of $12,000 were paid, plus interest of $625; no interest payable was accrued at June 30, 19X8.

16. The Transportation Revolving Fund purchased trucks for $9,000, of which $5,000 remains unpaid on open account.

17. The Transportation Revolving Fund charged the General Fund for transportation services applicable to General Fund activities in the amount of $3,000, at cost, including depreciation on trucks of $1,200; other operating expenses, all paid, totaled $1,600.

18. The Transportation Revolving Fund was paid $6,000 from the General Fund; accounts payable outstanding in the Revolving Fund at June 30, 19X8, were $2,000.

    (AICPA, adapted)

13

ENTERPRISE FUNDS; SUMMARY OF INTERFUND ACCOUNTING

Enterprise Funds are established to account for activities of a government that provide goods or services primarily to the public at large on a consumer charge basis. They should be distinguished from Internal Service Funds, which account for activities that provide goods or services to other departments of the governmental unit, and from activities of the general government that provide incidental services to the public for compensation. (Examples of the latter type of activities are those of libraries, highway departments, and police departments.)

Several tests have been suggested for determining whether Enterprise Funds should be created. The National Committee on Governmental Accounting suggested in 1968 a "principal revenues" test for determining whether an activity should be accounted for through an Enterprise Fund. Specifically, it suggested that:

> if a substantial amount of the revenues used to finance an activity or series of related activities in a single fund is derived from user charges, the fund can be appropriately classified and accounted for as an Enterprise Fund.[1]

Issuance of revenue bonds to finance an activity was also seen by the Committee as indicative of the self-supporting nature of an activity that should be accounted for through an Enterprise Fund.

The foregoing criteria did not provide for all of the cases in which municipal governing bodies found it desirable and appropriate to use proprietary accounting for their activities. In addition, the "principal revenues" test for determining whether an activity should be accounted for in the Enterprise Fund was not uniformly applied because there was no common understanding of what "principal" meant. Various percentages were suggested and applied in making deter-

---

[1] GAAFR (68), p. 50.

487

minations. Recognizing the need for revision of criteria, the National Council on Governmental Accounting more recently said that Enterprise Funds should be used:

> to account for operations (a) that are financed and operated in a manner similar to private business enterprises—where the intent of the governing body is that the costs (expenses, including depreciation) of providing goods or services to the general public on a continuing basis be financed or recovered primarily through user charges; or (b) where the governing body has decided that periodic determination of revenues earned, expenses incurred, and/or net income is appropriate for capital maintenance, public policy, management control, accountability, or other purposes.[2]

This new definition has much greater flexibility than did the old. The first part (a) may be described as "mandatory," since it sets up criteria that would require the use of Enterprise Funds. Part (b), on the other hand, may be described as "permissive." It provides wide discretion to the governing body in determining the circumstances under which the Enterprise Fund approach will be used. The "permissive" part (b) of the Enterprise Fund definition was included because some types of activities, such as mass transit systems, meet the part (a) criterion (supported primarily by user charges) in some years and do not meet it in others. By using the part (b) "permissive" part of the definition a government can account for its mass transit system consistently through the years as an Enterprise Fund. Further, some types of activities, such as city markets or convention centers, may never be supported primarily by user charges, yet city officials want them operated as Enterprise Funds in order to know their operating results on that basis as well as their expendable resource flows and balances. This discretion is likely to result in lack of uniformity, of course, and critics of governmental accounting and reporting may find such differences disturbing.

There do not appear to be any substantial restrictions on the types of businesses in which local governments may engage. Among the many types of activities of governments financed through Enterprise Funds are electric generation and/or distribution systems, water systems, natural gas distribution systems, sewer systems, public docks and wharves, hospitals, nursing homes, off-street parking lots and garages, toll highways and bridges, public housing, airports, garbage collection and disposal services, public transportation systems, liquor wholesaling and retailing operations, swimming pools, and golf courses.

A discussion of Enterprise Fund accounting principles and procedures comprises the principal topic of this chapter. The chapter is concluded by a summary review of interfund (or multifund) accounting concepts that is designed to assist the reader in (1) reviewing the material covered thus far, (2) integrating his knowledge of appropriate accounting principles and procedures for the various types of funds and account groups commonly employed by state and local governments, and (3) gaining conceptual dexterity in the application of appropriate accounting principles and procedures in the multiple entity accounting environment of governments.

[2] NCGAS 1, p. 7.

ENTERPRISE FUND ACCOUNTING

Enterprise activites may be administered through a department of a general purpose government, a separate board or commission under the jurisdiction of the government, or an independent special district not under the general purpose government's jurisdiction. Regardless of organizational location or the type of activity involved, certain characteristics, principles, and procedures are common to all Enterprise Fund accounting.

Characteristics of Enterprise Fund Accounting

For purposes of discussion, the major distinguishing characteristics of Enterprise Fund accounting may be categorized conveniently under the following headings: (1) accounting principles, (2) restricted asset accounts, and (3) budgeting and appropriations. Other features of certain enterprise situations (payments in lieu of taxes, Utility Acquisition Adjustment accounts, etc.) are discussed later in the chapter.

Accounting Principles. Enterprise Funds, like Internal Service Funds, are proprietary (nonexpendable) funds. Thus, it is essential that a distinction be maintained between capital contributions and revenues and that revenues and expenses be accounted for on an accrual basis so that periodic net income or loss can be determined. Fixed assets and long-term debt related to enterprise activities are accounted for in the Enterprise Fund, as are depreciation and amortization.

More specifically, the accounting principles or standards utilized should be those used in accounting for privately owned enterprises of similar types and sizes. Many municipally owned utilities are required by supervisory commissions to follow the same accounting as that prescribed for privately owned utilities of the same class. For financial reporting purposes the pronouncements of the Financial Accounting Standards Board (and its predecessors) are to be followed, where applicable.

Transactions between the enterprise and other governmental departments should be accounted for in the same manner as "outsider" transactions; i.e., they are quasi-external transactions. Therefore, goods or services provided by an Enterprise Fund to departments of the government financed from other funds should be billed at regular, predetermined rates; and all goods or services provided the enterprise by other governmental departments should be billed to it on the same basis that other users are charged. If this is not done, operating and position statements of all funds may be distorted.

A separate fund should be established for each governmental enterprise and all transactions or events relating to a specific enterprise should be recorded in the appropriate Enterprise Fund records. The major exception to this general rule occurs in the case of related activities, such as water and sewer utilities, which may be merged because of their complementary nature or because joint revenue bonds often are used in financing such operations.

Restricted Asset Accounts. Enterprise activities may involve transactions or relationships which, if encountered in a general government situation, would require the use of several separate and distinct fund entities. Thus, utilities may require customers to post deposits (Trust), may acquire or construct major capital facilities (Capital Projects), or may have sinking fund or other debt-related resources (Debt Service). In some cases, certain enterprise-related intrafund "funds" are required to be established under terms of bond indentures or similar agreements.

In keeping with its recommendation that governmental enterprises follow appropriate commercial accounting principles, the NCGA recommended that the term "funds" be interpreted in this instance in the usual commercial accounting connotation of restricted assets. Thus, Enterprise Funds may contain several "funds within a fund," since the use of distinctively titled intrafund restricted asset accounts (offset by liability or equity reserve accounts) is deemed preferable to the use of a series of separate fund entities in Enterprise Fund accounting. Application of the "funds within a fund" approach is demonstrated in the illustrative example in this chapter.

Budgeting and Appropriations. As in the case of Internal Service Funds, careful planning and realistic *flexible* budgeting should be considered prerequisites to sound Enterprise Fund management. It is not desirable, however, to control the expenditures of enterprises by means of rigid appropriations. Their levels of activities are controlled by the demands for their goods or services; as demand increases, revenues increase and expenses are likely to increase.

If flexible budgets are adopted, it is clear that, as in business enterprises, they are guides to action and means of managerial control, not fixed limitations as are the budgets of governmental funds. If fixed budgets are adopted because of legal requirements or the legislative body's desire to control some (e.g., capital outlay) or all expenditures, the budgets may be incorporated into the chart of accounts and used as they are used in governmental funds. Since the use of budgetary accounts in proprietary funds is illustrated in Chapter 12, we need not illustrate it for Enterprise Funds.

Enterprise Fund Accounting Illustrated

Services of the type generally referred to as "public utilities" are among the most common enterprise activities undertaken by local governments. Such activities invariably involve significant amounts of assets, liabilities, revenues, and expenses and are seldom considered in contemporary undergraduate accounting courses. For these reasons, we have chosen an electric utility example to illustrate Enterprise Fund accounting procedures. The illustrative example is presented in several topical phases.

Establishment of Fund and Acquisition of Plant. The acquisition of a utility may be financed wholly or partially by the sale of bonds to be retired from utility earnings, by contributions or grants from the governmental unit, and by contributions from prospective customers. If we assume that the acquisition of a utility plant is financed through a contribution from the General Fund of the governmental unit, the entry to record the receipt of the contribution and the establishment of the Fund is:

(1) Cash	400,000	
Residual Equity Transfer		
from General Fund		400,000
To record governmental unit's		
contribution for acquisition of		
utility.		

The next step is the acquisition of the plant. To simplify the discussion, let us assume further that a private electricity generation and distribution plant already in operation is acquired at book value. The entries to record the acquisition and payment therefor are:

(2) Land	50,000	
Buildings	100,000	
Improvements Other than		
Buildings	550,000	
Machinery and Equipment	150,000	
Accounts Receivable	62,000	
Inventory of Materials and Supplies.	10,000	
Allowance for Depreciation—		
Buildings		10,000
Allowance for Depreciation—		
Improvements Other than		
Buildings		70,000
Allowance for Depreciation—		
Machinery and Equipment		40,000
Allowance for Uncollectible		
Accounts		12,000
Bonds Payable		500,000
Vouchers Payable		10,000
Due to ABC Electric Company ..		280,000
To record the acquisition of the		
assets and liabilities of the ABC		
Electric Company.		
(3) Due to ABC Electric Company	280,000	
Cash		280,000
To record payment to ABC Electric		
Company.		

Note that the accounts for both original cost and accumulated depreciation of assets were brought forward from the books of ABC Electric Company. This practice is in keeping with recommendations of the National Association of Railroad and Utilities Commissioners (NARUC) that assets be accounted for at "original cost" to the utility *first* placing them in public service. This is the prevailing practice in regulated utility accounting. Alternatively, it is also acceptable to record the assets at their net cost to the Enterprise Fund and not to establish depreciation allowance accounts initially.

The practice of recording assets and accumulated depreciation on the books of the purchaser at book value to the seller (defined in regulatory accounting as "original cost") rather than at fair market value arose to curb abuses of depreciation accounting. In the absence of an "original cost" policy, for example, Utility A might (1) acquire new assets with an estimated useful life of twenty years; (2) depreciate them over a relatively short period, say five years, thus charging their full cost against revenues and—since a given level of earnings would be permitted by the regulatory body—to the consumer public; and (3) sell the fully depreciated (on the books) assets at fair market value to Utility B, which would charge its cost of the assets (fair market value) to depreciation expense and, ultimately, to the same consumer public. This sequence of events would constitute, in the view of many, a "double-charge" against the public. Thus, regulatory policies pertaining to fixed assets typically are based on the assumption that the public should be charged with depreciation of the original cost of specific assets only once; and many regulatory bodies require the rate of return permitted to be calculated on an "original cost" basis and/or allow only depreciation based on "original cost" to be deducted from revenues in determining net income for regulatory purposes. Such policies obviously are not justified by generally accepted accounting principles.

Had ABC Electric been purchased for $350,000, instead of at its $280,000 book value, the acquisition would have been recorded in the books of a *regulated* utility as follows:

Land	50,000	
Buildings	100,000	
Improvements Other than Buildings ...	550,000	
Machinery and Equipment	150,000	
Accounts Receivable	62,000	
Inventory of Materials and Supplies	10,000	
Utility Plant Acquisition Adjustments ..	70,000	
Allowance for Depreciation—		
Buildings		10,000
Allowance for Depreciation—		
Improvements Other than		
Buildings		70,000
Allowance for Depreciation—		
Equipment and Machinery		12,000
Allowance for Uncollectible Accounts .		40,000
Bonds Payable		500,000
Vouchers Payable		10,000
ABC Electric Company		350,000
To record acquisition of the assets and liabilities of the ABC Electric Company.		

The Utility Plant Acquisition Adjustments account is often improperly considered to represent goodwill. It is not designed to represent a payment for anticipated excess earnings, however, as does purchased goodwill. The Acquisitions Adjustment account merely shows the difference between the book value of the assets on the seller's books and their fair market value at the date of sale; it is necessary only because of the "original cost" accounting policy of regulatory bodies. The Acquisition Adjustments account is amortized in a rational and systematic manner over the lives of the assets that caused its establishment, i.e., over the lives of those assets whose fair market value exceeded their book value at the date of the sale. For regulatory reporting purposes, the amortization is shown as a nonoperating expense; the intent and effect is to exclude the amortization from the net income used by the regulatory commission for rate-making purposes. For reporting to the public, depreciation of the assets with which the amortization is identified is adjusted upward to show the depreciation expense of the enterprise on a purchase cost basis—in accordance with generally accepted accounting principles. Unless a Utility Plant Acquisition Adjustment account is required by the commission that regulates an enterprise, the account should not be used.

Accounting for Routine Operating Transactions. The following transactions and entries illustrate the operation of an Enterprise Fund for a utility. The accounting procedures for (1) the receipt and expenditure of bond proceeds, (2) utility debt service and related "funds," and (3) customers' deposits require use of intrafund restricted asset accounts and are discussed in a subsequent phase of the example. To simplify the discussion, all revenues, with the exception of interest revenues, are assumed to be credited to an Operating Revenues control account; and all expenses, with the exception of depreciation, taxes, and interest, are assumed to be charged to an Operating Expenses control account. A detailed operating expense statement is illustrated in Figure 13-4.

Additional Transactions

4. Total salaries and wages paid, $127,200.
5. Materials costing $59,000 were received.
6. Revenues billed during the year, $300,000.
7. Equipment costing $50,500 was purchased.
8. Telephone and telegraph bills paid, $500.
9. Rental due on equipment rented to the State Public Works Department, $7,000.
10. Fire insurance premiums paid, $1,000 (two-year policy).
11. Collection on accounts receivable, $290,000.
12. Bill received from Internal Service Fund for services rendered, $12,800.
13. Bonds paid, $50,000.
14. Interest paid, $20,000.
15. Interest received, $1,000.
16. Taxes paid, $10,500.
17. Vouchers payable of $70,000 were paid.
18. A subdivision electricity system, valued at $30,000, was donated to the utility by the subdivision developer.
19. Necessary adjusting entries were based on the following data:

a.	Accrued salaries and wages payable	$ 6,000
b.	Accrued interest payable	2,000
c.	Accrued interest receivable	200
d.	Accrued taxes payable	7,500
e.	Prepaid insurance	600
f.	Ending inventory of materials and supplies	30,000
g.	Estimated losses on accounts receivable	1,500
h.	Depreciation:	
	Buildings	5,000
	Improvements other than buildings	15,000
	Machinery and equipment	16,000
i.	Unbilled receivables	21,000

(4)	Operating Expenses	127,200	
	Cash		127,200
	To record payment of salaries and wages.		
(5)	Inventory of Materials and Supplies	59,000	
	Vouchers Payable		59,000
	To record purchase of materials.		
(6)	Accounts Receivable	300,000	
	Operating Revenues		300,000
	To record operating revenue.		
(7)	Machinery and Equipment	50,500	
	Vouchers Payable		50,500
	To record purchase of equipment.		
(8)	Operating Expenses	500	
	Cash		500
	To record telephone and telegraph expenses.		
(9)	Due from State Public Works Department	7,000	
	Nonoperating Revenues— Equipment Rental		7,000
	To record rental of equipment to State Public Works Department.		
(10)	Operating Expenses	1,000	
	Cash		1,000
	To record insurance premium payments.		
(11)	Cash	290,000	
	Accounts Receivable		290,000
	To record collection of accounts receivable.		
(12)	Operating Expenses	12,800	
	Due to Internal Service Fund		12,800
	To record cost of services rendered by Internal Service Fund.		
(13)	Bonds Payable	50,000	
	Cash		50,000
	To record retirement of part of issue of serial bonds.		
(14)	Interest Expense	20,000	
	Cash		20,000
	To record payment of interest.		
(15)	Cash	1,000	
	Interest Revenues		1,000
	To record receipt of interest revenues.		
(16)	Taxes Expense	10,500	
	Cash		10,500
	To record payment of taxes.		

(17)	Vouchers Payable	70,000	
	Cash		70,000
	To record payment of vouchers.		
(18)	Improvements Other than Buildings ...	30,000	
	Contribution from Subdividers		30,000
	To record dedication of subdivision distribution lines to the utility.		

(Tapping fees or similar charges paid by customers should also be credited to contributions from customers to the extent they exceed recovery of hookup costs.)

(19)	(a)	Operating Expenses	6,000	
		Accrued Salaries and Wages Payable		6,000
		To record salaries and wages accrued.		
	(b)	Interest Expense	2,000	
		Accrued Interest Payable		2,000
		To record accrued interest payable.		
	(c)	Accrued Interest Receivable	200	
		Interest Revenue		200
		To record accrued interest receivable.		
	(d)	Taxes Expense	7,500	
		Accrued Taxes Payable		7,500
		To record accrued taxes.		
	(e)	Prepaid Insurance	600	
		Operating Expenses		600
		To record unexpired insurance.		
	(f)	Operating Expenses	39,000	
		Inventory of Materials and Supplies		39,000
		To record operating expenses for materials used during year.		
	(g)	Operating Expenses	1,500	
		Allowance for Uncollectible Accounts		1,500
		To record estimated losses on accounts receivable.		
	(h)	Depreciation Expense	36,000	
		Allowance for Depreciation— Buildings		5,000
		Allowance for Depreciation— Improvements Other than Buildings		15,000
		Allowance for Depreciation— Machinery and Equipment		16,000
		To record depreciation for fiscal year.		
	(i)	Unbilled Accounts Receivable	21,000	
		Operating Revenues		21,000
		To record unbilled receivables and revenues at year end.		

Accounting for Restricted Asset Accounts. As indicated earlier, an enterprise's restricted assets are accounted for in the Enterprise Fund accounts rather than through separate fund entities. This is accomplished through use of distinctively titled restricted asset accounts, offset by liability or equity reserve accounts—by establishing "funds" within the Enterprise Fund—so that a single fund serves the purpose of several separate fund entities. Before studying the procedures that follow, note how the Trial Balance (Figure 13-1) and the Balance Sheet (Figure 13-2) presented at the conclusion of this example are designed to separate these intrafund "funds" from the unrestricted assets and other liabilities and equities.

The types of restricted asset situations that may be encountered in practice vary widely, from simple customer deposits "funds" to complex series of "funds" required under terms of bond indentures, through legislative decree, or for administrative purposes. Several of the more common restricted asset situations are presented here to illustrate the use of intrafund restricted asset accounts, sometimes referred to as "secondary account groups," in Enterprise Fund accounting. In the following illustrations we use distinctively titled asset and liability accounts for each "fund" and adjust the appropriate reserve accounts by inspection at period end. "Fund" revenues and expenses are recorded in the Electricity (Enterprise) Fund revenue and expense control accounts under the assumption that any "fund" detail needed is provided in subsidiary records. Alternatively, we might have used detailed "fund" revenue and expense accounts and closed them at period end either (1) directly to the appropriate reserve account, or (2) to the Retained Earnings account, followed by an entry adjusting the appropriate reserve account.

Customer deposits. A utility usually requires its customers to post deposits, on which it normally pays interest, as a partial protection against bad debt losses. The following transactions and entries illustrate the procedure in recording the deposits, earnings thereon, interest paid to depositors, forfeited deposits, and the return of deposits upon termination of service:

Transactions

20. Deposits of $11,000 were received.
21. Deposits in the amount of $10,000 were invested (assume that no premiums, discounts, or accrued interest purchases were involved).
22. Interest accrued on investments but not received, $200.
23. Interest accrued on deposits but not paid, $150.
24. A customer's deposit was declared forfeited for nonpayment of his account.
25. A customer moving to another town requested that his service be disconnected. His final bill was offset against his deposit and the balance remitted to him.
26. The appropriate reserve account was adjusted at period end to equal the net assets of the "fund."

(20)	Customers' Deposits—Cash	11,000	
	Customers' Deposits Payable		11,000
	To record receipt of customers' deposits.		
(21)	Customers' Deposits—Investments	10,000	
	Customers' Deposits—Cash		10,000
	To record investment of customers' deposits.		
(22)	Customers' Deposits—Accrued Interest Receivable	200	
	Interest Revenue		200
	To record interest revenues.		
(23)	Interest Expense	150	
	Customers' Deposits—Accrued Interest Payable		150
	To record interest expenses.		
(24) (a)	Customers' Deposits Payable	12	
	Customers' Deposits—Accrued Interest Payable	2	
	Allowance for Uncollectible Accounts	8	
	Accounts Receivable		22
	To record forfeiture of customers' deposit, offset against overdue receivable, and write-off of the uncollectible balance.		
(b)	Cash	14	
	Customers' Deposits—Cash		14
	To reclassify forfeited customer deposits' cash to unrestricted cash.		
(25)	Customers' Deposits Payable	15	
	Customers' Deposits—Accrued Interest Payable	3	
	Accounts Receivable		10
	Customers' Deposits—Cash		8
	To record offsetting of customers' final bill against his deposit account and remittance of the balance due him.		
(26)	Retained Earnings	60	
	Reserve for Earnings on Customers' Deposits		60
	To reserve Retained Earnings to indicate that net assets of the Customers' Deposits Fund are available only for customer deposit interest requirements.		

Construction financed by bond issue. Accounting for Enterprise Fund con-
ruction financed through the sale of bonds is not unlike that for private con-
ruction. Both the authorization of the bond issue and appropriations, if any, are
ormally recorded in memorandum form rather than formally within the accounts.

The following transactions and entries illustrate appropriate procedure in the typical case.

Transactions

27. Bonds of $200,000 (par) were sold at a premium of $2,000; the premium cash was reclassified as restricted for debt service.
28. A contract was entered into with Smith & Company for the construction of part of the project at a cost of $100,000.
29. Materials costing $41,000 were purchased by the utility and delivered to the construction site.
30. The bill for materials was paid.
31. A bill for $30,000 was received from Smith & Company.
32. Smith & Company was paid.
33. The utility paid $56,000, representing the cost of construction labor and supervisory expenses.
34. Smith & Company completed its part of the construction project and submitted its bill for $70,000.
35. Smith & Company was paid in full except for $10,000, which was retained pending final inspection and approval of the project.
36. The completed project was found to be satisfactory and was set up on the records as a fixed asset.
37. Smith & Company was paid the final amount due.
38. The remaining bond cash was transferred to the Enterprise debt service "fund."

Entries

(27a)	Construction—Cash	200,000	
	Cash	2,000	
	Unamortized Premiums on Bonds		2,000
	Bonds Payable		200,000
	To record sale of bonds at a premium.		
(27b)	Debt Service—Cash	2,000	
	Cash		2,000
	To record restriction of premium cash for debt service purposes.		
(28)	No entry is necessary to record entering into a contract; a narrative memorandum entry may be made.		
(29)	Construction Work in Progress	41,000	
	Construction Vouchers Payable		41,000
	To record cost of construction materials.		
(30)	Construction Vouchers Payable	41,000	
	Construction—Cash		41,000
	To record payment of bill for materials.		

(31)	Construction Work in Progress	30,000	
	Construction Contracts Payable		30,000
	To record receipt of bill from Smith & Company for part of cost of contract.		
(32)	Construction Contracts Payable	30,000	
	Construction—Cash		30,000
	To record payment of amount now due on contract.		
(33)	Construction Work in Progress	56,000	
	Construction—Cash		56,000
	To record cost of labor and supervisory expense.		
(34)	Construction Work in Progress	70,000	
	Construction Contracts Payable		70,000
	To record receipt of bill from Smith & Company to cover remaining cost of contract.		
(35)	Construction Contracts Payable	70,000	
	Construction—Cash		60,000
	Construction Contracts Payable— Retained Percentage		10,000
	To record payment of amount due on contract and retention of part of amount due pending final approval of project.		
(36)	Improvements Other than Buildings ...	197,000	
	Construction Work in Progress		197,000
	To close out Construction Work in Progress account and to set up cost of completed improvements.		
(37)	Construction Contracts Payable— Retained Percentage	10,000	
	Construction—Cash		10,000
	To record final payment to contractor.		
(38)	Debt Service—Cash	3,000	
	Construction—Cash		3,000
	To record transfer of unused bond proceeds to Debt Service Fund.		

Historically, interest expenses during the construction period on money borrowed to finance the construction have been capitalized in accounting for a privately owned regulated utility. And, even if the utility does not borrow money for construction, it may capitalize the interest (imputed) it would have paid if it had borrowed money for this purpose. The reason is that the utility is deprived of the use of the money for revenue-producing purposes until the project is completed and is in a position to earn revenue. Adding this "cost" to other project costs, and thus allowing it to enter the rate basis, will permit the utility to recover a like amount through additional depreciation charges against revenues or, where the allowable return is stated as a percentage of the book value of assets, to derive a higher dollar return during the asset's useful life.

The propriety of capitalizing interest expense incurred or imputed during construction was first addressed by the Financial Accounting Standards Board in SFAS 34[3] in 1979. It viewed such interest expense as a part of the historical cost of asset acquisition. SFAS 34 requires that the assets to whose cost interest is to be charged must require and be in a period of construction (a period of preparation for use in the revenue-producing operations of the enterprise or for sale or lease). The effect of the capitalization-expensing decision must be material. The interest to be capitalized must be incurred on debt; it may not be an imputed figure. The gross interest incurred—not offset by earnings from temporary investment of the debt issue proceeds—is to be capitalized. Where more than one construction-related debt is involved, the interest rate is to be a weighted average and must be computed from debt having explicit rates, or interest required (by Accounting Principles Board Opinion No. 21) to be imputed on certain payables, or interest on capitalized leases. In 1982, the FASB issued *SFAS 62*, which modifies the application of SFAS 34 to the acquisition of qualifying fixed assets financed by restricted tax-exempt debt issues, gifts, or grants—the usual government situation.[4] *SFAS 62* specifies that:

- Where the acquisition is financed by **tax-exempt debt** issues that are externally restricted for that purpose or to service related debt (1) *interest earned* (by temporarily investing the debt issue proceeds) *should be offset* against the interest costs incurred and the *net* interest cost capitalized, and (2) the *capitalization period* begins at the date of borrowing rather than at the beginning of construction.

- Where such acquisitions are financed by donor- or grantor-restricted **gifts or grants** (1) interest earned on temporary investments of the gift or grant proceeds should be considered additions to the gifts or grants, not offset against any project interest costs incurred, and (2) such assets are not subject to interest cost capitalization under SFAS 34.

In taking the described position on interest capitalization, the FASB took a middle road between expensing incurred interest and capitalizing interest, incurred or imputed, on all capital invested in the construction process.

1. If interest costs are expensed, interest is treated as a period cost of financing rather than a cost of the asset. This treatment disregards the argument that an implicit cost is involved, no matter what the source of financing.

2. If actual but not imputed costs are capitalized, an enterprise that uses borrowed capital will show a higher cost for an identical asset than would an enterprise that used capital contributed by the governmental unit. Most authorities would agree that interest costs are a part of the cost of constructed assets.

---

[3] *Statement of Financial Accounting Standards No. 34*, "Capitalization of Interest Costs" (Stamford, Conn.: FASB, 1979).

[4] Financial Accounting Standards Board, *Statement of Financial Accounting Standards No. 62*, "Capitalization of Interest Cost in Situations Involving Certain Tax Exempt Borrowings and Certain Gifts and Grants" (Stamford, Conn.: FASB, 1982)

3. If interest costs, whether imputed or actual, were required to be capitalized, comparative costs of assets would have the same basis, without regard to the method of financing. Many authorities believe that interest is a part of the cost of construction in all cases. Some would argue that imputation of interest costs is subjective and a departure from historical cost. With such divergence of opinion it appears unlikely that the last word on this subject has been spoken.

If interest incurred is to be capitalized, an accurate calculation, including appropriate treatments of premiums or discounts, must be made. For example, let us assume that interest accrued in the amount of $4,500 is attributable to a construction project that extended over the full year, and that the amount of premium to be amortized during the construction period is $100. The entry to record interest expense and the amortization of premiums is as follows:

Interest Expense	4,400	
Unamortized Premiums on Bonds	100	
Accrued Interest Payable		4,500
To record interest expense and		
reduction of same by amount of		
premium amortized.		

Subsequently an entry would be made capitalizing the net interest expense as follows:

Improvements Other than Buildings ...	4,400	
Interest Expense		4,400
To capitalize interest expense.		

Alternatively an account such as Interest Expense Capitalized may be credited, rather than Interest Expense, and deducted from gross interest expense in the Enterprise Fund Statement of Revenues, Expenses, and Changes in Retained Earnings (Figure 13-3).

Debt service and related accounts. A variety of intrafund "funds" related to bond issues may be required (in addition to a construction or Capital Projects "fund") under terms found in contemporary bond indentures. Among the most usual of these are:

1. *Term Bond Principal Sinking Fund.* Often referred to merely as a "Sinking" fund, its purpose is to segregate stipulated amounts of assets, and earnings thereon, for the eventual retirement of term bond principal.
2. *Revenue Bond Debt Service Fund.* This type of intrafund "fund," commonly referred to as an "Interest and Redemption," "Interest and Sinking," or "Bond and Interest" fund, is often required to assure timely payment of serial revenue bond interest and principal. A common indenture provision is that one-sixth of the next semiannual interest payment, plus one-twelfth of the next annual principal payment, be deposited monthly in a "fund" of this type.

3. *Principal and Interest Reserve Fund.* Often referred to simply as a "Reserve" fund, intrafund "funds" of this type are often required to provide bondholders an additional "cushion" or safety margin. "Funds" of this sort are usually required to be accumulated to a specific sum within the first 60 months after bonds are issued and are to be used (1) to pay matured bonds and interest if the resources in the Debt Service "fund" prove inadequate, or (2) if not required earlier to cover deficiences, to retire the final bond principal and interest maturities.

4. *Contingencies Fund.* This intrafund "fund," sometimes referred to as the "Emergency Repair" or "Operating Reserve" fund, is intended to afford bondholders even more security by providing in advance for emergency expenditures or for operating asset renewal or replacement. Thus, the bondholder receives additional assurance that the operating facilities will not be permitted to deteriorate in order that bond principal and interest requirements be met—or the utility be forced into receivership—because of such unforeseen expenditure requirements. Like the Principal and Interest Reserve "fund," the Contingencies "fund" is usually required to be accumulated in a specific amount early in the life of the bond issue.

The principles and procedures of accounting for both term and serial bond Debt Service Funds were covered in detail in Chapter 8 and are fully applicable to the first two types of intrafund "funds" listed above. The only difference is that such "funds" are accounted for on a "funds within a fund" basis within the Enterprise Fund—through use of a series of self-balancing restricted asset, liability, and equity reserve intrafund account groups—rather than through separate accounting entities.

In order to illustrate the operation and accounting for debt service-related "funds" within an Enterprise Fund, let us assume that Debt Service, Principal and Interest Reserve, and Contingencies "funds," as described in items 2, 3, and 4 above, are required under terms of an enterprise bond indenture. A total of $5,000 has already been classifed as Debt Service—Cash (Construction "fund" transactions 2 and 13) as a result of a bond issue premium ($2,000) and unused bond issue proceeds ($3,000). The following transactions illustrate typical activities related to these restricted asset accounts:

Transactions

39. The Debt Service "fund" was increased by $25,000; and $10,000 each was added to the Principal and Interest Reserve "fund" and to the Contingencies "fund."

40. Interest on bonds, $15,000, was paid.

41. A $7,000 unforeseen emergency repair was incurred and is to be paid from the Contingencies "fund."

42. Principal and Interest Reserve "fund" cash, $9,000, was invested.

43. Interest was earned on the investment above, $450, of which $300 was received in cash.

44. Bond interest payable had accrued at year end, $6,000; premium of $300 was amortized.

45. The appropriate reserve accounts were adjusted at year end to equal the net assets of the "funds."

Entries

(39)	Debt Service—Cash	25,000	
	Principal and Interest Reserve—Cash ..	10,000	
	Contingencies—Cash	10,000	
	Cash		45,000
	To record amounts restricted and set aside for these funds.		
(40)	Interest Expense	15,000	
	Debt Service—Cash		15,000
	To record payment of bond interest.		
(41)	Operating Expenses	7,000	
	Contingencies—Vouchers Payable		7,000
	To record liability for emergency repair expense.		
(42)	Principal and Interest Reserve—		
	Investments	9,000	
	Principal and Interest Reserve—		
	Cash		9,000
	To record investment of fund cash.		
(43)	Principal and Interest Reserve—Cash ..	300	
	Principal and Interest Reserve—		
	Accrued Interest Receivable	150	
	Interest Revenue		450
	To record interest earned and received.		
(44)	Interest Expense	5,700	
	Unamortized Premiums on Bonds	300	
	Debt Service—Accrued Bond		
	Interest Payable		6,000
	To record bond interest accrued and amortization of bond premium.		
(45)	Retained Earnings	22,450	
	Reserve for Bond Debt Service		9,000
	Reserve for Bond Principal and		
	Interest Payments Guarantee		10,450
	Reserve for Contingencies		3,000
	To adjust reserve accounts at year end.		

Retained Earnings reserves need to be adjusted to equal "fund" net assets only prior to statement preparation. Continuous adjustment merely constitutes "busy work," though such practice is technically correct and may occasionally be found. The purpose of these reserves is to indicate that restricted intrafund "fund" net assets are not available for "dividends" to the General Fund or for other purposes. The reserves also constitute the balancing accounts of the self-balancing "funds within a fund."

Adjusting Entries.   For ease of illustration, we have included most of the required adjusting entries in the various phases of our example in this chapter. Most of the adjusting entries required are similar to those common in commercial accounting; and, as in commercial accounting, those of an accrual nature would be reversed at the beginning of the subsequent period. The adjusting entries that may be less familiar to the reader, and therefore deserve special attention at this point, are those relating to unbilled receivables and amortization of the Utility Plant Acquisition Adjustments account.

Accurate determination of the revenue earned during a year requires that significant amounts of unbilled receivables be accrued at year end, particularly if the amount of such receivables varies materially from year to year. This is not to say that a cutoff point in the billing cycle cannot be used, or that other expediency methods that do not distort reported net income or financial position cannot be employed. Such methods should be used only after careful consideration of possible distortions or biases thereby introduced, however, and should be applied consistently each year.

As indicated previously, the Utility Plant Acquisition Adjustments account, when employed, is amortized in a systematic and rational manner. The amortization entry is as follows:

Amortization of Utility Plant Acquisition		
Adjustments	xx,xxx	
Accumulated Amortization of Utility Plant		
Acquisition Adjustments		xx,xxx
To record amortization of utility plant		
acquisition adjustments.		

The Accumulated Amortization of Utility Plant Acquisition Adjustments is a valuation account and is deducted from the Utility Plant Acquisition Adjustments account in the balance sheet. The Utility Plant Acquisition Adjustments account and the related allowance would be shown in the balance sheet as follows:

Utility plant acquisition adjustments	xx,xxx	
Less: Accumulated amortization of utility		
plant acquisition adjustments	xx,xxx	
Unamortized utility plant acquisition		
adjustments		xx,xxx

When assets are disposed of, any related balances in the Utility Plant Acquisition Adjustments and Accumulated Amortization of Utility Plant Acquisition Adjustments accounts should be removed in the same entry in which the "original cost" asset and accumulated depreciation accounts are reduced. Otherwise, the acquisition adjustments accounts will be overstated and the gain or loss reported on the disposal transactions will be misstated.

When the amortization process is completed, an entry may be made debiting the Accumulated Amortization of Utility Plant Acquisition Adjustments account and crediting the Utility Plant Acquisition Adjustments account for corresponding amounts to clear their balances. These amounts would then be added to the appropriate asset and accumulated depreciation accounts.

Recall again, however, that the Utility Plant Acquisition Adjustments account is peculiar to the *regulated* industry environment and is *not* a standard feature of Enterprise Fund accounting. Remember also that, although the Adjustments account and the related amortization and accumulated amortization accounts must appear in statements prepared for regulatory purposes, it may be necessary to allocate these to the asset and expense accounts relating to the properties being carried at "original cost" (that required the Acquisition Adjustments account to be established) and to prepare modified financial statements in order that general purpose financial statements present fairly the financial position and operating results of the Enterprise Fund in conformity with GAAP.

Preclosing Trial Balance. An adjusted, preclosing trial balance for the Electric (Enterprise) Fund, based on the journal entries in this chapter having numbers in parentheses by them, appears as Figure 13-1. In order to illustrate the "funds within a fund" approach common to Enterprise Fund accounting, this trial balance has been modified from the usual trial balance format in that (1) it is divided into two major sections, entitled "General Accounts" and "Restricted Accounts," respectively, and (2) subtotals have been included to indicate the self-balancing nature of many Enterprise Fund intrafund "funds."

This is not to say that all intrafund restricted account groups are self-balancing, for they need not be. Thus, had we not assumed in our example that the net assets of the Customers' Deposits "fund" were restricted to guarantee future interest liabilities to customers (1) there would have been no need to establish a Reserve for Earnings on Customers' Deposits, and (2) this "fund" would not be self-balancing.

Closing Entries. As observed earlier, any reasonable closing entry combination that brings the temporary proprietorship accounts to a zero balance and updates the Retained Earnings account is acceptable. Inasmuch as a multiple-step closing approach was illustrated in Chapter 12, the compound-entry approach is demonstrated here:

(46)	Residual Equity Transfer from General Fund	400,000	
	Operating Revenues	321,000	
	Nonoperating Revenue—Equipment Rental	7,000	
	Interest Revenue	1,850	
	Operating Expenses		194,400
	Depreciation Expense		36,000
	Taxes Expense		18,000
	Interest Expense		42,850
	Retained Earnings		38,600
	Contribution from municipality		400,000
	To close the temporary proprietorship accounts and update Retained Earnings.		

Financial Statements. In cases where it is necessary to present separately the financial position, operating results, and changes in financial position of each proprietary fund,[5] the NCGA has recommended three major statements: balance sheet; statement of revenues, expenses, and changes in retained earnings (or total equity); and statement of changes in financial position. Supplemental schedules

Figure 13-1

A GOVERNMENTAL UNIT
Electric (Enterprise) Fund
Preclosing (Adjusted) Trial Balance
(Date)

General Accounts:

Cash	86,814	
Accounts Receivable	71,968	
Allowance for Uncollectible Accounts		13,492
Unbilled Accounts Receivable	21,000	
Accrued Interest Receivable	200	
Due from State Public Works Department	7,000	
Inventory of Materials and Supplies	30,000	
Prepaid Insurance	600	
Land	50,000	
Buildings	100,000	
Accumulated Depreciation—Buildings		15,000
Improvements Other than Buildings	777,000	
Accumulated Depreciation— Improvements other than Buildings		85,000
Machinery and Equipment	200,500	
Accumulated Depreciation—Machinery and Equipment		56,000
Vouchers Payable		49,500
Due to Internal Service Fund		12,800
Accrued Salaries and Wages Payable		6,000
Accrued Interest Payable		2,000
Accrued Taxes Payable		7,500
Bonds Payable		650,000
Unamortized Premiums on Bonds		1,700
Contribution from Municipality		400,000
Contribution from Subdividers		30,000
Retained Earnings	22,510	
Operating Revenues		321,000
Operating Expenses	194,400	
Depreciation Expense	36,000	
Taxes Expense	18,000	
Nonoperating Revenue—Equipment Rental		7,000
Interest Revenue		1,850
Interest Expense	42,850	
Subtotal	1,658,842	1,658,842

---

[5] In some cases it may be satisfactory to present information for each fund only in combining and combined statements, or, conceivably, only in combined statements. See Chapter 14.

Figure 13-1 (Continued)

Restricted or Secondary Accounts:

	Customers' Deposits—Cash	978	
	Customers' Deposits—Investments	10,000	
	Customers' Deposits—Accrued Interest		
	Receivable	200	
Customers'	Customers' Deposits Payable		10,973
Deposits	Customers' Deposits—Interest Payable		145
"Fund"	Reserve for Earnings on Customers'		
	Deposits		60
	Subtotal	11,178	11,178
Debt	Debt Service—Cash	15,000	
Service	Debt Service—Accrued Interest Payable ...		6,000
"Fund"	Reserve for Bond Debt Service		9,000
	Subtotal	15,000	15,000
	Principal and Interest Reserve—Cash	1,300	
	Principal and Interest Reserve—		
Principal	Investments	9,000	
and	Principal and Interest Reserve—Accrued		
Interest	Interest Receivable	150	
"Fund"	Reserve for Bond Principal and Interest		
	Payments Guarantee		10,450
	Subtotal	10,450	10,450
Contin-	Contingencies—Cash	10,000	
gencies	Contingencies—Vouchers Payable		7,000
"Fund"	Reserve for Contingencies		3,000
	Subtotal	10,000	10,000
	Total	1,705,470	1,705,470

may be prepared showing the details of any segments of the principal statements that need additional explanation. Typical schedules of this type are for "operating expenses—budgeted and actual" and for fixed assets and depreciation, including changes therein. Schedules describing aspects of intrafund restricted account groups may also be desirable or required. For example, contractual requirements may dictate a statement of assets restricted for bond debt service. It may also be useful to prepare statements detailing changes in the cash and investment accounts of other intrafund restricted asset account groups.

Balance sheet. A Balance Sheet for the Electric (Enterprise) Fund is illustrated in Figure 13-2. Note that the balance sheet exhibited is similar to that of a profit-seeking public utility. Like the balance sheet of a business enterprise, or that of many Nonexpendable Trust and Internal Service Funds, this statement contains both fixed assets and long-term liabilities of the government enterprise.

The balance sheet presented in Figure 13-2 follows the arrangement recommended by the National Association of Railroad and Utilities Commissioners, in which fixed assets precede current assets and long-term debt precedes current liabilities. This arrangement of utility balance sheets is consistent with the usual relative importance of fixed assets and long-term liabilities in this "capital-inten-

Figure 13-2

A GOVERNMENTAL UNIT

Electric (Enterprise) Fund
Balance Sheet
(Date)

Assets

Plant and equipment:

Land		$ 50,000
Buildings	$100,000	
Less: Accumulated depreciation	15,000	85,000
Improvements other than buildings	$777,000	
Less: Accumulated depreciation	85,000	692,000
Machinery and equipment	$200,500	
Less: Accumulated depreciation	56,000	144,500

Total plant and equipment			$ 971,500
Current assets:			
Cash		$ 86,814	
Accounts receivable	$ 71,968		
Less: Allowance for uncollectible accounts	13,492	58,476	
Unbilled accounts receivable		21,000	
Accrued interest receivable		200	
Due from State Public Works Department		7,000	
Inventory of materials and supplies		30,000	
Prepaid insurance		600	
Total current assets			204,090
Restricted assets:			
Customers deposits:			
Cash	$ 978		
Investments	10,000		
Accrued interest receivable	200	$ 11,178	
Debt service:			
Cash		15,000	
Principal and interest reserve:			
Cash	$ 1,300		
Investments	9,000		
Accrued interest receivable	150	10,450	
Contingencies:			
Cash		10,000	
Total restricted assets			46,628
Total assets			$1,222,218

sive" industry—current assets and liabilities are often relatively insignificant by comparison. The familiar "order of liquidity" arrangement is also acceptable for utility balance sheets, however, and will normally be preferable for nonutility types of Enterprise Fund balance sheets. The balance sheet should be presented in comparative form, but in this case the Electric Fund is completing its first year of operation.

Figure 13-2 (Continued)

Liabilities and Fund Equity

Long-term liabilities:
Bonds payable	$650,000	
Unamortized premiums on bonds	1,700	
Total long-term liabilities		$ 651,700

Current liabilities (payable from current
   assets):
Vouchers payable	$ 49,500	
Due to Internal Service Fund	12,800	
Accrued salaries and wages payable	6,000	
Accrued interest payable	2,000	
Accrued taxes payable	7,500	
Total current liabilities (payable from current assets)		77,800

Liabilities payable from restricted assets:
Customers' deposits payable	$ 10,973	
Interest payable on customers' deposits	145	
Debt service—accrued bond interest payable	6,000	
Contingencies—vouchers payable	7,000	
Total liabilities payable from restricted assets		24,118
Total liabilities		$ 753,618

Fund equity:
  Retained earnings:
    Reserved:
Reserve for earnings on customers' deposits	$ 60	
Reserve for bond debt service	9,000	
Reserve for bond principal and interest guarantee	10,450	
Reserve for contingencies	3,000	
Total reserved		$ 22,510
Unreserved		16,090
Total retained earnings		$ 38,600

Contributions:
Contributions from municipality	$400,000	
Contributions from subdividers	30,000	
Total contributions		430,000
Total fund equity		$ 468,600
Total liabilities and fund equity		$1,222,218

*Note: This statement would be prepared in comparative form when data of the prior year
are available.*

Notice the asset categorization as among plant and equipment, current assets, and restricted assets in the Balance Sheet in Figure 13-2 and the parallel
division of liabilities into long-term liabilities, current liabilities payable from
current assets, and liabilities payable from restricted assets. Such intrastatement

categorization permits ready "across the balance sheet" comparisons and analyses.

The Contributions from Municipality account shows the amount of capital invested in the utility by the governmental unit. As indicated earlier, this account is credited for the amount expended by the governmental unit in acquiring the utility. Similarly, the account is credited for subsequent capital contributions made by the governmental unit to the utility, such as those to make up a deficit or to increase its capital. The NCGA position is that the Contributions from Municipality account should not be reduced by amounts transferred each year from the Enterprise Fund to the General Fund. (For example, the governmental unit may transfer all or a portion of utility profits to the General Fund each year.) Such transfers are deemed by the NCGA to first reduce Retained Earnings, since they usually are distributions of earnings rather than disinvestments of capital. Only when Retained Earnings has been reduced to zero are such transfers deemed to reduce the governmental unit's capital contribution. (A temporary advance to an Enterprise Fund should be recorded in "Advance To/From" accounts and the nature of the transaction should be documented in the minutes of the governing body.)

Statement of Revenues, Expenses, and Changes in Retained Earnings. A Statement of Revenues, Expenses, and Changes in Retained Earnings (or Equity) should be prepared annually and as necessary on an interim basis. Since this has been the first year of operation of the Electric Fund there are no data for the prior year, but the statement would ordinarily be prepared in comparative form.

The statement shown in Figure 13-3 illustrates the usual utility format in which (1) a distinction is maintained between operating revenues and expenses and nonoperating revenues and expenses, and (2) operating expenses are summarized, being supported by a Detailed Statement of Operating Expenses (Figure 13-4). Had there been many significant types of operating revenues, these too might have been shown in summary and supported by a detailed schedule.

The statement is prepared on the basis of **total** retained earnings and hence shows no changes in retained earnings reserves. If it had been prepared on the **unreserved** retained earnings basis, the "Illustrative General Purpose Financial Statements" prepared by the staff of the NCGA (but not approved by NCGA) to accompany *Statement 1* suggests that "any changes in the reserves during the year would be presented in an 'Other Changes in Unreserved Retained Earnings/Fund Balances' section after 'Net Income.' "[6] The suggested treatment would presumably result in a "Net changes in unreserved retained earnings" figure to which the beginning balance would be added to obtain the end-of-year balance. The authors prefer a treatment that parallels that of financial reporting for business:

Net income		$38,600
Unreserved retained earnings, beginning of year		0
Total		$38,600
Deduct changes in reserves:		
Increase in reserve for customers' deposits...	$	60
Increase in reserve for bond debt service ..		9,000

[6] NCGAS 1, p. 37.

Increase in reserve for bond principal and interest guarantee	10,450	
Increase in reserve for contingencies	3,000	
Total deductions		$22,510
Unreserved retained earnings, end of period .		$16,090

The principal causes of changes in the Retained Earnings account are, as in commercial accounting, (1) net income or loss, (2) "dividends" paid to the governmental unit, (3) increases or decreases in reserved retained earnings accounts, and (4) corrections of prior year errors. Note that the changes in contributed

Figure 13-3

A GOVERNMENTAL UNIT

Electric (Enterprise) Fund
Statement of Revenues, Expenses, and
Changes in Retained Earnings
For the Period Ended (Date)

Operating revenues:		
Residential sales	$155,200	
Commercial sales	91,300	
Industrial sales	62,500	
Public street lighting	12,000	
Total operating revenues		$321,000
Less: Operating revenue deductions:		
Operating expenses (Figure 13-4)	$194,400	
Depreciation*	36,000	
Taxes	18,000	
Total operating revenue deductions		248,400
Operating income*		$ 72,600
Add: Nonoperating revenues:		
Equipment rental	$ 7,000	
Interest revenue	1,850	
Total nonoperating income		8,850
Total operating and nonoperating income ..		$ 81,450
Less: Nonoperating expenses:		
Interest expense		42,850
Net income		$ 38,600
Retained earnings, beginning of period†		—
Retained earnings, end of period		$ 38,600

*Where net revenue is calculated on a cash basis for purposes of computing debt service coverage, an "Operating Revenue before Depreciation" figure is frequently presented, from which depreciation is deducted in determining "Operating Income."

†There is no beginning balance because this statement was prepared at the end of the first year of the enterprise's life.

Note: This statement would be prepared in comparative form when data for the prior year are available.

Figure 13-4

A GOVERNMENTAL UNIT

Electric (Enterprise) Fund
Detailed Statement* of Operating Expenses
For the Fiscal Year Ended (Date)

Production Expenses:
 Electric generating:
  Supervision .... $ 8,000
  Station labor 15,000
  Fuel 54,000
  Water 4,000
  Supplies and other expenses .... 8,400 $ 89,400

 Maintenance of plant and equipment:
  Supervision .... $ 4,000
  Maintenance of structures and
   improvements 8,000
  Maintenance of boiler plant equipment .. 10,000
  Maintenance of generating and electric
   plant equipment 10,000   32,000

 Power purchased   2,000

   Total production expenses $123,400
Distribution Expenses:
 Supervision .... $ 2,500
 Services on consumers' premises 4,500
 Street lighting and signal system 4,000
 Overhead system 18,200
 Maintenance and servicing of mobile
  equipment 3,000
 Utility storeroom expenses 4,000

   Total distribution expenses   36,200
Accounting and Collection Expenses:
 Customers' contracts and orders .... $ 2,500
 Meter reading 3,500
 Collecting offices 1,000
 Delinquent accounts—collection expense .. 2,000
 Customers' billing and accounting 4,000
 Provision for doubtful accounts 1,800

   Total accounting and collection
    expenses   14,800
Sales Promotion Expenses   1,000
Administrative and General Expenses:
 Salaries of executives .... $ 8,000
 Other general office salaries 3,500
 General office supplies and expenses 400
 Insurance 2,000
 Employees' welfare expenses 1,500
 Pension fund contributions 2,800
 Miscellaneous general expenses 800

   Total administrative and general
    expenses   19,000

Total operating expenses $194,400

Figure 13-4 (Continued)

*The detailed amounts in this statement cannot be derived from the example in the chapter. They have been hypothesized for illustrative purposes only.
Note: This statement would be prepared in comparative form when data for the prior year are available.

capital do not appear in this statement. Rather, they would be disclosed by footnote or in a separate statement of changes in contributed capital.

Statement of Changes in Financial Position. The third primary statement recommended for Enterprise Funds by the NCGA is the Statement of Changes in Financial Position. The AICPA Accounting Principles Board recommended in

Figure 13-5

A GOVERNMENTAL UNIT

Electric (Enterprise) Fund
Statement of Changes in (Working Capital) Financial Position
For the Period Ended (Date)

Sources of Working Capital

Operations:			
Net Income (Figure 13-3)		$ 38,600	
Add: Expenses not currently requiring working capital—			
Depreciation of facilities and equipment		36,000	
Deduct: Deductions from expense not currently providing working capital—			
Amortization of bond premium		(300)	
Total provided by operations			$ 74,300
Other Sources:			
Contribution from municipality		$400,000	
Contributions from subdividers		30,000	
Assumption of ABC bonds		500,000	
Issuance of bonds		202,000	
Total provided from other sources			1,132,000
Total provided			$1,206,300

Uses of Working Capital

Acquisition of land		$ 50,000	
Acquisition of buildings		90,000	
Acquisition of improvements other than buildings ..		707,000	
Acquisition of machinery and equipment		160,500	
Retirement of bonds		50,000	
Increase in net assets restricted for:			
Customers' deposits	$ 60		
Debt service	9,000		
Principal and interest reserve	10,450		
Contingencies	3,000	22,510	
Total uses			1,080,010
Increase in working capital			$ 126,290

Figure 13-6

A GOVERNMENTAL UNIT

Electric (Enterprise) Fund
Statement of Changes in (Unrestricted Cash) Financial Position
For the Period Ended (Date)

Sources of unrestricted cash:
Operations:

Net Income (Figure 13-3)		$ 38,600	
Add: Expenses not currently requiring unrestricted cash outlays—			
Depreciation of facilities and equipment	$ 36,000		
Increase in current liabilities	67,800	103,800	
Deduct: Deductions from expenses not affecting cash requirements:			
Amortization of bond premium ..	$ 300		
Increase in current receivables (net of allowance for uncollectible accounts)	36,676		
Increase in inventory of materials and supplies	20,000		
Increase in prepaid insurance	600	(57,576)	
Total provided by operations			$ 84,824
Other sources:			
Contribution from municipality		$400,000	
Assumption of ABC bonds payable		500,000	
Assumption of ABC vouchers payable		10,000	
Issuance of bonds		202,000	
Contribution from subdividers		30,000	
Total provided by other sources			1,142,000
Total provided			$1,226,824
Uses of unrestricted cash:			
Acquisition of land		$ 50,000	
Acquisition of buildings		90,000	
Acquisition of improvements other than buildings		707,000	
Acquisition of machinery and equipment		160,500	
Acquisition of initial accounts receivable		50,000	
Acquisition of initial inventory of materials and supplies		10,000	
Retirement of bonds		50,000	
Increases in net assets restricted for:			
Customers' deposits	$ 60		
Debt service	9,000		
Principal and interest reserve	10,450		
Contingencies	3,000	22,510	
Total uses			1,140,010
Increase in unrestricted cash			$ 86,814

Opinion 19 that the statement should be based on a broad concept of cash or working capital that embraces all changes in financial position and that the concept or basis of preparation should be clearly disclosed.

As noted in Chapter 12, considerable flexibility of both concept and format are permissible insofar as statements summarizing changes in financial position are concerned. It is imperative, however, that all important financing and investing activities be disclosed, even those that do not directly affect cash or other working capital elements. A Statement of Changes in Financial Position prepared on the working capital concept is illustrated in Figure 13-5. A Statement of Changes in Financial Position prepared on the cash concept is presented in Figure 13-6. A schedule of changes in working capital components (elements) should accompany or appear in Figure 13-5, but has been omitted in the interest of brevity since such a schedule is illustrated in Figure 12-4.

A detailed discussion of the underlying concepts and preparation techniques for the statement of changes in financial position is beyond the scope of this text. The reader desiring a detailed treatment of this topic is referred to Accounting Principles Board (APB) Opinions 3 and 19 and to any standard intermediate accounting textbook.

A GENERAL COMMENT ON REPORTING FOR PROPRIETARY FUNDS

The NCGA issued general guidelines for certain aspects of reporting for *all* proprietary funds as that reporting pertains to grants, entitlements, or shared revenues.[7] If receipts occur before the usual criteria for revenue recognition have been met, they should be shown as deferred revenues, a liability. When recognition criteria have been met, they are reported as nonoperating revenues unless they are externally restricted to capital acquisitions. In the latter case they should be reported as contributed capital in an appropriately descriptive caption, such as "Capital grants."

Assets acquired by a process that resulted in a credit to contributed capital are as subject to depreciation as are other fixed assets, and depreciation of all depreciable assets is a part of operating expenses. The Council permitted, but did not require,[8] the depreciation of assets acquired with intergovernmental grant resources externally restricted to capital acquisitions to be closed to the related contributed capital account, thus effectively transferring a portion of contributed capital to retained earnings. When the asset is fully depreciated, the related contributed capital would be eliminated.

Since there is no similar transfer process available for similarly acquired nondepreciable fixed assets, and since the using up of depreciable assets has no bearing on the fact of the contribution, there seems to be no theoretical justification for the process. However, many Enterprise Funds that were heavily grant financed had both large contributed capital balances and large retained earnings deficits. City officials with such Funds argued that (1) they would not have acquired

---

[7] NCGAS 2.
[8] Ibid., p. 3.

Figure 13-7

PROPRIETARY FUND BALANCE SHEET
EQUITY SECTION

Fund Equity:
Contributed capital:
Capital grants .... $xx
Less: amortization [Optional]   xx $xx

Government's contributions .....   xx $xx

Retained earnings   xx

Total Fund Equity .... $xx

Source: NCGAS 2, p. 3.

Figure 13-8

A GOVERNMENTAL UNIT
A PROPRIETARY FUND

Statement of Revenues, Expenses, and Changes in Retained Earnings
For the Fiscal Year Ended (Date)

Operating Revenues:	
(Detailed)	$ xx
Operating Expenses:	
(Detailed—includes depreciation on *all* depreciable fixed assets)	(xx)
Operating Income (Loss)	xx
Nonoperating Revenues (Expenses):	
(Detailed—nonoperating revenues include grants, entitlements, and shared revenues received for operations and/or such resources that may be used for either operations or capital outlay at the discretion of the recipient)	xx
Income (Loss) before Operating Transfers	xx
Operating Transfers:	
(Detailed)	xx
Net Income (Loss)	xx
Add depreciation on fixed assets acquired by grants, entitlements, and shared revenues externally restricted for capital acquisitions and construction that reduces contributed capital [Optional]	xx
Increase (Decrease in Retained Earnings	xx
Retained Earnings—Beginning of Period	xx
Retained Earnings—End of Period	$ xx

Source: NCGAS 2, p. 3.

the depreciable fixed assets, and thereby incurred the related depreciation expense, if grants had not been available, and (2) they would not replace the fixed assets unless grants were available. Thus they persuaded the NCGA to approve special grant accounting procedures for proprietary funds.

The effects of the alternative process on the financial statements were illustrated by the NCGA as shown in Figures 13-7 and 13-8.

SUMMARY OF INTERFUND ACCOUNTING

At this point all the types of funds and nonfund account groups commonly employed in state and local government accounting have been presented and discussed. It should be evident that the use of separate funds and account groups is the dominating characteristic of contemporary governmental accounting procedures. It is now appropriate to review and summarize the principal concepts that have guided the discussions of the procedures of the several types of funds and account groups.

Independent Fiscal and Accounting Entities. Each fund and nonfund account group is an independent fiscal entity and must be accounted for as such. The accounting system must be so devised that the assets, liabilities, capital or balances (reserves, unreserved fund balance, contributed capital, retained earnings), revenues, and expenditures or expenses are identified with the particular fund or nonfund account group entity to which they apply. It follows that each entity must have a self-balancing set of accounts. It does *not* follow that a separate ledger must be established for each fund and nonfund account group. The accounts required may be maintained either (1) in separate ledgers or (2) in a single ledger or computer file in which the fund and nonfund entities are distinguished through an appropriate account classification code.

A fund does not necessarily consist only of cash. It may also contain other assets—such as receivables, inventories, and even fixed assets—as well as the liabilities (either in total or those that have matured) that are to be discharged from its resources. Cash segregated for certain purposes does not necessarily constitute a fund, though it may constitute either a fund or a "fund" in the Enterprise Fund and commercial accounting sense.

Types of Independent Fiscal Entities. The NCGA used the following classifications of funds and account groups for accounting measurement purposes:

Governmental funds (expendable)
  General
  Special Revenue
  Capital Projects
  Special Assessment
  Debt Service
Proprietary funds (nonexpendable)
  Internal Service
  Enterprise
Fiduciary funds
  Government type (expendable)
    Expendable Trust
    Agency
  Proprietary type (nonexpendable)
    Nonexpendable Trust

Pension Trust
Nonfund account groups
General Fixed Assets
General Long-Term Debt

These classifications are useful because (1) many conceptual and procedural similarities are shared by the funds or nonfund account groups within each category, and (2) major conceptual and procedural characteristics distinguish each of the three categories. Thus, we have seen that (1) the primary focus of expendable fund accounting is upon flows (revenues and expenditures) and balances of appropriable resources, usually in relation to budgetary estimates or limitations, and that expendable funds are comprised primarily of current assets and related current liabilities; (2) the nonfund account groups provide accountability for non-appropriable (fixed) assets and for long-term liabilities that are not to be discharged from assets of a particular fund during the current accounting period; and (3) the nonexpendable funds are accounted for in generally the same manner as private commercial enterprises; i.e., the accounting focus is upon revenues and expenses (not expenditures) and both current and fixed assets and liabilities are included within the nonexpendable fund accounts.

Differences in Budgetary Control Emphasis. The revenue and expenditure transactions of most expendable funds are customarily planned and controlled through the use of rather rigid fixed dollar budgets and appropriations. This is particularly true of the General, Special Revenue, Capital Projects, and Debt Service Funds. In order to facilitate budgetary control and comparision in these funds, both budgetary and proprietary accounts are maintained within their account structures.

On the other hand, nonexpendable fund activities are more commonly planned through flexible budgeting techniques because their transactions are determined by the level of demand for their goods or services or by other factors. Thus, budgetary accounts are not usually included in their account structures. In those cases where nonexpendable funds are subject to budget and appropriation controls, budgetary accounts may be made a part of their accounting system but are not ordinarily combined with the proprietary accounts. Furthermore, usually only those budgetary constraints embodied in legal provisions are included as part of the nonexpendable fund accounting system; all other budgetary operations are recorded in budget memoranda accounts. For example, estimated revenues of nonexpendable funds rarely need to be recorded formally in the accounts.

Separation of Related Assets and Liabilities. The use of special purpose fund and nonfund account group entities often results in related assets and liabilities being accounted for through different accounting entities. For example, special assessment improvements are included in the General Fixed Assets accounts, whereas special assessment debt is shown as a liability of a Special Assessment Fund. Similarly, though bond issue proceeds are accounted for through a Capital Projects Fund, the related liability is included in the General Long-Term Debt Account Group.

Differences in Recording Assets and Liabilities. Because of the differing natures of the funds and account groups, identical types of assets and liabilities may be included in some funds and excluded from others. For example, fixed assets and bonds payable are included within an Enterprise Fund but not in the General Fund. Again, special assessment bonds payable are shown as a liability of the appropriate Special Assessment Fund, but the special assessment improvements are not capitalized therein.

Differences in the Basis of Accounting. Differences in the nature and accounting focus of the various funds also cause differences in the bases of accounting employed. The modified accrual basis is used for some, whereas the full accrual basis is employed for others.

In the funds subject to rigid budgetary control, the basis upon which appropriations are made *dictates* the basis of budgetary accounting that will be used during the budget period and the reporting that will indicate budget compliance. The modified accrual basis is recommended for all governmental (expendable) funds, but especially for those funds that are subject to formal budgetary control. It is obviously preferable, then, for budgets to be prepared on that basis. Financial statements prepared in conformity with GAAP will be prepared on the modified accrual basis no matter what the budgetary basis of accounting may be.

On the modified accrual basis revenues are recognized only when measurable appropriable resources become available. Expenditures are recognized in the period in which the fund liability is incurred, except that interest on general long-term debt is recognized in the period in which it will be paid, the period for which an appropriation will be made. In the Special Assessment Fund, interest on debt that is secured by interest-bearing special assessments should similarly be recognized when due, as is interest earned.

Even where the modified accrual basis of accounting is used, it may be necessary to adjust the asset and liability accounts at year end, and to increase or decrease the Fund Balance (either reserved or unreserved) accounts correspondingly, in order that the financial position of the fund may be reported properly. For example, inventory adjustments are handled in this manner when appropriations are based on inventory purchases rather than on usage. As suggested above, it may be necessary to issue supplementary financial statements when those prepared in conformity with GAAP do not provide a sufficient indication of compliance with legal requirements.

The accrual basis is used in accounting for nonexpendable funds because it is essential to determine periodic net income and measure preservation of capital of these funds. Under this basis, revenues are recorded as soon as they are earned, regardless of when they will be collected; and expenses are recorded when incurred, regardless of when they will be paid. Depreciation and other amortization expenses (and revenues) are recorded so that all revenues and expenses may be reported and all capital increments and decrements may be fairly presented.

Accounts of Funds v. Accounts of the Governmental Unit. Much of the foregoing summary points up a final observation. State and local government accounting and reporting suffers from an identity crisis: Which is the important entity? Is it the fund, the fund type, or the government as a whole? From a legal point of view the individual fund justifies, even requires, separate accounting and reporting. But many users of financial statements want an overall view of financial position and results of operation of a municipality or a state. The current resolution of this identity question is described in Chapter 14, and the matter is discussed further in Chapter 15. At this point it is sufficient to say that both needs must be and are being served.

▶ **Question 13-1.** How should one determine whether a particular activity should be accounted for through an Enterprise Fund?

Question 13-2. The garbage collection and disposal services of a local government might be accounted for through the General Fund, a Special Revenue Fund, a Special Assessment Fund, or an Enterprise Fund. Indicate the circumstances in which each of these fund types might be the appropriate accounting vehicle for such an activity.

Question 13-3. How does one distinguish between an Internal Service Fund and an Enterprise Fund?

Question 13-4. Contrast and explain the accounting distinction between revenues and capital investments (or disinvestments) in a nonexpendable (proprietary) fund such as the Enterprise Fund with that made in an expendable (governmental) fund.

Question 13-5. What is the purpose of reserves in Enterprise Fund accounting?

Question 13-6. An asset costing $10,000 was transferred from the General Fixed Assets Account Group of a governmental unit to the governmental unit's enterprise. What effect would this transfer have on the General Fund and the Enterprise Fund, respectively?

Question 13-7. Township City is located adjacent to a freeway leading to a nearby metropolitan area and has grown rapidly from a small village to a city of 75,000. Its population is expected to continue to double every ten years in the foreseeable future. The city has owned and operated the local electricity generation and distribution system since its inception many years ago and has never charged itself for electricity consumption. The newly employed comptroller of Township City seeks your advice in this regard. What is your response?

Question 13-8. (a) A utility bills its customers separately for services and for sales taxes. Should billings for sales taxes be included in Enterprise Fund revenues? (b) Suppose that the utility is not allowed to bill customers for the sales tax. However, rates have been raised by approximately the amount of the tax. Should the revenues be reduced by the amount of the sales tax? (c) Give the entries to show how the payment of the taxes by the governmental utility (enterprise) would be recorded in each of the above cases.

Question 13-9. A certain city, wishing to acquire a privately owned utility, had an appraisal made of the property. The appraisers valued the assets on the basis of original cost less accumulated depreciation and arrived at a value of $400,000. The owners refused to sell the plant for less than $425,000, however, and the municipality paid the full amount asked. Give the entry necessary to record the cash purchase of the utility by the municipality.

Question 13-10, Part I. A utility's engineer claims that no depreciation charges should be made during 19X1 on certain machines because these machines are operating with 95 percent efficiency, the same level as during the previous year. Are the engineer's claims correct?

Question 13-10, Part II. The engineers of a municipal utility claim that depreciation should not be charged since the city is spending money for maintaining the plant. Is their claim correct?

Question 13-11. It is sometimes claimed that to include depreciation among the expenses and to provide money out of earnings to retire bonds which were used to finance the acquisition of the assets being depreciated is to overcharge the current generation of customers. Through retiring the debt, the customers are paying for the old plant, and through depreciation charges they are paying for a new plant. Is this claim correct? Explain.

Question 13-12. Why is it not necessary to reserve Enterprise Fund Retained Earnings to the extent that assets are set aside in an equipment replacement intrafund "fund"? (Note particularly that this procedure is contrary to the practice followed in the case of a sinking "fund," where an amount corresponding to the addition made to the sinking fund is added to the appropriate reserve account.)

Question 13-13. Having been told repeatedly during his many years of service that depreciation was charged "in order to provide for the replacement of fixed assets," a member of a government's electric utility (Enterprise Fund) board of directors was visibly upset upon being advised by the controller that it would be necessary for the utility to go deeply in debt "in order to replace some of our fixed assets." "How can it be true," he asks, "that we have operated profitably each year, have an $850,000 Retained Earnings balance and total Accumulated Depreciation account balances of $6,000,000, have never made transfers to the General Fund, and yet have Cash and Investments totaling only $100,000?"

Question 13-14, Part I. A pension fund is maintained through contributions from both a municipal utility and its employees and is administered by an independent pension board. (a) Should such a fund be shown as part of the Enterprise Fund? (b) Would your answer be different if contributions were made only by the utility?

Question 13-14, Part II. A utility carries a pension fund as part of the Enterprise Fund. Should earnings on pension fund investments be included in Enterprise Fund revenues?

Question 13-15. A local government council has jurisdiction over the electricity generation and distribution franchise rights in its area. Having exhausted its taxing and general obligation debt issue authority, it is considering the possibility of terminating the franchise held by a privately owned regulated utility now serving the area. Certain members of the council have proposed that this be done, noting that a municipally owned utility is not subject to state or Federal regulation, state or local property taxes, and Federal or state income taxes. They suggest that the present owners of the utility be offered municipal utility revenue bonds in the amount of the unamortized original cost values of the fixed assets on the utility books; in addition, the present owners would be permitted to keep the cash and investments now held by the utility to the extent that they exceed its current liabilities, and the municipality would assume the outstanding bonds of the utility. The proponents of the plan further suggest that the excess of the receipts of the municipally owned utility over current expenses and debt service requirements be transferred to the General Fund and used to finance current operations of the municipality. Assuming that you are a newly elected member of the council, what questions would you raise with regard to the proposal?

Question 13-16. It is sometimes suggested that the amount contributed to a municipally-owned enterprise by the municipality or donated to it by others should be amortized to Retained Earnings as the property thereby acquired is depreciated in the accounts. Proponents of the amortization procedure believe that, in its absence, the Retained Earnings account is understated. Do you agree with the procedure proposed? Why?

Question 13-17. Does the term "accrual" refer to *what* is measured or to *when* measurement occurs? Explain.

Question 13-18. Why did the NCGA recommend the modified accrual basis of accounting for some funds and the accrual basis for others? Is this not inconsistent?

Question 13-19. A city controller has expressed his desire to convert the city's fund and nonfund account group records, now maintained in separate ledgers, to a system in which all accounts would be maintained within a single general ledger. Is this permissible? Explain.

Question 13-20. Which of the funds and nonfund account groups have what might be described as a budget? Explain.

Question 13-21. In governmental accounting, some funds are accounted for primarily on a period basis while the project is a more significant basis for reporting for others. State which basis is appropriate for each of the funds and nonfund account groups we have studied.

Question 13-22. Part I. In what funds may "Buildings" properly appear as an account title?

Question 13-22, Part II. For which types of funds are profit and loss (income determination) accounting procedures employed?

Question 13-23. Contrast and explain the differences in the accounting for bond premiums or discounts as among those arising upon the issue of general obligation construction bonds, special assessment bonds, and enterprise revenue bonds.

▶ **Problem 13-1.** The City of Lenn operates its municipal airport. The trial balance of the Airport Fund as of January 1, 19X0, was as follows:

Cash	$ 37,000	
Accounts Receivable	50,000	
Allowance for Uncollectible Accounts ..		$ 2,000
Land	200,000	
Structure and Improvements	700,000	
Accumulated Depreciation—Structures and Improvements		50,000
Equipment	250,000	
Accumulated Depreciation— Equipment		90,000
Vouchers Payable		48,000
Bonds Payable		800,000
Governmental Unit's Contribution		200,000
Retained Earnings		47,000
	$1,237,000	$1,237,000

The following transactions took place during the year:

1. Revenues collected in cash: aviation revenues, $340,500; concession revenues, $90,000; revenues from airport management, $30,000; revenues from sales of petroleum products, etc. (net revenue, after deducting all costs relating to the sales), $10,500.

2. Expenses, all paid in cash with the exception of $24,000, which remained unpaid at December 31, were: operating, $222,000; maintenance, $75,000; general and administrative, $73,000.

3. Bad debts written off during the year, $1,900.
4. The vouchers payable outstanding on January 1, 19X0, were paid.
5. Bonds paid during the year, $50,000, together with interest of $40,000.
6. The remaining accounts receivable outstanding on January 1, 19X0, were collected.
7. Accounts receivable on December 31, 19X0, amounted to $30,000, all applicable to aviation revenues, of which $1,400 is estimated to be uncollectible.
8. Accrued interest payable at the end of the year, $3,000.
9. Depreciation charges:

Structures and Improvements	$14,000
Equipment	21,000

Required:

(a) Prepare a worksheet to reflect the beginning trial balance, the transactions and adjustments during 19X0, the revenues and expenses of the year (or closing entries), and the ending balance sheet data.

(b) Prepare a Balance Sheet for the Airport Fund as of December 31, 19X0.

(c) Prepare a Revenue and Expense Statement for the Airport Fund for the fiscal year ended December 31, 19X0.

Problem 13-2. The following is a list of the accounts of the Electric Utility Fund of the City of Ditten as of June 1, 19X7:

Cash	$100,600	
Construction Fund—Cash	30,000	
Deposits Fund—Cash	2,000	
Construction Fund—Expenditures	100,000	
Construction Fund—Vouchers Payable.		$ 40,000
Bonds Authorized—Unissued	50,000	
Accounts Receivable	77,000	
Deposits Fund—Interest Payable		350
Deposits Fund—Interest Receivable ...	400	
Deposits Fund—Investments	10,000	
Deposits Funds—Surplus		2,050
Deposits Payable		9,000
Sinking Fund—Cash	20,000	
Sinking Fund—Investments	50,000	
Sinking Fund—Retained Earnings		5,000
Retained Earnings		139,000
Vouchers Payable		5,000
Inventory of Materials	10,000	
Allowance for Uncollectible Accounts ..		4,600
Appropriations		180,000
Reserve for Retirement of Sinking Fund Bonds (Actuarial Requirement).		65,000

You are given the following additional information:

The electric utility was formerly accounted for in the same manner as any other department. Beginning June 1, 19X7, the utility is to be accounted for as a self-supporting enterprise, no formal records are to be kept of appropriations or other authorizations, and proper account terminology is to be employed.

Fixed assets of the utility consist of the following:

Assets	Cost	Allowance for Depreciation
Land	$150,000	—
Structures and Improvements	320,000	$60,000
Equipment	105,000	30,000
	$575,000	$90,000

The utility began operations many years ago upon receiving a $360,000 cash contribution from the General Fund; the contribution was credited to Retained Earnings. Construction Fund expenditures were for construction work in progress. Bonds outstanding amount to $300,000 at June 1, 19X7.

Required:

(a) Prepare a worksheet from which to prepare a corrected Balance Sheet for the Electric Utility Fund of the City of Ditten at June 1, 19X7. Your worksheet columns should be headed as follows:

Columns	Headings
1–2	Ledger Balances, June 1, 19X7—Dr.
	Cr.
3–4	Adjustments and Corrections—Dr.
	Cr.
5–6	Balance Sheet, June 1, 19X7—Dr.
	Cr.
7–10	Balance Sheet: Detail—Dr. (Cr.)
	Operations ConstructionFund SinkingFund DepositsFund

(b) Prepare a Balance Sheet for the Electric Utility Fund of the City of Ditten as of June 1, 19X7, in proper and customary form.

Problem 13-3. The City of Larkspur provides electric energy for its citizens through an operating department. All transactions of the Electric Department are recorded in a self-sustaining fund supported by revenue from the sales of energy. Plant expansion is financed by the issuance of bonds which are repaid out of revenues. All cash of the Electric Department is held by the city treasurer. Receipts from customers and others are deposited in the treasurer's account. Disbursements are made by drawing warrants on the treasurer.

The following is the postclosing trial balance of the Department as at June 30, 19X7:

Cash on Deposit with City Treasurer ...	$ 2,250,000	
Due from Customers	2,120,000	
Other Current Assets	130,000	
Construction in Progress	500,000	
Land	5,000,000	
Electric Plant	50,000,000*	
Accumulated Depreciation—Electric Plant		$10,000,000
Accounts Payable and Accrued Liabilities		3,270,000

5% Electric Revenue Bonds Payable ...		20,000,000
Accumulated Earnings		26,730,000
	$60,000,000	$60,000,000

* The plant is being depreciated on the basis of a 50-year composite life.

During the year ended June 30, 19X8, the Department had the following transactions:

1. Sales of electric energy, $10,700,000.
2. Purchases of fuel and operating supplies, $2,950,000.
3. Construction expenditures relating to miscellaneous system improvements (financed from operations), $750,000.
4. Fuel consumed, $2,790,000.
5. Miscellaneous plant additions and improvements constructed and placed in service at midyear, $1,000,000.
6. Wages and salaries paid, $4,280,000.
7. Sale at par on December 31, 19X7 of twenty-year 5 percent Electric Revenue bonds, dated January 1, 19X8, with interest payable semiannually, $5,000,000.
8. Expenditures out of bond proceeds for construction of Larkspur Steam Plant Unit No. 1 and control house, $2,800,000.
9. Operating materials and supplies consumed, $150,000.
10. Payments received from customers, $10,500,000.
11. Expenditures out of bond proceeds for construction of Larkspur Steam Plant Unit No. 2, $2,200,000.
12. Warrants drawn on City Treasurer in settlement of accounts payable, $3,045,000.
13. The Larkspur Steam Plant was placed in service June 30, 19X8.
14. Interest on bonds paid during the year, $500,000.

Required:

(a) A worksheet for the Electric Department Fund showing:
1. The balance sheet amounts at June 30, 19X7.
2. The transactions for the year and closing entries. (Note: Formal journal entries are not required.)
3. The balance sheet amounts at June 30, 19X8.

(b) A Statement of Changes in Financial Position (working capital basis) of the Electric Department Fund during the year ended June 30, 19X8, accompanied by a Schedule of Changes in Working Capital.

Problem 13-4. The following information pertains to the operation of the Water Fund of the City of Marion. Included in the operations of this Fund are those of a Special Replacement Fund for the Water Department, the accounts of which are a part of the accounts of the Water Fund.

The balances in the accounts of this fund on January 1, 19X5, were as follows:

| Cash .... | $ 6,126 |
| Accounts Receivable (net of $1,200 estimated to be uncollectible) .... | 7,645 |

Stores	13,826
Investments—Replacement Fund	21,700
Property, Plant, and Equipment	212,604
Accumulated Depreciation	50,400
Vouchers Payable	4,324
Customers' Deposits*	1,500
Replacement Fund Reserve	21,700
Retained Earnings	21,977
Bonds Payable	60,000
Contributed Capital	102,000

No restrictions are placed on deposits received or investment income thereon; interest is not paid on deposits.

The following items represent all transactions of the fund for the year ended December 31, 19X5:

1.	Services billed	$146,867
2.	Accounts collected	147,842
3.	Uncollectible accounts of prior years written off; current provision made, $750	1,097
4.	Invoices and payrolls approved and vouchered for current expense	69,826
5.	Invoices approved and vouchered for water department stores purchased	31,424
6.	Stores issued for use in operation	32,615
7.	Supplies secured from General Fund stores and used in operation (cash paid to General Fund)	7,197
8.	Vouchers approved for payment of annual serial bonds maturity, including interest of $3,000	23,000
9.	Depreciation (replacement reserve and assets adjusted also "to fully reserve and fund" the accumulated depreciation)	10,600
10.	Deposits received	400
	Deposits refunded	240
11.	Invoices approved and vouchered for replacement of fully depreciated equipment which had cost $6,200	7,800
12.	Invoices approved and vouchered for additions to plant	12,460
13.	Interest received on investments; none is accrued at year end ..	1,102
14.	Purchased securities as necessary to fully invest the Replacement Fund to the nearest whole $100	compute
15.	Approved vouchers paid (general)	133,316
16.	Stores inventory per physical count at December 31, 19X5 (any shortages or overages are assumed to be related to operating expenses)	11,820

Required:

(a) A worksheet analysis of the beginning trial balance, transactions and adjustments during 19X5, revenues and expenses, and balance sheet at December 31, 19X5, of the Water Fund of the City of Marion.

(b) A Balance Sheet of the Water Fund as of December 31, 19X5.

(c) A Statement of Revenues, Expenses, and Changes in Retained Earnings for the Water Fund for the year ended December 31, 19X5.

(AICPA, adapted)

Problem 13-5. The following transactions or events are concerned with regulated utilities and with restricted asset intrafund "funds" within Enterprise Funds. Each is independent of the others unless stated otherwise.

1. Amortization of the Utility Plant Acquisition Adjustments account has been completed on an item of equipment still in service in Utility T. The equipment was acquired by Utility T from Utility X for $125,000; its cost new to Utility X was $175,000, and it had a book value of $90,000 when it was sold to Utility T. Both the original cost account and the accumulated depreciation account were recorded on Utility T's books at the time it acquired the equipment.

2. A machine bought by Utility B from Utility A for $300,000 (now 80 percent depreciated) was traded in on a replacement machine (list price $500,000); $450,000 difference was paid, $350,000 of this amount being paid from the Equipment Replacement Fund. Utility A had acquired the machine new at a cost of $400,000; the related accumulated depreciation account had a balance of $150,000 when the machine was acquired by Utility B, which recorded it at net book value in the Machinery and Equipment account at that time. The machine had a fair market value of $25,000 when it was traded in by Utility B. The Equipment Replacement Fund is fully reserved; the reserve is adjusted at the time a transaction affects it.

3. Same situation as transaction 2, but the replacement machine was bought on open account; no cash was disbursed at that time.

4. Depreciation and amortization adjustments for the year ended September 30, 19X8, were recorded by Utility F. Among its assets is a building acquired ten years ago from Utility N for $210,000, exclusive of land cost. At that time the building had a remaining useful life expectancy of 30 years and a net book value of $150,000 to Utility N, which had constructed it at a cost of $175,000.

5. Assume that the building referred to in transaction 4 was destroyed by fire on March 31, 19X2, and that insurance proceeds of $300,000 were accrued immediately.

6. Bond interest of $10,000 was paid at December 31, 19X9, the end of a utility's fiscal year, from the Bond Interest Payments Fund. An additional $2,000 was accrued, also to be paid from the Bond Interest Payments Fund, and bond discount of $350 was amortized.

7. A utility recorded accrued additional interest payable on customer's deposits of $9,600 (accrued during the year) at the end of 19X3 and accrued interest receivable on invested customers' deposits of $3,200. Interest earned on customers' deposits can be used only to pay interest thereon, and distinctively titled customers' deposits revenue and expense accounts are maintained in the utility's general ledger.

8. The customers' deposits accounts were closed. In addition to the information in transaction 7, assume that interest received of $10,000 on invested deposits had been recorded earlier, as had interest expense of $30 on the account of a consumer leaving the service area who was paid a total of $180 accumulated interest on his deposit. Further, assume that interest receivable on customers' deposits invested and additional interest payable on customers' deposits of $2,900 and $6,200 (additional), respectively, had been accrued at the close of the preceding year, at which time the total cumulative interest owed on customers' deposits was reported at $109,300.

Required:

Prepare general journal entries in compound form to record the transactions or events described. You may omit formal entry explanations, but should show all significant computations.

Problem 13-6. The Township of Hamlet finances its operation from revenues provided by property taxes, water distribution, fines levied by the municipal court, and interest. Hamlet maintains only a General Fund. You were engaged to conduct the audit for the year ended December 31, 19X6, and determined the following:

1. General Fund account balances on January 1, 19X6, were:

Cash in savings accounts	$ 62,030
Cash in checking accounts	38,450
Cash on hand (undeposited water receipts)	160
Water works supplies	2,640
Due from water customers	1,670
Fund balance	104,950

2. The budget for 19X6 adopted by the city commission and the transactions relating to the budget (with all current bills vouchered and paid on December 31, 19X6) for the year were:

	Budget	Transactions
Property taxes	$26,750	$26,750
Water works costs	66,500	64,360*
City constable and court fees	10,000	9,550
Water revenues	10,000	12,060†
Court fines	12,500	11,025
Commissioners' salaries and expenses	6,000	5,470
Interest on savings accounts	2,000	2,240
Miscellaneous expenses	1,200	2,610

*Cash expenditures.
†Billings.

3. The commissioners appropriated sufficient General Fund balance to equalize budgeted revenues and appropriations. The difference was caused by anticipated repairs to water mains. It was also necessary to transfer $15,000 from a savings account to a checking account to pay for these repairs during 19X6.

4. Your count of cash on December 31, 19X6, determined that there was $250 on hand that was not deposited until January 2, 19X7.

5. All billings for water during 19X6 were paid with the exception of statements totaling $1,230 which were mailed to customers the last week of December.

6. All water works supplies were consumed during the year on the repair of water mains. Hamlet's charter specifies that appropriation expenditures are to be based on purchases.

Required:

(a) Prepare a worksheet for the Township of Hamlet for the year ended December 31, 19X6. Column headings should provide for (1) a trial balance, (2) transactions for the year, (3) variances from budget, and (4) a balance sheet at December 31, 19X6. Formal statements and journal entires are not required. (Assume that the water distribution system may properly be accounted for in the General Fund.)

(b) Should a separate Enterprise Fund be established to account for the water distribution activity? Why?

(AICPA, adapted)

Problem 13-7. (Review Problem) The Village of Huttig was incorporated January 1, 19X0. You are to prepare worksheets for its several funds. Include the closing entries necessary to produce the correct year-end balances. The following transactions occurred during the year 19X0:

1. The council approved the following budget:

Revenues	$60,000
Expenditures:	
Current expenditures	$50,000
Sinking fund contribution	1,000
Equipment	8,500
	$59,500

2. The First Huttig State Bank loaned the village $10,000 on tax anticipation notes.

3. A General Fund transfer of $2,500 was made to establish an Internal Service Fund to provide a permanent investment in inventory.

4. The village decided to build a village hall and an issue of sinking fund term bonds, $30,000 par value, was authorized. The bonds bear interest at 6 percent and mature in 20 years.

5. The village decided to pave Main Street; a special assessment project was authorized to pave the street at a cost of $20,000.

6. The bond issue was sold at a price of 101 and accrued interest of $100.

7. The assessments were levied at the authorized total amount, less the village's share of $1,000. All assessments were collected during the year, together with the village's contribution.

8. Contracts were made for the paving, $20,000, and for the village hall, $28,000. The paving contract was completed but not approved at December 31; the contracter was paid all but 5 percent, which was retained to ensure compliance with the terms of the contract.

9. Property taxes of $50,000 were levied; it was expected that 1 percent of this amount would prove uncollectible.

10. Cash collections during the year were as follows:

Property taxes	$48,500
Miscellaneous revenues	9,000
	$57,500

11. The following purchase orders were issued during the year:

Various operating expenditures	$25,000
Various items of equipment	7,500
Stores for the IS Fund	2,000
	$34,500

12. The following schedule summarizes certain expenditures made during the year:

	Ordered	Vouchered
Various operating expenditures	$24,250	$48,000
Various items of equipment	7,500	7,400
Tax anticipation notes		5,000
Stores for the IS Fund	2,000	2,100
	$33,750	$62,500

13. The IS Fund purchases were paid for in full; General Fund payments of $50,000 were made on the vouchers above.

14. A local man was paid $250 from the IS Fund to operate the warehouse in his spare time. He issued materials which cost $1,800 to General Fund departments at a billed figure of $2,200. This bill was paid during the year from the General Fund.

15. The actuarial table prepared for the sinking fund showed a $1,000 contribution and earnings of $50 for 19X0. The contribution was paid. Securities were acquired for the sinking fund for $950 during the year and $40 of revenue was received therefrom.

16. The village hall was three-fourths completed according to the supervising architect. Payment of $20,500 was approved and paid. An additional $1,500 was paid to the General Fund to reimburse it for preliminary landscaping work done by employees paid from the General Fund.

17. The operating expenditures (see item 12) included withholding and FICA taxes which had been transferred to the Agency Fund on each payroll date (included in vouchers paid). The amount of these taxes was $750. At December 31, $500 had been paid out of the Agency Fund.

Problem 13-8. (Review Problem) The Village of Dexter was recently incorporated and began financial operations on July 1, 19X8, the beginning of its fiscal year.

The following transactions occurred during this first fiscal year, July 1, 19X8, to June 30, 19X9:

1. The village council adopted a budget for general operations during the fiscal year ending June 30, 19X9. Revenues were estimated at $400,000. Legal authorizations for budgeted expenditures were $394,000.

2. Property taxes of $390,000 were levied; it was estimated that 2 percent of this amount would prove to be uncollectible. These taxes are available as of the date of levy to finance current expenditures.

3. During the year a resident of the village donated marketable securities valued at $50,000 to the village under the terms of a trust agreement. The terms of the trust agreement stipulated that the principal amount is to be kept intact; use of revenue generated by the securities is restricted to financing college scholarships for needy students. Revenue earned and received on these marketable securities amounted to $5,500 through June 30, 19X9.

4. A General Fund transfer of $5,000 was made to establish an Internal Service Fund to provide for a permanent investment in inventory.

5. The village decided to install lighting in the village park and a special assessment project was authorized to install the lighting at a cost of $75,000.

6. The assessments were levied for $72,000, with the village contributing $3,000 out of the General Fund. All assessments were collected during the year, including the village's contribution.

7. A contract for $75,000 was let for the installation of the lighting. At June 30, 19X9, the contract was completed but not approved. The contractor was paid all but 5 percent, which was retained to ensure compliance with the terms of the contract. Encumbrances and other budgetary accounts are maintained.

8. During the year Internal Service Fund supplies were purchased at a cost of $1,900.

9. Cash collections recorded in the General Fund during the year were as follows:

$$\begin{array}{ll}
\text{Property taxes} \dots\dots\dots\dots\dots\dots\dots & \$386,000 \\
\text{Licenses and permits} \dots\dots\dots\dots\dots & 7,000
\end{array}$$

10. The village council decided to build a village hall at an estimated cost of $500,000 to replace space occupied in rented facilities. It was decided that general obligation bonds bearing interest at 6 percent would be issued. On June 30, 19X9, the bonds were issued at their face value of $500,000, payable June 30, 19Z9.

No contracts have been signed for this project and no expenditures have been made.

11. A fire truck was purchased for $15,000 and the voucher approved was paid from the General Fund. This expenditure was previously encumbered for $15,000.

Required:

Prepare journal entries to properly record each of the above transactions in the appropriate fund(s) or account groups of Dexter Village for the fiscal year ended June 30, 19X9. Use the following funds and account groups:

1. General Fund
2. Capital Projects Fund
3. Special Assessment Fund
4. Internal Service Fund
5. Trust Fund
6. General Long-Term Debt Account Group
7. General Fixed Assets Account Group

Each journal entry should be numbered to correspond with the transactions described above. Do not prepare closing entries for any fund.

Your answer sheet should be organized as follows:

Trans-action Number	Fund or Account Group	Account Titles and Explanations	Amounts	
			Debit	Credit

(AICPA adapted)

Problem 13-9. (Review Problem) The following transactions were among those affecting the City of Sterlington during 19X2:

1. The 19X2 budget was approved. It provided for $520,000 of General Fund revenues and $205,000 of School Fund revenues.

2. Appropriations were made for the General Fund, $516,000.

3. General taxes were levied, $490,000; approximately $10,000 of this amount will prove uncollectible or will be abated.

4. Contractors were paid $200,000 for construction of an office building. The payment was from proceeds of a general bond issue of 19X0.

5. Bonds of a general issue authorized previously were sold at par for $60,000.

6. Orders were placed for uniforms for the Police Department at an estimated cost of $7,500.

7. Payment of salaries of town officers was made in the amount of $11,200 (disregard withholding considerations.)

8. The uniforms ordered above (item 6) were received and vouchers approved for the invoice price of $7,480.

9. Fire equipment was purchased for $12,500 and a voucher approved in that (the encumbered) amount.

10. A payment of $5,000 was made from the General Fund to a fund for the redemption of general obligation bonds.

11. Of the taxes levied (item 3), $210,000 was collected during 19X2; the balance are now delinquent.

12. Supplies for general administrative use were requisitioned from the Stores Fund. A charge of $1,220 was made for the supplies; they cost the Stores Fund $1,150. (Supplies are accounted for on a perpetual basis in the Stores Fund; on a purchases basis in other funds.)

13. The General Fund advanced $30,000 cash to provide working capital for a fund out of which payment will be made for a new sewage system installation. Eventual financing will be by means of charges to property owners on the basis of benefit received; thus, the advance should be repaid within two or three years.

14. Equipment used by the Public Works Department was sold for $7,000 cash. This sale was not included in the budget. The equipment had been acquired ten years earlier, at which time its useful life was estimated at 20 years.

15. Receipts from licenses and fees amounted to $16,000.

16. A payment of $10,000 was made from the General Fund to a fund for the operation of a central printing service used by all departments of the municipal government. (This had not been budgeted and is not expected to be repaid.)

17. Taxes amounting to $1,240 written off as uncollectible in 19X0 were collected. No amount was budgeted for such collections.

18. A total of $1,000 of the payment made in item 16 was returned because it was not needed.

19. The city received a cash bequest of $75,000 for the establishment of a scholarship fund.

20. Previously approved and recorded vouchers for Police Department salaries of $6,200 and for the payment of $500 to the Police Pension Fund were paid.

Required:

(a) Set up an answer sheet like that illustrated on page 533.

(b) Indicate for each transaction (by means of the appropriate numerals) the accounts debited and credited in the General Fund. If two entries in the General Fund are required, place such entries one above the other.

(c) If a transaction requires an entry(ies) in a fund(s) or nonfund account group(s) other than the General Fund, indicate those affected by printing the appropriate letter symbol(s) in the column headed "Other Funds or Account Groups Affected." If no entry is required for a transaction, state "None," (Example: Payment by the General Fund of a bill owed by the Special Revenue Fund.)

ANSWER SHEET FORMAT

Transaction Number	General Fund		Other Funds or Account Groups Affected	"13" Account Explanation
	Dr.	Cr.		
Example	3	2	SR	
1.				
20.				

Symbol	Fund or Account Group	Number	Account Title
CP	Capital Projects	1	Appropriations
GLD	General Long-Term Debt	2	Cash
G	General	3	Due from Other Funds
GFA	General Fixed Assets	4	Due to Other Funds
DS	Debt Service	5	Encumbrances
SA	Special Assessment	6	Estimated Revenue
SR	Special Revenue	7	Expenditures
TA	Trust or Agency	8	Fund Balance
E	Enterprise	9	Reserve for Encumbrances
IS	Internal Service	10	Revenues
		11	Taxes Receivable—Current
		12	Vouchers Payable
		13	Other (explain)

Problem 13-10. (Review Problem) The transactions and events described below occurred in Joiner Junction Township during 19X5. Prepare all general journal entries necessary to reflect the transactions or events described, clearly indicating the fund or nonfund account group in which each entry is made. Omit subsidiary ledger entries and formal entry explanations; state any assumptions made concisely.

1. A $50,000, ten-year, 6 percent special-special bond issue of the Shady Lane Subdivision Improvement Fund was sold at 95 plus $250 accrued interest to finance the property owner's share of costs of construction. Neither the township nor the property owners will make up the deficiency; interest charged on deferred assessments should just cover the cash interest requirements of the bond issue.

2. Property owners involved in the Shady Lane Subdivision project were assessed $50,000, the amounts coming due equally over a ten-year period beginning in 19X5. The municipality's share of the cost, $10,000, was included in the General Fund budget and was set up as a liability of that Fund when property owners were assessed.

3. A $100,000 general obligation bond issue (5 percent, twenty-year term) sold at 102 plus $1,000 accrued interest. In accordance with terms of the bond issue

authorization, the premium and accrued interest were deposited directly to the Bond Principal and Interest Payments Fund.

4. A Central Equipment Repair Fund was established by transfer of $40,000 of the bond issue proceeds. This transfer is viewed as invested equity (rather than debt equity) in the new fund.

5. The township's share of the Shady Lane project cost was paid from the bond issue (item 3) proceeds rather than from the General Fund.

6. Sinking fund accounts were closed based on the following information:

	Budgeted (Actuarial) Requirements	Actual
General Fund transfers	$3,500	$1,800
Transfer of bond premium	—	2,000
Sinking fund earnings	200	150
Transfer of accrued interest	—	1,000
Interest payments	2,000	1,500

7. The Central Equipment Repair Fund billed the General Fund departments $1,000, and the Shady Lane Subdivision Improvement Fund $500, for services rendered.

8. The Joiner Junction Power Company was acquired by the municipality for $2,000,000. The cash remaining from the general obligation bond issue was transferred to the Electric Transmission Fund (not to be repaid) and revenue bonds were given power company shareholders for the balance of the purchase price.

	Power Company Books		
Asset	Cost	Accumulated Depreciation	Appraised Fair Market Value
Land and Rights-of-Way	$ 90,000	$ —	$ 480,000
Buildings and Improvements	60,000	30,000	360,000
Equipment	240,000	180,000	300,000
Transmission Lines	1,500,000	600,000	1,260,000
	$1,890,000	$810,000	$2,400,000

The utility will continue to be regulated by the Public Service Commission and must adhere to its "original cost" policies in regulatory reports and in rate determination cases.

9. The Shady Lane Subdivision Improvement Fund year-end closing entry was made based upon the following information (assume that adjustments required have been posted):

a. Construction activity to date (all projects are still in progress):

Expenditures	$25,000
Encumbrances outstanding	15,000

b. Interest expense and revenue:

Amounts paid/received	—
Accrued interest payable	1,000
Accrued interest receivable	600

10. Closing entries were made for the Shady School Memorial Trust Fund. This fund is nonexpendable as to principal. Sixty percent of the earnings inure to the "Shady School Student Assistance Fund" to provide low-interest loans to needy graduates of that school who wish to pursue higher education; the balance accrues to the "Shady School Maintenance Fund." Revenues of the Memorial Fund were: Rentals, $15,000; Interest, $10,000; Gain on Sale of Land, $6,000. Expenses were: Operating Expenses, $12,000; Depreciation (corpus), $4,000.

Problem 13-11. (Review Problem) Valle City had the following transactions in 19X7. Record transactions in all funds and account groups affected in general journal form, designating the fund or account group. The transactions are separate except where several appear under one Arabic numeral. Make all entries to which the transactions give rise.

1. General Fund current taxes of $85,000, subject to an estimated loss of $6,500, became delinquent.
2. A long-term advance of $500,000 was made from the General Fund to establish a fund to buy and hold stores and issue them to the City's various departments.
3. The annual General Fund contribution of $10,000 to the sinking fund for City Hall bonds became due and payable.
4. a. A trust that is expendable as to income and nonexpendable as to principal received $75,000 of rental payments from tenants of trust properties.
   b. Trust expenses of $60,000 were paid and depreciation of $5,000 was recorded.
   c. Land carried on the trust books at $16,000 was sold for $20,000.
   d. Trust books were closed at year end.
5. A 6 percent serial bond issue of $250,000 was sold at par to fund a General Fund deficit.
6. The General Fund liability of $7,500 for contributions to the employees' pension fund was accrued.
7. A lot appraised at $50,000 was received as a gift from an individual for the purpose of establishing a playground.
8. a. Furniture for the mayor's office estimated to cost $500 was ordered.
   b. The furniture and a bill therefor were received; the actual cost was $525.
9. Term (sinking fund) bonds of $100,000 matured, together with $2,000 interest thereon.
10. Term (sinking fund) bonds of $200,000 were sold at a premium of $1,000. They are 5 percent bonds and will mature in twenty years; the par amount is to be used to finance a general government office building construction project.
11. The office building construction project financed from the bonds referred to in the preceding transaction was completed. Construction expenditures of $197,000 were closed; proper disposition was made of the balance. (Prepare closing and disposition of balance entries.)
12. a. Special assessment improvements of $750,000 were authorized.
    b. Special assessment notes of $550,000 were sold at par.
    c. Assessments of $550,000, maturing in ten equal installments (the first installments coming due in six months), were levied on private property; the remainder of the cost is to be paid by the municipality.

d. The municipality authorized the issuance of bonds for the purpose of financing its share of the cost ($200,000).

e. The bonds were sold at a premium of $2,500.

f. The proceeds from the sale of the bonds, as well as the premium, were transferred to the proper fund or funds.

g. The municipality authorized the issuance of special assessment bonds of $550,000 to retire the special assessment notes.

h. The bonds were sold at par.

i. Construction expenditures during the first year amounted to $100,000; encumbrances at year end were $500,000.

j. Interest accrued at year end: on the bonds (e), $2,200; on the notes (b), $3,000; and on the bonds (g), $5,000. No interest payments were made during the year.

k. Interest accrued on deferred assessments at year end, $12,000; no interest collections were made during the year.

l. The books were closed at year end.

Problem 13-12. (Review Problem) You have been engaged by the Town of Nihill to examine its June, 30, 19X4, balance sheet. You are the first CPA to be engaged by the town and find that acceptable methods of municipal accounting have not been employed. The town clerk stated that the books had been closed and presented the following balance sheet:

TOWN OF NIHILL
Balance Sheet
June 30, 19X4

Assets

Cash	$ 36,200
Taxes receivable	21,900
Accounts receivable	9,000
Investments	84,200
Prepaid expenses	21,000
Fixed assets	245,400
Total	$417,700

Liabilities

Accounts payable	$ 6,500
Bonds payable	200,000
Fund balance	211,200
Total	$417,700

The Town of Nihill was formed as a separate political unit on July 1, 19X2. The town was formerly a real estate development within the Township of Hamton. Your audit disclosed the following information:

1. On July 1, 19X3, the town received a bequest of $50,000 in cash and a house with a fair market value of $40,000. The house was recorded on the books as an investment at its fair market value at July 1, 19X3. The bequest arose under the terms of a will which provided that the house would be used as a public library and the $50,000 would be established as a nonexpendable trust fund whose

income would be used to buy library books. Securities costing $49,200 were purchased in July 19X3 by the town for the trust fund and in June 19X4 securities with a cost of $5,000 were sold for $6,800. The trust fund had dividend and interest income of $2,100 during the year, of which $1,900 was expended. In addition, the town expended from general funds $9,000 for conversion of the house to library purposes and $19,000 for books; these last amounts were charged to expenditures. The town has no other investments. The decision was made to account for the library trust earnings in a separate fund.

2. Taxes levied for the year amounted to $84,300, of which $62,400 was collected and $800 has been identified as being illegal and requiring abatement. In addition, it is anticipated that $1,400 of the remaining 19X3–19X4 levy will prove uncollectible.

3. The water company that had been formed by the developer to service the real estate development was purchased by the town on July 1, 19X3. The seller accepted 5 percent general obligation bonds in settlement. Details of the sales contract follow:

Plant and equipment		$108,000
Assets and liabilities assumed:		
Prepaid expenses (inventories)	$19,000	
Accounts receivable	8,000	
Total	$27,000	
Accounts payable	5,000	22,000
Sales price		$130,000

Cash arising from the operation of the water plant, except for a $1,000 working fund, is used for the general purposes of the town. At June 30, 19X4, the following accounts pertain solely to the operation of the water plant: Accounts Receivable, Prepaid Expenses, and Accounts Payable.

4. A $300,000 issue of 5 percent general obligation bonds was authorized on July 1, 19X3. In addition to the settlement for the purchase of the water company, bonds in the amount of $70,000 were sold at 100 on that date, and $65,400 of the proceeds had been used up to June 30, 19X4, to obtain other equipment for the town. Interest is payable on June 30 and December 31; no interest payments are in arrears. Commencing June 30, 19X5, bonds of $10,000 are to be retired each June 30.

5. A shipment of supplies for the water plant was received in June 19X4 and included in Prepaid Expenses, but the invoice for $700 was recorded in July. An order was placed in June with a printer for stationery to be used by the town's governing body. The stationery was delivered in July and cost $500. The remaining composite life of the water company plant and equipment at July 1, 19X3, was estimated at 30 years.

Required:

Prepare a balance sheet worksheet to adjust the town clerk's account accumulations as of June 30, 19X4, and distribute them to the appropriate funds or nonfund account groups. The worksheet should be in the format of the town clerk's balance sheet and have the following column headings:

1. Balance per Books
2. Adjustments—Debits
3. Adjustments—Credits
4. General Fund
5. Library Endowment Principal Fund
6. Library Fund
7. General Fixed Assets
8. Enterprise Fund
9. Capital Projects Fund
10. General Long-Term Debt

(Formal journal entries are not required. Supporting computations should be in good form.)

(AICPA, adapted)

14

FINANCIAL REPORTING

The twelfth principle set forth by the National Council on Governmental Accounting states:

INTERIM AND ANNUAL FINANCIAL REPORTS

12. a. Appropriate interim financial statements and reports of financial position, operating results, and other pertinent information should be prepared to facilitate management control of financial operations, legislative oversight, and, where necessary or desired, for external reporting purposes.

b. A comprehensive annual financial report covering all funds and account groups of the governmental unit—including appropriate combined, combining, and individual fund statements; notes to the financial statements; schedules; narrative explanations; and statistical tables—should be prepared and published.

c. General purpose financial statements may be issued separately from the comprehensive annual financial report. Such statements should include the basic financial statements and notes to the financial statements that are essential to fair presentation of financial position and operating results (and changes in financial position of proprietary funds and similar Trust Funds).[1]

This chapter considers interim reporting briefly, then covers annual reporting comprehensively.

INTERIM REPORTING

Very few governments publish interim financial statements for external use as do most large business corporations. Rather, interim statements of governments are

[1] NCGAS 1, p. 18.

designed primarily to meet the needs of administrative personnel such as the chief executive, supervisors at the several levels of government, and budget examiners, though legislators may be interested in them as indications of whether budget plans are being followed. Interim statements help management determine how well the executive branch is complying with budgetary and other finance-related legal requirements. In addition, interim statements are important to controlling current operations—they disclose variations from plans that may require altering the plans or improving operating performance—and assist in planning future operations.

An interim balance sheet for a General Fund is presented in Figure 4-4. Interim operating statements presented earlier include a General Fund Statement of Actual and Estimated Revenue (Figure 5-11) and a Statement of Actual and Estimated Expenditures (Figure 6-5). Other interim statements commonly prepared include detailed budgetary statements and statements of cash receipts, disbursements, and balances for each fund.

The NCGA recognized the importance of good interim reporting both by including it in Principle 12a and as indicated by this excerpt from NCGA *Statement 1:*

> Interim financial reports are comprised principally of statements that reflect current financial position at the end of a month or quarter and compare actual financial results with budgetary estimates and limitations for the month or quarter and/or for the year to date. Interim reports typically are prepared primarily for internal use. Thus, they usually are prepared on the budgetary basis and often do not include statements reporting general fixed assets or general long-term debt. Further, they may properly contain budgetary or cash flow projections and other information deemed pertinent to effective management control during the year.
>
> The key criteria by which internal interim reports are evaluated are their relevance and usefulness for purposes of management control, which include planning future operations as well as evaluating current financial status and results to date. . . . Since managerial styles and perceived information needs vary widely, however, appropriate internal interim reporting is largely a matter of professional judgment rather than one to be set forth in detail here.[2]

Interim reporting typically is for internal use, and individual managers and environments require different types of interim reports. Thus, neither the NCGA nor any other recognized body has set forth what might be considered generally accepted principles of interim reporting.

ANNUAL REPORTING

Reporting is the last phase of the annual budget and accounting cycle for which the executive branch of the government is responsible. In the ideal annual financial report the executive branch (1) demonstrates its compliance with finance-related

---

[2] Ibid., pp. 18–19.

legal and contractual requirements, including fund and appropriation requirements, under which the government is operated, and (2) presents audited financial statements that conform with generally accepted accounting principles. The annual financial report is designed to inform the legislative body, creditors, investors, analysts, students of public finance, political scientists, and the general public.

The NCGA was emphatic that:

> Every governmental unit should prepare and publish, as a matter of public record, a *comprehensive annual financial report* (CAFR) that encompasses all funds and account groups. The CAFR should contain both (1) the *general purpose financial statements* (GPFS) by fund type and account group, and (2) *combining statements by fund type and individual fund statements*. The CAFR is the governmental unit's *official* annual report and should also contain introductory information, schedules necessary to demonstrate compliance with finance-related legal and contractual provisions, and statistical data.[3]

THE PYRAMID CONCEPT

The NCGA used a "pyramid" concept (Figure 14-1) in considering what types of annual reporting to require and in explaining the required reports and statements.

In studying the financial reporting pyramid (Figure 14-1) note that:

1. The top of the pyramid represents highly aggregated, consolidated financial statements, while the bottom of the pyramid represents highly detailed, voluminous reports that would include the details of virtually every transaction or event of a governmental unit. The Council opted for reports and statements between these two extremes. Thus neither "Condensed Summary Data" nor "Transaction Data" fall within the bounds of reports and statements to be prepared under generally accepted accounting principles.

2. A dual external reporting approach was chosen by the NCGA. The Comprehensive Annual Financial Report (CAFR) was selected as the primary report, the "official" annual report of the governmental unit, whereas the General Purpose Financial Statements (GPFS) in the CAFR may be issued separately for inclusion in official statements for bond offerings and for general widespread distribution to users apt to require less detail than is contained in the CAFR, provided the GPFS refer the reader to the CAFR should he need more detailed information.

3. The contents of the GPFS are limited to several combined statements, whereas the CAFR includes the combined statements, combining statements, and, perhaps, individual fund and account group statements. The dashed line in Figure 14-1 indicates the area where professional judgment is to be exercised by government finance officers and their auditors in determining when adequate disclosure has been

---

[3] Ibid., p. 19, emphasis added.

achieved without overwhelming the user of the CAFR with excessive detail.

4. It is essential (a) to distinguish between and among combined statements, combining statements, and individual fund and account group statements and schedules and (b) to realize that the data in combined statements are more summarized than that in the combining statements, which are more summarized than that presented in the individual fund and account group statements, which are more summarized than that presented in most individual fund and account group schedules. Thus the higher on the pyramid, the more summarized the data presented; and the lower on the pyramid, the more detailed the data presented.

Figure 14-1

THE FINANCIAL REPORTING "PYRAMID"

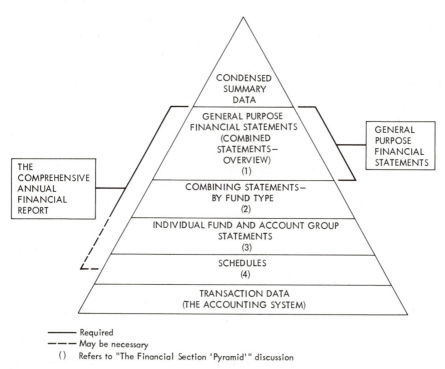

Required
May be necessary
() Refers to "The Financial Section 'Pyramid'" discussion

Source: NCGAS 1, p. 20.

The NCGA summarized its concept of the financial section pyramid as follows:

The Financial Section "Pyramid"

The financial section of the CAFR may be viewed as a "reporting pyramid" [Figure 14-1]. The governmental unit need go only as far down the reporting pyramid—in terms of increasing levels of detail—as necessary to report the financial position and operating results of its individual funds and account groups, to demonstrate compliance with finance-related legal and contractual requirements, and to assure adequate disclosure at the individual fund entity level. Those statements and schedules necessary for these purposes are *required;* others are *optional.*

The levels of the pyramid are:

1. *General Purpose Financial Statements (Combined Statements—Overview).* These basic financial statements provide a summary of the financial position of all funds and account groups and of the operating results of all funds. They also serve as an introduction to the more detailed statements and schedules that follow. Separate columns should be used for each fund type and account group.

2. *Combining Statements—By Fund Type.* Where a governmental unit has more than one fund of a given type (e.g., Special Revenue Funds), combining statements for all funds of that type should be presented in a columnar format. The total columns of these combining statements should agree with the amounts presented in the GPFS. (In some instances, disclosure sufficient to meet CAFR reporting objectives may be achieved at this level; in other cases, these statements "link" the GPFS and the individual fund statements.)

3. *Individual Fund and Account Group Statements.* These statements present information on the individual funds and account groups where (a) a governmental unit has only one fund of a specific type, or (b) sufficient detail to assure disclosure sufficient to meet CAFR reporting objectives is not presented in the combining statements. These statements may also be used to present budgetary and prior year comparative data.

4. *Schedules.* Data presented in schedules are not necessary for fair presentation in conformity with GAAP unless referenced in the notes to the financial statements. Schedules are used: (a) to demonstrate finance-related legal and contractual compliance (e.g., where bond indentures or grant provisions require specific data to be presented); (b) to present other information deemed useful (e.g., combined and combining schedules that encompass more than one fund or account group, such as a Combined Schedule of Cash Receipts, Disbursements, and Balances—All Funds); and (c) to provide details of data summarized in the financial statements (e.g., schedules of revenues, expenditures, transfers).

All four pyramid levels of detail may be required in some circumstances. On the other hand, adequate disclosure may require only one or two levels. Determining the appropriate level of detail and deciding what to present in statements, as opposed to schedules, are matters of professional judgment.[4]

THE COMPREHENSIVE ANNUAL FINANCIAL REPORT (CAFR)

The NCGA specified the following general outline and minimum contents of the CAFR in terms of (1) the Introductory Section, (2) the Financial Section, and (3) the Statistical Tables.

[4] Ibid., pp. 20–21.

1. Introductory Section
   a. Table of Contents
   b. Letter(s) of transmittal
   c. Other material deemed appropriate by management
2. Financial Section
   a. Auditor's Report
   b. General Purpose Financial Statements (Combined Statements—Overview)
      (1) Combined Balance Sheet—All Fund Types and Account Groups (Figure 14-5).
      (2) Combined Statement of Revenues, Expenditures, and Changes in Fund Balances—All Governmental Fund Types (Figure 14-6).
      (3) Combined Statement of Revenues, Expenditures, and Changes in Fund Balances—Budget and Actual—General and Special Revenue Fund Types (and similar governmental fund types for which annual budgets have been legally adopted) (Figure 14-7).
      (4) Combined Statement of Revenues, Expenses, and Changes in Retained Earnings (or Equity)—All Proprietary Fund Types (Figure 14-8).
      (5) Combined Statement of Changes in Financial Position—All Proprietary Fund Types (Figure 14-9).
      (6) Notes to the financial statements (Figure 14-10).

      [Trust Fund operations may be reported in (2), (3), (4), and (5) above, as appropriate, or separately.]
   c. Combining and Individual Fund and Account Group Statements and Schedules
      (1) Combining Statements—by Fund Type—where a governmental unit has more than one fund of a given fund type (e.g., Figures 4-9, 7-8, 7-9, 7-10, 8-2, and 8-4).
      (2) Individual fund and account group statements—where a governmental unit has only one fund of a given type and for account groups and/or where necessary to present prior year and budgetary comparisons.
      (3) Schedules.
         (a) Schedules necessary to demonstrate compliance with finance-related legal and contractual provisions.
         (b) Schedules to present information spread throughout the statements that can be brought together and shown in greater detail (e.g., taxes receivable, including delinquent taxes; long-term debt; investments; and cash receipts, disbursements, and balances).
         (c) Schedules to present greater detail for information reported in the statements (e.g., additional revenue sources detail and object of expenditure data by departments).

(Narrative explanations useful in understanding combining and individual fund and account group statements and schedules that are not included in the notes to the financial statements should be presented on divider pages, directly on the statements and schedules, or in a separate section.)

3. Statistical Tables

The Introductory Section

The introductory section of the CAFR includes a table of contents, letter(s) of transmittal, and other material deemed appropriate by management—e.g., organization chart, copy of current certificate of conformance awarded by the Municipal Finance Officers Association, roster of elected officials, and description of the government entity being reported on.

For many years only a single transmittal letter from the chief finance officer to the Mayor and Council was included. More recently a second transmittal letter, from the chief executive to the council and/or citizens, has become common in the introductory section of the CAFR. A transmittal letter from a mayor to the city-county council is presented in Figure 14-2; excerpts of a transmittal letter from the chief finance officer to the mayor are presented in Figure 14-3. The transmittal letter from the chief finance officer to the chief executive is an extremely important part of the CAFR. Indeed, like the president's letter in private corporation reports, most readers direct their attention here initially (perhaps exclusively) for an overview of the financial position of the city at year end and the results of operations for the year, expecting also that the major significant events that occurred during the year, whether good or bad, will be highlighted here.

The Financial Section

As indicated by the pyramid illustration and the general outline and content of the CAFR recommended by the NCGA, the financial section has three subsections: (1) the auditor's report, (2) the General Purpose Financial Statements (GPFS)—the combined statements and notes to the financial statements, and (3) the combining and individual fund statements and schedules.

The Auditor's Report. The auditor's report on the financial statements of the City of Indianapolis for the year ended December 31, 1980, appears in Figure 14-4. Note that this is a "dual opinion" in that it covers both the combined statements in the GPFS and the combining and individual fund statements in the CAFR equally, while covering the financial and budgetary schedules only as "accompanying" (supplemental) data presented for purposes of additional analysis. Note also that the auditor's opinion is qualified because the City accounts for city-administered police and firefighters' pension plans on a cash basis rather than on the accrual basis required by GAAP. The various audit scopes and typical auditor's reports are considered in depth in Chapter 21.

The Combined Statements (GPFS) and Notes. As noted previously, as few as five combined statements, accompanied by appropriate notes, may present fairly the financial position and results of operation of a city, county, or state (and

Figure 14-2

Mayor's Transmittal Letter
CITY OF INDIANAPOLIS
William H. Hudnut, III
Mayor

April 25, 1981

TO THE MEMBERS OF THE CITY-COUNTY COUNCIL:

This report has been prepared following the guidelines recommended by the Municipal Finance Officers Association of the United States and Canada. The MFOA awards Certificates of Conformance to those governments whose annual financial reports are judged to conform substantially with high standards of public financial reporting including generally accepted accounting principles promulgated by the National Council on Governmental Accounting. The City of Indianapolis was awarded a Certificate of Conformance for its annual financial report for the calendar year 1979. It is my belief that the accompanying 1980 financial report continues to meet program standards, and it will be submitted to the Municipal Finance Officers Association for review.

In accordance with the above-mentioned guidelines, the accompanying report consists of three parts.

(1) Introductory section, including the Controller's letter of transmittal.
(2) Financial section, including financial statements and supplemental data of the City accompanied by our independent auditor's opinion.
(3) Statistical section, including a number of tables of data depicting the financial history of the government for the past 10 years, information on overlapping governmental units, and demographic and other miscellaneous information.

The City of Indianapolis concluded 1980 in sound financial condition. There are, however, several external areas of concern which may require special attention by the Mayor's office and members of the City-County Council during the current fiscal period. Of concern to the City of Indianapolis, as well as all sectors of the economy, is the continued depressed status of the economy. While, to date, the economic slow-down has caused only minor concerns, a prolonged continuation of this depressed state may cause a need to reexamine the City of Indianapolis' priority of services.

The preparation of this annual financial report could not have been accomplished without the dedicated efforts of the City Controller and his entire staff, as well as many others. Their effort over the past years toward upgrading the accounting and financial reporting systems of the City of Indianapolis have lead substantially to the improved quality of the information being reported to the City-County Council and to the citizens of the City of Indianapolis.

Sincerely Yours,

William H. Hudnut III

Source: City of Indianapolis, Indiana, Annual Report, December 31, 1980.

---

the changes in financial position of its proprietary funds) under NCGA *Statement 1*. Since the data in combined statements are aggregated by fund type, not by individual fund, these statements have a "fund type" entity focus.

The combined statements in the GPFS are: (1) Combined Balance Sheet—All Fund Types and Account Groups; (2) Combined Statement of Revenues, Expenditures, and Changes in Fund Balances—All Governmental Fund Types;

Figure 14-3

Finance Officer's Transmittal Letter
CITY OF INDIANAPOLIS

William H. Hudnut, III
Mayor

April 25, 1981

Honorable Mayor William H. Hudnut, III
City of Indianapolis, Indiana

The Comprehensive Annual Financial Report of the City of Indianapolis (City), for the fiscal year ended December 31, 1980, is submitted herewith. . . . This report was prepared by the City's Finance Division of the Department of Administration. Responsibility for both the accuracy of the presented data and the completeness and fairness of the presentation, including all disclosures, rests with the City. We believe the data, as presented, is accurate in all material aspects; that it is presented in a manner designed to fairly set forth the financial position and results of operations of the City as measured by the financial activity of its various funds; and that all disclosures necessary to enable the reader to gain the maximum understanding of the City's financial affairs have been included.

Accounting system and budgetary control

In developing and evaluating the City's accounting system, consideration is given to the adequacy of internal accounting controls. Internal accounting controls are designed to provide reasonable, but not absolute, assurance regarding: (1) the safeguarding of assets against loss from unauthorized use or disposition; and (2) the reliability of financial records for preparing financial statements and maintaining accountability for assets. The concept of reasonable assurance recognizes that: (1) the cost of a control should not exceed the benefits likely to be derived; and (2) the evaluation of costs and benefits requires estimates and judgments by management.

All internal control evaluations occur within the above framework. We believe that the City's internal accounting controls adequately safeguard assets and provide reasonable assurance of proper recording of financial transactions.

Budgetary control is maintained at the Department and Agency object (character) level by the encumbrance of purchase orders against available appropriations. Capital projects reimbursable by grant revenues are encumbered for the total amount of the estimated project cost as of the purchase order date. Purchase orders which would result in an overrun of appropriated balances are not released until additional appropriations are made available. Open encumbrances are reported as reservations of the fund balance at December 31, 1980.

The reporting entity and its services

This report includes all of the funds and account groups of the consolidated City as defined by the consolidated First-Class Cities and Counties Act adopted by the 1969 Indiana General Assembly. [Reference to NCGA *Statement 3* now appropriate here.]

Figure 14-3 (Continued)

Financial Highlights

	1980	Increase (Decrease) (2)	Percent	1979	Increase (Decrease) [1979 (3)]	Percent	1978 (3)
Cash	$ 9,289,751	$ 3,502,935	60.5	$ 5,786,816	$ 1,134,300	24.4	$ 4,652,516
Investments	67,001,408	(32,338,911)	(32.6)	99,340,319	(11,178,568)	(10.1)	110,518,887
Total	$ 76,291,159	$ (28,835,976)	(27.4)	$ 105,127,135	$ (10,044,268)	(.9)	$ 115,171,403
Investment in general fixed assets	$ 313,802,930	$ 84,283,644	36.7	229,519,286	$ 57,148,203	33.2	$ 172,371,083
Encumbered fund balance	55,551,085	(70,592,080)	(56.0)	126,143,165	90,333,831	252.3	35,809,334
Unencumbered fund balance	(3,139,080)	41,604,825	93.0	(44,743,905)	(111,975,073)	(166.5)	67,231,168
Total	$ 52,412,005	$ (28,987,255)	(35.6)	$ 81,399,260	$ (21,641,242)	21.0	$ 103,040,502
Revenues	$ 272,683,193	$ 27,776,367	11.3	$ 244,906,826	$ 37,895,985	18.3	$ 207,010,841
Current expenditures	$ 166,979,592	$ 11,795,146	7.6	$ 155,184,446	$ (14,851,007)	(8.7)	$ 170,035,453
Bonding limit	791,102,581	228,441,570	40.6	562,661,011	96,981,712	20.8	465,679,299
Less bonds outstanding	212,362,000	(10,647,000)	(4.8)	223,009,000	(9,952,000)	(4.3)	232,961,000
Net bonding margin (1)	$ 578,740,581	$ 239,088,570	70.4	$ 339,652,011	$ 106,933,712	45.9	$ 232,718,299
Debt service	$ 22,623,305	$ 117,629	.5	$ 22,505,676	$ 3,682,122	19.6	$ 18,823,564
Capital outlays (2)	$ 103,698,581	$ 19,364,383	23.0	$ 84,334,198	$ 56,629,321	204.4	$ 27,704,877
Assessed valuation (Marion County)	$3,496,065,239	$1,021,369,659	41.3	$2,474,695,580	$ 80,169,770	3.4	$2,394,525,810

(1) The increased net bonding margin results from the March 1, 1979 re-assessment for taxes payable in 1980, the non-issuance of net debt in 1979 and 1980, and scheduled bond retirements in 1979 and 1980.

(2) The construction of the Advanced Wastewater Treatment facility, which is 85% funded by the United States Environmental Protection Agency and the State of Indiana, is the major capital project of the City and primarily accounts for the changes in cash, investments, investment in general fixed assets, encumbered and unencumbered fund balances, revenues and capital outlays.

(3) Certain of the above 1979 and 1978 amounts have been restated to give retroactive effect to the changes in the method of accounting for grant revenues, land sales revenues, and Agency Fund liabilities as described in Note 2 to the financial statements, elsewhere herein. In addition, the Pension Trust Funds have been reclassified with the Proprietary Fund Type operating statements for 1979 to conform with the 1980 presentation.

General governmental functions

The sources of revenue for 1980 and 1979 are as follows:

Revenue source	1980 Amount	1980 Percent of Total	Increase (Decrease) Amount	Increase (Decrease) Percent	1979 Amount	1979 Percent of Total
General property taxes	$ 69,731,742	25.6	$ 5,312,631	8.2	$ 64,419,111	26.2
State and local taxes	31,081,943	11.4	(4,590,892)	(12.9)	35,672,835	14.5
Federal funds	121,131,224	44.4	19,520,393	19.2	101,610,831	41.3
Fees and permits	3,455,255	1.2	318,641	10.1	3,136,614	1.3
Charges for service	18,212,035	6.7	586,772	3.3	17,625,263	7.2
Other	29,070,994	10.7	5,542,452	23.6	23,528,542	9.5
Total	$272,683,193	100.0	$26,689,997	10.8	$245,993,196	100.0

Figure 14-3 (Continued)

Expenditures for general governmental purposes for 1980 and 1979 are as follows:

Function	1980		Increase (Decrease)		1979	
	Amount	Percent of Total	Amount	Percent	Amount	Percent of Total
Protection of people and property	$ 63,722,974	21.7	$ 7,546,750	13.4	$ 56,176,224	21.4
Community cultural and recreation	11,075,128	3.8	(2,151,850)	(16.3)	13,226,978	5.0
Community development and welfare	39,002,629	13.3	14,109,503	56.7	24,893,126	9.5
Transportation and related services	22,112,721	7.5	(5,124,606)	(18.8)	27,237,327	10.4
Environmental services	25,230,458	8.6	(1,205,242)	(4.5)	26,435,700	10.1
Executive/Legislative affairs of government	1,112,337	.4	180,326	19.3	932,011	.4
Administrative services	4,723,345	1.6	(1,559,735)	(24.9)	6,283,080	2.4
Total current expenditures	166,979,592	56.9	11,795,146	7.6	155,184,446	59.2
Debt service	22,623,305	7.7	117,629	.5	22,505,676	8.6
Capital outlay	103,698,581	35.4	19,364,383	22.9	84,334,198	32.2
Total expenditures	$293,301,478	100.0	$31,277,158	11.9	$262,024,320	100.0

The annual budget process is a balanced budget concept projected six months in advance of the budget year. Accordingly, budgeted fund balances at January 1, 1980 are estimated not actual. The reduction in budget surpluses in the General, Special Revenue and Debt Service funds (approximately $27,250,000 and $28,725,000 at December 31, 1980 and 1979, respectively, on an accrual basis) results primarily from 1980 revenues and other additions less than expenditures and other deductions of approximately $1,470,000. Fund balances continue to indicate strong financial management controls by the administration.

Internal audit and audit committee

The internal audit division completed its fourth full year. The position of the Manager of Internal Audit held by Michael D. Humphreys, C.P.A., is a merit position reporting to both the Mayor and the President of the City-County Council. Appreciation is also expressed to him and his staff for their assistance.

Certificate of Conformance

The Municipal Finance Officers Association of the United States and Canada (MFOA) awarded a Certificate of Conformance in Financial Reporting to the City of Indianapolis for its comprehensive annual financial report for the fiscal year ended December 31, 1979.

In order to be awarded a Certificate of Conformance, a governmental unit must publish an easily readable and efficiently organized comprehensive annual financial report, whose contents conform to program standards. Such reports must satisfy both generally accepted accounting principles and applicable legal requirements.

A Certificate of Conformance is valid for a period of one year only. We believe our current report continues to conform to Certificate of Conformance Program requirements, and we are submitting it to MFOA to determine its eligibility for another certificate.

Acknowledgement

The Controller alone cannot prepare the report presented herein. A fine staff of capable accountants including deputy Mayor Hudnut, your continued interest and support of accounting and reporting in accordance with generally accepted accounting principles is most appreciated.

Respectfully submitted,

Fred L. Armstrong, P.A.

Fred L. Armstrong, P.A.
Controller

Source: City of Indianapolis, Indiana, Annual Report, December 31, 1980.

Figure 14-4

REPORT OF CERTIFIED PUBLIC ACCOUNTANTS

Mr. Fred L. Armstrong, P.A. Controller
City of Indianapolis, Indiana

We have examined the accompanying combined financial statements of the City of Indianapolis, Indiana and its combining and individual fund financial statements at December 31, 1980, and for the year then ended, listed under Part II Financial Statements, pages 2 through 55, in the preceding Table of Contents. Our examination was made in accordance with generally accepted auditing standards and, accordingly, included such tests of the accounting records and such other auditing procedures as we considered necessary in the circumstances.

As more fully described in Note 10 to the financial statements, the City is on the cash basis of accounting for pension expenses for the City administered police and firefighters plans. Annual contributions by the City and covered employees with respect to these plans currently approximate annual benefit payments. In our opinion, generally accepted accounting principles require that annual pension expense be reported on the accrual basis and include, at a minimum, normal cost (annual cost determined under an appropriate actuarial cost method), interest on unfunded prior service cost and, if applicable, a provision for vested benefits. As described in Note 10, pension expense reported in the accompanying financial statements is less than the minimum amount required under generally accepted accounting principles.

In our opinion, except for the effects of the accounting for pension expense referred to in the preceding paragraph, the combined financial statements mentioned above present fairly the financial position of the City of Indianapolis, Indiana at December 31, 1980, and the results of its operations and changes in financial position for the year then ended, in conformity with generally accepted accounting principles applied on a basis consistent with that of the preceding year after giving retroactive effect to the changes, with which we concur, in the method of accounting for grant revenues, land sale revenues, and Agency Fund liabilities as described in Note 2 to the financial statements. Also, in our opinion, except for the effects of the accounting for pension expense referred to in the preceding paragraph, the combining and individual fund financial statements mentioned above present fairly the financial position of the individual funds of the City of Indianapolis, Indiana at December 31, 1980, their results of operations, and the changes in financial position of individual proprietary funds for the year then ended, in conformity with generally accepted accounting principles applied on a basis consistent with that of the preceding year after giving retroactive effect to the changes, with which we concur, in the method of accounting for grant revenues, land sale revenues, and Agency Fund liabilities as described in Note 2 to the financial statements.

Our examination was made for the purpose of forming our opinion on the combined financial statements taken as a whole and on the combining and individual fund financial statements. The accompanying financial and budgetary schedules listed under Part II Financial Statements, pages 57 through 83, in the preceding Table of Contents are presented for purposes of additional analysis and are not a required part of the combined financial statements referred to in the preceding paragraph. The financial and budgetary schedules have been subjected to the auditing procedures applied in the examination of the combined, combining, and individual fund financial statements and, in our opinion, except as stated in the second preceding paragraph, are fairly stated in all respects material in relation to the combined financial statements taken as a whole.

April 2, 1981   *Arthur Young + Company*

Source: City of Indianapolis, Indiana, Annual Report, December 31, 1980.

(3) Combined Statement of Revenues, Expenditures, and Changes in Fund Balances—Budget and Actual—General and Special Revenue Fund Types (and similar funds for which an annual budget is adopted); (4) Combined Statement of Revenues, Expenses, and Changes in Retained Earnings (or Equity)—All Proprietary Fund Types; and (5) Combined Statement of Changes in Financial Position—All Proprietary Fund Types. The combined balance sheet includes all fund types and account groups. Separate operating statements are required for the governmental and the proprietary fund types, however, because governmental fund operations are measured on the expenditure basis while proprietary fund operations are measured on the expense basis. Trust Fund operations may be presented either separately or in the governmental and/or proprietary fund statements, as appropriate.

Combined Balance Sheet. A Combined Balance Sheet is presented in Figure 14-5. Note that the data in this statement are highly summarized since the purpose of the statement is to present an overview. The total and prior year comparative total are labeled "Memorandum Only" to signal that these totals do not purport to show data in conformity with GAAP as do the fund type columns in the statement.

Combined Statement of Revenues, Expenditures, and Changes in Fund Balances. Several aspects of this statement, illustrated in Figure 14-6, warrant attention: (1) It includes all of the governmental (expendable) funds and also the Expendable Trust Fund(s), as permitted by *Statement 1;* (2) the format of the statement is one of the acceptable options set forth in NCGA *Statement 1*—other financing resources are reported immediately after revenues and other financing uses follow expenditures; (3) the statement contains an interfund eliminations column, an option permitted by *Statement 1;* (4) all transfers appear to be operating transfers; and (5) the statement presents changes in *total* fund balances, not unreserved fund balances, and thus has no "changes in reserves" section.

Combined Statement of Revenues, Expenditures, and Changes in Fund Balances—Budget and Actual. The budget for the City of Indianapolis is prepared and administered on a cash basis. Thus, the amounts shown in the budgetary comparison statement in Figure 14-7 differ from those presented in the GAAP basis statement in Figure 14-6. In such cases a note to the financial statements should explain this difference and reconcile the major amounts in the two statements. Note also that (1) Debt Service Funds are presented in the budgetary comparison statement, indicating that they too are budgeted on an annual basis; and (2) that the headings of the statement differ from the budget-actual-variance heading illustrated in *Statement 1*, but have the advantage of partially reconciling Figures 14-6 and 14-7.

Combined Statement of Revenues, Expenses, and Changes in Retained Earnings/Fund Balances. This statement (Figure 14-8) resembles a combined income and retained earnings statement for a business concern, as it properly should under *Statement 1*. Note that Indianapolis (1) has no Internal Service Funds (if

Figure 14-5

CITY OF INDIANAPOLIS
All Fund Types and Account Groups
Combined Balance Sheet
December 31, 1980

	Governmental Fund Types				Proprietary Fund Type	Fiduciary Fund Type	Account Groups		Totals Memorandum Only (Note 1N)	
Assets and Other Debits	General	Special Revenue	Debt Service	Capital Projects	Enterprise	Trust and Agency	General Fixed Assets	General Long-Term Debt	1980	1979
Cash	$ 2,282,980	$ 2,964,623	$ 688,684	$ 2,790,762	$ 24,851	$ 537,851	$	$	$ 9,289,751	$ 5,786,816
Investment (Note 1H)	12,466,017	9,197,894	16,515,442	26,775,237		2,046,818			67,001,408	99,340,319
Cash and investments with fiscal agents				144,224		122,977			267,201	226,818
Taxes receivable (Note 1F):										
Property			49,914						49,914	2,393,242
Other local	256,169		87,253						343,422	616,556
Accounts receivable, less allowance of $350,000	1,949,375								1,949,375	1,717,549
Due from federal, state and local governments (Note 4)	1,369,064	1,702,794		12,056,169		3,178,804			18,306,831	15,712,593
Due from local sources			75,000	36,811					111,811	185,600
Due from other funds (Note 5)	1,929,016		1,409,587			800,000			4,138,603	5,205,272
Leases receivable, net (Notes 6A and 6C)	112,173		179,100		951,595				1,242,868	1,226,805
Long-term note receivable (Note 6E)	1,417,700								1,417,700	861,000
Long-term loans receivable (Note 6E)	3,432,209								3,432,209	
Inventories (Note 1C)	5,777,040								5,777,040	5,290,841
Land, buildings, and other fixed assets (Notes 1B and 7)					5,236,064	14,005	309,856,316		315,106,385	231,104,406
Land held for redevelopment							3,946,614		3,946,614	3,760,760
Amounts available in Debt Service Funds								2,578,092	2,578,092	3,253,019
Amounts to be provided for long-term leases (Note 6B)								11,442,996	11,442,996	10,528,722
Amounts to be provided for retirement of bonds (Note 8)								198,587,908	198,587,908	209,090,981
Total assets and other debits	$30,991,743	$13,865,311	$19,004,980	$41,658,979	$6,356,734	$6,700,455	$313,802,930	$212,608,996	$644,990,128	$596,301,299

Liabilities and Fund Equity

Liabilities:										
Matured bonds payable (Note 8)			$11,196,000						$11,196,000	$10,665,000
Matured interest payable (Note 8)			5,230,888						5,230,888	5,229,583
Accounts payable	1,968,455	72,949		28,412	18,407	6,774			2,094,997	3,051,427
Note payable		511,872							511,872	
Contracts payable	3,061,968	4,133,262		9,804,150		42,069			17,041,449	15,736,322
Contractor retainage payable				1,336,468					1,336,468	1,701,865
Accrued payroll and payroll taxes	2,533,417	269,153							2,802,570	3,382,801
Other accrued liabilities	2,562,920	3,231		6,716	6,056	1,846,105			4,425,028	4,939,615
Due to other funds (Note 5)	1,570,847	1,686,962		748,558		132,236			4,138,603	5,205,272
Deferred revenue (Note 1B)	1,805,766								1,805,766	861,000
Long-term leases payable (Note 6B)								11,442,996	11,442,996	10,528,722
Bonds payable (Note 8)					1,025,000			201,166,000	202,191,000	213,404,000
Total liabilities	13,503,373	6,677,429	16,426,888	11,924,304	1,049,463	2,027,184		212,608,996	264,217,637	274,705,607
Fund equity:										
Investment in general fixed assets (Note 1B)							313,802,930		313,802,930	229,519,286
Contributed capital					4,936,407				4,936,407	4,936,407
Retained earnings					370,864				370,864	449,898
Fund balances:										
Reserved for inventories (Note 1G)	5,777,040								5,777,040	5,290,841
Reserved for noncurrent loans receivable	3,432,209								3,432,209	
Reserved for encumbrances (Note 1E)	13,983,209	3,339,143		38,227,978		755			55,551,085	126,143,165
Reserved for pension benefit payments						41,036			41,036	
Unencumbered (overencumbered) (Note 1E)	(5,704,088)	3,848,739	2,578,092	(8,493,303)		4,631,480			(3,139,080)	(44,743,905)
Total fund equity	17,488,370	7,187,882	2,578,092	29,734,675	5,307,271	4,673,271	313,802,930		380,772,491	321,595,692
Total liabilities and fund equity	$30,991,743	$13,865,311	$19,004,980	$41,658,979	$6,356,734	$6,700,455	$313,802,930	$212,608,996	$644,990,128	$596,301,299

See the accompanying notes.

Source: City of Indianapolis, Indiana, Annual Report, December 31, 1980.

Figure 14-6

CITY OF INDIANAPOLIS

Governmental Fund Types and Expendable Trust Funds
Combined Statement of Revenues,
Expenditures and Changes in Fund Balances
Year Ended December 31, 1980

| | Governmental Fund Types | | | | Fiduciary Fund Type | | Totals Memorandum Only (Note 1N) | |
	General	Special Revenue	Debt Service	Capital Projects	Expendable Trust	Interfund Eliminations	1980	1979
Revenues:								
Taxes	$ 82,504,938	$ 5,397,274	$12,911,473	$	$	$	$100,813,685	$100,091,946
Licenses and permits	2,318,409						2,318,409	1,902,917
Charges for service	18,212,035						18,212,035	17,625,263
Federal revenue sharing					12,871,165		12,871,165	13,208,714
Other federal funds (Note 4)	19,350,829	42,508,748		61,732,787	336,325	(15,668,630)	108,260,059	88,402,117
Traffic violations and court fees	1,136,846						1,136,846	1,233,697
Other operating revenues	8,128,770	2,553,638	3,145,360	13,744,945	1,498,281		29,070,994	22,442,172
Total revenues	131,651,827	50,459,660	16,056,833	75,477,732	14,705,771	(15,668,630)	272,683,193	244,906,826
Other financing sources:								
Federal revenue sharing transfers (Note 5)	9,594,000					(9,594,000)		
Other transfers (Note 5)	197,751	2,656,670	5,221,113		68	(8,075,602)		
Total revenues and other financing sources	141,443,578	53,116,330	21,277,946	75,477,732	14,705,839	(33,338,232)	272,683,193	244,906,826

Expenditures:								
Current:								
Protection of people and property	63,722,974						63,722,974	56,176,224
Community cultural and recreation	11,075,128						11,075,128	13,226,978
Community development and welfare	11,050,688	43,620,571				(15,668,630)	39,002,629	24,893,126
Transportation and related services	17,971,059	4,141,662					22,112,721	27,237,327
Environmental services	25,127,006	103,452					25,230,458	26,435,700
Executive/Legislative affairs of government	1,112,337						1,112,337	932,011
Administrative services	4,723,345						4,723,345	6,283,080
Total current expenditures	134,782,537	47,865,685				(15,668,630)	166,979,592	155,184,446
Debt service	661,046	9,386	21,952,873				22,623,305	22,505,676
Capital outlay	5,510,455	5,747,945		92,440,181			103,698,581	84,334,198
Total expenditures	140,954,038	53,623,016	21,952,873	92,440,181		(15,668,630)	293,301,478	262,024,320
Other uses:								
Transfers (Note 5)	762,161	18,781		7,115,690	9,772,970	(17,669,602)		
Trust and Agency Funds disbursements					3,862,675		3,862,675	4,163,918
Total expenditures and other uses	141,716,199	53,641,797	21,952,873	99,555,871	13,635,645	(33,338,232)	297,164,153	266,188,238
Excess of revenues and other financing sources over (under) expenditures and other uses	(272,621)	(525,467)	(674,927)	(24,078,139)	1,070,194		(24,480,960)	(21,281,412)
Fund balances deficits at beginning of year (Notes 1A and 2)	17,760,991	7,713,349	3,253,019	53,812,814	3,561,650		86,101,823	107,383,235
Fund balances at end of year (Note 1A)	$ 17,488,370	$ 7,187,882	$ 2,578,092	$29,734,675	$ 4,631,844	$	$ 61,620,863	$ 86,101,823

See the accompanying notes.

Source: City of Indianapolis, Indiana, Annual Report, December 31, 1980.

555

Figure 14-7

CITY OF INDIANAPOLIS

General, Special Revenue and Debt Service Fund Types
Combined Statement of Revenues, Expenditures, and Changes in Fund Balances—Budget and Actual
For the Year Ended December 31, 1980

	General Funds			Special Revenue Funds			Debt Service Funds		
	Budget (Cash Basis)	Actual (Cash Basis)	Actual (Modified Accrual Basis)	Budget (Cash Basis)	Actual (Cash Basis)	Actual (Modified Accrual Basis)	Budget (Cash Basis)	Actual (Cash Basis)	Actual (Modified Accrual Basis)
Revenues:									
Taxes	$ 87,363,583	$ 85,291,908	$ 82,504,938	$ 5,903,279	$ 5,397,274	$ 5,397,274	$14,758,359	$14,393,947	$12,911,473
Licenses and permits	1,682,500	2,318,409	2,318,409						
Charges for services	19,342,000	18,368,275	18,212,035	53,824,696	44,228,301	42,508,748			
Other federal funds	33,481,232	19,248,291	19,350,829		2,609				
Traffic violations and court fees	2,242,900	1,136,846	1,136,846						
Other operating revenues	19,187,576	17,043,478	8,128,770	1,268,509	4,930,728	2,553,638	5,443,505	7,042,220	3,145,360
Total revenues	163,299,791	143,407,207	131,651,827	60,996,484	54,558,912	50,459,660	20,201,864	21,436,167	16,056,833
Other financing sources:									
Federal revenue sharing transfers (Note 5)	9,954,000	10,728,251	9,594,000						
Other transfers (Note 5)			197,751			2,656,670			5,221,113
Total revenues and other financing sources	173,253,791	154,135,458	141,443,578	60,996,484	54,558,912	53,116,330	20,201,864	21,436,167	21,277,946

556

Expenditures:									
Current:									
Protection of people and property	68,342,078	65,740,227	63,722,974	69,396,842	43,472,437	43,620,571			
Community cultural and recreation	13,680,015	11,418,844	11,075,128						
Community development and welfare	21,698,030	14,129,326	11,050,688						
Transportation and related services	23,249,483	19,286,352	17,971,059	5,460,332	4,233,657	4,141,662			
Environmental services	34,686,263	26,546,233	25,127,006	424,891	121,738	103,452			
Executive/Legislative affairs of government	1,157,644	1,077,997	1,112,337						
Administrative services	15,298,579	12,487,161	4,723,345						
Total current expenditures	178,112,092	150,686,140	134,782,537	75,282,065	47,827,832	47,865,685	21,297,555	21,420,568	21,952,873
Debt service (Note 8)	661,046	661,046	661,046	9,386	9,386	9,386			
Capital outlays	10,300,461	5,771,149	5,510,455	8,389,400	4,736,719	5,747,945			
Total expenditures	189,073,599	157,118,335	140,954,038	83,680,851	52,573,937	53,623,016	21,297,555	21,420,568	21,952,873
Other uses:									
Transfers (Note 5)			762,161			18,781			
Total expenditures and other uses	189,073,599	157,118,335	141,716,199	83,680,851	52,573,937	53,641,797	21,297,555	21,420,568	21,952,873
Excess of revenues and other financing sources over (under) expenditures and other uses	(15,819,808)	(2,988,877)	(272,621)	(22,684,367)	1,984,975	(525,467)	(1,725,691)	15,599	(674,927)
Fund balances at beginning of year (Notes 1A and 2)	15,819,808	13,418,229	17,760,991	22,684,367	10,055,228	7,713,349	1,725,691	16,884,806	3,253,019
Fund balances at end of year (Note 1A)	$ —	$ 10,435,352	$ 17,488,370	$ —	$12,040,203	$ 7,187,882	$ —	$16,900,405	$ 2,578,092

See the accompanying notes.

Source: City of Indianapolis, Indiana, Annual Report, December 31, 1980.

557

Figure 14-8

CITY OF INDIANAPOLIS

All Proprietary Fund Types and Similar Trust Funds
Combined Statement of Revenues, Expenses,
and Changes in Retained Earnings/Fund Balances
For the Year Ended December 31, 1980

	Proprietary Fund Type	Fiduciary Fund Type	Totals Memorandum Only (Note 1N)	
	Enterprise	Pension Trust	1980	1979
Operating revenues:				
Earned income on direct financing lease (Note 6A)	$ 42,926	$	$ 42,926	$ 44,554
Operating lease income	289,033		289,033	299,209
Contributions		13,258,294	13,258,294	12,986,463
Total operating revenues	331,959	13,258,294	13,590,253	13,330,226
Operating expenses before depreciation:				
Personal services	105,679		105,679	119,542
Contractual services	161,898		161,898	139,963

Supplies	8,825		8,825	5,957
Benefit payments		13,863,131	13,863,131	12,757,208
Other	33,725		33,725	18,480
Total operating expenses before depreciation	310,127	13,863,131	14,173,258	13,041,150
Operating income before depreciation	21,832	(604,837)	(583,005)	289,076
Depreciation	100,006		100,006	98,758
Operating income (loss)	(78,174)	(604,837)	(683,011)	190,318
Other income (expense):				
Interest income	46,840	57,986	104,826	34,036
Interest expense	(47,700)		(47,700)	(49,275)
Total other income (expense)	(860)	57,986	57,126	(15,239)
Net income (loss)	(79,034)	(546,851)	(625,885)	175,079
Retained earnings/fund balances at beginning of year	449,898	588,278	1,038,176	863,097
Retained earnings/fund balances at end of year	$370,864	$ 41,427	$ 412,291	$ 1,038,176

See the accompanying notes.

Source: City of Indianapolis, Annual Report, *December 31, 1980.*

it did, an Internal Service Fund column would be presented), and (2) chose to present its fiduciary fund statements with the governmental and proprietary fund statements, as appropriate, rather than separately.

Combined Statement of Changes in Financial Position. This statement (Figure 14-9) also resembles such statements prepared for business enterprises, and properly so. Accounting Principles Board *Opinion Number 19*, "Reporting Changes in Financial Position," is the authoritative guideline to preparing such statements for proprietary and similar fiduciary funds of governments as well as for business enterprises.

The Notes to the Financial Statements (GPFS). Since the GPFS can be issued separately from the CAFR, the GPFS and notes must be sufficiently complete to "stand alone," notwithstanding the disclosure in the GPFS that the CAFR is available for readers wanting more detailed data. Thus the NCGA required extensive notes to the GPFS and designated any further notes that may be needed to explain the combining and individual fund and account group statements and schedules "narrative explanations."

Statement 1 requires the following types of notes to the GPFS:

- Summary of significant accounting policies
- Contingent liabilities
- Encumbrances outstanding
- Significant effects of subsequent events
- Pension plan obligations
- Accumulated unpaid employee benefits (such as vacation and sick leave)
- Material violations of finance-related legal and contractual provisions
- Debt service requirements to maturity (formerly a required statistical table)
- Commitments under noncapitalized leases
- Construction and other significant commitments
- Changes in general fixed assets (formerly a required statement)
- Changes in general long-term debt (formerly a required statement)
- Any excess of expenditures over appropriations in *individual funds*
- Deficit balances of *individual funds*
- Interfund receivables and payables
- Any other disclosures necessary in the circumstances

and NCGA *Interpretation 6*, "Notes to the Financial Statements Disclosure,"[5] issued 1982, provides further footnote disclosure guidance, including references to footnote requirements of other NCGA *Statements* and *Interpretations*.

---

[5] National Council on Governmental Accounting, *Interpretation 6*, "Notes to the Financial Statements Disclosure" (Chicago: NCGA, 1982).

NCGA *Interpretation 2*, "Segment Information for Enterprise Funds,"[6] requires disclosure in the GPFS of certain specified information for each major Enterprise Fund. These disclosures may be accomplished in several ways, the most common being by a note to the financial statements that contains the information shown in Figure 14-10. Excerpts from the notes to the financial statements of the City of Indianapolis appear in Figure 14-11. Careful study of these selected notes yields many "real world" insights while illustrating some of the required note disclosures listed above.

The Combining and Individual Fund and Account Group Statements and Schedules. Combining and individual fund and account group statements and schedules have been presented in the preceding chapters both as integral parts of illustrative examples and as ancillary illustrations. NCGA *Statement 1* observes that:

> The major differences between the GPFS and the other statements in the CAFR relate to the reporting entity focus and the reporting on finance-related legal and contractual provisions that differ from GAAP. The CAFR includes (1) both individual fund and account group data and aggregate data by fund types, together with introductory, supplementary, and statistical information; and (2) schedules essential to demonstrate compliance with finance-related legal and contractual provisions. The GPFS present only aggregate data by fund type and account group, together with notes to the financial statements that are essential to fair presentation, including disclosures of material violations of finance-related legal and contractual provisions and other important matters that are not apparent from the face of the financial statements.[7]

The entity focus of the combining and individual statements is on the individual fund or account group—and combining statements also present total data for a fund type—whereas the GPFS entity focus is on aggregated fund type data. In summarizing its intent with respect to financial reporting under the pyramid concept, recall that the NCGA observed:

> The governmental unit need go only as far down the reporting pyramid—in terms of increasing levels of detail—as necessary to report the financial position and operating results of its individual funds and account groups, to demonstrate compliance with finance-related legal and contractual requirements, and to assure adequate disclosure at the individual fund [and account group] entity level.[8]

Thus, the purpose of the combining statements, individual fund and account group statements, and schedules is to "fill the gap," so to speak, between the GPFS which "present fairly" at the fund type entity level and the need in the CAFR

[6] National Council on Governmental Accounting, *Interpretation 2*, "Segment Information for Enterprise Funds," (Chicago: NCGA, 1980).

[7] NCGAS1, p. 19.

[8] Ibid., p. 20.

Figure 14-9

CITY OF INDIANAPOLIS

All Proprietary Fund Types and Similar Trust Funds
Combined Statement of Changes in Financial Position
Year Ended December 31, 1980

| | Proprietary Fund Type | Fiduciary Fund Type | Totals Memorandum Only (Note 1N) | |
	Enterprise	Pension Trust	1980	1979
Source:				
Net income (loss)	$(79,034)	$(546,851)	$(625,885)	$ 175,079
Depreciation—not affecting working capital in the current period	100,006		100,006	98,758
Reduction of direct financing lease receivable	40,416		40,416	35,446
	61,388	(546,851)	(485,463)	309,283
Application:				
Additions to fixed assets	3,045	1,150	4,195	3,985
Reduction in revenue bond payable	35,000		35,000	35,000
	38,045	1,150	39,195	38,985
Increase (decrease) in working capital	$ 23,343	$(548,001)	$(524,658)	$ 270,298

Changes in components of working capital:

Increase (decrease) in current assets:				
Cash	$ 3,991	$ (4,678)	$ (687)	$(140,881)
Investments		(179,997)	(179,997)	395,655
Cash and investments with fiscal agents	13,004		13,004	5,497
Rent and direct financing lease receivable	7,774		7,774	(4,823)
Due from other funds		(286,102)	(286,102)	92,226
	24,769	(470,777)	(446,008)	347,674
Increase (decrease) in current liabilities:				
Accounts payable	1,469	810	2,279	6,170
Accrued liabilities	(43)	8,222	8,179	(83,679)
Due to other funds		68,192	68,192	133
	1,426	77,224	78,650	(77,376)
Increase (decrease) in working capital	$ 23,343	$(548,001)	$(524,658)	$ 270,298

See the accompanying notes.

Source: City of Indianapolis, Indiana, Annual Report, December 31, 1980.

Figure 14-10

ILLUSTRATIVE ENTERPRISE FUND SEGMENT INFORMATION DISCLOSURE

The following example of notes to the financial statements disclosure of segment information is presented for illustrative purposes only. Alternative presentation formats may also be acceptable. This illustration assumes that there were no other material facts necessary to make the GPFS not misleading.

NOTE ( )—SEGMENT INFORMATION FOR ENTERPRISE FUNDS

The City maintains five Enterprise Funds which provide water, sewer, airport, golf and parking services. Segment information for the year ended December 31, 19X2 was as follows:

	Water Fund	Sewer Fund	Airport Fund	Other Enterprise Funds	Total Enterprise Funds
Operating Revenues	300,000	20,000	300,000	52,150	672,150
Depreciation, Depletion, and Amortization Expense	70,000	10,000	60,000	4,100	144,100
Operating Income or (Loss)	130,000	5,000	(35,000)	7,970	107,970
Operating Grants, Entitlements, and Shared Revenues	—	—	55,000	—	55,000
Operating Transfers:					
In	—	20,000	—	—	20,000
Out	(30,000)	—	—	—	(30,000)
Tax Revenues	—	10,000	—	—	10,000
Net Income or Loss	42,822	10,000	10,000	15,990	78,812
Current Capital:					
Contributions	682,666	—	—	—	682,666
Transfers	(10,000)	—	—	—	(10,000)
Plant, Property and Equipment:					
Additions	180,000	25,000	125,000	24,453	354,453
Deletions	(30,000)	—	—	(30,000)	(30,000)
Net Working Capital	167,491	35,812	43,187	41,773	288,263
Bonds and Other Long-Term Liabilities:					
Payable from Operating Revenues	1,598,000	—	—	—	1,598,000
Payable from Other Sources	200,000	—	—	—	200,000
Total equity	2,900,000	150,000	400,000	110,002	3,560,002

Source: *National Council on Governmental Accounting*, Interpretation 2, *"Segment Information for Enterprise Funds" (Chicago: NCGA, June 1980), p. 3.*

Figure 14-11

CITY OF INDIANAPOLIS

Notes to Financial Statements
December 31, 1980 and 1979

1. **Basis of presentation and summary of significant accounting policies**

The City maintains its accounting records on a cash basis to comply with statutory requirements of the State of Indiana and, except as to the accounting for certain pension costs as explained in part K of this Note and in Note 10, adjusts this data to an accrual or modified accrual basis to conform to generally accepted accounting principles applicable to governments as prescribed by Statements 1 and 2 of the National Council on Governmental Accounting (NCGA), effective for the City's current fiscal year. The City records transactions in several statutory funds that are consolidated into the funds and groups of accounts described elsewhere in this Note for financial reporting purposes. The following is a summary of the more significant policies:

A. Fund accounting

The accounts of the City are organized on the basis of funds and account groups, each of which is considered a separate accounting entity. The operations of each fund are accounted for with a separate set of self-balancing accounts that comprise its assets, liabilities, fund equity, revenues, and expenditures or expenses, as appropriate. Government resources are allocated to and accounted for in individual funds based upon the purposes for which they are to be spent and the means by which spending activities are controlled. The various funds are grouped, in the financial statements in this report, into three broad fund categories and six generic fund types as follows:

Noncurrent portions of long-term loans receivable due to governmental funds are reported on their balance sheets, notwithstanding their spending measurement focus. Special reporting treatments are used to indicate, however, that they should not be considered "available spendable resources," since they do not represent net current assets. Recognition of governmental fund type revenues represented by noncurrent receivables is deferred until they become current receivables. Noncurrent portions of long-term loans receivable are offset by fund balance reserve accounts.

Figure 14-11 (Continued)

Because of their spending measurement focus, expenditure recognition for governmental fund types is limited to exclude amounts represented by noncurrent liabilities. Since they do not affect net current assets, such long-term amounts are not recognized as governmental fund type expenditures or fund liabilities. They are instead reported as liabilities in the General Long-Term Debt Account Group.

C. Basis of accounting

Basis of accounting refers to when revenues and expenditures or expenses are recognized in the accounts and reported in the financial statements. Basis of accounting relates to the timing of the measurements made, regardless of the measurement focus applied.

All governmental funds and Expendable Trust Funds are accounted for using the modified accrual basis of accounting. Their revenues are recognized when they become measurable and available as net current assets. Taxpayer-assessed income, gross receipts and sales taxes are considered "measurable" when in the hands of intermediary collecting governments and are recognized as revenue at that time. Anticipated refunds of such taxes are recorded as liabilities and reductions of revenue when they are measurable and their validity seems certain.

Expenditures are generally recognized under the modified accrual basis of accounting when the related fund liability is incurred. Exceptions to this general rule include:

1. Accrued sick leave and vacation leave benefits, which are not accrued.
2. Serial bond principal and interest payments due on January 1, which are accrued on the preceding December 31.
3. Prepaid expenses are not recorded.

D. Budgets and budgetary accounting

The City budgets are prepared essentially on the cash basis of accounting. In addition, some interfund transactions are included in the budget as receipts and disbursements in more than one fund.

E. Encumbrances

Encumbrance accounting, under which purchase orders, contracts and other commitments for the expenditure of monies are recorded in order to reserve that portion of the applicable appropriation, is employed as an extension of formal budgetary [account] integration in the General Funds, Special Revenue Funds, Capital Projects Funds, and Expendable and Pension Trust Funds. Encumbrances do not lapse with the expiration of the budget period. Encumbrances outstanding at year end are reported as reservations of fund balances since they do not constitute expenditures or liabilities. Unencumbered fund balances represent fund balances available for future commitment. Overencumbrances reflect commitments in excess of available fund balances which will be financed from future revenue. Overencumbrances may occur in funds administering federally-funded projects because the related grant awards are not recognized as revenue until expenditures occur.

Transfers within fund types have been eliminated. Transfers between fund types during the years ended December 31, 1980 and 1979 were:

1980

| | Total Transfers Out | Transfers In | | | |
		General Funds	Special Revenue Funds	Debt Service Funds	Trust and Agency Funds
General Funds	$ 762,161	$	$ 686,193	$ 75,900	$ 68
Special Revenue Funds	18,781	18,781			
Capital Projects Funds	7,115,690		1,970,477	5,145,213	
Trust and Agency Funds	9,772,970	9,772,970			
	$17,669,602	$ 9,791,751	$2,656,670	$ 5,221,113	$ 68

1979

| | Total Transfers Out | Transfers In | | | |
		General Funds	Special Revenue Funds	Debt Service Funds	Trust and Agency Funds
General Funds	$ 355,451	$	$ 355,451	$	$
Special Revenue Funds	4,889,859	167,894		4,721,965	
Capital Projects Funds	6,809,554			6,805,355	4,199
Trust and Agency Funds	11,952,578	11,952,578			
	$24,007,442	$12,120,472	$ 355,451	$11,527,320	$4,199

Figure 14-11 (Continued)

6. **Leases and other financing transactions**

A. Financing lease receivable—parking garage:

The City has a direct financing lease expiring in July, 1997, for a parking lot and garage accounted for in the Enterprise Funds. The components of the net investment at December 31, 1980 and 1979 are as follows:

	1980	1979
Total minimum lease payments to be received	$1,326,666	$1,406,666
Estimated residual value	8,503	8,503
Less unearned income	(392,983)	(435,909)
Net investment in financing lease	$ 942,186	$ 979,260

At December 31, 1980, minimum lease payments for each of the five succeeding years are $80,000. Total minimum lease payments beyond five years amount to $926,666.

B. Capital leases payable—office building, parking lot and various equipment:

The City leases its office building and parking lot jointly with Marion County over a 40-year term expiring in December, 2001. The lease requires the City to make annual payments of $670,432 and to pay its share of building operation and maintenance costs ($1,644,732 in 1980 and $1,508,070 in 1979). The City and County will jointly obtain title to the building in the future. Accordingly, the City's portion of the lease is classified as a capital lease. The City also leases certain equipment under capital leases expiring in 1984. At December 31, 1980 the capitalized cost of the office building and parking lot was $13,373,254 and the capitalized cost of equipment was $2,630,190.

7. Changes in general fixed assets

A summary of changes in general fixed assets follows:

	Balance January 1, 1980	Additions	Transfers and Reclassifications	Reductions	Balance December 31, 1980
Land	$ 14,024,147	$ 21,800	$	$ 233,925	$ 13,812,022
Buildings	48,681,970	102,491	1,468,403		50,252,864
Improvements	44,918,169	45,061	500,040		45,463,270
Equipment	32,736,609	3,554,771	726,189	2,994,575	34,022,994
Land held for redevelopment	3,760,760	1,249,500		1,063,646	3,946,614
Construction in progress	61,393,783	83,602,167	(2,694,632)		142,301,318
Fixed assets held for investment	24,003,848				24,003,848
Total	$229,519,286	$88,575,790	$	$4,292,146	$313,802,930

8. Changes in long-term serial bonds

The following is a summary of bond transactions for the year ended December 31, 1980:

	General Obligation							
	Civil City	Redevelopment	Sanitary	Flood Control	Metropolitan Thoroughfare	Park	Revenue	Total
Bonds payable at January 1, 1980	$28,080,000	$9,670,000	$116,840,000	$12,006,000	$38,280,000	$18,133,000	$1,060,000	$224,069,000
Bonds retired	1,401,000	425,000	5,879,000	940,000	1,130,000	872,000	35,000	10,682,000
Bonds payable at December 31, 1980	$26,679,000	$9,245,000	$110,961,000	$11,066,000	$37,150,000	$17,261,000	$1,025,000	$213,387,000

Figure 14-11 (Continued)

9. Fund deficits

Fund balance deficits arise from the following:

	General Funds				Debt Service Funds	
	Consolidated County	Solid Waste	Police	Fire	Civil City Sinking	Flood Control Sinking
Anticipated Property tax distributions from the Marion County, Indiana, Treasurer not realized since the taxpayers have appealed their reassessed property values	$ 78,461	$183,188	$1,252,603	$1,121,840	$ 35,594	$19,391
Anticipated reimbursement from the Transportation General Fund for snow removal not realized		40,000				
Reduced court fees resulting from enactment of court fee rate increases later than anticipated			1,000,000			
Anticipated revenues from the sale of police vehicles not realized			170,000			
Anticipated pension plan membership contributions not realized			102,000			
Anticipated State of Indiana Pension Relief Act of 1977 revenues not realized			138,400			
Budgeted other operating income not realized					75,000	
Other, net	32,417	73,292	(31,780)	(207,387)	(6,131)	(3,636)
	$110,878	$296,480	$2,631,223	$ 914,453	$104,463	$15,755

Source: City of Indianapolis, Indiana, Annual Report, December 31, 1980.

to also "present fairly" under the individual fund and account group entity focus. Determining what financial statements and schedules must be presented in the CAFR beyond those of the GPFS requires careful consideration of the facts of each situation and professional judgment.

Combining statements are always required where a government has more than one fund of a fund type. Combining statements also may be presented in more detail than is possible in combined statements, often in sufficient detail to "present fairly" and thus avoid the need for several individual fund statements.

Individual fund statements are required wherever sufficient detail is not presented in combining statements or, in the case of the General Fund and the Account Groups, in the combined statements. They may also be needed to present budgetary comparisons in sufficient detail and/or to present prior year comparative data.

Schedules are used primarily to (1) demonstrate finance-related legal and contractual compliance, such as when bond indentures require certain data to be presented in the CAFR; (2) present other data management may wish to present, such as cash receipts and disbursements schedules for one, some, or all funds; and (3) present more detailed data than that appearing in the combined, combining, and individual fund and account group statements, such as detailed schedules of revenues and of expenditures. Schedules are not considered to be required by GAAP unless they are referenced in a statement or footnote. However, note that the notes to the financial statements (Figure 14-11) often include several schedules which are deemed essential to reporting in conformity with GAAP.

Narrative explanations are in essence additional notes to the combining and individual fund statements and schedules. They are not called notes under the dual reporting approach of the NCGA so they will not be confused with the notes to the GPFS, which are referred to as "Notes to the Financial Statements" in *Statement 1*. The NCGA summarized the nature and role of the narrative explanations in the CAFR as follows:

> Narrative explanations of combining and individual fund and account group statements and schedules should provide information *not* included in the financial statements, notes to the financial statements, and schedules that is necessary: (1) to assure an understanding of the combining and individual fund and account group statements and schedules, and (2) to demonstrate compliance with finance-related legal and contractual provisions. (In extreme cases, it may be necessary to prepare a separate legal-basis special report.) The narrative explanations, including a description of the nature and purpose of the various funds, should be presented on divider pages, directly on the statements and schedules, or in a separate section.[9]

Concluding Comments on Financial Reporting. The NCGA offered several other guidelines to financial reporting in *Statement 1*. At one point the Council noted that "Financial statements should present data summarized appropriately to their pyramid level."[10] This is an important point because, consistent with the pyramid concept, it emphasizes that combined statements are the most sum-

[9] Ibid., p. 24.
[10] Ibid., p. 22.

marized; combining statements should articulate with but be in more detail than the combined statements; and individual fund and account group statements should be in more detail than combining or combined statements.

At another point the Council noted that "a financial statement normally should not exceed two pages."[11] This both constrains and gives practical guidance to preparers of CAFRs. For example, we recommend that:

1. Combined statements must be in no more detail than can be presented on two pages. Some reduction is acceptable, but the published statements should be readable.

2. If a combining statement involves so many different funds that, after reduction, the statement would not be readily readable, a two-tier approach should be used. Under this approach the major funds of the type are presented and an "Other" column summarizes all of the other funds, which are presented in a second combining statement supporting the main combining statement.

3. Statements that would exceed two pages should be restructured so that the statement contains more summarized data, with the detail presented in the next lower level statement or in a schedule(s).

The NCGA also noted that combined statements may have total columns, but they must be labeled "Memorandum Only." Also, combined or combining statements may have an "interfund and similar eliminations" column or the total may be based on such eliminations even if the elimination column does not appear in the statement. Interfund and similar eliminations are a permissible option but, if made, must be apparent from the headings of the statement or disclosed in the notes and narrative explanations, as appropriate.

Finally, recall from Chapter 4 that there are several acceptable options for formats of statements of revenues, expenditures, and changes in fund balances prepared for governmental funds and similar trust funds. The NCGA illustrated one format, which is the basis for the illustrative example statement in Chapter 4; the City of Indianapolis selected another format, shown in Figure 14-6; and other acceptable approaches are discussed in Chapter 4 on pages 122–124.

Statistical Tables

The final section of the CAFR contains several types of statistical presentations. Some of the data are extracted from present and past financial statements, such as the table of General Government Expenditures by Function—Last Ten Years, to give the reader a historical and trend perspective of the government. Other data relate only to one year—such as the computation of legal debt margin and the computation of overlapping debt, discussed and illustrated in Chapter 10—to give the reader assurance that laws on how much debt can be incurred have been complied with, an idea of how much more debt could be issued before the legal debt ceiling is reached, or a perspective of the total local government tax load on the citizens in the government's jurisdiction. Other types of economic and demographic data are also presented here to give the reader a perspective

[11] Ibid.

on such matters as employment and unemployment, the major employees and taxpayers, and the general state of health of the local economy.

The NCGA specified that:

The following statistical tables should be included in the CAFR unless clearly inapplicable in the circumstances:
(1) General Governmental Expenditures by Function—Last Ten Fiscal Years. [Figure 14-11]
(2) General Revenues by Source—Last Ten Fiscal Years. [Figure 14-12]
(3) Property Tax Levies and Collections—Last Ten Fiscal Years. [Figure 14-13]
(4) Assessed and Estimated Actual Value of Taxable Property—Last Ten Fiscal Years. [Figure 14-14]
(5) Property Tax Rates—All Overlapping Governments—Last Ten Fiscal Years.
(6) Special Assessment Collections—Last Ten Fiscal Years.
(7) Ratio of Net General Bonded Debt to Assessed Value and Net Bonded Debt per Capita—Last Ten Fiscal Years. [Figure 10-13]
(8) Computation of Legal Debt Margin (if not presented in the GPFS). [Figure 10-11]
(9) Computation of Overlapping Debt (if not presented in the GPFS). [Figure 10-12]
(10) Ratio of Annual Debt Service for General Bonded Debt to Total General Expenditures—Last Ten Fiscal Years. [Figure 10-14]
(11) Revenue Bond Coverage—Last Ten Fiscal Years.
(12) Demographic Statistics.
(13) Property Value, Construction, and Bank Deposits—Last Ten Fiscal Years.
(14) Principal Taxpayers.
(15) Miscellaneous Statistics.[12]

The Council notes that not all of these presentations are needed in all circumstances and urges preparers to devise new types of statistical statements as needed.

Although space does not permit us to include illustrations of all fifteen of these statistical tables, the first four are illustrated in Figures 14-12 to 14-15. In addition, several of these statistical tables are illustrated in earlier chapters; e.g., Figure 10-11 presents a computation of legal debt margin; Figure 11-19 illustrates the computation of direct and overlapping debt; Figure 10-13 shows the ratio of net general debt to assessed value and net bonded debt per capita—last ten fiscal years; and Figure 10-14 reports the ratio of annual debt service for general bonded debt to total general expenditures—last ten fiscal years.

SUPPLEMENTAL AND SPECIAL PURPOSE REPORTING

A variety of special reports has emerged in recent years. Some are necessary because a government prepares its CAFR in accordance with GAAP but must also submit a non-GAAP report (possibly of cash receipts, disbursements, and balances)

[12] Ibid., p. 24.

Figure 14-12

CITY OF BIRMINGHAM

General Governmental Expenditures by Functions
Last Ten Fiscal Years

Fiscal Year	General Government	Public Safety	Streets and Sanitation	Culture and Recreation	Debt Service	Capital Outlay	Pensions
1971	$ 3,093,291	$12,888,715	$11,047,470	$ 4,603,112	$ 5,850,349	$14,235,804	$1,659,602
1972	3,970,538	16,543,900	14,180,486	5,908,535	8,076,012	21,244,977	1,848,348
1973	4,683,378	19,522,408	16,733,492	6,972,289	8,069,182	15,933,922	2,098,295
1974*	6,718,269	22,655,418	16,285,452	7,110,650	3,949,176	4,301,073	2,185,061
1975	6,296,746	31,057,756	17,792,747	9,491,544	7,786,143	8,721,719	2,899,794
1976	7,050,798	32,325,418	18,985,562	9,065,269	7,619,198	16,033,326	3,338,798
1977	8,936,734	33,815,796	22,316,780	8,622,106	8,508,859	19,388,112	3,949,169
1978	8,939,189	33,825,584	32,261,287	12,734,064	8,056,735	21,013,983	4,253,867
1979	15,139,443	40,105,139	28,472,391	11,261,335	17,209,338	20,053,393	4,836,619
1980	18,724,584	43,856,610	28,452,504	13,308,188	8,775,645	16,212,481	5,354,120

* Ten months.
Source: City of Birmingham, Alabama, Comprehensive Annual Financial Report, *Fiscal Year Ending June 30, 1980, p. 108.*

Figure 14-13

CITY OF BIRMINGHAM

General Government Revenues by Source
Last Ten Fiscal Years

Fiscal Year	Taxes	Licenses and Permits	Intergovernmental Revenue	Charges for Services	Fines and Forfeits	Miscellaneous Revenue	Bond Proceeds
1971	$20,822,841	$ 7,140,375	$ 9,267,681	$3,673,272	$ 1,794,635	$ 7,105,841	$15,700,000
1972	27,308,530	7,553,876	10,430,935	3,754,178	1,848,446	8,393,397	
1973	28,988,173	8,266,428	20,453,060	4,286,606	1,979,382	9,636,767	
1974*	26,730,228	8,667,893	18,965,265	3,878,359	1,526,807	8,329,980	5,050,000
1975	33,439,592	10,250,026	25,761,898	5,632,196	1,927,865	11,851,183	
1976	35,947,071	11,387,244	30,823,924	5,435,131	1,919,172	11,263,903	
1977	39,017,623	13,322,389	40,352,090	6,653,347	2,227,601	13,013,263	
1978	45,616,264	17,071,631	35,093,966	7,800,561	2,429,777	17,091,886	35,000,000
1979	50,147,212	17,871,212	30,675,274	8,816,910	3,029,580	21,233,950	7,454,482
1980	53,697,330	19,541,559	30,028,111	9,276,466	2,410,519	25,867,516	38,115,648

* Ten months.

Source: City of Birmingham, Alabama, Comprehensive Annual Financial Report, *Fiscal Year Ending June 30, 1980, p. 107.*

Figure 14-14

CITY OF BIRMINGHAM

Property Taxes Levied and Collected for Jefferson County, Alabama
Last Ten Years*

Beginning October 1	Assessed Valuation	Total Taxes Levied	Uncollected At Sale Date	
			Amount	Percentage
1970	$1,266,406,852	$40,386,869	$114,691	00.28
1971	1,341,285,006	43,087,020	107,414	00.25
1972	1,427,118,563	45,822,695	122,933	00.26
1973	1,200,817,471	49,057,218	80,895	00.16
1974	1,271,724,002	51,991,072	344,344	00.66
1975	1,372,133,142	59,792,816	258,891	00.43
1976	1,482,132,062	65,257,086	266,943	00.41
1977	1,579,281,481	69,377,503	287,011	00.41
1978	1,861,390,255	82,793,654	594,658	00.72
1979	1,628,403,755	93,038,643	800,494	00.86

All ad valorem taxes levied by the state, county and any municipality in Jefferson County are assessed by the Tax Assessor and collected by the Tax Collector of Jefferson County. The tax collection rate at the date of tax sale has exceeded 99.27% each year for the past ten fiscal years.
* From Jefferson County Tax Collector and Jefferson County Tax Assessor.
Source: City of Birmingham, Alabama, Comprehensive Annual Financial Report. *Fiscal Year Ending June 30, 1980, p. 109.*

to a state agency. This type situation was contemplated and discussed in NCGA *Statement 1.*

Another type of report that has emerged may be called "condensed summary reports" directed at the top of the NCGA pyramid. These vary from highly condensed (even consolidated) financial statements, perhaps presented in short booklets or brochures highlighting the key aspects of a city's operating results and status, to misleading presentations of selected data of only a few of a government's funds and account groups. In other words, some appear to be sincere efforts to communicate vital data at a more condensed level than that of the GPFS, whereas others appear to hide more than they disclose.

The NCGA considered at length whether any presentation more aggregated than the GPFS could be considered GAAP and concluded that it could not. At the same time the Council recognized that GAAP continually evolve and noted:

> Some governmental units have for many years published highly *condensed summary* financial data, usually as "popular" reports directed primarily to citizens. Often the data in such reports are presented in charts or graphs rather than in financial statements. More recently, several professional association committees and individuals have undertaken research and experimentation directed toward the design of highly condensed summary financial statements for governmental units. The Council encourages such research and experimentation, but believes that at the present time such statements should supplement, rather than supplant, the CAFR and the separately issued GPFS.

Further, the Council believes that the data in such highly condensed summary statements should be reconcilable with the combined, combining, and individual fund and account group statements, and that the reader of such statements should be referred to the CAFR and/or the separately issued GPFS of the governmental unit. The Council will continue to monitor experimentation with highly condensed summary statements and will consider such reporting in its subsequent research.[13]

Finally, the Council observed and instructed that:

The accounting principles and illustrative procedures in this volume are designed to enhance fiscal control, facilitate compliance with generally accepted accounting principles and finance-related legal and contractual requirements, and result in financial statements and reports that fulfill many user information needs. As such, they constitute the *minimum standards* of financial reporting for state and local governments.

The finance officer should assume responsibility for preparing supplemental fiscal data needed in reaching essential management decisions, formulating fiscal policy, informing the general and investing public, and submitting financial data to central compiling agencies such as national statistics bureaus. The finance officer should not assume that properly preparing a comprehensive annual financial report (CAFR), separately issuing general purpose financial statements (GPFS), and demonstrating finance-related legal and contractual compliance preclude additional reporting of fiscal data in total and/or on other than by fund types and funds. Neither generally accepted accounting principles nor finance-related legal and contractual requirements should be construed as establishing *maximum* reporting requirements. Supplementary information may be equally valuable in meeting other information needs and in providing a better understanding of the finances of the governmental unit.[14]

THE GOVERNMENT REPORTING ENTITY

Under what circumstances, if any, should one state or local governmental unit be considered a part of another state or local government and included in its general purpose financial statements and comprehensive annual financial report? Properly defining the government financial reporting entity presents problems primarily because units of general government—such as cities, counties, and states—often have various degrees of authority over and/or responsibilities for other legally separate governmental or quasi-governmental units—such as school districts, housing authorities, building authorities, fire districts, water districts, and transit authorities. Which of these, if any, should be included in the financial reports of an associated city, county, or state?

If an associated organization is included in the government's reporting entity the organization's assets, liabilities, equities, revenues, and expenditures or expenses will be reported in the government's financial statements as if the asso-

[13] Ibid., p. 26.
[14] Ibid.

Figure 14-15

CITY OF BIRMINGHAM
Assessed Value and Estimated True Value of All Taxable Property
Past Ten Fiscal Periods

Assessment Date October 1	Real Property*		Personal Property*		Automobile†		Total Assessed Value	Total Estimated True Value	Ratio Of Total Assessed Value to Total True Value
	Assessed Value	Estimated True Value	Assessed Value	Estimated True Value	Assessed Value	Estimated True Value			
1970	$469,863,417	$1,566,211,390	$145,843,175	$486,143,916	$46,841,515	$156,138,383	$662,548,107	$2,208,493,689	30
1971	495,234,991	1,650,783,303	153,595,828	511,986,093	47,764,030	159,213,433	696,594,849	2,321,982,829	30
1972	522,877,726	1,742,925,753	163,907,789	546,359,296	46,427,150	154,757,166	733,212,665	2,444,042,215	30
1973	431,162,223	1,853,444,561	150,033,911	564,156,296	49,498,800	164,997,000	630,694,934	2,582,598,362	Various
1974	437,627,891	1,867,881,346	162,416,482	623,030,428	53,370,735	177,902,450	653,415,108	2,668,814,224	Various
1975	451,404,234	1,924,948,981	183,817,215	710,484,303	69,174,815	276,699,260	704,396,264	2,912,132,544	Various
1976	466,700,303	1,984,198,500	205,777,235	792,109,860	65,727,000	262,908,000	738,204,538	3,039,216,360	Various
1977	479,232,349	2,034,588,831	215,299,194	830,204,056	65,312,600	261,250,400	759,844,143	3,126,043,287	Various
1978	558,190,505	2,702,836,434	231,460,718	925,842,872	67,538,580	270,154,320	857,189,803	3,898,833,626	Various
1979	502,189,800	2,736,848,430	152,068,306	763,786,580	69,627,620	278,510,480	723,885,726	3,779,145,490	Various

Ad valorem taxes are assessed and collected for the City of Birmingham by Jefferson County.
* From Tax Assessor of Jefferson County.
† From Director of Revenue, Jefferson County.
Source: City of Birmingham, Alabama, Comprehensive Annual Financial Report, *Fiscal Year Ending June 30, 1980*, p. 111.

ciated organization were a government department or agency. The associated organization's financial statements also may be issued separately.

If the associated organization is not included in the government's reporting entity, only its transactions with, receivables from, and obligations with respect to the associated organization will be reported in the government's financial statements and notes.

NCGA Statement 3

This difficult "government reporting entity" issue was addressed by the NCGA in *Statement 3*, "Defining the Governmental Reporting Entity," issued in December 1981.[15]

NCGA *Statement 3* recognizes that criteria for defining the government reporting entity are necessary to reduce both the possibility of arbitrary exclusions and inclusions of various associated organizations. However, it adopted a broad definition of the governmental reporting entity that is more apt to include than to exclude associated organizations.

The NCGA concluded that the basic criterion is whether a government's *elected* officials are *exercising oversight* responsibility over the associated organizations.[16] It noted that oversight responsibility is derived from one government's power over another and includes, but is not limited to:

- Financial Interdependency
- Selection of Governing Authority
- Designation of Management
- Ability to Significantly Influence Operations
- Accountability for Fiscal Matters

The NCGA stated that oversight responsibility connotes dependency of the associated organization on the governmental unit, and stated that the most significant "manifestation" of oversight responsibility, which usually is accompanied by one or more of the others, is financial interdependency. While "financial interdependency" is not defined in *Statement 3*, it is noted that "manifestations of financial interdependency include (1) responsibility for financing deficits, (2) entitlements to surpluses and (3) guarantees of or 'moral responsibility' for debt."[17]

The NCGA also concluded that there are situations where—even though the oversight responsibility criterion is not met—other factors in the associated organization-government unit relationship are so significant that excluding the associated organization from the government's reporting entity would make its financial statements misleading. These othese factors include:

- Scope of Public Service
  - • Where the activity is for the benefit of the reporting entity and/or its residents, and

---

[15] National Council on Governmental Accounting, *Statement 3*, "Defining The Governmental Reporting Entity" (Chicago: NCGA, December, 1981).

[16] Ibid., p. 3.

[17] Ibid., p. 3.

•• Whether the activity is conducted within the geographic boundaries of the governmental unit and is generally available to its citizens.
- Special Financing Relationships—such as housing and building authorities and the Municipal Assistance Corporation (MAC), New York City.[18]

The NCGA *Statement 1* government reporting entity criteria are summarized in Figure 14-16.

Finally, NCGA *Statement 3* requires that the notes to a government's financial statements disclose (1) the criteria used in determining its reporting entity, including how the specific elements of the criteria were considered and applied, and (2) any agency(ies) that met one or more of the criteria but was excluded from the government's reporting entity, and why it was excluded.[19]

Criticisms of NCGA *Statement 3*

The criteria set forth in NCGA *Statement 3* have been criticized from several perspectives. These criticisms, and an alternative proposal, are discussed in Chapter 15.

Figure 14-16

NCGA GOVERNMENT REPORTING ENTITY DEFINITION CRITERIA

EXERCISE OF OVERSIGHT RESPONSIBILITY
- *The "Basic" Criterion*
- *Elements or "Manifestations" of Exercise of Oversight* Responsibility include
   —*Financial Interdependency*—the most significant element, evidenced by
      —Responsibility for financing deficits
      —Entitlements to surpluses
      —Guarantees of or "moral responsibility" for debt
   —*The Other Elements*
      —Selection of Governing Authority
      —Designation of Management
      —Ability to Significantly Influence Operations
      —Accountability for Fiscal Matters

OTHER FACTORS—THE "SECONDARY" CRITERIA
- *Scope of Public Service*
   —Whether activity(ies) for benefit of the government and/or its residents
   —Whether activity(ies) conducted within geographic boundaries of the government and generally available to its citizens
- *Special Financing Relationships*
   —e.g., Housing and Building Authorities
   —e.g., Municipal Assistance Corporation (MAC), New York City

Source: National Council on Governmental Accounting, Statement 3, *"Defining the Governmental Reporting Entity" (Chicago: NCGA, December 1981).*

[18] Ibid., p. 4.
[19] Ibid., p. 14.

The "pyramid" reporting concept embraced in NCGA *Statement 1* has brought about major changes in annual financial reporting by state and local governments. Previously the reporting focus had been almost completely on individual fund and account group statements, with four statements typically required for each fund. By requiring only two statements for each governmental, proprietary, and fiduciary fund, and with many separate funds reported in combining statements, the NCGA facilitated the streamlining of the CAFR of many state and local governments to a fraction of its former size. Further, the CAFR is far more usable and understandable than before, since it permits users to begin with the combined overview statements—the General Purpose Financial Statements (GPFS)—and proceed to the more detailed combining and individual fund and account group statements in a logical manner.

Even more important, perhaps, is the dual reporting entity focus: (1) the GPFS, which includes data aggregated by fund type and account group; and (2) the CAFR, which includes combining and individual fund and account group data as well as the GPFS. The AICPA approved this dual reporting entity focus, as well as the separate publication of the GPFS, in AICPA SOP 80-2, discussed in Chapters 15 and 21.

The reporting changes made by the NCGA in *Statement 1* are more drastic than some wanted. On the other hand, others had urged the NCGA to develop and promulgate standards for consolidated financial statements for state and local governments and were disappointed that it did not do so. As is usually the case, the consensus required to establish generally accepted accounting principles (GAAP) was found between the extreme viewpoints.

Further discussion of the issues and controversies of financial reporting may be found in Chapter 15. With the Governmental Accounting Standards Board (GASB) assuming the primary role in determining GAAP applicable to states and local governments, it remains to be seen how quickly the GASB can address state and local government financial reporting and what changes, if any, it promulgates.

▶ **Question 14-1.** What standard(s) are prescribed by the NCGA for interim financial statements? Explain.

Question 14-2. Distinguish between the content and purpose(s) of the general purpose financial statements (GPFS) and the comprehensive annual financial report (CAFR).

Question 14-3. Explain the "pyramid" reporting concept utilized by the NCGA.

Question 14-4. Why is a good transmittal letter essential to the comprehensive annual financial report (CAFR)?

Question 14-5. Distinguish between combined statements and combining statements.

Question 14-6. Why are the totals columns of the Combined Balance Sheet (e.g., Figure 14-5) labeled "Memorandum Only"? Why is it not necessary to label the total(s) column(s) of combining statements "Memorandum Only?"

Question 14-7. Are interfund eliminations such as those reported in the Statement of Revenues, Expenditures, and Changes in Fund Balances in Figure 14-6 proper under generally accepted accounting principles? Explain.

Question 14-8. The format of the budgetary comparison statement in Figure 14-7 differs from that illustrated in NCGA *Statement 1* and discussed in this chapter. Is this format acceptable? Explain.

Question 14-9. What is the purpose(s) of the notes to the financial statements? The narrative explanations?

Question 14-10. What is the purpose(s) of schedules, as contrasted with statements?

Question 14-11. What is the purpose(s) of statistical tables as contrasted with that (those) of financial statements?

Question 14-12. Does the NCGA approve consolidated financial statements and consider them within the bounds of generally accepted accounting principles? Explain.

Question 14-13. Referring to the auditor's report in Figure 14-4, which data are (a) included fully in the auditor's scope and depth of examination, (b) included in the scope but reported on only in relationship to the data in (a), and (c) excluded from the auditor's scope?

Question 14-14. How can one quickly determine, by observation, whether a statement of revenues, expenditures, and changes in fund balances explains the changes in *total* fund balances or *unreserved* fund balances?

Question 14-15. Recast the following balance sheet so that it will show properly the financial condition of the City of K:

CITY OF K
General Fund Balance Sheet
March 31, 19X6

Assets

Current assets		$ 300,000
Fixed assets		8,196,000
		$8,496,000

Liabilities and Fund Balance

Liabilities:		
Current liabilities	$ 350,000	
Bonded indebtedness	3,400,000	$3,750,000
Fund balance		4,746,000
		$8,496,000

Question 14-16. Explain what is wrong with the following statement:

CITY OF X
General Fund Balance Sheet
December 31, 19X5

Assets

Cash		$82,000
Taxes receivable	$100,000	
Less: Allowance for uncollected taxes ..	100,000	
		$82,000

Liabilities and Fund Balance

Tax anticipation notes	$80,000
Fund balance	2,000
	$82,000

Question 14-17. What differences in classification of expenditures would you expect to find between an expenditure statement prepared primarily for the use of the city manager and one prepared for use by political scientists?

Question 14-18. A Lakesidites resident became concerned when reviewing the City of Lakesidites annual report because the amount of property taxes reported for the General Fund in the Combined Statement of Revenues, Expenditures, and Changes in Fund Balances—All Governmental Fund Types differed significantly from the amount of actual property taxes reported for that fund in the Combined Statement of Revenues, Expenditures, and Changes in Fund Balances—Budget and Actual—General and Special Revenue Funds. The resident is certain an error has occurred and calls it to the attention of the mayor, who immediately calls the chief accountant in to explain how such an error has occurred. Can such a discrepancy exist under generally accepted accounting principles applicable to governments? Explain.

▶ **Problem 14-1.** In connection with the audit of the City of Z, you are handed the following analysis of the changes in the Fund Balance account of the General Fund. The municipality is required to keep its accounts for both revenues and expenditures on the modified accrual basis.

CITY OF Z
General Fund
Statement of Changes in Fund Balance
For the Fiscal Year Ending June 30, 19X7

Fund Balance, June 1, 19X6		$ 75,000
Add: Excess of revenues over expenditures:		
Revenues	$350,000	
Less: Expenditures	305,000	45,000
Fund Balance, June 30, 19X7		$120,000

This statement can be analyzed as follows:

1. Among the revenues are included $15,000 estimated revenues not realized and $335,000 actual revenues, consisting among other items of cash receipts from the following sources:
   a. Collections applicable to the 19X8 tax levy, $3,000.
   b. Sale of fixed assets carried in the Enterprise Fund, $2,500.
   c. Special tax levy made for the purpose of establishing an Internal Service Fund, $75,000.
   d. Sale of general fixed assets which were financed by a general sinking fund bond issue still outstanding, $3,000.
   e. Sale of fixed assets originally financed 75 percent from special assessments and 25 percent from General Fund revenues, $1,500.
   f. A transfer from the Debt Service Fund to the General Fund, the money transferred to be used to retire sinking fund bonds, $150,000.
   g. Tax levy for the retirement of serial bonds, $15,000.
   h. Borrowed from the Enterprise Fund, $750.

2. The expenditures consist, among others, of the following items:
   a. Payments for the retirement of sinking fund bonds, $127,000.
   b. Payments for the retirement of serial bonds, $14,550.
   c. Repayment of a loan made from the Trust Fund, $450.
   d. City's share of cost of special assessment project, $3,000.
   e. Purchase of general fixed assets, $10,000.

3. Included also among the expenditures are unliquidated encumbrances of $22,000 outstanding on June 30, 19X7, as well as expenditures of $5,000 for which encumbrances amounting to $5,500 were outstanding on July 1, 19X6.

Required:

Prepare a corrected statement analyzing the changes in fund balance and showing separately each item and amount by which revenues or expenditures should be increased or decreased. Show also any other adjustments needed to show the correct fund balance on June 30, 19X7.

Problem 14-2, Part I. The following statement is taken from a state's financial report. (References are to schedules carried in the report but not reproduced here.)

STATE OF Y

Capital Balance Sheet
Assets, Investment, and Liabilities,
June 30, 19X9

Capital Assets

Debt Service Fund Assets		$ 23,528,921
Consisting of:		
(a) Cash in State Treasury (Schedule A1)	$ 774,145	
(b) Investments and Bonds (Schedule B1)	12,707,000	
(c) County Notes Receivable (Schedule B2)	10,047,776	
Investments in Railroad Stocks (Schedule B3) [*Assume that they apply to a trust fund.*]		5,233,584

	Par Value	Market Value
(a) X Railroad Stocks	$3,000,200	$ 4,410,294
(b) Atlantic and X Railroad Stocks	1,266,600	823,290
(c) Miscellaneous Stocks	775,080	—

Fixed Assets:
Consisting of:
State Highways, State Institutions,
Departmental Buildings, Real Estate,
Equipment, and other fixed assets $290,171,055

$318,933,560

Capital Liabilities

State Debt (Schedule B4)		$167,360,000
Consisting of:		
(a) State Highway Bonds	$97,171,000	
(b) General Fund Bonds	54,979,000	
(c) Special School Building Bonds	12,710,000	
(d) Veterans' Loan Bonds	2,500,000	

Total Capital Liabilities ....
Capital Surplus
(Value of Fixed Assets in excess of
Funded Debt of State) 151,573,560

$318,933,560

Required:

Recast this statement to show properly the financial condition of each fund and account group of the state. You may split up this statement into as many statements as you think desirable. Assume actuarial sinking fund requirements of $23,520,800.

Problem 14-2, Part II. In connection with the audit of the accounts of the City of X, you are handed the following balance sheet which has been prepared by the city comptroller:

CITY OF X

Balance Sheet
December 31, 19X8

Assets

	General Fund	Debt Service (Sinking) Fund
Cash	$ 58,000	$ 82,000
Taxes Receivable	155,000	17,500
Amount to Be Provided for Retirement of Bonds		168,000
Total	$213,000	$267,500

Bonds Payable		$250,000
Vouchers Payable .... $ 81,000		
Reserve for Uncollected Taxes 155,000		17,500
Operating Deficit 23,000*		
Total $213,000		$267,500

* *Red.*

Upon investigation you discover the following additional facts:

1. Estimated losses on taxes receivable are $10,000 in the General Fund and $1,000 in the Debt Service Fund.

2. Actuarial requirements of the Debt Service Fund at December 31, 19X8, $110,000.

3. Of the total bonds payable, $100,000 represents serial bonds payable (not matured); $15,000 represents matured serial bonds to be paid from the General Fund; and the remainder is represented by sinking fund bonds payable which have not yet matured.

4. Matured interest payable on sinking fund bonds, $2,700, and on serial bonds, $2,100, both to be paid from the General Fund.

5. Interest payable in future years on sinking fund bonds, $10,000, and on serial bonds, $30,000.

Required:

Prepare a columnar balance sheet on a *modified accrual basis* containing separate columns for the funds and account groups that you think it desirable to list separately. Your balance sheet should conform to generally accepted accounting principles applicable to municipalities.

Problem 14-3. The following Statement of Revenues, Expenditures, and Changes in Fund Balance has been prepared for a Special Revenue Fund of Greathouse County. You may assume that the format and amounts are correct.

GREATHOUSE COUNTY
Special Revenue Fund
Statement of Revenues, Expenditures, and Changes in Fund Balance
For the Year Ended December 31, 19X5

Revenues:	
Taxes	$ 500,000
Licenses and permits	200,000
Intergovernmental	100,000
Fines and forfeitures	65,000
Other	35,000
Total Revenues	900,000
Expenditures:	
Current Operating:	
Personal services	750,000
Materials and supplies	50,000
Contractual services	75,000

Other	25,000
Capital Outlay	80,000
Debt service:	
Principal retirement	50,000
Interest and fiscal charges	70,000
Total Expenditures	1,100,000
Excess of Revenues over (under) Expenditures	(200,000)
Other Financing Sources (Uses):	
Operating transfer from General Fund	400,000
Operating transfer to Capital Projects Fund	(20,000)
Total Other Financing Sources (Uses)	380,000
Excess of Revenues and Other Financing Sources over (under) Expenditures and Other Uses	180,000
Fund Balance—January 1:	
As originally reported	150,000
Correction of prior year error	(50,000)
As restated	100,000
Residual equity transfer from Debt Service Fund	70,000
Fund Balance—December 31	$ 350,000

Required:

(a) Recast the Greathouse County statement in two other acceptable formats, being careful to properly describe headings and subtotals. (Note: You need not detail the revenue and expenditure accounts in your solution.)

(b) Analyze and discuss the differing impressions statement users may have under each of the three alternative formats.

(c) Why must a governmental unit select one of the alternative formats in preparing statements of revenues, expenditures, and changes in fund balance for its governmental funds? Or must it do so?

(d) Which format is best suited for budgetary comparison statements? Explain.

(e) Which format typically is best suited for Capital Project Funds? Explain.

Problem 14-4. The controller of Points County has prepared the trial balance presented below and has asked your advice on which of the several alternative formats should be used in preparing the Statement of Revenues, Expenditures, and Changes in Fund Balance for the Points County Special Revenue Fund for the year ended June 30, 19X5.

POINTS COUNTY

Special Revenue Fund
Trial Balance
June 30, 19X5

Capital outlay	(160,000)
Contractual services	(150,000)
Correction of prior year errors	(100,000)
Debt service	(240,000)
Fines and forfeits	125,000
Fund Balance, 1/1/X4	300,000
Intergovernmental	200,000
Licenses and permits	400,000

Materials and supplies	(100,000)
Personal services	(1,400,000)
Operating transfer—Debt Service Fund	(40,000)
Operating transfer—General Fund	400,000
Other	60,000
Other	(50,000)
Residual equity transfer—Capital Projects Fund	5,000
Taxes	1,000,000
To balance	(250,000)
	—

Required:

(a) Prepare at least three Statements of Revenues, Expenditures, and Changes in Fund Balance for the Points County Special Revenue Fund for the year ended June 30, 19X5. Each should be in a different format acceptable to the National Council on Governmental Accounting. (Note: You must include the revenue and expenditure detail accounts on the first statement you prepare; thereafter they may be omi~ d.)

(b) Analyze each of the statements prepared and discuss the attributes of each format that might cause it to be preferred by certain people or in certain situations.

Problem 14-5. The General Fund Schedule of Revenues and Expenditures—Budgeted and Actual—for the year ended December 31, 19X7, for the City of Armstrong has been competently prepared and you may assume it is accurate. The budgetary basis employed is (1) cash receipts for revenues and (2) cash disbursements plus encumbrances outstanding for expenditures.

CITY OF ARMSTRONG
General Fund
Schedule of Revenues and Expenditures
Budgeted and Actual
for the Year Ended December 31, 19X7
(in Thousands)

	Budget (Revised)	Actual (Budgetary Basis)	Actual (Mod. Accrual Basis)
Revenues:			
Taxes	$ 77,500	$ 75,300	$ 72,500
Licenses	2,680	3,320	3,320
Charges for services	9,340	8,400	8,200
Fines and forfeitures	23,500	20,100	20,000
Other	1,980	2,880	980
	$115,000	$110,000	$105,000
Expenditures:			
Current operating:			
Protection of people and property	$ 58,900	$ 55,740	$ 53,722
Community cultural and recreation	13,900	11,500	11,400
Community development and welfare	11,700	10,900	9,400

Transportation and related services .	23,200	19,280	17,900
Administration	4,300	3,580	3,578
	112,000	101,000	96,000
Capital outlay	10,400	6,400	3,400
Debt service	6,600	6,600	6,600
	$129,000	$114,000	$106,000
Excess of revenues over (under) expenditures	$(14,000)	$ (4,000)	$ (1,000)

Required:

(a) Analyze the statement presented carefully and respond to the following questions:

1. How might it be possible for a city to budget an excess of fund expenditures over revenues? Is that bad practice? Is an excess of actual expenditures over revenues bad?

2. Why might the modified accrual and budgetary basis revenue data differ somewhat with respect to taxes, charges for services, and fines and forfeitures, yet be identical for licenses and permits?

3. Why might the modified accrual and budgetary basis expenditure amounts differ in most instances, yet agree on the debt service expenditure?

(b) After giving consideration to the following additional information, prepare a Statement of Revenues, Expenditures, and Changes in Fund Balance—Budgeted and Actual for the City of Armstrong General Fund for the year ended December 31, 19X7 in standard format. The numbers below are in thousands of dollars, as is the schedule and the statement you are to prepare.

1. The beginning of year fund balance was $4,000 (budgetary) and $3,000 (modified accrual).

2. A budgeted operating transfer of $20,000 was made to the General Fund from a Special Revenue Fund.

(c) Whenever the basis of the budget differs from GAAP, NCGA *Statement 1* requires that the difference(s) between the budgetary basis and GAAP be explained in the notes to the financial statements. Draft an appropriate note for this purpose.

Problem 14-6. The following statement was prepared by the new accountant at Fullerton City:

FULLERTON CITY

Statement of Revenues, Expenses, and Changes in Fund Balance
December 31, 19X8

Revenues:

Property taxes	$ 600,000
Sales taxes	400,000
Licenses and permits	100,000
Federal grant	300,000
Traffic violations and court costs	50,000
Internal Service Fund	75,000
Capital Projects Fund	25,000
Other	60,000
	$1,610,000

Expenses:

Salaries and wages	$ 645,000
Contractual services	130,000
Rentals	90,000
Prior year	40,000
Debt service	120,000
Enterprise Fund	125,000
Special Assessment Fund	160,000
Property taxes	5,000
Depreciation of general fixed assets	100,000
Other	30,000
	$1,445,000
Profit for the year	$ 165,000
Fund Surplus, beginning of year	200,000
Surplus receipts	135,000
Increase in Reserve for Contingencies	(100,000)
Fund Surplus, end of year	$ 400,000

Additional information:

1. The statement purports to present information for the General Fund of Fullerton City.

2. The Property Taxes revenue figure represents (a) collections during 19X8 of 19X7 taxes that were properly recorded as revenues and receivables in 19X7, $80,000; (b) the gross property taxes levied for 19X8, and (c) a $3,000 payment on 19X9 taxes by a property owner who plans an extended vacation overseas. The expenditure figure is for 19X7 property taxes written off during 19X8; some $20,000 of the current year property tax levy is expected to prove uncollectible. An allowance for uncollectible taxes has not been used in the past.

3. The Sales Taxes amount is the total of sales taxes collected during 19X8, $350,000; some $20,000 certified by the state as collected and due Fullerton City; and $30,000 estimated by the city controller to be due the city as a result of Christmas sales in November and December.

4. The Licenses and Permits data includes $85,000 of licenses and permits collected during 19X8 and $15,000 representing the final one-third payment of 19X8 business permit applications due January 15, 19X9.

5. The Federal grant amount is the total of a recently approved cost reimbursement grant to develop an improved water supply system for Fullerton City. Only $20,000 has been spent so far as the project is still in the preliminary stages.

6. Traffic Violations and Court Costs includes all fines and court costs collected during 19X8, $1,000 of which was on 19X7 offenses; and $6,000 of parking tickets issued during 19X8, of which $4,000 has been collected and $2,000 appears to be uncollectible.

7. The Internal Service Fund amount results from the repayment of an interfund advance.

8. The Capital Projects Fund figure represents the balance of a Capital Projects Fund returned to the General Fund at the end of the project so the Capital Projects Fund could be terminated.

9. Other revenues includes (a) $15,000 arising upon reinventorying the warehouse at the beginning of 19X0; the inventory was $60,000 rather than the $45,000 reported initially; and (b) $2,000 paid the General Fund from the Special As-

sessment Fund in reimbursement of contractual services expenditures initially made from the former but attributable to the latter.

10. Salaries and Wages includes the gross pay earned by employees during 19X8 and $25,000 of 19X7 gross wages that were not recorded as 19X7 expenditures.

11. Contractual Services includes consultation fees paid to individuals and firms, including $8,000 attributable to the Enterprise Fund and $10,000 for services rendered in 19X7 but not recorded as 19X7 expenditures. Some $18,000 of 19X8 consulting services had been rendered, but not formally billed, at the end of 19X8.

12. Rentals includes the aggregate rentals paid under a lease-purchase arrangement on city buildings used to house the city shop and warehouse. If this were a private business these capital lease payments would be reported as 75 percent interest and 25 percent principal reduction.

13. Prior Year represents the amount paid during 19X8 on 19X7 bills which had been recognized as expenditures and liabilities in 19X7.

14. Debt Service Fund indicates the amount paid from the General Fund to the Debt Service Fund as the annual contribution from the former to the latter.

15. The Enterprise Fund amount is (a) the amount (not expected to be repaid) that was transferred from the General Fund to acquire (with other borrowing) a local electric utility, and (b) the general government electric bills totaling $35,000.

16. The Special Assessment Fund amount arose from a ten-year loan from the General Fund to the Special Assessment Fund.

17. Other expenditures includes $20,000 of encumbrances at the end of 19X8.

18. Surplus Receipts is the amount realized from selling (during 19X8) a house the city owned.

19. The beginning of year Fund Surplus account was correct except for any errors noted in items 1 to 18.

Required:

(a) Identify the errors in the General Fund Statement of Revenues, Expenditures, and Changes in Fund Balance prepared by the new accountant at Fullerton City and prepare a schedule showing the uncorrected amounts, corrections and reclassifications, and correct classifications and amounts.

(b) Prepare a correct Statement of Revenues, Expenditures, and Changes in Fund Balance for the General Fund of Fullerton City for the year ended December 31, 19X8, in acceptable form.

CONTEMPORARY ISSUES, RESEARCH, AND DEVELOPMENTS

The state and local government (SLG) accounting and reporting model has deep roots historically and is firmly entrenched in practice. Formalized and formally adopted in this country by the National Committee on Municipal Accounting in the 1930s, the model has been evolved in several stages during the past 50 years, most recently as the result of its consideration by the National Council on Governmental Accounting.

How good is the SLG model? Opinions vary. At one extreme are its staunch advocates and defenders—who point to its heritage, note that it has proven practical and workable in practice, and cite the time-honored adage: "If it ain't broke, don't fix it." At the other extreme are its staunch critics who say that such an "old" model cannot serve today's needs—that the complexities of modern governments and of their financial transactions cannot be adequately accommodated by the model from either an accounting or a reporting standpoint—and that an entirely new SLG accounting and reporting model should be developed. As is so often the case, truth probably lies somewhere between these extremes.

Some of the unresolved conceptual and pragmatic issues relating to the SLG model are considered in this chapter, together with some of the recent research and publications bearing on these issues and the objectives of SLG accounting and reporting. This chapter is organized into five sections: (1) Contemporary Issues, (2) Recent Research and Publications, (3) Objectives of SLG Accounting and Reporting, (4) Who Should Set SLG Accounting and Reporting Standards?, and (5) Concluding Comments.

CONTEMPORARY ISSUES

A number of the more important contemporary issues related to state and local government financial accounting and reporting are considered briefly in this section. Some of the issues may appear on the surface to be standards problems, but most are conceptual or theoretical issues as well. The issues are presented in five subsections:

1. The Organizational Reporting Entity
2. Funds Flow v. Service Cost v.?
3. Pragmatic Problems with the SLG Model
4. The Financial Statement Entity
5. General Price-Level Adjustments

The Organizational Reporting Entity

In accounting for businesses, separate but related corporations are commonly treated as a single economic entity for general purpose external financial reporting purposes. The decision as to which, if any, other businesses are reported in a company's annual report depends upon whether the company can significantly influence or control the other businesses. To report its affairs properly, a company must include others it can significantly influence or control in its annual report.

There were no "economic entity" criteria for state and local government accounting and reporting until late 1981. Although many governmental and quasi-governmental organizations (e.g., special districts, school districts, and public authorities) are associated with cities, counties, or states—and some of them can be significantly influenced or controlled by the SLG unit, and thus possibly should be reported in the city, county, or state annual financial report—each typically was reported separately since each is a separate legal entity.

The NCGA recognized the importance of this issue while drafting *Statement 1* but could not agree on the solution. Thus, NCGA *Statement 1*, issued in 1979, addresses the issue only in a footnote:

> Certain funds or functions associated with, but not legally part of, the governmental unit may be reported on elsewhere rather than in the comprehensive annual financial report. This should be disclosed prominently, and the manner in which the user might obtain such separate reports should be noted. In this context, all special districts, authorities, or other activities bearing the name of the governmental unit in their name or which are to any significant extent under the jurisdiction of the governmental unit are deemed to be "associated."[1]

Note that this definition of "associated entity" includes the phrase "to any significant extent under the jurisdiction of the governmental unit," which might be interpreted as a move by the NCGA away from the legal entity criterion toward the "ability to exercise significant influence or control" criterion. But in *Statement 1* the NCGA stopped short of requiring associated entities to be reported upon in the SLG unit's CAFR, requiring only that they be disclosed and the reader be advised of how to obtain the separate reports of the associated entities.

Properly defining the entity for general purpose external financial reporting purposes (hereafter referred to as the organizational reporting entity or ORE) is one of the most fundamental conceptual and practical problems facing those con-

[1] NCGAS 1, p. 27 footnote 23.

cerned with SLG accounting and reporting. Yet, the profession has only recently become concerned with the ORE problem.

What constitutes the City of Minneapolis or the State of California seems intuitively obvious at first blush. There is a legal entity called the City of Chicago, for example. But that may comprise only part of the City of Chicago ORE. Over the years many special districts, authorities, commissions, and other quasi-governmental organizations have been formed—and are separate legal entities—within the bounds of many cities and states. Some, like building authorities, have as their sole function the borrowing of money with which to acquire buildings that are then leased to the city or state and that may become the property of the city or state when the lease expires and the related debt has been retired. Others involve functions such as redevelopment, mass transit, and sewage collection and disposal. Some were formed by the cities or states to bypass debt issue limitations; others were formed by residents of areas then outside the city limits and since annexed. Some operate completely independently from the city or state with which they are associated, while in other instances the city or state clearly has the ability to exercise significant influence or control over the satellite entities, for example, through appointing its officials and/or controlling its budget.

Clearly, some of these separate entities should be included in the city or state ORE and reported on in its GPFS and/or CAFR. Others should not, and need only be footnoted, at most; some appear to be borderline cases. What are needed, of course, are (1) a clear conceptual understanding of the matter, and (2) standards which set forth criteria for including or excluding such satellite entities.

The NCGA issued *Statement 3*, "Defining the Governmental Reporting Entity," in December 1981. Both the criteria set forth in *Statement 3* and its required footnote disclosures were discussed in Chapter 14.

We do not believe that *Statement 3* provides a satisfactory solution to the ORE problem for the following reasons:

1. *Statement 3* is not based on a logical, cohesive entity concept. For example, no logical underlying commonality or relationship is evident between or among its three types of criteria: (1) exercise of oversight responsibility, (2) special financing relationships, and (3) scope of public service.

2. The criteria are so broad as to be biased toward including virtually all associated organizations in the government ORE, notwithstanding the NCGA's recognition in *Statement 3* that improperly including an associated organization is as serious an error as improperly excluding such an organization.

3. The *ability* to exercise oversight responsibility is a far more logical and workable criterion than the *exercise* of oversight responsibility criterion of *Statement 3*. A government with the ability to exercise oversight might do so in some years and not do so in others. Should it be considered part of the government ORE in those years when oversight was exercised but excluded for those years when it was not? Surely not.

4. NCGA *Statement 3* does not indicate the degree or extent of exercise of oversight authority necessary to justify including an associated organization in the government ORE. While several "manifestations" of exercise of oversight responsibility are listed and discussed in *Statement 3*, it does not indicate at what point either (1) the individual manifestations of exercise of oversight responsibility sub-criteria, or (2) the overall basic "exercise of oversight responsibility" criterion, are met.

5. Financial interdependency—evidenced by governmental unit responsibility for financing deficits, entitlement to surpluses, and/or guarantees of or "moral responsibility" for debt—is cited in *Statement 3* as the most significant manifestation of the exercise of oversight responsibility. These factors do not necessarily indicate that the governmental unit can exercise significant influence or control over the associated organization or that it should be included in the government ORE. Any related assets and liabilities might better be reported in the government's financial statements and any contingencies disclosed in the notes to the financial statements.

6. The scope of public service criteria of *Statement 3*—which state that an associated organization should be included in the government ORE if its activities are for the benefit of the government unit and/or its residents or if its activities are conducted within the government's geographic boundaries and are generally available to its citizens—are not discriminating criteria. Most associated organizations—except government joint ventures—would meet those criteria. Indeed, if the scope of public service criteria are appropriate there seems to be little need for the other criteria.

7. Footnote 15 of NCGA *Statement 3* contains a major "loophole." While it requires disclosure of how the specific elements of exercise of oversight responsibility and other criteria were considered in determining the government ORE, it also permits the government to ignore the criteria so long as it discloses the reasons why associated organizations meeting the criteria were excluded from the government ORE.

The governmental reporting issue has been addressed by several different groups and individuals in recent years, and significantly different recommendations on its resolution have been made. Prior to issuance of *Statement 3*, criteria for defining the government reporting entity were proposed and/or used by several groups and individuals, including:

- The AICPA State and Local Government Accounting Committee—in its 1979 financial reporting experiment, "An Experiment in Government Accounting and Reporting by the AICPA State and Local Government Accounting Committee."[2]

---

[2] American Institute of Certified Public Accountants, State and Local Government Accounting Committee, *Experiment Booklet: An Experiment in Governmental Accounting and Reporting by the AICPA State and Local Government Accounting Committee.* (New York: AICPA, September 1979).

- The Council of State Governments State Accounting Project—in its working papers and, later, in its exposure draft of a research report, *Preferred Accounting Practices for State Governments, 1982.*[3]
- A Coopers & Lybrand study by James A. Hogan and Anthony J. Mottola, *Financial Disclosure Practices of the American Cities II: Closing the Communications Gap, 1978.*[4]
- An NCGA Research Report by William W. Holder, *A Study of Selected Concepts for Government Financial Accounting and Reporting, 1980.*[5]

Professor Craig D. Shoulders of Virginia Tech has done extensive conceptual and applied research on this topic. He concluded that the government reporting entity should be defined as follows:

> A governmental unit financial reporting entity should include all associated organizations for which the government has a degree of responsibility and accountability commensurate with treating the associated organizations as if they were city departments or agencies. A government's reporting entity should include (1) all associated organizations whose primary purpose is financing its capital acquisitions or operations and (2) all other associated organizations over which the government has the *ability* to impose its will with respect to (a) which programs, activities, and projects the organization can undertake to fulfill its purposes, and (b) the portion of associated organization resources which can be devoted to each program, activity, or project.[6]

The efforts to define the ORE have at least identified several factors that might be used in setting criteria:

1. The primary purposes of the associated organization
2. The degree of financial dependence of the associated organization on the city, county, or state
3. The constituency served by the associated organization
4. The selection of the governing board of the associated organization
5. The extent to which the city, county, or state can influence the operations of the associated organization
6. The extent of the city, county, or state's legal responsibility for the associated organization's actions

But despite the efforts and publications and progress on this issue, the fundamental question of which legal entities constitute the substantive economic entity to be reported on by a SLG unit remains unresolved.

[3] National Council on Governmental Accounting and State Government Accounting Project, *Preferred Accounting Practices for State Government: Exposure Draft of a Research Report* (Lexington, Kentucky: The Council of State Governments, 1982).

[4] Coopers & Lybrand, *Financial Disclosure Practices of the American Cities II: Closing The Communications Gap* (New York: Coopers & Lybrand, 1978).

[5] William W. Holder, *A Study of Selected Concepts for Government Financial Accounting and Reporting*, NCGA Research Report (Chicago, NCGA, 1980).

[6] Craig D. Shoulders, "Criteria for Identifying the Municipal Organizational Reporting Entity," Unpublished doctoral dissertation, Texas Tech University, 1982.

Funds Flow v. Service Cost v.?

Recall that for the proprietary (nonexpendable) funds of government both expenses (service cost) and sources, uses, and balances (funds flow) of working capital (or cash) are reported. But only sources, uses, and balances of fund financial resources (funds flow) are reported for the governmental (expendable) funds. Further, recall from NCGA *Principle 8* that an expenditure is recognized only when a *fund liability* is recognized—and that a major bond principal, interest, capital lease, or other expenditure required to be made early in 19X5 likely would not be recognized as a fund expenditure in 19X4, but in 19X5.

The basic issue here is whether expenditures and/or expenses should be reported for the "general government"—the governmental funds and account groups taken as a whole—as well as governmental fund expenditures. This very fundamental issue has been argued repeatedly since before the turn of the century. Some governments used "business-type" accounting systems in the early decades of this century. And the "xpense," "expenditure," or "expense and expenditure" issue was debated in the 1930s as the first authoritatively stated principles were drafted by the National Committee on Municipal Accounting. After the proponents of the "expense" or "expenditure and expense" viewpoint did not prevail at the NCMA, most governments converted to the NCMA approach and the issue lay dormant for over twenty years.

Although Wake Forrest Professor Delmer Hylton touched on the issue in a 1957 article, the issue resurfaced fully in a 1963 article on "Governmental Accounting: Funds Flow or Service Cost?" by Hawaii Professor Russell Taussig. [7] The issue then was considered by a series of American Accounting Association Committees, beginning with the 1968–1970 Committee on Accounting Practices of Not-for-Profit Organizations. [8] Individuals such as Professor Emerson O. Henke of Baylor University have long argued that both measurements are needed in governmental reports. The debate was focused even more when Harvard Professor Robert N. Anthony discussed the difference between fund expenditures, or "budgetary expenditures" as he called them, and "conventional expenditures." The distinction lies in whether expenditures are reported only when a liability is recognized in a specific governmental fund—which ordinarily must have an appropriation for the expenditure—or when the government as a whole incurs a liability. [9] He also considered the cost-of-service arguments. [10] Southern Cal Professor William W. Holder also considered the issue in his NCGA Research Re-

---

[7] Russell Taussig, "Governmental Accounting: Fund Flow or Service Cost?" *Accounting Review*, 38 (July 1963), pp. 562–567. See also Delmer Hylton, "Needed: More Understandable Financial Statements from Governmental Units," *Accounting Review*, 32 (January 1957), pp. 51–54.

[8] American Accounting Association, "Report of the [1968–1970] Committee on Accounting Practices of Not-for-Profit Organizations," *Accounting Review*, Supplement to Vol. 46 (1971), pp. 80–163. See also the reports of successor AAA Committees, e.g., "Report of the Committee on Not-for-Profit Organizations, 1972–73," *Accounting Review*, Supplement to Vol. 49 (1974), pp. 224–249, and "Report of the Committee on Nonprofit Organizations, 1973–74," *Accounting Review*, Supplement to Vol. 50 (1975), pp. 1–39.

[9] Robert N. Anthony, *Financial Accounting in Nonbusiness Organizations: An Exploratory Study of Conceptual Issues*, Research Report (Stamford, Conn.: Financial Accounting Standards Board, 1978), p. 84. Hereafter cited as Anthony Report.

[10] Ibid., p. 93.

port,[11] as have others. Perhaps the most lucid statement of the proponents of cost-of-service reporting was made in 1913:

> The answer . . . as to whether administration has been *efficient or inefficient* is found in contrasting *cost* with service *results* and judging the *accomplishments* by the best standards available.[12]

Note the similarity of some of the terms used in this 1913 book to those of the GAO audit standards (Chapter 21) and to those in the statements of the objectives of financial reporting for nonbusiness organizations (Chapter 1) and of accounting and reporting for state and local governments, discussed later in this chapter.

Finally, consider the possibility of some net asset "outflow" measure other than expense (cost), fund expenditures, and/or conventional expenditures. The ultimate outflow measure for SLG reporting may be some combination of these or some altogether new measure.

Pragmatic Problems with the SLG Model

Several matters of the type that typically concern governmental accounting practitioners and auditors more than theorists warrant at least passing mention at this point. Some of these have been discussed briefly in previous chapters, others have not. As each is discussed, consider whether it is purely a practice problem that could be solved, perhaps by changing current standards, or is a manifestation of a fundamental conceptual problem.

Proprietary or Governmental Fund?   Given the SLG model, the most fundamental practice issue that may arise is whether a given program, function, or activity should be accounted for in a proprietary fund or in a governmental fund (and perhaps in the GFA and GLTD accounts). Specifically, this issue may arise in two forms: (1) Enterprise Fund or governmental fund, and (2) Internal Service Fund or governmental fund? These are important issues since they will determine such things as (1) rates to be charged for goods and services, (2) whether depreciation is recognized, (3) whether expenses or expenditures are measured, and (4) in the case of Internal Service Funds, whether charges heretofore borne centrally will be charged to the user agencies. Also, the decision will determine whether the program, function, or activity is accounted for in a single proprietary fund entity or in several entities [governmental fund(s), GFA, GLTD].

The Enterprise Fund issue most often arises from the flexibility permitted in the two-part (mandatory and permissive) Enterprise Fund definition:

> *Enterprise Funds*—to account for operations (a) that are financed and operated in a manner similar to private business enterprises—where the intent of the governing body is that the costs (expenses, including depreciation) of providing goods or services to the general public on a continuing basis be financed or

---

[11] William W. Holder, *A Study of Selected Concepts for Government Financial Accounting and Reporting*, NCGA Research Report (Chicago: National Council on Governmental Accounting, 1980), pp. 22–23. Hereafter cited as Holder Study.

[12] Bureau of Municipal Research, *Handbook of Municipal Accounting* (New York: D. Appleton and Company, 1913), p. 85. (Emphasis added.)

recovered primarily through user charges; or (b) where the governing body has decided that periodic determination of revenues earned, expenses incurred, and/or net income is appropriate for capital maintenance, public policy, management control, accountability, or other purposes.[13]

Part (a) of this definition, the mandatory provision, is designed to include government owned utilities and other profitable or break-even activities. Its most critical aspect is determining the intent of the governing body. That intent may or may not have been expressed in the minutes or in discussions with knowledgeable persons. But actions can also imply intent, and if a governing board has consistently operated a function as an enterprise, setting rates to recover full cost and in other ways acting like the activity is an enterprise, it probably is one under either part (a) or part (b) of the definition.

Changes in intent can occur when membership and attitudes of a governing board change, of course, but it is clear that the NCGA did not intend for an activity to be accounted for as an enterprise one year, a governmental activity the next, and so forth. When a new activity is the center of the Enterprise Fund or governmental fund issue, persuading the proper people to agree upon and document the intent of the governing board may be the best approach. On the other hand, a strong finance officer will often make such decisions, then have the Council ratify them and place them in the minutes.

The "permissive" part (b) of the Enterprise Fund definition is intended to cover governmental bus lines, city markets, and other activities apt to incur losses. It does not pose as many problems as the "mandatory" part, since it takes positive action by a governing board—to state and document its intent that a given program, function, or activity that does not meet the usual Enterprise Fund definition is to be accounted for as an Enterprise Fund for one or more of the several possible reasons noted there. In such cases the usual reason is to see how much is being lost on a "full cost" basis as well as to know the sources, uses, and balances of the working capital or cash devoted to the activity.

The Internal Service Fund or governmental fund question may arise in connection with a variety of functions or activities, e.g., data processing, communications, purchasing, and materials storage and handling. There are two aspects of this decision, of which the first may be the easier: (1) Internal Service Fund or governmental fund, and (2) if Internal Service Fund, which costs are to be recovered through the fund and thus constitute "cost" in this situation?

Whether an activity is established as an Internal Service Fund—and thus its costs will be spread to those using its goods or services—is typically a policy decision. Often it begins with or is made by (with approval of superiors) the chief finance officer, who seeks to obtain better accountability for the function as well as better distribution and control of its costs to user agencies.

Assuming that an activity will be accounted for as an Internal Service Fund, there should be a determination of precisely which costs are to be charged to user agencies and on what basis. This should be agreed to by all agencies affected and documented.

The most significant problem arising from the proprietary fund or govern-

---

[13] NCGAS 1, p. 7.

mental fund issue is perhaps that of comparisons among governments. Assume that two governments have precisely the same activity and circumstances. Under current standards one government might account for an activity in a proprietary fund and another account for the same (hypothetically equivalent) activity in its governmental funds and account groups. The reason is that "intent" is the fundamental thread that runs throughout the proprietary or governmental fund issue. And intent varies among governments and may vary within one government through time.

Revenue Recognition. Ever since the AICPA audit guide (ASLGU) set forth the "susceptibility to accrual" criterion for revenue recognition in 1973— that a resource must be both "measurable" and "available" to be recognized as revenue[14]—both accounting and auditing practitioners and standards setters have wrestled with what "available" means and how to apply the "available" standard in practice. The AICPA issued SOP 75-3, "Accrual of Revenues and Expenditures by State and Local Governmental Units," two years after ASLGU was published in an attempt to clarify the "susceptible to accrual" criteria, particularly its "availability" aspect. But the SOP contains mostly illustrations and rules for specific cases rather than definitive guidelines that can be applied broadly.

The NCGA included the AICPA's "susceptible to accrual" criterion in NCGA *Statement 1*. It clarified the matter some, but also describes rather than defines the criterion. The NCGA has considered the matter further on several occasions, at first when a letter was received from a practitioner seeking specific answers to particular problems, and later in a series of letters and an interpretation on the matter.

The problem lies in the fact that the revenue recognition criterion is derived from a budgetary concept, as is much of the SLG model. The literature interprets "available" as being collected in cash during the year or soon enough thereafter to pay the current year's bills. When is soon enough after the year end to pay its bills? Is it 30 days, 60 days, or 90 days? Or should it be longer if the SLG can stall its creditors even longer? No doubt the criterion will need further consideration until it can be clearly defined; even then, however, a related standard might have to include an arbitrary cutoff, say 60 days, as does NCGA *Interpretation 3*, for the standard to be workable in practice.

Intermediate- to Long-Term Receivables. A practical problem related to the revenue recognition criterion and the SLG model arises when a SLG unit receives a twenty-year note receivable upon selling a building or enters into a thirty-year capital lease on one of its buildings. Accounting and auditing practitioners may be uncertain as to how to handle these transactions since (1) the General Fixed Assets Account Group cannot accommodate financial resources, yet (2) the General and Special Revenue Funds typically account only for current assets. Some have suggested that an Enterprise Fund should be established in such cases.

Fortunately, this type of problem can be solved by slightly "bending" the SLG model. Assume the note receivable is a $50,000, 10 percent, twenty-year

[14] AICPA Committee on Governmental Accounting and Auditing, *Audits of State and Local Governments* (New York: AICPA, 1973), pp. 14–15.

note received 1/2/19X1 for general government salvage sales, with equal principal payments each year end with interest on the unpaid balance. The proceeds of the note are unrestricted. The entries here would be in the General Fund:

1/1/19X1	Note Receivable	50,000	
	Deferred Revenues		50,000
	To record receipt of note.		
12/31/19X1	Cash	7,500	
	Deferred Revenues	2,500	
	Note Receivable		2,500
	Revenues		7,500
	To record collection of note payment.		
	Credit (Revenue Ledger):		
	Interest Revenues	5,000	
	Revenues from Sale of Property	2,500	
		7,500	

The "bending" required, of course, is accounting for a long-term note receivable in the General Fund. Since Deferred Revenues was credited and revenue is only recognized as it is available, in cash—and Fund Balance is not increased until revenue is recognized—no harm seems to be done to the model and the practitioner can handle the transaction in a relatively simple, familiar manner.

Expenditure Recognition. The issue of fund expenditure versus conventional expenditure recognition, discussed earlier, often crops up as a practice problem. For example, assume that a SLG unit leases a building from its owner under a twenty-year capital lease. The fair market value of the building is $300,000. The lease is entered into on 1/2/19X3 and calls for equal annual payments from the General Fund each December 31, beginning 12/31/19X3, of $35,237, calculated at 10% ($300,000 ÷ 8.513564 = $35,237).

How should this transaction be accounted for now and during its term? The inception of the lease should be recorded:

1/2/19X3	*General Fixed Assets:*		
	Building under Capital Lease	300,000	
	Investment in General Fixed		
	Assets		300,000
	To record acquisition of building		
	under capital lease.		
1/2/19X3	*General Long-Term Debt:*		
	Amount to be Provided	300,000	
	Obligation under Capital Lease		300,000
	To record liability assumed in capital		
	lease.		

At the end of the year when the annual capital lease payments are made the entries would be:

12/31/19X3	*General Fund:*		
	Expenditures	35,237	
	Cash		35,237

To record annual capital lease payment.

Debit (Expenditure Ledger):

Interest	$30,000
Principal	5,237
	$35,237

12/31/X3   General Long-Term Debt:

Obligation under Capital Lease	5,237	
Amount to be Provided		5,237

To record reduction of principal
of capital lease obligation.

Note that only the principal reduction is recorded in the GLTD accounts as a reduction of the obligation under the capital lease since only the principal of that obligation is recorded there.

What often concerns practitioners in this type of situation is that they want to see only the interest reflected as a General Fund expenditure since the balance of the payment is not "expense" but increases equity by reducing a debt. The answer, of course, is that the equity increase is recorded when the GLTD obligation is decreased and that General Fund accounting is expenditure-based, not expense-based.

A more difficult situation arises when the government as a whole may be said to have incurred a liability, and thus an expenditure should be recorded, but the expenditure cannot be recorded under current GAAP as reflected in the SLG model. To illustrate, assume that a state is billed $10,000,000 for its 19X6 contribution to the state pension plan, which is operated under the auspices of the state as a separate agency. However, the legislature in its wisdom appropriates only $4,000,000 after noting that the pension fund is reasonably sound actuarially and has a large amount of cash and investments while the state is in a tight financial situation overall.

How should we account for and report this situation? Should we record the $10,000,000 as a General Fund expenditure and report a $6,000,000 liability after making the $4,000,000 pension plan payment? That would overspend the appropriation granted, which is illegal; might cause the General Fund to end up in a deficit position, which also is probably illegal; and there is no assurance that the legislature will appropriate anything for pensions next year, although it may appropriate the same, more, or less.

About the best one can do in this situation under present GAAP is (1) record the $4,000,000 expenditure in the General Fund, (2) record the $6,000,000 liability in the General Long-Term Debt Account Group, and (3) disclose the situation in the notes to the financial statements. However, we believe that such a situation would be more properly recorded as:

General Fund:

Expenditures	10,000,000	
Due to Pension Trust Fund		4,000,000
Other Financing Sources—Increase in GLTD to Pension Trust Fund		6,000,000

To record pension expenditures, part of which are
recorded as liabilities in the GLTD accounts.

Amount to be Provided	6,000,000	
Liability to Pension Trust Fund		6,000,000

To record government's unfunded liability
to the Pension Trust Fund.

Pension Trust Fund:

Due from General Fund	4,000,000	
Amount to be Provided by Government	6,000,000	
Revenues		4,000,000
Deferred Revenues		6,000,000

To record accrual of current partial payment
of amount due from government and
recognition of balance in the GLTD accounts.

The General Fund budgetary comparison statements would be prepared on the budgetary basis, and the GAAP statements would be prepared on the basis suggested above.

Intermediate-Term Payables. NCGA *Statement 1* says that "general government" current liabilities should be accounted for in the governmental funds and that long-term liabilities should be reported in the General Long-Term Debt Account Group. What about "intermediate-term" debt that falls in the undefined zone between current and long-term liabilities?

It may be argued that "current" liabilities of governmental funds are those to be paid this year or very soon thereafter. Let us assume that the argument is valid since it is consistent with the revenue realization principle discussed earlier and recent NCGA pronouncements; and the usual one-year approach in business accounting makes no sense in the budget-driven government environment. Further, let us assume that five years is "long-term." We might as well have said ten years, since "long-term" is not defined in the authoritative literature.

What do you do accounting-wise when a city with excess money in the General Fund borrows money from a bank for five years? There are no ground rules in the authoritative literature for situations like this—but the practitioner must account and report for them as best he can from a professional, common sense perspective.

A practical answer to this dilemma might come from reading the Council's minute books or asking the finance officer or others involved in the decision to borrow when excess money was on hand. It may turn out that General Fund investments and excess monies were pledged against the loan—which was made because the General Fund investments yield a higher interest rate than the bank charges the City. In this case we suggest that the liability is a specific fund liability and should be recorded in the General Fund, with appropriate disclosure in the notes to the financial statements, notwithstanding NCGA *Statement 1* guidance that only current liabilities are to be recorded in the General Fund. There are exceptions, though they may be rare, to any general rule or guideline. On the other hand, if the city only appeared to have excess cash, but was faced with a major unexpected expenditure, say to upgrade its jail or school system, then it would appear appropriate to record the five-year note in the General Long-Term Debt accounts.

This type of "intermediate-term" debt issue arises frequently in practice. Although we wish that we could give definitive guidance on it, perhaps the best advice is that noted above: Learn all of the facts surrounding the situation and then do what seems right professionally and in terms of common sense—then disclose all pertinent facts in the notes to the financial statements.

Other types of "intermediate-term" debt often encountered in practice include Tax Anticipation Notes (TANs), Revenue Anticipation Notes (RANs), and Bond Anticipation Notes (BANs). TANs and RANs usually are payable from the collections of specified taxes or other revenue sources and are issued for one year or less. They may be payable in the middle or latter part of the year following issue, however, and on that basis some have suggested that they are not "current" liabilities properly recordable in a governmental fund. In the authors' opinions these are specific fund liabilities, not general long-term debt, since they are payable from the existing noncash assets of specific funds when those assets are converted to cash. On the other hand, BANs issued in contemplation of forthcoming general obligation bond issues are properly classified as general long-term debt and BAN proceeds are properly accounted for as "Other Financing Sources" in the Capital Projects Fund or other governmental fund involved. (An exception would be BANs issued to provide interim financing for Special Assessment Funds, since the BANs and bonds are specific liabilities of Special Assessment Funds.) When the general obligation bonds are sold, proceeds necessary to retire the BANs would be paid to a Debt Service Fund for that purpose and the balance would be paid to the Capital Projects Fund or other governmental fund involved.

Artificial Deficits. A situation often encountered in the project-oriented funds, the Capital Projects and Special Assessment Funds, is that expenditures and encumbrances incurred exceed revenues and other financing sources recognized, resulting in a fund balance deficit. The deficit may be "real," as when all financing sources available have been recognized, or it may be "artificial," as when other financing sources are available (e.g., transfers, debt issue proceeds, grants) but have not yet been recognized in the accounts.

To the extent that the artificial deficit results from encumbrances outstanding at year end, the problem can be solved by reporting the encumbrances outstanding in the notes to the financial statements rather than by a Reserve for Encumbrances in the financial statements. This is usually the solution in Special Assessment Funds where expenditures incurred result in recognition of equal amounts of revenue as we recommend. (However, as noted in Chapter 9, Special Assessment Fund revenue recognition criteria are debatable.)

This leaves us with the case often encountered in Capital Projects Funds where expenditures exceed revenues and other financing sources recognized, but other financing sources are assured—as when issuance of bonds or other debt securities has been deferred, perhaps in anticipation of lower interest rates being available later. Had BANs been issued, as discussed above, the "artificial deficit" might not occur. Prior to NCGA *Statement 1* it was considered proper to recognize assured future financing sources in the accounts, e.g., by debiting an account such as Projects Authorized or Bonds Authorized and crediting Fund Balance. This is no longer acceptable, however, and the project-oriented funds are forced into an annual reporting cycle. Thus, it is now necessary to report the artificial deficit in the financial statements and explain the situation in the notes to the financial statements. Since deficits are considered "bad"—and artificial deficits are a temporary phenomenon caused by forcing project-oriented funds into an annual accounting cycle—many people (including the authors) are not convinced that this "report the artificial deficit and explain its temporary nature" approach is a satisfactory solution to the problem.

SLG Pension Plans.   Many state and local governments administer their own pension plans. A unique problem they have faced since March 1980 is that there are two different approaches to SLG Pension Trust Fund accounting and reporting with substantial authoritative support. One is the approach in GAAFR (68) and in NCGA *Interpretation 4; Public Employee Retirement Administration,* authored in 1977 by the MFOA Committee on Public Employee Retirement Administration; and the MFOA's GAAFR (80) interpretation of how NCGA *Statement 1* should be applied. The other approach is that set forth by FASB *Statement 35,* "Accounting and Reporting by Defined Benefit Pension Plans," which the FASB says applies to SLG pension plans as well as those in the private sector. As noted earlier the effective date for state and local governments of FASB *Statement 35* and NCGA *Interpretation 4* was deferred by FASB *Statement 59* and NCGA resolution to fiscal years beginning after June 15, 1982 and ending after June 15, 1983.

Some SLGs are following the NCGA-MFOA approach, others the FASB approach; and some are reporting dually under both approaches. Hopefully, this dilemma will be resolved soon.

Notes to the Financial Statements.   With the issuance of NCGA *Statement 1* the primary financial statement reporting entity was shifted from individual fund data to the fund type data reported in the combined general purpose financial statements (GPFS). Individual fund data continue to be reported in the official comprehensive annual financial report (CAFR) of the SLG unit.

NCGA *Statement 1* provides that the notes to the financial statements are those applicable to the GPFS; additional notes that might be necessary at the individual fund level are referred to as "narrative explanations." *Statement 1* prescribes certain types of notes to the GPFS that must be included, some of which are individual fund disclosures, and states that "any other disclosures necessary in the circumstances should also be included."[15]

The problem here is that with such limited authoritative guidance practice appears to be varying considerably as to the disclosures presented in the notes to the financial statements. While the MFOA's GAAFR (80) contains an excellent discussion of what should be included in the summary of significant accounting policies and excellent illustrative notes, that source is not considered authoritative. Further, it does not set forth a listing (or checklist) of suggested or required notes other than the summary of significant accounting policies, though something of a listing may be implied from its illustrative examples. The NCGA provided some additional authoritative guidance with regard to the notes to the financial state-

[15] NCGAS 1, p. 24.

ments in NCGA *Interpretation 6*, "Notes to the Financial Statements Disclosure," issued in 1982.[16] Accounting and audit practitioners should use this guidance but also should review the notes to the financial statements in several good reports to help assure that they do not fail to include important notes to the financial statements.

Applicability of FASB and Predecessor Organization Pronouncements. A final problem facing the SLG practitioner is which pronouncements of the FASB and its predecessors, the Accounting Principles Board (APB) and the Committee on Accounting Procedure (CAP), should be applied to SLG financial reporting. The CAP noted that its pronouncements were *not* intended to apply to SLGs unless so stated in the document. In fact, none of its pronouncements were directed to SLG reporting. Its successor, the APB, followed a similar policy. Only one of its pronouncements, *Opinion 22*, "Disclosure of Accounting Policies," was directed to not-for-profit entities, including governments, as well as to business enterprises. It was quickly applied to SLG financial statements since all concerned agreed that the change improved SLG financial statements.

The AICPA state and local government audit guide has an appendix on "Applicability of Professional Pronouncements to Financial Statements of Governmental Units" which covers all CAP and APB pronouncements. The appendix concludes that most CAP and APB pronouncements are applicable to the proprietary funds of SLG units, and some are applicable to the governmental funds. Many of these properly apply, and can be applied, to the SLG model. Others, such as APB Opinion 8 on "Accounting for the Cost of Pension Plans," have caused problems in their application in the SLG environment—Opinion 8 focuses on expense (cost), whereas the governmental funds are accounted for on an expenditures basis. The result in practice has been that if a SLG unit did not report the proper *expense* amount as an *expenditure*, the auditor may feel forced to qualify his opinion on the SLG financial statements. This demonstrates the difficulty of forcing the application of an expense-focused pronouncement in the expenditure-focused SLG model.

No guidance exists as to whether (and how) the many pronouncements of the FASB issued in 1974 and later should be applied in SLG financial reports except for those cited in NCGA statements. A few FASB pronouncements are directed to SLG units, but most are directed toward business reporting. Thus, accounting and auditing practitioners should be aware of the FASB literature and sensitive to situations where it should be applied, together with the NCGA literature, but should not feel compelled to apply all, or even most, FASB and predecessor pronouncements to SLG financial reporting.

The Financial Statement Entity

The financial statement entity issue is primarily one of whether the principal data in SLG financial statements should be individual fund, fund type, or consolidated data.

---

[16] National Council on Governmental Accounting, *Interpretation 6*, "Notes to the Financial Statements Disclosure" (Chicago: NCGA, 1982).

NCGA *Statement 1* notes that:

> Historically, the individual fund and account group accounting entities have been considered to be the sole governmental financial reporting entity focus. This presumption has been questioned in recent years, however, and many accountants and financial statement users believe that fund type and account group data are sufficient to present fairly the government's financial position and operating results for general purpose financial reporting.

> The Council concludes that the individual funds and account groups should continue to be the basic entity reported upon in the CAFR, but that the primary reporting entity focus of separately issued GPFS should be upon fund type and account group financial information. The Council also concludes that the fund type and account group financial information included in the liftable GPFS (Combined Financial Statements—Overview) section of the CAFR constitutes "fair presentation in conformity with generally accepted accounting principles."[17]

AICPA Statement of Position 80-2 concurs and also gives the independent auditor several reporting scope options, including (1) the combined financial statements; (2) the combined financial statements, with the combining and individual fund statements reported on in relation to the combined statements; and (3) the combined statements and the combining and individual fund statements reported on equally.

The first aspect of the reporting entity controversy is that some believe the individual fund and account group data should continue to be the principal focus of SLG financial reports as they were for many years. They believe that combined fund type aggregations result in too much summarization and that important aspects of the SLG unit's operations or status are not adequately reported in combined statements. Thus they would like to reverse the *Statement 1* decision to have the combined statements be the "basic" statements reported by the SLG and, in most cases, reported on by the auditor.

A second aspect of the issue is raised by those who would require that the optional interfund and similar eliminations be made in the combined position and operating statements prescribed by *Statement 1* so that consolidated total columns would be presented. They believe that both the combined fund type data and the consolidated total data should be required, and that the total column need not be labeled "Memorandum Only" since appropriate interfund and similar adjustments would have been made. This would give the AICPA problems, of course, as its position has been that only one set of data can be the "basic" data, and hence the NCGA labeled the total columns in the GPFS "Memorandum Only." Notwithstanding the AICPA's problems, proponents of this view believe that both the fund type data and consolidated totals are essential for a fair presentation of the financial position and operating results of a SLG unit.

A third group would carry the aggregation one further step. They believe that only the consolidated data, as derived from the combined statements, are necessary and that the combined statements, as well as the combining and in-

---

[17] NCGAS 1, p. 25.

dividual fund statements, should be considered as back up detail for the consolidated statements.

The first three groups discussed would not change the basic NCGA accounting model. For example, even those wanting consolidated statements would want separate operating statements for governmental funds (and perhaps similar trust funds) and for proprietary funds (and perhaps similar trust funds). All three groups opt for the dual proprietary-type and governmental-type data reporting.

A fourth group would change the SLG model—and mix the aggregation and measurement issues—and report one balance sheet, one statement of revenues and expenses, and one statement of changes in financial position for the SLG unit. They believe this is the only way statements can fairly present the status and change of status of a city, county, or state.

No doubt there are other views as well, and SLG conceptual framework researchers and standards setters no doubt will be contending with this issue well into the future.

Price-Level-Adjusted Data

Whether governments should report data adjusted for changes in the general price level, for current replacement costs, or for other inflation or capital maintenance-related factors is *not* one of the most debated issues surrounding SLG accounting and financial reporting. Perhaps it should be. The FASB did not direct state and local governments to follow its *Statement 33* on general price-level-adjusted supplemental statements and replacement cost disclosures. Yet some are concerned with the effects of inflation and changing factor prices on the meaningfulness and propriety of SLG financial statements and statistical tables. At the least there needs to be some significant conceptual and applied research and experimentation in applying GPL adjustments, replacement cost data, or other inflation or capital maintenance data to SLG financial statements and statistical presentations. However, the authors are aware of no significant research and experimentation along these lines.

RECENT RESEARCH AND PUBLICATIONS

Where once few researchers focused on SLG accounting and reporting issues such as those noted above, many have done so in recent years, particularly since the New York City fiscal crisis. This section of the chapter provides a brief overview of some of the relevant research studies and position papers both to inform the reader and in hopes of stimulating him to seek out and explore in more depth some of the research reports, position papers, and articles mentioned here.

American Accounting Association Committees

Several American Accounting Committees in the 1960s and 1970s were concerned with governmental accounting and reporting and laid the ground work for later research. For example, the AAA Committee on Not-for-Profit Organizations, 1973[18] discussed at length some of the accounting and reporting problems (e.g., reporting entity, measurement) that have only recently become widely recognized as important issues. Its successor committee[19] delved deeply into such matters as users and uses of financial statements, measurement focus(es), and entity focus(es) and developed an approach to preparing consolidated SLG financial statements. Both committees drew heavily upon work of predecessor AAA Committees, as well as on a few classic[20] and recent[21] journal articles. Other AAA Committees since have also been concerned with public sector accounting and reporting, and the AAA Public Sector Section publishes working papers on public sector accounting, reporting, and auditing research.

The Research and Position Paper Era of the Mid-1970s

The mid-to-late 1970s saw a flurry of SLG-related research by academicians, practitioners, and standards setters, as well as position papers issued by public accounting firms. This era was kicked off by a national conference on "Municipal Accounting and Reporting: Issues for Research" sponsored by the University of Texas at Austin and the Municipal Finance Officers Association. UT Professor Michael Granof organized the conference and Alexander Grant & Co. provided financial support for the conference and published a summary of its proceedings.[22] The participants delved into numerous relevant issues and identified several needed research projects.

Several research studies and position papers appeared during the mid-1970s. Among them were:

1. Coopers & Lybrand and the University of Michigan, *Financial Disclosure Practices of the American Cities: A Public Report*[23]—in which, after reviewing their research of 46 city financial statements and the results of a conference, the authors recommend a new consolidated format for SLG reporting.

2. Sidney Davidson et al., *Financial Reporting by State and Local Government Units* (1977)—which considered the needs of users of SLG financial reports, consolidation, and what should be the applicable accounting principles, for example—and suggested a new format and approach to consolidated municipal reporting.[24]

[18] American Accounting Association, "Report of the Committee on Not-for-Profit Organizations, 1972–73," op. cit., pp. 224–249.

[19] American Accounting Association, "Report of the Committee on Nonprofit Organizations, 1973–74," op. cit., pp. 1–39.

[20] Hylton, op. cit., pp. 51–54; and Taussig, op. cit., pp. 562–567.

[21] Robert J. Freeman, "New Thoughts in Governmental Accounting," *Governmental Finance*, November 1972, pp. 2–8.

[22] "Municipal Accounting and Reporting: Issues for Research," Alexander Grant & Company, National Office, Sixth Floor, Prudential Plaza, Chicago, Illinois 60601.

[23] Coopers & Lybrand and the University of Michigan, *Financial Disclosure Practices of the American Cities: A Public Report*. Available from Coopers & Lybrand, P.O. Box 682, Times Square Station, New York City, New York 10036.

[24] Sidney Davidson et al., *Financial Reporting by State and Local Government Units* (Chicago: The University of Chicago, 1977).

3. Touche Ross & Company, *Public Financial Reporting By Local Government*[25]—a position paper that addresses topics such as the need for more understandable public reports, what should constitute GAAP applicable to municipalities, pension cost reporting, measurement objectives, and interim financial statements. Both short-run and longer-run recommendations are set forth.

4. Coopers & Lybrand, *Financial Disclosure Practices of the American Cities: Closing the Communications Gap*[26]—a position paper follow up on their prior report with the University of Michigan, this paper reports the results of some research but focuses principally on the C & L views on how to improve the communication of SLG statements and concludes by offering a revised model set of consolidated financial statements for a municipality.

5. Ernst & Whinney, *How Cities Can Improve Their Financial Reporting*[27]—which is based on a study of 100 city annual reports, contains analyses of the research findings, and provides practical guidance (including illustrations of better practices) to the city finance officer preparing financial statements under GAAP as applied to SLGs.

Other public accounting firms expended much time and effort on improving state and local government financial reporting. For example, Arthur Andersen & Co. published a position paper touching briefly on accounting but concerned mostly with management; and Arthur Young & Co. devoted its 1979 Professor's Roundtable[28] to SLG topics and its staff spent a great deal of time developing an evolutionary approach to consolidated reports that could be prepared relatively easily from existing GAAP data. Many other academicians and practitioners also have continued to research both pragmatic and conceptual issues.[29]

The Council of State Governments

The Council of State Governments (CSG) undertook an exhaustive, several-year research project which involved a large research team, led by Professor Relmond Van Daniker of the University of Kentucky (1) determining the state of the art of state accounting and reporting and publishing an *Inventory of Current*

[25] Touche Ross & Co., *Public Financial Reporting by Local Government: Issues and a Viewpoint* (n.p., 1977).

[26] Coopers & Lybrand, *Financial Disclosures of the American Cities: Closing the Communications Gap* (n.p., 1978).

[27] Ernst & Whinney, *How Cities Can Improve Their Financial Reporting* (Cleveland, Ohio: Ernst & Whinney, 1979).

[28] David Solomons (Ed.), "Improving the Financial Discipline of States and Cities," Proceedings of the Arthur Young Professor's Roundtable 1979 (Reston, Va.: The Council of Arthur Young Professors, 1980).

[29] See, for example, Frank M. Patitucci, "Governmental Accounting and Financial Reporting: Some Urgent Problems," *Public Affairs Report*, June 1977, reprinted in Robert W. Ingram, *Accounting in the Public Sector: The Challenging Environment* (Salt Lake City, Utah: Brighton Publishing Company, 1980), pp. 4–17.

State Government Accounting and Reporting Practices,[30] and (2) after preparing and discussing a series of issues papers, determining what it concluded were the "preferred" practices and approaches to state accounting and reporting, which were recommended to the NCGA for its consideration.[31]

The NCGA

The NCGA has consistently researched standards-oriented issues, but a HUD grant provided financial support for it to undertake significant conceptual framework research. The first published output of this research project was *A Study of Selected Concepts for Government Financial Accounting and Reporting,*[32] a research report prepared by Professor William W. Holder of the University of Southern California. This report was not commissioned to be impartial research. To the contrary, Holder's charge was to present and defend his personal views on what are the most critical conceptual problems that must be addressed in SLG accounting and reporting, together with his conclusions on those matters. He addressed the key issues, as agreed, and also presented a set of consolidating financial statements—which many viewed as being based on the business accounting model—for consideration by the NCGA. While his study was lauded by some, it was sharply criticized by the MFOA Committee on Accounting, Auditing, and Financial Reporting.[33]

Professor Allan R. Drebin of Northwestern University was the Principal Investigator of the major research study of the conceptual framework project, and James L. Remis was Project Director. They were assisted by Professor James L. Chan and Lorna Ferguson. The first phase of the project, concluded in 1981, was a major research study[34] which was the basis for NCGA *Concepts Statement 1,* "Objectives of *Accounting and Financial Reporting Objectives for Governmental Units,*[35] discussed later in this chapter.

The AICPA

The AICPA has had an active committee on state and local government accounting and auditing throughout the 1970s and early 1980s. That committee considered many of the same practice-oriented problems that confronted the NCGA—indeed, it established a subcommittee on each major NCGA agenda item and joint NCGA-AICPA Committee meetings were held annually.

---

[30] Council of State Governments, *Inventory of Current State Government Accounting and Reporting Practices* (Lexington, Ky.: CSG, 1980).

[31] National Council on Governmental Accounting and State Government Accounting Project, *Preferred Accounting Practices for State Governments,* Exposure Draft of a Research Report (Lexington, Ky: Council of State Governments, [1982]).

[32] Holder Study.

[33] MFOA Committee on Accounting, Auditing, and Financial Reporting, "A Response to the NCGA Holder Study," *Governmental Finance,* March 1981, pp. 26–31.

[34] Allan R. Drebin, James L. Chan, and Lorna Ferguson, *Objectives of Accounting and Financial Reporting For Governmental Units: A Research Study,* 2 vols. (Chicago: NCGA, 1981).

[35] National Council on Governmental Accounting, *Concepts Statement 1,* "Objectives of Accounting and Financial Reporting Objectives for Governmental Units" (Chicago: NCGA, 1981). Hereafter cited as NCGA Objectives.

In addition to its usual work, the AICPA undertook a major national research project in 1979. Often called simply "the experiment," the project involved a questionnaire to practicing finance officers (preparers of statements) who were also asked to recast their government's financial statements into the mold of the experimental consolidated statements presented by the AICPA Committee in its "Experimentation Booklet."[36] The response to the questionnaire was low, and relatively few SLG units recast their financial statements as requested. Perhaps the timing was bad, as the AICPA was asking people to experiment at a time when many probably were intent on understanding and conforming with NCGA *Statement 1.*

More recently, the AICPA Committee has begun extensive revision of its state and local government audit guide. The revised audit guide is scheduled for publication in 1985 or 1986.

The FASB

The FASB's concern for SLG accounting and reporting was heightened by criticism it received because of instances of poor state and local government reporting, many of which were not in compliance with NCGA standards. The FASB's interest in governmental accounting standards was heightened even further by the report of the Financial Accounting Foundation "Structure Committee," which stated:

> The Wheat Committee said the Board had to deal with all aspects of the standards-setting process if it were to be *the* standards-setting body. . . .If the Board tries to do all the work in-house, it must delay some projects (municipal accounting is a good example). . . .[37]

Further, the Chairman of the FAF structure committee also headed a major public accounting firm, which in 1977 issued a pamphlet saying, among other things, that the accounting profession should:

> Fix the responsibility for establishing authoritative accounting principles and reporting standards in a single public body responsive to all participants in this major segment of our economy but responsible solely to the users of reports. The Financial Accounting Standards Board, in our view, best meets this challenge.[38]

Deeply involved in its conceptual framework for business enterprises research, in 1977 the FASB commissioned Professor Robert N. Anthony of Harvard University to do an impartial exploratory study of the main conceptual issues of nonbusiness organization accounting and reporting. Working with a large task force of advisors (53), Anthony prepared *Financial Accounting in Nonbusiness*

---

[36] AICPA, State and Local Government Accounting Committee, "Experimentation Booklet: An Experiment in Government Accounting and Reporting by the AICPA State and Local Government Accounting Committee" (New York: AICPA, September 1979).

[37] Report of the Structure Committee, the Financial Accounting Foundation, *The Structure of Establishing Financial Accounting Standards*, April 1977, p. 26.

[38] Touche Ross & Co., op. cit., p. 1.

Organizations: An Exploratory Study of Conceptual Issues.[39] In the report, which most considered well and impartially done, he touched on topics such as user information needs, relating user information needs to financial statements, a series of selected issues, and the boundaries for nonbusiness accounting concepts. The FASB placed the objectives of nonbusiness reporting on its agenda at the conclusion of Anthony's project. The Anthony Report, as it came to be known, served as the integral part of a unique "wrap around" Discussion Memorandum issued by the FASB, which ultimately assumed responsibility for the accounting and reporting standards applicable to all nonbusiness organizations except governments.[40] Later, in December 1980, the FASB issued *Statement of Financial Accounting Concepts 4*, "Objectives of Financial Reporting by Nonbusiness Organizations,"[41] which was discussed briefly in Chapter 1 and is discussed further later in this chapter.

The Board also commissioned a research report by Peat, Marwick, Mitchell & Co. to determine the extent to which service efforts and accomplishments data were being publicly reported by nonbusiness organizations. The report of this endeavor, *Reporting of Service Efforts and Accomplishments*,[42] indicated over 1,000 instances of organizations reporting service efforts and accomplishments information in the 120 reports reviewed, some of which were state and local government reports.

OBJECTIVES OF SLG ACCOUNTING AND REPORTING

For years people have been concerned that there was no clear statement of objectives and other fundamental concepts to guide the development of accounting standards. Now there are two separate statements of the objectives of accounting and reporting for nonbusiness organizations, one of which is directed specifically to state and local governments. Both statements of objectives are considered here briefly, together with the role of such statements and their relationship to accounting and reporting standards.

FASB Objectives—Nonbusiness Organizations

FASB *Statement of Financial Accounting Concepts* No. 4, "Objectives of Financial Reporting by Nonbusiness Organizations," issued in December 1980, includes a preface describing the role of SFACs and its conceptual framework research project:

> This Statement of Financial Accounting Concepts is one of a series of publications in the Board's conceptual framework for financial accounting and re-

[39] Anthony Report.

[40] Financial Accounting Standards Board, *Statement of Financial Accounting Standards No. 32*, "Specialized Accounting and Reporting" (Stamford, Conn.: FASB, September 1979).

[41] Financial Accounting Standards Board, *Statement of Financial Accounting Standards No. 4*, "Objectives of Financial Reporting by Nonbusiness Organizations" (Stamford, Conn.: FASB, December 1980). Hereafter cited as FASB Nonbusiness Objectives.

[42] Paul K. Brace, Robert Elkin, Daniel D. Robinson, and Harold I. Steinberg, *Reporting of Service Efforts and Accomplishments*, Research Report (Stamford, Conn.: FASB, 1980).

porting. Statements in the series are intended to set forth objectives and fundamentals that will be the basis for development of financial accounting and reporting standards. *The objectives identify the goals and purposes of financial reporting. The fundamentals are the underlying concepts of financial accounting*—concepts that guide the selection of transactions, events, and circumstances to be accounted for; their recognition and measurement; and the means of summarizing and communicating them to interested parties. Concepts of that type are fundamental in the sense that other concepts flow from them and repeated reference to them will be necessary in establishing, interpreting, and applying accounting and reporting standards.

The conceptual framework is a coherent system of interrelated objectives and fundamentals that is expected to lead to consistent standards and that prescribes the nature, function, and limits of financial accounting and reporting. It is expected to serve the public interest by providing structure and direction to financial accounting and reporting to facilitate the provision of evenhanded financial and related information that helps promote the efficient allocation of scarce resources in the economy and society, including assisting capital and other markets to function efficiently.

Establishment of objectives and identification of fundamental concepts will not directly solve financial accounting and reporting problems. Rather, objectives give direction and concepts are tools for solving problems. . . .

Statements of Financial Accounting Concepts do not establish standards prescribing accounting procedures or disclosure practices for particular items or events, which are issued by the Board as Statements of Financial Accounting Standards. Rather, Statements in this series describe concepts and relations that will underlie future financial accounting standards and practices and in due course serve as a basis for evaluating existing standards and practices.[43]

Further, the Board states in the introduction to SFAC No 4:

1. This Statement establishes the objectives of general purpose external financial reporting by nonbusiness organizations. Those objectives, together with the objectives set forth in FASB Concepts Statement No. 1, *Objectives of Financial Reporting by Business Enterprises*, will serve as the foundation of the conceptual framework the Board is developing for financial accounting and reporting. Based on its review of the similarities and differences between those two sets of objectives, the Board has concluded that it is not necessary to develop an independent conceptual framework for any particular category of entities (e.g., nonbusiness organizations or business enterprises). Rather, its goal is to develop an integrated conceptual framework that has relevance to all entities and that provides appropriate consideration of any different reporting objectives and concepts that may apply to only certain types of entities. . . .

2. From its outset, the project leading to this Statement has included governmental units in its scope, and the Exposure Draft included governmental examples. On the basis of its study to date, the Board is aware of no persuasive evidence that the objectives in this Statement are inappropriate for general purpose external financial reports of governmental units. None-

---

[43] FASB Nonbusiness Objectives, pp. i–ii. (Emphasis added.)

theless, the appropriate structure for setting financial accounting and reporting standards for state and local governmental units continues to be discussed. Pending resolution of that issue, the Board has deferred a final decision on whether the objectives set forth in this Statement should apply to general purpose external financial reporting by state and local governmental units.

3. If the responsibility for standard setting was ultimately given to the Financial Accounting Standards Board, the Board would expect to consider the findings of research in process by the National Council on Governmental Accounting (NCGA), the Council of State Governments (CSG) . . . , and other intervening research. Before reaching a decision, it would also solicit additional views regarding the applicability of the conclusions in this Statement to general purpose external financial reporting of state and local governmental units.[44]

Recall that the objectives set forth for nonbusiness organization financial reporting by the FASB in SFAC No. 4 are:

- Financial reporting by nonbusiness organizations should provide information that is useful to present and potential resource providers and other users in making rational decisions about the allocation of resources to those organizations.
- Financial reporting should provide information to help present and potential resource providers and other users in assessing the services that a nonbusiness organization provides and its ability to continue to provide those services.
- Financial reporting should provide information that is useful to present and potential resource providers and other users in assessing how managers of a nonbusiness organization have discharged their stewardship responsibilities and about other aspects of their performance.
- Financial reporting should provide information about the economic resources, obligations, and net resources of an organization, and the effects of transactions, events, and circumstances that change resources and interests in those resources.
- Financial reporting should provide information about the performance of an organization during a period. Periodic measurement of the changes in the amount and nature of the net resources of a nonbusiness organization and information about the service efforts and accomplishments of an organization together represent the information most useful in assessing its performance.
- Financial reporting should provide information about how an organization obtains and spends cash or other liquid resources, about its borrowing and repayment of borrowing, and about other factors that may affect an organization's liquidity.
- Financial reporting should include explanations and interpretations to help users understand financial information provided.[45]

---

[44] Ibid., pp. 1–2.
[45] Ibid., pp. xiii–xiv.

NCGA Objectives—SLG Units

In the introductory part of its statement of objectives, the NCGA relates the objectives to NCGA *Statement 1:*

> In March, 1979, the National Council on Governmental Accounting (NCGA) published Statement 1, *Governmental Accounting and Financial Reporting Principles.* Statement 1 provides authoritative guidance to improve governmental accounting and reporting standards.
>
> In issuing Statement 1, however, the NCGA recognized that a much broader and fundamental effort was needed to meet future financial information needs. The council felt that a conceptual framework was necessary to permit the development of standards of accounting and financial reporting for governmental units that were logical, consistent and responsive to the needs of users. To accomplish this, the NCGA has conducted extensive research which, along with due process procedures, has led to the development of this statement.[46]

The NCGA statement of objectives also includes two definitions[47] that set the tone for the document:

> *Objectives* are statements of what is desired to be achieved by accounting and financial reporting. By nature they are broad and general, yet they should be helpful in evaluating whether particular practices are effective in accomplishing the objectives.
>
> *Accounting and financial reporting* refer to the collection, maintenance, processing and communication of information useful in making decisions or in assessing organizational performance. It is important to note that the objectives in this statement are not limited to information traditionally supplied by accounting systems. Thus, no reference is made to existing reporting media such as "General Purpose Financial Statements" or "Comprehensive Annual Financial Reports." Furthermore, nonmonetary information such as measures of service outputs is included within the scope of this statement.

Further, it contains an interesting pragmatic discussion of the role of objectives:

THE ROLE OF OBJECTIVES

If standards are to be developed to meet the needs of a wide range of potential users, it is first necessary to gain consensus concerning what standards are expected to achieve. The setting of standards is basically a legislative process. There are very few "truths" in accounting and financial reporting. If standards were set without agreement on objectives, there would be no basis for preferring one standard over another. If there were agreement on objectives, then it is possible to judge the effectiveness of alternative standards in terms of their impact on achieving the stated objectives.

If objectives are not explicitly stated and agreed upon, there may nevertheless be some "hidden" objectives pursued by proponents of particular points of view. Thus, some may advocate a particular standard based on an assumed

---

[46] NCGA Objectives, p. 1.

[47] Ibid., p. 3.

objective such as responding to the needs of a particular user, conforming to practices found in other segments of society or maintaining the status quo. Establishing objectives permits various interest parties to voice their agreement or disagreement as to the objectives, although as in any legislative process, there is no assurance that there will be unanimity regarding the objectives. Once the objectives are established, however, standards may be developed and evaluated in a rational fashion by reference to their impact on objectives.[48]

As noted earlier, the NCGA statement of objectives is directed specifically to state and local governments rather than to all nonbusiness organizations. The NCGA summary statement of governmental accounting and financial reporting objectives reads as follows:

OVERALL GOAL

8) The overall goal of accounting and financial reporting for governmental units is:

To provide: 1) financial information useful for making economic, political and social decisions, and demonstrating accountability and stewardship; and 2) information useful for evaluating managerial and organizational performance.

BASIC OBJECTIVES

9) The objectives of accounting and financial reporting for governmental units are (the order in which the objectives are listed is of no significance):

SHORT-TERM FINANCIAL RESOURCES

I) To provide financial information useful for determining and forecasting the flows, balances and requirements of short-term financial resources of the governmental unit.
   a) For determining and forecasting the balances and availability of short-term financial resources, including cash, for specific uses.
   b) For forecasting the need to obtain additional short-term financial resources.
   c) For forecasting the impact on short-term financial resources of specific revenue and other financing sources.
   d) For forecasting the impact on short-term financial resources of planned programs and activities.
   e) For forecasting the ability of the governmental unit to meet its short-term obligations as they come due.

FINANCIAL CONDITION

II) To provide financial information useful for determining and forecasting the financial condition of the governmental unit and changes therein.
   a) For determining and value and forecasting the service potential of resources held by the governmental unit.
   b) For determining whether the value and service potential of physical resources have been maintained during a period and forecasting the financial impact of maintaining or replacing service capacity.

[48] Ibid., pp. 3–4.

c) For forecasting the amounts and timing of future outflows resulting from existing commitments and the ability of the governmental unit to meet these when they come due.

d) For determining and forecasting the cost of programs or services provided by the governmental unit.

LEGAL, CONTRACTUAL AND FIDUCIARY REQUIREMENTS

III) To provide financial information useful for monitoring performance under terms of legal, contractual and fiduciary requirements.

a) For determining whether resources were utilized in accordance with legal and contractual requirements, including budgetary provisions.

b) For determining whether financial contributions of taxpayers, grantors and service recipients intended to support activities of a given time period were sufficient to recover the cost of those activities.

c) For determining whether fees or reimbursements are in accordance with legal, grant or contractual requirements.

d) For accounting for the use and disposition of resources entrusted to public officials.

PLANNING AND BUDGETING

IV) To provide information useful for planning and budgeting, and for forecasting the impact of the acquisition and allocation of resources on the achievement of operational objectives.

a) For forecasting the impact of program alternatives on short-term financial resources of the governmental unit.

b) For forecasting the impact of program alternatives on the financial condition of the governmental unit.

c) For forecasting the amount of financial contributions of taxpayers, grantors and service recipients needed to support activities of a given time period.

d) For forecasting the effectiveness, including the distribution of benefits among groups, of proposed programs and activities in achieving goals and objectives.

e) For forecasting the incidence of the burden of providing resources for governmental operations.

ORGANIZATIONAL AND MANAGERIAL PERFORMANCE

V) To provide information useful for evaluating managerial and organizational performance.

a) For determining the cost of programs, functions and activities in a manner which facilitates analysis and valid comparisons with established criteria, among time periods, and with other governmental units.

b) For evaluating the efficiency and economy of operations of organizational units, programs, activities and functions.

c) For evaluating the results of programs, activities and functions and their effectiveness in achieving their goals and objectives.

d) For evaluating the equity with which the burden of providing resources for governmental operations is imposed.

COMMUNICATION

VI) To communicate the relevant information in a manner which best facilitates its use.
   a) To present the information clearly and concisely.
   b) To make the information conveniently available, comprehensively and with full disclosure.
   c) To enhance the reliability of the information.
   d) To provide the information on a timely basis.
   e) To present the information in a comparable manner among entities and among time periods.[49]

The NCGA objectives statement obviously is more detailed than that of the FASB. Further, note that NCGA objectives I, Short-Term Financial Resources, and III, Legal, Contractual and Fiduciary Requirements, are rather well met by GAAP applicable to state and local government units. The other NCGA objectives are only partly met, at most, by contemporary SLG financial accounting and reporting principles and procedures.

WHO SHOULD SET SLG ACCOUNTING AND REPORTING STANDARDS?

The National Committee on Governmental Accounting and its predecessors were the sole, unchallenged body setting forth generally accepted accounting principles applicable to SLG units for 40 years. It became apparent when the AICPA audit guide for SLG units was being prepared that auditors also have an interest in accounting and reporting standards. The AICPA committee worked closely with numerous SLG accountants and auditors in finalizing ASLGU.

When the National Council on Governmental Accounting was established in 1974, three practicing CPAs were among its 21 part-time members; and the AICPA Committee and the NCGA each designated a liaison member to the other to assure open and continuous communication between the two bodies. The NCGA listened carefully to suggestions by the AICPA to assure that its pronouncements were agreeable to and understood by all concerned.

Thus, the AICPA had significant input to the NCGA standards-setting process. Indeed, to some extent it may be said that standards were being set jointly by the consensus approach followed by the AICPA and NCGA.

By 1978 the issue arose as to which of the following types of bodies should establish SLG accounting and reporting:

1. The NCGA, as then constituted
2. A reconstituted NCGA—smaller, better staffed, and perhaps full time
3. The FASB, as then constituted
4. The FASB, as reconstituted to add SLG members

---

[49] Ibid., pp. 4–6, subtitles from pp. 4–9.

5. A separate Governmental Accounting Standards Board (GASB) established either:

    a. Under the Financial Accounting Foundation, parallel to the FASB, or

    b. Under a separate foundation

6. Some other arrangement, e.g., a federally sponsored board.

The impetus for much of these discussions came from members of the NCGA who were concerned that a 21-member part-time board meeting two or three times annually could not keep up with the demands on the Council to conduct research and set standards on issues on a timely basis. Other views were expressed in a series of articles in the March 1979 *Journal of Accountancy*.

Informal discussions of various possibilities were held during 1978–1979 by various members of the NCGA, MFOA, AICPA, FAF, and FASB, as well as by others, including Federal government executives. During this same period Senator Harrison Williams began introducing bills to establish a Federal standards-setting agency that would have part-time members but a full-time staff.

In 1980 a Governmental Accounting Standards Board Organization Committee (GASBOC) was formed, which had a broader charge than its name implied. As explained in the introduction to the GASBOC exposure draft report[50] issued in February 1981:

> In April 1980 following a year of informal discussions, the American Institute of Certified Public Accountants (AICPA), Financial Accounting Foundation (FAF), Municipal Finance Officers Association (MFOA), National Association of State Auditors, Comptrollers, and Treasurers (NASACT), General Accounting Office (GAO), and National Council on Governmental Accounting (NCGA) established an ad hoc working committee, known as the Governmental Accounting Standards Board Organization Committee (GASBOC), to consider whether there is a need for a new structure to establish accounting and reporting requirements for state and local government and, if so, to develop detailed recommendations regarding the new structure, how it should be funded, how to bring about acceptance of the new structure's standards, and how the new structure should interface with the FAF/Financial Accounting Standards Board (FASB) structure. Professor Robert K. Mautz of the Paton Accounting Center agreed to serve as the chairman of the working committee. Besides those organizations named above, representatives of the following seven public interest groups participated in the Committee's deliberations:
>
> - Council of State Governments
> - International City Management Association
> - National Association of Counties
> - National Conference of State Legislatures
> - National Governors Association
> - National League of Cities
> - U.S. Conference of Mayors

---

[50] Report of the Governmental Accounting Standards Board Organization Committee, Exposure Draft, February 16, 1981, p. 1. Hereafter cited as GASBOC Report ED.

This group considered many matters, such as:

1. The several sources of SLG accounting principles: the NCGA; the AICPA, through ASLGU as modified by SOP 80-2; the FASB and its predecessors, particularly with relation to proprietary activities but to some extent on governmental activities; the Federal government, through its grant accounting and reporting regulations; and legal requirements affecting each SLG unit that affect its accounting and reporting.

2. That, in the absence of requirements such as those of the Securities and Exchange Commission regulating business, and in the absence of AICPA Rule 203 or equivalent recognition of NCGA standards, compliance with SLG accounting and reporting standards varies widely.

3. Whether a part-time voluntary body such as the NCGA could long continue to be the principal standards-setter for SLG units—because of its part-time membership; its limited resources; and because many perceived it as an arm of the MFOA, and thus as dominated by preparers of statements, rather than as truly independent.

4. The essential attributes of a sound standards-setting structure, which they listed as:

   1. *Independence*—the standard-setting body must be free of undue influence by any particular segment of its constituency.
   2. *Competence*—the standard-setting body must be highly knowledgeable in all areas of accounting and financial reporting with particular expertise in the governmental area, and must be supported by a technically competent research staff.
   3. *Appropriate procedures*—the standard-setting body must seek a broad range of views and thoroughly study the merits and consequences of the various alternatives before adopting standards.
   4. *Adequate resources*—the standard-setting body must have sufficient funds to support its work.
   5. *Authority/Compliance*—the board must be recognized as having the authority to set standards and failure to comply with its pronouncements must be generally considered unacceptable.[51]

If a new standards-setting body were to be considered:

1. Should one board (FASB) set standards for the governmental sector as well as for the private sector, or should a separate Governmental Accounting Standards Board (GASB) be established?
2. Should governmental accounting standards be established by government or by an independent body?
3. Assuming that a new GASB is created, should a single foundation have oversight responsibility for both FASB and GASB or should a Governmental Accounting Foundation (GAF) be established to oversee GASB operations?
4. Should GASB members serve full-time or part time?[52]

[51] Ibid., p. 5.
[52] Ibid.

The GASBOC initially concluded that:

1. A separate independent GASB should be created under a new foundation, rather than placing the GASB under the FAF which oversees the FASB, to assure acceptance by the SLG units and that sufficient time and resources would be devoted to SLG problems.
2. The GASB should be in the private sector rather than in the public sector to assure independence from political pressures, have the compensation and other flexibility to attract qualified board and staff members, and for other reasons.
3. The GASB should be comprised of five full-time members with adequate staff and other resources. [53]

The structure of the GASB proposal, as diagrammed in the GASBOC report exposure draft, is presented in Figure 15-1. The GASBOC Report ED also covered other matters, including the prospective relationship between the FASB and the GASB, the physical location of the GASB, assuring compliance with GASB standards, and the budget and funding for the GASB.

Hearings on the GASBOC Report ED were held in April and May 1981. Testimony for and against the GASBOC proposal was offered by over 100 persons and firms.

The GASBOC met again, formally and informally, during the summer of 1981 and worked out a compromise plan that was acceptable to at least the majority of its members. This plan included the following provisions, among others:

1. The GASB would be formed under the existing Financial Accounting Foundation (FAF) that oversees the FASB.
2. The FAF would be enlarged and three additional trustees representing state and local government would be appointed.
3. The FAF would be responsible for appointing GASB members, for financing the GASB operations, and for general oversight of the GASB in the same manner it exercises oversight of the FASB. Whether the GASB would be full time would be decided by the FAF, as would the GASB's location, staff support, and so on.
4. The National Council on Governmental Accounting would be changed to twenty members—including members from the college and university, public school, and hospital accounting organizations—representing various organizations and interests. The new NCGA would serve in a consultative and review capacity to the GASB much as the Financial Accounting Standards Advisory Council (FASAC) serves the FASB. Further, this new NCGA would have veto rights over the initial appointments of members to the GASB and over the selection of the first chairman and vice-chairman.
5. The GASB would have five members who would serve no more than two five-year terms.

In sum, the final proposal differed from the preliminary proposal principally in that (1) the FAF, rather than a separate foundation, would finance and oversee

[53] Ibid., pp. 5–8.

Figure 15-1

PROPOSED GOVERNMENTAL ACCOUNTING STANDARDS BOARD ORGANIZATION STRUCTURE

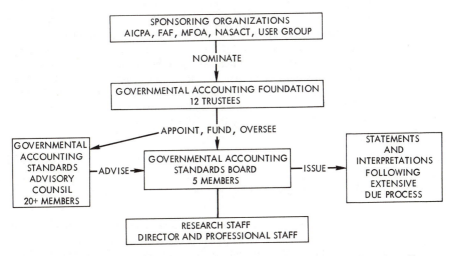

Source: Report of the Governmental Accounting Standards Board Organization Committee, Exposure Draft, February 16, 1981, p. 11.

the new GASB; (2) a new NCGA would serve as the Governmental Accounting Standards Advisory Council proposed by the GASBOC; and (3) the GASB members might serve part time rather than full time.

In establishing the GASB, the FAF tentatively decided that:

- The GASB chairman would serve full time, but the other four GASB members probably would serve part time, at least initially.
- A full time staff director and several full time staff members would assist the GASB.
- The initial GASB annual budget would be $1-$2 million.
- A Government Accounting Standards Board Advisory Council (GAS-BAC) would be formed, as originally recommended by the GASBOC, rather than reconstituting the NCGA to serve this function.
- The GASB offices would be located in Stamford, Connecticut, as is the FASB.

Two other aspects of the new GASB warrant attention (1) Jurisdiction of the GASB and FASB and (2) Mandatory structure review. As to jurisdiction it was agreed that:

> GASBOC recognizes the need for a close working relationship and a spirit of cooperation between the GASB and FASB, particularly on accounting issues that affect both governmental and nongovernmental reporting entities. The jurisdiction of the GASB in relation to the FASB should be as follows:
>
> 1. The GASB shall establish financial accounting standards for all state and

local governmental bodies not similar to privately owned entities such as utilities, hospitals, and universities. Financial reports by government entities that are similar to privately owned entities shall be subject to standards issued jointly only upon the mutual concurrence of the GASB and the FASB.

2. The FASB shall establish financial accounting standards for all privately owned nonprofit entities as well as for profit-seeking enterprises.

3. NCGA Statements and the AICPA Audit Guide, "Audits of State and Local Governmental Units" (as amended), shall be recognized by the GASB as being in force until such time as modified by standards issued by GASB. To the extent specified under these pronouncements, the standards of the FASB and its predecessors shall apply to government financial reporting unless and until modified by the GASB.

The FAF has the responsibility for resolving any conflicts between the GASB and the FASB.

The "mandatory structure review" provision is as follows:

> There shall be a mandatory review of the governmental accounting standard-setting structure after GASB has been in operation for approximately five years, including review of the future role of NCGA in the appointment process. The review shall be conducted by the Trustees of the FAF with heavy reliance on input from NCGA throughout the review.

Thus, even with the new GASB the controversy over who shall establish SLG accounting and reporting standards may continue, and may come to a head at the end of the first five years of the GASB's operations.

CONCLUDING COMMENTS

Controversy and change frustrate some persons. Others view them as positive signs that the attention of the accounting profession—including SLG finance officers, professors, and independent public accountants—is increasingly being directed toward the improvement of state and local government accounting and financial reporting. The latter is our view, though it admittedly is frustrating to realize that some aspects of our text are apt to be outdated soon after its release, perhaps even before.

Significant strides have been made toward resolution of important conceptual and practice issues, as well as in the standards-setting process. Too, important strides have been made toward agreeing on the proper objectives for SLG accounting and reporting, the starting point and essential ingredient in a conceptual framework for SLG accounting and reporting yet to be completed.

Accounting and reporting concepts and practices should and must evolve in all fields—business, nonbusiness, and government. Through the combined efforts of many persons and organizations, this evolution appears to be accelerating in the public sector.

▶ **Question 15-1.** Explain the Organizational Reporting Entity (ORE) issue thoroughly but concisely in a manner understandable to a nonaccountant.

Question 15-2. Briefly explain the funds flow versus service cost issue in a manner understandable to a layman city council member.

Question 15-3. Distinguish between "fund" expenditures and "conventional" expenditures.

Question 15-4. What problems do you foresee in applying the NCGA's "Enterprise Fund" definition in practice?

Question 15-5. What are the major problems in applying the "susceptibility to accrual" criteria to revenue recognition in practice?

Question 15-6. What is meant by the terms "short-term" or "current," "intermediate-term," and "long-term" in SLG accounting and reporting? What problems, if any, are associated with those terms?

Question 15-7. What is meant by the term "artificial deficits"? How may they arise? How can they be eliminated? If they cannot be eliminated, what should you do?

Question 15-8. Explain the several views of the reporting entity concisely. Which do you favor? Why?

Question 15-9. Why should state and local governments consider restating financial statements and statistical schedules for the effects of inflation?

▶ **Problem 15-1.** The City of Indy just leased a large tract of prime land it owned in downtown Indy to a hotel corporation for 50 years. The hotel corporation plans to build an ultra modern high-rise hotel on the property, and has an option to renew the lease for another 40 years if it wishes to do so. Under the terms of the lease, entered into on January 2, 19X0, the City will receive annual payments of $200,000 each December 31, beginning December 31, 19X0. Both the city and the hotel corporation agree that a 10 percent rate is implicit in this arrangement.

Required:

(a) Prepare the necessary general journal entries to record on the books of the City of Indy:

1. The inception of the lease
2. The first lease payment collection
3. The second lease payment collection

(b) What payments would have been required by the City if the fair market value of the property was agreed to be $6,000,000 and an interest rate of 12 percent per annum was agreed to by both parties at interest?

Problem 15-2. Proxy City leased an office building near city hall on January 2, 19X4. The twenty-year noncancellable lease requires the city to pay the owner of the property $60,000 per year each December 31. Had the City bought the building for $600,000 it would have borrowed money at 12 percent to do so.

Required:

(a) Prepare the general journal entries to record:
1. The inception of the lease at January 2, 19X4

2. The City's lease payment at December 31, 19X4

3. The City's lease payment at December 31, 19X5

(b) Should the city have leased the office building or bought it outright? Why?

Problem 15-3. The State of Confusion operates its own employee retirement trust fund. The Public Employee Retirement System (PERS) billed the General Fund $8,000,000 for its actuarially determined contribution for 19X8. However, the Legislature appropriated only $3,000,000 from the General Fund for this purpose.

Required:

(a) Prepare the general journal entries to record the billing and payment of the PERS expenditure in the General Fund and in any other fund or account group affected.

(b) The state auditor suggested that the entire $8,000,000 be reported as a General Fund expenditure and that a $5,000,000 transfer of debt to GLTD be added to the "Other Financing Sources" or as the last item in the General Fund Statement of Revenues, Expenditures, and Changes in Fund Balances for the year ended December 31, 19X8. Evaluate this suggestion.

Problem 15-4. (Research problem) Identify and explain the principal accounting and reporting differences between FASB *Statement 35*, "Accounting and Reporting by Defined Benefit Plans," and NCGA *Interpretation 4*, "Accounting and Financial Reporting for Public Employee Retirement Systems and Pension Trust Funds."

Problem 15-5. (Research problem) Locate as many of the research and position papers cited on pages 609–613 as possible.

(a) Prepare a brief abstract of each.

(b) Evaluate the strengths and weaknesses of each and its contribution to the profession.

Problem 15-6. (Research problem) (a) Analyze the Anthony Study carefully, research any articles in the literature related to it, and prepare a brief 10 to 20-page report of your findings and conclusions.

(b) Referring to part (a), do the same for the Holder Report.

Problem 15-7. (Research problem) Study the NCGA's statement of objectives of accounting and reporting for governmental units, including the research study, and compare them with the reporting objectives for nonbusiness organizations reporting set forth in FASB *SFAC No. 4*. Prepare a 10 to 20-page report summarizing your research and analyses, with particular emphasis being given to the similarities and differences of the FASB and NCGA approaches and conclusions.

16

COST ACCOUNTING, FINDING, AND ANALYSIS

Every organization, whether business, nonbusiness, or government, has only a limited amount of scarce resources at its disposal. Thus, every decision affecting future resource allocation—and each evaluation of past resource utilization—necessarily involves either implicit or explicit comparison of the costs incurred, or to be incurred, with the benefits received or expected. It is extremely important, therefore, that planners, decision makers, managers, and evaluators at all levels (including the citizenry) be provided reliable, relevant, and timely information on both past and prospective costs of governmental services, products, and activities.

Cost information recently has taken on added importance in California and other states where property or other taxes have been significantly reduced and future increases in such taxes are limited to specified or indexed amounts or percentages. Property taxes, in particular, have long been a mainstay of local government finance; alternative financing sources, such as fees for services, are often turned to when tax revenue is limited. The response of the citizenry or state government in several situations has been that all service fees must be "cost-justified," and any excess of fees over costs may be considered a tax that must be included in computing the maximum tax rate or amount permitted by law. Thus, governmental cost accounting and cost finding have taken on increased importance in recent years—for both (1) internal control, analysis, management, and planning, and (2) external service fee and tax rate justifications—and are apt to be even more important in the years ahead.

Any listing of the specific uses of cost information is necessarily incomplete—as its present and potential uses are both pervasive and dynamic. Among the more important specific uses of governmental cost information are:

1. *Budgeting:* Budgetary planning, preparation, and support—that is,

making decisions concerning the allocation of scarce resources among relatively unlimited demands. Appropriate cost records and forecasts are prerequisites to effective program or performance budgeting.

2. *Cost and efficiency analyses:* Interperiod, intraunit, and interunit analyses of costs and cost trends of selected activities, functions, or programs to determine their direction and to indicate relative efficiency.

3. *"Do or contract for" decisions:* Where goods or services are available from nongovernmental sources, whether the unit is effecting savings by providing the goods or performing the services or should contract for them.

4. *Fee determination and justification:* Determination and justification of service or product fee schedules, amounts to be assessed to property owners in special assessment projects, and costs reimbursable under terms of contracts or grants.

5. *Capitalization and analysis of construction projects:* Calculation of the total cost of assets constructed by the unit, for comparison with project cost estimates and as a basis for capitalizing the assets in the appropriate accounting records.

6. *Reporting:* Supplementing fund-based financial statements with data on total and/or unit costs of programs, projects, or other activities— either to inform statement users more completely or to demonstrate compliance with cost-based service fee, tax, or other restrictions.

Cost accounting may be broadly defined as the art of determining the cost of a product, service, or activity. We use the term *"cost accounting"* to refer to a continuous process of analyzing, classifying, recording, and summarizing costs within the discipline and controls of the formal accounting system and reporting them to users on a regular basis. The determination or estimation of costs by more informal procedures and/or on an irregular basis is referred to as *"cost finding."*

Following a brief introduction to cost concepts, terminology, and behavior, the remainder of this chapter is devoted primarily to cost accounting and cost finding in state and local governments. These topics normally comprise the subject of one or more separate courses in the contemporary collegiate accounting curriculum, of course, and this chapter should be viewed as introductory in nature. A detailed, complete presentation of the subject is beyond the scope of this book.[1]

---

[1] For a more complete treatment of cost accounting and cost finding, see Charles T. Horngren, *Cost Accounting: A Managerial Emphasis* (Englewood Cliffs, N.J.: Prentice-Hall, Inc., 1982) or another standard cost accounting textbook. Also see William W. Holder and Rick Kermer, *Cost Accounting For California Cities* (Sacramento: League of California Cities, 1981) and Robert J. Freeman, Harold H. Hensold, Jr., and William W. Holder, "Cost Accounting and Analysis in State and Local Governments," in Homer A. Black and James Don Edwards (Eds.), *The Managerial and Cost Accountant's Handbook* (Homewood, Ill.: Dow Jones–Irwin, 1979).

Differing concepts and measures of "cost" are relevant in differing analyses and decision situations. Imprecise usages of the term "cost" confuse and frustrate both the accountant and layman, however, and the term is best used only with an appropriate modifier.

Cost Concepts

One of the more common errors made in the interpretation of not-for-profit accounting data is considering expenditures to be synonymous with cost—and thus erroneously considering total or per unit expenditures to be equivalent to total or per unit cost of a product or service. The systems of appropriation-expenditure accounting for expendable governmental funds described in the earlier chapters of this book provide necessary records of the "things" (services, materials or supplies, debt service, fixed assets) for which a government incurs expenditures. The result is essentially a record of input—of funds (working capital) applied— and the systems described typically do not incorporate information on the goods or services actually rendered to the public or the total resources consumed in doing so. Rather, the emphasis of expendable fund accounting and reporting, especially that for the General Fund and Special Revenue Funds, is upon controlling the expenditure of appropriable resources.

Controlling governmental expenditures is an important aspect of public financial management and accountability, and the current operating expenditure data of General and Special Revenue Funds, in particular, provide important "controllable cost" information by organizational (department or agency) responsibility center and by object of expenditure. However, expenditure data of such funds are not intended to measure total costs since: (1) depreciation is not taken into consideration, (2) purchases of general fixed assets and retirement of general long-term debt are treated as current period expenditures, and (3) overhead costs are not likely to be assigned to operating units or activities.

In contrast to the working capital utilization, or input, approach of appropriation-expenditure accounting, cost accounting and cost finding usually are concerned with measurement of the total costs or expenses incurred by an organization or activity in producing goods or rendering services and, where possible, relating these costs to output in terms of volume and cost per unit of goods produced or services rendered. Both are akin to Enterprise and other proprietary and nonexpendable fund cost measurement rather than to expendable fund appropriable resource flow measurement.

The process of assigning all costs, direct and indirect, to measurable services or products distinguishes both cost accounting and cost finding from expenditure accounting. Calculation of the total and unit cost of the work done is the usual end product of both approaches to costing. Figure 16-15, discussed later, illustrates the relationship of current expenditures and total activity expenses or product costs.

When used without modifiers, both "cost accounting" and "cost finding" refer to the measurement or determination of total and/or per unit long-run historical costs incurred in producing an asset (a building, for example) or costs expired (expenses) in providing a service (e.g., garbage collection and disposal). Thus, long-run historical costing—often referred to as *"full"* or *"absorption"* costing—may be considered "general purpose" costing, and is the usual basis of cost accounting systems or cost finding calculations. Nonroutine or special situation decisions may require derivation of "special purpose" cost data, however, and the use of long-run cost data may be inappropriate and misleading in some circumstances.

Special purpose data of the types described in this and the remaining paragraphs of this section are not normally maintained in the accounts, but are derived on an "as needed" basis from a variety of sources. **Current replacement costs** are more relevant than historical costs in some situations, such as where one is planning to replace specific assets. Too, **opportunity costs**—the benefits forgone by using resources for one purpose rather than another—are often relevant in making choices among alternative courses of action, as when one must decide whether to use a structure for governmental purposes or to sell it and build another elsewhere (or use the sale proceeds for other purposes). In addition, differential or marginal costs often are more relevant to short-run decisions than are long-run full-cost data. **Differential costs** are the total "out-of-pocket" costs involved in changing the level or type of an activity. (**Incremental costs** refer to additional differential costs; **decremental costs** are decreases in differential costs.) **Marginal cost,** on the other hand, is the short-run cost change per unit of increasing or decreasing the level of an existing service or production activity.

Short-run data should be evaluated carefully and used cautiously in governmental decision-making, because decisions based on short-run costs and considerations often become built into the long-run scheme of things and have significant long-run cost effects. Thus, though the cost of paving an additional mile of street is relevant information, the estimated increased maintenance costs this will require in future years is equally relevant to the decision of whether to pave a particular street—and should not be overlooked in the decision process.

Another cost measure, of increasing importance to state and local governments in recent years, is that of allowable or **reimbursable costs.** These costs are those for which the organization will be reimbursed under terms of a grant or contractual agreement, usually with a higher level of government. Reimbursable costs usually are defined in the contract or grant document or by regulation or administrative directive, such as Office of Management and Budget (OMB) Circulars A-21 and A-87. A government's reimbursable cost accounting (or cost finding) situation is analogous to that of a commercial enterprise that must determine both net income for general purpose financial reporting and taxable income for special purpose reporting.[2] Where reimbursable costs are defined in a manner consistent with (or easily reconcilable with) generally accepted accounting principles (GAAP) applicable to either proprietary or governmental funds, they may be determined directly from available records or derived through supplementary

---

[2] It is also analogous to that of a hospital or nursing home that must substantiate medicare reimbursement requests as well as prepare general purpose financial statements, a regulated industry that must prepare both general purpose and prescribed financial reports, or a company whose securities are subject to SEC reporting requirements.

calculations. It is necessary to establish separate special purpose cost accounting records or cost-finding analyses, however, where reimbursable cost stipulations differ materially from applicable GAAP or costing principles. Both types of cost information are relevant in such situations, and one should not be permitted to supplant the other.

In summary, differing cost concepts and measures—either long-run or short-run, and on either a total or per unit basis—may be appropriate in different situations. The distinctions among the various cost concepts and measures, as well as their uses and limitations, should be borne in mind—and care should be exercised to assure that reliable cost data appropriate to the decision or evaluation at hand are made available on a timely basis. To summarize briefly, the four major cost concept categories discussed thus far are:

1. *Budgetary costs*—expendable fund expenditure data available from fund-based financial statements—provide valuable "controllable cost" information by responsibility center and type of expenditure, but do not constitute full costs, though they are often a convenient starting point in cost finding analyses.

2. *Special purpose or short-run costs*—such as replacement, differential, marginal, or opportunity costs—are not normally the basis of ongoing cost accounting systems but are determined on an "as needed" basis.

3. *Reimbursable costs*—stipulated or expressly defined costs—must be determined through cost accounting or cost finding. Reimbursable costs data should not supplant full-cost determinations, or other cost determination per GAAP, where they differ in concept.

4. *Full cost*—also referred to as "total cost" or "absorption cost"—is the cost concept or basis underlying most general purpose, ongoing cost accounting systems and cost finding determinations.

Again, the term "cost," when used without a modifier, should refer to full costing, the fourth cost concept noted above. This is the sense in which that term is used in the remainder of this chapter.

Cost Elements

The components of the total cost of producing a specific product or performing a specific service activity are commonly classified as follows:

1. **Direct labor:** labor costs incurred directly in the production of the good or service that are conveniently traceable thereto.

2. **Direct materials:** costs of materials used directly in the production of goods or services that are conveniently traceable thereto.

3. **Overhead:** indirect labor costs, indirect material costs, and all other costs (such as supervision, minor supplies, rent, utilities, small tools) reasonably associated with provision of the goods or services.

The total of direct labor and direct material costs are commonly referred to as "**prime**" costs; the total of direct labor costs and overhead costs, as "**conversion**" costs. These elements are illustrated in Figure 16-1.

Figure 16-1

COST ELEMENTS

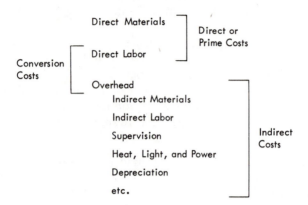

Cost Behavior

Costs may also be categorized according to their behavior patterns at various levels of activity for purposes of analysis, evaluation, and projection. (Such categories are not normally the basis for cost account classification or reporting.) The major classifications of cost by behavior, that is, by changes in total cost occasioned by a change in activity level, are variable, fixed, semivariable, and semifixed. These cost patterns are illustrated graphically in Figure 16-2.

A **fixed** cost factor is one that remains constant over a wide range of activity, that is, the total cost is fixed but the cost per unit of product produced or service provided decreases as the number of units increases. Equipment rental expense of $500 per month is a fixed cost. **Semifixed** or "step" costs are fixed at certain activity levels or ranges but increase to succeedingly higher plateaus as activity increases. Supervision costs, where one foreman is required for every ten laborers or for each shift, is an example of a semifixed or step cost. As more laborers are required or additional work shifts are necessitated by higher levels of activity, total supervision costs increase in steps—but are fixed within specified activity ranges.

Variable costs are fixed per unit within a wide range of activity and thus increase or decrease in direct proportion to the change in activity level. Material that costs $4 per unit or labor that costs $8 per hour are examples of variable costs. **Semivariable** costs are primarily variable but contain some elements of fixed costs at either the low or high end of the activity range. Labor costs, where hourly workers are guaranteed a minimum annual wage, is an example of semi-variable costs that are fixed on the low end of the range; social security or unemployment taxes, where most or all workers exceed the maximum earnings base on which such taxes are computed, illustrate semivariable costs fixed at the high end of the range. A costing system in which only variable costs are capitalized, and in which all fixed costs are considered "period costs" (current expenses), is referred to as "variable costing" or "direct costing." Many Capital Projects Funds are essentially accounted for on a variable cost or direct cost approach—only the

Figure 16-2

COST BEHAVIOR PATTERNS

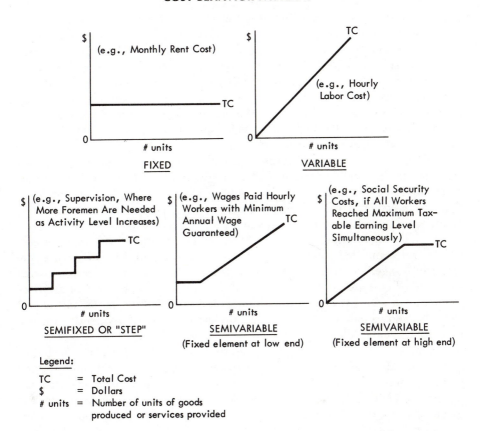

Legend:

TC   = Total Cost
$ = Dollars
# units = Number of units of goods
            produced or services provided

additional costs to the government that are directly related to the project are considered project costs. Reimbursable costs on grants may also be determined on a direct cost basis, with little or no provision for overhead. Variable or direct costing may also provide valuable insight for short-run decision-making purposes.

Where costs may be categorized reliably as between fixed and variable costs, one may readily determine the "break-even" point in situations where revenues are received in direct proportion to goods or services produced or provided. The break-even calculation is based on the assumption that production and sales are in equal quantities and that if one unit is sold another must be acquired to replace it in inventory. Thus, if fixed costs are to be recouped, or a profit realized, this must come from the "contribution margin," the difference between the revenue received per unit and the variable cost of acquiring an additional unit for inventory. For example, if goods or services have a variable cost of $3 per unit and are sold (or reimbursed for) at $5 per unit, the contribution margin is $2 per unit. If the activity through which they are produced incurs fixed overhead and other costs of $8,000 per year, then 4,000 units ($8,000 fixed costs ÷ $2 unit contribution margin) must be produced and/or sold during the year in order for the activity to break-even—for its revenues to exactly equal its total fixed and variable costs. Stated differently, it must have sales or other revenues of $20,000 (4,000 units × $5 unit sales price) in order to cover all costs. Should a profit of $1,000 be desired, one may simply view this as if it were added fixed costs to be recouped, that is, $8,000 fixed costs plus the $1,000 profit must be recouped through the contribution margin, and sales of 4,500 units ($9,000 ÷ $2 unit contribution margin) or $22,500 (4,500 units × $5 unit sales price) must be achieved. Similarly, if the activity receives a subsidy or for other reasons it is desired or necessary to cover only part of its fixed costs, the amount that must be covered by service fees or other charges may be divided by the unit contribution margin to determine the number of units that must be provided and/or sold and the total dollars of sales or other revenues required.

Two additional points concerning cost behavior warrant mention. First, most costs are either fixed or variable within narrow ranges. Thus, the semivariable costs (fixed element at low end) illustrated in Figure 16-2 would be considered fixed if the activity level was near the vertical axis. The more narrow the range of expected activity, therefore, the more likely are the costs to behave in a predictable manner. The expected activity level span over which fixed and variable cost classifications and computations are deemed to be reliable is known as the **"relevant range."** Second, cost behavior patterns are subject to change through time, either because of factor supply and demand shifts or because of a variety of internal or external factors. Both the classifications and dollar amounts of cost factors should be based on thorough analysis and reevaluated frequently to assure their accuracy and reliability.

The remainder of this chapter is devoted to a general discussion of (1) cost accounting, (2) cost finding, and (3) cost analyses. Again, a thorough and detailed presentation of these topics is beyond the scope of this book; the reader desiring a more complete understanding of these subjects is directed to one of the several excellent cost accounting texts available and to the monograph and periodical literature.

COST ACCOUNTING AND COST FINDING—OVERVIEW

The National Committee on Governmental Accounting defined cost accounting as:

> That method of accounting which provides for assembling and recording all the elements of cost incurred to accomplish a purpose, to carry on an activity or operation, or to complete a unit of work or a specific job.[3]

Recall that we earlier indicated a preference for the narrower interpretation of the term; that is, *cost accounting* is used here to refer to a continuous process of analyzing, classifying, recording, and summarizing cost data within the discipline and controls of the formal accounting system and reporting them to users

---

[3] GAAFR (68), p. 157.

on a regular basis. *Cost finding* is the determination or estimation of costs by less formal worksheet and other procedures and/or on an irregular basis.

The usefulness and importance of cost accounting and cost finding to governmental financial planning, management, and evaluation was noted in the introduction to this chapter. The observations of the American Accounting Association Committee on Accounting Practices of Not-for-Profit Organizations regarding society's interest in adequate governmental cost accounting appear equally relevant:

> Cost accounting has long been recognized by those in the profit-oriented environment as a useful tool for promoting efficiency. Yet cost accounting may be even more important in many NFP organizations than in the private sector because (1) all or a broader sector of society's interest may be involved than is the case for a single commercial enterprise, (2) the profit motive is lacking as a regulating device or a measure of operating efficiency in the NFP environment, (3) of the frequent lack of a powerful interest group (such as stockholders) to constantly review and evaluate management's effectiveness, and (4) some NFP organizations, particularly governments, have the power to enforce the extracting of revenues and thus ensure self-perpetuation even when they are inefficient.[4]

Despite widespread recognition of the usefulness of cost data, there is ample opportunity for further implementation of cost accounting systems and cost finding techniques within governments. The same American Accounting Association Committee observed that:

> The potentials of cost accounting techniques have scarcely begun to be realized in the NFP field. . . . NFP accounting has been tailored to fulfill legalistic fund and budgetary requirements and little attention has been given (outside the hospital field and in some NFP-owned utilities and other self-sustaining activities) to developing accrual-based cost accounting.[5]

The essential steps in both cost accounting and cost finding and reporting are to:

1. *Define* the *activities, programs,* or *products to be costed.* One does not do cost accounting or cost finding for "the state of Nebraska" or "Howard County," but for certain of their activities, programs, or products.
2. *Determine* the *relevant cost* measurement, e.g., full cost, direct cost, reimbursable cost, in the circumstances.
3. *Design* an accounting *system or* cost *assembly approach* to capture and accumulate the data needed.
4. *Accumulate* the cost data needed, either through a cost accounting system or by use of appropriate cost finding techniques and procedures.

[4] American Accounting Association, "Report of the Committee on Accounting Practices of Not-for-Profit Organizations," *Accounting Review,* Supplement to Vol. 46 (1971), p. 92.
[5] Ibid.

5. *Report* the cost information in an understandable manner to the appropriate person(s) at the appropriate time(s).

Cost Centers

The identification of cost centers and of activities or products to be costed is a critical step in developing any cost accounting system or cost finding approach. All governments are divided into organizational units. Each unit is typically responsible for a number of activities, and these activities are assigned to organizational subunits. Ideally each subunit would be assigned one activity or operation, and no more than one subunit would be engaged in a given activity. In the usual case the subunit is responsible for several operations or activities within an organizational unit, and two or more subunits are involved in some of the activities. Each cost center has both input and output relative to the activity or activities in which it engages, though the output, in particular, may not be objectively measurable. Many operations not now thought to be objectively measurable may later prove to be objectively measurable, however, and be brought under the control provided by unit cost accounting systems and analyses. Examples of operations and their units of measurement are given at several points later in this chapter.

Basic Costing Approaches

The appropriate approach to cost data accumulation for a cost center depends on the nature of the activity(ies) involved. One of two widely used approaches, referred to as "job order" and "process" costing, respectively, will fit most cost center activity patterns. In a few situations it may be necessary to use both approaches, or a combination of them, in accounting for a single cost center; but the basic nature of the approaches remains unchanged and universal, whether cost accounting or cost finding is involved.

The Job Order Approach. The *job order* approach, illustrated in Figure 16-3, is appropriate where the goods or services produced or provided are of a heterogeneous nature, that is, where they are "tailor made" or "special order" and are separable, discrete activities (jobs). The job order approach in governments is typified by cost accounting systems for construction projects, vehicle repair, and intergovernmental grant activities. It also has application in personal service activities such as building inspection and social welfare casework. Note in studying Figure 16-3 that the job order costing approach involves:

- Accumulating data on all of the costs applied to each job—e.g., data processing batch, social work case, fire inspection, etc.—in appropriate categories, usually direct labor, direct materials, and overhead and other costs.
- Tracking these costs from input to completion of the job being costed.
- Reporting the cost data in an understandable manner to the proper person(s) at the proper time(s).

If the activity costed is a capital project, such as a building, costs may stay in

Figure 16-3

JOB ORDER COSTING APPROACH
General and Subsidiary Ledgers

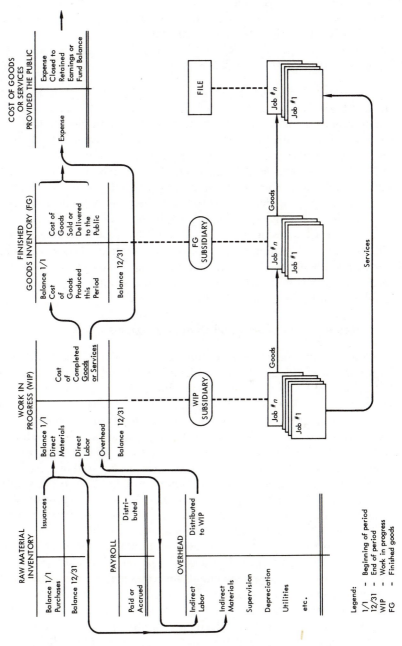

Legend:

1/1 – Beginning of period
12/31 – End of period
WIP – Work in progress
FG – Finished goods

work-in-process a year or more before being completed. If specific tangible items are being manufactured—as in an Internal Service Fund that finances office furnishings manufacture for a state—costs may be in work-in-process and finished goods inventory at most times. In the case of services, however, the costs associated with each client served continue to be recorded in the case record(s) as long as it is active, though the costs of each year may be summarized annually. Case service records are filed as either "active" or "inactive," and often contain service effort, medical, and other records as well as cost data.

The Process Approach. The *process costing* approach is used where many units of homogeneous goods or services are produced in or provided by a cost center characterized by a pattern of routine, repetitive activities, perhaps in mechanized work situations. The process costing approach is illustrated in Figure 16-4. Water purification and distribution systems, sewage collection and disposal, and garbage removal and disposal activities commonly fit this activity costing pattern, as do cashiering, accounting, data processing, and similar activities.

Observe in studying Figure 16-4 that the process being costed typically has several definable steps—e.g., water must be pumped from lakes or underground wells to purification stations, purified, and distributed to consumers, possibly with intermittent pumping and storage in watertanks before reaching its final destination. Should goods be involved, some may be in work-in-process or finished goods inventory at year end. Services, however, are either in process or completed and delivered to their beneficiaries.

Reconciliation of Cost and General Accounts

Cost determination is by definition an important aspect of the accounting for proprietary funds and Nonexpendable Trust Funds. Where activities financed and accounted for through proprietary funds or proprietary-type trust funds are to be costed, the cost accounts are readily made a part of and controlled by the usual accounting system. This is because such funds routinely measure expenses, not expenditures, and most cost accounting systems and cost finding methodologies—whether job order, process, or some combination—are expense-based. Thus, as illustrated in Figure 16-5, the cost accounting system is readily integrated into the proprietary fund financial accounting system. The cost accounting system general ledger accounts—e.g., Raw Material Inventory, Overhead, Work-in-Process, Finished Goods Inventory, and Cost of Goods or Services Provided—fit neatly within the other proprietary fund asset, liability, revenue, and expense accounts. Further, the general ledger accounts provide direct control over the cost accounting subsidiary ledger accounts by service client, project, or activity.

Cost accounting systems under governmental fund general ledger control may be designed and implemented readily (1) where all fixed assets are rented, either from sources external to the government or an Internal Service Fund, no long-term debt service is involved, inventories are accounted for by the consumption (use) method, and there are no significant other differences between fund expenditures and activity expenses; (2) for accumulating construction costs in Capital Projects and Special Assessment Funds, both of which are in large

Figure 16-4

PROCESS COSTING APPROACH
General Ledger

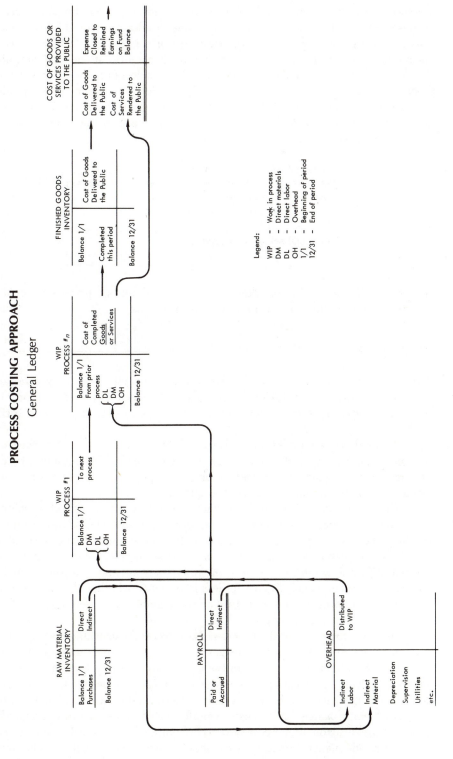

Legend:

WIP	–	Work in process
DM	–	Direct materials
DL	–	Direct labor
OH	–	Overhead
1/1	–	Beginning of period
12/31	–	End of period

measure cost-determination and -control funds; and (3) for reimbursable costing purposes, where the governmental (expendable) fund is accounted for on a basis consistent with grant- or contract-stipulated cost principles. Even where the costing and expenditure accounting bases do not totally conform, it may be practicable to gain effective general ledger control over the cost accounts by a reconciliation process. Assume, for example, that the only difference between proper costing and expenditure accounting in a given situation is that personal services expenditures are recorded on a cash basis. Personal services expenditures and expenses may be reconciled as follows in such a case:

Total personal services charged to expenditure accounts (on the cash basis)	$xxxxxx
Add: Accrued payroll, end of period	xx
Deduct: Accrued payroll, beginning of period	xxx
Total personal services charged to cost accounts	$xxxxxx

Such reconciliations, made on a total object basis, should be prepared regularly in order to assure effective control of the cost accounts.

COST STANDARDS AND VARIANCE ANALYSES

Total and unit cost and cost trend data provided by job order or process cost accounting systems constitute valuable financial management information. The ideal cost accounting system, however, also employs cost standards and variance analyses.

A "standard" is a predetermined criterion by which subsequent performance may be evaluated. A "cost standard" or "standard cost" is the minimum total or per unit cost necessary to complete a project, a phase of a project, or a given program, activity, or unit of work of the quality desired.

The use of poor or inappropriate standards may result in misleading analyses and erroneous evaluations of performance, so standard costs should be determined carefully and reviewed frequently. It is essential, for example, that cost standards established be both representative of efficient (or acceptable) levels of performance and realistically attainable in the work environment or situation subject to standard costing and variance analysis. It is of less importance whether the standards are integrated within the account structure or are maintained in memorandum form, though the former is usually preferable.

The self-study and evaluation necessary to establish viable cost standards is often of significant benefit to management. An even more significant financial management benefit can result from the added postevent evaluation capabilities afforded by variance analysis procedures. *Variance analysis* is the process of determining the nature, magnitudes, and causes of differences between planned and actual performance and/or costs of performance. Whereas only total and/or unit costs are available under cost systems not employing standards, standard cost systems provide information as to "what should have been" as well as "what was."

Figure 16-5

PROCESS COSTING APPROACH
Related to the Accounting Equation

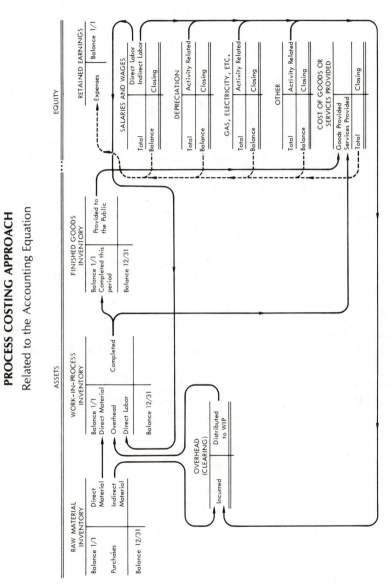

In other words, both the planned or expected and actual total and/or unit costs are known—and deviations between standard and actual costs may be analyzed for clues concerning inefficiency levels and causes, probable cost trends, and methods by which performance may be improved.

Although a detailed discussion of standard costing and variance analysis is beyond the scope of this book, a brief example of its application and usefulness is offered to illustrate its potential in governmental financial management.

Variance Analysis Example

The following simplified example (e.g., $2.00/hr wages) illustrates the essentials of standard cost variance analyses. Assume that a particular activity is deemed satisfactory if 10,000 units of output can be achieved at a cost of $2.00 per unit, or $20,000. This standard is based on the assumption that $\frac{1}{4}$ hour of labor ($2.00/hr) and 3 units of material (at $0.50) are needed to complete one unit. During 19XX 9,600 units were produced at a cost of $2.25 per unit, or $21,000. (Assume also that overhead costs are immaterial.)

The usual steps involved in variance analysis are explained, illustrated, and commented upon briefly below:

First step. Calculate the Total Variance:

Planned Total Cost (9,600 units @ $2.00)	=	$19,200
Actual Total Cost (9,600 units @ $2.25)	=	21,600
Total Variance (Unfavorable)		$ 2,400

(Note: Without a standard, the only data available would be the actual cost of $21,600. Had costs in the preceding year been $24,700, for example, it might appear that this year's performance was "good.")

Second step. The *Total Variance*, $2,400, can be further analyzed by cause through analysis of information on the actual time and material used and determination of unit costs and variances:

Planned cost per unit:
Materials	3@ $ .50	= $1.50	
Labor	$\frac{1}{4}$ hr @ $2.00	= .50	
		$2.00	

Actual cost per unit:
Materials	3 @ $ .60	= $1.80	$ .25 per unit
Labor	$\frac{1}{5}$ @ $2.25	= .45	Unfavorable (UF)
		$2.25	Variance

Unit Cost Variance may now be separated:

Materials:	$1.80 − $1.50 =	$ .30	UF
Labor:	$ .50 − $ .45 =	.05	Favorable (F)
		$ .25	UF

Third step. An analysis such as the following provides even more insight as to the underlying causes of these variances:

Materials

	Standard	at	Standard		
	3		.50	= $1.50	
	Actual	at	Standard		Use Variance = $0
	3		.50	= 1.50	
	Actual	at	Actual		Price Variance = $0.30 UF
	3		.60	= 1.80	

Total Materials Variance $ .30 UF per unit

Labor

	Standard	at	Standard		
	$\frac{1}{4}$		$2.00	= $ .50	
	Actual	at	Standard		Time Variance = $0.10 F
	$\frac{1}{5}$		$2.00	= .40	
	Actual	at	Actual		Pay rate
	$\frac{1}{5}$		$2.25	= .45	Variance = 0.05 UF

Total Labor Variance $ .05 F per unit

A Word of Caution

Although we emphasize the potential benefits of standard costing and variance analysis to governmental financial management, they do not constitute a panacea. Standard costing and variance analysis techniques can be no better than the standards themselves. Moreover, variance analyses do not provide "pat" answers, but offer clues or "leads" to areas warranting management attention.

An unfavorable variance is not always "bad," nor is a favorable variance always "good." One often must be intimately familiar with a specific project or activity to analyze the variances in sufficient depth to evaluate underlying causes of variation, their near-term significance, and their probable long-range implications. Thus, the unfavorable materials price variance in the example above could be the result either of inefficient purchasing or of excellent purchasing performance, such as by the purchasing department having provided the required quality of material at $0.60 per unit during a period in which the general market price of the item in question spurted to $0.70 per unit from the $0.50 per unit expected (standard) cost. Likewise, the favorable pay rate variance might reflect (1) increased efficiency resulting from use of more skilled workers whose greater productivity more than offsets the increased rate of pay they command, or (2) a temporary increase in productivity of the usual work force resulting from an overall wage boost—with the work force expected to return to lower, more normal productivity levels in the near future—which carries unfavorable long-range cost connotations.

COST FINDING

Many of the advantages of cost accounting may be obtained without a complete "full" cost accounting information system. Further, as noted earlier, "full" cost is not relevant to every decision or information need. For the preparation of the budget, for example, information and estimates based on the expenditure accounts may be more useful than costs containing elements (for example, depreciation) that are not budgeted. Similarly, control of costs by top administrators may be just as easy, or perhaps easier, if the costs for which a supervisor is held responsible consist only of those elements over which he has control ("controllable costs"). A supervisor can control such direct costs as personnel and materials; but depreciation expenses may have been determined by his superior or his predecessor, and overhead costs assigned to his operations usually are not subject to his control. Thus, control over costs at the point where they are incurred ordinarily does not require knowledge of total cost, though a "controllable cost" accounting system may be needed.

Attaining most of the other advantages of cost accounting noted at the beginning of this chapter requires knowledge of total costs, but having this information made available routinely through a formal cost accounting system may not be essential to effective day-to-day administration. Among the activities for which information need be available only periodically or occasionally are decisions as to whether the city's work force should do a job or whether it should be contracted; setting service charges and cost-justification of service charges; negotiating contracts for services rendered by the city to other governments, institutions, or major businesses; reporting to officials and the public; determination of the cost of fixed assets constructed; and determining the costs of certain activities or programs.

Basic Cost Finding Approaches

Cost finding, as contrasted with cost accounting, has been described as the determination or estimation of costs, however defined, by less formal procedures and/or on an irregular basis. In the usual case it involves taking available fund expenditure or other data and adjusting, recasting, supplementing, and manipulating it in order to derive the cost data or estimate sought.

The illustration in Figure 16-6, "Reconciliation of Expenditures and Costs or Expenses," might well have been titled "The Usual Governmental Cost Finding Approach," since it serves as a general cost finding model as well as to illustrate the reconciliation of expenditures and costs or expenses. To illustrate utilization of the cost finding approach, assume that the street maintenance function is financed through the General Fund, that it is desired to derive the *expense* of operating that department's vehicle fleet, and that the following information has been gathered from a variety of sources:

1. Total expenditures for vehicle acquisition, operation, and maintenance during the period were $72,000.
2. Of this total, $20,000 was for new vehicle acquisition and $8,000 was for major overhauls that should be capitalized; the balance was for routine maintenance.
3. Depreciation of the vehicles has been calculated at $84,000.
4. Maintenance expenditures of $1,000 were made for supplies not used this period; supplies acquired in prior periods but used for maintenance this period cost $4,000.

5. Insurance premiums for policies on all vehicles are paid through a Special Revenue Fund; the portion expired this period and applicable to the street maintenance vehicle fleet is determined to be $2,000.

Cost Calculation:

Total *Expenditures*, this period		$ 72,000
Less: Expenditures benefiting other periods:		
Acquisition of new vehicles	$20,000	
Major Overhauls	8,000	
Purchase of supplies not used this period	1,000	29,000
Current Period Expenditures		$ 43,000
Plus: Expenditures of other periods benefiting this period:		
Depreciation of vehicles	$84,000	
Supplies purchased previously but used this period .	4,000	
Insurance expense	2,000	90,000
Total *Expense*, this period		$133,000

This general approach is useful in all situations where the basic records available are expenditure-based and expense or cost data is desired. It is equally useful in determining reimbursable, controllable, direct (prime), variable, or other costs from expenditure-based data. Note also in the above example that total expenditures and total expenses were far different, indicating the severity of the potential error of anyone confusing these two very different concepts in either total or per unit calculations.

This general approach may also be used in reverse, that is, to convert expense data to expenditure data. This may be appropriate when considering whether to continue to account for an operation (e.g., a marginal enterprise) through a proprietary fund or to consider it a "general government" activity and account for it through the General or a Special Revenue Fund and the General Fixed Assets and/or General Long-Term Debt Account Groups.

More Complex Cost Finding Situations

In more complex cost finding situations it may be necessary, or at least helpful, to use one or more worksheets like that illustrated in Figure 16-7. This worksheet is designed to systematize the data accumulations and calculations illustrated in Figure 16-6. Where several departments participate in the activity being costed, a worksheet such as that illustrated in Figure 16-7 may be used to determine the relevant costs in each department, then to summarize the data for all departments to determine the total activity cost. The departmental worksheets should be supported by appropriate detailed schedules, such as of depreciation (4) and of expenses financed in other funds (6). In more complex cost-finding situations it often will be appropriate to prepare supporting schedules for most, if not all, of the columns numbered (2) to (6) in the worksheet in Figure 16-7. Further, standardized supporting schedule worksheets, such as the depreciation worksheet illustrated in Figure 16-8, may be helpful in more complex cost finding situations.

Care must be taken to include all relevant costs in cost finding exercises.

Figure 16-6

RECONCILIATION OF EXPENDITURES AND COSTS OR EXPENSES

(Activity Financed Through Expendable Fund)

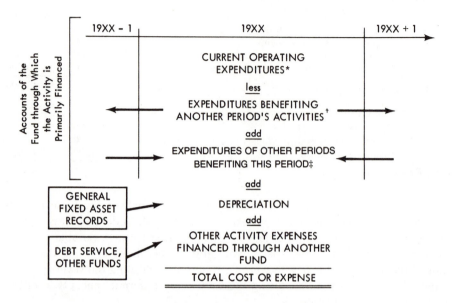

* *Excludes debt principal retirement and capital outlay expenditures.*

† *For example, prepaid insurance and inventory adjustments where expenditures are recorded on a "purchases" basis and other accrual and deferral adjustments for items reflected in the Expenditures account for the period that are applicable to previous or future periods.*

‡ *Adjustments for items such as those that are reflected in the Expenditures account in a previous or future period but are applicable to 19XX.*

For example, personnel costs recorded in a Special Revenue or Capital Projects Fund may not include payroll tax, pension, and other fringe benefit costs paid through the General Fund. Similarly, the materials and supplies expenditures may be recorded on the purchases basis rather than on the use basis. Further, some personnel and overhead costs properly allocable to the activity being costed may not be routinely allocated as an activity cost.

Allocating Costs to Activities

Two types of costs usually warrant careful attention and analysis in more complex cost finding situations: (1) personnel costs and (2) overhead costs.

Personnel Costs. Some personnel work full time in a single activity, whereas others work in several activities. Thus, assuming that all salary, wage, and related costs of personnel associated with an activity have been identified, there often remains the matter of determining the portion of one or more employee's time and payroll costs that should be allocated to the activity.

Public sector employees often do not keep detailed records of how their time is utilized. Thus, it may be necessary to use the best estimates available to

Figure 16-7

CITY OF _____

Cost Allocation Plan
Schedule for the Conversion of Expenditures to Expenses

| Department/Program | Total Expenditures (1) | Deductions | | | Additions | | Total Expenses (7) |
		Capital Outlay (2)	Other Period Expenses Paid in Current Period (3)	Depreciation (4)	Current Period Expenses Paid in Other Period (5)	Expenses Financed in Other Funds (6)	
Total							

Source: William W. Holder and Rick Kerner, _Cost Accounting for California Cities_ (Sacramento: League of California Cities, 1981), p. 62.

Figure 16-8

DEPRECIATION WORKSHEET

Program/Department _____

Cost Center _____

FY _____

Group	Assets					Depreciation			
	Begin. (1)	Add (2)	Deduct (3)	Ending (4)	Accum. Begin. (5)	Rate (6)	Current Year Add (7)	Deduct (8)	Accum. Ending (9)
Buildings						0.03			
Improvements other than building landscaping						0.20			
Subtotal						///			
Machinery and Equipment									
Office furniture						0.10			
Office equipment (including data processing)						0.20			
Vehicles						0.33			
Maintenance and grounds equipment						0.20			
Radios						0.20			
Recreation and park equipment						0.20			
Computer software						0.33			
Subtotal						///			
"Public Domain" Fixed Assets									
Street surfaces						0.10			
Curbs, gutters, and sidewalks						0.04			
Storm drains—concrete						0.02			
Sewers—concrete						0.02			
Street lights						0.04			
Traffic signals						0.10			
Subtotal						///			
Total						///			

Source: William W. Holder and Rick Kermer, *Cost Accounting for California Cities* (Sacramento: League of California Cities, 1981), p. 61.

prorate their time and costs among the various activities in which they are engaged. Often the best estimate is not the officially budgeted allocation of the person's time but that person's estimate of how his time has been spent.

Overhead Costs. Two problems are associated with overhead cost allocation. The first is which overhead costs should be allocated to the activity; the second is how the overhead costs should be allocated.

The issue of which overhead costs should be assigned to an activity is best explained by an example. Assume that the activity being costed is one of several in the police department. Is the office of the Chief of Police to be considered a separately reportable cost (e.g., administration) or should it (and other administrative activities) be considered part of the overhead costs to be allocated to the several direct service activities of the police department? If the latter, should only the direct costs of police department administration be considered allocable to police activities, or should part of the city's overall administrative costs be allocated to the police department administrative costs and the total then allocated to the police department direct service activities?

There are two theoretical viewpoints on this question. The first is that (1) all activities are either direct services activities or supporting services activities, and (2) all costs should be calculated for both direct services and supporting services activities, then the costs of the supporting services activities should be allocated in a systematic and rational manner to the direct services activities. The other view is that at least the major administrative activities, such as those of the mayor and council, are direct services activities and their cost should not be allocated to other activities. Supporters of this view also note that attempting to allocate all supporting services costs, including administration, to direct services activities involves so many arbitrary allocations that the resulting data may be of limited value.

The correct view, in the authors' opinion, depends on the objective of the cost finding endeavor. If it is to produce a highly condensed report to the public of the costs of the several major functions or programs comprised of the numerous activities costed, then it would seem that accounting and most other administrative activities should be allocated to the direct services activities. However, city leadership costs (mayor, commission, council, etc.) probably should be reported as direct services activities. If the objective is to determine the cost of a specific activity(ies) for internal decision-making use, it would seem that only the "relevant" costs, those that would change if the activity(ies) were discontinued, should be of concern. In any event, it clearly is important that a policy decision on this matter be made early in the cost finding process.

Assuming that the costs of the various activities of a government have been determined—and the activities have been categorized as either direct services or supporting services—there remains the matter of how the costs of the supporting services activities should be allocated to the direct services activities. Several approaches of varying complexity and accuracy are available:

- *Simultaneous equations method.* This method recognizes that supporting services activities serve each other as well as the direct services activities. An equation describing each supporting service—in terms of its cost and the percentage of each other supporting service it re-ceives—is written, together with equations for each direct services activity based on its cost and the percentages of each supporting services activity it utilizes. The allocations of supporting service costs among each other, and then to the direct services activities, are accomplished by solving these simultaneous equations. This method is conceptually the most accurate but is complex and requires use of computerized techniques when many equations are involved.

- *"Step-down" method.* This method allocates the costs of the supporting services activities receiving the least services from the other support-ing services activities, in order, to the other supporting services and direct services activities until all costs have been allocated to the direct services activities. This method is less accurate, and less complex, than the simultaneous equations method, usually yields reasonable results, and is perhaps the most widely used allocation method in practice.

- *Direct method.* This method allocates supporting services costs directly to direct services activities, ignoring the fact that supporting services activities render services to, or receive them from, other supporting services activities. The direct allocation method is simpler, but less accurate, than the step-down method, but may yield reasonable results in some situations.

- *Consolidated method.* Under this method all government overhead costs are "pooled" and allocated to all direct services cost centers as a uniform percentage of some cost common to all direct services centers (such as payroll cost) or by the ratio that the direct costs of each services cost center is to the total direct costs of all direct services centers. This method is the least reliable, but simplest, of the four methods.

Detailed consideration of each of these allocation methods is beyond the scope of this text.[6] It is important, however, that an appropriate method that yields reasonable results be selected.

CONCLUDING COMMENTS

As noted at the first of this chapter, governmental cost accounting, finding, and analysis have taken on increased importance in recent years and are apt to be even more important in the years to come. Yet, though many governments have sophisticated proprietary fund cost accounting systems, the development of gov-ernmental cost accounting, finding, and analysis generally has lagged behind their development in private business.

Governments, like businesses, must be able to adapt quickly to rapidly changing economic conditions and political climates. Cost accounting, finding, and analysis are extremely helpful tools to government managers seeking ways to understand and evaluate existing activities, increase productivity, establish and justify reasonable service charges, make reasoned "make or buy" and "do or

[6] For an excellent discussion and illustration of these methods, see Holder and Kermer, op. cit.

contract" decisions, adapt to decreased grant funding or a declining tax base, and generally better manage state and local governments.

Finally, although this chapter is addressed specifically to cost accounting, finding, and analysis for state and local governments, the major concepts and techniques discussed are equally applicable to the Federal government, colleges and universities, hospitals, and other not-for-profit organizations discussed in later chapters of this book. Cost accounting, finding, and analysis are extremely important to (and well developed in) hospitals, for example, and Chapter 18 includes a hospital cost finding example. The Federal government agency accounting model includes cost (expense) accounts and is very adaptive to cost accounting, as is that used by voluntary health and welfare and other nonprofit organizations; and the current funds of colleges and universities, expendable funds like the General and Special Revenue Funds of state and local governments, are particularly suited for cost finding and analysis.

▶ **Question 16-1.** Explain the meaning of the statement made in the chapter that "every decision affecting future resource allocation—and each evaluation of past resource utilization—necessarily involves either implicit or explicit comparison of the costs incurred, or to be incurred, with the benefits received or expected."

Question 16-2. What is the principal difference between financial accounting generally and cost accounting? Between cost accounting and cost finding?

Question 16-3. How do *budgetary* costs differ from *full* costs?

Question 16-4. Fixed costs are variable per unit and variable costs are fixed per unit. Explain.

Question 16-5. Distinguish between the following terms:

(a) Replacement cost and opportunity cost

(b) Marginal cost and differential cost

(c) Incremental cost and decremental cost

(d) Process costs and controllable costs

(e) Reimbursable costs and job order costs

(f) Fixed costs and variable costs

(g) Semifixed costs and semivariable costs

(h) Direct costs and indirect costs

(i) Prime cost and conversion cost

(j) Short-run costs and long-run costs

(k) Absorption costing and variable (or "direct") costing

(l) Relevant cost center and relevant range

Question 16-6. Discuss the desirability of a cost accounting system as compared with a cost finding system.

Question 16-7. Do you think that a cost finding system should be used in a municipality? For all activities? Characterize the types of activities for which you think cost finding is suitable.

Question 16-8. Mention at least three factors that are likely to make the unit cost of collecting and hauling garbage in two cities differ.

Question 16-9. What are cost *standards* and of what value are they in municipal cost accounting?

Question 16-10. What are the major benefits and limitations of standard costing?

Question 16-11. "The existence of an effective costing system is a prerequisite to an effective performance budgeting system." Discuss.

Question 16-12. Why is it important that reimbursable costing, though necessary, not be permitted to supplant cost determination on another basis?

Question 16-13. A city operates both an electric utility and a water utility. The electric utility uses water to generate steam, and the water utility uses electricity for pumping purposes. If both utilities make a sufficient profit each year from sales of services to customers to provide the money necessary for the retirement of bonds, should the charges made by the electric utility to the water utility (or vice versa) for services be sufficiently high to yield a profit or should they be limited to the cost of rendering the service (exclusive of profits)?

Question 16-14. Indicate some of the dangers inherent in relying upon short-run cost data in decision-making.

Question 16-15. After reading an article you recommended on cost behavior, your client asks you to explain the following excerpts from it:

(a) "*Fixed costs* are variable per unit of output and *variable costs* are fixed per unit of output (though in the long run all costs are variable)."

(b) "*Depreciation* may be either a fixed cost or a variable cost, depending on the method used to compute it."

Required:

For each excerpt:

(a) Define the terms in italics. Give examples where appropriate.

(b) Explain the meaning of the excerpt to your client.

   (AICPA, adapted)

▶ **Problem 16-1.** (Cost finding methodology) The City of Marianne finance director wants to prepare expense-based condensed summary financial statements to supplement the county's 19X4 annual financial statements prepared in conformity with generally accepted accounting principles. The cost categories in the report are to be: City Management and Administration, Fire, Police, Court, Recreation, and Other. The City of Marianne fiscal year is the calendar year.

Additional information:

1. General Fund expenditures for the year were:

	Current Operations	Capital Outlay	Debt Service	Total
Court	$ 124,500	$ 6,400		$ 130,900
Council/Mayor	88,400	8,600		97,000

	Current Operations	Capital Outlay	Debt Service	Total
Manager	93,700	6,700		100,400
Finance	123,400	12,400	$7,000	142,800
Personnel	51,600	6,700		58,300
Building and Maintenance	104,900	44,300		149,200
Fire	$1,259,800	241,000		1,500,800
Police	1,400,700	24,700		1,425,400
Recreation	89,900	12,900		102,800
Other	177,600	4,800		182,400
	$3,514,500	$368,500	$7,000	$3,890,000

2. The police, fire, and recreation departments are in separate buildings; all other departments and functions are housed in the city hall. The debt service on these facilities, paid through Debt Service Funds, and the depreciation on the buildings, calculated from General Fixed Assets records, are:

Building	Principal	Interest	Depreciation
City Hall	$300,000	$200,000	$435,000
Police	—	—	187,500
Fire	200,000	100,000	193,000
Recreation	60,000	40,000	62,000

The $7,000 debt service charged against the Finance Department was for open note borrowing during the year and should be reported as "Other."

3. Building and Maintenance current operations expenditures include annual fire insurance premiums for all buildings, which were paid July 1, 19X4; the rates of the preceding year were 10 percent lower than those for 19X4.

Building	One-Year Insurance Policy Premium
City Hall	$ 5,000
Fire	3,500
Police	3,500
Recreation	2,000
	$14,000

4. Amounts of current operating expenditures constituting prepayments of subsequent year expenses, excluding insurance premiums, were:

	12/31/X3	12/31/X4
Court	$ 1,500	2,500
Council/Mayor	—	4,000
Manager	1,000	—

Finance	2,000	3,500
Personnel	1,500	—
Building & Maintenance	4,000	1,000
Fire	6,400	8,500
Police	7,500	3,300
Recreation	1,500	2,000
Other	—	1,000
	$25,400	$25,800

5. Depreciation of equipment was calculated from General Fixed Assets records as follows:

Court	$ 10,000
Council/Mayor	15,000
Manager	18,000
Finance	74,000
Personnel	31,000
Building & Maintenance	5,000
Fire	37,000
Police	38,500
Recreation	12,500
Other	20,000
	$261,000

The city's policy is to record no depreciation in the year a fixed asset is acquired and a full year's depreciation in the year of its replacement or retirement.

6. Payroll costs are reflected in the expenditure data in item 1, but employee hospital insurance, retirement system contributions, and other fringe benefit payments by the city on behalf of city employees were paid through another fund. These were:

Court	$ 24,600
Council/Mayor	19,500
Manager	20,200
Finance	24,400
Personnel	11,300
Building & Maintenance	21,000
Fire	249,400
Police	261,600
Recreation	13,100
Other	4,900
	$650,000

7. The city hall is divided approximately as follows:

	Percent
Court	14
Council/Mayor	8

	Percent
Manager	15
Finance	22
Personnel	24
Other	17
	100

The finance director considers it appropriate to allocate all building-related expenses in accordance with space usage. Maintenance of the police, fire, and recreation buildings is included in expenditures for these departments.

8. Expenses of the Council/Mayor, Manager, Finance, and Personnel departments are allocable as follows:

Department	Court	Fire	Police	Recreation	Other	City Mgt.
Council/Mayor	10	10	10	10	10	50
Manager	5	15	15	15	10	40
Finance	15	20	20	15	10	20
Personnel	10	25	25	20	15	5

Required:

(a) Prepare a schedule, such as that illustrated in Figure 16-7, to convert the expenditure data to expense data for the ten departments.

(b) Allocate the expenses to cost categories specified by the finance director and prepare a Cost of Services statement to accompany the 19X4 GAAP financial statements.

Problem 16-2. (Cost projection) In 19X1 the Hometown Construction Company was awarded a contract to construct a civic center for the City of Lyleston. The contract was for $2,730,000, with an escalator clause for changes in labor rates. The contract price was based on estimated costs plus a 5 percent markup, and contained a provision to the effect that "in no event shall Hometown Construction Company be reimbursed for less than its reasonable total costs" of constructing the facility. At year end the following information is available:

1. Construction labor was originally estimated at 92,000 hours at an average rate of $7.00 per hour. To date 65,800 hours have been expended by the labor force and it is estimated that an additional 65,000 will be needed to complete the job.

2. Effective January 1, 19X2, the construction force union contract provides for a 4 percent increase in the basic hourly rate.

3. Material costs were originally estimated at $1,375,000. Purchase orders totaling $1,250,000 for 90 percent of the material have been placed. The remaining materials will cost 7 percent more than originally estimated because of general price increases.

4. The electrical work estimated at $130,000 was subcontracted for $127,500.

5. In a supplemental contract it was agreed that the air-conditioning equipment

installed would be modified at a contract price of $42,000. The subcontractor estimated his cost at $40,000 for this extra work.

6. Costs incurred to date aggregate $1,605,500.

Required:

Prepare an estimate at December 31, 19X1, of the probable final cost of the civic center to the City of Lyleston.

(AICPA, adapted)

Problem 16-3. (Revenue and expense estimates; pro forma operating statement) The Metropolitan Area Transit Authority, Inc., has been established to inaugurate express bus service between the City of Thorne and a nearby suburb (one-way fare $.50) and is considering the purchase of either 32- or 52-passenger buses, on which pertinent estimates are as follows:

	32-Passenger Bus	52-Passenger Bus
Number of each to be purchased	6	4
Useful life	8 years	8 years
Purchase price of each bus	$80,000	$110,000
Mileage per gallon of fuel	5	3
Salvage value per bus	$ 6,000	$ 7,000
Drivers' hourly wage	$ 5.50	$ 6.20
Price per gallon of fuel	$ 1.30	$ 1.30
General and administrative expenses ...	$44,000	$ 44,000
Other annual cash expenses	$ 5,000	$ 3,000
Maintenance cost per mile	$ 0.12	$ 0.15

The buses would be in operation five days per week generally, but the routes would not be run during weekends or on major holidays. During the four daily rush hours all buses would be in service and are expected to operate at full capacity (state law prohibits standees) in both directions of the route, each bus covering the route twelve times (six round trips) during that period. During the remainder of the sixteen-hour day, it is estimated that 500 passengers would be carried and Thorne would operate only four buses on the route. Part-time drivers would be employed to drive the extra hours during the rush hours. A bus traveling the route all day would go 480 miles and one traveling only during rush hours would go 120 miles a day during the 260-day year.

Required:

Prepare a pro forma (estimated) statement of annual operations (revenue and expense) for the Thorne Metropolitan Area Transit Authority, Inc., accompanied by schedules of estimated annual revenue, estimated annual drivers' wages, and estimated annual cost of fuel.

(AICPA, adapted)

Problem 16-4. (Cost and revenue projection: marginal income; break-even) The Ruidoso County Park and Recreation Authority operates a ski shop, restaurant, and lodge during the 120-day ski season from November 15 to March 15. The administrator is considering changing the manner of operations and keeping the lodge open all year. Results of the operations for the year ended March 15, 19X7, were as follows:

	Ski Shop		Restaurant		Lodge	
	Amount	Percent	Amount	Percent	Amount	Percent
Revenue:	$27,000	100	$40,000	100	$108,000	100
Costs:						
Cost of goods						
sold	$14,850	55	$24,000	60		
Supplies	1,350	5	4,000	10	$ 7,560	7
Utilities	270	1	1,200	3	8,640	8
Salaries	3,620	13	12,000	30	32,400	30
Insurance	810	3	800	2	9,720	9
Property taxes						
on building ..	540	2	1,600	4	6,480	6
Depreciation ...	1,080	4	2,000	5	28,080	26
Total costs ...	$22,520	83	$45,600	114	$92,880	86
Net income or						
(loss)	$ 4,480	17	$(5,600)	(14)	$15,120	14

1. The lodge has 50 rooms and the rate from November 15 to March 15 is $20 per day for one or two persons. The occupancy rate from November 15 to March 15 is 90 percent.

2. The administrator is considering keeping the lodge open from March 15 to November 15. The ski shop would be converted into a gift shop if the lodge should be operated during this period with conversion costs of $1,000 in March and $1,000 in November each year. It is estimated that revenues from the gift shop would be the same per room occupied as revenues from the ski shop. The occupancy rate of the lodge at a room rate of $10 per day is estimated at 50 percent during the period from March 15 to November 15 whether or not the restaurant is operated.

Required:

(Use 30 days per month for computational purposes.)

(a) Prepare a projected income statement for the ski shop and lodge from November 15, 19X7, to March 15, 19X8, assuming that the restaurant is closed during this period and all facilities are closed during the remainder of the year.

(b) Assume that all facilities will continue to be operated during the four-month period of November 15 to March 15 of each year.

  1. Assume that the lodge is operated during the eight months from March 15 to November 15. Prepare an analysis which indicates the projected marginal income or loss of operating the gift shop and lodge during the 8-month period.

  2. Compute the minimum room rate which should be charged to allow the lodge to break even during the eight months from March 15 to November 15 assuming the gift shop and restaurant are not operated during this period.

(AICPA, adapted)

Problem 16-5. (Variance analysis) You are preparing your report in connection with the examination of City Gas Company at December 31, 19X7. The report will include an explanation of the 19X7 increase in operating revenues. The following information is available from the company records:

	19X6	19X7	Increase (Decrease)
Average number of customers	27,000	26,000	(1,000)
MCF sales	486,000	520,000	34,000
Revenue	$1,215,000	$1,274,000	$59,000

Required:

Prepare an explanation of the 19X7 increase in operating revenues, accompanied by an analysis accounting for the effect of changes in:

1. Average number of customers
2. Average gas consumption per customer
3. Average rate per MCF sold (MCF = thousand cubic feet)

Problem 16-6. (Cost determination; cost statements) The City of Y operates a central equipment bureau, renting out the equipment to various departments as needed. The following is a condensed statement of the expenses and miles or hours of use of each piece of equipment for the year ending December 31, 19X0:

Equipment No.	Operating Expenses	Mainte- nance Expenses	Other Expenses	Miles or Hours* Used	Rental Rate per Mile or Hour*
1	$ 93	$ 71	$284	4,210	$0.1215
2	135	142	187	7,812	0.0903
3	127	99	260	2,712*	0.4464*
4	436	347	149	5,140*	0.3600*
5	288	124	178	3,260*	0.3402*
6	161	70	209	11,140	0.0560
7	355	650	693	541*	2.0028*

The equipment was used during the year by the following departments, among others, which were charged at the rental rates indicated above:

Equipment No.	Department Using the Equipment	Miles or Hours* Used
1	Mayor	4,210
2	Department of Public Safety:	
	Division of Weights and Measures .	3,712
	Department of Health:	
	Food and Sanitary Division	4,100
3	Department of Public Works:	
	Division of Construction and Repairs:	
	Job B	600*
	Job C	300*
	Job D	1,500*

4	Department of Public Works:	
	Bureau of Streets and Alleys	5,112*
5	Department of Public Works:	
	Bureau of Streets and Alleys	1,210*
	Bureau of Sewers	1,712*
6	Department of Health:	
	Nursing Division	5,200
	Board of Elections	2,315
	Department of Law	3,625
7	Department of Public Works:	
	Bureau of Street Cleaning:	
	Street A	150*
	Street B	175*
	Street C	200*

Required:

(a) Prepare a statement showing the cost of operating each piece of equipment, the earnings for each piece, and the net profit or loss, for the year ending December 31, 19X0.

(b) Prepare a statement showing for each organization unit the number of miles or hours worked for it by each piece of equipment, the amount charged to it on account of the use of each piece, and the total charges to it on account of equipment use.

(c) Prepare a statement showing the amounts charged to the various construction and repair jobs and to the streets cleaned.

Problem 16-7. (Cost finding and unit cost determination) On the basis of the following data, prepare a statement for the City of R for the year ending June 30, 19X1, showing the total cost of refuse collection and the cost per ton or cubic yard, as the case may be (carry unit costs to three decimal places).

	Garbage	Rubbish
By City Forces:		
Salaries and wages	$512,000	$215,000
Materials and supplies	$ 32,000	$ 28,800
Equipment use*	$116,050	$ 70,500
Tons collected	193,000	—
Cubic yards collected	—	312,000
By Contract:		
Cost	$ 81,600	$ 16,400
Tons collected	27,000	—
Cubic yards collected	—	26,000

Includes depreciation and rentals, but excludes capital outlays of $231,586. The equipment has a composite useful life of seven years.

Overhead is calculated at an additional 12 percent of total direct costs in the case of city force collection and 5 percent in the case of collection by contract.

PART II

FEDERAL AND INSTITUTIONAL ACCOUNTING AND REPORTING

17

FEDERAL GOVERNMENT ACCOUNTING

The Federal Government of the United States is engaged in an unparalleled number and variety of functions, programs, and activities both here and abroad. It is the country's biggest employer and its biggest consumer. One of every 33 citizens is an employee of its myriad agencies. Federal disbursements were estimated at $564 billion during 1980, up about twelve-fold from 1950, and now exceed $750 billion. Federal Government purchases of goods and services now comprise about 24 percent of our gross national product.

Federal accounting is similar to that of state and local governments because it is heavily influenced by law and regulation. It serves as a major tool of fund and appropriation control at both the central government and agency levels. But it is noticeably different in that (1) the agency or department is generally considered the primary accounting entity, (2) agency accounting provides—via "dual-track" systems—for both expenditure and expense accounting and reporting, and (3) accounting is concerned with budgetary and financial operations (and financial position) of the Government as a whole *and* of individual agencies.

Thus, the accounting system of the Federal Government must be, and is, composed of many sets of systems and subsystems. Complete financial data are to be maintained for each agency by its system; financial reports are to be prepared by the agency. Financial reports for the Government as a whole are compiled by the Treasury Department's Bureau of Financial Operations from the central accounts and from monthly reports submitted to it by the agencies.

THE FEDERAL FINANCIAL MANAGEMENT ENVIRONMENT

The importance of budgeting, accounting, and reporting to governmental financial management and accountability was recognized by those drafting the Constitution

663

of the United States. Thus, they included a mandate (Article I, Section 9) that:

> No money shall be drawn from the treasury, but in consequence of appropriations made by law; and a regular statement and account of the receipts and expenditures of all public money shall be published from time to time.

From the outset, therefore, financial management was seen as a shared function of the legislative and executive branches of the Federal Government. Then as now, the "power of the purse string" was vested in Congress, while the executive branch was charged with administering the activities of the Government and reporting on its stewardship both to the Congress and to the public.

Financial Management Roles and Responsibilities

The general outlines of the individual and shared financial management roles and responsibilities within the Federal Government, apparent in the legislation cited above, are summarized in Figure 17-1. The major financial management roles and responsibilities of the legislative and executive branches are discussed below briefly in the following order:

> Legislative Branch
>   Congress
>   General Accounting Office (Comptroller General)
>   Congressional Budget Office
> Executive Branch
>   President
>   Office of Management and Budget
>   Secretary of the Treasury
>   Federal Agencies
> Joint
>   Joint Financial Management Improvement Program

Congress. Authority for all programs of the executive branch rests with the Congress, which also provides for their financing through the enactment of appropriations. Although the President *proposes* programs and appropriations through the executive budget, the Congress enacts the *actual* budget, which is invariably different from the executive budget.

Congress also exercises general oversight over the executive branch by means of committee investigations, budgetary and other hearings, and audits and other studies by the General Accounting Office.

General Accounting Office (GAO). A multitude of roles and responsibilities have been assigned to the GAO—headed by the Comptroller General of the United States—since its inception in 1921. Among these roles and responsibilities are:

> 1. *Assisting the Congress in the general oversight of the executive branch.* Though all GAO activites are related to this purpose, specific activities related hereto include (a) assigning staff members to assist Congres-

Figure 17-1 FEDERAL FINANCIAL MANAGEMENT ROLES AND RESPONSIBILITIES—A SUMMARY

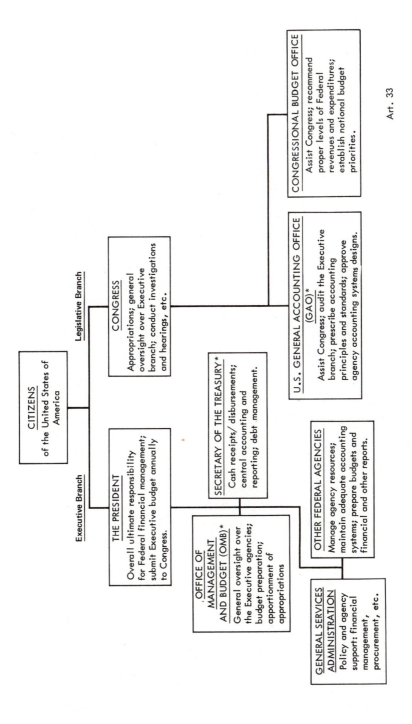

Executive Branch

Legislative Branch

CITIZENS
of the United States of America

THE PRESIDENT
Overall ultimate responsibility for Federal financial management; submit Executive budget annually to Congress.

CONGRESS
Appropriations; general oversight over Executive branch; conduct investigations and hearings, etc.

OFFICE OF MANAGEMENT AND BUDGET (OMB)*
General oversight over the Executive agencies; budget preparation; apportionment of appropriations

SECRETARY OF THE TREASURY*
Cash receipts/ disbursements; central accounting and reporting; debt management.

GENERAL SERVICES ADMINISTRATION
Policy and agency support: financial management, procurement, etc.

OTHER FEDERAL AGENCIES
Manage agency resources; maintain adequate accounting systems; prepare budgets and financial and other reports.

U.S. GENERAL ACCOUNTING OFFICE (GAO)*
Assist Congress; audit the Executive branch; prescribe accounting principles and standards; approve agency accounting systems designs.

CONGRESSIONAL BUDGET OFFICE
Assist Congress; recommend proper levels of Federal revenues and expenditures; establish national budget priorities.

Art. 33

* *Members, with the Director, Office of Personnel Management, of the Joint Financial Management Improvement Program Steering Committee.*

sional Committees, and (b) conducting special studies and investigations at the request of Congress. For example, the Congressional Budget and Impoundment Control Act of 1974 (31 U.S.C. 1301) specifies a number of ways for the GAO to assist Congress in considering Presidential requests for rescissions of budget authority.

2. *Serving as the independent legislative auditor of the Federal Government.* The GAO audit staff conducts audits of all branches of the Government, both here and abroad.

3. *Prescribing principles and standards for Federal agency accounting systems.* This is done through the *General Accounting Office Policy and Procedures Manual For Guidance of Federal Agencies*, published in looseleaf form and updated periodically.

4. *Assisting agencies in accounting systems design.* To this end the GAO (a) provides technical assistance upon request to Federal agencies designing or modifying accounting systems, (b) approves those agency statements of principles and agency system designs which comply with requirements set forth in the GAO *Manual*, (c) includes recommendations for systems improvement in its audit reports, (d) conducts an on-going program of agency system review, and (e) circulates illustrative examples of suggested and notable accounting and reporting practices among the agencies.

5. *Reporting to Congress on the status of agency accounting systems.* This is done through providing members of Congress copies of all audit reports and through an annual summary report to Congress on this subject.

Congressional Budget Office (CBO). This newest of the financial offices was established by the Congressional Budget Office Act of 1974 (88 Stat. 302; 2 U.S.C. 601). The purpose of the Act was to revise Congress's consideration of the budget. The CBO was created to provide the Congress with information regarding the budget and related issues. Its specific duties include:

1. *Economic forecasting and analysis of fiscal policy.* Unlike the budgets of lesser organizations, that of the nation has important effects on the economy. Analyzing and forecasting the effects of alternative levels and locations of revenues and expenditures is designed to assist Congress to make valid decisions.

2. *Accumulating and reporting information about the actions taken by the Congress while those actions are being made and immediately thereafter.* This information permits comparisons of the results of actions with the targets Congress sets for itself before it makes specific appropriations.

3. *Cost estimates.* The CBO develops five-year projections of the costs of carrying out any public bill reported by a committee and of the costs of extension of existing spending and taxation policies.

4. *An annual report on the budget.* By April 1 of each year the CBO must give Congressional Committees a report discussing alternative

revenue levels, spending levels, sources of revenue, and expenditure programs and functions, all from the viewpoints of national needs, growth, and development.

5. *Special studies.* The CBO prepares special studies on budget-related topics at the request of Congressional Committees.

President. The President of the United States has ultimate responsibility for financial management and accountability of the executive branch of the Government. In fulfilling his responsibilities he relies heavily upon the heads of the executive agencies, particularly the Treasury and OMB, to which a great deal of authority is delegated.

Though the President can only suggest to Congress the appropriations he desires, he has the power to veto appropriation bills passed by the Congress. He cannot modify a bill, however, but must approve or disapprove it in its entirety. A Presidential veto can be overridden only by a two-thirds vote of Congress.

Until the passage of the Congressional Budget and Impoundment Control Act of 1974 there had been uncertainty as to whether appropriations were authorizations to obligate the Government or legislative orders to do so. Presidents had in fact instructed the OMB to "impound" ("reserve") appropriations for purposes they did not approve. The Act provides that the President is to ask Congress for a rescission of budget authority if he believes that all or some part of an appropriation should not be used for the specified purpose or, more generally, if he believes expenditures should be withheld for fiscal policy or other similar reasons. If Congress does not act on the President's request for rescission within 45 days, the authorization must be made available for obligation.

Although there are some flaws in the Act, principally related to the timeliness of requests for rescission and Congressional action on them, it did settle the argument. Appropriations are orders to obligate.

Office of Management and Budget (OMB). An agency within the Executive Office of the President, the OMB has broad financial management powers as well as the responsibility of preparing the executive budget. Among the other duties assigned OMB are:

- To study and recommend to the President changes relative to (a) the existing organizational structure of the agencies, their activities and methods of business, etc., (b) appropriations, (c) the assignment of particular activities or tasks within the executive branch, and (d) any need for reorganization of the executive branch.
- To apportion appropriations (enacted) among the agencies and establish "reserves" in anticipation of cost savings, contingencies, etc.
- To develop programs and regulations for improved gathering, compiling, and disseminating of statistical data pertaining to the Government and its agencies.
- Upon request, to furnish statistical data and other assistance to Congress.

Numerous bulletins, circulars and other directives relating to Federal budgeting, accounting, and reporting have been issued by OMB.

Secretary of the Treasury.   The Secretary of the Treasury is both the chief accountant and the banker of the Federal Government. His functions include:

- Central accounting and reporting for the Government as a whole.
- Cash receipt and disbursement management—including supervision of the Federal depository system and disbursing cash for virtually all civilian agencies.
- Management of the public debt—including the scheduling of borrowing to meet current needs, repayment of principal, and meeting interest requirements.
- Investment of Trust Funds.
- Supervision of agency borrowing from the treasury.

Numerous directives issued by the Secretary of the Treasury affect Federal accounting and reporting, the most comprehensive being the *Treasury Department Fiscal Manual for Guidance of Departments and Agencies.*

Federal Agencies.   The efficacy of Federal financial management is determined by the economy, efficiency, and effectiveness achieved at the agency or department level. Similarly, Federal budgeting, accounting, and reporting can be no better than that of the related departmental or agency systems and subsystems upon which the central systems are dependent. Among the many accounting-related functions and activities of the agencies are these:

- To prepare agency budget requests for submission to the President through OMB.
- To establish and maintain effective systems of accounting and internal control in conformity with the principles and standards prescribed by GAO.
- To furnish reports and other information requested by the Treasury, OMB, and GAO.
- With OMB assistance, to achieve insofar as possible (a) consistency in accounting and budgetary classifications, (b) synchronization between accounting and budgetary classifications and the agency's organizational structure, and (c) adequate support of budget requests by data on performance and program costs, by organizational units.
- To report to Congress on actions taken pursuant to recommendations for improvement contained within GAO reports.

Though they are to comply with the broad principles and standards set forth by the GAO, agency accounting systems are "tailor made" to the needs of the agency and vary widely in design and procedure. Most agencies have developed accounting policies and procedures manuals that serve both as a guide to agency personnel and as valuable reference material to others interested in the systems and procedures of a particular agency.

Most Federal agencies have Inspector Generals or similar internal audit and investigation officers who continually study and evaluate the agency's activities.

The Inspector General Act of 1978 created the office for a number of departments and agencies. Each Inspector General is appointed by the President with the advice and consent of the Senate. He is to report to the head of the organization or his chief deputy. He must prepare a semiannual report on his findings, and the organization must forward the report to appropriate Congressional Committees within seven days.

Joint Financial Management Improvement Program. The Joint Financial Management Improvement Program (JFMIP) is a Government-wide cooperative effort to coordinate and improve financial management within the Federal complex. Begun informally in 1947, and officially authorized by the Budget and Accounting Act of 1950, the JFMIP operates under the joint leadership of the Comptroller General, the Secretary of the Treasury, the Director of OMB, and the Chairman of the Office of Personnel Management.

A steering committee comprised of representatives of each central agency coordinates the JFMIP activities. It meets regularly to consider problem areas, initiate research projects, and evaluate financial management progress throughout the Government. The JFMIP has played a major coordinative role and provides an essential vehicle for carrying out joint endeavors such as those contained in the Legislative Reorganization Act of 1970 to the effect that the Secretary of the Treasury and the Director of OMB, in cooperation with the Comptroller General, are to develop, establish, and maintain:

- Insofar as practicable, a standardized information and data processing system for budgetary and fiscal data.
- A standard classification of programs, activities, receipts, and expenditures of Federal agencies.

Fund Structure

Fund structures employed in Federal Government accounting may be broadly classified as (1) funds derived from general taxing and revenue powers and from business operations, also known as "Federal" or "Government-owned" funds, and (2) funds held by the Government in the capacity of custodian or trustee, sometimes referred to as "Not Government-owned" or "Trust and Agency" funds. Six types of funds are employed within these two broad categories:

Government-Owned or "Federal" Funds	Trust or Custodian Funds
General Fund	Trust Funds
Special Funds	Deposit Funds
Revolving Funds	
Management Funds	

General Fund. The General Fund of the Federal Government is similar in many respects to that of a state or local government. There is only one General Fund; it is used to account for collections that are not dedicated to specific purposes; and the bulk of Congressional appropriations or other authorizations to the various agencies are financed through it.

Special Funds. Special Funds are much like Special Revenue Funds of municipalities. They are established to account for the receipt and expenditure of appropriable resources (1) earmarked by law or contractual agreement for some specified purpose, but (2) not generated by operations for which continuing authority to reuse such receipts has been granted. There are many Special Funds in the Federal Government, though most involve relatively small amounts of money.

Revolving Funds. Revolving Funds are employed to account for the continuous cycles of commercial-type operations of the Federal Government in which revenues generated are, for the most part at least, automatically available for agency use without need for further action by Congress. There are two types of funds within this category:

1. *Public Enterprise Funds*—the revenues of which are derived primarily from user charges levied outside the Federal Government. These are similar to Enterprise Funds of municipalities.
2. *Intragovernmental Industrial or Working Capital Funds*—also known as "Stock" Funds—financed by charges to user agencies within the Government. These are similar to Internal Service Funds of municipalities.

Management Funds. Management Funds are established to facilitate the financing of and accounting for—on a "suspense" or "clearing account" basis—agency operations that ultimately will be charged to two or more appropriations. Management Funds are used, for example, to account for central payment of transportation vouchers and for research projects conducted jointly by several agencies.

Trust Funds. Trust Funds are established to account for the receipt and expenditure of resources by the Federal Government in the capacity of trustee for the benefit of specific individuals or classes of individuals. The Federal Old-Age and Survivors Insurance Trust Fund, the National Service Life Insurance Fund, and the Highway Trust Fund are examples of Federal Trust Funds. The principles of Trust Fund accounting discussed in Chapter 11 are generally applicable to Federal Trust Fund accounting.

Deposit Funds. These Funds, similar to municipal Agency Funds, are employed to facilitate the accounting for collections either (1) held in suspense temporarily and later refunded or paid into some other Federal fund, or (2) held by the Government as a banker, or in some other agency capacity, and to be paid out at the direction of the owner.

THE BUDGETARY PROCESS

Federal agencies may incur obligations requiring either current or future disbursements from one or more of the Government's funds only if Congress has granted budgetary authority to do so. Budgetary authority is usually granted in the form of appropriations, though it may also be granted in the form of "contract authorizations"—which permit obligations to be incurred in either a definite or indefinite amount, but require a subsequent appropriation to liquidate the obligations—or in a variety of other forms.

Most appropriations for current operations provide obligational authority only within the year for which they are granted (one-year or annual appropriations), though disbursements to liquidate them may occur in the two following years. In some cases—such as where major facility construction or research are involved—the appropriation continues as valid obligational authority for several years (multiple-year appropriations) or until expended (no-year appropriations). Occasionally appropriations are made on a permanent basis (permanent appropriations), particularly for activities financed from Revolving and Trust Funds, and agency receipts are available to the agency without additional authorization from Congress. Similarly, Congress may authorize an agency to spend debt receipts, a form of authority sometimes referred to as "back-door financing." Should the new fiscal year begin before an agency's appropriations are enacted—which has occurred with increasing frequency in recent years—Congress passes a "continuing resolution" authorizing the agency to incur obligations under the assumption that the current year appropriations will be identical to those of the prior year.[1]

A Federal agency therefore may have several types of obligational authority available during a given year—e.g., from different appropriations, some definite and some indefinite in amount, some one-year and others multiple-year or no-year, and so on. Thus, budgetary accounting in a Federal agency may be far more complex than in a municipality.

The Budget Cycle

The Federal budget cycle, like that of municipalities and states, has four stages: (1) formulation of the executive budget, (2) Congressional action, (3) execution of the enacted budget, and (4) budgetary reporting and auditing. We shall not give a complete description of the Federal budget process but will present some of the salient characteristics, particularly where they differ from the process described in the budgeting chapter of this text.

Formulation of the Executive Budget. Budget preparation and presentation of the budget to Congress in January of each year is a Presidential responsibility. Preparation requires continuous exchange of information, proposals, evaluations, and policy determination among the President, central financial agencies, and operating agencies.

The process of executive budget formulation may be described concisely.

---

[1] One reason why Congressional appropriations often are not finalized by the October 1 start of the new fiscal year is that an appropriation may not be enacted prior to enactment of legislation authorizing the agency to conduct the program(s) for which budget authority is sought. Thus, not only must new programs be authorized, but many prior year program authorizations expire each year and must be considered for renewal before the budget requests may be considered and appropriations made. For these and other reasons, the use of continuing resolutions has increased in recent years. (Some agencies have operated for the full fiscal year on this basis.)

1. During the spring, each agency evaluates its programs, identifies policy issues and prepares budgetary estimates and projections for the fiscal year to begin in 1 to 1½ years—taking into account both anticipated program changes and alternative means of achieving its objectives.

2. After review in the agency and by OMB, and OMB-agency conferences on major issues or questions involved, preliminary budget plans are transmitted to the President.

3. The President reviews the preliminary agency budget plans—together with preliminary projections of the economic outlook and revenue estimates provided him by the Treasury Department, the Council of Economic Advisors, and OMB—and issues general budgetary and fiscal policy guidelines for the fiscal year in question. The agencies then receive tentative policy decisions and planning parameters to serve as guidelines for preparing formal agency budget requests.

4. Agency budgets compiled in accordance with these guidelines are reviewed by OMB. After OMB hearings and additional OMB–agency conferences to resolve questions or differences remaining, revised agency budgets are submitted to the President.

5. After the President again reviews the overall economic outlook, revised revenue estimates, and individual agency requests, he orders the executive budget to be finalized for presentation to the Congress.

Congressional Action.   The Congressional Budget Act of 1974 (88 Stat. 302; 2 U.S.C. 601) created the present procedure by which the Congress determines the annual Federal budget. At the beginning of consideration, by concurrent resolution, it establishes target levels for overall expenditures, budget authority, budget outlays, broad functional expenditure categories, revenues, the deficit, and the public debt. As action is taken through bills on the foregoing topics, the Congressional Budget Office compares and reports the differences between targets and actions.

Congressional appropriations are not based directly on expenditures, but on authority to obligate the Government ultimately to make disbursements for expenditures or loans. Thus, an agency's total "budget authority" (BA) is comprised of "new obligational authority" (NOA)—authority to incur obligations for agency programs—and "loan authority" (LA)—authority to incur obligations covering the principal of loan programs.

Execution of the Enacted Budget.   When Congress has approved an appropriation bill, an appropriation warrant is drawn by the Treasury, countersigned by the GAO, and forwarded to the agency. The agency revises its plans and sends a request for apportionment to OMB. The OMB makes apportionments to the agency, reserving funds for contingency, savings, timing, or policy reasons. (But note that the Impoundment Control Act of 1974, discussed under "President" on page 667, limits the "reserving" process.) The agency carries on its programs with the apportioned appropriations through allotments to programs and activities, obligating and expending money, and the provision of services. It reports to OMB on its activities, on its use of resources, and on its costs and accomplishments. OMB in turn reports to the President concerning budget status and managerial accomplishments of the agencies. The agency prepares vouchers for expenditures and submits them to the Treasury for payment.

One aspect of the description above bears repetition and emphasis: An agency has only a part of its annual obligational authority available to it at any time—the apportioned part. The agency head, in turn, allots its apportioned obligation authority to its programs and/or organizational subunits. Only the allotted apportionments are valid obligational authority at the agency field office level.

Reporting and Audit. Agency accounting, internal auditing, and reporting are responsibilities of agency management. In addition to preparing financial and managerial reports for internal use and for others interested in its activities and status, the agency also prepares such reports as may be required by the Treasury, the Congress, or OMB. Again, the central reporting function (for the Government as an entity) is carried out by the Treasury Department, based on its central accounting records and the monthly reports filed with it by the agencies.

Independent legislative audit of the executive agencies is performed by the GAO. The GAO audit is also viewed as an integral part of the agency management process, and it has increasingly been management-assistance oriented in recent years. GAO findings and recommendations for corrective action are reported to the President, the Congress, and the agencies—and the agencies must respond to the GAO reports and inform Congress as to their progress and plans relative to the implementation of GAO suggestions.

ACCOUNTING PRINCIPLES AND STANDARDS FOR FEDERAL AGENCIES

The accounting principles and standards for Federal agencies prescribed by the Comptroller General are contained in Chapter 2, "Accounting Principles and Standards," of Title 2—"Accounting," of the GAO *Manual for Guidance of Federal Agencies.* A portion of Title 2 is published separately as *Accounting Principles and Standards for Federal Agencies* (revised 1978). Selected major aspects of these principles and standards are discussed below.

Objectives

The objectives of Federal agency accounting set forth in the Budget and Accounting Procedures Act of 1950 are:

- Full disclosure of the financial results of agency activities.
- Production of adequate financial information needed for agency management purposes.
- Effective control over and accountability for all funds, property, and other assets for which each agency is responsible.

- Reliable accounting reports to serve as the basis for preparation and support of agency budget requests, for controlling the execution of budgets, and for providing financial information required by OMB.
- Suitable integration of agency accounting with the central accounting and reporting operations of the Treasury Department.

Proper accounting is an inherent responsibility of agency management. Though the agency head may delegate the authority for accounting systems design and operation, he must bear the ultimate responsibility for the systems. Thus, he should assure himself that:

- A proper accounting system is established based on the accounting principles and standards prescribed by the Comptroller General.
- The information provided by the accounting system lends itself to effective use and is used:
  -To provide information necessary for effective and economical management of its operations and the resources entrusted to it.
  -To enable the management to report on the discharge of its responsibilities for the resources and operations for which it is accountable.

Standards for Internal Management Control

Among the more important objectives of an agency's internal management control system are to:

- Promote efficiency and economy of operations.
- Restrict obligations and costs, consistent with efficiently and effectively carrying out the purposes for which the agency exists, within the limits of congressional appropriations and other authorizations and restrictions.
- Safeguard assets against waste, loss, or improper or unwarranted use.
- Insure that all revenues applicable to agency assets or operations are collected or properly accounted for.
- Assure the accuracy and reliability of financial, statistical, and other reports.[2]

Twelve standards for internal management control are prescribed by the Comptroller General:

1. *Policies.* Management policies adopted for carrying out agency functions should be clearly stated; systematically communicated throughout the organization; conformed to applicable laws and external regulations and policies; and designed to promote the carrying out of authorized activities effectively, efficiently, and economically.
2. *Organization.* A carefully planned organizational structure should be established under which responsibility for the performance of all duties

[2] Comptroller General of the United States, *Accounting Principles and Standards for Federal Agencies*, 1978 Revision, (Washington, D.C.: U.S. Government Printing Office, 1978), p. 35.

necessary to carry out the functions for which the agency exists is clearly defined and specifically assigned, and appropriate authority for such performance is delegated.

3. *Segregation of duties and functions.* Responsibility for assigned duties and functions should be appropriately segregated, as among authorization, performance, keeping of records, custody of resources, and review, so as to provide proper internal checks on performance and to minimize opportunities for carrying out unauthorized, fraudulent, or otherwise irregular acts.

4. *Planning.* A system of forward planning, embracing all significant parts of the agency, is needed for determining and justifying needs for financial, property, and personnel resources and for carrying out operations effectively, efficiently, and economically.

5. *Procedures.* Procedures adopted to carry out agency operations should be as simple, efficient, and practicable as circumstances permit, considering the nature of the operations and the applicable legal and regulatory requirements. Such factors as feasibility, cost, risk of loss or error, and availability and suitability of personnel must be considered.

6. *Authorization and record procedures.* An adequate system of authorization and record procedures must be devised to (1) promote compliance with prescribed requirements and restrictions of applicable laws, regulations, and internal management policies, (2) prevent illegal or unauthorized transactions or acts, and (3) provide proper accounting records for the assets, liabilities and appropriations, obligations, receipts and revenues, expenditures, costs, and disbursements of the agency.

7. *Information system.* An adequate and efficiently operated information system should exist to promptly provide essential and reliable operating and financial data to decisionmakers or those reviewing performance.

8. *Supervision and review.* The performance of all duties and functions should be under proper supervision. All performance should be subject to adequate review under an effective internal audit program so as to provide information as to whether performance is effective, efficient, and economical; management policies are adhered to; applicable laws and prescribed regulations are complied with; and unauthorized, fraudulent, or otherwise irregular transactions or activities are prevented or discovered.

9. *Qualifications of personnel.* The qualifications of officials and other personnel as to education, training, experience, competence, and integrity must be appropriate for the responsibilities, duties, and functions assigned to them.

10. *Personal accountability.* Each official and employee must be fully aware of his assigned responsibilities and understand the nature and consequences of his performance. Each person must be held fully accountable for the faithful, honest, and efficient discharge of his duties and functions, including where applicable the custody and administration of public funds and property and compliance with requirements of law, regulations, or other prescribed policies applicable to their conduct or performance.

11. *Expenditure control.* Adequate control over expenditures requires that effective procedures be devised to provide assurance that needed goods and services are acquired at the lowest possible cost; that goods and services paid for are actually received; that quality, quantity, and prices

are in accordance with the applicable contracts or other authorizations; that such authorizations are consistent with applicable statutes, regulations, and policies; and that effective use is made of all acquired resources.

12. *Safeguarding of resources.* All funds, property, and other resources for which the agency is responsible should be appropriately safeguarded to prevent misuse, misappropriation, or unwarranted waste, deterioration, or destruction.[3]

Standards for Accounting Systems

Agency accounting systems must not only assist in demonstrating compliance with statutory requirements, including the principles and standards set forth by the Comptroller General, but must fulfill the needs of Congress, of higher-level executive agencies such as the OMB and the Treasury Department, and of agency managers. Thus, an agency's accounting system must meet all recurring internal and external needs for cost and other financial data for planning, programming, budgeting, control, and reporting. Stated differently, the accounting system must provide not only the basis for control over funds, property, and other assets, but must provide an accurate and reliable basis for developing and reporting costs of performance in accordance with (1) major organizational segments, (2) budget activities, and (3) program structures.

Several other broad accounting system principles or standards also are prescribed:

1. *Usefulness.* The financial data produced by the system should be useful. It must be promptly presented and clearly reported so that its significance is understood by both internal and external users.

2. *Accounting for responsibilities.* The system should be designed so that major assignments of responsibility can be reported on readily.

3. *Consistency of account classifications.* Planning, programming, budgeting, and accounting classifications should be consistent with each other and synchronized with the agency's organization structure to the extent practicable.

4. *Technical requirements.* The system should provide complete and reliable records of the resources and operations of the agency entity. The records should embrace all agency assets, as well as its liabilities and obligations, receipts and revenues, expenditures, and costs (expenses). Financial transactions should be adequately supported by pertinent documents available for audit. Furthermore, interfund and interagency transactions and balances should be separately identified in agency records and statements to facilitate the preparation of consolidated financial reports for the Government.

5. *Qualified personnel.* Agency officials are entitled to and should demand a high degree of technical competence in selecting and retaining top accounting personnel.

6. *Truthfulness and honesty.* The highest standards of truthfulness and

[3] Ibid.

honesty should be applied in agency accounting. Accordingly, financial transactions should not be recorded in a manner that will produce materially inaccurate, false, or misleading information.

7. *Simplicity.* Accounting procedures should be as simple and understandable as practicable. Excessive details and unnecessary refinements in the accounting records should be avoided.

8. *Accuracy, reliability, and materiality.* In determining the degree of precision to be sought in making allocations of cost (expense) or revenues, or in computing other items where judgments and estimates are employed, the materiality and relative significance of the items involved should be considered carefully. Meticulous procedures which do not produce materially more accurate results or provide other offsetting benefits should be avoided.

9. *Updating needed.* Agency accounting systems should be (a) reviewed from time to time to assure that they continue to meet the test of usefulness to users, and (b) modified as appropriate in light of changing circumstances.

The Accrual Basis of Accounting

Federal agencies are required by law to maintain accounts on the accrual basis. Appropriate records on obligations incurred and liquidated must be kept to provide information to assist in expenditure control and disbursement planning and for reporting on the status of appropriations and funds. Agency accounting systems that provide information primarily in terms of obligations (encumbrances) and disbursements are incomplete if they cannot also produce the data needed to properly disclose information on financial and property resources, liabilities, revenues and expenditures, and costs (expenses) of operations by major areas of responsibility and activity.[4]

A Federal agency's accounting system therefore must include data on "obligations" (encumbrances), "expended appropriations" (expenditures), "applied costs" (expenses), and cash disbursements—not one or the other. This requirement may be illustrated by the purchase and use of materials:

1. When an order is placed, an *obligation* (encumbrance) is recorded.
2. When the materials are delivered, an *expended appropriation* (expenditure) is recorded.
3. When the materials are used, an *applied cost* (expense) is recorded.
4. When the payment for the materials is made, a cash *disbursement* is recorded.

Fund Control

"Fund control" refers to management control over the use of fund authorizations to assure that (1) funds are used only for authorized purposes, (2) they

[4] The accrual basis may be followed in day-to-day accounting procedures or the system may be maintained on a cash or obligation basis and converted to the accrual basis periodically (at least monthly) prior to statement preparation.

are used economically and effectively, and (3) obligations and disbursements do not exceed the amounts authorized. The last of these is important not only because of constitutional requirements related to disbursements and the fact that Congressional appropriations are in terms of obligational authority, but also to assure compliance with the Antideficiency Act—which forbids incurring obligations or making disbursements which would create deficiencies in appropriations and funds. Thus, each agency accounting system must record its appropriations and other authorizations, apportionments, and allotments—as well as its related obligations, expenditures, and disbursements.

Accounting Entity and Account Structure

Federal agency accounting entities may be the entire agency, subdivisions thereof, or one or more legally established funds. The preferred entity and account structure is one in which accounts relating to all sources of funds used to finance agency activities are incorporated into a single, integrated accounting system. Thus, while fund entities are of paramount importance at the central accounting level, the agency or subunit is normally the primary accounting entity at the agency level—and fund detail is maintained within that accounting entity. The basic structure of a Federal agency's accounts usually is:

Balance Sheet Accounts	Assets Liabilities Investment of the U.S. Government
Temporary Accounts	Revenues Costs (expenses) Budgetary accounts

The accounting equation and the basic accounting procedures of a typical agency are illustrated both graphically and by a case example later in this chapter.

Assets. For the most part, the principles and standards of asset accounting set forth by the Comptroller General relate to standard intermediate accounting topics such as cash, receivables, and property—including determination of the cost of property upon acquisition, treatment of purchase discounts as deductions from cost rather than as revenue, accounting for materials on a consumption basis rather than on a purchase basis, and the need for taking inventory periodically. Two points deserve special mention, however.

The first relates to the Cash accounts. Since the Treasury Department disburses cash for most Federal agencies, agency Cash accounts (Fund Balances with U.S. Treasury) are segregated by fund and appropriation. As will be explained later, this is a principal manner in which fund control is exercised in the accounts; and the Cash accounts (other than Petty Cash and Cash on Hand) offset the budgetary accounts in the agency ledger.

Second, though the Comptroller General stops short of requiring depreciation accounting in all agencies and in all situations, depreciation accounting is clearly encouraged. Specifically, the *Principles and Standards* document states:

A basic responsibility of agency management is to fully and fairly account for all resources entrusted to or acquired by the agency. This responsibility extends to the consumption of those resources through use in carrying out operations and is just as applicable to long-lived physical facilities as it is to expendable materials. . . .

Although depreciation is not represented by current expenditures of funds, and although there is no precise way to arrive at an accurate measure of depreciation as a current cost, it is nonetheless a real cost. However, the activities of the Federal Government are so varied that a uniform requirement to account for depreciation of capital assets cannot be justified.

Procedures shall be adopted by each agency to account for depreciation . . . whenever a need arises for a periodic determination of the cost of all resources consumed in performing services. This information is needed when:

1. The financial results of operations, in terms of costs of performance in relation to revenue earned, if any, are to be fully disclosed in financial reports.
2. Amounts to be collected in reimbursement for services performed are to be determined on the basis of the full cost of performance pursuant to legal requirements or administrative policy.
3. Investment in fixed assets used is substantial and there is a need to assemble total costs to assist management and other officials in making comparisons, evaluating performance, and devising future plans.
4. Total cost of property constructed by an agency is needed to determine the amount to be capitalized.[5]

The Comptroller General's emphasis on the need for cost information (discussed below) would seem to require depreciation accounting in most situations.

Liabilities. Principles and standards relating to agency liability accounting include requirements that (1) liabilities incurred be accounted for and reported irrespective of whether funds are available or authorized for their payment, and (2) the accounting system provide for separate identification of funded and unfunded liabilities. Other topics include the need to disclose all contingent liabilities; the necessity in accounting for Federal insurance, pension, and similar programs requiring actuarial basis measurement to disclose the current costs of such programs as they accrue and the estimated liabilities accrued at the reporting date, irrespective of the degree to which funds have been appropriated or otherwise obtained for such payments; the requirement that real property acquired under lease-purchase contracts be recorded as an asset (and a corresponding liability be established) upon acceptance of the property; the need to account for liabilities under construction or other contracts on a "constructive receipt" basis rather than only upon project completion or cash disbursement; and accounting for Working Fund advances and employee leave costs.

Investment of the U.S. Government. The Investment of the U.S. Government represents the residual equity of the Federal Government in the agency. The major causes of change in this account are:

[5] Comptroller General of the United States, op. cit., pp. 35–36.

Additions:
   Congressional appropriations
   Property and services obtained from other Federal agencies without
       reimbursement
   Donations received
   Net income from operations
Reductions:
   Funds returned to the U.S. Treasury
   Property transferred to other Federal agencies without reimbursement
   Net loss from operations

These changes in the residual equity are recorded in separate temporary accounts
as necessary for proper reporting. The Federal agency accounting equation is
summarized in Figure 17-2.

Revenues.   The discussion of the nature, control, use of the accrual basis
of accounting, and reporting of revenues in the *Manual* is similar to that commonly
found in intermediate accounting texts. It is important to note that appropriations
are *not* considered revenues but are considered to be capital contributions when
expended. The term refers to agency operating revenues such as from billings for
services and to gains from property disposal.

Costs (Expenses).   The term "cost" is defined as the financial measure of
resources consumed in accomplishing a specified purpose, carrying out an activity,
or completing a unit of work or a specific project. This topic is covered extensively
in the *Principles and Standards* document; Public Law 84-863 requires Federal
agencies to install accounting systems that produce appropriate data on the cost
of operations.
   The importance attributed to cost accounting and cost finding by the Comptroller General is indicated by the following excerpts from the *Principles and
Standards* document:

> Cost information provides a common financial denominator for the measure-
> ment and evaluation of efficiency and economy in terms of resources used in
> performance.
>
> The production and reporting of significant cost information are essential in-
> gredients of effective financial management. Such information must be avail-
> able to agency management officials, the Office of Management and Budget,
> and the Congress for devising and approving realistic future financial plans
> [budgeting]. It is needed in making meaningful comparisons and in keeping
> costs within limits established by law, regulation, or agency management
> policies.
>
> Every expenditure should be conceived as a cost of some essential, planned
> activity. Because costs furnish important measures of performance, they de-
> serve the unremitting attention of management officials.
>
> Efficient use of resources is a management responsibility. The use of cost
> information to achieve this objective places positive emphasis on the receipt
> of value for resources used. In turn, this emphasis results in giving greater
> prominence to cost aspects in the planning of operations as opposed to placing

exclusive emphasis on not exceeding budgetary authorizations with a resulting lack of emphasis on value received.[6]

Cost accounting or cost finding systems of Federal agencies should provide for accumulation of cost information by (1) major organizational segments, (2) budget activities, and (3) program structure of the agency. In order to facilitate cost (expense) determination, expenditures should be categorized according to whether they pertain to current expenses or the acquisition of assets and by object, e.g., labor, materials, and contractor services.

Financial Reporting

Although agency managers determine the internal reports needed, four basic financial statements are required of all Federal agencies: (1) Statement of Assets and Liabilities (Balance Sheet), (2) Statement of Operations, (3) Statement of Sources and Application of Funds, and (4) Statement of Changes in the Investment of the United States. These and other statements are illustrated in the final section of this chapter. Furthermore, agencies must report on the status of all appropriations or other authorizations, separate statements should be prepared for each fund, and the agencies must prepare any other financial reports required by the Congress, its committees, or the central agencies. Combined or consolidated statements should be prepared where they will throw further light on the financial condition or financial operations of the agency.

Reporting standards prescribed relate to (1) Fairness of Presentation, (2) Compliance with Prescribed Requirements, (3) Timeliness, and (4) Usefulness.

The standards relating to *fairness* of presentation may be summarized as follows:

1. *Completeness and clarity.* All essential facts are to be included and disclosed adequately.
2. *Accuracy, reliability, and truthfulness.* Not only should reports be accurate, reliable, and truthful, but all appropriate steps should be taken to avoid bias, obscurement of significant facts, and presentation of misleading information.
3. *Accounting support.* The financial reports are assumed to be supported in the accounts unless other data sources are disclosed and explained.
4. *Excluded costs.* The exclusion of any significant costs should be explained in the notes to the statement.
5. *Form, content, and arrangement.* This shall be as simple as possible and emphasize communication of significant information to report users.
6. *Extent of detail.* While detail should be sufficient to provide a clear and complete report, unnecessary detail should be avoided—especially where its inclusion obscures significant financial data.
7. *Performance under limitations.* Financial performance should be reported in relation to statutory or other limitations prescribed by higher

---

[6] Ibid., pp. 44–45.

authorities, particularly where these affect operational economy, efficiency, or effectiveness.

8. *Consistency.* Data reported are assumed to be based on accounting records maintained on a consistent basis unless material changes in accounting policies and methods are disclosed and their effects are explained.

9. *Terminology.* This should be consistent and nontechnical.

The *compliance* standard states that reports must comply with (1) applicable laws and regulations relative to the nature, accounting basis, content, frequency, and distribution of reports, and (2) applicable restrictions pertaining to information that is classified for national security purposes. The *timeliness* standard requires that reports be produced promptly in order to be of maximum usefulness, while the *usefulness* standard calls for reports to be carefully designed with an eye to their usefulness and suggests that unnecessary reports be abolished.

FEDERAL AGENCY ACCOUNTING AND REPORTING ILLUSTRATED

This concluding section of the chapter contains (1) an overview of the Federal agency accounting equation and the usual account and ledger relationships, (2) a case illustration of Federal agency accounting, and (3) illustrative agency financial statements. Although specific methods of accounting vary among agencies, as do their functions and financing methods, the approach illustrated is typical and serves to highlight the major aspects of Federal agency accounting and reporting.

Overview of the Federal Agency Accounting Equation

Figure 17-2 contains a graphic illustration of the accounting equation and the usual account and ledger relationships of a Federal agency financed through General Fund appropriations and billings for services rendered.

1. The accounting equation may be expressed as "Assets = Liabilities + Investment of the United States Government."

2. The equity section, the Investment of the United States Government, is subdivided into Invested Capital and Unexpended Appropriations subsections. The former is proprietary in nature, whereas the latter is budgetary.

3. The budgetary account credit balances are offset by the Fund Balance with U.S. Treasury and Estimated Appropriation Reimbursements (estimated operating revenues) accounts initially. Subsequently they are offset by these accounts and the Reimbursements to Appropriations (actual operating revenues) account.

4. Revenues and Expenses (Applied Costs) are accounted for, as well as

Expended Appropriations (Expenditures)—which is viewed as both an expenditure and a capital increment account.

Other capital increments and decrements also are accounted for separately from Revenues and Expenses. Thus, the typical Federal agency accounting system is a dual system in which (1) budgetary and proprietary accounting occur simultaneously, and (2) the distinction between capital transactions, including appropriation expenditures, and current revenues and expenses is maintained.

The illustration in Figure 17-2 warrants careful study and should be reviewed from time to time in conjunction with the case example and the illustrative financial statements that follow.

A Case Illustration

In order to illustrate the principal aspects of Federal agency accounting, let us assume that (1) a newly created agency began its first year of operations on October 1, 19X0, concluding it on September 30, 19X1; and (2) its activities are financed through a single General Fund appropriation and reimbursements for services rendered. To simplify the illustration, we also (1) assume that general ledger control accounts similar to those in Figure 17-2 are employed, (2) limit our presentation to general ledger entries, and (3) in order to demonstrate the entire cycle, make summary entries where similar transactions typically recur throughout the year.

Description of the Agency. The agency's primary function is rendering services to other agencies. Reimbursements received or accrued are available to the agency without further appropriation and are thus credited to its appropriation accounts. The agency renders personal services for the most part, but also acquires and uses materials and equipment; it has no field offices. Reimbursable expenses are billed to user agencies monthly on the basis of direct labor and materials costs incurred and estimated overhead (based on a predetermined percentage of direct cost).

The agency maintains both a general accounting system and a job-order (work order) cost accounting system. A perpetual inventory system is employed, as is the accrual basis of accounting. The Allotment-Expenditure subsidiary ledger format typically used is shown in Figure 17-3.

Illustrative Transactions and Entries. Most of the remainder of this chapter is devoted to the presentation of a series of selected illustrative transactions or events and the entries made to record their effects.

Summary of Transactions and Events/Entries

1. Congress appropriated $175,000 from the General Fund to finance the agency during the fiscal year; in addition, appropriation reimbursements from charges for services to be rendered during the year are estimated at $40,000.

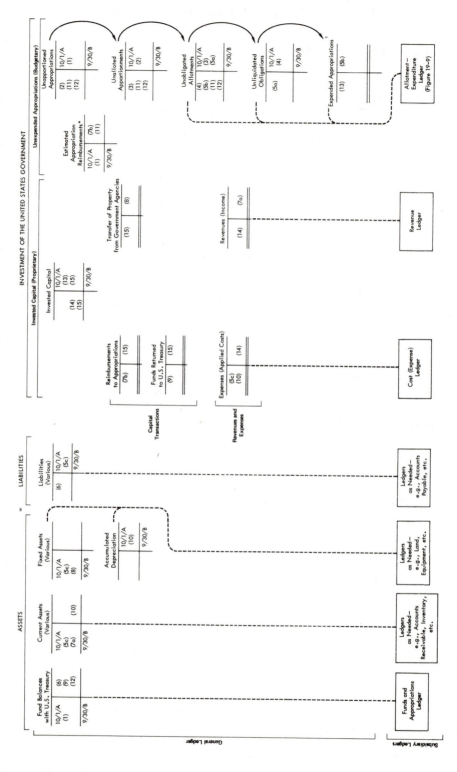

Figure 17-2

NOTES

* This account may be considered an asset (or "assets and other debits") account rather than a budgetary account.

† This account is more properly classified under "capital transactions"; it is shown in the "Unexpended Appropriations" section here to better illustrate Federal agency budgetary accounting.

Legend:

10/1/A—Beginning-of-period balances

Budgetary and Operating

1. Unapportioned Appropriations enacted by Congress and Estimated Appropriation Reimbursements (estimated agency operating revenues) are established in the accounts.

2. Appropriations are apportioned to Agency by OMB.

3. Apportioned appropriations are allotted (usually by months or quarters) to Agency programs, field offices, etc. by Agency top management.

4. Allotted appropriations are obligated (encumbered) for goods or services ordered or other commitments made.

5. Goods or services are received or other expenditures are made: (a) Obligation entry is reversed; (b) the Expended Appropriations (Accrued Expenditures) are recorded and Unobligated Allotments is reduced accordingly; and (c) the related assets or expenses and liabilities are established in the accounts.

6. Liabilities are paid through Treasury disbursement officer.

7. Revenues usable by the Agency without the need for further Congressional action are received or accrued: (a) Asset (Cash or receivable) and revenue are recorded, and (b) The Reimbursements to Appropriations and reductions in Estimated Appropriation Reimbursements yet to be received or accrued are reflected. [Note: The debit in Reimbursements to Appropriations will be closed to Invested Capital to offset the credit to that account upon the Expended Appropriations account being credited thereto in closing—in order that only the expended Congressional appropriations serve to increase the Invested Capital Account. See entry 15 below.]

Capital Transactions

8. Fixed assets are transferred to the Agency from another Agency at no cost to the recipient Agency. [This would be reflected as Transfers of Property To Government Agencies on the books of the transferor Agency.]

9. Cash in excess of the Agency's needs was released to the Treasury for other uses. (This constitutes a U. S. Government *disinvestment* in this Agency.)

Adjusting Entries

10. Depreciation and other asset consumption charges are recorded as Expenses (Applied Costs).

11. Estimated Appropriation Reimbursements is adjusted to the balance properly carried forward to the succeeding year and corresponding adjustments are made to the Unapportioned Appropriations, Unallotted Apportionments and Unobligated Allotments accounts.

12. Unobligated appropriations that lapse at year end are recorded as reductions of the Fund Balances with U. S. Treasury, Unapportioned Appropriations, Unallotted Apportionments and Unobligated Allotments.

Closing Entries

13. Expended Appropriations (Accrued Expenditures) for the period are closed to Invested Capital to reflect the additional investment by the U. S. Government in the Agency financed through appropriations.

14. Agency Expenses, net of Revenues (Income) from Agency operations, are closed to Invested Capital at year end.

15. Other Invested Capital increment and decrement accounts are closed at period end.

9/30/B—Balances at period end, after closing.

Figure 17-3

ALLOTMENT—EXPENDITURE LEDGER

Allotment Class/Code _____
Division or Activity _____
Apportioned Appropriation _____

Allotments: 1st Quarter _____
2nd Quarter _____
3rd Quarter _____
4th Quarter _____

Date	Explanation	Document Reference	Object Code	Accrued Expenditures	Obligations		Allotments	Unobligated Allotments
					Liquidated	Incurred		

(1)	Fund Balances with U.S. Treasury	175,000	
	Estimated Appropriation		
	Reimbursements	40,000	
	Unapportioned Appropriations		175,000
	Unallotted Apportionments		40,000
	To record appropriation and estimated		
	appropriation reimbursements.		

Were the $40,000 Estimated Appropriation Reimbursements subject to OMB apportionment, the entire $215,000 would be credited to Unapportioned Appropriations.

2. The OMB apportioned $170,000 of the Congressional appropriation, reserving $5,000 for possible cost savings and contingencies.

(2)	Unapportioned Appropriations	170,000	
	Unallotted Apportionments		170,000
	To record OMB apportionments of		
	appropriations.		

3. Administrative allotments were made by agency management as follows:

First quarter	$ 55,000
Second quarter	58,000
Third quarter	44,000
Fourth quarter	50,000
	$207,000

(3)	Unallotted Apportionments	207,000	
	Unobligated Allotments		207,000
	To record allotment of apportioned		
	appropriations.		

This is a summary entry. In practice an entry would be made each quarter; the $207,000 is the total of the allotments made during the year.

4. Purchase orders were placed for materials estimated to cost $37,000.

(4)	Unobligated Allotments	37,000	
	Unliquidated Obligations		37,000
	To record obligations outstanding for		
	materials on order.		

The Unliquidated Obligations account—sometimes called Unfilled Orders—is similar to the Encumbrances account used in municipal accounting.

5. Materials estimated to cost $30,000 were received; the invoice was for $30,500.

(5)	(a)	Inventories	30,500	
		Accounts Payable—Nonfederal ..		30,500
		To record cost of materials		
		purchased and the liability		
		therefor.		

(b)	Unliquidated Obligations	30,000	
	Unobligated Allotments		30,000
	To reverse estimated obligations previously recorded.		
(c)	Unobligated Allotments	30,500	
	Expended Appropriations		30,500
	To charge allotment with cost of materials purcased.		

Entries (b) and (c) may be combined as follows:

Unliquidated Obligations	30,000	
Unobligated Allotments	500	
Expended Appropriations		30,500
To record the expenditure for materials, remove the obligation previously recorded, and reduce the allotment by the excess of actual materials cost over that estimated.		

Similarly, had the order cost less than estimated, the Unobligated Allotments account would be credited for the difference between estimated and actual cost.

6. Materials costing \$25,000 were used by the agency.

(6)	Direct Costs	25,000	
	Inventories		25,000
	To record direct materials used.		

7. A one-year insurance policy was purchased at mid-year at a cost of \$200.

(7)	(a)	Prepaid Expenses	100	
		Overhead Expenses	100	
		Accounts Payable—Nonfederal ..		200
		To record liability for insurance policy acquired.		

Alternatively, the entire \$200 might be set up as Prepaid Expenses and an adjusting entry made at period end for the portion consumed.

(b)	Unobligated Allotments	200	
	Expended Appropriations		200
	To charge allotment with the cost of insurance acquired.		

8. Travel advances made to agency employees totaled \$1,000.

(8)	Travel Advances	1,000	
	Fund Balances with U.S. Treasury ...		1,000
	To record travel advances to employees.		

9. An employee submitted an expense report for $300, of which $200 was covered by travel advances; he is to be reimbursed for the remaining $100.

(9)	(a)	Overhead Expenses	300	
		Travel Advances		200
		Accounts Payable—Nonfederal ..		100
		To record travel expenses, reduction of travel advances, and liability for expenses not advanced previously.		
	(b)	Unobligated Allotments	300	
		Expended Appropriations		300
		To charge the allotment with travel expenses incurred.		

10. Overhead expenses of $26,450 were incurred, of which $1,330 is payable to other Federal Government agencies.

(10)	(a)	Overhead Expenses	26,450	
		Accounts Payable—Federal		1,330
		Accounts Payable—Nonfederal ..		25,120
		To record overhead expenses incurred.		

Federal agencies separate Federal and nonfederal payables and receivables to assist in the preparation of consolidated reports.

	(b)	Unobligated Allotments	26,450	
		Expended Appropriations		26,450
		To charge allotment with overhead expenses incurred.		

11. Equipment estimated to cost $10,200 was ordered.

(11)	Unobligated Allotments	10,200	
	Unliquidated Obligations		10,200
	To record obligation incurred for equipment ordered.		

12. The equipment arrived, together with an invoice for $10,000.

(12)	(a)	Equipment	10,000	
		Accounts Payable—Nonfederal ..		10,000
		To record acquisition of equipment.		
	(b)	Unliquidated Obligations	10,200	
		Unobligated Allotments		10,200
		To reverse estimated obligation recorded when equipment was ordered.		

(c) Unobligated Allotments   10,000
        Expended Appropriations   10,000
     To charge allotment for cost of
     equipment purchased.

Alternatively, entries (b) and (c) may be combined, with the $200 excess of estimated over actual costs being credited to Unobligated Allotments. See entry 5.

13. Equipment was transferred from another Federal Government agency at no cost to this (recipient) agency. The equipment had originally cost $5,750 and accumulated depreciation of $750 had been recorded on the transferor agency's books.

(13) Equipment   5,750
        Accumulated Depreciation—
          Equipment   750
        Transfers of Property from
          Government Agencies   5,000
      To record transfer of equipment from
      another agency at book value.

14. Equipment that originally cost $1,000, on which accumulated depreciation of $100 had been recorded, was sold for $950 cash.

(14) Undeposited Collections   950
        Accumulated Depreciation—
          Equipment   100
          Equipment   1,000
          Other Income   50
      To record sale of equipment for more
      than book value.

15. The proceeds of the equipment sale were transferred to the U.S. Treasury.

(15) Funds Returned to U.S. Treasury   950
        Undeposited Collections   950
      To record transfer of equipment sale
      proceeds to the prescribed
      miscellaneous receipts account of the
      Treasury.

Had the proceeds been needed to finance equipment replacement in the current or succeeding year, they might have been retained by the agency. If this were the case, the proceeds would be placed in a Deposit Fund of the Treasury and the appropriate budgetary account credited. Here it is assumed that the proceeds were transferred to the Treasury for general Government use.

16. The agency's liability for employees' annual leave accrued during the year amounted to $9,600.

(16)	Overhead Expenses	9,600	
	Liability for Accrued Leave		9,600

To charge accrued employee leave cost
as an expense.

Accrued employee leave costs are established as expenses and liabilities as earned. During the payroll period in which the leave is taken, the liability is reduced by the amount of leave taken and the leave costs, together with other payroll costs, are charged against the allotment. See entry 17.

17. Direct labor costs incurred during the year totaled $108,000. With-holdings that must be matched by the agency amounted to $10,150; income taxes withheld were $19,000; and employee leave taken amounted to $8,100.

(17)	(a)	Direct Costs	108,000	
		Overhead Costs	10,150	
		Liability for Accrued Leave	8,100	
		Accounts Payable—Federal		39,300
		Accounts Payable—Nonfederal ..		86,950

To record payroll and related costs
and reduce the liability for
employee leave by the amount
taken during the payroll period.

Accounts Payable—Federal are as
follows:

Income Taxes Withheld	$19,000
Retirement Withheld	10,150
Matching Retirement	10,150
Total	$39,300

	(b)	Unobligated Allotments	126,250	
		Expended Appropriations		126,250

To charge the allotment with
payroll and related expenditures.

18. Agency billings for services rendered to other Federal agencies were $39,000.

(18)	(a)	Accounts Receivable—Federal	39,000	
		Billings for Services (or Sales) ...		39,000

To record billings for services
rendered.

	(b)	Reimbursements to Appropriations .	39,000	
		Estimated Appropriation		
		Reimbursements		39,000

To record reimbursements to
appropriations resulting from
billings for services and reduce the
Estimated Appropriations
Reimbursements account by the
amount of the actual
reimbursements.

The Estimated Appropriation Reimbursements account balance should reflect the amount estimated *yet* to be received. Had reimbursements arising from billings for services exceeded the estimate recorded at the beginning of the year—for example, had they amounted to $42,000—the entry would appear as follows:

(a)	Accounts Receivable—Federal	42,000	
	Billings for Services (or Sales) ...		42,000
	To record billings for services.		
(b)	Reimbursements to Appropriations.	42,000	
	Estimated Appropriation Reimbursements		40,000
	Unallotted Apportionments		2,000
	To record appropriation reimbursements, reduce the Estimated Appropriation Reimbursements account to zero, and record the additional authorization arising upon actual reimbursements exceeding those estimated.		

Note the additional appropriation recorded in this situation.

19. Accounts receivable collected during the period totaled $36,500.

(19)	Undeposited Collections	36,500	
	Accounts Receivable—Federal		36,500
	To record collection of receivables.		

20. Collections of receivables were deposited intact with the U.S. Treasury.

(20)	Fund Balances with U.S. Treasury	36,500	
	Undeposited Collections		36,500
	To record deposits with Treasury.		

21. Vouchers scheduled for payment by the depository during the year were as follows: to Government agencies, $37,780; to others, $152,220.

(21)	Accounts Payable—Federal	37,780	
	Accounts Payable—Nonfederal	152,220	
	Fund Balances with U.S. Treasury ...		190,000
	To record scheduling of vouchers for payment by disbursing officer.		

22. Depreciation of agency equipment during the year was estimated at $1,500.

(22)	Overhead Expenses	1,500	
	Accumulated Depreciation—Equipment		1,500
	To record depreciation of equipment.		

23. Direct salary costs of $4,000 were accrued at year end; the physical inventory was in agreement with the perpetual records.

(23) (a) Direct Costs 4,000
    Accrued Liabilities   4,000
    To record accrued salaries.

  (b) Unobligated Allotments 4,000
    Expended Appropriations   4,000
    To charge the allotment for
    accrued salaries.

24. Deposits with the U.S. Treasury in the amount of $1,500 had not been confirmed by the depository to the agency at period end, nor had payments of $800 of vouchers scheduled for payment.

(24) Deposits in Transit 1,500
   Disbursements in Transit   800
   Fund Balances with U.S. Treasury ...   700
   To record deposits for which no
   depository confirmation has been
   received at period end and vouchers
   scheduled for payment for which
   payment notification has not been
   received at period end.

Deposits in Transit and Disbursements in Transit, the latter being equivalent to checks outstanding, are set up formally—rather than only in reconciliations—at period end. This is done both for control purposes and to assist in the preparation of government-wide financial reports.

25. Unobligated appropriations lapse at year end; all reimbursable costs have been billed and no further appropriation reimbursements are expected to result from this year's activities.

(25) Unapportioned Appropriations 5,000
   Unallotted Apportionments 3,000
   Unobligated Allotments 2,300
   Estimated Appropriation
    Reimbursements   1,300
   Fund Balances with U.S. Treasury ...   9,300
   To record lapsed appropriations and
   reduce appropriations by the excess of
   estimated over actual reimbursements.

It is assumed here that the appropriation is of the annual or one-year type. Had any unobligated appropriations not lapsed, only the lapsed portions would be canceled. Similarly, were further reimbursements expected from this period's activity, a portion or all of the Estimated Appropriation Reimbursements account would be carried forward to the succeeding period. Note that the Unliquidated Obligations account is carried forward as it serves as expenditure and disbursement authority during the two years following the year in which the obligations are incurred.

26. Closing entries were prepared at the end of the period.

(26)	(a)	Invested Capital	146,050	
		Billings for Services (or Sales)	39,000	
		Other Income	50	
		Direct Costs		137,000
		Overhead Expenses		48,100

To close revenue and expense accounts and reduce Invested Capital by the excess of expenses over revenues.

	(b)	Expended Appropriations	197,700	
		Reimbursements to		
		Appropriations		39,000
		Invested Capital		158,700

To close the expenditures and reimbursements accounts and increase the Invested Capital account by the net additional investment of the U.S. Government during the period that was financed through current appropriations.

Observe that closing the Billings for Services account in entry 26(a) increased the Invested Capital account by $39,000; the identical $39,000 balance in the Reimbursements to Appropriations account serves to avoid double counting this amount by causing the Invested Capital to be increased in entry 26(b) only by those expenditures financed through current appropriations, exclusive of reimbursements.

	(c)	Transfers of Property from		
		Government Agencies	5,000	
		Funds Returned to U.S.		
		Treasury		950
		Invested Capital		4,050

To close other capital investment and disinvestment accounts and increase the Invested Capital account accordingly.

Reporting. The principal financial statements prepared for Federal agencies, both on an interim basis and at year end, include the following:

1. Statement of Assets and Liabilities (Figure 17-4)

2. Statement of Changes in the Investment of the United States Government (Figure 17-5)

3. Statement of Expenses (Figure 17-6)
4. Statement of Sources and Applications of Funds (Figure 17-7)
5. Statement of Status of Appropriations (Figure 17-8)
6. Reconciliation of Program Costs with Obligations (Figure 17-9)

As noted earlier, the first four statements listed above are required of all agencies. The latter two are primarily for internal and intragovernmental use.

Except where a report or statement format is prescribed, agency managers have considerable latitude both as to the financial statements to be prepared for the agency and statement format. Thus, both the statements issued and the statement formats may vary somewhat from those illustrated here, and additional statements may be prepared to fulfill agency management purposes or requests of OMB, Treasury, or Congress.

Figure 17-4

ILLUSTRATIVE FEDERAL AGENCY
Statement of Assets and Liabilities
September 30, 19X1

Assets

Current Assets:		
Fund balances with U.S. Treasury	$10,500	
Deposits in transit	1,500	
Accounts receivable—Federal	2,500	
Travel advances	800	
Inventories	5,500	
Prepaid expenses	100	$20,900
Fixed Assets:		
Equipment	$14,750	
Less: Accumulated depreciation	2,150	12,600
Total Assets		$33,500

Liabilities and Investment of the United States Government

Current Liabilities:		
Disbursements in transit	$ 800	
Accrued liabilities	4,000	
Accounts payable—nonfederal	650	
Accounts payable—Federal	2,850	$ 8,300
Other Liabilities:		
Liability for accrued leave		1,500
Total Liabilities		$ 9,800
Investment of the United States Government (Figure 17-5):		
Invested capital	$16,700	
Unexpended appropriations	7,000	23,700
Total Liabilities and Investment of the United States Government		$33,500

Figure 17-5

ILLUSTRATIVE FEDERAL AGENCY

Statement of Changes in the Investment of
the United States Government
For the Fiscal Year Ended September 30, 19X1

Balance of Investment of the United States Government, October 1, 19X0		$ —
Add:		
Appropriations*	$175,000	
Revenues (Figure 17-6)	39,050	
Transfer of property from Government Agencies .	5,000	$219,050
Less:		
Expenses (Figure 17-6)	$185,100	
Funds returned to U.S. Treasury	950	
Unobligated appropriations lapsing during the year	9,300	195,350
Balance of Investment of the United States Government, September 30, 19X1		$ 23,700

Composed of:			
Invested Capital		$ 16,700	
Unexpended appropriations:			
Unapportioned appropriations† .	$ —		
Unallotted apportionments†	—		
Unobligated allotments†	—		
Unliquidated obligations	7,000	7,000	$ 23,700

Alternatively, the Expended Appropriations and Unliquidated Obligations balances may be added in lieu of adding total appropriations and deducting unobligated appropriations lapsing during the year.

† *Accounts having zero balances normally are excluded from the financial statements. These accounts are shown here to illustrate how they would appear on interim statements and, if all unobligated appropriations do not lapse, at year end.*

Figure 17-6

ILLUSTRATIVE FEDERAL AGENCY

Statement of Expenses (Net)
For the Fiscal Year Ended September 30, 19X1

Expenses:		
Direct Costs:		
Direct labor	$112,000	
Direct material	25,000	$137,000
Overhead expenses:		
Salaries and wages	$ xx	
Heat, light, and power	xx	
Rent	xx	
Printing	xx	
Travel	300	
Depreciation	1,500	
Annual leave	9,600	
etc.	xx	48,100
Total expenses		$185,100

Figure 17-6 (continued)

Revenues:		
Billings for services	$ 39,000	
Other income	50	
Total revenues		39,050
Net expenses (or Excess of expenses over revenues)		$146,050

Figure 17-7

ILLUSTRATIVE FEDERAL AGENCY

Statement of Sources and Applications of Funds
(Statement of Changes in Financial Position—Working Capital Basis)
For the Fiscal Year Ended September 30, 19X1

Funds provided by:			
Appropriation from Congress	$175,000		
Less Appropriations lapsing during the year.	9,300	$165,700	
Revenues—Billings for services		39,000	
Sale of equipment		950	
Total funds provided			$205,650
Funds applied to:			
Cost of current year's operations:			
Expenses (Figure 17-6)		$185,100	
Adjustments to derive working capital effect—			
Deduct: Depreciation	$ 1,500		
Leave earned but not taken ..	1,500	3,000	
		$182,100	
Purchase of equipment		10,000	
Funds returned to U.S. Treasury		950	
Total funds applied			193,050
Increase in working capital			$ 12,600

The increase in working capital is accounted for as follows:

	10/1/19X0	9/30/19X1	Increase (Decrease)
Current Assets:			
Fund balances with U.S. Treasury	$ —	$ 10,500	$ 10,500
Deposits in transit	—	1,500	1,500
Accounts receivable—Federal	—	2,500	2,500
Travel advances	—	800	800
Inventories	—	5,500	5,500
Prepaid expenses	—	100	100
	$ —	$ 20,900	$ 20,900
Current Liabilities:			
Disbursements in transit	—	800	800
Accrued liabilities	—	4,000	4,000
Accounts payable—nonfederal	—	650	650
Accounts payable—Federal	—	2,850	2,850
Working Capital	$ —	$ 12,600	$ 12,600

Figure 17-8

ILLUSTRATIVE FEDERAL AGENCY

Statement of Status of Appropriations
September 30, 19X1

Current Fiscal Year Appropriation

Appropriation(s)	$175,000	
Reimbursements	39,000	
Total appropriation and reimbursements		$214,000
Less: Appropriations lapsing during the year		9,300
		$204,700
Less: Unexpended appropriation at September 30, 19X1:		
Unapportioned appropriations	$ —	
Unallotted apportionments	—	
Unobligated allotments	—	
Unobligated balance of appropriation	$ —	
Unliquidated obligations	7,000	
Unexpended balance of appropriation		7,000
Current appropriation expended in the current fiscal year		$197,700

Prior Fiscal Years' Appropriations

Unliquidated obligations, October 1, 19X0	$ —	
Less: Unliquidated obligations, September 30, 19X1	—	
Prior year appropriations expended in current fiscal year		—
Total appropriation expended		$197,700

Figure 17-9

ILLUSTRATIVE FEDERAL AGENCY

Reconciliation of Program Costs with Obligations
For the Fiscal Year Ended September 30, 19X1

Total expenses (Figure 17-6)		$185,100
Equipment purchases		10,000
Total program costs (including capital outlays)		$195,100
Less: Expenses not chargeable to current appropriation:		
Depreciation	$1,500	
Leave earned but not taken	1,500	3,000
Total adjusted program costs		$192,100
Add: Increase in inventories	$5,500	
Increase in prepaid expenses	100	5,600
Expended appropriations (Figure 17-8)		$197,700
Add: Increase in unliquidated obligations		7,000
Obligations incurred		$204,700

Note: Key terms are set in boldface for illustrative purposes.

▶ **Question 17-1.** Governmental accounting is said to involve two fundamental objectives: managerial control and accountability. Explain.

Question 17-2. List the major types of data that a Federal agency accounting system should provide on a routine, recurring basis.

Question 17-3. Explain the meaning of the following terms in Federal accounting:

(a) Apportionment

(b) Reserves (by OMB)

(c) Allotment

(d) Obligation

(e) Expended Appropriations

(f) Obligation Incurred

(g) Cost (or Applied cost)

(h) Reimbursements to Appropriations

(i) Fund Balance with U.S. Treasury

Question 17-4. Distinguish among and between the following: obligations, expended appropriations, disbursements, and applied costs.

Question 17-5. (a) List the Federal fund types. (b) In a parallel column, list the types of municipal funds in a manner that "matches" the municipal funds to the Federal funds to the extent practicable.

Question 17-6. Why are intragovernmental transactions and balances (receivables and payables) of a Federal agency distinguished in the accounts from those not involving other Federal agencies?

Question 17-7. Briefly state the Comptroller General's position with respect to depreciation accounting by Federal agencies.

Question 17-8. List the types of financial statements issued by Federal agencies.

Question 17-9. How is fund accounting accomplished in a Federal agency where the agency is the accounting entity?

Question 17-10. Explain the following types of appropriations or other types of obligational authority: (a) contract authorization; (b) multiple-year appropriations; (c) no-year appropriations; (d) permanent appropriations; and (e) continuing resolutions.

Question 17-11. Audits performed by the U.S. General Accounting Office are considered both part of the reporting and audit phase of Federal financial management and an integral part of agency management. Explain.

Question 17-12. Compare the Investment of the United States Government or Invested Capital account with (a) the Fund Balance account of a municipal expendable fund, and (b) the Contributions and Retained Earnings accounts of a municipal Enterprise Fund.

Question 17-13. What types of problems might you expect to encounter in accounting for (a) expended appropriations on the basis of constructive receipt, and (b) personal income tax accruals?

Question 17-14. Compare the manner in which budgetary accounting is accomplished in a Federal agency with that of a municipality.

Question 17-15. What are the principal duties of the Congressional Budget Office?

Question 17-16. What is the nature of a Congressional appropriation to the executive branch, and how does its nature affect the concept of "impounds"?

Question 17-17. Describe the function of a Federal agency's inspector general. To whom and in what manner does the agency inspector general report?

▶ **Problem 17-1.** The trial balance of Able Agency at October 1, 19X6, the start of its 19X7 fiscal year, was as follows:

Fund Balances with U.S. Treasury	40,000	
Inventories	10,000	
Equipment	25,000	
Accumulated Depreciation		5,000
Unliquidated Obligations—19X6		30,000
Invested Capital of the U.S. Government		40,000
	75,000	75,000

The following transactions and events occurred during the month of October 19X6:

1. Able Agency was notified that its fiscal 19X7 appropriation was $2,500,000.
2. The Office of Management and Budget apportioned $600,000 to Able Agency for the first quarter of the 19X7 fiscal year.
3. Able Agency's chief executive allotted $500,000 of the first quarter appropriation apportionment.
4. Obligations incurred during the month for equipment, materials, and program costs amounted to $128,000.
5. Goods and services ordered during the prior year were received:

	Obligated for:	Actual Cost
Materials	$ 20,000	$ 21,000
Program A costs	7,000	7,000
Program B costs	3,000	3,000
	$ 30,000	$ 31,000

6. Goods and services ordered during October 19X6 were received:

	Obligated for:	Actual Cost
Materials	$ 6,000	$ 5,000
Equipment	10,000	10,000
Program A costs	30,000	32,000
Program B costs	80,000	81,000
	$126,000	$128,000

7. Depreciation for the month of October was estimated at $200, chargeable to Overhead.

8. Materials issued from inventory during October were for: Program A, $18,000; Program B, $7,000; and general (Overhead), $3,000.

9. Liabilities placed in line for payment by the U.S. Treasurer totaled $145,000.

10. Other accrued expenditures at October 31, 19X6, not previously recorded, were: Program A, $1,000; Program B, $6,000; and general (Overhead), $1,500.

Required:

(a) Prepare the general journal entries necessary to record the transactions and events affecting Able Agency during the month of October 19X6. (Key entries to problem data; omit entry explanations.)

(b) Prepare a trial balance for Able Agency at October 31, 19X6. (Assume that closing entries are made annually.)

(c) What is the invested capital of the U.S. Government in Able Agency at October 31, 19X6? The total investment of the U.S. Government?

Problem 17-2. From the information in Problem 17-1:

(a) Prepare a worksheet summarizing the activities of Able Agency during the month of October 19X6. Your worksheet should be cross-referenced to the numbered items in that problem and should be headed as follows:

Columns	Heading
1–2	Trial Balance, October 1, 19X6
3–4	Entries during October, 19X6
5–6	Trial Balance, October 31, 19X6

(b) Prepare a Statement of Status of Appropriations for Able Agency at October 31, 19X6.

Problem 17-3. The trial balance accounts of X Agency at September 30, 19X1, the end of its first year of operations, appears below. The data are adjusted for all items except the lapsing of appropriations.

Accounts Payable—Federal ...	8,000	Inventories	700
Accounts Receivable—		Liability for Accrued Leave ...	1,200
Nonfederal	12,000	Overhead	30,000
Accrued Liabilities	500	Prepaid Expenses	200
Accumulated Depreciation	1,000	Reimbursements to	
Deposits in Transit	3,000	Appropriations	18,000
Depreciation	1,000	Revenues	18,000
Direct Costs	79,300	Transfer of Property from	
Disbursements in Transit	4,000	Government Agencies	15,000
Equipment	20,000	Travel Advances	400
Estimated Appropriation		Unallotted Apportionments ...	10,000
Reimbursements	1,500	Unapportioned Appropriations..	12,000
Expended Appropriations	114,000	Undeposited Collections	2,500
Fund Balances with U.S.		Unliquidated Obligations	7,000
Treasury	25,100	Unobligated Allotments	3,000

Additional information:

1. All appropriations are one-year appropriations.

2. No further reimbursements on account of this year's activities are expected.

3. The transfer of property from government agencies consisted of equipment.

Required:

(a) Entries to adjust the appropriations (budgetary) accounts and to close the books on September 30, 19X1.

(b) A Statement of Assets and Liabilities of X Agency at September 30, 19X1.

(c) A Statement of Changes in the Investment of the United States Government in X Agency for the year ended September 30, 19X1.

(d) A Reconciliation of Program Costs with Obligations for X Agency for the year ended September 30, 19X1.

Problem 17-4. Innovative Agency, established during 19X2, is financed by no-year appropriations and from billings for certain of its services. Its trial balance at the beginning of 19X3 was as follows:

	Debit	Credit
Fund Balances with the U.S. Treasury	15,000	
Accounts Receivable—Federal	9,000	
Materials and Supplies	41,000	
Plant and Equipment	60,000	
Accumulated Depreciation		2,000
Accounts Payable—Federal		8,000
Invested Capital		100,000
Unobligated Allotments		10,000
Unliquidated Obligations		5,000
	125,000	125,000

A summary of the transactions and events affecting Innovative Agency during 19X3 follows:

1. Additional appropriations of $500,000 were made for the agency. Billings for services, available to the agency without further appropriation, were estimated at $200,000.

2. All but 5 percent of the current year's appropriation was apportioned to the agency by the OMB.

3. Agency management allotted all but $50,000 of the increased obligational authority available to the agency.

4. Billings for services totaled $215,000, all to Federal agencies; collections amounted to $210,000, all deposited with the U.S. Treasury to the credit of Innovative Agency by payor agencies.

5. Purchase orders were placed for materials, supplies, and equipment estimated to cost $183,000.

6. Equipment was transferred to the agency at no cost from another agency. The equipment had originally cost $70,000; accumulated depreciation of $40,000 had been recorded thereon by the transferor agency.

7. The equipment received by transfer (item 6) proved unsatisfactory and was sold for cash at book value.

8. The equipment sale proceeds were returned to the U.S. Treasury for general government use.

9. Orders were received from industrial suppliers as follows:

	Estimated Cost	Actual Cost
Materials and supplies	$ 66,000	$ 68,000
Equipment	120,000	120,000

10. Employee annual leave earned amounted to $25,000.

11. Employee salaries amounted to $400,000, including $12,000 annual leave taken. Withholdings that must be matched totaled $24,000; income taxes withheld were $40,000; and withholdings on private insurance plans totaled $14,000.

12. Materials and supplies used during the year cost $90,000.

13. A two-year insurance policy costing $1,000 was purchased at midyear.

14. Depreciation of agency plant and equipment during the period was recorded, $16,000.

15. Vouchers were scheduled for payment by the U.S. Treasurer as follows: Federal, $88,000; nonfederal, $530,000.

16. All deposits were confirmed by the U.S. Treasury, but $14,000 of disbursements were in transit at year end.

Required:

From the above information for Innovative Agency, prepare:

(a) A worksheet summarizing the financial activities during 19X3. Your worksheet should be keyed to the problem data items and should be headed as follows:

Columns	Heading
1–2	Trial Balance, Beginning of 19X3
3–4	Transactions and Adjustments—19X3
5–6	Preclosing Trial Balance, End of 19X3 (Optional)
7–8	Closing Entries, End of 19X3
9–10	Postclosing Trial Balance, End of 19X3

(b) A Statement of Assets and Liabilities (Balance Sheet) at the end of 19X3.

(c) A Statement of Changes in the Investment of the United States Government during the 19X3 fiscal year.

(c) A Reconciliation of Program Costs with Obligations for the 19X3 fiscal year.

18

ACCOUNTING

FOR HOSPITALS

The scope and complexity of the hospital environment have undergone swift and dramatic changes in recent years. Correspondingly, hospital financial management and accounting practices have evolved rapidly and significantly to keep abreast of the changes in their environment.

Environmental changes include:

1. Increases in the volume of services to meet demand.
2. Increases in the range of services offered, based on:
   a. Continuing improvements in health care techniques and equipment.
   b. Broadened expectations of hospital clientele.
3. Increases in hospital costs:
   a. Increases in hospital personnel and their level of training.
   b. Introduction of new technology.
   c. Inflationary pressures on all cost components.
4. Decrease in the percentage of support by local governments and philanthropists for expansion of facilities.
5. Increase in the proportion (today, approximately 90 percent) of hospital charges paid by third-party payers.

Because it is more difficult than in the past to generate funds by operations—because government grants and gifts from philanthropists for construction have decreased, and for other reasons as well—hospitals have found it necessary to turn to the capital markets for loans for expansion. Audited financial statements are highly desirable, if not mandatory, to support borrowing activities; CPAs have therefore had an upsurge of influence on the reporting practices of hospitals. The

Hospital Audit Guide,[1] published by the AICPA, is now recognized to constitute, together with applicable pronouncements of the FASB and its predecessors, generally accepted accounting principles for hospitals.

Two industry professional associations—the American Hospital Association (AHA) and the Hospital Financial Management Association (HFMA)—have been dominant forces in the development and improvement of hospital financial management, accounting, and reporting. Accounting and statistical manuals, data processing services, symposiums and workshops, advisory services, and recognized journals are provided for the industry on a regular basis through one or both of these associations.[2] These organizations encourage their members to follow generally accepted accounting principles in reporting and to have annual audits.

FUNDS

The *Guide* recognizes only two major classes of funds: unrestricted and restricted. If the governing board may use assets (resources) for whatever purpose it chooses, the assets should be accounted for in the Unrestricted Fund. If donors or other third parties have placed restrictions on the discretion of the board in using assets, then the assets should be accounted for in a Restricted Fund.

Unrestricted Funds

There are three types of resources in the Unrestricted Fund: (1) current (sometimes called "operating"), (2) board-designated, and (3) plant. The board may "designate" (not "restrict") some of the unrestricted resources for specific purposes. Board designations might be established, for example, for expansion of the physical plant, to retire debt, or even to serve as an endowment for the hospital. Board designation of assets for specified purposes does not remove the assets from the unrestricted status and does not create separate funds. In essence it creates a segregation of the Unrestricted Fund balance similar to appropriations of retained earnings. From the point of view of the management of the hospital the designation creates restrictions as valid as those of donors. Hospital management may use the resources only for those purposes specified by the board. *But,* to repeat, since the board has the power to remove its designation, the resources are not contractually or legally restricted and should be accounted for in the Unrestricted Fund.

All fixed assets are recorded in the Unrestricted Fund. The theory is that the board can use its discretion in deciding how these assets are to be used and that readers of the financial statements should be presented with a total of all assets subject to discretionary use.

---

[1] Subcommittee on Health Care Matters, American Institute of Certified Public Accountants, *Hospital Audit Guide,* 3rd. ed. (New York: AICPA, 1980). (Including Statements of Position issued by the Auditing Standards Division.)

[2] *Hospitals* is the official journal of the American Hospital Association; *Hospital Financial Management* is that of the Hospital Financial Management Association (formerly the American Association of Hospital Accountants).

Restricted Funds

The term "restricted" is reserved for resources that are restricted as to use by the donor, grantor, or other source of the resources. Examples of purposes for which resources may be restricted are (1) specific operating purposes, (2) additions to fixed assets, (3) endowment, (4) loan, (5) annuity, and (6) life income.

Funds restricted to specific operating purposes should be accounted for as deferred revenue in the Unrestricted Fund or placed in a Restricted Fund (sometimes called a Specific Purpose Fund) until appropriate expenditures occur. At that time the expenditures should be recorded in the Unrestricted Fund and the restricted resources should be transferred to the Unrestricted Fund as "other operating revenue." Exactly when an expenditure satisfies the terms set by the donor (and agreed to by the hospital board) is a matter for careful interpretation.

Resources that are given to the hospital to be used only for additions to fixed assets should be considered to increase the hospital's permanent capital and should be credited to fund balance in a Restricted Fund (frequently called a Plant Replacement and Expansion Fund). When expenditures that satisfy the donor's terms are made, the assets and the related fund balance amount should be transferred to the Unrestricted Fund by a debit to the asset and a credit to Unrestricted Fund Balance.

Endowment Funds, including income therefrom, should be accounted for in accordance with the terms of the donor. Income may be unrestricted, in which case it goes to the Unrestricted Fund as "nonoperating revenue." The principal of term endowments may become available to the board for either unrestricted or restricted use upon occurrence of a specific event or fulfilment of a condition. The financial statements should disclose the essential terms of the endowment— length; uses of resources; restrictions, if any, on the use of income; and the like.

INCOME DETERMINATION AND ASSET VALUATION FEATURES

Although hospital accounting is fund-based, the excess of revenues over expenses of the hospital as a whole is calculated and reported. This does not mean that all hospitals are profit-seeking organizations. Rather, it reflects the predominant view that (1) hospitals are "going concerns," even if "not-for-profit," and (2) revenues must cover all expenses (not merely *expenditures*) if the hospital's capital is to be maintained intact. Hospital generally accepted accounting principles are a blend of the principles of financial accounting for businesses and of fund accounting, and some hospital transactions are more like those of not-for-profit organizations than those of business enterprises. Several income determination and asset valuation features need to be discussed.

Figure 18-1, based on the American Hospital Association's *Chart of Accounts for Hospitals*,[3] presents the major revenue and expense accounts and account groupings that hospitals use. Some of the characteristics of hospital accounting

[3] American Hospital Association, *Chart of Accounts for Hospitals* (Chicago: AHA, 1978), pp. 32–39.

Figure 18-1

SELECTED MAJOR REVENUE (R) AND EXPENSE (E) CATEGORIES

Nursing and Other Professional Services:

E	Nursing Administration
RE	Nurses' Stations (inpatient services): by location, patient classification, and/or type of medical service
RE	Hemodialysis
RE	Labor and Delivery Services
RE	Surgical Services: by type of surgery
RE	Emergency Services
RE	Central Services
RE	Laboratory Services: by type of analysis
RE	Electrodiagnosis:
RE	Electrocardiology
RE	Electromyography
RE	Electroencephalography
RE	Radiology—Diagnostic
RE	Radiology—Therapeutic
RE	Nuclear Medicine—Diagnostic
RE	Nuclear Medicine—Therapeutic
RE	Pharmacy
RE	Anesthesiology
RE	Rehabilitation Services: by types of service
RE	Clinic Services: by medical specialty
RE	Home Health Care
RE	Social Services
E	Medical Records
E	Medical Library

Other Operating Revenues:

R	Transfers from restricted funds for research, education, or other operating expenses
R	Tuition: by class of student
RE	Cafeteria
RE	Laundry and/or Linen Service
R	Services to Other Organizations: by type of service

Deductions from Revenue:

R	Provision for Bad Debts: by type of patient
R	Contractual Adjustments: by type of payer
R	Charity Services
R	Other Deductions

Other Services:

E	Research
E	Nonphysician Education: by type of student
E	Medical Staff Service and Education: by type of staff

General Services:

E	Dietary Service
E	Kitchen
E	Patient food service
E	Cafeteria
E	Plant Operation and Maintenance
E	Housekeeping Service
E	Laundry and Linen Service

Fiscal and Administrative Services

E	Fiscal Services: by type of service

E   Administrative Services: by type of service
E   Medical Care Evaluation
   Unassigned Expenses
E   Depreciation
E   Leases and Rentals
E   Insurance
E   Licenses and Taxes
E   Interest
E   Employee Benefits
E   Other Operating Expenses: by type of expense
RE Nonoperating Revenues and Expenses
E   Federal Income Tax—Current
E   Federal Income Tax—Deferred
E   State Income Tax—Current
E   State Income Tax—Deferred
R   General Contributions
R   Donated Services
R   Donated Commodities
R   Income and Gains from [Unrestricted Fund] Investments
R   Unrestricted Income from Endowment Funds
R   Unrestricted Income from Other Restricted Funds
R   Term Endowment Funds Becoming Unrestricted

Source: Adapted from American Hospital Association, *Chart of Accounts for Hospitals (Chicago: AHA, 1978)*, pp. 32–39.

are exemplified by the listed revenue and expense accounts. Look for the accounts named in Figure 18-1 as hospital accounting characteristics are discussed below.

Classes of Revenue

Hospital revenues are classified broadly into two major categories:

1. *Operating Revenues:*
   a. *Patient Service Revenues:* the *gross* revenues, measured at regularly established standard rates, earned in the several revenue-producing centers through rendering inpatient and outpatient services.
   b. *Deductions from Patient Service Revenues:* the reduction in gross revenues collectible occasioned by charity services rendered, contractual adjustments arising from third-party payer agreements or regulations, policy discounts such as are often extended patients who are themselves members of the medical profession, administrative adjustments, and bad debts.
   c. *Other Operating Revenues:* those usual, day-to-day revenues that are not derived from patient care and service. Major sources are student tuition and fees derived from schools that a hospital operates and grants for such specific purposes as research and education. Miscellaneous sources are typified by rentals of hospital plant, sales of scrap, cafeteria sales, sales of supplies to physicians and employees, and fees charged for copies of documents.

2. *Nonoperating Revenues:* revenues "not directly related to patient care, related patient services, or the sale of related goods."[4] Major sources are unrestricted gifts and grants and unrestricted income from Endowment Funds. Miscellaneous sources are typified by donated services, interest on investments of Unrestricted Funds, gain on sale of hospital properties and investments of Unrestricted Funds, and rentals of property not used in the operation of the hospital.

Items 1a and 1b relate to patient services, the major source of revenues for most hospitals. The full normal charge for services rendered is credited to revenues in order to present the total market value of the services without regard to ultimate collectibility and to facilitate the preparation and evaluation of data concerning gross revenue trends. Deductions from gross revenue are accounted for separately for purposes of control and evaluation. These deductions are for (1) uncollectible accounts and (2) allowances. Allowances are the differences between gross revenues billed at established rates and the lesser amounts that certain patients are to pay. Patients may not pay the established rates because they are indigent or because they are members of groups (doctors, clergymen, employees, or employees' dependents) that receive allowances. Patients' bills that are paid to the hospital by third party payers may not be paid at established rates because the contracts between the hospital and third parties set lower rates.

When third parties (usually Medicare, Medicaid, and Blue Cross) contract with hospitals to pay patients' bills, agreed reimbursement rates are likely to be based on cost. For example, the Medicare Act, passed in 1965, provides that reimbursement is to be the cost of providing services to patients. Established hospital rates are not necessarily based on cost; indeed, they are not likely to represent cost. Hence when Medicare patients are billed at established rates, a contractual allowance is needed to reduce gross revenues to amounts actually received.

Donations

Hospitals receive several kinds of donations. Unrestricted gifts, grants, and bequests are recorded as nonoperating revenue of the Unrestricted Fund. Hospitals may receive donations in the form of services. For them to be recorded as revenues (nonoperating), there must be an employer-employee relationship and the value of the services must be objectively determinable. Gifts of supplies and commodities fall into the same category of revenue.

Resources whose donors specify the uses to which they may be put are ordinarily recorded as deferred revenue in the Unrestricted Fund or as additions to fund balance in a Restricted Fund, as previously discussed. When the terms of the gift (or grant) have been satisfied by appropriate expenditures, the nonoperating revenue should be recognized in the Unrestricted Fund.

When a donor specifies that resources are to be used for the acquisition of fixed assets, he is presumed to have added to the permanent capital, and the resources are recorded as an increase in the fund balance of a Restricted Fund.

[4] Subcommittee on Health Care Matters, AICPA, op. cit., p. 34.

Upon appropriate expenditure of the resources, a transfer of fund balances from the Restricted Fund to the Unrestricted Fund would occur. If the donation consists of fixed assets, they should be recorded directly in the Unrestricted Fund with a credit to fund balance. Presumably the rationale for not recognizing revenue is that a restricted gift has been made. A more practical reason might be to avoid the distortion of reported revenues that would result from the gift of a major asset.

Timing of Revenue Recognition

As we have seen, a significant feature of hospital accounting is that revenue is recognized in the period in which the related assets become available for *unrestricted* use by the governing board or are *expended* for the donor-specified restricted purposes. Unrestricted revenues are recognized on the accrual basis. Assets to be expended for specified purposes, such as research grants, are considered realized in the period of expenditure.

Two arguments can be given favoring the described delay of recognition of revenue for restricted assets. First, it permits recognition of revenues in the same period as related expenses are incurred. Second, it can be said that externally restricted resources are not truly "earned" until they are used for their designated purpose.

Another occasion for revenue deferral arises when a hospital's contract with a third-party payer calls for the use of allowable costs that differ from costs used for GAAP reporting. A hospital may contract with third-party payers to use a form of accelerated depreciation to calculate "allowable costs" but elect to use, say, straight-line depreciation in its accounts. In such a case a portion of the reimbursement will be allocable to depreciation expense not yet reported in the financial statements. This portion of revenue should be deferred, to be recognized in subsequent years when straight-line depreciation exceeds the accelerated depreciation. Other costs for which "allowable" costs may exceed reported costs include pensions and vacation pay. The effects of the resulting "timing differences" should appear in the financial statements in conformity with the treatment prescribed for deferred income taxes set out in APB Opinion No. 11.

Accounts Receivable

Hospital accounts receivable are classifiable under four main headings:

- Inpatients not discharged
- Inpatients discharged
- Outpatients
- Other accounts receivable

The patient classes are then subdivided according to the payer:

- Blue Cross/Blue Shield
- Medicare

- Medicaid
- Compensation and liability cases
- Other

Thus, patient receivables are likely to be accounted for under some fifteen controls. The "other accounts receivable" category includes such receivables as government appropriations, allocations from the Community Chest or United Fund, tuitions and fees, and pledges.

Property, Plant, and Equipment

Hospital fixed assets should be recorded and depreciated on the historical cost basis. If appropriate records have not been maintained, the assets should be inventoried, appraised on the basis of historical cost, and recorded. The basis of fixed asset valuation should be disclosed among the accounting policies, of course, as should the depreciation policy.

Assets used by the hospital may be owned outright, rented from or made available by independent or related organizations, or provided by a governmental agency or hospital district. The nature of such relationships must be disclosed in the financial statements, and the accounting therefor should be in conformity with GAAP. Specifically, the provisions of APB Opinion No. 5, "Reporting of Leases in Financial Statements of Lessee," and of FASB Statement 13, "Accounting for Leases," as amended, should be followed in accounting for leases.

Marketable Equity Securities

The discussion in this section is based on AICPA *Statement of Position 78-1*, "Accounting by Hospitals for Certain Marketable Equity Securities," issued May 1, 1978. SOP 78-1 has the same authority for members of AICPA as do the Audit Guides. Only the aspects of the pronouncement that require interpretation in the hospital environment will be discussed; for example, changes of securities from current to long-term status and disclosure requirements are not discussed.

The Financial Accounting Standards Board issued *Statement of Accounting Standards (SFAS) No. 12*, "Accounting for Certain Marketable Securities," in 1975, stating that it did not apply to not-for-profit organizations. Thus, it *is* applicable to profit-seeking hospitals. SOP 78-1 does two things: (1) it makes SFAS No. 12 applicable to not-for-profit hospitals, and (2) it specifies how SFAS No. 12 is to be applied in hospital accounting and reporting.

SFAS No. 12 provides for a distinction between current asset and long-term investments in marketable equity securities. In general, hospitals hold long-term securities for income and appreciation; the discussion of long-term investments in SOP 78-1 deals only with marketable equity securities held for those purposes.

SFAS No. 12 requires explanation in the hospital environment primarily because of the use of fund accounting. Figure 18-2 indicates the essence of the reporting of marketable equity securities portfolios and transactions. The footnotes are a vital part of the presentation.

Figure 18-2

REPORTING OF
MARKETABLE EQUITY SECURITIES OF
HOSPITALS

Type of Asset	Unrestricted Fund*	Restricted Funds
Current: Asset	Portfolio A at lower of cost or market†	Portfolio C at lower of cost or market†
Realized Gain or Loss	Nonoperating revenues section of statement of revenues and expenses	Statement of changes in fund balance unless restrictions dictate other treatment‡
Changes in Valuation Allowance	Nonoperating revenues section of statement of revenues and expenses	Statement of changes in fund balance
Accumulated Changes in Valuation Allowance	Undisclosed in fund balance	Disclosed in fund balance
Noncurrent: Asset	Portfolio B at lower of cost or market†	Portfolio D at lower of cost or market†
Realized Gain or Loss	Nonoperating revenues section of statement of revenues and expense	Statement of changes in fund balance unless restrictions dictate other treatment‡
Changes in Valuation Allowance	Statement of changes in fund balance	Statement of changes in fund balance
Accumulated Changes in Valuation Allowance	Disclosed in fund balance	Disclosed in fund balance

*Board designation of funds does not alter their unrestricted status.
† Marketable equity securities should be grouped into portfolios as indicated. A separate portfolio should be set up for each type of fund in the restricted group. Comparisons of cost and market should be based on aggregate values for each portfolio. The excess of aggregate cost over aggregate market of the portfolios should be shown in appropriate valuation allowance accounts.
‡ If realized gains or losses go to and are required to be made up by Unrestricted Funds, they would be shown in the nonoperating revenues section of the Statement of Revenues and Expenses of the Unrestricted Fund.

Pooling of Investments

There are substantial advantages, in terms of total investment return, to placing all the investments of all hospital funds in a single pool. Where hospitals have several funds with investments, and where investments and disinvestment transactions occur frequently, it is essential that the accounting for the pool be on a current value basis. The pool and its operation and accounting closely resemble a mutual fund (open-end investment trust), which should record all transactions on a current value basis. This position does not alter the application of GAAP to marketable securities in the accounts of the several funds and in the financial statements.

ILLUSTRATIVE TRANSACTIONS AND ENTRIES ————————

Accounting for the varied, complex, and voluminous transactions of a hospital requires many subsidiary ledgers and other similar records. Examples of this complexity have already been presented in the discussion of accounts receivable, and many of the revenue and expense accounts in Figure 18-1 either control subsidiary ledgers or are divided into several accounts. In this illustrative case we deal only with the general ledger accounts.

The case example presented here relates to Alzona Hospital, a medium size, not-for-profit, general short-term health care facility financed from patient services fees, donations, and investment earnings. The Balance Sheet of Alzona Hospital at October 1, 19A, the beginning of the fiscal year to which the example relates, is presented as Figure 18-3.

Summary of Transactions and Events

UNRESTRICTED FUND:

1. Gross charges to patients at standard established rates were $4,400,000.

(1) Accounts and Notes Receivable	4,400,000	
Patient Service Revenue		4,400,000
To record gross billings for services at established rates.		

2. The following amounts were credited to receivables:

	Amounts Accrued 10/1/19A	Applicable to Fiscal 19B Revenues	Total
Contractual adjustments	10,000	265,000	275,000
Charity adjustments	5,000	125,000	130,000
	15,000	390,000	405,000

The balance in the Allowance for Uncollectible Receivables and Third-Party Contractuals at October 1, 19A, was comprised as follows:

Figure 18-3

ALZONA HOSPITAL
Balance Sheet
October 1, 19A

Unrestricted Funds

Assets		
Current:		
Cash		$ 175,000
Accounts and notes receivable	$ 700,000	
Less: Estimated uncollectibles and allowances	85,000	615,000
Due from Specific Purpose Fund		145,000
Inventories		165,000
Total current assets		$1,100,000
Other:		
Investments		100,000
Land	$ 130,000	
Land improvements	80,000	
Buildings	5,000,000	
Fixed equipment	600,000	
Major movable equipment	90,000	
Total property, plant, and equipment	$5,900,000	
Less: Accumulated depreciation	2,450,000	
Net land, property, plant, and equipment		3,450,000
Total		$4,650,000

Liabilities and Fund Balances		
Current:		
Notes payable		$ 150,000
Accounts payable		175,000
Total current liabilities		$ 325,000
Long-term debt:		
Mortgage payable		100,000
Total		$ 425,000
Fund balance		4,225,000
Total		$4,650,000

Restricted Funds

Specific Purpose Fund:			Specific Purpose Fund:	
Cash	$ 20,000		Due to Unrestricted Fund	$ 145,000
Investments	360,000			
Due from Endowment Fund	20,000		Fund balance	255,000
Total	$ 400,000		Total	$ 400,000
Endowment Fund:			Endowment Fund:	
Cash	$ 25,000		Due to Specific Purpose Fund	$ 20,000
Investments	475,000		Fund balance	480,000
Total	$ 500,000		Total	$ 500,000
Plant Replacement and Expansion Fund:			Plant Replacement and Expansion Fund:	
Cash	$ 25,000		Fund balance	$ 325,000
Investments	300,000			
Total	$ 325,000		Total	$ 325,000

Uncollectibles	$70,000	
Contractual adjustments	10,000	
Charity adjustments	5,000	
	$85,000	

(2) Allowance for Uncollectible Receivables and Third-Party Contractuals	15,000	
Contractual Adjustments	265,000	
Charity Services	125,000	
Accounts and Notes Receivable		405,000
To record deductions from gross revenues and receivables.		

3. Collections of accounts receivable totaled $3,800,000.

(3) Cash	3,800,000	
Accounts and Notes Receivable		3,800,000
To record collections of accounts receivable.		

4. Accounts receivable written off as uncollectible during the year totaled $125,000.

(4) Allowance for Uncollectible Receivables and Third-Party Contractuals	125,000	
Accounts and Notes Receivable		125,000
To record write-off of accounts deemed uncollectible.		

5. Year-end estimates of required allowances were as follows:

Uncollectible accounts	$65,000	
Contractual adjustments	15,000	
Charity adjustments	10,000	
	$90,000	

(5) Provision for Bad Debts	120,000	
Contractual Adjustments	15,000	
Charity Services	10,000	
Allowance for Uncollectible Receivables and Third-Party Contractuals		145,000
To adjust deductions from gross revenue and the allowance accounts to appropriate year-end balances.		

6. Materials and supplies, including food, purchased on account during the year totaled $600,000. A perpetual inventory system is in use.

(6) Inventories 600,000
      Accounts Payable 600,000
    To record inventory purchases on
    account.

7. Materials and supplies were used by major functions as follows:

Nursing services	$170,000
Other professional services	50,000
General services	319,000
Fiscal services	8,000
Administrative services	3,000
	$550,000

(7) Nursing Services Expense 170,000
    Other Professional Services Expense ... 50,000
    General Services Expense 319,000
    Fiscal Services Expense 8,000
    Administrative Services Expense 3,000
      Inventories 550,000
    To record inventory usage.

8. Accounts payable paid during the year were $725,000; purchase discounts of $7,000 were allowed. Cash disbursed was $718,000.

(8) Accounts Payable 725,000
      Other Operating Revenue 7,000
      Cash 718,000
    To record payment of accounts payable.

(Purchase discounts are, of course, reductions in the cost of purchases; but they are treated as other revenue in hospital accounting to simplify inventory control. The treatment is satisfactory as long as the amount of discounts is immaterial.)

9. Salaries and wages paid during the year were for the following:

Nursing services	$1,316,000
Other professional services	828,000
General services	389,000
Fiscal services	102,000
Administrative services	65,000
	$2,700,000

(9) Nursing Services Expense 1,316,000
    Other Professional Services Expense ... 828,000
    General Services Expense 389,000
    Fiscal Services Expense 102,000
    Administrative Services Expense 65,000
      Cash 2,700,000
    To record salaries and wages paid.

10. Expenses other than for salaries and materials and supplies paid during the year were chargeable as follows:

Nursing services	$ 86,000
Other professional services	79,000
General services	221,000
Fiscal services	44,000
Administrative services	327,000
	$757,000

(10) Nursing Services Expense	86,000	
Other Professional Services Expense	79,000	
General Services Expense	221,000	
Fiscal Services Expense	44,000	
Administrative Services Expense	327,000	
Cash		757,000
To record expense payments.		

11. Salaries and wages accrued at year end were for the following:

Nursing services	$ 35,000
Other professional services	21,000
General services	19,000
Fiscal services	6,000
Administrative services	2,000
	$ 83,000

(11) Nursing Services Expense	35,000	
Other Professional Services Expense	21,000	
General Services Expense	19,000	
Fiscal Services Expense	6,000	
Administrative Services Expense	2,000	
Accrued Salaries and Wages Payable		83,000
To record accrued expenses at year end.		

12. Interest expense on notes payable was $8,000, of which $1,000 was accrued at year end; the principal was reduced by $20,000.

(12) Notes Payable	20,000	
Interest Expense	8,000	
Accrued Interest Payable		1,000
Cash		27,000
To record interest payment and accrual and reduction of principal of notes payable.		

13. Interest earned during the year on Unrestricted Fund investments was $5,000, of which $2,000 was accrued at year end.

(13) Cash	3,000	
Accrued Interest Receivable	2,000	
Income and Gains from Unrestricted		
Fund Investments		5,000
To record interest earned on		
Unrestricted Fund investments.		

14. *Unrestricted* earnings on Specific Purpose Fund investments, $24,000, received and accounted for directly in the Unrestricted Fund.

(14) Cash	24,000	
Unrestricted Income from Specific		
Purpose Fund		24,000
To record unrestricted interest		
earnings on Specific Purpose Fund		
investments deposited directly in the		
Unrestricted Fund.		

15. Money collected as agent for special nurses for services rendered by them amounted to $48,000.

(15) Cash	48,000	
Due to Special Nurses		48,000
To record fees collected as agent for		
special nurses.		

16. Of the total collected for special nurses, $45,000 was paid to them; the balance has not yet been claimed.

(16) Due to Special Nurses	45,000	
Cash		45,000
To record payment of fees collected in		
an agency capacity to special nurses.		

17. Professional services donated to the hospital were objectively valued and charged as follows:

Nursing services	$17,000
Other professional services	3,000
	$20,000

(17) Nursing Services Expense	17,000	
Other Professional Services Expense ...	3,000	
Donated Services		20,000
To record the value of donated services		
received.		

18. Other revenues collected during the year were from the following:

Cafeteria sales	$45,000
Television rentals	30,000
Medical record transcript fees	15,000
Vending machine commissions	5,000
	$95,000

(18) Cash	95,000	
Cafeteria Sales		45,000
Television Rentals		30,000
Medical Record Transcript Fees		15,000
Vending Machine Commissions		5,000
To record receipt of miscellaneous revenues.		

19. General contributions received in cash, $100,000.

(19) Cash	100,000	
General Contributions		100,000
To record receipts of unrestricted contributions.		

20. Accrued interest on bonds payable at year end (see transaction 21) was $30,000.

(20) Interest Expense	30,000	
Interest Payable		30,000
To record interest accrued at year end on bonds outstanding.		

21. Bonds were issued at par, $3,000,000, to be used to pay for a new building wing and to retire the mortgage payable.

(21) Cash	3,000,000	
Bonds Payable		3,000,000
To record sale of bonds at par.		

22. The mortgage notes were paid and the contractor was paid $2,700,000 on the $2,900,000 contract; the balance is being held pending final inspection of the new wing.

(22) Buildings	2,900,000	
Mortgage Payable	100,000	
Contracts Payable—Retained Percentage		200,000
Cash		2,800,000
To record payment of mortgage payable and the building contractor, less percentage of contract retained pending final inspection of new wing.		

23. Fixed equipment costing $100,000, on which there was accumulated depreciation of $60,000, was sold for $30,000.

(23) Cash	30,000	
Accumulated Depreciation	60,000	
Loss on Disposal of Fixed Assets	10,000	
Fixed Equipment		100,000
To record the sale of fixed equipment		
at a loss.		

24. Depreciation expense for the year was $300,000.

(24) Depreciation Expense	300,000	
Accumulated Depreciation		300,000
To record depreciation expense.		

25. The board of directors designated $200,000 for future plant replacement and expansion. Although this action is binding on hospital management, it does not remove resources from the Unrestricted Fund.

> No entry is required. The board's action could be disclosed either in a footnote or in the financial statements. The following entry would be acceptable:

(25) Fund Balance	200,000	
Board-Designated Reserve for Plant		
Replacement and Expansion		200,000
To record the board's setting up a		
reserve for plant replacement and		
expansion.		

26. The charges to General Services Expense were found to include $5,000 for major movable equipment. No depreciation need be taken in the current year.

(26) Major Movable Equipment	5,000	
General Services Expense		5,000
To capitalize equipment previously		
charged to expense.		

SPECIFIC PURPOSE FUND:

27. A grant of $400,000 to defray specific operating costs was received.

(27) Cash	400,000	
Specific Purpose Fund Balance		400,000
To record receipt of a grant to be used		
to pay certain operating costs.		

28. Investments made during the period were $300,000.

(28) Investments	300,000	
Cash		300,000
To record investments during the		
period.		

29. Investments maturing during the period, $150,000, had been originally purchased at par.

(29)	Cash	150,000	
	Investments		150,000
	To record the maturity of investments		
	originally purchased at par.		

30. Earnings on investments, restricted to specified purposes, were $15,000. (Compare this transaction with transaction 14.)

(30)	Cash	15,000	
	Specific Purpose Fund Balance		15,000
	To record receipt of investment income		
	that is restricted to specific purposes.		

ENDOWMENT FUND:

31. A benefactor gave rental properties valued at $300,000, and subject to a $100,000 mortgage, to the hospital. The corpus is to be maintained intact; earnings may be used for general operating purposes.

(31)	Rental Properties	300,000	
	Mortgage Payable		100,000
	Endowment Fund Balance		200,000
	To record a gift of properties, subject		
	to mortgage assumed. The corpus is to		
	be maintained intact; earnings are not		
	restricted as to use.		

32. Rentals received in cash were $45,000.

(32)	Cash	45,000	
	Rental Revenues		45,000
	To record receipt of rentals.		

33. Depreciation of rental property was $6,000.

(33)	Depreciation Expense	6,000	
	Accumulated Depreciation		6,000
	To record depreciation.		

34. Other expenses related to rental property, paid in cash, were $9,000.

(34)	Other Rental Expenses	9,000	
	Cash		9,000
	To record payment of rental expenses.		

PLANT REPLACEMENT AND EXPANSION FUND:

35. Earnings on Plant Replacement and Expansion Fund investments, $16,000, are restricted to plant expansion.

(35) Cash 16,000
      Fund Balance   16,000
    To record earnings owned on plant
    fund investments; these earnings are
    restricted to use for plant expansion.

INTERFUND:

36. Specific Purpose Fund investments costing $165,000 were sold for $170,000; proceeds from gains on these investments are available for unrestricted use.

SPECIFIC PURPOSE FUND:

(36) Cash 170,000
      Investments   165,000
      Due to Unrestricted Fund   5,000
    To record sale of investments at a gain
    and the resulting liability to the
    Unrestricted Fund.

UNRESTRICTED FUND:

(36) Due from Specific Purpose Fund 5,000
      Unrestricted Income from Specific
        Purpose Fund   5,000
    To record gain on sale of Specific
    Purpose Fund investments and a
    receivable therefor.

(Had the proceeds of the sale in excess of cost not been available for unrestricted use, the $5,000 would have been credited to Specific Purpose Fund Balance; no entry would have been made in the Unrestricted Fund and no revenue would have been recognized at this time.)

37. Cash was transferred as necessary to settle the beginning of year interfund receivables and payables.

UNRESTRICTED FUND:

(37) Cash 145,000
      Due from Specific Purpose Fund   145,000
    To record settlement of interfund
    balances at the beginning of the year.

SPECIFIC PURPOSE FUND:

(37) Due to Unrestricted Fund 145,000
      Due from Endowment Fund   20,000
      Cash   125,000
    To record settlement of interfund
    balances at the beginning of the year.

ENDOWMENT FUND:

```
(37) Due to Specific Purpose Fund ..........   20,000
        Cash .......................................           20,000
     To record settlement of interfund
     balances at the beginning of the year.
```

38. A $300,000 transfer from the Specific Purpose Fund to the Operating Fund was authorized to reimburse the latter for specified expenses incurred; $200,000 of this amount was paid by the Specific Purpose Fund.

UNRESTRICTED FUND:

```
(38) Cash .........................................   200,000
        Due from Specific Purpose Fund ........   100,000
        Transfers from Specific Purpose
            Fund ...................................           300,000
     To record revenue transfer.
```

SPECIFIC PURPOSE FUND:

```
(38) Specific Purpose Fund Balance ..........   300,000
        Due to Unrestricted Fund ............           100,000
        Cash ......................................           200,000
     To record transfer to Unrestricted
     Fund.
```

39. Endowment rental property earnings were established as a liability to the Unrestricted Fund.

ENDOWMENT FUND:

```
(39) Rental Revenues ...........................   45,000
        Depreciation Expense ..................            6,000
        Other Rental Expenses .................            9,000
        Due to Unrestricted Fund .............           30,000
     To close operating accounts and record
     liability to Unrestricted Fund for
     earnings.
```

UNRESTRICTED FUND:

```
(39) Due from Endowment Fund .............   30,000
        Unrestricted Income from
            Endowment Fund ....................           30,000
     To record net rental income due from
     Endowment Fund.
```

40. Major movable equipment was purchased for $18,000; it was reimbursed by the Plant Replacement and Expansion Fund.

UNRESTRICTED FUND:

| (40) Major Movable Equipment .... | 18,000 | |
| Cash .... | | 18,000 |

To record purchase of equipment.

| Cash .... | 18,000 | |
| Fund Balance .... | | 18,000 |

To record reimbursement for purchase
of equipment.

PLANT REPLACEMENT AND EXPANSION FUND:

| (40) Fund Balance .... | 18,000 | |
| Cash .... | | 18,000 |

To record reimbursement of the
Unrestricted Fund for purchase of
equipment.

41. Restricted earnings received on Endowment Fund investments, $25,000, were recorded as a liability to the Specific Purpose Fund.

ENDOWMENT FUND:

| (41) Cash .... | 25,000 | |
| Due to Specific Purpose Fund .... | | 25,000 |

To record restricted earnings due to
the Specific Purpose Fund.

SPECIFIC PURPOSE FUND:

| (41) Due from Endowment Fund .... | 25,000 | |
| Specific Purpose Fund Balance .... | | 25,000 |

To record restricted purpose earnings
due from the Endowment Fund.

CLOSING:

42. Closing entries were made at year end:

UNRESTRICTED FUND:

(42) Patient Service Revenues	4,400,000
Cash Discounts on Purchases	7,000
Cafeteria Sales	45,000
Television Rentals	30,000
Medical Record Transcript Fees	15,000
Vending Machine Commissions	5,000
Transfers from Specific Purpose Fund ..	300,000
Unrestricted Income from Endowment Fund	30,000
Income and Gains from Unrestricted Fund Investments	5,000

Unrestricted Income from Specific Purpose Fund	29,000	
Donated Services	20,000	
General Contributions	100,000	
Excess of Expenses over Revenues	2,000	
Provision for Bad Debts		120,000
Contractual Adjustments		280,000
Charity Services		135,000
Nursing Services Expense		1,624,000
Other Professional Services Expense		981,000
General Services Expense		943,000
Fiscal Services Expense		160,000
Administrative Services Expense		397,000
Interest Expense		38,000
Loss on Disposal of Fixed Assets		10,000
Depreciation Expense		300,000
To close accounts at year end.		

Revenues and expenses of the other funds have been closed in preceding entries or carried directly to fund balance. Thus no closing entries are required for the Specific Purpose, Endowment, or Plant Replacement and Expansion Funds.

FINANCIAL STATEMENTS

The financial statements that a hospital should prepare for use by the public include a balance sheet, a statement of revenues and expenses, a statement of changes in fund balance, and a statement of changes in financial position. Statements should be comparative in form to provide maximum information to readers.

Notes to Financial Statements

Notes to the financial statements are an essential part of the statements. If the hospital management thinks it appropriate, supplemental schedules may also be presented to show more detailed information on segments of the statements such as patient service revenue and operating expenses.

Footnotes should describe the accounting policies of the hospital and provide information not included in the statement descriptions and amounts. Examples of subjects of footnotes include cost prices and market values of investments; bases for classifying assets and liabilities as current or otherwise; method or methods of depreciation; details of property, plant, and equipment and accumulated depreciation; information regarding bonds and related mortgages; information on capital and other leases; and pension plan descriptions and liabilities.

Balance Sheets

Figures 18-3 and 18-4 provide Balance Sheets of the Alzona Hospital at the beginning and end of the year that has been used as the example for hospital operations. Since Figure 18-3 does not contain comparative data, Figure 18-4 should be considered the better example.

The style of the two statements is often referred to as "pancake," since data for the several funds are provided in self-balancing layers. Major divisions of the layered balance sheets are labeled "Unrestricted" and "Restricted." All the funds in the latter group are externally restricted as to use, i.e., the governing board can only administer the funds in accordance with the terms established by a donor, grantor, or other provider of the funds. On the other hand, the resources in the "Unrestricted" category may be used by the board as it sees fit. Some of the resources may be "board-restricted" to a specific purpose; but, from the point of view of a third party, the board is accountable for the proper administration of all funds subject to its control.

Statement of Revenues and Expenses

Alzona Hospital's Statement of Revenues and Expenses, Figure 18-5, is based on the operations of the Unrestricted Fund. Increases and decreases in other funds are considered "changes in fund balance" rather than revenues and expenses. Only when these amounts affect the Unrestricted Fund are they treated as revenues and expenses. (Note that amounts restricted by donors or grantors to plant expansion and replacement are never recorded as revenues. When they are expended for the designated purposes, the assets are recorded in the Unrestricted Fund with a corresponding increase in fund balance.)

Donations or grants made to the hospital for the care of charity patients should be deducted from the cost of charity service. The cost of charity service should be shown net of the contributions and the amount of contributions should be shown on the face of the statement or in the footnotes.

Statement of Changes in Fund Balances

The Statement of Changes in Fund Balances is usually shown in conventional pancake form (Figure 18-6). An alternative form for the Unrestricted Fund is shown in Figure 18-7, Statement of Revenues, Expenses, and Changes in Fund Balance. The latter form provides (1) a complete presentation of the changes in the Fund for the year, and (2) a distinction among activities identified with hospital operations, plant, and other. Although the distinction does provide additional information, it may be primarily a bow to the past, when separate funds for the three were generally accepted as desirable. In fact, the basic accounting may acceptably be done with separate funds for operations, for plant, and for other board-designated groupings. We have not demonstrated such separate fund accounting because it serves internal purposes only and would result in statements identical to those we have presented.

Statement of Changes in Financial Position

The Statement of Changes in Financial Position, Figure 18-8, is conventional for enterprise-type organizations. Note that it relates only to the Unrestricted Funds because these resources are the only ones subject to control by the board.

Figure 18-4

ALZONA HOSPITAL
Balance Sheet
September 30, 19B
With Comparative Figures for September 30, 19A

Unrestricted Fund

Assets	September 30 19B	September 30 19A
Current:		
Cash	$ 573,000	$ 175,000
Receivables	$ 770,000	$ 700,000
Less: Estimated uncollectibles and allowances	90,000	85,000
	$ 680,000	$ 615,000
Interest receivable	$ 2,000	
Due from Endowment Fund	$ 30,000	
Due from Specific Purpose Fund .	$ 105,000	$ 145,000
Inventories	$ 215,000	$ 165,000
Total current assets	$1,605,000	$1,100,000
Other:		
Investments	$ 100,000	$ 100,000
Land	$ 130,000	$ 130,000
Land improvements	80,000	80,000
Buildings	7,900,000	5,000,000
Fixed equipment	500,000	600,000
Major movable equipment	113,000	90,000

Liabilities and Fund Balances	September 30 19B	September 30 19A
Current:		
Notes payable	$ 130,000	$ 150,000
Accounts payable	50,000	175,000
Interest payable	31,000	
Salaries and wages payable	83,000	
Due to special nurses	3,000	
Contracts payable, retained percentage	200,000	
Total current liabilities	$ 497,000	$ 325,000
Long-term debt:		
Mortgage payable		100,000
Bonds payable	3,000,000	
Fund balance	4,241,000	4,225,000

Total property, plant, and equipment	$8,723,000	$5,900,000
Less: Accumulated depreciation	2,690,000	2,450,000
Net property, plant, and equipment	$6,033,000	$3,450,000
Total assets	$7,738,000	$4,650,000

Restricted Funds

Specific Purpose Fund:

Cash	$130,000	$20,000
Investments	345,000	360,000
Due from Endowment Fund	25,000	20,000
Total assets	$500,000	$400,000

Specific Purpose Fund:

Due to Unrestricted Fund	$105,000	$145,000
Fund balance	395,000	255,000
Total	$500,000	$400,000

Endowment Fund:

Cash	$66,000	$25,000
Investments	$475,000	475,000
Rental properties	$300,000	
Less: Accumulated depreciation	6,000	
Net rental properties	$294,000	
Total assets	$835,000	$500,000

Endowment Fund:

Due to Specific Purpose Fund	$25,000	$20,000
Due to Unrestricted Fund	30,000	
Mortgage payable	100,000	
Total liabilities	$155,000	
Fund balance	680,000	480,000
Total	$835,000	$500,000

Plant Replacement and Expansion Fund:

Cash	$23,000	$25,000
Investments	300,000	300,000
Total assets	$323,000	$325,000

Plant Replacement and Expansion Fund:

Fund balance	$323,000	$325,000
Total	$323,000	$325,000

Figure 18-5

ALZONA HOSPITAL

Statement of Revenues and Expenses
For the Year Ended September 30, 19B
With Comparative Figures for 19A

	September 30	
	19B	19A*
Patient service revenues	$4,400,000	
Less: Deductions from patient service revenues:		
Contractual adjustments	$ 280,000	
Charity service	135,000	
Provision for bad debts	120,000	
Total deductions from patient service revenues	$ 535,000	
Net patient service revenues	$3,865,000	
Other operating revenues:		
Cafeteria sales	$45,000	
Television rentals	30,000	
Medical record transcript fees	15,000	
Vending machine commissions	5,000	
Discounts on purchases	7,000	
Transfers from Specific Purpose Fund	300,000	
Total other operating revenue	$ 402,000	
Total operating revenue	$4,267,000	
Operating expenses:		
Nursing services	$1,624,000	
Other professional services	981,000	
General services	943,000	
Fiscal services	160,000	
Administrative services	397,000	
Depreciation	300,000	
Loss on disposal of assets	10,000	
Interest expense	38,000	
Total operating expenses	$4,453,000	
Loss from operations	$ 186,000	
Nonoperating revenues:		
Unrestricted income from Endowment Fund	$ 30,000	
Income and gain from Unrestricted Fund investments	5,000	
Unrestricted income from Specific Purpose Fund	29,000	
Donated services	20,000	
General contributions	100,000	
Total nonoperating revenues	$ 184,000	
Excess of expenses over revenues	$ 2,000	

Although the hospital operated in fiscal 19A, the figures for that year's activities were not needed for the example in the chapter and we provide none here.

Figure 18-6

ALZONA HOSPITAL

Statement of Changes in Fund Balances
For the Year Ended September 30, 19B
With Comparative Figures for 19A

	Year Ending September 30	
	19B	*19A**
Unrestricted Fund:		
Balance, beginning of year	$4,225,000	
Transferred from Plant Replacement and Expansion Fund to finance expenditure for property, plant, and equipment	18,000	
Excess of expenses over revenues	(2,000)	
Balance, end of year	$4,241,000	
Restricted Funds:		
Specific Purpose Fund:		
Balance, beginning of year	$ 255,000	
Specific purpose grant	400,000	
Investment income of Specific Purpose Fund	15,000	
Investment income from Endowment Fund—restricted to a specific purpose ..	25,000	
Transferred to Unrestricted Fund as other operating revenue	(300,000)	
Balance, end of year	$ 395,000	
Endowment Fund:		
Balance, beginning of year	$ 480,000	
Endowment received, net of mortgage assumed	200,000	
Balance, end of year	$ 680,000	
Plant Replacement and Expansion Fund:		
Balance, beginning of year	$ 325,000	
Investment income—restricted to plant expansion	16,000	
Transferred to Unrestricted Fund to finance expenditure for property, plant, and equipment	(18,000)	
Balance, end of year	$ 323,000	

Although the hospital operated in fiscal 19A, the figures for that year's activities were not needed for the example in the chapter and we provide none here.

Figure 18-7

ALZONA HOSPITAL

Statement of Revenues, Expenses, and
Changes in Unrestricted Fund Balance
(Alternative Presentation)
For the Year Ended September 30, 19B
With Comparative Figures for 19A

	19B				19A*
	Operations	*Other*	*Plant*	*Total*	
Patient service revenues	$4,400,000			$4,400,000	
Less: Deductions from patient service revenues:					
Contractual adjustments	$ 280,000			$ 280,000	
Charity service	135,000			135,000	
Provision for bad debts	120,000			120,000	
Total deductions from patient service revenues	$ 535,000			$ 535,000	
Net patient service revenues	$3,865,000			$3,865,000	
Other operating revenues (including $300,000 from Specific Purpose Fund)	402,000			402,000	
Total operating revenues	$4,267,000			$4,267,000	
Operating expenses:					
Nursing services	$1,624,000			$1,624,000	
Other professional services	981,000			981,000	
General services	943,000			943,000	
Fiscal services	160,000			160,000	

Administrative services	397,000			397,000
Depreciation	300,000			300,000
Loss on disposal of assets	10,000			10,000
Interest expense	38,000			38,000
Total operating expenses	$4,453,000			$4,453,000
Loss from operations	$ 186,000			$ 186,000
Nonoperating revenues:				
Unrestricted income from Endowment Fund		$ 30,000		$ 30,000
Income and gain from Unrestricted Fund investments		5,000		5,000
Unrestricted income from Specific Purpose Fund		29,000		29,000
Donated services	$ 20,000			20,000
General contributions		100,000		100,000
Total nonoperating revenues	$ 20,000	$164,000		$ 184,000
Excess of revenues over expenses	$ (166,000)	$164,000		$ (2,000)
Fund balance, beginning of year	775,000	100,000	$3,350,000	4,225,000
Transferred from restricted funds			18,000	18,000
Intrafund transfers	499,000	(164,000)	(335,000)	—
Fund balance, end of year	$1,108,000	$100,000	$3,033,000	$4,241,000

*Although the hospital operated in fiscal 19A, the figures for that year's activities were not needed for the example in the chapter and we do not provide them here.

Figure 18-8

ALZONA HOSPITAL

Unrestricted Funds
Statement of Changes in Financial Position
For the Year Ended September 30, 19B
With Comparative Figures for 19A

	19B	19A*
Funds provided:		
Operations:		
Excess of expenses over revenues	$ (2,000)	
Add: Expenses not requiring funds:		
Depreciation	300,000	
Loss on sale of fixed equipment	10,000	
Funds provided by operations	$ 308,000	
Sale of fixed equipment	30,000	
Issuance of bonds payable	3,000,000	
Transferred from Plant Replacement and		
Expansion Fund	18,000	
Total funds provided	$3,356,000	
Funds applied:		
Additions to property, plant, and equipment	$2,923,000	
Reduction of mortgage	100,000	
Increase in working capital	333,000	
Total funds applied	$3,356,000	
Changes in working capital:		
Increase (decrease) in current assets:		
Cash	$ 398,000	
Receivables	65,000	
Interest receivable	2,000	
Due from Endowment Fund	30,000	
Due from Specific Purpose Fund	(40,000)	
Inventories	50,000	
Increase in current assets	$ 505,000	
Increase (decrease) in current liabilities:		
Notes payable	$ (20,000)	
Accounts payable	(125,000)	
Interest payable	31,000	
Salaries and wages payable	83,000	
Due to special nurses	3,000	
Contracts payable, retained percentage	200,000	
Increase in current liabilities	$ 172,000	
Increase (decrease) in working capital	$ 333,000	

Although the hospital operated in fiscal 19A, the figures for that year's activities were not needed for the example in the chapter and we do not provide them here.

RELATED ORGANIZATIONS[5]

Hospitals have a variety of contacts with foundations, auxiliaries, and guilds. They have in some cases created "separate organizations, frequently referred to as foundations, to raise and hold certain funds for hospitals."[6] In at least some cases the purpose of the foundations is to segregate resources so that their availability will not cause external forces (governmental programs and controls) to require their use to subsidize services other than those the hospital board would select.

Such organizations are "related" if the hospital controls the separate organization's operations *or* if the hospital is the organization's sole beneficiary. Reference to Accounting Research Bulletin No. 51, "Consolidated Financial Statements," will provide guidance as to whether the financial statements of the hospital and its related organizations should be consolidated or combined.

If the statements are not consolidated but a high degree of relationship (both the "control" and "sole beneficiary" tests are met) exists, the hospital must provide substantial footnote information about the organization. A description of the nature of the relationship, together with summary data from the related organizations' financial statements regarding assets, liabilities, fund balance, and changes therein, including results of operation, should be included in the hospital's statements.

If the financial statements have not been consolidated and the disclosures described in the preceding paragraph have not been made because the relationship tests have not been met, there may be circumstances that require *some* disclosures. Specific reference to SOP 81-2 is recommended.

A HOSPITAL COST FINDING EXAMPLE

The American Hospital Association recommends that hospitals use a "controllable cost" accounting system to control day-to-day activities and that full and reimbursable costs be determined by use of cost finding techniques.[7] Data for budgeting and current control over costs are produced by use of cost accounting centers, for which are accumulated the direct costs that are controllable by the department head or lower-level supervisor. These cost centers traditionally are referred to as *special service* or *patient service* departments or activities if their services are rendered directly to patients; they are referred to as *general service* departments or activities if they provide services to the hospital as a whole. In recent years they have increasingly been categorized simply as "revenue producing" or "nonrevenue producing." A system of worksheet (or computerized)

---

[5] This section is based on the AICPA Subcommittee on Health Care Matters, *Statement of Position No. 81-2*, "Reporting Practices Concerning Hospital Related Organizations" (New York: AICPA, 1981). Hereafter cited as SOP 81-2.

[6] Ibid., Paragraph 1.

[7] *Cost Finding and Rate Setting for Hospitals* (Chicago: The Association, 1968), p. 1. This AHA book contains extensive discussions on, and a comprehensive illustration of, hospital cost finding. The illustration in this chapter is necessarily brief and general.

procedures is then utilized to provide for the allocation and accumulation of cost data so that information equivalent to that produced by a full-cost accounting system is produced.

Methods of Cost Allocation

Three methods, known by various terms or simply by number, are currently accepted and widely used for making the cost allocations. The results produced by the methods differ enough to require that a single method should be adopted and used consistently if period-by-period comparisons are to be made.

Under Method 1, often referred to as the "direct" or "single step" method, the costs of nonrevenue producing (general service) cost centers are distributed only to the revenue producing (special service and patient service) cost centers. Revenue producing patient service cost centers—classified here as Inpatients, Nursery, Outpatients, Emergency, and Private Ambulatory—are not the cost centers to which most costs are charged directly. However, all costs are ultimately charged to them by the worksheet procedure.

Under Method 2, often termed the "step-down" method, a nonrevenue producing (general service) department's costs may be distributed to other non-revenue producing (general service) departments as well as to revenue producing (special service and patient service) cost centers. After a department's costs have been distributed, it does not receive distributions from other departments, how-ever, even though it may benefit from their services. Therefore an attempt is made to allocate departmental costs in such an order that the inaccuracies will be minimized; that is, the departments that receive the least service from the others will be closed out first.

Under Method 3, sometimes known as the "double step" or "double dis-tribution" method, the costs of each nonrevenue producing (general service) department are distributed to every other department it serves. Again, an attempt is made to distribute first the costs of the departments that receive the least service from others. Even though a department's costs have been allocated, it may receive distributions from other departments during the "first round" allo-cation process. The amounts are then reallocated as in Method 2.[8]

Method 3 is the most accurate of those described above; Method 1, the least accurate. Method 2 is a widely used compromise and is used in a further de-scription of cost allocation worksheet technique.

The usual worksheet procedures involve three basic steps: (1) rearrangement of direct costs, (2) allocation of nonrevenue producing (general service) department costs, and (3) allocation of revenue producing (special service) department costs. Each of these steps is discussed in the following paragraphs.

---

[8] A fourth method, which may be called the "mathematical" or "scientific" method, is more accurate than any of the three common methods discussed but appears to be used rather infrequently, possibly due to its use of complex simultaneous equations to apportion costs among all departments and ultimately allocate all general service costs to special service and patient cost centers. Mathematical solution of a distribution involving as many unknowns as are present in a hospital usually is not feasible in the absence of computer capability; hence this method is not discussed in detail here.

Rearrangement of Direct Costs

In some cases direct cost centers established because of supervisory assignments contain costs allocable to two or more identifiable activities. For example, budgeting and day-to-day cost control may dictate the use of a dietary cost center. All raw food and food preparation costs are assigned to this center and are the responsibility of the dietitian. But for allocation purposes it must be recognized that a hospital cafeteria usually serves individuals or groups in addition to inpatients. Hence, before the allocation of dietary costs to other departments is begun, they must be separated into those costs applicable to the cafeteria, those applicable to the nursery, and those applicable to inpatients. The separation should be based on priced requisitions of food and analysis of payroll costs incurred for cafeteria and other dietary functions. The cost center data that are the basis of succeeding steps in this example may be assumed to already reflect rearrangements of direct costs such as that just described.

Allocation of Nonrevenue Producing (General Service) Department Costs

The following is a list of typical nonrevenue producing (general service) departments and their usual bases of allocation to other nonrevenue producing (general service) departments and to revenue producing (special service and patient service) cost centers:

Nonrevenue Producing (General Service) Cost Center	Basis of Allocation
Provision for Depreciation	For Buildings: Floor Space
	For Equipment: Equipment in Use
Employee Health and Welfare	Dollars of Payroll
Operation of Plant	Floor Space
Maintenance of Plant	Floor Space
Laundry and Linen Service	Pounds of Laundry Used
Housekeeping	Hours of Service
Dietary—Raw Food	To Cafeteria: Priced Requisitions
	To Inpatients: Meals Served
Dietary—Other	To Cafeteria: Percent of Raw Food Costs
	To Inpatients: Meals Served
Cafeteria	Sales Value of Meals Served
Maintenance of Personnel	Number of Employees Housed
Nursing Service	Hours of Service
Medical Supplies and Expense	Priced Requisitions
Pharmacy	Priced Requisitions
Medical Records	Hours of Service
Social Service	Hours of Service
Nursing School	Hours of Service
Intern–Resident School	Hours of Service
Administration and General	Accumulated Costs of Other Centers

A worksheet illustrating the allocation of Nursing Service costs to other centers is given in Figure 18-9. Nursing staff hours for the period were 100,000;

Figure 18-9

A HOSPITAL
Cost Apportionment

Schedule No.: <u>B–11</u>
Cost Center: <u>Nursing Service</u>
For Fiscal Year: _____
Basis of Apportionment: <u>Nursing Staff Hours</u>

Cost Center	Statistical Data	Cost Apportionment
Inpatients	75,000	$712,500
Nursery	25,000	237,500
Total	100,000	$950,000

---

total cost was $950,000. By dividing $950,000 by 100,000 an hourly rate of $9.50 is produced; this rate times the nursing hours spent in a cost center produces the nursing service allocation to that center. A similar worksheet allocation is prepared for each general service cost center.

Data provided by the worksheet allocations described in the preceding paragraph are summarized on the "Cost Apportionment—General Services" worksheet, Figure 18-10. Note that the provision for depreciation is distributed first (in column 3) and that depreciation becomes a part of the total cost of the employee health and welfare center which is distributed. As a further example note that the direct cost of nursing service is $910,000 (column 1) but that the amount distributed in column 13, $950,000, includes cost distributions made in preceding columns.

The result of the distributions made in Figure 18-10 is the accumulation of total costs for special service centers and partial costs for patient service centers. A comparison of the statistics on output of the special service centers with their accumulated total costs will produce total unit costs. These data may be reported for the purposes previously cited in a statement such as "Special Services Costs," Figure 18-11.

Allocation of Special Service Department Costs

After total costs have been computed for special service departments they are distributed to the patient cost centers. A worksheet such as that illustrated in Figure 18-9 for the apportionment of nursing service costs is prepared for each of the special service centers. The apportionments are made on the bases indicated in Figure 18-11, the report of "Special Services Costs," except that if some of the units are not uniform, a weighting process may be used. That is to say, if certain kinds of physical therapy treatments are more expensive than others, the more expensive ones may be appropriately weighted to allocate the total cost of treatments more accurately.

A worksheet for accumulation of total patient center costs is illustrated in Figure 18-12. The data from the allocation worksheets for each special service cost center are entered in it to accumulate total costs.

After total costs have been computed they may be compared with statistical data concerning output of the patient centers to arrive at total unit costs. Reporting of these data is illustrated in Figure 18-13, "Inpatient and Outpatient Costs."

Hospitals are not, of course, the first organizations to use cost finding. Broadly speaking, any special study of costs is "cost finding," as is a system of cost accounting. However, the formal acceptance of cost finding as a preferred solution to the problem of obtaining total cost is unusual; the usefulness of the approach for hospital administration indicates that it may be useful in other areas of fund accounting.

▶ **Question 18-1.** Prepare a list of the funds recommended for use by a hospital. Opposite the funds indicate the fund(s) or account group(s) recommended for municipalities by the National Council on Governmental Accounting that is most nearly comparable in nature.

Question 18-2. What is the Unrestricted Fund treatment accorded transfers from funds restricted to use for specific operating purposes? From funds restricted to use for fixed asset additions? Explain the difference.

Question 18-3. What is the difference between funds designated by hospital boards for specific purposes and those designated by outside donors for specific purposes? What are the accounting effects?

Question 18-4. What kind of fund should be used to account for a hospital that is the property of a government? What are the differences, if any, between the accounting for a government-owned hospital and that for a hospital that is an entity in itself? Explain.

Question 18-5. Why is it important to distinguish between "unrestricted" and "restricted" assets in hospital accounting? (Define these terms in your answer.)

Question 18-6. Explain the increase of the influence of the AICPA over hospital accounting.

Question 18-7. List the principal classifications of hospital revenues.

Question 18-8. What have been the principal effects of the rapidly expanded role and the significance of third party payers on hospital accounting and reporting?

Question 18-9. What are the advantages of showing billings at standard rates and showing allowances as deductions from gross revenues rather than showing the net amount billed as revenues without disclosing the amounts of deductions?

Question 18-10. Discuss the advisability of comparing the unit costs of one hospital with those of another hospital.

Question 18-11. Diagnostic and analysis equipment developed by the Federal government at a cost of $1,000,000 per unit was donated to Peoples' Hospital for medical and research use. Similar equipment is available from a commercial supplier at a cost of $600,000 new or for $400,000 if used and of about the same age as that received. The hospital will

Figure 18-10

A HOSPITAL
Cost Apportionment—General Services
For Fiscal Year

Cost Center	Total	Provision for Depreciation	Employee Health and Welfare	Nursing Service	Social Service
1	2	3	4	13	17
General Service Cost Centers					
Provision for Depreciation....	$ 45,000	$45,000			
Employee Health and Welfare	40,000	$ 50	$40,500		
Operation of Plant	65,000	600	$ 200		
Maintenance of Plant	35,000	400	1,300		
Laundry and Linen Service .	30,000	800	1,350		
Housekeeping	60,000	300	2,300		
Dietary—Raw Food	46,000				
—Other.............	61,000	800	2,500		
Cafeteria	52,000	1,200	800		
Maintenance of Personnel ...	5,000	7,050	200		
Nursing Service.............	910,000	400	11,300	$950,000	
Medical Supplies and Expense	85,000	800	1,200		
Pharmacy	50,000	450	400		
Medical Records............	20,000	600	900		
Social Service	10,000	300	300		$12,500
Nursing School	27,000	2,550	1,050		
Intern-Resident Service	48,000	150	1,850		
Administration and General .	160,000	2,500	4,300		
Cost of Meals Sold					
Cost of Rooms Rented					
Special Service Cost Centers					
Operating Service...........	76,000	4,500	2,550		
Delivery Room	20,000	850	850		
Anesthesia	12,000	350			
Radiology	56,000	2,200	1,850		
Laboratory	81,000	1,200	2,850		
Blood Bank	34,000	300	400		
BMR—EKG	8,000	200	100		
Oxygen Therapy	6,000	400	50		
Physical Therapy	25,000	800	600		
Cost of Medical Supplies Sold					
Cost of Drugs Sold					
Inpatient Cost Centers					
Inpatients		12,150		$712,500	$ 6,500
Nursery	2,000	850		237,500	
Outpatient Cost Centers					
Outpatients	15,000	1,500	500		5,500
Emergency.................	20,000	750	800		500
Total	$2,104,000	$45,000	$40,500	$950,000	$12,500

Figure 18-10 (continued)

Subtotal	Deduct Recovery of Expenses	Nursing School	Intern-Resident Service	Subtotal After Deductions	Administrative and General	Total
18	19	20	21	22	23	24
$ 85,000	$ 8,500	$76,500				
75,000			$75,000			
202,000				$ 202,000		
23,500	23,000			500		
6,500	6,700			(200)	$202,300	
108,000		$ 7,500	$10,000	125,500	$ 20,742	$ 146,242
36,000		6,500	7,500	50,000	8,264	58,264
14,000			8,000	22,000	3,636	25,636
66,000				66,000	10,908	76,908
86,000				86,000	14,214	100,214
34,000				34,000	5,619	39,619
9,000				9,000	1,487	10,487
7,000				7,000	1,157	8,157
31,000				31,000	5,124	36,124
4,500				4,500		4,500
35,000				35,000		35,000
570,500		52,000	36,000	658,500	108,835	1,173,585
51,000		4,500		55,500	9,173	258,423
29,500		3,600	7,000	40,100	6,628	46,728
30,500		2,400	6,500	39,400	6,513	45,913
$2,104,000	$38,200	$76,500	$75,000	$1,465,800	$202,300	$2,065,800

Figure 18-11

A HOSPITAL

Special Services Costs
For the Fiscal Year

Special Service Cost Center	Total Costs	Units of Service Rendered	Average Cost per Unit
Operating Service	$146,242	5,879 hours	$24.88
Delivery Room	58,264	1,167 deliveries	49.92
Anesthesia	25,636	6,555 hours	3.91
Radiology	76,908	29,015 films	2.65
Laboratory	100,214	70,780 examinations ...	1.42
Blood Bank	39,619	1,752 transfusions	22.61
BMR—EKG	10,487	1,772 examinations ...	5.92
Oxygen Therapy	8,157	8,526 hours	.96
Physical Therapy	36,124	1,111 treatments	3.25
Cost of Medical Supplies Sold	4,500		
Cost of Drugs Sold	35,000		

use the equipment extensively, but the administrator doubts that it will be replaced when it is worn out or obsolete due to its high cost.

(a) Should the contribution be accounted for as either revenue or contributed capital by the hospital? Explain.

(b) Should depreciation be recorded and, if so, on what "cost" basis?

Question 18-12.

(a) Should depreciation be charged on the fixed assets of a hospital if these assets have been financed from contributions but are intended to be replaced from hospital revenues?

(b) Assume that the replacement of the fixed assets is intended to be financed from contributions. Should depreciation be charged on such fixed assets?

Question 18-13. The XYZ Hospital has an appropriation for *Clerical Help* which includes the salaries of clerks in the administrator's office, admissions office, accounting office, and outpatient clinic. Discuss the implications of this arrangement for cost accounting and cost finding purposes.

Question 18-14. A county hospital derives its revenues solely from a special tax levy made for this purpose. Would the accounting procedures outlined throughout this chapter apply to such a hospital? If not, indicate the fund or funds in which the financial transactions of the hospital should be recorded.

▶ **Problem 18-1.** The Community Hospital began operations in early January 19X0 in facilities financed largely by donations from the James family. No capital expenditures were made during 19X0 and no fixed assets were retired. By action of the board of trustees, the administrator is responsible for funding depreciation unless excused by action of the board. No such action has been taken.

The Edna May James Fund has been established for the special purpose of making loans to X-ray students. The Julian James Fund has been established to buy additional X-

Figure 18-12

A HOSPITAL

Cost Apportionment—Special Services

For the Fiscal Year

Cost Center	Accumulated Costs*	Inpatients	Nursery	Outpatients	Emergency	Private Ambulatory
1	2	3	4	5	6	7
Special Service Cost Centers:						
Operating Service	$ 146,242	$ 137,442	$ 8,800			
Delivery Room	58,264	58,264				
Anesthesia	25,636	24,600	1,036			
Radiology	76,908	34,200	1,708	$ 2,200	$ 5,300	$33,500
Laboratory	100,214	80,500	1,500	7,914	700	9,600
Blood Bank	39,619	37,400	500		1,719	
BMR—EKG	10,487	7,800	100	500	100	1,987
Oxygen Therapy	8,157	6,100			557	
Physical Therapy	36,124	11,200	1,500	9,924		15,000
Cost of Medical Supplies Sold	4,500	4,100	400			
Cost of Drugs Sold	35,000	26,600	200	2,800	1,100	4,300
Inpatient Cost Centers:						
Inpatients	1,173,585	1,173,585				
Nursery	258,423		258,423			
Outpatient Cost Centers:						
Outpatients	46,728			46,728		
Emergency	45,913				45,913	
Private Ambulatory						
Total	$2,065,800	$1,601,791	$274,167	$70,066	$55,389	$64,387

*From Column 24, Figure 18-10.

Figure 18-13

A HOSPITAL

Inpatient and Outpatient Costs
For the Fiscal Year

Cost Center	Total Costs*	Units of Service Rendered	Average Cost per Unit
Inpatient Cost Centers:			
Inpatients	$1,601,791	53,161 patient days	$30.13
Nursery	274,167	7,393 newborn days .	37.08
Outpatient Costs Centers:			
Outpatients	70,066	9,886 visits	7.09
Emergency	55,389	5,518 visits	10.04
Private Ambulatory .	64,387	13,025 visits	4.94

*From "Total" line, Figure 18-12.

ray equipment. $10,500 in cash and $12,000 in securities were donated to form the Julian James Fund and these assets were combined with other cash and securities intended for plant building use.

The books were closed on December 31, 19X0. No financial statements have ever been prepared, but the list of accounts shown is in balance.

Required:

From the information available to you, prepare a worksheet that provides balance sheet information for each of the necessary funds. (A formal balance sheet is not required.) Include, in the worksheet, columns for the December 31, 19X0, trial balance, adjustments, nd adjusted balances for the necessary funds.

Schedule of Account Balances

Accounts payable	7.000
Accounts receivable	70,000
Accrued interest payable	20,000
Accrued salaries and wages payable	10,000
Accrued taxes payable	500
Accumulated depreciation—buildings	30,000
Accumulated depreciation—equipment	37,500
Allowance for doubtful accounts	7,800
Allowance for uncollectible pledges	20,000
Buildings	1,500,000
Building drive pledges receivable	115,000
Capital	2,660,400
Cash—Building drive fund	73,000
Cash—Edna May James	700
Cash—Operating fund	41,500
Cash—Payroll account	2,500
Equipment	600,000
Inventory	20,000
Investments—Building drive fund	840,000
Investments—Edna May James	2,000
Land	25,000

Mortgage payable	500,000
Petty cash	500
Prepaid expenses	2,500

(FHFMA, adapted)

Problem 18-2. The following transactions and events relate to the operation of a hospital. Prepare journal entries to record the effects of these transactions and events in the general ledger accounts of the appropriate fund(s). Explanations of entries may be omitted, but indicate the fund in which each is made.

1. Total billings for patient services rendered, $85,000; it was estimated that bad debt losses on these billings would be $1,000 and that contractual adjustments would amount to $6,000.

2. A transfer from the Heart Research Fund to the Unrestricted Fund was authorized, $15,000, to defray such expenses previously recorded in the Unrestricted Fund. The cash will be transferred later in the year.

3. An item of fixed equipment (cost, $8,000; accumulated depreciation, $5,000) was sold for $1,000.

4. Depreciation expense on buildings was recognized, $18,000.

5. Earnings of the Endowment Fund are restricted to use for intern education. The net income of the Endowment Fund (revenues, $18,000; expenses, $4,000) was established as a liability to the appropriate fund.

6. Unrestricted income on Endowment Fund investments, $3,500, was received and recorded directly in the Unrestricted Fund.

7. An $11,000 transfer from the Unrestricted Fund was authorized (not yet paid) to partially fund depreciation expense.

8. Of the billings for patient services rendered (see item 1), $1,000 was written off, $600 of which was found to relate to charity cases.

Problem 18-3. A newly elected board of directors of Central Hospital, a not-for-profit corporation, decided that effective January 1, 19X4:

1. The existing general ledger balances are to be properly adjusted and allocated to two separate funds (Unrestricted Fund, John Central Endowment Fund).

2. The totals of the John Central Endowment Fund and the Allowance for Accumulated Depreciation are to be fully invested in securities.

3. All accounts are to be maintained in accordance with the principles of hospital accounting. The board engaged you to determine the proper account balances for each of the funds.

The balances in the general ledger at January 1, 19X4, were:

	Debit	Credit
Cash	$ 50,000	
Investment in U.S. Treasury bills	105,000	
Investment in common stock	417,000	
Interest receivable	4,000	
Accounts receivable	40,000	
Inventory	25,000	
Land	407,000	
Building	245,000	
Equipment	283,000	
Allowance for accumulated depreciation		$ 376,000
Accounts payable		70,000
Bank loan		150,000

John Central Endowment Fund Balance		119,500
Surplus		860,500
Totals	$1,576,000	$1,576,000

The following additional information is available:

1. Under the terms of the will of John Central, founder of the hospital, "the principal of the bequest is to be fully invested in trust forevermore in mortgages secured by productive real estate in Central City and/or in U.S. Government securities . . . and the income therefrom is to be used to defray current expenses."

2. The John Central Endowment Fund Balance account consists of the following:

Cash received in 18Z6 by bequest from John Central ..	$ 81,500
Net gains realized from 19T2 through 19W5 from the sale of real estate acquired in mortgage foreclosures	23,500
Income received from 19W6 through 19X3 from U.S. Treasury Bill investments	14,500
Balance per general ledger on January 1, 19X4	$119,500

3. The Land account balance was composed of:

18Z6 appraisal of land at $10,000 and building at $5,000 received by donation at that time. (The building was demolished in 19R6)	$ 15,000
Appraisal increase based on insured value in land title policies issued in 19T3	380,000
Landscaping costs for trees planted	12,000
Balance per general ledger on January 1, 19X4	$407,000

4. The Building account balance was composed of:

Cost of present hospital building completed in January 19T2 when the hospital commenced operations (41 years ago)	$300,000
Adjustment to record appraised value of building in 19U3 (30 years ago)	(100,000)
Cost of elevator installed in hospital building in January 19V9 (14 years ago)	45,000
Balance per general ledger on January 1, 19X4	$245,000

The estimated useful lives of the hospital building and the elevator when new were 50 years and 20 years, respectively.

5. The hospital's equipment was inventoried on January 1, 19X4. The cost of the inventory agreed with the Equipment account balance in the general ledger. The Allowance for Accumulated Depreciation account at January 1, 19X4, included $158,250 applicable to equipment and that amount was approved by the board of directors as being accurate. All depreciation is computed on a straight-line basis.

6. A bank loan was obtained to finance the cost of new operating room equipment purchased in 19X0. Interest on the loan was paid to December 31, 19X3.

Required:

Prepare a worksheet to present the adjustments necessary to restate the general ledger account balances properly and to distribute the adjusted balances to establish the required fund accounts at January 1, 19X4. Formal journal entries are not required.

DEXTER HOSPITAL

Balance Sheet

As of December 31, 19X5

Assets | _Liabilities and Fund Balances_

Unrestricted Fund

Current:			Current:			
Cash		$ 20,000	Accounts payable			$ 16,000
Accounts receivable	$ 37,000		Accrued expenses			6,000
Less allowance for uncollectible			Total current liabilities			$ 22,000
accounts	7,000	30,000	Mortgage bonds payable			150,000
Inventory of supplies		14,000	Fund balance			2,158,000
Total current assets		$ 64,000				
Other:						
Land		$ 400,000				
Buildings	$1,750,000					
Less accumulated depreciation	430,000	1,320,000				
Equipment	$ 680,000					
Less accumulated depreciation	134,000	546,000				
Total other assets		$2,266,000				
Total		$2,330,000	Total			$2,330,000

Endowment Fund

Cash		$ 6,000	Fund balance	$266,000
Investments		260,000		
Total		$266,000	Total	$266,000

Plant Replacement and Expansion Fund

Cash		$ 53,800	Fund balance	$ 125,000
Investments		71,200		
Total		$125,000	Total	$ 125,000

Computations should be in good form and should be referenced to the worksheet adjustments which they support. In addition to trial balance columns, the following columnar headings are recommended for your worksheet:

Adjustments		Unrestricted Fund		John Central Endowment Fund	
Debit	Credit	Debit	Credit	Debit	Credit

Problem 18-4. The combined balance sheet of Dexter Hospital as of December 31, 19X5 is presented on page 747.

During 19X6 the following transactions occurred:

1. Gross charges for hospital services, all charged to accounts receivable, were as follows:

Room and board charges	$780,000
Charges for other professional services	321,000

2. Deductions from gross revenues were as follows:

Provision for uncollectible receivables	$30,000
Charity service	15,000

3. The Unrestricted Fund paid $18,000 to retire mortgage bonds payable with an equivalent par value.

4. During the year the Unrestricted Fund received general contributions of $50,000 and income from Endowment Fund investments of $6,500. The Unrestricted Fund has been designated to receive income earned on Endowment Fund investments.

5. New equipment costing $26,000 was acquired. An X-ray machine which originally cost $24,000, and which had an undepreciated cost of $2,400, was sold for $500.

6. Vouchers totaling $1,191,000 were issued for the following items:

Administrative service expenses	$120,000
Fiscal service expense	95,000
General service expense	225,000
Nursing service expense	520,000
Other professional service expense	165,000
Supplies	60,000
Expenses accrued at December 31, 19X5 .	6,000

7. Collections on accounts receivable totaled $985,000. Accounts written off as uncollectible amounted to $11,000.

8. Cash payments on vouchers payable during the year were $825,000.

9. Supplies of $37,000 were issued to nursing services.

10. On December 31, 19X6, accrued interest income on Plant Replacement and Expansion Fund investments was $800. Income is donor-restricted to plant replacement and expansion.

11. Depreciation of buildings and equipment was as follows:

Buildings	$44,000
Equipment	73,000

12. On December 31, 19X6, an accrual of $6,100 was made for fiscal service expense on bonds.

Required:

For the period January 1, 19X6, through December 31, 19X6, prepare journal entries to record the transactions described above for the following funds of Dexter Hospital:

Unrestricted Fund (UF)
Endowment Fund (EF)
Plant Replacement and Expansion Fund (PREF)

Each journal entry should be numbered to correspond with the transaction described. Indicate by appropriate initials the fund in which the entry is made.

(AICPA, adapted)

Problem 18-5. The Z Society, a fraternal order which operated X County Hospital for indigent members of the community, donated it on September 1, 19X5, to the Village of H, in which it is located. The gift included all of the securities in the Endowment Fund (the hospital's principal source of income), as well as the real estate, equipment, and other assets. Since the village had made no appropriation for the operation and maintenance of a hospital, and no fees are charged the patients, gifts from public-spirited citizens supplemented the Endowment Fund income to provide for operating costs during the first year of its operation by the village, which coincided with the village fiscal year. No part of the principal of endowments may be used for operations. By the end of the year, preparations were under way for a drive to raise funds to enlarge and improve the plant.

The following transactions occurred during the first year:

Contributions and Receipts

1. Hospital site—value	$ 25,000
2. Hospital buildings—value	200,000
3. U.S. Treasury bonds contributed as endowment, principal amount	100,000
4. Accrued interest on U.S. bonds at August 31, 19X5	1,250
5. Stocks and bonds contributed as endowments (no accrued dividends or interest)—market value	1,300,000
6. Equipment—value	60,000
7. Life insurance policies irrevocably assigned to hospital as endowments—	
Cash value .... $ 5,000	
Face amount 150,000	
(The hospital is to pay the premiums on this policy; however, it may not borrow against or cancel the policy, but must await collection of the face amount upon the donor's death.)	
8. Contributions from X County for hospital operations	10,000
9. Contributions from numerous individuals for hospital operations	20,000
10. Proceeds from sponsored charity bazaar	500
11. Interest received from U.S. Treasury bonds	2,500
12. Dividends from stocks	44,000
13. Interest from bonds, other than U.S. Treasury	12,000
14. Sale of stocks included in endowments at $27,000	52,000

Disbursements

15. Building improvements	$ 20,000

16.	Equipment	15,000
17.	Salaries	15,000
18.	Food and dietary supplies	10,000
19.	Medicinal supplies	20,000
20.	Life insurance premium paid	2,000
21.	Property insurance	5,000
22.	Light, heat, and water	1,000
23.	Expenses of charity bazaar, announcements, etc.	15
24.	Other operating expenses	4,000

Other Information

25.	Cash value of life insurance held for benefit of hospital at August 31, 19X6	$	6,500
26.	Contributions subscribed but not collected		5,000
27.	Prepaid insurance on property at end of year		500
28.	Balance in bank per bank statement of the Unrestricted Fund at end of period		51,085
	Outstanding checks amount to $3,300 and the last day's deposit of $1,200 is not included on the bank statement.		
29.	Upon completion of the $20,000 improvements to the hospital building it was appraised at $250,000.		
30.	There were no material amounts of accrued wages, inventories, or similar items at year end.		

Required:

Prepare a worksheet(s) to reflect the transactions of the various funds of X County Hospital for the year ended August 30, 19X6. Your worksheet headings should appear as follows:

Transactions and Adjustments 9/1/19X5–8/31/19X6		Revenues and Expenses during 19X6		Balance Sheet August 31, 19X6	
Debit	Credit	Debit	Credit	Debit	Credit

Problem 18-6. Hospital M has not previously kept its accounting records by funds, and the following balances appear in its general ledger as of January 1, 19X9:

	Debits	Credits
Cash on hand and in banks	$ 143,866	
Accounts receivable—patients	48,740	
Sundry accounts receivable	508	
Inventory of supplies	17,583	
Prepaid insurance	3,294	
Stocks and bonds	3,702,010	
Other investments	225,950	
Land	25,000	
Buildings (net of $90,456 accumulated depreciation) ...	402,305	
Equipment (net of $63,500 accumulated depreciation) .	106,500	
Allowance for loss on accounts receivable		$ 10,385
Accounts payable		29,227
Other current liabilities		38,014
Bonds payable—first mortgage,* 5 percent		300,000
Advance payment by patients		6,364
Balance		4,291,766
	$4,675,756	$4,675,756

* The mortgage is against the building, the construction of which was financed partially by bonds.

From the following information and summary of the transactions for the year ended December 31, 19X9, you are to prepare worksheets showing by appropriate funds all information needed for (a) a statement of revenues and expenses for the year and (b) a balance sheet for each fund as of December 31, 19X9. Changes in fund balances should be shown in additional columns and/or in notes to the worksheets.

1. The stocks and bonds, together with $112,150 of the cash, belong to Endowment Funds, the income of which may be used for general purposes of the hospital. An additional $12,150 of cash belongs to expendable Specific Purpose Funds. Buildings and equipment are stated net of accumulated depreciation, which has been charged to the current expenses of each year. There is no intention to provide a fund for replacement of assets. The other investments belong to Endowment Funds. The income from these funds may be used only for the purposes designated.

2. Cash income from Endowment Fund stocks and bonds amounted to $138,710. Income from other investments amounted to $11,765.

3. Cash donations received amounted to $41,305, all except $10,500 of which was for current use. The $10,500 was expendable only for a designated purpose.

4. Services billed to patients amounted to $930,480, all of which was recorded through accounts receivable—patients.

5. Cash collected from patients and prospective patients amounted to $925,428, of which $12,890 represented advance payments.

6. Cash of $1,375 was collected on sundry accounts receivable.

7. The allowance for loss on accounts receivable was increased by $10,000. Patients' accounts totaling $6,302 were considered to be uncollectible and were written off.

8. Depreciation on the buildings was $11,307; depreciation on equipment was $18,541.

9. The following vouchers were approved:
   Storeroom supplies—$78,240; Insurance—$11,624; General operating expenses—$979,731; Maintenance—$7,488; Replacement of equipment—$11,432; Interest on bonds—$15,000; Retirement of bonds—$10,000. Other current liabilities were credited with $505,212 of these $1,113,515 of vouchers.

10. The book value of equipment replaced was $2,710; it had originally cost $10,000 but was now obsolete and had no market value.

11. Free services rendered during the year amounted to $108,000; of this, 75 percent was for charity cases and the balance was a result of policy discounts.

12. Services rendered patients (see item 4) were covered by advance payments amounting to $14,105.

13. Cash disbursements of $502,701 were made in payment of other current liabilities and $610,043 in payment of accounts payable. Discounts taken on accounts payable amounted to $2,305.

14. Storeroom supplies of $72,578 were issued for general use and $1,073 of supplies were sold to employees at cost and charged to sundry accounts receivable. Insurance expired amounted to $10,445.

15. Cash expenditures for equipment from Specific Purpose Funds were $5,875.

16. Cash receipts for the year included unexpendable cash contributions of $50,000 (income therefrom is unrestricted), proceeds from sale of stocks and bonds of $502,164 and proceeds from sale of other investments of $52,125. There was a loss of $7,354 sustained on the sale of stocks and bonds and a $9,978 loss sustained on the sale of other investments.

17. Cash disbursements not vouchered consisted of $507,892 for purchase of stocks and bonds and $48,100 of the proceeds from sale of other investments, which was invested in bonds.

18. Inventory of supplies on hand at year end, at cost, amounted to $21,500.

(AICPA, adapted)

Problem 18-7. McClusky Hospital, a general care facility, had the following trial balances at January 1, 19X6:

Unrestricted Fund

Cash	$ 24,000	
Accounts Receivable	35,000	
Allowance for Uncollectible Accounts		$ 500
Due from Specific Purpose Fund	3,000	
Investments	6,000	
Buildings	840,000	
Accumulated Depreciation—Buildings		10,000
Equipment	370,000	
Accumulated Depreciation—Equipment		30,000
Land	90,000	
Accounts Payable		12,000
Fund Balance		1,315,500
	$1,368,000	$1,368,000

Specific Purpose Fund

Cash	$ 6,500	
Due to Unrestricted Fund		$ 3,000
Fund Balance		3,500
	$ 6,500	$ 6,500

Endowment Fund

Cash	$ 46,000	
Investments—Certificates of Deposit	110,000	
Endowment Fund—Balance A		$ 81,000
Endowment Fund—Balance B		75,000
	$ 156,000	$ 156,000

Plant Improvement and Replacement Fund

Cash	$ 14,000	
Investments	6,000	
Fund Balance		$ 20,000
	$ 20,000	$ 20,000

The following transactions took place during the year:

1. Bills rendered to patients: $500,000 for daily patient services, $400,000 for other nursing services, and $600,000 for other professional services; of these billings $10,000 is estimated to be uncollectible, $3,000 of which is attributable to

expected contractual adjustments and $2,000 to expected policy discounts allowed.

2. Expenditures for salaries and wages and for materials (all paid for in cash) were as follows:

Department	Amount
Professional care of inpatients (nursing services, etc.) ..	$737,000
Outpatient and emergency services	28,000
Dietary services	205,000
Administrative and general	139,000
Household and property maintenance	291,000

3. Accounts receivable of $1,480,000 were collected; bad debts of $4,800 were written off; and contractual and policy adjustments made amounted to $2,700 and $1,900, respectively.

4. An Unrestricted Fund billing in the amount of $10,000 was rendered to the Specific Purpose Fund for its share of the cost of recreational activities included in the expenditures above.

5. Accounts payable outstanding on January 1, 19X6, were paid.

6. The $3,000 due from the Specific Purpose Fund on January 1, 19X6, was paid to the Unrestricted Fund.

7. Mortgage interest in the amount of $3,200 was paid.

8. The cafeteria (operated as a separate corporation) paid to the Unrestricted Fund $20,000 representing its net income for the year.

9. The following liabilities and accruals remained unpaid at December 31, 19X6:

Accounts payable (for materials and supplies used; to be charged to professional care of inpatients)	$ 5,000
Accrued interest on mortgage	800
Accrued salaries and wages chargeable as follows:	
Administrative and general	3,000
Dietary services	1,200
Household and property maintenance	4,800
Professional care of inpatients	13,000
Outpatient and emergency services	1,000

10. Annual depreciation charges:

Buildings	$30,000
Equipment	50,000

11. A cash donation of $25,000 was received to be used for recreational purposes only.

12. A donation of $75,000 was received in cash for the purpose of establishing an Endowment Fund (hereafter referred to as Endowment Fund C), the income from which is to be used to provide special services for patients.

13. The money was invested in bonds which were purchased at par.

14. Stocks with a market value of $100,000 were donated to the hospital for the purpose of establishing an Endowment Fund (hereafter referred to as Endowment Fund D), the income from which is to be available for general purposes.

15. Bonds with a par value of $3,000 were sold at a loss of $300.

16. Stocks with a book value of $5,000 were sold at a profit of $500.

17. Interest income was received on certificates of deposit, $6,240. Earnings on Endowments A and B accumulate for 20 more years, at the end of which time the entire Fund Balances may be used to acquire equipment or furnishings in honor of the donors.

18. The cost of constructing and equipping a major addition to the hospital was financed by a grant of $1,250,000 and borrowing on mortgage notes of $100,000. The cost is distributed as follows: land, $80,000; building, $950,000; equipment, $320,000.

19. A restricted donation of $10,000 in cash and $10,000 (market value) in stocks was received. The donation is to be used to finance improvements and replacements.

20. Dividends (restricted) on the above stock in the amount of $500 were received in cash.

21. Equipment costing $6,000 was purchased for cash from the Plant Improvement and Replacement Fund.

Required:

(a) Prepare worksheets for 19X6 for each of the funds to show beginning balances, transactions and adjustments, and postclosing balances. For the Unrestricted Fund there should also be columns for revenues and expenses.

(b) Using the foregoing worksheets, prepare for McClusky Hospital a balance sheet at December 31, 19X6, and statements of revenues and expenses, changes in fund balances, and changes in financial position for the year then ended.

Problem 18-8. The City of Titusville built a municipal hospital on land previously owned by the city. The building was completed on March 1, 19X0. Since that date the hospital has been under the control of a superintendent. He has rendered monthly reports to the town mayor, but these reports have been on a cash basis and have not shown separation of amounts by funds. You have been employed by the city government to prepare financial statements for the ten months ending December 31, 19X0, and to do certain other work in connection with setting up an accounting system for the hospital operations. The city wants the financial statements to be on an accrual basis, to the extent such basis is appropriate, and to follow usual hospital accounting practices. From the information presented below, you are to prepare statements showing revenues and expenses, changes in fund balances, and financial position; supporting computations or worksheet(s) should be in good form.

1. The total contract price of the buildings was $240,000. The contractor was paid in the following manner:
   a. Cash of $120,000, which was a contribution by the Federal government toward the hospital cost.
   b. Cash of $25,000 contributed by the county government toward the cost.
   c. Hospital bonds issued by the city to the contractor in the amount of $100,000. These bonds are 5 percent bonds dated 1/1/19X0, due in ten years, interest payable semiannually. They are general obligation bonds of the city but the hospital is primarily liable for them and is to service them.

2. Equipment was initially obtained as follows:
   a. Purchased by the city for cash—$35,300.
   b. Purchased out of cash donations made by citizens for that purpose—$9,800.
   c. Donated equipment which had an estimated value of—$11,000.

3. The statement of cash receipts and disbursements, exclusive of items described above, for the ten months was as follows:

Received from patients:

Rooms and meals	$105,314
Laboratory and other fees	6,170
Outpatients	4,201
Miscellaneous income from meals, etc.	515
Received from estate of James Johnson, M.D.	25,000
Miscellaneous donations	10,410
Received from Beulah Jenkins	32,500
Donations from churches	1,850
Received from county for county charity patients—room and meals	940
Income from rents	2,000
Income from bonds	2,125
Total cash received	$191,025
Payroll and taxes thereon paid	$ 96,200
Stores and supplies purchased	34,180
Equipment purchased	27,250
Expense of operating rented property	700
Miscellaneous expenses (including bond interest of $2,500)	4,170
Total cash disbursed	$162,500
Balance of cash, 12/31/19X0	$ 28,525

4. Investigation revealed the following additional information:
   a. Patients' accounts on the books as of December 31, 19X0, amounted to $9,403, distributed as follows: for room and meals—$7,310; for laboratory and other fees—$1,095; for outpatients—$998. It is estimated that $500 of these accounts will never be collected.
   b. As of December 31, 19X0, accrued unpaid wages amounted to $5,234; unpaid supply invoices amounted to $6,810 and accrued utilities amounted to $174. The analysis of miscellaneous expenses shows that there is $330 of prepaid insurance. Kitchen and other supplies on hand amounted to $1,760 at cost.
   c. It has been decided to charge current income with depreciation on general hospital property at the following annual rates based on the year-end balance of the asset accounts:

   Buildings .... 2 percent
   Equipment .... 10 percent and 20 percent

   All equipment will take the 10 percent rate except for $18,500 of minor items of equipment, which will be depreciated at the 20 percent rate. Depreciation is to be computed for a full year and is not to be funded.
   d. The following facts were determined in respect to the donations:
      (1) The donation from the estate of James Johnson, M.D., was received July 1, 19X0. It consisted of two houses and $25,000 in cash. The terms of the bequest provided that the cash is to be invested and that the income therefrom and from the houses is to be used for the purchase of surgical

equipment. The houses had a market value of approximately $30,000, of which amount $5,000 was for the land. The estimated life of the properties from date of the gift was 25 years. (Depreciation does not reduce rental earnings available for purchase of surgical equipment.) The houses were rented and, in addition to the $2,000 of rent received, there was $150 rent receivable as of December 31, 19X0. All expenses on the houses for the year have been paid and are included in the disbursements. No purchase of surgical equipment has been approved.

(2) The miscellaneous donations were made for general purposes of the operation of the hospital.

(3) The Beulah Jenkins donation received June 1, 19X0, consisted of cash and of $50,000 face value of X Corporation 4¼ percent bonds. Interest dates are June 1 and December 1. The provisions of the gift were: "The amounts are to be invested by said trustees in accordance with applicable law governing trust investments and the income derived therefrom is to be used to defray or help to defray the necessary hospitalization costs of such indigent women as the trustees shall designate upon application by their physician." The trustees were designated in the document. These trustees have accepted their appointments but have never met or transacted any business.

(4) The donations from churches are to apply toward purchase of an "iron lung." No order has yet been placed for such equipment.

(AICPA, adapted)

Problem 18-9. (a) From the following information, compute the minimum average billed charges per day which the Peoples' Hospital must experience in order to recover the total cost of care for the year 19X8. (Submit computations in clear-cut form.)

1. Number of days of care	10,000
2. Operating expenses:	
Payroll	$1,200,000
Supplies	800,000
Depreciation	100,000
Total	$2,100,000
3. Classification of Accounts (in days):	
Charity Cases	600
Contractual Cases	1,200
Uncollectible Accounts	200
Full-Pay Patients	8,000
Total	10,000
4. Estimated Collections per Day:	
Charity Cases	None
Contractual Cases	$240,000
Uncollectible Accounts	None
Full-Pay Patients	Billed charges

(b) After computing the minimum average billed charges, summarize the data and present the dollar amounts in the following form:

        Revenue from services to patients .... $_____
        Deductions from revenue .... $_____

Net revenue from services to patients ..	$___	
Operating expenses	$___	
Net income	$___	

(FHFMA, adapted)

Problem 18-10. Good Hope Hospital completed its first year of operation as a qualified institutional provider under the health insurance (HI) program for the aged and wishes to receive maximum reimbursement for its allowable costs from the government. The hospital engaged you to assist in determining the amount of reimbursement due and furnished the following financial, statistical, and other information:

1. The hospital's charges and allowable costs for departmental inpatient services were:

Departments	Charges for HI Program Beneficiaries	Total Charges	Total Allowable Costs
Inpatient routine services (room, board, nursing)	$425,000	$1,275,000	$1,350,000
Inpatient ancillary service departments:			
X-ray	56,000	200,000	150,000
Operating room	57,000	190,000	220,000
Laboratory	59,000	236,000	96,000
Pharmacy	98,000	294,000	207,000
Other	10,000	80,000	88,000
Total ancillary	280,000	1,000,000	761,000
Total	$705,000	$2,275,000	$2,111,000

2. For the first year the Reimbursement Settlement for Inpatient Services may be calculated at the option of the provider under either of the following apportionment methods:
   a. *The Departmental RCC (ratio of costs-to-charges) Method* provides for listing on a departmental basis the ratios of beneficiary inpatient charges to total inpatient charges with each departmental beneficiary inpatient charge ratio applied to the allowable total cost of the respective department.
   b. *The Combination Method (with cost finding)* provides that the cost of routine services be apportioned on the basis of the average allowable cost per day for all inpatients applied to total inpatient days of beneficiaries. The residual part of the provider's total allowable cost attributable to ancillary (nonroutine) services is to be apportioned in the ratio of the beneficiaries' share of charges for ancillary services to the total charges for all patients for such services.

3. Statistical and other information:
   a. Total inpatient days for all patients 40,000
   b. Total inpatient days applicable to HI beneficiaries (1,200 aged patients whose average length of stay was 12.5 days) 15,000
   c. A fiscal intermediary acting on behalf of the government's HI program negotiated a fixed "allowance rate" of $45 per inpatient day subject to retroactive adjustment as a reasonable cost basis for reimbursement of covered services

to the hospital under the HI program. Interim payments based on an estimated 1,000 inpatient-days per month were received during the twelve-month period subject to an adjustment for the provider's actual cost experience.

Required:

(a) Prepare schedules computing the total allowable cost of inpatient services for which the provider should receive payment under the HI program and the remaining balance due for reimbursement under each of the following methods:
  1. Departmental RCC method
  2. Combination method (with cost finding)

(b) Under which method should Good Hope Hospital elect to be reimbursed for its first year under the HI program assuming the election can be changed for the following year with the approval of the fiscal intermediary? Why?

(c) Good Hope Hospital wishes to compare its charges to HI program beneficiaries with published information on national averages for charges for hospital services. Compute the following (show your computations):
  1. The average total hospital charge for an HI inpatient
  2. The average charge per inpatient day for HI inpatients

(AICPA, adapted)

Problem 18-11. The accountant for the Unrestricted Fund of D Village Hospital accumulated the information on the following pages from the December 31, 19X4, trial balance and other 19X4 sources.

Required:

Prepare the following for the year ended December 31, 19X4:

(a) A worksheet showing the apportionment of the cost of the Provision for Depreciation to other centers.

(b) A worksheet showing the apportionment of Nursing Service costs to other centers (see Figure 18-9). Note: You must proceed with requirement (d) until total Nursing Service costs are obtained before you can fulfill requirement (b). Total Administrative and General costs must be similarly obtained in order to fulfill requirement (c).

(c) A worksheet showing the apportionment of Administrative and General costs to other centers.

(d) A worksheet showing "Cost Apportionment—General Services" (see Figure 18-10).

(e) A statement of "Special Services Costs" (see Figure 18-11).

(f) A worksheet showing the "Cost Apportionment—Special Services" (see Figure 18-12).

(g) A statement of "Inpatient and Outpatient Costs" (see Figure 18-13).

(Round to the nearest whole dollar; and round the final figure in a column where necessary.)

	Trial Balance Amounts	Square Feet of Floor Space Occupied	Cost of Equipment in Use	Pounds of Laundry Used	Hours of Nursing Service	Amount of Priced Requisitions	
						Medical Supply	Pharmacy
Provision for Depreciation:							
Building	$ 10,000						
Equipment	10,000						
Operation and Maintenance of Plant	40,000	2,000	$ 3,000				
Laundry Service	15,000	500	1,000				
Housekeeping	72,000	500	1,000	1,000			
Dietary (Service to inpatients only)	55,000	3,000	5,000	3,000			
Nursing Service	160,000	500	1,000	—	8,000		
Medical Supply	46,000	1,500	4,000	5,000			
Pharmacy	25,000	1,500	2,000	1,000			
Medical Records	5,000	500	1,000				
Administration and General	48,000	2,000	5,000				
Operating and Delivery Service	42,000	15,000	20,000	20,000	20,000	$10,000	$ 4,000
Radiology	22,000	5,000	25,000	3,000	10,000		1,000
Laboratory Services	65,000	10,000	10,000	2,000			1,000
Cost of Drugs Sold							30,000
Inpatients		45,000	25,000	100,000	200,000	34,000	6,000
Nursery	1,000	5,000	5,000	6,000	34,000	2,000	1,000
Outpatients	8,000	5,000	4,000	4,000	20,000	1,000	1,000
Emergency Room	10,000	3,000	8,000	5,000	8,000	3,000	1,000
Private Ambulatory							
	$634,000	100,000	$120,000	150,000	300,000	$50,000	$45,000

Patient days	42,079
Newborn days	8,305
Outpatient visits	12,046
Emergency visits	5,156
Private ambulatory visits	5,491
Prescriptions filled	8,328

	Hours of Operating and Delivery Room Use	Number of X-Ray Films (Radiology)	Number of Laboratory Examinations	Retail Price of Drugs Sold	Hours of Housekeeping Service	Hours of Service on Medical Records
Medical Supply					500	
Pharmacy					500	
Medical Records					2,000	
Administration and General					8,000	
Operating and Delivery Service					2,000	
Radiology					2,000	
Laboratory Services					3,500	
Cost of Drugs Sold						
Inpatients	19,000	23,000	107,000	$40,000	49,000	5,000
Nursery	1,000	1,000	2,000	1,000	1,000	
Outpatients		2,000	5,000	5,000	5,000	1,500
Emergency Room		5,000	1,000	2,000	1,500	500
Private Ambulatory		19,000	10,000	2,000		
	20,000	50,000	125,000	$50,000	75,000	7,000

19

ACCOUNTING FOR COLLEGES AND UNIVERSITIES

The development of accounting and reporting principles for colleges and universities followed a pattern almost identical to that of municipalities. A few publications on the subject appeared during the 1910–1935 era; the first attempt at standardization, undertaken cooperatively by the various regional associations of college and university business officers, was published in 1935; there followed a series of twenty interpretive and advisory studies by the Financial Advisory Service of the American Council on Education (ACE) during the 1935–1942 period.

A National Committee on the Preparation of a Manual on College and University Business Administration—formed in 1949 of representatives from the various regional business officer associations, the ACE, and the U.S. Office of Education—prepared *College and University Business Administration*. This two-volume work, published by the ACE in 1952 and 1955, respectively, was the first authoritative publication covering all areas of higher education business administration. In 1963 The Committee to Revise Volumes I and II, *College and University Business Administration* (The Committee) was formed of representatives of the National Association of College and University Business Officers (NACUBO)[1], the AICPA, the U.S. Office of Education, and ACE. Assisted by several special consultants, this committee prepared a one-volume revised edition of *College and University Business Administration*[2] (*CUBA*). Published in 1968 by the ACE, the revised edition of *CUBA* was described by The Committee as "a

---

[1] The various regional associations formed the National Federation of College and University Business Officers Associations in 1950, which in 1960 became the National Association of College and University Business Officers (NACUBO). NACUBO and the American Council on Education (ACE) have been instrumental in the continuing development and improvement of college and university financial management, accounting, and reporting.

[2] *College and University Business Administration*, revised edition (Washington, D.C.: American Council on Education, 1968). Specifically, see Part 2, "Principles of Accounting and Reporting"; Appendix A, "The Chart of Accounts"; and Appendix B, "Illustrative Forms."

761

painstakingly achieved consensus of leading experts in the field."[3] *College and University Business Administration* found widespread acceptance in practice, and its recommendations formed the basis of modern textbooks on college and university accounting.

Several significant events affecting college and university accounting and reporting occurred in the early 1970s. First, the AICPA Committee on College and University Accounting and Auditing prepared *Audits of Colleges and Universities*,[4] an industry audit guide issued in 1973. The audit guide basically endorsed CUBA as a primary authoritative source of generally accepted accounting principles but took exception to several practices suggested or permitted in CUBA. The AICPA committee was aware that the Accounting Principles Committee of NACUBO was preparing a revision of *CUBA* and, related to that task, was holding discussions with the National Center for Higher Education Management Systems (NCHEMS) concerning the classification of revenues and expenditures in college and university accounting and reporting. As a result, a small AICPA Accounting Standards Task Force on Colleges and Universities, comprised of several members of the committee that prepared the audit guide, was formed and worked in a consultative capacity with both the NACUBO and NCHEMS committees. The result was a Joint Accounting Group (JAG) that worked to achieve consensus on numerous matters related to higher education accounting and reporting. That consensus was reached and in 1974:

1. NACUBO issued the third edition of *College & University Business Administration*[5] (CUBA), the fifth part of which deals with "Financial Accounting and Reporting,"

2. the *Report of the Joint Accounting Group*[6] was published, and

3. the AICPA issued Statement of Position 74-8[7], which amended the audit guide to recognize the revenue classifications by source and expenditure classifications by function in the 1974 edition of CUBA, completing the reconcilation of differences between the 1974 edition of CUBA and the audit guide.

The FASB recently assumed responsibility for all nonbusiness organization (except government) accounting and reporting standards and designated those in the audit guide "preferable" standards pending any FASB statements on college and university accounting and reporting.[8]

[3] Ibid., p. v.

[4] Committee on College and University Accounting and Auditing, American Institute of Certified Public Accountants, *Audits of Colleges and Universities* (New York: AICPA, 1973).

[5] National Association of College and University Business Officers, *College & University Business Administration*, 3rd ed. (Washington, D.C., NACUBO, 1974). Specifically, see Part 5, "Financial Accounting and Reporting." Hereafter cited as CUBA.

[6] Report of the Joint Accounting Group (Boulder, Colo.: Western Interstate Commission for Higher Education, March 1974.)

[7] Accounting Standards Division, American Institute of Certified Public Accountants, *Statement of Position 74-8*, "Financial Accounting and Reporting by Colleges and Universities" (New York: AICPA, August 31, 1974).

[8] Financial Accounting Standards Board, *Statement of Financial Accounting Standards No. 32*, "Specialized Accounting and Reporting Principles and Practices in AICPA Statements of Position and Guides on Accounting and Auditing Matters" (Stamford, Conn.: FASB, September 1979).

Thus, the 1974 edition of *College and University Business Administration* and the 1973 AICPA audit guide, as amended, are the most authoritative sources of college and university accounting and reporting principles. Accordingly, this chapter is based on those recommendations.

OVERVIEW

College and university accounting and reporting may be visualized as a *composite* of selected aspects of municipal and hospital accounting and reporting. Among the features shared with both municipalities and hospitals is the fund principle.

Fund Groups

The Committee endorsed the use of the following fund groups by colleges and universities:

Fund Group	Major Subdivisions
1. Current Funds	Current Funds—Unrestricted
	Current Funds—Restricted
2. Loan Funds	
3. Endowment and Similar Funds	Endowment Funds ("pure" or "true")
	Term Endowment Funds
	Quasi-Endowment Funds (Funds Functioning as Endowment)
4. Annuity and Life Income Funds	Annuity Funds
	Life Income Funds
5. Plant Funds	Unexpended Plant Funds
	Funds for Renewals and Replacements
	Funds for Retirement of Indebtedness
	Investment in Plant
6. Agency Funds	

These fund groups are based on the restrictions on or the purposes of the funds. A college or university may (1) establish several separate fund entities of each type, as needed, but prepare its financial reports on a fund group basis, or (2) maintain only one fund accounting entity for each fund group and account for the subfunds on an intrafund "funds within a fund" basis. Either approach is acceptable; however, within each of the fund groups each fund must, as a minimum, have separate accounts to show the balance of the fund and the results of its operations. These fund groups are discussed and illustrated more fully following a brief comparison of the major features of college or university accounting and reporting with those of municipalities and hospitals.

Comparison with Municipal Accounting and Reporting

College and university accounting and reporting is like that for the governmental funds and account groups of municipalities in the following respects:

1. Both are concerned primarily with the measurement and reporting of revenues and *expenditures*—funds flows and balances—rather than with the determination of net income of the organization.

2. Depreciation is *not* normally recorded except where required by law or agreement (e.g., to assure that the principal of endowments or other nonexpendable trusts is maintained intact) but accumulated depreciation may be recorded in the General Fixed Assets accounts of governments or in college and university Plant Funds.

3. Statements analyzing the changes in fund balances are the major operating statements of both.

4. The current period expenditures of both may be controlled by budgets or appropriations, and statements setting forth the revenues and expenditures of a period in detail may include budgetary or year-to-year comparisons.

5. Combined balance sheets and operating statements are presented.

6. Both follow similar accounting and reporting for quasi-external transactions, reimbursements, and transfers.

7. Both account for and report encumbrances.

8. As noted earlier, some colleges and universities establish a separate accounting entity for each identifiable fund (subfund) within the fund groups, as do municipalities.

A summary comparison of the fund structures of colleges or universities and municipalities is presented in Figure 19-2.

Comparison with Hospital Accounting and Reporting

College and university accounting and reporting also resembles that for hospitals in many respects. For example:

1. A distinction is maintained between restricted and unrestricted resources.

2. Restricted contributions and earnings are accounted for by colleges and universities in much the same way as they are by hospitals, that is, they are recognized as revenues only in the period in which they are expended for their designated purposes.

3. The funds structures of colleges and universities are quite similar to those of hospitals, as shown in Figure 19-2.

4. Though colleges and universities primarily account for funds flows and balances rather than net income, the principal operating statement of a college or university is the Statement of Current Funds Revenues, Expenditures, and Other Changes, in which all operating revenues and expenditures recognized by the institution are reported.

5. As in hospitals, the principal operating statements of funds other than the Current Funds of colleges and universities are statements analyzing changes in the fund balances.

6. The value of donated services and facilities may be recognized by colleges and universities operated by religious orders.

7. As in hospitals, long-term investments of college and university fund

groups may be recorded either at cost or revalued periodically to fair market value.

8. As noted earlier, colleges and universities, like hospitals, present a combined balance sheet rather than separate balance sheets for each fund or fund group.

Summary

Many of the principal aspects of college and university accounting and reporting may be observed from the presentations in Figures 19-1 and 19-2. Highlights of college and university accounting and reporting are noted in Figure 19-1; a summary comparison of fund structures—colleges and universities with municipalities and hospitals—appears in Figure 19-2. The reader may find it helpful to return to these figures from time to time as he studies the remainder of this chapter; they may be useful also as a review and summarization of the chapter.

Chapter Overview

Each of the fund groups commonly found in college and university accounting is discussed more fully in the following pages. These discussions are illustrated by means of a continuing case example. For simplicity of illustration we assume that "A University" is in its first full year of operation, though some of the physical plant was acquired in the preceding year.

CURRENT FUNDS

Current Funds available for current operations may be either restricted or unrestricted. Typically they may be used either for general educational purposes or for auxiliary enterprises. A careful distinction should be maintained between *Unrestricted* Current Funds and *Restricted* Current Funds, as the accounting and reporting procedures are quite different for these two subgroups of Current Funds.

Unrestricted Current Funds

The *Unrestricted* Current Funds subgroup includes those financial resources of the institution that are expendable for any legal and reasonable purpose agreed upon by the governing board in carrying out the primary purposes of the institution (e.g., instruction, research, public service) *and* that have *not* been designated *externally* (by grantors, donors, etc.) for specific purposes. Thus, the Unrestricted Current Funds are similar to the General Fund of a government. Resources restricted by donors, grantors, or outside agencies for specific current operating purposes are accounted for in the *Restricted* Current Funds.

Unrestricted Current Funds designated by the governing board to serve as loan or quasi-endowment funds, or to be expended for plant purposes, are usually included in the Loan, Endowment, and Plant Funds, respectively. Such unrestricted amounts are distinguished from the restricted portions of those funds by using Fund Balance—Unrestricted and Fund Balance—Restricted accounts. Un-

Figure 19-1

OVERVIEW OF COLLEGE AND UNIVERSITY ACCOUNTING AND REPORTING

FUND GROUPS

	Currently Available for Expenditure		Not Currently Available for Operating Expenditure				
	Unrestricted Current Funds	Restricted Current Funds	Loan	Endowment and Similar	Annuity and Life Income	Plant	Agency

Fund Groups

Revenue Realization Rules or Conventions

Unrestricted Current Funds: Revenues and expenditures recognized in the period earned or incurred.

Restricted Current Funds: Earnings, contributions, or transfers are credited to fund balances. Revenue recognized only to the extent resources are expended.

Loan / Endowment and Similar / Annuity and Life Income / Plant: Earnings, contributions, or transfers are credited to fund balances. Expendable earnings or other resources are transferred to Unrestricted or Restricted Current Funds, as appropriate, unless for capital outlay or debt service, which are accounted for in the Plant Funds.

Agency: No revenue—custodian relationship only.

Principal Financial Statements

Statement of Current Funds Revenues, Expenditures, and Other Changes Statement(s) of Changes in Fund Balances

Statements of Changes in Fund Balances

Balance Sheet (Combined)

Figure 19-2

SUMMARY COMPARISON OF FUND STRUCTURES

Colleges and Universities with Municipalities and Hospitals

Primary Purpose of Funds and Account Groups	Municipalities	Colleges and Universities	Hospitals
Finance current operations	General Special Revenue (and Expendable Trust)	Unrestricted Current Restricted Current*	Unrestricted (Operating) Specific Purpose

Fiduciary responsibilities	Nonexpendable
	Trust
	
	Agency
		Loan
		Endowment and
		Similar:
		  Endowment (true)
		  Term Endowment
		  Quasi-Endowment
		Annuity and Life
		Income:
		  Annuity
		  Life Income
		Agency†
			Endowment
			"Board-Created"
			Endowment

Acquisition of and accountability for major fixed assets and related long-term debt	Capital Projects‡
	Debt Service
	General Fixed
	  Assets/General
	  Long-term Debt
		Plant:
		  Unexpended
		  For Renewals and
		    Replacements
		  For Retirement of
		    Indebtedness
		  Investment in Plant
			Plant
			  Replacement
			  and Expansion§

* Restricted Current Funds revenue is considered realized, and hence is recognized as revenue, only to the extent that it has been expended for the specified purpose. Thus, the realization rule here is similar to that of a hospital Specific Purpose Fund: (1) restricted earnings or contributions are credited to fund balance, then (2) in the period of expenditure, fund balance is debited and an appropriate revenue account is credited.

† Hospitals usually account for agency relationships in the Unrestricted (Operating) Fund rather than by setting up separate Agency Funds.

‡ Funds for renewals and replacements of municipal fixed assets may be accounted for in the General Fund or in Capital Projects, Expendable Trust, or Special Revenue Funds, as appropriate to the restrictions on or purpose of these resources and their materiality.

§ Hospital fixed assets and long-term debt are accounted for in the Unrestriced (Operating) Fund.

restricted Current Funds designated by the governing board for specific current operating purposes should be accounted for in the *Unrestricted* Current Funds, either as formal appropriations or as allocations, designations, or reservations of the fund balance, as appropriate.

Several features of Unrestricted Current Fund accounting should be noted:

1. Where a portion of the standard tuition and fee charges is waived, as is common for students on scholarships and fellowships, the full amount of the standard tuition and fees is recognized as revenues and

the amounts waived are recorded as expenditures for scholarships and fellowships.

2. Where the *full amount* of specific fees or other revenue sources is legally or contractually pledged (externally restricted) to nonoperating purposes (such as debt service or plant construction or renovation), the revenues are not reported in the Unrestricted Current Funds but are recorded as additions to the fund balance of the appropriate other fund, e.g., the Plant Funds in the examples cited above.

3. Where *only part of* specific fees or other revenue sources is legally or contractually pledged for nonoperating purposes (such as for debt service or plant construction or renovation), the full amount of the revenue is reported in the Unrestricted Current Funds and the pledged amount is reported as a *mandatory transfer* to the appropriate other fund, e.g., the Plant Funds in the examples cited above.

4. Where the governing board has allocated part of an unrestricted revenue source(s) for purposes such as debt service or plant construction or renovation, the entire amount of the revenue is recognized in the Unrestricted Current Funds and a *nonmandatory transfer* to the other fund(s) is reported.[9]

5. Significant amounts of inventory should be reported in the year-end balance sheet, and Expenditures should be increased or reduced, as appropriate, by the amount of the inventory change during the year. (This compares with the "consumption" or "use" method of inventory accounting by state and local governments.) Similarly, if significant amounts of service costs benefit the next period they should be recorded as deferred charges and the Expenditures account reduced.

6. Residual balances of Endowment and Similar Funds and of Annuity and Life Income Funds paid to the Unrestricted Current Funds at the conclusion of the trust, annuity, or life income arrangement should be reported as a separate revenue item in the Statement of Current Funds Revenues, Expenditures, and Other Changes (see Figure 19-8).

7. The return of unrestricted resources which had previously been transferred to a Quasi-Endowment Fund or to the Plant Funds, for example, should be reported as a transfer, not as revenue, in the Statement of Current Funds Revenues, Expenditures, and Other Changes.

Restricted Current Funds

The *Restricted* Current Funds subgroup is used to account for resources that are expendable for operating purposes but are restricted by donors, grantors, or other outside agencies to expenditure for specific operating purposes. They are similar to Specific Purpose Funds of hospitals, and similar revenue realization conventions apply to both. Earnings or contributions of *Restricted* Current Funds are not recognized as revenue until expended for their intended purpose. Amounts

---

[9] Note that part of the total debt service transfer, for example, may be reported as "mandatory" and the balance reported as "nonmandatory."

received or accrued are credited initially to a Fund Balance account. Prior to preparation of financial statements, an amount equal to that expended for the restricted purpose is deducted from the appropriate Fund Balance account and added to the appropriate Revenue account.[10]

The more common additions to *Restricted* Current Funds include (1) restricted gifts for specific operating purposes; (2) restricted endowment income; and (3) grants received from private organizations or governments for research, public service, or other specific purposes. Reductions of *Restricted* Current Funds balances are occasioned by (1) expenditures charged to the funds, when corresponding amounts are recognized as revenues to "match" the revenues and expenditures; (2) refunds to donors and grantors; and (3) transfers of unrestricted revenues to the Unrestricted Current Funds representing indirect cost recoveries on sponsored programs. Alternatively the indirect cost recoveries on sponsored programs may be recorded directly in the Unrestricted Current Funds. The Fund Balance accounts are titled according to restricted use or source, such as:

> Fund balances:
> Restricted Income from Endowment Funds
> Gifts Restricted for Operating Purposes
> Federal Government Grants for Research
> Auxiliary Enterprises

The Fund Balance accounts may be separately titled in the general ledger, the subsidiary ledger, or in both ledgers. Further, the governing board may designate portions of these balances for specific purposes or projects permissible under the restrictions placed on them, which may require that more detailed Fund Balance accounts be established.

"Board-Restricted" or "Board-Designated" Current Funds

Some colleges and universities include "Board-Restricted" or "Board-Designated" Current Funds in the *Restricted* Current Funds. This is appropriate in some instances, as where restricted resources have been transferred to a Quasi-Endowment Fund and the earnings, also restricted as to use, are added to the Restricted Current Funds. But "Board-Restricted" or "Board-Designated" *Unrestricted* Current Funds should be accounted for in the *Unrestricted* Current Funds, since the distinction between the balances that are externally restricted and those that are internally designated (but otherwise unrestricted) should be maintained in the accounts and disclosed in the financial statements. Further, Unrestricted "Board-Restricted" or "Board-Designated" Funds revenue should be recognized when it is earned; revenue recognition should not be deferred until the resources are expended.

---

[10] Alternatively, all earnings or contributions may be credited to Revenues; prior to statement preparation, an appropriate amount is added to or deducted from Revenues and deducted from or added to Fund Balances so that the amount of revenues recognized equals the expenditures during the period.

Account Classifications

The asset and liability accounts of Current Funds are almost exclusively current assets and current liabilities. Revenues and expenditures of Current Funds are usually classified by function for external reporting purposes; expenditures are classified by department and object for internal reporting and control purposes. The major functional classifications used by most colleges or universities are (1) Educational and General, and (2) Auxiliary Enterprises, Hospitals, and Independent Operations. Appropriate detailed accounts would be provided, of course.

The major Revenue, Expenditure, and Transfer accounts recommended in *CUBA* are presented in Figure 19-3. More detailed accounts would be established in practice, of course—in the general ledger, the subsidiary ledger(s), or in both ledgers. For ease of illustration, we use only general ledger control accounts in the illustrative entries in this chapter.

Figure 19-3

CLASSIFICATION OF CURRENT FUNDS
REVENUES, EXPENDITURES, AND TRANSFERS

Revenues	*Expenditures and Transfers*
Tuition and Fees	Educational and General
Appropriations	Instruction
Federal	Research
State	Public Service
Local	Academic Support, e.g.,
Grants and Contracts	Computing Services
Federal	Libraries
State	Student Services, e.g.,
Local	Counseling and Career Guidance
Private Gifts, Grants, and Contracts	Dean of Students
Endowment Income	Financial Aid Administration
Sales and Services of	Intramural Athletics
Educational Activities, e.g.,	Institutional Support, e.g.,
Film Rentals	Legal Counsel
Testing Services	Alumni Office
Sales and Services of Auxiliary	Purchasing
Enterprises, e.g.,	Operation and Maintenance of Plant
Residence Halls	Scholarships and Fellowships
Food Services	Mandatory Transfers
College Union	Nonmandatory Transfers
Athletic Programs	Auxiliary Enterprises, Hospitals, and
Sales and Services of Hospitals	Other
Other Sources	Auxiliary Enterprises
Independent Operations	Hospitals
	Independent Operations

Source: National Association of College and University Business Officers, *College and University Business Administration*, 3rd ed. (Washington, D.C.: NACUBO, 1974), pp. 211–214.

Budgetary Accounts—Current Funds

Budgetary accounts may be incorporated in the ledger of either Unrestricted or Restricted Current Funds in a manner similar to that used in the General Fund of a municipality. Slightly different accounts titles are commonly used by colleges or universities, as compared with municipalities, and the difference between estimated revenues and estimated expenditures is usually carried in an "Unassigned Budget Balance" or "Unallocated Budget Balance" account—similar to the Budgetary Fund Balance account used by some governments—during the period rather than being closed to the Fund Balances account. The budgetary entry for a college or university Current Fund would appear as follows:

Estimated Revenues (or Unrealized Revenues)	1,000,000	
Expenditures and Other Changes Allocations (or Budget Allocations for Expenditures and Other Changes)		990,000
Unallocated Budget Balance (or Unassigned Budget Balance)		10,000
To record the college or university budget.		

These amounts would be reversed from the accounts at year end when their purpose has been served. Inasmuch as budgetary accounting for colleges and universities closely parallels that of a municipal General Fund, it is not illustrated further in this chapter.

Some Terminology Matters

The terms "mandatory transfer" and "nonmandatory transfer" were used earlier in the text and appear in Figure 19-3. These terms are unique to college and university accounting and reporting and are defined and explained in CUBA as follows:

> *Mandatory transfers.* This category should include transfers from the Current Funds group to other fund groups arising out of (1) binding legal agreements related to the financing of educational plant, such as amounts for debt retirement, interest, and required provisions for renewals and replacements of plant, not financed from other sources; and (2) grant agreements with agencies of the federal government, donors, and other organizations to match gifts and grants to loan and other funds. Mandatory transfers may be required to be made from either unrestricted or restricted current funds.
>
> *Nonmandatory transfers.* This category should include those transfers from the Current Funds group to other fund groups made at the discretion of the governing board to serve a variety of objectives, such as additions to loan funds, additions to quasi-endowment funds, general or specific plant additions, voluntary renewals and replacements of plant, and prepayments on debt principal. It also may include the retransfer of resources back to current funds.[11]

[11] CUBA, p. 189.

Another term mentioned above and in Figure 19-3 is "auxiliary enterprise." That term is defined and explained in CUBA as follows:

> *Auxiliary enterprises.* An "auxiliary enterprise" is an entity that exists to furnish goods or services to students, faculty, or staff, and that charges a fee directly related to, although not necessarily equal to, the cost of the goods or services. The distinguishing characteristic of auxiliary enterprises is that they are managed as essentially self-supporting activities. Examples are residence halls, food services, intercollegiate athletics (only if essentially self-supporting), college stores, faculty clubs, faculty and staff parking, and faculty housing. Student health services, when operated as an auxiliary enterprise, also should be included. The general public may be served incidentally by auxiliary enterprises. Hospitals, although they may serve students, faculty, or staff, are separately classified because of their relative financial significance.[12]

Note that even though auxiliary enterprises are called an entity, their operating accounts are carried in the Unrestricted Current Funds, Restricted Current Funds, or both, and related fixed assets and long-term debt are accounted for in the Plant Funds. Note also that—though the term "enterprise" is used and reference is made to auxiliary enterprises being self-supporting—auxiliary enterprises are not accounted for on a revenues and expenses basis like proprietary funds of government but on a revenues, expenditures, and fund balances basis.

Another term, "Deductions from Fund Balances," may be encountered in higher education accounting and reporting. Such transactions as refunds to donors and grantors and the return to the state of unencumbered or unexpended balances of lapsed appropriations are recorded and reported as deductions from fund balances rather than as expenditures.

Finally, while Figure 19-3 contains an excellent classification of Current Funds Revenues, Expenditures, and Transfers accounts, in our illustrative examples we use an even simpler general ledger approach for ease of illustration.

Transactions and Entries—Unrestricted Current Funds

Assume for purposes of illustration that two Current Fund accounting entities—an Unrestricted Current Fund and a Restricted Current Fund—are in use and that most auxiliary enterprises are accounted for as part of the Unrestricted Current Fund. The following are some typical Unrestricted Current Fund transactions and the entries to record them. Transactions 10, 11, and 12 require entries not only in the Unrestricted Current Fund but also in the Plant Funds; entry 13 requires an entry in the Endowment and Similar Funds; and entry 15 corresponds with entry 3 in the Restricted Current Fund illustration.

Transactions and Entries

1. Educational and general revenues earned during the year amounted to $2,600,000, of which $2,538,000 has been collected, $12,000 is covered by tuition scholarships, and the balance is outstanding receivables.

---

[12] Ibid., pp. 189–190.

(1) Cash	2,538,000	
Expenditures—Educational and		
General	12,000	
Accounts Receivable	50,000	
Revenues—Educational and		
General		2,600,000
To record educational revenues		
earned.		

2. It is estimated that $2,000 of the accounts receivable will never be collected.

(2) Expenditures—Educational and		
General	2,000	
Allowance for Uncollectible		
Accounts		2,000
To record provision for uncollectible		
accounts.		

3. Other revenues of $700,000 were collected through auxiliary enterprises.

(3) Cash	700,000	
Revenues—Auxiliary Enterprises		700,000
To record revenues of auxiliary		
enterprises.		

4. Total purchases of materials and supplies for the year amounted to $600,000, of which $560,000 has been paid.

(4) Inventory of Materials and Supplies	600,000	
Cash		560,000
Accounts Payable		40,000
To record purchases of materials and		
supplies.		

5. Materials and supplies used during the year amounted to $550,000, of which $250,000 is chargeable to educational and general activities and $300,000 to auxiliary enterprises.

(5) Expenditures—Educational and		
General	250,000	
Expenditures—Auxiliary Enterprises ...	300,000	
Inventory of Materials and		
Supplies		550,000
To record cost of materials and		
supplies used.		

6. Salaries and wages paid amounted to $2,200,000, of which $1,920,000 is chargeable to educational and general activities and $280,000 to auxiliary enterprises.

(6) Expenditures—Educational and
    General 1,920,000
    Expenditures—Auxiliary Enterprises ... 280,000
    Cash 2,200,000
    To record salaries and wages paid.

7. Legal fees, insurance, interest on money borrowed temporarily for operating purposes, and telephone and telegraph expenditures, all chargeable to educational and general activities, amounted to $100,000; all had been paid by the end of the year.

(7) Expenditures—Educational and
    General 100,000
    Cash 100,000
    To record legal and insurance
    expenditures, interest on money
    borrowed for operating purposes, and
    telephone and telegraph expenditures.

8. Other expenditures chargeable to auxiliary enterprises and paid for totaled $10,000.

(8) Expenditures—Auxiliary Enterprises ... 10,000
    Cash 10,000
    To record expenditures of auxiliary
    enterprises other than those for
    materials and supplies or for salaries.

9. Student aid cash grants totaled $8,000.

(9) Expenditures—Educational and
    General 8,000
    Cash 8,000
    To record student aid granted.

10. Unrestricted current funds of $25,000 were transferred to the Funds For Retirement of Indebtedness to pay an installment of the mortgage note carried as a liability in the Investment in Plant accounts. This transfer is required under terms of the loan agreement. (See entry 1, Funds for Retirement of Indebtedness.)

(10) Mandatory Transfers to Plant Funds 25,000
     Cash 25,000
     To record payment of mortgage note
     carried as a liability in the Plant
     Funds.

11. A $30,000 nonmandatory transfer was made from the Unrestricted Current Fund to the Unexpended Plant Fund for the purpose of financing additions to the plant. (See entry 2, Unexpended Plant Funds.)

(11) Nonmandatory Transfers to Plant
      Funds 30,000
      Cash 30,000
To record transfers to Plant Funds for
purposes of making additions to plant.

12. Unrestricted current funds of $10,000 were spent for equipment. (See entry 3, Investment in Plant Fund.)

(12) Nonmandatory Transfers to Plant
      Funds 10,000
      Cash 10,000
To record cost of plant additions
financed from the Unrestricted
Current Fund.

13. In accordance with a resolution of the board of trustees of the university, $100,000 was transferred from the Unrestricted Current Fund to the Endowment and Similar Funds group for the purpose of establishing a fund which is to function as an endowment. (See entry 10, Endowment and Similar Funds.)

(13) Nonmandatory Transfers to Endowment
      and Similar Funds 100,000
      Cash 100,000
To record transfer of cash to Endowment
and Similar Funds group for the purpose
of establishing a fund which is to function
as an endowment.

14. The board of trustees voted to reserve $75,000 of the Unrestricted Current Fund resources for a computer use survey during the subsequent year.

(14) Fund Balances—Unallocated 75,000
      Fund Balances—Allocated 75,000
To establish a fund balance reserve for
the estimated cost of a computer use
survey to be made during the
subsequent period.

15. Indirect overhead recovery on sponsored research, $8,000, was paid from the Restricted Current Fund to the Unrestricted Current Fund. (See entry 3, Restricted Current Fund.)

(15) Cash 8,000
      Revenues—Educational and General
                         8,000
To record receipt of indirect cost recovery on sponsored research from the Restricted Fund.

16. Revenue, expenditure, and transfer accounts were closed at year end.

(16)		
Revenues—Educational and General	2,608,000	
Revenues—Auxiliary Enterprises	700,000	
Expenditures—Educational and General		2,292,000
Expenditures—Auxiliary Enterprises..		590,000
Mandatory Transfers to Plant Funds .		25,000
Nonmandatory Transfers to Plant Funds		40,000
Nonmandatory Transfers to Endowment and Similar Funds		100,000
Fund Balances—Unallocated		261,000
To close out revenues, expenditures, and transfers.		

Statement of Changes in Fund Balances—Unrestricted Current Funds

A statement analyzing the changes in fund balances of the Unrestricted Current Fund is illustrated in Figure 19-4. The excess of revenues over expenditures and transfers shown in this statement corresponds with the Fund Balances—Unallocated credit in entry 16 and with the amount shown in the statement illustrated in Figure 19-6.

Figure 19-4

A UNIVERSITY

Unrestricted Current Funds
Statement of Changes in Fund Balances
For Fiscal Year

	Total	Unallocated	Allocated
Balances, beginning of year*	$ —	$ —	$ —
Additions—			
Excess of revenues over expenditures and transfers (Figure 19-6)	261,000	261,000	
Transfers between unallocated and allocated—allocation for computer use survey	—	(75,000)	75,000
Balances, end of year	$261,000	$186,000	$75,000

The illustrative example in this chapter is for the initial year of operations of A University. Otherwise, there would in all likelihood have been a beginning-of-year balance.

Transactions and Entries—Restricted Current Funds

The following are typical transactions of this fund group and the entries made to record them.

Transactions and Entries

1. Cash receipts during the year were as follows:

Federally Sponsored Research (grant)	$100,000	
Gifts—Library Operations	200,000	
Endowment Income—Supplemental Salary Payments*	62,400	
Endowment Income—Student Aid*	15,600	$378,000
Endowment Income—Auxiliary Enterprises*		9,700
		$387,700

See also Endowment and Similar Funds, transaction 5.

(1) Cash	387,700	
Fund Balances—Federally Sponsored Research		100,000
Fund Balances—Gifts—Library Operations..		200,000
Fund Balances—Endowment Income— Supplemental Salary Payments		62,400
Fund Balances—Endowment Income— Student Aid		15,600
Fund Balances—Endowment Income— Auxiliary Enterprises		9,700
To record resources received.		

(Fund Balances subsidiary accounts usually show the sources and purposes of the resources received or accrued. Alternatively, a series of Fund Balances general ledger accounts may be used, as is done here for clarity of illustration.)

2. Expenditures were incurred as follows, of which $7,000 remained unpaid at year end:

Sponsored Research	$ 40,000
Library Operations	130,000
Instruction and Departmental Research (Supplemental Salary Payments)	50,000
Auxiliary Enterprises	2,000
Student Aid	12,000
	$234,000

(2) Expenditures—Educational and General	232,000	
Expenditures—Auxiliary Enterprises	2,000	
Accounts Payable		7,000
Cash		227,000
To record expenditures incurred.		

3. Recovery of indirect costs of $8,000, associated with the $40,000 of sponsored research expenditures, was transferred to the Unrestricted Current Fund. (See also Unrestricted Current Fund, transaction 15.)

(3) Fund Balances—Federally Sponsored
     Research 8,000
     Cash 8,000
To record payment to Unrestricted Current
Funds of indirect cost recovery under
provisions of research grant.

(The indirect cost recovery revenue is recognized in the Unrestricted Current Fund in entry 15. Alternatively, indirect cost recoveries may be recorded directly in the Unrestricted Current Fund rather than being recorded initially in the Restricted Current Fund.)

4. Income due from the Endowment and Similar Funds group at year end was as follows:

For Supplemental Salary Payments	$25,000
For Student Aid	5,000
	$30,000

(See also Endowment and Similar Funds, transaction 9.)

(4) Due from Endowment and Similar Funds 30,000
    Fund Balances—Endowment Income—
      Supplemental Salary Payments 25,000
    Fund Balances—Endowment Income—
      Student Aid 5,000
To record resources due from endowment
earnings.

5. Revenue for the period was recognized and fund balances adjusted accordingly at year end.

(5) Fund Balances—Federally Sponsored
     Research 40,000
    Fund Balances—Gifts—Library Operations ... 130,000
    Fund Balances—Endowment Income—
      Supplemental Salary Payments 50,000
    Fund Balances—Endowment Income—
      Student Aid 12,000
    Fund Balances—Endowment Income—
      Auxiliary Enterprises 2,000
      Revenues—Educational and General 232,000
      Revenues—Auxiliary Enterprises 2,000
To recognize revenues to the extent that
restricted resources were expended during
the period.

(Compare this entry to entry 2. Note again that revenues are recognized only to the extent that the restricted resources are expended for the purposes or functions designated by donors, grantors, or outside agencies.)

6. Closing entries were made.

(6) Revenues—Educational and General 232,000
Revenues—Auxiliary Enterprises 2,000
  Expenditures—Educational and General ...   232,000
  Expenditures—Auxiliary Enterprises   2,000
To close the Revenues and Expenditures
accounts at year end.

(Obviously, the entries to close the Revenue and Expenditures accounts must be in corresponding amounts in the case of Restricted Current Funds, because revenue is realized only upon expenditure of the restricted resources.)

In each case above, less resources were expended (and recognized as revenue) than were received or accrued. Had fund balances been brought forward from prior years, the opposite might have been true. Again, as in the case of Specific Purpose Funds of hospitals, the logic of the realization (revenue recognition) convention employed in Restricted Current Funds accounting—as recommended in *CUBA* and as done in most colleges and universities—is that the resources have not been earned until they have been expended for their designated purposes.

Two alternative approaches that may be found in practice warrant brief mention here. First, some colleges and universities do not observe the "revenue recognition deferral" convention with respect to Restricted Current Funds. Rather, they (1) account for the Restricted Current Funds in the same manner as the Unrestricted Current Funds during the year, and (2) at year end, they close the Revenues and Expenditures accounts to appropriately titled Fund Balance—Reserved or Fund Balance—Restricted accounts. Second, some colleges and universities account for both restricted and unrestricted resources available for current expenditures in a single Current Funds general ledger. In this case it is necessary that the fund balance accounts (and related subsidiary records) be clearly identified as between Fund Balances—Unrestricted and Fund Balances—Restricted.

The Statement of Changes in Fund Balances of A University's Restricted Current Fund for the fiscal year is presented as Figure 19-5. Note the format and content of this statement and use it to review the Restricted Current Funds illustration.

Operating Statement—Current Funds

A Statement of Current Funds Revenues, Expenditures, and Other Changes, based on the journal entries for the two Current Funds subgroups, is presented in Figure 19-6. It shows the total revenues from each source and the total amount spent for each major activity, both classified as to whether they pertain to Unrestricted or Restricted Current Funds.

Since detailed revenue and expenditure accounts are not used in the journal entries in this chapter, the most common accounts (see Figure 19-3) are listed in Figure 19-6. The amounts presented in the Restricted Current Funds columns

Figure 19-5

A UNIVERSITY

Restricted Current Funds
Statement of Changes in Fund Balances
For Fiscal Year

| | Total | Educational and General | | | | |
		Sponsored Research	Library Operations	Supplemental Salary Payments	Student Aid	Auxiliary Enterprises
Balance, beginning of year*	$ —	$ —	$ —	$ —	$ —	$ —
Additions:						
Sponsored reasearch	$100,000	$100,000				
Gifts	200,000		$200,000			
Endowment income	117,700			$87,400	$20,600	$9,700
	$417,700	$100,000	$200,000	$87,400	$20,600	$9,700
Deductions:†						
Expenditures (Figure 19-6)	$234,000	$ 40,000	$130,000	$50,000	$12,000	$2,000
Indirect cost recoveries on sponsored programs transferred to Unrestricted Current Funds	8,000	8,000				
	$242,000	$ 48,000	$130,000	$50,000	$12,000	$2,000
Balances, end of year	$175,700	$ 52,000	$ 70,000	$37,400	$ 8,600	$7,700

*The illustrative example in this chapter is for the initial year of operations of A University. Otherwise, there would in all likelihood have been a beginning-of-year balance.

†The "Deductions" section reports those amounts (1) reported simultaneously as revenues and expenditures on the Statement of Current Funds Revenues, Expenditures, and Other Changes (Figure 19-6), and (2) refunds of restricted resources because of the lapsing of a governmental appropriation, because they are not needed for the restricted purpose, etc.

Figure 19-6

A UNIVERSITY

Statement of Current Funds Revenues,
Expenditures, and Other Changes
For Fiscal Year

	Total	Unrestricted	Restricted
Revenues:			
Tuition and fees	$1,358,000	$1,358,000	—
State appropriations	1,000,000	1,000,000	—
Federal grants and contracts	40,000	—	$ 40,000
State grants and contracts	—	—	—
Local gifts, grants, and contracts	132,000	130,000	2,000
Private gifts, grants, and contracts	130,000	—	130,000
Endowment income	62,000	—	62,000
Sales and services of educational activities .	70,000	70,000	—
Sales and services of auxiliary enterprises ..	700,000	700,000	—
Expired term endowment	—	—	—
Other sources (if any)	50,000	50,000	—
	3,542,000	3,308,000	234,000
Expenditures and mandatory transfers:			
Educational and general:			
Instruction	922,000	872,000	50,000
Research	140,000	100,000	40,000
Public service	50,000	50,000	—
Academic support	330,000	200,000	130,000
Student services	150,000	150,000	—
Institutional support	400,000	400,000	—
Operation and maintenance of plant	500,000	500,000	—
Scholarships and fellowships	32,000	20,000	12,000
Total educational and general expenditures	2,524,000	2,292,000	232,000
Mandatory transfers for:			
Principal and interest	25,000	25,000	—
Renewals and replacements	—	—	—
Loan fund matching grant	—	—	—
Total educational and general	2,549,000	2,317,000	—
Auxiliary enterprises:			
Expenditures:	592,000	590,000	2,000
Mandatory transfers for:			
Principal and interest	—	—	—
Renewals and replacements	—	—	—
Total auxiliary enterprises	592,000	590,000	2,000
Total expenditures and mandatory transfers	3,141,000	2,907,000	234,000

Figure 19-6 (continued)

Other transfers and additions (deductions):			
Excess of restricted receipts over transfers			
to revenues	175,700	—	175,000
Nonmandatory transfers to plant funds	(40,000)	(40,000)	—
Nonmandatory transfer to Endowment and			
Similar Funds	(100,000)	(100,000)	—
Net increase in fund balance	$ 436,700	$ 261,000	$175,700

are properly classified, as are the mandatory and nonmandatory transfers and auxiliary enterprises revenues and expenditures. The other amounts in the Unrestricted Current Funds columns have been allocated (arbitrarily) among the more common revenue and expenditure accounts solely for instructional purposes. Also, some accounts with zero balances are included for illustrative purposes. Schedules showing the details of current revenues and expenditures, and of the transfers, should be prepared in support of these major elements of the statement for internal uses. For example, details of the operations of each department should be shown, and a separate statement of revenues and expenditures should be prepared for each of the auxiliary activities.

BALANCE SHEET—FOR THE UNIVERSITY

A balance sheet for the university at the close of the fiscal year is presented in Figure 19-7. Data from the transactions already presented for the Unrestricted Current and Restricted Current Funds are the bases of the balance sheet for the Current Funds group. The year-end balance sheets of the other funds or fund groups (after the transactions discussed later) are added to the Balance Sheets of the two types of funds already discussed.

This "pancake" form of the university-wide balance sheet seems to be the preferred form, though college and university balance sheets are often presented in columnar form. Even though like balances of the several fund groups are placed on the same line using a columnar format, no total column is usually provided. This recognizes that assets and liabilities of the fund groups are in most cases subject to legal or donor restrictions and other obligations that may make it misleading to show totals for the university as a whole.

LOAN FUNDS

Loan Funds are used to account for funds that may be loaned to students and, in some cases, to faculty and staff. If only the fund's income may be loaned, the principal is included in the Endowment and Similar Funds group and only the income is included with the Loan Funds. It is desirable to classify the fund balances in appropriate ways. For example, some may come from appropriations, others from private donors, and still others from Unrestricted Current Funds set aside for this purpose by the college or university governing board. Some may be refundable to donors under specified conditions.

Loan funds have become major activites requiring professional management at many higher education institutions. Some have raised large sums for loan purposes through gifts and many participate in the National Direct Student Loan (NDSL) Program and the Federally Insured Student Loan (FISL) program. Both federal programs must be administered in accordance with many regulations, and the NDSL requires the college or university to contribute 10 percent of the total loan fund balance.

Covering such programs, which are subject to change, is beyond the scope of this text. Rather, especially since loan funds of governments were covered earlier, accounting for loan losses in colleges and universities is discussed briefly and a simplified example of a college or university Loan Fund is presented.

Loan losses may be accounted for in one of two ways. Under one method, an Allowance for Loan Losses is deducted from the total loans and the Loan Funds Balance in the year-end balance sheet. It is reversed at the start of the new year and loan losses are charged against specific Loan Fund Balance accounts. Under the second method, an allowance method, estimated losses are deducted from the Loan Funds Balance accounts to which they are expected to relate and an Allowance for Loan Losses is established. Loan losses incurred are charged against the allowance account.

In reviewing the following transactions assume that a Loan Fund was established to make interest-free loans and that (1) income on Fund investments is to be added to the principal of the Fund, and (2) the total assets of the Fund, both the original principal and that from earnings, may be loaned.

Transactions and Entries

1. A donation of $100,000 was received for the purpose of making loans to students.

(1)	Cash	100,000	
	Fund Balance		100,000
	To record donation received for the purpose of setting up Loan Fund.		

2. Loans of $50,000 were made.

(2)	Loans Receivable	50,000	
	Cash		50,000
	To record loans made.		

Figure 19-7

A UNIVERSITY

Balance Sheet

At Close of Fiscal Year

Assets		Liabilities and Fund Balances	
Current Funds:		Current Funds:	
Unrestricted:		Unrestricted:	
Cash	$ 203,000	Accounts payable	$ 40,000
Accounts receivable, less allowance for uncollectible accounts of $2,000	48,000	Fund balances (Figure 19-4)	261,000
Inventory of materials and supplies	50,000		
Total unrestricted	$ 301,000	Total unrestricted	$ 301,000
Restricted Funds:		Restricted Funds:	
Cash	$ 152,700	Accounts payable	$ 7,000
Due from endowment and similar funds	30,000	Fund balances (Figure 19-5)	175,700
Total restricted	$ 182,700	Total restricted	$ 182,700
Total current funds	$ 483,700	Total current funds	$ 483,700
Loan Funds:		Loan Funds:	
Cash	$ 25,400	Fund balances*	$ 99,900
Loans receivable	49,500		
Investments	25,000		
Total loan funds	$ 99,900	Total loan funds	$ 99,900

Endowment and Similar Funds:

Assets other than fixed:
Cash .... $ 205,800
Investments:
Preferred stocks, at cost
(market value $625,000) ...... $ 500,000
Common stocks, at cost (market
value, $1,215,000) 1,065,000
Bonds, at cost (market value
$465,000) 454,700
Held in trust by others—cost,
$200,000 (market value,
$234,000) .... —
$2,019,700
$2,225,500

Fixed assets:
Land .... $ 100,000
Buildings, less allowance for depreciation of $6,000 594,000
Equipment, less allowance for depreciation of $14,000 136,000
$ 830,000
Total endowment and similar funds $3,055,500

Annuity and Life Income Funds:
Cash .... $ 10,000
Investments, at cost (market value, $177,000) 176,000
Total annuity and life income funds .... $ 186,000

Endowment and Similar Funds:
Due to restricted current funds ..... $ 30,000
Fund balances:*
Endowment $2,925,500
Quasi-Endowment 100,000
3,025,500

Total endowment and similar funds $3,055,500

Annuity and Life Income Funds:
Annuities payable .... $ 161,589
Fund balances—Annuities* 24,411
Total annuity and life income funds .... $ 186,000

Figure 19-7 (continued)

Plant Funds:

			Plant Funds:		
Unexpended:			Unexpended:		
Cash		$ 18,000	Fund balances—Unrestricted*		$ 18,000
Investments, at cost (market value $22,100)		20,000	Fund balances—Restricted		20,000
Total unexpended		$ 38,000	Total unexpended		$ 38,000
For retirement of indebtedness:			For retirement of indebtedness:		
Investments		$ 25,000	Fund balances—Restricted*		$ 225,000
Sinking Fund—Bank Trustee		200,000			
Total for retirement of indebtedness		$ 225,000	Total for retirement of indebtedness		$ 225,000
Investment in plant:			Investment in plant:		
Land		$ 300,000	Mortgage payable		$ 370,000
Buildings		4,000,000	Net investment in plant*		4,951,000
Improvements other than buildings		12,000			
Equipment		809,000			
Library books		200,000			
Total investment in plant		$5,321,000	Total investment in plant		$5,321,000
Total plant funds		$5,584,000	Total plant funds		$5,584,000

*Statements analyzing changes in the balances of each fund group should be presented in the financial report.

3. The sum of $25,000 was invested in bonds. The bonds were purchased at par plus accrued interest of $100.

(3)	Investments	25,000	
	Accrued Interest on Investments		
	Purchased	100	
	Cash		25,100

To record investments and accrued
interest purchased.

4. A $500 check in payment of three months' bond interest was received.

(4)	Cash	500	
	Accrued Interest on Investments		
	Purchased		100
	Fund Balance		400

To record receipt of semiannual
interest payment.

5. A student died and it was decided to write off his loan of $500 as uncollectible.

| (5) | Fund Balance .... | 500 | |
| | Loans Receivable .... | | 500 |

To write off loan as uncollectible.

ENDOWMENT AND SIMILAR FUNDS

These Funds are used to account for assets which, at least at the moment, cannot be expended, although usually the income from them may be. Funds donated by outsiders fall into two categories: (1) those that have been given in perpetuity, Endowment Funds, sometimes referred to as "true" or "pure" Endowment Funds; and (2) those for which the donor has specified a particular date or event after which the funds may be expended, "Term Endowment Funds."

The appropriate policy-making body of an institution may also set aside available funds for the same purposes as those donated as endowments. These are called "Quasi-Endowment Funds" or "Funds Functioning As Endowments," and, of course, are subject to reassignment by the authority that created them.

Donors may choose to make the income from endowment-type funds available to a university but to leave the principal in the possession and control of a trustee other than the university. Such funds usually are not included among the Endowment and Similar Funds of the university, but should be disclosed in the financial statements by an appropriate footnote. Unrestricted income from such funds is reported as revenue in the Unrestricted Current Funds. If restricted to specific operating purposes, the income is recorded as an addition to the Restricted Current Funds balance. When expended, it is reported there as Endowment Income if the trust is irrevocable; if it is a revocable trust, the income recognized should be reported there as Gifts. If the income is restricted to plant or debt service uses, it is recorded in the appropriate Plant Funds.

Determining and Reporting Income

One of the most debated issues in Endowment Fund accounting is: What is Endowment Fund income? At least four views on the matter have found their way into practice. Considerable attention is given to this subject in CUBA and it warrants our attention before delving into the illustrative example that follows.

Most higher education institutions have followed the classical trust or fiduciary principle that "yield" on investments includes dividends, rents, royalties, interest, and the like but does not include appreciation (realized or unrealized) of the market value of the endowment or trust principal (corpus) assets. In other words, under the trust fund theory the principal includes appreciation of the value of the assets held in trust as well as the original assets and any subsequent enhancements by donations.

Another view is that the corporate law—where all realized gains and losses affect income—should prevail. This is the opposite view, of course, from the trust principle or theory discussed above.

Still another approach may be followed in the several states that have adopted the model Uniform Management of Institutional Funds Act (UMIFA) which permits the "prudent" use of appreciation in the value of investments over their original historic cost. This is very near the "corporate law" principle discussed above, although that concept presumes that the investment had been sold and the gain realized, which is not necessary under the UMIFA. On the other hand, the UMIFA is more stringent in requiring "prudent" use of the appreciation.

Finally, many universities have adopted various "total return" approaches under which they consider as income (and spend) a "prudent *portion*" of the appreciation—unrealized, realized, or both—as well as the yield. Various spreading and averaging approaches are instituted to minimize the effects of short-term fluctuations in the value of the investments; some are applied only to realized gains, others to unrealized gains, and others to both.

After considering the wide variation in Endowment and Similar Funds management, accounting, and reporting—and particularly the "total return" methods—the following is concluded in *CUBA:*

> The concept of "principal" is often indecisive; there is no clear redefinition of income; the exercise of prudence is subjective and not susceptible to measurement in an accounting sense; and the "spending rate" is often related to the market value of securities rather than to the total return actually experienced.
>
> Until a general practice in the application of the total return concept evolves that produces results that are objectively determinable, institutions should report any *appreciation* utilized from investment of endowment and similar funds as a *transfer.* To the extent such a transfer is added to current funds, it should be reported separately from the traditional income from endowment and similar funds and should *not be included in total current funds revenues.*[13]

---

[13] Ibid., p. 193. (Emphasis added.) Much of the discussion above is paraphrased from CUBA, pp. 192–193.

The AICPA college and university audit guide contains a lengthy discussion of the history and application of the "total return" concept and the AICPA committee concluded by concurring with the *CUBA* conclusions and recommendations cited above.[14]

Thus, both *CUBA* and the AICPA prefer the conservative, traditional, objectively determinable classic trust or fiduciary method of determining income of Endowment and Similar Funds, which is reported as follows:

1. If the income must be used for specified *restricted* purposes, it is credited to appropriate Fund Balance accounts in the Restricted Current Funds, Loan Funds, Endowment and Similar Funds, or Plant Funds, as specified by terms of the gift agreement.

2. If the income is *unrestricted*, it is credited to Unrestricted Current Funds revenues.

Under this approach, unrealized gains are not considered income; realized gains typically are considered income only if that is the donor's wish.

Transactions and Entries—Endowment Funds

The following transactions and entries illustrate the operation of Endowment and Similar Funds, which are similar to municipal Nonexpendable Trust Funds.

Transactions and Entries

1. Cash was donated by a family during the year to establish three separate endowments, as follows:

Endowment A (for Supplemental Salary Payments)	$1,000,000
Endowment B (for Supplemental Salary Payments)	600,000
Endowment C (for Student Aid)	400,000
	$2,000,000

These endowments included a provision that any earnings in excess of $78,000 be dedicated to the athletic program, an auxiliary enterprise of the university.

(1) Cash	2,000,000	
Endowment Fund A Balance		1,000,000
Endowment Fund B Balance		600,000
Endowment Fund C Balance		400,000
To record receipt of money for the purpose of establishing three endowments.		

---

[14] Committee on College and University Accounting and Auditing, op. cit., pp. 37–40.

2. It was decided to invest this money in securities that were to be pooled. The following securities were acquired at the prices indicated:

Preferred stocks	$ 500,000
Common stocks	1,000,000
Bonds:	
Par value	200,000
Premiums	10,000
Bonds:	
Par value	250,000
Discounts	5,000
Accrued interest on investments	
purchased	1,000

(2) Preferred Stocks	500,000	
Common Stocks	1,000,000	
Bonds	450,000	
Accrued Interest on Investments		
Purchased	1,000	
Unamortized Premiums on		
Investments	10,000	
Unamortized Discounts on		
Investments		5,000
Cash		1,956,000
To record purchase of pooled investments.		

3. Cash received on these investments for the year was as follows:

Dividends on preferred stocks	$20,000
Dividends on common stocks	60,000
Interest	9,000

No material amounts of investment income were accrued at year end.

(3) Cash	89,000	
Income on Pooled Investments		88,000
Accrued Interest on Investments		
Purchased		1,000
To record income received as follows:		

Dividends on preferred stock		$20,000
Dividends on common stock		60,000
Interest received	$9,000	
Less—Interest purchased	1,000	8,000
		$88,000

4. Premiums on investments in the amount of $500 and discounts in the amount of $200 were amortized at the end of the year.

(4)	Unamortized Discounts on Investments	200	
	Income on Pooled Investments	300	
	Unamortized Premiums on		
	Investments		500
	To record amortization of premiums		
	and discounts.		

5. The earnings on Endowments A, B, and C exceeded $78,000. Thus, $78,000 was paid to the Restricted Current Funds for the primary purposes of these endowments and the remainder of the net income from pooled investments was paid to the Restricted Current Funds for auxiliary enterprise purposes. (See also transaction 1, Restricted Current Fund.)

(5)	Income on Pooled Investments	87,700	
	Cash		87,700
	To record payment of endowment		
	income to the Restricted Current		
	Funds as follows:		

Fund	Fund Balance*	Percentage of Total	Income Apportioned
A	$1,000,000	50	$39,000
B	600,000	30	23,400
C	400,000	20	15,600
	$2,000,000	100%	$78,000
Earnings			87,700
Balance—for auxiliary enterprises			$ 9,700

It is assumed that market values and book values of the several funds are in this case identical.

6. Common stock with a book value of $10,000 was sold for $10,500.

(6)	Cash	10,500	
	Common Stock		10,000
	Endowment Fund A Balance		250
	Endowment Fund B Balance		150
	Endowment Fund C Balance		100
	To record sale of common stock at a		
	gain of $500 and the addition of the		
	gain to the balance of each Endowment		
	Fund as follows:		

Fund	Fund Balance	Percentage of Total	Gain Apportioned
A	$1,000,000	50	$250
B	600,000	30	150
C	400,000	20	100
	$2,000,000	100%	$500

7. An individual donated common stock which had cost him $65,000 (hereafter referred to as Endowment Fund D). At the time of the donation the stock had a market value of $75,000. The income from these securities is unrestricted and may be used for any university purposes.

(7) Common Stock	75,000	
Endowment Fund D Balance		75,000
To record donation of common stock		
with a market value of $75,000; the net		
income of Endowment D is		
unrestricted.		

8. An individual had a small apartment complex constructed and equipped and then turned it over to the university with the specification that the net income therefrom was to be used $\frac{1}{6}$ for student aid and $\frac{5}{6}$ for supplemental salary payments (hereafter referred to as Endowment Fund E). The total cost was $850,000, divided as follows:

Land	$100,000
Building	600,000
Equipment	150,000

(8) Land	100,000	
Building	600,000	
Equipment	150,000	
Endowment Fund E Balance		850,000
To record gift of an apartment complex		
as an endowment, the net income of		
which is restricted to certain purposes.		

9. Gross income from the apartments (Endowment Fund E) for the current year was $170,000; and total expenses were $120,000, exclusive of depreciation of $20,000 (building, $6,000; equipment, $14,000). No receivables or payables were outstanding at year end and the net income of Endowment Fund E was established as a liability to the Restricted Current Fund. (See transaction 4, Restricted Current Fund.)

(9) Cash	50,000	
Allowance for Depreciation—		
Building		6,000
Allowance for Depreciation—		
Equipment		14,000
Due to Restricted Current Fund		30,000
To record results of Endowment E		
operations for the period and liability		
to the Restricted Current Fund for the		
net income, after depreciation, of		
Endowment E.		

10. The sum of $100,000 was received from the Unrestricted Current Fund for the purpose of establishing a fund functioning as an endowment (Quasi-Endowment Fund) in accordance with a resolution adopted by the university's Board of Trustees. (See transaction 13, Unrestricted Current Fund.)

```
(10) Cash ..........................................   100,000
        Quasi-Endowment Fund Balance .....              100,000
     To record receipt of money from
     Unrestricted Current Fund for purpose
     of setting up a fund to function as an
     Endowment Fund in accordance with
     resolution adopted by the university's
     Board of Trustees.
```

11. An individual set up a trust (to be administered by the Village National Bank) in the amount of $200,000, the income from which is to go to the university.

```
(11) No entry, or purely memorandum entry. The trust would be
     disclosed in the notes to the financial statements.
```

Commentary—Endowment Funds Transactions and Entries

The following points should be noted with respect to the foregoing transactions and entries.

1. Three types of nonexpendable funds were illustrated: (a) "pure" endowment funds, exemplified by transactions and entries 1 to 9, (b) funds being accounted for as endowments through action of the Board of Trustees of the university, illustrated by transaction and entry 10, and (c) funds turned over by a donor to a trustee or trustees with the stipulation that the income therefrom is to go to the university, exemplified by transaction 11, which requires no entry in the Endowment and Similar Funds group.

2. The investments of several Endowment Funds have been pooled and premiums, discounts, and accrued interest purchases are involved.

3. Since investment earnings may fluctuate from year to year, it may be desirable to establish a Reserve for Income Stabilization. If unrestricted earnings are held in the Endowment and Similar Funds for this purpose, Current Funds revenues will be understated.[15] Thus, all Endowment and Similar Funds earnings should be distributed each year. If a Reserve for Income Stabilization is desired, it should be established in the Unrestricted Current Funds.

4. Since the objective of the investment pool is the production of income,

---

[15] Reserves for Income Stabilization that result in understatement of periodic revenue are not in accordance with generally accepted accounting principles.

income should be computed on an accrual basis. Accordingly, both premiums and discounts on investments have been amortized in the illustrative case and any material receivables would have been accrued.

5. Since Endowment and Similar Funds are normally operated on the principles of accounting for trusts, losses or gains on the sale of pooled investments are not elements in the income calculation but are adjustments of the balances of the Endowment and Similar Funds. If the equities in pooled investments of the participating funds are maintained on a book value (cost) basis, losses or gains on the sale of pooled investments may be treated in two ways: (a) Gains may be credited and losses charged to a Reserve for Gains or Losses on Pooled Investments account, which eventually is closed out into the principal of each participating fund. (b) Gains may be credited and losses charged to the investment pool equity (and the fund principal) of each participant fund as they occur. If there are many sales of pooled securities, the first method if desirable; if there are few sales the second method may be employed.

6. If there are changes in the market value of pooled investments, and if the several participating funds make contributions to the pool that are not proportionate to their original investments, the book value method demonstrated in the example will not result in equitable assignments of gains or losses on the sale of investments and of income on pooled investments. Consequently, The Committee (CUBA) endorsed the use of the market value method of accounting for the equities of the several funds and pooled investments—as used by Regulated Investment Trusts (mutual funds)—whether or not changes in investment market values are recorded in the accounts. Under the market value method the initial balances of the participating funds are divided by some arbitrary value, say $10, that is to be assigned to a share in the pool. A fund with a $5,000 balance, then, would have 500 shares. If the market value of investments in the pool doubled, the unit value would increase to $20, but the fund with a $5,000 initial balance would still have 500 shares. A new fund being admitted to the pool would have its number of shares determined by dividing the market value of its contribution, whether in cash or investments, by $20. The number of shares then would become the basis for allocating realized gains or losses, as well as income from the pool, among the funds.

Withdrawals of participating funds from the investment pool are made at market value. If the market value of shares has increased, the payment to the withdrawing fund will result in a cash payment in excess of the fund balance, assuming it is carried at cost. This excess is composed of unrealized gains in the market value of investments, together with any undistributed realized gains or losses. Consequently it is appropriate to charge this share adjustment, the excess of market value over cost, to the account for (realized) gains and losses on investments.

Realized gains and losses might properly be distributed to the balances of the several funds in proportion to their numbers of shares. The same may be said of the share adjustments arising from unrealized appreciation of the investment portfolio. In practice the balances of the Undistributed Gains and Losses on Investment Transactions and Undistributed Share Adjustments accounts may be accumulated, although it would be equitable to distribute the former, at least, to the funds on the basis of their shares. In no event, however, should the undistributed Gains and Losses on Investment Transactions account be used to postpone the reporting of revenue.

The necessity for the Undistributed Share Adjustments account arises from the use of the cost basis in accounting for investments and fund balances. Both *CUBA* and the AICPA college and university audit guide[16] permit recording the market value in the accounts. Recognition in the accounts of the market value of investments, which appears to be increasing in practice, permits recognition of unrealized increments or decrements, which in turn eliminates the need for the share adjustment account. However, realized and unrealized gains must be carefully distinguished, as should gains and losses considered income and those attributable to principal.

7. Transaction and entry 7 illustrate that securities should be recorded at their market value at the date they are donated.

8. Transaction and entry 9 illustrate that depreciation charges must be taken into account in computing the income of an Endowment Fund that has investments in the form of fixed assets if the Fund is to remain nonexpendable. It illustrates further that it is essential to retain cash (initially) equal to depreciation charges in the Endowment Fund, and transfer only the net income to the Restricted Current Funds. If prices are rising, these depreciation charges retained, even if invested, may not provide sufficient resources to replace the fixed assets. But these charges will at least assure that the original cost is replaced and that the fund principal will, in dollar terms, remain intact. If the donor desires it, provision can be made for additional charges sufficient to replace the depreciated fixed assets. If the supplementary charges are made, the resulting credit would not be to an Allowance for Depreciation account but rather to an account representing an increase in fund balance. A donor could, of course, specify that depreciation would not be recognized or, more properly, that income before depreciation be used for the specified purpose(s). If the gift is accepted, the terms of the gift must be followed.

ANNUITY AND LIFE INCOME FUNDS

Annuity and Life Income Funds are used to account for assets given to the institution with the stipulation that the institution either (1) make annuity payments to designated recipients for a specified period (Annuity Funds), or (2) pay the income from the assets to a designated recipient(s) during his lifetime (Life Income Funds). Since the specified period of an annuity could be the life of the beneficiary, the most fundamental distinction between these two types of funds is that one assures the beneficiary of a fixed dollar payment periodically (Annuity Funds) and the other pays the beneficiary variable amounts according to the earnings of the fund (Life Income Funds). After the specified period (Annuity Funds) or upon the death of the donor (Life Income Funds) the principal is

[16] Committee on College and University Accounting and Auditing, op. cit., p. 8.

transferred to the fund group specified by the donor or, if unrestricted, to the Unrestricted Current Funds.

Accounting for Annuity and Life Income Funds is similar to that for Endowment and Similar Funds. If these funds are immaterial in amount, they may be reported with the Endowment and Similar Funds.

Annuity Funds

CUBA explains Annuity Funds as:

> funds acquired by an institution under agreements whereby money or other property is made available to an institution on condition that it bind itself to pay stipulated amounts periodically to the donors or other designated individuals, which payments are to terminate at the time specified in the agreement.[17]

The Internal Revenue Code and regulations state the conditions under which an annuity trust may be accepted and must be administered from an income tax standpoint, and several states also regulate annuity trusts. Too, since the institution accepts some risk by guaranteeing the beneficiary a fixed amount for a specified period, perhaps for life or even for the lifetime of two or more persons, the governing board will want assurances (1) that the assets donated should generate sufficient income to pay the specified amounts, or (2) if not, and some of the payments must come from principal, that a significant residual balance should be available to the institution at the end of the annuity period.

When the Annuity Fund is established the assets should be recorded at their fair market value, together with any liabilities against the assets assumed by the institution. The liability for the annuity payments is recorded at its present value, based on the expected earnings rate and, if appropriate, life expectancy tables. Any difference between the assets and liabilities should be debited or credited, as appropriate, to Annuity Fund Balances.

To illustrate Annuity Funds accounting, assume that an individual donated $20,000 cash and investments worth $180,000 to A University on January 2, 19X3, with the stipulation that he be paid $25,000 each December 31 for the next ten years. Any remaining net assets should then be used to remodel the business and public administration building. The university finance officer expects to earn at least 7 percent on the fund's assets during each of the next ten years. The entry to record creation of this Annuity Fund would be:

Cash	20,000	
Investments	180,000	
Annuities Payable		175, 589
Annuity Fund Balance		24,411

To record establishment of Annuity
Fund. Calculation of annuity payable:
$25,000 × 7.023582, the present value
of an ordinary annuity of $1 for 10
periods at 7 percent, is $175,589.

[17] CUBA, p. 194.

Investment earnings and gains are credited, and annuity payments and losses are debited, to Annuities Payable. Thus, on December 31, 19X3, the end of the university's fiscal year, the following entries would be made:

Annuities Payable	25,000	
Cash (or Annuities Currently Payable)		25,000
To record the annual annuity payment.		
Investment Earnings	13,000	
Investment Gains	3,000	
Investment Losses		5,000
Annuities Payable		11,000
To close the investment earnings, gains, and losses accounts at year end.		

The logic underlying this approach is that (1) investment gains and losses, as well as investment earnings, should enter the determination of the fund's yield; and (2) if the actual yield equals the expected yield each year, the net decrease in the Annuities Payable account will equal the decrease in its present value. The present value of the annuity liability should be recomputed periodically—using revised yield estimates and, where appropriate, revised life expectancies—and the Annuities Payable and Annuity Fund Balance accounts should be adjusted accordingly.

At the end of the annuity period any remaining balance would be disposed of in the manner specified by the donor. In this example the balance should be transferred to the Plant Renewal and Replacements Fund since the donor specified that it should be used to remodel the business and public administration building.

Life Income Funds

Life Income Funds are defined in *CUBA* as:

> funds acquired by an institution under agreements whereby money or other property is made available to an institution on condition that it bind itself to pay periodically to the donors or other designated individuals the income earned by the assets donated, usually for the lifetimes of the income beneficiaries.[18]

A Life Income Fund might also be established where the beneficiary is to receive only a part of the earnings, say half, with the balance to be used for some specified or unspecified university purpose(s).

Life Income Funds are subject to Internal Revenue Code and regulation provisions, as are Annuity Funds, and may be subject to state regulations. Since

[18] Ibid., p. 195.

only the earnings inure to the beneficiary(ies) of Life Income Funds, and no fixed payment is guaranteed, the college or university does not take an earnings risk as in the case of Annuity Funds.

The accounting for Life Income Funds is not as complex as that for Annuity Funds. All that is involved is: (1) at its inception record the assets at fair market value and record any liabilities assumed; the difference is credited to Life Income Fund Balance; (2) during the term of the fund record fund revenues, expenses, gains, and losses—following donor instructions or, in the absence of instructions, applicable law in determining whether gains or losses affect income or the principal—and distribute the earnings to the beneficiary(ies); and (3) upon the death of the beneficiary(ies), distribute the net assets of the fund as specified by the donor or, in the absence of such instructions, to the Unrestricted Current Funds.

PLANT FUNDS

The Plant Funds consists of four fund subgroups:

1. *Unexpended Plant Funds:* to account for resources to be used for the acquisition of institutional fixed assets.
2. *Funds for Renewals and Replacements:* to account for resources to be used for the remodeling, renovation, or replacement of existing fixed assets.
3. *Funds for Retirement of Indebtedness:* to account for resources to be used to service the debt incurred in relation to the physical plant.
4. *Investment in Plant:* to account for the institution's fixed assets, related indebtedness, and net investment in plant.

The Unexpended Plant Funds and the Funds for Renewals and Replacements are similar to Capital Projects Funds of municipalities; the Funds for Retirement of Indebtedness compare to Debt Service Funds of municipalities; and the Investment in Plant subgroup is like a combination of the General Fixed Assets and General Long-Term Debt Account Groups of a municipality.

All but the Investment in Plant subgroup are used to account for financial resources (cash, investments, etc.). Sometimes these financial resources are reported directly in the Plant Funds, as when (1) resources are dedicated by donors for plant purposes, and (2) specific student fees are assessed under binding external agreements for plant improvement or related debt service purposes. Other restricted financial resources may come from the Endowment and Similar Funds; and unrestricted resources may be transferred to the Plant Funds from the Unrestricted Current Funds. The distinction between unrestricted and restricted (externally) resources should be maintained in the accounts and reports (1) to assure that the restricted funds are used for the proper purposes, and (2) because the governing board can transfer unrestricted resources back to the Unrestricted Current Funds or to the Endowment and Similar Funds.

For external reporting purposes all Plant Funds subgroups may be reported either separately or combined, as long as the separate fund balances are reported.

Any encumbrances outstanding should be disclosed by a Reserve for Encumbrances or in the notes to the financial statements. The results of the transactions and entries of each Plant Funds subgroup are shown in the Balance Sheet presented in Figure 19-7.

Unexpended Plant Funds

The purpose of the Unexpended Plant Funds is to account for the inflows, uses, and balances of financial resources (and any related liabilities) obtained from various sources to finance the acquisition of new long-lived plant assets. Most expenditures from this fund will ultimately be capitalized in the Investment in Plant accounts.

If debt is issued to finance a project the debt is *initially* accounted for in the Unexpended Plant Funds. Expenditures are debited to Construction in Progress unless they are noncapitalizable, in which case they are debited to Fund Balance.

The capital expenditures, the related liabilities, and any associated fund balance should be removed from the Unexpended Plant Funds to the Investment in Plant accounts either (1) at each year end, or (2) at the conclusion of the project. When this is done at the end of each year, equal amounts of Construction in Progress and liabilities are moved to the Investment in Plant accounts until all liabilities have been transferred; thereafter, Unexpended Plant Fund Balance is reduced. In our example we assume that the reclassification occurs at the conclusion of the project.

Some typical Unexpended Plant Funds transactions and the related entries are given below. Transaction and entry 3 also affect the Investment in Plant accounts.

Transactions and Entries

1. A donation of preferred stocks valued at $20,000 was made by an individual for the purpose of financing additions to the plant.

(1) Investments	20,000	
Fund Balances—Restricted		20,000
To record investments donated for the		
purpose of financing additions to plant.		
(The Fund Balances account controls		
accounts for separate funds in this		
group.)		

2. Cash in the amount of $30,000 was transferred from the Unrestricted Current Fund to this fund for the purpose of financing additions to the plant. (See transaction 11, Unrestricted Current Fund.)

(2) Cash	30,000	
Fund Balances—Unrestricted		30,000
To record receipt of cash from the		
Unrestricted Current Fund for the		
purpose of financing additions to plant.		

3. A small house trailer costing $12,000 was purchased for cash. (See transaction 3, Investment in Plant.)

> (3) Fund Balances—Unrestricted 12,000
>   Cash 12,000
>   To record purchase of a house trailer.

4. A $500,000 loan was secured to finance a building addition.

> (4) Cash 500,000
>   Notes Payable 500,000
>   To record borrowing to finance a
>   building addition.

5. By year end $240,000 of building addition expenditures had been incurred, of which $200,000 had been paid.

> (5) Construction in Progress 240,000
>   Cash 200,000
>   Accounts Payable 40,000
>   To record capitalizable construction
>   expenditures and the related payments
>   and liability.

Funds for Renewals and Replacements

The Funds for Renewals and Replacements are accounted for in much the same way as the Unexpended Plant Funds. The essential difference is that the expenditures of this fund are for renewals and replacements of plant assets, most of which are charged to Fund Balance rather than being capitalized. In practice it is often difficult to distinguish betterments and improvements, which are capitalized, and expenditures for renewals and replacement, which are not capitalized. In any event, some of the expenditures of the Funds for Renewals and Replacements may properly be capitalized in the Investment in Plant accounts.

Since the accounting and reporting for Funds for Renewals and Replacements are identical to that for the Unexpended Plant Funds, we assume that A University does not have such a fund yet and do not illustrate any transactions or entries for the Funds for Renewals and Replacements subgroup.

Funds for Retirement of Indebtedness

The purpose of the Funds for Retirement of Indebtedness subgroup is to account for the accumulation and expenditure of financial resources to service the institution's plant-related indebtedness. Payments of debt principal, interest, and fiscal agent fees are made from this Fund, as well as payments to trustees of externally administered sinking funds. If the debt instruments require the accumulation of university-managed sinking funds, payments made to the sinking fund involve intrafund transfers between assets of the Funds for Retirement of Indebtedness; that is, sinking fund assets remain as assets of the Funds for Retirement of Indebtedness. As principal payments are made from the Funds for Retirement of Indebtedness, the additional net investment of university funds in fixed assets should be recognized in the Net Invested in Plant account in the Investment in Plant subgroup.

The following are some typical transactions of this Fund and the related entries. Transaction 2 affects not only this Fund but also the Investment in Plant accounts.

Transactions and Entries

1. A mandatory transfer of $25,000 was received from the Unrestricted Current Funds. (See entry 10, Unrestricted Current Funds.)

   (1) Cash 25,000
        Fund Balances—Restricted   25,000
       To record receipt of mandatory transfer
       from Unrestricted Current Funds.

2. The $25,000 received from the Unrestricted Current Funds was used to pay an installment of the mortgage note, $5,000 of which represents interest. (See entry 1, Investment in Plant.)

   (2) Fund Balances—Restricted 25,000
        Cash   25,000
       To record payment on mortgage note,
       including $5,000 interest.

3. A donation of $15,000 was made for the purpose of paying a $10,000 mortgage installment falling due during the current year, plus $5,000 interest.

   (3) Cash 15,000
        Fund Balances—Restricted   15,000
       To record receipt of money to pay
       mortgage installment falling due during
       the current year.

4. The money was used for this purpose. (See transaction 4, Investment in Plant.)

   (4) Fund Balances—Restricted 15,000
        Cash   15,000
       To record payment of mortgage
       installment: $5,000 interest and
       $10,000 principal.

5. A donation of $25,000 was made for the purpose of paying a mortgage installment falling due next year.

(5) Cash 25,000
      Fund Balances—Restricted   25,000
      To record receipt of money to pay part
      of mortgage installment falling due
      during the following year.

6. The cash received in transaction 2 was invested.

(6) Investments 25,000
      Cash   25,000
      To record investing the cash received
      from the Unrestricted Current Fund.

7. A $100,000 gift was received with the stipulation that the funds be managed as a debt service sinking fund by the Last National Bank. The donor is attempting to get others to match his gesture so a major building program may be begun.

(7) (a) Cash 200,000
         Fund Balances—Restricted   200,000
         To record gift to be used to set up
         sinking fund at the Last National
         Bank.
  (b) Sinking Fund—Last National Bank . 200,000
         Cash   200,000
         To record payment to the Last
         National Bank to establish a debt
         service sinking fund.

Investment in Plant

The asset accounts in the Investment in Plant subgroup contain the book values of the institutional plant properties except for any that are accounted for in Endowment and Similar Funds. Depreciation on these assets is normally not recorded, but accumulated depreciation may be reported in the Investment in Plant balance sheet and the periodic depreciation provision may be reported in the statement of changes in fund balance. The liabilities incurred in the acquisition or construction of plant, including those arising from capital leases, also are accounted for here—with increments of construction in progress and related liabilities being added each year, or with the total liability and asset cost being added here at the conclusion of the project. The net equity in fixed assets is maintained in the Net Invested in Plant account, which may be kept in such detail as seems necessary. For example, separate categories might be maintained for net investment from gifts; appropriations; Federal, state, and local grants; Current Funds; and other funds.

The balances in the Investment in Plant accounts at the beginning of the period were as follows:

	Debit Balances	Credit Balances
Land	$ 300,000	
Buildings	4,000,000	
Equipment	800,000	
Library Books	200,000	
Mortgage Payable		$ 400,000
Net Invested in Plant		4,900,000
	$5,300,000	$5,300,000

Originating in:

1. FUNDS FOR RETIREMENT OF INDEBTEDNESS (see transaction 2 in that Fund):Mortgage notes carried as a liability of the Investment in Plant Fund, $20,000, were paid from Funds for Retirement of Indebtedness.

   (1) Mortgage Payable 20,000
        Net Invested in Plant   20,000
        To record payment of mortgage
        principal from the Funds for
        Retirement of Indebtedness.

2. UNRESTRICTED CURRENT FUND (See transaction 12 in that Fund): Equipment was purchased for $10,000.

   (2) Equipment 10,000
        Net Invested in Plant   10,000
        To record purchase of equipment out
        of the Unrestricted Current Fund.

3. UNEXPENDED PLANT FUND (See transaction 3 in that fund): A house trailer costing $12,000 was purchased for cash.

   (3) Improvements Other than Buildings ... 12,000
        Net Invested in Plant   12,000
        To record purchase of house trailer out
        of the Unexpended Plant Funds.

4. RETIREMENT OF INDEBTEDNESS FUND (See transaction 4 in that Fund): An installment of the mortgage note in the amount of $10,000 was retired.

   (4) Mortgage Payable 10,000
        Net Invested in Plant   10,000
        To record payment of part of mortgage
        payable from the Retirement of
        Indebtedness Fund.

5. INVESTMENT IN PLANT ACCOUNTS: A piece of uninsured equipment financed from current revenues and costing $1,000 was destroyed by fire.

   (5) Net Invested in Plant 1,000
        Equipment   1,000
        To remove the original cost of
        equipment destroyed.

AGENCY FUNDS

A university usually serves as a depository and fiscal agent for a number of student, faculty, and staff organizations. It holds funds belonging to others in these cases, and only the usual asset and liability accounts of Agency Funds need be maintained, since there is no Agency Fund balance.

FINANCIAL REPORTING

The three basic financial statements recommended in CUBA and in the AICPA audit guide for colleges and universities are:

1. Balance Sheet
2. Statement of Changes in Fund Balances
3. Statement of Current Funds Revenues, Expenditures, and Other Changes

Both a balance sheet (Figure 19-7) and a Statement of Current Funds Revenues, Expenditures, and Other Changes (Figure 19-6) have been presented for the A University example. Further, Figures 19-8 and 19-9 present the "models" of the Statement of Changes in Fund Balance and the Statement of Current Funds Revenues, Expenditures, and Other Changes agreed to by both the AICPA audit guide authors and those who wrote *CUBA*, which relate to a more complex university than illustrated in the chapter. Studying those statements carefully should further enhance one's knowledge of higher education accounting and reporting.

In studying the Statement of Current Funds Revenues, Expenditures, and Other Changes (Figures 19-6 and 19-9) note particularly the additions to Restricted Current Funds balances—such as through gifts and investment earnings—that would be reported as revenue immediately were it not for the convention of recognizing revenue only to the extent the restricted resources are expended. Similarly, in studying the Statement of Changes in Fund Balances (Figure 19-8) note the additions to the Endowment and Similar Funds that will not be recognized as revenue until such time, if ever, that the investment earnings are expended for operating purposes.

The primary statements should be accompanied by detailed supporting schedules and footnotes appropriate to assure full disclosure and fair presentation of the operations and balances of the various fund groups and subgroups. *CUBA* suggests the following types of supplemental schedules for consideration:

1. Schedule of current funds expenditures and mandatory transfers and resources *utilized.* (This schedule would be especially useful to institutions employing the total return concept or managing unrestricted gifts as separate resources.)
2. Schedule of current funds revenues.
3. Schedule of current funds expenditures.
4. Summary of gifts received—by source and purpose.

Figure 19-8

SAMPLE EDUCATIONAL INSTITUTION

Statement of Changes in Fund Balances
For the Year Ended June 30, 19—

Revenues and other additions:	Current Funds		Loan Funds	Endowment and Similar Funds	Annuity and Life Income Funds	Plant Funds			
	Unrestricted	Restricted				Unexpended	Renewal and Replacement	Retirement of Indebtedness	Investment in Plant
Educational and general revenues	$5,300,000								
Auxiliary enterprises revenues	2,200,000								
Expired term endowment revenues	40,000								
Expired term endowment—restricted						50,000			
Gifts and bequests—restricted		370,000	100,000	1,500,000	800,000	115,000		65,000	15,000
Grants and contracts—restricted		500,000							
Governmental appropriations—restricted						50,000			
Investment income—restricted		224,000	12,000	10,000		5,000	5,000	5,000	
Realized gains on investments—unrestricted				109,000					
Realized gains on investments—restricted			4,000	50,000		10,000	5,000	5,000	
Interest on loans receivable			7,000						
U.S. Government advances			18,000						
Expended for plant facilities (including $100,000 charged to current funds expenditures)									1,550,000
Retirement of indebtedness									220,000

Figure 19-8 (continued)

	Unrestricted	Restricted	Loan Funds	Endowment and Similar Funds	Annuity and Life Income Funds	Unexpended	Renewal and Replacement	Retirement of Indebtedness	Investment in Plant
Accrued interest on sale of bonds								3,000	
Matured annuity and life income funds restricted to endowment				10,000					
Total revenues and other additions	7,540,000	1,094,000	141,000	1,679,000	800,000	230,000	10,000	78,000	1,785,000
Expenditures and other deductions:									
Educational and general expenditures	4,400,000	1,014,000							
Auxiliary enterprises expenditures	1,830,000								
Indirect costs recovered		35,000	10,000						
Refunded to grantors		20,000	1,000						
Loan cancellations and write-offs			1,000						
Administrative and collection costs			1,000					1,000	
Adjustment of actuarial liability for annuities payable					75,000				
Expended for plant facilities (including noncapitalized expenditures of $50,000)						1,200,000	300,000		
Retirement of indebtedness								220,000	
Interest on indebtedness								190,000	
Disposal of plant facilities									115,000
Expired term endowments ($40,000 unrestricted, $50,000 restricted to plant)				90,000					

	(1)	(2)	(3)	(4)	(5)	(6)	(7)	(8)	(9)
Matured annuity and life income funds restricted to endowment					10,000				
Total expenditures and other deductions	6,230,000	1,069,000	12,000	90,000	85,000	1,200,000	300,000	411,000	115,000
Transfers among funds—additions/(deductions)									
Mandatory:									
Principal and interest	(340,000)							340,000	
Renewals and replacements	(170,000)						170,000		
Loan fund matching grant	(2,000)		2,000						
Unrestricted gifts allocated	(650,000)		50,000	550,000		50,000			
Portion of unrestricted quasi-endowment funds investment gains appropriated	40,000			(40,000)					
Total transfers	(1,122,000)		52,000	510,000	50,000		170,000	340,000	
Net increase (decrease) for the year	188,000	25,000	181,000	2,099,000	715,000	(920,000)	(120,000)	7,000	1,670,000
Fund balance at beginning of year	455,000	421,000	502,000	11,901,000	2,505,000	2,120,000	380,000	293,000	36,540,000
Fund balance at end of year	$ 643,000	446,000	683,000	14,000,000	3,220,000	1,200,000	260,000	300,000	38,210,000

Source: Committee on College and University Accounting and Auditing, American Institute of Certified Public Accountants, *Audits of Colleges and Universities* (New York: AICPA, 1973), pp. 64–65.

Figure 19-9

SAMPLE EDUCATIONAL INSTITUTION

Statement of Current Funds Revenues, Expenditures, and Other Changes
For the Year Ended June 30, 19—
With Comparative Figures for 19—

	Current Year			Prior Year Total
	Unrestricted	Restricted	Total	
Revenues:				
Educational and general:				
Student tuition and fees	$2,600,000		2,600,000	2,300,000
Governmental appropriations	1,300,000		1,300,000	1,300,000
Governmental grants and contracts	35,000	425,000	460,000	595,000
Gifts and private grants	850,000	380,000	1,230,000	1,190,000
Endowment income	325,000	209,000	534,000	500,000
Sales and services of educational departments	90,000		90,000	95,000
Organized activities related to educational departments	100,000		100,000	100,000
Other sources (if any)				
Total educational and general .	5,300,000	1,014,000	6,314,000	6,080,000
Auxiliary enterprises	2,200,000		2,200,000	2,100,000
Expired term endowment	40,000		40,000	
Total revenues	7,540,000	1,014,000	8,554,000	8,180,000
Expenditures and mandatory transfers:				

Educational and general:				
Instruction and departmental research	2,820,000	300,000	3,120,000	2,950,000
Organized activities related to educational departments	140,000	189,000	329,000	350,000
Sponsored research		400,000	400,000	500,000
Other separately budgeted research	100,000		100,000	150,000
Other sponsored programs		25,000	25,000	50,000
Extension and public service	130,000		130,000	125,000
Libraries	250,000		250,000	225,000
Student services	200,000		200,000	195,000
Operation and maintenance of plant	220,000		220,000	200,000
General administration	200,000		200,000	195,000
General institutional expense	250,000		250,000	250,000
Student aid	90,000	100,000	190,000	180,000
Educational and general expenditures	4,400,000	1,014,000	5,414,000	5,370,000
Mandatory transfers for:				
Principal and interest	90,000		90,000	50,000
Renewals and replacements	100,000		100,000	80,000
Loan fund matching grant	2,000		2,000	
Total educational and general	4,592,000	1,014,000	5,606,000	5,500,000
Auxiliary enterprises:				
Expenditures	1,830,000		1,830,000	1,730,000
Mandatory transfers for:				
Principal and interest	250,000		250,000	250,000
Renewals and replacements	70,000		70,000	70,000
Total auxiliary enterprises	2,150,000		2,150,000	2,050,000
Total expenditures and mandatory transfers	6,742,000	1,014,000	7,756,000	7,550,000

Figure 19-9 (continued)

	Current Year			Prior Year Total
	Unrestricted	Restricted	Total	
Other transfers and additions/(deductions):				
Excess of restricted receipts over transfers to revenues		45,000	45,000	40,000
Refunded to grantors		(20,000)	(20,000)	
Unrestricted gifts allocated to other funds	(650,000)		(650,000)	(510,000)
Portion of quasi-endowment gains appropriated	40,000		40,000	
Net increase (decrease) for the year	$ 188,000	25,000	213,000	160,000

Source: Committee on College and University Accounting and Auditing, American Institute of Certified Public Accountants, *Audits of Colleges and Universities* (New York: AICPA, 1973), pp. 66–67.

5. Summary of investments.
6. Summary of property, plant, and equipment.
7. Schedule of long-term debt.
8. Details of balances of each fund and changes therein during the period.
9. Schedule of operations of auxiliary enterprises.
10. Schedule of operations of hospitals.
11. Schedule of operations of independent operations.[19]

CONCLUDING COMMENTS

Accounting and reporting for colleges and universities has evolved rapidly in recent years, and may be expected to evolve still further in the future. The efforts of the AICPA, NACUBO, and NCHEMS committees, which ultimately led to the Joint Accounting Group (JAG) Report, were extensive and impressive. The results of their labors were equally impressive, as numerous major improvements in college and university accounting and reporting resulted from the joint, arduous efforts by preparers, auditors, and users of higher education financial reports.

Some contend that further changes are needed in college and university accounting and reporting. For example, some believe that the Current Funds should be combined, with the restricted fund balances reported as deferred revenues in the one Current Fund; others question the propriety of deferring revenue recognition in Restricted Current Funds until resources are expended; and some contend that all unrestricted funds, including those in Quasi-Endowment and Plant Funds, should be reported as part of the Current Funds.

The future of college and university accounting standards now rests with the FASB. It will be interesting to see what conceptual and procedural changes in college and university accounting and reporting are prescribed by that Board, and at what pace it moves.

▶ **Question 19-1.** Prepare a list of the funds recommended for use by a college or university. Opposite the funds indicate the funds or account groups recommended for municipalities by the National Council on Governmental Accounting which are most nearly comparable in nature.

Question 19-2. The Main City College is financed solely from a special tax levy. The construction of the building was financed from the sale of bonds. These bonds, as well as the interest thereon, are also being paid from the special tax levy. Would the accounting procedure outlined in the chapter also apply to this college? Indicate the fund or funds in which these financial transactions of the college should be recorded.

Question 19-3. The American Hospital Association recommends that depreciation be recorded on all fixed assets of hospitals, whereas NACUBO recommends that, with certain exceptions, no depreciation be recorded on the fixed assets of colleges. Do you think there is a better reason for charging depreciation on the fixed assets of hospitals than on the fixed assets of colleges?

Question 19-4. What is the purpose of charging depreciation on the fixed assets of an Endowment Fund? Explain.

[19] Ibid., p. 202.

Question 19-5. Under what circumstances are resources expendable for operating purposes accounted for in Restricted Current Funds? At what point should contributions to Restricted Current Funds be recognized as revenue? Justify your response.

Question 19-6. List the funds recommended for use by a hospital down the center of a sheet of paper. To the left of the hospital funds indicate the funds or account groups recommended for municipalities by the National Council on Governmental Accounting which are most nearly comparable in nature; to the right, do a similar comparison between hospital funds and those employed by colleges and universities. At the bottom of the page list those municipal and college and university funds and account groups for which there is no reasonably close parallel in hospital accounting.

Question 19-7. Name three differences between the accounting procedures of colleges and those of hospitals.

Question 19-8. Why is it necessary to distinguish "restricted" and "unrestricted" balances in the Endowment and Similar Funds and in the Plant Funds.

Question 19-9. Student tuition, fees, and other assessments may be restricted, in whole or in part, to debt service or plant acquisition, renewal, or replacement. How should these amounts be accounted for by a college or university?

Question 19-10. Distinguish between mandatory and nonmandatory transfers and how they are reported in higher education financial statements.

Question 19-11. What is an auxiliary enterprise? How are they accounted for and reported on by colleges and universities?

Question 19-12. When are earnings of Endowment and Similar Funds reported as revenue? Might the principal of such funds also be reported as revenue? Explain.

Question 19-13. Summarize the key issues regarding the determination of Endowment Fund distributable income, e.g., the classical trust "yield" principle, the corporate law view, the Uniform Management of Institutional Funds Act, and the "total return" approaches.

Question 19-14. Distinguish between the key accounting aspects of Annuity Funds and of Life Income Funds.

Question 19-15. Should plant-related long-term debt and construction in progress be accounted for in the Unexpended Plant Funds or the Plant Funds for Renewal and Replacement until completion of the project, or should appropriate amounts be reclassified to the Investment in Plant Accounts at the end of each year?

Instructor's Note: Problems 19-1 to 19-4 relate to X University. These problems may be assigned separately, while together they comprise a comprehensive review problem.

▶ **Problem 19-1, Part I.** The trial balance of the Unrestricted Current Funds of X University on September 1, 19X0, was as follows:

Cash	$155,000	
Accounts Receivable	30,000	
Allowance for Uncollectible Accounts		$ 2,000
Inventory of Materials and Supplies	25,000	
Vouchers Payable		23,000
Fund Balance		185,000
	$210,000	$210,000

X University's dormitory and food service facilities are operated as auxiliary enterprises.

The following transactions took place during the current fiscal year:

1. Collections amounted to $2,270,000, distributed as follows: tuition and fees, $1,930,000; Federal grants, $170,000; sales and services of educational activities, $115,000; other sources, $25,000; accounts receivable, $30,000.

2. Receivables at end of the year were $29,000, consisting entirely of tuition and fees revenues.

3. It is estimated that tuition receivable of $3,000 will never be collected.

4. Revenues from auxiliary enterprises were $300,000, all collected in cash.

5. Materials purchased during the year for cash, $500,000; on account, $50,000.

6. Materials used amounted to $510,000, distributed as follows:

Educational and general:		
Institutional support	$ 30,000	
Research	5,000	
Instruction	305,000	
Academic support	7,000	
Other	53,000	$400,000
Auxiliary enterprises		110,000
		$510,000

7. Salaries and wages paid:

Educational and general:		
Institutional support	$ 170,000	
Research	63,000	
Instruction	1,212,000	
Academic support	80,000	
Other	85,000	$1,610,000
Auxiliary enterprises		90,000
		$1,700,000

8. Other expenditures paid:

Educational and general:		
Institutional support	$10,000	
Research	2,000	
Instruction	53,000	
Academic support	3,000	
Other	7,000	$75,000
Auxiliary enterprises		20,000
		$95,000

9. Interest expenditures chargeable to Institutional Support, $3,000, were paid.

10. Vouchers payable paid, $40,000.

11. A transfer of $20,000 was made to the Fund for Retirement of Indebtedness, as required by the bond indenture.

12. The board of trustees of the university passed a resolution authorizing the transfer of $150,000 to a fund which is to function as an endowment, and the transfer was made.

13. Some $30,000 was transferred from the Unrestricted Current Fund, one-half for additions to the plant and one-half for plant renewals and replacements.

Required:

Prepare and complete an eight-column Unrestricted Current Funds work-sheet with headings as follows:

Columns	Heading
1–2	Balances, September 1, 19X0
3–4	19X0–19X1 Transactions
5–6	19X0–19X1 Operating Results
7–8	Postclosing Trial Balance, August 31, 19X1

Alternatively, with your instructor's permission:

(a) Prepare journal entries for the Unrestricted Current Funds for the 19X0–19X1 fiscal year.

(b) Post the opening trial balance and journal entries to T-accounts.

Problem 19-1, Part II. The trial balance of the Restricted Current Funds of X University on September 1, 19X0, was as follows:

Cash	$32,000	
Vouchers Payable		$ 2,000
Fund Balance*		30,000
	$32,000	$32,000

The Fund Balance was from private gifts to be used only for academic support.

The following transactions took place during the current fiscal year:

1. Cash was received as follows for the purposes noted:

Educational and general:	
Endowments—Institutional service and research .	$ 75,000
Private gifts—Research	40,000
Federal grants—Instruction	150,000
State grant—Student services	20,000
	$285,000
Auxiliary enterprises	130,000
	$415,000

2. Expenditures paid in cash:

<table>
<tr><td>Educational and general:</td><td></td><td></td></tr>
<tr><td>   Institutional support ....</td><td>$ 40,000</td><td></td></tr>
<tr><td>   Research ....</td><td>30,000</td><td></td></tr>
<tr><td>   Instruction ....</td><td>125,000</td><td></td></tr>
<tr><td>   Student services ....</td><td>20,000</td><td>$215,000</td></tr>
<tr><td> Auxiliary enterprises ....</td><td></td><td>90,000</td></tr>
<tr><td></td><td></td><td>$305,000</td></tr>
</table>

3. Investments of $100,000 were made.

Required:

(a) Prepare and complete an eight-column Restricted Current Funds worksheet with the headings set forth in the requirements to Problem 19-1, Part I. Alternatively, with your instructor's permission, you may:

1. Prepare journal entries.
2. Post the opening trial balance and journal entries to T-accounts.

(b) Prepare a combined balance sheet of the Unrestricted Current Funds and Restricted Current Funds as of August 31, 19X1.

(c) Prepare a statement of current funds revenues, expenditures, and other changes for the two funds for the fiscal year ended August 31, 19X1.

Problem 19-2. X University had no Endowment Funds prior to September 1, 19X0. The following transactions took place in the Endowment Funds of X University during the fiscal year ended August 31, 19X1:

1. At the beginning of the year, a cash donation of $900,000 was received to establish Endowment Fund X, and another donation of $600,000, also in cash, was received for the purpose of establishing Endowment Fund Y. The income from these funds is restricted for specific purposes. It was decided to invest this money immediately; to pool the investments of both funds; and to share earnings, including any gains or losses on sales of investments, at the end of the year based on the ratio of the original contributions of each fund.

2. Securities with a par value of $1,000,000 were purchased at a premium of $10,000.

3. Securities with a par value of $191,500 were acquired at a discount of $2,000; accrued interest at date of purchase amounted to $500.

4. The university trustees voted to pool the investments of a new endowment, Endowment Fund Z, with the investments of Endowment Funds X and Y under the same conditions as applied to the latter two Funds. The investments of Endowment Fund Z at the date it joined the pool at midyear amounted to $290,000 at book value and $300,000 at market value. (Hereafter, the investment pool earnings are to be shared 9:6:3.)

5. Cash dividends received from the pooled investments during the year amounted to $70,000, and interest receipts amounted to $5,500.

6. Premiums of $500 and discounts of $100 were amortized.

7. Securities carried at $30,000 were sold at a gain of $2,400.

8. Each fund was credited with its share of the investment earnings for the year (see transactions 1 and 4).

9. A provision of Endowment Fund Y is that a minimum of $75,000 each year, whether from earnings or principal or both, is to be paid to the Restricted Current Funds to support specified institutional services and research projects. The payment was made.

10. An apartment complex comprised of land, buildings, and equipment valued at $800,000 was donated to the university, distributed as follows: land, $80,000; buildings, $500,000; equipment, $220,000. The donor stipulated that an endowment fund (designated as Endowment Fund N) should be established and that the income therefrom should be used for a restricted operating purpose.

11. $150,000 was received from Unrestricted Current Funds as a quasi-endowment (or fund functioning as an endowment) and was designated Fund O.

12. A trust fund in the amount of $350,000 (cash) was set up by a donor with the stipulation that the income was to go to the university to be used for general purposes. This fund was designated Endowment Fund P.

Required:

Prepare and complete a four-column worksheet with these column headings:

Columns	Heading
1–2	19X0–19X1 Transactions
3–4	Postclosing Trial Balance, August 31, 19X1

Alternatively, with your instructor's approval:

(a) Prepare journal entries.

(b) Post to T-accounts.

(c) Prepare a balance sheet of the Endowment Funds as of August 31, 19X1.

Problem 19-3. The following transactions affected the Annuity and Life Income Funds and the Loan Funds of X University during the fiscal year ended August 31, 19X1:

Annuity and Life Income Funds

1. A gift of $500,000 cash, from the Lobo family, was received by X University on September 3, 19X0. According to the terms of the bequest, the University must pay the donor, or her estate should she die, $50,000 on each August 31 for twenty years, beginning in 19X1. The balance remaining at the end of the twenty-year period is to be used to supplement the income of outstanding professors at X University. The chief finance officer expects to earn an average of at least 9 percent on investments over the next twenty years.

2. Another gift, from the Mann family, was received, comprised of:

Office Building	Donor's Cost	Fair Market Value
Land	$ 50,000	$ 70,000
Building	300,000	400,000
Equipment	80,000	40,000
Common Stock	100,000	90,000
	$530,000	$600,000

The University is to pay the income (as conventionally determined) from these assets to the donor or his spouse as long as either lives. Their combined life expectancy is fifteen years according to recognized life expectancy tables.

3. The $500,000 cash received from the Lobo family was invested.

4. The Lobo investments earned $55,000 during the year, all received in cash.

5. The Mann investment earnings were (a) office complex: revenues, $900,000; expenses of $700,000, including $30,000 depreciation on the building and $4,000 depreciation on the equipment; an amount equal to net income before depreciation was received by X University; (b) common stock: dividends of $75,000, all received in cash.

6. The appropriate payments were made to the Lobo and Mann families and appropriate closing entries, if any, were made.

Loan Funds:

1. A donation of $150,000 was received in cash for the purpose of making loans to students.

2. Cash in the amount of $50,000 was invested in bonds acquired at par.

3. Loans of $60,000 were made to students.

4. Interest on investments, $300, was received in cash.

5. Student loans of $1,000 were written off as uncollectible.

Required:

Prepare and complete a four-column worksheet for each fund or fund group with these column headings:

Columns	Heading
1–2	19X0–19X1 Transactions
3–4	Postclosing Trial Balance, August 31, 19X1

Alternatively, with your instructor's approval:

(a) Prepare journal entries.

(b) Post to T-accounts.

(c) Prepare a balance sheet for each fund as of August 31, 19X1.

Problem 19-4. The trial balance of the Investment in Plant Fund of X University as of September 1, 19X0, was as follows:

Land	$ 200,000	
Buildings	3,300,000	
Equipment	1,200,000	
Mortgage Payable		$ 250,000
Investment in Plant from Federal Grants		800,000
Investment in Plant from Unrestricted Funds		650,000
Investment in Plant from Gifts		3,000,000
	$4,700,000	$4,700,000

The following transactions took place during the year:

1. A cash donation of $40,000 was received from an individual for the purpose of financing new additions to the business and public administration building.
2. The money was invested in securities acquired at par.
3. Cash was received from the Unrestricted Current Funds as follows:

For retiring indebtedness	$20,000
For plant improvements and renovations	15,000
For plant additions	15,000
	$50,000

4. Of the money received from the Unrestricted Current Fund, $10,000 was used to finance the acquisition of additional equipment.
5. A $1,000,000 addition to the business and public administration building was begun. Expenditures of $600,000 were incurred (and paid) by August 31, 19X1, financed by a loan (note) in that amount from the Last National Bank pending the receipt of more donations. X University's accounting policy is to account for construction in progress and related debt in the Investment in Plant Fund.
6. Some $13,000 was spent in remodeling an art building classroom.
7. A cash donation of $75,000 was received for the purpose of paying part of the mortgage.
8. A mortgage installment of $35,000 ($10,000 principal and $25,000 interest) which became due during the year was paid from the above donation.
9. An uninsured piece of equipment costing $5,000 and financed from the Unrestricted Current Fund was destroyed.

Required:

(a) Prepare and complete appropriate worksheets for the several types of Plant Funds, *or*

    1. Prepare journal entries for the several types of Plant Funds, as needed.
    2. Post the opening trial balance and entries to T-accounts.

(b) Prepare a combined balance sheet for the Plant Funds as of August 31, 19X1.

Problem 19-5. From the following information relating to Prep School, prepare a worksheet showing opening balances, transactions, and adjustments for the year ended June 30, 19X5, and trial balances as of June 30, 19X5, for each of the appropriate funds and fund subgroups. The balances of the general ledger accounts as at July 1, 19X4, are as follows:

Cash—for general use	$ 1,000	
Cash—from alumni subscriptions for new dormitory	2,000	
Cash—endowment	45,000	
Cash—for student loans	1,000	
Tuition receivable	12,500	
Investments—temporary investments of general cash	4,000	
Investments—endowment	250,000	
Inventory of supplies	15,000	
Alumni pledges for new dormitory (due September 30, 19X6)	8,000	
Student loans receivable	3,500	
Education plant:		
Financed from original and subsequent endowments	600,000	
Financed from tuition	50,000	
Financed from alumni pledges	200,000	
Financed by Federal government grants ...	50,000	
Accounts payable (for supplies)		$ 3,500
Unpaid costs of alumni pledge campaign. ..		1,000
Balance		1,237,500
	$1,242,000	$1,242,000

1. Endowment investments and $40,000 of the endowment cash represent principal of Endowment Funds held under terms providing that the income therefrom shall be used only for operating expenditures of the school. The balance of Endowment Fund cash represents accumulated income not transferred from the endowment to the Unrestricted Current Fund.

2. Student population was 150 students. The tuition rate was $1,000 per school year per student except for six full scholarships and three partial (one-half) scholarships.

3. Ninety percent of current tuition was collected and $100 of the balance is considered uncollectible.

4. Tuition receivable of prior years was collected, $12,000, and the balance is considered uncollectible.

5. Charges for operating expenditures incurred and supplies purchased during the year totaled $135,000.

6. Inventory of operating supplies at June 30, 19X5, amounted to $13,500.

7. Accounts payable for operating supplies and other expenditures amounted to $2,000 at June 30, 19X5.

8. All temporary investments of general cash were sold on July 1, 19X4, for $4,300 and accrued interest of $100.

9. Endowment investments having a book value of $25,000 were sold for $27,500, including accrued interest of $500.

10. Investments were purchased by the Endowment Fund trustees at a cost of $50,000.

11. Interest on Endowment Fund investments not sold during the year amounted to $20,500 for the year, all collected in cash.

12. The Endowment Fund trustees transferred $22,500 to the Unrestricted Current Funds bank account.

13. As a result of the continued alumni subscription campaign, additional pledges of $65,000 were received for the purpose of providing a new dormitory. These subscriptions were payable one-fifth at the date of the pledge and one-fifth quarterly beginning January 15, 19X5.

14. Ten percent bonds in the amount of $50,000 were issued for cash on January 1, 19X5, to provide funds for immediate construction of the new dormitory. Interest is payable annually.

15. Contracts in the amount of $70,000 were let for construction of the new dormitory, to be paid from pledges.

16. The contract for construction of the new dormitory was 50 percent completed on June 1, 19X5, and payment for one-half of the total amount, less a retained percentage of 10 percent, was made on that date.

17. All alumni pledges of the current year were paid on the due dates; those due previously were also paid in full.

18. Tuition revenues amounting to $5,000 were used to build additional bleachers at the athletic stadium.

19. A riding stable costing $4,000 and financed during a previous year from tuition revenues was destroyed by fire. Insurance recovery was $4,500; the building will not be replaced.

20. Student loans amounting to $3,500 were made.

21. Student loan collections amounted to $4,000, including $200 interest.

Problem 19-6. Presented on page 821 is the Current Funds balance sheet of Burnsville University as of the end of its fiscal year ended June 30, 19X7.

The following transactions occurred during the fiscal year ended June 30, 19X8:

1. On July 7, 19X7 a gift of $100,000 was received from an alumnus. The alumnus requested that one-half of the gift be used for the purchase of books for the university library and the remainder be used for the establishment of a scholarship fund. The alumnus further requested that the income generated by the scholarship fund be used annually to award a scholarship to a qualified disadvantaged student. On July 20, 19X7, the board of trustees resolved that the funds of the newly established scholarship fund would be invested in savings certificates. On July 21, 19X7, the savings certificates were purchased.

2. Revenue from student tuition and fees applicable to the year ended June 30, 19X8, amounted to $1,900,000. Of this amount, $66,000 was collected in the prior year and $1,686,000 was collected during the year ended June 30, 19X8. In addition, at June 30, 19X8, the university had received cash of $158,000 representing fees for the session beginning July 1, 19X8.

3. During the year ended June 30, 19X8, the university had collected $349,000 of the outstanding accounts receivable at the beginning of the year. The balance

BURNSVILLE UNIVERSITY

Current Funds Balance Sheet

June 30, 19X7

Assets

Current Funds:

Unrestricted:

Cash	$210,000	
Accounts receivable-student tuition and fees, less allowance for doubtful accounts of $9,000	341,000	
State appropriations receivable	75,000	$626,000

Restricted:

Cash	7,000	
Investments	60,000	67,000
Total current funds		$693,000

Liabilities and Fund Balances

Current Funds:

Unrestricted:

Accounts payable	$ 45,000	
Deferred revenues	66,000	
Fund balances	515,000	$626,000

Restricted:

Fund Balances		67,000
Total current funds		$693,000

was determined to be uncollectible and was written off against the allowance account. At June 30, 19X8, the allowance account was increased by $3,000.

4. During the year interest charges of $6,000 were earned and collected on late student fee payments.

5. During the year the state appropriation was received. An additional unrestricted appropriation of $50,000 was made by the state, but had not been paid to the university as of June 30, 19X8.

6. An unrestricted gift of $25,000 cash was received from alumni of the university.

7. During the year investments of $21,000 were sold for $26,000. Investment income amounting to $1,900 was received.

8. During the year unrestricted operating expenditures of $1,777,000 were recorded. At June 30, 19X8, $59,000 of these remained unpaid.

9. Restricted current funds of $13,000 were spent for authorized purposes during the year.

10. The accounts payable at June 30, 19X7, were paid during the year.

11. During the year, $7,000 interest was earned and received on the savings certificates purchased in accordance with the board of trustees resolution, as discussed in item 1.

Required:

(a) Prepare journal entries to record in summary the above transactions for the year ended June 30, 19X8. Each journal entry should be numbered to correspond with the transaction described above.

Your answer sheet should be organized as follows:

| | Current Funds | | | | | |
| | Unrestricted | | Restricted | | Endowment Fund | |
Accounts	Dr.	Cr.	Dr.	Cr.	Dr.	Cr.

(b) Prepare a statement of changes in fund balances for the year ended June 30, 19X8.

(AICPA, adapted)

Problem 19-7. You are to (a) prepare a four-column worksheet, with separate sections for each fund type, and record the following transactions of the County College for 19X0, and (b) prepare a trial balance, *including all accounts used even though they do not have a balance*. In entering the transactions, key them to the transaction numbers given; enter the journal entries required in the first two columns and the trial balance in the last two columns. Allow two or three lines for each account heading, except that one cash account (Endowment Funds) requires seven lines.

January 1:

County College, which previously held no endowment funds, received five gifts as a result of an appeal for funds. The campaign closed December 31 and all gifts received are to be recorded as of January 1. Gifts were as follows:

1. From A. B. Smith, $10,000, the principal to be held intact and the income to be used for any purpose that the Board of Control of County College should indicate.
2. From C. D. Jones, $20,000, the principal to be held intact and the income to be used to endow scholarships for worthy students.
3. From E. F. Green, $30,000, the principal to be held intact and the interest to be loaned to students. All income is to be again loaned, and all losses from student loans are to be charged against income.
4. From G. H. White, $200,000. During the lifetime of the donor, semiannual payments of $9,000 are to be made to him. Upon his death, the fund is to be used to construct or purchase a residence hall for housing men students. Mr. White's life expectancy is twenty years and investments are expected to earn 10 percent annually.
5. From I. J. Brown, 1,000 shares of XYZ stock, which had a market value on this date of $150 per share. Such shares are to be held for not more than five years and all income received thereon held intact. At any date during this period, designated by the Board of Control, all assets are to be liquidated and the proceeds used to build a student infirmary.
6. The Board of Control consolidated the Smith and Jones funds as to assets into a Merged Investments account (in the proportion of their principal accounts) and purchased $25,000 of 10 percent Electric Power Company bonds at par. Interest dates, January 1 and July 1.
7. The cash of the Green fund was used to purchase $30,000 of 12 percent bonds of the Steam Power Company at par and accrued interest. Interest dates, April 1 and October 1.
8. The $200,000 cash of the White fund was used to purchase $200,000 of 11 percent U.S. Treasury notes at par. Interest dates, January 1 and July 1.

July 1

9. All interest has been received as stipulated on bonds owned and $4,000 of dividends were received on XYZ stock.
10. Payment was made to G. H. White in accordance with the terms of the gift.
11. $20,000 par of Electric Power Company bonds were sold at 102. No commission was involved.
12. Loan made to M. N. Black, $300, from the Green student loan fund.

October 1

13. Notice was received of the death of G. H. White. There is no liability to his estate.
14. A scholarship award of $200 was made to G. P. Gray from the Jones scholarship fund.
15. $200,000 par of U.S. Treasury notes held by the White fund were sold at 101 and accrued interest.
16. Interest due on bonds was received.

December 31

17. M. N. Black paid $100 principal and $5 interest on his student loan.
18. The Board of Control purchased a building suitable for a residence hall for $250,000, using the available funds from the G. H. White gift as part payment therefor and giving a twenty-year mortgage note payable for the balance.

   (AICPA, adapted)

20

ACCOUNTING
FOR OTHER
NOT-FOR-PROFIT
ORGANIZATIONS

As recognized in preceding chapters, authoritative pronouncements of accounting principles and reporting requirements have been issued by appropriate standards-setting bodies for state and local governments, hospitals, and colleges and universities. Other not-for-profit organizations—including voluntary health and welfare organizations and a myriad of other nonprofit organizations—were not covered by universally recognized accounting and reporting standards until late 1979.

An American Institute of Certified Public Accountants (AICPA) committee issued an audit guide, *Audits of Voluntary Health and Welfare Organizations*, in 1966 and issued a revised audit guide in 1974.[1] Audit guides are not binding on the profession under the Institute's Rules of Conduct, however, but are published "for the guidance" of members of the Institute. Similarly, the Accounting Standards Division of the AICPA issued *Statement of Position (SOP) 78-10*, "Accounting Principles and Reporting Practices for Certain Nonprofit Organizations,"[2] at the end of 1978. SOPs, like audit guides, do not establish standards enforceable under the AICPA Rules of Conduct but are issued "for the general information of those interested in the subject." Further, SOP 78-10 was issued without an effective date since the Financial Accounting Standards Board (FASB) had a project on "nonbusiness" accounting and reporting on its agenda.

In 1979 the FASB assumed responsibility for setting accounting and reporting standards for all nonbusiness organizations except governments. The Board agreed to accept responsibility for the specialized accounting and reporting

[1] Committee on Voluntary Health and Welfare Organizations, American Institute of Certified Public Accountants, *Audits of Voluntary Health and Welfare Organizations* (New York: AICPA, 1974). Hereafter cited as VHWO audit guide.

[2] Accounting Standards Division, American Institute of Certified Public Accountants, *Statement of Position 78-10*, "Accounting Principles and Reporting Practices for Certain Nonprofit Organizations" (New York: AICPA, December 31, 1978). Hereafter cited as SOP 78-10.

principles and practices in the AICPA SOPs, audit guides, and accounting guides in *Statement of Financial Accounting Standards No. 32.*[3] While the Board stopped short of fully endorsing all such AICPA publications as constituting generally accepted accounting principles, and thus making them enforceable under the AICPA Rules of Conduct, it (1) announced its intention to study these publications and, after due process, release them (or modifications of them) as FASB standards covered by Rule 203 of the AICPA Rules of Conduct; and (2) in the interim, stated that the principles and practices in the audit guides, accounting guides, and SOPs listed in FASB *Statement 32* are "preferable" accounting principles for purposes of justifying a change in accounting principles under *Accounting Principles Board Opinion 20*, "Accounting Changes," and revised *Opinion 20* accordingly.

Both *Audits of Health and Welfare Organizations* and AICPA SOP 78-10, "Accounting Principles and Reporting Practices for Certain Nonprofit Organizations," are covered by FASB Statement 32. Thus, these are the most authoritative pronouncements on accounting and reporting for these types of organizations. Both were widely accepted in practice prior to FASB *Statement 32* and have become even more accepted since its issuance. Accordingly, this chapter is based on the guidance and illustrations in the VHWO audit guide and in SOP 78-10.

This chapter is organized in three sections: (1) Voluntary Health and Welfare Organizations, (2) Other Nonprofit Organizations, and (3) Summary Comparisons and Illustrative Entries. The similarities of the accounting and reporting for these organizations to each other and to other types of nonbusiness organizations are emphasized, as are their distinctive features.

VOLUNTARY HEALTH AND WELFARE ORGANIZATIONS

Voluntary health and welfare organizations (VHWOs) are formed to provide various kinds of health, welfare, and community services voluntarily (for no fee or a low fee) to various segments of society. They are tax exempt, organized for the public benefit, supported largely by public contributions, and operated on a not-for-profit basis. The United Way—or another federated community contribution solicitation and allocation organization—is active in most cities and is perhaps the most widely recognized type of VHWO in the United States. Numerous other VHWOs exist in most cities, however, many of which are financed wholly or partially by allocations from the United Way or equivalent organizations. Among the many types of services provided through VHWOs are child care for working mothers, family counseling, nutritious meals and recreation for the elderly, family planning assistance, care and treatment of mentally and/or physically handicapped persons, protection of children from parental or other abuse, halfway houses for criminal or drug offenders, and sheltered workshops for physically and/or mentally

---

[3] Financial Accounting Standards Board, *Statement of Financial Accounting Standards No. 32*, "Specialized Accounting and Reporting Principles and Practices in AICPA Statements of Position and Guides on Accounting and Auditing Matters" (Stamford, Conn.: FASB, September 1979).

handicapped citizens. Most VHWOs charge modest fees to those who can afford to pay them, using a sliding fee schedule based on family size and income.

Purpose of Accounting and Reporting

The VHWO audit guide states that:

> A fundamental purpose of the financial statements . . . should be to disclose how the entity's resources have been acquired and used to accomplish the objectives of the organization. Thus, the organization's financial statements should, to the extent possible, reflect the total resources available to carry out the various program services to which it is committed and the use made of those resources.[4]

The guide notes that a wide variety of persons and groups are interested in the reports of VHWOs:

- Contributors to the organization
- The organization's trustees or directors
- Executives of the VHWO
- Governments that have authority to control (or regulate) charitable solicitation through legislation and the local, state, and Federal governments which grant tax exemptions to charitable organizations.[5]

The *accrual* (not the modified accrual) basis of accounting is deemed essential to develop and report cost of services data, and is required for VHWO financial statements to be prepared in conformity with generally accepted accounting principles (GAAP).

The accounting principles and reporting procedures specified in the VHWO audit guide are something of a blend of college or university accounting and reporting with that for hospitals. Yet they constitute a distinctive approach unique to VHWOs.

Fund Structure

The audit guide does not require VHWOs to use fund accounting, but notes that most have restrictions placed on some of their resources and use fund accounting. The guide does not set forth a specific fund structure that must be used, but notes that the most commonly used funds are:

1. *Current Unrestricted Fund:* to account for all unrestricted resources which the governing body may use as it sees fit, consistent with the organization's charter and bylaws, except for unrestricted amounts invested in land, buildings, and equipment that are accounted for in the Land, Buildings, and Equipment (or Plant) Fund.

2. *Current Restricted Fund(s):* to account for restricted resources that are expendable, and are available for use, but may be expended only for operating purposes specified by the donor or grantor.

[4] VHWO audit guide, p. 1.
[5] Ibid., p. 24.

3. *Endowment Fund(s):* to account for the principal of gifts and bequests accepted with donor stipulations that (a) the principal is to be maintained intact in perpetuity, for a specified period, or until a specified event occurs, and (b) only the income on the fund's investments may be expended for general purposes or for purposes specified by the donor.

4. *Custodian Fund(s):* to account for assets received that are to be held for, or disbursed only on instructions from, the person or organization from whom they were received.

5. *Loan and Annuity Fund(s):* to account for assets held for purposes of making loans or paying annuities to recipients, typically with the provision that the VHWO is the "remainderman" of the annuity trust.

6. *Land, Buildings, and Equipment (or Plant) Fund:* to account for (a) unexpended restricted resources to be used to acquire or replace land, buildings, or equipment for use in operating the organization; (b) land, buildings, and equipment used in operating the organization; (c) mortgages or other liabilities relating to the land, buildings, and equipment used in operations; and (d) the net investment in land, buildings, and equipment (or plant).

In studying this fund structure, note that:

- The *Current Unrestricted Fund* is comparable to the Unrestricted Current Funds of colleges and universities and to the General Fund of state and local governments.

- The *Current Restricted Fund(s)* is comparable to the Restricted Current Funds of a college or university.

- *Endowment Fund(s)* parallel those found in colleges and universities and, on occasion, in hospitals; they also are like Nonexpendable Trust Funds of state and local governments.

- *Custodian Fund(s)* are equivalent to Agency Funds of state and local governments, hospitals, and colleges and universities.

- *Loan and Annuity Fund(s)* are comparable to those in colleges and universities and occasionally found in state and local governments and in hospitals.

While each of the usual VHWO funds has one or more parallels in state and local government, hospital, and college and university accounting, there also are several distinctive features of VHWO fund accounting. These are noted as we discuss the basic financial statements prepared for VHWOs.

Financial Statements

The financial statements required for VHWOs are the (1) Balance Sheet(s); (2) Statement of Support, Revenue, and Expenses and Changes in Fund Balances; and (3) Statement of Functional Expenses. A statement of changes in financial position is *not* required by the VHWO audit guide since the information normally presented in a statement of changes in financial position "will, in most cases, be readily apparent from [the] other financial statements."[6] Further, the statements illustrated are viewed as guidelines rather than mandates, and the VHWO audit guide states that: "Modifications to the financial statements illustrated should be made to fit the facts and circumstances of each specific organization."[7]

Balance Sheet(s). A balance sheet(s) for Voluntary Health and Welfare Service appears in Figure 20-1. This balance sheet may be viewed as one combined balance sheet or as a series of separate fund balance sheets. If there are more than one fund of a type, a combining statement(s) by fund type should be presented. Also, the balance sheet could be presented in columnar form, rather than layered, and "memorandum only" totals could be presented in either format. The notes to the financial statements appear in Figure 20-4.

Investments. Investments of VHWOs are recorded initially at cost, except that donated securities are recorded at their fair market value at the date of the gift. Thereafter they may be accounted for at cost (or lower of cost or market) or at market value. All investments of the VHWO should be accounted for on the same basis; but transfers of investments between funds should be recorded at fair market value, with gain or loss reported in the transferor fund (see note 2, Figure 20-4).

If investments are carried at cost, it may be appropriate to recognize declines in their fair market value below cost by establishing an account such as "Allowance for Decline in Market Value" and charging an appropriate loss account. If investments are carried at market value, the unrealized appreciation or depreciation of investment values should be separately identified (as *unrealized* gain or loss) and included in the fund's revenues or expenses as appropriate, in the statement of support, revenues, expenses and changes in fund balances.

Where investments are carried at cost, their market value should be reported parenthetically or by footnote. Similarly, where investments are carried at market, their cost should be disclosed parenthetically or by footnote. In either case, the unrealized appreciation (or depreciation) of investments at the beginning and end of the year should be disclosed in the footnotes (see note 2, Figure 20-4).

Finally, VHWOs may establish investment pools. Such pools should be accounted for on a fair market basis—to assure equitable allocations of pooled investment income or loss—though the investments, including the investment in the pools, may be accounted for on a cost or market basis in the several funds. Recall, however, that the investments of all funds (excluding the investment pool) of the VHWO must be accounted for on the same basis, either cost or market.

Pledges. Pledges receivable should be recognized in the accounts and an appropriate allowance for uncollectible pledges should be established. If the charge for uncollectible pledges is made to an expense account, the gross amount pledged is reported as revenue. Alternatively, only the net expected pledge collections may be recognized as revenue. Pledges for contributions for future periods should be recorded as deferred support.

[6] Ibid., p. 33.
[7] Ibid.

Figure 20-1

VOLUNTARY HEALTH AND WELFARE SERVICE

Balance Sheets
December 31, 19X2 and 19X1

Current Funds
Unrestricted

Assets	19X2	19X1
Cash	$2,207,000	$2,530,000
Investments (Note 2):		
For long-term purposes	2,727,000	2,245,000
Other	1,075,000	950,000
Pledges receivable less allowance for uncollectibles of $105,000 and $92,000	475,000	363,000
Inventories of educational materials, at cost	70,000	61,000
Accrued interest, other receivables and prepaid expenses	286,000	186,000
Total	$6,840,000	$6,335,000

Liabilities and Fund Balances	19X2	19X1
Accounts payable	$ 148,000	$ 139,000
Research grants payable	596,000	616,000
Contributions designated for future periods	245,000	219,000
Total liabilities and deferred revenues	989,000	974,000
Fund balances:		
Designated by the governing board for:		
Long-term investments	2,800,000	2,300,000
Purchases of new equipment	100,000	—
Research purposes (Note 3)	1,152,000	1,748,000
Undesignated, available for general activities (Note 4)	1,799,000	1,313,000
Total fund balance	5,851,000	5,361,000
Total	$6,840,000	$6,335,000

Cash	$ 3,000	$ 5,000
Investments (Note 2)	71,000	72,000
Grants receivable	58,000	46,000
Total	$ 132,000	$ 123,000
Fund balances:		
Professional education	$ 84,000	$ —
Research grants	48,000	123,000
Total	$ 132,000	$ 123,000

Land, Building, and Equipment Fund

Cash	$ 3,000	$ 2,000
Investments (Note 2)	177,000	145,000
Pledges receivable less allowance for uncollectibles of $7,500 and $5,000	32,000	25,000
Land, buildings, and equipment, at cost less accumulated depreciation of $296,000 and $262,000 (Note 5)	516,000	513,000
Total	$ 728,000	$ 685,000
Mortgage payable, 8% due 19XX	$ 32,000	$ 36,000
Fund balances:		
Expended	484,000	477,000
Unexpended—restricted	212,000	172,000
Total fund balance	696,000	649,000
Total	$ 728,000	$ 685,000

Endowment Funds

Cash	$ 4,000	$ 10,000
Investments (Note 2)	1,944,000	2,007,000
Total	$1,948,000	$2,017,000
Fund balance	$1,948,000	$2,017,000
Total	$1,948,000	$2,017,000

See accompanying notes to financial statements.

Source: VHWO audit guide, pp. 46–47.

Land, buildings, and equipment. Fixed assets of VHWOs are recorded at cost or, if donated, at fair market value at donation. Fixed assets used in current operations are recorded in the Land, Building, and Equipment (or Plant) Fund. Sales of fixed assets are also recorded there, together with losses and gains on sales. Sales proceeds may remain in the fund or be transferred to the Current Unrestricted Fund.

Donated fixed assets may not be immediately usable or salable because of donor restrictions or conditions. These fixed assets are reported as contributions to the Current Restricted Fund(s) or another restricted fund. When the donor restrictions expire, or donor conditions have been met, the fixed assets are transferred to the Land, Buildings, and Equipment Fund if they are to be used in VHWO operations. If they are to be sold or held to produce income, the fixed assets are recorded in the Current Unrestricted Fund, if the income and/or sale proceeds are unrestricted, or in the Current Restricted Fund if the income and/or sale proceeds are restricted as to use. Sales of such fixed assets, together with the gain or loss upon sale, are recorded in the fund in which the fixed asset is recorded.

Depreciation expense and accumulated depreciation are recorded for exhaustible fixed assets in operating use or held to produce income. Depreciation is not recorded on fixed assets held for sale (see note 5, Figure 20-4).

Liabilities. All VHWO liabilities are reported in the fund to which they relate, if that is apparent, or in the Current Unrestricted Fund(s). Contributions restricted to use in future periods are reported in the liability section as deferred support. Long-term debt usually relates to the Land, Buildings, and Equipment Fund or to the Endowment Fund(s). However, liabilities against fixed assets held for income or sale would be reported with the assets in the Current Restricted Fund(s) or the Current Unrestricted Fund(s), as appropriate.

Fund balance. The fund balances of the Current Unrestricted Fund(s) and the Current Restricted Fund(s) of a VHWO may be "designated" by the governing board, as in Figure 20-1, for specific purposes and projects or for investment. Such designations do not constitute, and should not be confused with, donor restrictions. The board can change or reverse its designation action at will, and designations report only tentative plans that may be changed, (see note 4, Figure 20-4).

Fund Balances of Current Restricted Fund(s) are identified according to the purposes for which they may be used. Endowment Fund balances may also be reported according to purpose, donor, or otherwise. Finally, note that the Fund Balance of the Land, Buildings, and Equipment (or Plant) Fund is separated between its expended and unexpended components, and the unexpended balance is further classified as to whether it is restricted or unrestricted.

Statement of Support, Revenue, and Expenses and Changes in Fund Balances. The major VHWO operating statement is the Statement of Support, Revenue, and Expenses and Changes in Fund Balances (Figure 20-2). Note that the major components of this statement are:

1. Public Support and Revenue
   a. Public support (listed by source)

> **b.** Revenue (listed by source)
> Total support and revenue

2. Expenses
   a. Program services (listed by functions)
   b. Supporting services (listed by functions)
   Total expenses
   Excess (deficiency) of public support and revenue over expenses

3. Other Changes in Fund Balances

4. Fund Balances, beginning of year

5. Fund Balances, end of year

Each fund should be clearly identified in the heading, although similar funds can be combined, and presentation of prior year comparative data is suggested (but not required) in the VHWO audit guide.

Public support and revenue. The term "public support" indicates resources provided by donors in nonreciprocal transactions. Current contributions to fund-raising drives, special fund-raising events, legacies and bequests, and contributions from federated (e.g., United Way) and other fund-raising campaigns are typical major support sources of VHWOs. Note that only the net contributions—gross contributions less costs incurred—of special fund-raising events are reported as "Public Support."

"Revenues" include such items as membership dues (often really "public support"), investment income, gains and losses on disposal of fixed assets or investments, and fees for services rendered. Investment income may be reported on either the cost or market value approach, as noted earlier, and the gains and losses reported should be consistent with the investment accounting method employed.

The fair market value of significant amounts of donated materials should be reported as support when the materials are received and expenses when the materials are used if (1) their omission would cause the statement of support, revenue, and expenses and changes in fund balances to be misleading; and (2) the organization has an objective, unbiased basis of estimating their fair market value. The same is true for donated (free) use of facilities and other assets. Donated services should also be reported both as public support and expense if:

1. The services performed are a normal part of the program or supporting services and would otherwise be performed by salaried personnel.

2. The organization exercises control over the employment and duties of the donors of the services.

3. The organization has a clearly measurable basis for the amount.[8]

Expenses. VHWO expenses (not expenditures) are reported in two broad categories: (1) Program Services and (2) Supporting Services. *Program service expenses* should be classified by functions using terms that best convey the primary

---

[8] Ibid., pp. 20–21.

Figure 20-2

VOLUNTARY HEALTH AND WELFARE SERVICE

Statement of Support, Revenue, and Expenses
and Changes in Fund Balances
Year Ended December 31, 19X2
With Comparative Totals for 19X1

	Current Funds		Land, Building, and Equip- ment Fund	Endowment Fund	Total All Funds	
19X2	Unrestricted	Restricted			19X2	19X1
Public support and revenue:						
Public support:						
Contributions (net of estimated uncollectible pledges of $195,000 in 19X2 and $150,000 in 19X1)	$3,764,000	$162,000	$ —	$ 2,000	$3,928,000	$3,976,000
Contributions to building fund	—	—	72,000	—	72,000	150,000
Special events (net of direct costs of $181,000 in 19X2 and $163,000 in 19X1)	104,000	—	—	—	104,000	92,000
Legacies and bequests	92,000	—	—	4,000	96,000	129,000
Received from federated and nonfederated campaigns (which incurred related fund-raising expenses of $38,000 in 19X2 and $29,000 in 19X1)	275,000	—	—	—	275,000	308,000
Total public support	4,235,000	162,000	72,000	6,000	4,475,000	4,655,000
Revenue:						
Membership dues	17,000	—	—	—	17,000	12,000
Investment Income	98,000	10,000	—	—	108,000	94,000
Realized gain on investment transactions	200,000	—	—	25,000	225,000	275,000

	A	B	C	D	E	F
Miscellaneous	42,000	—	—	—	42,000	47,000
Total revenue	357,000	10,000	—	25,000	392,000	428,000
Total support and revenue	4,592,000	172,000	72,000	31,000	$4,867,000	$5,083,000
Expenses:						
Program services:						
Research	1,257,000	155,000	2,000	—	$1,414,000	$1,365,000
Public health education	539,000	—	5,000	—	544,000	485,000
Professional education and training	612,000	—	6,000	—	618,000	516,000
Community services	568,000	—	10,000	—	578,000	486,000
Total program services	2,976,000	155,000	23,000	—	3,154,000	2,852,000
Supporting services:						
Management and general	567,000	—	7,000	—	574,000	638,000
Fund raising	642,000	—	12,000	—	654,000	546,000
Total supporting services	1,209,000	—	19,000	—	1,228,000	1,184,000
Total expenses	4,185,000	155,000	42,000	—	$4,382,000	$4,036,000
Excess (deficiency) of public support and revenue over expenses	407,000	17,000	30,000	31,000		
Other changes in fund balances:						
Property and equipment acquisitions from unrestricted funds	(17,000)	—	17,000	—		
Transfer of realized endowment fund appreciation	100,000	—	—	(100,000)		
Returned to donor	—	(8,000)	—	—		
Fund balances, beginning of year	5,361,000	123,000	649,000	2,017,000		
Fund balances, end of year	$5,851,000	$132,000	$696,000	$1,948,000		

See accompanying notes to financial statements.

Source: VHWO audit guide, pp. 42–43.

thrust of programs of the VHWO. Program service expenses include both *direct expenses* that are clearly identifiable with the program or function and *allocations of indirect costs*, presumably in a rational and systematic manner. *Supporting service expenses* include management and general, fund-raising, and other costs not associated directly with rendering program services. Analysts and regulators of VHWOs pay close attention to the relationship of supporting services expenses to program services expenses and total expenses. In particular, fund-raising costs are often compared among organizations and for one VHWO through time.

Accounting for expenses (and expenditures) during the year may center on departmental responsibility and type (object) of expense or expenditure incurred rather than on functions. Further, some personnel may work in more than one function and some expenses may involve several functions. In such cases it is necessary to maintain time and activity records by function, and other records where appropriate, so that all expenses can be assigned, directly or by allocation, to the functions of the VHWO.

Other changes in fund balances.   Other changes in fund balances include direct and indirect interfund transfers, as well as certain external transactions. Direct interfund transfers occur when money or other assets are transferred directly from one fund to another, as in the case of the transfer of realized Endowment Fund appreciation in Figure 20-2. Transfers from the Current Unrestricted Fund(s) to the Land, Buildings, and Equipment Fund would also constitute direct transfers, as would transfers of fixed asset sale proceeds from the Land, Buildings, and Equipment Fund to the Current Unrestricted Fund.

Indirect transfers are illustrated by the "Property and equipment acquisitions from unrestricted funds" item in Figure 20-2. Rather than transfer the money to the Land, Buildings, and Equipment Fund, the property and equipment was acquired directly from the Current Unrestricted Funds but capitalized in the Land, Buildings, and Equipment Fund. External transfers are illustrated by the "Returned to donor" item in Figure 20-2.

Note that the Statement of Support, Revenue, and Expenses and Changes in Fund Balances presented in Figure 20-2 explains the changes in *total* fund balances. The VHWO audit guide makes no provision for "reserves" or for "reserved" and "unreserved" fund balances, and designations are not the equivalent of reserves. Hence the emphasis on total fund balance seems proper, although an explanation of changes in designations during the year might be necessary (or at least useful) in many VHWO situations.

Statement of Functional Expenses.   The Statement of Functional Expenses, illustrated in Figure 20-3, presents a detailed analysis of the "Expenses" section of the Statement of Support, Revenue, and Expenses and Changes in Fund Balances in Figure 20-2 by object class or type of expenditure. Note that (1) the headings correspond to the "Program Services" and "Supporting Services" expense categories of the Statement of Support, Revenue, and Expenses and Changes in Fund Balances in Figure 20-2, and that (2) a "Total expenses before depreciation" subtotal is presented, followed by "Depreciation of buildings and equipment" and "Total expenses." The total before depreciation data provides

Figure 20-3

VOLUNTARY HEALTH AND WELFARE SERVICE

Statement of Functional Expenses
Year Ended December 31, 19X2
with Comparative Totals for 19X1

| | Program Services | | | | | Supporting Services | | | Total Expenses | |
| | 19X2 | | | | | | | | | |
	Research	Public Health Education	Professional Education and Training	Community Services	Total	Management and General	Fund Raising	Total	19X2	19X1
Salaries	$ 45,000	$291,000	$251,000	$269,000	$ 856,000	$331,000	$368,000	$ 699,000	$1,555,000	$1,433,000
Employee health and retirement benefits	4,000	14,000	14,000	14,000	46,000	22,000	15,000	37,000	83,000	75,000
Payroll taxes, etc.	2,000	16,000	13,000	14,000	45,000	18,000	18,000	36,000	81,000	75,000
Total salaries and related expenses	51,000	321,000	278,000	297,000	947,000	371,000	401,000	772,000	1,719,000	1,583,000
Professional fees and contract service payments	1,000	10,000	3,000	8,000	22,000	26,000	8,000	34,000	56,000	53,000
Supplies	2,000	13,000	13,000	13,000	41,000	18,000	17,000	35,000	76,000	71,000
Telephone and telegraph	2,000	13,000	10,000	11,000	36,000	15,000	23,000	38,000	74,000	68,000
Postage and shipping	2,000	17,000	13,000	9,000	41,000	13,000	30,000	43,000	84,000	80,000
Occupancy	5,000	26,000	22,000	25,000	78,000	30,000	27,000	57,000	135,000	126,000
Rental of equipment	1,000	24,000	14,000	4,000	43,000	3,000	16,000	19,000	62,000	58,000
Local transportation	3,000	22,000	20,000	22,000	67,000	23,000	30,000	53,000	120,000	113,000
Conferences, conventions, meetings	8,000	19,000	71,000	20,000	118,000	38,000	13,000	51,000	169,000	156,000
Printing and publications	4,000	56,000	43,000	11,000	114,000	14,000	64,000	78,000	192,000	184,000
Awards and grants	1,332,000	14,000	119,000	144,000	1,609,000	—	—	—	1,609,000	1,448,000
Miscellaneous	1,000	4,000	6,000	4,000	15,000	16,000	21,000	37,000	52,000	64,000
Total expenses before depreciation	1,412,000	539,000	612,000	568,000	3,131,000	567,000	650,000	1,217,000	4,348,000	4,004,000
Depreciation of buildings and equipment	2,000	5,000	6,000	10,000	23,000	7,000	4,000	11,000	34,000	32,000
Total expenses	$1,414,000	$544,000	$618,000	$578,000	$3,154,000	$574,000	$654,000	$1,228,000	$4,382,000	$4,036,000

See accompanying notes to financial statements.

Source: VHWO audit guide, pp. 44–45.

much of the information on uses of working capital (or cash) normally provided by the statement of changes in financial position, and is one reason why the statement of changes in financial position is not a required VHWO statement.

Notes to the Financial Statements. The notes to the financial statements presented for Voluntary Health and Welfare Service in the VHWO audit guide appear in Figure 20-4. Although most of them have been referred to in discussing the financial statements, they should be reviewed in their entirety, together with the financial statements, before proceeding to the next section of this chapter.

Figure 20-4

VOLUNTARY HEALTH AND WELFARE SERVICE
Notes to Financial Statements
December 31, 19X2

1. *Summary of Significant Accounting Policies.* The financial statements include the accounts of the Service and its affiliated chapters. The Service follows the practice of capitalizing all expenditures for land, buildings, and equipment in excess of $100; the fair value of donated fixed assets is similarly capitalized. Depreciation is provided over the estimated useful lives of the assets. Investments are stated at cost. All contributions are considered to be available for unrestricted use unless specifically restricted by the donor. Pledges for contributions are recorded as received and allowances are provided for amounts estimated to be uncollectible. Policies concerning donated material and services are described in Note 6.

2. *Investments.* Market values and unrealized appreciation (depreciation) at December 31, 19X2 and 19X1 are summarized as follows:

	(Thousands of Dollars)			
	December 31, 19X2		December 31, 19X1	
	Quoted Market Value	Unrealized Appreciation	Quoted Market Value	Unrealized Appreciation (Depreciation)
Current unrestricted fund:				
For long-term purposes .	$2,735	$ 8	$2,230	$ (15)
Other	1,100	25	941	(9)
Current restricted funds ...	73	2	73	1
Endowment funds	2,125	181	2,183	176
Land, building, and equipment fund	184	7	153	8

Interfund transfers include $100,000 for 19X2, which represents the portion of the realized appreciation ($25,000 realized in the current year and $75,000 realized in prior years) in endowment funds that, under the laws of (a state), were designated by the governing board for unrestricted operations. At December 31, 19X2, $200,000 of realized appreciation was available in endowment funds, which the governing board may, if it deems prudent, also transfer to the unrestricted fund.

If the organization accounts for its investment on the market value basis, the first part of the above note might be worded as follows:

Cost and unrealized appreciation (depreciation) at December 31, 19X2 and 19X1 are summarized as follows:

Figure 20-4 (continued)

| | December 31, 19X2 | | December 31, 19X1 | |
	Cost	Unrealized Appreciation	Cost	Unrealized Appreciation (Depreciation)
Current unrestricted fund:				
For long-term purposes .	$2,727	$ 8	$2,245	$ (15)
Other	1,075	25	950	(9)
Current restricted funds ...	71	2	72	1
Endowment funds	1,944	181	2,007	176
Land, building, and equipment fund	177	7	45	8

3. *Research Grants.* The Service's awards for research grants-in-aid generally cover a period of one to three years, subject to annual renewals at the option of the governing board. At December 31, 19X2, $1,748,000 had been designated by the board for research grants, of which $596,000 had been awarded for research to be carried out within the next year.

4. *Proposed Research Center.* The XYZ Foundation has contributed $50,000 to the Service with the stipulations that it be used for the construction of a research center and that construction of the facilities begin within four years. The Service is considering the construction of a research center, the cost of which would approximate $2,000,000. If the governing board approves the construction of these facilities, it is contemplated that its cost would be financed by a special fund drive.

5. *Land, Buildings and Equipment and Depreciation.* Depreciation of buildings and equipment is provided on a straight-line basis over the estimated useful lives of the assets. At December 31, 19X2 and 19X1, the costs of such assets were as follows:

	19X2	19X1
Land	$ 76,000	$ 76,000
Buildings	324,000	324,000
Medical research equipment	336,000	312,000
Office furniture and equipment	43,000	33,000
Automobiles and trucks	33,000	30,000
Total cost	812,000	775,000
Less accumulated depreciation	296,000	262,000
Net	$516,000	$513,000

6. *Donated Materials and Services.* Donated materials and equipment are reflected as contributions in the accompanying statements at their estimated values at date of receipt. No amounts have been reflected in the statements for donated services inasmuch as no objective basis is available to measure the value of such services; however, a substantial number of volunteers have donated significant amounts of their time in the organization's program services and in its fund-raising campaigns.

7. *Pension Plans.* The organization has a non-contributory pension and retirement plan covering substantially all of its employees. Pension expense for the current year and the prior year was $_____ and $_____, respectively, which includes amortization of prior service cost over _____ year period. The Service's policy is to fund pension cost accrued. At December 31, 19X2, the actuarially computed value of the vested benefits in the plan exceeded the fund balance of the plan by approximately $_____.

Figure 20-4 (continued)

8. *Leased Facilities.* Most of the buildings used by the organization for its community services programs are leased on a year-to-year basis. At December 31, 19X2, fifteen such buildings were being leased for an annual cost of approximately $12,000.

Source: VHWO audit guide, pp. 48–50.

OTHER NONPROFIT ORGANIZATIONS

As noted earlier, the most authoritative source of accounting principles and reporting standards for the many types of not-for-profit organizations other than VHWOs is AICPA *Statement of Position 78-10,* "Accounting Principles and Reporting Practices for Certain Nonprofit Organizations." SOP 78-10 applies to all nonprofit organizations except those covered by an AICPA audit guide—hospitals, colleges and universities, state and local governments, and voluntary health and welfare organizations—except those nonprofit organizations that operate essentially as business enterprises for the direct economic benefit of their members or stockholders. Thus, whereas SOP 78-10 does *not* apply to employee benefit and pension plans, mutual insurance companies or banks, agricultural cooperatives, or similar member benefit organizations, it *does* apply to the following types of organizations and to other truly nonprofit organizations (NPOs):

- Cemetery organizations
- Civic organizations
- Fraternal organizations
- Libraries
- Museums
- Other cultural institutions
- Performing arts organizations
- Political parties
- Private and community foundations
- Private elementary and secondary schools
- Professional associations
- Religious organizations
- Research and scientific organizations
- Social and country clubs
- Trade associations
- Zoological and botanical societies

General Attributes of "Other" NPO Accounting and Reporting

Several general attributes of NPO accounting and reporting warrant attention at this point. These include (1) Purposes of Financial Statements, (2) Basis of Financial Reporting, (3) Fund Accounting, and (4) Financially Interrelated Organizations.

Purposes of Financial Statements. Financial statements of these organizations, as described in this chapter, are designed for those who are interested in the organizations as "outsiders," not members of management. Presumably the latter group has access to whatever data they may want. But the organization's contributors, beneficiaries of services, employees, creditors and potential creditors, related organizations, and even the trustees or directors need information that comes in a complete package ready for their appropriate uses. The same can be said of representatives of governments that may have jurisdiction over not-for-profit organizations.

The financial statements should provide information that describes and discloses the following:[9]

1. The nature and amount of available resources.
2. The degree of control exercised by donors and the amount of freedom management has in determining which resources will be used and how they will be used.
3. The uses made of resources, including identification of the nature and costs of the principal programs.
4. The net changes in fund balances during the reporting period.
5. A basis for evaluating management's performance.
6. A basis for evaluating the likelihood that management can carry out its prescribed or announced programs with available resources.

Basis of Financial Reporting. The financial statements should be prepared on the *accrual* basis of accounting. It is acceptable to keep the accounts on some other basis, such as cash, and make period-end adjustments to bring them into conformity with GAAP.

There may be organizations for which the accrual basis is not necessary because statements that use the cash receipts and disbursements basis do not differ materially from those that would be prepared on the accrual basis. These statements can be said to be in conformity with GAAP. Cash-basis statements for more complex operations are special reports, however, and are not in conformity with GAAP. The provisions of AICPA *Statements on Auditing Standards No. 14,* "Special Reports," should be used by an auditor in determining the nature of his report following the audit of such statements. They have been prepared on a comprehensive basis other than GAAP, constitute special purpose financial statements, and do not purport to present financial position and results of operations in conformity with GAAP.

Fund Accounting. Fund accounting should be used in most cases where the organization has restricted funds that must be indentified and segregated from other resources. Where more than one fund of a type is used, "combining" statements should be prepared for each such groups of funds. "Combined" statements showing totals for all fund groups are desirable but are not required by SOP 78-10.

[9] Adapted from SOP 78–10, p.9.

Where complexities of resources restrictions might justify fund accounting, an acceptable alternative is classifying the accounts on a restricted-unrestricted basis. Under either alternative the financial statements must make clear the restrictions placed on resources by third-party providers and should indicate the expendable-nonexpendable status of the resources.

The preceding discussion assumes that the restrictions referred to are imposed by "outside authority" such as donors or grantors. Restrictions imposed by management, including a board of trustees or directors ("internal" restrictions), may be removed by the same management authority that created them. They therefore do not impose restrictions as to when or how the resources may be used and should not be presented in the financial statements as restrictions. Resources that are internally restricted (designated) should be included among the unrestricted resources in the balance sheet.

SOP 78-10 does not specify the fund structure to be used by nonprofit organizations using fund accounting, leaving that decision to the organization and its auditors. However, commonly used funds in the illustrative financial statements in Appendix C of SOP 78-10 are:

- Operating Funds—Unrestricted
- Operating Funds—Restricted
- Plant Funds
- Endowment Funds
- Annuity and Life Income Funds
- Deposit and Loan Funds

These are virtually identical to those prescribed in the VHWO audit guide, and fund accounting for "other" nonprofit organizations with complex operations requiring fund accounting closely parallels that for VHWOs.

Financially Interrelated Organizations. When a group of organizations is financially interrelated, the entity assumption indicates that a single set of financial statements for the group should be made available to the public. Nonprofit organizations have many kinds of relationships, ranging from outright control to association only in terms of a similarity of purpose. The SOP poses two tests for determining the desirability of combined statements:

1. Control, which means "the direct or indirect ability to determine the direction of management and policies through ownership, by contract, or otherwise."[10]
2. Compatible purpose (which was left undefined).

Both of the tests must be affirmative for combined statements to be justified.

More specifically, if any of the following relationships exist in combination with control, as defined above, combined statements should be presented:

a. Separate entities solicit funds in the name of and with the expressed or implicit approval of the reporting organization, and substantially

---

[10] Ibid., p. 17.

all of the funds solicited are intended by the contributor or are otherwise required to be transferred to the reporting organization or used at its discretion or direction.

b. A reporting organization transfers some of its resources to another separate entity whose resources are held for the benefit of the reporting organization.

c. A reporting organization assigns functions to a controlled entity whose funding is primarily derived from sources other than public contributions.[11]

Financial statements of included entities may of course be presented in addition to combined statements. The disclosures required by *Statements on Auditing Standards No. 6,* "Related Party Transactions," should be made, but contributions made to a nonprofit organization by related parties need be disclosed only if there are "reciprocal economic benefits" between the parties.

Certain national and international organizations have local chapters, affiliates, and so on, that may or may not meet the tests for statement combination. Examples of characteristics of relationships that would not require combination are local determination of programs, financial independence, and control of assets. Even where combined statements are not required, it is appropriate to disclose the existence of affiliates and the nature of their relationships with the reporting entity.

"Other" NPO Financial Statements

The basic financial statements prescribed by SOP 78-10 are:

- Balance Sheet
- Statement of Activity (including changes in fund balances)
- Statement of Changes in Financial Position

Specific titles and formats for these statements are not prescribed in the SOP. Rather, each organization should develop the statement formats most appropriate to its situation and needs in conformity with the principles discussed in the SOP. Each of the basic financial statements is discussed and illustrated, and the underlying accounting principles are explained, in the following sections. The Sample Independent School illustrative statements and notes (from Appendix C to SOP 80-10) serve as the primary illustrations and appear in Figures 20-5 to 20-8.

Balance Sheet. Although the SOP does not prescribe a specific balance sheet format, it sets forth numerous asset, liability, and fund balance accounting and reporting guidelines, many of which also affect the statement of activity.

Restricted v. unrestricted. The balance sheet should clearly distinguish *externally restricted* assets, related liabilities, and fund balances from *unrestricted* assets, related liabilities, and fund balances available to the organization. This may be done by columnar presentation of fund data, as in Figure 20-5, or by use

[11] Ibid., p. 18.

Figure 20-5

SAMPLE INDEPENDENT SCHOOL
Balance Sheet
June 30, 19X1

	Operating Funds	Plant Funds	Endowment Funds	Total All Funds
Assets				
Cash	$ 87,000	$ 15,000	$ 19,000	$ 121,000
Accounts receivable, less allowance for doubtful receivables of $3,000	34,000	—	—	34,000
Pledges receivable, less allowance for doubtful pledges of $10,000	—	75,000	—	75,000
Inventories, at lower of cost (FIFO) or market	7,000	—	—	7,000
Investments (Note 2)	355,000	10,000	100,000	465,000
Land, buildings, equipment, and library books, at cost less accumulated depreciation of $980,000 (Note 3)	—	2,282,000	—	2,282,000
Other assets	17,000	—	—	17,000
Total assets	$500,000	$2,382,000	$119,000	$3,001,000
Liabilities and Fund Balances				
Accounts payable and accrued expenses ...	$ 13,000	—	—	$ 13,000
Deferred amounts (Note 6)				
Unrestricted	86,000	—	—	86,000
Restricted	27,000	$ 100,000	—	127,000
Long-term debt (Note 4)	—	131,000	—	131,000
Total liabilities	126,000	231,000	—	357,000
Fund balances:				
Unrestricted:				
Designated by the governing board for long-term investment	355,000	—	—	355,000
Undesignated	19,000	—	—	19,000
	374,000	—	—	374,000
Restricted—nonexpendable	—	—	$119,000	119,000
Net investment in plant	—	2,151,000	—	2,151,000
Total fund balances	374,000	2,151,000	119,000	2,644,000
Total liabilities and fund balances ..	$500,000	$2,382,000	$119,000	$3,001,000

Source: SOP 78-10, p. 47.

---

of restricted-unrestricted or expendable-nonexpendable balance sheet classifications.

The SOP recognizes that many NPOs have land, buildings, equipment, art collections, rare books and manuscripts, religious artifacts, and similar items that were acquired with a combination of unrestricted and restricted resources. These and similar Plant Fund assets may make it impractical to report separately Plant Fund balances other than as "expended" (or invested) and "unexpended"; i.e., the expended (invested) balance cannot reasonably be reported as between "restricted" and "unrestricted." The SOP also provides that "the plant fund may be reported separately or combined with either the unrestricted or restricted funds, as appropriate."[12]

Current v. noncurrent. NPOs having only unrestricted assets, liabilities, and fund balances should classify the assets and liabilities as either "current" or "noncurrent" (or "fixed," "long-term," etc.). NPOs with both restricted and unrestricted assets, related liabilities, and fund balances should also classify the assets and liabilities as "current" or "noncurrent" unless the fund structure adequately indicates the current or noncurrent status of the assets and liabilites.

Investments. SOP 78-10 permits NPOs to account for investments in the following manners:

- *Marketable debt securities*—where there are both the intent and ability to hold such securities to maturity—should be reported at (1) amortized cost, (2) market value, or (3) lower of amortized cost or market value.
- *Marketable debt securities* not expected to be held to maturity and *marketable equity securities* should be reported at either (1) market value or (2) lower of cost or market value.
- *Other type of investments*, such as real estate, oil and gas, and other interests, should be reported at either (1) fair value or (2) lower of cost or fair value.[13]

The same valuation method should be used for all investments in each of these categories, however, and interfund sales, exchanges, and transfers should be recorded at fair value if a restricted fund is involved. The investment valuation method(s) used should be disclosed in the notes to the financial statements, which should also contain a summary of the total realized and unrealized investment gains, losses, and income.

Fixed assets. Fixed assets should be recorded at cost, if purchased, or at fair market value when donated. If historical cost or fair market value data are not available, fixed assets may be capitalized at amounts determined by any reasonable basis, such as cost-based appraisals, insurance appraisals, replacement costs, or property tax appraisals adjusted to approximate market value. In such cases the valuation method(s) used should be disclosed in the notes to the financial statements.

Depreciation and accumulated depreciation of *exhaustible* fixed assets should be recorded. Depreciation and accumulated depreciation need not be recorded on *inexhaustible* fixed assets—such as landmarks, monuments, cathedrals, and historical treasures—or on structures used primarily as houses of worship.

Inexhaustible collections owned by museums, art galleries, botanical gardens, or other NPOs are not required to be valued or capitalized, but they should be cataloged and controlled. If inexhaustible collections are not recorded in the

---

[12] Ibid.. p. 12.
[13] Adapted from ibid., p. 27.

accounts they should be listed on the balance sheet, with no valuation indicated, with a reference to a note to the financial statements that describes the collections. Although capitalization of inexhaustible collections is not required by the SOP, it is encouraged—at any reasonable estimate of cost, fair market value, or other valuation. Further, *exhaustible* collections, such as some exhibits, should be capitalized and depreciated.

Deferred support and revenue. Assets that are otherwise unrestricted but (1) are intended by donors to finance operations of future years or (2) result from prepayments of service charges or other revenues should be reported as deferred support or revenue, as appropriate. Resources that are restricted for specified operating purposes should also be reported as deferred support or revenue, as appropriate, until the restrictions are met. Restrictions are considered to have been met to the extent that expenses have been incurred during the year for the purpose specified by the donor or grantor.

Deferred capital additions. Capital additions are defined as:

> nonexpendable gifts, grants, and bequests restricted by donors to endowment, plant, or loan funds, either permanently or for extended periods of time. Capital additions also include legally restricted investment income and gains or losses on investments that must be added to the principal. Capital additions do not include donor-restricted gifts for program or supporting services.[14]

Capital additions of Endowment, Loan, and similar funds are reported as "capital additions" or "capital contributions" in the statement of activity (Figure 20-6) for the year in which the gift or grant is received or the restricted income is earned. However, gifts or grants restricted for acquiring plant assets should be reported as "Deferred Capital Support" in the Plant Fund balance sheet until they are expended for that purpose, at which time they are reported as capital additions in the statement of activity.

Future interests. Future interests should be appropriately reported in the balance sheet. The most common types of future interests given NPOs, like colleges and universities, are annuity and life income gifts.

In an *annuity* gift the NPO receives assets but assumes an obligation to pay a specified person(s) a specified sum each year for a fixed or determinable number of years. The excess of the assets received in an annuity gift over the present value (actuarially determined) of the liability assumed should be reported as support at the date of the gift only if such excess is unrestricted and may be used immediately. Otherwise, the excess should be reported as (unrestricted or restricted) deferred support or capital additions, as appropriate, until the terms of the annuity gift have been met.

Similarly, the principal of *life income* gifts—where a specified person(s) is to receive the income from the assets for life or another determinable period of

[14] Ibid., p. 19.

time—should be reported as (unrestricted or restricted) deferred support or capital additions, as appropriate, until the terms of the life income gift have been met.

Other balance sheet guidance. Several other matters relating to NPO balance sheets are discussed in SOP 78-10. These include:

- *Pledges* that can be legally enforced should be recorded as assets, together with an appropriate allowance for uncollectible pledges.
- *Investment pools* should be operated on a market value basis to assure equitable allocation of both realized and unrealized gains and losses to investor funds.
- *Interfund borrowings* should be disclosed when restricted funds have been loaned or when the liquidity of either fund is in question. Also, any unauthorized or illegal interfund loans should be disclosed, and interfund loans should be reported as transfers when it is evident that repayment is unlikely.
- *Designations of fund balances* for specific purposes may be made by NPO management. Designations should not be reported as expenses and/or liabilities; they should not be reported in the statement of activity but in the balance sheet as part of the unrestricted fund balance.
- *Funds held in trust by others* that are in neither the possession nor the control of the NPO are not reported in the balance but are disclosed, either parenthetically in the Endowment Fund(s) balance sheet or in the notes to the financial statements.
- *Other funds* used by a NPO that are not recognized or discussed in SOP 78-10 may be reported separately in the balance sheet or be reported as part of another fund. The data of these funds should be precisely classified in either event so that liabilities—such as for agency, custodial, or self-administered pension funds—are clearly distinguished from fund balances.

Many of these principles and those discussed earlier are illustrated in the Sample Independent School balance sheet (Figure 20-5) and the notes to the financial statements (Figure 20-8). The balance sheet is organized on a fund basis; the Operating, Plant, and Endowment Funds used are explained in note 1; and both the "unrestricted-restricted" and "current-noncurrent" status of its assets are apparent from the balance sheet and the notes. The "Deferred Amounts—Restricted" reported in the Operating and Plant Funds indicate that revenue recognition is being deferred until pertinent restrictions have been met; and the unrestricted deferred amount indicates that certain otherwise unrestricted assets have been received in advance of the year in which they may be expended. Changes in deferred restricted accounts are disclosed in note 6.

Fund balance designations are properly reported as part of unrestricted fund balances in Figure 20-5. The simple "Net Investment in Plant" account indicates that dividing the amount into "restricted" and "unrestricted" components is not practicable. Note also that the composition of the Plant Fund fixed assets is disclosed in note 3, Long-term debt is detailed in note 4, and investment accounting policies and other disclosures are made in note 2.

Statement of Activity. The statement of activity reports the support, revenue, capital or nonexpendable additions, expenses, transfers, and other changes in fund balances. Alternatively, a NPO may present a statement of activity that excludes the changes in fund balances, but must also present a separate statement of changes in fund balances that reconciles the beginning and ending balances.

The statement of activity may be titled as the NPO sees fit, as long as the title appropriately describes the nature and content of the statement. Note that the statement of activity for Sample Independent School (Figure 20-6) is appropriately titled "Statement of Support and Revenue, Expenses, Capital Additions, and Changes in Fund Balances." Note also that the "Support and Revenue" and "Expenses" sections of this statement are identical to the VHWO Statement of Support, Revenue, and Expenses and Changes in Fund Balances. Both report support and revenue by source; expenses, classified as between program services and supporting services, by function; and an excess or deficiency of revenue and support over (under) expenses. They differ only in that (1) the VHWO statement presents all "other changes in fund balances" in a section immediately before beginning and ending fund balances, whereas (2) the other NPO statement reports capital additions separately before beginning fund balance and reports interfund transfers between the beginning and ending fund balances. The format of the VHWO and other NPO operating statements may be summarized as follows:

	Other NPO	VHWO
(Public) Support and Revenue	X	X
Public Support		X
Listed by source	X	X
Revenue		X
Listed by source	X	X
Total Support and Revenue	X	X
Expenses	X	X
Program Services	X	X
Listed by function	X	X
Supporting Services	X	X
Listed by function	X	X
Total Expenses	X	X
Excess (Deficiency) of Support and Revenue over (under) Expenses	X	X
Other Changes in Fund Balances (e.g., Capital Additions, Transfers)		X
Capital Additions	X	
Excess (Deficiency) of Support and Revenue over Expenses after Capital Additions	X	
Fund Balances, Beginning of Year	X	X
Transfers	X	
Fund Balances, End of Year	X	X

Support and revenue. The deferral of revenue and support items by NPOs until pertinent restrictions or other conditions are met was discussed in the preceding section. Support and revenue recognized in the statement of activity includes:

- *Unrestricted* contributions, gifts, bequests, service fees, investment income, and the excess of annuity gifts of the period over the present value of related liabilities.

- Support and revenue classified as deferred in prior periods because they relate to the current period.

- *Restricted* contributions, gifts, bequests, service fees, investment income, and other items which may be recognized in the current period because they have been expended for the specified purposes or other restrictions or conditions have been met.

Pledges, membership dues, etc. Revenues from legally enforceable pledges may be reported gross, with the estimated uncollectible amount charged to expense when the allowance for uncollectible pledges is increased. Alternatively, gross revenues may be reduced by the amount of the estimated uncollectible pledges and only the net expected pledge collections reported as revenue. Further, where membership dues or subscription fees relate to several periods, they usually should be recognized as revenues of those periods. However, fees from life memberships may be recognized currently, unless significant future costs are involved, as may dues, assessments, and similar items that are in substance contributions.

Investment income and gains/losses. Investment income reported and gains and losses recognized on investment transactions are determined partly by the investment valuation method(s) used. If investments are reported at the lower of cost or market (or fair value), declines are recognized when their *aggregate* market value, by fund or fund group, is less than the carrying amount of the investments. Recoveries of aggregate market values in subsequent periods should be recognized only to the extent of previous write-downs. Where the market value method of investment accounting is used, the changes in market value, as well as interest and dividends, are reported as investment income. Recall, however, that only unrestricted investment income is recognized immediately; that restricted to specific operating or capital uses is recorded as deferred support or capital additions, as appropriate, until the related conditions or restrictions have been fulfilled. In either event (1) interfund sales, exchanges, or transfers of investments should be reported at fair value, with gain or loss recognized in the transferor fund, and (2) the notes to the financial statement should contain a summary of the total realized and unrealized investment gains, losses, and income of all funds except life income and custodial funds (since the investment earnings, gains, and losses of such funds do not inure to the NPO).

Figure 20-6

SAMPLE INDEPENDENT SCHOOL

Statement of Support and Revenue, Expenses,
Capital Additions, and Changes in Fund Balances
Year Ended June 30, 19X1

	Operating Funds			Plant Funds	Endowment Funds	Total All Funds
	Unrestricted	Restricted	Total			
Support and revenue						
Tuition and fees	$ 910,000	—	$ 910,000	—	—	$ 910,000
Contributions	104,000	$ 80,500	184,500	—	—	184,500
Endowment and other investment income	23,000	1,500	24,500	—	—	24,500
Net loss on investment transactions	(8,000)	—	(8,000)	—	—	(8,000)
Auxiliary activities	25,000	—	25,000	—	—	25,000
Summer school and other programs	86,000	—	86,000	—	—	86,000
Other sources	26,000	—	26,000	—	—	26,000
Total support and revenue	1,166,000	82,000	1,248,000	—	—	1,248,000
Expenses						
Program services						
Instruction and student activities	798,000	43,000	841,000	$ 69,000	—	910,000
Auxiliary activities	24,000	—	24,000	—	—	24,000
Summer school and other programs	91,000	—	91,000	7,000	—	98,000
Financial aid	—	37,000	37,000	3,000	—	40,000
Total program services	913,000	80,000	993,000	79,000	—	1,072,000
Supporting services						
General administration	147,000	2,000	149,000	13,000	—	162,000
Fund raising	12,000	—	12,000	1,000	—	13,000
Total supporting services	159,000	2,000	161,000	14,000	—	175,000
Total expenses	1,072,000	82,000	1,154,000	93,000	—	1,247,000

			Land, Building, and Equipment	Endowment	Total
Excess (deficiency) of support and revenue over expenses before capital additions	94,000	—	(93,000)	—	1,000
Capital additions					
Contributions and bequests	—	—	80,000	$ 30,000	110,000
Investment income	—	—	5,000	—	5,000
Net gain on investment transactions	—	—	1,000	2,000	3,000
Total capital additions	—	—	86,000	32,000	118,000
Excess (deficiency) of support and revenue over expenses after capital additions	94,000	—	(7,000)	32,000	119,000
Fund balances at beginning of year	387,000	—	2,047,000	91,000	2,525,000
Transfers					
Equipment acquisitions and principal debt service payments	(111,000)	—	111,000	—	—
Realized gains on endowment funds utilized	4,000	—	—	(4,000)	—
Fund balances at end of year	$ 374,000	—	$2,151,000	$ 119,000	$2,644,000

Source: SOP 78-10, pp. 48-49.

Donated and contributed materials, facilities, and services. Donated *services* are recorded as support and as expense if *all* of the following conditions are met:

1. The services performed are significant, comprise an integral part of the organization's efforts, would otherwise be performed by a salaried person, and will be continued by the NPO.
2. The NPO controls the employment and duties of the service donor.
3. The NPO has a clearly measurable basis for determining the amount of the support and expense to be reported.
4. The services of the NPO are not primarily for the benefit of its members.

These criteria are rather restrictive, and preclude recording most volunteer service, e.g., in fund raising or in assisting NPO staff work with agency clients. Too, the fourth requirement generally precludes religious organizations, professional and trade associations, labor unions, political parties, fraternal organizations, social and country clubs, and other "member benefit" NPOs from recording donated services. In any event, the notes to the financial statements should disclose (1) the method used by the NPO in valuing, recording, and reporting donated or contributed services and (2) the donated or contributed services for which values have and have not been recorded.

Donated *materials and facilities* should be recorded at their fair value, provided they are significant (material) and the NPO has a clearly measurable and objective basis for determining their value. However, neither donated materials (such as used clothing or furniture) that cannot be reasonably valued nor items that are merely passed through the organization to the beneficiaries (the NPO serving only in an agency capacity) should be recorded as contributions and expenses.

Expense Classification. Expenses of NPOs that receive significant support from the general public should be appropriately categorized (as in VHWOs) as between "program expenses," which relate directly to the primary missions of the NPO, and "supporting services," which do not relate directly to the primary missions and include such costs as general administration, membership development, and fund raising. Further, as in VHWOs, the expenses are to be reported by major programs or functions within these two categories.

Program services. Expenses directly related to rendering program services should be reported using program services descriptors that clearly convey the primary service thrusts of the agency. Some NPOs remit a portion of their receipts to an affiliated state or national organization. A NPO that in essence serves as a collecting agency for the state or national affiliate—e.g., one that must remit a percentage of all collections to the affiliate—should report such payments as deductions from total support and revenue. Other organizations should report dues and other remittances to affiliates as program expenses.

Management and general costs. Management and general costs are not identifiable with a specific program or fund-raising activity but are necessary to the organization's existence and effectiveness. They include such costs as board meetings, business management, record keeping, budgeting, accounting, and overall direction and leadership. To the extent that some of these costs are directly related to the primary programs, they should be allocated to those program costs in a systematic and rational manner.

Fund-raising and other supporting services. Fund-raising costs are incurred to induce contributions of money, securities, real estate or other properties, materials, or time to the NPO. Fund-raising efforts and costs vary widely among the many types of NPOs, but fund-raising costs such as the following are often incurred: mailing lists, printing, mailing, personnel, occupancy, newspaper and other media advertising, and costs of unsolicited merchandise sent to encourage contributions.

Fund-raising costs paid directly by a contributor should be recorded by the NPO as both a contribution and a fund-raising expense. When fund-raising banquets, dinner parties, theater parties, merchandise auctions or drawings, and similar events are held, only the net (after related direct costs) proceeds of such functions should be reported as support. However, costs of the fund-raising merchandise, meals, or other direct benefits to donors should be disclosed in the notes to the financial statements. Where several fund-raising efforts are undertaken with mixed success it may be appropriate to summarize the results of each fund-raising activity in the statement of activity or in the notes to the financial statements.

Fund-raising costs usually are expensed each year. However, if pledges or restricted contributions received in a fund drive are appropriately recorded as deferred support, directly related fund-raising costs may be deferred if the donor(s) is aware that the contribution could be used to cover fund-raising costs. Similarly, costs of literature, materials, and so on, incurred in one year to be used in fund raising the next year should be deferred and recognized as fund-raising costs of that year.

Costs of soliciting grants from foundations or government agencies should be reported as separate categories of fund-raising expenses. Similarly, the costs of membership development efforts should be reported as a separate item of "supporting services."

Other expense-related matters. Some NPOs make grants to other organizations. Grants should be recorded as expenses and liabilities at the time the recipient is entitled to them, normally when the board approves the grant and the grantee is notified of its approval. Multiple year grants subject to only minimal grantee performance requirements and not requiring subsequent review and approval for continuance should be recorded as expenses and liabilities in the year the grant is awarded. However, if the grantor reserves the right to revoke the grant, only the amounts that the grantee is clearly entitled to should be recorded as expenses and liabilities. Grants subject to periodic renewal are recorded as expenses and liabilities upon renewal and the remaining commitment is disclosed in the notes to the financial statements.

Finally, the expenditure and/or expense accounts of many NPOs are maintained during the year on a departmental responsibility center and object-of-expenditure basis rather than by functional classifications. Also, some costs incurred benefit more than one function, and some employees are involved in more than one function. In such cases it is necessary to keep such time, cost, and related records as may be needed to allocate the costs incurred to functions in a systematic and reasonable manner at year end.

Capital additions. Capital additions were defined earlier to include:

- Nonexpendable gifts, grants, and bequests restricted, either permanently or for an extended period of time, to endowment, plant, or loan funds.
- Legally restricted income, gains, and losses on investments held by such funds that must be added to fund principal.

These are illustrated in Figure 20-6, where both the Plant and Endowment Funds report restricted contributions and bequests and restricted net gains on investment transactions. The Plant Funds also report restricted investment income. All of these restricted amounts are usable only for the purposes of each fund, and only within the confines of the constraints as to the use of those assets.

Transfers. Transfers are defined in SOP 78-10 as "Moving fund balances from one fund to another, usually as a result of an intended change in the use of the assets."[15] Since transfers are neither revenues, support, nor expenses, NPO interfund transfers should be reported after the beginning fund balance in the statement of activity. Transfers required under contractual arrangements and those required upon expiration of a term endowment fund should be separately disclosed.

Note in Figure 20-6 that the "transfers" section is appropriately placed. Note also (1) the indirect transfer reported as the result of Plant Funds assets having been acquired directly from Unrestricted Operating Funds resources and (2) the (assumedly legal) transfer of realized gains on Endowment Fund investments to the Unrestricted Operating Fund.

Statement of Changes in Financial Position. The statement of changes in financial position, which may be prepared on either a working capital or cash basis, should summarize all changes in financial position of the NPO and its funds, including (1) capital additions, (2) changes in deferred support and revenue, and (3) financing and investing activities. Note that the Sample Independent School Statement of Changes in Financial Position (Figure 20-7):

- Begins appropriately with the "Excess (deficiency) of support and revenue *before* capital additions." This "links" the Statement of Changes in Financial Position with the Statement of Activity.

[15] Ibid., p. 43.

Figure 20-7

SAMPLE INDEPENDENT SCHOOL

Statement of Changes in Financial Position
Year Ended June 30, 19X1

	Operating Funds	Plant Funds	Endowment Funds	Total All Funds
Resources provided				
Excess (deficiency) of support and revenue over expenses before capital additions	$ 94,000	$(93,000)	—	$ 1,000
Capital additions				
Contributions and bequests	—	80,000	$ 30,000	110,000
Investment income	—	5,000	—	5,000
Net gain on investments .	—	1,000	2,000	3,000
Excess (deficiency) of support and revenue over expenses after capital additions	94,000	(7,000)	32,000	119,000
Items not using (providing) resources				
Provision for depreciation.	—	93,000	—	93,000
Net (gain) loss on investment transactions	8,000	(1,000)	(2,000)	5,000
Decrease in inventories	2,000	—	—	2,000
Increase in deferred amounts	3,000	75,000	—	78,000
Proceeds from sale of investments	160,000	2,000	47,000	209,000
Total resources provided	267,000	162,000	77,000	506,000
Resources used				
Purchases of equipment	—	145,000		145,000
Reduction of long-term debt	—	52,000	—	52,000
Purchases of investments ...	210,000	6,000	136,000	352,000
Increase in other assets	1,000	—	—	1,000
Increase in accounts and pledges receivable	3,000	60,000	—	63,000
Decrease in accounts payable and accrued expenses	3,000	—	—	3,000
Total resources used ...	217,000	263,000	136,000	616,000
Transfers				
Equipment acquisitions and principal debt service payments	(111,000)	111,000	—	—
Realized gains on endowment funds utilized	4,000	—	(4,000)	—
Total transfers	(107,000)	111,000	(4,000)	—
Increase (decrease) in cash	$ (57,000)	$ 10,000	$ (63,000)	$(110,000)

Source: SOP 78-10, p. 50.

- Reports capital additions, then comes to the "Excess (deficiency) of support and revenue over expenses *after* capital additions." This also "links" the Statement of Changes in Financial Position with the Statement of Activity.

- Adjusts the revenue and expense data used as the starting point for the statement to cash flow data, e.g., depreciation expense and gains (losses) on investment transactions are revenue and expense items but do not cause current period cash inflows or outflows.

- Lists other sources and uses of cash, including the effect of the increase in deferred amounts.

- After presenting total resources provided and used, separately presents the interfund transfers—which affect the financial position of certain funds but not that of the school as a whole—before presenting the net increase (decrease) in cash.

Notes to the Financial Statements.   The notes to the financial statements presented for Sample Independent School appear in Figure 20-8. Although most of the notes have been referred to in discussing the financial statements, they should be reviewed in their entirety, together with the financial statements, before proceeding to the next section of this chapter.

Figure 20-8

SAMPLE INDEPENDENT SCHOOL
Notes to Financial Statements
Year Ended June 30, 19X1

Note 1—Summary of Significant Accounting Policies
The financial statements of Sample Independent School have been prepared on the accrual basis. The significant accounting policies followed are described below to enhance the usefulness of the financial statements to the reader.

Fund Accounting
To ensure observance of limitations and restrictions placed on the use of resources available to the school, the accounts of the school are maintained in accordance with the principles of fund accounting. This is the procedure by which resources for various purposes are classified for accounting and reporting purposes into funds established according to their nature and purposes. Separate accounts are maintained for each fund; however, in the accompanying financial statements, funds that have similar characteristics have been combined into fund groups. Accordingly, all financial transactions have been recorded and reported by fund group.

The assets, liabilities, and fund balances of the school are reported in three self-balancing fund groups as follows:

- Operating funds, which include unrestricted and restricted resources, represent the portion of expendable funds that is available for support of school operations.
- Plant funds represent resources restricted for plant acquisitions and funds expended for plant.

Figure 20-8 (continued)

- Endowment funds represent funds that are subject to restrictions of gift instruments requiring in perpetuity that the principal be invested and the income only be used.

Expendable Restricted Resources

Operating and plant funds restricted by the donor, grantor, or other outside party for particular operating purposes or for plant acquisitions are deemed to be earned and reported as revenues of operating funds or as additions to plant funds, respectively, when the school has incurred expenditures in compliance with the specific restrictions. Such amounts received but not yet earned are reported as restricted deferred amounts.

Plant Assets and Depreciation

Uses of operating funds for plant acquisitions and principal debt service payments are accounted for as transfers to plant funds. Proceeds from the sale of plant assets, if unrestricted, are transferred to operating fund balances, or, if restricted, to deferred amounts restricted for plant acquisitions. Depreciation of buildings and equipment is provided over the estimated useful lives of the respective assets on a straight-line basis.

Other Matters

All gains and losses arising from the sale, collection, or other disposition of investments and other noncash assets are accounted for in the fund that owned the assets. Ordinary income from investments, receivables, and the like is accounted for in the fund owning the assets, except for income derived from investments of endowment funds, which is accounted for, if unrestricted, as revenue of the expendable operating fund or, if restricted, as deferred amounts until the terms of the restriction have been met.

Legally enforceable pledges less an allowance for uncollectible amounts are recorded as receivables in the year made. Pledges for support of current operations are recorded as operating fund support. Pledges for support of future operations and plant acquisitions are recorded as deferred amounts in the respective funds to which they apply.

Note 2—Investments

Investments are presented in the financial statements in the aggregate at the lower of cost (amortized, in the case of bonds) or fair market value.

	Cost	Market
Operating funds	$355,000	$365,000
Plant funds	10,000	11,000
Endowments funds	100,000	109,000
	$465,000	$485,000

Investments are composed of the following:

	Cost	Market
Corporate stocks and bonds	$318,000	$320,000
U.S. government obligations	141,000	159,000
Municipal bonds	6,000	6,000
	$465,000	$485,000

Figure 20-8 (continued)

The following tabulation summarizes the relationship between carrying values and market values of investment assets.

	Carrying Value	Market Value	Excess of Market over Cost
Balance at end of year	$465,000	$485,000	$20,000
Balance at beginning of year	$327,000	$335,000	8,000
Increase in unrealized appreciation			12,000
Realized net loss for year			(5,000)
Total net gain for year			$ 7,000

The average annual yield exclusive of net gains (losses) was 7% and the annual total return based on market value was 9% for the year ended June 30, 19X1.

Note 3—Plant Assets and Depreciation
A summary of plant assets follows.

Land'	$ 255,000
Buildings	2,552,000
Equipment	340,000
Library books	115,000
	3,262,000
Less accumulated depreciation	980,000
	$2,282,000

Note 4—Long-Term Debt
A summary of long-term debt follows.

7½% unsecured notes payable to bank due in quarterly installments of $2,500	$ 29,000
8½% mortgage payable in semiannual installments of $3,500 through 19X7	102,000
	$131,000

Note 5—Pension Plans
The school has noncontributory pension plans covering all personnel. Total pension expense for the year ended June 30, 19X1, was $60,000, which includes amortization of prior service costs over a period of twenty years. The school's policy is to fund pension costs accrued. The actuarially computed value of vested benefits as of June 30, 19X1, exceeds net assets of the pension fund by approximately $100,000.

Note 6—Changes in Deferred Restricted Amounts

	Operating Funds	Plant Fund
Balances at beginning of year	$ 24,000	$ 25,000
Additions		
Contributions and bequests	79,000	158,000
Investment income	6,000	1,000
Net gain on investment transactions	—	2,000
	109,000	186,000
Deductions—funds expended during		
the year	82,000	86,000
Balances at end of year	$ 27,000	$100,000

Note 7—Functional Allocation of Expenses
The costs of providing the various programs and other activities have been summarized on a functional basis in the statement of support and revenue, expenses, capital additions, and changes in fund balances. Accordingly, certain costs have been allocated among the programs and supporting services benefited.

Note 8—Commitments
The school has entered into various agreements aggregating approximately $80,000 for the purchase of equipment to be received subsequent to June 30, 19X1.

Source: SOP 78-10, pp. 51–54.

SUMMARY COMPARISONS AND ILLUSTRATIVE ENTRIES

The accounting and reporting for voluntary health and welfare organizations (VHWOs) and other nonprofit organizations (ONPOs) is markedly similar. The authors of AICPA SOP 78-10 were obviously very familiar with the VHWO audit guide, and the functions and activities of many of the ONPOs covered by SOP 78-10 are similar to those of many VHWOs.

A summary comparison of the key similarities and differences in the accounting and reporting for VHWOs and ONPOs is presented in Figure 20-9. Careful study of Figure 20-9 should help clarify many points brought out in the preceding sections of this chapter and bring them into sharper focus and perspective.

Finally, a series of illustrative VHWO and ONPO transactions and general journal entries is presented in Figure 20-10. These selected transactions and entries do not constitute a comprehensive illustrative problem but are designed to reinforce and illustrate the distinctive features of VHWO and ONPO accounting and reporting summarized in Figure 20-9 and discussed throughout this chapter. The illustrative transactions and entries in Figure 20-10 assume (1) that fund accounting is used in the manner specified in the VHWO audit guide and as discussed and illustrated in AICPA SOP 78-10, and (2) that 19X1 is not the first year of VHWO/ONPO activities. Account terminology used is sufficiently neutral to be appropriate to both VHWO and ONPO accounting and reporting, and most types of transactions and events commonly encountered in VHWOs and ONPOs are included in the illustrative transactions and entries in Figure 20-10.

Figure 20-9

SUMMARY COMPARISON

Accounting and Reporting Standards—Voluntary Health and Welfare Organizations
and Other Nonprofit Organizations

Attributes	Voluntary Health and Welfare Organizations (AICPA VHWO audit guide)	Other Nonprofit Organizations (ONPOs) (AICPA SOP 78-10)	Comments
Fund Structure	Most commonly used funds: 1. Current Unrestricted. 2. Current Restricted. 3. Land, Buildings, and Equipment (Plant). 4. Endowment. 5. Custodian. 6. Loan. 7. Annuity.	Fund accounting recommended for most, but fund structure not specified. Alternatively, may classify as restricted-unrestricted or expendable-nonexpendable. Funds in illustrations parallel VHWO fund structure.	Fund structures of most VHWOs and ONPOs are similar to those recommended in VHWO audit guide.
Basis of Accounting	Accrual	Accrual	*Not modified accrual*
Basic Financial Statements	1. Balance Sheet. 2. Statement of Support, Revenue, and Expenses and Changes in Fund Balances. 3. Statement of Functional Expenses (details of expenses reported in 2 by object.)	1. Balance Sheet 2. Statement of Activity (May issue separate statements of (1) Activity and (2) Changes in Fund Balance). 3. Statement of Changes in Financial Position (Cash or working capital basis).	1. Identical "status" statements. 2. Operating statements identical except for reporting of "other" changes in fund balances. 3. Statement of Changes in Financial Position *not* required for VHWOs; Statement of Functional Expenses considered a "supplemental schedule" for ONPOs.

Investments	1. Initially recorded at cost or, if donated, at fair market value when donated.	Same for VHWOs and ONPOs.
	2. Thereafter at (1) cost, (2) market, or (3) lower of cost or market.	VHWOs and ONPOs have several alternative investment accounting policy options.
	2. Thereafter: (1) marketable debt securities (MDS) to be held to maturity at (a) amortized cost, (b) market, or (c) lower of amortized cost or market; (2) other MDS and marketable equity securities (MES) at (a) market or (b) lower of cost or market; and (3) other investment at (a) fair value or (b) lower of fair value or cost.	
	3. All investments must be accounted for on the same method or basis.	3. All investments *in each group* must be accounted for on the same method or basis.
	4. Interfund exchanges and transfers of investments must be accounted for at market.	4. Interfund exchanges and transfers of investments must be accounted for at market *if a restricted fund is involved.*
	5. Investment pools should be accounted for on the market method or an equivalent method that assures equity in allocating investment pool income, gains, and losses.	ONPOs have slightly more latitude in selecting an investment accounting policy(ies). ONPOs can account for investment transfers or exchanges at cost if no restricted fund(s) involved. Same for VHWOs and ONPOs.

	6. Disclosures:
	  a.) Basis(es) of investment accounting;
	  b.) Market value of investments if carried at cost; and
	  c.) Cost of investments if carried at market.
		6. Disclosure:
		  a.) Basis(es) of investment accounting; and
		  b.) A summary of total realized and unrealized investment income, gains, and losses.
		
		ONPO disclosure (b) would be appropriate, though not required, in VHWO notes to the financial statements.

Pledges (receivable)	Should be recorded, net of allowance for uncollectible pledges.	Should be recorded, net of allowance for uncollectible pledges, *if legally enforceable.* ONPOs record pledges *only if legally enforceable.*

Figure 20-9 (continued)

Attributes	Voluntary Health and Welfare Organizations (AICPA VHWO audit guide)	Other Nonprofit Organizations (ONPOs) (AICPA SOP 78-10)	Comments
Fixed Assets	1. Initially recorded at cost or, if donated, at fair value at donation. 2. If historical cost or fair market data not available, may estimate cost or market by a reasonable method. 3. Fixed assets used in operations capitalized in Plant (or equivalent) Fund. Those not immediately usable for operations or which are held to produce income or for resale are recorded in the appropriate unrestricted or restricted fund. 4. Depreciation and accumulated depreciation is recognized on *exhaustible* fixed assets used in operations or held to produce income. 5. Depreciation and accumulated depreciation are *not* recognized on (1) inexhaustible fixed assets, including collections, or on houses of worship; or (2) fixed assets held for resale or for future operations use.	6. Inexhaustible collections preferably capitalized, but capitalization not required. If not capitalized, should list on balance sheet, with no valuation, and describe in the notes to the financial statements.	Most fixed asset accounting and reporting requirements are the same, or nearly so, for both VHWOs and ONPOs.
Future Interests		1. Future interests—as from annuities, life income, or similar gifts—should be recorded at fair market value at receipt, and any associated liabilities should be recorded at present value.	The VHWO audit guide does not contain guidance for these types of situations. The ONPO guidance would seem appropriate for VHWOs also.

2. If "excess" of assets received over liabilities assumed is immediately usable for unrestricted purposes it is recorded as support; otherwise is recorded as deferred support or deferred capital additions, as appropriate.

Liabilities

1. All liabilities should be recorded in the funds to which they relate.
2. Long-term debt typically relates to Plant, Endowment, and/or Annuity Funds.

VHWO and ONPO guidance identical.

Deferred Support and Revenue

1. Reported as liabilities of the appropriate restricted or unrestricted funds.
2. Arises in *unrestricted funds* primarily from asset receipt or accrual prior to the period in which the assets may be used, e.g., pledges for future year support and prepaid (unearned) revenues.
3. Arises in *restricted funds* for the reasons noted in (2) and also because restrictions or other conditions on assets and expenditures have not yet been met. [Restrictions typically met by expenditure of assets for specified purpose(s).]

VHWOs include Deferred Capital Support or Additions in this category.

Deferred Capital Contributions

1. Includes gifts, grants, etc., restricted for Endowment, Loan, and Plant Funds and similarly restricted investment income, gains, and losses.
2. Initially recorded as Deferred Capital Contributions in the Plant, Loan, and Endowment Funds.
3. When restrictions or conditions are met, as by expending resources for

No parallel guidance in the VHWO audit guide. VHWOs include Deferred Capital Contributions in Deferred Revenue and Support, and report as Support when restrictions or conditions are met. ONPO Statement of Activity has section for Capital Additions; VHWO operating statement does not have such a section.

Figure 20-9 (continued)

Attributes	Voluntary Health and Welfare Organizations (AICPA VHWO audit guide)	Other Nonprofit Organizations (ONPOs) (AICPA SOP 78-10)	Comments
Deferred Capital Contributions (continued)		specified capital purposes, reported as Capital Contributions or Capital Additions.	
Fund Balance		1. Neither the VHWO audit guide nor SOP 78-10 mention or illustrate fund balance reserves.	Same for WHWOs and ONPOs.
		2. Management may make Fund Balance "designations," including those for encumbrances outstanding. Such designations are reported as part of *unrestricted* fund balance since management can change or reverse them.	
		3. Fund Balance should be reported as between "restricted" and "unrestricted" where appropriate and feasible.	
Public Support and Revenue		1. Public support (or support) refers to nonreciprocal donations of money or other assets to VHWOs and ONPOs.	Same for VHWOs and ONPOs.
		2. Only the net proceeds (after related costs) of fund-raising banquets, auctions, and similar functions are recognized as support.	
		3. Revenue arises in reciprocal transactions, such as from charges for services rendered or interest on money invested and from gains on disposals of investments, fixed assets, or other assets.	
		4. Items initially recorded as Deferred Revenue and Support are recognized as Revenue or Support, as appropriate, when time, expenditure, or other restrictions or conditions are met.	
		5. Investment income, gains, and losses should be recognized in a manner consistent with the investment accounting policies adopted.	
Donated Materials, Facilities, and Services	1. Fair value of donated *materials, facilities, and other assets* is recognized as support and as asset or expense, as appropriate, *if* (1) the fair	1. Donated *materials and facilities* are recorded at fair value as support and as assets or expenses, as appropriate, *if* (1) they are significant and (2)	VHWO criteria for recording donated materials, facilities, etc., are more restrictive than ONPO criteria.

value can be objectively and reasonably estimated *and* (2) not recording them would cause the Statement of Support, Revenue, and Expenses and Other Changes in Fund Balances to be misleading.

2. Donated *services* are recognized as support, and also as an expense, *only if:* (1) the services are a normal part of the VHWO programs and supporting services, and would otherwise have been performed by paid personnel; (2) the VHWO exercises control over the employment and duties of the services donor; *and* (3) the VHWO has a reasonable basis for valuing the donated services.

the ONPO has a clearly measurable and objective basis for determining their value.

2. Donated *services* are reported as support and expense *only if all of these four conditions are met:* (1) the services are significant, an integral part of the ONPO efforts, otherwise would be performed by a paid person(s), and will continue to be performed; (2) the ONPO controls the employment and duties of the services donor; (3) the ONPO has a measurable basis for valuing the services; and (4) ONPO services are *not* primarily for member benefit.

The first three VHWO and ONPO criteria are very similar, though the ONPO criteria are more restrictive. The fourth ONPO criteria effectively precludes "member benefit" ONPOs—e.g, religious organizations, professional and trade associations, labor unions, political parties, fraternal orders, and social and country clubs—from recording donated services as support and expenses.

3. Fund-raising costs paid directly by donor should be recorded both as support and fund-raising expense.

Not mentioned in VHWO audit guide, but would appear reasonable to apply this guidance to VHWOs also.

Same for both VHWOs and ONPOs.

Expenses

1. Expenses are reported in two categories: (1) Program Services and (2) Supporting Services.
2. Program Services and Supporting Services expenses should be reported by function in the basic operating statement.
3. Organizations may account by organizational lines and object-of-expenditure during the year, then convert such data to

If this approach is used the organization must keep time,

Figure 20-9 (continued)

Attributes	Voluntary Health and Welfare Organizations (AICPA VHWO audit guide)	Other Nonprofit Organizations (ONPOs) (AICPA SOP 78-10)	Comments
Expenses (continued)			activity, and other records necessary to derive functional expense data at year end.
	4. If contractually required to remit a portion of their support or revenues to a national or state affiliated organization: (1) report payments where the VHWO or ONPO serves in an agency capacity for the affiliate as deductions from gross support and revenues; and (2) report payments where goods or services were received as assets or expenses, as appropriate, with expenses classified by function.	5. Significant fund-raising costs that directly relate to, and are expected to benefit, future periods should be reported as prepaid (deferred) expenses.	The VHWO audit guide has no such provision, but it would seem appropriate to follow this approach in VHWOs also.
		6. The full amount of multiyear grants awarded should be recorded as expenses and liabilities in the year the grant is awarded *unless* the ONPO has the right to not renew the grant.	
Capital Additions	1. Recorded as "Support" when restrictions and conditions are met.	1. Recorded as "Capital Additions" when the restrictions or conditions have been met.	
	2. Reported with and as "Support" in the operating statement.	2. Reported in "Capital Additions" section of the Statement of Activity.	
Other Changes in Fund Balance	Includes interfund transfers as well as external transactions, such as contribution refunds.	The ONPO Statement of Activity has no "Other Changes in Fund Balance" section.	ONPO interfund transfers reported in a "Transfers" section, as noted below.

	VHWO	ONPO
Transfers	VHWO interfund transfers reported as "Other Changes in Fund Balances," as noted above.	Interfund transfers are reported in a "Transfers" section of the Statement of Activity.	ONPO "Transfers" section should be after the beginning fund balance.
Miscellaneous		1. Interfund borrowing should be disclosed if (1) restricted funds have been loaned or (2) the liquidity of either fund is in question. Interfund loans should be reported as transfers when repayment of the loan is unlikely. 2. Funds held in trust by others, that are in neither the possession nor the control of the ONPO, are not reported as assets in the balance sheet but should be disclosed in the notes to the financial statements. 3. Other funds may be used by an ONPO that are not discussed in SOP 78-10. These may be reported separately in the balance sheet or reported as part of another fund. In either event the data should be properly classified so that liabilities—e.g., for agency, custodial, or self-administered trust funds—are clearly distinguished from fund balances.	No similar guidance in VHWO audit guide, but (1) and (2) seem reasonable for VHWOs also.

Figure 20-10

ILLUSTRATIVE TRANSACTIONS AND ENTRIES
VHWOs and ONPOs—For the Year 19X1

No.	Descriptions of 19X1 Transactions and Events	Fund	Accounts	Dr.	Cr.
1.	The following cash gifts were received: $5,000 Unrestricted; 10,000 Unrestricted (for 19X2); 30,000 Restricted to education use; 100,000 Restricted for capital additions; 55,000 For endowment for scholarships; $200,000	Current Unrestricted	Cash	15,000	
			Support—Contributions		5,000
			Deferred Support—Contributions		10,000
		Current Restricted	Cash	30,000	
			Deferred Support—Education		30,000
		Plant	Cash	100,000	
			Deferred [capital] Support*—Contributions		100,000
		Endowment	Cash	55,000	
			Fund Balance—Scholarships		55,000
2.	A $200,000 building addition was completed and paid for using the $100,000 gift (in 1) for this purpose and $100,000 paid directly from the Current Unrestricted Fund	Current Unrestricted	Transfer to Plant Fund	100,000	
			Cash		100,000
		Plant	(a) Buildings and Improvements	200,000	
			Cash		100,000
			Transfer from Current Unrestricted Fund		100,000
			(b) Deferred [Capital] Support—Contributions*	100,000	
			[Capital] Support—Contributions*		100,000
			(c) Fund Balance—Unexpended	100,000	
			Fund Balance—Expended		100,000
3.	Pledges were received as follows: $200,000—19X1—Unrestricted; 100,000—19X1—Restricted for education use	Current Unrestricted	Pledges Receivable	250,000	
			Allowance for Uncollectible Pledges		25,000
			Support—Contributions		180,000
			Deferred Support—Contributions		45,000

50,000—19X2—Unrestricted

$350,000

Experience indicates that 10% of pledges prove to be uncollectible. All pledges are legally enforceable.

Fund	Account	Dr.	Cr.
Current Restricted	Pledges Receivable	100,000	
	Allowance for Uncollectible Pledges		10,000
	Deferred Support—Contributions		90,000

4. Education expenses, $70,000, were incurred and vouchered.

Fund	Account	Dr.	Cr.
Current Restricted	(a) Expenses—Education	70,000	
	Vouchers Payable		70,000
	(b) Deferred Support—Contributions	70,000	
	Support—Contributions		70,000

5. Depreciation expense for 19X1 is recognized as follows:

$25,000 Plant assets
15,000 Endowment assets
$40,000

Fund	Account	Dr.	Cr.
Plant	Depreciation Expense	25,000	
	Accumulated Depreciation		25,000
Endowment	Depreciation Expense	15,000	
	Accumulated Depreciation		15,000

6. Fixed assets were sold as follows:
a. Plant equipment, cost $75,000, 60% depreciated, for $40,000, to be retained in Plant Fund.
b. Donated lot and building, held for resale, unrestricted, for $150,000 book value.

Fund	Account	Dr.	Cr.
Plant	(a) Cash	40,000	
	Accumulated Depreciation	45,000	
	Gain on Sale of Equipment		10,000
	Equipment		75,000
	(b) Fund Balance—Expended (Invested)	40,000	
	Fund Balance—Unexpended		40,000
Current Unrestricted	Cash	150,000	
	Land and Building		150,000

7. Received an annuity gift, $300,000. The present value of the annuity liability is $160,000. Terms of the gift are that half of the excess can be used immediately, 60% for unrestricted uses and 40% for services for handicapped clients of the agency. The portion of the gift that can be used immediately is recorded as an interfund payable in the Annuity Fund.

Fund	Account	Dr.	Cr.
Annuity	Cash	300,000	
	Annuities Payable		160,000
	Deferred Support—Gifts		70,000
	Due to Current Unrestricted Fund		42,000
	Due to Restricted Current Fund		28,000
Current Unrestricted	Due from Annuity Fund	42,000	
	Support—Gifts		42,000
Current Restricted	Due from Annuity Fund	28,000	
	Deferred Support—Gifts		28,000

Figure 20-10 (continued)

No.	Descriptions of 19X1 Transactions and Events	Fund	Accounts	Dr.	Cr.
8.	Upon an order by the Board, proceeds of the equipment sale (transaction 6) were transferred to the Current Unrestricted Fund.	Plant	Transfer to Current Unrestricted Fund..	40,000	
			Cash		40,000
		Current Unrestricted	Cash	40,000	
			Transfer from Plant Fund		40,000
9.	Investment income was received as follows:	Current Unrestricted	Cash [$20,000 + 0.4 ($35,000)]	34,000	
			Revenue—Investment Income		34,000
		Current Restricted	Cash [$10,000 + 0.3 ($35,000)] ......[+]	20,500	
	Fund Amount		Revenue—Investment Income[+]		20,500
	Current Unrestricted .... $ 20,000	Endowment	Cash (.3) ($35,000)	10,500	
	Current Restricted 10,000		Revenue—Investment Income[+]		10,500
	Endowment 35,000	Plant	Cash	15,000	
	Plant 15,000		Revenue—Investment Income[+]		15,000
	Annuity 40,000	Annuity	Cash	40,000	
	$120,000		Revenue—Investment Income		40,000
	Endowment earnings are dedicated to building the endowment base (30%) and for scholarships (30%); the balance is unrestricted.				
10.	A ten-year term endowment matured and the balance is available for use as follows:	Endowment	(a) Transfer to Current Unrestricted Fund	40,000	
			Transfer to Plant Fund	60,000	
	$ 40,000 Unrestricted		Cash		100,000
	60,000 Capital outlay		(b) Fund Balance	100,000	
	$100,000		Transfer to Current Unrestricted Fund		40,000
	The cash is transferred and the term endowment fund is terminated.		Transfer to Plant Fund		60,000
		Current Unrestricted	Cash	40,000	
			Transfer from Endowment Fund ..		40,000
		Plant	Cash	60,000	
			Transfer from Endowment Fund[+].		60,000

11. A fund-raising banquet was held. Proceeds were $75,000 and related costs of $45,000 were incurred and paid.

Current Unrestricted

	Debit	Credit
Cash	75,000	
Revenue—Special Events		30,000
Cash		45,000

12. Investments of the Current Unrestricted Fund, which cost $90,000, were written down to $75,000 market (lower of cost or market) at the end of 19X0. At the end of 19X1 the market value of the investments is $113,500.

Current Unrestricted

	Debit	Credit
Allowance for Market Decline of Investments	15,000	
Revenue—Recovery of Market Decline of Investments		15,000

(Note that under the lower of cost or market method investment market value appreciation is recognized as gain only to the extent of market losses recognized previously.)

13. Donated materials and contributed use of facilities that are recordable in 19X1 were:

a. $10,000 Materials (40% in inventory; 60% used on fund-raising project)

b. $ 8,000 Facilities (60% used for research offices; 40% for record keeping)

Current Unrestricted

	Debit	Credit
(a) Inventory of Materials	4,000	
Expenses—Fund Raising	6,000	
Support—Donated Materials		10,000
(b) Expenses—Research	4,800	
Expenses—Management and General	3,200	
Support—Donated Facilities		8,000

14. Donated services that are recordable include the time of:
(1) A CPA, who audited the agency at no cost, $6,000;
(2) An attorney, who did necessary legal work at no cost, $1,000; and
(3) A medical doctor, who assisted in a research project, $3,000.

Current Unrestricted

	Debit	Credit
Expenses—Management and General ..	7,000	
Expenses—Research	3,000	
Support—Donated Services		10,000

Figure 20-10 (continued)

No.	Transactions and Events	Fund	Accounts	Dr.	Cr.
15.	Payments from the Plant Fund included: 1. $100,000 On mortgage principal 60,000 Interest on mortgage 140,000 Equipment purchased $300,000	Plant	(a) Mortgage Payable .... Expenses—Interest .... Equipment .... Cash .... (b) Fund Balance—Unexpended .... Fund Balance—Expended	100,000 60,000 140,000 240,000	 300,000 240,000

(Entry b is necessary now, or by year end, since Plant Fund Balance is classified as "Unexpended" and "Expended.")

*ONPOs segregate capital additions from other support and report capital additions in a separate statement of activity section.

†Could be credited to *Deferred Revenue—Interest* pending being expended for scholarships.

‡ONPOs report as "Capital Addition."

CONCLUDING COMMENTS

VHWOs and ONPOs encompass a myriad of diverse types of not-for-profit organizations. Yet, despite some differences, their accounting and reporting—a unique blending of the accrual basis and the traditional expendable-nonexpendable, restricted-unrestricted fund structure—are markedly similar.

Whereas separate AICPA committees largely determined what now constitutes GAAP in the VHWO/ONPO environment, the FASB has now assumed this responsibility. It will be interesting to observe what influence, if any, the VHWO/ONPO model(s) has as the FASB reconsiders the broader question of what should constitute GAAP for nongovernment not-for-profit organizations.

▶ **Question 20-1.** Compare the fund accounting structure of voluntary health and welfare organizations (VHWOs) with that for other nonprofit organizations (ONPOs).

Question 20-2. Compare the basic financial statements required for VHWOs with those required for ONPOs. Explain how and why they differ.

Question 20-3. Although most VHWOs and ONPOs use fund accounting, both use the accrual basis of accounting rather than the modified accrual basis. Why do you suppose this is so?

Question 20-4. VHWOs and ONPOs have considerable latitude in deciding upon their investment accounting policies. Explain these options and indicate why, in your opinion, so many investment accounting options are available to VHWOs and ONPOs.

Question 20-5. Contrast the investment-related disclosures that must be made, parenthetically or in the notes to the financial statements, by VHWOs and ONPOs.

Question 20-6. VHWOs and ONPOs are given great latitude in determining the amounts at which fixed assets are capitalized. Explain the options available to them and why, in your opinion, they have such latitude.

Question 20-7. All fixed assets of VHWOs and ONPOs may not be recorded in the Plant (or equivalent) Fund and depreciated. (a) In which other VHWO and ONPO funds might fixed assets properly be carried? (b) In which circumstances would it be proper to not recognize depreciation and accumulated depreciation of fixed assets?

Question 20-8. Inexhaustible collections of ONPOs are not required to be capitalized, much less depreciated. Why is this so, and what accounting and reporting recognition, if any, is given such inexhaustible collections?

Question 20-9. Gifts, contributions, and bequests to VHWOs and ONPOs may be restricted to use for specified operating or capital outlay purposes. Explain how restricted gifts, contributions, and so on, are accounted for (a) at receipt, and (b) upon expenditure, by VHWOs and ONPOs.

Question 20-10. Distinguish between fund balance "reserves" and "designations."

Question 20-11. VHWOs and ONPOs may receive unrestricted contributions and service fees, yet properly account for them as deferred support and deferred revenues rather than as support and revenues. Explain.

Question 20-12. Distinguish between the terms "support" and "revenue" as they are used in VHWO and ONPO accounting and reporting.

Question 20-13. When VHWOs and ONPOs hold fund-raising banquests, auctions, bazaars, and similar events only the net amount raised, after deducting related costs, is accounted for as "support." Why is this so?

Question 20-14. Donated materials, facilities, and services are sometimes given accounting recognition—and at other times are not given accounting recognition—in the accounts and statements of VHWOs and ONPOs. Explain why some are given accounting recognition and others are not. (Do not list the criteria.)

Question 20-15. Some VHWOs and ONPOs remit portions of their support and revenue to affiliated state or national VHWOs and ONPOs. How should they account for and report such remittances?

Question 20-16.

(a) What is meant by "capital additions" as that term is used in accounting and reporting for ONPOs?

(b) How are "capital additions" accounted for and reported by ONPOs?

Question 20-17.

(a) What is meant by "other changes in fund balances" as that term is used in accounting and reporting for VHWOs? (b) How are "other changes in fund balances" reported by VHWOs?

▶ **Problem 20-1** The VHWO, Inc., Current Unrestricted Fund preclosing trial balance at the end of 19X4 included the following accounts, listed in alphabetical order:

	Dr. (Cr.)
Community Services	670,000
Contributions	(2,800,000)
Fund Balance	(1,900,000)
Fund Raising	400,000
Gains on Investments	(200,000)
General and Administrative	580,000
Investment Income	(100,000)
Legacies and Bequests	(150,000)
Public Education	700,000
Rehabilitation Services	1,050,000
Research	400,000
Special Events	(250,000)
Transfer to Plant Fund	300,000
Transfer from Endowment Fund	(50,000)
United Way Allocation	(450,000)
Total—Net Balance	1,800,000)

Required:

(a) Prepare in good form a statement of support, revenue, and expenses and changes in fund balance for the VHWO, Inc., Current Unrestricted Fund for 19X4.

(b) If VHWO, Inc., were an ONPO, how would the Statement of Activity prepared for its Current Unrestricted Fund differ from the statement prepared at requirement (a)?

Problem 20-2. The West Texas Zoological and Botanical Society bookkeeper prepared the following balance sheet:

West Texas Zoological and Botanical Society

Balance Sheet
December 31, 19X5

Assets

Cash	$ 350,000
Accounts receivable	120,000
Allowance for doubtful accounts	(20,000)
Pledges receivable	700,000
Allowance for doubtful pledges	(100,000)
Inventories	300,000
Investments	14,500,000
Land	1,000,000
Buildings and Improvements	35,000,000
Equipment	2,000,000
Accumulated depreciation	(10,000,000)
Other assets	150,000
	$44,000,000

Liabilities and Fund Balance

Accounts payable	$ 525,000
Accrued expenses payable	100,000
Deferred revenue—unrestricted	75,000
Deferred support—restricted	4,500,000
Deferred capital additions	1,200,000
Long-term debt	5,500,000
	$11,900,000

Fund Balance:	
Invested in plant	$22,000,000
Endowment	2,850,000
Restricted—Specified Programs	1,000,000
Unrestricted	6,250,000
	$32,100,000
	$44,000,000

Additional information:

1. The Endowment Fund consists solely of investments, except for $50,000 of cash, and has no liabilities.
2. The Plant Fund has $10,000 cash and some investments. No receivables or other assets relate to the Plant Fund, which has no current liabilities.
3. The Current Restricted Fund has $115,000 cash, the pledges receivable, and $25,000 of accounts payable, in addition to investments.

Required:

Prepare in good form a corrected balance sheet for the West Texas Zoological and Botanical Society at December 31, 19X5. Use a columnar format.

Problem 20-3. Prepare the general journal entries needed to record the following transactions and events in the general ledger accounts of the appropriate funds of an ONPO. The ONPO has the following funds: Operating—Unrestricted, Operating—Restricted, Plant, and Endowment.

1. Contributions were received as follows:

a. Cash:

$	700,000	for general operations
	600,000	for building addition
	200,000	for aid to the elderly
	500,000	as an endowment, the income to be used for assisting handicapped persons
$2,000,000		

b. Pledges:

$	750,000	for aid to the handicapped
	950,000	for building additions
	150,000	for general operations.
$1,850,000		Experience indicates that 10 percent will prove uncollectible

2. A building addition was completed at a cost of $1,500,000. The $600,000 received in item 1 was paid the contractor, and the balance is owed on a five-year, 12 percent note.

3. Expenditures, all paid, were made as follows:

From:	For:	Amount
Operating—Unrestricted	Fund Raising	$100,000
	General and Administrative	80,000
	Program A	320,000
		$500,000
Operating—Restricted	Aid to Elderly (Program B)	$200,000
	Aid to Handicapped (Program C)	400,000
		$600,000
Plant	1/10 of the principal	$ 90,000
	and six months' interest	54,000
	on the note payable (2)	$144,000
Endowment	Investments	$450,000

4. Equipment costing $300,000 was purchased from the Operating—Unrestricted Fund.

5. An older piece of equipment, original cost $100,000, accumulated depreciation $65,000, was sold for $40,000. The cash received was recorded in the Operating—Unrestricted Fund.

6. A lot and building, estimated fair market value $700,000, were donated to the ONPO on the condition that they be sold and the proceeds used for Program D, which serves physically and mentally handicapped babies and children.

7. The lot and building (6) sold immediately for $850,000.

8. Received a $500,000 cash annuity gift. The present value of the liability assumed in accepting the gift is $400,000. Half of the difference (excess) is immediately usable for general unrestricted purposes; the other half is to be retained in the fund as a "buffer" to assure that the obligations can be met.

9. Investment earnings were accrued and received as follows:

Operating—Unrestricted Fund	$ 40,000	accrued
Operating—Restricted Fund	60,000	accrued
Endowment Fund	65,000	cash
[Restricted: see 1 above]		
Plant Fund [Restricted for capital		
outlay purposes]	35,000	cash
	$200,000	

10. A fund-raising bazaar, tasting bee, and banquet were held. Receipts were:

$100,000	Unrestricted
170,000	Restricted for Program D
30,000	Restricted for Program A
$300,000	

Costs incurred—including food, gifts, kitchen help, and waiters—totaled $60,000. They would have been higher but the hotel waived their normal charge ($10,000) and a local supermarket donated food and other merchandise valued at $7,500.

11. To assure that the babies, young children, and elderly clients are receiving proper medical attention, a local doctor gives each a thorough physical examination annually. He has a young child in one of the ONPO programs and refuses to accept payment for his services, conservatively valued at $30,000. Similarly, a clinical psychologist, who also has a child in the program, assures that each child is properly tested (e.g., intelligence, aptitudes, progress) on a timely basis. His time would be conservatively valued at $15,000. Both the doctor and the psychologist have assigned duties, keep regular hours, maintain case records on each child, and call to the attention of ONPO staff persons each child's status, potential, and psychological or medical needs. Both of their time is spent approximately 30 percent on Program A, 20 percent on Program B, and 50 percent on Program C clients.

12. The family that donated the lot and building (in item 7) was so pleased that it sold that they donated land and a small building adjacent to the ONPO offices for use as an infant nursery and playground. The land and building are conservatively appraised at:

Land	$100,000
Building	250,000
	$350,000

However, there is an old 6 percent $50,000 mortgage note payable on the building, which the ONPO assumed.

Problem 20-4. Modern Museum, which has been in operation for many years, presented the following "operating" statement for its Operating Fund for the year ended September 30, 19X3:

Modern Museum, Inc.

Operating Statement

September 30, 19X3

Income:

Auxiliary activities	$ 510,000
Admissions	135,000
Investment Income	300,000
Investment Gains on Sales	120,000
Gifts	550,000
Grants for Equipment	440,000
Membership Dues	60,000
City Contribution	125,000
Life Memberships	30,000
Transfer from Endowment Fund	200,000
	$2,470,000

Expenses:

Curatorial and Conservation	$ 625,000
Accession of Art Collection	300,000
Management and General	70,000
Fund Raising	400,000
Exhibits	110,000
Education	145,000
Fellowships	75,000
Public Information	30,000
Membership Development	25,000
Transfer to Plant Fund	120,000
Mandatory Transfer to Plant Fund	100,000
	$2,000,000
Net Income	$ 470,000
Fund surplus, beginning of year	1,130,000
Fund surplus, end of year	$1,600,000

Additional information:

1. The equipment grant was received in 19X3.
2. The mandatory transfer to the Plant Fund is for debt service and is required by a mortgage loan agreement.
3. The nonmandatory transfer to the Plant Fund is to reimburse it for expenditures for equipment covered by the grant.
4. Modern Museum elects not to capitalize art collection expenditures.
5. Membership dues and life memberships are in substance "support."
6. Of the gifts, $150,000 was given for library book purchases.
7. Half of the investment income is restricted to developing a new artifacts collection.

Required:

(a) Prepare a statement of activity, in proper form, for the Modern Museum, Inc., Current Unrestricted Fund for the year ended September 30, 19X3.

(b) Prepare the general journal entries necessary to correct the general ledger accounts of the various funds for any errors noted in completing requirement a assuming that (1) the accounts for 19X3 have not been closed, and (2) the accounts for 19X3 have been closed.

PART III

PUBLIC
SECTOR
AUDITING

AUDITING

Auditing is the process of collecting and evaluating evidence to formulate an independent, professional opinion about assertions made by management. The typical readers of a financial or operational report issued by management have no opportunity to review the operations in question or to assess the credibility of management's representations, and few could do a good job given the opportunity. The auditor's review provides an expert's independent, professional judgment on the matters covered in his report. The purpose of the opinion is to add credibility to those representations properly made by management and to reduce the credibility of those that the auditor does not consider appropriate. These representations may take the form of financial statements, reports on the activities of organizations in carrying out programs assigned by legislative action, or implied representations regarding the carrying out of basic managerial responsibilities. For example, management is responsible for compliance with legal requirements, for maintaining adequate internal controls, and for carrying out programs economically and efficiently. The auditor may be asked to give his opinions on such matters even when management's representation is an implied one.

OVERVIEW

Classifications of Audits

The term *preaudit* has been used to characterize the work done to control the accuracy of the collecting and recording of revenues and the incurring and recording of expenditures and disbursements. Preaudit work is part of the accounting and control processes and therefore is not included in the definition of auditing as that term is used here. *Postaudits*, examinations conducted after transactions and events have occurred, are the principal focus of this chapter.

Audits may be classified as *internal* or *external* on the basis of the relationship of the auditor to the agency being examined. Internal auditing is defined by the Institute of Internal Auditors as:

> an independent appraisal activity within the organization for the review of operations as a service to management. It is a management control which functions by measuring and evaluating the effectiveness of other controls.[1]

Management customarily uses internal auditors—who are employees of the agency being audited—to review the operations of the agency, including employee compliance with managerial policies, and to report to management on these matters. Although the internal auditor's responsibility is ordinarily of the postaudit type (i.e., he is not directly involved in the accounting processes), he is employed by and reports to top management of the agency. External auditors are independent of the auditee agency and are responsible to the legislative body, the public, and other governmental units.

The National Committee on Governmental Accounting further divided postaudits into general or special categories:

> General audits are those which embrace all financial operations and records of a governmental unit and are made after the close of an accounting period. Special audits are those which are restricted to some segment of the unit's financial transactions or which cover all financial transactions for a period of time shorter or longer than the normal operating period (usually a fiscal year).[2]

Another useful classification of audits is the *financial* audit as opposed to the *operational* or *managerial* or *performance* audit. Perhaps they may best be described by analyzing the purposes of audits.

Purposes of the Audit

A governmental audit performed by an independent external auditor will have one or more of the following four major purposes:

1. To ascertain whether, in the auditor's opinion, the financial statements *present fairly* the financial position and results of operations of the organization in conformity with generally accepted accounting principles applied on a basis consistent with that of the preceding year. The typical examination of financial statements has this objective, together with the following one.

2. To determine *compliance* with legal provisions relating to finances— the *regularity* of fiscal operations. These two purposes include a determination of the adequacy of accounting records and procedures and a verification of the financial stewardship of the organization's management. An audit having these two objectives would be characterized

[1] GAAFR (80), p. 86.
[2] GAAFR (68), p. 127.

as a "financial and compliance" audit or as a "fiscal" audit. Although the contract for a financial audit engagement may not provide for recommendations for improvement, the professional auditor will make suggestions to management regarding the possible improvements that have come to his attention during the audit. Many believe that such audits also serve as control devices to prevent the loss of public funds through fraud or inefficiency.

3. To evaluate the *effectiveness* of the operations of an agency in attaining the objectives of the agency's programs (*program results*). This may include evaluating whether the activities contemplated in the statutes are properly designed to attain legislative intent as well as evaluating the program's operations.

4. To evaluate the *economy and efficiency* of the agency management in carrying out its programs. Technically, economy deals with a minimization of expenditure, whereas efficiency implies a maximization of benefits for costs consumed. An audit having either or both of the third and fourth objectives is called an "operational" or "performance" audit.

All of the foregoing purposes have to do with an evaluation of the responsibility and accountability of public officials. The first two deal with compliance with fiscal requirements. The last two emphasize managerial effectiveness. An audit intended to fulfill all these purposes or objectives may be referred to as a "comprehensive" audit. The scope of a comprehensive audit, and the components to which a given audit may be limited, are summarized in Figure 21-1.

Few audits of governments today are intended to include all aspects of the comprehensive audit in depth. Rather, audits are increasingly being designed to meet the specific needs of agency managers, other governments, investors, and the public in a given situation. Thus, while some attention may be given to all areas of the comprehensive audit, one aspect may receive the principal thrust of the audit effort while the others receive secondary attention. The primary thrust of most contemporary general audits of governments is upon the financial and compliance (fiscal) aspects, though special audits are often directed toward the efficiency and economy or program results (effectiveness) aspects. These various audit aspects (or thrusts) are not mutually exclusive, but overlap significantly. The alternate thrusts of public sector auditing, the overlapping nature of these alternate audit thrusts, and the minimum governmental auditing coverage deemed to be acceptable by most authorities today are illustrated graphically in Figure 21-2.

Management's Representations

In giving an opinion on the fairness of financial statements the auditor is dealing with representations specifically made by management. Assuming that the representations made are proper, the purpose of an opinion on these statements is clearly to add credibility to these representations. However, the same thing may be said of the other three objectives. If it does not publicly address itself to the other matters, management implicitly asserts that it has complied with the law, has achieved agency and program objectives or made reasonable

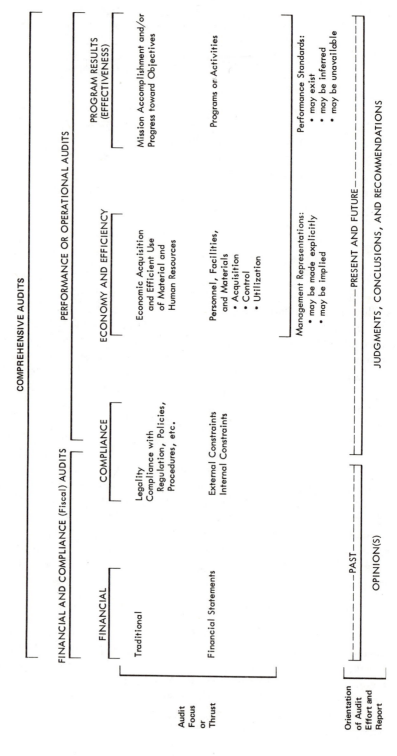

Figure 21-1

POTENTIAL SCOPE OF A GOVERNMENTAL AUDIT

COMPREHENSIVE AUDITS

FINANCIAL AND COMPLIANCE (Fiscal) AUDITS

PERFORMANCE OR OPERATIONAL AUDITS

FINANCIAL

COMPLIANCE

ECONOMY AND EFFICIENCY

PROGRAM RESULTS (EFFECTIVENESS)

Traditional

Legality
Compliance with Regulation, Policies, Procedures, etc.

Economic Acquisition and Efficient Use of Material and Human Resources

Mission Accomplishment and/or Progress toward Objectives

Financial Statements

External Constraints
Internal Constraints

Personnel, Facilities, and Materials
• Acquisition
• Control
• Utilization

Programs or Activities

Management Representations:
• may be made explicitly
• may be implied

Performance Standards:
• may exist
• may be inferred
• may be unavailable

Audit Focus or Thrust

Orientation of Audit Effort and Report

-------PAST------- -------PRESENT AND FUTURE-------

OPINION(S)

JUDGMENTS, CONCLUSIONS, AND RECOMMENDATIONS

Figure 21-2

ALTERNATIVE THRUSTS OF PUBLIC SECTOR AUDITING

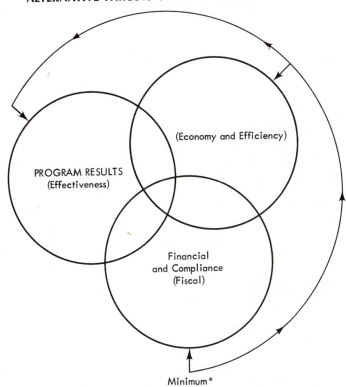

(Economy and Efficiency)

PROGRAM RESULTS
(Effectiveness)

Financial
and Compliance
(Fiscal)

Minimum*

* Most authorities believe that the *minimum* acceptable scope of contemporary public sector audits should include in-depth consideration of the financial and compliance (fiscal) aspects plus review and comment upon significant aspects relative to the economy and efficiency and program results (effectiveness) aspects that come to the auditor's attention during the course of his fiscal audit work. Others believe that certain economy and efficiency and program results aspects should be included in the *minimum* acceptable scope (and procedural steps) of public sector audits.

progress toward them, and has operated economically and efficiently. Although these representations may not be as specific as those regarding finances, they may still be evaluated and the auditor's opinion may be as useful as if specific representations had been made.

Classification of External Auditors

External audits are performed by persons who are independent of the administrative organization of the unit audited. There are three groups of independent auditors: (1) those who are officials of the governmental unit being examined, (2) those who are officials of a government other than the one being examined, and (3) independent public accountants and auditors.

Most states and a few municipalities have an independent auditor either elected by the people or appointed by the legislative body. In such cases the auditor is responsible directly to the legislative body or to the people; *he is not responsible to the chief executive* or anyone in the executive branch of the government. Election of the independent auditor works well in some jurisdictions; but in others only minimal qualifications are needed to seek the office and the auditor may be elected "on the coattails of" the governor. The elected auditor's independence and effectiveness are impaired significantly in the latter situation.

The term "auditor" is sometimes applied to the principal accounting officer of a state. In such cases he is not, of course, an independent external auditor. In other cases the external auditor is vested with some of the preaudit responsibilities; for example, he may be required by law to rule upon the legality of proposed expenditures upon request by the operating agencies. Such a provision is unsound. The constructive accounting processes are a part of the executive function; assigning a portion of them to an auditor who is not responsible to the chief executive represents a division of the chief executive's authority and, hence, his responsibility. In addition, the provision results in the auditor reviewing his own work as he performs the audit function.

State audit agencies in some states are responsible for auditing local governmental units, either at or without the request of the units. Such audit agencies do not necessarily audit any of the state agencies, though some do. Most local governmental audits are made by independent certified public accountants, however, and state agencies increasingly are concerning themselves with (1) setting standards for the scope and minimum procedures of local government audits in their jurisdiction, (2) reviewing reports prepared by independent auditors to assure that they are in compliance with these standards, (3) performing "spot check" or test audit procedures where audit coverage appears to be insufficient, and (4) accumulating reliable and useful statewide statistics on local government finance for use by both the executive and legislative branches of the state government.

Selection of the Auditor

The auditor should be selected by the legislative body on the basis of the quality of work that he may be expected to do. Many governments attempt to select an auditor by competitive bidding, but most accountants feel that this device imposes unprofessional pressures upon the auditors and is not conducive to selection of the best qualified auditor. Commodities for which precise specifications may be prepared may be profitably acquired by competitive bids, but professional qualities cannot be so defined.

The inappropriateness and adverse effects of securing professional audit services on the basis of competetive bidding were set forth in a *Joint Statement on Competetive Bidding for Audit Services in Governmental Agencies* by the American Institute of Certified Public Accountants and the Municipal Finance Officers Association of the United States and Canada. Issued in 1955 and revised in 1961, this statement reads, in part, as follows:

> Competitive bidding . . . is not an effective procedure in arranging for an independent audit.

It is not effective for the simple reason that an audit is not something which can be covered by rigid specifications. *An audit is a professional service requiring professional independence, skill, and judgment. An independent auditor should have as much latitude as he may find necessary* to be assured that the records are in order and that the system of accounts is functioning properly. . . .

This statement is not intended to challenge the right of government officials to obtain some estimate of their auditing expenses. Once a governmental agency has decided to engage an independent auditor, it ought to discuss the engagement with the auditor it believes to be the best qualified to render the most satisfactory service. After the independent auditor has surveyed the fiscal records and identified the principal problems, it should be possible to develop an understanding on the scope of his audit and on the length of time which will be required for its completion. The independent auditor should then be in a position, if required, to give an estimate of the cost of the service which is not likely to be exceeded unless he encounters unforeseen problems.

This approach to the selection of an auditor, reflecting a legitimate concern for costs, is perfectly reasonable and acceptable. But *no one gains—indeed, everyone is likely to lose—when auditors are selected by competitive bidding on the basis of the lowest possible price.*

It would be in the best interest of all concerned for political subdivisions employing a certified public accountant or a firm of certified public accountants to do so in the same way in which they would select an attorney, doctor, or other professional advisor—choose the one in whom they have the most confidence, discuss the work to be done, and agree on the basis for the fee.[3]

The position of the National Committee on Governmental Accounting, consistent with the logic of the *Joint Statement* cited above, was that independent auditors:

> should be selected only on the basis of professional competence and experience. This will not only mean that the auditor should be a certified public accountant authorized to practice in the jurisdiction being audited, but that he should have appropriate experience in the audit of governmental units and a demonstrated high level of attainment in such a professional practice. There must be a clear recognition on the part of both public officials concerned and independent accountants that auditing services are truly professional in nature. This being the case, the audit services should be compensated on the basis of professional fees agreed upon in advance of the engagement and not on the basis of competitive bids. . . .[4]

Selection of independent public auditors by means of competitive bids appears to have decreased significantly in local governments following issuance of the *Joint Statement* and the NCGA position statement. However, several Federal agencies, in particular, have insisted upon securing audit services on the basis

[3] Ibid., p. 129. (Emphasis added.)
[4] Ibid, p. 128.

of competitive bids in recent years, and the auditors of many state and local governments and agencies are selected by competitive bid.

The National Intergovernmental Audit Forum, an organization of Federal, state, and local government audit executives, offers this advice:

> Governmental agencies, . . . contracting for audits by other than government employed auditors, should be encouraged to engage public accountants by competitive negotiations that take into consideration such factors as the experience, plans, qualifications and price of the offeror. The weights to be assigned to each factor should be tailored to the particular tasks to be performed.[5]

The Audit Contract

To assure that there is no misunderstanding as to the nature, scope, or other aspects of the independent auditor's engagement, the contract should be in written form. Frequently, correspondence is simply exchanged, though formal contracts are generally considered preferable. Among the matters to be covered in the contract are: (1) the type and purpose of the audit—including a clear specification of the audit scope, any limitation of the scope, and the parties at interest; (2) the exact departments, funds, agencies, and the like to be audited; (3) the period the audit is to cover; (4) approximate beginning and completion dates and the date of delivery of the report; (5) the number of copies of the report; (6) the information and assistance that the auditee will provide for the auditor; (7) the means of handling unexpected problems, such as the discovery of fraud, which require a more extensive audit than was agreed upon, and the manner by which—and to whom—the auditor is to report fraud, malfeasance, and so on, coming to his attention; (8) the terms of compensation and reimbursement of the auditor's expenses; and (9) the place at which the audit work will be done.

Preliminary steps in the audit of an organization that uses fund accounting include familiarization with the nature of the organization, investigation of its system of internal control, and familiarization with the appropriate principles of accounting and financial reporting. The auditor must also acquaint himself with the legal and contractual provisions that govern the agency's fiscal and reporting activities. These include the restrictions governing the provision and disbursement of revenues and those controlling the funds and budget practices to be used. Some of these steps, or portions of them, often must be taken before the auditor can determine whether he should accept the engagement or before the terms of the engagement may be intelligently agreed upon.

AUDITING STANDARDS

AICPA Auditing Standards

The American Institute of Certified Public Accountants has approved a set of standards of quality for the performance of an audit.

---

[5] GAAFR (80), p. 90.

GENERAL STANDARDS

1. The examination is to be performed by a person or persons having adequate technical training and proficiency as an auditor.
2. In all matters relating to the assignment an independence in mental attitude is to be maintained by the auditor or auditors.
3. Due professional care is to be exercised in the performance of the examination and the preparation of the report.

STANDARDS OF FIELD WORK

1. The work is to be adequately planned and assistants, if any, are to be properly supervised.
2. There is to be a proper study and evaluation of the existing internal control as a basis for reliance thereon and for the determination of the resultant extent of the tests to which auditing procedures are to be restricted.
3. Sufficient competent evidential matter is to be obtained through inspection, observation, inquiries and confirmations to afford a reasonable basis for an opinion regarding the financial statements under examination.

STANDARDS OF REPORTING

1. The report shall state whether the financial statements are presented in accordance with generally accepted principles of accounting.
2. The report shall state whether such principles have been consistently observed in the current period in relation to the preceding period.
3. Informative disclosures in the financial statements are to be regarded as reasonably adequate unless otherwise stated in the report.
4. The report shall either contain an expression of opinion regarding the financial statements, taken as a whole, or an assertion to the effect that an opinion cannot be expressed. When an overall opinion cannot be expressed, the reasons therefor should be stated. In all cases where an auditor's name is associated with financial statements the report should contain a clear-cut indication of the character of the auditor's examination, if any, and the degree of responsiblity he is taking.[6]

The auditor also is guided by many detailed audit standards set forth in AICPA Statements on Auditing Standards (SASs).

Audit procedures must be distinguished from audit standards. Standards deal with quality, while procedures are the actual work that is performed. Standards govern the auditor's judgment in deciding which procedures will be used, the way they will be used, when they will be used, and the extent to which they will be used. No listing of audit procedures will be attempted here. Many of the procedures for a government audit are essentially the same as those for the examination of a profit-seeking organization; however, the procedures used must be tailored to the characteristics of the organization, which include legal requirements and restrictions, generally accepted accounting principles, and the objec-

---

[6] Committee on Auditing Procedure, American Institute of Certified Public Accountants, *Statement on Auditing Standards*, Codification of Auditing Standards and Procedures No. 1 (New York: AICPA, 1973) paragraph 150.02, p. 5.

tives of the audit. The AICPA standards are applicable to examinations of financial statements of organizations that use fund accounting, but some interpretation seems desirable. For example, an auditor may have adequate technical training and proficiency to audit a profit-seeking enterprise but lack the knowledge of governmental accounting or of the laws of a specific government that is necessary for an adequate audit of a government. In such a case he should refuse the engagement or acquire the necessary knowledge. (Special applications of the "Standards of Reporting" are discussed later in the chapter.) Additional guidance and interpretation are provided by the governmental auditing standards set forth by the Comptroller General of the United States.

Governmental Auditing Standards

Though there are many similarities between auditing profit-seeking and governmental organizations, there are also many differences. Further, there was no comprehensive statement of governmental auditing standards prior to issuance of *Standards for Audit of Governmental Organizations, Programs, Activities & Functions*[7] by the Comptroller General of the United States in 1972.

The Comptroller General noted in the foreword of that *Standards* document that:

> Public officials, legislators, and the general public want to know whether governmental funds are handled properly and in compliance with existing laws and whether governmental programs are being conducted efficiently, effectively, and economically. They also want to have this information provided, or at least concurred in, by someone who is not an advocate of the program but is independent and objective.
>
> This demand for information has widened the scope of governmental auditing so that such auditing no longer is a function concerned primarily with financial operations. Instead, governmental auditing now is also concerned with whether governmental organizations are achieving the purposes for which programs are authorized and funds are made available, are doing so economically and efficiently, and are complying with applicable laws and regulations. The standards contained in this statement were developed to apply to audits of this wider scope.[8]

In the foreword of the 1981 revision of the *Standards* the Comptroller General observed:

> In the past few years, we have seen an unprecedented interest in government auditing. Public officials, legislators, and private citizens want and need to know not only whether government funds are handled properly and in compliance with laws and regulations, but also whether government organizations are achieving the purposes for which programs were authorized and funded and are doing so economically and efficiently.

---

[7] Comptroller General of the United States, *Standards for Audit of Governmental Organizations, Programs, Activities & Functions* (Washington, D.C.: U.S. General Accounting Office, 1972).
   [8] Ibid., p. i.

Forty years ago auditors concentrated most of their efforts on auditing the vouchers which support expenditures. But today, auditors are also concerned with the economy, efficiency, and effectiveness of government operations.[9]

These standards are intended for application in audits of all governmental organizations, programs, activities, and functions—whether they are performed by auditors employed by Federal, state, or local governments; independent public accountants; or others qualified to perform parts of the audit work contemplated under the standards. Similarly, they are intended to apply to both internal audits and audits of contractors, grantees, and other external organizations performed by or for a governmental agency. Moreover, the Office of Management and Budget (OMB) includes the Comptroller General's standards as basic audit criteria for Federal agencies in OMB Circular A-73 and incorporates them by reference in OMB Circular A-102, as revised by Attachment P on October 22, 1979 dealing with the "Single Audit," discussed later in this chapter. Several state and local government audit agencies have adopted these standards, and the AICPA has issued guidance to its members, discussed later in this chapter, concerning the GAO standards.

The standards set forth by the Comptroller General recognize and incorporate the standards of the AICPA. The AICPA standards are recognized as being necessary and appropriate to financial statement audits, but insufficient for the broader scope of governmental auditing. The governmental auditing standards are built around the three elements of a comprehensive audit discussed earlier:

1. *Financial and compliance*—determines (a) whether the financial statements of an audited entity present fairly the financial position and the results of financial operations in accordance with generally accepted accounting principles and (b) whether the entity has complied with laws and regulations that may have a material effect upon the financial statements.
2. *Economy and efficiency*—determines (a) whether the entity is managing and utilizing its resources (such as personnel, property, space) economically and efficiently, (b) the causes of inefficiencies or uneconomical practices, and (c) whether the entity has complied with laws and regulations concerning matters of economy and efficiency.
3. *Program results*—determines (a) whether the desired results or benefits established by the legislature or other authorizing body are being achieved and (b) whether the agency has considered alternatives that might yield desired results at a lower cost.[10]

Provision for such a broad audit scope is not intended to imply that all audits are or should be of such an extensive scope. Indeed, the introduction to the *Standards* notes that:

The audit standards are more than the mere codification of current practices, tailored to existing audit capabilities. They include concepts and areas of audit

[9] Comptroller General of the United States, *Standards for Audit of Governmental Organizations, Programs, Activities, and Functions* (Washington, D.C.: U.S. Government Printing Office, 1981), p. i.
[10] Ibid, p. 3.

coverage which are still evolving and are vital to the accountability objectives sought in auditing governments and their programs.

An audit of a government entity may include all three elements or only one or two. It is not intended or even feasible or desirable that every audit include all three. The expanded scope audit should not be conducted routinely, but instead [should be] selected when it will meet the needs of expected users of the audit results.

The above expansion of the definition of "auditing" highlights the importance of a clear understanding of the audit scope by all interested parties. This takes on added importance when a public accountant is engaged to perform the audits. The engagement agreement between a government unit and the public accountant should specify the scope of the work to be done as defined in the standards, to avoid misunderstandings.[11]

Since the standards are structured so that any one of the three elements can be performed separately, if this is deemed desirable, it is *essential* (1) that audit contracts or letters of engagement specifically identify which of the three elements are to be covered and (2) that the auditor's report indicate which were included in the audit. Obviously, in the governmental environment "an audit" is not necessarily synonymous with "an audit"—as the scope of audit engagements varies considerably.

The standards of governmental auditing set forth by the U.S. Comptroller General, as revised in 1981, are summarized as follows:

SUMMARY OF STANDARDS

A. Scope of Audit Work

The expanded scope of auditing a government organization, a program, an activity, or a function should include:

1. *Financial and compliance*—determines (a) whether the financial statements of an audited entity present fairly the financial position and the results of financial operations in accordance with generally accepted accounting principles and (b) whether the entity has complied with laws and regulations that may have a material effect upon the financial statements.
2. *Economy and efficiency*—determines (a) whether the entity is managing and utilizing its resources (such as personnel, property, space) economically and efficiently, (b) the causes of inefficiencies or uneconomical practices, and (c) whether the entity has complied with laws and regulations concerning matters of economy and efficiency.
3. *Program results*—determines (a) whether the desired results or benefits established by the legislature or other authorizing body are being achieved and (b) whether the agency has considered alternatives that might yield desired results at a lower cost.

In determining the scope for a particular audit, responsible audit and entity officials should consider the needs of the potential users of audit findings.

[11] Ibid, pp. 3–4.

B. General Standards

1. Qualifications: The auditors assigned to perform the audit must collectively possess adequate professional proficiency for the tasks required.
2. Independence: In all matters relating to the audit work, the audit organization and the individual auditors, whether government or public, must be free from personal or external impairments to independence, must be organizationally independent, and shall maintain an independent attitude and appearance.
3. Due professional care: Due professional care is to be used in conducting the audit and in preparing related reports.
4. Scope impairments: When factors external to the audit organization and the auditor restrict the audit or interfere with the auditor's ability to form objective opinions and conclusions, the auditor should attempt to remove the limitation or, failing that, report the limitation.

C. Examination and Evaluation (Field Work) and Reporting Standards for Financial and Compliance Audits

1. AICPA Statements on Auditing Standards for field work and reporting are adopted and incorporated in this statement for government financial and compliance audits. Future statements should be adopted and incorporated, unless GAO excludes them by formal announcement.
2. Additional standards and requirements for government financial and compliance audits.
   a. Standards on examination and evaluation:
      (1) Planning shall include consideration of the requirements of all levels of government.
      (2) A review is to be made of compliance with applicable laws and regulations.
      (3) A written record of the auditors' work shall be retained in the form of working papers.
      (4) Auditors shall be alert to situations or transactions that could be indicative of fraud, abuse, and illegal expenditures and acts and if such evidence exists, extend audit steps and procedures to identify the effect on the entity's financial statements.
   b. Standards on reporting:
      (1) Written audit reports are to be submitted to the appropriate officials of the organization audited and to the appropriate officials of the organizations requiring or arranging for the audits unless legal restrictions or ethical considerations prevent it. Copies of the reports should also be sent to other officials who may be responsible for taking action and to others authorized to receive such reports. Unless restricted by law or regulation, copies should be made available for public inspection.
      (2) A statement in the auditors' report that the examination was made in accordance with generally accepted government auditing standards for financial and compliance audits will be acceptable language to indicate that the audit was made in accordance with these standards. (See ch. V, par. 2b for AICPA-suggested language.)
      (3) Either the auditors' report on the entity's financial statements or a separate report shall contain a statement of positive assurance on

those items of compliance tested and negative assurance on those items not tested. It shall also include material instances of noncompliance and instances or indications of fraud, abuse, or illegal acts found during or in connection with the audit.

(4) The auditors shall report on their study and evaluation of internal accounting controls made as part of the financial and compliance audit. They shall identify as a minimum: (a) the entity's significant internal accounting controls, (b) the controls identified that were evaluated, (c) the controls identified that were not evaluated (the auditor may satisfy this requirement by identifying any significant classes of transactions and related assets not included in the study and evaluation), and (d) the material weaknesses identified as a result of the evaluation.

(5) Either the auditors' report on the entity's financial statements or a separate report shall contain any other material deficiency findings identified during the audit not covered in (3) above.

(6) If certain information is prohibited from general disclosure, the report shall state the nature of the information omitted and the requirement that makes the omission necessary.

D. Examination and Evaluation Standards for Economy and Efficiency Audits and Program Results Audits

1. Work is to be adequately planned.
2. Assistants are to be properly supervised.
3. A review is to be made of compliance with applicable laws and regulations.
4. During the audit a study and evaluation shall be made of the internal control system (administrative controls) applicable to the organization, program, activity, or function under audit.
5. When audits involve computer-based systems, the auditors shall:
   a. Review general controls in data processing systems to determine whether (1) the controls have been designed according to management direction and known legal requirements and (2) the controls are operating effectively to provide reliability of, and security over, the data being processed.
   b. Review application controls of installed data processing applications upon which the auditor is relying to assess their reliability in processing data in a timely, accurate, and complete manner.
6. Sufficient, competent, and relevant evidence is to be obtained to afford a reasonable basis for the auditors' judgments and conclusions regarding the organization, program, activity, or function under audit. A written record of the auditors' work shall be retained in the form of working papers.
7. The auditors shall:
   a. Be alert to situations or transactions that could be indicative of fraud, abuse, and illegal acts.
   b. If such evidence exists, extend audit steps and procedures to identify the effect on the entity's operations and programs.

E. Reporting Standards for Economy and Efficiency Audits and Program Results Audits

1. Written audit reports are to be prepared giving the results of each government audit.

2. Written audit reports are to be submitted to the appropriate officials of the organization audited and to the appropriate officials of the organizations requiring or arranging for the audits unless legal restrictions or ethical considerations prevent it. Copies of the reports should also be sent to other officials who may be responsible for taking action on audit findings and recommendations and to others authorized to receive such reports. Unless restricted by law or regulation, copies should be made available for public inspection.

3. Reports are to be issued on or before the dates specified by law, regulation, or other special arrangement. Reports are to be issued promptly so as to make the information available for timely use by management and by legislative officials.

4. The report shall include:
   a. A description of the scope and objectives of the audit.
   b. A statement that the audit (economy and efficiency or program results) was made in accordance with generally accepted government auditing standards.
   c. A description of material weaknesses found in the internal control system (administrative controls).
   d. A statement of positive assurance on those items of compliance tested and negative assurance on those items not tested. This should include significant instances of noncompliance and instances of or indications of fraud, abuse, or illegal acts found during or in connection with the audit. However, fraud, abuse, or illegal acts normally should be covered in a separate report, thus permitting the overall report to be released to the public.
   e. Recommendations for actions to improve problem areas noted in the audit and to improve operations. The underlying causes of problems reported should be included to assist in implementing corrective actions.
   f. Pertinent views of responsible officials of the organization, program, activity, or function audited concerning the auditors' findings, conclusions, and recommendations. When possible their views should be obtained in writing.
   g. A description of noteworthy accomplishments, particularly when management improvements in one area may be applicable elsewhere.
   h. A listing of any issues and questions needing further study and consideration.
   i. A statement as to whether any pertinent information has been omitted because it is deemed privileged or confidential. The nature of such information should be described, and the law or other basis under which it is withheld should be stated. If a separate report was issued containing this information it should be indicated in the report.

5. The report shall:
   a. Present factual data accurately and fairly. Include only information, findings, and conclusions that are adequately supported by sufficient evidence in the auditors' working papers to demonstrate or prove the bases for the matters reported and their correctness and reasonableness.
   b. Present findings and conclusions in a convincing manner.
   c. Be objective.
   d. Be written in language as clear and simple as the subject matter permits.

e. Be concise but, at the same time, clear enough to be understood by users.

f. Present factual data completely to fully inform the users.

g. Place primary emphasis on improvement rather than on criticism of the past; critical comments should be presented in a balanced perspective considering any unusual difficulties or circumstances faced by the operating officials concerned.[12]

The seven basic premises underlying the standards serve to highlight the objectives of the standards, and place them in perspective:

1. The term "audit" is used to describe not only work done by accountants and auditors in examining financial statements but also work done in reviewing (a) compliance with applicable laws and regulations, (b) economy and efficiency of operations, and (c) effectiveness in achieving program results.

2. Public office carries with it the responsibility to apply resources efficiently, economically, and effectively to achieve the purposes for which the resources were furnished. This responsibility applies to all resources, whether entrusted to public officials by their own constituency or by other levels of government.

3. Public officials are accountable both to other levels of government for the resources provided to carry out government programs and to the public. Consequently they should provide appropriate reports to those to whom they are accountable. Unless legal restrictions, ethical considerations, or other valid reasons prevent them from doing so, audit organizations should make audit findings available to the public and to other levels of government that have supplied resources.

4. Financial and compliance auditing is an important part of the accountability process since it provides independent opinions on whether the entities' financial statements present fairly the results of financial operations. Economy and efficiency audits and program audits can assist government operations by identifying needed improvements.

5. The interests of individual governments in many financially assisted programs often cannot be isolated because the resources applied have been commingled. Different levels of government share common interests in many programs. Therefore, an audit should to the extent practicable be designed to satisfy both the common and discrete accountability interests of each contributing government.

6. Cooperation by Federal, State, and local governments in auditing programs of common interest with a minimum of duplication benefits all concerned and is a practical method of auditing intergovernmental operations.

7. Auditors should rely upon the work of other auditors to the extent feasible if they satisfy themselves as to the other auditors' independence, capability, and performance by appropriate tests of their work or by other acceptable methods.

An assumption underlying all the standards is that governments will cooperate in making audits in which they have mutual interests. This is especially true when one government receives funds from several others and each has a

---

[12] Ibid., pp. 6–11.

continuing need for a basic financial and compliance audit. In these circumstances, audits should be made on an organizationwide basis whenever possible, rather than on a grant-by-grant basis, and in a manner that will satisfy the audit needs of the participating governments.[13]

AUDITING PROCEDURES

An authoritative coverage of municipal auditing procedures is contained in *Audits of State and Local Governmental Units*,[14] as amended, an AICPA industry audit guide. The municipal auditor should be thoroughly familiar with this publication since it contains much useful information. Guidance also is provided in the "Auditing Governmental Organizations" chapter of GAAFR (80).[15] In addition, several states and state CPA societies prescribe or recommend minimum audit programs or procedures. Audit guides are also available for many Federal programs. These should be studied carefully by the auditor in formulating his audit program. The *Audit Guide and Standards for Revenue Sharing Recipients*[16] has almost universal significance in governmental auditing. The auditor should inquire as to the existence and availability of audit guides pertinent to other Federal programs in which the auditee organization participates—audit guides are available for most of the larger ones—as they not only provide useful guidance but may impose specific accounting, auditing, and/or reporting requirements. Finally, guidelines are available for those performing financial and compliance audits, economy and efficiency audits, and program results audits. These are cited in the following sections.

THE FINANCIAL AND COMPLIANCE (FISCAL) AUDIT

Legal compliance is considered an integral part both of managerial responsibility and accountability and of the fiscal audit of governments. The legal constraints under which governments operate and the control orientation of governmental accounting systems have been commented upon at numerous points throughout this book. Obviously, the accountability process is incomplete if the audit of the financial statements does not include the legal compliance aspects within its scope or these are not included in the auditor's report.

Auditing Standards

The AICPA standards are designed for the financial aspects of the fiscal audit and have been incorporated in the Comptroller General's standards. The laws, regulations, or other legal constraints under which the government operates establish the standards against which legal compliance is measured.

[13]Ibid., pp. 4–5.
[14] Committee on Governmental Accounting and Auditing, American Institute of Certified Public Accountants, *Audits of State and Local Governmental Units*, (New York: AICPA, 1973).
[15] GAAFR (80), pp. 86–93.
[16] Department of the Treasury, Office of Revenue Sharing, Audit Guide and Standards for Revenue Sharing Recipients (Washington, D.C.: U.S. Goverment Printing Office, October 1973).

Audit Procedures

The procedures commonly employed in financial auditing are covered adequately in the several standard auditing textbooks available.

Specific guidance for audits of governments, hospitals, colleges and universities, voluntary health and welfare organizations, and other nonprofit organizations is available in the several AICPA audit guides for these types of organizations, cited at various points in this text. The most detailed guidance to the procedural aspects of fiscal audits generally is contained in *Guidelines for Financial and Compliance Audits of Federally Assisted Programs*,[17] a 1980 publication of the U.S. General Accounting Office. This guidebook covers topics such as audit standards to be applied, audit procedures to be followed, audit report to be prepared, planning the audit, audit workpapers, compliance with legal and regulatory requirements, study of internal control, tests of account balances, and other audit procedures. An AICPA committee is preparing—with GAO and OMB cooperation—a fiscal audit guide to update and supersede the GAO *Guidelines*.

The procedures involved in auditing legal compliance will vary with the circumstances. Either the government's attorney or the auditor must determine the legal provisions of laws, ordinances, bond indentures, grants, and so on, that are applicable in the situation. The auditor then determines the extent to which they have been complied with and the adequacy of the disclosure in the financial statements in this regard. The auditor must also assure himself that the auditee has not incurred significant unrecorded liabilities through failure to comply with, or through violation of, pertinent laws and regulations.

The Audit Report

The auditor's report on his fiscal examination is discussed under four headings: (1) Scope, (2) Statements, (3) Opinion, and (4) Comments. Operational or performance audit reporting follows a similar pattern, though it typically is longer and includes additional topics.

Scope. In the first paragraph of the "Auditor's Short Form Report" (Figure 21-3) the auditor describes the scope of his examination. The wording in Figure 21-3, "the examination was made in accordance with generally accepted auditing standards," means that a satisfactory examination has been performed for the specified statements. If the scope of his examination was unsatisfactory in any respect, the auditor must decide whether the alternative procedures (if any) that he employed were satisfactory and what the effect on his opinion has been.

It is essential that the auditor indicate the statements on which he is rendering an opinion. This is usually done by referring to those statements as listed in the table of contents of the report. The typical annual report contains both financial and statistical statements, as well as schedules or other statements accompanying the basic financial statements. Ordinarily, the auditor does not give an opinion on the statistical statements, and his scope paragraph should state whether they are covered by his opinion. The auditors may take full, partial, or

---

[17] U.S. General Accounting Office, *Guidelines for Financial and Compliance Audits of Federally Assisted Programs* (Washington, D.C., February 1980).

Figure 21-3

Auditor's Report

Unqualified Opinion on Combined Financial Statements

We have examined the combined financial statements of the City of Example, Any State, as of and for the year ended December 31, 19X2, as listed in the table of contents. Our examination was made in accordance with generally accepted auditing standards and, accordingly, included such tests of the accounting records and such other auditing procedures as we considered necessary in the circumstances.

In our opinion, the combined financial statements referred to above present fairly the financial position of the City of Example, Any State, at December 31, 19X2, and the results of its operations and the changes in financial position of its proprietary fund types for the year ended, in conformity with generally accepted accounting principles applied on a basis consistent with that of the preceding year.

Source: Audit Standards Division, American Institute of Certified Public Accountants, *Statement of Position 80-2*, "Accounting and Financial Reporting by Governmental Units" (New York: AICPA, June 30, 1980), p. 9.

no responsibility for certain statements and schedules. Some auditors insert a disclaimer in front of those statements to which the opinion does not apply to further assure that the reader is not confused in this regard.

Statements. As has already been emphasized, the statements on which the auditor gives an opinion are the primary responsibility of the administration of the unit being audited. In many instances, the statements are prepared by the auditor, but both he and the officials involved should recognize that the latter are responsible for their fairness. The auditor should secure for his work papers an affirmation from the officials indicating that the statements present fairly the organization's financial condition and results of operations.

If the auditor's contract requires that he prepare (as well as audit) the financial reports, the auditor will prepare and present the statements in the same form as would the officials. In this case, his report will also constitute his letter of transmittal.

Opinion. The second paragraph of the "Auditor's Short Form Report" (Figure 21-3) contains the model language suggested by the American Institute of Certified Public Accountants for an "unqualified" opinion—that is, an opinion based on an examination of financial statements conducted in conformity with generally accepted auditing standards applied to statements that acceptably meet the terms set out in the second paragraph—adapted to the state and local government environment. If the audit or the statements are less than satisfactory in some material respect, the auditor must give a qualified opinion or an adverse opinion or, if he is unable to form an opinion, he must disclaim an opinion. In giving a "qualified" opinion the auditor states that, in spite of the audit's scope or procedures or the statements' content being less than satisfactory in some specified respect, he has arrived at an overall opinion on the statements. If the statements are not fairly presented in conformity with generally accepted accounting principles and standards, the auditor must specify the flaw or flaws and express an "adverse" opinion—state that the statements are *not* fairly presented.

Because of major omissions of auditing procedures or because of major uncertainties regarding one or more statement items, the auditor may not know whether the statements are fairly presented. He will therefore disclaim an opinion (issue a "disclaimer") on the fairness of the statements taken as a whole.

A number of factors affect the type of opinion that an auditor should render. Generally speaking, if the problem is not so great that referring to it and taking exception to it would negate an expression of opinion on the statements taken as a whole, he will render a qualified opinion. If the problem that he cites is so grave that a qualified opinion is not appropriate, he must express an adverse opinion if the problem is one of fairness or he must disclaim an opinion if the problem is one of uncertainty. If the auditor's name is associated with a set of statements, the responsibility that he assumes must be clearly stated.

The auditor's report presented in Figure 21-3 relates only to the general purpose financial statements (GPFS) of a state or local government. This opinion may have resulted from an engagement to audit only the GPFS, which is not condoned by the NCGA. Alternatively, this opinion may accompany the separately issued GPFS and be derived from and consistent with the auditor's report on the financial statements in the comprehensive annual financial report (CAFR).

Figures 21-4 and 21-5 present unqualifed opinions for two different levels of scope of audit and auditor responsibility. In Figure 21-4 the auditor takes full responsiblity only for the GPFS and states that the combining, individual fund, and account group statements and schedules are presented only for purposes of additional analyses, though such information has been subjected to the auditing procedures applied and is *fairly stated in all material respects in relation to the combined financial statements taken as a whole*. Thus, this is a two-tier auditor's report where (1) full responsiblity as an auditor is taken for the GPFS, but (2) much less responsibility is assumed for the other statements and schedules in the financial section of the CAFR.

The auditor's report in Figure 21-5, on the other hand, constitutes an unqualified opinion on both the GPFS and the combining, individual fund, and account group financial statements, with a lesser opinion rendered on the related schedules.

The auditor's reports in Figures 21-3, 21-4, and 21-5 are from *AICPA Statement of Position 80-2*. The document also contains other guidance to auditors of governments, including additional examples of the type of report the auditor should render in varying circumstances.

Figure 21-4

AUDITOR'S REPORT

Unqualified Opinion on Combined Financial Statements Presented with Combining, Individual Fund, and Account Group Financial Statements and Supporting Schedules

We have examined the combined financial statements of the City of Example, Any State, as of and for the year ended December 31, 19X2, as listed in the table of contents. Our examination was made in accordance with generally accepted auditing standards and, accordingly, included such tests of the accounting records and such other auditing procedures as we considered necessary in the circumstances.

Figure 21-4 (continued)

In our opinion, the combined financial statements referred to above present fairly the financial position of the City of Example, Any State, at December 31, 19X2, and the results of its operations and the changes in financial position of its proprietary fund types for the year then ended, in conformity with generally accepted accounting principles applied on a basis consistent with that of the preceding year.

Our examination was made for the purpose of forming an opinion on the combined financial statements taken as a whole. The combining, individual fund, and account group financial statements and schedules listed in the table of contents are presented for purposes of additional analysis and are not a required part of the combined financial statements of the City of Example, Any State. The information has been subjected to the auditing procedures applied in the examination of the combined financial statements and, in our opinion, is fairly stated in all material respects in relation to the combined financial statements taken as a whole.

Source: Audit Standards Division, American Institute of Certified Public Accountants, *Statement of Position 80-2,* "Accounting and Financial Reporting by Governmental Units" (New York: AICPA, June 30, 1980), p. 9.

Figure 21-5

AUDITOR'S REPORT

Unqualified Opinion on Combined Financial Statements and Combining, Individual Fund, and Account Group Financial Statements Presented with Supporting Schedules

We have examined the combined financial statements of the City of Example, Any State, and the combining, individual fund, and account group financial statements of the city as of and for the year ended December 31, 19X2, as listed in the table of contents. Our examination was made in accordance with generally accepted auditing standards and, accordingly, included such tests of the accounting records and such other auditing procedures as we considered necessary in the circumstances.

In our opinion, the combined financial statements referred to above present fairly the financial position of the City of Example, Any State, at December 31, 19X2, and the results of its operations and the changes in financial position of its proprietary fund types for the year then ended, in conformity with generally accepted accounting principles applied on a basis consistent with that of the preceding year. Also, in our opinion, the combining, individual fund, and account group financial statements referred to above present fairly the financial position of the individual funds and account groups of the City of Example, Any State, at December 31, 19X2, and the results of operations of such funds and the changes in financial position of individual proprietary funds for the year then ended, in conformity with generally accepted accounting principles applied on a basis consistent with that of the preceding year.

Our examination was made for the purpose of forming an opinion on the combined financial statements taken as a whole and on the combining, individual fund, and account group financial statements. The accompanying financial information listed as supporting schedules in the table of contents is presented for purposes of additional analysis and is not a required part of the combined financial statements of the City of Example, Any State. The information has been subjected to the auditing procedures applied in the examination of the combined, combining, individual fund, and account group financial statements and, in our opinion, is fairly stated in all material respects in relation to the combined financial statements taken as a whole.

Source: Audit Standards Division, American Institute of Certified Public Accountants, *Statement of Position 80-2,* "Accounting and Financial Reporting by Governmental Units" (New York: AICPA, June 30, 1980), p. 9.

Comments. The auditor's reports in Figures 21-3 to 21-5 point out that both the government engaging the auditor and the auditor should clearly understand the scope of the audit to be made and that it be clearly communicated to the readers of audited financial statements.

The NCGA position on the matter is that:

> Independent audit of state and local government financial statements is an essential element of financial control and accountability. Accordingly, the Council recommends independent annual audits of the financial statements of all state and local governments in accordance with generally accepted auditing standards.
>
> The establishment, evaluation, and enforcement of generally accepted auditing standards and guidelines for financial audits is an important function of the American Institute of Certified Public Accountants and is not within the purview of the National Council on Governmental Accounting. At the same time, since the auditor expresses his or her opinion in terms of the extent to which financial statements are fairly presented in conformity with generally accepted accounting principles, the Council's conclusions have important implications for the scope and nature of financial audits.
>
> The GPFS . . . are designed to present fairly the financial position of the fund types and account groups, the results of operations by fund type, and the changes in financial position of the proprietary funds in conformity with generally accepted accounting principles. Thus, the GPFS comprise the minimum acceptable scope of annual audits.
>
> The Council recommends that the scope of the annual audit also encompass the combining and individual financial statements of the funds and account groups. Although presentation of individual fund data of homogeneous funds is not necessary for fair presentation in conformity with generally accepted accounting principles, the Council believes that the individual funds should be subjected to the audit tests and other procedures. Further, the Council believes that the auditor's opinion with respect to individual fund statements should, as a minimum, make reference to their fairness in all material respects in relation to the GPFS. Statistical tables are normally excluded from the audit scope, since they cover many years and include nonaccounting data.[18]

Thus, the NCGA would not be pleased with an audit such as that reported on in Figure 21-3 unless it was an opinion derived from a more complete audit such as one indicated by the reports in Figures 21-4 and 21-5. In the NCGA view an audit like that reported on in the auditor's report in Figure 21-4 as the *minimum* acceptable scope and thus would also approve of an audit report like that in Figure 21-5.

While the independent auditor is engaged primarily to give an opinion on the financial statements and the extent of legal compliance, one of his most valuable services can be to provide analyses and recommendations on matters that came to his attention in the process of his examination. This additional information typically is presented in a letter to responsible officials known as the

[18] NCGAS 1, p. 25.

"management letter." In the management letter the auditor provides discussions, analyses, and recommendations on operational matters such as accounting systems and procedures; protection, utilization, and disposition of assets; number of funds; cash management; organizational arrangements; and insurance and bonding practices. The auditor may also comment on compliance or lack of compliance of officials with legal and contractual requirements. Officials should not be criticized for using a procedure that complies with the law; if the auditor believes that the procedure is subject to criticism, he should criticize the legal requirements. Similarly, he may have to criticize officials for efficient procedures if they are not in strict compliance with the law, and he may recommend changes in the law.

THE SINGLE AUDIT

A recent movement spawned by the rapid expansion of federal grants to and contracts with state and local governments, universities, hospitals, and other not-for-profit organizations is known as the "single audit." In the absence of a single audit, an organization may be subjected to numerous different audits by various Federal and state audit agencies and independent public accountants. Most of the audits are limited in scope to different facets of the organization's operations, e.g., a research grant, the food stamp program, or a day care center. The basic notion of the "single audit" is that one audit can satisfy the major aspects of the many audits now done of an organization, and do so more economically and efficiently.

Recently, the U.S. President and the Office of Management and Budget (OMB) ordered the evolution of a single-audit approach to government financial and compliance audits. These new single audits are expanded financial and compliance audits which include selected program compliance audit elements. *Guidelines for Financial and Compliance Audits of Federally Assisted Programs*, popularly known as the "red book," cited earlier, is the official single-audit guidebook. Also, the major grantor Federal agencies have been assigned "cognizant agency" responsibilities to oversee and coordinate the move toward single audits of all state governments; provision has been made for a cognizant agency to be assigned for any city, village, or county that wants a single audit; and the key program aspects of the major Federal programs that should be tested in a single audit have been decided upon and codified.

The single audit notion has been evolving for several years, but was ordered by Attachment P to OMB Circular A-102, published in the October 22, 1979, *Federal Register*. Several experimental single audits were performed in 1979 and 1980, and single audits have increased significantly since 1980. But as noted in GAAFR (80):

> A viable single audit concept will require agreement at the federal level on a finite list of standardized program compliance requirements sufficient to meet the legitimate informational needs of numerous federal departments and agencies providing intergovernmental revenues to state and local governments. An effective single audit will also require clarification and coordination on the part of state legislatures and state government oversight bodies in

specifying those finance-related legal and contractual provisions with which auditors must be concerned in performing single audits.[19]

Successful implementation of the single-audit concept may also involve the formaton of audit teams comprised of federal auditors, state auditors, and independent public accountants—with each member focusing on his area of expertise but with one member having overall "in-charge" responsibility for the single audit. The single-audit concept is excellent and will no doubt continue to evolve in practice as additional auditor guidance is provided.

THE OPERATIONAL (PERFORMANCE) AUDIT

Audit work of professional quality requires the preexistence of a number of factors. There must be a body of competent auditors who are willing to express an opinion. These individuals must be equipped with techniques of evidence gathering that are satisfactory for the requirements of the audit. The existence of a professional organization implies self-imposed standards of performance that control the quality of audit work. There must be persons interested in receiving and using the opinions that the auditors render, whatever the subject of the audit may have been. Finally, there must be standards of performance by which the organization can be judged, and there must be explicit or implicit representations of compliance with these standards made by the management of the audited entity.

The outstanding example of a governmental organization engaged in operational auditing is the United States General Accounting Office. Its work exemplifies the requirements for operational audit work of professional quality. In the past the GAO's audits were generally performed by employees who were certified public accountants. They brought with them the generally accepted auditing standards of the accounting profession. The accountants were assisted in their audit work by lawyers, whose duties included the review of the legality of proposed and actual executive department expenditures. Increasing emphasis upon audits of managerial performance has led to the recruiting of engineers and others whose technical backgrounds are useful in evaluating operations. The GAO reports to the Congress of the United States, and Congress has increasingly assigned the evaluation of executive branch performance to the GAO.

Recently, other Federal audit organizations, such as that within the Department of Health and Human Services, have done some outstanding operational or performance audits. More recently, independent public accountants have been requested to perform or participate in audits to evaluate government economy, efficiency, and program results.

Several important guidelines to performing operational or performance audit (or review) engagements have been issued recently. Two of these are published by the U.S. General Accounting Office: (1) *Guidelines for Economy and Efficiency Audits of Federally Assisted Programs, 1981,* and (2) *Comprehensive Approach for Planning and Conducting a Program Results Review, 1981.* Another is *Guide-*

---

[19] GAAFR (80), p. 87.

lines for CPA Participation in Government Audit Engagements to Evaluate Economy, Efficiency, and Program Results, published by the AICPA in 1977.[20]

Standards of Managerial Performance

Standards of operational performance are not nearly so well defined as are those of financial auditing, nor are managerial representations as to operational performance likely to be so definite. Performance auditing is concerned with administrative activities designed to achieve the objectives of the functions, programs, and activities that have been assigned to the audited agencies by legislative action. Accordingly, the standards of performance must deal with how well the organization is managed and, concomitantly, whether the agency has achieved the objectives set out for it by legislative action.

In financial auditing the standards of agency performance are reasonably explicit—compliance with generally accepted accounting principles and compliance with laws, policies, and procedures that govern fiscal operations. In the field of operational auditing there may be occasional explicit representations by management as to accomplishment, but more often there is no explicit representation but only the implicit managerial responsibility for economical, efficient, and effective performance.

Operational auditing performance standards are derived from and implied by many different sources. One of the most important sources is legislative statement of policy. When legislation creates programs and activities and provides financing for them, the appointed agency has the responsibility of carrying out legislative direction; it may properly be held accountable through the audit process for compliance and accomplishment. It is important to note that legislative prescription is not always best designed to achieve legislative intent. A proper function of an auditor who reports to the legislative body is to comment upon achievement of legislative intent as well as compliance of the agency with programs and activities the legislature designed to achieve its objectives. For example, the GAO was requested by the Congress to evaluate the efficacy of the Head Start program. In such circumstances the auditor has a responsibility to evaluate both administrative compliance with legally prescribed programs and the efficacy of well-administered programs in achieving legislative objectives.

Many professional organizations formally state desirable policies and levels of performance in their fields of proficiency. The auditor may properly look to such statements for standards to be used in evaluating the performance of agencies operating in such professional fields.

The auditor may also use comparisons as standards of quality and achievement for the operation to be examined—accomplishments of the audited agency in the past and of other organizations, trends, statistics of accomplishment at the national or local levels, and the like may form the basis for such comparisons. Statistical data measuring the output of the agency are particularly useful.

The principles of management may be used as criteria for managerial per-

[20] American Institute of Certified Public Accountants, *Guidelines for CPA Participation in Government Audit Engagements to Evaluate Economy, Efficiency, and Program Results*, Management Advisory Services Guideline Series Number 6 (New York: AICPA, 1977).

formance. Management should explicitly plan its objectives, programs, policies, standards, and organizational arrangements. It must assign responsibility and delegate authority. It must set up procedures that will provide for proper use and control of its resources. It must set up record keeping and reporting systems and provide for internal audit of its activities. It must select personnel of appropriate quality.

Management's own statements of standards, goals, objectives, and other criteria of success, together with reports thereon, are useful standards and sources of evaluation, respectively.

Finally, there are certain common sense standards of performance that the agency must expect to be used in judging it. Duplication of effort, backlogs of work, failures to enforce agreements, failure to use good management techniques, obsolete or excessive inventories, use of government property for private benefit, failure to coordinate activities with agencies doing related work—all of these are indications of operational misfeasance or malfeasance that should be used by the auditor who is evaluating performance.

Auditing Standards

The generally accepted auditing standards developed by the American Institute of Certified Public Accountants for the guidance of members in conducting and reporting upon examinations of financial statements have in general been used by its members in both management services and auditing engagements, including those involving operational auditing. The "General Standards" and "Standards of Field Work" have been accepted as directly pertinent, while the standards of reporting clearly must be evaluated with respect to specific engagements. For example, the first AICPA standard of reporting says that "the report shall state whether the financial statements are presented in accordance with generally accepted principles of accounting." This standard is clearly inapplicable for a report on an operational auditing examination. On the other hand, AICPA standard of reporting number four concludes with this sentence: "In all cases where an auditor's name is associated with financial statements the report should contain a clearcut indication of the character of the auditor's examination, if any, and the degree of responsibility he is taking." With appropriate modifications to recognize that financial statements are not the matters being examined, this statement is clearly applicable to operational auditing.

Since performance auditing involves activities traditionally considered management advisory services (MAS) or consulting, the AICPA's MAS practice standards may also be applicable.

However, the *Standards for Audit of Governmental Organizations, Programs, Activities and Functions* include the AICPA audit standards and go beyond them. Thus, they are the primary source of professional audit and review standards in government performance audits. Not only are these standards designed specifically for governmental audits, but the Federal government has the authority to require their implementation wherever Federal funds are involved—that is, most state and local governmental units and many nongovernment and quasi-governmental organizations. As noted earlier, these standards are normative rather than descriptive; i.e., they portray what should be or might be, not necessarily the level of current practice. They provide guidelines for the upgrading of governmental audit practice, at least, and probably point the direction of the evolution of governmental auditing in the future. The relationship of AICPA standards and those of the GAO is discussed further in *Guidelines for CPA Participation in Government Audit Engagements to Evaluate Economy, Efficiency, and Program Results.*[21]

Audit Procedures

The techniques of operational auditing are in many ways similar to those of financial audits. The auditor's objective is to find sufficient evidence to support his opinion. He must review the legal background of agency operations, the administrative requirements of laws or contracts, the policies of the agency, and the management controls and systems, including financial and operating reports. He must examine organizational arrangements, flows of financial and operational data, and documentary evidence. He must analyze, inspect, observe, count, trace, compare, question, and obtain confirmations. The collection of evidence by these methods, and others, must be directed to the specific objectives of the audit, whether they be those of a financial audit, an operational audit, or a comprehensive audit covering all aspects of agency operation and representations of management.

One way of viewing the nature of performance audit findings is:

ELEMENTS OF PERFORMANCE AUDIT FINDINGS

Element	Definition
Authority	Legal or administrative authority to conduct the activity under audit
Goal	What the activity under audit is intended to achieve
Condition	Extent to which objectives are being achieved
Effect	Beneficial results from achieving objectives or the loss in dollars or in effectiveness caused by failing to meet objectives
Procedures and practices	Establish ways of performing tasks and achieving objectives
Underlying causes	Reasons why procedures and practices are effective if goals are being achieved or the reasons why they are ineffective if goals are not being achieved.

Source: GAAFR (80), p. 89.

The auditor's findings of fact, cause, and effect will ordinarily be divisible into two categories: a group of findings that is favorable to the management of the auditee agency and a group that is not. When the auditor identifies a problem that is not favorable to the management, he will want to determine how widespread it is in the agency. He will want to evaluate the materiality of the problem and its effects on costs, both directly and indirectly. He must attempt to determine

[21] Ibid.

the causes of inefficiency and consider and evaluate the options for eliminating them. The problem must be related to the personnel responsible for it, and the auditor will want to discuss his findings and his proposed options with the management personnel who are responsible. Their review is exceedingly important because of their intimate relationship with and knowledge of the agency. Only after the auditor has gone through this process is he is a position to select the option that he wants to recommend and to formulate his report.

Reporting

The audit report should clearly state the scope of the examination, including its objectives. For example, the auditor might be expected to ascertain the extent to which the objectives set out in legislation have been achieved or whether the administration of the act has been carried out economically and efficiently. Certainly the organization or organizations subject to examination must be identified. In some cases programs that have common or similar goals or similar patterns of activities may and probably should be examined by audits that cross organizational lines.

Another section of an operational audit report will include the findings of fact and, to the extent they can be identified, the causes and effects of the situations or events described in the findings. This is an appropriate spot for commendations of especially good management and results. It is essential here that the auditor assess the efficacy of managers within the environment in which they work, not some hypothetical ideal environment, and that he evaluate their actions in terms of the information available at the time decisions had to be made. This is crucial to a fair, undistorted evaluation, since "hindsight is always 20/20."

A third section of the report should contain the auditor's recommendations for improvement. These should flow out of the statements of fact, cause, and effect that will already have appeared in the report. Frequently, the auditor will have worked with agency personnel to solve problems; full credit should be given to the agency for its suggested solutions and for taking prompt action on those recommendations that have already been put into effect. Recommendations that have not been implemented may well be divided into those that are capable of implementation without additional legislation and those that are not. Special attention is justified for (1) recommendations of prior audits that the auditee agency has not put into effect, and (2) recommendations with which the auditee agency management disagrees.

The work of the auditor may well be justifiable by means of specific accomplishments. The auditor should summarize dollars collected and dollars saved because of his recommendations where such summarization is possible. Mention of financial or other benefits that are not measurable in quantitative terms also may be appropriate.

CONCLUDING COMMENT

Both the theory and the practice of governmental auditing are evolving rapidly. A major factor underlying this rapid evolution, or "quiet revolution," has been the widespread realization that the traditional financial audit has limited utility in governments—that the accountability process remains incomplete in the absence of an independent audit of at least certain aspects of legal compliance, economy and efficiency, and effectiveness. What is taking place, in effect, may be described as an effort to meld the traditional financial audit with legal compliance evaluation and with selected techniques of systems analysis, operations research, value engineering, and other tools of the modern internal auditor, mathematician, engineer, and management consultant—and to bring these to bear in the management and evaluation of governments through the audit process. The ultimate results of this significant change in scope and emphasis remain to be seen, but great strides already have been made in several Federal, state, and local audit agencies, as well as by the American Institute of Certified Public Accountants and many independent public accounting firms.

▶ **Question 21-1.** Compare the responsibilities of a municipality's officers and its independent auditor for the financial report.

Question 21-2. In the course of an audit of the books of a municipality, you find that the financial statements, when prepared on the basis required by law, do not reflect the true financial condition or financial operations of the municipality. What would be your procedure?

Question 21-3. In making an audit, how would you ascertain that expenditures were properly appropriated for?

Question 21-4. You are called in to audit the books of a municipality for which taxes are collected by a county. How would you verify that taxes receivable controlling accounts are correct?

Question 21-5. In your audit of the taxes receivable of a county which collects both its own taxes and taxes for other units, how would you verify that the taxpayers' individual account balances, as shown in the records, are correct?

Question 21-6. A municipal golf course charges $4.00 for eighteen holes played during regular hours but only $1.50 for nine holes played in the 2½ hours prior to dusk. It has been found that the clerk has been charging players at the daytime rate but recording the receipts as twilight-hour receipts and pocketing the difference. What steps would you recommend to ensure that all receipts will be properly accounted for hereafter?

Question 21-7. Describe briefly the contents of the audited comprehensive annual financial report of a governmental unit.

Question 21-8. A municipality requires auditors to submit bids as to how much they would charge for the annual audit. The audit contract is awarded to the lowest bidder. What is wrong with this method of engaging auditors?

Question 21-9. Upon completion of your audit and presentation of the report to a city council one of the councilmen takes exception to the phrase "in our opinion" which appears in your audit. He states that you were engaged to make a sufficiently complete and detailed examination to determine all pertinent facts about the city; that if you have not completed all the work necessary to that end, you should continue your investigation as long as necessary, but that he wants a certificate consisting of positive statements of fact, without any qualification or questions of "opinion." Discuss the logic of the councilman's remarks and the position which you would take. (AICPA, adapted)

Question 21-10. A councilman requests that you, an independent public accountant, render an opinion on the budget presented to the council by the city manager. Discuss the position which you would take with respect to his request. (AICPA, adapted)

Question 21-11. The comptroller of D City is responsible for approval of all receipts of city funds and all disbursements thereof. The city council takes the position that, since he is auditing both receipts and disbursements for accuracy and legality, no additional audit by independent accountants is necessary. What position would you, a new councilman, take?

Question 21-12. The state auditor has for years been responsible for examinations of the financial operations of all state agencies. A bill is under consideration to add to his duties those of the chief accounting officer of the state. You are testifying before a legislative committee which is considering the bill. What is the tenor of your testimony?

Question 21-13. Auditing has been defined as the process of collecting and evaluating evidence in order to formulate an opinion about assertions made by management. About what assertions is the external auditor giving his opinion as the result of a fiscal audit? About what assertions is the external auditor giving his opinion as the result of an operational audit?

Question 21-14. What are the factors required if there are to be audits of professional quality, whether they be fiscal audits or operational audits?

Question 21-15. By what standards of performance may the auditor evaluate the efficacy and efficiency of management in government?

Question 21-16. The auditor's report on a fiscal audit has scope and opinion sections. What sections would you expect to find in the audit report of an operational audit?

Question 21-17. Describe the nature of a "single" audit of a state or local government.

Question 21-18. How would the thrust of audit or review on the economy and efficiency of a government program differ from that directed to the effectiveness of the program?

The purpose of the auditing chapter is to impress students of governmental accounting with the proper functions of the independent auditor and with the principles which guide the auditor. In view of this limited objective, no problems have been provided.

INDEX

911